CAREERS
2013
9th edition

trotman | t

Careers 2013

This ninth edition published in 2012 by Trotman Publishing, an imprint of Crimson Publishing Ltd, Westminster House, Kew Road, Richmond, Surrey TW9 2ND.

© Trotman Publishing 2012

Contributors: Matthew Charley, Victoria Daniel, Francesca Jaconelli, Lucy Smith, Jessica Spencer, Abigail Van-West and Libby Walden.

British Library Cataloguing in Publication Data
A catalogue record for this book is available from the British Library

ISBN: 978–1–906041–88–5

The information in this book was correct to the best of the publisher's belief at the time of going to press. However, if you would like to contact the publisher to report any recent changes please do so at the following address: editorial@trotman.co.uk

Typeset by IDSUK (DataConnection) Ltd
Printed and bound in the UK by Ashford Colour Press, Gosport, Hants

CONTENTS

WELCOME TO *CAREERS 2013*

When you first start choosing your future career it can seem a daunting and complicated process. There are so many different jobs with new ones emerging all the time; how do you begin to search for something that would suit you?

Finding all the information you need to help with your career choices can therefore be difficult – and when you find it, it is not always easy to understand.

We all have different values, interests and ambitions so *Careers 2013* lists all of the most important aspects for young people searching for a future career to help make the process of choosing a career path much easier.

Within *Careers 2013* you will find brief but detailed entries on hundreds of different jobs, each of which includes entry requirements, advantages and disadvantages, working conditions, your future prospects, a description of the type of person suited to the area of work and a money guide.

Although you can go straight to the pages on the jobs you're already interested in, to get the most from using *Careers 2013* we suggest you first read the opening section, as this will explain more about the content and how to use the publication.

We are confident that *Careers 2013* offers a new approach, is interesting and is easy to use. More importantly, however, it will help you to find the answers to the questions that matter to you.

- Which careers will suit me?
- What qualifications will I need?
- How much can I hope to earn?
- What's the future likely to hold?
- Will the studying be worthwhile?

Take a look at the sample job profile overleaf to see how you can use this book to find out exactly what you need to know.

We hope you enjoy using *Careers 2013* and wish you all the best with your future career choices.

The Trotman team.

An example job profile

All of the job profiles in *Careers 2013* are laid out in the same style with the same sections. This is an example job profile showing you what each section refers to and the information it contains.

Heading/job title

This refers to the title of the job you will find on the page. Some job profiles are very closely linked so they have been merged together, so the heading will have each job title that is going to be covered in the profile.

CRCI

(Connexions Resources Centre Index)

These codes show you where you will be able to find additional information about the job title within school, college, university or community-based careers information areas.

Qualifications and courses

This section looks in detail at the most common ways to enter a profession and the qualifications and courses you will need to take. If there are different qualifications available depending on whether you live in England, Scotland, Wales or Northern Ireland, these variations will be listed here too.

As qualifications and courses change often, we would recommend that you use the Further information section to get more advice on which qualifications you will need to give yourself the best chance of entering your chosen career.

What the work involves

These opening points will give you a quick overview of what the job is like.

Type of person suited to this work

Within this category you will find lots of information to help you match your own strengths, weaknesses, likes and dislikes to the individual job.

Sadly it is very common for someone to start a job not knowing what they will be expected to do. They might then be confronted with something they find either too hard or not enjoyable; this might mean leaving a job they studied a long time for. To make sure this doesn't happen to you, think carefully about the information provided here and whether it matches your skills, experience and personality. If you think it does, then you should also do some further research to get more detailed and comprehensive information.

Working conditions

This section explains where you can expect to work, whether it's outside or inside, in an office or travelling around the country, for the career that interests you. It also tells you the typical working hours you can expect and whether you will be expected to work at weekends, evenings and on shifts. This will give you a good idea of the day to day life you can expect on the job.

QUALITY MANAGER — ENTRY LEVEL 5

ADMINISTRATION, BUSINESS, OFFICE AND FINANCIAL SERVICES

CRCI: AA

Qualifications and courses

Most entrants hold a degree or postgraduate degree. Depending on the industry that you want to move into, useful subjects may include polymer science/technology, textile technology, business/management, engineering or physical/mathematical/applied science. You can also complete an HND in a similar subject or in materials science/technology, printing, clothing technology, or food science/technology.

The general entry requirements for an HND are 1 A level and 4 GCSEs (A*–C) or equivalent.

Entry without a degree or HND is often possible when an applicant is moving across from another vocational field involving quality or management. The qualifications provided by the Chartered Quality Institute (CQI) would provide the necessary skills for a manager qualified in an area such as accountancy, law, engineering or marketing. These qualifications are the Certificate in Quality Management (Level 3) and the Diploma in Quality Management (Level 5). The Chartered Management Institute (CMI) also offers qualifications which may be beneficial.

What the work involves

Quality managers are employed by an organisation to ensure that quality assurance aims are met in relation to products or services; this includes legal compliance levels and customer expectations.

Practices include monitoring and advising on existing systems in order to consistently improve current standards, and publishing data and reports that inform management.

Quality managers must ensure that the company they are working for is applying the required level of environmental and health and safety standards. Encouraging staff to adhere to new doctrines and legislation is fundamental.

Type of person suited to this work

This job is suited to someone that has an interest in securing and improving standards of quality. In order to do this, it is necessary to have good communication skills in order to influence and persuade others to follow set regulations and uphold required standards. Problems may arise owing to complicated legislation and staff lacking interest and so quality managers must be resilient and create ways in which models of quality can be easily understood and adhered to. An organisation's customers must be listened to and so quality managers must be adaptable and approachable.

Working conditions

Normal working hours apply when employed by the government or a bank, although a position in engineering, production or retail could involve shift work. Offices and laboratories are where most are based, although those with experience often become consultants to smaller firms once they have gained enough experience to be self-employed.

It may be necessary to travel to different clients during the working day, or even to stay overnight.

Future prospects

There are around 25,000 quality managers in the UK, with employment opportunities ranging across business, production, commerce and public sector organisations. Opportunities for progression to managerial and board room levels are ever increasing owing to the rising importance of health and safety, and customer expectation.

Quality managers can decide whether to specialise in a particular area or whether to progress to a position of management in other sectors; these include production, health and safety, technical sales, and customer relations.

Advantages/disadvantages

Quality managers have high levels of responsibility and so the work they undertake can be both rewarding and respected.

Career progression or movement to self-employment is possible.

Quality legislation is constantly changing so entrants must be willing to remain up to date with developments in the field.

Money guide

Quality managers can expect a starting salary in the region of £18,000–£23,000.

As you gain experience and progress to a senior role, you can achieve earnings of £35,000 to £60,000.

Those who reach director level can earn up to £70,000.

Salaries vary according to the sector you are working in, company size and geographical location.

Related opportunities

- Project Manager p43
- Quality Control Inspector p000
- Statistician p000

Further information

British Quality Foundation
www.quality-foundation.co.uk

Chartered Management Institute
www.managers.org.uk

Chartered Quality Institute
www.thecqi.org

44

Entry level

This number corresponds to the *Careers 2013* level of qualification you need to start your career in a particular job. For more information about what the entry levels in *Careers 2013* mean, see the next page.

Future prospects

This section shows you where you could progress to within a certain career. This may be in terms of climbing the career ladder, or branching into new territory as a career sector develops and changes. Of course, no one can predict the future of any career sector completely but important changes to the economy, reductions and increases in the labour force as well as technological advances will have an impact upon how a sector develops. This information will give you a balanced view of where your future could take you in any given career.

Advantages/disadvantages

It's important that, when choosing a career, you have a well-rounded and honest view of what the work will be like. This section gives you some of the most common good and bad points about a job so that you can decide if a job matches up to your expectations.

Money guide

For some people one of the most important things they'll consider before undertaking a new course, qualification or a career is 'how much can I expect to earn?'

To help you we have included:

■ the most up-to-date information about pay scales

■ where possible, what you can expect at entry, intermediate and senior levels

■ any regional differences.

Related opportunities

This section lists jobs that are similar in style and the skills that they require to the job profile you are looking at. This is to give you lots of options to choose from if you haven't decided which career interests you the most.

You might not have considered or heard of some of these before, so it will help you to broaden out your ideas further.

Further information

Listed here are the websites of organisations that can help you continue your research into your chosen job areas.

Qualifications: what do the entry levels in *Careers 2013* mean?

You will see that every job profile in this book has an entry level number, ranging from 1 to 8, assigned to it. This refers to the lowest qualification level that you need to achieve in order to enter the profession.

The number shown indicates the level of qualification you are most likely to need:

■ to enter the job and

■ to enter the job and to train while working.

The qualifications grid

Opposite is a grid which shows what the levels in *Careers 2013* refer to in terms of qualifications that you can take in England, Wales, Northern Ireland and Scotland.

The information from three qualifications frameworks has been incorporated into this table: the Qualifications and Credit Framework (QCF), the Scottish Credit and Qualifications Framework (SCQF) and the Framework for Higher Education Qualifications (FHEQ).

Because the frameworks all have their own levels please be aware that this grid cannot accommodate subtle differences between the frameworks and you should refer directly to the websites below for more information.

The Qualifications and Credit Framework (QCF)

The QCF has now replaced the NQF (National Qualifications Framework) and is the basis of the qualifications grid on the following page. The framework contains both academic and vocational qualifications offered in England, Wales and Northern Ireland from Entry level to Level 8.

The Framework for Higher Education Qualifications (FHEQ)

The FHEQ includes higher education qualifications from Certificates of Higher Education through to Doctoral degrees. It applies to qualifications offered in England, Wales and Northern Ireland and includes five levels, each indicated by a letter corresponding with the initial of the main qualification offered at that level.

The Scottish Credit and Qualifications Framework (SCQF)

The SCQF is a 12-level framework including vocational, occupational and academic qualifications offered in Scotland. It covers all levels including further and higher education, from Access through to Doctoral degrees.

Further information

Each framework is under continuous review, but information in this book was correct at the time of writing.

For further details and the most up-to-date information, refer to the following websites:

■ QCF: www.ofqual.gov.uk
www.wales.gov.uk; www.ccea.org.uk

■ FHEQ: https://qaa.ac.uk/academicinfrastructure/fheq

■ SCQF: www.scqf.org.uk

Key

Qualifications that are available in England, Wales, Northern Ireland and Scotland.

Qualifications that are available in England, Wales and Northern Ireland.

Qualifications that are available in Scotland.

Careers 2013 level	Rough equivalent framework level	General and academic qualifications	Vocational and occupational qualifications
Entry level	QCF Entry Level Skills for Life at entry level SCQF Access Levels 1–3	**Entry Level Certificate SQA Access 1, 2 Access 3, Foundation Standard Grade National Certificate**	**National Progression Award (start at SCQF Level 2)**
1	QCF Level 1 SCQF Level 4	GCSE grade D–G 14–19 Foundation Diploma Skills for Life Key Skills Level 1 **Intermediate 1 General Standard Grade National Certificate**	NVQ/SVQ Level 1 BTEC Introductory Certificate/ Diploma Level 1 Certificate OCR Nationals **National Progression Award**
2	QCF Level 3 SCQF Level 5	GCSE grade A*–C 14–19 Higher Diploma Skills for Life Key Skills Level 2 **Intermediate 2 Credit Standard Grade National Certificate**	NVQ/SVQ Level 2 Level 2 Certificate/Diploma BTEC First Certificate/Diploma Apprenticeship BTEC Nationals OCR Nationals **National Progression Award**
3	QCF Level 3 SCQF Level 6	A level Key Skills Level 3 14–19 Advanced Diploma Advanced Extension Award Mathematics Extended Project International Baccalaureate **Scottish Higher**	NVQ/SVQ Level 3 A levels in applied subjects Level 3 Certificate/Diploma BTEC National Award/Certificate/ Diploma Advanced Apprenticeship (England) BTEC Nationals OCR Nationals City & Guilds Level 3 **Modern Apprenticeship (Scotland, Wales, Northern Ireland) Professional Development Award**
4	QCF Level 4 FHEQ Level C SCQF Level 7	Certificate of Higher Education Key Skills Level 4 **Scottish Advanced Higher Higher National Certificate**	NVQ/SVQ Level 3 Level 4 Certificate/Diploma BTEC Professional Diplomas, Certificates and Awards City & Guilds Licentiateship **Professional Development Award**
5	QCF Level 5 FHEQ Level I SCQF Levels 8 and 9	Bachelor's degree Diploma of Higher Education Diploma of Further Education Foundation Degree Higher National Diploma	NVQ/SVQ Level 4 Higher National Certificate/Diploma (HNC/HND) BTEC Professional Diplomas/ Certificates/Awards National Diploma in Professional Production Skills Level 5 Certificate/Diploma City & Guilds Full Technological Certificate (FTC) **Professional Development Award**
6	QCF Level 6 FHEQ Level H SCQF Level 10	Bachelor's degree with Honours Graduate Diploma Graduate Certificate	NVQs Level 6 Certificate/Diploma BTEC Advanced Professional Diplomas/Certificates/ Awards City & Guilds Graduateship **Professional Development Award**
7	QCF Level 7 FHEQ Level M SCQF Level 11	Master's degree Postgraduate Diploma (PgDip) Postgraduate Certificate (PgCert) Integrated Degree Diploma in Translation	NVQ/SVQ Level 5 Level 7 Diploma/Fellowship Level 7 Advanced Professional Certificate BTEC Advanced Professional Diplomas/Certificates/Awards City & Guilds Membership **Professional Development Award**
8	QCF Level 8 FHEQ Level D SCQF Level 12	Doctorate	Specialist awards and diplomas from professional bodies City & Guilds Fellowship **Professional Development Award**

Job families

The jobs in this book have been divided into job families to make it easy for you to go straight to the right section and find the job you are interested in. At the beginning of each job family section is an introduction to the career sector and a list of all the jobs that will appear in the section. You will also find information on other similar job families and where to find them in the book.

There are 20 job families in *Careers 2013* which are:

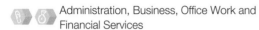 Administration, Business, Office Work and Financial Services

Building and Construction

Catering and Hospitality

Computers and IT

Design, Arts and Crafts

Education and Training

Engineering, Manufacturing and Production

Environment, Animals and Plants

Healthcare

Languages, Information and Culture

Legal and Political Services

Leisure, Sport and Tourism

Marketing, Advertising, Media, Print and Publishing

Performing Arts

Personal and Other Services including Hair and Beauty

Retail, Sales and Customer Services

Science, Mathematics and Statistics

Security, Emergency and the Armed Forces

Social Work and Counselling Services

Transport and Logistics

What do the icons mean?

The icons used in this book are the same as those used in the CRCI (Connexions Resources Centre Index) and they will appear at the beginning of each section to make it easy and clear to see exactly which job families are being covered.

Administration, Business, Office Work and Financial Services

To work in this sector you often need to have a great head for numbers and be very good at managing your time effectively. The variety of jobs in this family is huge, so you could work in a large, busy office or you could work for yourself dealing with clients from a host of different professions. Many jobs require you to have an eye for detail as you could be compiling reports and advising organisations on how they could work more effectively or safely or organising other people's time and schedules. In all cases, you should be highly motivated and organised. If you enjoy this responsibility and like the idea of the challenge of keeping a business running like clockwork there are many jobs that would suit you in this sector.

For a full list of jobs in this section turn to page 15.

Building and Construction

The jobs in this sector are very varied; some require a high level of personal fitness, while for others, a creative flair is essential. You may be interested in working on a construction site with a team of people and for this you would need to demonstrate excellent personal safety and be happy to work outside in all weathers. Alternatively, maybe your interest lies in buying and selling property or maybe working in an office is more your sort of thing. All the jobs in the sector require someone with a great eye for detail who is very good at working with others.

For a full list of jobs in this section turn to page 69.

Catering and Hospitality

Working in this sector, you will meet a wide variety of people and probably need to be a very strong team player. For some of the jobs, you need to be outgoing, confident and sociable and may end up working early mornings or late nights. For many jobs in this sector you need to be very meticulous when it comes to standards of cleanliness and tidiness. Workers in the sector thrive on providing an impeccable service and ensuring customers are completely satisfied and are given a wonderful experience whether that be in a restaurant, hotel or bar.

For a full list of jobs in this section turn to page 133.

Computers and IT

This sector is still fairly new and so it is expanding all the time, creating new jobs for a whole range of people. You may have a mathematical brain or a real creative ability – or a bit of both! Essentially, you must be passionate about computers to consider working in this sector. You could be working directly with clients and customers, helping them to rectify problems with their computers or you could be researching and developing the latest console for the games market. In all cases you need to keep right up to date with the latest technologies and IT developments as well as people's tastes, interests and hobbies to enjoy working in this sector.

For a full list of jobs in this section turn to page 149.

Design, Arts and Crafts

The idea of turning your arts and crafts hobby into a career may be one you like the thought of. Jobs in this sector can involve working in any medium, from textiles to jewellery to metalwork or children's toys. Some jobs may involve you researching current styles and trends and creating your own designs whereas others will involve working to a set brief set out by your customer to create a bespoke product. You may find yourself working for a company but many people in this industry are self-employed working for a range of clients. This means you need to be very organised and have brilliant communication skills to ensure you can give your clients exactly what they want. People working in this industry are extremely passionate about their careers and have a real sense of perfectionism to produce a beautiful finished article.

For a full list of jobs in this section turn to page 167.

Education and Training

To work in this sector you need to be motivated and enthusiastic about other people's learning, whether it's adults or children. There are jobs suitable for people with all levels of qualification, but whatever your entry level you will need to be interested in keeping up to date on the latest developments in education and will enjoy working with other people. If you choose to teach, the range of subjects available is huge so whatever your interest – languages, art, sciences, cooking, sports – you can become a teacher in that field. Jobs in this sector require a multitude of skills including: creativity, imagination, numerical skills, good communication and organisational skills and, in some cases, having a lot of patience!

For a full list of jobs in this section turn to page 189.

Engineering, Manufacturing and Production

There are a number of highly-skilled jobs available in this job family and workers need to be creative and methodical, combining brilliant technical skill with spatial awareness. Engineers are very well qualified indeed so you should be willing to study hard for good qualifications. Jobs in this sector can take you into a range of different fields, from scientific research to car production to working out at sea; there's something for anyone who has an inquisitive mind and a high level of technical capability. Another attractive element of this industry is that you can work with an enormous variety of different materials. You may be interested in food production but equally your passion could lie in working with aircraft or marine manufacture. People in these professions share the ability to concentrate for long periods of time and work meticulously on a job to finish it to a

high standard. Some will also be highly trained with specialist equipment which may sometimes be hazardous to use so a high level of personal safety awareness is vital.

For a full list of jobs in this section turn to page 209.

Environment, Animals and Plants

Some people working in this sector spend a lot of their time outdoors. This means the jobs are perfect for those of you who don't want to spend every day behind a desk in an office, although this is not to say that you will not need to spend time writing reports and keeping a log of research findings or clients' information. Workers in this sector are passionate about animals or about caring for and maintaining the environment. You will sometimes work in unpredictable settings, especially if you are working outside or have close contact with animals. You should also have brilliant people skills especially if you find yourself responsible for the welfare of someone else's animal. You should be someone who is very observant and interested in the natural world, not just from a welfare point of view but also from an economic one; many jobs in this sector involve using the environment for financial gain but increasingly industry is interested in doing so responsibly.

For a full list of jobs in this section turn to page 249.

Healthcare

If you are keen to pursue a career in healthcare you must be compassionate and enjoy either caring for people or deciding what treatment they should receive. There is such a wide variety of jobs available in this sector simply because you can specialise in absolutely any aspect of human healthcare. Maybe you're interested in working with athletes or perhaps working with children interests you more. You could be part of the rehabilitation process after an illness or injury or find yourself working as a mental health nurse. Many jobs require a lot of training and you can expect to work in some highly-pressurised and sometimes distressing situations. Workers in healthcare are extremely dedicated and enthusiastic about their careers, which rarely constitute a 9–5 job. You can expect every day to be different and you should relish the challenges working with people of all ages can bring.

For a full list of jobs in this section turn to page 287.

Languages, Information and Culture

If you are really interested in history or perhaps would like to use another language as part of your career, a job in this sector could be right for you. The jobs in this family are quite varied in terms of whether you would work with other people or by yourself. You could find yourself working in a range of different places, from museums to antiques fairs to conferences. Some of the jobs in this family are more unusual and are perfect for those of you who want a fascinating job that allows you to indulge in your passion for historic artefacts and artwork or languages and foreign countries. To excel in this sector you should have an inquisitive mind, be meticulous in your work and enjoy carrying out research. If you are keen to work with languages you should also be willing to travel in order to improve your language and your knowledge of the culture and history.

For a full list of jobs in this section turn to page 343.

Legal and Political Services

Are you interested in justice and fairness for all? Do you relish the opportunity to speak out for what's right and enjoy the challenge of persuading others that everyone needs an equal voice? Maybe you find the law a fascinating subject and you feel you would enjoy a challenging career where the rewards are a good salary and a real sense of achievement when your hard work pays off. If so, a job in this sector could be what you are looking for. Workers in this sector are fiercely passionate about their careers and have more often than not, completed a lot of training and worked hard to establish themselves in this competitive field. You need to be driven and thrive on pressure and tight deadlines; this is a sector for someone who is ambitious and very talented at working tactfully with people.

For a full list of jobs in this section turn to page 359.

Leisure, Sport and Tourism

This sector relies on a motivated, upbeat and outgoing workforce for its success. You will need to show that you can work very well with other people, providing them with an excellent service when they want to enjoy themselves on holiday or if they are keen to improve their fitness and sporting ability. If you are keen to work with professional sports players or become one yourself you should be very aware of how to keep the body fit while avoiding injury. It's also important that you can keep a level head as you will often be responsible for other people's welfare. You should be warm and friendly but also able to maintain a high level of professionalism at the same time. You should also demonstrate you have patience and tact and be clued up on health and safety regulations.

For a full list of jobs in this section turn to page 377.

Marketing, Advertising, Media, Print and Publishing

Do you consider yourself to be a great communicator? Are you interested in working in an exciting and often fast-paced environment with passionate, driven and ambitious individuals? If so, a career in this industry could be right for you. People who work in this sector are exceptionally motivated and are willing to put in long hours often on low starting wages because of their love of the job. While you need to be good at preparing your work alone, people who work in this sector tend to be very good at working with others and build up strong professional relationships as part of their job. You should have a great sense of creativity and imagination and be good at putting your ideas on paper, but you will often also need strong business acumen as many of your decisions will be made from an economical point of view as well as a creative one.

For a full list of jobs in this section turn to page 395.

Performing Arts

This job family contains a wide range of exciting jobs for those of you who want to work in theatre, music, on screen or behind the scenes. People working in this sector do so because they are passionate and creative and love the arts. Jobs can be scarce, so you will need to demonstrate that you are willing to work very hard but the rewards of being part of a fantastic production can be huge. You won't necessarily be confined to working in one place as your job may take you on tour all over the world. There are also jobs available in this sector for those of you who are more technically minded – sound and lighting engineers also play a vital role in this industry as do people who have trained in fashion and textiles. Make-up artists also play an important part in theatre, television and music production.

For a full list of jobs in this section turn to page 429.

Personal and Other Services including Hair and Beauty

This is a very wide job family and covers everything from hairdressing and beauty to cleaning to wedding consulting. You can enter this career sector with a host of different skills and qualifications. What all of the jobs have in common is that they provide a particular service that a customer has asked for so you need to be good at listening to others and giving customers exactly what they want – people in this sector have a brilliant way with people. You should also demonstrate creativity and strong practical and technical skills as many of the jobs in this family require you to use specialist equipment, and have knowledge of health and safety.

For a full list of jobs in this section turn to page 453.

Retail, Sales and Customer Services

Jobs in this sector are suited to those of you who are very good at communicating with others and are interested in making your customers happy. Maybe you're interested in working with food and want to give your customers high quality, fresh produce. Your interest may lie in fashion retail and you could spend your time providing style advice. You should also be commercially minded and think about how your work relates to the success of the company you work for. Jobs in this sector also involve maintaining standards such as safety and quality to ensure guidelines are met, so a practical outlook can be useful.

For a full list of jobs in this section turn to page 473.

Science, Mathematics and Statistics

Do you have a very mathematical brain? Are you logical in how you approach tasks? Maybe you are fascinated by scientific advances and would like to be involved in future discoveries? People who work in this sector can spend long periods of time carrying out meticulous research. You may find yourself working for a variety of employers, from the health service to a cosmetics company or even a charity. You should be willing to work on your own but also be happy to present your findings in reports to others. People in this sector are very highly skilled individuals who have often been through a lot of training, and possess a questioning and inquisitive mind.

For a full list of jobs in this section turn to page 501.

Security, Emergency and the Armed Forces

Working in this sector may give you many incredible experiences and opportunities not open to most people. You need to be an excellent team player and in some instances you may find yourself in a potentially dangerous situation. Working in this sector you can expect to spend your day absolutely anywhere! Some roles involve a lot of office work whereas others can involve spending a lot of your time on the road, or even at sea. If you're looking for a job that will be exhilarating but are able to remain calm and professional under pressure this sector could offer you a lot of opportunities.

For a full list of jobs in this section turn to page 539.

Social Work and Counselling Services

People who work in this sector are dedicated to caring and talking through people's problems and anxieties to improve their general well-being and their future prospects in life. The work requires a lot of patience, an open mind and a friendly and approachable personality. You could be helping people who are distressed and need help and guidance but equally you may be helping people who want to move on to the next stage in their careers or educational choices. Either way, you should be someone who enjoys helping people change their lives for the better. If you are interested in working in this field you need to show that you are compassionate and very good at communicating with people from all walks of life and of all ages. You should also be someone who can maintain a strong sense of professionalism as you could be in a position of trust and you must be very respectful of your clients' privacy.

For a full list of jobs in this section turn to page 567.

Transport and Logistics

The jobs in this sector are immensely varied because of the wide range of transport and communication links that exist today to keep our lives running. You could need a high level of technical knowledge in this sector especially for jobs such as pilot or train driver. But you could also be great at keeping attention to detail and maintaining schedules if logistics is more where your interest lies. Jobs in transport and logistics require very efficient and practical people to ensure that our infrastructure continues to run smoothly and safely. You may need to cope well under pressure. As you will probably have contact with the general public you should be good with people, and have a calm, professional manner.

For a full list of jobs in this section turn to page 589.

Where to go for more help

Below is a brief explanation with some contact details of the main organisations that can help you find out more about the career you are interested in.

England

Speak to the careers adviser at your school or college. Alternatively there is a wide range of information on the National Careers Service website. You can also contact a trained careers adviser by phone or text or through their website with an email or by using the webchat service. The website also has moderated chatrooms and message boards.

Tel: Freephone 0800 100 900
Text: 07766 413219
Email: use the contact form on the National Careers Service website

www.nationalcareersservice.direct.gov.uk

Northern Ireland

If you want advice from a careers adviser you can attend one of the local careers offices throughout Northern Ireland. Here you will get information on all aspects of work, education and employment issues. Careers Advisers visit schools regularly and you should speak to your careers teacher to arrange a careers interview. If you have left school you should contact your local JobCentre to make an appointment to speak to a Careers Adviser. The Careers Service NI website is also packed with information.

Tel: 028 9044 1781

www.careersserviceni.com

Scotland

Skills Development Scotland

Skills Development Scotland is available to both young people and adults looking for information about careers, education or employment options.

For more information contact: 0845 8 502 502

www.myworldofwork.co.uk
www.skillsdevelopmentscotland.co.uk

Wales

Careers Wales

Offering help to both young people and to adults, Careers Wales provides advice on any issues you have related to careers, work, education or training. Talk to your Careers Adviser in school or visit the website for more information.

Tel: Freephone 0800 100 900

www.careerswales.com

England, Wales and Northern Ireland

learndirect

If you need advice on any aspect of your careers, training or educational options try contacting learndirect. learndirect has trained advisers who can discuss your options over the phone or you can attend one of the many learndirect centres available throughout England, Wales and Northern Ireland. Their help is available to anyone of any age, although it is mainly aimed at adults.

If you want some more information or advice contact:
0800 101 901
www.learndirect.co.uk and www.learndirect-advice.co.uk

Administration, Business, Office Work and Financial Services

To work in this sector you need to have a great head for numbers and be very good at managing your time effectively. Jobs in business and finance can be fast-paced and exciting and workers in all four of these areas are highly motivated and enjoy working in an office environment.

The jobs featured in this section are listed below. For similar jobs to this job family please go to the section: *Legal and Political Services* on page 359.

- Accountant p16
- Accounting Technician and Accounts/Finance Clerk p18
- Actuary p19
- Auditor p22
- Bank Cashier/Customer Adviser p23
- Bank Manager p24
- Business Adviser p25
- Chartered/Company Secretary p26
- Civil Service Administrative Officer p27
- Civil Service Executive Officer p28
- Company Director p29
- Compliance Officer p30
- Credit Analyst p31
- Debt Collector p32
- Diplomatic Services Operational Officer p33
- Economist p34
- Education Officer p35
- Environmental Health Practitioner/Officer p36
- Equality and Diversity Officer p37
- Ergonomist p38
- Estates Officer p39
- Financial Adviser p40
- Health and Safety Adviser p41
- Human Resources/Personnel Officer p42
- Insurance Broker p43
- Insurance Risk Surveyor p46
- Insurance Underwriter p47
- Investment Analyst p48
- Legal Secretary p49
- Loss Adjuster p50
- Management Consultant p51
- Medical Receptionist p52
- Payroll Manager p53
- Pensions Administrator p54
- Pensions Adviser p55
- Personal Assistant p56
- Project Manager p57
- Quality Manager p58
- Receptionist p59
- Recruitment/Employment Agency Consultant p60
- Regeneration Manager/ Economic Development Officer p61
- Registrar of Births, Deaths, Marriages and Civil Partnerships p62
- Risk Manager p63
- Secretary p64
- Stock Market Trader p65
- Stockbroker p66
- Telephonist p67
- Training Development Officer p68

ACCOUNTANT

ENTRY LEVEL 5

Qualifications and courses

Most people start with a degree (usually 2.2 classification or higher) and then study for professional qualifications. If your degree is in accounting or a related subject you may be exempt from certain papers for some of the professional qualifications. Owing to an increase in global companies, graduates with language degrees are in high demand.

The minimum entry requirements for a degree are normally 2 A levels/3 H grades and 5 GCSEs/S grades (A*–C/1–3) including maths and English, or equivalent. An HNC/HND in accounting or a business-related subject followed by a top-up degree may be another route into the profession although bigger firms do tend to favour traditional degrees.

Although most trainee accountants are graduates, it is possible for school leavers, with a minimum of 4 GCSEs/S grades, including English and maths, to follow a vocational training route. This is normally offered by the Association of Accounting Technicians (AAT) and the Chartered Institute of Management Accountants (CIMA). There are varied exam requirements depending on the qualifications you already have.

Accountants hold a qualification from one of the recognised accountancy bodies: Association of Chartered Certified Accountants (ACCA), Institute of Chartered Accountants in England and Wales (ICAEW), Institute of Chartered Accountants of Scotland (ICAS), Institute of Chartered Accountants in Ireland (ICAI), Association of International Accountants (AIA).

The Chartered Institute of Management Accountants (CIMA) and the Institute of Financial Accountants (IFA) provide qualifications for management accountants and financial accountants working in all sectors. To become a qualified chartered management accountant (ACMA), you will have to pass the CIMA Professional Qualification and complete at least 3 years of relevant work experience. To achieve the CIMA Professional Qualification you will need to take 3 exams at Operational level, 3 exams at Management level, 3 exams at Strategic level and a 2-part Test of Professional Competence in Management Accounting, based on practical experience and a case study.

Accountants working in the public sector usually hold the Chartered Institute of Public Finance and Accountancy (CIPFA) qualification.

It is becoming increasingly difficult to secure a training contract with an employer that is approved by the institutes listed above so it is useful to gain pre-entry work experience.

What the work involves

Accountancy involves providing a company or individual with trustworthy information about their financial records.

By analysing a company or individual's finances, accountants identify ways to maximise profits. They provide professional advice on financial planning and development, tax returns and future costs and budgets.

You will keep detailed accounts, carry out internal audits and produce regular statements on whether the company's systems are efficient and cost effective.

There are 3 main areas of accounting and within each sector you can become either a certified or a chartered accountant. Chartered accountants work to a globally recognised standard and are often sponsored by their employer to achieve this qualification.

Industrial and commercial

Employed directly by a company, you will provide them with a range of services.

You will help to plan the company's development by predicting costs, benefits and risks.

You may be expected to make business decisions along with other managers.

Private practice

You will work for a specialist accountancy firm that offers services to clients.

Smaller practices usually work for local businesses. However, accountancy firms can be huge and some companies provide services to multinational corporations.

Your clients can vary from small businesses that do not employ their own in-house management accountant to large companies or wealthy individuals.

Public sector

Working for public bodies such as the NHS, universities and local authorities, you will offer advice on tax, financial problems, raising money, financial IT systems and management consultancy.

Your role will be to help provide an efficient, quality service that is within the budgets set by the government.

You will play an important part in making sure that public money is spent properly.

Type of person suited to this work

As you will be giving presentations and working with people at all levels, you will need excellent written and verbal communication skills.

Much of your work will involve dealing with confidential reports and financial information so reliability, honesty and integrity are essential attributes.

Time management and organisational skills are key as you must be able to work under pressure and meet deadlines.

As you are required to study whilst working and remain up to date with developments in the field, it is important to be self-motivated and committed to your career.

Confidence working with numbers and an interest in how businesses work is essential.

You will need problem-solving and research skills and the ability to process and analyse complicated financial information.

Working conditions

You could work in an organisation of any size and will generally be office based, spending a lot of time using IT, sitting at a desk or meeting clients. Smart dress will be required.

Depending on your role, you might have the opportunity to travel both in this country and abroad to meet clients so a driving licence could be useful.

Although you will normally work office hours from Monday to Friday, you might need to work extra hours at busy times, especially during February to April (the end of the financial year).

Flexible working is possible (once you are qualified) and there is the opportunity to set up as an independent practitioner.

Future prospects

The growing importance of information technology is having a major impact on the accountancy sector. Access to faster communication systems means that more companies are becoming global, which in turn will have an impact on the numbers required within the accountancy sector.

It is recommended that you think carefully about the area within accountancy that you would like to focus on at an early stage of your career as this may enable you to specialise in that field.

There are lots of structured routes for progression and an accountant can often become a manager after just 2 years and a senior manager 3 years after that. The next level is partner and although this is very competitive in certain firms, it is possible to acheive this 8–15 years after qualifying.

In the long term you could choose to become self-employed, offering consultancy services to clients.

There is also the opportunity to progress to general management roles within business.

Industrial and commercial
There is a high demand for trainees with opportunities throughout the country but as you would probably be working for a larger organisation, you will be based in a city. Once you are qualified and experienced you could move into highly paid senior management positions, or you could choose to move to a larger company for promotion.

Private practice
You could work for a small company, offering a personal service to local businesses and individuals or for a huge multinational firm. Job opportunities are good and there is high demand for qualified accountants.

Public sector
The public sector covers a wide range of services, including education, healthcare and social services. Government changes mean that budgets are increasingly held at local level, opening up opportunities across the country.

If you do well, you can move into high-level management jobs.

Advantages/disadvantages

Accountancy is a varied career and there are many opportunities both in this country and abroad.

You must be prepared to cope with a lot of responsibility, stress and pressure.

You will need to be committed and determined to manage training, studying and taking exams whilst you work.

Salaries in this field tend to be extremely high and progression can be quite rapid.

Money guide

Your salary will depend a lot on your level, experience and location.

The highest salaries are within London and the south-east of England; the lowest are in Northern Ireland, Scotland and the north-east of England.

Graduates usually receive higher salaries than school leavers during their training.

Industrial and commercial
Whilst you are training you could earn between £18,000 and £30,000 a year, depending on the stage you have reached in your training.

Once qualified, accountants in this sector can earn between £30,000 and £50,000.

Depending on the company's size, finance managers and directors can earn between £50,000 and £100,000.

Private practice
During their training, graduates can earn between £18,000 and £28,000 per year depending on their location.

Recently qualified graduates earn between £29,000 and £50,000.

When fully qualified, with several years' experience and perhaps a specialist area of work, salaries can reach in excess of £80,000.

Public sector
A trainee usually starts on £17,000–£25,000 per year. On completion of training you could earn between £28,000 and £50,000.

Fully qualified senior managers can earn £50,000–£150,000 per year, while directors could earn £150,000+.

Related opportunities

- Accounting Technician and Accounts/Finance Clerk p18
- Actuary p19
- Auditor p22
- Financial Adviser p40
- Insurance Broker p43

Further information

Association of Chartered Certified Accountants
www.acca.co.uk

Institute of Chartered Accountants in England and Wales
www.icaew.co.uk

Institute of Chartered Accountants of Scotland
www.icas.org.uk

Institute of Financial Accountants
www.ifa.org.uk

ACCOUNTING TECHNICIAN AND ACCOUNTS/FINANCE CLERK

Qualifications and courses

There are no formal academic requirements to train to be an accounting technician, but some GCSEs/S grades (A*–C/1–3), including English and maths, are desirable. Other useful qualifications include the Diploma in Business, Administration and Finance, A levels, BTEC Awards and HNC/HNDs in subjects such as accounting, finance and business. City & Guilds also offer Levels 1 and 2 in Book-keeping and Accounts.

The Association of Accounting Technicians (AAT) and the Association of Chartered Certified Accountants (ACCA) award accounting technician qualifications, which are usually studied part time at college or work. These are available at 3 NVQ/SVQ stages: Level 2 (Foundation), 3 (Intermediate) and 4 (Technician). You might be exempt from some levels if you have relevant qualifications or experience.

The AAT also offers a diploma for those who are unable to find a work placement whilst they study. This has 3 stages: Certificate in Accounting (Foundation), Advanced Certificate in Accounting (Intermediate) and Diploma in Accounting (Technician). Technician status is awarded on completion of all 3 components.

Alternatively, the Certified Accounting Technician (CAT) qualification, awarded by the ACCA, combines a year's practical experience with exams at 3 levels.

What the work involves

Accounting technicians are responsible for financial issues including company expenditure, tax returns and payroll. Your work will include collecting and analysing information, keeping records and writing reports.

In a large firm, you will probably work as part of a team and support qualified accountants. In a smaller company, you might cover a wider range of tasks and be responsible for most of the finances.

Once you are qualified you could specialise in a specific financial area, for example insolvency or tax analysis.

Type of person suited to this work

You will need to be confident with numbers, and have the ability to gather, analyse and record information accurately when under pressure from deadlines. Good ICT skills are also important, as most of the work is computer based.

Good verbal and written communication skills are essential, as you will often have to explain complicated financial issues to clients in a clear manner.

You must be willing and committed to further study in order to pass your technician exams. You will be expected to continue learning throughout your career, as it is important for accounting technicians to keep up to date with changes in financial law.

Working conditions

You will normally work standard office hours from Monday to Friday, however at busy times you might need to put in extra hours over evenings or weekends.

Most work will be office based, although you may also travel to meetings with clients within your working day so a driving licence could be useful.

Future prospects

Although the finance industry employs a lot of people, the majority do not hold many professional qualifications. This means there is a skills shortage within the sector, so the higher the qualifications you gain the better your career prospects.

Prospects for promotion are good, and working in a smaller company may also give you the opportunity to take on more responsibility and work at a more senior level earlier in your career. Alternatively, you could choose to become self-employed, or train as a chartered accountant.

Advantages/disadvantages

You will usually be working in a team environment, which means that you will build strong relationships.

The work can be slightly monotonous.

Money guide

As a trainee accounting technician you can expect to earn between £12,000 and £22,000 per year.

When fully qualified, earnings range from £14,000 to £32,000.

Once you have gained experience and progressed to a management level, or if you are successfully self-employed, you could earn up to £49,000.

Salaries tend to be higher in southern England, particularly in London.

Related opportunities

- Accountant p16
- Bank Cashier/Customer Adviser p23
- Pensions Administrator p54

Further information

Association of Accounting Technicians
www.aat.org.uk

Association of Chartered Certified Accountants
www.acca.co.uk

ACTUARY

Qualifications and courses

Most employers prefer candidates to have achieved a 2.1 classification or higher, preferably in maths or a related subject, such as statistics or economics. Some entrants have a postgraduate qualification in actuarial science or a professional qualification from the Institute of Actuaries (England and Wales) or the Faculty of Actuaries (Scotland).

Normal entry requirements for a degree course are 2 A levels/3 H grades and 5 GCSEs/S grades (A*–C/1–3), or equivalent. For a degree in maths, this will include an A level/H grade in the subject.

To qualify as an actuary you need to enrol as a student member of the Faculty and Institute of Actuaries while working and studying for professional exams at the same time. A trainee post usually lasts 3 to 6 years.

Trainees with a degree or diploma in actuarial science/ studies may be exempt from some elements of the training. Other degree disciplines may provide exemption from certain exam papers.

What the work involves

Actuaries calculate financial risk. Using statistics and knowledge of investments, law, business and economics, they make financial predictions to help design products such as insurance and pensions.

As an actuary you would help set insurance prices based on statistics, probability and risk. You would also use your knowledge to help companies make long-term financial decisions.

You might work in insurance, life assurance, pensions, investments or for the government.

Type of person suited to this work

You must be good with numbers and enjoy solving complicated mathematical problems. You should also be analytical, able to think logically, and be skilled at problem-solving.

You will need to have excellent communication skills as you must explain complicated financial issues in a clear and understandable way to clients.

Actuaries must pay close attention to detail and work to deadlines. You must keep up to date with new developments, such as the laws governing the industry. You will be expected to dress formally and have excellent ICT skills.

Working conditions

Most actuaries work within life assurance companies and numbers in general insurance are increasing rapidly. Although the profession is growing, entry is competitive and you will most likely need relevant work experience. Jobs are available throughout the country but most are based in Edinburgh, London and the south-east of England.

As a trainee you will have to study in your own time but once you are qualified you could work abroad and might be able to work part time.

Future prospects

As a fully qualified actuary you can work within a specialism or in a consultancy, or you could travel as your qualifications will be recognised all over the world. Within larger companies there are opportunities for promotion to very senior positions.

Advantages/disadvantages

Training after university takes up to 6 years and involves studying while working full time.

Actuaries have good long-term career prospects and opportunities for promotion.

UK qualifications are recognised everywhere so you have the option to work abroad.

Money guide

As a graduate trainee you can expect a salary between £25,000 and £35,000 per year.

Salaries for newly qualified actuaries range from £40,000 to £55,000.

Senior staff typically earn in excess of £100,000.

Salaries vary based on location and specialism, and are likely to be higher in London and the south-east of England.

Related opportunities

- Financial Adviser p40
- Risk Manager p63
- Stockbroker p66

Further information

Association for Consulting Actuaries
www.aca.org.uk

Institute and Faculty of Actuaries
www.actuaries.org.uk

Actuarial careers

THE ACTUARIAL PROFESSION

Who are actuaries?

Actuaries use their knowledge of mathematics, statistics, economics and business to assess financial risks and probabilities. Traditionally their work is concerned with finance and investment, risk management, general insurance, life insurance, pensions and healthcare.

They create statistical and mathematical models to analyse past events and predict the financial outcome of different situations; especially when the amount of a future payment or the timing of when it will be paid is uncertain.

What do actuaries do?

The work that actuaries do is very diverse due to the nature of the role and the huge variety of practise areas that they work in. In insurance they may look at what brand of car you drive, and the likelihood of you having an accident to ensure that there are sufficient funds to cover liabilities but still make a profit for the insurance company. In consultancy, actuaries provide specialist services to business of every kind. They advise on business recovery, acquisitions and employee benefit schemes. Central government also has its own actuarial department, which provides actuarial support and information across government, its agencies and the NHS. Actuaries are also key in the area of enterprise risk management helping to identify and calculate risks to ensure businesses make well-informed strategic decisions. Actuaries are also employed in the marketing and development of financial products.

How do you become an actuary?

To qualify as an actuary you must become a student member of the Actuarial Profession; it will take around 3–6 years. Most employers will look for a Maths A level at grade A or B and a degree at 2:1 level. If you have a degree or postgraduate qualification in actuarial science, statistics or economics, you may be exempt from some of the exams. Most employers will give you a day off in the week to study and work with you to meet the work-based skills requirement.

What skills do I need?

You must have excellent maths and statistical skills and be able to understand and explain complex information. You should have a thorough understanding of business and economics, be a good communicator, and work well within a team. The roles of actuaries are diverse so your skill set will depend on the company and role you apply for.

How much should I expect to earn?

This is a highly rewarding career path with trainee actuaries earning between £25,000 and £30,000. Newly qualified actuaries can earn up to £45,000. As you then move up the career path you can earn well over £120,000 as a senior practice director.

Where can I find out more?

If you want to find out more about becoming an actuary, visit the Actuarial Profession's website at www.actuaries. org.uk/becoming-actuary/pages/becoming-actuary. You'll find profiles of actuaries and details of actuarial employers offering placements and graduate opportunities. Visit our Facebook page to engage with current student actuaries to discuss your future as an actuary.

Case study

THE ACTUARIAL PROFESSION

Name: Graham Jones

University: Strathclyde University

Degree: BSc Honours in Mathematics, Statistics and Finance.

Role: Actuarial Trainee

Office: Glasgow

Employer: Hymans Robertson

I have been employed with Hymans Robertson as an actuarial trainee since September 2010. I was offered this position after a successful 3 month internship following my penultimate year at university.

The internship was a very positive experience. The employees were very welcoming and always willing to explain and assist me with anything I was unsure of, allowing me to settle in and focus on the challenging work I was presented with. The internship is an excellent opportunity to understand the career you are interested in and help you decide if this is the correct route for you.

No two days are the same working at Hymans Robertson and this makes work both interesting and stimulating. In the short time since I started, I have been involved in numerous projects such as valuations, producing accounting disclosures and carrying out transfer value calculations. The support I received from my colleagues has given me an understanding of the key concepts that are essential when working in this role.

It is my intention to undertake my actuarial exams whilst getting involved in as many areas of the business as I can. Gaining exposure to varying areas of work, members of the team and clients will be beneficial as it will allow me to strengthen and build on the core knowledge I have gained so far within pensions. Working with different people will also enhance my development not only in the technical side but at a professional level too.

As I was offered my present position following my summer internship, the interview process was slightly different. The interview was much shorter and included a meeting with a senior actuarial consultant and a member of HR. I was asked a range of questions based on my experiences from university and my views on current issues in pensions. It is important to have an understanding of the changes pensions have gone through recently and what is currently happening in the area, as well as examples of when you have worked in a team, shown leadership qualities and other basic competencies.

Finding a work life/study balance has proved quite challenging especially when exams are imminent! My working hours are generally 9am–5pm, with one day off a week for studying. It is important to keep up with your studying even when exams are not just around the corner. Managing your time well and putting together a study plan is extremely helpful.

Initially, I found it quite challenging adapting to the work environment. Things which I now take for granted seemed daunting at first. For example, sending a simple internal email was something I was unsure of at first, but I soon realised that I just had to ask and everyone was happy to help. Not being afraid to ask questions is definitely the key to progressing when you first start.

AUDITOR

Qualifications and courses

In order to become an auditor, you will need to obtain a professional accountancy qualification and most entrants to this profession are graduates.

A chartered accountancy qualification with either the Chartered Institute of Public Finance and Accountancy (CIPFA), the Association of Chartered Certified Accountants (ACCA), the Institute of Chartered Accountants in England and Wales (ICAEW), the Institute of Chartered Accountants of Scotland (ICAS), the Institute of Chartered Accountants in Ireland (ICAI), the Association of International Accountants (AIA) or the Chartered Institute of Management Accountants (CIMA) is required to work in either private or public sector auditing.

External auditors join a company as a graduate and study for a professional qualification with one of the above accountancy bodies. A degree in maths, accountancy or economics may be useful.

Candidates keen to work in internal auditing can come from a variety of academic backgrounds. Prior experience in finance or business is an advantage. The Diploma in Internal Audit Practice is offered by the Chartered Institute of Internal Auditors; entry is either with a degree or recommendation by an employer.

Alternatively, the National Audit Office has a 5 year programme for school leavers who achieve 300 UCAS points at A level. During the scheme, trainees study for professional accountancy qualifications whilst working.

What the work involves

You will be a fully qualified accountant specialising in audit work, exploring all aspects of a business, talking to staff and ensuring that the paperwork and accounts give a true picture of the company's finances.

Internal auditors work for a company preparing their accounts for external auditors to check. They are also responsible for assessing other risks, not just finances. All businesses and government departments must be externally audited by law.

As an external auditor you will create an independent report for a company, stating that the accounts are true and accurate and recommending possible improvements to the business.

Type of person suited to this work

You must be happy working with numbers and interpreting statistics and be a thorough and methodical person.

As you will be using your skills and experience to solve financial problems you need to enjoy researching all aspects of a business.

It is important that you have excellent communication skills so that you can present your findings clearly, both verbally and in writing. You should also be able to work effectively as part of

a team and with the company you are auditing. You should be well organised, able to work under pressure, meet deadlines and have excellent ICT skills.

Working conditions

Large companies have internal auditors who prepare their accounts for inspection. External auditors are based temporarily in the firms they are auditing, so they may have to travel and stay away from home. A driving licence can be useful.

You will work normal office hours but might have to work evenings and weekends.

Future prospects

There is an increasing demand for qualified auditors. As an internal auditor you could work for a business or government department, work for yourself or as a consultant.

External auditors are employed by accountancy firms, the National Audit Office (the Accounts Commission in Scotland) auditing central government departments, or the Audit Commission working with public sector organisations such as local authorities or the NHS.

Advantages/disadvantages

Accountancy training takes 3–5 years and involves studying in your own time.

You will usually need work experience to support an application.

There are opportunities to work abroad during a secondment.

Money guide

Trainees on the National Audit Office's school leaver scheme earn £22,274 per year.

Graduates can expect a salary of £15,000–£25,000 during training.

This could rise to £30,000–£45,000 a year when you are qualified.

A senior audit manager can earn between £50,000 and £100,000.

Salaries can be up to 20% higher in London.

Related opportunities

- Actuary p19
- Chartered/Company Secretary p26
- Financial Adviser p40

Further information

Association of Chartered Certified Accountants
www.acca.co.uk

Chartered Institute of Management Accountants
www.cimaglobal.com

Institute of Internal Auditors
www.iia.org.uk

BANK CASHIER/CUSTOMER ADVISER

ENTRY LEVEL 2

ADMINISTRATION, BUSINESS, OFFICE WORK AND FINANCIAL SERVICES

CRCI: IE

Qualifications and courses

You need a minimum of 4 GCSEs/S grades (A*–C/1–3) including English and maths, or equivalent qualifications.

Other useful qualifications include City & Guilds' Awards in Customer Service (Levels 1, 2 and 3), City & Guilds' Certificate/Diploma in Business and Administration (Levels 2 and 3), the IFS Certificate/Diploma in Financial Studies (Level 3), a BTEC Nationals in Business or Personal and Business Finance, and the CCN Professional Bankers qualifications (Level 3).

Most banks offer a variety of trainee programmes for A level or graduate entrants. You will usually need either 2 A levels/3 H grades or a minimum 2.1 degree in any subject. Competition for places is intense, so relevant work experience in finance, sales or marketing could be helpful.

You can also enter this career by completing an Apprenticeship in Providing Financial Services.

What the work involves

Bank cashiers/customer advisers work for banks and building societies, and are the first point of contact for customers with enquiries or complaints.

You may be working in a branch dealing with customers face to face, or you could be based in a contact centre liaising with them over the phone or by email.

You will be handling customers' accounts, including the paying in and withdrawing of money using computerised systems. You will also be expected to sell the company's products and services, which will involve working to set sales targets.

Type of person suited to this work

You will need excellent customer service skills so that you can process their requests efficiently, and also gain their trust in order to advise them on a range of financial products.

You must be confident working with figures and ICT, and working to targets. As you will be handling money, you should be trustworthy and able to work accurately, paying close attention to detail.

Since you will be working as part of a team, a helpful and positive attitude coupled with the ability to use your own initiative is valuable.

Working conditions

In a branch you will probably work normal office hours, and Saturdays if the bank is open. Call centres usually offer a 24 hour service, so you should expect to work shifts that include nights and weekends.

Part-time and flexible working hours are commonly available.

You should be well presented, and will usually be required to wear a uniform.

Future prospects

Despite the recent economic downturn which has affected some areas of the financial sector, there are still opportunities in retail banking available, especially at entry level.

You could specialise in an area such as mortgages or pensions, or gain further professional qualifications in order to train as a financial adviser or bank manager.

Advantages/disadvantages

Looking after customers and helping to solve their queries can be interesting and rewarding.

Banks offer well-structured training programmes on entry and you will have a clear route for career progression.

Owing to the economic downturn, entry into this profession is more competitive than ever before.

Money guide

The starting salary for a trainee ranges between £8,750 and £10,500, rising up to a possible £16,000 once qualified.

With several years' experience you could be earning up to £24,000.

Senior customer advisers, especially those who have specialised in a certain financial area, can earn £30,000+.

You may receive bonuses for meeting sales targets and most employers offer packages that include cheaper mortgages, pensions, loans and insurance.

Related opportunities

- Bank Manager p24
- Financial Adviser p40
- Pensions Adviser p55

Further information

Financial Services Skills Council
www.fssc.org.uk

IFS School of Finance
www.ifslearning.ac.uk

23

BANK MANAGER

Qualifications and courses

Entrants typically hold a degree or equivalent qualification. Most employers offering graduate management training schemes require candidates to have at least a 2.1 classification. Relevant subjects such as maths, business studies, economics or accountancy may be an advantage but employers often welcome applicants from a range of degree disciplines. It is advisable to study a foreign language if you wish to apply to an international bank.

Training schemes usually last 18–24 months. For degree entry you will need at least 2 A levels/H grades and 5 GCSEs/S grades.

School leavers with GCSEs/S grades (A*–C/1–3) have the option to start work in a bank in a service role and then progress to management by studying for professional qualifications. The IFS School of Finance Certificate in Personal Finance (Level 2), Certificate/Diploma in Financial Studies (Level 3) or the Professional Banker Certificate/Diploma offered by the Chartered Institute of Bankers in Scotland (CIOBS) may all be useful.

What the work involves

Bank managers are responsible for running branches of retail, commercial or corporate banks. You will be accountable for staff recruitment, motivation and training, as well as meeting budget and sales targets for products and services.

You will be required to keep up to date with a range of financial products, and market your services to individuals and businesses.

Attending meetings and preparing reports on branch operations for both staff and head office will also be important tasks.

Type of person suited to this work

Bank managers work with people at all levels, so excellent verbal and written communications skills are essential.

You will be expected to deal with customers on a daily basis, as well as leading and motivating your team, both of which require confidence, organisation, negotiation skills, initiative and the ability to think on your feet.

You should be comfortable working with numbers as you will have to meet budget and sales targets, and calculate profits.

Working conditions

You will usually work normal office hours and occasional Saturdays, in keeping with the opening hours of your bank. If you manage a call centre, you will probably be required to work shifts in order to provide a 24 hour service to customers.

As well as working in an office, you will occasionally travel to visit clients at their business premises, so a driving licence could be useful.

Future prospects

Despite recent bank mergers, the number of management positions has stayed quite stable. As a branch manager, you could progress to become a regional manager, or use your skills and experience to work in the company's head office. You could also specialise in areas such as training, human resources or marketing.

London is one of the leading financial centres of the world and offers the best opportunities for pursing a high-level career. There are also numerous roles located overseas.

Advantages/disadvantages

This challenging, fast-moving industry offers roles in various sectors such as telephone and internet banking.

Most towns have bank branches so there are opportunities to work throughout the UK.

Within investment and merchant banking you can earn extremely high salaries.

You will need to meet challenging targets in an increasingly competitive market which is sensitive to changes in the national and global economy.

Money guide

Graduates on bank management training schemes can expect to make £19,500–£28,000.

With qualifications and experience this increases to £26,000–£50,000.

Senior staff, such as area managers, can earn salaries of up to £100,000. Merchant and investment bankers can earn higher salaries still.

You may get bonuses for meeting targets. Additional benefits usually include cheaper mortgages, pensions, loans and insurance.

Related opportunities

- Accountant p16
- Bank Cashier/Customer Adviser p23
- Financial Adviser p40
- Insurance Broker p43

Further information

Chartered Institute of Bankers in Scotland
www.charteredbanker.com

IFS School of Finance
www.ifslearning.ac.uk

BUSINESS ADVISER

Qualifications and courses

There are no specific entry qualifications but advisers must have a proven track record in business. Many advisers have prior experience running a business or working as a management consultant. Others have expertise in a key area of business, such as project management, marketing, human resources or finance.

You may want to start off with GSCEs/S grades and A levels/H grades in applied business or business studies before gaining practical experience in the industry. Business-related degree courses and diplomas that include a year in industry are recommended.

The Institute of Consulting (IC) provides various entry level qualifications: a Certificate in Management Consulting Essentials, a Certificate/Diploma in Business Support and a Diploma in Management Consultancy. IC also offers higher level qualifications such as Certified Management Consultant (CMC) and Certified Business Advisor (CBA).

Bodies such as IC, Technology Means Business and the Small Firms Enterprise Development Initiative (SFEDI) have begun regulating and accrediting business advisers. You will be required to purchase professional indemnity insurance before offering your services.

What the work involves

Business advisers provide independent advice to an array of small and medium-sized businesses or enterprises in order to improve their success.

You will provide advice on prospective business plans and recommend relevant specialist services and suppliers that could support the venture. You may run workshops and seminars that offer basic support and information for new or existing businesses.

You will need to be informed about numerous areas of business but you will often choose to specialise in a specific area, such as marketing and public relations (PR), accountancy and taxation or law.

Type of person suited to this work

You will need to have a good understanding of a variety of business environments and sizes. You must be able to use your knowledge to offer advice on current business issues, geographical trends and financial help available to support new or failing businesses.

You need to be logical and objective, yet approachable and enthusiastic. You will need the ability to manage a variety of projects whilst consistently meeting tight deadlines.

Working conditions

Hours tend to follow the national average of between 37 and 40 hours a week, working 9am–5.30pm, Monday to Friday. Occasionally you might be required to attend weekend or evening events.

You will be mostly office based, with occasional visits to clients' premises, suppliers or networking events. If you became a self-employed consultant then you would have the opportunity to work from home.

Future prospects

With approximately 12,000 business advisers in the UK, this is a thriving industry with nationwide opportunities. Vacancies are posted on enterprise and business support organisations' websites and on the IC database.

It is important to gain accreditation, such as the IC's internationally recognised CMC and CBA qualifications, which you can apply for after gaining 3 years' practical experience. Business advisers are then eligible to join the national register for business support professionals.

Advantages/disadvantages

Employment as a business adviser enables you to work autonomously and use your initiative.

You will work on a variety of projects and have the opportunity to build relationships with a range of people.

It is necessary to have a wealth of business experience before you can become a business adviser.

It is important to gain recognised awards, such as those offered by the Institute of Consulting, in order to prove to clients that you are a certified adviser.

Money guide

Business advisers can expect to earn £20,000 a year.

After several years' experience salaries increase to around £35,000.

Those in senior positions can achieve £60,000.

Related opportunities

- Company Director p29
- Management Consultant p51
- Project Manager p57

Further information

Institute of Consulting
www.iconsulting.org.uk

National Enterprise Network
www.nationalenterprisenetwork.org

CHARTERED/COMPANY SECRETARY

Qualifications and courses

You will need a degree, Foundation degree, HNC/HND or equivalent to enter and train in this career. At least 1 A level/2 H grades or equivalent are required for entry onto an HNC/HND course, while degree courses require 2 A levels/3 H grades and 5 GCSEs/S grades (A*–C/1–3) or equivalent.

This sector is open to all graduates but entrants with degrees in law, business/management or accountancy/finance may be preferred. For those pursuing the HNC/HND route, a business, legal or political subject may be beneficial.

You will need to become a member of the Institute of Chartered Secretaries and Administrators (ICSA) by passing the Chartered Secretaries Qualifying Scheme. This has 2 levels, each with 4 modules, some of which you may be exempt from depending on your existing qualifications.

To become an Associate member of the ICSA, you will need at least 3 years' work experience (6 if you have not got a degree). You are eligible to become a Fellow of the Institute when you reach a senior level and have 8 years' work experience.

ICSA offer courses for extra qualifications which can be done full or part time depending on your job and responsibilities.

What the work involves

This is a vital administrative and managerial role. You will have a high level of responsibility. You will be in a very senior position advising executives and directors on finance and company law.

You will be responsible for the legal reports all companies are required to keep, reporting to Companies House and other institutions such as the Stock Exchange.

You will be responsible for running board meetings and could be responsible for financial planning, accounts, wages, human resources and all administrative and ICT systems.

Type of person suited to this work

You will need excellent communication skills to be able to work with people at all levels. You should be interested in business and have a thorough knowledge of how your organisation works. You will need to understand complicated legal and financial issues and be able to use your knowledge to solve problems, maximise efficiency and advise ways of improving and developing the company.

You should be highly organised, able to deal with several tasks at once and pay close attention to detail. You will analyse figures and accounts and work to strict legal guidelines. You must be confident giving presentations to high-level staff.

Working conditions

Most of your work will be office based, attending lots of meetings, including working at other sites and outside organisations, which could involve some travel and possibly going abroad.

You will normally work office hours but will have a heavy workload and a lot of responsibility; you will need commitment and dedication to work overtime and meet deadlines.

To be successful, a high level of personal and professional integrity is important.

Future prospects

The Companies Act 2008 means that private companies are no longer legally required to have a company or chartered secretary. Despite this change, businesses will still have to meet a range of legal requirements so most will continue to employ a company secretary.

An experienced company secretary will have opportunities to work in highly paid jobs in a range of organisations, and you could go on to specialise or could become a self-employed consultant.

Advantages/disadvantages

This is a high-level career which is interesting, varied and challenging. You will use a wide range of skills and knowledge, prospects are good and earnings can be high. But you will have to take on a lot of responsibility and work long hours; you might have to prepare information for directors if the company is doing badly.

Money guide

Graduates starting out as a company secretarial assistant earn between £28,000 and £42,000 per year.

Once fully qualified, a chartered secretary working in the private sector can achieve a salary of £55,000+.

Experienced secretaries working for FTSE 100 companies have an average wage of £193,105.

Related opportunities

- Accountant p16
- Barrister/Advocate p361
- Company Director p29

Further information

Companies House
www.companieshouse.gov.uk

Council for Administration
www.cfa.uk.com

Institute of Chartered Secretaries and Administrators
www.icsa.org.uk

CIVIL SERVICE ADMINISTRATIVE OFFICER

Qualifications and courses

Each department within the civil service organises its own recruitment and sets its own entry requirements. Some departments do not require specific qualifications and instead it is necessary for applicants to take aptitude tests in areas such as teamwork, communication skills or numeracy.

School leavers with Level 2 qualifications can go straight into the civil service, although they will usually begin by working as an office junior and train on the job to become an administrator. 5 GCSEs/S grades (A*–C/1–3) are normally required, including English and maths. Equivalent qualifications such as an NVQ/SVQ Level 1 or 2 in Administration are accepted.

Many entrants have a degree or an HNC/HND. Degrees in related subjects such as business and management, legal studies, social administration, social policy or politics may be an advantage.

To work for the civil service you will need to be a British national, a Commonwealth citizen or have dual nationality (with one nationality being British).

A Civil Service Fast Stream scheme is open to all graduates, which allows a more focused and rapid career progression from administrative to management level.

What the work involves

Administrators deal with paperwork including filing, photocopying and faxing, and also store and update information on computer systems.

Civil service administrators work for specific national government departments, such as planning or environmental, or the central administrative, policy and support services. If you work in local government, you are more likely to work across a range of areas such as leisure, environment and public health.

There are also some opportunities in departments such as human resources, neighbourhood renewal, social justice and European and international relations.

Type of person suited to this work

You will need excellent organisational skills as you will be responsible for administering numerous important projects at a time. The ability to use your initiative, prioritise your workload, and work on your own are also essential.

A high level of accuracy and attention to detail is required in order to keep good records and produce clear correspondence.

Since you will be liaising with team members and the public daily, excellent verbal and written communication skills are vital. You will also need to have an understanding of some specialist terminology.

Working conditions

You will probably work normal office hours, and offices may operate a flexitime policy. There are also opportunities for part-time work.

Future prospects

Although job opportunities may be affected by recent budget cuts to local government authorities, the civil service has an established training and development programme, and is keen to reward hard work and effort with promotion or pay rises in keeping with their grading system.

Local government administrators can continue working upward to a senior administrative level, or diversify into a different career. For example, if you became interested in housing policy, you could undertake appropriate training to become a housing officer or similar.

Advantages/disadvantages

Public sector work offers good holidays, flexible working hours and excellent perks.

Even without advanced qualifications there are opportunities to progress into higher level jobs.

In the initial stages of employment and training, work can be repetitive.

Money guide

Administrative assistants begin their career with an annual salary of around £12,000.

Administrative officers can expect to receive £14,500 a year.

Salaries increase to £16,000–£20,000 with experience.

Graduates on the Civil Service Fast Stream scheme receive a starting salary between £25,000 and £27,000.

After 4 to 5 years' experience, graduates may earn up to £45,000 after promotion.

Increases in pay are based upon performance.

Related opportunities

- Personal Assistant p56
- Project Manager p57
- Secretary p64

Further information

Civil Service Fast Stream
www.faststream.gov.uk

Local Government Association
www.lga.gov.uk

CIVIL SERVICE EXECUTIVE OFFICER

Qualifications and courses

Entry requirements vary between the different civil service departments. Some departments require 2 A levels (or equivalent) while others do not ask for formal qualifications.

Prospective employees will be invited to attend an interview and may be required to complete a range of tests designed to highlight ability in numeracy, writing, communication and interpersonal skills, along with decision-making and analytical skills.

Candidates who hold a 1st or 2nd class Honours degree can apply for the 4 year Fast Stream scheme which will lead to senior management positions. Applicants from all degree disciplines will be considered although some departments may prefer subjects relevant to their work.

Entrants may be recruited directly at executive level or can work their way up from the administrative grade.

What the work involves

Civil servants work for one of the many departments and agencies that provide services directly to the public and the government, such as industry and agriculture or benefits and pensions.

A civil service executive officer is the equivalent of a junior manager, with specific activities including the managing of a small team, helping with staff training, advising members of the public and investigating those that are believed to be breaking the law.

Type of person suited to this work

You should have a neutral interest in governmental affairs, and enjoy providing a service to members of the public. You will need to understand government legislation, and to be able to explain it clearly to others.

You must be able to work both independently and as part of a team, as much of the work requires liaising with different departments. Those wishing to become executive officers should have excellent management, leadership and communication skills.

Much of the information that you will be coming into contact with is of a confidential nature and so you must be appreciative of privacy rules.

Working conditions

Civil servants usually work between 35 and 37 hours a week, Monday to Friday, although hours may increase during busier periods. There are flexitime schemes in place for all government employees, which allow staff to work overtime to gain extra holiday time. Currently, 20% of employees work part time and job share is also widely available.

These positions are office based, but it is occasionally necessary for executive officers to visit members of the public or organisations.

There tends to be a relaxed office environment that aims to support employees and reduce stress. There are opportunities for career breaks or secondment, which allow employees to gain experience in a different department and 25 days' holiday are usually available.

Future prospects

The civil service offers a clearly defined promotion structure, with experienced executive officers being able to apply for senior posts after a period of working in their contracted position. Promotion is often awarded after 3–5 years when employees join the civil service through the Fast Stream entry plan.

If an executive officer has at least 2 years of experience and was not employed through the Fast Stream service, they are eligible to be nominated as an applicant to the In-service Fast Stream system.

Advantages/disadvantages

There are various promotion opportunities on offer, alongside rewarding salaries and the opportunity to help members of the public.

Limited budgets sometimes mean an increased workload when colleagues go on leave or progress to other positions and funds are not available for their replacement.

Money guide

Starting salaries are between £21,000 and £24,000 a year.

Those on the Civil Service Fast Stream scheme will commence their career with a salary of £25,000–£27,000.

Higher salaries are available in London.

All employees of the civil service receive a variety of benefits, such as a pension scheme and discounts on sports and social facilities.

Related opportunities

- Civil Service Administrative Officer p27
- Diplomatic Services Operational Officer p33
- Project Manager p57
- Quality Manager p58

Further information

Civil Service Fast Stream
www.faststream.gov.uk

Government Skills
www.government-skills.gov.uk

National School of Government
www.nationalschool.gov.uk

COMPANY DIRECTOR

Qualifications and courses

There is no set route to becoming a company director but you will usually need experience at senior management level. You could enter the company at any level and then, as you gain qualifications and work experience, you can progress up to management roles and eventually become company director.

Entrants often have a degree, either in a business-related subject, or a specialist subject relevant to the company's business area. After completing a degree or Level 3 qualifications, candidates could start on a management trainee scheme.

The Institute of Directors (IOD) and the Chartered Management Institute (CMI) offer courses for the professional development of managers. CMI offer both Apprenticeships and higher level qualifications. The Accelerated Certificate in Company Direction is one of the many courses available at the IOD.

Once you have got management experience you could take a Master's of Business Administration (MBA).

You may be able to do NVQs/SVQs in Management at Levels 3 and 4 on a management training scheme. Level 5 NVQs/SVQs are available in specialist areas.

What the work involves

As company director you will have responsibility for every aspect of your business. You will be responsible for setting the company's aims and polices and ensuring that it achieves these as efficiently as possible.

You might own the company or head a board of directors. In a large company you will probably lead a team of managers who specialise in specific areas such as sales, finance or product development but you will have overall responsibility.

Type of person suited to this work

The ability to analyse problems, find solutions, make decisions and think through their long-term effects is vital. You will need excellent communication skills to motivate staff and help sell your ideas, products and services to your customers and investors.

You should be highly motivated and prepared to work long hours. You must be able to prioritise, work to deadlines, supervise others, take advice and respond to change.

An excellent knowledge and understanding of your business and its markets will be necessary to make your company successful.

Although you will probably be advised by a team of experienced and knowledgeable managers, you will make the final decision and must be prepared to take risks and accept consequences.

Working conditions

You will probably be office based but will attend a lot of meetings with customers, financial and legal advisers, and staff. You should be prepared to work long hours and to travel in the UK and abroad.

Future prospects

Once you are at manager level, you can take professional courses to develop your skills and become a member of the Institute of Directors. IOD members may become qualified as Chartered Directors. There is the opportunity for progression to chief executive and then chair of an organisation. You could also become a part-time non-executive director for other organisations.

If you are successful, there is no limit to what you can achieve.

Advantages/disadvantages

You can get enormous rewards and satisfaction from seeing the company grow and succeed.

You could start your own business based on a personal interest or skill.

You will have huge responsibility and need to be dedicated, hard working and able to cope with failure as well as success.

Money guide

Earnings will vary enormously depending on the size and success of the business.

A trainee manager starts on about £20,000 a year.

With 1–2 years' experience, salaries can rise to around £40,000+.

Directors of large private companies can earn between £50,000 and £1.5 million plus huge bonuses.

As the owner of your own successful company you could become extremely rich.

Salaries tend to be higher in London.

Related opportunities

- Accountant p16
- Financial Adviser p40
- Management Consultant p51

Further information

Chartered Management Institute
www.managers.org.uk

Institute of Directors
www.iod.com

COMPLIANCE OFFICER

Qualifications and courses

While there are no set qualifications for this profession, most employers prefer candidates with a relevant degree in accountancy, auditing or law. Professional qualifications in investments, insurance or banking are also useful. Entry requirements for financial degree programmes vary but are usually a minimum of 2 A levels/3 H grades and 5 GCSEs/S grades (A*–C/1–3) including maths and English.

Many employers offer in-house training programmes. Trainees will work under the supervision of an experienced colleague, whilst gaining qualifications through part-time study, including distance learning.

Should you wish to train before entering the workplace, there are a number of professional bodies that offer relevant qualifications. Recommended courses include the Certificate/Diploma/Advanced Diploma in Financial Planning offered by the Chartered Insurance Institute or the IFS School of Finance's CeFA, CertRCC or DipFA.

Several compliance qualifications are also available through the International Compliance Association (ICA). These vary from short introductory courses to a bachelor's degree in management with compliance.

What the work involves

Compliance officers work for financial services organisations, and are responsible for aiding senior management in ensuring that their firm is complying with the rules set by the Financial Services Authority (FSA).

Alongside this you will investigate complaints from clients that relate to possible breaches of these rules.

You will explore the ways in which business efficiency can be improved within the FSA rules through the monitoring of sales processes, checking of paperwork and telephone recordings.

Type of person suited to this work

You will need to have an enquiring, analytical mind, enjoy analysing information and be interested in the legal aspects of selling financial products.

It is important that you are an easily approachable person with good communication skills and excellent report writing skills.

The job may be quite demanding and so you should be able to work well under pressure and be capable of working on a variety of projects at one time, whilst remaining organised and informed.

Working conditions

Compliance officers are generally office based, with attendance at meetings being a regular occurrence. They might have to travel around the country, or even overseas for an international company.

Generally, a compliance officer will work in the region of 37 hours a week, 9am to 5pm, Monday to Friday. However, changes to FSA policy may mean that extra hours need to be worked in order to implement changes.

Future prospects

Competition for FSA training posts is high, however you will be entering one of the fastest growing areas in financial services. There are around 9,000 compliance officers in the UK and many other positions involved with compliance, which highlights that the future is alive with prospects.

As you progress within this role you will have the opportunity to experience greater levels of responsibility and roles within management.

Advantages/disadvantages

There are chances for progression within this vocation and opportunities to work from home as a consultant.

You may feel under pressure at times and will often be asked to explain changes to the financial system in a clear and concise way.

Money guide

Graduates on a compliance officer training scheme can expect a starting salary of £18,000–£24,000.

With increased experience, you can earn £30,000–£60,000.

Should you wish to progress further, you can earn £50,000–£80,000 in a senior role and £90,000+ as a head of compliance.

Related opportunities

- Auditor p22
- Financial Adviser p40
- Risk Manager p63

Further information

Compliance Institute
www.complianceinstitute.co.uk

Financial Services Authority
www.fsa.gov.uk

International Compliance Association
www.int-comp.org

CREDIT ANALYST

Qualifications and courses

Credit analysts usually have a degree (preferably a 2.1 or higher) and enter the profession through a graduate training scheme. Suggested degree courses include economics, business studies, maths, accounting and statistics. Other subjects that include a high level of numerical content are also recommended, for instance computer science, physics and electronics. Professional qualifications in areas such as accountancy improve career prospects.

In order to be accepted onto one of the above degree courses, prospective students need at least 5 GCSEs/S grades (A*–C/1–3) and 2 A levels/3 H grades. However, most degree courses will ask for qualifications above this minimum suggestion.

The larger commercial and investment banks offer career training programmes for mature candidates. There are also some professional bodies that offer relevant qualifications, such as the IFS School of Finance, the Chartered Financial Analyst Institute (CFA) and the Institute of Credit Management (ICM).

Credit analysts are expected to take part in continuing professional development (CPD), which involves reading relevant journals and undertaking skills-related courses.

What the work involves

Credit analysts deal with both personal and business credit. They assess the individual circumstances of the application, using statistical and accounting criteria in order to decide the extent of the risk involved when lending.

Much of the work involves administration and figure work, owing to a need for the analysis of given data and the writing of reports and presentations.

To thoroughly assess an application, an analyst must have an understanding of legal, compliance and business issues. For instance, a business application would be considered against economic growth and the country's financial stability.

Type of person suited to this work

You should have an interest in the financial sector and have a general and varied knowledge of the business world. Much of the work deals with statistics and so analysts need computer skills and the ability to work with spreadsheets and specialist statistical software packages.

You need to have good organisational and both verbal and written communication skills so that you can explain concepts to non-specialists.

Working conditions

Daily working hours range from 9am to 5pm or 5.30pm, Monday to Friday. There may be times when you will be required to work extra hours. However, there are also opportunities for part-time working.

Generally, credit analysts are based in offices, with much of their work involving computer based activities and the monitoring of the financial markets, with the occasional need to present changes in the market to senior staff.

Future prospects

There are currently more vacancies than applicants, with job opportunities being stable. This profession holds many avenues for promotion or progression into other areas of banking. Most opportunities are available in London, West Yorkshire, Cardiff and Scottish cities.

Advantages/disadvantages

There are many opportunities for promotion and progression within this career.

Salaries tend to be very rewarding.

Credit analysts must be able to handle high levels of pressure and responsibility as they often have to make difficult decisions about awarding or denying credit.

Money guide

Credit analysts usually receive a starting salary of £22,000–£25,000 a year.

Salaries rise to between £40,000 and £60,000 a year with experience.

A senior analyst for a major corporation can expect to earn in the region of £80,000–£100,000 a year.

Additional benefits could include subsidised mortgages, pensions and private healthcare.

Related opportunities

- Bank Manager p24
- Economist p34
- Insurance Broker p43

Further information

Chartered Financial Analyst Institute
www.cfainstitute.org

Financial Services Skills Council
www.fssc.org.uk

IFS School of Finance
www.ifslearning.ac.uk

DEBT COLLECTOR ENTRY LEVEL 2

Qualifications and courses

This role does not require specific qualifications. However, employers may look for GCSEs/S grades (A*–C/1–3) in English and maths.

If you want to progress to management roles you will need a degree with an element of credit management. For degree entry you will need at least 2 A levels/3 H grades and 5 GCSEs/S grades (A*–C/1–3).

There are a variety of vocational courses available, with the Institute of Credit Management (ICM) providing professional qualifications, such as the ICM Certificate/ Diploma in Credit Management. The Credit Services Association (CSA) offers awards, certificates and diplomas in debt collection. These courses include information on how to deal with abusive debtors and telephone collection techniques.

Prospective debt collectors could also take Credit Management Training courses, with topics including cash collection, the psychology of a debtor and legal actions. CMT also offer a Level 4 Diploma in Credit Management accredited by NCFE. This awards participants with first year membership of the Association of Credit Professionals and the designated letters MACP to use after their name.

What the work involves

Debt collectors are employed to recover assets for the organisation that is owed the money. The debtor is firstly contacted by letter or telephone, they then receive a personal visit should this not work, and are finally contacted by a solicitor if the matter remains unresolved.

The 5 areas of specialism include consumer debt collection, commercial debt collection, international collection, legal collection and debtor tracing.

Specific activities include helping debtors by arranging payment through instalments and becoming involved with debt collections that have entered the legal system.

Type of person suited to this work

The job of a debt collector can often be challenging and sometimes confrontational, so a person entering this profession needs to be resilient, determined and skilled in all forms of communication. Empathy with the debtor's situation is required at times and is often just as important as assertiveness and the ability to negotiate a suitable solution for both parties.

Debt collectors require commercial awareness and an understanding of consumer and credit law, should they be involved in legal collections. Knowledge of the financial and credit industries, and numeracy and IT skills will also be of benefit.

Working conditions

Commercial debt collectors work from 9am until 5pm, Monday to Friday. It may sometimes be necessary to work extra hours, in this case in order to meet monthly collection targets.

In comparison, consumer debt collectors may work from 8am to 9pm, Monday to Saturday. However, these hours are usually part of a flexible shift system.

Most debt collectors will be office based and work in teams; in comparison field agents are often based at home and are self-employed, often visiting debtors' homes or places of work.

Future prospects

You will be entering an ever increasing profession that employs around 10,000 people, with employment opportunities existing throughout the UK.

Owing to the UK being a capitalist, consumer society, overdue debt is a constant problem, with this allowing for good opportunities in the future of debt collecting.

This is one of few professions that will benefit from the current economic crisis.

Advantages/disadvantages

The job can often be confrontational and challenging, with consumer debt collectors sometimes working unsociable hours.

However, the salary is often rewarding and helping debtors arrange more manageable repayments can often be gratifying.

Money guide

The average starting wage for a debt collector is about £14,000 a year.

As you gain experience, your salary can increase to £30,000.

If debt collectors become self-employed and establish a successful business, they can earn in excess of £35,000 a year.

Debt collectors employed by a company can receive target-related bonuses on top of basic salaries.

Related opportunities

- Bailiff/Enforcement Agent p360
- Debt Counsellor/Money Advice Caseworker p570
- Financial Adviser p40

Further information

Credit Management Training Ltd
www.cmtltd.co.uk

Credit Services Association
www.csa-uk.com

Institute of Credit Management
www.icm.org.uk

DIPLOMATIC SERVICES OPERATIONAL OFFICER

Qualifications and courses

Operational posts within the Diplomatic Service are available to those with a minimum of a 2.2 Honours degree. Candidates from all degree disciplines are considered. If you want to specialise as an economist in the Diplomatic Service, you must have a 2.1 classification in an economics degree. As the job involves working abroad, language skills are beneficial but not essential.

All applicants must be British citizens and meet the British Foreign & Commonwealth Office (FCO)'s residency requirements. You must also pass a security vetting process which could take up to 9 months.

Graduates can join the Civil Service Fast Stream scheme as Policy Entrants. The application process has various stages which involve aptitude tests, assessment centres and interviews. Competition for places on the scheme is tough so it is worth being persistent and applying again if you are unsuccessful.

For the European Fast Stream, which will prepare you to work for the EU, you will also need French or German at A level/H grade (A–C).

What the work involves

Candidates on the Civil Service Fast Stream for Diplomatic Service will spend their first 2 years working at the Foreign and Commonwealth Office in the UK. The role involves delivering policy and delivering services. You could spend your time dealing with security issues, working to improve human rights abroad or assisting British citizens who are overseas.

Candidates will then work abroad, in one of the 200+ British embassies, for a 3–4 year posting. You will promote British interests overseas, providing advice and support to ministers developing UK foreign policy in many areas including politics and commerce.

For school leavers interested in joining the FCO, there are opportunities to work as an administrative assistant (providing clerical support) or an executive assistant (drafting letters, handling accounts and invoices, and providing clerical support).

Type of person suited to this work

An interest in foreign policy and international issues is essential, as is a willingness to work abroad and adapt to other cultures.

You will need to have excellent organisational and communication skills and be able to prioritise conflicting tasks and deadlines.

You will need to be highly literate and numeracy is important for posts where you will be handling accounts. Strong customer service and IT skills are also essential.

It would be an advantage to speak another language, or have the ability to learn new languages.

Working conditions

You work in the UK for the first few years of your career and then have the opportunity to work in various different countries.

Approximately two-thirds of your career will be spent abroad.

You would generally work normal office hours (9am–5pm, Monday–Friday) but if you are working overseas these may vary according to the culture of the country.

Future prospects

The Civil Service Fast Stream opens for applications in mid-September.

Promotions are based on performance. Working in the Fast Stream Programme, you could reach senior management in as little as 4–5 years.

The British government is currently encouraging and promoting career opportunities for British Citizens at EU level.

Advantages/disadvantages

The government provides good benefit schemes and officers receive a range of allowances such as rent-free accommodation and travel expenses when posted abroad.

The regular hours in the UK allow for a good work/life balance.

You will have the opportunity to live in many different countries and cultures, although frequent relocation could be disruptive to family life.

Money guide

Graduates recruited from the Civil Service Fast Stream receive a starting salary of £25,000–£27,000.

If entrants perform well, their salary can rise to £45,000 within 5 years.

Related opportunities

- Civil Service Administrative Officer p27
- Civil Service Executive Officer p28
- Politician p375

Further information

Civil Service Fast Stream
www.faststream.gov.uk

Foreign and Commonwealth Office
www.fco.gov.uk

ECONOMIST

Qualifications and courses

You will need a 2.1 degree or higher in economics. A joint degree in economics and another related subject such as law, politics, finance, maths, or even a business studies degree with a high economics content, is often acceptable. Those studying for a joint degree should try to ensure that the majority of their modules are in economics. Many employers are also increasingly requiring candidates to hold a postgraduate economics qualification.

Entry onto a degree course usually requires at least 2 A levels/3 H grades, including maths and preferably economics. Five GCSEs/S grades (A*–C/1–3) including maths and English are necessary prior to this. For entry onto a postgraduate degree you will need a 2.1 Honours degree.

On top of academic achievement, knowledge of a foreign language may aid employment prospects, as would relevant work experience. With regard to this, the Government Economic Service offers work experience placements, as does the Bank of England. These include internships, sponsorships, sandwich placements, gap year placements and vacation work placements.

What the work involves

Economists play a vital role in a country's financial stability, with the government, financial institutions and major businesses taking heed of their advice.

Economists research and analyse a variety of mathematical modelling techniques and data, with the information received being used to identify and predict economic changes.

Many economists work alone, although much of their work will be through consultation with statisticians, civil servants and marketers.

Type of person suited to this work

The work of an economist takes into account many factors and so it is necessary for them to have an interest in current affairs, politics, social welfare and business, alongside economics. Much of the job centres on the researching and analysing of market trends, so a methodical and accurate, self-reliant nature is essential, as often they are required to advise and report on situations through their own interpretation. Economic information reported in an unambiguous way will be sought; owing to this economists must be able to communicate their understanding of a situation in a clear and concise way.

Working conditions

Economists tend to work regular office hours, between 9am and 5.30pm, Monday to Friday. However, some related

sectors could require extended hours owing to the work topic being unpredictable. For those that work in the Civil Service and similar sectors, flexibility may be allowed in relation to hours worked, with part-time work and job sharing being an option.

Economists are mostly office based, with the occasional need to travel to meet clients or to be present at conferences and seminars, to which they may need to contribute.

Future prospects

This profession holds many exciting opportunities, such as the chance to progress to an economic adviser after only 3 to 4 years, based on your ability and drive. Many economists choose to become self-employed or to work abroad with multinational companies after gaining experience and establishing a reputation.

Advantages/disadvantages

This job offers fantastic career prospects, with there being opportunities for progression in a short amount of time once training has been completed.

The salary is highly competitive, when compared to other professions, and the working hours are relatively average.

Tight deadlines, political pressure and the need to juggle different projects can make the job a demanding one.

Money guide

Economists usually have a starting salary ranging from £25,000 to £35,000.

After 10–15 years' experience in the role, economists typically earn £40,000 to £52,000.

Those at senior level can achieve earnings of up to £72,500.

Salaries vary greatly between those employed in industry and those working for government departments.

Related opportunities

- Accountant p16
- Actuary p19
- Mathematician/Mathematics Research Scientist p525

Further information

Bank of England
www.bankofenglandjobs.co.uk

Government Economic Service
www.ges.gov.uk

Royal Economic Society
www.res.org.uk

EDUCATION OFFICER

Qualifications and courses

In the role of an education officer you will need to be educated to degree or HND level. The normal minimum entry requirements for degrees are 2 A levels/3 H grades and 5 GCSEs/S grades (A*–C/1–3), and for Foundation degrees or HNC/Ds, 1 A level/2 H grades and 3 GCSEs/S grades (A*–C/1–3).

Qualifications and/or experience in teaching or community education are useful, and may be required. Relevant work experience is essential in order to secure a paid position.

To work as an education officer in a museum or gallery, useful degree/HND subjects include history, archaeology, anthropology, museum studies, cultural studies, history of art and education.

An environmental education officer will require a degree in a biological or environmental science, eg ecology or zoology. It is also possible to enter this position with an HND in a related area such as countryside management.

What the work involves

Education officers will prepare educational materials and resources to highlight and raise awareness for a particular issue or promote a certain gallery, museum or organisation. It will be your responsibility to increase public awareness about new exhibitions and/or events, and to update the educational sections of your website.

You will be responsible for teaching a wide range of age groups and liaising with communities and companies on a variety of topics. You will construct and be expected to run educational campaigns, talks, workshops and activities in line with the ethos of your organisation.

Type of person suited to this work

You will need self-confidence and an ability to talk to people in a way that will interest and excite them. You must be bright, interesting, humorous, have lots of patience and a willingness to listen.

You will always be busy, so you will need good organisational skills, as well as excellent written and verbal communication skills. An understanding of ICT and confidence in handling budgets will also be useful.

Working conditions

Your time will be spent in an office, lecture room or working within the community where you will represent your organisation. You might be expected to wear a uniform or protective clothing.

Depending on your organisation you might spend some of your time outdoors in all weathers, for example at a zoo or community farm. You might do some evening work, especially if you work with community groups.

Future prospects

Entry to this profession is very competitive, but there is a steady increase in the number of educational jobs available in organisations.

Alongside traditional exhibits, learning through demonstrations, videos, talks and other presentations is being introduced by education officers as interactive experiences increase in popularity.

Advantages/disadvantages

This offers an opportunity to be involved in teaching without being in the classroom as well as learning effective marketing and events organisation.

You will contribute to making a visit to your company a more memorable experience for everyone and raising a positive public profile.

You will be juggling lots of different tasks at once.

Money guide

Starting salaries typically range from £15,000 to £23,000.

For senior level posts where officers have approximately 10 years' experience salaries will rise to between £22,000 and £40,000.

For management positions within private organisations where you are responsible for developing policy and a multidisciplinary team, salaries can reach up to £50,000.

Related opportunities

- Arts Administrator/Manager p347
- Environmental Health Practitioner/Officer p36
- Learning Mentor p196
- Museum/Art Gallery Curator p355

Further information

GEM
www.gem.org.uk

ENVIRONMENTAL HEALTH PRACTITIONER/OFFICER

Qualifications and courses

To become an environmental health practitioner you will need a BSc or MSc in environmental health accredited by the Chartered Institute of Environmental Health (CIEH) or the Royal Environmental Health Institute of Scotland (REHIS).

Entry to an undergraduate degree normally requires 2 A levels/3 H grades including a science subject, plus 5 GCSEs/S grades (A*–C/1–3) including English, maths and science, or equivalent. Entry to the MSc requires an undergraduate degree in a relevant science or technology subject accredited by the CIEH/REHIS.

It is also necessary to complete a 9–12 month work placement. This can be incorporated into an undergraduate degree through a sandwich year or completed after graduation in England and Wales. Candidates receive a Certificate of Registration from the Environmental Health Registration Board when they suuccessfully complete the training requirements and professional exams.

In Scotland, the REHIS scheme consists of a 48 week placement with a local authority. Training may be undertaken during university holidays or after graduation. Successful completion of all the training requirements and professional exams leads to the REHIS Diploma in Environmental Health.

What the work involves

Some environmental health practitioners are responsible for all aspects of environmental health in their local areas, while others specialise in either food safety, housing conditions, workplace health and safety, or environmental conditions.

Your tasks might include developing public health policies, carrying out inspections in premises such as restaurants, houses and workplaces to identify any hazards and ensure that relevant laws are being followed and educating and advising the public and businesses.

You will also carry out investigations of accidents or outbreaks and contaminations.

Type of person suited to this work

You must be interested in finding ways of improving public health, and will need a scientific and logical approach to collect and assess evidence and use it to identify and solve problems. Excellent written and verbal communication skills are vital for explaining regulations clearly and simply to a wide range of people.

You have to be able to handle challenging situations, for example when confronting noisy neighbours. You must be able to enforce the law when necessary.

You need to be comfortable working both alone and as part of a team.

Working conditions

You will be office-based, but spend a lot of time visiting homes and businesses such as restaurants and factories in your local area. Some of the places you visit will be smelly, dirty or potentially dangerous and you will sometimes have to wear protective clothing.

You will probably work a normal working week from Monday to Friday, but you will occasionally need to work evenings and at weekends.

Future prospects

Job opportunities are good as there is a strong demand for environmental health practitioners. Most jobs are with local authorities, but you could also work for central government agencies such as the Food Standards Agency, or for environmental protection consultancies, the NHS, holiday companies or the food industry.

With experience, you could progress to higher levels such as senior, principal or chief environmental officer. Self-employment and working abroad are also options.

Advantages/disadvantages

It can be challenging dealing with people who are angry, for example when enforcing regulations.

You will have the satisfaction of protecting the health and safety of people and improving their quality of life.

You may have to face some distressing sights.

Money guide

Starting salaries range from £20,000 to £30,000.

Once you have gained experience and achieved a senior level, salaries increase to between £30,000 and £60,000.

Environmental health practitioners working for private companies typically earn more than employees in the public sector.

Related opportunities

- Health and Safety Adviser p41
- Health Promotion/Education Specialist p306
- Trading Standards Officer p496

Further information

Chartered Institute of Environmental Health
www.cieh.org

Royal Environmental Health Institute of Scotland
www.rehis.org

EQUALITY AND DIVERSITY OFFICER

ENTRY LEVEL 5

Qualifications and courses

Most people enter this profession with a degree, HNC/HND or equivalent. Degrees and HNCs/HNDs in education, law, business/management and human resources are all useful for this career. Relevant work experience is very beneficial and it is advisable to seek opportunities with your local government, in the faith or community sectors, or to become involved with equality and diversity societies whilst at university.

Most people enter this role through experience working in law, human resources, social work or teaching. Many equal opportunities advisers are members of the Chartered Institute of Personnel and Development (CIPD).

Relevant postgraduate courses include race relations or disability studies. These qualifications can be beneficial in acquiring a senior level position.

The CIPD offer short courses for further study, such as Discrimination and the Law and Managing Diversity. A number of short courses are also run by colleges and training centres and include equal opportunities (good practice) and equal opportunities (legislation).

What the work involves

Your role is to ensure that businesses and public organisations do not discriminate on disability, race, gender, sexuality, age or religion. You will make sure that services such as education and health are accessible to everyone.

You will promote positive images of all groups and promote diversity in all company literature.

You will advise on how to attract job applicants from all sections of the local community and ensure the company is following all the relevant legislation.

Type of person suited to this work

You should be committed to working for change, be persuasive and good at negotiating. At the same time you need to be a good listener, be sensitive and diplomatic in the way you deal with people and situations.

You will need excellent communication skills and should be confident in giving presentations, advising management and delivering training.

You will need to be able to understand all the relevant equal opportunities laws and regulations and be able to apply them to all policies and procedures within the company, offering advice on any new developments and how to implement them. For some jobs you might need specialist skills such as being able to speak another language.

Working conditions

Much of your time will be office based, working normal office hours. However, you will probably do quite a bit of evening and weekend work too, organising special events and working with community groups.

You may visit other businesses and organisations, so a driving licence may be useful.

Future prospects

Opportunities are increasing but competition is strong. Government departments, local authorities, universities, trade unions and large companies employ specialist equal opportunities advisers. In smaller companies the work is covered by the human resources department.

You could progress into management and will develop specialist knowledge and experience, so you could work for yourself offering a consultancy service to companies who want to ensure they are working within equal opportunities legislation.

Many public services are focusing upon delivering services to asylum seekers and immigrants. This means many organisations are employing officers to work specifically with these minority groups.

Advantages/disadvantages

You will be working for a cause you feel passionately about and could be making a real difference to people.

The work can be stressful – you will be dealing with sensitive issues and may be working with people who do not share your beliefs or who have no desire to change.

Money guide

Starting salaries can be between £17,000 and £25,000 per year.

With experience you can expect approximately £30,000–£45,000.

Those in managerial roles within large companies can earn in excess of £50,000.

Related opportunities

- Human Resources/Personnel Officer p42
- Training Development Officer p68
- Welfare Benefits Adviser/Welfare Rights Caseworker p584

Further information

Equality & Human Rights Commission
www.equalityhumanrights.com

Equality Commission for Northern Ireland
www.equalityni.org

ERGONOMIST

Qualifications and courses

Entry to this profession requires either a BSc degree in ergonomics from Loughborough University or a degree in a related subject such as biology, engineering, design, medicine or psychology. If you graduate in one of the above degrees you will need to follow this up with a postgraduate course in ergonomics.

For a BSc degree in ergonomics you will need at least 3 A levels/4 H grades. Useful subjects include maths, physics, biology and psychology.

Relevant work experience is recommended as entry onto degree courses and into the industry is competitive.

Graduates of degree courses accredited by the Institute of Ergonomics & Human Factors (IEHF) can join the Institute as Graduate Members and this is a useful way to make contacts within the industry.

The IEHF encourages students and newly qualified ergonomists to take part in their work experience scheme 'Opening Doors'. Many other organisations across the UK also offer schemes that are helpful to those entering the profession.

What the work involves

An ergonomist creates designs that aid society, such as a comfortable chair or a social environment that accounts for the disabled and the elderly.

People within this profession aim to improve the health, safety and efficiency of different equipment and systems.

Designs are informed by biomechanics, physiology, psychology, engineering, industrial design and IT. Ergonomists consult with other professionals including design/production engineers, health and safety practitioners, computer specialists and industrial physicians.

Type of person suited to this work

An interest in the human body and mind, and the ways in which designs can aid quality of life, is an important part of this profession. Ergonomists must be analytical, observant and able to conduct detailed research into the needs of society.

As the role involves creating high quality designs and solutions, entrants need to have problem-solving skills, attention to detail and persistence.

Interaction with clients is frequent so good communication and negotiation skills are a must.

Working conditions

Those within the profession usually work normal office hours, 9am to 5pm, Monday to Friday. However, overtime or weekend work may be required depending on the project and deadline.

Working environments are variable and involve a combination of office, laboratory and fieldwork.

Ergonomists are often required to travel within the working day, with occasional overnight stays and trips abroad.

Future prospects

Developing a specific area of interest early in your career can be useful and can lead to opportunities within specialist consultancies.

Self-employment as a consultant is a common option for ergonomists and it is also possible to move into a research role with universities or organisations.

Those keen to progress within the industry are more likely to gain promotion by changing employer and so a willingness to be geographically mobile is helpful.

Advantages/disadvantages

Ergonomics is a fairly small professional community so there are opportunities to become actively involved with industry bodies and network with your colleagues.

As the technology and industry is constantly changing, ergonomists must be willing to continue learning and training throughout their careers.

The work can be stressful as you are required to meet the varying demands and deadlines of your clients.

Money guide

Graduates entering the profession can expect to earn between £20,000 and £25,000 a year.

After about 5 years' experience, ergonomists have an average salary of £25,000–£40,000.

If you reach a senior level within the field, you can achieve a salary in excess of £60,000.

Salaries vary with the size of the company and geographical location.

Related opportunities

- Consumer Scientist p510
- Health and Safety Adviser p41
- Product Designer p183

Further information

Loughborough University
www.lboro.ac.uk

The Institute of Ergonomics & Human Factors
www.ergonomics.org.uk

ESTATES OFFICER

Qualifications and courses

There are no set minimum entry requirements but most employers will require at least five GCSEs (A*–C), possibly A levels/ Scottish Highers and an increasing number of applicants hold a relevant degree, often in surveying or housing management.

You may choose to do an Apprenticeship in surveying and follow the surveying track or the property and maintenance track. There is also the option of on-the-job training, working towards NVQ/SVQ Level 4 in property management or housing.

You can also work towards professional qualifications through the Royal Institution of Chartered Surveyors (RICS) or the Institute of Revenues, Rating and Valuation (IRRV).

A list of relevant qualifications is available on the Asset Skills website at www.assetskills.org.

What the work involves

Estates officers manage, refurbish and uphold land and property that belongs to private landlords, local authorities and organisations involved in land and property owning.

Specific activities include the management of an organisation's property portfolio, such as ensuring the amount of rent being paid is sufficient, dealing with tenancy agreements/applications, checking that properties are not being maltreated, and organising any necessary building repair or environmental work.

Letting, buying and management are areas of specialism.

Type of person suited to this work

This job is suitable for someone who is able to communicate well in order to co-ordinate the work of colleagues, and has good negotiating skills when discussing tenancy agreements and the terms of a contract.

Organisation is of importance when overseeing a portfolio of properties for a client, with an appreciation for detail being paramount when examining a property, proposed legal documents or finances.

It is often necessary to be analytical when dealing with written and numerical information, and the ability to write clear and concise reports and presentations is an important requirement of the job.

Working conditions

Working hours tend to be from 9am to 5pm, Monday to Friday.

As with many jobs, extra hours may need to be worked in order to attend committees or meet deadlines, although there are also opportunities for flexitime, job sharing and part-time work.

This job is mostly office based, although site visits to portfolio buildings may involve being outside in all weathers, a lot of walking, and the climbing of ladders.

Future prospects

Self-employment or employment with a commercial business may be the most sustainable career path for estate officers, owing to local authorities privately contracting work to outside companies.

Health authorities, civil service departments, university estates departments, charities and the Office of Government Commerce also provide work opportunities.

Opportunity for promotion is more likely in larger estates businesses and departments, with progression leading to appointment as the head of a unit, a specialist area, or department.

Advantages/disadvantages

This position holds a fair amount of responsibility, with the use of leadership qualities and organisational skills on a regular basis increasing the chances of promotion.

Although mostly office based, estate officers often have to make visits to buildings within their remit, which may mean having to work outside in all types of weather.

Money guide

A junior estates officer can expect to earn £18,000–£26,000 per year.

Through gaining experience and further qualifications, this amount may rise to £33,000 per year.

Heads of units, specialist areas or departments often have an income of c. £43,000 per year.

Related opportunities

- Chartered Surveyor p82
- Facilities Manager p97
- Health Service Manager p308

Further information

Chartered Institute of Housing
www.cih.org

College of Estate Management
www.cem.ac.uk

Institute of Revenues Rating and Valuation
www.irrv.org.uk

Royal Institution of Chartered Surveyors
www.rics.org

ADMINISTRATION, BUSINESS, OFFICE WORK AND FINANCIAL SERVICES

CRCI: AC

FINANCIAL ADVISER

ENTRY LEVEL 3

Qualifications and courses

There are no specific entry routes, and requirements depend on the employer. Two A levels/3 H grades and 5 GCSEs/S grades (A*–C/1–3), including English and maths, are usually the minimum requirements. Communication and personal skills are also essential.

This area of work is open to degree students of all disciplines but students of finance, business management and accountancy may be at an advantage. Other useful qualifications include the BTEC National Award in Personal and Business Finance, the BTEC National Award in Business and the Edexcel Level 3 Award in Providing Financial Advice. Apprenticeships in Providing Financial Services with a track in general insurance or retail banking are available.

On-the-job training is provided, with additional study undertaken part time or through distance/online learning. This is regulated by the Financial Services Authority.

The Chartered Insurance Institute, Chartered Institute of Bankers in Scotland and Institute of Financial Services offer more specialised qualifications, for example the Certificate in Mortgage Advice and Practice.

What the work involves

Financial advisers offer client consultations on a wide range of financial issues including mortgages, pensions and investments.

You will also be producing reports and annual summaries for clients to keep them up to date with their financial situation.

Tied advisers work for a financial institution, like a bank, advising clients on their services. Independent advisers sell products and services offered by a range of companies.

Type of person suited to this work

Good communications skills are essential in order to explain complex financial matters simply to your clients. You will need to enjoy working with numbers, and have the ability to analyse and understand technical financial information.

You should be honest and reliable. This will allow you to gain the trust of your clients and subsequently sell your products. You must be self-motivated and organised with good ICT skills.

You will also need an understanding of the relevant financial laws, and to keep up with changes in the industry.

Working conditions

You will usually work standard office hours, but you should be prepared to work longer hours at busy times.

Tied advisers usually work some Saturdays, and independent advisers may have to work evenings and weekends to suit their clients.

You will be expected to dress formally, and to visit clients in their homes or offices so a driving licence would be useful. Jobs are available throughout the UK, but the majority are based within London and the south-east of England.

Future prospects

The demand for financial advisers is growing as people increasingly take charge of their own pensions and finances.

Financial advisers work in insurance companies, banks and other businesses, and there is also the option of being self-employed.

Promotion prospects are good, and there are opportunities to take additional qualifications and move into management jobs. You could also specialise in a particular area, perhaps training others or marketing products.

Advantages/disadvantages

Pay and prospects are good; you can specialise in specific financial areas, such as savings or pensions, or become self-employed.

The job comes with a high level of responsibility, and you will be under pressure to sell products and meet targets.

Money guide

Entry level salaries at trainee adviser level vary from £22,000 to £30,000.

A typical salary for a qualified adviser is £30,000–£40,000.

Senior level financial advisers can earn £40,000–£70,000.

For the most successful advisers, a salary of £80,000–£120,000 is possible. Bonuses may also be offered and these can be uncapped.

Related opportunities

- Bank Manager p24
- Business Adviser p25
- Stockbroker p66

Further information

Chartered Institute of Bankers in Scotland
www.charteredbanker.com

Chartered Insurance Institute
www.cii.co.uk

Financial Services Skills Council
www.fssc.org.uk

IFS School of Finance
www.ifslearning.ac.uk

HEALTH AND SAFETY ADVISER

ENTRY LEVEL 3

ADMINISTRATION, BUSINESS, OFFICE WORK AND FINANCIAL SERVICES

CRCI: AA

Qualifications and courses

Entry to this career normally requires an industry-recognised qualification, which can be a degree or equivalent professional qualification. The main professional qualifications are the newly revised National Diploma awarded by the National Examining Board in Occupational Safety and Health (NEBOSH), and the NVQ/SVQ Level 4 in Occupational Health and Safety Regulation.

Entry to the NEBOSH Diploma requires an approved qualification in health and safety accredited at Level 3 or above. Evidence of relevant work experience may also be needed.

It is possible to gain experience first or alongside taking qualifications, for example at an operational level, in a scientific or technical field. Health and safety advisers are normally corporate members of the Institute of Occupational Safety and Health (IOSH).

Many local authorities and councils also offer Advanced Apprenticeships in Occupational Health and Safety providing relevant training with an employer.

What the work involves

You will help maintain a safe workplace by developing and implementing health and safety policies and procedures.

You will inspect premises and ways of working, ensuring all relevant regulations are followed.

The work involves investigating and reporting on accidents and giving specialist advice and training to staff on health and safety issues such as fire regulations and dealing with dangerous chemicals.

Type of person suited to this work

You must be investigative, diplomatic and able to visualise the big picture of how a company works and how they can improve.

You will need to understand technical and operational processes and be able to explain your findings and recommendations in a clear and straightforward way.

You should be thorough, methodical and able to understand and apply relevant regulations. You will also need good ICT and administrative skills and need to be reasonably fit for working safely on large outdoor and industrial sites.

Working conditions

You will be office based but depending on where you work, may have to spend a lot of time visiting factories and building sites. This could mean having to wear protective clothing, working outdoors in all weathers and at heights or in hot, noisy conditions.

You will work normal office hours but may need to be on-call at other times in case of emergencies.

Future prospects

The government and European Union are producing more regulations and guidelines to help companies ensure a safe working environment for staff. This means that opportunities are increasing as employers need help implementing and monitoring new legislation.

Many health and safety advisers work in engineering, construction and manufacturing; there are also opportunities to specialise or do consultancy work. It might be necessary to switch jobs in order to be promoted.

Advantages/disadvantages

The work can be varied and you will be instrumental in helping to save people's lives.

You will be dealing with important issues that affect people's safety and wellbeing, so there is a lot of responsibility.

The conditions you have to work in will sometimes be dangerous, dirty and noisy. You may also have to work in extreme weather.

Money guide

Starting salaries can range from £18,000 to £24,500 per year.

At senior level, with a minimum of 10 years' experience, the average salaries are around £33,000–£36,000.

Levels do vary according to sector. In areas such as local government you could earn up to £30,000 a year, but with experience and working in a high-risk industry such as construction or oil and gas, you could earn over £35,000 a year.

Related opportunities

- Human Resources/Personnel Officer p42
- Road Safety Officer p614
- Trading Standards Officer p496

Further information

British Safety Council
www.britishsafetycouncil.co.uk

Health & Safety Executive
www.hse.gov.uk

Institute of Occupational Safety and Health
www.iosh.co.uk

41

HUMAN RESOURCES/ PERSONNEL OFFICER

ENTRY LEVEL 2

Qualifications and courses

There are no minimum entry requirements for this career, but most human resources officers have a degree or postgraduate qualification. Relevant subjects include business studies, human resource management, management, social administration and psychology. Employers are likely to ask for 5 GCSEs/S grades (A*–C/1–3), including English and maths, and some A levels/H grades.

Some companies offer a graduate training scheme. Usually a 2.2 or 2.1 in any subject is required for these schemes, although degrees in human resources and business may be more relevant.

Personnel assistants or administrators can take the Chartered Institute of Personnel and Development's Certificate in Human Resources Practice while working, or prior to searching for employment. Taking this certificate makes you eligible for Associate Membership of the CIPD.

With a degree or HND you train on the job, usually taking CIPD professional qualifications. Some degrees and postgraduate qualifications give exemptions from parts of the Professional Development Scheme (PDS). The PDS has 4 parts: Leadership and Management, People Management and Development, Specialist and Generalist Personnel and Development, and Applied Personnel and Development.

What the work involves

Human resources officers are responsible for recruiting the right staff for jobs at all levels and helping them get the training and development that they and the company need.

You will be involved with negotiations between staff and trade unions on issues such as pay and conditions.

You will also be involved with discipline, complaints and redundancy.

Type of person suited to this work

You will work with people at all levels, including staff who could be angry or upset, so you will need excellent communication skills. You should be interested in people and be able to solve problems. You will need to help with negotiations between staff and managers over issues such as pay and conditions.

You may be involved with disciplinary procedures and redundancies which can be very stressful. In these situations you will need to be tactful and diplomatic.

You will have to understand and implement employment legislation, manage a budget, write clear and accurate reports, be organised and methodical and be able to work under pressure.

Working conditions

You will work standard office hours, 9am–5.30pm, Monday to Friday, although you might need to work extra hours during busy periods. You will visit the different locations and sites of your organisation so that people get to know and trust you, which could also involve being outdoors or in noisy, dirty places.

You must be able to work well with others as you will probably be working as part of a human resources team.

Future prospects

All types of businesses employ HR staff but it's a popular and competitive career so work experience is vital. Many HR officers have a degree but you could work your way up from an administrative role.

You may get more responsibility in a small company but have better prospects in a larger one. You will need to take professional qualifications and could work abroad or become a self-employed consultant.

Advantages/disadvantages

This is a rewarding career if you are interested in people and helping them to develop their skills.

You can study for professional qualifications and gain promotion.

You will be involved in solving disputes between staff and the company, which can be stressful and you might have to make staff redundant.

Money guide

Salaries vary considerably between employers, sectors, office locations and job roles.

Starting salaries can range from £22,000 to £25,000 and up to £30,000–£37,000 with some experience.

Typical salaries at senior level can range from £35,000 to £65,000.

HR directors or heads of department can earn £45,000–£80,000 per year.

Related opportunities

- Recruitment/Employment Agency Consultant p60
- School Administrator/Secretary p201
- Work-based Training Instructor p207

Further information

Chartered Institute of Personnel and Development
www.cipd.co.uk

People Management
www.peoplemanagment.co.uk

INSURANCE BROKER

ENTRY LEVEL 3

Qualifications and courses

Although there are no formal entry requirements, most organisations prefer at least 2 A levels/3 H grades and 2 GCSEs/S (A*–C/1–3), including English and maths for entrance to a junior position.

Many candidates are graduates in related subjects including accounting, maths, finance, business and economics. Larger companies offer specialised training schemes for graduates.

Some previous work experience in customer service or the financial sector, whilst not essential to a new entrant, is looked upon favourably by employers.

Apprenticeships at Levels 2 and 3 in Providing Financial Services are also available as an entry route with options to pursue financial advice, general insurance or long-term care insurance.

The Chartered Insurance Institute (CII), the Institute of Financial Services (IFS), and British Insurance Brokers' Association (BIBA) run relevant courses for new entrants. Additional qualifications are offered by the IFS, which are particularly relevant for those seeking to work in financial planning. Recruiters generally look for entrants with no criminal record.

What the work involves

Insurance brokers act as an agent between clients and insurance companies. You will advise on the best policies to meet the client's needs and negotiate deals. You could advise individuals or business clients.

You will have to research policies from many different insurance providers and so you must be impartial. You will have to negotiate with these insurance companies to get policies at the best terms for your client.

You could advise people on all types of insurance, or you could specialise in just one main area, such as motor insurance. You will also collect premiums and process all of your accounts.

Type of person suited to this work

Brokers need excellent verbal and written communication skills in order to obtain information, negotiate deals, sell policies and explain complicated financial issues to clients in simple terms. It is essential to be detail oriented and good with numbers.

You will also need to be personable, honest and trustworthy in order to gain the confidence of your clients. It is essential to be persuasive as well as you want to secure the best deal for your client. You should be able to manage your time well as you will work on multiple projects at once. Good ICT skills are also important.

Working conditions

Brokers could work in a high-street location, selling policies to the public, or in an office where customers call for quotes or claims updates. You will spend a lot of time on the phone, visiting customers and sourcing new business.

Although you will work normal office hours you might need to work the occasional Saturday to meet the needs of your clients.

Smart dress is important as you must be presentable when meeting with clients.

Future prospects

As a broker you could work in a small company, dealing with a wide range of services, or specialise in a specific area such as household or risk management insurance within a larger organisation.

With experience you might choose to move into a management role or become an account executive dealing with more complex claims and visiting clients on their own sites. You also have the option to train further and become a chartered broker.

Eligibility for chartered status requires at least 5 years' experience. CII qualifications are very well regarded and have become essential rather than optional to ensure recognised professional status. The development of regulation under the Financial Services Authority (FSA) has made the drive for qualifications, and continuing professional development (CPD), increasingly important.

Advantages/disadvantages

The insurance industry offers good career prospects and chances for promotion.

Insurance qualifications gained in the UK are respected worldwide allowing you to work abroad.

The work can involve a lot of responsibility and stress as you will be dealing with huge sums of money and sometimes major disasters.

Money guide

Trainee insurance brokers with mainly administrative duties start on £15,000 to £23,000 per year.

This could increase up to £40,000 with 3 to 5 years' experience.

You could earn up to £100,000 as a senior insurance broker. Your pay may vary based on where you live, with higher salaries normally in London. Your salary may also be based on commission.

Related opportunities

- Financial Adviser p40
- Insurance Underwriter p47
- Loss Adjuster p50

Further information

British Insurance Brokers' Association
www.biba.org.uk

Chartered Insurance Institute
www.cii.co.uk

Financial Services Skills Council
www.fssc.org.uk

Organisation profile
INSURANCE

CII

Insurance is about understanding risk and managing it. Everything in the world has a risk attached to it, whether it's the 2012 Olympic stadium, an oil pipeline or a sports star's body.

The CII is the world's largest professional body for insurance and risk, with more than 105,000 members in over 150 countries (it is also the UK's largest professional body for financial advice and planning, with more than 30,000 members).

You can join our profession from school, college or university. Wherever you start, there is nothing to stop you earning a very large salary and working around the world.

From school or college, you could take an Apprenticeship that includes a CII professional qualification. More companies are offering Apprenticeships than before and value them as an alternative to graduate schemes. You can find out more about this by visiting www.cii.co.uk/apprenticeships.

If you want to go to university, it's your personality – your communication, negotiation and problem-solving skills – rather than the subject you study that will get you on the graduate scheme. That's why you can find engineering, religious studies and geography graduates working in risk alongside those with degrees in business, finance and languages.

Larger employers have well-established graduate schemes which offer two approaches – the rotational scheme to expose you to different business areas; and the specialist scheme which builds you expertise in one area from day one.

Don't overlook smaller companies – they may only offer one or two graduate roles but they will allow you to grow within a business and gain an understanding of the broader business operations.

In most cases, your company will pay for you to study CII's professional qualifications. These are available at three levels – Certificate, Diploma and Advanced Diploma. Many graduate schemes will include the Advanced Diploma in Insurance, completion of which gives you the designatory letters ACII. These letters are globally recognised and valued by employers. Find out more about CII qualifications by visiting www.cii.co.uk/qualifications.

With the ACII and at least five years' experience under your belt, you can apply for Chartered status, the pinnacle of a profession.

The variety of roles is vast – brokers and underwriters negotiate on risks to be insured; claims experts and loss adjusters deal with the aftermath of events; risk analysts and catastrophe modellers run programmes to understand the potential impact of events on people and the landscape; there are also professionals in marketing, IT, HR and many more business support areas.

The CII's Discover Risk website www.discoverrisk.co.uk is an invaluable resource of case studies and useful information.

Discover membership is a low-cost way for students at UK universities to find out more about the sector. For just £35 a year you receive access to local networking events, podcasts, as well as member-only data that reveals the key companies. In a people profession, your network can be almost as important as your knowledge and skills.

Email discover@cii.co.uk for all your enquiries.

Case study

DISCOVERING RISK: INSURANCE

Here's Stef Parker's story

Stef is a Trainee Client Executive within Marsh's Risk Management Practice, which deals with Marsh's largest multinational accounts.

What were you doing before this role?

'Having spent a year travelling after studying Emergency and Disaster Management for my undergraduate degree, I returned home and did a Masters in Business Management, which allowed me to combine the knowledge I had in risk with knowledge of the world of business.'

What do you do in a typical working day?

'A Client Executive's typical day includes liaising with clients; co-ordinating service teams and brokers around the globe; providing wider risk management services beyond insurance to clients and prospects; and managing market account relationships. As a graduate I am being thrown in the deep end and am learning the role by engaging in aspects of all of the above!'

What do you enjoy most about your job?

'The interesting and varied nature of the work, as every client has a unique set of risks. It is currently a steep learning curve, but the sociable nature of the profession makes it a great one to be getting involved in. I rarely have a day where I don't meet someone new. The swanky office and sharp suits are a bonus too!'

What do you need to be successful in your role?

'Having confidence, good communication skills and the ability to adapt goes a long way. The more willing you are to throw yourself in at the deep end the more you will learn. Generally being a people person is a plus, as much of the role is about building and maintaining good relationships, with both your clients and the insurers.'

Have you taken any professional qualifications?

'Since joining Marsh I have gained the CII Certificate in Insurance, and am on schedule to achieve the CII Advanced Diploma in Insurance (ACII) within the next 18 months. It is hard work but a great way to learn about the profession. Everything you read about in the textbooks is going on around you on a daily basis, making it interesting and easy to learn quickly. I am also lucky that Marsh offer great financial incentives which helps to soften the blow of the hard work!'

What are the main benefits of working in risk?

'The opportunities for career development within insurance and risk management are endless. There are so many different roles to choose from, and many transferable skills to be learnt. As a global industry, beginning a career in the area means that the world is your oyster!'

Why did you choose a career in risk?

'It allows me to work in an environment filled with interesting people, variety, competitiveness, and constant change. It is an area which will remain dynamic and interesting. There will always be something new to learn and new people to meet.'

To find out more about graduate schemes, Apprenticeships and other job opportunities, visit www. discoverrisk.co.uk

INSURANCE RISK SURVEYOR

Qualifications and courses

Generally, this is not considered to be an entry-level position. To become an insurance surveyor you will need to have gained experience in the insurance industry, usually as an underwriter. Qualifications and experience in a related, specialised profession like building surveying is also accepted.

Most employers will expect you to have a degree or HND. Subjects such as science and risk management will be useful. If you want to specialise in engineering insurance you will need an engineering degree.

Although requirements vary between universities and colleges, most degree courses require at least 5 GCSEs/S grades (A*–C/1–3) and 2 A levels/3 H grades. You may apply for a graduate training scheme at many large insurance companies. These will require a 2.2 degree or equivalent.

If you complete a Higher Diploma in Business, Administration and Finance you may be able to get a job as an assistant and be promoted to insurance surveyor while studying for professional qualifications such as the CII Diploma in Insurance.

All trainees are expected to qualify as Chartered Insurance Institute (CII) Associates. The qualifications can be studied at Diploma (Dip CII), Advance Diploma (ACII) and Certificate (Cert CII) level and many candidates will already be at this level through roles in underwriting.

What the work involves

You will provide insurance companies with relevant information about a site that may affect their decision to accept requests for insurance cover.

You will investigate sites that need to be insured and prepare reports detailing the risks and recommend ways underwriters can reduce these.

Your reports will enable underwriters to decide whether or not to accept these risks and what terms and conditions should go into their policies. You may specialise in one of four areas: engineering, fire and perils, burglary or liability.

Type of person suited to this work

You will come into contact with a diverse range of people and must be able to communicate complicated and technical information in a clear way. You should be honest in order to build your clients' trust and you should have excellent negotiation skills.

An investigative nature will help you survey a variety of risks and you will need to be able to pay close attention to detail and work efficiently under pressure when writing up your reports for insurance companies. Workloads can be heavy so you should be self-motivated and organised.

Good ICT skills are essential.

Working conditions

Most of your time will be spent investigating a variety of sites which could include industrial plants, engineering plants, oil rigs and construction zones. These can be potentially dangerous and polluted and may require you to work at heights. You will need to wear business attire when greeting your customers but change into protective gear when surveying the site.

You will most likely work Monday to Friday during normal office hours but might need to work evenings or weekends depending on the avilability of your customers. Working from home will give you greater flexibility and is increasingly favoured over being office based.

Future prospects

Career prospects may be affected by the financial climate. However, insurance risks are a high priority for many companies and jobs are available.

You may choose to specialise in one area of risk such as business interruption or travel overseas to work for a global insurer dealing in international risks.

You could be promoted to corporate risk manager or head of department but this will mean a less hands-on role. Many surveyors also move out of insurance and into the public sector.

Advantages/disadvantages

You will always be developing and growing in knowledge as no two days will be alike. You also have the chance to meet new people and to travel the world.

Sometimes customers may prove difficult to work with. Visiting hazardous sites on a regular basis can be physically and emotionally demanding.

Money guide

Starting out, insurance surveyors earn between £20,000 and £22,000 a year.

With a few years of experience and professional qualifications you can earn between £30,000 and £50,000.

If you are a specialist, for example in liability insurance, a manager or head of department, you can earn up to £65,000. This could rise to £100,000 if you work in London.

Many employers also offer additional benefits such as medical insurance.

Related opportunities

- Building Surveyor p77
- Civil/Construction Engineer/Civil Engineering Technician p83
- Insurance Underwriter p47

Further information

Chartered Insurance Institute
www.cii.co.uk

Lloyd's of London
www.lloyds.com

INSURANCE UNDERWRITER

Qualifications and courses

Most companies require you to at least have GCSEs/S grades (A*–C/1–3), including English and maths, for entrance to a junior position.

Many companies offer graduate training schemes that require a 2.1 degree for entry. Degrees in business, statistics, law, accounting, financial services and economics are useful.

A Level 2 Apprenticeship and Level 3 Advanced Apprenticeship in providing financial services are also available as entry routes with options to pursue general insurance.

The Chartered Insurance Institute (CII) offers certificates, diplomas and advanced diplomas in insurance for new entrants. You will need to complete the Lloyd's and London Market Introductory Test (LLMIT) if you wish to work in London.

What the work involves

Underwriters decide whether or not applications for insurance cover (risks) should be accepted, as well as assessing the size of risks to work out premiums.

In all negotiations you should make a profit for your company and protect them from losses.

In order to do this you will need to research, interview specialists, analyse statistics and write up policy wording, often inserting additional conditions. You should always keep records of the policies you write.

Type of person suited to this work

Underwriting is a specialist job that requires an in-depth knowledge of risk in order to make predictions from applications. You will need excellent attention to detail, along with numeracy skills, in order to solve complex problems and prepare accurate and detailed reports.

You must be able to work well under pressure and make quick, difficult decisions. You should have a good sense of judgement and be trustworthy when handling confidential information.

Negotiation and communication skills are essential when arranging deals with brokers.

Working conditions

Underwriters' work is mainly office based and travel is rare although commercial underwriters will occasionally travel to meet clients. You will work Monday to Friday but might need to stay late at the office to meet deadlines. Most underwriters do have the option to work on flexitime which means you can shape your hours around what works best for you.

You will spend most of your time at a computer researching and writing up reports. You may need to investigate dangerous or distressing situations at times.

Future prospects

As you gain experience you will attract more difficult and complicated cases, enabling you to earn a promotion or switch companies more easily. Many underwriters choose to move into management or training roles or specialise in one type of insurance such as aviation.

You may wish to set up your own broking company, switch to reinsurance or train in sales and sell insurance packages which can prove to be a profitable option.

Advantages/disadvantages

Underwriters are constantly researching risks and are therefore learning new information every day which makes the job exciting. It offers excellent benefits.

You may feel under pressure as you must make difficult decisions regarding risks often at short notice. Insurance can be a tough industry to work in during a recession.

Money guide

Starting salaries for underwriters range from £17,000 to £30,000 a year.

If you're experienced and have a Diploma in Insurance you can reach a salary of £50,000.

With an Advanced Diploma in Insurance and managerial duties you can expect to earn in excess of £70,000. Lloyd's of London underwriters can earn in excess of £300,000.

Benefit packages are also common including discounted personal insurance and subsidised mortgages.

Related opportunities

- Actuary p19
- Insurance Broker p43
- Insurance Risk Surveyor p46

Further information

Chartered Insurance Institute
www.cii.co.uk

Financial Services Skills Council
www.fssc.org.uk

International Underwriting Association of London
www.iua.co.uk

INVESTMENT ANALYST

Qualifications and courses

To enter this profession you usually need at least a 2.1 degree. Relevant subjects are economics, accountancy, maths and statistics, with a second language being recommended. In order to be accepted on to a desired degree course, most applicants will need at least 2 A levels/3 H grades and 5 GCSEs/S grades (A*–C/1–3).

A relevant postgraduate qualification is also recommended. The internationally recognised Chartered Financial Analyst (CFA) qualification or a Master of Business Administration (MBA) are recommended. Alongside this, internships in the summer of the second year of a degree can help; as many as 60%–95% of interns are offered full-time employment.

Should you choose not to study for a degree, possible entry routes are as a junior researcher or administrator, which allows for progression to a position as an analyst. Applicants should ensure that they have good A levels/H grades and relevant commercial experience.

What the work involves

The main job of an investment analyst is to inform other professionals, such as stockbrokers, traders and fund managers, about the best and worst investments for making a profit.

Sell-side analysts assess an individual company's financial output and report this to private investors and unit trust fund managers. Buy-side analysts research investment opportunities for pension funds, investment banks, and insurance and life assurance companies.

Activities include analysing the economic stability of various countries, predicting the movement of share prices and taking account of the economic implications of events, for example, warfare.

Type of person suited to this work

This job is suitable for someone that has an interest in current affairs and the impact these have on the financial markets. A certain amount of research is required in order to make informed, accurate decisions on possible financial opportunities. You will be expected to present your findings and this requires tenacity and self-belief. The pressured environment, and constant need to be reliable, requires someone who can be resilient and trustworthy when calculating risks and forecasting trends.

In order to present findings in an effective way, employees need to be good communicators who have initiative and are numerically skilled.

Working conditions

This profession requires employees to work long hours, often starting work before 7am in preparation for the opening of the London Stock Exchange and closure of Far Eastern markets, and working until after 6pm. These hours could change, or even increase, for analysts who need to cover markets operating in different time zones.

Future prospects

Although employment prospects have been significantly affected by the recent economic downturn, there are still annual recruitment opportunities for graduates with large companies. Application deadlines usually occur in November or December of the year before the graduate programme starts.

Opportunities for promotion are related to individual performance, with 7 to 8 years of service seeing an analyst progressing to the position of company vice-president; or executive director after 10 to 15 years. Should an individual or team appear to be performing extremely well, there are often competing companies that will poach successful employees.

Advantages/disadvantages

This is an extremely well paid job that allows for progression within a relatively short period of time.

Owing to the fast moving stock market and the responsibility for vast sums of money, this job can often be highly pressured, yet rewarding.

An extremely high level of concentration is needed.

Money guide

A junior analyst can expect to be paid between £25,000 and £40,000 a year.

With experience, an analyst's income could rise to between £50,000 and £80,000 a year.

A senior analyst (usually a vice president or director) can earn around £130,000.

In addition to this, analysts often receive performance-related pay, with there being the possibility of substantial bonuses, low-rate mortgages, medical insurance, and life and pension cover.

Related opportunities

- Credit Analyst p31
- Economist p34
- Stockbroker p66

Further information

Association of Certified International Investment Analysts
www.aciia.org

Financial Services Authority
www.fsa.gov.uk

Securities & Investment Institute
www.sii.org.uk

LEGAL SECRETARY

ENTRY LEVEL **2**

Qualifications and courses

There are no set entry qualifications, although many employers look for GCSEs/S grades (A*–C/1–3) in English and maths. A lot of employers also ask for previous administrative experience or a relevant qualification.

You could take an NVQ at Levels 1–4 or a City & Guilds qualification at Levels 2 and 3 in business. A City & Guilds Diploma is also available in Keyboarding, Text Production Skills and Office Procedures, as well as an OCR Certificate in Text Processing.

You could also study for The Institute of Legal Secretaries and PAs Legal Secretaries Diploma or take a course in Conveyancing, Family Law or Wills, Probate and Administration.

The Institute of Legal Executives also provides the Level 2 Certificate and the Level 3 Diploma for Legal Secretaries.

What the work involves

Secretaries provide help with administrative tasks such as arranging meetings, making travel arrangements and updating filing systems.

You will also help lawyers, legal executives and paralegals with specialist tasks such as studying different parts of the law for cases and making notes at court, police stations and appointments with clients.

You will be responsible for typing legal documents and arranging statements and paperwork for court. Secretaries may also manage cases in fields such as debt recovery.

Type of person suited to this work

You will need to be very organised, have fast typing skills and a good grasp of spelling, grammar and punctuation.

You must also have good eye for detail as you will be checking and handling confidential legal documents.

A legal secretary will have to be aware of different legal terminology and processes and possess excellent research skills.

You should be able to work to tight deadlines and be friendly, polite and helpful at all times.

Working conditions

You will work normal office hours (9am to 5pm) and will spend a great deal of time using a computer as well as other office equipment.

You may also have to attend court to make notes, deliver legal documents and attend meetings, at which times you will need to be well presented.

You could also make visits to police stations. This job may also require you to show clients around the organisation.

Future prospects

After gaining 2 years of experience, it is possible to become an Associate member of the Institute of Legal Secretaries and PAs.

You could progress to a role as senior secretary, personal assistant or office manager.

In a bigger organisation, there is a higher chance of promotion into a senior role.

With further training, you can become a legal executive, paralegal or licensed conveyancer.

Some secretaries study for a law degree in order to become a solicitor or barrister.

Advantages/disadvantages

Part-time work is available.

With further qualifications, there is the opportunity to progress into related legal careers.

The job can be repetitive. Tight deadlines and a heavy workload can be very stressful.

Money guide

Salaries depend on the location and size of the employer. Higher salaries are often available in London and other big cities.

A legal secretary in their first job can expect between £13,000 and £16,000 a year.

With experience, this can rise to £25,000.

Legal secretaries with extensive experience and qualifications can earn up to £37,000.

Related opportunities

- Bilingual Secretary p348
- Personal Assistant p56
- Receptionist p59

Further information

Institute of Legal Executives
www.ilex.org.uk

Institute of Legal Secretaries and PAs
www.institutelegalsecretaries.com

National Association of Licensed Paralegals
www.nationalparalegals.com

ADMINISTRATION, BUSINESS, OFFICE WORK AND FINANCIAL SERVICES

CRCI: AD

LOSS ADJUSTER

Qualifications and courses

All entrants must have GCSEs/S grades (A*–C/1–3) in English and maths. Entry without a degree or HND is possible with many candidates starting in the claims handling department of insurance companies. However, most candidates are increasingly graduates/HND holders. A degree in a subject such as accountancy, insurance studies, law, statistics, surveying, economics or business studies could put you at an advantage.

However, relevant practical experience is equally as important as academic qualifications. You could start out as a claims technician and with experience and professional qualifications gained on the job you can progress to a loss adjuster; loss adjusting is frequently a second career.

Most qualified loss adjusters become Associate members of the Chartered Institute of Loss Adjusters (CILA). To take the CILA exams, you need to be an ordinary member of the CILA, have at least 2 years' work experience in the office of a member company, and have a relevant professional qualification. To become an ordinary member of the CILA, you need to be aged 21 or over and working for a company or an independent loss adjusting firm.

What the work involves

Loss adjusters are independent specialists who work for insurance companies, investigating and advising on large or complicated claims or where there is a dispute.

During your work you will visit premises, check damage and inspect reports from other professionals such as the fire service or police force to assess whether loss resulting from an incident is covered by the insurance policy.

On completing your research, you will recommend the size of payments and offer advice to both claimants and insurers.

You could be investigating numerous claims which can involve a lot of responsibility and stress, dealing with huge sums of money and sometimes being drafted in following major incidents such as plane crashes.

Type of person suited to this work

You will be communicating with distressed claimants on a daily basis, so you will need excellent communication skills in order to be sympathetic whilst maintaining a professional distance.

Part of your job will be resolving disputes between organisations and/or individuals, which will require you to be calm and focused in order to make impartial decisions based on evidence.

You could be dealing with a number of complex cases at once, so good time management and organisational skills are an attribute.

Working conditions

You will usually work normal office hours, although it is not uncommon for adjusters to be called to look at premises in the evening or at weekends in emergency cases.

The majority of work is office based, but you will have to travel to sites within the local area or overseas to make assessments.

You may be asked to assess the potentially distressing aftermath of situations such as fires, earthquakes, train crashes and robberies, in which case you must be emotionally prepared. You will be required to wear relevant safety equipment when on site.

Future prospects

Loss adjustment is a highly competitive area of work but opportunities are increasing.

You could work in a large firm, which may allow you to focus on a particular area of interest early on and could create an excellent route of career progression into a management role.

Smaller insurance firms usually hire loss adjusters on a case-by-case basis, so you also have the opportunity of working on a freelance basis. With experience, you could set up your own firm.

Advantages/disadvantages

Loss adjusters who specialise in major risks can earn extremely high salaries.

Insurance is a major industry in the UK and overseas, so this career offers plenty of international opportunities.

Money guide

The starting salary for a junior loss adjuster is £18,000–£24,000.

Typical salaries with three to 5 years' experience are £25,000–£40,000.

With further experience and the relevant professional qualifications this can increase to £40,000–£60,000.

Related opportunities

- Accountant p16
- Actuary p19
- Financial Adviser p40

Further information

Chartered Institute of Loss Adjusters
www.cila.co.uk

Financial Services Skills Council
www.fssc.org.uk

Qualifications and courses

Entry to this profession generally requires a degree (minimum 2.1 Honours). Any subject is usually acceptable, but if you have a degree in business, management, maths, economics or a related area, this can be an advantage. Typical minimum entry requirements for a degree are 2 A levels/3 H grades and 5 GCSEs/S grades (A*–C/1–3).

A postgraduate qualification, such as an MBA (Master of Business Administration), can be an advantage; entry usually requires a good first degree and substantial work experience may also be required.

Mature entry may also be possible through relevant work experience in management or a related area. Some entrants have an accountancy qualification with one of the main accountancy bodies.

Training is usually provided on the job, which may include the chance to study for an employer-sponsored MBA. The Institute of Consultancy (IC) offers professional training courses, including the Certified Management Consultant Award (CMC). For the latter, candidates need to be Associate members of the IC with appropriate qualifications and at least 3 years of experience as a management consultant.

What the work involves

You will work with organisations and companies to help and advise them on developing and improving their efficiency, services, products or staffing.

This might involve observing and evaluating working practices, researching information, training staff or developing new ways of operating. You will need extensive knowledge of the sector you are working within.

Consultants can work for a private consultancy organisation, be members of a specialised team or be freelance/self-employed.

Type of person suited to this work

You must be dynamic, confident and self-motivated. You will need to be able to research information, talk to staff and develop a thorough knowledge of an organisation. You must be good at identifying problems and problem-solving. You may need to develop training programmes.

You will need excellent communication skills for writing reports, dealing with staff and presenting information.

You may have to review budgets and make savings, which may result in redundancies or spending cuts. Therefore you will need to have good financial skills, be able to justify your decisions and cope with any criticism.

Working conditions

A lot of your time will be spent travelling to different companies, so you will probably have to spend time away from home.

Working to deadlines can be stressful. The work can be pressured as you will have to taking responsibility for high-level decisions which could have far-reaching consequences.

You could be self-employed, work for a private consultancy service or be part of a team of company improvement specialists.

Future prospects

The consultancy market in the UK has grown to become the largest in Europe as many private and government organisations have reduced costs by cutting management staff and employing consultants for specific tasks. Many different types of organisations require management consultants, but competition is intense.

To succeed you will need to deliver an excellent service, build a reputation and be able to secure new contracts and work to deadlines.

Advantages/disadvantages

This is a rewarding, varied and interesting career with lots of opportunities.

Salaries can be high and you may be able to travel.

This job can be stressful and demanding, and hours can be long and unpredictable.

Money guide

If you are freelance or self-employed you will probably be paid per day and your earnings will depend on your success.

Entry level consultants may earn up to £30,000.

With several years of experience this can rise to around £50,000.

Senior consultants can earn over £90,000 and may also receive commission and bonuses.

Related opportunities

- Equality and Diversity Officer p37
- Financial Adviser p40
- Human Resources/Personnel Officer p42

Further information

Chartered Management Institute
www.managers.org.uk

Institute of Consulting
www.iconsulting.org.uk

Management Consultancies Association
www.mca.org.uk

MEDICAL RECEPTIONIST

Qualifications and courses

There are no minimum entry requirements, although employers may ask for 5 GCSEs/S grades (A*–C/1–3), including English and maths or NVQs/SVQs at Levels 1 or 2.

Work experience in an office or in customer service may be helpful.

The Diploma in Business Administration or Society, Health and Development, City & Guilds Level 2 Certificate in Medical Reception or EDEXCEL Level 2 NVQ in Support Services in Health Care may be useful.

Apprenticeships/Skillseekers in Business and Administration may be available for candidates aged 16 and 24.

Medical receptionists are trained on the job, and may be encouraged to undertake further training. The Association of Medical Secretaries, Practice Managers, Administrators and Receptionists offers several training courses including the Certificate in Health Service Administration and the Intermediate Diploma in Medical Reception.

What the work involves

Medical receptionists book appointments for patients, organise the appointment diaries, answer the telephone and take messages.

You will be responsible for greeting patients when they arrive, making sure they are in the right place, and answering their queries.

You will also carry out some general administrative work, such as preparing patients' notes and files, dealing with post and typing letters.

Type of person suited to this work

It is important that you are well presented, friendly and reassuring. You will be the first point of contact for patients, so need to make a good first impression.

Excellent communication skills are required as you will be interacting with patients and other medical staff all day, in person and by telephone.

Most receptionists are required to have a good working knowledge of basic computer programmes as the majority of work is computer based.

You will need to be well organised and efficient, as you might be dealing with several queries at once and will need to make sure they are all dealt with as quickly and accurately as possible.

As you will be helping sick, ill or distressed patients it is important to be sympathetic when dealing with their problems.

You will often be dealing with confidential information and so it is important that you are respectful and professional.

Working conditions

You will be working standard office hours, Monday to Friday. However you may work shifts including the weekends and evenings if your place of work offers extended opening hours.

You will spend most of your time in an office, sitting at a desk, and looking at a computer screen.

Future prospects

Medical receptionists are needed all over the UK, so there are good job prospects. Most are employed by the NHS but there are opportunities in the private sector.

Progression in this career is relatively easy. With some training you could become a medical secretary or move into a supervisory or managerial role.

Advantages/disadvantages

Helping people, who are sick or distressed, will bring great job satisfaction.

You will have to deal with patients who could be angry or distressed which could be upsetting.

This job will be great for you if you enjoy meeting new people.

Part-time work is widely available.

You will work in accordance to surgery hours which can sometimes mean finishing late with extended opening hours and weekend work.

Money guide

Starting salaries are around £14,000 a year.

With experience this could increase to about £16,000.

Those in senior positions or with extra responsibilities might be paid around £20,000.

Related opportunities

- Hotel Receptionist p142
- Personal Assistant p56
- Secretary p64

Further information

Association of Medical Secretaries, Practice Managers, Administrators and Receptionists
www.amspar.com

Council for Administration
www.cfa.uk.com

PAYROLL MANAGER

Qualifications and courses

You will not be required to have any specific qualifications to become a payroll clerk, supervisor or manager. However, employers prefer candidates with GSCEs (A*–C) or equivalent including English and maths.

The Diploma in Business, Administration and Finance, the City & Guilds' Award/Certificate in Providing Financial Services or the Levels 1–3 qualifications in Payroll from the International Association of Book-keepers (IAB) could all be useful for entry into this line of work.

Both Intermediate and Advanced Apprenticeships are available in Payroll.

You will train on the job. The Chartered Institute of Payroll Professionals (CIPP) offers various different qualifications and short courses in this field, including the Diploma in Payroll Management. Further qualifications also include BTEC Advanced Certificates in Payroll Techniques or Payroll Procedures and a BTEC Diploma in Payroll Management.

What the work involves

Payroll managers are employed by organisations to arrange and manage employees' salaries. You will ensure that each member of staff receives the correct amount on the correct date. When doing this you will take into account laws regarding tax, national insurance, sick pay and maternity/paternity leave.

Your tasks will include keeping records of hours worked, calculating repayments for salary advances or student loans, calculating pay, pensions and tax deductions.

As you progress from payroll clerk to payroll supervisor and payroll manager you will gradually take on more responsibilities, such as managing and delegating tasks to a team of payroll clerks, and creating and documenting payroll policies.

Type of person suited to this work

As you will be in contact with many employees and work alongside other payroll staff, you must enjoy working with other people and be able to work in a team. You should be sensitive in your approach to discussing earnings with employees, and treat their information with confidentiality.

As you will be responsible for maintaining records and large amounts of information you must be organised and methodical in your work.

You will need strong numerical and IT skills as you will be working with figures and working on computerised systems. You should also be able to multi-task and work to tight deadlines.

Working conditions

From Monday to Friday you will work around 37 hours per week. You might have to work overtime, especially at the end of a financial year which can be a busy time.

You might have the option of working part-time or flexible hours and there may even be opportunities for job-sharing.

You will be largely office based. You will have a desk from which you will answer the phone, send emails and make calculations. You may have to attend meetings at times.

Future prospects

You will enter this profession as a payroll clerk and after you have gained a few years' experience and qualifications you will be able to progress to payroll supervisor and payroll manager.

These roles will involve more responsibility and managerial tasks such as liaising with HM Revenue & Customs, organising training for other members of payroll staff and being involved in business strategy.

Advantages/disadvantages

You will build relationships with a variety of people as you will potentially be working with each employee within an organisation.

At times the administrative nature of your work may become repetitive and monotonous.

Money guide

As a payroll clerk your starting salary can be around £13,000 to £18,000 per year.

With experience you can progress to a supervisory position and earn between £20,000 and £25,000 a year.

The salary for a payroll manager ranges from £20,000 to £40,000 depending on the size of the team and your responsibilities.

Related opportunities

- Accounting Technician and Accounts/Finance Clerk p18
- Bank Cashier/Customer Adviser p23
- Pensions Administrator p54

Further information

Association of Accounting Technicians
www.aat.org.uk

Chartered Institute of Payroll Professionals
www.cipp.org.uk

International Association of Book-keepers
www.iab.org.uk

PENSIONS ADMINISTRATOR

Qualifications and courses

The entry requirements can vary widely. The minimum academic requirement is at least 4 GCSEs/S grades (A*–C/1–3) including English and maths.

Advanced Apprenticeships in Providing Financial Services are available. Following this route can lead to a career as a pensions administrator, pensions team leader or pensions manager.

You might be required to gain professional qualifications as you work. The Pensions Management Institute (PMI) has numerous options, including an Award/Certificate in Pensions Essentials, a Certificate/Diploma in Pensions Administration and a Diploma in Pension Calculations (DPC). The PMI also provides Associateship examinations that cover the whole of pension management and administration. For more information visit the PMI website.

If you are an administrator involved with personal pension schemes you might need to gain one of the following qualifications: the Chartered Insurance Institute (CII) Certificate in Financial Administration or the PMI Diploma in Member Directed Pension Scheme Administration (MDPSA).

What the work involves

As a pensions administrator you will be responsible for the general management and maintenance of pension schemes and life insurance policies.

You will answer queries from customers by telephone or email and complete the necessary associated administration. This can include information on policies in general, tax relief entitlement, cash sums on retirement and options for benefit transfer.

You will undertake a variety of administrative tasks such as calculating pension forecasts, processing pension contributions and keeping up-to-date records. When a policy has to be paid out, in case of retirement or a death, you will organise all of the paperwork and arrange the payment of lump sums.

Type of person suited to this work

You should enjoy methodical, detailed work. You will need strong mathematical and IT skills in order to work out calculations and check databases for information.

As you will be dealing with the public a great deal you should be friendly and polite and be able to explain detailed policies in laymen's terms. You should have an interest in the financial sector and tax regulations and keep up to date with economic developments.

As you will be maintaining records and referring back to them frequently you must have excellent organisation skills. You must be able to multi-task and prioritise your workload.

Working conditions

You will work Monday to Friday, 35 hours a week. At times you may be required to work overtime at weekends or in the evenings. You are likely to be able to work part-time or flexible hours or organise job sharing.

You will be office-based which will have certain benefits depending on the organisation you work for.

You will have a mainly sedentary working lifestyle, sitting at a desk using computers and answering the telephone.

A good deal of on-the-job assessment and training is required throughout your career, for example pensions companies must assess staff involved in pension schemes owing to the Financial Services Authority (FSA) requirements.

Future prospects

With experience and further qualifications you may be promoted to team leader or a management position. There may also be opportunities to move across to pension advice or consultancy where you will provide information and guidance regarding financial planning and employee benefits.

Advantages/disadvantages

Each day you will have to deal with a variety of different queries from customers.

Some aspects of your work may be repetitive.

Money guide

As a trainee pensions administrator you can earn from £13,000 to £19,000 per year.

For experienced pensions administrators, annual salaries are typically £20,000–£30,000.

In a senior role or as a team leader you can earn up to £40,000 per year.

Related opportunities

- Bank Cashier/Customer Adviser p23
- Insurance Broker p43
- Pensions Adviser p55

Further information

Chartered Insurance Institute
www.cii.co.uk

Pensions Management Institute
www.pensions-pmi.org.uk

PENSIONS ADVISER

Qualifications and courses

You will usually need to have a degree, Foundation degree, diploma or at least an HND. Relevant subjects include business, accountancy and finance. Some organisations run graduate training programmes requiring a 2.1 degree. For entry to a degree you will need at least 2 A levels/3 H grades and 5 GCSEs/S grades (A*–C/1–3) including English and maths.

An Apprenticeship in Providing Financial Services or in Advising on Financial Products may be useful.

Before being able to give advice, all pensions advisers and managers need to be registered with the Pensions Management Institute (PMI), pass professional qualifications and be at least 18 years old.

Professional qualifications from the Chartered Insurance Institute (CII) include the Certificate/Diploma in Financial Planning and the Certificate in Life and Pensions. You can also take an NVQ in Providing Financial Advice and the IFS School of Finance's Certificate for Financial Advisers. PMI also offers a range of qualifications.

It is sometimes possible to start out as an administrator within the industry and then progress to pensions adviser or manager with experience and professional qualifications.

What the work involves

Pension advisers help individuals and organisations to choose, create and manage a pension plan that is most suited to their needs.

You will work in-house, or as a consultant for businesses and other organisations, to set up and maintain pensions that will suit all employees whilst remaining within budget.

As you will work with and train a team of pension advisers and administrators you will need to understand and keep up to date with the latest changes in financial and tax regulations.

Type of person suited to this work

As you will be working closely with the public you should have excellent communication and interpersonal skills in order to explain complex policies in laymen's terms in a polite, friendly manner. You should have a genuine interest in answering consumers' financial queries.

You must have strong numerical skills in order to make accurate financial estimates and economic forecasts and IT skills to keep records of current policies and procedures.

You should be able to lead a team as you may manage a group of advisers and administrators. You must have excellent organisational skills and pay attention to detail.

Working conditions

You will work around 40 hours a week, Monday to Friday. You may have to be flexible with your hours to suit clients who need weekend or evening appointments.

You will be mainly office based but you might occasionally have to travel within the UK to meet with clients and organisations or to liaise with other financial advisers.

Future prospects

As the financial sector is constantly changing and adjusting its regulations, and you must be aware of new developments, you will be subject to training and continuing professional development (CPD).

You may be promoted to senior roles, progress to other advisory roles in financial areas in actuarial firms, with accountants or solicitors for example. You may also be able to become self-employed.

Advantages/disadvantages

Your work will be diverse as you will meet with different customers on a daily basis and tailor your advice to each new client.

Some aspects of your work might be stressful, particularly if you are on performance-related pay.

Money guide

In a trainee or graduate role you might have a starting salary of £15,000–£20,000.

With 5 years' experience you can earn £25,000–£50,000 a year.

If you work in a senior role for a large firm you can earn up to £80,000.

You may also be eligible for performance-related pay and some bonuses.

Related opportunities

- Accountant p16
- Actuary p19
- Financial Adviser p40

Further information

Pension Careers
www.pensioncareers.co.uk

Pensions Management Institute
www.pensions-pmi.org.uk

PERSONAL ASSISTANT

Qualifications and courses

There are no specific qualifications required although some GCSEs/S grades (A*–C/1–3), including English and maths, may be advantageous. Some employers may expect a bachelor's degree or equivalent. A business-related BTEC, HND or degree could help you find a position with greater responsibilities.

You may find it useful to have NVQ Level 2 and/or 3 in Business and Administration or a City & Guilds Certificate/Diploma in Business and Administration. Advanced Apprenticeships are also available in Business and Administration.

Previous experience in other administrative or clerical roles is vital. For this reason, graduates are unlikely to enter directly into a PA position. To show your commitment to the career, it may be beneficial to take the Private Secretary's Diploma offered by LCCI International Qualifications or Pitman Training's Executive PA Diploma.

You should be computer literate and able to use a variety of computer software. Extra skills such as shorthand, audio typing or a foreign language can also be helpful.

What the work involves

Personal Assistants ease the workload of senior managers and directors, allowing businesses to run more efficiently.

PAs are responsible for administrative and secretarial duties.

You will work on a one-to-one basis with your manager, often making decisions on their behalf and representing them at events.

It will be your job to organise efficient administrative systems, both paper and ICT based. You will maintain diaries, take minutes, answer phone calls, greet visitors, write letters and arrange meetings and travel.

Type of person suited to this work

Excellent organisational skills are essential. The role involves juggling several things at once so you need to be adaptable, efficient and able to work to deadlines. You will have to follow instructions but also use your initiative and manage your own workload.

You will need a good knowledge of the company you work for and you may have to deal with budgets. Strong written and verbal communication skills are a must.

You should be discreet and reliable as you may be dealing with confidential information. Excellent IT skills are essential in this role.

Working conditions

You will work in an office and your hours will mainly be 9am–5pm but occasionally you may have to work overtime to meet deadlines.

As the role involves frequent contact with colleagues and clients, you will be expected to dress quite formally.

Future prospects

With experience, PAs can progress rapidly to senior roles with increased responsibility and the possibility of managing junior employees.

PAs gain insight into all aspects of a business and these skills can be transferred to roles in other sectors, such as human resources or public relations.

There are opportunities to work throughout the UK and, if you have language skills, abroad.

Experienced PAs can become self-employed as 'virtual assistants', working from home for a range of clients.

Advantages/disadvantages

The job can be varied and interesting with a lot of responsibility.

If you have a good working relationship with your manager then the role can be very rewarding.

As you work in a support role, it can be frustrating if your contribution is not recognised within the company.

Money guide

Salaries vary according to the size and type of company you work for and your level of responsibility.

Wages tend to be higher in London and south-east England.

A starting salary is around £20,000–£24,000 per year.

With experience, personal assistants can earn between £25,000 and £33,000.

A senior personal assistant in a large company could achieve a salary of up to £50,000.

Related opportunities

- Public Relations Officer p416
- Receptionist p59
- Secretary p64

Further information

Council for Administration
www.cfa.uk.com

Institute of Professional Administrators
www.inprad.org

Qualifications and courses

There are no formal academic requirements but all entrants need experience in commerce, business, management, engineering, construction, IT or science. This experience could range from an Apprenticeship to a postgraduate degree.

A Foundation degree, degree or postgraduate qualification in project management combined with construction or civil engineering would be useful.

Entry to degrees requires at least 2 A levels/3 H grades and 5 GCSEs/S grades (A*–C/1–3), or equivalent.

There are options to study while you are working by taking online or part-time courses. The Association for Project Management (APM), The Chartered Institute for IT (BCS) and the Project Management Institute (PMI) all offer a range of professional qualifications which are suitable for both entry-level and experienced project managers. Further training on the job may include studying for the PRINCE2 qualifications.

What the work involves

Many project managers specialise in a particular area, such as the managing of commercial business improvements.

In the course of a job, a project manager will liaise with the client, create a timescale, a budget plan that keeps to agreed standards, and choose a capable project team.

You will need to access specialist software for scheduling, risk analysis, costing and estimating.

Type of person suited to this work

The project manager is relied upon to co-ordinate the operations of his team and solve any problems that may arise. Owing to this, it is necessary for people thinking of entering this profession to enjoy teamwork and have strong people management, communication, and organisational skills. In order to solve any problems which may arise, a project manager must be logical and methodical, especially when under pressure.

In addition to this, the job of a project manager requires good computer skills and an ability to understand complex information and control budgets, whilst working on several other projects.

Working conditions

A certain amount of variation must be allowed for from these hours owing to variety in projects. However, generally, hours range from 9am to 5pm, Monday to Friday. Like many jobs, the meeting of deadlines may mean these hours are occasionally increased.

Managers are often office based, with the occasional need to visit sites or clients to check progression. Should a manager be working on a project abroad, it may be necessary to spend prolonged periods of time away from home.

Future prospects

By becoming a project manager you will be joining a growing industry, with the Association for Project Management (APM) having over 18,000 members. Upon entering the profession, most people will make up part of the project support team, progressing to team leader after the gaining of experience, which gradually leads to a position as project manager. There are promotional opportunities to senior management posts from here, although this may mean changing companies, with some managers setting up their own consultancy business.

Advantages/disadvantages

This job allows for variety owing to there being many different projects to work on. Although this may cause the employee to feel pressured, the rewards of the completed project may be of greater benefit.

Salaries are very rewarding and the expansion of the industry indicates that this is fast becoming a thriving industry with long term employment prospects.

Money guide

For people entering this profession, the starting salary ranges from around £20,000 to £27,000 a year.

As you gain experience as a project manager, the salary rises to £30,000–£62,500 a year.

Senior project managers can achieve a salary in excess of £72,000.

There are often opportunities for bonuses when a deadline or objective has been met.

Freelance project managers may be paid around £300–£400 per day.

Related opportunities

- Business Analyst p150
- Construction Supervisor/Manager p88
- Risk Manager p63

Further information

Association for Project Management
www.apm.org.uk

Chartered Management Institute
www.managers.org.uk

QUALITY MANAGER

ENTRY LEVEL 5

Qualifications and courses

Most entrants hold a degree or postgraduate degree. Depending on the industry that you want to move into, useful subjects may include polymer science/technology, textile technology, business/management, engineering or physical/mathematical/applied science. You can also complete an HND in a similar subject or in materials science/technology, printing, clothing technology, or food science/technology.

The general entry requirements for an HND are 1 A level and 4 GCSEs (A*–C) or equivalent.

Entry without a degree or HND is often possible when an applicant is moving across from another vocational field involving quality or management. The qualifications provided by the Chartered Quality Institute (CQI) would provide the necessary skills for a manager qualified in an area such as accountancy, law, engineering or marketing. These qualifications are the Certificate in Quality Management (Level 3) and the Diploma in Quality Management (Level 5). The Chartered Management Institute (CMI) also offers qualifications which may be beneficial.

What the work involves

Quality managers are employed by an organisation to ensure that quality assurance aims are met in relation to products or services; this includes legal compliance levels and customer expectations.

Practices include monitoring and advising on existing systems in order to consistently improve current standards, and publishing data and reports that inform management.

Quality managers must ensure that the company they are working for is applying the required level of environmental and health and safety standards. Encouraging staff to adhere to new doctrines and legislation is fundamental.

Type of person suited to this work

This job is suited to someone that has an interest in securing and improving standards of quality. In order to do this, it is necessary to have good communication skills in order to influence and persuade others to follow set regulations and uphold required standards. Problems may arise owing to complicated legislation and staff lacking interest and so quality managers must be resilient and create ways in which models of quality can be easily understood and adhered to. An organisation's customers must be listened to and so quality managers must be adaptable and approachable.

Working conditions

Normal working hours apply when employed by the government or a bank, although a position in engineering, production or retail could involve shift work. Offices and laboratories are where most are based, although those with experience often become consultants to smaller firms once they have gained enough experience to be self-employed.

It may be necessary to travel to different clients during the working day, or even to stay overnight.

Future prospects

There are around 25,000 quality managers in the UK, with employment opportunities ranging across business, production, commerce and public sector organisations. Opportunities for progression to managerial and board room levels are ever increasing owing to the rising importance of health and safety, and customer expectation.

Quality managers can decide whether to specialise in a particular area or whether to progress to a position of management in other sectors; these include production, health and safety, technical sales, and customer relations.

Advantages/disadvantages

Quality managers have high levels of responsibility and so the work they undertake can be both rewarding and respected.

Career progression or movement to self-employment is possible.

Quality legislation is constantly changing so entrants must be willing to remain up to date with developments in the field.

Money guide

Quality managers can expect a starting salary in the region of £18,000–£23,000.

As you gain experience and progress to a senior role, you can achieve earnings of £35,000 to £60,000.

Those who reach director level can earn up to £70,000.

Salaries vary according to the sector you are working in, company size and geographical location.

Related opportunities

- Project Manager p57
- Quality Control Inspector p238
- Statistician p533

Further information

British Quality Foundation
www.quality-foundation.co.uk

Chartered Management Institute
www.managers.org.uk

Chartered Quality Institute
www.thecqi.org

RECEPTIONIST

Qualifications and courses

There are no minimum entry requirements, although employers are likely to ask for 5 GCSEs/S grades (A*–C/1–3) including English and maths or NVQs/SVQs at Levels 1 or 2.

IT skills and previous office experience will also be a distinct advantage.

City & Guilds offer several training courses such as the Diploma/Advanced Diploma in Reception Operations and Services. Additional options are the NCFE Level 1 Certificate in Customer Service and Level 2 Certificate in Customer Service Knowledge.

An Intermediate Apprenticeship in Business and Administration may be available for candidates aged 16–24 who are interested in becoming a receptionist.

Once entrants obtain a position, training will be provided on the job by a senior receptionist and many employers encourage further study. Courses available include the NVQ in Customer Service (Levels 1–4), the NVQ/SVQ in Business and Administration (Levels 1–4) and the Certificate/Diploma in Business and Administration (Levels 2 and 3).

What the work involves

You will be greeting visitors, signing them in and out of the building, checking they know where they are going and answering any queries.

You will be responsible for answering the telephone, transferring calls and taking messages, as well as managing queries via email.

You may also manage incoming and outgoing post and handle cash transactions.

Type of person suited to this work

You will create the first impression of your organisation, so it is vital that you should be friendly, welcoming, outgoing and well presented.

Excellent communication skills are essential as you will be solving problems and queries for visitors and other members of staff.

You will need to be able to remain calm under pressure and balance a heavy workload, as the reception desk could get very busy at times.

Good organisation skills and efficiency are needed for dealing with visitors' queries swiftly and accurately.

Working conditions

Receptionists are based at a reception desk, with access to a phone and computer.

You will normally work standard office hours Monday to Friday, but this does depend on the opening hours of your place of work. You may need to work evenings and weekends.

There are usually opportunities to work part time or temporary contracts.

Future prospects

All types of organisations employ receptionists including law firms, banks, garages, leisure centres and veterinary practices; therefore there are good job prospects across the UK.

Reception work offers progression into other areas such as office or customer service work; you will develop a good range of transferable skills.

You may be able to progress to a managerial role or supervisory position after a few years' experience and further training.

Advantages/disadvantages

This is a great job if you enjoy meeting people and providing good customer service.

Some people you encounter may be rude or angry if they have a problem with the company you work for.

There are good opportunities to enter other professions such as office or secretarial work.

Money guide

Starting salaries are around £12,000–£15,000.

With experience this can increase to £16,000–£21,000 a year.

Senior receptionists with extra responsibilities may earn £25,000 or more.

Related opportunities

- Medical Receptionist p52
- Personal Assistant p56
- Secretary p64

Further information

Council for Administration
www.cfa.uk.com

London Chamber of Commerce and Industry
www.londonchamber.co.uk

RECRUITMENT/EMPLOYMENT AGENCY CONSULTANT

ENTRY LEVEL 2

Qualifications and courses

You can enter this career with qualifications at Level 2 but people often have qualifications up to Level 5. Entrants come from various backgrounds such as sales, marketing or customer service and work experience in one of these fields is beneficial.

Graduate schemes are available and although most subjects are welcome, a degree in human resources or business can improve your chances.

Employees receive training on the job and may take courses accredited by the Recruitment and Employment Confederation (REC). The Institute of Recruitment Professionals (IRP)'s Certificate in Recruitment Practice is designed for new entrants or those who have no formal training or qualifications. The Diploma in Recruitment Practice is aimed at experienced recruitment consultants. Passing the Diploma gives you full membership of the REC and eligibility to study the master's degree in Recruitment Practice at Middlesex University Business School. These qualifications may be useful but are not essential.

The REC and the Chartered Institute of Personnel and Development (CIPD) both offer various courses to help you develop throughout your career.

What the work involves

Working for an agency, you will help companies recruit the right staff for permanent and temporary jobs through advertising, networking, headhunting and referrals.

Your work will include carrying out a preliminary interview and background check and then helping suitable candidates to find work to suit their skills and experience.

You will assess people's skills to help them decide on the type of work they want, and may suggest further training, which could be available through your company. You will spend time making contacts with new companies to sell your agency's services.

Type of person suited to this work

You will be selling your agency's services so will need to be well presented with excellent sales ability.

You will probably be working on commission so should be able to remain calm when working to tight deadlines.

You will need to be persuasive as it is essential that employers continue to use your agency. You may need to be persistent if they do not respond after a first approach.

Working conditions

Office hours will often be long as you might have to speak to clients outside working hours.

You will be doing a lot of work on the phone and some agencies are internet based. You may need to visit employer premises, so could need a driving licence. You will probably work in a team and be expected to dress smartly.

Future prospects

Opportunities depend on the economy and which sectors are hiring new staff.

You could work for a specialist agency, for example supplying medical staff but may need experience within that sector first. Some people work as 'head hunters', actively searching out people for specific high-level jobs.

With good results you could be promoted to senior consultant and then branch manager. You may go on to start your own agency or you could move into a related area such as human resources.

Advantages/disadvantages

You will meet people at all levels and will get satisfaction from helping them find the right job or career.

Working on commission can be stressful and clients and businesses can be demanding. This is a very competitive career and your success will depend on your sales ability.

Money guide

Trainees start on a basic salary between £14,000 and £20,000 per year.

The average salary for an experienced recruitment consultant is £26,000.

Senior consultants can earn £32,000 and managers with 10–15 years' experience can achieve over £40,000.

Recruitment consultants often work on commission and receive bonuses for meeting sales targets. This means that you could earn considerably more than your basic salary if you perform well.

Wages are higher in London and the south-east of England.

Related opportunities

- Human Resources/Personnel Officer p42
- Marketing Manager/Director p408
- Secretary p64

Further information

Chartered Institute of Personnel and Development
www.cipd.co.uk

Recruitment & Employment Confederation
www.rec.uk.com

Qualifications and courses

You will need a degree and possibly experience within regeneration. Recommended subjects are urban studies, housing and planning, with related subjects including geography, social studies and economics. Entry for a degree requires at least 2 A levels/3 H grades plus 5 GCSEs/S grades (A*–C/1–3), including English and maths. Postgraduate study may be beneficial.

Foundation degrees in regeneration, sustainable communities and community development are also available.

You should also gain relevant work experience or voluntary environmental work in order to improve career and employment prospects. Areas such as housing, planning, urban design or surveying would be best. Knowledge of government regeneration policy and the main sources of funding will also strengthen applications. Voluntary placements are available with organisations such as Groundwork and the Prince's Regeneration Trust.

Some companies and local governments offer graduate schemes. With entry-level roles it is common to develop your skills while you work and through in-house training.

What the work involves

Regeneration managers aim to improve living environments in areas such as: dilapidated residential areas where local industries have closed down, areas of low income and high unemployment, and areas with poor access to healthcare and education.

Specialist fields include economic development, planning, surveying and housing.

The extent of involvement ranges from the presentation of an idea, to ensuring that the project is completed on time and on budget and the generation of financial support and planning permission.

Type of person suited to this work

It is necessary to have an interest in the ways in which communities and living environments can be improved when deciding upon whether to become a regeneration manager. Owing to this profession involving a lot of negotiation with a variety of people, you will need good communication skills and should be able to influence people towards contributing in a positive way. Regeneration managers often need to be strict with budgets and able to solve problems that may arise; both of which need a strong will and an ability to deliver results in a set amount of time.

Working conditions

Generally, working hours are typical of those for an office job, with the amount of hours worked usually being around 37 a week, with the occasional need to attend a residency meeting during the evening or at weekends. Employment with local councils tends to be employee focused, with most offering part-time or job-sharing contracts, alongside flexitime schemes.

Although mostly based in an office, regeneration managers will need to travel to sites that are undergoing the regeneration process in order to meet with residents, clients and agencies.

Future prospects

The government is currently committed to improving community areas through regeneration schemes, making this a very positive vocation to get involved with; especially whilst there is a current shortage of people who have the combination of skills required for this job.

Opportunities are available within the following employers: local authorities and government agencies, regional development agencies and English Partnerships, the government's national regeneration agency. There are also employment possibilities with private consultancies, housing associations and property developers.

Advantages/disadvantages

Both the public and private sector are becoming involved in regeneration projects, with opportunities opening up in senior management roles for those with experience.

This job may be extremely challenging when you have to convince people that regeneration is positive, especially when they have lived in a location for a certain number of years.

Money guide

Initially regeneration managers can expect to earn approximately £22,000 a year.

Salaries steadily increase to £30,000–£40,000 as you gain experience.

Those in senior management roles can achieve a salary of up to £60,000 a year, depending on their level of responsibility.

Related opportunities

- Building Conservation Officer p75
- Chartered Surveyor p82
- Project Manager p57

Further information

British Urban Regeneration Association
www.bura.org.uk

English Partnerships
www.englishpartnerships.co.uk

Improvement and Development Agency for Local Government
www.idea.gov.uk

REGISTRAR OF BIRTHS, DEATHS, MARRIAGES AND CIVIL PARTNERSHIPS

ENTRY LEVEL 2

Qualifications and courses

In England and Wales there are no set entry requirements for this career. A good general standard of education is expected, including English and maths. GCSEs are increasingly preferred and if working in Wales, candidates should have GCSE Welsh.

Applicants from certain professions are prohibited from becoming registrars, including doctors, midwives, ministers of religion, funeral directors and anyone working in the life assurance industry.

In Scotland, candidates need 3 GCSEs/S grades (A*–C/1–3) including English. Assistant registrars must be at least 18 years old and registrars must be 21. Candidates take the examination of the Association of Registrars in Scotland and obtain a Certificate of Proficiency in the Law and Practice of Registration. At least 2 years' experience is required before the certificate can be awarded.

In England and Wales, training is undertaken on the job and coordinated by the General Register Office. Trainees will learn about registration law in detail. Studying for the Registrar General's Certificate of Competence in Registration Law and Practice could enhance your career prospects.

What the work involves

Registrars record all births, stillbirths, marriages, civil partnerships and deaths in their local area, making sure all details are accurate.

After a birth you will interview parents, record the baby's name and date of birth and issue a birth certificate. After a death you will interview relatives before providing a death certificate and informing the coroner or procurator fiscal if anything seems suspicious.

You will interview people planning to marry or enter a civil partnership to check that they are legally eligible to do so and you will conduct marriage and civil partnership ceremonies.

Type of person suited to this work

You will need to be a good listener and have the ability to communicate effectively with a wide range of people.

As you will often be dealing with people in difficult circumstances, discretion, tact and patience are essential attributes.

Confidence with public speaking is important for conducting marriages and civil partnerships.

Attention to detail, accuracy and the ability to work neatly are all vital when completing forms and ensuring that all legal requirements have been met.

You must be able to use your initiative and judgement to assess whether someone is withholding information.

Working conditions

You will be based in the registrar's office for your district and much of your day will be spent interviewing people by appointment.

You will work a 37 hour week which will often include Saturdays. You may also need to be on-call to work evenings, Sundays or bank holidays.

You may travel to conduct marriages or civil partnership ceremonies so a driving licence is useful. You will conduct ceremonies in various locations such as hotels, civic buildings and other public places.

Future prospects

Vacancies within this field only arise occassionally.

The usual career path is to progress from assistant registrar to deputy registrar and then from registrar to superintendent.

You will have opportunities for in-house training and you could move into other administration-based careers.

Advantages/disadvantages

The work is varied and no two days are the same.

You have the opportunity to meet many different people who will be at their happiest or saddest moments.

You will work some weekends and bank holidays and may be on-call at other times.

This is regarded as an important community position to hold so you are likely to be well respected.

Money guide

Registrars have a starting salary of £15,000–£16,000.

A superintendent registrar could expect to earn £17,000–£25,000.

With increased responsibilities and experience, a registrar can achieve annual earnings up to £32,000.

Related opportunities

- Court Administrative Officer p365
- Legal Executive p370
- Magistrates' Court Legal Adviser/Sheriff's Clerk p372

Further information

Association of Registrars of Scotland
Local Government Careers

General Register Office
www.gro.gov.uk

Local Government Careers
www.lgcareers.com

RISK MANAGER

Qualifications and courses

Entry without a degree is possible and would entail following the career path from administration to a risk assistant position and, finally, to a risk management role. However, the majority of risk managers do have a degree.

Any degree subject is relevant but it may be an advantage to have a degree in risk assessment, finance, statistics or law. Entry to a degree is with a minimum of 2 A levels/3 H grades and 5 GCSEs/S grades (A*–C). If your first degree is not in a relevant subject or as a way to strengthen your application you can study the Institute of Risk Management (IRM) Certificate in Risk Management or for a postgraduate degree.

Training is organised by the employer and further study is required. The IRM offers the International Certificate in Risk Management and the International Diploma in Risk Management which leads to IRM membership. Risk managers working in insurance can study towards the Chartered Insurance Institute Advanced Diploma, and others choose to study towards the National Examination Board for Occupational Safety and Health qualifications.

As a risk manager it is important to commit to continuing professional development; the IRM has a programme that can be followed and leads to Fellowship.

What the work involves

Risk managers are responsible for assessing the viability and risks of a business, or project within a business. They identify, analyse, control and monitor each risk for the safety of the business.

Risks can be different in each organisation; financial companies are concerned with market risks and even the health service needs to identify risks to patients and staff.

You will be doing a variety of tasks including risk surveys, designing strategies to prevent risks, and presenting all of your findings to the head of the business.

Type of person suited to this work

You will need to have in-depth knowledge of the organisation that you work for and excellent research skills to be able to identify potential risks.

Good problem-solving skills will be essential for creating strategies as will knowledge of regulations which are relevant to your company.

It is important to have good communication skills, both written and verbal, as you will need to write up reports of your findings and present these back to your colleagues or clients. Being persuasive and tactful will help you convince people to support your view of how to deal with a potential risk.

Working conditions

You will be working around 37 hours a week, Monday to Friday; however a heavy workload might require longer hours.

Although the majority of your time will be spent in an office, you might need to visit sites which could be dangerous, or industrial locations such as engineering plants and building sites.

It would be helpful to have a driving licence and your own vehicle for travelling between sites.

Future prospects

There are jobs available across the UK, with risk managers being employed in both the private and public sector; these may include banks, local authorities, engineering firms and the emergency services. There is currently a shortage of financial risk managers.

Promotions are possible from risk manager to chief risk officer; you might need to move around different companies though to gain enough experience. You can also go into self-employment as a consultant or trainer. There are promotional possibilities to senior positions through the gaining of experience, with opportunities increasing throughout the UK when specialising in a technical field or industry sector.

Advantages/disadvantages

This is an exciting and varied career as you can work in a range of sectors from financial to the emergency services.

There could be dire consequences if you make a mistake and neglect a risk.

There are opportunities to be self-employed as a consultant and to travel abroad.

Money guide

Starting salaries for risk analysts are usually £22,000–£30,000.

Salaries at manager level increase to around £30,000–£60,000.

At director level it is possible to reach a salary in excess of £70,000, particularly within areas such as finance.

Related opportunities

- Chartered Surveyor p82
- Insurance Broker p43
- Insurance Risk Surveyor p46

Further information

Association of Insurance and Risk Managers
www.airmic.com

Institute of Risk Management
www.theirm.org

SECRETARY

ENTRY LEVEL 2

Qualifications and courses

Employers look for GCSEs/S grades (A*–C/1–3), including English. A GCSE in business studies could be helpful.

School leavers often study for a secretarial or business administration qualification, including NVQs in Business and Administration at Levels 1–4, the OCR Higher Diploma in Administrative and Secretarial Procedures or the Pitman Diploma and Advanced Diploma in Secretarial Studies. Foundation degrees in business and finance, BTEC National Certificates and Apprenticeships are also available.

You could also study for a degree or HND in secretarial studies, government/public administration, or business/management. There are also secretarial courses for graduates at private colleges.

However, relevant experience is often more highly valued than specific, formal qualifications but excellent ICT skills are a must and candidates should have a typing speed of 45 wpm.

Senior or executive secretaries are often members of the Institute of Chartered Secretaries and Administrators or take a course approved by the Chartered Institute of Personnel and Development.

What the work involves

Secretaries are responsible for giving clerical assistance to professionals in order to ensure the efficient running of an organisation.

Your job will include typing letters and reports, setting up and updating filing systems, taking care of diaries and travel arrangements as well as coordinating meetings and appointments.

Type of person suited to this work

You must be organised, efficient and able to multi-task.

You will need a good grasp of spelling, grammar and punctuation as well as a fast typing speed. It is important that you are IT literate, have a good attention to detail and are able to work to tight deadlines.

You should have excellent communication skills and be friendly, helpful and discreet, especially when dealing with confidential information.

The ability to work on your own, as well as part of a team, is also essential.

Numerical skills are an advantage as your role may include dealing with financial tasks.

Working conditions

Your working hours will typically be from 9am to 5pm, with longer hours during busy periods.

Part-time and temporary work is widely available.

You will probably be located in an open plan office, and you will spend the majority of your day on the phone and working at a computer.

Future prospects

You could progress in a bigger company to a job with a more senior manager, or to a role as a personal assistant.

You could find a role in human resources, sales or marketing.

With experience, many secretaries are working as a virtual assistant from home.

Advantages/disadvantages

You can use your experience in a particular company or department to gain a promotion.

Part-time and temporary work is widely available in this line of work.

This job could be a practical way of using your skills and interests.

Tight deadlines and a heavy workload can make this job stressful. It can be repetitive.

Money guide

You can expect a starting salary of £13,000–£18,000 when working outside London, and £17,000–£22,000 in London.

After significant experience and responsibility salaries increase to around £25,000–£30,000.

Roles in banking and finance are more highly paid than those in the media, charities and smaller companies.

Related opportunities

- Bilingual Secretary p348
- Personal Assistant p56
- Receptionist p59

Further information

Council for Administration
www.cfa.uk.com

Institute of Chartered Secretaries and Administrators
www.icsa.org.uk

STOCK MARKET TRADER

Qualifications and courses

You will need at least a 2.1 degree or higher, in a subject that has a strong numerical focus to it, such as economics, business studies, accountancy, maths, science or engineering. Minimum requirements for degree courses are often at least 2 A levels/3 H grades and 5 GCSEs/S grades (A*–C/1–3), including English and maths, or equivalent qualifications.

As the selection process is demanding, it is a good idea to try and gain an internship or financial work experience, alongside the submission of a speculative application, which shows you have researched the industry. Major investment banks offer graduate training schemes.

The Institute for Fiscal Studies (IFS) Certificate or Diploma in Financial Studies could be useful.

Entry without a degree or HND is incredibly difficult but possible if you work your way up through the administrative roles and make contacts.

What the work involves

Traders use their knowledge of the market to make the highest possible profit on behalf of investors by buying and selling shares, bonds and other assets.

There are three types: market traders operate on behalf of clients; sales traders highlight new financial ideas, but take direct orders from clients; and proprietary traders make investments for banks.

You will deal with large sums of money, so your decisions must be quick and well-informed; because of this, you will need to build strong contacts in order to be successful in this business.

Type of person suited to this work

You should have enthusiasm for the financial sector and enjoy a working environment that is highly performance related.

Alongside this, you will need to be extremely confident and full of informed initiative, whilst having the ability to cope with the constant pressure of trading with large sums of money that belong to other people.

As well as demanding accuracy, skilled analysis and responsibility, the job also requires that you are physically forceful and competitive, an excellent verbal communicator and a team player.

Working conditions

Traders often need to begin work at 7am in order to be informed about developments that have happened in foreign markets overnight and to be ready for the 8am opening of the London Stock Exchange, often not finishing their working day until 5pm.

The highly pressurised trading arena involves the monitoring of markets on a screen, and the making of deals on a phone.

This communicative tool has made the environment less noisy, although it still remains competitive and ruthless.

Future prospects

Given the current financial climate, opportunities for traders may be limited, however prospects are improving as the economy stabilises.

Once in the industry however, there are many opportunities for progression. The gaining of experience and qualifications allows for promotion to an analyst, being put in charge of a team or gaining the responsibility of a new trading desk. These positions often lead to associate, senior associate and director level. International offices are common with investment banks, bringing an opportunity to work in foreign arenas.

Many traders change career after a few years owing to the highly pressurised working environment.

Advantages/disadvantages

This is an exciting and often hugely rewarding job that would never become boring owing to the constant changes in the financial market.

The highly pressurised environment can often be stressful and means the professional duration of a stock market trader is generally less than those in another profession.

Money guide

The starting salary of a stock market trader is usually £30,000–£45,000 per year, plus a small signing-on bonus.

A typical, experienced trader will be earning £45,000–£75,000.

An associate with experience selling credits can expect a salary around £140,000 per year in a top tier bank or around £230,000 if working in more lucrative markets. (However it must be noted that these are figures for markets in London, and other regions will sometimes pay far less than these top figures.)

In addition to these impressive salaries are large bonuses, up to 100% of a salary, non-contributory pensions and mortgage subsidies.

Related opportunities

- Investment Analyst p48
- Risk Manager p63
- Stockbroker p66

Further information

Financial Services Authority
www.fsa.gov.uk

Financial Services Skills Council
www.fssc.org.uk

London Stock Exchange
www.londonstockexchange.com

STOCKBROKER

Qualifications and courses

You will normally need at least a 2.1 degree, particularly in such subjects as economics, business studies, maths, physics, accountancy or law. Increasingly, in a very competitive market, possession of a postgraduate qualification such as an MBA (Master of Business Administration) or a master's in subjects such as business or economics, together with another language, will prove very useful.

Typical entry requirements for a degree course are 2 A levels/3 H grades and 5 GCSEs/S grades (A*–C/1–3) or equivalent; specific subjects may be required. Many companies have their own, very detailed selection procedures, including psychometric and aptitude testing. New entrants must be registered by their employer as an 'authorised person' with the Financial Services Authority (FSA).

Individuals with relevant experience may be able to move into stockbroking from an analytical, research or investment banking role and graduates are allowed to register for the Chartered Financial Analyst (CFA) Institute exams before starting in stockbroking. Advanced Apprenticeships are also possible.

Graduate trainee positions are available on an annual basis from major investment banks. It is important to apply in late October/early November for these roles starting the following summer or autumn.

What the work involves

Stockbrokers work for individuals or companies investing their clients' money to make them a profit by buying and selling stocks, bonds and shares.

You will be managing investments, advising your clients on investing their money and trading on behalf of your clients, often dealing with huge amounts of money.

You will have to keep up to date with economic trends, interpret market information, and predict how a company's stocks and shares are likely to perform.

Type of person suited to this work

To succeed as a stockbroker you must be confident, determined, competitive and outgoing.

You will have to predict trends in a constantly changing market and take risks with huge sums of money so must be decisive and able to remain calm under pressure. You will need to be personable, trustworthy and honest with a good reputation.

You will need excellent ICT skills and will be expected to work long hours and to dress smartly.

Working conditions

You will be office based, acquiring much of your market information from computers and doing much of your work by telephone. Hours are long: you will probably start early and finish late in order to accommodate international markets in different time zones. You will most likely work over the weekend as well. Much of your day will be spent in a very busy, tense and pressurised environment.

Future prospects

You could be working for a firm which specialises in this work or for other financial institutions such as banks or building societies. Your career will develop by taking on more responsibilities and more important clients.

Competition for jobs is intense so work experience is vital. Economic changes can happen fast so jobs are not always secure.

This is a high pressure job and many stockbrokers finish their careers in their 40s. You could move into other areas within finance such as fund management or become self-employed as a consultant.

Advantages/disadvantages

The hours are long and the work is very pressurised and stressful.

It is a very competitive job and you will need to be tough and determined to succeed.

The work can be exciting and rewarding and is extremely well paid.

Money guide

You could earn £24,000–£35,000 a year when you first start work and training after university, with a fairly small number of clients.

With experience you could earn between £45,000 and £80,000. After many years of experience and depending on location, some stockbrokers can earn over £150,000. In addition to their salary, stockbrokers also receive bonuses on the trade they do and can earn substantially more.

Related opportunities

- Accountant p16
- Bank Manager p24
- Economist p34

Further information

Financial Services Authority
www.fsa.gov.uk

London Stock Exchange
www.londonstockexchange.com

TELEPHONIST

Qualifications and courses

There are no formal entry requirements for this work, but 5 good GCSEs/S grades (A*–C/1–3), including English language and maths, are a distinct advantage. Basic computing skills or an ICT qualification are also useful.

Many colleges offer courses in customer service and telephone skills at Levels 1–3.

Most training is done on the job. Your employer may support studying the NVQ at Levels 1–4 in Customer Service.

What the work involves

Telephonists work at a switchboard, answering calls, connecting callers to the right person and advising them on which department or person they need to speak to.

You will be responsible for a caller's first impression of your company.

Your job will include taking messages, testing phone lines and reporting faults. You may need to respond to out-of-office calls left on answering machines.

You might do other reception duties such as meeting and dealing with visitors, taking deliveries and other clerical work.

Type of person suited to this work

You will need a professional and friendly telephone manner, a clear and polite voice and good listening skills.

Excellent customer service is essential. You must be assertive with impatient and rude callers while at the same time remaining calm and understanding even when you are busy.

You should be someone who enjoys working with people in a team and who can work quickly and accurately.

It's also important to have a good understanding of how your organisation works in order to answer calls effectively.

Working conditions

Most of your work will be in an office or telephone room, probably with other people. You might be based at a reception desk.

Although you will probably work normal office hours, you might need to be at work to take calls before the company opens.

Some switchboards provide a 24-hour service which means working shifts including nights and weekends.

You will be wearing a headset and using computer databases and automated switchboards.

Future prospects

Most large or medium-sized companies need people to answer their phones and provide a reception service, so job opportunities are good.

You could work in finance, industry, schools, government, NHS, emergency services or transport companies and call centres.

You may lead a team of other telephonists or move into a job in telesales. You could become a senior telephonist receiving training in customer service skills and gaining administrative experience.

You could then move into a wide range of jobs working in business administration in offices or with the public.

Advantages/disadvantages

On a busy switchboard you will be working under pressure and could be working shifts.

Dealing with the public means staying polite and calm no matter what happens.

You will gain valuable customer service and administration skills to help you progress.

Money guide

As a trainee your starting salary is normally around £12,000 per year.

With more experience this rises to between £16,000 and £19,000.

Earnings could reach in excess of £17,000 for a senior switchboard operator with experience. This could then rise to in excess of £21,000 for a senior switchboard operator who has experience and more responsibility, such as supervising other staff.

Related opportunities

- Court Administrative Officer p365
- Receptionist p59
- Secretary p64

Further information

Council for Administration
www.cfa.uk.com

e-skills UK
www.e-skills.com

Institute of Customer Service
www.instituteofcustomerservice.com

TRAINING DEVELOPMENT OFFICER

Qualifications and courses

There are no formal requirements for entry into this profession, but some employers may require relevant vocational qualifications, such as an NVQ/SVQ at Level 3 in Direct Training and Support, or a degree or HND in a subject such as business studies, management, training or personnel.

Training managers are often trained in house but there are some relevant courses of study. The Chartered Institute of Personnel and Development (CIPD) offers a range of relevant courses, including: the Advanced Certificate in Learning and Development Practice, the Advanced Certificate in Managing Organisational Learning, and a professional development scheme. The latter consists of four modules, completion of which allows the candidate to become a graduate member of the CIPD.

Other relevant NVQs/SVQs include: Management and Development of Learning Provision, and Training and Development Strategy at Level 5.

Postgraduate qualifications in training and development are also available. Entry usually requires a degree, a relevant professional qualification, or equivalent work experience.

What the work involves

You will be responsible for making sure your company's staff have the skills and knowledge they need to make the business as efficient as possible.

Some of your work will involve looking at how to provide the best training at the lowest cost – from different options such as in-house, distance learning, ICT packages or college courses.

You will also deliver training yourself or organise other trainers to do this. You will have to write reports and make presentations assessing the value of training.

Type of person suited to this work

You should be interested in people and in helping them to develop and improve their skills. You will need to be able to pass on your knowledge and expertise in a lively, interesting way by designing imaginative and varied training that appeals to everyone.

You will need to be organised and able to plan ahead, meet deadlines and assess the effectiveness of training. To do this you will need excellent ICT skills and an understanding of costs and budgets.

Working conditions

You will usually do normal office hours but may have to work longer at busy times or attend residential, evening or weekend events.

You will be based in an office, probably working as part of a team, but will spend a lot of your time out and about – delivering training, finding training venues, going to meetings and visiting staff in their work places.

Future prospects

Training managers come from a variety of backgrounds as they often become experts in their own field before moving into training people within the industry, but it is possible to start as a graduate trainee.

There are opportunities all over the country as all types of organisations have training managers. Developments in new technology and more on-the-job training have increased the need for staff training. More companies are using consultants to deliver training to their staff so opportunities to become a self-employed consultant are increasing. It is also possible to gain promotion or move into related areas.

Advantages/disadvantages

The work can be varied and you will have the satisfaction of passing on your expertise to help people learn and develop.

You may need to work hard to motivate staff who are having to do training they are not interested in or do not feel they need.

Money guide

Starting salaries are normally between £20,000 and £30,000 per year.

As an experienced and qualified training officer you can earn between £32,000 and £55,000. This could rise to £60,000 a year in some companies for a training manager with responsibility for other staff.

Salaries will vary, depending on experience and the size of the company.

Related opportunities

- Further Education Lecturer p195
- Human Resources/Personnel Officer p42
- Work-based Training Instructor p207

Further information

Chartered Institute of Personnel and Development
www.cipd.co.uk

Lifelong Learning UK
www.lluk.org

Building and Construction

Are you interested in working on a construction site with a team of people? Maybe your interest lies in buying and selling property and working in an office is more your sort of thing. All the jobs in the sector require someone with a great eye for detail, creative flair and someone who is very good at working with others.

The jobs featured in this section are listed below. For similar jobs to the ones in this section why not have a look at *Engineering, Manufacturing and Production* on page 209.

ARCHITECT

Qualifications and courses

Professional architects must have chartered membership of the Royal Institute of British Architects (RIBA) and registration with the Architects Registration Board (ARB). The main route to qualification is via a RIBA/ARB-recognised degree. Minimum entry requirements are 2 A levels/3 H grades which should be drawn from academic fields of study. In addition you must have passed at least 5 GCSEs/S grades including English, maths and science. Equivalent qualifications such as a National Certificate/Diploma may be accepted.

Candidates without the usual entry requirements for a degree may be able to take a foundation year at a school of architecture instead.

Training as an architect takes 7 years. Candidates spend 3 years studying for an undergraduate degree in architecture (RIBA Part 1) and then undertake a year's practical training in an architect's office. Two years are spent studying for a diploma, further degree or master's in architecture (RIBA Part 2). After completing another 12 month work placement, trainees are then eligible to take the RIBA Part 3 exam in professional practice and management.

If you have passed Part 1, you may be able to join an architectural practice as an architectural technician.

What the work involves

Architects design new buildings and the spaces around them. They also design changes to existing buildings.

Your work will include agreeing design briefs with clients, researching development sites, deciding which materials to use for particular buildings and drawing technical plans. You will also be responsible for testing new ideas, obtaining planning permission and inspecting building work while it is in progress.

You could specialise in a particular field such as building heritage and conservation, sustainable and environmental design, or project management.

Type of person suited to this work

You must be able to produce creative, detailed designs that meet the needs and wishes of your clients and other people in the community.

You will need excellent verbal communication skills for working with other professionals, such as surveyors, planners and builders, and for presenting your ideas to them and your clients. You also have to be organised and have good research and problem-solving skills.

As you will use computer-aided design (CAD) in your work, ICT skills are also useful.

Working conditions

Although architects are based in offices, you will go out to visit construction-sites and meet clients. You will need to pay attention to health and safety regulations when on-site. A driving licence may be necessary.

You are likely to work regular office hours, although to meet deadlines you might have to do some work at weekends and during the evenings.

Future prospects

Generally, you would start work in a private architect's practice to gain wide experience of the work, but you may also work for other employers, such as local or central government, later on.

Self-employment is common for qualified and experienced architects.

In the long term, your career will be dependent on your experience, ability and competence. If you decide to remain in private work you could progress to associate level and possibly become a partner. Some of the larger architectural practices win international contracts so you could work on projects abroad.

Advantages/disadvantages

There may be problems to overcome when making design decisions. For example, there might be conflicting needs and views to deal with.

There is personal satisfaction in dealing with these problems and creating designs for buildings that will influence the landscape for many years to come.

Money guide

Graduates who have completed Part 1 of their training can expect a starting salary of £15,000–£20,000.

Upon completion of Part 2, salaries rise to £20,000–£26,000.

Once fully qualified as an architect, you can earn £26,000–£35,000 a year.

Those who reach senior level or become a partner in a firm can achieve a salary ranging from £35,000 up to £80,000.

Related opportunities

- Architectural Technician p71
- Architectural Technologist p72
- Construction Supervisor/Manager p88

Further information

Architects Registration Board
www.arb.org.uk

Royal Incorporation of Architects in Scotland
www.rias.org.uk

Royal Institute of British Architects
www.architecture.com

Qualifications and courses

The most common route into this career is to complete an HNC/HND or a Foundation degree in a relevant subject such as architecture or building technology. HNC/HNDs are available in both Architectural Design and Architectural Technology. HNC/HND courses usually require applicants to have at least 1 A level/2 H grades (relevant subjects include physics and maths) as well as a GCSE/S grade (A*–C/1–3) in your A level/H grade subject. You should also have another 3 or 4 GCSEs (A*–C) or equivalent including maths, English and a science subject.

You can also complete a degree but most employers will not expect applicants to be graduates.

To become a qualified architectural technician (TCIAT) you will need to apply to become an Associate member (ACIAT) of the CIAT. To pass the required Architectural Technician Professional and Occupational Performance (POP) Record, candidates must undertake 2 years of supervised work experience and be assessed against CIAT's professional standards.

What the work involves

This is essentially a support role; you will be providing assistance to the other members of the team including architects, architectural technologists, surveyors and engineers enabling them to complete their work as efficiently as possible. You will be responsible for liaising between the construction and design teams, making sure everyone is up to date with the latest project developments.

You will gather and organise all of the technical information required throughout the project.

You will prepare drawings, plans and specifications using CAD (computer-aided design) software and also by hand.

Type of person suited to this work

You need good drawing skills, both hand and CAD. You will need an ability to visualise in three dimensions.

You must also be able to develop a scientific and technological knowledge of building materials. You will need to understand building regulations and techniques and be able to explain them to others.

You will need to be able to work well alone, as well as having good verbal communication skills for working with other professionals, such as architects, surveyors and engineers. Your organisational, research and problem-solving skills will need to be excellent.

Working conditions

Architectural technicians are based in offices, but you may visit sites to inspect work in progress. You will need to be aware of health and safety regulations when on-site and will be expected to wear safety clothing. When working on site you will be outdoors in all weathers and may need to climb ladders or scaffolding. You may need a driving licence. You are likely to work normal office hours (9am–5pm, Monday to Friday), although you might have to work late and at weekends on some projects.

Future prospects

An architectural technician may take further CIAT-accredited training to develop their skills and apply to work as an architectural technologist.

You could choose to work in private practice or alternatively within the public sector in an area such as local government, research practices, education or central government. You may need to change employers in order to progress.

There is also the possibility to work freelance or on short contracts.

Advantages/disadvantages

As you are the main point of contact between contractors and clients, you will be at the centre of any confrontations that arise.

If you work for a larger company you will have the opportunity to work on a range of projects which will keep your job interesting.

Money guide

Architectural technicians usually receive a starting salary of £15,000–£18,000.

After 3 years' experience you could earn between £20,000 and £25,000 a year.

Architectural technicians employed on a freelance/self-employed basis can expect to earn a higher hourly rate than those in full-time employment.

Earnings vary widely depending on location and the individual employer.

Related opportunities

- Architectural Technologist p72
- Surveying Technician p124
- Town Planner/Planning Technician p127

Further information

Chartered Institute of Architectural Technologists
www.ciat.org.uk

Chartered Institute of Building
www.ciob.org.uk

ConstructionSkills
www.cskills.org

ARCHITECTURAL TECHNOLOGIST

Qualifications and courses

The preferred route to becoming an architectural technologist is to complete a degree which has been accredited by the Chartered Institute of Architectural Technologists (CIAT). There are currently over 30 accredited degree programmes and they are listed on CIAT's website. Candidates who take an accredited degree benefit from exemptions when they study for their Professional and Occupational Performance (POP) Record which is a necessary requirement to become a chartered architectural technologist (MCIAT).

You could alternatively complete an NVQ/SVQ Level 4 in Architectural Technology or a related industry degree such as architecture, architectural engineering, building services engineering, building/construction, built environment studies, civil and structural engineering, computer-aided engineering or surveying.

Completion of an HNC/HND in Construction or a Foundation degree in architectural technology will enable you to become a qualified architectural technician. Once you have had more than 10 years' experience and after successful completion of CIAT's professional standards assessment you could become an architectural technologist.

Relevant work experience would be extremely beneficial.

What the work involves

You will be responsible for ensuring that the architect's design is translated into a functioning building. You will be involved right from the start, helping to liaise with the client and the architect and advise them on any issues that might affect the build.

You will make sure that the more practical elements of the build run smoothly, by ensuring that the right materials are used and that all legal requirements and building regulations are met.

You will have a leading role within the construction team including developing project briefs, coordinating, negotiating contracts and providing guidance.

Type of person suited to this work

You need good drawing skills, both hand and computer-aided design (CAD). You will need an ability to visualise in three dimensions.

You must also be able to develop a scientific and technological knowledge of building materials. You will need to understand planning regulations and construction law, and be able to explain them to others.

You will need good communication skills for working with other professionals. Your organisational, management,

research and problem-solving skills will need to be excellent.

Working conditions

Architectural technologists are based in offices, but you may visit sites to inspect work in progress. You will generally be working 9am–5pm but you might need to work extra hours to meet deadlines. You will need to be aware of health and safety regulations when on-site and will wear safety clothing. On-site work can be cold and wet, or hot and dusty as you will be outdoors in all weathers. You may need a driving licence.

Future prospects

Architectural technologists, with CIAT qualifications and experience, may set up their own practice or work in a partnership with other architectural technologists or architects.

It is also possible to progress within private firms to more senior positions or move to other companies which attract larger and possibly international contracts. Promotion is generally easier within larger firms but you may still need to change employers in order to progress.

Advantages/disadvantages

There may be problems to solve at any time during the architectural process, for example, issues with the supply of the right materials.

It is rewarding to make your contribution to the design and construction of buildings that will influence the landscape for many years to come.

Money guide

Generally salaries are higher in London and the south of England.

A junior technologist typically has a starting salary of £15,000–£23,000 a year.

After 3 years' experience you should be earning between £24,000 and £28,000 a year.

Once you are in a senior position and have been working for 10 years, you could achieve a salary of £30,000–£45,000.

Related opportunities

- Architect p70
- Cartographer p80
- Town Planner/Planning Technician p127

Further information

Chartered Institute of Architectural Technologists
www.ciat.org.uk

ConstructionSkills
www.cskills.org

Qualifications and courses

There is no specific entry route for this career, although you will need a degree in land management or a property-related subject to join a company as a trainee. You could study for a degree in property and valuation accredited by the Royal Institution of Chartered Surveyors (RICS) and join a surveying firm or you could enter a different area, such as estate management, and train as a chartered surveyor on the job. Entry to a degree is normally with 5 GCSEs/S grades (A*–C/1–3) and a minimum of 2 A levels/3 H grades.

Training is done on the job, under the supervision of a senior consultant. The National Association of Valuers and Auctioneers (NAVA) offer property auction workshops to help develop trainees' skills. The National Federation of Property Professionals (NFoPP) has a Level 3 Technical Award in Real Property Auctioneering, which is available through distance learning.

It is important to commit to a continuing professional development programme to keep your skills and knowledge of property law and auctioning methods up to date.

What the work involves

You will be responsible for valuing property and land, from listed buildings to new builds, assessing the current market and organising the property or land to be auctioned off.

You will be meeting prospective clients, researching their property or land, attending the auction and getting the best price for the client.

You will need to make detailed reports of the property you value, and report back to your client. You might also have other duties such as advising clients how auctions work and of any other services your company offers.

Type of person suited to this work

You will need excellent communication skills to successfully run an auction, and be firm when settling a bid.

Being lively, outgoing and confident will help when you have to address a large crowd of people; a clear and authoritative voice will be beneficial.

You will need good observational skills for valuing land and property, with a good knowledge of the property market. You will need to keep up to date with current property laws.

Working conditions

You will work around 37 hours a week, Monday to Friday, with the possibility of working evenings and weekends, depending on when the auction is.

You will spend a lot of time in an office, but you will be out and about on a daily basis, meeting clients and valuing properties. You will need to work in all weather conditions, and travel around regularly – a driving licence and vehicle will be very useful.

Future prospects

There are jobs available across the UK, with international auction houses being based in London. There is currently a need for property auctioneers owing to the increase in popularity of property auctions, therefore job prospects are good.

You can progress into a senior auction role, or managerial position. It may be possible to move into different areas of auctioning, such as livestock or antiques.

Advantages/disadvantages

Auctions are fast paced and lively events; this job offers an exciting day's work!

It could be frustrating when an auction does not go the way you planned and profit is not made.

You get great job satisfaction when you successfully auction off a property.

Money guide

The amount that you earn depends on which type of organisation you work for and where it is located. For example, an auction house may pay less than a private chartered surveyor company.

Starting salaries can be between £18,000 and £23,000 a year.

With experience, earnings can rise to £24,000–£36,000.

Chartered land and property valuers can earn around £40,000 a year.

Those who are particularly successful can achieve in excess of £60,000.

Related opportunities

- Auctioneer p475
- Estate Agent p95
- Surveying Technician p124

Further information

National Federation of Property Professionals
www.nfopp.co.uk

Royal Institution of Chartered Surveyors
www.rics.org

BRICKLAYER

Qualifications and courses

Apprenticeships/Skillseekers are open to those aged 16–24. Some GCSEs/S grades (A*–E/1–5) are normally required in subjects such as English, maths, science and technology. In England and Wales, a Construction Apprenticeship Scheme allows you to study for NVQ Levels 2 and 3.

There is no upper age limit for this scheme. Vocational qualifications include: BTEC Introductory Certificate and Diploma in Construction; BTEC First Certificate and Diploma in Construction; City & Guilds Certificate in Basic Skills (6081). Bricklayers who train on the job can work towards NVQs/SVQs in Trowel Occupations at Levels 1–3 specialising in Bricklaying.

ConstructionSkills' On-Site Assessment and Training (OSAT) programme or the Experienced Worker Practical Assessment (EWPA) offer unqualified bricklayers the opportunity to receive a nationally recognised NVQ.

New Deal offers taster courses and placements with an employer for at least 26 weeks. It may be possible to stay on and study for NVQs/SVQs. To qualify you must be aged 18–24 and unemployed for more than 6 months, or 25 or over and unemployed for 18 months.

What the work involves

Bricklayers build and repair external and internal walls.

You will use a range of materials including bricks, stones and mortar as well as specialist tools to build walls that often include ornamental and decorative effects.

Jobs include building houses as well as office buildings, other public venues, shopping centres and stadiums. You will spend a lot of your time outside doing manual work.

Type of person suited to this work

As the work requires you to move around a lot and lift materials, you must be physically fit. And you must not mind working at heights.

You need to be able to follow plans and work with accuracy and attention to detail, so that the walls you build are structurally perfect and create the right visual effect.

You also need to work in a team with other bricklayers and those in other construction trades and professions.

Working conditions

You will often be working outdoors and in all weather conditions. This can mean being cold and wet in the winter and hot and dusty in the summer.

To keep yourself and others safe you will need to observe health and safety regulations, which will include wearing protective clothing.

You are likely to work a normal working week, although weekend and evening work is common.

Future prospects

There are currently plenty of opportunities to enter bricklaying as construction is the largest industry in the UK.

In the long term, you could progress to technical, supervisory and managerial roles. You can also become an instructor in a training school. The construction industry has one of the highest percentages of self-employment and bricklayers are no exception. Many have set up their own businesses, often working on smaller, local contracts.

Advantages/disadvantages

The work can be physically demanding for some people.

Bricklayers are in demand particularly in the south-east of England.

This is a great career if you like being outdoors, doing practical and creative work.

Money guide

Salaries for trainees/labourers start at £7,000–£13,000, according to the level of training.

Once NVQ/SVQ Level 2 qualifications have been achieved, salary expectations can rise to £16,000–£23,000.

Experienced and qualified bricklayers can earn £30,000.

Overtime is often available, and on some projects there are bonuses based on outputs, which can lead to higher earnings. If you are self-employed you have more freedom to negotiate your rate of pay with your clients.

Related opportunities

- Building Technician p78
- Dry Stone Waller p91
- Stonemason p122

Further information

ConstructionSkills
www.cskills.org

Federation of Master Builders
www.fmb.org.uk

Scottish Building Apprenticeship and Training Council
www.sbatc.co.uk

BUILDING CONSERVATION OFFICER

Qualifications and courses

Most entrants are graduates and will have studied relevant subjects such as planning, building, construction, civil engineering, surveying, architecture, design or history of art. Courses in architectural heritage and conservation and building conservation and management are offered by some universities. Many graduates will have a postgraduate degree as it is quite a specialist area.

Entry with an HND is possible, or alternatively you can enter as a planning technician and after gaining experience and training become a historic buildings inspector or a conservation officer.

Training is usually provided on the job but employers look for candidates with experience. You could volunteer with the National Trust or a national amenity society. The Society for the Protection of Ancient Buildings also runs a lecture series each year aimed at professionals in the industry and runs several courses for continuing personal development (CPD).

What the work involves

Building conservation officers protect and restore buildings of special historical or architectural interest, such as houses, churches, windmills, factories and lighthouses.

You will be involved in planning the development of listed buildings and sites, recommending buildings for conservation, writing reports on their condition, making schedules and estimates for work required and giving advice to architects, local authorities or planning committees on building conservation.

You might have to source suppliers or craftspeople who work with specialised or traditional building materials.

Type of person suited to this work

You will be working to restore historical buildings and sites so it is important that you are interested in history, architecture and construction. An understanding of historical architecture, building methods and techniques would be very useful.

You will need excellent communication skills as you will coordinate the many different aspects involved in the development of one site. You must have excellent verbal and written skills to give presentations to planning authorities or government agencies to persuade them to follow your advice.

Working conditions

Your work is occasionally office based, but much takes place outdoors on site. This can be dusty and dirty, working at heights and confined spaces in adverse weather conditions. Protective clothing, including hard hats and safety boots, is necessary as you may be visiting buildings in poor repair.

Travel during the day with the occasional overnight stay may be necessary. Working as a consultant may involve travel all over the UK or visiting sites in remote areas so a car and driver's licence are useful. Working hours include regular extra hours but not weekends or shifts.

Future prospects

Positions as a historic inspector or conservation officer can be found in local authorities, district and county councils. You may be promoted to senior conservation officer or managerial roles. Promotions are limited in small organisations.

There are many opportunities in national government organisations such as English Heritage and charities such as the National Trust, the Victorian Society or the Georgian Group.

As a qualified and experienced professional you can be self-employed. With substantial experience and industry contracts you can become involved in consultancy work which focuses on advisory and design work.

Advantages/disadvantages

You will gain a great deal of satisfaction from working to ensure the survival of listed buildings.

Buildings are often in a poor state of repair and building sites may be hazardous.

Money guide

Starting as a trainee or in an entry level position you can expect a salary of between £18,000 and £24,000 per year, dependent on your experience.

With experience and/or qualifications, earnings can rise to between £26,000 and £36,000 per year. Local authority trainees' salaries are generally lower than those of historic buildings inspectors employed by central government bodies.

At senior level, with 10 to 15 years in a role, you can earn in excess of £40,000.

Related opportunities

- Architect p70
- Architectural Technologist p72
- Building Surveyor p77

Further information

Institute of Historic Building Conservation
www.ihbc.org.uk

Society for the Protection of Ancient Buildings
www.spab.org.uk

BUILDING SERVICES ENGINEER

Qualifications and courses

To enter this profession you will need a relevant degree; subjects include building services engineering, mechanical engineering, maths and physics. Entry to a degree is usually with 2 A levels/3 H grades with at least one in maths or a science.

Accredited HNDs or Foundation degrees in engineering or technology can be used to progress to full degree courses or trainee posts.

As a trainee you will need to complete Initial Professional Development (IPD) to become a professional engineer. You can train for this through your employer.

You can then work towards Incorporated Engineer (IEng) or Chartered Engineer (CEng) status, and commit to a continuing professional development (CPD) programme to keep your skills up to date.

What the work involves

Building services engineers are responsible for each aspect of energy-using building services such as lifts, lighting, heating, air-conditioning, water supply, ventilation and electrical supply.

You will design and plan services that are efficient, cost effective, sustainable and in the interest of public safety. You will also be responsible for organising and supervising the installation and maintenance of these services, working with architects and clients to reduce the environmental impact.

Although the industry is becoming increasingly multidisciplinary, you will probably specialise in mechanical engineering, electrical engineering or public health.

Type of person suited to this work

You should have a good grasp of maths and physics as you will have to plan each stage of a building service system.

You will need excellent problem-solving, communication and interpersonal skills. Teamworking skills are essential so that you can work with those involved in other aspects of each project's design and construction.

You should have an aptitude for design and technical drawing, model making and show proficiency working with computers and computer-aided design (CAD) software.

Working conditions

Your time will be divided between office-based work, such as planning, designing and estimating costs of projects, to spending time on-site, coordinating installation or managing existing systems.

You may work on sites such as airports, hospitals, industrial plants, domestic housing, leisure pools, hotels and cinemas. For this you might need specialist skills.

You will usually be expected to work more than the average office hours but not weekends or shifts. Some roles require on-call availability in case of emergencies. You may have to travel within a day but overnight stays are uncommon.

Future prospects

Opportunities in this field are numerous, with demand for building services engineers usually exceeding supply.

Promotion to a managerial role such as team leader, project manager or department manager is likely, which will involve pay increases. You can then go on to become a company director or partner.

As a chartered engineer you may establish yourself as an independent consultant.

Advantages/disadvantages

The profession has been traditionally separated into electrical and mechanical roles, but it is now becoming increasingly multidisciplinary.

This profession depends heavily on the economic climate of the construction industry, so you need to be aware of this as it will affect your chances of employment.

Money guide

Your starting salary could range from £20,000 to £24,000.

With experience your salary can rise to between £25,000 and £35,000.

At senior level it is possible to earn more than £40,000 and as a partner of a consultancy firm it is possible to earn in excess of £65,000 a year.

Related opportunities

- Architect p70
- Civil/Construction Engineer/Civil Engineering Technician p83
- Electrical Engineer p219

Further information

Chartered Institution of Building Services Engineers
www.cibse.org

Institution of Engineering and Technology
www.theiet.org

BUILDING SURVEYOR

Qualifications and courses

All building surveyors hold a relevant degree on entry to the profession. You may study full time at university for a Royal Institution of Chartered Surveyors (RICS) accredited degree in a relevant subject. The Chartered Institute of Building (CIOB), the Association of Building Engineers (ABE), and the British Institute of Facilities Management (BIFM) also offer professional qualifications.

Candidates with a non-accredited degree, or a degree in a non-vocational subject, can take a postgraduate conversion course that has been accredited by the RICS. It is also possible to enter the industry at technical surveyor level with a relevant HND such as building surveying or building/construction.

The Chartered Surveyors Training Trust offers work-based training for young people aged 16–24 in London and the south-east of England. Applicants must have a minimum of 4 GCSEs (A*–C) or equivalent.

Graduates who have completed a year in industry as part of their degree have an advantage in the job market.

What the work involves

Building surveyors work on new building projects, and also suggest ways to improve or enhance existing structures.

You could work on residential and commercial building projects, and will advise on a number of areas including design, restoration, sustainability and repairs.

You may also be responsible for ensuring that buildings meet health, safety and access regulations.

Type of person suited to this work

Since the job involves explaining ideas and negotiating with industry professionals and clients, good communication skills are vital. You will produce detailed reports, so a good standard of written English is required.

You will need excellent time management skills and a head for figures to ensure that projects come in on time and within budget.

You will need a logical, analytical and practical approach to work, along with the ability to organise and manage a team. As much of the work involves computers and electronic equipment, you will need to have good ICT skills.

Working conditions

Working hours are normally 9am–5pm, although longer hours and evening meetings with clients are not uncommon. Most surveyors divide their time equally between office-based work and external client meetings, site visits and surveys. These travel commitments mean it is helpful to have a driving licence and transport.

When on-site you will need to stick to health and safety regulations and be prepared to get muddy, wet and cold.

You may occasionally be called to give evidence in court proceedings concerning a breach of building regulations.

Future prospects

At the moment prospects are not as good as they once were as the sector has been affected by the financial crisis.

You could work for a variety of employers including surveying practices, construction companies, government departments, and mortgage and property companies, both throughout the UK and internationally. Freelance and consultancy work are also a possibility.

With experience, you could become a partner in a company or establish your own firm. You could also specialise in an area that interests you, such as advising on the restoration and improvement of historical or architecturally valuable buildings.

Advantages/disadvantages

Surveying provides a varied career as each day is different and there are a range of areas to work in.

Many surveyors are self-employed and enjoy the flexibility of working freelance.

Sometimes you will need to work extra hours to meet deadlines, or if you are working towards promotion.

Money guide

Graduate surveyors can expect a salary of £20,000–£26,000, which can rise in London-based roles.

Chartered surveyors can expect to earn up to £32,000 and if you became a partner in a firm this could rise to in excess of £70,000.

Some companies offer additional benefits such as a company car, mobile phone and pension scheme.

Related opportunities

- Civil/Construction Engineer/Civil Engineering Technician p83
- Quantity Surveyor p114
- Rural Property/Practice Surveyor p117

Further information

Chartered Institute of Building
www.ciob.org.uk

Royal Institution of Chartered Surveyors
www.rics.org

BUILDING TECHNICIAN

Qualifications and courses

Building technicians normally need to train to NVQ/SVQ Levels 3 or 4. It is possible to train as a building technician with an employer as a construction apprentice. Apprenticeship schemes require a minimum of 4 GCSEs/S grades (A*–C/1–3), including maths and science or technology, or equivalent. Most apprentices start between the ages of 16 and 18, though entry is possible after this.

HNDs in building studies or similar subjects can be studied over 2 years full time. Applicants should ideally have a science A level/H grade. Introductory courses to a career at technician level include BTEC National Certificate/Diploma or Scottish Group Award in Construction.

You can apply for a ConstructionSkills Inspire Scholarship if you plan to pursue a construction-related degree. This includes a 10 week placement as well as a grant to support university study.

Many companies offer training schemes, day-release study (for HNC and Chartered Institute of Building exams), time spent on building sites, in-house training courses, and the Construction Industry Training Board (CITB) Technician Training Scheme.

What the work involves

Building technicians support the work of construction professionals including surveyors and construction managers.

Your work will vary depending on your employer, but might include planning work schedules, drawing up plans and estimating project costs.

A building technician is also responsible for buying materials, checking that plans meet building regulations, measuring and preparing construction sites, and supervising work on site.

Type of person suited to this work

Organisational skills are essential as you ensure each construction job is completed accurately and efficiently. Mathematical and ICT skills are important for calculating costs, taking measurements and using computer-aided design.

You must have an understanding of the technical aspects of construction. You must be dependable and will need strong communication skills for working with suppliers, site teams and other professionals.

Working conditions

You may work on construction sites or in an office. Building technicians often divide their time between the two. When on site you will need to wear a safety helmet, overalls and boots at all times.

You are likely to work regular hours, but you may also have to start early, finish late or work at weekends on occasion as well as spend time away from home for various projects.

Future prospects

There are about 20,000 building technicians in the UK and currently a shortage of qualified applicants for the steady supply of vacancies.

Building technicians work for employers such as contractors, construction companies, property developers, surveyors' practices as well as the public sector. You may also have the opportunity to work abroad.

With experience and further qualifications, you may be promoted to a higher position such as building/construction manager. You may also choose to specialise in an area of expertise such as buying or drafting.

Advantages/disadvantages

It can be stressful having to work to deadlines.

Your work will be varied and interesting and you will be an integral part of the team producing all sorts of different buildings.

Money guide

Entry level salaries are typically £14,000–£17,000 but can increase to £23,500 with greater experience.

Up to £30,000 is possible for experienced senior building technicians.

Related opportunities

- Architectural Technologist p72
- Construction Supervisor/Manager p88
- Surveying Technician p124

Further information

Association of Building Engineers
www.abe.org.uk

Chartered Institute of Building
www.ciob.org.uk

ConstructionSkills
www.cskills.org

CARPENTER/JOINER ENTRY LEVEL 1

Qualifications and courses

There are no formal entry requirements for this career, although GCSEs/S grades in maths, English and technology will be helpful for calculations, measurements and theory. Most employers will require some on-site experience or a recognised qualification. City & Guilds offer Certificates in Basic Construction Skills such as Carpentry and Joinery (6217-02) and Woodworking (6217-05) for young learners under the age of 16. Once employed, you can work towards NVQs/SVQs in Carpentry, both on the job and at college.

Three-year Apprenticeships in Construction Building are available for school leavers. Diplomas and NVQs can be studied without an Apprenticeship, or alongside practical working, by attending a training centre or college.

NVQs in wood occupations are available, such as the Diploma in Site Carpentry (Levels 2 and 3) and the Certificate in Shopfitting Site Work (Levels 2 and 3).

The Construction Awards Alliance (CAA) runs a Foundation Certificate in Building Craft Occupations. Young Apprenticeships for 14–16 year olds may be available through the Construction Industry Training Board (CITB).

What the work involves

Carpenters/Joiners make, put in place or repair the wooden parts of buildings.

You may make and install floorboards, skirting boards, cupboards, partitions, windows and doors.

You will work with different types of wood and use specialist hand tools such as hammers, chisels and planes, as well as power tools like jigsaws and sanders. You will work either in a workshop or on site with other building professionals.

Type of person suited to this work

You must have good practical skills and enjoy working with your hands and different tools.

You will be expected to follow plans and work carefully with attention to detail so that the structures you make fit into place correctly. As you will need to take measurements and calculate angles and dimensions, you will have to be good at maths and be accurate.

You should be physically fit in order to move around and lift materials. You must also be able to work in a team with other carpenters and those from the other construction trades.

Working conditions

You may work in a workshop or on construction sites, or divide your time between the two.

This can be heavy, dangerous and dusty work. You will need to keep to health and safety regulations, which may include wearing protective gear such as safety goggles and a mask. You are likely to work a normal working week, usually with an early start, although weekend work may also be required.

Future prospects

Across the UK there are around 240,000 carpenters/joiners, but employers are finding it difficult to recruit well-qualified and experienced carpenters. Many qualified carpenters are self-employed or work as sub-contractors.

With experience, you could move into a related occupation like shopfitting, kitchen fitting or furniture making, or you may progress to training, technical, supervisory and managerial levels.

Advantages/disadvantages

Work can be seasonal: working fewer hours in the winter or having jobs cancelled is common.

You will develop a lot of new skills and you can specialise in certain areas such as listed buildings.

You get a sense of achievement when you see your woodwork in a building.

Money guide

Trainees start on a salary of £13,000–£16,000.

Qualified carpenters can earn anything in the range of £17,000–£26,000 per year.

Very experienced joiners could have an income of £35,000+.

The Building and Allied Trades Joint Industrial Council (BATJIC) agrees minimum wages annually.

Overtime is often available and on some projects you will receive bonuses based on output which can increase your earnings.

Self-employed carpenters will negotiate their own rates of pay.

Related opportunities

- Building Technician p78
- Construction Operative p86
- Window Fitter p131

Further information

British Woodworking Federation
www.bwf.org.uk

Institute of Carpenters
www.instituteofcarpenters.com

CARTOGRAPHER

Qualifications and courses

The usual entry requirement for a cartographer is a relevant degree. Useful degree subjects include geography, geographical information systems, urban/land studies, surveying and mapping sciences. GCSE/S grade maths is generally needed for entry to these degrees and an A level/H grade in science, maths or geography might be required. It is also useful to hold a postgraduate qualification in a relevant subject, for example, cartography, geographical information systems or remote sensing.

Entrants receive on-the-job training in relevant software and techniques. Government departments that employ cartographers have their own training schemes. It is also possible to work towards an NVQ/SVQ at Levels 3 and 4 in Spatial Data Management.

The minimum entry requirements for a cartographic technician are GCSEs/S grades (A*–C/1–3), including maths, English and a science. In practice, most entrants have A levels/H grades and some enter with a National Certificate/Diploma or HNC/HND in a relevant area.

The Royal Air Force and Ordnance Survey may have opportunities for school leavers to study for a Certificate/Diploma or HNC/HND in cartography by day release while training on the job.

What the work involves

Cartography involves collecting, evaluating and displaying information gained from a variety of sources, including satellite technology, to create or update maps and navigation charts. This is achieved by using artistic, scientific, and technological methods.

Owing to advances in information technology, geographical information systems and digital mapping techniques are now frequently used in this sector. You will use a range of sophisticated technology in all aspects of your work.

Type of person suited to this work

You will need to have strong IT, scientific and mathematical skills and an interest in geography.

Owing to the nature of the work, it is essential that you have good spatial awareness, colour vision and an eye for layout and design. One sheet of a map can take months to produce, so you must be patient and dedicated to your work. A high level of accuracy and attention to detail is needed so that the map provides the best possible information for the user.

You must be willing to keep up with developments in the field and experiment with new ways of producing maps.

Working conditions

You are likely to work normal office hours at a workstation where you will have access to a computer.

At a senior level you will have more opportunity to meet and interact with colleagues and clients.

Part of your job will involve travelling around the UK to carry out surveys.

Future prospects

Most work is available in government departments, such as Ordnance Survey, the Hydrographic Office and the Meteorological Office. You could also work for local authorities, universities, councils, commercial map publishers, oil companies and motoring organisations.

With experience, you could become a freelance cartographer, provide consultancy services or work within higher education as a tutor.

Willingness to be geographically mobile can improve your chances of career progression.

If you are interested in living abroad, there are opportunities to work in cartography all over the world.

Advantages/disadvantages

Producing a map that looks good, is user friendly and is likely to be used by many people is a very satisfying and rewarding experience.

As you near project deadlines, there is a higher level of pressure and you may be required to work late.

The work is varied and combines a variety of subject areas, from design to geography to maths.

Money guide

Starting salaries are usually between £15,000 and £18,000.

After 3–5 years' work experience, your earnings could increase to £20,000–£25,000.

It is possible for experienced or senior cartographers to achieve a salary of £30,000–£45,000.

Earnings vary depending on the size of the company and whether you work in the public or private sector.

Related opportunities

- Geographer p517
- Land/Geomatic Surveyor p106
- Town Planner/Planning Technician p127

Further information

Association for Geographic Information
www.agi.org.uk

British Cartographic Society
www.cartography.org.uk

The Survey Association
www.tsa-uk.org.uk

CEILING FIXER

Qualifications and courses

No specific qualifications are required, although GCSEs/S grades or a BTEC in Construction and the Built Environment may be helpful. Maths, design and technology, science and English are useful subjects.

You will be trained on the job while working towards qualifications. This may also involve going to a college or training centre on day or block release.

NVQs/SVQs in Interior Systems (Construction) Ceiling Fixing (Levels 1–3) are available. The Construction Specialist Apprenticeship may be available for those aged 16–24 who are looking to become a ceiling fixer.

You can also train by doing one of the Construction Industry Training Board (CITB)'s ConstructionSkills Apprenticeships which involves both studying and on-site experience.

Many employers require you to have the CSCS card issued by the Construction Skills Certification Scheme as proof of your competence working on site.

What the work involves

As a ceiling fixer you will fit suspended ceilings into new and existing commercial or public buildings.

Your work will involve fitting a ceiling grid in place and inserting tiles by using tools such as metal cutters and screwdrivers. The ceiling is fitted to the concrete floor of the room above and may hide wiring and air conditioning systems.

As the job requires you to work at heights and on construction sites, your safety training must be up to date.

Type of person suited to this work

You will need to be comfortable working at heights and you must be physically fit to do the necessary climbing, carrying and bending.

You need to be thorough and accurate. An understanding of technical plans is essential and you must be able to follow instructions but also use your initiative. Numeracy skills are important to measure materials and calculate weights. As you will work alongside other ceiling fixers, electricians, heating and ventilating fitters, painters and decorators you need to be a good team player.

Working conditions

You will need to travel to various construction sites so a driving licence will be useful. The sites you work on will mainly be indoors and you will most likely work from a ladder in confined spaces.

You will need to take safety precautions for yourself and your colleagues and you will be expected to wear protective clothing such as a hard hat, boots and overalls. You are likely to work Monday to Friday, normal office hours, although overtime may be available at the weekends.

This could be dusty work which might be difficult if you suffer from some allergies.

Future prospects

There is currently a shortage of qualified ceiling fixers in the construction industry.

You will most likely start out as a tradesperson. With experience, you may progress to a supervisory or managerial position, or perhaps run your own company. You could become a subcontractor.

Advantages/disadvantages

Working at heights and in confined spaces may be stressful for some people.

It is satisfying to see the transformation that takes place when you have worked on fitting a ceiling.

You will have the opportunity to work on a variety of projects in different types of buildings.

Money guide

Trainees can earn up to £13,000 a year.

When starting out as a newly qualified ceiling fixer you can expect a salary of around £18,000 per year.

With a Level 3 NVQ, your earnings can reach up to £22,000.

Ceiling fixers with extensive experience can achieve a salary of £28,000.

Those who do contract/temporary work may receive a higher hourly/daily rate than those in full-time employment.

There are often opportunities to increase your earnings through shift allowances, working overtime and receiving performance-related bonuses.

Related opportunities

- Construction Operative p86
- Plasterer p111
- Roofer p116

Further information

Association of Interior Specialists
www.ais-interiors.org.uk

ConstructionSkills
www.cskills.org

CHARTERED SURVEYOR

Qualifications and courses

You must become a member of the Royal Institution of Chartered Surveyors (RICS). For this you must complete an RICS-accredited degree course or a postgraduate conversion course. Degree entry requires 5 GCSEs/S grades (A*–C/1–3) and 3 A levels/4 H grades, or the relevant BTEC/SQA national awards. After completing an RICS-accredited course you must gain practical experience and undertake training before you will be fully qualified.

If you do not have the appropriate A levels or GCSEs you can take HNC/HND courses or Foundation degrees which can then be supplemented by an RICS-accredited degree course.

You can also train on the job as part of the Chartered Surveyors Training Trust scheme. This is available to those aged 16–24 who have 4 GCSEs (A*–C) or equivalent. This programme involves a 2 year Apprenticeship which will grant you Associate membership of the RICS. You then have the option to study for an accredited degree and take the RICS Assessment of Professional Competence to become a chartered surveyor.

You will be required to undertake continuing professional development (CPD) to keep up to date with surveying trends and skills.

What the work involves

As a chartered surveyor you will offer professional advice within the particular field of surveying that you choose to specialise in. This can be in building, construction, planning, the environment or quantity surveying. You will also spend time negotiating and explaining design/construction issues to clients.

You will have a variety of tasks to do such as examining plans, designs and project briefs, taking measurements, recording and analysing data and interpreting it through charts, maps or diagrams.

You may oversee entire construction projects, where you will ensure that specifications are met, calculate supplies needed and advise clients on the purchase, sale or development of property or land.

Type of person suited to this work

You should have an interest in construction, architecture, landscape and the environment.

As you are required to liaise with construction workers and clients, you must have excellent communication, negotiation and problem-solving skills and the ability to delegate tasks.

You need to be highly organised, methodical in your work and have a keen eye for detail as you may be coordinating several complex projects at the same time.

Working conditions

You will probably work 9am–5pm, Monday to Friday. You may have to work longer hours to meet deadlines. Part-time work is available.

You will primarily be based in an office but you will also spend a considerable amount of time on site.

Depending on your field of specialisation, you might have to work in various weather conditions and wear protective clothing when on site.

You may have to travel for your work, both abroad and within the UK. For this reason a driving licence is strongly recommended.

Future prospects

You may follow a formal promotion structure to gain senior management roles.

You could choose to become self-employed or to join a private practice.

As a qualified chartered surveyor and member of the RICS you will have to take part in Continuing Professional Development (CPD). For this you must accumulate 60 hours of CPD every 3 years.

Advantages/disadvantages

Employers may provide benefits such as a company car, mobile phone, bonuses and pension scheme.

There is significant competition for graduates wishing to gain entry to some areas of chartered surveying.

Money guide

As a graduate your starting salary may range from £19,000 to £25,000 a year.

Once fully qualified, you can expect to earn £32,000–£40,000.

Those in a senior role with extensive experience can achieve £70,000–£100,000.

Salaries vary with geographical location and tend to be higher in London.

Depending on the type of project you are working on, very generous bonuses may be available.

Related opportunities

- Land/Geomatic Surveyor p106
- Surveying Technician p124
- Town Planner/Planning Technician p127

Further information

Association of Building Engineers
www.abe.org.uk

Chartered Surveyors Training Trust
www.cstt.org.uk

Royal Institution of Chartered Surveyors
www.rics.org

Qualifications and courses

Entrants to civil engineering are usually graduates, although there are opportunities to progress from a craft or technical level.

The main route to becoming an engineer is a degree in the relevant branch of engineering or a closely related subject. It is recommended that you study a civil engineering course which is accredited by the Institution of Civil Engineers (ICE). The normal minimum entry requirements for an engineering degree are 3 A levels or 5 H grades including maths and a science, usually physics or chemistry. Equivalent qualifications such as BTEC/SQA National qualifications may be accepted.

Candidates who do not have the relevant A levels or equivalent may gain entry to an engineering degree by taking a 1 year foundation course. Foundation courses are offered by universities and are sometimes taught at local partner colleges.

It is possible to enter engineering after taking GCSEs/S grades and progress to technician or professional level by studying part time for an HNC/HND or NVQ/SVQ Levels 4 or 5. You will need GCSEs/S grades (A*–C/1–3) in English, maths and science. There are also BTEC and SQA National Certificates or Diplomas which will give you the relevant qualifications and which can be studied at any age.

Many engineering technicians gain entry to the career by firstly working through an engineering Apprenticeship scheme. To gain a place you may need 4 GCSEs with grades A*–C in subjects including maths, science or design and technology, or equivalent qualifications. The availability of Apprenticeship schemes depends on the job market of your local area and on the skills needed by your local employers.

Professional engineers can be chartered or incorporated members of one of the engineering professional bodies, such as ICE or the Chartered Institution of Building Services Engineers (CIBSE).

The usual requirement for chartered status is an accredited MEng degree or equivalent. For incorporated status, a 3 year accredited BEng or BSc degree or an HND or equivalent, plus an additional period of learning is required.

Undertaking a summer work experience placement or choosing a degree course with a year in industry can be useful ways to develop contacts within engineering and extend your knowledge.

What the work involves

Civil engineer (consulting)
You will be designing and developing plans for construction projects such as roads, tunnels, bridges, railways, reservoirs, pipelines and major buildings.

Your work could span many areas including waste management, coastal development and geotechnical engineering.

Your job will involve communicating with clients and once you have gained significant experience, you can run projects as a project manager.

Civil engineer (contracting)
You will take the consulting civil engineer's designs and make them into a reality at ground level, overseeing and managing the construction project.

This will include recruiting a team, sourcing materials, managing budgets and ensuring that the project is completed on time.

Contractors will sometimes create a design and build a team themselves. The roles of consultants and contractors are therefore not always entirely different from one another.

Civil engineering technician
You will be responsible for providing technical support to the civil engineer, which may include producing costing and timing estimates for a project and helping with recruitment.

The role will also include aspects of land and quantity surveying, as well as the production of design drawings.

Projects in which you are involved will fall under the categories of structural, transportation, environmental and maritime.

Type of person suited to this work

Regardless of the area you decide to work in, you will need to enjoy finding creative but workable solutions to problems.

You will need to be confident when using computers to produce designs, work out budgets and undertake research.

You should also be good at maths and science so that you can make accurate calculations and understand the different building materials available to you.

You must be able to think three dimensionally so that you can visualise and design different buildings and structures.

Written and verbal communication skills are important as you will have to write reports, explain your designs to clients and other professionals and supervise construction staff. You will work as part of a team so you must be able to communicate and cooperate with people at all levels.

An understanding of environmental building issues, such as the use of energy efficient materials and land protection, is of increasing importance.

Working conditions

Working hours are typically longer than the average working week and can include early morning and evening work on site.

Weekend or shift work is rare for civil engineers, although civil engineering technicians can be required to remain on 24 hour call for some projects.

Your work will involve being both indoors and out on-site. When working on site you will need to stick to health and safety regulations and be aware of your own and colleagues' safety. You will have to wear safety clothing including a helmet.

You could spend time in dangerous places or in difficult environments, for example you may have to work up ladders or on scaffolding.

When you are in your office, you will be based at a workstation where you will use a computer with specialised software and possibly a drawing board. You will attend meetings and speak to clients on the phone or in person.

It is also likely that you will have to work away from home occasionally, both within the UK and abroad, but the extent of this will depend on the size of the company you work for and the type of contracts they attract.

Future prospects

Around 100,000 professional civil engineers work in the UK for a range of employers including health trusts, local authorities, central government, energy suppliers (including water, gas, nuclear and electricity companies), contractors, consultancies and transport networks.

Work is available on a variety of projects including the building of new schools, hospitals and the upgrading of public transport networks.

Many UK civil engineering companies also operate globally, increasing the opportunities to work overseas. The range and size of opportunities open to you will depend on the size of the company you work for and the types of contracts won.

Civil engineering technicians can undertake job-related training and study for more qualifications to become a civil engineer.

There is scope to undertake further study and specialise in areas such as environmental engineering, coastal and marine engineering, geotechnics or tunnelling.

With experience, you can progress into management or possibly associate/partnership positions within UK or international companies. Within the public sector, there are opportunities for management and chief engineer jobs. Another career option is to become self-employed or to provide training or consultancy services.

Advantages/disadvantages

You will play an important part in the design and construction of buildings and structures throughout the world so you are likely to be well-respected.

Seeing a project come to completion can be very satisfying.

Having an engineering background and qualifications opens up opportunities to enter other non-engineering careers at senior levels.

There is the opportunity to become self-employed or work overseas.

Work is varied, each day is different and you will be meeting and dealing with a wide range of people.

The pace of work varies quite extensively as you will alternate between a heavy workload and quieter periods.

There is a high level of responsibility in this field so the work can be demanding and occasionally stressful.

Money guide

Starting salaries for civil engineers, either contracting or consulting, are between £17,000 and £24,000.

As you gain between 2 and 5 years' experience, earnings range from £25,000 to £31,000.

Civil engineers in more senior roles average between £32,000 and £45,000.

Qualifying as a member or fellow of the Institution of Civil Engineers (ICE) can see salaries for civil engineers rise to over £60,000.

Civil engineering technicians start on about £17,000–£19,000.

With experience, earnings increase to £20,000–£26,000 a year.

Senior technicians can earn £33,000 or more and if you train as a civil engineer your earning potential will increase as above.

Earnings are likely to be considerably higher in London and they vary depending on the size of the company.

Many employers offer additional benefits including a pension scheme, life insurance, a healthcare package and possibly a company car.

Related opportunities

- Architect p70
- Building Surveyor p77
- Insurance Risk Surveyor p46
- Town Planner/Planning Technician p127

Further information

Engineering Council UK
www.engc.org.uk

Institution of Civil Engineers
www.ice.org.uk

The Engineering Careers Information Service
www.enginuity.org.uk

WISE
www.wisecampaign.org.uk

CONCRETER

Qualifications and courses

You can work as a trainee concreter and learn on the job as soon as you leave school. Apprenticeships are available. It would be helpful to have GCSEs/S grades (A*–E/1–5) including maths, design, technology and English.

You can work towards NVQs in Trowel Occupations (Levels 1 and 2), Erection of Precast Concrete (Level 2) and Specialist Concrete Occupations such as Concrete Repair, Sprayed Concrete or Concrete Drilling (Level 2).

Foundation Construction Awards in Trowel Occupations are available if obtaining experience in the workplace for NVQs is a challenge. Colleges offer these awards alongside an Apprenticeship.

What the work involves

Your job will aid in the construction of drives and pathways, floor slabs, foundations, columns and beams.

You will initially level and compact the ground to prepare it for concreting.

You will take early-morning deliveries of concrete, place it on the prepared ground, vibrate it to remove air trappings, and wrap it in polythene sheeting in order to cure it.

At times you might need to mix cement, stone and water to make concrete.

Type of person suited to this work

You should have a careful, methodical approach to your work and have good hand skills.

Maths skills are important as you will be calculating quantities for materials.

You should enjoy working outdoors, as part of a team or on your own. Being fit and active is essential as you will be required to work long and at times hard hours.

You need to be aware of health and safety requirements when working on site.

Working conditions

Your work will be site based, largely undertaking manual labour in dirty or dusty surroundings.

You will work 37 hours a week, including some early mornings and late nights.

You could work on a building site, motorway, private driveway or the interiors of large buildings.

Protective clothing is needed, as the work is messy and at times, potentially dangerous.

You will use traditional hand tools such as shovels as well as machinery such as cement mixers and drillers.

Future prospects

You can move into specialised areas of work such as concrete spraying or concrete repair. It is also possible to progress to a managerial or supervisory role.

After gaining experience, many concreters choose to become self-employed. You could start your own company or work on a labour-only basis for a contractor.

You can work for building and engineering contractors, local authorities and public organisations. Job opportunities are also available abroad, as well as throughout the UK.

Advantages/disadvantages

You have the opportunity to earn good money if you work hard.

There is an increased risk of injury on construction sites. The cement in concrete can cause burning or inflammation and you should avoid contact with the skin.

The work is physically draining, as it involves a great deal of practical work and, at times, heavy lifting.

Money guide

As a trainee you can expect to earn around £12,500.

With experience this can rise to £20,000–£25,000.

Concrete sprayers with a lot of experience can earn up to £30,000.

Salaries can be boosted by bonuses and overtime.

You may earn more if you set up your own contracting firm.

Related opportunities

- Bricklayer p74
- Construction Operative p86
- Plasterer p111

Further information

Chartered Institute of Building
www.ciob.org.uk

The Concrete Centre
www.concretecentre.com

Women and Manual Trades
www.wamt.org

CONSTRUCTION OPERATIVE

ENTRY LEVEL 1

Qualifications and courses

Your training will be mainly on the job by experienced labourers/construction operatives and tradespeople.

There may be opportunities while you are working to study for NVQs/SVQs (Levels 1 and 2) in Construction and Civil Engineering or Specialised Plant and Machinery Operations.

City & Guilds offer Certificates in Basic Construction Skills (6217) for young learners under the age of 16 and an Award/Certificate/Diploma in Basic Construction Skills for 14–19 year olds. BTEC Certificates and Diplomas are available in Construction as well as a Foundation Certificate in Building and Craft Occupations.

You can also train to be a construction operative via a 2 year Construction Civil Engineering Apprenticeship scheme and choose to do an extra year for a Level 3 Construction Diploma.

If you are a full-time student doing a construction-related course you can qualify for a programme-led apprenticeship (PLA) and can gain experience up to NVQ Level 2.

Many employers require you to have the CSCS card issued by the Construction Skills Certification Scheme as proof of your competence working on site.

What the work involves

Construction operatives support the work of other construction workers by doing various practical tasks.

Your work might include digging trenches, moving building materials and tools, putting up signs and safety barriers, helping to lay drains, and paving roads.

You will also mix and lay cement as well as operate construction equipment and vehicles.

Type of person suited to this work

As the work requires you to lift heavy materials and be on the move a lot you must be physically fit. You must also not mind working at great heights or depths.

You need to be able to follow and carry out instructions and work well in a team with other labourers and professionals.

It is essential to be hands on, flexible and trustworthy.

Working conditions

You will be working both indoors and outdoors in all weather conditions.

The work is often dusty and dirty and may be difficult for people suffering from allergies.

You will need to pay attention to both your own and your colleagues' health and safety. You will be expected to follow procedures for each type of work you do, including the wearing of protective clothing.

You may work a normal week, although evening and weekend work may also be available, and you might need to start early or finish late for some projects as well as work away from home at times.

Future prospects

Building projects, new builds and renovations can't happen without construction operatives so they are in strong demand when business is doing well.

You could work for the public sector, contractors or local authorities.

You may progress to a specialist craft career such as carpentry or bricklaying or advance to a supervisory role. You have the option of becoming self-employed or working abroad.

Advantages/disadvantages

The work can sometimes be physically demanding.

You have the opportunity to learn a wide range of skills and work on a different project every day.

Your role on site is important as you pave the way for tradespeople to complete their tasks.

Money guide

As a trainee starting out you can expect a salary of around £9,000–£15,500 per year.

As a skilled construction operative you could earn £17,000–£20,000.

Depending on the project they are working on, skilled operatives may receive more than £24,000 a year.

Overtime is often available for those who wish to increase their earnings.

On some projects there are bonuses based on outputs which can lead to higher earnings.

Related opportunities

- Bricklayer p74
- Building Technician p78
- Mastic Asphalter p107

Further information

ConstructionSkills
www.cskills.org

Federation of Master Builders
www.fmb.org.uk

Women and Manual Trades
www.wamt.org

CONSTRUCTION PLANT OPERATOR

Qualifications and courses

There are no set academic entry requirements, although GCSEs/S grades or equivalent in English, maths and science or technology are useful, along with equivalent vocational qualifications. It is also possible to take NVQs/SVQs in Specialised Plant and Machinery Operations (Levels 1 and 2) and Foundation, Intermediate and Advanced certificates in Maintenance of Construction Plant.

The minimum age to operate plant and equipment is 18 but 17-year-olds may work under supervision while they are training.

Construction Civil Engineering Apprenticeships may be available for those over the age of 16 who wish to train as a construction plant operator. Another option is to train as an apprentice in Crane Operation or Plant Operations with the National Construction College. This route involves practical training and studying for the NVQ Diploma and Certificate in Plant Operations (Level 2).

The Construction Plant Competence Scheme (CPCS) card is required to operate most categories of plant, including cranes. New applicants must pass a health and safety test and technical test for a red CPCS card which allows trainees to work on site. After working 300 hours and completing an NVQ/SVQ you can obtain a blue card.

What the work involves

Construction plant operators operate and maintain different forms of plant (machinery) used for tasks such as moving soil and building materials, flattening the earth and preparing concrete.

You may operate bulldozers, excavators, diggers, cranes and fork-lift trucks.

In larger organisations you may specialise in operating one type of plant. For example, crane operators control the machine to load and unload materials, working in conjunction with a signaller on the ground.

Type of person suited to this work

As you will often handle large and complex machines, you need to be good with your hands and have keen safety awareness. You will also need good mechanical knowledge.

You need to stay focused and communicate with your workmates so that you can operate safely. If you are working on cranes, you need to be comfortable working at heights, be alert and be a skilled driver.

Working conditions

You will work outdoors and on a variety of sites. Expect to get hot, dusty and dirty in the summer and cold, muddy and wet in the winter. You will have to stick to health and safety regulations and wear a protective helmet and boots.

You are likely to work a normal working week from Monday to Friday but you may also work extra hours at weekends. Some construction firms operate longer hours during the summer months and shorter during the winter. You might have to travel away from home on some contracts.

A driving licence (often a large goods vehicle category C licence) is essential for crane operators.

Future prospects

Work is available across the UK with crane-hire companies, manufacturers, local authorities and construction companies. For operators specialising in engineering work there is a high concentration of jobs available in the Midlands and in the north of England.

With experience, you may progress to using a wider range of plant and you may supervise or train plant operators or work as a safety inspector. You may also choose to specialise in operating one type of plant.

With experience and financial backing, it may be possible to start your own construction plant operation or hire business.

Advantages/disadvantages

Working on construction sites can be noisy, dusty and dirty although you will have safety equipment/clothing such as ear protectors. Working at heights may be demanding for some people.

It is a skilled and varied career where you are responsible for some impressive machinery. It can be satisfying to be able to control the machinery efficiently and safely.

Money guide

Trainee construction plant operators typically have a starting salary of £13,000.

As you gain qualifications, your earnings can increase to £15,000–£19,000 a year.

Very experienced plant operators or those with specialist skills can achieve £20,000–£28,000.

It is possible to increase your earnings through bonuses and working overtime.

Related opportunities

- Construction Operative p86
- Demolition Operative p90
- Highways Maintenance/Road Worker p103

Further information

Association of Building Engineers
www.abe.org.uk

ConstructionSkills
www.cskills.org

CONSTRUCTION SUPERVISOR/ MANAGER

Qualifications and courses

The normal entry qualification to be a construction manager is a degree, HND or Foundation degree. Relevant subjects include construction project management, building services engineering and building technology. For entry to a degree, 5 GCSEs/S grades (A*–C/1–3) including maths and science and 2 A levels/3 H grades are normally required.

It may be possible to work your way up from technician level. The NVQ/SVQ in Construction Site Supervision (Level 3) and Construction Site Management (Level 4) are open to anyone with experience in building site supervision and management. Technicians can also study part time towards an HNC or degree.

The Chartered Institute of Building (CIOB) offers qualifications at Levels 3 and 4 in Site Management and Site Supervisory Studies which could improve your career prospects.

Recently qualified graduates are likely to continue training on programmes designed for professional and managerial staff. The CIOB runs a Professional Development Programme (PDP) leading to Chartered Membership of the Institute.

What the work involves

Construction supervisors/managers run both new build and maintenance construction sites. Your duties will include planning the build, preparing the site, arranging deliveries, and checking quality and cost of building materials and equipment.

You will also have the responsibility for overseeing the construction project, hiring and managing staff, making sure everyone is safe on site, and solving problems when they arise.

You will need to report directly to whoever is paying for the work to be done and keep them updated on progress.

Type of person suited to this work

You have to be able to plan ahead and have good management and problem-solving skills so that projects run smoothly. Numeracy skills are important in order to budget your projects.

You need to be a good communicator, energetic, hard working and diplomatic in order to motivate and manage your staff effectively. You must be able to develop an in-depth knowledge and understanding of all aspects of the construction business. You will use computer software packages to plan workflow, so ICT skills are also useful.

Organisational skills are essential and you should be prepared to take responsibility for anything that happens on your site.

Working conditions

You will be based on construction sites and are likely to work from a portable office. You will work outdoors in all weathers.

You may work a normal working week, but you may also have to start early, finish late or work at weekends on some projects. As some companies win contracts all over the UK, you might have to work away from home.

Future prospects

There is a shortage of qualified construction managers and supervisors across the UK. There are opportunities on a wide range of projects including multi-million pound builds. You may also be able to work abroad.

You may work for contractors, construction companies, project management companies, surveyors' practices, public services, utility companies or retailers.

With experience, you may be promoted to work as a contract manager on bigger and more prestigious projects. You could teach or work as a health and safety inspector.

Advantages/disadvantages

There is a great deal of satisfaction to be obtained from knowing that you have the ability to begin with an empty piece of land and leave a finished construction behind.

When there is a tight deadline to meet and a problem arises, the work can be stressful – particularly as many projects are on large but tightly planned budgets.

Money guide

Trainee construction managers usually have an annual salary of £14,000–£19,000.

Once you have gained experience as a manager, your earnings can rise to between £25,000 and £40,000.

For managers running the largest projects £70,000+ is possible.

Earnings vary depending on geographical location and your particular employer.

Related opportunities

- Architectural Technician p71
- Building Surveyor p77
- Civil/Construction Engineer/Civil Engineering Technician p83

Further information

Chartered Institute of Building
www.ciob.org.uk

ConstructionSkills
www.cskills.org

DAMP PROOFER

Qualifications and courses

There are no set academic requirements. However GCSE/S grade English and maths (A*–E/1–5) are an advantage as you will need to calculate quantities, make estimates and keep written records.

No colleges provide apprenticeships specifically for damp proofing. Some private companies, involved in Investors in People, may consider apprenticeships.

On-the-job training is provided by experienced damp proofers. Damp-proof installer companies may provide courses on safety awareness.

Technicians can take short courses at the British Wood Preserving and Damp Proofing Association. You can study for the Level 2 NVQ in Insulation and Building Treatments. You must have a Construction Skills Certification Scheme card to work on a building site.

What the work involves

You will provide guidance and solutions to people in residential or commercial properties who experience damp problems.

You also may need to install damp-proof courses to buildings. This is a horizontal layer of water-repellent/proof material that prevents moisture rising from the ground up the walls.

You will need to be able to install damp-proof courses to old and new buildings. In new buildings this is laid as walls are constructed by the bricklayers.

Type of person suited to this work

As you will be working on buildings or engineering projects, you should have an interest in construction and architecture. You should also be in good health and have an understanding of health and safety protocol.

You should have good problem-solving skills and relish new challenges. You should be able to work in a team and cooperate with colleagues and customers. You will need good written and communication skills to give and follow instructions and guidelines.

You need to have a keen eye for detail and have good practical skills to operate drills and specialist machinery such as moisture meters to check damp levels. You should also be willing to travel.

Working conditions

You will usually work 38 hours a week, Monday to Friday. You may have to work overtime and this could include evenings and weekends. These hours will vary depending on where you are working, who you are working for and even the weather.

You will have to do a lot of travelling to each new site. A driving licence and car would be useful.

Your work will be largely outdoors, so can be affected by the weather.

Future prospects

You can find job opportunities with the 1500 damp proofing contractors across the UK. You can also find employment in related fields such as timber treatment, waterproofing and pest control.

With experience you will be eligible for promotion to remedial treatment surveyor or supervisory posts. The BWPDA runs its own training courses for surveyors and technicians and with an NVQ/SVQ Level 2 in Insulation and Remedial Maintenance you can apply for occupational assessment under the Construction Skills Certification Scheme (CSCS Card).

You may become self-employed.

Advantages/disadvantages

As a damp proofer you will have plenty of opportunities to travel around the UK and abroad.

You may have to work in uncomfortable weather conditions and antisocial working hours.

Money guide

Starting salary can range between £12,000 and £15,000 a year.

With experience, this can rise to £25,000 a year.

With specialised skills and training you can earn up to £35,000 or more.

Related opportunities

- Building Technician p78
- Concreter p85
- Thermal Insulation Engineer p126

Further information

Institute of Specialist Surveyors and Engineers
www.isse.org.uk

Wood Protection Association
www.wood-protection.org

DEMOLITION OPERATIVE

Qualifications and courses

No formal qualifications are required to be a demolition operative. However GCSEs/S grades (A*–E/1–5) in maths, science subjects and English or a background in general construction may be useful for calculations, measurements and theory. The Edexcel Diploma in Construction and the Built Environment may be relevant for this job.

You can enter via the ConstructionSkills Demolition Plant Operation Apprenticeship, if you are under 16, but you need to be at least 18 to work as a demolition operative. There is also a specialist Apprenticeship, for people who work in demolition but do not handle machinery.

Most training is done on the job, with special attention given to health and safety – including accident prevention, manual handling, noise control and fire control/prevention. You can study for the NVQ at Level 2 in Demolition and Demolition Plant. Other NVQs are available for specialist work such as the Level 2 in Removal of Hazardous and Non-Hazardous Waste.

You will need a Certificate of Competence of Demolition Operatives (CCDO) card to prove you are qualified to carry out the job.

What the work involves

Demolition operatives demolish or dismantle buildings and structures. The job can be highly dangerous if the right precautions are not taken so you will be responsible for assessing structures and planning for the safest and most efficient way to demolish them.

You will prepare sites, put up fencing and scaffolding, strip out fittings, and remove, sort and grade reusable materials.

You will use a variety of tools such as chisels, crowbars and axes for hand demolition of brick and stone and you may also use specialised machinery including pneumatic drills, steel girders, chain saws and even explosives for bigger jobs.

Type of person suited to this work

As you will be involved in the construction industry you should have an interest in building, construction and the environment.

You should have a high level of fitness as your work can be quite physical at times, lifting and carrying, and you should be able to work at heights. You will also need good manual skills to operate equipment and tools and an aptitude for more delicate tasks such as hand demolition.

You should have a strong eye for detail and able to follow health and safety instructions rigorously.

You should be willing to work as part of a team and be conscious of your safety and that of those around you.

Working conditions

You will normally work 39 hours per week. This will frequently include weekends and overtime.

As you will be working on construction sites you should be willing to work outdoors in dirty, dusty, noisy conditions in all weathers. This will also involve lifting, bending and working at heights.

You will need to wear protective equipment including helmets, boots, gloves and goggles which will be provided by the employer. You may also be required to wear breathing equipment for some jobs.

Future prospects

There are opportunities for demolition operatives on many building and development projects throughout the UK. You can find employment in specialist companies which may be based nationally but many companies are based in urban and traditionally industrial areas of the UK.

Advantages/disadvantages

Although it is unusual to be self-employed in this profession, with experience you can set up your own contracting business.

At times your work can be strenuous and potentially hazardous if you do not follow safety procedures.

Money guide

Demolition operatives have nationally recommended minimum rates of pay.

Starting salaries are around £12,500 a year.

With experience this can rise to £18,000.

As a senior operative you can earn up to around £23,000. You may earn significantly more with overtime or for operating plant machinery.

Related opportunities

- Construction Operative p86
- Quarry Worker p240
- Scaffolder p118

Further information

ConstructionSkills
www.cskills.org

National Federation of Demolition Contractors
www.demolition-nfdc.com

DRY STONE WALLER

Qualifications and courses

No specific qualifications are required. You can train with an experienced dry stone waller or do a land-based training course that includes dry stone walling.

Lantra Certificates at Levels 1 and 2 are available in Dry Stone Walling.

The Dry Stone Walling Association of Great Britain (DSWA) runs a National Certification scheme at 3 levels (Initial, Intermediate and Advanced), which is open to anyone, including complete beginners.

What the work involves

Dry stone walls are built as boundaries in rural landscapes, and sometimes in gardens and parks. Unlike other walls, they are built without the use of mortar or cement.

You will build new walls and maintain and rebuild existing walls, using the existing or newly quarried stone.

You will prepare foundations, set up a frame and lay stones, as well as strip out any existing wall or stones. You will need to be able to use tools such as hammers, sledgehammers, pick axes and tape measures.

Type of person suited to this work

You need to be thorough, methodical and good with your hands.

Being physically fit is essential as you will be lifting and carrying heavy stones. You will also need endurance and self-motivation as you will most likely be self-employed.

An eye for design is useful for creating decorative effects. You may also need to work in a team with other dry stone wallers.

You will need to respect the plants, animals and insects that live within, on or around the walls and other parts of your working area so having an interest in conservation and the environment is useful. You should also be aware of health and safety regulations.

Working conditions

Your work will be physically demanding and take place outdoors in most weather conditions. The work may also be dusty and dirty.

You will need to wear protective gear such as boots, strong gloves and safety goggles.

Your working hours are likely to vary according to daylight hours and when the work is available. You may need to work weekends.

Future prospects

Dry stone walling is prospering owing to the increased interest in conserving walls and the growth in artistic landscape projects.

With a demand for walls on farms, parks and gardens, work is available in all rural areas of the UK for skilled dry stone wallers.

Employment is possible with organisations such as National Parks and The National Trust – although most experienced dry stone wallers are self-employed.

You can begin by working for an experienced dry stone waller and gain the necessary skills before working for yourself.

Many experienced wallers travel around the UK to complete projects. A few wallers combine this work with traditional bricklaying work.

Advantages/disadvantages

The work can be physically demanding.

It is rewarding to use craft skills to build dry stone walls that are not only functional, but also enhance the landscape and become part of our heritage.

You also have the chance to be creative when producing decorative effects.

Money guide

The normal starting point for new entrants is around £8,000 per year.

For dry stone wallers with some experience, earning between £10,500 and £14,500 is possible.

For very skilled dry stone wallers up to £21,000 is likely. Earnings vary widely across the UK.

Related opportunities

- Blacksmith p214
- Construction Operative p86
- Stonemason p122
- Thatcher p125

Further information

Dry Stone Walling Association of Great Britain
www.dswa.org.uk

Lantra
www.lantra.co.uk

ELECTRICIAN

Qualifications and courses

An appropriate Level 3 NVQ and a technical certificate are needed. The most common route is through an Electrotechnical Advanced Apprenticeship. As part of this route you will take an NVQ in Electrotechnical Services and there are options to specialise in areas such as Electrical Installation and Electrical Maintenance.

Entry requirements are 3 GCSEs/S grades (A*–C/1–3) including English, maths and science.

Entry to the profession is quite competitive and you must pass a colour vision and selection test.

The City & Guilds' Certificate in the Requirements for Electrical Installations helps to ensure that those practising in the electrical industry are up to date with the latest safety regulations.

Those experienced in areas like electronics may qualify for entrance onto a training course. Colleges and private organisations offer their own courses but candidates must show practical work ability. Other qualifications include the City & Guilds NVQ in Engineering Maintenance and the BTEC National Certificate in Engineering.

What the work involves

Electricians install and inspect the wiring systems in all kinds of buildings (residential and commercial) and mechanical equipment.

You will follow detailed diagrams and plans when checking and installing new systems. Once installed you will test them to make sure they are safe.

You may work on quite complex wiring systems, ranging from security circuits and computer networks to traffic lights and other street lighting.

Type of person suited to this work

Normal colour vision is essential. You must also have the practical skills to be able to use tools such as pliers, screwdrivers and drills. You should have the ability to follow wiring diagrams and work within strict safety regulations. Knowledge of maths and physics is beneficial.

You will need to be physically fit as the work involves bending, stretching, kneeling and generally being active. It can also involve working at heights, so you must be comfortable with this.

You may work alone or in a team but either way you will be talking to customers and explaining electrical problems, so good communication skills are an asset.

Working conditions

You may work a normal working week from Monday to Friday, but most electricians work 37–40 hours including evenings and weekends to accommodate the needs of their customers.

Electricians work in a variety of locations from people's homes to offices or building sites. You will almost certainly need a driving licence. The work can be dusty and dirty.

You will need to keep to health and safety regulations otherwise working with electricity can be exceedingly dangerous.

Future prospects

Employment prospects for new trainees are good, although the job market may be affected by the recent economic downturn.

Work is available in housing associations, general building companies and public services such as local authorities and health trusts.

With further qualifications and experience, you can progress to approved grade and then technician grade, which will increase your earning potential. You may hold a supervisory or management position and owning your own company is also an option. There may be opportunities to work abroad.

Advantages/disadvantages

You are providing a vital service and it is particularly rewarding to solve problems for people.

Many electricians are self-employed so you could have increased control over your work–life balance.

You may be required to work long hours and sometimes in physically difficult circumstances.

Money guide

The Joint Industry Board (JIB) for the Electrical Contracting Industry sets salary rates for apprentices and qualified electricians.

Trainees usually start on about £9,000–£10,000.

Once qualified, salaries rise to between £14,000 and £20,000.

Earnings increase with experience and those who specialise in a certain area can make £30,000–£40,000 a year.

Related opportunities

- Bricklayer p74
- Carpenter/Joiner p79
- Plumber p112

Further information

Scottish Electrical Charitable Training Trust
www.sectt.org.uk

SummitSkills
www.summitskills.org.uk

Organisation profile

NICEIC

About NICEIC

NICEIC is the UK's leading voluntary regulatory body for the electrical contracting industry. It has been assessing the electrical competence of electricians for over 50 years and currently maintains a roll of over 26,000 registered contractors.

Choosing an NICEIC registered electrician is a householder's best way to ensure a safe job. Electricians registered with NICEIC are assessed on a regular basis to ensure high standards and their work is checked against the IEE Wiring Regulations BS7671 as well as other standards.

Why choose an NICEIC registered electrician?

NICEIC operates an independent complaints procedure governing the technical standards of its Approved Contractor and Domestic Installer Schemes. If the work of a registered contractor is found to be below the accepted technical standard, NICEIC can require the contractor to correct the work at no additional cost to the customer.

Approved contractors undergo a rigorous assessment process, covering a representative sample of their work, their premises, documentation, equipment, and the competence of their key supervisory staff. They are then re-assessed on a regular basis to ensure continued compliance.

Once registered with the NICEIC, contractors can access a range of support services, including technical advice, industry recognised training, industry literature and contractor insurance.

NICEIC regularly promotes the importance of employing an approved contractor to homeowners. Aside from the assurance of safety and competence of work, additional benefits to the consumer include guaranteed compliance with building regulations, an insurance-backed warranty and access to an independent complaints procedure, should a problem arise.

Looking after the industry

NICEIC is committed to improving standards within the industry and in September 2010 NICEIC set up an apprenticeship scheme as part of its commitment to training the workforce of the future.

NICEIC believe apprenticeships make industries more effective, productive and competitive by addressing the skills gap directly. They are the proven way to train the workforce of the future.

The NICEIC Apprentice Academy gives those just starting out on their careers the knowledge to complete electrical installations in line with current and future working practices. Run in partnership with Bedford College, trainee electricians complete a series of fortnightly courses over 2 years before embarking on a final year of professional development under the guidance of NICEIC.

NICEIC is also committed to improving opportunities for women in the electrical contracting industry. Women are severely under-represented in most trade professions with less than one in every thousand electricians a female – despite their now being a valid business case to employ more women.

In response to this NICEIC launched its Jobs for the Girls campaign. Through its extensive media coverage the campaign has raised awareness of the opportunities available to women in the industry. It also garnered the support of a cross party band of MPs and in 2011 NICEIC was invited to Westminster to host a parliamentary reception about the campaign.

For more information or to find a qualified electrician in your area, visit www.niceic.com.

Case study

ELECTRICIAN

Steven Bastien, NICEIC Approved Contractor

When I was younger, during the weekends I would accompany my electrician uncle on his jobs in London, to earn extra pocket money. I was about 14 and I found it interesting working in different types of buildings and areas. The excitement and adventure of going to different places and meeting different people made it enjoyable.

Until the age of 16 I continued working with my uncle at weekends. I learnt how to install new electrical installations and rewire properties. At first, the jobs I did were mainly manual, moving furniture, lifting up carpets and floorboards etc. Sometimes I would get the opportunity to chase out walls to bury cables. I also had to pack away the tools at the end of the day, and make sure none were missing!

As time went on, I realised I really enjoyed electrical work. It made me feel important and made me feel valued. I felt good about myself. I felt I was doing something which was a skilled trade…so becoming an electrician was a straightforward choice. I was advised by my careers adviser and teachers what subjects would be best to study; these subjects were science, maths, English, history and geography.

After leaving school, I studied at college for two years, taking relevant City & Guilds qualifications. I studied very hard to make sure I would pass – which I did with a distinction and passes. I then applied to electrical companies for an electrical apprenticeship. I was successful and offered a 5-year JIB Apprenticeship. It was here I gained a vast amount of experience in the electrical field, working in offices, schools, factories and shops. I carried on at college where I continued my studies to gain more qualifications in Electrical Installations.

Three years later I became a Qualified Electrician. I then decided to become even more adventurous by becoming self-employed. This gave me the opportunity to work on major building projects throughout the UK. I worked in a variety of places such as Fleet Street working for different newspapers. I even worked on a building which had a helicopter pad on top of it. That was quite exciting! I also worked on the first tower block of Canary Wharf. I worked on Tower Bridge, the NEC in Birmingham, the first Toyota car factory in the UK, and many more.

I then started working for local authorities, carrying out maintenance work as well as emergency callouts. Callouts give you a good feeling as you have helped someone.

Recently, I have formed my own company – Facelift Electrical Services Ltd and successfully became an NICEIC Domestic Installer. I then become an NICEIC Approved Contractor which involved me taking more qualifications.

I can now say to any young person who would like to become an electrician, that it's a very enjoyable and satisfying career. It's great when you see the beginning of the project and see it through to the end. It's great to know you were part of that project being completed.

For further information visit www.niceic.com or call 0870 013 0382.

ESTATE AGENT

Qualifications and courses

No formal qualifications are required to become an estate agent. However, it is useful for entrants to have 5 GCSEs/S grades (A*–C/1–3). Most entrants start as a trainee negotiator and undertake an NVQ qualification in the Sale of Residential Property (Level 2). However, a degree, Foundation degree or HND in subjects like property management and real estate management can increase your chances of employment.

Training can be done on the job. It may involve studying for Technical Awards offered by the National Federation of Property Professionals (NFoPP), such as the Sale of Residential Property, Residential Letting and Property Management and Commercial Property Agency. NFoPP also offer Certificates in the Sale of Residential Property, Residential Letting and Property Management and Commercial Property Agency which are intended for those with around 3 years' experience. Both the Technical Awards and the Certificates may be studied by distance learning or part-time at a college.

School leavers looking to become an estate agent administrator can enrol on the Intermediate Apprenticeship in Property Services and those who want to become an estate agent could consider the Advanced Apprenticeship.

What the work involves

Estate agents are responsible for selling or letting residential or commercial properties on behalf of their clients.

Properties are valued based upon factors such as their condition, location, comparison to other properties and the current housing market.

Estate agents market a property, show prospective buyers around and negotiate prices to ensure the best deal for their client.

During the selling process you will have to liaise with banks, surveyors, mortgage brokers and solicitors.

Type of person suited to this work

You will need excellent speaking and listening skills so that you can recommend suitable properties to potential buyers. You also have to be good at negotiating so that you can help buyers and sellers to agree prices for properties.

You must be confident dealing with people and prepared to work hard to achieve sales.

As you will be dealing with figures when valuing properties or negotiating prices, you will need numeracy skills and an interest in keeping up to date with what is happening in the housing and property markets.

Working conditions

Some of your time will be spent in the branch office, and the rest of the time you will be visiting properties, so a driving licence is needed.

Estate agency branches are often modern and open-plan with up-to-date equipment. You will spend a lot of your time working at a computer and speaking to your customers on the phone.

This can be very stressful work as you will have sales targets to reach and your earnings will depend on your selling ability. You are likely to need to work at weekends and evenings (with some time off during the week instead).

Future prospects

Estate agents are located throughout the UK but there tend to be fewer opportunities in a poor housing market.

If you do well and gain experience and qualifications, there are opportunities for promotion – especially in larger estate agencies. For example, you may move from trainee to negotiator, then to senior negotiator and on to branch manager.

Advantages/disadvantages

The work can be stressful if you are finding it hard to meet sales targets, especially if you are working on a commission-only basis in a slowing housing market.

When the property market is booming, or for those who are very skilled in sales, the financial rewards can be high.

Money guide

Estate agents' earnings are usually a combination of a basic salary plus commission based upon their sales figures. Some estate agents work for commission only.

You may be entitled to a performance-related bonus.

Starting salaries for new entrants are between £12,000 and £20,000.

With experience you can expect to earn about £25,000 a year.

Those employed at a managerial level can achieve up to £55,000.

Related opportunities

- Auction Property Consultant p73
- Planning and Development Surveyor p110
- Property Valuer p113

Further information

Asset Skills
www.assetskills.org

National Association of Estate Agents
www.naea.co.uk

Qualifications and courses

There are no specific entry qualifications. However GCSEs or S grades (A*–E/1–5) in English and maths are useful. Science and design and technology are useful as you must have an understanding of calculations, measurements and theory.

ConstructionSkills may provide apprenticeships. You will be assessed on literacy and your ability to work at heights. You will take an aptitude exercise on maths and problem-solving.

Construction apprentices learn practical skills under the supervision of skilled fabricators, as well as taking courses at a college or training centre. These include NVQs/SVQs such as Level 1 in Construction and Civil Engineering Services, Level 2 and 3 in Fabrication and Welding Engineering, Level 2 and 3 in Carpentry and Joinery and Level 4 in Construction Site Management.

A Construction Skills Certification Scheme card is needed to work on a building site.

What the work involves

Fabricators manufacture, assemble and install structural frames of buildings.

You will extend and adapt existing buildings or work on manufacturing the entire framework for new ones. This may include houses, public buildings, swimming pools, airport terminal buildings and caravans.

Your work will be influenced by architectural demands and advances. The need for thermal performance, speed and versatility in architecture means that traditional forms of construction such as concrete, steel and glass are being replaced with new, more efficient materials. You will probably work with a diverse range of materials such as aluminium, PVC foam, timber, natural stone and fibreglass.

Type of person suited to this work

As a fabricator you should have an interest in machinery and the construction industry.

You will be working on site or in a manufacturing plant; as this may include physical labour you should be fit and have good manual skills.

You should also enjoy working in a team and have excellent knowledge and awareness of health and safety practices. You should be organised and know how to plan ahead.

Working conditions

You will typically work 39 hours per week, Monday to Friday. This may vary depending on the project you are working on. You may also be required to do shifts and overtime or work evenings and weekends.

You may work in a variety of locations; outdoors, indoors and at heights. Weather conditions may make this work uncomfortable or delay work.

As a fabricator you might have to operate machinery such as mobile cranes.

Future prospects

As you gain experience you will have the opportunity to specialise in a certain area of fabrication. This could be as an aluminium fabricator (curtain walls, windows and frames), a conservatory fabricator (working with timber, aluminium or PVC to erect conservatories), or a window fabricator (working with frame makers and door makers building offsite manufactured rooms that can be assembled onsite).

As you accumulate experience you can progress to a higher level position such as a supervisor or you may also choose to become self-employed.

Advantages/disadvantages

New and exciting developments and improvements in materials and technology mean that your work is likely to include scope for diversity and creativity.

Your work at times may be very physically demanding.

Money guide

Your starting salary may be around £15,000 a year.

With experience, you could earn between £29,000 and £35,000 per year, although the average salary of a fabricator is £24,500.

Related opportunities

- Building Technician p78
- Carpenter/Joiner p79
- Ceiling Fixer p81

Further information

ConstructionSkills
www.cskills.org

National Association of Shopfitters
www.shopfitters.org

FACILITIES MANAGER

Qualifications and courses

Many entrants to this profession are graduates who have studied property and land-based subjects such as estate management or surveying. Others gain experience in relevant fields such as construction, building services, engineering or hospitality to acquire skills for facilities management.

You can take vocational courses in facilities management. These include appropriate NVQs/SVQs or professional qualifications from the British Institute of Facilities Management (BIFM). You can also study for a Foundation degree (developed by Asset Skills), or an HND in facilities management.

Work experience is recommended and employers will seek candidates with good experience. For graduates year-long placements are invaluable.

Entrants to facilities management also come from other areas of employment using relevant skills and experience. Many of these entrants have backgrounds in office management and administration, building services and engineering, customer services and the Armed Forces.

What the work involves

Facilities managers are responsible for the management and administration of premises, including offices, schools and commercial properties. You will provide a safe and efficient work environment for staff by implementing procedures to improve facilities, reduce costs and increase productivity.

Your day-to-day work will depend on the type of organisation you work for, but will include a broad spectrum of tasks such as coordinating and managing central services, organising mail receipt and despatch, arranging contractors for security or supervising cleaning and catering.

You must be able to respond to all problems that arise unexpectedly, and react to them appropriately and efficiently.

Type of person suited to this work

As you will be coordinating many different aspects of an organisation, or many organisations in one location, you need to be highly organised. You should be able to meet deadlines and have strong problem-solving skills.

You will lead a team so you should have excellent negotiation skills and strong written and verbal communication ability. As you will be working with a variety of different people you should have good customer service skills.

You should also be aware of environmental issues affecting premises and how budgets are planned and controlled.

Working conditions

Your hours will vary depending on the organisation you work for but on average you will work from 9am to 5pm. You will mainly be office based, but you will move around a lot to inspect and supervise various projects throughout the location you work in.

You may have a permanent contract or work on a fixed-term contract. At times you may be required to be available at any time in the event of emergencies.

Future prospects

You may begin as an assistant in a particular support field such as IT, HR, finance or purchasing or health and safety and then progress to functional manager, senior manager and director positions.

You can work as a facilities manager in-house or join a facilities management provider or consultancy. This will provide a variety of projects and responsibilities but will not have the same level of stability.

It is recommended that you seek opportunities in different organisations to secure promotion.

Advantages/disadvantages

Prospects for career development can be excellent. If you are hardworking, flexible, and efficient, have commercial acumen and the ability to juggle tight budgets you can progress to higher level management jobs.

You may find it difficult to move from an in-house role to a position with a service provider as there is a perceived difference in outlook and experience.

Money guide

Starting salaries may range from around £16,000 to £20,000 per year.

An experienced facilities manager can earn between £25,000 and £34,000 a year.

Senior and regional facilities managers can earn in excess of £60,000.

Related opportunities

- Building Services Engineer p76
- Health and Safety Adviser p41
- Quality Manager p58

Further information

British Institute of Facilities Management
www.bifm.org.uk

Chartered Management Institute
www.managers.org.uk

Qualifications and courses

No specific qualifications are required, although a common route is through Apprenticeships where GCSEs/S grades (A*–E/1–5) in maths, design and technology, science and English are a requirement.

You will be trained on the job while working towards qualifications. You may go to a college or training centre on day or block release. The Construction Industry Training Board (CITB) offers an Apprenticeship Scheme in Floor Covering, which will provide you with a Level 2 Construction Diploma in Floor Covering and a Level 2 NQV in Flooring Occupations.

Fast-track short courses from independent providers like the Flooring Industry Training Association and NVQs/SVQs in Floor Covering at Levels 1–3 are also available.

Many employers on construction sites require workers to have a Construction Skills Certification Scheme (CSCS) card. This demonstrates that the holder has health and safety training.

What the work involves

Floor layers fit various rooms and buildings with many different types of flooring, such as vinyl, wood, carpet, tiles, rubber or plastic. You will decide on the best material to use for the particular type of floor.

You will use various tools to prepare the surface, cut the flooring material to size and lay the floor.

You will work from technical plans and diagrams in order to lay and fit each floor correctly.

Type of person suited to this work

To do this work you will need accurate numerical skills in order to calculate the exact amount of flooring material you will need for each job.

You should be physically fit as you will spend a lot of time lifting and carrying materials, or working on your hands and knees.

You may work alone for some smaller jobs, but you must also be able to work in a team with other construction professionals for larger jobs. Good planning skills are helpful when organising your workload, and you should be happy meeting and talking to lots of different people.

Working conditions

You will usually work normal Monday to Friday office hours, but you may also need to work through the night or over weekends on some contracts, so that you can lay floors without disrupting the work of shops and businesses.

Most of your work will be spent indoors in a variety of locations including people's homes, hospitals, offices and construction sites, some of which will be dirty and dusty. This is mobile work, so a driving licence is useful.

Some contracts may involve absence from home overnight or for longer periods of time.

Future prospects

There are good prospects for finding work as a trainee floor layer because there is a shortage of floor layers nationwide. Once you have qualified, work will be available within small or large flooring companies or contractors across the UK.

You may choose to specialise in using one type of flooring material such as tiles or laminates.

With experience, you can progress to technical, supervisory or managerial posts. Or you could set up on your own as a self-employed floor layer.

Advantages/disadvantages

An attractive and well-laid floor can transform a room. The ability to use your skills and a range of materials to create this effect can give you great job satisfaction.

You will spend a lot of time travelling to and from jobs, and may need to spend time away from home on big flooring projects.

Money guide

Starting rate for trainees is around £12,500 per year.

With an NVQ earnings can rise to £14,500, and as a fully qualified floor layer you could earn from £20,000 to £25,000.

Highly skilled, experienced floor layers can earn salaries of up to £30,000.

Earnings vary among employers and in different parts of the country. Salaries in London are higher. Many floor layers are self-employed and earnings will depend on the ability to win contracts.

Related opportunities

- Carpenter/Joiner p79
- Plasterer p111
- Roofer p116

Further information

ConstructionSkills
www.cskills.org

Flooring Industry Training Association
www.fita.co.uk

Case study
THE FLOORING TRADE

Matthew Blackbourn's Story

On the job training has formed a key part of 26 year old Matthew's journey into the flooring trade fitting all types of flooring in the domestic and commercial sectors. He firmly believes that ensuring you begin your working life with a reputable, established company is vital. Matthew has supplemented the experience he has gained on site with training courses through FITA, after which he applied to become a "Masterfitter" in Carpet via the NICF. Although he has a passion for installation and gets a true buzz from a job well done, Matthew hopes to grow more in to the management side. However, his positive experience of training has also led him to have ambitions to become an instructor and put something back in the industry.

For Matthew the future in flooring is bright and full of opportunity.

- Master Fitter in different disciplines other than carpet e.g. Vinyl Tiles & Laminate, also a fitter in Wood & Resilient;
- QA card accredited, leading to more work e.g. M&S and also Contractors looking for quality commercial installers;
- Training to be a FITA Instructor;
- Training two apprentices with our company;
- Being part of the NICF has got me involved with some very interesting installation such as London fashion week. Also a carpet company who make handmade 100oz luxury carpets with borders for very wealthy clients around the country;
- Now doing more with the day to day running of our company, working with customers, selling in the showroom, estimation and quoting, site surveys etc.;
- Installing a wide range of floor coverings for the family business.

What the job entails

Working for a small business in the domestic market, means that the range of tasks involved are enormous. "I generally find myself fitting floors during the day and enjoy the diversity of products and skills I have to employ really interesting. I also like working with the public and when we are busy I tend to help out with measures in the evenings. More recently, I have started to get involved with pricing and ordering stock etc."

The commercial sector is of course slightly different with work typically taking place in offices hospitals and schools. Generally on a bigger scale, some of the contracts involved have materials worth many thousands of pounds. Main contractors are often working to tight timescales and obviously floor layers have to enjoy working in a team in what is often essentially a construction environment. As well as a craft and a skill, floor laying is increasing technical and finding the solution to meet the needs of a client (many working on fast track projects) are some of the demands and challenges of the "on site" role.

What you need to succeed

Flexibility, good communication, as well as an obvious natural tendency towards good practical skills, are all qualities required to succeed in the flooring industry. The ability to use your own initiative, as well as work in a team, is often an advantage.

Practical on site experience will always be required, but formal qualifications such as an NVQ level 2 in floor laying are recognised qualifications that can currently be gained through a number of routes including a modern apprenticeship. This can be supplemented with short training courses through organisations such as FITA as both an introduction, as well as a career building strategy.

For further information or advice contact:
The Contract Flooring Association (CFA)
Telephone: 0115 941 1126

The Flooring Industry Training Association (FITA)
Telephone: 0115 950 6836

The National Institute of Carpet & FloorLayers (NICF)
Telephone: 0115 958 3077

GAS SERVICE TECHNICIAN

Qualifications and courses

At least 4 GCSEs/S grades (A*–C/1–3) including English, maths and sometimes science or technology subjects are normally required to enter this career. Practical subjects such as metalwork and woodwork are useful.

Apprenticeships/Skillseekers are available for people aged 16–24. An Advanced Apprenticeship in The Gas Industry is a good route for those who wish to become a gas service engineer. Apprentices work towards the NVQ/SVQ in Domestic Natural Gas Installation and Maintenance and Emergency Services Operations (Levels 2 and 3) awarded by City & Guilds. Gas service companies also run their own apprenticeship schemes.

Trainees must gain registration with the Gas Safe Register. To become registered, trainees need to work towards the above City & Guilds NVQ/SVQ or complete equivalent in-house training with a company. Technicians with qualifications or training other than the NVQ/SVQ must complete ACS (Accredited Certification Scheme) assessments.

Gas service technicians have to demonstrate their gas safety competence on a 5-year cycle by successfully completing nationally agreed ACS assessments.

What the work involves

Your job will be to install, maintain, repair and test gas appliances such as fires, cookers, heating systems, shower units and industrial equipment. You will carry out scheduled maintenance checks on systems and equipment once installed.

You could work in private homes or on business premises.

You may also have to give customers quotes for costs and timescales, sell additional company services and deal with complaints.

As a trained professional, you will be required to give advice on the safety and efficiency of gas systems and equipment.

Type of person suited to this work

You will need excellent practical and problem-solving skills as you will be required to investigate and fix faults.

Gas appliances are potentially dangerous so you should be very thorough, reliable and aware of safety practices.

As you will be visiting clients' homes, you should be personable and presentable.

Working conditions

Working hours are generally 8am to 5pm, Monday to Friday. However, if your employer offers 24-hour emergency cover, you may have to undertake shift work.

Although most of your work will take place in customers' homes or business premises, you will also need to work on many different construction sites. You will need to wear protective clothing, such as a hard hat, goggles and gloves.

A driving licence is essential as you will be required to travel to jobs in a van which stores your parts and equipment.

Future prospects

There is currently a shortage of trained gas service technicians.

You can work for national or private companies. In larger companies you can apply for training posts at local colleges or within private organisations.

Once you have gained enough experience, you could progress into gas engineering, a supervisory/management role or become self-employed. You could specialise in a specific area such as energy efficiency.

Advantages/disadvantages

If your employer offers 24-hour emergency cover, you may have to work some unsocial hours.

The job can be strenuous and can involve working at heights or in confined spaces.

There is a high demand for gas service technicians and career progression opportunities are good.

Successfully repairing a potentially dangerous gas leak can be a rewarding experience.

Money guide

During your Apprenticeship, you can expect to earn between £12,000 and £15,000 per year.

Salaries for experienced gas service technicians range from £18,000 up to £40,000.

Those who become self-employed and manage their own company and employees can achieve in excess of £40,000.

It is also possible to increase your earnings through overtime and shift work.

Related opportunities

- Gas Network Engineer p226
- Heating and Ventilating Engineer p102
- Plumber p112

Further information

Energy and Utility Skills
www.euskills.co.uk

Gas Safe Register
www.gassaferegister.co.uk

GLAZIER

Qualifications and courses

GCSEs (or equivalent) or vocational qualifications can improve your chances of getting work. Maths, English and technology subjects are useful for the parts of the job that involve measurements and calculations, and for theoretical training. Apprenticeships in the Glass Industry, which last 2 to 3 years, are also available at both Intermediate and Advanced Levels.

To work as a glazier you need to have a Construction Skills Certification Scheme (CSCS) card or be registered with an affiliated scheme. This scheme requires an NVQ Level 2 and the completion of a health and safety test.

You can train and gain vocational qualifications while you work. You will be taught practical skills and may spend time off-site at a college or training centre.

You are likely to work towards NVQs in glass-related subjects. These include Glazing, Automotive Glazing, and Fenestration Installation and Surveying at both Levels 2 and 3.

What the work involves

Glaziers use specialist cutting and fixing tools to cut glass to the correct size and fit it into place.

You might fit glass into houses, shop fronts, office blocks or roofs.

You might be working on new buildings or replacing existing or broken glass.

You will use your knowledge to choose a suitable type of glass for each job.

Type of person suited to this work

You will be measuring and cutting glass accurately so that it fits perfectly into the frame. As you will be using different hand tools a practical ability will be necessary.

You will also need to be physically fit so that you can carry glass and be comfortable working at heights (sometimes extreme heights).

You may work alone for some jobs, such as in people's homes, but you must also be able to work and communicate with other glaziers, especially when working on large jobs with big, heavy panes of glass.

Working conditions

You will work indoors and outdoors in many different locations. A driving licence may be useful.

You will need to work safely and be aware of your own, the public's and your colleagues' safety when carrying, cutting and fixing glass.

You may work normal working hours during the week, but you may also need to work at weekends and during evenings, possibly offering emergency cover for households and businesses when replacing broken glass.

Future prospects

Work is available with glazing and construction companies throughout the UK and the demand for trained glaziers is high.

The range of jobs in glazing work is also increasing to include specialist areas, for example automotive glass repair and replacement.

After gaining sufficient experience, you may progress to technical or supervisory levels, or you could decide to start your own glazing business. The majority of glaziers are self-employed.

Advantages/disadvantages

Working at extreme heights may be demanding for some.

You will get to work in a variety of locations on a wide range of projects.

Cutting tools and glass can be dangerous, so you will have to be aware of health and safety regulations.

You could be called out at all hours for emergency jobs but the rates of pay for this type of work will be higher.

Money guide

Newly qualified glaziers earn between £12,500 and £16,000.

With qualifications, glaziers can expect to earn up to £18,000.

Those who are highly skilled, with experience and extra responsibilities such as emergency call-outs, might achieve anything from £20,000 to £35,000.

Shift allowances and the opportunity to work overtime can supplement your income.

Related opportunities

- Building Technician p78
- Ceiling Fixer p81
- Window Fitter p131

Further information

Glass and Glazing Federation
www.ggf.co.uk

Glass Qualifications Authority
www.glassqualificationsauthority.com

Proskills UK
www.proskills.co.uk

HEATING AND VENTILATING ENGINEER

Qualifications and courses

Most employers train young entrants through Apprenticeships/Skillseekers. Apprenticeships in Heating and Ventilation are available at Intermediate and Advanced Level. 4 GCSEs/S grades (A*–C/1–3) including maths, English and a science subject may be required for entry to these. You will also need to pass a colour vision test and selection test.

Training for Apprenticeships/Skillseekers includes attending college on day or block release. You will work towards NVQ/SVQ Level 2 in Mechanical Engineering Services – Heating and Ventilating, progressing to NVQ/SVQ Level 3. NVQs/SVQs cover industrial, commercial and domestic installation and maintenance of components. The same NVQs are available to adults but you may need to have relevant work experience.

Other training includes: City & Guilds Certificate in Energy Efficiency for Domestic Heating (6084) for domestic fitters and the Oil Firing Technical Association (OFTEC)'s training scheme for those working with oil-fired equipment.

It is also possible to achieve higher level qualifications including NVQ Level 4 and foundation and master's degrees which can lead to professional membership of the Chartered Institution of Building Services Engineers (CIBSE).

What the work involves

Heating and ventilating engineers install equipment such as pipework and boilers for systems including central heating, hot and cold water services, and gas supplies in industrial and commercial buildings.

Your work will include cutting, bending and joining pipes that will need to withstand high pressures, so welding is an important part of the work.

When you have installed a system, you will test it to make sure that everything is working properly.

Type of person suited to this work

You must be a practical person so that you can use the equipment for the job. Understanding and following diagrams is an essential part of the work, so you need a logical, mechanically minded approach to your work. You will also need to be good at maths for making calculations.

It can be physically demanding work, as you will be bending, kneeling and working in tight spaces. You also need a head for heights and a safety-conscious attitude, because you will often be working from ladders and scaffolding.

Teamwork and communication skills are also important when you are installing large systems.

Working conditions

A lot of your time will be spent indoors, but you will also need to work on various construction sites when you will need to wear safety protective clothing.

You may work a normal working week, but there may be times when you will work weekends and evenings to avoid disruption to clients or if you provide emergency cover. You may also be expected to work away from home on various contracts.

Future prospects

There is currently a shortage of skilled heating and ventilating engineers with around 56,000 currently working in the UK.

Once you are qualified, work will be available with specialist heating and ventilation companies, or organisations such as the NHS or local authorities. Many qualified fitters also become self-employed, joining up with other engineers to offer sub-contracting services.

There are good prospects for advancement to supervisory roles and it is possible for you to become a heating and ventilating technician. If you take additional qualifications and higher education, progression to professional engineering level is also possible. There are also opportunities to work overseas.

Advantages/disadvantages

Working in cramped and awkward spaces can be uncomfortable.

Transforming a building from an empty shell into a warm, comfortable environment can be rewarding.

Career progression opportunities are excellent and there is demand across the country for work in this area.

Money guide

As an apprentice your starting salary could be between £9,100 and £11,250.

A newly qualified engineer could expect to earn £20,000–£24,000.

With experience and additional responsibilities, you could achieve £30,000–£40,000.

Working overtime and receiving bonuses could increase your pay.

Related opportunities

- Gas Network Engineer p226
- Gas Service Technician p100
- Thermal Insulation Engineer p126

Further information

Building Engineering Services Training
www.best-ltd.co.uk

Heating and Ventilating Contractors' Association
www.hvca.org.uk

SummitSkills
www.summitskills.org.uk

Qualifications and courses

There are no formal entry requirements for this work but GCSEs/S grades in maths, English and design and technology may be helpful. Personal skills and physical fitness are usually more important than qualifications. Employers may also want you to have some on-site experience.

Your training will mainly be given on the job by experienced road workers. Whilst you are in employment, you may be able to study at a local college on day or block release. You could work towards an NVQ in Construction and Civil Engineering (Level 2), an NVQ Certificate/Diploma in Highways Maintenance (Level 2), an NVQ Diploma in Roadbuilding (Level 2) and City & Guilds Winter Maintenance Operations (Level 2).

To become a fully qualified site operative, you need to register with the Street Works Qualifications Register by studying for either a City & Guilds certificate in Streetworks Excavation and Reinstatement, an SQA national award in Excavation and Reinstatement or a Street Works Excavation and Reinstatement qualification awarded by CABWI.

If working with plant machinery, you will need to be 18 or over. A driving licence will also be required and an LGV licence may be needed for some jobs.

What the work involves

Road workers' tasks include building new roads, re-routing or widening existing roads, and repairing potholes and cracks in roads.

You will also have other duties such as putting up warning signs and barriers, controlling the movement of traffic near the work site, laying kerbstones and pavements, and gritting roads in the winter.

You will work with numerous building materials including concrete, tarmac and paving slabs. You will use a range of tools and equipment in your work, including specialised, heavy machinery such as diggers and rollers.

Type of person suited to this work

You must have a good standard of fitness, as the work involves a lot of hard, physical work and requires you to lift and carry heavy materials.

Practical ability with tools such as picks and shovels is useful, as is experience of operating equipment such as cement mixers, diggers and rolling machines.

As much of your work will be undertaken as part of a team of road workers and supervisors, it is important that you can get along with colleagues at all levels.

Working conditions

You are likely to work a normal 37 hour working week, although you may also work weekends and evenings to avoid disrupting traffic.

You will need to be aware of the danger of traffic and health and safety for yourself and your colleagues. Onsite, you will wear protective clothing such as a safety helmet, fluorescent jacket and boots.

Future prospects

Road workers may work for local authorities or, as work is increasingly contracted out, for specialist road-building or civil engineering companies.

Work is available across the UK. Some work is short term or seasonal. You could become self-employed and work on contract basis.

As you develop and gain experience and qualifications, you may go on to lead a small team or become a supervisor.

Advantages/disadvantages

You will be helping to maintain and improve the safety of the roads in your local area which can be personally rewarding.

You will be carrying out physically demanding work outdoors during all weathers so you can expect to get hot in the summer and cold in the winter.

Money guide

Trainee road workers have a starting salary of £10,500–£14,000.

As you gain experience, you could earn £15,000–£18,000.

Road workers with additional responsibilities, such as supervisory duties, can achieve a salary in excess of £20,000.

Those who operate plant machinery may receive additional payments.

You can increase your earnings with overtime and shift work.

Related opportunities

- Bricklayer p74
- Concreter p85
- Construction Operative p86

Further information

ConstructionSkills
www.cskills.org

Street Works Qualification Register
www.swqr.org.uk

HOUSING OFFICER

Qualifications and courses

It is possible to enter at an administrative level with GCSEs/S grades (A*–C/1–3) and study part time while working. Many people enter with an HNC/HND, Foundation degree, degree or postgraduate qualification in housing studies and social policy.

The National Certificate in Housing Studies is often taken before the HNC in Housing. For entry to a Foundation degree in Housing Studies, at least 2 A levels/3 H grades are required.

Housing officers whose degrees do not include a work placement will be expected to gain appropriate industrial experience before they become a member of the Chartered Institute of Housing (CIH). Vacation or voluntary work with local authority housing departments, previous experience in a customer service role or experience within your community as a member of a tenants' committee could all be useful.

The CIH also offers courses which can be studied part time and through distance learning; these include the Certificate in Housing Practice (Level 2), the Award/Certificate/Diploma in Housing Practice (Level 3) and the Certificate for the Housing Profession (Level 4).

What the work involves

You will manage and maintain rented housing, usually for a housing association or local authority. Tasks include assessing housing needs in an area and making policies to provide for them, allocating housing to applicants and planning property maintenance and repair.

You will also need to set rent rates, deal with tenants who are behind with their payments, resolve neighbourhood disputes and answer tenants' enquiries.

You will find yourself working with a variety of different people, ranging from vulnerable members of the community to those in challenging economic situations.

Type of person suited to this work

As most of your work will involve talking and listening to people, you will need excellent communication and negotiation skills. You should have an interest in working with diverse social groups and be sensitive to the needs of tenants and colleagues.

Maths and numeracy skills are useful for dealing with rental payments, maintenance and repair costs, and budgets.

It is important to keep up with developments in a range of housing and tenant welfare issues, be flexible and have the ability to solve problems as and when they arise. You will also need to be capable working both independently and as part of a team.

Working conditions

Many housing officers are based in an office but regularly travel to make property inspections, visit tenants or attend meetings. As some of your work will involve travelling, a driving licence and your own vehicle is often required. Although you will normally work standard office hours, you might have to do some weekend work or unsocial hours.

You should be prepared to deal with rude and aggressive tenants.

Future prospects

Social housing is currently a growth area, with organisations taking on a number of new trainees as well as experienced staff. Work is available in towns and cities throughout the UK.

Employers look favourably on work experience or voluntary work in housing.

Most housing officers work for local authorities and housing associations but you may also work for other employers such as voluntary organisations, property companies, private landlords and housing trusts. You may be able to specialise in a particular area such as neighbourhood management or welfare benefits.

After gaining experience, you could progress into a more senior role such as principal housing officer or housing manager.

Advantages/disadvantages

You will be responsible for resolving complicated issues, such as misuse of property, and disputes between residents.

Helping people find a home can be personally rewarding.

Money guide

Housing officers usually have a starting salary ranging from £17,500 to £27,000, depending on location.

Those who become housing managers can expect to earn £20,000–£35,000.

At senior manager level, you can achieve earnings in excess of £50,000.

Related opportunities

- Residential Support Worker p578
- Social Worker p579
- Welfare Benefits Adviser/Welfare Rights Caseworker p584

Further information

Chartered Institute of Housing
www.cih.org

Scottish Federation of Housing Associations
www.sfha.co.uk

LAMINATOR

Qualifications and courses

No formal qualifications are normally required. However some GCSEs/S grades might be useful as you must have an understanding of design technology and calculations.

Some employers will take on apprentices. Apprenticeships require 4 GCSE/S grades (A*–C/1–3) in maths, science or technology. CITB-ConstructionSkills provides guidance on apprenticeships.

On the job training is provided. You can also undertake further training at college through courses that focus on the theoretical parts of your job, first aid, and health and safety. Available courses are NVQs at Level 2 in Polymer Processing Operations and Performing Engineering Operations and BTEC National Certificates/Diplomas in Polymer Processing and Materials Technology.

With 4 years' experience, relevant NVQs/SVQs or a BTEC certificate/diploma, you could apply for membership of the Institute of Materials, Minerals and Mining.

There is a shortage of laminators, so many employers seek adults with previous relevant experience and will provide further training to technician level following an NVQ/SVQ Level 3 training route.

What the work involves

Laminators work with polymer composite materials to make a variety of products such as hockey sticks, snowboards, canoes, car bodies, yachts and aircraft cabin interiors.

You will follow a brief for the design of a product, taking into consideration any requirements regarding strength, colour and finish. You will then choose the appropriate material to be pressed, sprayed or poured into a mould, prior to it being shaped into the final product.

You will work with traditional materials such as wood laminates, fibre glass and resin, and new products such as Kelvar.

Type of person suited to this work

You should have a keen interest in design and technology, engineering and materials science.

You should like practical work and have practical skills to handle tools and use specialist machinery. You need to be reasonably fit and have good vision for monitoring quality and noticing detail.

You should have initiative, follow a brief and work to a deadline. You should also be interested in, and keep up to date with, technological advancements in laminate materials. You should like to work in a team.

Working conditions

Your working hours will depend heavily on the project you are working on. Typically it can range from 37 to 40 hours but will vary according to the rate of your work and deadlines.

You will usually work in an environmentally controlled building. This means that the temperature is controlled and maintained to help resin harden quickly. Air is changed frequently to remove dust and the strong smell of resin.

You will be required to wear full protective clothing.

Future prospects

You may be employed by an engineering consultancy that undertakes installation projects for companies.

With experience and training there are opportunities to be promoted to roles such as technician and senior technician, or to move into design, research or development work for specialist composite laminate manufacturers.

Advantages/disadvantages

You may have the opportunity to work on products that are on the cutting edge of design such as speed boats, Formula 1 racing cars and craft for the air force and the military.

Your work will frequently be dusty and involve the use of strong industrial chemicals which may be hazardous if handled incorrectly.

Money guide

A salary for an apprentice laminator starts at around £7,000 per year.

With further experience and qualifications this may increase to £18,000 per year.

A senior laminator can earn up to £25,000 per year.

Related opportunities

- Carpenter/Joiner p79
- Marine Craftsperson p230
- Polymer Technologist p237

Further information

British Plastics Federation
www.bpf.co.uk

Institute of Materials, Minerals and Mining
www.iom3.org

BUILDING AND CONSTRUCTION

CRCI: BC

Qualifications and courses

Most entrants have completed a Royal Institution of Chartered Surveyors accredited degree in subjects like surveying and mapping science, geomatics or geographic information systems as well as a period of supervised instruction. An HND or Foundation degree in applied science, land/estate surveying or civil engineering is also accepted, although you would start in a slightly lower position in a company.

If you wish to specialise in a particular area, such as offshore engineering, a postgraduate qualification may be helpful.

Once qualified, many surveyors work towards achieving chartered status and undertake further courses and assessment through bodies such as the Institution of Civil Engineering Surveyors (ICES) and the Royal Institution of Chartered Surveyors (RICS). This usually takes between 4 and 5 years. Regardless of your position, it is advisable to become a student member of the Royal Institution of Chartered Surveyors (RICS) or Chartered Institution of Civic Engineering Surveyors (ICES) in order to keep up to date with developments in the industry and aid continuing professional development(CPD).

Apprenticeships in Land/Geomatics Surveying are also available. You will work towards gaining an NVQ.

What the work involves

Land/geomatic surveyors collect and analyse information to map the land and/or sea, which is then used when planning construction and civil engineering projects.

You will use satellite images, GPS, digital mapping and other equipment to produce surveys that record features such as contours, materials below the Earth's surface and man-made objects.

You will use technical software such as computer-aided design (CAD) to record and present the data you have gathered. You will also have to interpret data from maps and plans and explain it to clients.

Type of person suited to this work

You will be working with clients and other professionals on a daily basis, so excellent verbal and written communication skills will be needed to present and explain complex information.

As much of the work involves using technical equipment and producing maps, plans and reports using specialist computer software, you will need to have very strong analytical and ICT skills with specific knowledge of geographical information systems (GIS) and AutoCAD.

Working conditions

Working hours are usually 9am to 5pm, but you might need to work unsocial hours to ensure projects are finished on time. Weekend or shift work can also be needed for certain projects.

You will often work away from home. You will be paid more for overseas work and most contracts are on a short-term basis, although multinational companies offer good long-term opportunities.

Self-employment is an option, but finding work is not always easy so most surveyors choose to work in salaried employment.

Future prospects

Prospects are good as there is a national shortage of land/geomatic surveyors. Most graduates start as a junior surveyor, from which there is a natural progression to surveyor and then on to a team management position. You could alternatively undertake further study and gain a qualification as a chartered surveyor.

You can specialise in a number of areas including offshore engineering and exploration or cartography.

Advantages/disadvantages

You will have the opportunity to travel throughout the UK and overseas.

You could be playing a key role in land and environmental development.

A considerable amount of time is spent outdoors so be prepared to get cold, wet and muddy.

Money guide

Starting salaries for non-graduates are between £13,000 and £16,000 per year.

For newly graduated land surveyors salaries fall between £20,000 and £23,000.

If you also hold a qualification in chartered surveying, your starting salary would rise to between £27,000 and £34,000.

With several years' experience you could earn between £40,000 and £50,000.

At a senior level, either as a manager or a partner, salaries can reach between £44,000 and £72,000.

Salaries are highest in London or if you work overseas.

Related opportunities

- Planning and Development Surveyor p110
- Rural Property/Practice Surveyor p117
- Town Planner/Planning Technician p127

Further information

Chartered Institution of Water and Environmental Management
www.ciwem.org

Institution of Civil Engineering Surveyors
www.ices.org.uk

MASTIC ASPHALTER

Qualifications and courses

To train in this field, it is useful to have some GCSEs/S grades (A*–E/1–5) in English, maths, design and technology. Alternatively, vocational qualifications such as the Diploma in Construction and the Built Environment, the BTEC Introductory, First Diploma or Certificate in Construction or Foundation, Intermediate and Advanced levels in Construction Awards may prove useful.

Most entrants complete the Construction Industry Training Board (CITB) Construction Apprenticeship Scheme in Mastic Asphalting. This scheme takes 2 to 3 years and apprentices complete either an NVQ Level 2 or 3 in Mastic Asphalt or the CSkills Awards Level 2 Diploma in Mastic Asphalting.

If you decide to specialise in roofing, it would be helpful to undergo examinations from the Institute of Roofing.

Mastic asphalters employed on construction sites require a Construction Skills Certification Scheme (CSCS) card. This demonstrates that the holder has health and safety training, as well as aiming for competence in a particular occupation (usually requiring an appropriate NVQ or equivalent).

What the work involves

You will work with material called mastic asphalt, a mixture of limestone and bitumen which turns to liquid when heated. You will inspect a site, clean it, lay out membranes and guides and then spread hot liquid asphalt onto the area. It will cool into a protective waterproof surface.

You will work on surfaces such as dams, landfills, riverbank protection, car parks, bus stations, pathways and the roofs of buildings.

You will use various specialised tools such as boilers, mixers and cylinders in order to prepare surfaces and apply the asphalt.

Type of person suited to this work

You need to have good practical skills to be able to spread and form the mastic asphalt. Maths skills will be useful too, for calculating quantities of materials.

It is important to be able to understand plans, follow instructions and work well in a team.

As it is an active job you must be physically fit, and you must be happy climbing and working at heights. Agility is essential and you should be able to work quickly but accurately.

Working conditions

You will mainly work outdoors, although some of the work may be under cover. You will travel regularly between sites. You will need to wear protective gear such as a safety helmet, gloves and boots.

If you suffer from claustrophobia, vertigo or breathing problems, this work might be difficult for you.

You are likely to work a normal working week, although you might need to work evenings and weekends as well.

Future prospects

Most opportunities are with specialist mastic asphalt contractors. Self-employment is also common if you are skilled.

You can work your way up to become a supervisor, manager or trainer in large companies. Alternatively, you could set up your own contracting business.

You may need to move between employers for promotion.

Advantages/disadvantages

Working at heights on roofs, or in cramped conditions when working in tanks or underground spaces, can be demanding for some people. There is the possibility of fumes and accidental burns in this line of work.

You will develop a range of skills and work on a variety of surfaces.

Money guide

£10,000 per year is average for a trainee starting in this work.

With experience you could earn around £25,000.

In excess of £30,000 is possible for supervisory workers.

Overtime is often available, and on some projects there are bonuses based on outputs, which can lead to higher earnings. Travelling expenses will be reimbursed.

Related opportunities

- Floor Layer/Finisher p98
- Roofer p116
- Thatcher p125

Further information

ConstructionSkills
www.cskills.org

Mastic Asphalt Council
www.masticasphaltcouncil.co.uk

NAVAL ARCHITECT

Qualifications and courses

You must have a degree in engineering, marine technology, naval architecture or another similar subject; many degrees are accredited by the Royal Institution of Naval Architects (RINA). Generally 2 A levels/H grades including physics and maths, and 5 GCSEs/S grades (A*–C/1–3) are needed to enter onto a degree course.

If you have a BTEC HND/NHC you can transfer to an engineering degree. A master's degree in engineering can improve your chances of finding a job. The Ministry of Defence has a Defence Engineering and Science Group Graduate Scheme, although it is competitive. You may be able to join a marine engineering Apprenticeship straight from school, through the Royal Navy or local ship builders.

On-the-job training is provided, with extra courses available to reach fully qualified naval architect. A number of specialist conferences are also available on a range of subjects including historic ships, technical and material challenges of the work. These are run by the RINA and the Institute of Marine Engineering, Science and Technology.

After significant work experience, membership of RINA and registration as a Chartered or Incorporated Engineer with the Engineering Council UK is possible.

What the work involves

As a naval architect you will be responsible for the design, construction and repair of marine vessels and offshore structures, including merchant ships, submarines and offshore drilling platforms. You will have to coordinate a team of engineers working on a project.

You will ensure that the structure you are working on is safe and seaworthy, within budget and to the specifications laid out in the design brief.

Your work will depend on the specialism you choose, but you could prepare architectural designs, work with computer or 3D models, source materials or evaluate the safety of the design.

Type of person suited to this work

As you will be working with others and as part of a team you will need to have good written and verbal communication skills.

As you will be coordinating various aspects of a project such as budget, location and facilities you must be organised and efficient in your work. You must also be able to lead a team and work to a deadline.

You should also have strong ICT and numeracy skills and a keen eye for detail.

Working conditions

You will work average office hours, 5 days a week. However you might have to work extra hours to meet deadlines.

You may be office based while working on design work or visiting construction sites, docks and shipyards within the UK or overseas. Shipyards, docks and marinas can be noisy and dirty. If you are working onboard a craft you may encounter fumes, heat and noise and have to work in all weather conditions. You may be required to wear protective clothing.

Future prospects

As a naval architect you can become self-employed, work for a company or organisation, or work as a design consultant.

Organisations such as the Royal Institution of Naval Architects (RINA) provide continuing professional development (CPD) courses which are essential for progression in this job.

You can move up from technical roles to general management roles and then senior roles or directorships. Your career development will depend on the qualifications you have and the specialism you choose to go into.

Advantages/disadvantages

There is a lot of opportunity to work abroad for a ship surveying company, on contract, or you may work on a large scale project abroad.

Competition for jobs as a naval architect is high.

Some aspects of the work may involve working in difficult and physically demanding conditions.

Money guide

Your starting salary as a naval architect can be from £22,000 to £28,000 a year.

With experience this can increase to £35,000.

Extensive experience can increase earnings to £75,000.

Salaries do vary considerably based on employer, specialist skills, type of work and location.

Related opportunities

- Aerospace Engineer p212
- Marine Engineer p231
- Merchant Navy Engineering Officer p605

Further information

Defence Engineering Science Group
www.desg.mod.uk

Royal Institution of Naval Architects
www.rina.org.uk

WISE
www.wisecampaign.org.uk

Qualifications and courses

It is useful to have some GCSEs/S grades (A*–E/1–5) in subjects such as maths, design and technology and English. You could also enter with a vocational qualification, such as a BTEC Introductory Certificate/Diploma in Construction.

Construction Apprenticeships offer a training programme leading to NVQ/SVQ Level 3. Apprenticeships are validated by the Construction Industry Training Board (CITB).

Most training is done on the job whilst attending college, to obtain qualifications such as NVQs/SVQs in Painting and Decorating (Levels 2/3), CITB Cskills Diplomas in Decorative Finishing and Industrial Painting Occupations (Levels 1/2), or City & Guilds (6217–03) Level 1 Certificate in Basic Construction Skills (Painting and Decorating).

A Construction Skills Certification Scheme (CSCS) card is mandatory for painters and decorators working on construction sites. All applicants need to have a relevant NVQ/SVQ qualification and to pass a health and safety test. Trainees who are working towards an NVQ Level 2 or a construction award can apply for a Trainee Card (Craft and Operative).

What the work involves

Painters and decorators improve the interior and exterior of people's homes and other new or old buildings. They also paint large structures such as bridges.

Your work will include preparing surfaces by making sure they are clean and smooth, applying primers, undercoats and topcoats of paint and putting up wall coverings such as wallpaper.

You will use a range of tools including brushes, rollers and spraying equipment.

Type of person suited to this work

You need to be good with your hands, and particularly skilful when using fine decoration techniques. You will also need an eye for colour and design and an interest in décor and current trends.

You need to be friendly, personable and able to work well in a team. You will need to be fit and active as you will have to climb ladders and carry tools and equipment. You should not mind working at heights.

You must be able to measure accurately so that you can work out how much paint and other material you will need.

Working conditions

Most of the work is indoors, but some is outdoors. You will regularly work on ladders or on scaffolding. It is important that you follow health and safety regulations, which might include wearing a mask to prevent you from breathing in paint fumes.

You are likely to work a normal working week, although weekend work and overtime is common. You may need a driving licence.

Future prospects

There are good employment opportunities for painters and decorators in the UK at the moment.

You can work for painting and decorating companies or building contractors. Painting and decorating companies may offer a range of work or may specialise in work such as domestic, commercial, new build or industrial.

After gaining experience, it is possible to progress to a supervisory role or become self-employed.

Advantages/disadvantages

Working at extreme heights may be difficult for some people.

It can be rewarding to see the improved look of a newly painted building or structure and you have the opportunity to be creative.

Money guide

Apprentices under the age of 19 can earn up to £14,439 a year.

New entrants/trainees can expect to earn between £13,500 and £16,500 per year.

NVQ Level 2 or 3 qualified painters and decorators can earn between £18,000 and £21,500.

Decorators with specialist skills and supervisory duties can earn £25,000 or more.

Overtime is often available, and on some projects there are bonuses based on outputs.

Related opportunities

- Construction Operative p86
- Plasterer p111
- Wall/Floor Tiler p128

Further information

Painting & Decorating Association
www.paintingdecoratingassociation.co.uk

PLANNING AND DEVELOPMENT SURVEYOR

Qualifications and courses

This profession is open to all graduates, although further academic and vocational qualifications from the Royal Institution of Chartered Surveyors (RICS) must be gained before you can qualify as a chartered planning and development surveyor.

Some RICS-accredited degree and HND subjects offer exemption from the academic stages of the RICS assessment, and these include surveying, planning and land/estate/property management. Entry requirements for most degree/HND courses are a minimum of 5 GSCEs/S grades (A*–C/1–3), 3 A levels/H grades or the relevant BTEC/SQA National Awards (or equivalent).

If you have a non-accredited degree, you will need to take an RICS-approved conversion course prior to your training. Occasionally, larger organisations will employ graduates with unrelated degrees and allow them to undertake a conversion course during their employment, via day release or distance learning.

Once employed you should work towards chartered status by taking the Assessment of Professional Competence with the RICS or registering with the Chartered Institute of Building (CIOB)'s Faculty of Architecture and Surveying.

What the work involves

Planning and development surveyors develop and manage new building or refurbishment projects. You will create proposals and oversee projects from conception through to completion.

You will be responsible for recruiting team members for each project, as well as liaising with external industry professionals throughout.

You will also give valuations on properties and developments, advise clients on financing options for their building plans, and prepare their applications for planning permission.

Type of person suited to this work

As you will be managing team members, briefing other professionals and dealing with clients on a daily basis, well-developed communication and negotiation skills are required.

Good numeracy skills, coupled with scientific aptitude, are essential to successfully write proposals and manage financial details within a project. An understanding of legal matters within the building and construction industries is helpful, as is an interest in the environment, architecture, history or preserving the natural landscape.

Working conditions

You may have to work longer than the standard 35 hour week, but weekend and shift work is unusual.

Although there is some day to day travelling involved, overnight stays are uncommon.

Most jobs are found in cities where there is a high level of commercial activity. You could work for public sector or private companies, which range in size from very small practices up to large multinational firms. Work in the public sector is becoming increasingly flexible, with part time work and career breaks available.

Future prospects

Your career progression should be very straightforward; from graduate trainee, to surveyor, to senior surveyor, and up to associate or partner with several years' experience. If you progress to become an equity partner you will earn a high salary and also get a cut of the company's profits.

If you work in the public sector, you could enhance your career prospects with a Royal Town Planning Institute (RTPI) qualification, or develop a more specialised career in an area of surveying in which you are particularly interested.

Advantages/disadvantages

Work is varied and you have the opportunity to travel within the UK and overseas.

Although you might need to work extra hours, weekend work is rare.

You will have a lot of responsibility which can be stressful at times.

Money guide

New graduates can start on salaries between £20,000 and £24,000, the higher end of which is usually for London-based positions.

Fully qualified and experienced surveyors can earn £24,000–£38,000 per year.

Chartered surveyors with a wealth of experience can achieve a salary over £40,000.

Partners in a surveying firm often earn £70,000–£80,000, with an additional share of profits on top.

Related opportunities

- Land/Geomatic Surveyor p106
- Rural Property/Practice Surveyor p117
- Town Planner/Planning Technician p127

Further information

Chartered Institute of Building
www.ciob.org.uk

Institution of Civil Engineering Surveyors
www.ices.org.uk

Royal Institution of Chartered Surveyors
www.rics.org

Qualifications and courses

To be eligible for an Apprenticeship you will need some GCSEs/S grades in subjects such as English, maths, and design and technology. Construction Specialist Apprenticeships are available at both Intermediate and Advanced Level and offer a structured training programme leading to NVQ/SVQ Level 3. Apprenticeships are validated by the Construction Industry Training Board (CITB) and last 3 years in England and Wales, and 4 years in Scotland.

Most training is done on the job whilst attending college to obtain qualifications such as NVQs/SVQs in Plastering (Levels 1–3) or the City & Guilds Certificate in Basic Construction Skills – Plastering (6217-04). NVQ Level 3 will enable you to qualify for craftsperson status. Further options available through City & Guilds include the Foundation Construction Award (Level 1) and the Intermediate Construction Award (Level 2). A Diploma in Construction and the Built Environment is also relevant for plasterers.

Construction Skills Certification Scheme (CSCS) cards are required by plasterers employed on construction sites to demonstrate that they have health and safety training and are competent in their field.

What the work involves

There are three types of plastering that you could do: solid, fibrous or dry lining. Solid plastering involves the application of plaster or cement to internal and external walls, ceilings and floors.

Fibrous plastering involves making ornamental plaster work, such as the kind you see on decorative ceilings.

Dry lining involves the use of plasterboard to construct walls or partitions and then skimming over the joins with plaster making them ready for decoration.

Type of person suited to this work

To be able to use your tools skilfully, you need to be good with your hands. An ability to use basic maths for calculating the amounts of materials you will need for a job is also helpful.

You will need to be able to work in a team with other plasterers, and with those in other construction trades.

You should be physically fit, as the work is very active and can be tiring. It can also be dusty when working with the plaster powder; this may be difficult if you suffer from certain allergies. You will be climbing ladders and possibly scaffolding, so you must not mind working at heights.

Working conditions

Solid/dry lining

Most of the work for solid plasterers and those doing dry lining work is indoors, although you might have to work outdoors if working on exteriors. You will work from ladders and scaffolding.

Fibrous

Most fibrous plasterers work in workshops, although you may also install your work on-site.

All plastering requires an understanding and appreciation of health and safety regulations, which includes wearing protective gear. You may work a normal working week, although you might need to start early or finish late, and weekend work may also be available.

Future prospects

Because the building industry is cyclical there may be less of a demand for plasterers during a recession. Shortages of qualified plasterers do exist however in the south and south-east of England. Besides being employed by specialist plastering firms and building contractors, you can also work in the cultural heritage or public sectors.

After you have gained sufficient experience, you could progress to technical, supervisory or managerial roles or become self-employed.

Advantages/disadvantages

Working at heights may be difficult for some people.

As a solid plasterer you will be able to work in a variety of locations and those in fibrous plaster work have opportunities to be creative.

Money guide

As a trainee you could earn around £14,000–£17,000 per year.

Once qualified, salaries can rise to £17,000–£25,000 and experienced plasterers can achieve up to £35,000.

Overtime, shift allowances and performance-based bonuses can all increase earnings.

Self-employed plasterers may earn more as they negotiate their own rates.

Related opportunities

- Building Technician p78
- Mastic Asphalter p107
- Wall/Floor Tiler p128

Further information

ConstructionSkills
www.cskills.org

Federation of Plastering and Drywall Contractors
www.fpdc.org

Scottish Building Apprenticeship and Training Council
www.sbatc.co.uk

PLUMBER

Qualifications and courses

To train as a plumber, either on the job or via an Apprenticeship, you will normally need 3 or 4 GCSEs/S grades (A*–C/1–3) preferably including English, maths, and science and technology. Equivalent qualifications may also be accepted. Entrants for Apprenticeships or training schemes will need to pass a selection test and have their colour vision tested. For those over the age of 16, an Apprenticeship in Plumbing and Heating may be available at Intermediate or Advanced level.

As of April 2011, in order to become a qualified plumber you will need to complete the new City & Guilds NVQ Diploma in Plumbing and Heating (6189) at Levels 2 and 3 or the Excellence, Achievement & Learning Limited (EAL)'s NVQ Diploma in Plumbing and Heating (Level 2) and NVQ Diploma in Domestic Plumbing and Heating (Level 3).

Once you have passed recognised qualifications and gained practical experience, it is possible to become a member of the Chartered Institute of Plumbing and Heating Engineering (CIPHE).

Gas Safe registration and possession of a Gas Safe ID card is a legal requirement for anyone installing or repairing gas fittings or appliances.

What the work involves

Plumbers install, maintain and repair plumbing, heating and water systems in various locations including people's homes and public buildings.

You will use a range of hand and power tools, such as wrenches, cutters and welding equipment. You will also be responsible for routine check-ups on appliances such as boilers.

When you have completed a job, you will need to test the system to make sure that everything is working properly.

Type of person suited to this work

Good practical skills are essential. You must be careful and accurate and follow instructions to ensure that systems work properly and safely. Analytical and problem-solving skills are also important.

You might be bending, kneeling and squeezing into tight spaces so it would help if you were physically fit. You need to be comfortable working at heights.

You need to be a team player but also willing to work alone. You should keep a good appearance and have excellent communication skills when dealing directly with customers.

Working conditions

You will work both indoors and outdoors, possibly within confined spaces and at heights. Travelling will be required for jobs so it would be useful to have a driving licence and your own vehicle.

You may work a normal working week but, if your organisation offers a 24/7 call-out service, you need to be available at all times of the day or night, any day of the week.

Future prospects

Work is available across the UK, though the job market is more competitive in London.

With additional training and Gas Safe registration, you could move into gas central heating installation and repair. You could also move into a related career such as heating and ventilation, refrigeration or air conditioning.

You can progress to supervisory, training or managerial positions after a few years' experience. Also, many plumbers choose to set up their own business.

Advantages/disadvantages

You could be called out at any time of the night or day to deal with plumbing emergencies which can be difficult for those with family commitments.

Being able to solve a difficult problem and make a customer happy can be very rewarding.

Money guide

Trainee plumbers typically start on £10,000–£15,000 per year.

Once qualified, earnings increase to £16,500–£18,500.

Experienced plumbers can expect to earn anything from £21,000 up to £40,000.

Earnings for self-employed plumbers can be much higher as they negotiate their own rates of pay.

Salaries are highest in London and the south-east of England.

Overtime is often available and those who attend emergency call-outs can receive higher pay for working unsociable hours.

Related opportunities

- Gas Network Engineer p226
- Heating and Ventilating Engineer p102
- Refrigeration Engineer/Technician p115

Further information

Chartered Institute of Plumbing and Heating Engineering
www.ciphe.org.uk

SummitSkills
www.summitskills.org.uk

PROPERTY VALUER

Qualifications and courses

Although entry requirements vary depending on employer, candidates normally hold a degree or professional qualification approved by the Royal Institution of Chartered Surveyors (RICS). You will find a full list of accredited degree and diploma courses on the RICS website.

If you hold an HND or HNC you could enter the profession as a surveying technician and take further study to fully qualify.

Once employed, you should become a member of a professional body such as the RICS or the Institute of Revenues Rating and Valuation (IRRV). Graduates of an RICS-accredited degree are required to complete the Assessment of Professional Competence (APC), which involves practical experience and assessments, before they can become a member of the RICS.

Those who have not studied a degree in a relevant subject can take an RICS-accredited postgraduate degree or diploma course in an auctioneering/valuation subject. You may have to combine these courses with work experience and further professional qualifications.

The IRRV offers qualifications and training for continuing professional development (CPD).

What the work involves

As a property valuer you will assess the value of property (buildings, land or personal items) for a client and advise them on how the property may be sold, loaned, taxed, acquired by a company or made part of a compensation claim. Local authorities also use these valuations to help set council tax and rating levels.

You will assess new commercial and industrial property and reassess existing property that has been altered and improved.

You will provide reports on your valuations which may be important if property becomes part of legal negotiations or insurance claims. You may have to run live auctions where you will sell items that you have valued or you may pass them to a specialist.

Type of person suited to this work

You should have a keen interest in property valuation law and taxation.

You must have strong numerical skills to make accurate calculations, such as working out taxes or analysing accounts. As you may be hired by a company on a freelance basis, you will also need to be organised and able to use your initiative.

You need to have excellent written and verbal communication skills in order to communicate with clients, employers and government bodies.

Working conditions

You will work about 35–40 hours per week, Monday to Friday. You may have to work weekends depending on the project or your employer.

You will mainly be office-based but will frequently have to visit and inspect properties or meet clients.

As you might need to travel locally, a driving licence is recommended.

Future prospects

There are many opportunities in the UK. You may work for an estate agent in order to value property that is being sold, rented or mortgaged. You may find opportunities in the Valuation Office Agency assessing property for local authorities and government departments.

Valuers are also needed by HM Revenue & Customs (HMRC) where you will value property and land that must be taxed when it is sold or bought.

Once you have gained sufficient experience, you could become a project manager, company partner or work as a freelance consultant.

Advantages/disadvantages

The job tends to be diverse and interesting as you will usually combine your role as a valuer with other areas such as estate management, surveying and even auctioning.

Property and land valuations may become part of compensation claims which involve a lengthy legal process.

Occasionally, property viewings and auctions will take place on evenings and weekends.

Money guide

Your starting salary can be £19,000–£23,000 a year.

With experience, earnings can increase to between £24,000 and £36,000.

The average earnings of an RICS member are £50,250.

Freelance land and property valuers charge in accordance with their experience and type of contract.

Related opportunities

- Auction Property Consultant p73
- Insurance Risk Surveyor p46
- Loss Adjuster p50

Further information

Institute of Revenues Rating and Valuation
www.irrv.org.uk

National Association of Valuers and Auctioneers
www.nava.org.uk

Royal Institution of Chartered Surveyors
www.rics.org

QUANTITY SURVEYOR

Qualifications and courses

Most employers look for candidates who have a degree that is accredited by the Royal Institution of Chartered Surveyors (RICS), particularly in quantity surveying. If you hold a non-accredited degree, or you study another subject at undergraduate level, you will need to take a postgraduate conversion course that is recognised by the RICS. First degree subjects which may be useful include geography, maths and economics.

An HND in a related subject such as building/ construction, civil engineering or urban and land studies is also valued by employers and may gain you employment as a surveying technician. You can then progress to quantity surveyor level by studying, either part time or via distance learning, for RICS-recognised qualifications.

Entry without a degree or HND is sometimes possible, although unusual. You would have to work your way up through the industry, undertaking relevant courses and gaining qualifications as you go.

Once you are in employment, you will need to become a member of the RICS. This is achieved by attaining an approved degree in quantity surveying and completing the Assessment of Professional Competence (APC) which requires at least 2 years' practical, work-based experience.

What the work involves

Quantity surveyors are responsible for calculating costs, issuing contracts, keeping projects to time and within budget, managing subcontractors and arranging payments for work.

You will need a good understanding of building regulations to ensure that projects meet the required standards of quality and safety.

You could work on a wide variety of projects from residential developments to hospitals or sports stadiums.

Type of person suited to this work

You must have a high level of numeracy and the ability to manage financial projects as you will be responsible for all the financial details of projects. Good negotiation skills are also important, as you must agree contracts and prices with workers and contractors.

Excellent verbal and written communication skills are vital for leading and motivating the onsite team, liaising with clients and subcontractors, and producing accurate and detailed progress reports.

Finally, a good understanding of business and legal matters in relation to the building and construction industry is needed, since you will be responsible for ensuring that all projects meet current regulations and standards.

Working conditions

Working hours are slightly longer than average and will include early starts, late evenings and weekend work.

You will usually be office based, although it is not uncommon for the office to be in the form of a temporary hut onsite. Travel to client meetings and other projects is also expected.

Self-employment is possible, and many companies use freelance quantity surveyors on projects. There is also the opportunity to travel overseas.

Future prospects

Your opportunities are likely to lie within local authority or government departments, private practices, building contractors, property companies or commercial organisations both in the UK and abroad.

With experience, you can undertake a more comprehensive project management role and have the satisfaction of taking a job through from conception to completion. There is also a natural progression from quantity surveying to commercial management.

Advantages/disadvantages

Working on numerous projects and with a range of people makes the job varied.

There are good opportunities for career progression and specialisation.

Hours are longer than average, with occasional weekend work.

Money guide

Starting salaries for quantity surveyors can range from £17,000 to £25,000.

Those in senior roles can achieve salaries of £35,000–£50,000 and partners in private firms can expect considerably more.

Obtaining chartered status and/or further qualifications significantly improves your career prospects and earnings.

Benefits can include shift and site allowances, pension schemes, healthcare packages and a company car.

Related opportunities

- Civil/Construction Engineer/Civil Engineering Technician p83
- Insurance Risk Surveyor p46
- Town Planner/Planning Technician p127

Further information

ConstructionSkills
www.cskills.org

Royal Institution of Chartered Surveyors
www.rics.org

REFRIGERATION ENGINEER/ TECHNICIAN

Qualifications and courses

Entry is usually through apprenticeship. To qualify you are likely to need 4 GCSEs/S grades (A*–C/1–3) in English, maths, physics and design and technology.

Apprentices can gain NVQs, Levels 2 and 3, in Mechanical Engineering Services and Refrigeration and Air Conditioning, alongside health and safety procedures. Arrangements for apprenticeships are different in Scotland, Wales and Northern Ireland.

Further qualifications such HNCs/HNDs in Refrigeration and Air Conditioning, the BTEC national certificate/ diploma, and Foundation degrees in building services engineering are available. You can also apply to be a member of the Institute of Refrigeration.

What the work involves

Your work as a refrigeration engineer will involve the design, installation and repair of refrigeration equipment and air conditioning systems. You will be called out to undertake repairs and maintenance, estimate costs of construction and installation projects, carry out inspections on existing equipment, and give advice on adjustments and improvements.

Refrigeration engineers aim to create and maintain comfortable working/living environments in offices and homes that are both energy-efficient and safe.

Your work in commercial buildings and factories will be to provide refrigeration systems that keep food at the correct, safe temperature.

Type of person suited to this work

It is important that you like hands-on work and have a practical approach to problem-solving.

You should be interested in the building services industry and keep up to date with relevant developments in legislation and technology.

Written and spoken communication skills are important as you will be in contact with clients and planning projects. You should also have an aptitude for maths and physics and have strong technical skills.

Working conditions

You will normally work around 37 hours a week and how this is spread over a week may vary. However you might have to work longer hours during the summer which is peak time for refrigeration engineers.

You will be office based to plan visits to sites and organise jobs, but you will also visit various locations such as offices, shopping centres or factories. This will be to complete practical jobs such as maintenance, repair and installation.

You may also work in refrigeration transport, on specially adapted vehicles such as trucks, aircraft and fishing vessels or in vehicle workshops. On certain visits you might have to wear protective clothing or equipment.

Future prospects

As you gain experience in the field you will find opportunities for progression to supervisory and managerial roles.

To improve your skills you may take further qualifications such as NVQs in Building Services Engineering at Levels 3 and 4 or in other refrigeration and air conditioning specific topics. Such courses act as a stepping stone to the Chartered Institution of Building Services Engineers (CIBSE).

You can add further experience with further qualifications and work towards becoming an incorporated or chartered engineer.

Advantages/disadvantages

There are opportunities to work abroad as UK qualifications are internationally respected.

You may also be required to do overtime work and to be on-call overnight and on weekends.

Money guide

First year apprentices normally earn around £10,000 a year.

Starting salaries, once you have qualified, are around £20,000 to £27,000 a year.

This can increase to around £30,000 and above with experience and qualifications.

Salaries can be as high as £50,000 per year.

Related opportunities

- Civil/Construction Engineer/Civil Engineering Technician p83
- Electrical Engineer p219
- Electrician p92

Further information

Institute of Refrigeration
www.ior.org.uk

ROOFER

Qualifications and courses

To train as a roofer it is useful to have some GCSEs/S grades (A*–E/1–5) or a vocational qualification. Maths, English, craft, design and technology are all relevant subjects.

You could also enter this profession through an apprenticeship programme. ConstructionSkills offers specialised roofing apprenticeships through the National Construction College (NCC) that lead to NVQ/SVQ Level 2 qualifications.

Most training is done on the job whilst attending college to obtain qualifications such as NVQs/SVQs in Roofing Occupations and City & Guilds Certificates.

Many employers on construction sites require workers to have a Construction Skills Certification Scheme (CSCS) card. This demonstrates that the holder has health and safety training.

What the work involves

Roofers remove old roofs and replace them, cover new roofs and repair existing ones. You will have a choice of roofing materials to work with, such as tile, slate, felt, thatch and sheet. You could specialise in flat or pitched (sloping) roofs or work on both.

When working on flat roofs you will need to spread a waterproof bitumen layer. On all types of roofs your work will involve measuring and cutting materials, layering them on the roof and using mortar or cement to seal it.

You could also conduct lead work or liquid applied roofing.

Type of person suited to this work

You need to have good practical skills and be physically fit, so that you can climb ladders and scaffolding and carry roofing materials. You must be comfortable working at heights.

It is important to be able to understand plans and follow instructions. You should be a team player with good communication skills when dealing with customers.

It will also be useful to be interested in building construction and to enjoy being outdoors.

Working conditions

You will work outdoors on roofs in various locations from people's homes to historic cathedrals and construction sites. The work can be dusty and dirty.

As you will be working up ladders, on scaffolding or on the roof itself, you will need to pay close attention to all health and safety procedures, which includes wearing protective gear such as a safety helmet and boots.

You are likely to work a normal working week, although extra work may be available at weekends.

Future prospects

There is a good demand for qualified roofers across the UK at the moment. Work is available within roofing companies, contractors, local authorities, roofing material suppliers and other public organisations. Self-employment is common.

You can decide to specialise in using one type of roofing material (such as slate) or you can train to become skilled in using several types.

You may work your way up to technical, supervisory and managerial levels. After you have gained enough experience, you could start your own roofing company.

Advantages/disadvantages

Working at heights may be difficult for some people.

You could get to work on some impressive projects such as fitting the roof on a new football stadium. It is satisfying to produce a lasting structure that is functional and looks good.

You will gain an understanding of other construction work, such as joinery.

Money guide

Trainee salaries are about £13,500 per year. After NVQ/SVQ qualifications this rises to around £16,000.

As a trained roofer with qualifications you can earn £16,500–£25,000.

In excess of £26,000 is possible for very experienced roofers who are self-employed.

Overtime is often available and on some projects there are bonuses based on outputs.

Related opportunities

- Construction Operative p86
- Scaffolder p118
- Thatcher p125

Further information

ConstructionSkills
www.cskills.org

Institute of Roofing
www.instituteofroofing.co.uk

Qualifications and courses

This sector is open to all graduates, although a degree in a related subject such as agriculture, forestry, estate management or land management is particularly useful. Most degree courses require 5 GSCEs/S grades (A*–C/1–3), 2 A levels/3 H grades or relevant BTEC/SQA national awards (or equivalent). Degree courses accredited by the Royal Institution of Chartered Surveyors (RICS) will reduce the length of time you will have to spend in professional training by a year.

If your first degree was in an unrelated subject, the College of Estate Management offers a postgraduate conversion course that can be studied by distance learning.

If you have a relevant HND or Foundation degree, in land and property studies for example, then you can qualify for Associate/RICS status. However, a degree is necessary to become a fully chartered surveyor.

Once qualified, you will need to complete the Assessment of Professional Competence during your first 2 years of employment, in order to gain Chartered status.

What the work involves

Rural property/practice surveyors manage properties in the countryside such as farms and estates. You will give professional and technical advice to rural landowners on how to develop their assets – land and property – as well as providing business and resource management and consultancy for land, construction and property industries.

Giving advice on the buying and selling of properties, on farming grants and subsidies and how national and EU law affects their business is a typical example of work involved.

However, jobs do vary between those who work for corporations who deal with several clients and those who manage estates. You can also choose to specialise in specific areas, such as auctioneering or environmental sustainability, but this can limit employability to an extent.

Type of person suited to this work

Excellent communication skills are needed as you will need to negotiate and liaise with people of all ages and backgrounds.

You must have an analytical mind and a clear, concise writing style in order to explain detailed statistical information.

A good understanding of rural issues, including knowledge of crops, is essential in order to assess a client's economic viability with accuracy. Problem-solving and forward-planning skills are also essential to keep on top of a heavy workload.

Working conditions

The average working week can be 40+ hours and early morning and weekend work is common as you need to adapt around clients as well as rural events such as harvests.

You will mostly work outdoors, regardless of the weather. If you are office based, it will usually be in rural market towns or villages. You should be prepared to drive and travel regularly as work will often cover a large geographical area.

Future prospects

Your career path is narrow but progression can occur very quickly. In larger companies, there may be the opportunity to specialise in areas such as agriculture or renewable energy use in the countryside. By contrast, a smaller company could give you a greater range of projects which will build broader experience. With 10–15 years of experience, you could become a partner in a firm.

Advantages/disadvantages

You will be based in peaceful rural locations.

You will be instrumental in developing the future of the countryside and rural industries.

Hours can be long and you should expect to regularly work early mornings and weekends.

Money guide

Average earnings for new graduates are £20,000–£23,000.

With experience, this can increase to £38,000.

A senior chartered surveyor can receive a salary in excess of £45,000. Compared with other surveying roles, rural property salaries are fairly low and the opportunity to earn more than £50,000 is rare.

Additional benefits such as a company car or health insurance are sometimes offered by employers, and subsidised accommodation may be available for surveyors managing a farm or estate.

Related opportunities

- Auction Property Consultant p73
- Building Surveyor p77
- Civil/Construction Engineer/Civil Engineering Technician p83

Further information

Agricultural Development and Advisory Service
www.adas.co.uk

Department for Environment, Food and Rural Affairs
www.defra.gov.uk

Royal Agricultural College
www.rac.ac.uk

SCAFFOLDER

Qualifications and courses

There are no set entry requirements but some GCSEs/S grades (A*–E/1–5) or a vocational qualification, such as the BTEC Introductory Certificate or Diploma in Construction (Level 1) are useful. Training is normally on the job with part-time attendance at college to get qualifications. Employers often expect some on-site experience so it may be useful to work as a labourer first.

The Construction Industry Scaffolders Record Scheme (CISRS) operates a card system, which is the recognised qualification for scaffolding. The CISRS card system ensures that operatives are properly trained and sufficiently experienced to work safely and correctly. An 18 month Apprenticeship will provide you with the CISRS Scaffolder card and the QCF CSkills Awards Diploma in Scaffolding (Level 2). You can also qualify for the CISRS Scaffolder card with 6 months' scaffolding experience, the CISRS Scaffolding courses (Parts 1 and 2) and the NVQ Diploma in Accessing Operations and Rigging (Construction) – Scaffolding (Level 2).

For the Advanced CISRS Card, scaffolders must have a Scaffolder Card, 12 months' subsequent experience and complete the 10-day Advanced Scaffolding course provided by CISRS and the NVQ Diploma in Accessing Operations and Rigging (Construction) – Scaffolding (Level 3).

What the work involves

Scaffolders put up scaffolding so that new constructions, or the maintenance of existing buildings and structures such as bridges, can take place. You will put together metal tubes, fittings and wooden or metal platforms to create the scaffolding.

You will use tools such as swivel spanners and spirit levels in your work.

You may also put up spectator stands, stages and rigging for outdoor concerts and events.

Type of person suited to this work

Safety is the main priority in scaffolding. You need to ensure that it is safe for the people who will be working on it, passers-by, workmates and yourself. For this reason, you have to be able to keep your concentration, have good practical skills, be well organised and be able to follow instructions and take measurements accurately.

You must be physically fit so that you can lift and carry equipment up and down ladders and, of course, you must be happy working at heights.

You also need to be able to work as part of a team of scaffolders.

Working conditions

You will be working mainly outdoors in most weather conditions, often at great heights.

You will need to wear protective equipment such as a hard hat, boots and a safety harness.

You may work a normal working week from Monday to Friday, although you might need to start work early or finish late. Extra hours at weekends may also be available.

Future prospects

There is a good demand for scaffolders across the UK and opportunities with specialist scaffolding firms and building contractors as well as oil and power companies.

You may progress from basic to advanced scaffolder, and then on to supervisory and managerial positions. Some experienced scaffolders set up their own businesses. If you possess computer-aided design skills, progression to project design and management is possible.

You may also work in other countries.

Advantages/disadvantages

This job can be physically challenging and working at heights can be demanding for some people.

You will get to work in a variety of locations and you might have the chance to put up scaffolding for major sports and music events or for film sets.

Money guide

Starting as an Apprentice or trainee, you can earn from £7,100 to £13,000 per year.

Once qualified as a scaffolder, salaries range from £16,600 up to £23,000.

Those with extensive experience or supervisory duties can achieve £25,000–£38,000.

Self-employed or contract scaffolders can often negotiate higher rates of pay.

Overtime is frequently available and on some projects there are performance-related bonuses which can lead to higher earnings.

Related opportunities

- Building Technician p78
- Construction Operative p86
- Roofer p116

Further information

ConstructionSkills
www.cskills.org

National Access and Scaffolding Confederation
www.nasc.org.uk

SHOPFITTER

Qualifications and courses

You can begin as a trainee in a specific role such as shopfitting joiner, wood machinist or metal fabricator.

No formal academic qualifications are required but some employers might expect entrants to have GCSEs/S grades (A*–E/1–5) in English, maths and a science. GSCEs in art, design and technology might also be useful. The BTEC Introductory Certificate and Diploma in Construction (Levels 1 and 2) and City & Guilds NVQ in Woodmachining (Levels 2 and 3) are also relevant.

You could begin as an apprentice with a shopfitting company. This leads to NVQs/SVQs in Shopfitting (Levels 2–4) which will include training, on-site work, bench work and site management. Apprenticeships in Construction Building are available at both Intermediate and Advanced Levels.

With experience you can apply for membership of the National Association of Shopfitters (NAS) for further training provided by the Shopfitting Independent Training Forum (SITF).

Many employers require you to have the CSCS card issued by the Construction Skills Certification Scheme as proof of your competence working on site.

What the work involves

As a shopfitter you will create and install the interiors and exteriors of commercial buildings such as shops, banks, offices, restaurants and hotels. You may be working from designs made by an architect or designer, or you might have to research and prepare your own design drawings.

You will prepare, assemble and finish joinery and metalwork according to the design, before bringing each part together and assembling them on site.

You will probably specialise in a particular area. These include a metal fabricator, cutting and shaping metal components; a wood machinist, using specialist machinery to cut precise parts for joiners.

Type of person suited to this work

As you will be working in a workshop or on site you should have a keen interest in practical work and have good hand skills. You should also be interested in design and construction.

You should have an eye for detail and a high level of concentration, but you will also need a certain level of fitness as you will be required to work long and at times, hard hours.

As you will be taking measurements and making calculations frequently you should have good spatial awareness and an aptitude for maths.

Working conditions

You will normally work around 40 hours per week. Your work may be in an office, a workshop, a machine shop or a paint shop. You may have to travel to work onsite and this may involve working away from home at times. You can often do overtime work.

You may have to work irregular hours, overnight or at weekends to accommodate clients – work may need to be done during the night when premises are closed.

Onsite work may be dusty, dirty and noisy and usually involves physical work such as lifting and bending.

Future prospects

Once you are qualified and have built up experience, you could progress to a supervisory or managerial role.

It is possible to establish your own shopfitting business.

The skills that you develop as a shopfitter could be utilised in various other building trades.

Advantages/disadvantages

Shopfitting is a diverse profession as your work will change according to the project that you are working on. This could include working with a variety of materials such as wood, glass, aluminium and plastic.

You will meet and work with many other professionals involved in construction such as engineers, architects, electricians and plumbers.

The job is physically demanding and you may be required to work long or unsocial hours.

Money guide

Your starting salary may be around £13,500 to £16,000 a year.

With experience and qualifications, earnings can rise to between £17,000 and £24,000.

As a shopfitter with supervisory duties you may be able to earn around £30,000 per year.

Related opportunities

- Builders' Merchant/Assistant p477
- Carpenter/Joiner p79
- Furniture Manufacturing Operative p225

Further information

ConstructionSkills
www.cskills.org

National Association of Shopfitters
www.shopfitters.org

SITE MANAGER/CLERK OF WORKS

Qualifications and courses

There are no set qualifications to become a clerk of works/site manager. However, experience in a relevant industry is necessary, perhaps at craft or technician level in construction or civil engineering. It is not normally a profession that you can enter when you first leave school.

As well as experience, you might need certain construction and civil engineering qualifications. These might include City & Guilds Award, Certificate and Diploma in Basic Construction Skills (Level 1), NVQs Level 2 or 3, a BTEC/SQA National Award, a BTEC Higher National Award or a Foundation or Honours degree.

When you are working you can gain NVQs in Site Inspection (Levels 3 and 4). As you accumulate qualifications you can achieve different levels of membership with the Institute of Clerks of Works and Construction Inspectorate (ICWCI). Although this membership is not essential, it is increasingly sought by employers. To enter each level of membership you will need to have a relevant qualification, a report of your professional history and a materials identification test.

Graduates may be taken on by companies as apprentices where they will learn on the job.

What the work involves

As a site manager/clerk of works you will be responsible for supervising all the on-site aspects of a construction contract.

You must ensure that good standards are maintained and that work is carried out efficiently and on time.

You will inspect and monitor materials, procedures and work so that the client is guaranteed quality and value for money. You will also act as a superintendent, advising contractors about aspects of work and solving problems as they arise.

Type of person suited to this work

You should have an interest in construction and should enjoy working outdoors and in all weather conditions. You will need to be physically fit and have a head for heights.

You need to be responsible, organised and honest as you may be in control of projects involving large teams of workers and a variety of materials. You will need a keen eye for detail and to be thorough and vigilant in maintaining quality standards of work and material.

You should have excellent communication skills, be able to lead a team and to establish appropriate working relationships with contractors' staff.

Working conditions

You will usually work around 40 hours a week, Monday to Friday. However you will frequently have to work at the weekend and during the evening depending on deadlines.

You will be based in a site office which will usually be a temporary structure. You will have to spend much of your time outdoors in all weather conditions.

You may have to climb ladders and scaffolding or in tunnel construction, work underground. When you are inspecting a site you might have to wear protective clothing such as a hard hat and work boots.

Future prospects

As an experienced clerk of works you must undertake continuing professional development. This is so that you can keep up to date with advances in areas such as new materials, practices, law and regulations, and health and safety issues.

Clerks of works can move up to roles in site management or other management roles in the construction industry.

You may have the opportunity to become self-employed and to work abroad.

Advantages/disadvantages

You can choose to specialise in particular areas such as building, civil engineering or mechanical and electrical installations.

On-site inspection may be dusty, dirty and noisy.

Money guide

Starting salaries are typically £18,000–£20,000 a year.

With experience, a clerk of works can earn about £25,000.

Senior clerks of works can achieve salaries of £30,000 to £35,000.

Related opportunities

- Building Surveyor p77
- Civil/Construction Engineer/Civil Engineering Technician p83
- Construction Supervisor/Manager p88

Further information

Chartered Institute of Building
www.ciob.org.uk

Institute of Clerks of Works
www.icwgb.org

Qualifications and courses

There are no formal entry qualifications for this job but you will find it useful to have GCSEs/S grades (A*–E/1–5) in maths, English, science and technology for calculations and measurements.

Young entrants can train on the job with an employer or as an apprentice with an approved Apprenticeship scheme. CITB ConstructionSkills provide opportunities for apprentice steeplejacks to study at the National Construction College. Entrants will take aptitude tests in maths and problem-solving and will be assessed in literacy and their ability to work at heights. Apprentices are sponsored by an employer and spend 6 months, over a 2–3 year period, at the residential National Construction College. Qualifications acheived will include NVQs in Accessing Operations and Rigging (Levels 2 and 3), Functional Skills (Level 1) and various other CITB courses such as Health and Safety, Employment Responsibilities and Rights, First Aid certification, and Working at Heights certification.

Many employers require you to have the CSCS card issued by the Construction Skills Certification Scheme as proof of your competence working on site.

What the work involves

Steeplejacks work on high structures including power station chimneys, cooling towers, oil refineries, factories and church spires. Your work on these structures will involve climbing to high places with your tools to complete routine maintenance, repairs or renovation projects.

You will plan each job carefully. To ensure a safe and accessible working environment you will put in ladders, specialist scaffolding or industrial rope access (abseiling), work platforms (cradles) and bosun's seat (harness) and fall-arrest devices.

You will be working on both historic buildings and modern constructions, in urban and rural areas.

Type of person suited to this work

You should be organised as you will have to make sure in advance that you have the right safety equipment and tools to complete the job. The ability to work well as part of a team is also important.

You must be comfortable working at heights or in confined spaces, have a good sense of balance and be physically fit. Good coordination and practical skills are required to use the tools of the trade.

You should enjoy working outdoors in all weather conditions and you must be very conscious of, and committed to, health and safety procedures.

Working conditions

Your working hours and shifts can vary and you might have to work during the evenings and weekends.

Your work will be physically demanding as it will involve rigging, climbing, carrying ladders and tools and working with your hands. You will need to wear protective clothing and headgear. You may have to work on industrial chimneys which can be extremely dusty, requiring respiratory equipment.

A driving licence is useful as you may have to travel.

Future prospects

As a steeplejack you will probably work for construction firms that specialise in steeplejacking. These tend to be based in London, Middlesbrough, Manchester, Nottingham, Bristol, Cardiff, Edinburgh and Glasgow, and are likely to seek local employees.

With experience you will be eligible for promotion to a role as a supervisor or manager within a firm. With significant experience you can become self-employed, although this is not common.

There are increasing opportunities to work abroad.

Advantages/disadvantages

There are currently between 800 and 1000 steeplejacks in the UK. As a qualified steeplejack you may find work easily and there are plenty of opportunities in this area.

Your work may be hampered by weather conditions, for example, high winds may prevent access to structures and delay completion of projects.

Money guide

The starting salary for a trainee steeplejack usually ranges from £12,500 to £15,000.

Once qualified, you can earn around £17,000 and this will increase to about £21,000 as you gain experience.

Those who take on extra responsibilities, become a senior engineer or specialise in a particular area can earn £25,000–£35,000 a year.

Related opportunities

- Bricklayer p74
- Scaffolder p118
- Stonemason p122

Further information

Association of Technical Lighting and Access Specialists
www.atlas.org.uk

ConstructionSkills
www.cskills.org

STONEMASON

ENTRY LEVEL **1**

Qualifications and courses

There are no formal entry requirements to train as a stonemason but an interest in art and design is desirable and it may be useful to have GCSEs/S grades (A*–D/1–4) in English, maths and technology.

Training is provided on the job with part-time attendance at college or training centres to gain relevant NVQs/SVQs. Apprenticeships/Skillseekers at both Intermediate and Advanced Levels may be available for those aged 16–24.

Relevant qualifications in stonemasonry are offered by the Construction Awards Alliance (CAA) – a partnership between ConstructionSkills and City & Guilds. Courses offered include NVQ Diplomas (Levels 2 and 3) in Banker Masonry, Memorial Masonry, Stone Fixing and Stone Cladding. Further options are the NVQ Diploma in Heritage Skills (Construction) – Mason (Level 3) or the City & Guilds NVQ in Stonemasonry (Level 3).

Many employers on construction sites require workers to have a Construction Skills Certification Scheme (CSCS) card.

Those with experience in the field may wish to demonstrate their expertise by studying for one of the NVQ Diplomas (Level 4) in Senior Crafts (Construction) – Stone Masonry.

What the work involves

There are three types of stonemason. Banker masons cut, shape and carve the stone, fixer masons assemble and fix stones into place and monumental masons make things such as plaques and headstones.

While the work is manual and strenuous it is also highly creative. You may work on new buildings but could also work on restoring and repairing old buildings.

Type of person suited to this work

Banker mason
As a banker mason, you have to be good with your hands to cut, shape and carve stone accurately. You also need artistic skills for producing decorative finishes.

Fixer mason
You must be physically fit so that you can lift the stones, although you will use special equipment to lift the heaviest ones. You must not mind working at heights.

Monumental mason
In this sector, you will be working closely with the funeral industry, so you need to be sensitive to people's requirements and have a good eye for design. It is also useful to be interested in architecture and history, as much of the work involves restoring old buildings.

Working conditions

Banker masons mainly work in a workshop, while fixer masons work on-site in all weather conditions and restoration masons work on monuments and listed buildings, often at heights.

All masonry work can be dusty, noisy and unsuitable for people who have allergies. You will need to follow health and safety procedures and wear protective clothing.

You will normally work a 39-hour week but overtime may be required when nearing a project deadline.

Future prospects

There is good demand for stonemasons in the UK.

You can choose to work for stonemasonry companies and larger building contractors. If you work for a small stonemasonry company you are likely to have to do both banking and fixing work.

After training, you may wish to specialise in restoration work or new buildings.

There are opportunities to take on supervisory or managerial roles.

Advantages/disadvantages

The physical nature of the job, including working at heights, may be strenuous for some people.

You may have the opportunity to work on impressive restoration projects, for example in cathedrals or stately homes.

It can make you proud to produce work on a building that will be admired for many years.

Money guide

As a new entrant you could earn £12,000–£15,000 per year.

With experience, your salary could be £20,000–£25,000.

Senior stonemasons can achieve up to £33,000.

Overtime and performance-based bonuses are often available.

Related opportunities

- Bricklayer p74
- Building Technician p78
- Dry Stone Waller p91

Further information

National Heritage Training Group
www.nhtg.org.uk

Stone Federation Great Britain
www.stone-federationgb.org.uk

STRUCTURAL ENGINEER

Qualifications and courses

Entrants normally have a degree in structural or civil engineering. Graduates who have studied another engineering subject or a highly numerate science degree can enter the profession but their career progression may be slower or more limited.

For a degree course in engineering you will need at least 5 GCSEs/S grades (A*–C/1–3) and 2 or 3 A levels/H grades. This should include maths and any science subject, although physics is sometimes specifically requested. Colleges and universities may also accept a relevant Access to Higher Education Diploma for entry onto some courses.

It is possible to enter this career after studying for an HNC/HND or Foundation degree in engineering. You will have to enter at technician level and work your way up to engineer status by training on the job.

Graduate structural engineers are advised to pursue membership with the Insitution of Structural Engineers (IStructE) as this can greatly improve your employability and salary. Associate members are required to have an accredited bachelor's degree, complete an Initial Professional Development (IPD) programme and pass a Professional Review Interview (PRI) and exam. In addition to these requirements, those who wish to acquire Chartered status must hold an accredited master's degree.

What the work involves

Structural engineers design structures that are able to withstand the high pressure they are placed under.

You will work with architects on the design and construction of a variety of structures including bridges, tunnels, domestic houses, office blocks or sports stadia.

Among other tasks you will calculate the loads and stresses of a structure, analyse potential problems and test digital models to examine how they will endure influences such as wind, gravity and earth tremors. You will investigate soil conditions, visit construction sites, and undertake projects that involve demolition or repair of a structure.

Type of person suited to this work

You will need to be good at technical drawing and have 3D concept skills. You must have a keen eye for detail and accomplish your work efficiently and with the utmost accuracy.

You should have an aptitude for problem-solving and analytical thinking. You should also have strong skills in maths, physics and ICT.

You must be able to work in a team as well as being able to work with other professionals from across the construction industry.

Working conditions

You will work a total of approximately 40 hours a week, Monday to Friday. At times you might have to work on the weekend.

You will work both in an office and on-site. This can be in all weather conditions and you will have to wear protective clothing such as a hard hat.

You will frequently have to travel from site to site and a driving licence may be useful for this.

Future prospects

Many employers provide training schemes for new structural engineers which allow you to work towards achieving professional status.

You may follow a formal progression structure within an engineering organisation.

You can become self-employed although chartered status is necessary if you want to start up your own business.

Advantages/disadvantages

Despite the recent decline in the construction industry, many projects are planned in London and the south-east of England.

You should be prepared to work in all weather conditions.

Travel within a working day is common and you may be required to work away from home sometimes.

This is an important job with high levels of responsibility so you are likely to be well-respected.

Money guide

Graduate trainees have a starting salary of £19,000–£23,000.

After several years' experience in the role a structural engineer could earn £32,000–£40,000.

Senior level employees, particularly those who have achieved chartered status, could receive up to £70,000 a year.

Salaries vary depending on location and company size.

Related opportunities

- Architect p70
- Quantity Surveyor p114
- Surveying Technician p124

Further information

Association for Consultancy and Engineering
www.acenet.co.uk

ConstructionSkills
www.cskills.org

Institution of Structural Engineers
www.istructe.org.uk

Qualifications and courses

Entry to this profession is usually with a degree or diploma, preferably one that is accredited by the Royal Institution of Chartered Surveyors (RICS). For a degree course, the usual qualifications needed are a minimum of 2 A levels/3 H grades or a relevant BTEC/SQA National Award.

You could also obtain a job by studying towards Level 4 NVQs in Quantity Surveying Practice, Valuation, Spatial Data Management or Town Planning whilst doing work experience.

To become a chartered member of RICS you need to complete a 2 year Assessment of Professional Competence (APC) which involves training and practical experience.

The Chartered Surveyors Training Trust (CSTT) offers work-based training for young people aged 16–24, living in England. Applicants must have a minimum of 4 GCSEs (A*–C) or equivalent. CSTT apprentices train for 2 years and then have the option to study for an RICS-accredited degree. Another route for school leavers is to apply for the Advanced Apprenticeship in Surveying.

Once you have qualified as a surveying technician, further training is possible in the form of NVQs. This may lead you to specialise in a particular area of surveying.

What the work involves

Surveying technicians work alongside chartered surveyors, providing hands-on support across the full range of surveying specialisms including building, land, rural and commercial.

You will be expected to carry out a range of administrative tasks associated with each project, such as putting together contracts and writing reports.

You will also be using complex computer programs and technical equipment both onsite and in the office in order to create reports and survey drawings, and to assess various aspects of each project.

Type of person suited to this work

You will be working closely with other professionals and clients at all levels, so the ability to communicate both verbally and in written documents is vital.

Because you will be dealing with very specific technical issues in each project, you will need to have an accurate and methodical approach to work, good numerical skills and the ability to multi-task and think on your feet.

You will need a good level of ICT skills, and confidence in using the wide range of sophisticated equipment required for the job. Knowledge of business, law and health and safety-related regulations is also desirable.

Working conditions

Working hours usually follow those of a normal office job, but you will occasionally be called to work early mornings, evenings and at weekends during busy times or for certain site visits.

Most of the work is office based, but you will also spend time working onsite. This means you must be prepared to get cold, wet, muddy and dusty, and wear appropriate safety equipment at all times.

You will be carrying out a lot of complex technical tasks which require excellent concentration and can be quite tiring.

Future prospects

You could work with central or local government, large construction firms, smaller surveying companies or even financial businesses, and art and antiques auction houses.

You could progress to become a consultant, a partner in a firm or even move into related sectors such as town planning or chartered surveying with the right qualifications. Self-employment is also an option.

Advantages/disadvantages

Job satisfaction is likely to be high as you will provide invaluable support on a number of important projects.

There is the opportunity to become self-employed or work overseas.

Earning potential is not as high as some other roles in surveying and hours can be long and unpredictable at busy times.

Money guide

Starting salaries range from £16,000 to £21,000 per year.

With experience, earnings could rise to about £25,000.

The highest earning senior technicians can achieve in excess of £31,000.

Salaries are generally higher in London.

Related opportunities

- Civil/Construction Engineer/Civil Engineering Technician p83
- Construction Supervisor/Manager p88
- Quantity Surveyor p114

Further information

Association of Building Engineers
www.abe.org.uk

Chartered Surveyors Training Trust
www.cstt.org.uk

Royal Institution of Chartered Surveyors
www.rics.org

Qualifications and courses

There are no set entry requirements for this profession. It may help to have GCSEs/S grades (A*–E/1–5) in English, maths and ICT as these could be useful if you become self-employed and run a small business.

There are no formal Apprenticeship schemes for thatching so it is recommended that you contact master thatchers to try and secure a training or apprentice role. To try and make contacts within the industry, it may be useful to look at the websites of the National Society of Master Thatchers, the National Council of Master Thatchers Associations or the Thatch Advice Centre.

Those who wish to gain further training and experience could study for the NVQ in Roofing Occupations (Construction) – Thatching at Level 2 or 3.

What the work involves

Thatching is the covering of roofs with plant stems such as water reed, combed wheat reed and long straw. Your tasks will include thatching new roofs and repairing or re-thatching existing thatched roofs.

Your work will involve using many different tools, including mallets, hooks, needles, knives and shears.

As thatchers work outside all year round, your hours will differ depending on the season.

Type of person suited to this work

You need to have good practical skills to use the specialised equipment and to develop an expertise in the craft. You must be physically fit so that you can climb ladders and scaffolding whilst carrying thatching materials. You will need to be comfortable working at heights.

It is important to be able to measure roofs accurately so you can work out the required amount of thatching material. Communication skills are necessary for talking to customers and planning officers. You will also need to be interested in learning a traditional rural craft.

Working conditions

You will work outdoors on roofs in rural locations in most weather conditions. The work can be dusty, which can be difficult if you suffer from certain allergies.

It is important that you follow health and safety procedures closely when working on roofs.

Your working hours are likely to vary according to when the work is available. This can be seasonal work, meaning you will be busiest during the spring and summer months when the weather is best.

Future prospects

There are approximately 500 thatcher businesses in the UK and, as about half of all thatched buildings need to be re-roofed every 15–20 years, there is a steady demand for thatching work. However, there is fierce competition for training vacancies and some thatchers have another job to supplement their income. Not all areas of the UK have thatched buildings so you might have to relocate to find work.

It can take a number of years to become highly skilled. Many thatchers become self-employed once they are fully trained.

Advantages/disadvantages

It is rewarding to practise an ancient craft and create thatched roofs that are both functional and decorative.

The job involves being active and working outdoors.

Working at heights may be demanding for some people and potentially dangerous.

You may need a second job to supplement your earnings.

Money guide

Earnings vary according to the county and employer.

Trainees will usually receive the minimum wage during their apprenticeship.

Upon completion of an apprenticeship, thatchers could earn £14,000–£20,000.

An experienced thatcher's salary could be about £23,000.

Self-employed thatchers who have established a good reputation amongst their clients can achieve up to £35,000.

Related opportunities

- Dry Stone Waller p91
- Roofer p116
- Stonemason p122

Further information

Lantra
www.lantra.co.uk

National Heritage Training Group
www.nhtg.org.uk

Thatching Advisory Services
www.thatchingadviseryservices.co.uk

THERMAL INSULATION ENGINEER

Qualifications and courses

Although no formal qualifications are required, employers usually require GCSEs/S grades in English, maths, science and an engineering or construction subject. It is possible to enter this career from an Apprenticeship opportunity if you are aged 16–24.

You will have to pass an entry test after which you will undertake on-the-job and off-the-job training at college. Your employer could use a training programme provided by the Insulation and Environmental Training Agency (IETA). It is also helpful if you can provide evidence of some practical work experience when applying.

NVQs/SVQs in Thermal Insulation Engineering are available at Levels 2–3. Completing a Level 2 certificate in Thermal Insulation or a Key Skills in Communication, Application of Number and IT could also improve your employability.

Many employers on construction sites require workers to have a Construction Skills Certification Scheme (CSCS) card. This demonstrates that the holder has health and safety training.

What the work involves

You will use various types of insulation to either prevent heat loss or keep heat out within different types of products and equipment, such as boilers, pipework, refrigeration or air conditioning. The types of insulation you will use will be dependent on the actual project but could involve silicate or foam.

You will measure, cut and shape insulating materials to fit around pipes, boilers and duct work. Once the item is insulated, you will cover it using sheet metal or another cladding material.

You will assess clients' needs and advise them on the best plan to solve their insulation problem.

Type of person suited to this work

You may be exposed to some potentially dangerous materials, so you must follow health and safety regulations carefully.

You should be able to understand instructions, have a practical approach to your work and enjoy using manual skills, particularly for cutting and fitting materials. Mathematical skills are useful for measuring and working out quantities.

Much of the work involves strenuous lifting, balancing and climbing up scaffolding, so you will have to be physically fit, as well as able to work within confined spaces and at height.

The ability to work in a team and get on with other people will be important as you will often work alongside other professionals from the construction and engineering industries.

Working conditions

You could be working indoors or outside at heights, in places that are cramped or difficult to access.

You may be exposed to harmful substances and be working in dusty and dirty environments, so you will wear protective clothing, like goggles and sometimes a face mask.

You will normally work a standard 38-hour week, but overtime and evening or weekend work might be required. Travelling around the country to visit different sites and projects may be necessary.

Future prospects

The energy conservation industry is expanding and there is growth in the demand for qualified thermal insulation engineers to work on a wide range of engineering and construction projects.

After gaining training and experience, you could find a job within building, building service engineering or specialised energy conservation companies.

Within the larger companies it might be possible to progress into supervisory posts and work abroad can be available.

Advantages/disadvantages

You will be working alongside people from different industries. Opportunities are good and overseas work may be possible.

You will need many different skills to complete one job.

You may need to stay away from home – this could be difficult if you have family commitments.

Money guide

Training salary is usually £10,000–£16,000 a year.

With qualifications this rises to £17,000– £22,000 a year.

Senior thermal insulation engineers can earn up to £30,000.

Contract work is common and this could lead to expense payments for working away or bonus for early completion.

Related opportunities

- Damp Proofer p89
- Gas Network Engineer p226
- Heating and Ventilating Engineer p102

Further information

ConstructionSkills
www.cskills.org

Insulation and Environmental Training Agency
www.tica-acad.co.uk

TOWN PLANNER/PLANNING TECHNICIAN

Qualifications and courses

Town planning technician

There are no set qualifications, but at least 4 GCSEs/S grades (A*–C/1–3) including English and maths, are usually required. Many entrants also have A levels, Foundation degrees or other qualifications. Planning technicians are trained on the job and may also undertake part-time study. Technical Membership of the Royal Town Planning Institute (RTPI) requires a recognised qualification at NVQ Level 3 or higher and 2 years' work experience.

Town planner

You will need to have an accredited qualification such as a first degree or a postgraduate qualification. For degree entry you will need at least 2 A levels/H grades. For entry to a postgraduate course, a degree in a related subject such as geography, architecture or statistics is required. Full membership of the RTPI is given after completion of an accredited qualification and 2 years' relevant work experience.

Continuing Professional Development (CPD) forms an essential part of advancement in your career. Once you have qualified you will be expected to undertake relevant courses, 50 hours' worth of development, and keep a 2–year written record of your progress.

What the work involves

Town planner

You will manage and develop urban or rural areas to best serve the population. When deciding how to use the land you will take into account commercial, social, environmental and heritage needs.

Town planning technician

You will support the work of town planners.

You will carry out surveys, map areas, record information, analyse and present reports and provide advice on planning permission.

Type of person suited to this work

You will need excellent communication skills as you will need to explain your ideas clearly and produce comprehensive written reports.

You must be organised with good research, problem-solving and analytical skills to investigate the potential effects of different proposals for land use.

Specialist skills required include competency in graphic design, desktop publishing and familiarity with computer-aided design (CAD), geographical information systems (GIS) and cartography.

Working conditions

Regular office hours are likely, although you may sometimes need to attend meetings in the evening.

Most town planners are based in offices but often go out on site visits. A driving licence might be necessary.

Future prospects

There is a huge demand for more qualified planners in the UK and overseas.

Most employers are local authorities and planning consultancies, but opportunities also exist within central government, construction companies and environmental organisations. With experience, you may be promoted to senior or chief town planner, or move into related careers such as recreation management, market research or property development.

Advantages/disadvantages

It is satisfying to deal with public problems and to improve the environment in which people live and work.

It can be frustrating to compromise on planning initiatives.

Dealing with angry or upset members of the public can be difficult.

Money guide

Starting salaries for trainee technicians range from £14,000 to £18,000 per year; this can reach about £25,000 once qualified.

Experienced technicians can earn up to £32,000.

Newly graduated town planners could earn between £16,000 and £28,000. This will be more if you are a registered member of the Royal Town Planning Institute (RTPI).

Senior planners can earn between £20,000 and £34,000.

Principal planners or heads of a team can earn between £29,000 and £41,000.

Chief planning officers, heads of department and company directors can earn between £50,000 and £80,000.

Related opportunities

- Land/Geomatic Surveyor p106
- Planning and Development Surveyor p110
- Quantity Surveyor p114

Further information

Royal Town Planning Institute
www.rtpi.org.uk

WALL/FLOOR TILER

Qualifications and courses

No specific qualifications are required, although GCSEs/S grades (A*–E/1–5) in subjects like maths, technology or English may be useful. Similar subjects may be needed to be eligible for an Apprenticeship or equivalent vocational qualifications like the Edexcel Introductory Certificate. Certain schools also offer 14–16-year-olds the Foundation Certificate in Building Craft Operations by the Construction Awards Alliance (CAA).

You will be trained on the job while working towards qualifications. This may also involve going to a college or training centre on day or block release. NVQs in Wall and Floor Tiling at Levels 2 and 3 are available.

Apprenticeships may be available to those aged 16–24. In Scotland, applicants for a construction Apprenticeship need to take a selection test.

It is becoming increasingly necessary to have a Construction Skills Certification Scheme (CSCS) card to work in construction. Eligibility for this card depends on your qualifications and experience. Check the CSCS website for more details on this scheme.

What the work involves

You will fit tiles in various locations, from bathrooms and kitchens to hospitals and swimming pools. You may work with many kinds of tile including ceramic, stone, glass, terracotta, granite, marble and mosaic.

First you will set out(known as marking) an area by calculating the amount of tile and adhesive needed. You will then use bench-mounted or hand tools to cut the tiles to the correct size and shape.

You will level the surface with plaster, cement or sand, fix the tiles in the correct position and then fill in the gaps with grout.

Type of person suited to this work

Maths skills are essential as you will need to measure and calculate how much material you will need. You must work carefully and accurately. It is important to match colours and patterns, so a flair for design is useful.

You need to be physically fit for carrying the materials and for working on your hands and knees.

You need to be able to work on your own initiative as well as in a team. You should be presentable and pleasant when dealing with customers.

Working conditions

You will work mainly indoors in a variety of locations, ranging from a client's home to offices, factories and construction sites. A driving licence might be useful.

You may work a normal working week, but you may also need to work evenings or weekends so that you can tile walls and floors without disrupting businesses.

As you will use special cutting tools and adhesives you will need to be aware of health and safety procedures.

Future prospects

Work is available with specialist tiling companies and building contractors, or you may choose to become self-employed, providing services to individuals or sub-contracting to organisations. Demand for tilers depends on the economy.

It is possible to specialise in using one type of tiling, for example flooring tiles, mosaic work or bathrooms.

With experience, you may progress to technical, supervisory or managerial positions.

Advantages/disadvantages

You will be on your hands and knees, sometimes working in dusty, dirty or cramped conditions.

The work is varied and you can achieve spectacular results using coloured and textured tiles to decorate walls and floors.

Money guide

Salaries are around £17,000 per year and this can rise to £23,000 with experience.

£40,000 is possible for the highest earners.

Overtime is often available, and on some projects there are bonuses based on outputs, which can lead to higher earnings.

Related opportunities

- Building Technician p78
- Construction Operative p86
- Floor Layer/Finisher p98

Further information

ConstructionSkills
www.cskills.org

The Tile Association
www.tiles.org.uk

WASTEWATER TREATMENT PLANT OPERATOR

Qualifications and courses

There are no formal academic qualifications required to become a wastewater treatment plant operator. However, some companies seek employees with a minimum of 4 GCSEs/S grade (A*–E/1–5) in maths, English and a science or technology subject. Most enter the industry through a Water Industry Apprenticeship. The minimum age for apprentices is generally 18.

You can also take a course with City & Guilds to improve your skills, including the Level 2 Certificate for Water Sector Competent Operators. Another important qualification is the NVQ Level 2 in Operating a Process Plant (Water/Waste Water/Sludge). You can also gain an NVQ Level 2 in Utilities Control Centre Operations.

You may choose to pursue an HND/C or degree which will qualify you for more senior roles.

What the work involves

Water treatment plant operators monitor wastewater as it goes through various treatment processes which remove harmful substances. They ensure that treated water is returned to the water cycle and that wastewater is removed and destroyed as appropriate.

You will be responsible for the operation and maintenance of the plant, ensuring that septic tanks, filters and screens are disinfected, checking water samples, and adding treatment micro-organisms and chemicals to the water when necessary.

You will conduct tests on samples, take readings from monitors and adjust treatment equipment as necessary. You will work with a team composed of a supervisor, senior technicians, engineers and a manager.

Type of person suited to this work

You need to have a passion for the environment, science and technology. You also need to be happy to work with new technology which you will use on a daily basis.

You must be able to communicate effectively and work well in a team. You will have to follow health and safety regulations. It is important that you are fit and active as you may be doing practical strenuous work at times, such as cleaning and maintenance.

You must be organised and methodical as you will be testing samples to ensure that harmful substances are removed from the water cycle.

Working conditions

You will work approximately 37 hours a week. Overtime may be possible but part-time work is rare. You will probably have to work shifts as water treatment plants operate 24 hours a day. You may have to join a call-out rota to cover nights and weekends.

You will be based indoors in control rooms but some of your work will involve being outside in all weather conditions. You may also have to carry out work at heights or in confined spaces.

Protective clothing is provided. This may include a breathing apparatus, and should be worn to prevent contact with harmful substances.

Future prospects

After gaining experience, you could progress to a role as a supervisor and from there to roles as an inspector, a superintendent or a plant manager. You may also choose to move into a related area such as treatment plant design.

You can also take a Higher National Certificate, Diploma or degree which will allow you to move to higher positions.

Advantages/disadvantages

You may find opportunities to increase wages by taking extra shifts, going on stand-by and doing overtime.

Your working environment in the plant may be smelly and wet.

You may sometimes be called into work if there is an emergency situation.

Money guide

Your salary as a trainee can start at around £12,000 a year.

With experience you can earn between £18,000 and £25,000.

Supervisors and department leaders can earn between £25,000 and £32,000.

Overtime and extensive shift work can greatly increase salary.

Related opportunities

- Brewery Worker p215
- Energy Engineer p221
- Water/Sewerage Network Operative p130

Further information

City & Guilds
www.cityandguilds.com

Energy and Utility Skills
www.euskills.co.uk

Water UK
www.water.org.uk

WATER/SEWERAGE NETWORK OPERATIVE

Qualifications and courses

There are no formal entry requirements, but you might need 4 GCSEs/S grades (A*–C/1–3) including maths, English, science or technology.

Relevant experience, for example in site maintenance work, is useful. Registration in an appropriate safety passport scheme could be required by many employers for you to be able to work on-site.

Entrants are trained on the job, and may work towards vocational qualifications. An NVQ/SVQ Level 2 is available in Water Distribution. The Certification and Assessment Board for the Water Industry (CABWI) offers a range of relevant NVQs, including Distribution Control Level 2, Operating Process Plant (Water) Level 2, Leakage Control Level 3 and Maintaining Water Supply Level 3.

Apprenticeships/Skillseekers may be available for people aged 16–24. The scheme starts with basic preliminary training, with apprentices usually working towards NVQs/ SVQs at Level 2 in subjects such as customer care, water distribution, construction and technical drawing.

What the work involves

Water/sewerage network operatives lay, maintain and repair the pipework that carries drinking water, waste water and sewage.

Your tasks might include digging trenches in roads and relaying them afterwards, putting up barriers and warning signs, laying pipes, repairing leaks, clearing blockages and installing water meters.

You will use a range of tools such as welding equipment to join pipes together and machinery such as mechanical diggers.

Type of person suited to this work

You must have good practical skills and be mechanically minded so that you can use tools, equipment and machinery effectively. You must be able to follow health and safety regulations as working on-site can be dangerous. You will have to follow plans and instructions accurately, so that systems are installed correctly and safely.

You must be fit and active for bending, kneeling and carrying materials and equipment.

You will have to deal with complaints from the public, who might be upset that their water services are disrupted. You must also be able to work in a team with other water/ sewerage network operatives. You may need a driving licence.

Working conditions

You will work outdoors in all weather conditions. The work can be dusty, dirty and wet, as well as smelly.

You will need to follow strict health, safety and hygiene regulations, which may include wearing a breathing apparatus, a safety helmet, boots and gloves.

You may work normal working hours or shifts, but the particular hours you work will vary according to the needs of the job and the hours of daylight available. You may be on-call 24/7 in case of the need for emergency repairs.

Future prospects

There is strong demand for water/sewerage network operatives because the privatised water companies, who manage water supply and sewerage disposal, are investing money in developing their systems.

You can find work with water companies and construction firms across the UK. After gaining experience, you could progress to a role as a team leader or supervisor.

You could move into related areas such as water distribution inspection work.

Advantages/disadvantages

The work can be physically demanding for some people, and it can get smelly if you are working on sewerage systems.

Helping to provide people with an essential service can be rewarding.

Money guide

Trainees earn around £10,000–£11,000 a year. This can rise to £17,000 for fully trained operatives with 1 year's experience.

With additional experience earnings can increase to £25,000 or more.

Earnings vary depending on your employer and in which part of the country you work.

Related opportunities

- Construction Operative p86
- Gas Network Engineer p226
- Plumber p112

Further information

Energy and Utility Skills
www.euskills.co.uk

Water UK
www.water.org.uk

WINDOW FITTER

Qualifications and courses

There are no formal entry requirements, but you might need some GCSEs/S grades; English, maths and technology, or equivalent qualifications, are useful.

Apprenticeship/Skillseekers may be available for people aged between 16 and 24. Applicants normally need GCSEs/S grades (A*–E/1–5), or an equivalent qualification such as Intermediate GNVQ or First Diploma. Proskills, the Sector Skills Council, is currently promoting Apprenticeships in the glass industry.

Initial training is provided by employers and covers removing and fitting window frames, health and safety, customer relations and relevant paperwork.

You can gain vocational qualifications while you work. You will be taught practical skills and may work towards NVQs/SVQs in Fenestration Installation at Level 2, Fenestration Installation and Surveying at Level 3 and Glazing Installation and Maintenance at Levels 2–3. Glass Training Limited (GTL) provides a list of relevant glass related NVQs on their website.

What the work involves

Window fitters install windows into new and existing buildings.

You will use hand and power tools to take out any old windows and fit new ones. You will work with materials such as glass, plastic and wood.

Once you have fixed a new window into the allocated space, you will need to give it a weatherproof seal. Your job may also involve fitting doors, conservatories and weatherboarding.

Type of person suited to this work

You will need good practical hand skills for using tools and you will need to be physically fit as you will be lifting and carrying windows. Maths skills are essential in order to make accurate calculations and fit frames properly.

You should be safety conscious and comfortable working on ladders.

You may work on your own for some jobs, but you will often work with one other window fitter, or in a small team so you must be able to work with others. You should also be able to get on with customers because you will spend a lot of time on their premises.

Working conditions

You will work indoors and outdoors in a variety of locations, and you will be working in most weather conditions. A driving licence may be useful.

You will need to pay attention to health and safety, especially when working with glass, and be happy clearing up after your work has finished.

You are likely to work normal working hours during the week, but overtime may be available at weekends.

Future prospects

Work is available throughout the UK. There is an increasing demand for double-glazed windows and for conservatories so job prospects are high.

After gaining sufficient experience, you may progress to team leader or supervisory positions. You could also run your own window-fitting business. You may choose to specialise in fire-proof glazing or film application (applying film to glass for privacy).There are also openings within the sales and marketing sides of the industry.

Advantages/disadvantages

Lifting and carrying windows and working at heights may be difficult for some people.

You will get to travel to many different locations in your job.

It is satisfying to make customers happy by improving the appearance, value and function of their buildings by installing and repairing windows.

Money guide

You can expect a salary of between £14,000 and £18,000 per year once you have qualified.

A salary of between £22,000 and £26,000 is likely to be earned by a competent window fitter.

£30,000 could be earned by supervisors or managers.

Earnings will depend on where you work and the size of the organisation.

Related opportunities

- Carpenter/Joiner p79
- Ceiling Fixer p81
- Glazier p101

Further information

Glass and Glazing Federation
www.ggf.co.uk

Proskills UK
www.proskills.co.uk

Catering and Hospitality

Working in this sector, you will meet a wide variety of people and probably need to be a very strong team player. Workers in the sector thrive on providing an impeccable service and ensuring customers are completely satisfied and are given a wonderful experience whether that is in a restaurant, hotel or bar.

The jobs featured in this section are listed below. For similar jobs to the ones in this section why not have a look at *Leisure, Sport and Tourism* starting on page 377 and *Retail, Sales and Customer Services* from page 473.

- Bar Manager/Licensee/ Publican p134
- Catering/Restaurant Manager/Maître d'Hôtel p135
- Cellar Technician p136
- Chef/Sous Chef p137
- Concierge p138

- Food Safety Officer p139
- Hotel Manager p140
- Hotel Porter p141
- Hotel Receptionist p142
- Hotel/Accommodation Room Attendant p143

- Housekeeper/Accommodation Manager p144
- Kitchen Assistant/ Supervisor p145
- Waiting Staff p146

BAR MANAGER/LICENSEE/ PUBLICAN

Qualifications and courses

You can start as a bar person from the age of 18 and train on the job, progressing to a supervisory or management position. NVQs/SVQs are available in Bar Service (Level 2), Food and Drink Service (Level 2) or Hospitality Supervision (Level 3). The BTEC Level 2 Firsts in Hospitality or the BTEC Level 3 Nationals in Hospitality are also relevant. City & Guilds offers the Diploma and Certificate in Professional Food and Beverage Service (7103). School leavers could apply for the Intermediate Apprenticeship in Licensed Hospitality.

You could study for an HNC/HND, Foundation degree or degree in a related subject such as hospitality and licensed retail management. Some of the larger pub companies offer graduate schemes where trainees follow a structured programme to gain practical experience and progress to a management role. Employers may consider graduates from all disciplines but relevant work experience is often required.

In England and Wales, new entrants to on-licensed premises are required by law to take the Level 2 National Certificate for Personal Licence Holders. This is available from the British Institute of Innkeeping Awarding Body (BIIAB). In Scotland, you must take the Scottish Certificate for Personal Licence Holders (SCPLH) from the BIIAB.

What the work involves

Your duties will include the recruitment, training and management of staff. You will also deal with the accounts, stock replenishment, and maintaining links with suppliers and business development.

You will need to keep up to date with any changes to licensing laws and other legal requirements such as health and safety or fire safety regulations, and ensure that your customers and staff adhere to them.

In addition, you will demonstrate a high level of customer service to ensure client satisfaction.

Type of person suited to this work

It is essential to have excellent communication skills and to enjoy meeting and speaking to people of all ages. A confident, professional attitude is needed to deal with customer or supplier problems.

Being physically fit and able to stay on your feet all day is helpful. You should be practical, flexible and good at multi-tasking.

Good numeracy skills are expected as you will be managing cash on a daily basis. Finally, you should keep up to date with legal requirements, and enforce those that affect you.

Working conditions

Although pubs, clubs and bars can remain open for 24 hours a day, most only extend their hours at weekends or for special events.

You will work long hours in an environment which can be busy, noisy and hot. You will be required to stand for lengthy periods and lift and carry heavy items such as barrels.

You may have to deal with demanding or difficult customers who are intoxicated. Changes to smoking legislation have resulted in the need to provide outside facilities, where problems might occur.

Future prospects

Despite the recent economic downturn, the hospitality industry continues to grow, so job prospects are good.

A publican can own, lease or become a tenant of their premises. You can be a manager on behalf of a brewery of different premises like high street chains, family establishments, café bars or themed pubs and restaurants across the country.

Advantages/disadvantages

The hours will be long and irregular which might affect your personal life.

You will have to deal with drunk customers, who may be difficult or aggressive, on a fairly regular basis.

The working atmosphere is informal and enjoyable.

You may have the opportunity to live on the pub premises which can reduce your living expenses.

Money guide

Assistant managers can expect a starting salary in the region of £14,000–£21,000.

Once you reach manager or licensee level, you could earn £20,000–£35,000.

Those who work in a very successful or large establishment, or become area managers for a pub company, can achieve earnings of £40,000–£50,000.

Earnings vary according to the type, size and location of the premises you work in.

Related opportunities

- Brewery Worker p215
- Hotel Manager p140
- Waiting Staff p146

Further information

British Beer and Pub Association
www.beerandpub.com

British Institute of Innkeeping
www.biiab.org

Wine & Spirit Education Trust
www.wset.co.uk

Qualifications and courses

There are no formal entry requirements for this profession. School leavers could start as a kitchen assistant, waiter/waitress, chef or cook and gradually progress to management level. City & Guilds offer various qualifications that are suitable for new entrants and those with experience in the industry. These include the NVQ in Hospitality and Catering (Level 2), the NVQ in Hospitality Supervision (Level 3), the Award in Hospitality Supervision and Leadership Principles (Level 3) and the Higher Professional Diploma in Hospitality and Catering (Level 4).

Many hotel and restaurant chains offer training schemes. It may be possible to join a scheme with A levels/H grades or equivalent but the usual requirement is a degree or HNC/HND in a relevant subject, such as hospitality management, hospitality and catering, hotel management or international hospitality management. Candidates without a relevant degree subject may be considered but they will usually need experience in a customer service environment or the catering industry. Minimum requirements for degree entry are usually 5 GCSEs/S grades (A*–C/1–3) and 2 A levels or 3 H grades. Postgraduate courses are also available.

What the work involves

You will manage, train and employ staff in a kitchen or restaurant. A maître d'hôtel is specifically responsible for running a hotel restaurant.

Part of your work will involve planning menus, checking stocks of food and drink and ordering fresh supplies when needed. You will be expected to handle paperwork, manage budgets and organise staff rotas.

You will be responsible for the health and safety of both your staff and customers.

Type of person suited to this work

You will be dealing with kitchen staff, suppliers and other business professionals so you must be confident and have excellent communication skills. It is essential to provide good customer service at all times.

As you will be preparing food for the public, you will be required to follow and keep up to date with health and safety laws. You will also need an interest in service delivery and food.

Good management skills, including an understanding of the different roles undertaken by your staff, are essential. Exceptional organisational abilities and good numeracy skills are also important.

Working conditions

Much of your time will be spent in your kitchen or restaurant, which can get very hot and busy. Expect to be on your feet for long periods of time.

You might wear a uniform or protective clothing and regularly work unsocial hours. It is important to follow high standards of food safety and hygiene.

It is possible to work as a catering manager in the Armed Forces, in which case you might find yourself working in challenging environments, anywhere in the world, in a variety of climates.

Future prospects

Currently there is a shortage of restaurant managers across the UK so prospects are good. The sector offers a wide range of career opportunities and quick progression. However, it will help your career if you work in increasingly bigger and well-known premises.

Some restaurant/catering managers move on to running their own businesses, either a restaurant or private contract catering company.

Advantages/disadvantages

You will be working in a fun and lively atmosphere and you might have the chance to organise the catering for special events such as weddings or parties.

This can be a very busy job where you will be doing several tasks at the same time.

Hours are long and will include weekend or evening work.

Money guide

Starting salaries for assistant managers range from £15,000 to £18,000.

Experienced managers can earn £20,000–£28,000 a year.

Senior managers in large or very successful premises can achieve anything from £40,000 to £70,000.

Salaries vary significantly depending on the type of establishment you work in.

The highest salaries are in London and the south-east of England.

Related opportunities

- Events and Exhibition Organiser p404
- Food Safety Officer p139
- Kitchen Assistant/Supervisor p145

Further information

Institute of Hospitality
www.instituteofhospitality.org

People 1st
www.people1st.co.uk

CELLAR TECHNICIAN

Qualifications and courses

A useful starting point is to have GCSEs/S grades (A*-C/1–3) in maths, science or technology subjects and some employers will require this.

It is necessary to have a British Institute of Innkeeping Awarding Body (BIIAB) Certificate in Cellar Service Installation and Maintenance (Level 2). This involves classroom and on-the-job training while candidates study for 5 units.

Once you have acquired the BIIAB certificate, you could take the City & Guilds Certificate/Diploma in Drinks Dispense Systems (Levels 2 and 3) or the NVQ Diploma in Drinks Dispense Systems (Level 3).

Qualifications in engineering, and in particular electrical engineering, may also be useful. These include NVQs, City & Guilds courses and BTEC First or National Certificates.

Employers provide training that covers areas such as health and safety, customer care, refrigeration, checking systems and working with equipment.

Experience working in a bar is useful and many cellar technicians work their way up from bar staff level. Cask Marque offers a 1-day course in Cellar Management Training for those already employed in the sector.

What the work involves

You will set up and maintain the systems that keep alcoholic and soft drinks at a consistent quality in pubs, hotels and other sites.

Visiting a range of locations, you will install equipment such as high-pressure gas systems, and check that they are compatible with existing water, electricity supply or drainage systems.

You will undertake regular maintenance checks to make sure that everything works properly, train the staff on how to operate it and deal with any problems.

Type of person suited to this work

You will need good practical skills and the confidence to work and operate different systems quickly and efficiently.

As you will be handling heavy equipment, a good level of physical fitness is helpful.

Good communication skills are useful, as is a confidence in your ability to do the job well.

As you will be providing a service on behalf of your company for lots of different licensed premises you will need to have excellent customer care skills.

Working conditions

You will spend lots of time driving from site to site.

Some of your work will be attending emergency call-outs which could include evenings and weekends. The extended pub opening hours might mean this includes 24-hour call-out duties.

You will work in dark, cramped conditions using specialist tools and equipment such as electrical testing devices.

Future prospects

There is a steady demand for experienced cellar technicians.

The main employers are breweries, drink-dispensing equipment manufacturers and soft drinks manufacturers.

Many applicants come from the licensed trade who have watched the job and become interested. It is therefore useful to have pub experience or relevant qualifications before applying.

With experience you can apply for senior/managerial posts or move into other areas of the licensed or food and drink sector such as sales.

Advantages/disadvantages

This job combines meeting and training people with lots of practical work.

You might have to travel long distances to reach customers.

You might work in uncomfortable conditions, for example when fitting a new dispensing system in a cellar.

Money guide

Starting salaries for cellar technicians range from £12,300 up to £18,000 per year.

With experience, earnings can increase to £20,000–£30,000.

The highest salary for a cellar technician is about £35,000.

You might be paid overtime for emergency call-out duties or for working evenings/weekends.

Related opportunities

- Bar Manager/Licensee/Publican p134
- Brewery Worker p215
- Plumber p112

Further information

British Soft Drinks Association
www.britishsoftdrinks.com

People 1st
www.people1st.co.uk

CHEF/SOUS CHEF

Qualifications and courses

No academic qualifications are required to enter this profession. Most training is on the job and you will be taught by an experienced chef whilst you work in the kitchen. It is possible to work your way up to chef level with enough kitchen experience.

You could take a GCSE in Hospitality and Catering, a City & Guilds Diploma in Professional Cookery (Levels 1–3) or an NVQ Diploma in Professional Cookery (Levels 2 and 3). Intermediate and Advanced Apprenticeships may be available for 16–24 year olds looking to enter this industry. You can also study for NVQs/SVQs (Levels 1–3) in Food Preparation and Cooking.

Many employers will require you to have health and safety and/or food hygiene certificates so it would be useful to study for these while training as a chef.

Further qualifications are also available, including degrees or foundation degrees in professional culinary arts and culinary arts management.

What the work involves

Chefs and sous chefs cook for restaurants, cafés, bars, cruise ships and catering firms. Some also work for specialist food companies, helping to create new products. You will coordinate kitchen activities and supervise the preparation of food by your team of kitchen staff.

Commis chefs are trainee chefs. Sous chefs are second-in-command of the kitchen. They will be required to recruit and train kitchen staff.

Planning new menus and dishes, checking stocks of food and drink and dealing with suppliers are also included in the sous chef role.

Type of person suited to this work

Kitchens can be hot and hectic environments, therefore you need to be able to remain calm under pressure.

Good teamwork, communication and multi-tasking skills are important to ensure the smooth running of the operation. As you are responsible for the health and safety of your team, you must also be vigilant at all times.

You should have excellent cooking skills, be very creative and have a passion for food. This role would suit someone who is keen to try out new things and set trends. Good numeracy skills are also required to manage budgets and stock levels.

Working conditions

Most of your work will be in a kitchen which will be hot, busy and noisy. You will be required to use equipment that can be dangerous if not used correctly.

As you will be preparing food, you will need to wear protective clothing and pay attention to health and hygiene.

Hours are typically 40 per week in a shift pattern and include evenings and weekends. Part-time work can be found.

Future prospects

With an increased number of establishments opening, there is currently a shortage of qualified chefs in many areas of the UK.

Starting as a commis chef you will help in different sections of the kitchen. With experience you can progress to sous chef, where you act as deputy to the chef and manage your own section, or head chef.

Gaining significant experience may allow you to open your own business or even become a lecturer.

Advantages/disadvantages

Preparing high-quality food that your customers enjoy is very rewarding.

You will have the opportunity to combine creativity with practical skills.

You will work long, unsocial hours when you will be on your feet in a hot and busy environment.

Money guide

A commis chef has a starting salary of £12,000–£16,000.

Sous chefs usually earn around £22,000–£25,000 a year.

A head chef can achieve up to £35,000.

Executive head chefs in very successful establishments could earn £40,000–£60,000.

Salaries vary significantly depending upon the size, reputation and location of the restaurant, with the highest salaries in London and the south-east of England.

Related opportunities

- Catering/Restaurant Manager/Maître d'Hôtel p135
- Food Safety Officer p139
- Kitchen Assistant/Supervisor p145

Further information

Institute of Hospitality
www.instituteofhospitality.org

People 1st
www.people1st.co.uk

CONCIERGE

Qualifications and courses

There are no formal academic requirements for this profession. The ability to speak a foreign language would be very beneficial. Useful qualifications include the BTEC Award in Principles of Customer Service in Hospitality, Leisure, Travel and Tourism (Level 2), the NVQ in Hospitality (Levels 1 and 2) or the NVQ in Multi-skilled Hospitality Service (Level 2).

You will usually start in a front of house role, such as a porter, bellboy or receptionist, and with experience progress to the role of concierge. You could train in-house or through an Apprenticeship in Hospitality.

You will learn and train as you work. This may include gaining knowledge of the establishment's policies and techniques in waiting and room service. It is also important that you have good local knowledge of the area where you work.

Previous work experience in catering or hospitality is recommended.

What the work involves

Concierges work as part of the front of house team in a hotel, apartment block or corporate organisation. You will be responsible for greeting guests, assisting with their baggage, answering questions, giving advice or directions and generally making them feel as comfortable as possible.

If you work in a hotel you must keep up to date with events and functions in the hotel and you may be asked to book tickets or organise travel for guests.

You may manage a team of other concierges, reception or door staff. Some organisations may require you to undertake extra services such as shopping and pet walking/sitting.

Type of person suited to this work

As you will be the first port of contact for guests and visitors to the establishment, you should look presentable, enjoy meeting new people and thrive in a busy environment.

You must be polite, friendly, helpful and informative at all times. You should have an interest in the catering and hospitality industry.

You need to have a practical approach to problem-solving and be able to remain calm. As you will be entrusted with important errands and messages, you must be responsible, reliable and trustworthy.

You should also have a certain level of strength and fitness to carry bags and work long shifts.

Working conditions

On average, you will work 40 hours a week. This will mainly be shifts of 12 hours and will include working at night, early mornings and weekends.

You may have a desk or an office where you will use the telephone or computer but you will spend the majority of your time on your feet in the reception area, meeting and helping guests or running errands within the establishment or around the local area. You may be required to lift heavy bags.

Your employer will usually provide you with a uniform.

Future prospects

Establishments may have formal progression routes and this could involve moving up from a position as a porter to deputy head concierge, head concierge and then up again to front office management positions.

You could transfer to another discipline within hospitality or even set up your own business.

There are international opportunities within certain establishments so you may be able to live abroad.

Advantages/disadvantages

You will have the opportunity to meet a variety of new people from different countries each day.

You will be responsible for a wide variety of guests or visitors and their requirements.

You may have to work long and unsociable hours.

Money guide

Your starting salary as a concierge can be around £12,000.

As you gain experience over the years you can earn £17,000–£21,000.

If you reach the position of head concierge in a four or five star establishment, you could achieve up to £29,000.

Related opportunities

- Customer Services Assistant/Manager p480
- Personal Assistant p56
- Receptionist p59

Further information

Institute of Hospitality
www.instituteofhospitality.org

People 1st
www.people1st.co.uk

Qualifications and courses

To become a food safety officer in England, Wales or Northern Ireland, you will first need to train as an environmental health officer.

You will need a BSc or MSc in environmental health/science accredited by the Chartered Institute of Environmental Health (CIEH). Entry to a degree normally requires 2 A levels/3 H grades including a science subject, plus 5 GCSEs/S grades (A*–C/1–3) including English, maths and science. Entry to the MSc requires a first degree in a relevant science or technology subject. Before qualifying as an environmental health officer, graduates must complete an Experiential Learning Portfolio (ELP) to provide evidence of their work-based learning and pass professional exams. CIEH also offer a wide range of food safety qualifications at Levels 1–4 which may be useful. These awards cover food safety issues within catering, manufacturing and retail.

Food safety officers in Scotland must meet the requirements of the Scottish Food Safety Officers' Registration Board. Candidates for the Higher Certificates in Food Premises Inspection and Food Standards Inspection must have a minimum of an HND in Food Science or Food Technology. Candidates undertake 6 months' structured practical training with a local authority and complete written assessments.

What the work involves

You will advise those working in catering/food premises by providing information on the safe presentation, preparation and storage of food for public consumption.

Your role will be to investigate outbreaks of food-related illnesses and implement hazard warnings in places such as butchers, retailers and restaurants.

You will enforce accurate food labelling. You will also advise schools and businesses on food regulations as well as nutritional awareness.

Type of person suited to this work

You need excellent communication skills as you will be advising and educating people of all backgrounds on food safety and nutrition. You should be able to explain technical information in a simple and clear way. You must also be tactful when investigating food poisoning and other hazardous issues.

It's important to be analytical and methodical in your work. Good attention to detail is essential. You need to be able to juggle many different jobs at once and be a confident decision maker.

Working conditions

Although you will be office based, most of your time will involve travelling to businesses, restaurants, schools and homes, following up complaints and giving advice. A driving licence is essential.

The places you investigate may be smelly and unpleasant at times. You will need to wear protective clothing such as masks, hair protection and boots. You will work normal office hours, but some evenings and weekends may be required.

Future prospects

Owing to the rise in mass manufacturing of food and fast food outlets, the need for food safety officers has remained steady. You may be employed by a local authority or by a food company.

Outside of Scotland, most food safety officers begin as environmental health officers and specialise later. In Scotland, inspection and food hygiene is undertaken by registered food safety officers.

With experience you can progress to senior positions within food safety or return to other areas of environmental health. You could also set up your own consultancy.

Advantages/disadvantages

This job offers flexibility (as there are options for part-time work or job shares) and variety (as you will be visiting a range of different premises).

You have a chance to make a difference to public health.

Investigations can occasionally be stressful if you have to enforce regulations or close down a business.

You will sometimes have to visit dirty or unpleasant establishments.

Money guide

Starting salaries for food safety officers are usually £20,000–£30,000.

With several years' experience, you could earn £30,000–£40,000.

Food safety officers employed at a senior or managerial level can achieve up to £60,000.

Those employed by private companies earn more than workers in the public sector.

Related opportunities

- Environmental Health Practitioner/Officer p36
- Health and Safety Adviser p41
- Meat Hygiene Inspector p486

Further information

Chartered Institute of Environmental Health
www.cieh.org

Royal Environmental Health Institute of Scotland
www.rehis.org

CRCI: AA   CATERING AND HOSPITALITY

139

HOTEL MANAGER

Qualifications and courses

No specific academic qualifications are required as it is possible to enter the industry at a lower level and work your way up. Knowledge of a foreign language could be useful.

You can study part time towards NVQs/SVQs in Hospitality (Levels 1 and 2), the NVQ in Hospitality Supervision (Level 3) or City & Guilds Award in Hospitality Supervision and Leadership Principles (Level 3).

School leavers could apply for an Advanced Apprenticeship in Hospitality and Catering which involves on-the-job training and the opportunity to study for some of the above NVQs.

Existing employees, graduates or those with previous hotel experience may be eligible for one of the fast track training schemes offered by some of the larger hotel companies.

The Institute of Hospitality provides a range of qualifications for those pursuing a management or leadership role within the hospitality industry.

Many entrants to this profession have a degree, HNC/HND or postgraduate qualification and enter as management trainees. Relevant degree subjects include hospitality management, business or travel and tourism.

What the work involves

You will manage the services and staff of your hotel, ensuring that it is a successful business and gains new customers to make a profit.

You will be responsible for checking that the buildings and grounds of your hotel meet health and safety and other standards.

Your work could involve promoting and developing the hotel to increase numbers of customers. You could work in all types of hotel, from a small private one up to large national or international chains.

Type of person suited to this work

As you will manage budgets and cash flow, you will need a good level of numeracy and the confidence to handle large quantities of money. Communication skills are very important as you will be organising staff and dealing with guests. You will be working in a sociable and busy environment, so you will need to enjoy meeting lots of different people.

You should be well organised and able to meet targets. Strong customer service and good business skills are essential, as is flexibility, as you will be working long and unsocial hours.

A knowledge of tourism is useful.

Working conditions

This work involves working long hours that include evenings and weekends. You might spend some of your evenings living-in so you can be on-site in case of emergencies. You are also likely to work shifts.

Some members of the public can be rude and aggressive so you will need to maintain a calm professional manner at all times.

You will need to have a smart appearance and you might have to wear a uniform.

Future prospects

Hospitality is a developing sector and there are about 46,000 hotels of all kinds throughout the UK employing over 280,000 people. After a difficult period the hotel sector is showing signs of growth with around a fifth of hotel staff reaching managerial roles.

With experience, you could work overseas, open your own hotel or progress from hotel management into other areas of a company such as human resources, finance and IT.

Advantages/disadvantages

There are opportunities to travel and work overseas.

You can progress to be a manager of a large hotel relatively quickly.

As you are responsible for the welfare and happiness of the guests, there will be a lot of pressure and demands.

Money guide

Salaries will depend on the size, reputation and location of the hotel in which you work.

Assistant or trainee managers have a starting salary of £12,000–£21,000 per year.

Managers of small hotels or deputy managers of large hotels could earn £21,000–£35,000.

Senior managers can achieve £60,000 or more and salaries for those employed in large, global hotels can be considerably higher.

Benefits can include pension schemes, healthcare, live-in accommodation and discounts on staying in other hotels.

Related opportunities

- Bar Manager/Licensee/Publican p134
- Holiday Representative p384
- Housekeeper/Accommodation Manager p144

Further information

Institute of Hospitality
www.instituteofhospitality.org

Springboard UK
www.springboarduk.net

HOTEL PORTER

Qualifications and courses

There are no minimum entry requirements for this job but some employers prefer individuals with a good general education.

Communication skills, IT skills and some previous experience in a customer service field would be useful.

A driving licence can be helpful. Some employers prefer individuals to be over 18 years of age as you may be required to serve alcohol.

Many hotels will provide training to new staff, whether or not they have previous experience. This is usually gained over a period of several weeks or longer, under the supervision of a more experienced member of staff. As you are required to lift and carry luggage, some of the training may be concerned with health and safety and risk assessment for manual handling.

It is possible to gain qualifications whilst working, including City & Guilds Award in Introduction to Employment in the Hospitality Industry (Level 1), the NVQ in Front Office (Levels 1 and 2) and City & Guilds Award in Principles of Customer Service in Hospitality, Leisure, Travel and Tourism (Level 2).

What the work involves

As a porter, you will greet hotel guests, answer the phone, take reservations and deal with general enquiries.

You will also be responsible for moving guests' luggage to and from rooms.

If you work as a night porter, you will look after the security and safety of the hotel site.

As a head porter in a large hotel, you will be responsible for a team of porters that will include night, conference and kitchen porters.

Type of person suited to this work

You will need excellent customer service skills, a smart appearance and extensive knowledge of the local area. Good communication and teamwork skills are also important.

You may be asked to undertake duties at short notice so you will need a flexible and enthusiastic attitude.

You must be fit and active as you will do a lot of lifting and carrying.

Being responsible for the security of the hotel site and guests' belongings means that you must be honest, reliable and aware of security issues.

Working conditions

The work can be physically demanding as you will spend a lot of time on your feet and lifting luggage. You will primarily be based inside the hotel but you may be required to greet guests outside in all weather conditions.

You may work shifts or standard hours. If you work as a night porter your working hours may affect your personal life. If you live in the hotel you might be on-call.

You might have to wear a uniform which should be provided by your employer.

Future prospects

You can work in hotels all over the country and possibly abroad. Part-time and seasonal work is also available.

Smaller hotels tend to employ one porter so you would need to move to larger hotels if you want to progress. For this reason, willingness to be geographically mobile could be helpful.

In larger companies, you could work towards a job as a head porter or a reception-based role.

Advantages/disadvantages

In some hotels you would be required to live on-site.

If you find a seasonal position this job can fit around educational commitments but some hotels prefer to employ mature individuals.

You will have the opportunity to meet and help many different people so your work will be rewarding and interesting.

Money guide

Salary levels vary according to the type of hotel you work for and geographic location.

Starting salaries are about £9,000–£12,000 per year.

As you gain experience, your annual earnings can increase to about £16,000.

Head porters in large hotels can achieve up to £22,000.

Shift allowances, overtime work and tips from guests can increase your earnings.

Related opportunities

- Concierge p138
- Hotel/Accommodation Room Attendant p143
- Receptionist p59

Further information

Institute of Hospitality
www.instituteofhospitality.org

People 1st
www.people1st.co.uk

HOTEL RECEPTIONIST

Qualifications and courses

There are no minimum entry requirements, although employers are likely to ask for 5 GCSEs/S grades (A*–C/1–3) including English and maths.

Having some office or customer service-based work experience and computer skills would be helpful for this career.

Further training is usually provided by the employer and new entrants often work under the supervision of more experienced reception staff.

If you wish to demonstrate your knowledge and skills in this field, there are various qualifications available. These include City & Guilds Award in Introduction to Employment in the Hospitality Industry (Level 1), the NVQ in Front Office (Levels 1 and 2), the NVQ in Multi-Skilled Hospitality Services (Level 2) and City & Guilds Award in Principles of Customer Service in Hospitality, Leisure, Travel and Tourism (Levels 2 and 3).

The Intermediate Apprenticeship in Hospitality and Catering would be useful for those seeking a reception role and candidates keen to progress to head of reception could take the Advanced Apprenticeship.

What the work involves

You will be responsible for welcoming guests to the hotel, checking them in and out, managing any requests and allocating them a room. You will also prepare guests' bills, take payments and handle foreign exchange. You will answer the telephone, take messages and bookings and inform guests about the local area.

Hotel receptionists work closely with other members of staff to ensure the smooth running of the hotel. In a large hotel you might work within a team of receptionists whereas in a small hotel you may work alone and have extra duties including housekeeping and waitressing.

Type of person suited to this work

You should be a friendly, welcoming and well-presented person as you will be the first point of contact for hotel guests.

Good communication skills are essential as you will be interacting with all types of people and a polite telephone manner will be necessary when making calls and taking messages.

You will be very busy at times but will have to stay calm and polite even under pressure, making sure that each guest gets the service they expect.

It would be helpful to be knowledgeable about the local area and the hotel. Being able to speak a foreign language would also be desirable, as you might have foreign guests staying at the hotel or you may want to work overseas.

Working conditions

Hotels are open 24/7 so you will probably do shift work to ensure the reception desk is manned at all times. There are opportunities to work part time or seasonally.

You will work behind the reception desk the majority of the time, where you will have access to a computer and a telephone. You might be provided with a uniform.

Future prospects

Job opportunities are available throughout the UK as tourism is a growth industry. The majority of hotels are in the south-east of England, Scotland and the West Country.

As a hotel receptionist you could progress to being a supervisor or manager of a team of receptionists, or you move to a different area of the hotel industry, such as event organisation.

Your transferable skills would enable you to work as a receptionist in other sectors.

Advantages/disadvantages

You will be responsible for dealing with complaints and disturbances which could be stressful or frustrating.

This is a varied and active role which will suit those who like to keep busy and meet new people.

You could have the opportunity to work in hotels overseas.

Money guide

Your salary may depend on the location and size of the hotel you work for.

Starting salaries range from £10,000 to £12,500.

With experience, you can expect to earn about £15,000.

Senior receptionists or those in supervisory roles can achieve £20,000–£25,000.

Additional benefits may include meals and accommodation.

Related opportunities

- Personal Assistant p56
- Secretary p64
- Travel Agent p394

Further information

Institute of Hospitality
www.instituteofhospitality.org

People 1st
www.people1st.co.uk

HOTEL/ACCOMMODATION ROOM ATTENDANT

Qualifications and courses

There are no minimum entry requirements for this job. Some companies prefer to employ people over the age of 18. Employers look for people who are honest, reliable and hardworking.

The Intermediate Apprenticeship in Hospitality and Catering could provide a route into this line of work.

Once you find a position as a room attendant, you will receive on-the-job training, usually under the supervision of a more experienced member of staff. This could include aspects such as safe lifting methods and furniture and carpet cleaning.

Employers may encourage you to complete qualifications, such as the NVQ in Cleaning and Support Services (Levels 1 and 2), the NVQ in Housekeeping (Level 2) or City & Guilds IVQ in Accommodation Operations and Services (Levels 1–3).

The City & Guilds Award, Certificate and Diploma in Cleaning and Cleaning Supervision (Levels 1–3) or the NVQ in Hospitality Supervision (Level 3) may be useful for those who wish to progress to the role of staff supervisor or accommodation manager.

What the work involves

You will clean, tidy and prepare guest rooms to a high standard. This could include cleaning bathroom and toilet areas and other parts of the hotel.

Work involves stocking up levels of supplies as they are used and keeping records of any items of lost property left in rooms.

Using a trolley or cart, you will move supplies of linen, towels and other items around the hotel. You will also check for maintenance problems or damage to hotel property.

Type of person suited to this work

As much of the work involves cleaning areas of the site and moving supplies around, you will need a good level of physical fitness.

You must be well organised, enthusiastic and able to work quickly to get all your tasks completed on time. In order to keep up standards of cleanliness, you need a good eye for detail.

A polite and friendly manner when liaising with guests is essential. As you will be cleaning areas around guests' personal belongings, it is important to respect their privacy.

Working conditions

This is physical work so expect to be on your feet for much of the time, using cleaning equipment and pushing a cart from room to room.

You will be working with cleaning fluids and other cleaning equipment on a daily basis which could affect those with skin problems.

You will probably work shifts and may need to work early mornings, late at night and at weekends.

Future prospects

Despite the recent economic downturn, the hospitality industry is growing so job prospects are good. You could work in a hotel, bed and breakfast or leisure facility. Larger employers provide staff with good training and development support.

You may have opportunities to work abroad for an international hotel or in a resort.

With experience, you could go on to work as an accommodation manager or housekeeper and have responsibility for other staff.

Advantages/disadvantages

Some employers allow you to live on site and will provide your meals.

There are opportunities to gain seasonal/holiday work and this type of job is available on a part-time basis.

The work is quite physically demanding and involves bending, stretching and some heavy lifting.

During busy periods when many guests are staying at the hotel, you will have to work efficiently to meet tight deadlines.

Money guide

Earnings vary according to employer and location.

Some room attendants may receive an hourly rate which can range from the National Minimum Wage to about £7 an hour.

Starting salaries are usually £10,000–£11,000 and can rise to £15,000 with experience.

Guests often leave tips for room attendants.

Overtime work or shift allowances could increase earnings.

Related opportunities

- Cleaner p460
- Hotel Manager p140
- Hotel Porter p141

Further information

Institute of Hospitality
www.instituteofhospitality.org

People 1st
www.people1st.co.uk

HOUSEKEEPER/ACCOMMODATION MANAGER

Qualifications and courses

It is possible to enter this career without academic qualifications but employers will want to see evidence that you are organised and have good customer service skills. Many entrants start out as room attendants and work their way up. Most employers will require you to be at least 18 years old to start work. Intermediate or Advanced Apprenticeships in Hospitality and Catering are available to those aged 16–24.

HNCs/HNDs, Foundation degrees or degrees in subjects such as hospitality or hotel management can be useful. You will need a degree if you want to be accepted onto a management training scheme at a large hotel chain.

Training usually takes place on the job. You can study for qualifications through the Institute of Hospitality, including the Diploma in Hospitality and Tourism Operations (Level 2), the Diploma in Hospitality and Tourism Management (Level 3) and the Diploma in Advanced Hospitality and Tourism Management (Level 4).

Other relevant qualifications include City & Guilds Award in Supervising Customer Service Performance in Hospitality, Leisure, Travel and Tourism (Level 3) and the NVQ in Hospitality Supervision and Leadership Principles (Level 3).

What the work involves

You will be in charge of a team of cleaners and will ensure that all rooms on your premises are clean, tidy and hospitable.

You may work in hotels, conference centres, private households, hospitals, care homes and university halls of residence.

You will manage a housekeeping budget, recruit and train staff, and organise work rotas and duties.

On a day-to-day basis you will inspect rooms, take care of repairs, and ensure linens, soaps, towels and other necessities are always in stock.

You will also be responsible for sorting out lost property and filing maintenance reports.

Type of person suited to this work

As you will be in charge of a team, good organisational, delegation and management skills are essential, as is the ability to motivate and encourage staff. You should be capable managing budgets and solving problems.

Strong verbal communication skills are important as you will interact with both customers and staff.

Working conditions

Although you will have an office, you will be on your feet for the majority of the time.

Some establishments will require you to live on-site and you might have to work shifts or unsocial hours.

Future prospects

There is scope to develop a career in management in this area but you have to work your way from junior or deputy housekeeper to senior housekeeper.

In larger hotels, you could progress to a role in head office, in areas such as human resources or training. There are also opportunities in facilities management.

International companies could provide the opportunity to work overseas. With enough experience, you could go on to own and run a hotel.

Advantages/disadvantages

Larger hotel and leisure companies often provide staff with leisure and restaurant discounts.

You will be responsible for generating customer satisfaction which can be very rewarding.

Depending on the size and location of the establishment, the work may be seasonal.

Money guide

Salaries vary significantly depending on the size, reputation and location of the establishment.

Starting salaries are usually £12,000–£14,000.

A graduate trainee accommodation manager will start on £17,000–£21,000 per year.

Senior housekeepers can expect to earn £20,000–£28,000.

Those employed in the largest and most successful hotels can achieve up to £40,000.

If accommodation is provided, salaries might be reduced to cover rent and living expenses.

Related opportunities

- Cleaner p460
- Hotel Porter p141
- Hotel/Accommodation Room Attendant p143

Further information

Institute of Hospitality
www.instituteofhospitality.org

People 1st
www.people1st.co.uk

Springboard UK
www.springboarduk.net

Qualifications and courses

Kitchen assistant

There are no minimum qualifications but previous catering experience is helpful. Most employers provide on-the-job training.

Qualifications such as the GCSE in food technology, City & Guilds Award in Introduction to Employment in the Hospitality Industry (Level 1) and City & Guilds Certificate in Hospitality and Catering/Food Studies (Levels 1 and 2) are useful. In Scotland the SQA National Qualification in Health and Food Technology is available.

Kitchen supervisor

There are no formal requirements to become a supervisor but you will need previous experience as a fully trained chef.

The City & Guilds Diploma in Professional Cookery (Levels 1–3), the NVQ in Hospitality and Catering (Level 2) and the City & Guilds Certificate in Hospitality and Catering Principles (Levels 2 and 3)may be useful. BTEC Specialist Qualifications in Hospitality and Catering Principles are available in areas such as Food Production and Cooking, Professional Cookery and Kitchen Services. HNC/HND and degree qualifications in hospitality will increase your chances of getting a job.

What the work involves

Kitchen assistant

You will keep the kitchen clean, wash up equipment, peel and chop fruits, vegetables and meat and check on stock levels. You will also prepare quick, simple dishes.

Kitchen supervisor

Kitchen supervisors are experienced, trained chefs who oversee the running of a kitchen and hire, train and manage all kitchen staff.

You will plan menus, order ingredients, oversee food preparation, presentation and quality control and contact suppliers to place orders and negotiate prices.

Type of person suited to this work

As a supervisor you need to be assertive, patient and composed as you will have to delegate tasks, resolve disputes, negotiate prices, keep records and stay in control of a team. You also need to have good teamwork, communication and multi-tasking skills and must adhere to and impose strict health and safety procedures and hygiene standards.

Kitchen assistants need to be on time for work, able to follow directions and to work efficiently at a fast pace.

Working conditions

Most kitchen assistants work part time on a shift system including split shifts and overtime. Supervisors generally work a 40-hour week. All kitchen staff should be prepared to work holidays and weekends.

Kitchens can be noisy, clammy and cramped places to work. You will need to wear protective clothing to ensure food is not contaminated.

While both kitchen assistants and supervisors will spend most of their time standing and lifting heavy items, supervisors will also have a small office in which they organise their paperwork.

Future prospects

Kitchen workers are constantly in demand. You may work in a wide range of settings from restaurants, bars and hotels to hospitals, schools or the Armed Forces.

Kitchen assistant

You may progress to an assistant chef or move into food service or bar work.

Kitchen supervisor

You may be promoted to general manager or head office manager. You may also choose to set up your own independent restaurant or catering company.

Advantages/disadvantages

Working with a team in a fast-paced kitchen can be fun and exciting.

You may need to work long shifts at unsocial times.

The work can be stressful and physically demanding.

Money guide

Kitchen assistant

If you work a 40-hour week your salary can range from £10,000 to £12,500. With experience you may earn up to £15,000.

Kitchen supervisor

The starting salary for a chef is about £14,000.

Kitchen supervisors can earn £16,000–£25,000.

Related opportunities

- Catering/Restaurant Manager/Maître d'Hôtel p135
- Chef/Sous Chef p137
- Waiting Staff p146

Further information

Institute of Hospitality
www.instituteofhospitality.org

Qualifications and courses

Waiter/waitress

No minimum qualifications are required. However, communication and numeracy skills are important. School leavers could apply for an Intermediate Apprenticeship in Hospitality and Catering.

It is possible to study for NVQs/SVQs in Hospitality (Levels 1 and 2), an NVQ in Food and Drink Service (Level 2) or the City & Guilds Diploma and Certificate in Professional Food and Beverage Service (Levels 1 and 2).

High profile employers may require staff with experience in fine dining and silver service. The Academy of Food and Wine Service provides short courses such as the Licence to Work in Banqueting Service.

Butler

No formal academic qualifications are required but hospitality experience is essential. Qualifications in general hospitality and catering are well regarded. It may be beneficial to take the NVQs/SVQs in Hospitality (Levels 1 and 2), an NVQ in Food and Drink Service (Level 2) or an NVQ in Hospitality Supervision (Level 3). The City & Guilds Diploma for Butlers (Levels 2 and 3) would also be a useful qualification.

Some large institutions such as hotel chains provide formal training. You will probably need a driving licence and a second language may be useful.

Sommelier

There are no minimum qualifications but you must be 18 years or over to serve alcohol. Relevant experience working in a bar or restaurant would be useful, as would fluency in a foreign language, especially French.

The Wine & Spirit Education Trust (WSET) offer qualifications in wines, spirits and wine service ranging from Level 1 Awards up to a Level 5 Honours Diploma. Employers may require you to have completed some of these courses.

Another specialist training option is the Professional Connoisseur Series: Senses, Service & Skills – An Introduction to Sommellerie course offered by the Academy of Food and Wine Service.

The NVQ in Food and Drink Service (Level 2) and the City & Guilds Diploma and Certificate in Professional Food and Beverage Service (Levels 1 and 2) may also be relevant.

What the work involves

Waiter/waitress

You will take food orders from customers and provide meals through table or counter service. You will supply accurate bills for meals and take payment from customers. Before and during your shift you will probably have to keep the eating area clean and prepare tables for customers.

Butler

You will work in a private household where you will be responsible for arranging travel and security, providing and serving food and welcoming visitors. You will usually work within a wealthy household, including those of celebrities or royalty.

Sommelier

You will be responsible for the provision of wines or other alcoholic beverages such as spirits. You will be expected to attend tastings and to design a wine list or cocktail menu. It is important to understand how beverages complement food in order to aid customer selection. You will need to serve beverages correctly at the expected temperature.

Type of person suited to this work

Waiter/waitress

As you will be working with the public, you should possess a polite attitude, a neat appearance and good customer service skills. You may have to explain parts of the menu to customers so an interest in food and drink is useful.

You will need a good memory and communication skills to take food orders correctly from customers and pass them on to kitchen staff. You should be happy to work as part of a team.

The ability to work with numbers and deal with cash is important. You must work to a high standard of health and hygiene at all times.

Butler

In addition to the above skills, you should be impeccably presented, honest and reliable. Your employers will expect you to be dedicated, loyal and discrete as you will be responsible for their day-to-day security, their home and their personal affairs.

Sommelier

It is essential that you are enthusiastic about wines and have an interest in food. You should understand tasting notes, have a good palate and demonstrate a thorough knowledge of wines and beverages from all over the world.

Working conditions

Waiter/waitress

This role involves shift work and you will have to work unsocial hours including evenings and weekends. It is essential to have lots of energy as you will be on your feet most of the time, carrying heavy plates and dishes.

Most waiting staff serve a number of tables at once and have to remember different customer requests. It is important to have the ability to remain calm in the face of customer complaints.

You will be required to wear a uniform and may be exposed to a hot, noisy kitchen environment. You will be expected to work to a high standard of cleanliness at all times.

Butler

You will probably work within luxurious surroundings in the UK or abroad and will normally live-in and have your own quarters.

You may be required to care for the home whilst your employer is away and you may also escort them overseas.

Sommelier

You will probably wear a uniform and work shifts, including weekends and evenings, until the early hours of the morning.

You will spend most of your time front of house and should be energetic and have high hygiene standards.

You may have the opportunity to travel domestically and internationally to attend tastings.

Future prospects

Waiter/waitress

The hospitality industry is growing in the UK, with further expansion predicted. As a result there is a strong demand for waiting staff with good customer service skills and experience. Opportunities to work abroad are also available.

Once you gain experience, you could become junior or head waiter. Larger employers such as hotel chains increasingly provide formal training and support for staff and may allow inter-departmental movements.

Butler

Opportunities to become a butler are increasing. You are more likely to get a job if you are willing to be flexible and take on other responsibilities, such as those of a personal assistant or providing some childcare services. Many catering firms have butler services and there is demand from contract caterers, hotels and financial institutions.

Many of the jobs are overseas and the most successful butlers are willing to be geographically mobile.

Sommelier

There are a growing number of opportunities to work in a variety of outlets in the UK and abroad. An increasing number of women are entering the profession.

With experience it is possible to progress to a higher managerial position in the hospitality industry or start your own business in the wine sector.

Advantages/disadvantages

Waiter/waitress

Catering staff are often provided with uniforms, free meals and accommodation.

The role can be physically draining.

Butler

Your job could include lots of travelling and the opportunity to live in the luxurious homes of the rich and famous.

This job can affect your personal life as it is difficult to be off-duty.

Sommelier

You may have the opportunity to travel within the UK and abroad.

Working long and unsociable hours can affect your personal life.

Money guide

Waiter/waitress

Salaries will depend on the location, size and reputation of your employer.

Starting salaries are usually £11,900–£14,500.

With experience and extra responsibilities you can achieve £15,000–£19,000.

Your income can be supplemented by tips from customers.

Butler

Your salary will depend on your experience and your employer.

Starting salaries are around £15,000–£17,000.

Your salary will increase as you gain experience and the most successful butlers working in the private sector can receive £50,000–£100,000.

In addition, you may be provided with free accommodation and meals.

Sommelier

Salaries will depend on the location, size and reputation of the organisation you work for.

A trainee can expect around £13,000 per year.

Salaries increase to £20,000–£30,000 as you gain experience.

A head sommelier could earn £40,000+

Benefits may include tips, bonuses, free meals and accommodation.

Related opportunities

- Concierge p138
- Cruise Ship Steward/Purser p595
- Housekeeper/Accommodation Manager p144
- Kitchen Assistant/Supervisor p145

Further information

Institute of Hospitality
www.instituteofhospitality.org

Springboard UK
www.springboarduk.net

Wine & Spirit Education Trust
www.wset.co.uk

Computers and IT

This sector is still fairly new and so it is expanding all the time, creating new jobs for a whole range of people.

You may have a mathematical brain or a real creative ability – or a bit of both! Essentially, you must be passionate about computers to consider working in this sector. You need to keep right up to date with the latest technologies and IT developments as well as people's tastes, interests and hobbies to enjoy working in this industry.

The jobs featured in this section are listed below. For similar jobs to the ones found in this section have a look at *Administration, Business, Office and Financial Services* on page 15 and *Retail, Sales and Customer Services* starting on page 473.

Qualifications and courses

Most entrants have a degree, Foundation degree or HNC/HND in a relevant subject, such as e-business/commerce, accountancy, business studies or computer science.

A sponsored degree in Information Technology Management for Business (ITMB) from e-skills UK is available. This is focused on learning through project work in teams with external mentors from sponsoring organisations such as BT, Ford, IBM, Deloitte, Unilever and Sainsbury's. The opportunities to network with industry professionals could be invaluable when pursuing a graduate career.

The normal minimum entry requirements for degrees are 2 A levels/3 H grades and 5 GCSEs/S grades (A*–C/1–3). For Foundation degrees or HNCs/HNDs, 1 A level/2 H grades and 3 GCSEs/S grades (A*–C/1–3) are necessary. Maths might be a required subject.

The Higher Apprenticeship in ICT may be available as a funded route and leads to a full Honours degree in addition to vocational, technical and Key Skills qualifications and work experience.

A BTEC National Diploma in an IT or business-related subject could be helpful. The Chartered Institute for IT (BCS) offers business analysis certifications at various levels.

What the work involves

You will be responsible for inspecting businesses, to see if there are any improvements to be made or current problems that can be solved using information technology. Your aim is to generate higher efficiency and profits for the company.

You will work with managers in order to learn more about the organisation structure and the technology it uses. You will map out a new business plan and train staff on how to implement it.

You will ensure that project deadlines and budgets are met on time.

Type of person suited to this work

Your understanding of how businesses work is the key to being a successful business analyst – you will be aware of the need to balance costs with solutions.

You will also need to be a good negotiator, able to influence managers who may not understand how the new solutions or products you are suggesting can benefit their businesses.

Excellent communication skills are crucial because you will need to put across your ideas in meetings and in written reports. You will also need a strong knowledge of what is available in the technology market and how it works in order to develop project briefs.

Working conditions

You will work standard office hours, although work at evenings and weekends will be necessary when projects are near to completion. You will spend a lot of time working with other members of the project team. It is likely that your job will also involve travelling to meet clients at all stages of the project.

Future prospects

There are vacancies in all areas of business including finance and retail. Employers also include specialist management consultancies, software houses and computer companies.

There is a growing market for business analysts with the right combination of skills and talents. Analysts with e-commerce technology skills and experience are in particular demand, owing to the continued growth of internet use in business.

Progression is possible into senior analyst jobs and on to project management or consultancy work.

Advantages/disadvantages

You can get a real sense of satisfaction from producing successful solutions that transform a business.

There often has to be a trade-off between the solution you would like to recommend and the limitations set by your client's budget.

Entry to this profession can be quite competitive.

You will have the opportunity to meet a range of people and gain exposure to various business sectors.

Money guide

Starting salaries can range from £17,000 to £25,000.

Earnings rise to £30,000–£45,000 with experience.

Senior business analysts can achieve £60,000–£80,000.

Salaries vary greatly depending on location and are highest in London.

Additional benefits may include profit sharing, performance-related pay and a company car.

Related opportunities

- Software Developer/Programmer p159
- Systems Analyst p161
- Technical Sales Specialist p162

Further information

BCS, The Chartered Institute for IT
www.bcs.org

e-skills UK
www.e-skills.com

Institute for the Management of Information Systems
www.imis.org.uk

COMPUTER GAMES DESIGNER

Qualifications and courses

Many employers will ask for a minimum of a degree and although entry into the industry is possible with a HND, many developers are graduates. A portfolio of game projects or designs is also beneficial although this is largely dependent on the kind of job you apply for; depending on either artistic or programing requirements. Relevant industry experience is a must and many people work initially as a tester of quality assurance in a games studio.

Useful degree subjects include computer games technology, computer arts or computer animation. The computer games industry is constantly developing, and as games grow closer to traditional cinema, developers may value knowledge of cinematography or a flair for storytelling. At least 2 A levels/3 H grades or equivalent might be required or preferred for entry to related degrees.

A funded route that may be on offer in your area is the Higher Apprenticeship in IT. This leads to a full Honours degree in addition to vocational, technical and Key Skills qualifications and work experience. An Apprenticeship in Quality Assurance and Games Production is also available. Training programmes are on offer for graduate entrants from any discipline.

What the work involves

Using storyboards and flowcharts, you will present your ideas for a new computer game to a panel for acceptance or rejection.

If it is accepted you will manage all aspects of the playing experience, from scripts to programming and from animation to sound effects and music.

You will work with a team of specialists, such as programmers and graphic artists, to produce a prototype. Once a computer games playtester has picked out any flaws and if the panel think it is a winner, it will go into full development by your team.

Type of person suited to this work

To be a top-class computer games designer you will need creativity and an ability to see how ideas fit together. You will also have a passion for and knowledge of the computer games market.

Your ideas need to be technically viable and cost effective, so you will need a broad understanding of computers and games consoles, multimedia and the internet.

You will need to be a team player to work with specialists such as graphic designers to make sure that their part of the project fits in with the final version of the game.

Working conditions

You will be mainly based in an office or studio working with other members of the games project team.

Although you will work Monday to Friday, you might need to work overtime on evenings and weekends to meet deadlines.

Future prospects

Employers are specialised companies producing games for PCs or games consoles such as Wii, Kinect, Nintendo DS, Xbox or PS3. This market is expected to grow as the computer games industry is a profitable global business.

It is a popular career choice so entry is competitive. You will need talent and project/people management skills in order to be promoted from junior to designer and then to lead designer.

There may be opportunities to work abroad. Progression is possible into management or consultancy work.

Advantages/disadvantages

Games designers say it is enjoyable creating entertainment for a living. It is a young business and the rewards can be high.

It can be tough when a game does not sell or receives poor reviews.

It is stressful producing a game for a timed release such as the Christmas market.

Money guide

£20,000 per year is usual for starting/training salaries in this area of work for designers with prior industry experience.

This can then rise to between £25,000 and £35,000 with more experience.

Between £35,000 and £55,000 is possible for senior games designers.

Additional benefits usually include profit sharing and performance-related pay or a bonus.

Related opportunities

- Interactive Media Designer p155
- Online/Web Content Manager p158
- Software Developer/Programmer p159

Further information

BCS, The Chartered Institute for IT
www.bcs.org

Institute of IT Training
www.iitt.org.uk

COMPUTER HARDWARE ENGINEER

Qualifications and courses

The majority of employers look for prospective employees to have a degree when recruiting for this position. However, it is possible to start at basic technical support level and work your way up.

Useful degree subjects include computer systems engineering or electronic engineering.

The normal minimum entry requirements for degrees are 2 A levels/3 H grades and 5 GCSEs/S grades (A*–C/1–3). For technical degrees, maths, technology or a science subject may be required.

You may choose to enter this career through an Apprenticeship in IT and Telecoms Professionals.

Training programmes are on offer for graduate entrants from any discipline. Engineers must ensure their technical knowledge is always up to date by completing continuing professional development (CPD) courses. Once qualified, computer hardware engineers register with the Engineering Council as an Incorporated Engineer (IEng) or Chartered Engineer (CEng). Registration can aid career advancement and CPD, as it can expose you to networkng, training and job opportunities.

What the work involves

You will be responsible for developing, installing and repairing computer hardware – the computer itself rather than the applications or software.

You will be designing computer components, including microchips and circuit boards, and testing these systems.

When repairing a fault or upgrading a machine you will open up the computer and use tools to install upgrades or replace faulty parts.

You may specialise in installing new computer systems and training the people who use them.

Type of person suited to this work

You will need both technical skills and practical ability. Building your own computer system and repairing friends' machines is something you will probably already be doing in your spare time.

You should be a good problem solver. You will need to be able to identify what is wrong and put it right within a strict deadline, especially as your customer may be losing money while you do the repair.

It is important to be inquisitive and adaptable as you will need to absorb new information quickly in order to solve many repairs.

You should pay close attention to detail and be thorough and accurate in your work. Often working on your own, you will also need to be reliable and able to work unsupervised.

Working conditions

You might be based in a workshop or in an office, but many engineers travel to individual customers' premises or homes.

You will work a 37 to 40 hour week, but as businesses generally need major work to be done in the evenings and at weekends, you will have to work shifts or be on a call-out rota.

Future prospects

Computer hardware engineers are employed by computer manufacturers, computer service firms and by a range of large organisations such as banks, hospitals and universities.

This is a stable area of work because computers need regular repairs or upgrades to improve performance or capacity.

Promotion could be to team leader or supervisor and then on to senior engineer. Self-employment as a freelance/consultant engineer is possible.

Advantages/disadvantages

Your job will be varied as few technical problems are ever the same.

It is rewarding to get a computer up and running again.

Your customer may have a service agreement requiring you to put the problem right in a fixed period of time, which can be stressful.

Money guide

When you begin work as a computer hardware technician you can expect your starting/trainee salary to be around £18,000 per year.

This could then increase once you have experience to between £19,000 and £25,000.

Salaries can rise to between £35,000 and £40,000 at senior level.

Related opportunities

- Computer Technical Support Person/Helpdesk Adviser p153
- Software Developer/Programmer p159
- Software Engineer p160

Further information

e-skills UK
www.e-skills.com

Tomorrow's Engineers
www.tomorrowsengineers.org.uk

COMPUTER TECHNICAL SUPPORT PERSON/HELPDESK ADVISER

ENTRY LEVEL 2

Qualifications and courses

It is possible for school leavers to enter this profession via an Intermediate Apprenticeship for IT, Software, Web and Telecoms Professionals. Those with limited IT experience can also obtain qualifications in customer service and support from the Help Desk Institute (HDI). However, some employers may prefer you to have relevant qualifications, such as a BTEC First or National in IT or a degree or HNC/HND in computing.

For computer technical support staff, the Computer Technology Industry Association (CompTIA) provides the A+ Certification. The Service Desk Institute (SDI) also offers qualifications suitable for both entry level and experienced IT support workers.

Other acceptable entry qualifications include the City & Guilds NVQ for IT Practitioners/Professionals (Levels 1–4), the OCR iPRO Certificate and Diploma in ICT Systems Support and courses offered by the Chartered Institute for IT (BCS).

Microsoft, Linux, Unix, Oracle and Cisco offer certification courses in their own products, such as the Microsoft Certified Solutions Associate (MCSA) and the Microsoft Certified Solutions Expert (MCSE). These qualifications are the most broadly accepted technical certifications.

What the work involves

Computer helpdesk advisers answer telephone calls or emails from computer users who are having technical problems and will advise the customer on how to correct the fault.

A computer technical support person will also try to solve customers' technical problems by phone or email, and will also go to the user's workstation to fix the problem if it is more complex. You might also install new systems and upgrades and train staff in their use.

Type of person suited to this work

You will need to be both technical and practical to resolve hardware or software problems.

You will also need to be a good communicator – able to explain technical language to inexperienced users.

You need to cope well with stress and deadlines. You will be under pressure to get the problem sorted quickly so that staff can get back to work. A keenness to stay up to date is vital – you will be expected to be the expert.

Working conditions

You will probably be based in an office with a technical workshop attached.

You may have to work shifts to cover your employer's hours of operation, which may be 24/7, or to install or repair equipment outside office hours.

The employers of computer technical support staff may have several sites you need to travel between, sometimes in different parts of the UK.

Future prospects

Computer helpdesk advisers are mostly employed by computer hardware and software manufacturers or internet service providers, who offer support to their customers. The main employers of computer technical support staff are large organisations such as banks, retail chains and hospitals.

With experience, promotion for a computer technical support person could be to team leader, network manager/administrator or on to network development. You could also become self-employed. For a computer helpdesk adviser, promotion to supervisory and management work is possible.

The number of technical support positions has reduced, owing to the shift in ICT companies offering remotely managed services and the recession. Similarly, employers sometimes source helpdesks outside the UK to reduce costs.

Advantages/disadvantages

Computer technical support can lead to jobs at a higher level in the IT industry as you develop useful, transferable computer skills.

It is a rewarding experience to help people and solve problems.

The job can be stressful because customers might be angry and frustrated.

Money guide

Starting salaries for computer helpdesk advisers range from £14,000 to £21,000.

As you gain experience earnings can rise to £18,000–£27,000.

Those who take on managerial responsibilites can achieve £30,000–£42,000.

Entrants to computer technical support may begin on a salary of £17,000–£22,000.

At senior level, you could achieve up to £45,000.

Related opportunities

- Computer Hardware Engineer p152
- Network Manager p157
- Technical Sales Specialist p162

Further information

BCS, The Chartered Institute for IT
www.bcs.org

e-skills UK
www.e-skills.com

Institute of IT Training
www.iitt.org.uk

DATABASE ADMINISTRATOR

Qualifications and courses

Entrants to this work normally have a degree, Foundation degree or HNC/HND in a relevant subject, for example, computer science, software engineering, operational research, e-commerce, technology or maths. Other qualifications may be acceptable, such as BTEC National Diplomas and NVQs/SVQs.

The normal minimum entry requirements for degrees are 2 A levels/3 H grades and 5 GCSEs/S grades (A*–C/1–3). For Foundation degrees or HNCs/HNDs you need 1 A level/2 H grades and 3 GCSEs/S grades (A*–C/1–3). For technical degrees, maths or science may be required.

A funded route for school leavers is the Advanced Apprenticeship for IT, Software, Web and Telecoms Professionals. Entrants will receive practical and technical training in database administration and have the opportunity to work towards relevant qualifications.

Entry without a degree may be possible if you have significant programming experience and knowledge. Graduates are also advised to gain experience by undertaking vacation work or a sandwich degree in the computer industry.

Database managers may also take courses in particular operating systems/packages offered by the manufacturers.

What the work involves

Your job is to ensure that databases are accurate, accessible and secure. A database will be used if a huge amount of information needs to be stored with the capacity to search and access specific parts of the data. For example, a hospital uses a database to manage information about its patients.

To keep the data secure you will back up the content regularly, train users and issue them with passwords.

You may also be responsible for setting up and testing a new database.

Type of person suited to this work

Databases function to provide people with the information they require to do their jobs, so you will need effective communication skills.

You should be a good negotiator. To train users to input or access a new or modified database you will need to be able to convince them that these changes will benefit them.

To set up or develop a database you will need to be very technical with a high level of programming knowledge. You will also need to be a good listener, able to find out what the database users want including the new design they wish to achieve.

Working conditions

You will be based mainly in your own office although in some cases the work can be carried out at home or in a place of your choice using laptops and broadband wireless technology.

Your employer may have several sites you need to travel between, sometimes in different parts of the UK.

You may have to be on-call to deal with problems outside your normal working hours.

Future prospects

The main employers of database administrators are large organisations, such as banks and retailers. You could also work for a specialist ICT firm providing a complete database service to customers.

This is a growth area because increasing numbers of businesses are developing databases for their websites to allow customers to look at information about their goods online and then go on to buy them.

With experience, you could specialise in network development or move into consultancy work.

Advantages/disadvantages

If you are methodical and analytical you will enjoy the complex job of creating a new database.

It can be frustrating when database users cause problems by not keeping their information up to date or by leaving out vital parts.

The job can be flexible as there are often opportunities for freelance and part-time work, self-employment and working from home.

Money guide

Starting salaries for graduates in this field can be up to £25,000.

As you gain experience, your earnings will increase to about £32,500 a year.

The average salary for a database administrator with several years' experience is £45,000.

Those employed at a senior level can achieve up to £55,000.

Related opportunities

- IT Trainer p156
- Network Manager p157
- Software Developer/Programmer p159

Further information

BCS, The Chartered Institute for IT
www.bcs.org

e-skills UK
www.e-skills.com

INTERACTIVE MEDIA DESIGNER

Qualifications and courses

Entrants often have a degree, Foundation degree or HNC/HND in an art and design-related subject such as graphic or multimedia design.

The normal minimum entry requirements for degrees are 2 A levels/3 H grades and 5 GCSEs/S grades (A*–C/1–3). For Foundation degrees or HNCs/HNDs you usually need 1 A level/2 H grades and 3 GCSEs/S grades (A*–C/1–3). For technical degrees, maths or science may be required.

Entry without a degree, Foundation degree or HNC/HND is possible for those with IT skills and creative talent. The BTEC National Diploma in Art and Design (Interactive Media) (Level 3) could be beneficial. Alternatively, you may choose to do the Advanced Apprenticeship for IT, Software, Web and Telecoms Professionals to gain qualifications and practical training.

All entrants should try to get as much experience in the field as possible and it is essential that you compile a portfolio with relevant samples of your interactive media work, produced either at home or during a work placement.

The Chartered Institute for IT (BCS) and the Institute for the Management of Information Systems (IMIS) also offer qualifications which may be useful.

What the work involves

Interactive media designers use a mix of visuals, sounds, animation, text and effects to produce multimedia and communication tools such as apps, interactive websites and DVDs.

You will work with a team to develop a brief, finding out what your client wants and determining how to find the best solution. You will create simulations along the way to show the client your ideas.

Your role will also involve planning, coordinating and overseeing the whole project as well as testing, integrating and, if needed, installing at the customer's site.

Type of person suited to this work

Your creative skills need to be outstanding for this job. Every project will be different and you will need the vision to be able to think about what a client wants to achieve with a multimedia project and then develop ideas to produce a solution.

You need to be good at working in a team and motivating others to achieve tight deadlines. You must be organised, have a keen eye for detail and possess good drawing skills.

You should have excellent presentation and communication skills, as you might need to bid against other designers to win contracts for new projects.

Working conditions

You will spend time at your workstation, working in an office or studio, but you will also be working with your project team and meeting customers and may also have the opportunity to work from home.

You may have to travel regularly to clients, to meet and present your solutions to them.

Although you will work normal hours from Monday to Friday, you may need to work overtime when a deadline is approaching.

Future prospects

Employers include specialist multimedia consultancies, internet service providers, e-learning specialists, mobile phone companies, software houses and hardware manufacturers.

Interactive media is a growing industry and designers who have an understanding of both technical and creative aspects are currently in demand.

Once experienced you could become self-employed, or work on a contract or consultancy basis. You could also move into management or training.

Advantages/disadvantages

This is a young, vibrant industry where you will be using cutting-edge technology.

Seeing people use apps and websites that you have created is very rewarding.

The fast pace of development in this field means that you will have to continue learning to remain up to date.

Money guide

Starting salaries are usually between £15,500 and £22,000.

Experienced interactive media designers can expect around £30,000–£35,000.

Those who are highly experienced could earn in excess of £50,000.

Salaries are usually higher in London and the south-east of England.

Related opportunities

- Online/Web Content Manager p158
- Software Developer/Programmer p159
- Software Engineer p160

Further information

British Interactive Multimedia Association
www.bima.co.uk

e-skills UK
www.e-skills.com

IT TRAINER

Qualifications and courses

To work as an IT trainer you need to first gain the relevant skills and experience in IT yourself.

Although no set qualifications are required, it might be an advantage to have a degree, Foundation degree or HNC/D in a relevant subject, for example computer science, e-business/commerce or software engineering. The normal minimum entry requirements for degrees are 2 A levels/3 H grades and 5 GCSEs/S grades (A*–C/1–3). For Foundation degrees or HNC/Ds you need 1 A level/2 H grades and 3 GCSEs/S grades (A*–C/1–3). You could enter this job without a degree if you have got significant experience and training in IT.

The Institute of IT Training is the certification awarding body for a range of courses in e-learning training skills offered by the Training Foundation. Through the Institute of IT Training you can qualify as Certified Training Practitioner.

Once you have qualified, it is advisable that you join the Chartered Institute for IT (also known as the British Computer Society); this will give the opportunity to interact with others in the industry and pursue courses to continue your professional development. Through the BCS it will also be possible to keep up to date with the latest developments in what is a continually evolving industry.

What the work involves

IT trainers give people user skills, for example, in applications such as Word, Excel or desktop-publishing packages. You may also train people in advanced computer skills such as programming languages.

Planning courses, preparing learning materials and setting up the computers ready for a session will be part of your typical day. You will give presentations and network some materials. You will demonstrate the software being taught and assist students with any problems.

Evaluating what has been learned and changing future learning materials as required will also be part of your job.

Type of person suited to this work

The constant release of new IT products guarantees a future for trainers but only if you are keen to stay up to date. You will need lots of self-discipline to do research and prepare learning materials.

As e-learning and virtual classroom technology expands, more students are being taught over the internet. Therefore, you will need to be up to date with e-learning tools, technologies and processes.

This job is about helping others to learn. Whether you train face to face or by virtual technology, you will need strong interpersonal and communication skills. Students can be sensitive to criticism and need to be motivated and encouraged.

Working conditions

You may be based in a training centre or you may travel to clients' premises to train their staff on-site.

Although your hours will be usually Monday to Friday, you will need to spend time preparing learning materials and working some evenings and weekends to fit in with students' timetables.

Future prospects

Employers such as hardware and software manufacturers, IT consultancies, training organisations and colleges employ IT trainers. There is a strong demand for trainers, especially in the south-east of England.

This is not considered to be an entry-level post. Most trainers have gained experience in other areas of computing first.

Experienced IT trainers can move into self-employment as consultants. Promotion into supervisory or management roles may be possible.

Advantages/disadvantages

It can be personally rewarding when you succeed in making a student understand a difficult subject.

This job can be badly affected when the economy is depressed as training is often the first thing businesses cut back on in difficult times.

Money guide

Starting salaries are usually between £18,000 and £23,000 per year.

The current national average salary is £28,750 and £32,000 for Greater London.

At senior levels, with management responsibilities, it is possible to earn in excess of £40,000.

Self-employed trainers, who work for set fees either per day or per training course, can earn over £30,000.

Related opportunities

- Business Analyst p150
- Secondary School Teacher p203
- Work-based Training Instructor p207

Further information

BCS, The Chartered Institute for IT
www.bcs.org

Institute of IT Training
www.iitt.org.uk

Qualifications and courses

Entry is usually by means of a degree, Foundation degree or HNC/D in a relevant subject, for example control and network computing, software engineering, artificial intelligence or computer science. The normal minimum entry requirements for degrees are 2 A levels /3 H grades and 5 GCSEs/S grades (A*–C/1–3), and for Foundation degrees or HNC/Ds, 1 A level/2 H grades and 4 GCSEs/S grades (A*–C/1–3). For technical degrees, maths/science may be required.

Network manager candidates will also need prior experience. This can be gained through a Higher Apprenticeship in IT. For entry onto a Higher Apprenticeship you will need qualifications at Advanced level or Level 3, such as A levels/H grades, or a level 3 NVQ.

Training programmes on offer to graduates from any discipline include the Graduate Professional Development Award. This offers training and accreditation to ICT professionals in work.

Other useful qualifications include the City & Guilds Level 4 Higher Professional Diploma in Information Management using ICT, the Institute for the Management of Information Systems Foundation Diploma or accredited qualifications from CISCO and Microsoft.

What the work involves

You will design, set up and maintain a network of computers and any linked equipment such as printers. This could be in just one building or extend across different sites. It will be your responsibility to solve the network users' problems.

Managing access to and the security of your network, you will put in place and monitor firewalls, password systems and antivirus software.

In large organisations you could manage a team of ICT technicians and carry out duties such as training staff, organising work rotas and allocating staff duties.

Type of person suited to this work

You need to have excellent communication skills in order to explain technical issues clearly and simply to computer users who need to get back onto the network.

Technical ability and determination are needed for this job. You might develop and write software programs for your network and need to be logical to work out how to sort out any problems.

Network solutions are developing very quickly so you will need to be prepared to carry on learning to keep up your expert status.

Working conditions

You will work standard office hours, though longer hours can be required when installing systems or on-call.

You will use a computer to manage the system. You may need to work in the same room as a noisy mainframe server.

You may have to move around your company's site to attend meetings, train staff and resolve problems.

Future prospects

Most organisations use networks to enable their staff to work together, communicate and share resources from their own workstations. Employers include industry, retailers, schools and universities, hospitals, local and central government and financial companies. You could work within an organisation as a network manager, or as part of an external IT agency and work in many different companies.

Promotion could be into the job of senior network manager and then project manager. A talented network manager could also move into freelance or network design consultancy work. Other possibilities include lecturing or training.

Advantages/disadvantages

You will feel valued because communication and the sharing of information are central to the effective running of any organisation.

This job can be stressful as problems will need to be solved quickly so that users can go back to work.

Money guide

Starting salaries are usually from about £24,000 per year.

With experience you could earn from £33,500 to £47,000.

Senior network managers can earn in excess of £50,000.

Additional benefits may include profit sharing or performance-related pay.

Related opportunities

- Computer Hardware Engineer p152
- Computer Technical Support Person/Helpdesk Adviser p153
- Database Administrator p154

Further information

BCS, The Chartered Institute for IT
www.bcs.org

e-skills UK
www.e-skills.com

CRCI: D   COMPUTERS AND IT

Qualifications and courses

The usual entry qualification for this work is a degree, Foundation degree or HNC/HND in a relevant subject, such as e-business/commerce, e-systems design/technology, 3D design, graphic design or computer science.

The normal minimum entry requirements for degrees are 2 A levels/3 H grades and 5 GCSEs/S grades (A*–C/1–3). For Foundation degrees or HNCs/HNDs you will be expected to have 1 A level/2 H grades and 3 GCSEs/S grades (A*–C/1–3).

A funded route that may be on offer for school leavers is the Advanced IT Application Specialist Apprenticeship. Entrants will gain practical training and relevant qualifications which will help them to secure a suitable role within this industry.

Training will be provided on the job but any experience that you have working with web content management systems or particular programs, packages or operating systems would be an advantage. Vacation work or voluntary placements within the sector would also provide useful experience and enable you to develop industry contacts.

What the work involves

You might work in or supervise a team of staff who design, programme and maintain the various pages that make up an internet site.

In a small company, you might be the programmer, designer and master/manager of the site.

You might write content or develop a content management program for authorised staff to contribute material.

Type of person suited to this work

You must have good attention to detail and be able to carefully check your work. You will need to set up secure data entry checking systems and regularly test them for faults. You must be able to respond quickly and calmly when faults occur, such as the wrong prices being matched to the wrong products on a shopping site, and be able to work efficiently to fix them.

It will be your responsibility to create your own website or maintain one from the group of sites you work with. Creativity is important, as is accuracy; you need to make sure the site is easy to use.

Excellent management and communication skills are vital as you may be required to lead a project team at senior level.

Working conditions

You will mainly be office based, using a computer to manage the website. You may have to move around your company's premises to train, meet with managers and discuss website improvements.

You will work a 37–40 hour week, normally Monday to Friday, but if you are working to maintain and support a 24/7 site you will work shifts as part of a team to cover all hours.

Future prospects

Websites are big business, with growing numbers of organisations using them to share information, market themselves, sell goods or services and advertise jobs.

You could work for web-based retailers, travel companies, the multimedia industry, local and central government and financial companies.

After gaining experience, you could progress to project management level. A talented web content manager could move into freelance or website development consultancy work.

Advantages/disadvantages

This is an expanding market with high rewards on offer if you are creative and have technical skills.

As you are responsible for your company's website, the work will sometimes involve high levels of pressure.

The skills that you will develop in this role are transferable and could open up opportunities to work for a variety of companies.

Money guide

The starting salary for a web content manager would usually be in the region of £17,000 to £24,000.

Those with experience in the field could expect to earn £25,000–£35,000 a year.

Senior web managers with additional responsibilities could achieve £40,000–£50,000.

Related opportunities

- Database Administrator p154
- Network Manager p157
- Software Developer/Programmer p159

Further information

British Interactive Media Association
www.bima.co.uk

e-skills UK
www.e-skills.com

Qualifications and courses

Entry is usually by means of a degree, Foundation degree or HNC/D in a relevant subject, for example programming, software engineering or computer science, or a degree with modules in computer graphics or html and Java programming. The normal minimum entry requirements for degrees are 2 A levels/3 H grades and 5 GCSEs/S grades (A*–C/1–3), and for Foundation degrees or HNC/Ds, 1 A level/2 H grades and 3 GCSEs/S grades (A*–C/1–3). For technical degrees, maths or science may be required.

Entry with a degree in an unrelated subject area is possible; larger employers recruit graduates from all disciplines. However as the industry is competitive it may be beneficial to take a conversion course or postgraduate course in a computing subject.

Entry without a degree, Foundation degree or HNC/D is unusual unless you have substantial experience in programming work and experience of designing or programming websites using new media. A strong portfolio will be required.

Further study is available, from in-house training to professional qualifications. These include the BCS, Chartered Institute for IT Professional Certification.

What the work involves

You will be designing, developing and testing computer software for your clients to improve their business's productivity and efficiency.

You may also improve existing software by analysing and fixing any problems.

Your clients could be companies from the finance, insurance, retail or building industries.

You will work closely with a team of other programmers and designers to develop a detailed specification for the software and present this back to your client.

You will write the programming code for the new software from scratch or adapt an existing code.

You will then be responsible for testing and maintaining the software, and making sure your client is happy with the new system.

Type of person suited to this work

You will need to have excellent ICT skills, with an in-depth knowledge of up to date packages and software coding techniques.

You must be a good communicator, as you will be working with other ICT professionals and members of staff.

Being logical and having a knack for problem-solving will be vital in this work, as you will need to come up with new programming codes and restore existing ones.

Working conditions

Most software developers/programmers work normal office hours. If there is a deadline to meet you might work overtime or at the weekend.

You will be based in an office, but you might need to travel around the country when meeting clients.

Future prospects

Software developers/programmers are employed by a variety of industries; these include retail, finance, engineering and government bodies.

You can progress into senior or management roles, or work as a contracted IT consultant.

Some software developers/programmers become self-employed or become trainers.

Advantages/disadvantages

You will need to keep up to date with new and developing ICT techniques; this could prove difficult if you wanted a career break.

There are great opportunities for promotion, leading to senior management roles and consultancy.

Money guide

Starting salaries may be around £20,000–£26,000.

This can increase to £28,000–£40,000 once you have gained several years' experience.

Senior and management roles can pay up to £70,000.

Related opportunities

- Interactive Media Designer p155
- Online/Web Content Manager p158
- Website Designer p164

Further information

British Interactive Media Association
www.bima.co.uk

COMPUTERS AND IT

CRCI: D

SOFTWARE ENGINEER

Qualifications and courses

The usual entry qualification is a degree or a master's in a relevant subject, for example computer science, artificial intelligence or electronic engineering. The normal minimum entry requirements for degrees are 2 A levels/3 H grades and 5 GCSEs/S grades (A*–C/1–3). Required subjects usually include maths and physics.

Should you have no formal qualifications, there may be the opportunity of an Apprenticeship in IT within your area. Otherwise Access courses are generally available if you wish to progress to a degree.

Training programmes are on offer for graduate entrants from any discipline. Engineers must ensure their technical knowledge is always up-to-date by completing continuing professional development courses.

What the work involves

Software engineers test and evaluate software that helps computers to run effectively.

You may also develop new software such as computer games, operating systems and business applications.

As well as providing technical support to businesses and organisations, you may also build new computer systems for them from scratch.

You will debug software when it is faulty and constantly research new technologies to find the best solutions.

You will work with computer codes and will usually specialise in either systems or applications.

Type of person suited to this work

You will need technical, practical and creative ability. It will be useful if you write your own programs or have built your own computer system.

You should be an excellent problem solver. You will need to be able to anticipate problems and work out ways to prevent them.

You must be patient and methodical to be able to produce accurate work when your deadline is close and your tests are not going well.

Your teamwork and communication skills should be strong as you will be working with a project team. At higher levels you will be giving presentations or lectures.

Working conditions

You may be based in a laboratory, a research and development unit, or a workshop.

At project management level you may travel nationally and internationally to meetings and conferences.

You will work a 37 to 40 hour week but you will need to be flexible and put in extra hours at key times.

Future prospects

There is a strong demand for software engineers in many sectors, including academia, government research, computer manufacturing, software development and electronics and telecommunications.

You will have more opportunities if you are both creative and technical.

You will start work as a junior member of a project team. With experience you could move into lecturing or project management. You might also choose to become an IT consultant or work as a contractor.

Advantages/disadvantages

Your team's work could make the headlines. New products and cutting-edge research, such as the building of world-class supercomputers, are of international interest.

Solutions to problems do not happen quickly. It can be really frustrating to retest hundreds of times and still not get the result you are looking for.

Money guide

The average starting salary is £27,000 per year.

With experience you may earn between £35,000 and £38,000.

At senior levels you can earn £40,000 and this often can rise to be in excess of £60,000 including bonuses.

Related opportunities

- Computer Hardware Engineer p152
- Interactive Media Designer p155
- Software Developer/Programmer p159

Further information

e-skills UK
www.e-skills.com

Institution of Analysts and Programmers (IAP)
www.iap.org.uk

SYSTEMS ANALYST

Qualifications and courses

A degree, Foundation degree or HNC/HND is usually required. Useful degree subjects include computer science, information technology and e-systems design and technology. Minimum entry requirements for these degrees are usually 2 A levels/H grades (including maths). Entry to the profession is still open to those with unrelated degrees but a postgraduate conversion course in IT may be needed.

A sponsored degree in Information Technology Management for Business (ITMB) from e-skills UK is available. This is focused on learning through project work in teams with external mentors from sponsoring organisations such as BT, Ford, IBM, Deloitte, Unilever and Sainsbury's.

The Higher Apprenticeship for IT, Software, Web and Telecoms Professionals involves practical training. For entry onto a Higher Apprenticeship you will need qualifications such as A levels/H grades or NVQ Level 3.

Relevant courses include the NVQ in Communication Technology for Practitioners and Professionals (Levels 1–4), City & Guilds Advanced Diploma for IT Professionals (Level 3), the BTEC National in IT (Level 3) or the BTEC Higher National in Computing and Systems Development (Levels 4 and 5).

What the work involves

You will prepare a brief of what your client wants a computer system to do and then translate this brief into recommendations for IT solutions.

To determine the system needed you will use performance monitoring or sizing tools. You will then design, cost and recommend suitable hardware/software solutions.

If purpose-built software is needed, you may write it or brief a programmer on your team. You will go on to install and test the configuration you have developed.

Type of person suited to this work

An excellent all-round knowledge of ICT, including hardware and software, is vital. You will also have to keep up to date with new ICT products as you will be expected to be the technical expert.

Your teamwork and communication skills will need to be good as you will be working with business clients and colleagues such as business analysts and programmers to produce the best value system as a team.

To make systems that work well and enhance profitability and efficiency for your customer, you will also need to be a problem solver who understands how businesses work.

Working conditions

You will be mainly based in an office, working with other members of the project team. You will have to travel to clients at all stages of the project and may be away for several days when installing and testing the new system.

Although your hours will be usually Monday to Friday, you will need to work some evenings and weekends to meet deadlines.

Future prospects

Employers include software and systems houses, ICT consultants as well as organisations in sectors such as commerce, finance and banking, retail and health.

You could move from this broad-based job either to specialise in offering ICT solutions for business, or into a technical area such as software or website development.

Progression is possible into a senior analyst role, project management or consultancy work. The speed of advancement depends upon the size and type of organisation you work for. You could also become an independent consultant.

Advantages/disadvantages

It is rewarding to combine hardware and software to create a unique solution designed for your customer.

You will have the opportunity to meet a range of people and work on a variety of IT projects.

Trying to work to strict deadlines and a tight budget can involve high levels of pressure.

You have full responsibility for meeting your clients' needs which could be stressful.

Money guide

Graduates usually receive a starting salary of £20,000–£27,000.

Experienced systems analysts can expect to earn £30,000 to £45,000.

Those in a senior position can achieve in excess of £60,000 and a project manager could earn over £80,000.

Salaries tend to be higher in London, the south-east of England and the Midlands.

Related opportunities

- Database Administrator p154
- Network Manager p157
- Software Developer/Programmer p159

Further information

e-skills UK
www.e-skills.com

Institute for the Management of Information Systems
www.imis.org.uk

Institute of IT Training
www.iitt.org.uk

Qualifications and courses

You will usually need a degree, Foundation degree or HNC/D in a computer-related subject to enter this job. The normal minimum entry requirements for degrees are 2 A levels/3 H grades and 5 GCSEs/S grades (A*–C/1–3), and for Foundation degrees or HNC/Ds, 1 A level/2 H grades and 3 GCSEs/S grades (A*–C/1–3). Maths and physics are often required subjects for entry.

A funded route that may be on offer in your area is the IT and Telecoms Professionals Apprenticeship.

Experience in sales is extremely useful. If you have a sales background and want training in IT you can pursue a City & Guilds Level 4 Higher Professional Diploma in Information Management using ICT or a BTEC National Certificate/Diploma for IT Practitioners. Recently, a new degree course has been founded in partnership with several successful IT companies; the Information Technology Management for Business (ITMB) BSc integrates a BSc Honours degree with learning, teaching and assessment aspects.

Initial training is usually intense as you will need to gain a thorough technical knowledge of your employer's products and their preferred communication style.

What the work involves

You will talk to customers interested in your product, finding out what they are looking for, answering technical questions and explaining how the product works.

You will then present what the client requires to an in-house technical team and work on adapting the product to suit the client.

Presentation of the finished product to your client is an important part of making the sale.

Type of person suited to this work

It is essential to be personable and persuasive. You will also need good verbal and written communication skills as you will be dealing with customers as well as writing up reports and proposals.

You must be able to clearly explain technical jargon to customers who may have no technical knowledge. Equally, you will need to understand all the technical specifications of your products as some of your customers will be experts.

It is a competitive market so you will need to be good at selling, negotiating and building customer loyalty. You will also need to be up to date with all the products out there so that you know the competition.

Working conditions

You might be based in an office, dealing with customers by phone or email, or in a retail outlet, selling direct.

If you specialise in selling to retail chains or organisations, you will spend a lot of time driving and in meetings. A driving licence will be useful.

Your hours will depend on your customers. Your employer may operate a shift system to deal with queries and sales from early until late, 7 days a week.

Future prospects

Employers include large ICT companies producing and retailing products such as mobile phones, computer hardware and software. Large specialist ICT retailers also employ technical sales staff.

The demand for new ICT products continues to grow but new competitors are always entering the market. Strong areas of demand include secure wireless broadband and mobile working.

You might be able to gain promotion to a supervisory or sales management role, or work as an IT consultant, a lecturer or contractor.

Advantages/disadvantages

If you close a deal at a good price or sell extras such as a service contract, you could be paid a bonus.

Selling can be very stressful, with high sales targets to achieve.

It can be frustrating if you spend a lot of time with a customer without it resulting in a purchase.

Money guide

Starting salaries are usually £16,000–£24,000 per year.

This could rise to £40,000 with experience.

Sales managers can earn more than £70,000.

Additional benefits may include profit sharing, performance-related pay, mobile phone, laptop and a car.

Related opportunities

- Business Analyst p150
- Computer Technical Support Person/Helpdesk Adviser p153
- IT Trainer p156

Further information

BCS, The Chartered Institute for IT
www.bcs.org

e-skills UK
www.e-skills.com

Institute of Sales & Marketing Management
www.ismm.co.uk

TELECOMMUNICATIONS TECHNICIAN

Qualifications and courses

You can enter this profession as an apprentice, where you will be supervised by a qualified telecommunications technician. Apprenticeships usually last for 2 years. You can work towards NVQs Level 2–3.

The IT and Telecoms Professionals Apprenticeship requires that candidates have 4 GCSES/S grades (A*–C/1–3) which must include English, maths, science, technology or a BTEC First diploma in a relevant subject.

You can also take a vocational course such as a BTEC National Certificate or Diploma, HND or a Foundation degree in a relevant subject such as telecommunications, technology, electronics or computing. City & Guilds also offer a Level 2 Award in Communications Cabling and a Level 3 Diploma in ICT Communications Systems.

Depending on the company you work for, continuing in-service training may be available. This can be combined with specific manufacturers' courses and vendor qualifications such as the networking qualifications offered by CISCO and Microsoft.

What the work involves

Telecommunications technicians install, test and repair networking and communications technology and systems across a range of applications, including mobile phones, telephones, satellite and radio networks and aerials.

Your day to day tasks will vary but you may be assembling, installing and testing telecommunications equipment; laying copper and fibre optic wire in the street or other sites; setting up or repairing networks.

You may also be involved in designing or consulting on plans for telecommunications systems.

Type of person suited to this work

You should be interested in maths, IT, electronics and communications.

As you will be working in a team and explaining technical terms to customers you should have good communication and customer service skills. You should also have good writing skills to write up reports and produce statistics.

As you may be installing systems and laying wires which may involve heavy lifting and carrying, digging or using ladders, you should be fit and have a good head for heights.

Working conditions

You will work between 9am and 5pm, Monday to Friday. You may be required to work shifts which may include evenings, weekends or to be available on-call. Overtime may be necessary to complete projects or meet deadlines.

You may be based in a factory workshop or in a control centre from where you will travel to complete projects. These may be in homes, offices or outdoors.

Future prospects

To progress as a telecommunications technician you can apply to become a professionally recognised engineering technician (EngTech) or ICT technician (ICTTech).

With experience and qualifications you may be promoted to senior technician or supervisor. With further experience, qualifications and skills you can apply for incorporated and chartered engineer status.

You can become self-employed, or work on a contract basis. There are also numerous opportunities to work abroad.

Advantages/disadvantages

You may be in a diverse working environment as new and exciting developments in technology are occurring rapidly.

You may have to work outdoors in uncomfortable weather conditions.

Money guide

Your starting salary will be around £12,000 a year.

With experience and qualifications you can earn up to £25,000.

The most experienced technicians can earn in excess of £30,000.

Related opportunities

- Computer Hardware Engineer p152
- Electrical Engineer p219
- Network Manager p157

Further information

Institute of Telecoms Professionals
www.theitp.org

Institution of Engineering and Technology
www.theiet.org

WEBSITE DESIGNER

ENTRY LEVEL 3

COMPUTERS AND IT

CRCI: D

Qualifications and courses

There are no specific qualifications needed to become a web designer, although most designers have experience in other design fields, or have taken training in web design. Most employers will expect you to have some experience and to have a related qualification such as a Foundation degree, computer related Honours degree or HND that covers internet technology, graphic or interactive design. On-the-job training is common, but you will also need to keep up date with the latest developments in the field.

A good working knowledge of HTML is essential. It could be useful to have experience working with Dreamweaver, Photoshop, Flash and Fireworks, CSS, Javascript and .Net. Professionally accredited training courses and online tutorials are also available from a number of recognised institutions such as The British School of Computing.

You could also study for qualifications such as the BTEC Interactive use of Media levels 1 to 3, OCR ITQ Levels 1 to 3, OCR Creative iMedia Levels 1 to 3 and City & Guilds E-Quals IT Users awards Level 2 (Diploma) and Level 3 (Advanced Diploma).

You could also take a higher level course, for example a Foundation degree, BTEC HNC/HND or degree in a design or multimedia subject.

What the work involves

Web designers build new or improve existing websites. You will be responsible for dealing with the visual image of the website but, you will not necessarily be involved with coding the website or making it function.

You will meet with clients and discuss what they want their website to look like and who it is aimed at. You will then have to use their requirements to create the design.

Type of person suited to this work

You will need excellent communication skills, as you have to understand the requirements of your client and create a design from their instructions.

You will need a great deal of creativity, to make the page as attractive as possible, but it is also essential to have a good understanding of consumer needs, in order to make the design comprehensible and functional.

Good time management is necessary, as you will be working to very strict deadlines.

Working conditions

You will usually work 37 to 40 hours a week, Monday to Friday, although you will sometimes have to work extra hours to meet a deadline, or when problems occur with a website.

Most of your time will be spent indoors in an office, or at home on your own computer if you are self-employed. When meeting clients, it may sometimes be necessary to travel.

Future prospects

You could work for web design companies, in the IT departments of large public and private organisations, or as a freelance designer.

Working for a company could give you the opportunity to work your way up into a design team management post, or expand your skills to become a web content manager.

Once you have gained enough experience, you could set up your own web design business.

Advantages/disadvantages

If you enjoy being creative, web designing will give you the opportunity to express your passion on a daily basis.

You will also feel a sense of achievement when you are able to see your finished piece being put to use.

Your clients could be relying on you to create a website that will generate them more business which could mean a lot of pressure to do an excellent job.

You will have to work to strict deadlines and this could mean working extra hours.

Money guide

Starting salaries begin at around £15,000 for non-graduates and at between £18,000 and £20,000 for graduates.

Experienced designers can earn up to £30,000.

Senior designers and those with specialist skills can earn in excess of £40,000.

Related opportunities

- Business Analyst p150
- Interactive Media Designer p155
- Online/Web Content Manager p158
- Website Developer p165

Further information

BCS, The Chartered Institute for IT
www.bcs.org

British Interactive Multimedia Association
www.bima.co.uk

e-skills UK
www.e-skills.com

UK Web Design Association
www.ukwda.org

WEBSITE DEVELOPER

Qualifications and courses

You do not necessarily need qualifications to become a web developer, but you will need a good knowledge of how to make the site attractive, easy to use and how to make it function.

Employers will also look for evidence of your experience. You should therefore keep a portfolio of your work. Developing and designing sites for local community groups or voluntary agencies could be a useful way to get your portfolio started.

It is important to be familiar with a number of areas, including common operating systems and servers, databases and web programming, networking and security, graphics, animation and web design software.

You should also have an understanding of the World Wide Web Consortium (W3C) standards for website accessibility.

Many who are just starting out in this career now have either a Foundation degree, BTEC HNC/HND award or degree, usually in an IT-related subject. However employers are equally open to those with a degree or other qualification in a related subject such as sicence or maths. A logical mind and good problem-solving skills are highly valued.

Owing to the evolving nature of the IT industry generally, you should try to keep up to date with industry developments and continued continuing professional development(CPD), through courses run by larger companies or membership of The Chartered Institute for IT, is advised.

What the work involves

As a web developer, you will be in charge of working with a client, learning what they require from their website and then programming the website to make sure it functions as it should.

You will often work alongside a web designer to work on the site's appearance.

You will have to make sure that the site can be smoothly integrated into the client's existing network and also find and fix any 'bugs' before the site goes 'live'.

Type of person suited to this work

Excellent web and database programming skills are essential. These should coincide with good problem-solving skills.

You will need to be committed to working to deadlines and to keeping up to date with developments in the latest technology.

It is also very important to have good communication skills, as you will be working with clients and listening to their requirements, before ensuring that their website functions in the way they desire.

Working conditions

Normal working hours are 37 to 40 hours a week, Monday to Friday. Near to deadlines some evening and weekend work may be necessary.

Although self-employment means hours are flexible, you will still need to work whatever hours are necessary to complete the job, which could result in working more hours.

Work is mostly office based. If you work for a company, this will usually mean working on one site, but self-employed web developers will often have to work from home or from the client's premises.

Future prospects

The internet and e-commerce are constantly expanding and consequently, you could find opportunities in a range of industries.

Once you have gained enough experience, you could specialise in a particular area, such as e-commerce.

You could also progress to more senior roles, such as project leader or lead programmer.

Advantages/disadvantages

It is extremely satisfying to see your finished website up and running.

You need to make sure you are up to date with new design trends and software, which could be challenging.

You will also face a lot of pressure from clients, who wish to see their website completed to a deadline and to a high standard.

Money guide

Salaries start at around £20,000 a year.

With experience this can rise to £30,000.

Lead developers could earn around £40,000.

Related opportunities

■ Interactive Media Designer p155
■ Software Developer/Programmer p159
■ Website Designer p164

Further information

BCS, The Chartered Institute for IT
www.bcs.org

e-skills UK
www.e-skills.com

Design, Arts and Crafts

The idea of turning your arts and crafts hobby into a career may be one you like the thought of. Jobs in this sector can involve working in any medium, from textiles to jewellery to metalwork or children's toys. You may find yourself working for a company but many people in this industry are self-employed working for a range of clients. This means you need to be very organised and have brilliant communication skills to ensure you can give your clients exactly what they want.

The jobs featuring in this section are listed below. For similar jobs to these have a look at these sections: *Marketing, Advertising, Media, Print and Publishing* on page 395 and *Performing Arts* starting on page 429.

Qualifications and courses

Entry usually requires an HND, Foundation degree or degree in animation, art and design, or a related area; a relevant postgraduate qualification can be an asset. Entry requirements vary so it is best to check with individual institutions.

A portfolio of relevant work, demonstrated by a show reel, is essential. Unpaid work experience as a general or animation assistant for a company is a good way to build up relevant skills.

Entry to the profession without a degree/HND may be possible, by starting off as a runner fulfilling basic tasks for an employer, however most are graduates.

With experience, you could work towards an NVQ/ SVQ Level 3 in Animation Assistance; Skillset vocational courses for the industry are also available in Design for the Moving Image at Levels 2, 3 and 4. Continuing professional development (CPD) is also possible, with much learning done on the job, and the Skillset website contains a list of relevant additional qualifications that are available. However the fees for many of these courses are funded by the candidates alone.

What the work involves

Animators produce images that appear to come to life on the screen, both creatively and commercially, for use by TV companies, games developers, in advertising, on websites, and in films.

There are 4 specialisms: traditional (2D drawn), 2D computer generated, 3D computer generated and stop frame or stop motion. In all of these styles you will work to create a continuous story.

Type of person suited to this work

You will need strong creative flair and imagination to develop new ideas for animated stories and characters.

You must have excellent computer skills; a knowledge of software such as Flash, Maya and After Effects is essential. However modelling and life drawing are still important.

You must be patient, have a keen eye for detail and be able to work in a team as well as under pressure. Problem-solving skills are also necessary in a job where you might need to adapt to technical challenges.

Working conditions

Your working environment will depend on the type of animation you do. In some jobs, you will work with tools to hand-create images or forms in different materials. You could be on your feet (using your hands) all day: bending, lifting and shaping models.

Many new animation jobs involve work with specialist computer-aided design (CAD) packages at a computer console; this can be done individually or as part of a team. Most of your work will be done during normal office hours except when projects have tight deadlines!

Future prospects

This is a highly competitive field. Although there are some opportunities for traditional drawing-based animators, the main area of growth is in computer generation. Most recruiting now comes from games developers.

Once within the industry, contracts are usually short term, but it is possible to move from working as a key animator, to an animation director role. At senior levels, you would have more creative input and be less directly involved with the technical side. With experience, you could set up as a freelance animator or start your own company.

Advantages/disadvantages

This type of work can be highly satisfying, providing opportunities to develop your own creative ideas and style. Animation is rising in popularity amongst the public. Many animated films are highly successful at the box office.

In more commercial jobs, you would need to produce work under pressure to meet a client's requirements.

Money guide

The Broadcasting, Entertainment, Cinematograph and Theatre Union (BECTU) sets minimum wage guidelines for the industry.

Animators negotiate their own rates and may receive more depending on the project. On avaerage, a new animator can expect to earn £20,000 a year.

An experienced animator could earn £30,000.

Senior animators can expect to earn in excess of £40,000. Contact BECTU for details of current freelance salaries.

Related opportunities

- Cartoonist p169
- Fine Artist/Sculptor p172
- Graphic Designer p175

Further information

Broadcasting Entertainment Cinematograph and Theatre Union
www.bectu.org.uk

Creative Skillset
www.creativeskillset.org

CARTOONIST

Qualifications and courses

A strong portfolio and relevant experience are usually more important than formal qualifications. Most entrants have an HNC/HND or degree in an art and design subject, such as graphic design, illustration or fine art.

There are a small number of cartooning qualifications available through distance learning courses, including a Cartooning Diploma course. These can help you develop your cartooning skills and provide feedback on your work but are not a necessity for employment.

In England, Wales and Northern Ireland, many students take a 1-year art Foundation course as preparation for entry to an art and design degree course. 5 GCSEs/S grades (A*–C/1–3) and a relevant A level/H grade are usually required. In Scotland the first year of an art and design degree course equates to the Foundation year.

What the work involves

You will plan and draw original cartoons and captions. These can be single images, whole cartoon strips or entire books. You will promote and market your work, for example by sending out samples to newspapers and advertising through the internet.

Cartoonists create images for greetings cards, adverts, book illustrations, magazines, newspapers and websites.

A small number of cartoonists are employed to run regular cartoon features in newspapers or other media but others maintain a web comic of their work.

Type of person suited to this work

Creativity and an excellent sense of humour are essential. You should have a wild imagination and be up to date with current trends. Cartoon ideas often draw on situational humour or arise in quick response to headline news.

Even if you use a software art package, good drawing skills are very important. You may have to work to deadlines so need to be well organised, with good business management skills. Self-motivation is important.

As you will be sending out examples of your work to potential employers, you will need to be able to deal with rejection and have the confidence to persevere.

With commissioned work you will need to be able to stick to a design brief and show awareness of the target market as well as incorporating your unique flair.

Working conditions

Most professional cartoonists work on a freelance basis, either in a studio or from home. This can be isolating as many work alone. Much of your time will be spent at a drawing board or a computer where you will either sit or stand using the materials required.

If you are self-employed you will have the freedom to set your own working hours. You might need to attend meetings with clients or potential employers, which could involve travelling long distances and working longer hours.

Future prospects

Most cartoonists work on a freelance basis for a number of employers at the same time. Some work as animators for companies that develop games and other ICT resources.

You could also be employed by publishers, advertising agencies, television studios, newspapers, magazines or theme parks. With experience you could run workshops in schools, libraries and museums. You could also specialise in one form of cartoon such as political or comic strips.

You could also move into other areas such as illustration or graphic design.

Advantages/disadvantages

As cartoonists are usually paid for individual pieces of work they have little job security, especially at the start of their careers.

You would have the satisfaction of creating original work and seeing it in print.

If you are working from home, set up costs are relatively low.

Money guide

Salaries vary greatly owing to the freelance heavy nature of the industry and cartoonists are usually paid on a one-off basis for commissioned work.

However, those starting out in full-time employment can expect to earn around £15,000–£20,000 per year. If you become established, well known, and are in demand for your work, you could earn up to £50,000.

It is possible to earn higher levels of pay by doing commercial work for greetings cards and adverts. Cartoonists creating work to illustrate books can earn royalties from sales.

Related opportunities

- Animator p168
- Fine Artist/Sculptor p172
- Graphic Designer p175

Further information

Arts Council England
www.artscouncil.org.uk

Creative and Cultural Skills
www.ccskills.org.uk

The Cartoon Art Trust
www.cartoonmuseum.org

Qualifications and courses

Most people have a Foundation degree, degree or postgraduate diploma in a relevant subject such as art, costume design, fashion, theatre design or performing arts (production). Most entrants begin their career as a wardrobe assistant or costume maker and progress as they develop experience and build contacts.

Useful courses include the City & Guilds qualification in Design and Craft – Theatre Costume (Levels 2 and 3) and the National Open College Network (NOCN)'s QCF qualifications in Making it in Fashion (Level 1), Skills for the Fashion Industries (Level 2) and Employment in the Fashion Industries (Level 3).

The Royal Academy of Dramatic Art (RADA) offers a 2-year vocational course in Theatre Costume. Those interested in film and TV could apply for the BBC Design Trainee Scheme.

Work experience is invaluable as it helps you to build up a portfolio or showreel of your design work. As well as contacting theatres and film/TV companies, you could become involved in student productions or amateur theatre.

Joining the Society of British Theatre Designers or the Costume Society might facilitate networking and lead to work experience opportunities.

What the work involves

You will design, buy or hire the clothes and accessories worn by casts in films, plays and TV shows.

You will read scripts, research the period and setting of a production and come up with original sketches to best represent the director's vision. You will then decide which fabrics and materials to use. You could also be involved with making costumes or overseeing costume production.

You will be responsible for organising fittings and ensuring that costumes are delivered on time, are comfortable and within budget. Depending on the size of the production, you may also manage a team of costume professionals.

Type of person suited to this work

Creativity and originality are essential. Having the skills to draw designs by hand and to use specialist computer-aided design (CAD) software when required is also important.

You should have a meticulous eye for detail and demonstrate a passion for costume history, fashion and the arts. It is important to be a good communicator and to work well in a team.

You must be organised to ensure that projects are carried out on time, within budget and as requested. As deadlines can be tight, you need the ability to work well under pressure.

Working conditions

Hours are long and irregular, including evenings and weekends. It is possible to work for production companies but most costume designers are freelancers who travel around the UK and sometimes overseas.

You will normally work in a studio using drawing tables, computers, cutting tables and sewing machines.

It is likely that you will be standing for long periods of time and you may do some heavy lifting.

Future prospects

Costume designer vacancies are rarely advertised and most work is centred in major cities such as London and Manchester. It is essential for costume designers to have a strong portfolio and to build up good contacts.

If you work for a large organisation such as the BBC you could progress to head of department or to head of wardrobe for a theatre company.

Advantages/disadvantages

It is rewarding to see your original work on the stage or screen, providing enjoyment for viewers.

You might be able to work flexible hours but they could also be unsocial.

You will often be required to work to tight deadlines which could be stressful.

Money guide

Industry salaries vary depending on the type of employer and geographical location.

Earnings in film and TV are generally higher than in theatre.

The starting salary for a costume designer is typically between £13,000 and £18,000.

As you gain experience, you could earn up to £28,000.

Senior costume designers can achieve £35,000–£40,000.

Freelancers in film and TV can expect to earn about £700 per week.

Related opportunities

- Fashion Designer/Milliner p171
- Tailor/Dressmaker p243
- Visual Merchandiser p187

Further information

Costume Society of Great Britain
www.costumesociety.org.uk

Department for Culture, Media and Sport
www.culture.gov.uk

Design Council
www.designcouncil.org.uk

Qualifications and courses

Entants to this profession usually have a degree, Foundation degree or HNC/HND in a relevant subject such as fashion, textiles or millinery. A postgraduate degree will help those who wish to specialise in a particular area.

Candidates without a degree or graduates from non-related subjects can sometimes enter this industry but they must have relevant work experience and be able to demonstrate expertise and interest in fashion.

City & Guilds teach specific skills such as tailoring, pattern cutting, textile decoration and millinery. The National Open College Network (NOCN) provide QCF qualifications in Making it in Fashion (Level 1), Skills for the Fashion Industries (Level 2) and Employment in the Fashion Industries (Level 3).

All entrants are strongly advised to pursue work experience, either voluntary or paid, to build up their portfolio of designs, technical drawings and garments. Placements show commitment to the profession and provide opportunities to make industry contacts.

Some graduates gain experience with European or American designers before aiming to break into the UK market.

What the work involves

Using your design sense and knowledge of textiles and other materials you will develop clothing, shoes and accessories. A milliner specialises in creating headwear.

You could work in haute couture, ready-to-wear or high street fashion. You will be responsible for analysing trends in fabrics, colours and shapes.

As well as creating initial designs by hand and with computer-aided design (CAD), you may also oversee the manufacture of these items.

Type of person suited to this work

It is essential to have the creativity and the imagination to develop original designs. Having the skills to draw designs by hand and to use specialist CAD software is also important, as are technical skills, such as pattern cutting, and a good eye for design, colour and detail.

These abilities should be balanced with good business sense and the competence to see a project through.

You will also need excellent communication, negotiation and organisational skills to ensure that projects are carried out on time, within budget and as requested.

Working conditions

You will usually work alone or in a small team in a studio. The environment can be dusty and you will be using specialist equipment such as cutting tools and sewing machines.

Hours could be irregular including overtime in the run-up to shows when changes to designs might need to be made at the last minute.

You will also spend some of your time visiting textile producers and clients at their premises which could be overseas.

Future prospects

Most designers work in and around the fashion hub of London.

Career progression depends upon the individual's talent and reputation. You will most likely start as a design assistant and progress to a role as a designer. With experience, it is possible to become a senior or head designer or work in an area such as style consultancy or fashion journalism. There are fewer opportunities for promotion in millinery owing to the smaller size of the industry.

The UK fashion industry has an excellent international reputation, offering the chance to work overseas if desired.

Advantages/disadvantages

Seeing your original ideas in the public eye is satisfying.

You will have the opportunity to travel and meet interesting people of different nationalities.

Working to tight deadlines in the lead-up to shows can be stressful.

Money guide

Salaries vary according to the company type and location.

Newly qualified designers can expect to earn £14,000 to £20,000 per year.

After several years' experience, you could have a salary of £22,000–£45,000.

Senior designers can achieve in excess of £60,000.

Your salary will be determined by your success and the most famous designers have very high incomes.

Related opportunities

- Illustrator/Technical Illustrator p176
- Interior Designer p177
- Visual Merchandiser p187

Further information

Design Council
www.designcouncil.org.uk

Qualifications and courses

There are no specific entry requirements as artistic talent is the most important attribute. However, the majority of artists choose to pursue formal qualifications to increase their chance of success. A degree in fine art or an HNC/HND in art and design would be useful. Postgraduate qualifications in fine art are also available. Sculptors usually have a fine art degree with a specialisation in sculpture.

Entry requirements for degree courses vary. Some institutions require A levels/H grades in relevant subjects, while others accept students on the strength of their portfolio. Some entrants choose to complete a Foundation Diploma in art and design before applying for further education.

Various short courses are available, including evening or weekend classes, 1-week intensive classes, certificates and diplomas.

Graduates who undertake voluntary work experience or work shadowing in the creative industries can improve their employment prospects.

For sculptors, training usually occurs on the job under the supervision of an experienced professional.

What the work involves

Fine artists work with various media such as oil paints and charcoal to create 2D pieces of various sizes. Sculptors create 3D pieces and use materials like clay, stone and metal.

You will be responsible for promoting your work to sponsors, galleries and other organisations by networking or issuing publicity material.

You might organise solo or joint exhibitions in a variety of venues to showcase your work. Some residencies are available in institutes such as schools and prisons.

Type of person suited to this work

You will be creating original works of art so need strong artistic and technical skills, well-developed powers of observation and a vivid imagination.

Self-belief and motivation are important as it takes perseverance to turn an original idea into a finished piece. Sculptors will also require a high level of manual dexterity.

Many artists are self-employed, necessitating good business sense and organisational skills. Strong communication skills will help you to negotiate exhibitions with galleries and network with contacts in the art world.

Working conditions

You will work in a studio, or on location or teach workshops at a residency. Much of your time will be spent alone and you will set your own hours.

Many artistic materials are dusty, oily or may stain and, even wearing overalls, you can expect to get dirty. You might have to work with solvents and other chemicals.

Sculptors will work with dangerous tools such as knives, chisels and welding equipment.

Future prospects

This job demands confidence and persistence as few artists and sculptors earn their living from art alone. You could earn additional income by working in related areas such as arts education, community development and in art galleries.

A developing artist should join networks to make contacts. It is possible to sell your work through a number of galleries, shops, workshop co-operatives, studios and the internet. You could progress from showcasing your work in a group exhibition to securing a solo exhibition. You could eventually have your own studio, secure an agent and have your work displayed in national and international art fairs.

Advantages/disadvantages

The job is fulfilling as you will have the pleasure of seeing customers enjoy and appreciate your art.

It can be an isolated way of life and you may not always receive recognition for your work.

Money guide

Artists' earnings differ depending on their talent, experience and reputation.

It is possible to earn a regular income from your work but many artists have another job to provide a more stable source of income.

The Artists Information Company have an artist's fees toolkit on their website which provides guidance on the rates artists should charge for their work.

Sculptors who secure a post as a sculptor in residence can earn £28,000 per year.

Related opportunities

- Cartoonist p169
- Graphic Designer p175
- Illustrator/Technical Illustrator p176

Further information

Arts Council England
www.artscouncil.org.uk

Department for Culture, Media and Sport
www.culture.gov.uk

Scottish Arts Council
www.scottisharts.org.uk

GEMMOLOGIST

Qualifications and courses

There are no set entry requirements, however many entrants are graduates of relevant subjects such as art, craft, earth sciences, geology, sciences, physics in particular, and technology.

If you have a qualification in a geological subject, and experience in a relevant field such as diamond mining, you could train as a gemmologist. Other useful qualifications include a degree in a geoscience subject such as geology, geophysics or geochemistry. An HND in Gemmology is available from Birmingham City University.

You are likely to train on the job and study for qualifications on a part time basis. This may take 1–4 years. The Gemmological Association (GEM-A) offers qualifications which combine theoretical and practical work.

Jewellery courses and qualifications are available in many institutions throughout the UK.

What the work involves

Gemmologists work with diamonds, gems, precious stones and other ornamental materials. You will identify such materials and examine their quality. This may involve assessing or grading the cut of the stone, or identifying flaws or imitations (stones that are made of synthetic or artificial materials).

You are likely to work for a jewellery house where you will be involved in making evaluations for customers and clients, and buying and selling stones.

You may also be employed by an insurance company where you will make appraisals for those who wish to insure their jewellery.

Type of person suited to this work

It is important that you have an interest in rocks, gems and crystals, design, the earth sciences and geology. You should also have a keen eye for detail as you will have to look for the slightest qualities to make valuations and identify stones.

As your work will mainly be hands-on you should be good with your hands and have good eyesight and memory.

You should be trustworthy and happy to work in high-security environments.

Working conditions

Your working hours will depend on the type of organisation that you work for. If working for a retail jeweller, you might work around 40 hours a week, including weekends.

You could work in an office, laboratory, workshop or studio. If you become involved in mining or travelling to gem markets you might have to work in remote and uncomfortable conditions.

You will use specialist equipment such as lenses, refractometers, spectroscopes and microscopes to examine gemstones. Owing to the nature of your work, you will have to adhere to strict security protocol, including locked doors, barred windows, armed guards, CCTV surveillance and alarm systems.

Future prospects

After you have finished your training and gained qualifications and experience, you may move up to senior management positions.

You may find opportunities in wholesale organisations, retail operations such as jewellery houses, and insurance companies. There may be opportunities to work abroad.

With significant experience and good contacts you may become self-employed, work as a consultant or set up your own business as a jewellery maker or designer.

Advantages/disadvantages

As a self-employed gemmologist your work may involve travel to mines, markets and international gem-selling centres such as Africa, Russia, Australia, Thailand, Brazil or Madagascar.

As you may be working with valuable materials you might have to work in restricted, high security environments.

Money guide

Starting salaries for gemmologists are around £12,000 a year.

As an experienced gemmologist you can earn between £25,000 and £35,000 a year.

You can earn more than £50,000 a year in a senior position.

Related opportunities

- Gold/Silversmith/Engraver p174
- Jeweller p484
- Materials Scientist p524

Further information

GEM-A The Gemmological Association of Great Britain
www.gem-a.info

Jewellery and Allied Industries Training Council
www.jaitc.org.uk

Qualifications and courses

No formal qualifications are required but GCSEs/S grades in art and design or design and technology are useful.

Many different qualifications in design crafts and art and design are available. Entrants could take a City & Guilds Award/Certificate/Diploma in Creative Techniques (Levels 1–3), a UAL Foundation Diploma in Art and Design, a BTEC First in Art and Design (Level 2), a BTEC National in Art and Design (Level 3) or a BTEC Higher National in 3D Design (Levels 4 and 5). Foundation degrees in applied art and 3D design might also be useful.

For the creative side of engraving, there are degrees and master's degrees in metalwork, jewellery making, goldsmithing and silversmithing. Entry for a degree usually requires a portfolio of work, an art and design Foundation course and/or a relevant BTEC National Diploma.

The National Association of Goldsmiths has created many distance learning courses designed to complement a traineeship. Training is done on the job, working with an experienced goldsmith, silversmith or engraver. There is no age limit for entry to training. Alternatively, the Goldsmiths' Company offer Apprenticeships, which involve practical training and qualifications, for those aged 16–21.

What the work involves

Gold/silversmiths create large and small items such as boxes, figures, picture frames and clocks in gold and silver.

Engravers will create and insert or engrave images, words or patterns onto stone, glass, metal or wood. You will be required to work with your hands and use specialist equipment.

You may create objects commissioned by jewellers or individual clients, or develop your own craft pieces to sell through galleries and craft shops.

Type of person suited to this work

This job demands dexterity and conscientiousness. A technical and creative approach is useful to help you plan a piece and decide on the amount of material needed.

An artistic flair is essential in this type of work, as is the ability to see a project through from start to finish. You will need considerable patience to undertake delicate and sometimes repetitive work with specialist materials and equipment.

If you run your own business you will need a confident and determined approach in order to promote yourself and your products. Financial and business skills are also needed.

Working conditions

You will probably work in a workshop or studio – either with other craftspeople or on your own. You may work in a shop and have meetings with customers to discuss pieces of work.

You will use specialist tools for heating, cutting, bending and shaping the metals, which can be dangerous if used incorrectly. You will therefore need to wear eye, face, hand and possibly ear protection for some jobs.

Future prospects

This is a competitive area owing to the high cost of silver and gold and the limited demand for glass and metal engraving.

However, stone engravers are sought by stone masonry firms which are doing less hand-carving than before.

You could work for a specialist company or a shop. With experience and funding, you could set up your own studio/ shop to sell individual pieces.

Advantages/disadvantages

This type of work provides the intense satisfaction of creating attractive and lasting objects.

Working with expensive materials such as glass and metal can be challenging, time-consuming and allows little room for mistakes.

Money guide

It is quite common for a goldsmith/silversmith in the early stages of their career to supplement their income with another job.

Earnings for freelance goldsmiths/silversmiths vary depending upon their sales and reputation.

Trainees could expect to earn about £12,000.

Graduates could have a starting salary of £16,000.

With experience, your earnings might rise to £20,000– £28,000.

The salary progression for an engraver is similar and increases with experience.

Related opportunities

- Gemmologist p173
- Jewellery Designer p178
- Model Maker p180

Further information

British Jewellers' Association
www.bja.org.uk

Crafts Council
www.craftscouncil.org.uk

Institute of Professional Goldsmiths
www.ipgold.org.uk

GRAPHIC DESIGNER

Qualifications and courses

Most entrants have a degree in a visual arts subject such as graphic design, fine art, illustration or 3D design. Minimum requirements for a degree are usually 2 A levels/3 H grades including an art-related subject. It is also recommended to complete a foundation diploma or BTEC National in art and design as entry to an undergraduate art degree without these qualifications is rare.

School leavers have the option to apply for an Apprenticeship in Design and train to become a graphic design assistant or junior graphic designer.

Competition within this industry is strong so you are advised to undertake a work experience placement or internship. Networking with graphic designers during a placement could help you to secure employment in the future. Work experience will also allow you to build up a portfolio of your design work which is essential for interviews. Creating a website to showcase your work is also advised.

In the absence of formal qualifications, a keen interest and an exceptional portfolio may secure a trainee post.

A working knowledge of computer design software such as Quark Xpress, FreeHand, Illustrator or Photoshop is beneficial.

What the work involves

Graphic designers produce original images and designs for use in published or other materials such as leaflets, brochures, websites, logos and stationery. Most work is now done on computer, although manual techniques are occasionally used.

You will need a thorough understanding of clients' needs in order to develop appropriate designs for specific projects.

You will be responsible for producing time and budget schedules and ensuring that they are adhered to.

Type of person suited to this work

It is essential to have a strong creative flair, the imagination to develop original designs and a good eye for layout. Having the skills to draw designs by hand and to use industry-specific graphics or multimedia software packages is also important.

You need good communication skills and the confidence to present ideas to colleagues and clients. It is likely that you will work in a fast-paced environment with tight deadlines so you need to be able to multi-task and work well under pressure.

Organisational skills are essential to ensure that projects are carried out on time, within budget and as requested.

Working conditions

Most of your work will take place at a computer and drawing board within a studio. However, you may undertake external research in order to gain inspiration for a project and you will also be required to attend client meetings to present your ideas.

The majority of graphic designers work 37 hours a week, Monday to Friday. You will be expected to work overtime in order to meet deadlines. Part-time work is available and many experienced designers become freelancers.

Future prospects

In the UK there are about 40,000 businesses in this growing sector, with over half in London and the south-east of England. The diversity of graphic design qualifications available has resulted in increased competition for positions.

There is the possibility to work for a range of clients in an agency or in-house for a large organisation such as a bank. Junior designers can progress to senior level and eventually a director role. With experience there are many freelance opportunities.

Advantages/disadvantages

Creating original work and seeing your ideas being used in the public eye is satisfying.

Competition is becoming increasingly fierce as the number of available qualifications in this field rises.

Money guide

Earnings vary according to the type and size of employer and geographical location.

A junior designer can expect to earn £14,000–£20,000 at the start of their career.

As you gain experience in the field, your salary could increase to £25,000–£35,000.

Senior graphic designers or creative directors can earn between £45,000 and £65,000.

It is possible for a highly regarded freelancer to earn up to £40 per hour.

Related opportunities

- Advertising Art Director p397
- Animator p168
- Illustrator/Technical Illustrator p176

Further information

D&AD
www.dandad.org

Department for Culture, Media and Sport
www.culture.gov.uk

Design Council
www.designcouncil.org.uk

Qualifications and courses

Most professional illustrators have an HNC/HND, Foundation degree or a degree in art and design related subjects such as graphic design, fine art and fashion. A strong portfolio is essential, and an excellent portfolio can be a substitute for academic qualifications.

Technical illustrators are required to demonstrate a good knowledge of science and/or technology depending on your desired specialisation.

Training is provided on the job, and can lead to specialisation in areas such as technical illustration or medical illustration.

The Association of Illustrators (AOI) offers practical advice to illustrators and runs training seminars on business and computer related subjects.

What the work involves

You will create original illustrations for published material such as books, magazines and greetings cards. You may also create images for TV and the internet.

You will work with specialist design software, pen and ink and other media to develop strong designs. Your work will include attending client meetings, agreeing payments and contracts, and working to fulfil specific clients' requirements.

Technical illustrators design accurate graphics or illustrations to accompany and clarify often complex technical information in product and systems manuals, training information, presentations and technical websites.

Type of person suited to this work

You will need strong design skills, a creative flair and imagination for illustration work. You should also be able to work well with computer design software. You will require a good knowledge of legal issues in order to protect your copyright and licence rights.

Technical illustration necessitates high attention to detail and strong technical drawing skills to plan and create accurate images.

Sharing ideas and working around another person's vision or 'brief' demands good communication skills. As many illustrators/technical illustrators work on a self-employed basis, you will need the confidence to promote your services as well as good business and financial sense.

Working conditions

You are likely to work in a shared studio or at your own premises. Technical illustrators occasionally work in offices, and some illustrators are employed in publishing or design houses, but freelancing is increasing.

You will probably use paints and adhesives which may cause respiratory problems or skin allergies for susceptible people.

Future prospects

The internet and email have made it easier for illustrators to promote themselves and find work, and it is now possible to gain work from clients based overseas.

Some people choose to specialise in competitive areas such as medical, botanical or technical illustration.

To subsidise their income, some illustrators also teach, lecture or work in other related areas. A small number write and illustrate their own books. Others supplement their salary by selling illustrations and paintings through galleries.

Advantages/disadvantages

This type of work provides the satisfaction of seeing your work in print and often in the public domain.

Working on a freelance, job-by-job basis can be an insecure way to make a living. Generally, illustrators have a second job to support them during quiet periods.

Money guide

Salaries vary according to employers and individual projects. Projects can range from one image to a series of illustrations.

Illustrators may be paid per project, by the hour or by the day. Hourly pay is around £35 to £45.

Income for employed new entrants is around £14,000 to £18,000 per year.

Experienced illustrators could earn £20,000–£30,000.

With 10 years' experience the best known can earn in excess of £40,000 per year.

Related opportunities

- Cartoonist p169
- Graphic Designer p175
- Medical Illustrator p179

Further information

Association of Illustrators
www.theaoi.com

Institute of Scientific and Technical Communicators
www.istc.org.uk

INTERIOR DESIGNER

Qualifications and courses

The preferred route is to take a degree in interior design, interior architecture or spatial design. Another option is to study for an HNC/HND in interior design or art and design. 5 GCSEs/S grades (A*–C/1–3) and 2 relevant A levels/3 H grades are usually required for degree entry. Many applicants also complete a Foundation Diploma in art and design before applying for higher education.

Voluntary or part-time work experience is usually required prior to securing full-time employment. Placements will enable you to become familiar with computer design software and build up your porfolio of design work. The British Institute of Interior Design, the Chartered Society of Designers and the Directory of Design Consultants provide contact details for interior designers which may be useful when looking for work placements.

In the absence of formal qualifications, an applicant with relevant experience, enthusiasm and an exceptional portfolio may secure a trainee post within a design consultancy or architectural firm.

The City & Guilds Award/Certificate/Diploma in Creative Techniques – Interiors (Levels 1–3) would be useful for developing practical skills.

What the work involves

Interior designers create specific, coordinated styles for homes, commercial spaces and other buildings.

You will be required to assess spaces, produce detailed designs, increasingly using computer-aided design (CAD) software, and choose suitable materials for the project which may include upholstery, wallpaper, furniture and decorative objects.

You will need to get a good understanding of the client's needs and negotiate fees with them. You will provide supervision to ensure that the project is completed accurately and in accordance with the budget and schedule.

Type of person suited to this work

It is essential to have a strong creative flair and the imagination to develop original designs. Having the skills to draw designs by hand and use specialist CAD software are also very important.

You will be required to keep up to date with changes in design and architecture, and to understand building regulations. You also need good business sense and the competency to see a project through.

You should have good communication, negotiation and organisational skills to ensure that projects are carried out on time, within budget and as requested.

Working conditions

The main employers in this sector are design and architectural firms. However, many designers are self-employed and part-time work is possible.

Client meetings often occur in the evenings and at weekends. You could be working on several contracts at the same time and tight deadlines can result in overtime.

Your work will be divided between meeting clients in their own premises and working in your studio or other work space. Smart dress is expected and protective clothing may be required on site.

Future prospects

The contribution of design towards the UK economy is very important and the significance of this intensely competitive sector continues to grow.

Although many interior designers work for design and architectural companies, some are freelance and many choose self-employment, either immediately after graduation or once they have gained experience.

After several years you could progress to a partner role in a consultancy. The UK industry has an excellent international reputation so you could work overseas.

Advantages/disadvantages

Creating original work and seeing your ideas being used in a practical or decorative way is satisfying.

Working as a freelance designer can result in greater flexibility.

Meeting deadlines and budgets can be stressful.

Money guide

A junior/trainee interior designer would usually start on £15,000–£20,000.

Those with experience can expect to earn £20,000–£35,000 a year.

Senior designers can achieve £45,000–£60,000.

Freelance designers set their own rate based upon their reputation and experience.

Related opportunities

- Illustrator/Technical Illustrator p176
- Model Maker p180
- Visual Merchandiser p187

Further information

British Institute of Interior Design
www.biid.org.uk

Chartered Society of Designers
www.csd.org.uk

Design Council
www.designcouncil.org.uk

DESIGN, ARTS AND CRAFTS

CRCI: E

177

DESIGN, ARTS AND CRAFTS

CRCI: E

Qualifications and courses

There are no academic requirements in order to become a jewellery designer. However many courses and programmes are available which may help you to develop your skills.

You can take GCSEs/S grades and A levels/H grades in art and design or design and technology, which will help you to gain entry to this profession or to higher level courses. These include HNDs, Foundation degrees or degrees in art and design or craft making such as goldsmithing, silversmithing and jewellery design. It may be possible to move across from another relevant subject such as fashion design, textile design, fine art or applied arts if you build up a suitable portfolio.

If you are interested in gold and silver craftwork specifically you may benefit from a BTEC National Certificate or Diploma course in Design Crafts which are available at some colleges.

However, qualifications are not as important as craft skills. Work placements can help you to accumulate experience of the jewellery industry and build up a network of contacts which will help you to develop skills and find buyers and sellers for your work.

What the work involves

Jewellery designers are involved in each aspect of the production of decorative pieces of jewellery of various types, including those with materials such as gold, silver, precious metals and stones.

You will research the design and the function of a piece; its symbolism, the materials used, the cost, the potential buyer and even current trends.

You will prepare detailed drawings which you or a craftworker will construct using traditional crafting methods or using high-tech machinery. A design may be for a one-off piece or part of a range of pieces. You will undertake tasks such as stone cutting and setting, model-making, mounting, engraving, enamelling, welding, chain-making, cleaning and polishing.

Type of person suited to this work

You should have a strong interest in art, design and craftwork. As your sales may be influenced by the current design marketplace, you should keep up to date with jewellery fashion and design trends.

You must have a keen eye for detail and patience as you will be working with small scales and intricate and delicate designs.

You will need to be organised and self-motivated as you will probably be working on a variety of projects at the same time. You should also be able to visualise 2D designs as 3D objects.

Working conditions

If you are employed by a company you will usually work 35–40 hours a week, Monday to Friday, including late nights or weekend work when deadlines are approaching.

You can also work on a freelance basis or become self-employed. If you are self-employed you are likely to work on commission and produce designs specifically tailored to the client's requirements.

You may work in a studio which can be bright and airy or in a large workshop, which may be noisy and dusty. You must wear protective clothing.

Future prospects

As you gain experience and build up a good reputation you may be able to become self-employed. To stay ahead in the industry you should attend trade fairs and exhibitions.

As an employed goldsmith or silversmith you may be able to progress to management positions or retail positions such as international buyer.

Advantages/disadvantages

You may be able to work from your own designs and see your creations become popular pieces.

As a self-employed jewellery designer you may find that without the right support system in areas such as promotion, marketing and sales it can be difficult to become established.

Money guide

As a graduate your salary can start at around £15,000 per year.

This can increase to anywhere between £25,000 and £45,000 or more with experience.

Your salary will depend greatly on factors such as whether or not you are self-employed, experienced and have enough success to gain a reputation within the industry.

Related opportunities

- Fashion Designer/Milliner p171
- Gold/Silversmith/Engraver p174
- Product Designer p183

Further information

Crafts Council
www.craftscouncil.org.uk

178

MEDICAL ILLUSTRATOR

Qualifications and courses

To work as a medical illustrator you need A levels/H grades and a relevant degree. Medical illustrators usually enter the profession as trainees and learn on the job while working towards a medical illustration qualification.

The Medical Artists' Educational Trust postgraduate Diploma in Medical Art is available in Manchester and London. Entrants need a degree and a relevant portfolio. Once you complete the course you automatically become a member of the trust.

A voluntary national register for medical illustrators was formed in 2010 by the Committee for the Accreditation of Medical Illustration Practitioners (CAMIP). The register was formed in anticipation of required state registration with the Health Professions Council (HPC). At present registration with HPC is not mandatory to practise medical illustration, but legislation is currently moving towards this goal.

Qualified clinical illustrators will need to have a degree or postgraduate degree in clinical photography.

What the work involves

Medical illustrators create annotated or labelled images to provide visual information to professionals and trainees working in medical care, research and education.

You may also work as a medical photographer or video producer (digital technician), or combine all these functions in one role.

You will have to record images of patients and develop graphics for health/medical publications such as information leaflets and websites. You could work in wards, operating theatres, pathology labs, mortuaries and clinical exam centres.

Type of person suited to this work

Good visual sense and attention to detail is very important. You should have excellent technical skills to work with equipment such as videos and cameras, and will have to work creatively yet accurately with computer design packages.

As you will have to record images of patients, a sensitive, tactful and ethical approach is necessary. You should also have a knowledge of physiology and anatomy.

Also required is the ability to communicate with all sorts of people, some of whom could be very ill. You must be able to cope with upsetting situations and sights, for example, if visiting someone who is terminally ill.

Working conditions

You may be based within a group of hospitals and other centres and have to travel regularly between these. During the day you will visit theatres, wards, training centres and mortuaries – all of which could involve distressing sights and intense odours. You may have to be on-call at night to photograph emergency operations.

Using a computer and software design packages, you will work within an office or studio to prepare and produce images and visual information. You may also have to record laboratory results.

Future prospects

Whilst this is a relatively small and quite competitive area of work, there is a steady need for accurate medical visual information.

Gaining a range of technical skills and experience rather than specialising in one area could open more opportunities.

After training, it is possible to progress within one organisation to head of department or you could go on to provide freelance services for medical establishments or medical and scientific publications.

Advantages/disadvantages

This job gives the satisfaction of providing valuable visual information to help medical professionals and their patients.

You may have the opportunity to freelance, which offers flexibility.

You will work with sick and sometimes distressed patients and may have to deal with upsetting sights. You may also have to be on-call at night in order to photograph emergency operations.

Money guide

Trainee illustrators can expect to earn between £21,000 and £27,000 a year.

With experience, senior medical illustrators can earn around £30,000.

Up to £55,000 is possible for a head of department in a university teaching hospital.

Medical illustrators in large university teaching hospitals could be employed on a number of pay scales covering technicians, medical laboratory officers, or sterile services technicians. Check with the university teaching hospitals for more details.

Related opportunities

- Fine Artist/Sculptor p172
- Graphic Designer p175
- Photographer p412

Further information

Association of Illustrators
www.theaoi.com

Health Professions Council
www.hpc-uk.org

Institute of Medical Illustrators
www.imi.org.uk

DESIGN, ARTS AND CRAFTS

CRCI: E

MODEL MAKER

Qualifications and courses

There are no formal entry requirements. However, most entrants complete a model-making course and a portfolio of work is usually required.

The ability to work with your hands, using specialist tools, is required.

There are a wide variety of courses available including a City & Guilds Level 2 Certificate in Engineering, ABC Level 3 Award in Model Making and Presentation, and degrees in 3D design. Entry requirements vary but are very competitive and most institutions will expect some GCSEs/S grades in subjects such as maths, design and technology, and physics. At least 2 A levels (or equivalent) in a relevant subject are required for degree courses.

Foundation courses are available in art and design which can help applicants to build up a portfolio of work. Entry via an Apprenticeship/Skillseekers programme may also be possible in your area.

Professional bodies such as the Design Council and the Design and Art Direction (D&AD) provide various opportunities for continuing professional development (CPD). A number of workshops are available and improvement is driven through design award schemes. The Institution of Engineering Designers operates a membership scheme with events and classes for its members.

What the work involves

Working with materials such as fibreglass, resin, wood and rubber you will create 3D images or models.

You will construct detailed and accurate models of buildings, prototypes of items, engineering products and figures for museums and TV or film companies.

You will work with clients to develop their ideas into a convincing and practical model, deciding which materials to use. You will plan the model using technical drawings or computer software.

Type of person suited to this work

You will need a strong creative flair to visualise and develop models. Producing detailed models out of fragile materials demands tremendous patience and good technical skills. You should have a logical approach in order to plan and create accurate work.

The tasks will demand great attention to detail and good eyesight. A feel for, and interest in, design will enable you to create well-planned models.

You will also need a basic knowledge of maths and the ability to understand technical drawings. The capacity to work effectively with computer design packages is increasingly important in this area of work.

Working conditions

Most model makers work standard office hours, but evening and weekend work may be required to meet deadlines.

Your work will be carried out in a studio, where you will wear protective clothing to suit the materials and tools you are using. This could include eye, ear and skin protection. Sometimes you may be based in an office, planning models with specialist design software.

You may need to travel around the UK or overseas to meet clients and assemble or install models for them.

Future prospects

Most model makers work within London and the south-east of England. Whilst this is quite a small area of work, demand is stable.

You could focus on architectural model making and work for a large architectural practice, or work for museums to create historical models for display purposes. However, most model makers work on a freelance basis and are paid contract by contract.

Some model makers choose to set up their own business after developing a strong portfolio and good reputation.

Advantages/disadvantages

This job can provide the satisfaction of developing original work.

You will need to create highly detailed work to fairly limited deadlines, which can be stressful.

Some of the materials you work with may produce unpleasant or dangerous fumes.

Money guide

Starting salaries are between £19,000 and £20,000 per year.

With experience this rises to between £23,000 and £30,000.

At senior level, with many years of experience, you could earn up to £45,000.

Related opportunities

- Fine Artist/Sculptor p172
- Graphic Designer p175
- Toymaker/Designer p186

Further information

Creative and Cultural Skills
www.ccskills.org.uk

D&AD
www.dandad.org

Design Council
www.designcouncil.org.uk

Qualifications and courses

There are no set qualifications for this type of work; however you will require the specialist skills to make/repair your particular type (family) of instruments.

BTEC awards in Music Technology are available and courses in musical instrument making are available up to degree level from specific colleges and universities, such as London Metropolitan University. Entry requirements for these courses vary, but it will be necessary to have relevant GCSEs/S grades and A levels/H grades for some courses. For full details of course providers visit the National Association of Musical Instrument Repairers website.

When you begin employment you may receive on the job training from an experienced instrument maker/repairer and develop skills through part-time, specialist courses.

What the work involves

You will make, repair and service musical instruments such as pianos, flutes and violins but normally will specialise within one family.

The work will include building new instruments and working with specialised equipment and materials, replacing worn-down or broken parts of instruments and checking for the cause of specific faults by undertaking assessments. This could range from fine tuning to significant maintenance work.

You will work with customers, dealing with repair requests or commissions for new instruments.

Type of person suited to this work

A passion for music and a practical understanding of how musical instruments function is essential. They are complex objects so you will need a good eye for detail, excellent hearing and a patient approach.

Strong technical skills will enable you to design, create or repair instruments. You will need to be dexterous and confident in working with your hands and in using materials such as wood and glue.

You need to have excellent communication and interpersonal skills in order to deal with customers, particularly if you are self-employed.

Working conditions

You will work with a range of specialised tools in the workshop of a specialist company or from home if self-employed.

You will normally work a 40-hour week, Monday to Friday, however if you are self-employed you will often have to adapt your working hours to meet demand and client's timetables.

With larger instruments, such as pianos, organs or timpani, you will need to visit private homes and other locations (such as concert halls, theatres or music studios) to do repairs on-site.

It would be useful to have your own driving licence and transport.

You need to have strong manual handling skill. This job may be difficult for people with skin or respiratory conditions owing to some of the specialist materials used.

Future prospects

This is a specialised area of work, but you could work for educational music departments, major orchestras, opera houses and theatres, rehearsal studios, retailers, and individual musicians.

Specialising in a specific area such as classical guitars or making unusual instruments from commissions can enhance your reputation and build a strong client base in niche markets.

You may also be able to sell instruments to enhance your income as you will have ready access to the market.

A lot of people are self-employed and some music shops will publicise local repairers, instrument makers and tuners, rather than employing their own.

Advantages/disadvantages

Many musical instrument repairers/makers are freelance and work on a project-by-project basis, which can create some job insecurity.

This career has excellent fringe benefits as you could work for some of the best musical talents in the UK.

Money guide

In some parts of the country there is not sufficient work for full-time employment so earnings for instrument makers/repairers will depend on your location, the local music scene and your specialism.

Work permitting, you could earn around £16,000–£20,000 per year once trained.

The most experienced people can earn up to £30,000 a year.

Related opportunities

- Art Therapist p292
- Musician p442
- Private Music Teacher p200

Further information

British Violin Making Association
www.bvma.org.uk

Crafts Council
www.craftscouncil.org.uk

Institute of Musical Instrument Technology
www.imit.org.uk

National Association of Musical Instrument Repairers
www.namir.org.uk

DESIGN, ARTS AND CRAFTS

CRCI: E

PICTURE FRAMER

Qualifications and courses

There are no formal educational requirements. However, gaining relevant qualifications will help you to learn the specific skills and techniques that the job requires. Courses are available from local colleges and education services. These could be residential, weekend or part-time courses and they might last from 8 weeks up to a year.

An interest and experience in woodwork, metalwork or textiles would be useful. GCSEs/S grades, A levels/H grades, certificates, diplomas, NVQs, Foundation degrees or degrees can also be an advantage; relevant subjects include art and design, creative arts and contemporary crafts.

Training is usually done on the job alongside an experienced professional. In order to work with high-value items, framers need to be trained to conservation standards.

Picture framers are able to work towards the Guild Commended Framer (GCF) qualification from the Fine Art Trade Guild, which involves both practical and written assessments. This qualification sets an internationally recognised standard for picture framers.

What the work involves

You will plan and create attractive and protective surrounds or frames for prints, paintings, photographs and three-dimensional objects. Working with specialist equipment and materials you will create strong, high-quality frames.

Helping customers choose the most suitable style and size of frame will be part of your job and you will advise them on the most practical and appropriate method of framing and glazing the artwork.

If you work on a self-employed basis you will need to promote your services to potential customers.

Type of person suited to this work

Creativity is essential in order to design the frame. You will also need good customer service skills. Technical skills and the ability to work safely with potentially dangerous equipment are highly important.

Paying attention to detail and taking a pride in your work will ensure that you produce high-quality frames. You will need to be able to work under pressure as short deadlines can be a part of this job. You should also be commercially aware. If self-employed, you will require business, financial and marketing skills to be successful.

Working conditions

You could work in a shop or workshop. When working in the shop you will have to deal with customers who can sometimes be rude or confrontational if dissatisfied. Workshops can be noisy and busy.

Picture framers generally work 40 hours a week, with weekend work often needed and overtime during busy periods. Many picture framers work on a part-time basis.

Picture framers work with potentially dangerous equipment such as specialist cutting machinery so you will need to be aware of health and safety requirements and wear protective clothing.

Future prospects

Success depends upon the skills and reputation of the individual.

Many picture framers set up their own studios or shops where they also sell works of art and artists' materials. Others work solely in framing and are employed in larger workshops, mass-producing framed prints and mirrors. There is the possibility of promotion to a supervisory or managerial role in bigger companies. Some picture framers take additional training so that they can teach part time.

Advantages/disadvantages

This job provides the satisfaction of creating enduring and high quality items.

If you are employed in a gallery or museum, you will have the opportunity to work with famous and valuable pieces of art.

The nature of the work requires you to be precise, careful and patient.

Money guide

The starting salary for a picture framer is usually about £12,000 to £14,000.

With experience, your earnings could rise to £15,000–£20,000.

Specialists who work with high value artwork in a gallery or museum could achieve £20,000–£25,000.

Earnings for self-employed framers vary depending on location, expertise and the success of their business.

Related opportunities

- Conservator/Restorer p349
- Gold/Silversmith/Engraver p174
- Model Maker p180

Further information

Fine Art Trade Guild
www.fineart.co.uk

Institute of Conservation
www.icon.org.uk

PRODUCT DESIGNER

ENTRY LEVEL **5**

DESIGN, ARTS AND CRAFTS

CRCI: E

Qualifications and courses

Entry to this profession usually requires an HNC/HND, Foundation degree or degree in product design, industrial design or a related subject. Some degree courses include an industrial placement. Design courses can be centred on the art or engineering sides of product design. Students should check which universities offer modules in areas they would like to specialise in. Those choosing the art-based route sometimes take a 1-year Foundation course in art and design before their degree.

Entry requirements for a degree are usually 2 A levels/3 H grades and 5 GCSEs/S grades (A*–C/1–3). For an HND you need 1 A level/H grade in an art and design subject and 3 GCSEs/S grades (A*–C/1–3). A BTEC qualification in art and design or 3D design could also be useful.

A postgraduate qualification enables you to specialise in a specific area and may provide an advantage when working with certain European clients.

Previous experience through industrial placements, freelance work or design competitions is invaluable. This sector is very competitive so you should make contacts during work placements or by joining the Chartered Society of Designers. Employers will look for a strong portfolio which showcases your design work.

What the work involves

Product designers create new products and improve the design, functionality or cost efficiency of existing products. These could be day-to-day products like tables or specialist ones like medical equipment.

You will decide upon a design brief with your client and carry out research into similar products and consumer behaviour. You will use both traditional drawing techniques and specialist computer software to develop appropriate designs.

You will select materials, produce prototypes and ensure that the project is completed on time and to budget.

Type of person suited to this work

This job requires both creativity and technical expertise. You should have a good eye for design as well as technical drawing and IT skills. It is important to understand how different materials and production methods function.

You need good communication skills and an understanding of clients' needs and consumer behaviour.

Problem-solving and organisational skills are essential to ensure projects are completed on time and within budget.

Working conditions

The majority of product designers work 37 hours a week, Monday to Friday. You will be expected to work extra hours in order to meet deadlines. Part-time and freelance work is quite common.

Most of your work will take place in a bright, clean studio or office. However, you will undertake some experiments and material testing in lab conditions, using specialist tools and equipment. You might also have to visit production factories which may be dusty and noisy.

Future prospects

Product designers work in manufacturing firms and design companies which produce material for a variety of sectors. Employment is available all over the UK but most design consultancies are based in London and the south-east of England.

There is strong competition for entry level jobs but there is a shortage of experienced product designers with a high level of technical expertise. Experienced designers may have the opportunity to work abroad or freelance. You could progress to a senior or managerial level.

Advantages/disadvantages

You will have the opportunity to use your imagination and technical skills.

Creating original work that is used by the public is satisfying.

Competition for entry level jobs is fierce.

Working to tight budgets and project deadlines can be stressful.

Money guide

Earnings vary according to the geographical location, type and size of employer.

Starting salaries for junior designers are around £14,000–£20,000.

Those with experience typically earn £25,000–£40,000 per year.

Senior product designers can achieve £45,000–£65,000.

Contract or freelance designers set their own rates depending upon their reputation and client contacts.

Related opportunities

- Manufacturing/Production Engineer p229
- Toolmaker p246
- Toymaker/Designer p186

Further information

Chartered Society of Designers
www.csd.org.uk

183

SIGNWRITER/ SIGNMAKER

Qualifications and courses

There are no formal educational requirements, but relevant vocational qualifications can be useful. NVQs/ SVQs at Levels 2 and 3 are available in Signmaking.

Training is usually done on the job.

Many employers offer Apprenticeships/Skillseekers for people aged between 16 and 24. Applicants normally require 4 GCSEs/S grades (A*–D/1–4), including maths, English language, a science and an art and design subject, or other evidence of aptitude.

It is also possible to take a full- or part-time course in signwriting and signmaking.

You can specialise in this area after taking a general art and design course such as a Foundation degree or a HND/C.

What the work involves

You will design, plan and produce signs with graphic images, lettering and logos to publicise companies, attract customers and draw attention to specific locations.

You will work closely with customers to develop appropriate, appealing designs that match their requirements.

You could work with any number of different materials and methods; from plastics to glass to sketching as well as computer-aided design (CAD).

You will produce signs for shop fronts, roadsides, hospitals, vehicles and even boats!

Type of person suited to this work

As you will be creating signs to interest or warn people, you will need strong graphic design skills. A creative flair and drawing skills are also important.

You will need an understanding of the materials you work with and good manual skills.

You must be methodical and have strong attention to detail. Technical skills will allow you to work with a range of equipment. ICT skills and an ability to use programs such as Omega are becoming increasingly important.

Good written and verbal communication skills, along with excellent people skills, will help you to meet clients' requirements accurately and avoid expensive errors.

Working conditions

You could work within a studio or manufacturing site, which can get messy and noisy.

You might attend meetings with customers and make site visits. Much of your time will be spent drafting signs at a computer using special software.

You may work with large or small-scale specialist equipment, with printing inks and chemical finishes, which can affect people with skin or respiratory conditions.

Future prospects

This is a fairly competitive area; however, the demand for high-quality signs from a range of organisations means that there are many opportunities.

You could work in the more commercial side of signwriting, within a specialist company on the design or manufacturing side, or you could work within the more creative, hand-crafted side of the industry.

Some signwriters go into set design for theatre. With experience, you could start your own business – perhaps specialising in pub or restaurant signs.

Advantages/disadvantages

This kind of work can provide opportunities to be creative and to use your imagination to help customers, for example when designing a company logo.

You might need to travel frequently to visit a range of locations, to take measurements or photographs, with the option of working abroad.

Money guide

Trainees and apprentices are most likely to start at around £12,000.

With experience, signwriters can earn £17,000–£24,000 per year.

With management responsibilities you could earn up to £30,000.

Self-employed signwriters will earn more.

Related opportunities

- Cartoonist p169
- Fine Artist/Sculptor p172
- Graphic Designer p175

Further information

British Sign and Graphics Association
www.bsga.co.uk

Creative and Cultural Skills
www.ccskills.org.uk

Faversham House Group
www.fhgmedia.com

Qualifications and courses

It is possible to enter the industry as a craft assistant in a design studio and work your way up. However, most people have an HND, a degree, or postgraduate diploma in theatre design or a related art and design subject.

For a degree you should have 2 A levels/3 H grades or a BTEC national diploma/certificate in a relevant subject, 5 GCSEs/S grades (A*–C/1-3) and a good portfolio. For an HNC/D you are normally required to have 1 A level/H grade.

A design qualification is useful as it enables you to further build your portfolio which will be essential when securing employment. You also must demonstrate a passion and commitment to stage and set design.

It is helpful to obtain experience before entering this highly competitive profession as it highlights commitment to the industry. This can be achieved by means of an unpaid placement, freelance work and involvement in student productions or design competitions.

What the work involves

Stage/set designers are responsible for the visual elements of a theatre (stage designer), TV or film production (set designer) including sets, locations and possibly props and costumes.

From background research, you will be required to create original ideas which accurately reflect the relevant style and historical period of the piece.

Working closely with the production team, you will oversee the development and installation of the sets and ensure that everything is delivered on time and within budget.

Type of person suited to this work

It is essential to have a strong creative flair and a good eye for design. Having the skills to use specialist computer-aided design (CAD) software, to draw designs by hand and to create scale models when required is also very important.

You should be detail driven and demonstrate a passion for history, culture and the performing arts. These abilities should be balanced with good communication skills to aid leadership and self-promotion.

Organisational skills are important to ensure that projects are carried out on time, within budget and as requested. As deadlines can be tight, you should also have the ability to work well under pressure.

Working conditions

Designers either work directly for the production company or freelance. Working hours are long and unsociable and travel may be involved. You will be expected to work supplementary hours in order to meet deadlines.

Your work will be divided between being in a studio designing and building models of the sets, and consequent supervision or involvement in their creation. Normally this happens behind the scenes in theatres, television studios or purpose-built warehouses.

You will work on large pieces, which necessitate the use of ladders and scaffolding.

Future prospects

Stage designers work for theatres and opera houses and may have the opportunity to oversee a travelling production. There is fierce competition for entry level positions.

Set designers can work for the BBC or one of the 1500 production firms in the country.

Part-time work is difficult to find and although there are many freelancers in the industry, work can be sporadic.

Advantages/disadvantages

The creation of original work and seeing your ideas being used in the public eye and in high profile productions is satisfying. Working as a freelancer can also result in greater flexibility.

Competition for entry level jobs is fierce and a strong portfolio and good networking skills are important.

Meeting tight deadlines can result in high stress levels.

Money guide

Most designers work freelance as very few companies have resident designers now.

Earnings will be dependent on individual ability, location and the contract size.

Newly qualified assistant designers in a theatre can expect to earn about £15,600 per year. On a film set, designers will earn the equivalent of around £14,000 a year.

This can rise to between £20,000 and £40,000 with experience. Very well-established designers can earn considerably more.

Contact the Broadcasting Entertainment Cinematographic and Theatre Union (BECTU) or Equity for information on minimum pay guidelines.

Related opportunities

- Costume Designer p170
- Interior Designer p177
- TV, Film and Radio Production Assistant/Runner p426

Further information

Broadcasting Entertainment Cinematograph and Theatre Union
www.bectu.org.uk

Design Council
www.designcouncil.org.uk

Society of British Theatre Designers
www.theatredesign.org.uk

DESIGN, ARTS AND CRAFTS

CRCI: E

Qualifications and courses

There are no formal entry requirements but many entrants have a background in art and design. An HND or degree can be an advantage and relevant subjects include art and design, product design, graphic design or 3D design. Institutions sometimes have links with toy manufacturers which can provide a useful first step into the industry. Minimum entry requirements for a degree are usually 2 A levels/3 H grades or equivalent.

Coventry University offers either a BA or MDes degree in product design with the opportunity to specialise in toy design and making.

In England, Wales and Northern Ireland many students take a 1-year Foundation course as preparation for entry to an art and design degree; 5 GCSEs/S grades (A*–C/1–3) and a relevant A level/H grade are also usually required. In Scotland, the first year of a degree equates to the Foundation year.

Alternatively, those who do not wish to pursue a degree could take relevant courses such as the City & Guilds Award/Certificate/Diploma in Creative Techniques (Levels 1–3), the BTEC Award/Certificate/Diploma in Design Crafts (Level 3) or the BTEC Higher National in 3D design (Levels 4 and 5).

What the work involves

You will design, plan, test and create toys for babies, children and even adults!

As a traditional toymaker, you could use early designs to make toys by hand, such as doll houses and rocking horses. If you work for a large manufacturer you will develop new products based on original ideas and sketches.

You will spend time promoting your work and design services to clients and customers. Your work could be sold in shops or at craft and toy fairs.

Type of person suited to this work

You will need creative flair to develop original ideas. Practical design skills and an active imagination will help you create long-lasting and functional toys. A genuine interest in how individuals respond to toys will help you design appealing items that sell well.

If creating objects by hand, as many toymakers do, you will need good manual handling skills and an understanding of the materials you work with. Knowledge of 3D design is fast becoming essential.

If self-employed, you will also need good business and financial skills and the confidence to promote your work.

Working conditions

Most toymakers/designers spend a lot of time in a workshop, planning and developing their products. Some of the materials used can be dangerous so you might need to wear protective clothing.

If employed as a toy designer by a manufacturer, you may work purely with computer design software and create, rather than construct, your designs.

Future prospects

Public interest in traditional toys and games is growing. You could work on a self-employed basis, making and designing toys. Some toymakers/designers own shops where they sell their own handmade toys. A growing number sell their products at craft fairs, on the internet or by mail order. A small number of toymakers also restore antique toys.

There is steady demand for innovative toys in high street shops and you will always have an emerging potential market for new products. There may be opportunities in buying, marketing and business development with larger toy manufacturers.

Advantages/disadvantages

Creating fun, attractive toys which will be enjoyed by children and adults alike is a rewarding career.

It is satisfying to see your original designs come to life as a finished product.

Competition is high and vacancies for toy designers are limited at manufacturing companies.

Those who become self-employed can expect it to take time and hard work to establish a business.

Money guide

Starting salaries for toy designers working for toy manufacturers range from £10,000 to £15,000 per year.

Those with experience who work in a large company can expect £23,000–£35,000.

The most successful designers of popular toys can achieve in excess of £45,000.

Traditional toymakers are usually self-employed and salaries will depend on the success of the business.

Related opportunities

- Animator p168
- Carpenter/Joiner p79
- Picture Framer p182

Further information

British Toymakers Guild
www.toymakersguild.co.uk

Crafts Council
www.craftscouncil.org.uk

Design Council
www.designcouncil.org.uk

Qualifications and courses

There are no formal entry requirements for this type of work but many candidates will have studied for relevant qualifications in design or retail.

Many different courses are available at Level 5 in display or design, marketing or retail. Degree courses in visual merchandising usually require 2 A levels/H grades and 5 GCSEs/S grades (A*–C/1–3) or equivalent. Foundation degrees typically require 1 A level/H grade and 5 GCSEs/S grades (A*–C/1–3) or equivalent.

Other relevant qualifications include City & Guilds Diploma in Retail – Visual Merchandising (Level 3), the Fashion Retail Academy's Diploma in Visual Merchandising (Level 4) and the Certificate in Display and Visual Merchandising from the British Display Society. ABC also offer a Diploma in Retail Skills (Visual Merchandising) at Level 3.

The Intermediate Apprenticeship in Retail involves training for the visual merchandiser role and you can progress to the level of visual merchandiser supervisor by taking the Advanced Apprenticeship.

A portfolio of art and design work is usually required by employers. Experience in display and the retail/exhibition sector can also be helpful.

What the work involves

Using your technical design skills, you will plan and design eye-catching window or shop front displays for shops, businesses and other organisations. You will work closely with clients to make sure that your designs meet their requirements.

Once you have identified materials and props for a window display, you will design an arrangement to create a striking theme or effect.

You might also provide advice to other shop branches or organisations on successful display design.

Type of person suited to this work

It is important to have strong creative ability, as well as excellent technical drawing and computer-aided design (CAD) skills. You need to have excellent communication skills to be able to balance your vision with that of your client and work with a wide range of people.

Certain roles will require you to keep up with new trends and products in fashion and culture. You must also be numerate, as one of your responsibilities will be to manage project budgets. A good level of fitness is also needed as assembling displays can be tiring.

Working conditions

Normally, you will be working indoors with different hand tools, materials, fabrics and the products to be displayed in the window or display. The work can often be pressured owing to strict deadlines. You might have to work late especially in the build up to holiday seasons such as Christmas.

The job can involve a great deal of manual work. You will do lots of lifting and be on your feet for long periods, which can be very tiring. A driving licence would be useful as you will have to travel to meet suppliers and visit exhibitions and different company stores.

Future prospects

There are a range of opportunities, for example working for specialist display consultancy firms, large retailers, museums and other visitor attractions.

You will probably start as a junior and progress to a more senior position as supervisor, head designer, merchandiser and possibly department manager.

If you work for a multinational company, the opportunity may arise to work abroad. You could also go on to teach or lecture in design-related subjects. With experience, some display designers set up their own businesses or provide consultancy support to other organisations.

Advantages/disadvantages

This type of work can involve high levels of pressure owing to tight deadlines.

You will have the satisfaction of seeing people enjoying your displays and giving you positive feedback.

You could have the opportunity to work with special effects like animatronics.

Money guide

Starting salaries are usually in the range of £12,000 to £16,000.

Once you have gained experience, your salary could rise to £20,000–£25,000.

Those who reach a senior level earn about £45,000.

The most successful designers can achieve up to £60,000.

Related opportunities

- Interior Designer p177
- Model Maker p180
- Retail Buyer p489

Further information

British Display Society
www.britishdisplaysociety.co.uk

Design Council
www.designcouncil.org.uk

DESIGN, ARTS AND CRAFTS

CRCI: E

Education and Training

To work in this sector you need to be motivated and enthusiastic about other people's learning, whether it is adults or children. If you chose to teach, the range of subjects available is huge so whatever your interest – languages, art, sciences, cooking, sports – you can become a teacher in that field. Jobs in this sector require a multitude of skills including: creativity, imagination, numerical skills, good communication and organisational skills and, in some cases, having a lot of patience!

The jobs featured in this section are listed below. For similar jobs to the ones in this sector turn to *Social Work and Counselling Services* on page 567.

- Community Education Officer p190
- Dance Teacher p191
- Early Years Specialist/Nursery Nurse p192
- Education and Childcare Inspector p193
- Education Welfare Officer p194
- Further Education Lecturer p195
- Learning Mentor p196
- NVQ/SVQ Assessor p197
- Play Worker/Hospital Play Specialist p198
- Primary School Teacher p199
- Private Music Teacher p200
- School Administrator/Secretary p201
- School Business Manager/Bursar p202
- Secondary School Teacher p203
- Special Educational Needs Teacher p204
- Teacher of English to Speakers of Other Languages p205
- Teaching Assistant/Learning Support Assistant p206
- Work-based Training Instructor p207

COMMUNITY EDUCATION OFFICER

ENTRY LEVEL 5

Qualifications and courses

You can gain entry to this profession with a degree, a diploma or an HND/Foundation degree. A qualification in a relevant subject such as community education, sociology, social sciences, educational studies or youth work may give you an advantage. Some undergraduate and postgraduate courses provide part-time or distance learning and many employers will support you while you are studying.

Employers usually seek candidates who have combined their qualification with paid or voluntary community experience. Some entrants come from a teaching background, while others have experience in the youth and community sector.

If you have no qualifications but you have accumulated significant experience then it may be possible for you to secure a post in the voluntary sector. However, it is likely that you will be required to have academic qualifications to reach a senior level.

You can gain experience, learn about the sector and decide if it is an area you would like to work in by volunteering when you are a student. Information and advice about voluntary work is available from YouthNet, the Workers' Educational Association (WEA) and local volunteer centres. Paid vacancies could arise from voluntary placements.

What the work involves

Community education officers provide all members of the community with information on, and access to, educational and developmental programmes. You may work in areas of social deprivation or high unemployment, or with certain disadvantaged groups such as ethnic minorities or the homeless.

You will identify the needs and interests of the community, and sensitively and creatively organise a variety of suitable activities and courses to improve learning, career and personal development opportunities.

You will plan projects and outreach programmes, liaise with community and local authority groups, and recruit and train staff. At a senior level your job will involve developing policies and negotiating funding.

Type of person suited to this work

You should have a genuine interest in helping people and charitable work. As you will be liaising with communities, government departments and voluntary bodies, you must be able to communicate with a variety of different people, in both casual and formal situations, whilst maintaining a professional approach.

You should be a good listener and have a practical, optimistic approach to problem-solving.

You will need to show initiative and be able to work as part of a team. Patience is essential as many projects are long-term developments rather than quick-fix solutions.

Working conditions

Many posts are short-term contracts because their existence is heavily dependent on funding. This can be difficult as projects often require long-term support. There is plenty of opportunity for part-time work and flexible hours but these may involve working during the evening and at weekends.

You will have an office based in a community centre, a local authority or a college, from which you will travel to the surrounding region. A driving licence is useful.

Future prospects

Once you have secured a post you will receive formal training consisting of short courses that will develop skills or examine new issues such as health development.

You may find that postgraduate programmes in community studies and education are beneficial to your progress. NVQs and diplomas in relevant subjects such as youth and community work will boost your opportunities for progression.

Willingness to be geographically mobile will enhance your career prospects.

Advantages/disadvantages

Providing communities with the educational opportunities they require for personal or career growth can be highly rewarding.

You will have the opportunity to work with a variety of people from different backgrounds.

Limited funding may prevent you from providing the courses and programmes that you wish to which can be frustrating.

Money guide

Starting salaries are usually between £20,000 and £25,000.

Those employed at a senior level can achieve £26,000–£30,000.

Salaries in the voluntary sector are usually lower than in the public sector.

Related opportunities

- Social Worker p579
- Volunteer Manager p583
- Youth and Community Worker p585

Further information

Workers' Educational Association
www.wea.org.uk

DANCE TEACHER

ENTRY LEVEL 5

Qualifications and courses

The usual entry route for a dance teacher is to study for a degree, HND or Foundation degree in a dance-related subject.

If you want to teach dance in a state school you will need to obtain Qualified Teacher Status (QTS). This can be achieved by doing a postgraduate certificate in education (PGCE) after your degree or, alternatively, some undergraduate degrees in dance subjects incorporate study for QTS.

Those who wish to become a dance teacher in the private sector can take vocational qualifications available at certain dance and performing arts institutions. The Royal Academy of Dance (RAD) offers diplomas, bachelor's degrees and master's degrees which provide students with RAD Registered Teacher Status (RTS). The Imperial Society of Teachers of Dancing (ISTD) also have teaching qualifications at both initial and advanced level.

Once qualified as a dance teacher for the private sector, you should become accredited by the Council for Dance Education and Training (CDET). Your details can then be listed on the CDET UK Directory of Registered Dance Teachers.

What the work involves

You will plan dance lessons for pupils that adhere to a syllabus or curriculum set out by a school. In the private sector you will train and prepare pupils for dance exams.

You will help your pupils to develop their fitness and agility, ensuring that they do so safely without causing injury to themselves or others.

You will choreograph dance routines, as well as choosing music and costumes.

Type of person suited to this work

You need to have a high level of fitness and stamina and be able to demonstrate complicated dance moves and positions to your pupils.

You should also be very enthusiastic about music and the performing arts in general and possess good rhythm and balance.

As a teacher of any subject it is imperative that your communication skills are impeccable but for dance teachers this is especially important because you need to ensure that everyone in your class is dancing safely.

Creativity and self-discipline are very important traits to possess as well.

Working conditions

If you are employed in the state school sector you will be working during the school day but it is likely that you will also run classes after school in the early evening. This is certainly true of the private sector.

If you are a freelance teacher you can expect to travel as you will work at a variety of different venues; from schools and colleges to theatres and community centres.

Future prospects

As a dance teacher you can progress to becoming self-employed and even to running your own dance school.

There are also other performing arts sectors you could branch into such as choreography.

For experienced dance teachers there is the possibility to move into community work as a dance therapist.

Advantages/disadvantages

The job is very active so you will stay fit and healthy.

Your work will often be fun as it is a very creative and expressive art form.

You may injure yourself from constantly dancing and this could jeopardise how much you can work.

Preparing for a big performance can be stressful, especially if you are working with children who can be unpredictable.

Money guide

Earnings vary according to whether you work for a state school or in the public sector.

Newly qualified teachers in state schools start on a salary of about £21,500.

As state teachers gain experience and increased responsibilities, they can earn up to £31,500.

Earnings for dance teachers in the private sector depend upon the size, type and reputation of the dance school.

Self-employed dance teachers charge an hourly rate which can range from £12 to £50. These fees have to cover the cost of hiring a venue.

Related opportunities

- Choreographer p433
- Dancer p436
- Primary School Teacher p199

Further information

Council for Dance Education and Training
www.cdet.org.uk

Imperial Society of Teachers of Dancing
www.istd.org

National Dance Teachers Association
www.ndta.org.uk

EDUCATION AND TRAINING

CRCI: F

EARLY YEARS SPECIALIST/NURSERY NURSE

Qualifications and courses

Academic qualifications are not necessary, although GCSEs/S grades (A*–C/1–3), especially in English and maths are helpful.

There is a framework of nationally accredited nursery nurse qualifications in England and Wales. Typical qualifications include CACHE Level 3 Diploma in Child Care and Education; BTEC National Diploma in Children's Care, Learning and Development and NVQ/SVQ Level 3 in Children's Care, Learning and Development. Apprenticeships in Children's Care, Learning and Development may also be available.

In Scotland, registration of nursery workers has been introduced. Early years practitioners with qualifications such as SVQ Level 3 or an HNC can register with the Scottish Social Services Council (SSSC).

All applicants must pass a Criminal Records Bureau check.

What the work involves

Within a nursery or private home, early years specialists/ nursery nurses look after young children, from newborn babies up to the age of 8, ensuring they are safe and comfortable.

Much of your work will involve feeding, changing, dressing and bathing babies, and helping older children to develop in areas such as language, art, practical skills and music.

You will plan the day to include play, exercise, meals and rest, to keep children healthy and mentally stimulated.

Type of person suited to this work

It is essential to enjoy caring for young people and to be outgoing, with a friendly manner towards children and adults alike. You also need to be patient and tolerant to deal with different types of behaviour.

Planning activities needs imagination and creativity, and it is helpful to be good at art, practical tasks and singing.

You will need to be flexible, enjoy working in a team and be comfortable working with many different types of people from all cultures and backgrounds.

You will also need excellent communication skills as you will need to discuss the children's development and progress, and any other issues, with their parents or carers.

Working conditions

The majority of nursery nurses work 40 hours a week, however hours can vary depending on parents' requirements.

Most of your work will be indoors in a nursery, school, hospital or private home. You may 'live in' if you are a nanny in a private home.

The work involves bending, lifting and playing with children so you need to be physically fit.

Future prospects

Nursery nurses work in nurseries, schools and hospitals, and as nannies in private homes. You can start to train straight from school or after gaining experience in other types of work.

With the large rise in working mothers, there is high demand for qualified childcare staff throughout the UK. Sometimes, there are opportunities to travel, particularly in private work.

Promotion prospects are limited. After gaining experience and further specialist qualifications you could become a Nursery Manager or you could take further training to enter paediatric nursing or primary school teaching.

Advantages/disadvantages

The work is varied and rewarding.

As well as children, you will have the opportunity to work with adults.

The hours can be long, particularly in nanny work, and you might have to work shifts and weekends.

Money guide

Expect to start on around £10,000–£12,000 per year.

With experience earnings can increase to £14,000–£18,000.

Salaries can rise to £35,000 for a management post in a nursery.

Related opportunities

- Childminder p567
- Children's Nurse p294
- Teaching Assistant/Learning Support Assistant p206

Further information

CACHE
www.cache.org.uk

Care Commission
www.carecommission.com

EDUCATION AND CHILDCARE INSPECTOR

Qualifications and courses

Registered inspectors in England and Wales, and inspectors in Scotland, must be qualified as teachers and have 5 years' experience working in education.

Qualified Teacher Status (QTS) is gained through Initial Teacher Training (ITT). The two main routes are a first degree followed by a Postgraduate Certificate in Education (PGCE) or a first degree (BEd/BA/BSc) leading to QTS.

Registered inspectors also need to have 3 years' experience in a leadership or a managerial role. Many inspectors are ex-head teachers or childcare managers.

Training for inspectors is provided by the Office for Standards in Education (Ofsted) in England, Estyn in Wales, HM Inspectorate of Education in Scotland, and the Department of Education for Northern Ireland. This includes, in England, additional courses which run for up to the first year of employment.

In Wales, candidates undertake a 3-day course on which they are taught and assessed on the Common Inspection Framework. You can then undertake a further 2 days' training in a chosen specialism. Successful participants are then placed on a 'tender list' to bid for additional work.

All assessors, throughout the UK and Scotland, will be expected to keep their knowledge up to date through continuing professional development (CPD).

What the work involves

You will use your extensive experience gained from working in schools, colleges, nurseries or youth service settings to undertake inspections.

You might inspect early years learning, or focus on secondary education and preparation-for-work organisations. Inspections cover special schools and out-of-school learning units.

Inspectors look at the quality of teaching, curriculum, standard of leadership and pupils' achievement levels. During the visit you will contribute to the inspection report, which is then made available for everyone to read on the internet.

Type of person suited to this work

You must be knowledgeable about the types of organisations you will be inspecting. You should be observant and possess a high level of integrity. Strong analytical skills are essential. You will be gathering evidence and interviewing a variety of people so you need to be an effective communicator and be able to make appropriate and fair judgements.

It's important to work to a high standard but also to work quickly and to deadlines. Good ICT and report writing skills are also important.

Working conditions

You will visit organisations across the country and will need to spend long periods of time away from home.

Most of the work takes place in classrooms or offices where you will speak to head teachers, pupils, parents, governors and the other professionals linked to the organisation.

Most inspectors are freelance.

Future prospects

You could be working for Ofsted, Tribal Inspections, Serco Education and Children's Services or the Centre for British Teachers Education Trust. These organisations have offices in London, Bristol and Manchester although most inspectors work from home.

Inspectors working for Ofsted are called HMIs (Her Majesty's Inspectors). AIs (Additional Inspectors) work for other organisations under contract to Ofsted. Early years inspectors specialise in education for under-5s. AIs can apply to be HMIs, and early years inspectors can be promoted to adult and senior children's services. There is also the chance to be promoted to managerial level in all groups.

Advantages/disadvantages

This job offers you the chance to use your experience to make sure that the right quality of provision is in place in an institution.

You have the chance to travel around the country.

It's challenging when you need to give an 'inadequate' judgement to an institution.

Money guide

Pay varies, depending on the level of work.

Early years inspectors are usually employed by private organisations; salaries vary but as a guide starting salaries are around £28,000.

HMIs can earn £48,500–£62,000 per year for full-time employment, with pro rata for part time.

AIs can earn £300–£500 per day and have expenses paid.

Related opportunities

- Education Officer p35
- Secondary School Teacher p203
- Work-based Training Instructor p207

Further information

HM Inspectorate of Education in Scotland
www.hmie.gov.uk

Ofsted
www.ofsted.gov.uk

EDUCATION WELFARE OFFICER

Qualifications and courses

There are a number of routes into this profession. Candidates generally have relevant work experience in areas such as special education, teaching, counselling or youth work.

Employers often expect you to have, or be studying for, a qualification in social work. Qualifications in education welfare, teaching or youth and community work may also help you gain entry to this profession. Degree courses usually require a minimum of 2 A levels/3 H grades and 5 GCSEs/S grades (A*–C/1–3) or equivalent including English and maths.

Those without a professional qualification who have extensive experience working with children/young people and their families may be accepted but they will usually be expected to have at least A levels or equivalent. An NVQ in Learning, Development and Support Services for Children, Young People and Those who Care for Them (Levels 3 and 4) is also available.

Candidates are advised to gain as much experience as possible by seeking opportunities through Community Service Volunteers (CSV). Experience in caring for people or advising/counselling work and skills in communication, IT and teamwork would also be valuable. You need Criminal Records Bureau (CRB) clearance to work with children.

What the work involves

You will work with young people who are not attending school, and their families, to support them back into education.

It will be your responsibility to issue education supervision orders, school attendance orders and truancy schemes. You may have to prosecute parents of children who continue to truant despite your efforts to help the children to return to school.

You will help families get all the benefits they are entitled to, such as free school meals, clothing or transport. As a link between families and schools, you will try to improve existing relationships – writing reports, attending meetings and case conferences.

Type of person suited to this work

As there can be many reasons for poor attendance at school, such as fear of bullying, caring responsibilities at home or difficulty in coping with school work, it is important to be open minded and to listen impartially to school staff and parents. You will also need to be strong enough to prosecute a family if it becomes necessary.

You must enjoy working with young people and see the value in education, because you might have to convince parents who do not share your views.

You will also have to keep up to date with legislation and you must be able to work on your own and as part of a team.

Working conditions

You will have an office base, but most of your time will be spent visiting young people and their families at home or looking for young people in the local area, so a driving licence is useful.

You may go to other agencies' offices to attend meetings and case conferences.

Families may view your interventions as interfering rather than assisting; you must always consider your safety.

Future prospects

There are about 4500 education welfare officers in England, Wales and Northern Ireland. In Scotland, they are called attendance officers.

There is a promotion structure within local authorities and you can become a senior education welfare officer, team leader or manager. There is also the opportunity to become a specialist, for example dealing only with primary school pupils. With further training, you can do similar work in care and social services.

Advantages/disadvantages

You will have the satisfaction of helping people – sometimes quite profoundly.

You may have to work in the evenings to meet parents when they are available.

Some people may be abusive and you could find yourself in stressful situations.

Money guide

Your starting salary could be £18,000–£21,000 per year.

With experience you could earn up to £30,000.

Those with relevant qualifications are likely to receive higher salaries.

Wages vary depending on your geographical area and the local authority you work for.

Related opportunities

- Careers Adviser p566
- Social Worker p579
- Youth and Community Worker p585

Further information

General Social Care Council
www.gscc.org.uk

Northern Ireland Social Care Council
www.niscc.info

FURTHER EDUCATION LECTURER

Qualifications and courses

New entrants need a relevant degree, Foundation degree or HND. You can also apply if you have significant work experience and a qualification at Level 3 in the subject you wish to teach. You will need to register with the Institute for Learning (IfL).

In England and Wales, within 5 years of commencing teaching you need a Certificate in Teaching in the Lifelong Learning Sector (CTLLS), a Diploma in Teaching in the Lifelong Learning Sector (DTLLS), a Certificate in Education (Cert Ed) or a Postgraduate Certificate in Education (PGCE). Those who get a lecturing job without a teaching qualification must gain the Preparing to Teach in the Lifelong Sector award (PTLLS) within their first year.

To qualify as a full teacher you must take the DTLLS, Cert Ed or PGCE. You will generally need a QCF Level 4–6 qualification for entry to the DTLLS or CertEd programme and a degree for entry to a PGCE. To qualify as an associate teacher with fewer responsibilities you need the CTLLS.

What the work involves

You will teach students aged 16+ on vocational or academic courses at a further education college.

Your work will involve planning and preparing lessons, setting assignments and marking pupils' work. You will also undertake administrative tasks and keep records of students' progress.

As well as teaching your main subject, you will arrange work placements, visit students to assess their progress, act as a student mentor and meet colleagues to develop courses.

Type of person suited to this work

Lecturers need to be interested in teaching people of all ages. You must be comfortable talking to large groups of students.

You need extensive knowledge of your subject and the ability to explain things to students at a level that they will understand.

You should be creative to devise lectures, activities and materials which will interest your students. Planning and organisation skills are essential.

Working conditions

HE lecturers mostly teach in lecture theatres, classrooms, labs or workshops. If you teach a practical subject you may work outdoors sometimes. Occasionally you might take students on field trips.

When you are not teaching, you will be researching, writing papers and marking students' work. Consequently, you will have to work some evenings and weekends.

Depending on the institution you are employed by, you will usually work during term time and have school holidays off.

Future prospects

Further education lecturers could progress to more senior roles such as senior lecturer, curriculum manager, head of department or divisional manager. However, tight college budgets have led to a reduction in the number of management positions. For this reason, you will need a willingness to be geographically mobile if you are keen to gain a promotion.

You could move into other areas of education, for example, you could take further training to become a higher education lecturer.

You could also progress to a non-teaching position in college management.

Advantages/disadvantages

You are able to teach in a less formal environment than a school.

Witnessing students' progression is rewarding.

You will be required to spend a lot of time planning lessons and marking work, which may interfere with your personal life.

Money guide

Starting salaries for full-time FE lecturers are £18,000 to £23,000, depending on whether or not they have qualified.

With several years' experience or promotion to senior level, earnings rise to around £35,000.

Hourly rates for part-time lecturers range from £14 to over £20.

Salaries are dependent on your experience and expertise, and the size and status of your college.

Salaries are typically £3,000 per year higher in London.

Related opportunities

- Primary School Teacher p199
- Secondary School Teacher p203
- Work-based Training Instructor p207

Further information

Lifelong Learning UK
www.lluk.org

University and College Union
www.ucu.org.uk

EDUCATION AND TRAINING

CRCI: F

195

Qualifications and courses

There are no formal entry requirements for this career. However, nearly all entrants have a degree, HND or equivalent vocational qualification.

The NVQ Level 3 in Learning, Development and Support Services for Children and Young People is a minimum requirement for many local authorities.

Relevant degree subjects include social sciences, psychology and National Curriculum subjects.

Experience of working with young people is required, and experience in a related area such as social work, counselling or teaching is useful.

There is the opportunity to participate in mentor schemes at some universities which provides good experience.

The majority of newly appointed learning mentors will participate in a standardised induction programme aimed at support staff in education.

You will also receive specific mentor training, usually from the area learning mentor coordinator.

It is also common for newly appointment mentors to keep a portfolio of evidence detailing their work.

The NVQ/SVQ Level 4 is normally required to become a learning mentor coordinator. All candidates are required to undergo a Criminal Records Bureau check.

What the work involves

You will support people while they are learning to overcome obstacles and meet their targets.

Your work will be complementary to teachers and other school support staff as well as parents.

Working on a one-to-one basis, you will listen to your mentee's difficulties and offer various solutions.

You will help everybody you work with to succeed in and enjoy their learning experience.

You will cover a range of topics from bullying to abuse to gifted and talented students.

Type of person suited to this work

To be a good learning mentor, you will need to have experience of the subject you mentor, along with an understanding of different styles of studying.

You should enjoy helping and listening to people and have good communication skills. You should be patient and willing to listen.

The best mentors are those who can be a critical friend, know the benefits of learning and can explain them to the people they work with.

You should be able to handle emotional stress, be adaptable, non-judgemental and encouraging.

Working conditions

You can work on a part- or full-time basis with people at school, home or sometimes at a college, university or training centre.

You might be employed on a term-time only basis or all year round. Some of your work might involve weekends and evenings – this will depend on the organisation you work for.

You will meet in a quiet, confidential area where you will examine workbooks and essays, talk over any issues and offer help.

Future prospects

There are opportunities to progress to management roles or even to head of year at some schools.

You may choose to study further and become a teacher, youth worker or social worker.

You could also specialise in various areas including working with refugee families or children with behavioural disorders.

As the profession is still developing, current learning mentor coordinators have often come from other professions such as careers advisory roles or social work but it is possible to progress from a learning mentor to coordinator through experience and further training.

Advantages/disadvantages

This job involves a variety of roles – friend, confidence builder and motivator.

Results have shown how important this job can be in helping learners to succeed.

You will be working with students without being a teacher.

Money guide

Within schools, salaries for newly appointed mentors range between £14,000 and £17,000 per year. As you gain experience, you can expect this to increase to between £20,000 and £25,000. If you take on managerial responsibilities it is possible to earn up to £27,000.

The salary can vary a lot between different settings. The professionalism of the role is somewhat contentious and whilst some employers recognise the expertise (and therefore salary) as similar to a new teacher or social worker, others only view the role as a supporting role.

Related opportunities

- Careers Adviser p566
- Learning Disabilities Nurse p314
- Special Educational Needs Teacher p204
- Youth and Community Worker p585

Further information

Mentoring and Befriending Foundation
www.mandbf.org.uk

NVQ/SVQ ASSESSOR

Qualifications and courses

It is necessary to have between 2 and 4 years' occupational experience, and often a vocational qualification, in the subject or work area to be assessed. For this reason it is not possible for school or college leavers to enter this area straight away.

It is necessary to have an assessor qualification. You may study for Level 3 Awards in Assessing Competence in the Work Environment and Assessing Vocationally Related Achievement, or a Level 3 Certificate in Assessing Vocational Achievement. Each of these will include a knowledge and understanding unit (Level 3 Award in Understanding Principles and Practices of Assessment) and a practical application unit.

Some courses only accept candidates who have been nominated by their employer and have extensive experience in the specialist area and a Level 2 qualification (or higher) in the area.

Qualified assessors can carry out further training to work as NVQ/SVQ verifiers. A number of Level 4 Awards and Certificates are available for both internal and external verifiers.

Once you begin your training you can join the Institute of Assessors and Internal Verifiers (IAV) as an Associate member. After gaining 12 months' experience you can apply for Licentiate membership and you will be added to the IAV's National Register and after 5 years you can apply for Fellowship.

What the work involves

NVQ/SVQ assessors work alongside trainees to ascertain their current knowledge, and from this formulate a plan for their development.

You will offer feedback on their progress as they gain experience and take their NVQ/SVQ qualifications.

You will observe how trainees perform different tasks and measure their achievements against the standards for the qualification. You will also read through each trainee's portfolio of evidence, checking that tasks are undertaken.

Type of person suited to this work

It is essential to demonstrate an interest in other people and a commitment to helping them to progress. You will need to motivate and encourage all kinds of individuals – some of whom will not have enjoyed school and find training difficult.

Excellent communication skills are important for the amount of speaking, questioning, listening and reporting that is involved.

In addition you should be organised and able to interpret the different standards in ways that are helpful to those who are learning. You should also have an interest in the area you are assessing.

Working conditions

You will have access to an office where you will use a computer to update learner records and check portfolios. You will also spend lots of time travelling to meet employers and trainees at their places of work.

Depending on your specialist area you could have very early starts (for example assessing bakers at work) or late finishes (assessing car finishers working nights).

It is necessary to keep up to date with the changes and developments in your occupational area.

It is possible to work freelance.

Future prospects

The government is currently encouraging learning through work-based qualifications and school/college leavers now have more opportunities to pursue Apprenticeships, National Traineeships or Skillseekers.

There is currently a national shortage of skilled professionals in this area, and there will be increasing need for NVQ/SVQ assessors in the future. This may result in more firms and organisations having a team of specialists who train other employees in their particular area of expertise, eg health and safety.

It is possible to expand your role by becoming an internal or external verifier. With experience, it is also possible to move into further education teaching or training.

Advantages/disadvantages

This work involves being at the centre of improving the skills levels of the workforce. You will spend lots of your time meeting, speaking to and getting to know other people.

Depending on your specialist area, you might have to work unsociable hours in order to assess candidates in their workplace.

It can be challenging to motivate and encourage candidates who do not enjoy learning towards a qualification.

Money guide

Average starting salaries are between £14,000 and £20,000.

More experienced assessors can expect to earn up to £24,000 per year which can increase beyond £35,000 for the most senior positions.

Freelance rates vary.

Related opportunities

- Education and Childcare Inspector p193
- Further Education Lecturer p195
- Training Development Officer p68

Further information

Chartered Institute of Personnel and Development
www.cipd.co.uk

Lifelong Learning UK
www.lluk.org

The Institute of Assessors and Internal Verifiers
www.iavltd.co.uk

Qualifications and courses

Most people enter this career as a play assistant for which you will need an NVQ Level 3 qualification in Childcare.

Relevant courses include the CACHE Certificate in Playwork and NCFE Certificate in Playwork, both at Level 2, and the CACHE Certificate and Diploma in Childcare and Education. NVQs/SVQs are available.

To become a registered hospital play specialist, you must be aged 20 or over and will need a Foundation degree in hospital play specialism, approved by the Hospital Play Staff Education Trust. To be accepted onto the Foundation degree course applicants must have an appropriate qualification in a subject such as childcare, nursery nursing, drama or music therapy, teaching or social work, and at least 2 years' recent experience of working in a related field.

The 2-year course is delivered by means of formal teaching and practical experience with a mentor. Once this is completed you can apply for a licence to practise from the Hospital Play Staff Education Trust (HPSET).

There are also Apprenticeships available in health and social care and children's care which would be useful starting points when entering this career.

What the work involves

Play workers and hospital play specialists are responsible for ensuring that children between the ages of 5 and 15 play in a safe environment.

You will encourage children and young people to learn through play by giving them the freedom to explore and get to know themselves.

Hospital play specialists use play to entertain children and help them to deal with their experiences in hospital. This includes using play to prepare them for treatments and diverting their attention from unpleasant procedures. You may work with severely disabled children.

Type of person suited to this work

Imagination and creativity are needed to do this job well. It is essential that you like being with children of all ages, understand what they like to do and recognise how they change as they develop.

You should be positive and patient with lots of energy and stamina. As the safety of the children will be your responsibility, you will need high levels of concentration and to stay alert at all times.

A hospital play specialist needs to be sympathetic to the needs and issues of each child, have some understanding of medical conditions, and must be able to cope with distressing situations.

Working conditions

As many opportunities operate after school or during holidays you will normally work in the early evening, at weekends and in school holidays. Many jobs are seasonal and most are part time.

Hospital play specialists work in children's hospitals, children's wards and outpatients' clinics. You may take children on trips or visit them in their homes, so you might need a driving licence.

Future prospects

This area of work is rising in importance and is part of the National Childcare Strategy, which recognises the significance of giving young people opportunities to improve their lives through education, sport and leisure.

With the increased number of working parents, the need for out-of-school carers has grown.

There is currently an increase in the number of hospital play specialist posts available nationally. Most opportunities are with NHS hospitals but you could also work in hospices or community paediatric teams.

Advantages/disadvantages

Helping children who are ill to enjoy themselves can be extremely rewarding.

Hospital play specialists may have to deal with sad and distressing situations.

Money guide

Starting salaries for hospital play specialists range from £17,700 to £20,820.

With experience or promotion, salaries can increase up to £26,800.

As a senior manager, it is possible to achieve salaries up to £35,000.

Related opportunities

- Childminder p567
- Teaching Assistant/Learning Support Assistant p206
- Youth and Community Worker p585

Further information

CACHE
www.cache.org.uk

National Association of Hospital Play Staff
www.nahps.org.uk

Qualifications and courses

You can enter this career with a Bachelor of Education (BEd) degree or a BA/BSc degree with Qualified Teacher Status (QTS).

Alternatively, after obtaining an Honours degree, you could complete a Professional Graduate Certificate in Education (ProfGCE) or, at master's level, a Postgraduate Certificate in Education (PGCE). In Scotland you can complete a Professional Graduate Diploma in Education (PGDE).

Another option is to study for qualifications whilst working in a school. In England and Wales, if you have a degree it is possible to apply for the Graduate Teacher Programme (GTP). This takes between 3 months and a year to complete. Students are employed by a school and earn a salary while they train. Competition for the limited places available on the GTP is high so entrants are advised to gain as much classroom experience as possible.

All entrants, no matter which route they are following, are required to have GCSEs/S grades (A*–C/1–3) in English, maths and a science subject. During their training they must also pass numeracy, literacy and IT skills tests and obtain clearance from the Criminal Records Bureau (CRB).

What the work involves

You will teach young children the key subjects of English, maths and science as well as IT, history, religious education, geography, art, languages and physical education.

In a state school, you will teach young children reading, writing and numeracy following the frameworks outlined in the National Curriculum. Private schools can set their own teaching guidelines. You will prepare resources for structured play and social development work.

Primary schools admit pupils aged 5–11 and have children of a wide range of abilities in the same class.

Type of person suited to this work

You must be calm and caring in order to deal with different types of behaviour. You should also be assertive and able to uphold discipline within the class.

Planning activities requires creativity. You need to have excellent organisation skills and be able to communicate with children, parents and colleagues. It is also important to be able to encourage and motivate your students – no matter how small their achievements are.

Working conditions

The majority of primary school teachers work 50+ hours a week. Teachers have 12–13 weeks' holiday per year when the school closes. However, preparation for lessons and marking is often completed during this time, as well as at evenings and weekends during term-time. Extra responsibilities include parents' evenings, after-school activities and school inspections.

You will be based in a classroom and will have a great deal of freedom over your teaching timetable for the day. It is also possible to gain part-time supply work.

Future prospects

You could become a coordinator of your specialist subject or work with teachers in nearby schools as an advanced skills teacher (in England and Wales) or a chartered teacher (in Scotland). The National College for Leadership of Schools and Children's Services provides programmes which offer greater salaries and responsibilities to gifted teachers. Progression to deputy head/head can be achieved in 10 years.

Other options include jobs in local or national government, such as an Ofsted inspector. Some teachers offer private tutoring or prepare educational texts.

Advantages/disadvantages

Being responsible for your students' educational development can be very rewarding.

The job is demanding as you will have to carry out many duties, such as marking and preparing lessons, and you will be required to complete this work in the evening and at weekends.

Money guide

The main pay scale for qualified teachers in England and Wales ranges from £21,588 to £31,552.

Teachers on the main pay scale move up to the next point each year if their performance has been satisfactory.

Those who take on additional responsibilities can earn £34,181–£36,756.

Advanced skills teachers have a salary of £37,461–£56,950 and those in senior roles can earn considerably more.

Earnings in Scotland are comparable and also operate on a pay scale system.

Related opportunities

- Secondary School Teacher p203
- Teaching Assistant/Learning Support Assistant p206
- Work-based Training Instructor p207

Further information

Training and Development Agency for Schools
www.tda.gov.uk

EDUCATION AND TRAINING

CRCI: F

PRIVATE MUSIC TEACHER

ENTRY LEVEL 4

Qualifications and courses

For private music teachers there are no set qualifications, however most do have a degree. It is also useful to study for further teaching and performance and theory qualifications. The most important qualification though is excellent music competence and knowledge of your instrument, usually grade 7/8 from an Associated Board on a first instrument and grade 6 on a second.

Private music teachers can join the Incorporated Society of Musicians (ISM) (as long as they meet the criteria) which lists available teachers and their credentials. The ISM can also provide Approved Private Teacher status which involves obtaining a Criminal Records Bureau check, a reference from a current pupil or their parent/guardian and adhering to the ISM Code of Practice for Private Music Teachers.

There are also a wide range of courses available for music teachers. Rockschool offers a music educator course, which will help to demonstrate your commitment to the teaching and learning process.

For private music teachers who want to work in state schools, Qualified Teacher Status (QTS) could help the application. QTS can be achieved through a first degree followed by a Postgraduate Certificate in Education (Professional Graduate Diploma of Education in Scotland) or a BEd degree that includes QTS.

What the work involves

Private music teachers provide vocal, instrumental and theoretical music training for a range of people and ages. You will work at a variety of different levels and with both individuals and groups.

Your teaching may take place in a classroom, either in a primary or secondary school, in a community setting, at your pupil's home or from your own home. You will be expected to plan lessons, organise groups such as orchestras, and you might have to prepare students for external exams.

You may be hired by a particular local authority music service, schools, a music centre or be self-employed and many private music teachers work in a combination of these settings and roles.

Type of person suited to this work

You should be patient, have a caring attitude towards others and an interest in drawing out and developing an individual's potential in learning about music.

Excellent communication skills are important, as are firmness and commitment, imagination and creativity. You have to be well organised, flexible and able to change plans and the sequence of lessons to accommodate unexpected events.

It is important to be comfortable in maintaining discipline and be confident when speaking to large groups of young people and other professionals.

Working conditions

Music teachers work indoors in all kinds of settings within public and private sector schools and learning centres, and in their own or pupils' homes as tutors.

Work in schools will usually be between 8.45am and 3.45pm, with some evening and weekend work required for tuition, rehearsals and concerts.

It is likely that you will work evenings and weekends, and part-time work is common. You should expect to carry out some travelling and you may be expected to lift and carry heavy musical instruments.

Future prospects

Many private teachers combine their teaching work with composing, performing or directing choirs/orchestras, and career breaks are common. If you can play the piano and have excellent sight reading, you could accompany students at examinations and recitals.

Advantages/disadvantages

Teaching is a rewarding profession in which you can witness a student's progression.

You will be kept very busy with preparation, classes, assessing your students, communicating with examining bodies, meetings and ordering materials.

Money guide

For private teachers the Musicians' Union recommends a rate of £29 an hour.

For teachers visiting schools pay varies between £24 and £35 an hour, depending on reputation, experience, qualifications and location.

After considerable experience, at least 10–15 years, private music teachers can expect to earn in the range of £30 to £50 an hour.

Related opportunities

- Dance Teacher p191
- Primary School Teacher p199
- Secondary School Teacher p203
- Teaching Assistant/Learning Support Assistant p206

Further information

Incorporated Society of Musicians
www.ism.org

Musicians' Union
www.musiciansunion.org.uk

Rockschool Ltd
www.rockschool.co.uk

Qualifications and courses

There are no formal entry requirements but you will probably need 5 GCSEs/S grades (A*–C/1–3) or equivalent and a good standard of maths and English. Adult entry is common and many entrants have several years of office experience.

You will need keyboard and word-processing skills. Other IT skills and shorthand are also useful. Training is mostly on the job and some schools will require you to undergo external training.

It is possible to study for the National Certificate in Educational Administration (Level 3) at the School of Educational Administration (SEA). This course can be undertaken in 1 year by distance learning and it covers topics such as government policies, education and the law, and business management.

In addition, an NVQ in Business and Administration (Levels 1–4) is available, and City & Guilds offer an Award/Certificate/Diploma in Support Work in Schools (Levels 2 and 3).

What the work involves

School administrators/secretaries are responsible for greeting visitors and answering telephone calls.

You will develop administrative systems (both paper and IT based) to keep information organised and easily accessible.

In some schools you might also collect money for lunch and school trips and you could be in charge of the medical room.

Type of person suited to this work

You will be highly organised and efficient with excellent written and verbal communication skills. You should be confident dealing with people at all levels, including teachers, students and their guardians. You might need to work with people who are ill, angry or upset.

You should have an excellent telephone manner and possess keyboard skills and knowledge of IT packages and information systems.

You must be responsible, flexible, and able to prioritise your workload and use your initiative. You should also be able to work calmly under pressure, meet deadlines and handle confidential information discreetly.

Working conditions

You will usually be office based, doing normal school hours (8.30am–4pm). You will use a range of office equipment, including computers, photocopiers, telephones and fax machines.

School offices are open to visitors and pupils and can be very busy. On a reception desk you will be responsible for greeting visitors and showing them to their meeting room or contacting colleagues. Business dress is often required.

Many school secretaries work part time and do not work at all during the school holidays.

Future prospects

In the UK there are about 55,000 administrators employed in nursery, primary and secondary schools. There are job opportunities in all areas of the country, although jobs can be competitive as the working hours and holidays are appealing.

Much of the work is part time and there are not many opportunities for promotion. However, you could work your way up to become a school business manager/bursar or move into secretarial work outside the education sector.

Advantages/disadvantages

The working hours, holiday allowances and opportunities for part-time work make this job ideal for someone with family commitments.

You will learn key, transferable skills that could be used in many other jobs and sectors.

The work can be routine and repetitive.

Money guide

In a state school, you would usually receive a starting salary of £11,500–£16,500.

With experience in the role, or if you take on additional responsibilities, your earnings could increase to £20,000–£25,000.

Salaries in large secondary schools and private schools may be higher.

Related opportunities

- Arts Administrator/Manager p347
- Personal Assistant p56
- Receptionist p59
- School Business Manager/Bursar p202

Further information

School of Educational Administration
www.admin.org.uk

EDUCATION AND TRAINING

CRCI: F

Qualifications and courses

Most entrants have experience in a related field and many hold a degree or professional qualification in a business or finance-related subject. Management experience in education, accountancy or personnel would be useful. Those seeking entry to this career may find it an advantage to study for the NVQ/SVQ in Business and Administration (Levels 1-4) or the NVQ/SVQ in Management and Team Leading (Levels 2–5).

For those already employed as a school business manager/bursar, the National College for School Leadership offers a professional development programme. The Certificate of School Business Management (CSBM) is an entry level qualification aimed at newly appointed bursars or those in school administration posts, and the Diploma of School Business Management (DSBM) is intended for experienced bursars/business managers.

The Independent Schools' Bursars Association offers induction courses for new bursars working in independent schools and a series of professional development seminars.

The National Association of School Business Management (NASBM) provides the MSc in Educational Leadership (School Business Management) for those with relevant professional qualifications (CSBM or DSBM) and experience.

What the work involves

You will be responsible for the financial and strategic planning, human resources and environmental issues of a school or college.

The term 'bursar' is common in independent schools; in the state sector you might also be called a school business manager or finance manager.

Your role will involve organising staff pay and recruitment, as well as managing contracts with cleaning and maintenance companies. You will have to keep all the school premises' insurance documents up to date. In independent schools, you will also set fees and distribute bursaries, scholarships and awards.

Type of person suited to this work

You need a polite yet firm approach and excellent communication skills as you will deal with the head teacher and senior staff, other professionals (auditors, company managers, etc) as well as parents and students.

You should have a head for figures and be happy using computers and financial software. You need to be very organised in order to oversee all of your responsibilities.

Working conditions

Normally, you will work in an office sitting at a desk. You will have access to a computer and spend lots of time talking to people – both in or outside of your organisation.

You will attend lots of meetings with the head teacher and other professional staff – sometimes staying late to give reports to your school's governing body.

You may also need to work during the evenings and in school holidays.

Future prospects

Most bursars progress to the role after working in a private financial organisation or as an accountant. Some bursars work their way up within a school or college, possibly from secretary level.

With experience, bursars can move to larger organisations or return to the private sector. You could also work in British schools overseas.

Posts are advertised in local and national publications such as the *Times Educational Supplement*. Jobs are also posted on the National Association of School Business Management (NASBM)'s website.

Advantages/disadvantages

The role is varied and you will be able to use your initiative.

You will have the opportunity to work with people of all ages and backgrounds.

You are usually required to work during the school holidays.

There is a high level of responsibility involved in this job so your work may occasionally be stressful.

Money guide

Salaries for bursars vary greatly depending on the size, type and geographical location of the institution you work in.

The average starting salary in a state school or college ranges from £16,000 to £25,000.

As you gain experience, you could expect to earn between £30,000 and £50,000.

Salaries are higher in the independent sector and it is possible to achieve up to £90,000.

Related opportunities

- Accountant p16
- Accounting Technician and Accounts/Finance Clerk p18
- Financial Adviser p40

Further information

Independent Schools' Bursars Association
www.theisba.org.uk

National Association of School Business Management
www.nasbm.co.uk

SECONDARY SCHOOL TEACHER

Qualifications and courses

You can take a Bachelor of Education (BEd) degree or a BA/BSc degree with Qualified Teacher Status (QTS). Alternatively, you can do an undergraduate degree and then a Postgraduate Certificate in Secondary Education (PGCE) or a Professional Graduate Diploma in Education (PGDE) if you live in Scotland. You should study for a degree related to the subject you wish to teach.

Employment-based routes to QTS are also available for those who want to work in school whilst they qualify. The school-centred initial teacher training (SCITT) is a 1-year course open to graduates who hold a degree in the subject they wish to teach. Alternatively, the Graduate Teacher Programme (GTP) is available for graduates and takes 3 months to 1 year to complete. GTP students are employed by a school and earn a salary while they train on the job.

Teach First offers a 2-year Leadership Development Programme in which graduates study for a PGCE whilst training on the job. On completion of this scheme, candidates can remain in teaching or move into business or other public sector jobs.

All entrants, no matter which route they follow, must have GCSEs/S grades (A*–C/1–3) in English and maths and must pass a Criminal Records Bureau (CRB) check.

What the work involves

You will be a specialist in 1 or 2 subjects and teach students aged 11–19.

You will also take on the role of form tutor and be responsible for encouraging personal development and good behaviour.

In state schools, you will follow the National Curriculum. Private and independent schools are free to set their own educational standards.

Type of person suited to this work

You must be patient, caring and have excellent communication skills in order to relate to and teach your pupils. You should also be assertive and able to maintain discipline with large groups of young people.

You must be imaginative and creative to design lessons which capture your students' attention.

It is important that you are highly organised as this jobs involves a lot of marking and lesson planning.

Working conditions

You will be based in a classroom and will teach classes from about 9am until 3 or 4pm. However, you will have to come in early, stay late and work from home in order to carry out preparation for lessons and finish marking pupils' work.

Schools are usually open for 39 weeks of the year but teachers often carry out preparatory work during the holidays.

Teachers sometimes go on school trips or visit students on work placements. Modern foreign language and PE teachers should be prepared to go on school trips overseas.

Future prospects

There are shortages of maths, science, IT, design technology and religious education teachers in secondary education.

You could progress to a role as a Key Stage coordinator, the head of a department or year group, or work with teachers as an advanced skills teacher (chartered teacher in Scotland).

You could also go into teacher training, advisory work or become a school inspector. The National College for School Leadership provides opportunities for gifted teachers to develop skills and improve their leadership.

Advantages/disadvantages

Helping your students to learn and progress can be very rewarding.

The holiday allowance is very generous.

Pupils can sometimes be difficult and disruptive.

You will have to work from home in order to finish marking and preparing lessons.

Money guide

The main pay scale for qualified teachers in England and Wales ranges from £21,588 to £31,552.

Teachers on the main pay scale move up to the next point each year if their performance has been satisfactory.

Those who take on additional responsibilities can earn £34,181–£36,756.

Advanced skills teachers have a salary of £37,461–£56,950 and those in senior roles can earn considerably more.

Earnings in Scotland are comparable and also operate on a pay scale system.

Related opportunities

- Education and Childcare Inspector p193
- Primary School Teacher p199
- Teaching Assistant/Learning Support Assistant p206
- Work-based Training Instructor p207

Further information

General Teaching Council Scotland
www.gtcs.org.uk

Training and Development Agency for Schools
www.tda.gov.uk

Qualifications and courses

It is generally necessary to have teaching experience in a mainstream school before you can work as a teacher for pupils with special educational needs. In England and Wales it is necessary to have qualified teacher status (QTS) or a teaching qualification in Scotland. In order to obtain these you should have a Postgraduate Certificate in Education, a Bachelor of Education (BEd), or a BA or BSc with QTS.

The Training and Development Agency for Schools provides courses that cover ways of teaching different subjects, such as maths and science, to children with special educational needs. It also offers courses which raise awareness of special educational needs (SEN) teaching methods and practices.

Postgraduate qualifications are available in subjects such as special educational needs, specific learning difficulties (dyslexia), and visual impairment. You can study part time or by distance learning.

You must have relevant qualifications if you are teaching children with visual, hearing or multi-sensory impairments. Qualified teachers of hearing impaired pupils require CACDP Stage 1 in sign language, or equivalent. Qualified teachers of visually impaired pupils must be proficient in Braille.

What the work involves

Teachers for special educational needs help children with disabilities, learning difficulties or emotional or behavioural problems to achieve their best. You might also work with exceptionally gifted children.

Working with educational psychologists, social workers, other teachers and learning support workers, you will assess each child's individual needs and draw up an Individual Education Plan (IEP).

In each of these teaching jobs, you will accompany students on visits and trips, help them understand the world around them, and teach life skills to give them greater independence.

Type of person suited to this work

You must be patient and determined in order to deal with challenging behaviour and solve communication problems with pupils. You should be observant and must be able to recognise and praise efforts and achievements, however small.

You need to be kind and have excellent communication skills as well as a commitment to drawing out and developing individuals' potential in learning. You have to be well organised, flexible and able to change plans and the sequence of lessons to accommodate unexpected events.

Working conditions

There are opportunities all over the UK. You may be based in one school or work in teams covering a number of institutions. Part-time work is possible if you are registered with your local authority. Freelance or self-employment is less common.

You will work 39 weeks a year in school. Hours are usually 9am to 4pm Monday to Friday. Additional hours will be required to create lesson plans and attend meetings.

Future prospects

There are over 150,000 SEN teachers in the UK. Most work in mainstream schools, whilst others work in special schools like hospital schools, pupil referral units, youth custody centres and community homes. There is a shortage of skilled candidates.

SEN teachers working in a mainstream school may have the opportunity to be promoted to special education needs co-ordinator. You could also progress to a role as a special needs assessor in a local education authority.

Advantages/disadvantages

Helping children with disabilities, learning difficulties or emotional or behavioural problems and knowing that you helped them to progress is extremely rewarding.

You will be kept very busy with duties including preparation, classes, marking and assessing, analysing coursework, communicating with examining bodies, meetings and ordering materials, which can be stressful.

Money guide

Salaries are based on the teaching pay scale and range from £21,102 to £30,842. In inner London the range is higher, between £26,000 and £35,568.

Once you reach the top of the main salary scale you can apply to be assessed for the upper salary scale which ranges from £33,412 to £35,929 or £40,288 to £43,692 in inner London.

Related opportunities

- Education and Childcare Inspector p193
- Further Education Lecturer p195
- Work-based Training Instructor p207

Further information

National Association for Special Educational Needs
www.nasen.org.uk

Qualifications and courses

It is becoming increasingly necessary to have a degree to enter this occupation, especially in England. Useful degree subjects include English, linguistics, modern foreign languages and education.

In addition, you will need either the Level 5 Certificate in Teaching English to Speakers of Other Languages (CELTA) from Cambridge ESOL or the Level 5 Certificate in Teaching English to Speakers of Other Languages (CertTESOL) from Trinity College London.

Higher-level courses are also available for people with an initial language qualification (such as CELTA or CertTESOL) and at least 2 years' TEFL/TESOL experience. Cambridge ESOL offer the Level 7 Diploma in Teaching English to Speakers of Other Languages (DELTA) or Trinity College London provide the Level 7 Licentiate Diploma in Teaching English to Speakers of Other Languages (DipTESOL).

Experienced teachers with a degree and/or TESOL qualification can also study for a master's in TESOL.

Candidates who wish to teach in a state school must have Qualified Teacher Status (QTS) which can be obtained from studying for a BA/BSc with QTS or a Postgraduate Certificate in Education (PGCE).

What the work involves

You may be based in the UK or overseas and will teach English to students who are not native speakers. The term Teachers of English to Speakers of Other Languages (TESOL) is only used when the students are in the UK. Teaching English as a Foreign Language (TEFL) is used if you are teaching students abroad.

You will teach pupils of all ages who want to learn to speak English for educational, cultural or business reasons.

It is your responsibility to demonstrate your passion for the English language as well as inspiring and encouraging your students.

Type of person suited to this work

It is essential that you have an excellent grasp of the English language. You should be patient and have an interest in developing individuals' learning potential. Good communication skills are important, as is commitment and imagination.

You have to be well organised and flexible. You must be able to recognise and praise efforts and achievements.

You should be comfortable in maintaining discipline and be confident when speaking to large groups.

Working conditions

If you teach English as a foreign language, you may work in this country or abroad, teaching in community and learning centres or commercial and industrial settings.

Hours vary according to the employer, however evening and weekend work is common.

Future prospects

There is always a need for English language teachers to cope with the high demand of people who wish to learn English. However, competition is fierce for full-time positions. Most English language teachers are employed overseas on temporary contracts during the academic year. They may return to the UK to teach during the summer.

It is possible to progress to become a course director or course co-ordinator. With experience, you could get involved in teacher training or set up your own private language school.

Advantages/disadvantages

This is a very busy and demanding job as you will have to deal with preparation, teaching, marking and different examining bodies.

Teaching is a rewarding profession in which you can witness a student's progression and know that you played a major role in helping them master the English language.

Money guide

Teaching English in a UK commercial language school, you can expect a starting salary of £13,000–£18,000.

Experienced teachers or those in a senior role can earn £18,000–£30,000.

It is possible to achieve up to £36,000 if you take on management responsibilities.

Those who work on a part-time or seasonal basis usually receive an hourly or weekly rate.

If you work outside the UK, your salary is likely to be much lower.

Incentives offered by overseas language schools may include flights and accommodation.

Related opportunities

- Education and Childcare Inspector p193
- Further Education Lecturer p195
- Teaching Assistant/Learning Support Assistant p206

Further information

Cambridge ESOL
www.cambridgeesol.org

EDUCATION AND TRAINING

CRCI: F

Qualifications and courses

There are no specific academic requirements for entry to this career as local education authorities set their own requirements. Candidates need to be at least 18 years old to apply and must obtain clearance from the Criminal Records Bureau (CRB). Previous relevant experience, for example in nursing, childcare or youthwork, is an advantage.

CACHE, NCFE and Edexcel (BTEC) offer the Certificate in Support Work in Schools (Level 2) which may be useful. The Apprenticeship in Supporting Teaching and Learning in Schools is available to school leavers at both Intermediate and Advanced Level and leads to NVQs at Levels 2 or 3.

You will be trained on the job and local authorities in England and Wales may encourage you to study for professional qualifications while you work. Upon entry you can study for the NVQ in Supporting Teaching and Learning in Schools (Levels 2 and 3) or the SVQ in Supporting Teaching and Learning in Schools (Classroom Assistants) (Levels 2 and 3). Another option is the City & Guilds vocational Certificate in Supporting Teaching and Learning in Schools (Levels 2 and 3).

Experienced teaching assistants in England can work towards Higher Level Teaching Assistant (HLTA) status.

What the work involves

Teaching/classroom assistants help pupils to learn by supporting the teacher and, sometimes, by describing the work in a more visual way or reading questions aloud.

You may be required to plan and deliver parts of a lesson for the main teacher, working together to make the best use of time and resources.

Some teaching/classroom assistants will offer one-to-one support to students with learning difficulties or disabilities.

Type of person suited to this work

In this work, you need to like children to help them make the most of their time in school.

You will need lots of patience and possess the ability to stay calm, as all pupils have their off-days when they are noisy or upset.

Sometimes, you will work with students who need extra help so you should have an interest in young people who have special needs.

Working conditions

Many learning support assistants work in mainstream schools, but some are employed in independent schools, in residential institutions for students with special needs or specialist colleges.

You will normally work between 8.30am and 4.30pm, although you might have to attend meetings after this and sometimes at weekends.

Future prospects

Recent changes to teachers' workload have involved freeing them from some administrative tasks so they have more classroom time. This has increased the need for teaching assistants working across the UK.

You can progress to become a Higher Level Teaching Assistant (HLTA), which involves increased responsibility.

Experienced teaching assistants often train to become teachers themselves and there are Initial Teacher Training courses especially for teaching assistants.

Special needs learning assistants may specialise in helping young people with a particular disability.

Advantages/disadvantages

This can be a very rewarding job as you will witness students' educational development and growth.

You might help students take steps towards independent living.

You will be very busy and will have limited time to hold meetings with colleagues.

Money guide

Wages are set by local education authorities so the rates can vary across regions.

The starting salary for a teaching assistant ranges from £12,000 to £17,000.

Experienced HLTAs can achieve £16,000–£21,000 per year.

Related opportunities

- Childminder p567
- Play Worker/Hospital Play Specialist p198
- Primary School Teacher p199

Further information

CACHE
www.cache.org.uk

Training and Development Agency for Schools
www.tda.gov.uk

WORK-BASED TRAINING INSTRUCTOR

Qualifications and courses

You can work towards relevant qualifications whilst in employment, including NVQs/SVQs in learning and development at Levels 3, 4 and 5. The Chartered Institute of Personnel and Development (CIPD) offers a Certificate in Learning and Development Practice which is equivalent to NVQ/SVQ Level 3. The higher level NVQs/SVQs and the CIPD Professional Development Scheme are appropriate for people in training manager posts.

Postgraduate qualifications are available in subjects such as education and training management, training and development, mentoring and coaching. These can usually be studied part time or by distance learning. Entry requirements are a degree or equivalent professional qualification.

Training practitioners can also work towards gaining NVQ assessor qualifications. Entry requirements are at least 2 years of occupational experience in the subject or work area to be assessed.

Associate teachers at further education colleges or organisations funded by the government need a Certificate in Teaching in the Lifelong Learning Sector. Full teachers need to take a 1-year course to obtain the Diploma in Teaching in the Lifelong Learning Sector.

What the work involves

You will work alongside employees, in their workplace or in a training centre, and teach them new skills or develop their existing skills.

You will liaise closely with the employer's training or human resources manager in order to ascertain the type of training needed and organisational aspects.

It is likely that you will specialise in an area such as IT, management, personal development, customer service or craft.

Type of person suited to this work

It is essential to demonstrate a real interest in helping people to learn and progress.

You must be patient, organised and up to date with the latest developments in your occupational area. Good ICT skills will also be helpful.

Excellent communication skills are important for the large amount of speaking, questioning, listening and reporting that are involved.

Working conditions

You will work in an office where you will use a computer to prepare lessons and update learner records. However, you will also spend lots of time travelling to meet employers and learners at their workplaces.

You will work normal office hours, Monday to Friday.

Future prospects

New media and different ways of working mean that there is a continual need to help businesses and industry develop the right people to carry out new work tasks.

All companies today are expected to develop their workforces and the government is currently encouraging learning through work-based qualifications. Additionally, school/college leavers now have a wider range of opportunities to pursue such as Apprenticeships.

Promotion to a training manager or consultant is possible with experience and further qualifications such as NVQs at Levels 4 and 5.

Advantages/disadvantages

This work involves being at the centre of improving the skills levels of the workforce.

You constantly have the opportunity to learn new things.

It can be challenging to motivate trainees who do not have an interest in studying towards a qualification.

Money guide

Salaries vary depending on the type and size of employer and location. Larger salaries are possible if the specialised skill you teach is in high demand.

Starting salaries are about £16,000 a year.

With experience this can rise to between £18,000 and £20,000.

Top earners can expect £30,000.

Related opportunities

- Further Education Lecturer p195
- Human Resources/Personnel Officer p42
- Training Development Officer p68

Further information

Chartered Institute of Personnel and Development
www.cipd.co.uk

EDUCATION AND TRAINING

CRCI: F

Engineering, Manufacturing and Production

There are a number of highly skilled jobs available in this job family and workers need to be creative and methodical and combine brilliant technical skill with spatial awareness. You may be interested in food production but equally your passion could lie in working with aircraft or marine manufacture. People in these professions share the ability to concentrate for long periods of time and work meticulously on a job to finish it to a high standard. Some will also be highly trained with specialist equipment which may sometimes be hazardous to use so a high level of personal safety awareness is vital.

The jobs featured in this section are listed below.

Organisation profile

ROLLS-ROYCE APPRENTICESHIPS

'The best part of the Rolls-Royce apprenticeship is you're learning from the best to be the best.'

Gurjit Johal – Plant Design Engineer

Join the team that sets the standard

Why Rolls-Royce?

Because we set the standard, that's why.

Others may talk about achieving the impossible; we go out there and do it.

We've broken the sound barrier, produced engines that fly passengers around the world in record time and transported rescuers to previously unreachable places. We've even designed turbines that generate enough energy to power a city the size of New York.

It takes 39,000 people, including some of the world's most respected engineers, to make all this possible. Each one of us shares a fascination with how things work, and a passion for wanting to make them work better. Want to join us?

Go further with the Rolls-Royce of apprenticeships

The Rolls-Royce Apprenticeship Scheme, which was recently described as 'outstanding' by Ofsted inspectors, is designed to help you reach your full potential.

As one of our apprentices, you'll carry out mission-critical work, earning while you learn from the engineers and scientists behind the world's most important power systems.

Studying theory one day, the next putting it into practice, you'll have real responsibility from day one – and a steep learning curve. At the same time, you'll have the support you need to help you succeed. Plus the privilege of working with some of the world's best technology and practices.

Start your journey to becoming a world-renowned engineer

You can join us at just 14 as a Young Apprentice, combining your apprenticeship with school work, or wait until you're 16 and over and become a full-time apprentice. You can also opt for a Practical Apprenticeship, where you'll be hands-on, or a Technical Apprenticeship where you'll be mostly on the computer, problem solving.

Either way, you'll earn while you learn and there's a high possibility that we'll sponsor you for your degree.

What's more, when your apprenticeship finishes, you'll be off to a fantastic start – with all the skills, experience and confidence you need for a full-time role. Plus, with the retention rate for Rolls-Royce apprenticeships currently 98% (the national average is 65%), you can look forward to an exciting career with us.

See where a Rolls-Royce apprenticeship could take you, visit www.rolls-royce.com/apprenticeships

Trusted to deliver excellence

Case study

ROLLS-ROYCE APPRENTICESHIP

'I'm furthering my education while gaining invaluable work experience and being paid.'

Rachel Freestone
Advanced/Modern Apprenticeship in Mechanical Engineering

Rolls-Royce's apprenticeships are a genuine alternative to university. Combining classroom study with on-the-job training, they offer two routes to becoming a world-renowned engineer – practical and technical.

Rachel Freestone chose the practical route. She explains why. 'The Technical Apprenticeship is more theoretical. You're in the office, on the computer, which isn't me. I'm more hands-on and like being on the shop floor.'

Now in the second year of her 3.5-year apprenticeship, it's easy to see Rachel loves what she does. She comes alive when she talks about engines and it's surprising to think that, when younger, she wanted to be a hairdresser.

'This is much better than being a hairdresser,' Rachel confides. 'It's great to work with an engine from the start – from stripping it – to the end where it's tested. You learn about the engine in depth, especially since you're taught by amazing engineers who really know their stuff. You study one day; the next you put what you've learnt into practice. It's brilliant.'

So what's the biggest highlight of her apprenticeship so far? Rachel smiles, 'It's got to be when I first helped assemble the EJ200, a gas turbine engine which powers the Eurofighter Typhoon. It was the first engine I worked on in my career – amazing!'

Rachel concludes, 'I never really saw myself going to university. But, with Rolls-Royce, I'm currently studying for my HNC – and they may even sponsor my degree. The way I see it: what's the point of getting into debt at uni when you can earn while you learn with a good job at the end?'

See where a Rolls-Royce apprenticeship could take you, visit www.rolls-royce.com/apprenticeships

Qualifications and courses

Most entrants are graduates, and many have studied aeronautical engineering as a degree. Bachelor of Engineering degrees (BEng) last 3 years and Master of Engineering degrees (MEng) last 4. You will need at least 5 GCSEs/S grades (A*–C/1–3) and 2 A levels/Highers, including maths and physics, for entry to a degree. A postgraduate degree will give you an advantage; an appropriate Master's degree is a requirement to qualify as a chartered engineer. Prior work experience, for example doing a voluntary work placement at an industrial company, would be helpful.

It is possible to enter at a lower level by training as a craft or technician straight from school. Apprenticeship schemes usually require good GCSE/S grades in English, maths and physics.

Many companies offer graduate training schemes and some are accredited by a professional body such as the Royal Aeronautical Society. There is also the chance to work towards an engineering licence through the Civil Aviation Authority.

What the work involves

Aerospace engineers research, design and manufacture space vehicles, satellites, missiles and aircraft. You can specialise in mechanical, electrical or electronics engineering, and within these areas you can focus on airframes, hydraulics, materials and structures, or engines.

Your work might involve research, design and manufacture, or experimenting with new materials.

You may also undertake flight test programmes, and maintain and improve fleets of aircraft all over the world.

Type of person suited to this work

You should have a logical mind and be good at problem-solving. You should also be good at maths, and be able to produce good drawings and diagrams, as well as being able to interpret them well.

Your verbal and written communication skills should also be good, as you will need to communicate ideas effectively. Teamworking skills are essential, but you must also be able to take on responsibility and work independently.

You will be expected to keep up to date with new technology and developments in the industry, and for some roles you need to have normal colour vision.

Working conditions

It is usual to work 37–40 hours a week, but this depends a lot on project deadlines and what is currently taking place: hours can be longer.

Work usually takes place in clean quiet laboratories, but visits to production areas are essential and these areas are usually dirty and noisy.

Visits to airfields also take place, where you might be required to inspect and test the functions of the aircraft.

Future prospects

There are good opportunities for promotion in aerospace engineering. The skills you will require will make you suitable for higher positions even in other branches of engineering, and many aerospace engineers move into management positions or research roles as their career progresses.

Some aerospace engineers work independently as consultants, and others find work abroad for foreign governments or aircraft construction companies.

Advantages/disadvantages

You may have to work long hours, evenings and weekends. Stress levels can also be high if you are trying to meet deadlines.

The starting salary is relatively high, and you can work your way up to a good wage with time and experience.

Money guide

Starting salaries for graduates tend to range from £20,000 to £25,000 per year.

Depending on your professional status, you can work your way up to £40,000 per year as an experienced engineer.

Senior engineers might earn over £65,000.

Related opportunities

- Electrical Engineer p219
- Marine Engineer p231
- Mechanical Engineer p233

Further information

Institution of Engineering and Technology
www.theiet.org

Royal Aeronautical Society
www.aerosociety.com

The Engineering and Technology Board
www.etechb.co.uk

ASSEMBLER

ENTRY LEVEL 1

Qualifications and courses

There are no formal entry requirements for this work. Key Skills, GCSEs/S grades in English, maths and practical subjects or vocational qualifications in engineering/manufacturing can be useful.

You may have to undertake an entry test at interview that will assess your practical, reading and writing skills.

Apprenticeships/Skillseekers may be available to enter this area of work.

Training is on the job; you will be instructed on company policies such as health and safety, whilst working alongside a more experienced member of staff who will train you on the numerous assembly stages.

What the work involves

You will work on an assembly line within a factory or workshop, or at a bench. You could work on products within sectors as diverse as: engineering, furniture production, soft furnishings, domestic electrical equipment, vehicles or electrical circuit boards.

Assembly line

You will assemble products or components as they arrive at your work area. Sometimes they may not stop, but keep moving along a belt or route in the factory. As the line needs to keep going at a set speed, you will be required to work at the same pace as everyone else.

Bench

Using hand tools, and in some cases simple machinery, you will carry out specific assembly tasks or create a finished product.

Type of person suited to this work

You will need to have practical skills and enjoy making or repairing items. In order to construct your product or components, you will have to follow diagrams and instructions and be able to work quickly and precisely.

You need good interpersonal skills and a solid work ethic.

As it can be repetitive work you must be able to focus on the same task many times a day.

Working conditions

Assembly line

You can expect to be in a large factory – in some sectors this could be noisy, dirty and busy and in others, such as the electronics industry, it would be clean and dust-free.

Some assembly lines require 24/7 production; if so, you will normally work a shift pattern.

Bench

You will be sitting or standing using the tools and machinery positioned around you. If you need to use a soldering iron for assembly it can be hot work and may cause fumes. You can also work part time.

Future prospects

The largest employers of assemblers are the electrical, electronic and information technology industries.

As machines are increasingly replacing some of the assembly work that used to be done by people, jobs are reducing. However there is still demand for assemblers to work on assembling products that are too intricate to be done by machine, or for assembling very small batches of goods.

With experience, you may be able to progress into a supervisory role or other areas of manufacturing such as quality control. You could also go on to train as an engineering craft worker.

Advantages/disadvantages

Whilst carrying out repetitive tasks, you must be able to concentrate and maintain a fast pace of work for long periods of time.

Your surroundings may be dirty and noisy.

Owing to advances in technology, the need for workers will continue to drop.

Part-time work is also available, which is attractive to people with families wanting to supplement their income.

Money guide

Starting salaries for assemblers are on average between £10,000 and £12,000 per year.

For experienced assemblers salaries can range from £13,500 to £17,000.

Very skilled and experienced assemblers in certain parts of the industry, such as automotive assembly, or those with supervisory responsibilities can earn around £20,000 a year.

Salaries may vary if you work on piece rates (pay for each product produced).

There is the potential for overtime or for shift work.

Related opportunities

- Food Processing Operative p224
- Mechanical Engineer p233
- Welder p248

Further information

Proskills UK
www.proskills.co.uk

Semta
www.semta.org.uk

ENGINEERING, MANUFACTURING AND PRODUCTION

CRCI: NJ

213

BLACKSMITH

Qualifications and courses

You can enter this career by completing an Apprenticeship and training on the job. To gain access to an Apprenticeship, you will need to approach individual employers and see if they are willing to take you on. Consequently, availability is not guaranteed and will depend on your local jobs market.

Alternatively, you can complete a college course. Some courses may require specific GCSEs/S grades and forge-work experience. HNDs and degrees in creative aspects of blacksmithing are available. To gain entry, you will need 2 A levels/3 H grades and 5 GCSEs/S grades (A*–C/1–3).

The National Crafts Training Programme combines on-the-job training with periods of block-release study at college. This takes from 2 to 3 years to complete.

Herefordshire College of Technology offers a degree and diplomas in blacksmithing and metalwork, as well as a farriery access programme. As contacts are so important in this field for securing work, it may be beneficial to join a professional body such as the British Artist Blacksmiths Association (BABA) to attend relevant courses and make new contacts in the industry.

What the work involves

You will shape and join metals like steel, iron, copper and bronze to produce decorative pieces, such as gates and furniture or functional objects for use by companies, such as fire escapes and security screens. You may also restore antique iron work.

You may create specially commissioned pieces such as a stairway for a building project or specialise in an area such as agricultural engineering or security.

If you specialise in artistic work, you are likely to be self-employed. Your job will therefore include all of the administrative tasks needed to run a business, alongside the general work as a blacksmith. You will also have to find business and this may involve attending craft shows and fairs.

Type of person suited to this work

Blacksmiths mostly work alone so you should be able to use your initiative.

Much of your time will be spent on your feet using different hand tools, often near to the forge which will be very hot. You will need to be very responsible, as the tools and materials that you will be working with can be dangerous.

Having a creative flair will help you to use your materials imaginatively. You will also need an understanding of the way products function and how different metal properties will affect the end product.

Working conditions

You will work with various metals and use different hand and bench tools and a forge. This will result in conditions that can be noisy, dirty and sometimes cramped. You will spend much of the time on your feet and you will wear protective clothing such as gloves, ear protectors and goggles.

You could work in rural areas or in mines, docks and with engineering companies.

Future prospects

With experience you may move on to work for a museum or heritage centre.

If you work within a company, you might progress to supervisory or managerial posts. Most blacksmiths however are self-employed. Future success will rely on your ability to gain orders and build a reputation.

Advantages/disadvantages

Much of the work is done alone and can be isolating.

The work is tiring, but when you have created what a customer requires it can be satisfying too.

If you are involved in a creative project such as a commissioned sculpture, it can be very rewarding.

Money guide

There are currently no agreed minimum rates for apprentice blacksmiths so salaries can vary widely.

Starting salaries generally range from £12,000 to £16,000 a year.

Once training has been completed you could earn in excess of £25,000 depending on regional differences.

Highly experienced blacksmiths earn over £50,000.

Related opportunities

- Bricklayer p74
- Farrier p265
- Sheet Metal Worker p242

Further information

British Artist Blacksmiths Association
www.baba.org.uk

National Association of Farriers, Blacksmiths and Agricultural Engineers
www.nafbae.org

Worshipful Company of Blacksmiths
www.blacksmithscompany.org.uk

Qualifications and courses

There are no set entry requirements for this career. Having GCSEs/S grades in English, maths and science may be helpful. Sometimes it is possible to start with a role in packaging operations and progress to brewery worker.

There may be an Apprenticeship/Skillseekers available in your area in food manufacture which leads to this career.

Brewery workers can train on the job and study for NVQs at Levels 1, 2 and 3 in food manufacture. Brewing Research International (BRI) offers the opportunity to progress into the more technical side of the industry, though this requires you to be educated to degree level. The Institute of Brewing and Distilling also offers short courses in drink manufacture.

It may be helpful to complete the NVQ Level 3 in Food Manufacture if you wish to progress to a supervisory post. There are also several courses are run by the Institute of Brewing and Distilling.

What the work involves

You will make and package beer, stout and lager for a variety of outlets including shops and pubs.

You could be involved in the whole beer making process or just certain stages.

You will work as part of a team supervised by a technical brewer. Your jobs will include weighing and mixing ingredients, monitoring quality, labelling and packing the product and loading the beer ready for dispatch.

Type of person suited to this work

You will need to enjoy working in a team, and be aware of the health and safety regulations to keep yourself and others safe at work.

The work is quite physically demanding; you will be lifting and operating heavy machinery so will need to be fit and healthy.

Good numeracy skills will be helpful when measuring out ingredients and checking the amount of products produced.

Working conditions

Most large breweries have a shift system in place for their workers. You will usually work around 40 hours a week, and can work overtime if necessary.

You will be working with machinery and fermenting ingredients, therefore overalls, gloves and goggles may be worn to limit contamination and to keep you safe.

You will have to work through all weather conditions, loading products and unloading raw materials.

Future prospects

After a few years of experience you can move into a supervisory or management role, in charge of a team of brewery workers.

Often brewery workers study further to become craft technical brewers.

Jobs traditionally carried out by brewery workers are increasingly being completed by computerised machinery. However, jobs such as weighing and measuring, sterilising equipment, cleaning the work area and keeping records of ingredients still need to be done by brewery workers.

Advantages/disadvantages

Owing to the decline in breweries across the UK, it can be difficult to find work; many smaller breweries are family run, employing very few staff.

Working in a brewery can be smelly, hot and physically demanding; this may be stressful or tiring at times. However, working in a team of other brewery workers creates a lively and fun atmosphere.

Making beer, stout and lager is a satisfying job role as you know you are creating beverages that people enjoy drinking.

Money guide

The amount you earn does depend on the location and size of the brewery you work for.

Average starting salaries can be up to £15,000, with this rising to £22,000 with a few years' experience.

Senior brewery workers or those in supervisory roles may earn £29,000+.

Related opportunities

- Cellar Technician p136
- Craft Technical Brewer p218
- Food Processing Operative p224

Further information

Institute of Brewing and Distilling
www.ibd.org.uk

ENGINEERING, MANUFACTURING AND PRODUCTION

CRCI: NC

CAD DRAUGHTSPERSON

Qualifications and courses

You can enter this job as a trainee technician by learning from an employer through the Advanced Apprenticeship in Engineering Manufacture (Craft and Technician). Most entrants are aged 16–19 but entry is possible up to the age of 24. Applicants require 4 GCSEs/S grades (A*–C/1–3) or equivalent including maths and science or technology.

The Engineering Construction Industry Training Board (ECITB) also offer 3-year Apprenticeships for Design and Draughting Technicians.

Alternatively, you can take relevant pre-entry qualifications such as the City & Guilds Awards and Certificates in Computer Aided Design and Manufacturing (Levels 1–3), the City & Guilds Award in Computer Aided Design and Parametric Modelling (Levels 1–3), the BTEC First in Engineering (Level 2) or the BTEC National in Engineering (Level 3).

Qualifications that can be obtained through on-the-job training include NVQs/SVQs at Level 3, BTEC National Certificates or Diplomas, or a City & Guilds Certificate.

What the work involves

You will produce the drawings and instructions that will enable others to create structures, equipment or components.

Using a computer-aided design (CAD) workstation you will draw up technical drawings for components or sections of a structure, or for different products.

Depending on the specialism of the company you work for, you may design part of a structure as large as a factory or bridge, or a component as small as an electronic circuit.

Type of person suited to this work

You should be patient, accurate and have a good understanding of different production processes.

You need to be organised and methodical in your work and able to work to tight deadlines.

Good IT, technical drawing and numerical skills are essential. You will need to be able to solve design problems in a creative way and you should be comfortable and confident communicating your work to others.

Working conditions

Most of your work will be done sitting in front of your computer or drawing board in an office or design area.

You will work normal office hours but you might need to work overtime when deadlines are close.

Sometimes you will visit the shop floor or factory area where the product you are designing is being made and conditions could be noisy, hot and dirty. However, your own workspace will be quiet as a lot of concentration is required.

Future prospects

A wide range of employers recruit CAD draughtspeople including aeronautical, civil, electrical, mechanical and marine engineering companies, central and local government and the public utilities such as water and electricity supply.

All construction and manufacturing companies across the UK need trained draughtspeople which means they are in constant demand.

You can progress to senior, supervisory and team-leader work with experience and training. With further qualifications you could become an architect or a chartered engineer. There are also opportunities to work abroad.

Advantages/disadvantages

As much of your work involves using your drawing board or computer, your eyes could get tired and strained.

If you want to progress, you can move to supervisor level within your own company or elsewhere.

With experience, it may be possible to work on a freelance basis, being contracted by smaller companies who do not employ their own draughtsperson.

Money guide

Earnings will be affected by the type of industry you work in and your geographical location.

Starting salaries are typically between £15,000 and £20,000 per year.

With experience, you can expect to earn £23,000–£30,000.

High earners employed at a senior level can achieve up to £40,000 a year.

Related opportunities

- Architectural Technician p71
- Architectural Technologist p72
- Graphic Designer p175

Further information

Chartered Institute of Architectural Technologists
www.ciat.org.uk

Tomorrow's Engineers
www.tomorrowsengineers.org.uk

Qualifications and courses

This career is open to graduates with a degree in physical or applied sciences, or engineering. Specific subjects such as chemistry, chemical engineering, applied chemistry and polymer science may improve your chances further. HNDs in similar subjects are also considered although you might have to start as a technician and work up to the position of chemical engineer as you gain further qualifications. You will need a minimum of 5 GCSEs/S grades (A*–C/1–3) including English, maths and science, and 2 A levels/H grades in order to gain a place on an engineering or related degree/HND course.

Your degree or HND must be accredited by the Institution of Chemical Engineers (IChemE) if you want to qualify as a Chartered Chemical Engineer (CEng). Becoming chartered can significantly enhance your career prospects.

Entry without a degree or HND is uncommon, although you may be able to secure an Apprenticeship in engineering, which could lead to a role as an engineering technician and may provide the opportunity to study for a relevant degree.

Chemical engineers need to commit to a programme of continuing professional development (CPD) to make sure their skills are kept up to date throughout their career.

What the work involves

You will devise low-cost, safe and environmentally friendly methods that will transform raw materials into products such as fuel, pharmaceuticals, plastics and toiletries.

You might research ways to improve the future of our planet which could include discovering renewable energy sources or producing replacement human organs.

You might work in manufacturing and help design and construct plants for mass production of products. You will then oversee the running of the plant and the quality of its products.

Type of person suited to this work

You will need to have good oral and written communication skills in order to brief colleagues and compile extensive reports from research you have undertaken. Project management skills are also very important.

An analytical mind and the ability to problem solve are helpful when designing and testing products or equipment in the plant itself.

You will also need to be creative in order to come up with cost-effective products and solutions to problems.

An aptitude and interest in chemistry is also recommended, as is a good understanding of engineering and maths.

Working conditions

Working hours are normally standard office hours from Monday to Friday, although you might have to work overtime on occasion (including evenings and weekends), particularly if you are developing a new product.

You will usually work in a plant, laboratory or research establishment so conditions can vary from peaceful, sterile labs to noisier factory floors.

You might need to wear appropriate safety equipment for certain aspects of the job.

Future prospects

Jobs are available across the UK in a range of industries, from pharmaceuticals to oil and gas.

Opportunities for progression and promotion are good; you could obtain a position in senior management or a project leader role.

Chemical engineers are encouraged to achieve chartered or incorporated status.

Advantages/disadvantages

You will continue to learn new skills and gain qualifications throughout your career.

You will have the opportunity to work in a range of industries and possibly abroad.

Some of the conditions that you work in could be distracting or challenging.

Money guide

Typical graduate starting salaries range from £20,000 to £28,000.

Experienced engineers can expect to earn £30,000–£55,000.

Senior chemical engineers can achieve in excess of £60,000.

Earnings will be higher for those who have achieved chartered status.

Related opportunities

- Environmental Engineer p223
- Manufacturing/Production Engineer p229
- Mechanical Engineer p233

Further information

British Chemical Engineering Contractors Association
www.bceca.org.uk

Institution of Chemical Engineers
www.icheme.org

Semta
www.semta.org.uk

The Career Engineer
www.thecareerengineer.com

ENGINEERING, MANUFACTURING AND PRODUCTION

CRCI: GD

Qualifications and courses

Trainee technical brewers usually have a degree or postgraduate qualification. Degrees in brewing and distilling, food studies, biochemistry and biology are all relevant. Entry requirements for a degree are 5 GCSEs/S grades and at least 2 A levels/H grades.

Starting out as a brewery worker or production assistant and progressing to technical brewer may also be possible. Usually only GCSEs/S grades are needed to start in these roles.

Work experience in a brewery will help an application as a technical brewer.

Technical brewers usually have further training when they begin work. The Institute of Brewing and Distilling offers a range of courses for general brewing and specialist subjects; these include a general certificate in brewing, distilling and packaging, a diploma in brewing modules and master brewing modules.

What the work involves

You will be overseeing the whole brewing process, managing the brewery workers and monitoring the condition of the brewing equipment.

Technical brewers are responsible for checking the quality of raw materials and testing the product regularly for texture, taste and appearance.

In a large brewery you may specialise in a certain area of brewing, such as fermentation, packaging or quality control, whereas in a small brewery you are likely to be involved with all aspects of the brewing process.

You will be responsible for developing new brewing methods, and designing and developing new beers, stouts and lagers.

Type of person suited to this work

You will need to be scientific, with an enquiring mind and a particular interest in biochemistry. Both a practical ability and an interest in engineering are also useful.

Leadership and interpersonal skills are needed as you will be managing a team of brewers. Good communication skills are also needed as you will be responsible for writing reports, keeping records and presenting new brewery methods to your colleagues.

Working conditions

As brewing is a continuous process, you will work shifts including nights and weekends. Usually you will work no more that 40 hours a week.

Some technical brewers will need to be on their feet all day, checking the brewing process, in hot and noisy conditions.

Some time will be spent in an office organising paperwork and making reports on production, stock quality and budgets.

Future prospects

Owing to the decline in breweries in the UK, competition for positions is high. The highest concentration of jobs is in the east of England and London; this may mean relocating.

You can progress to managerial roles and senior brewer positions in a large brewery. Some brewers can choose to set up their own microbrewery.

There are opportunities to work abroad.

Advantages/disadvantages

This is an interesting and diverse role, which can lead to good promotions and self-employment.

Working night shifts in a hot and smelly environment may be tiring and stressful.

Money guide

Starting salaries are generally between £15,000 and £19,000 per year; this can increase to £30,000 with some experience.

Senior brewers working in a large brewery may earn up to £40,000.

Related opportunities

- Biotechnologist p505
- Brewery Worker p215
- Cellar Technician p136

Further information

Brewing Research International
www.brewingresearch.co.uk

Institute of Brewing and Distilling
www.ibd.org.uk

Qualifications and courses

You will need a degree in a subject such as electrical or electronic engineering, mechanical engineering, applied physics or computer science. For degree entry you will need at least 2 A levels/H grades and 5 GCSEs/S grades (A*–C/1–3) including maths and science. Graduate schemes are available from many employers.

You could train to become an electrical engineering technician straight from school through the Advanced Apprenticeship in Engineering Manufacture (Craft and Technician) or the Higher Level Apprenticeship in Engineering Manufacture (Senior Technician). You will need good GCSEs/S grades (A*–C/1–3) in English, maths, science or technology. However, in order to become an engineer, you will need to study for a degree.

Scholarships, sponsorships and placements are available and the Institution of Engineering and Technology (IET) provides further information on these schemes.

Undertaking work experience or a vacation placement may be advantageous.

Those with a BEng or equivalent can apply for incorporated engineer (IEng) status and those who have studied to master's level can gain chartered engineer (CEng) status.

What the work involves

Electrical engineers research, design and develop a range of electrical equipment. You will be making, testing and servicing all types of electrical equipment and machinery, and as such you will be involved in projects from conception to completion.

You will usually work on projects with a team of professionals, including contractors and engineers from other industries.

You will also be liaising with clients and contractors about the development of each project, which will involve preparing reports and giving presentations.

Type of person suited to this work

You should have excellent mathematical ability and a very analytical mind in order to successfully design and develop complicated new electrical systems. A logical approach to problem-solving is also beneficial.

You will need good communication skills, both verbal and written, for working alongside team members and clients. This will involve explaining and talking through projects, as well as compiling written reports and leading presentations.

You must have normal colour vision and natural manual dexterity.

Working conditions

Although electrical engineers usually work within the normal working week, you may find that you need to work additional or unsocial hours in order to solve problems and meet project deadlines.

Your time will be divided between office-based and on-site work. You can expect to travel on a daily basis so a driving licence is useful.

Conditions on site can often be dirty, cramped and potentially hazardous so you should be prepared to get your hands dirty and wear safety equipment.

Future prospects

There are no set pathways of career progression for electrical engineers and many decide to stay in a purely engineering role for the duration of their working life.

Alternatively, there are possibilities to move into project management, become a consultant or take on a more managerial role within a company.

Advantages/disadvantages

Your work will be undertaken at a variety of indoor and outdoor locations so you will not be confined to an office environment.

You will play an instrumental role in developing new and increasingly safe electrical equipment for a variety of important functions.

Hours can be long and unpredictable, especially when nearing completion of a project.

Money guide

The starting salary for a graduate electrical engineer can range from £20,000 to £25,000.

Experienced incorporated engineers are likely to earn £28,000–£38,000 a year.

Experienced chartered engineers usually receive a salary of £40,000–£50,000.

Salaries vary according to the size, type and geographical location of a company.

Some companies offer excellent benefit packages and bonus schemes in addition to a basic wage.

Related opportunities

- Civil/Construction Engineer/Civil Engineering Technician p83
- Mechanical Engineer p233
- Telecommunications Engineer p244

Further information

Institution of Engineering and Technology
www.theiet.org

ELECTRICITY DISTRIBUTION WORKER

Qualifications and courses

Most people start in this career as an apprentice. Although there are no set qualifications, most employers look for a minimum of 4 GCSEs/S grades (A*–C/1–3) including English, maths and a related subject such as science, design and technology or engineering. The Advanced Apprenticeship in Engineering Manufacture (Craft and Technician) may be available. Apprenticeships are open to those aged 16–24 and could last up to 4 years. You will undertake a mixture of on-the-job practical training and college-based study.

Relevant qualifications include the City & Guilds NVQ in Electrical Power Engineering (Levels 2 and 3) and the BTEC National in Electrical/Electronic Engineering (Level 3).

On completion of your training, you could work towards becoming a registered engineering technician (EngTech) with the Engineering Council, which will improve your earning potential and career prospects.

What the work involves

Electrical distribution workers are responsible for installing, checking and maintaining all machinery and equipment that supplies electricity to commercial and residential properties. You will be working on a variety of projects from small-scale domestic problems to regional electrical concerns.

You will be working on the overhead lines, masts and underground cables that run from power stations and connect all the electricity networks together.

You could work as a cable jointer who mainly works on the underground cables, an overhead line worker or an electrical fitter who installs, tests and repairs equipment in the regional electricity substations.

Type of person suited to this work

You will need to be practical and good with your hands as you will be using a variety of tools and undertaking fiddly tasks. You must have normal colour vision and pay meticulous attention to detail.

You should be reasonably fit with a head for heights, as some jobs may require lifting and carrying heavy equipment or working high above the ground.

Since you will be working with live electricity, you must be aware of your own safety and that of others around you. You may need to wear protective equipment at times.

Working conditions

Although you will usually work an average of 37 hours a week, these may involve shift patterns including evenings and weekends. You should also expect to work overtime on occasion in order to complete projects on time.

The work can be physically demanding as you will be bending and carrying large cables and equipment. You may work outdoors in damp and muddy trenches and you can expect to be carrying out tasks in cramped conditions sometimes.

Future prospects

As an electricity distribution worker, you will have various options available as you progress in your career. You may go on to become a supervisor or manager and be responsible for a team of workers. Alternatively, you could move into another related job within the industry.

Your career prospects could be improved by studying for additional qualifications as you work, such as an NVQ Level 4 in electrical engineering, or even a relevant degree.

Advantages/disadvantages

You will be on site for the majority of your time so you will not be confined to an office environment

Possibilities for career progression or diversification are good.

Conditions can be unpleasant owing to extreme weather or space constraints.

You may have to work irregular/unsocial hours.

Money guide

Apprentices typically earn between £11,000 and £15,000 per year, depending on the stage of their training.

The starting salary for a qualified electricity distribution worker is usually about £18,000–£22,000.

Experienced workers, who are employed in a senior or managerial role, can achieve £30,000–£45,000.

Related opportunities

- Electrical Engineer p219
- Electrician p92
- Gas Network Engineer p226

Further information

Engineering Council UK
www.engc.org.uk

Institution of Engineering and Technology
www.theiet.org

ENERGY ENGINEER

Qualifications and courses

This career is open to all graduates with a degree in engineering, maths, chemistry or physics. Specific subjects such as petroleum engineering, mineral engineering, mechanical engineering or structural engineering may improve your chances further. Entry might be possible with a degree in geology or natural science. For non-accredited degrees, graduates will need to complete a conversion course to upgrade their qualifications. There is a wide variety of dedicated postgraduate courses in engineering which may help secure a more senior position.

Most entrants to graduate training programmes for the larger oil companies will have gained a high 2.1 in their subject, and MEng degrees are preferred. A postgraduate MSc in offshore or petroleum engineering may increase your chances of employment.

Experience is also important so a summer internship or work experience will also be beneficial. As some jobs may be off-shore or take place overseas, a basic knowledge of another language could be helpful.

Entry requirements for engineering or related degrees are a minimum of 5 GCSEs/S grades (A*–C/1–3) including English, maths and science, and 3 A levels/Highers. Alternative entry qualifications may include relevant BTEC National Diplomas or Access courses.

What the work involves

You will be involved with the extraction of oil and gas and the production of energy from renewable or sustainable sources, such as wind power, solar power or biofuels.

You will have to calculate how much oil or gas a well will produce and decide how to extract as much as possible and also oversee the drilling operations on an offshore rig.

You could also have to research new ways of generating energy, whilst developing ways of improving existing processes.

Type of person suited to this work

Excellent communication and interpersonal skills are needed for teamwork and to build strong relationships with other professionals and clients.

You should have a high level of numeracy and good IT skills, as well as scientific understanding of related fields such as geology and chemistry.

You will need to have excellent planning, organisational and problem-solving skills to successfully run a project.

Working conditions

If you become involved with power plant or drilling operations, you could work on a 7-day shift system, which would include nights and weekends, whereas, working in design, research and development will mean working more standard office hours.

The work is both mentally and physically demanding and conditions onsite are often noisy, wet, cold and inhospitable.

Some jobs may involve international travel and long stays away from home.

Future prospects

You could be employed in the oil and gas industry, energy production companies or move into the education field through government and university research.

The renewable energy industry is expanding, owing to increased interest in environmental issues, the greater demand for oil and gas and the pressure on businesses to reduce their carbon footprint.

With experience, you could move into planning, policy development, or freelance consultancy.

Advantages/disadvantages

Oil drilling in particular operates in some of the most dangerous and hostile areas of the world, so your safety could be threatened on a daily basis.

It will be rewarding to know that you have helped to minimise environmental damage.

You will have to be prepared to spend some time away from home.

Money guide

Salaries for graduates typically range from £22,000 to £30,000, with the larger salaries coming from the big oil companies.

After 5 years, you could earn between £30,000 and £60,000.

Engineers in managerial roles could earn up to £100,000.

Salaries are performance based, and the location of your projects will influence the amount you are paid. Most companies give additional benefits or allowances for overseas work.

Related opportunities

- Civil/Construction Engineer/Civil Engineering Technician p83
- Environmental Engineer p223
- Mechanical Engineer p233

Further information

Engineering Council UK
www.engc.org.uk

Oil Careers
www.oilcareers.com

ENGINEERING, MANUFACTURING AND PRODUCTION

CRCI: GI

ENGINEERING CRAFT MACHINIST

Qualifications and courses

Entry into this career is usually between the ages of 16 and 18 via the Advanced Apprenticeship in Engineering Manufacture (Craft and Technician). Most employers require candidates for Apprenticeships to have at least 4 GCSEs/S grades (A*–C/1–3) including English, maths, a science subject and either technology, engineering or a related subject.

As an apprentice, you will undertake several months of training away from the workplace to develop your skills. You will then spend 2–3 years working for a company whilst also attending college and studying towards relevant professional qualifications. These could include the BTEC First in Engineering (Level 2), the NVQ in Mechanical Manufacturing Engineering (Levels 2 and 3) and the BTEC National in Mechanical Engineering or Manufacturing Engineering (Level 3).

Entry for older candidates is possible, although they must be able to demonstrate some relevant experience and skills. Some employers will be willing to support you in working towards an NVQ Level 3 qualification.

What the work involves

Engineering machinists make engineered parts from various materials, such as metals or heavy and lightweight plastics. You could make parts for a variety of products, from domestic appliances and machines to wind turbines and aeroplane engines.

You will be using a range of machinery, including grinding and cutting machines, drills and presses. Increasingly, computer numerically controlled (CNC) machinery is being used which combines some of the manufacturing processes.

You will need to interpret complicated engineering drawings in order to assess which materials, tools and machines to use to produce each part.

Type of person suited to this work

You will need to have good eyesight, excellent coordination and sound practical ability in order to operate machinery safely and accurately.

Good mathematical skills and the ability to read complicated engineering drawings and interpret them into a 3D part are essential.

You should have strong communication skills as you will mainly be working in a team environment. A good level of physical fitness is also beneficial as the job involves lifting heavy materials and standing or bending over machinery for the majority of the day.

Working conditions

Working hours are usually around 38 per week, Monday to Friday, although you will usually start early in the morning and finish early in the afternoon.

Some larger companies operate 24-hour production and would require you to work shifts including evenings and weekends. Conditions in factories and workshops are usually fairly pleasant, although it can be noisy at times.

As you are operating machinery, you will need to wear appropriate safety equipment at all times.

Future prospects

There are jobs available for machinists throughout Britain, although the majority are found in larger cities and within general mechanical engineering companies.

With experience, you could be promoted to become team leader or supervisor and if you gain further qualifications you could go on to specialise in areas such as design.

Job prospects are good as there is currently a shortage of machinists in the engineering sector.

Advantages/disadvantages

Jobs are available throughout the UK and there is little travelling involved so you will rarely be absent from home.

It is a physically demanding role, with large amounts of time spent standing or bending over machinery and lifting heavy materials and equipment.

You may have to work unsocial hours owing to early starts or unpredictable shift patterns.

Money guide

Starting salaries for trainees are usually between £12,000 and £15,000.

With experience, your earnings can rise to £17,000–£25,000.

Those employed in a senior position with supervisory responsibilities can achieve up to £30,000 a year.

Related opportunities

- Motor Vehicle Technician p234
- Sheet Metal Worker p242
- Toolmaker p246

Further information

Semta
www.semta.org.uk

ENVIRONMENTAL ENGINEER

ENTRY LEVEL 4

Qualifications and courses

Most employers require a degree in a relevant subject such as civil or environmental engineering. You may be considered if you have studied another engineering subject, or something related such as physics, applied physics or maths. You will need at least 2 A levels/ Highers and 5 GCSEs/S grades (A*–C/1–3), including maths and physics, for degree entry.

You can also enter with an HND in a relevant subject such as general engineering, civil engineering, environmental engineering, applied physics or computing and IT. Some employers do prefer graduates, however, so supplementing your HND with work experience is highly recommended.

Some companies offer a sponsorship scheme for candidates who have completed their A levels/Highers. This sponsorship consists of financial support to the candidate throughout their degree programme and the offer of an apprenticeship upon graduation.

To become a professional engineer, you will need to take a Master's degree to gain Incorporated Engineer (IEng) or Chartered Engineer (CEng) status.

What the work involves

Environmental engineers work on projects concerning waste management, land reclamation and pollution control, and liaise with a variety of clients from local authorities to private property developers.

You will visit and assess numerous sites in relation to their environmental impact, and will explain your findings to clients via presentations and reports.

You may also communicate the environmental issues of a project or site to the general public, green groups and regulatory authorities.

Type of person suited to this work

You should have excellent mathematical ability and a very analytical mind in order to successfully carry out complicated procedures and calculations to assess sites and projects. A swift and logical approach to problem-solving is also needed when dealing with often unforeseen environmental complications.

Good both verbal and written communication skills are essential for working alongside team members and clients.

Negotiation skills are also helpful as you might need to reach compromises over projects with local government officials, residents or clients.

Working conditions

You will usually work 35–40 hours from Monday to Friday, although additional or unsocial hours are not uncommon should problems occur or if deadlines need to be met on a project.

Your time will be divided between office-based and on-site work, so you can expect to travel on a daily basis. A driving licence is essential.

You will work in all weather conditions on-site, so should be prepared to get cold and muddy. You will also have to adhere to site safety regulations and wear relevant protective clothing.

Future prospects

As environmental concerns become an increasingly important aspect of construction projects across the globe, there are good prospects and opportunities within this field for career progression.

With experience, you could move into consultancy and set up your own firm. Alternatively, you could specialise in an area such as treatment of industrial waste, or provision of drinking water in developing countries.

You could work in a small company, or in much larger multinational firms. There are also numerous opportunities to work on projects abroad.

Advantages/disadvantages

You will be responsible for minimising the environmental impact of building projects and protecting the wellbeing of the natural surroundings, which will be rewarding.

Working on potentially controversial developments could lead to confrontations with local residents or clients.

There are excellent opportunities to work overseas, or set up your own company.

Money guide

The starting salary for an environmental engineer can range from £18,000 to £24,000.

With a few years' experience, your salary could rise to £30,000–£40,000.

Senior environmental engineers can earn £60,000+.

Related opportunities

- Environmental Health Practitioner/Officer p36
- Marine Engineer p231
- Mechanical Engineer p233

Further information

Chartered Institution of Water and Environmental Management
www.ciwem.org

Engineering Council UK
www.engc.org.uk

The Career Engineer
www.thecareerengineer.com

CRCI: TD/ BB

Qualifications and courses

There are no set qualifications. Some employers will ask for basic levels of literacy and numeracy. If you want to progress into a supervisory role, you might need GCSEs/S grades (A*–C/1–3) in English, maths, science or food technology. Some companies will require you to be 18 or over to start work.

An Apprenticeship in Food Manufacture may also be useful.

Most training will take place on the job. Practical skills will be taught, as well as general health and safety with food safety. You can improve your skills by taking an NVQ/SVQ (Level 1–4) in Food and Drink Manufacturing Operations.

With time, you can work towards progressing to a management role or supervisory position. At an operative level, you can choose to move to different areas of food production, such as baking, freezing or brewing.

What the work involves

Food processing operatives can be involved in one of many areas of food processing. These include freezing, canning, baking, drying, cooking, chilling, pasteurising or a combination of several of these processes.

Since much of the work above is carried out by machines, you may be involved in operating the machinery, and you might also be expected to carry out basic maintenance on it.

You might be involved in the production of the food, for example placing different components of foodstuffs in containers. Packaging and labelling are other tasks that you might be required to carry out.

Type of person suited to this work

It is helpful if you have an interest in food and food processing.

You should be good at working in a team, and be able to respond quickly to problems that may arise. You need to be able to stay alert and perceptive at all times, even if tasks are mundane or boring. A good ability to concentrate and observe what is going on around you will really help with this.

Good literacy and numeracy skills are also essential, and you will need to be able to follow instructions easily, both written and spoken. A thorough understanding of health and safety requirements is also an advantage.

Working conditions

You will be working in a factory environment most of the time. This will involve standing in a production line, as well as bending and lifting. Temperature in the factory varies according to the processes taking place, and could be very warm or quite chilly.

You will almost certainly be required to wear special clothing, such as overalls and hats, and a high level of personal hygiene is essential.

You can expect to work 37 to 40 hours a week, usually on a shift system which may include weekends. Overtime is often available.

Future prospects

Progression within the food and drink industry is relatively common, and if committed you stand a good chance of moving up in your company or moving to others.

You can progress to supervisory and management positions quite quickly. Most managers in this sector started out as a food processing operative or something similar.

Advantages/disadvantages

The working environment may not always be pleasant: it can be very hot or very cold. Work may be mundane at times, and the salary is not very high.

There are usually plenty of jobs available in this sector, and prospects for promotion are good. If you work your way up jobs become more interesting and better paid.

Money guide

Salaries start at about £11,900 per year, but some apprentices might earn less.

This can rise to £16,500 as you gain experience.

Supervisors and managers can earn in excess of £18,000.

Related opportunities

- Brewery Worker p215
- Food Safety Officer p139
- Meat Process Worker p232

Further information

Food and Drink Federation
www.fdf.org.uk

Improve Ltd
www.improveltd.co.uk

Scottish Food and Drink Federation
www.sfdf.org.uk

Qualifications and courses

Most employers do not require any specific qualifications, but some ask for GCSEs/S grades (A*–C/1–3). You may need to pass an eyesight and colour vision test.

Apprenticeships in Wood Making and in Making and Installing Furniture are available.

Training usually occurs on the job. As a trainee you could follow a part-time course in college and gain a relevant qualification. This could be a City & Guilds Certificate in Furniture Production, or one of many NVQ qualifications in furniture manufacturing.

What the work involves

Furniture manufacturers construct pieces of furniture; they may either use machinery, or construct furniture by hand.

This involves cutting and shaping individual parts of each piece, then assembling them to make a finished item. You may then have to smooth and finish items, getting them ready for sale.

You will usually then be asked to add handles and hinges, and sometimes to upholster the furniture too.

Type of person suited to this work

You must be practical and good with your hands.

You should also have excellent eyesight and full colour vision. Hand-to-eye coordination is a must.

Some jobs will also require artistic ability. You must be accurate, careful, and above all patient.

Your physical strength should be reasonably good, as you will need to lift and carry things.

You must be able to take orders, and work under supervision. It is also important to be able to work in a team.

Tasks may become repetitive, but you need to be able to stay focused at all times.

Working conditions

You will be working in a factory, so the environment may be noisy. Most jobs require you to stand in a production line all day, and the air may be dusty and smell strongly of the products used to treat finished furniture.

Protective clothing is usually worn, including ear protectors and face masks for many jobs. Many jobs involve standing for long periods, lifting heavy weights, and bending.

It is normal to work a 39 hour week. Shift work might be required and overtime is common during seasonal peaks or when the factory has a delivery deadline.

Future prospects

Promotion is a possibility, and many manufacturers move into more senior roles within companies, managing projects and gaining responsibility.

Others choose to specialise in specific areas of furniture manufacture, for example furniture restoration, craft cabinet making or even furniture design.

Some furniture manufacturers choose to teach their craft or set up their own business.

Advantages/disadvantages

If you are interested in your craft and willing to put a little time in, a career in furniture manufacture can really grow, and so can your salary.

This job can be satisfying if you enjoy building and making things and are good at DIY.

Working on constructing the same item over and over again can get repetitive.

Money guide

Most operatives start on a salary of around £11,000 per year.

Once you have gained some experience, this might increase to about £15,000 per year.

If you become highly skilled, you can expect to earn £20,000 upwards.

Related opportunities

- Carpenter/Joiner p79
- Ergonomist p38
- Shopfitter p119

Further information

Association of Master Upholsterers and Soft Furnishers
www.upholsterers.co.uk

British Furniture Manufacturers Association
www.bfm.org.uk

British Woodworking Federation
www.bwf.org.uk

GAS NETWORK ENGINEER

Qualifications and courses

You will normally start as a trainee or an apprentice. There are no formal qualifications required for traineeships but a good standard of education would be expected. For entry onto a gas network engineering apprenticeship you will need a minimum of 4 GCSEs/S grades (A*– C/1–3), in maths, science, English and a practical technical subject.

Once employed you can start working towards NVQs at Level 1, 2 and 3 in Gas Network Operations (Mains Laying, Service Laying or Craft). After completing an NVQ Level 3 it is possible to apply for a HND/ degree or higher level NVQs. Graduate engineering and management training schemes are also available. It is also possible to undertake a 3-year National Grid Advanced Apprenticeship.

Employers will consider it necessary for you to have a safety passport from an appropriate industry scheme, with Energy and Utility Skills for example.

What the work involves

Gas is transported from its supply points (called beaches) to domestic and industrial customers by a network of pipes and meters that will be your responsibility to fit and maintain.

To gain access to pipework you will probably need to dig a hole in a road, garden or pavement. This can be a physically demanding job. You will be using digging and excavating tools and pipe-laying equipment.

You will be responsible for the safety of yourself and others when carrying out work. This will include putting up warning signs, barriers and traffic control if needed. You may have to deal with emergency gas leaks.

Type of person suited to this work

You will normally work in a small team, so you should enjoy working with and be able to get on with people. You will be meeting new customers each day, so being polite and courteous are also important skills.

An ability to follow instructions and an understanding of technical language and drawings is essential as these will be used to tell you what you need to do on a daily basis.

When the job is complete, you will have to ensure the finished surface is safe and as good as it was when you started, so you should be tidy and efficient.

Working conditions

You will be working in a team outdoors in all weathers. You will normally work a 37–40 hour week, overtime and weekend work will be expected on a rota basis.

You will be using equipment which can be physically demanding and you will get dirty. As this can be dangerous work you will wear protective clothing such as high-visibility and fireproof clothing, steel toe-capped boots and head gear.

Future prospects

The National Grid coordinates and monitors the gas distribution network in the UK. There are 4 gas distribution companies; National Grid Distribution, Wales and West Utilities, Northern Gas Networks and Scotia Gas Networks (operating in the south of England as Southern Gas and in Scotland as Scotland Gas Networks). There is currently a demand for gas network engineers owing to an extensive 30-year pipeline replacement programme.

With experience and training, you could progress to a technician, supervisory or management position where you would be responsible for a number of teams.

Advantages/disadvantages

You will be working outside in all weathers.

You may have to deal with complaints from angry customers about holes in their road.

Giving the public a gas supply for their homes and businesses can be rewarding.

Money guide

Whilst training, workers can earn around £11,000 per year.

With qualifications and experience this can rise to £18,000–£25,000 per year.

As a team leader or with more responsibility you can expect your salary to increase to £25,000–£32,000 per year.

Salaries may be boosted significantly with payment for overtime and shift work.

Related opportunities

- Construction Operative p86
- Construction Plant Operator p87
- Water/Sewerage Network Operative p130

Further information

Energy and Utility Skills
www.euskills.co.uk

Energy and Utility Skills Register
www.eusr.co.uk

Northern Gas Networks
www.northerngasnetworks.co.uk

Scotland Gas Networks
www.scotiagasnetworks.co.uk

Qualifications and courses

This career is open to all graduates with a degree in engineering. Subjects such as agricultural engineering, environmental engineering, electrical engineering or mechanical engineering may improve your chances. HNDs in similar subjects are also considered for entry level positions and some employers may be willing to support further study to take you to degree level. You will need a minimum of 5 GCSEs/S grades (A*–C/1–3) including English, maths and science, and 2 A levels/H grades for degree entry.

Your degree or HND must be accredited by the Institution of Agricultural Engineers (IAgrE), or a similar licensed body of the Engineering Council, if you would like to progress to qualifying as a Chartered (CEng) or Incorporated (IEng) Engineer. Those with an accredited bachelor's degree or HND are eligible for IEng status and those who have studied to master's level can pursue CEng status. These qualifications will significantly enhance your career prospects and earning potential.

For those looking to work as a technician, the Intermediate or Advanced Apprenticeship in Land-based Engineering may be available. However, if you wish to become a fully qualified engineer, you will need to study for a degree.

What the work involves

Land-based engineers design, develop, test and modify agricultural and horticultural equipment in order to ensure that these industries stay up to date.

You will need to carry out extensive research into the needs of those using the equipment you are producing, as well as assessing and limiting the environmental impact of your projects.

You will also be required to compile reports, undertake presentations on your work and offer expert advice to clients and other professionals.

Type of person suited to this work

You will need great ingenuity in order to find solutions to problems or design new equipment to aid agricultural and horticultural processes.

Excellent communication skills are required to understand the needs of your clients and translate them into designs and instructions for your team.

Good IT skills, problem-solving abilities and a flexible approach to work are also essential in order to cope with the various demands of differing projects.

Working conditions

You will usually work a normal working week, although occasional overtime may be necessary to meet project deadlines.

Although you will be office based for the majority of the time, there will be some on-site and fieldwork so that you can assess projects and carry out tests on equipment.

You may find that you have to work outdoors in unpredictable weather or cold, wet and muddy conditions. You will also need to wear relevant safety equipment whilst on site.

Future prospects

There are opportunities for land-based engineers to work all over the world, undertaking a variety of projects from food production in the UK to creating effective water supplies in areas of the developing world.

You could work in a large multinational organisation or a smaller company. Larger firms offer greater scope for career progression and you could soon be managing your own projects and moving up the career ladder. Smaller firms offer less opportunity for progression, so you might have to move to another company to develop in your field.

Advantages/disadvantages

Each day will present new problems and challenges so the work will always be interesting and stimulating.

You will be working with a variety of people from many professional sectors and areas of the community.

On average, you will earn less than engineers in other industries.

Money guide

Starting salaries for land-based engineers are usually between £18,000 and £25,000.

Once you have gained 10–15 years' experience, you could expect earnings in the range of £35,000–£50,000.

Chartered land-based engineers can earn in excess of £60,000.

Salaries vary depending on geographical location.

Additional allowances and benefits are usually given for overseas work.

Related opportunities

- Agricultural Scientist p253
- Environmental Engineer p223
- Land/Geomatic Surveyor p106

Further information

British Agricultural and Garden Machinery Association
www.bagma.com

Engineering Council UK
www.engc.org.uk

ENGINEERING, MANUFACTURING AND PRODUCTION

CRCI: GB

LOCKSMITH

Qualifications and courses

There are no specific educational requirements but most applicants will be expected to hold GCSEs/S grades (A*–C/1–3) in English, maths and preferably a practical subject such as craft or technology.

There are no formal apprenticeship schemes for locksmithing but you may be able to start as a trainee within a company. Candidates are advised to contact local locksmiths and ask if there are any trainee positions available. The 'Find a Locksmith' database on the Master Locksmiths Association (MLA)'s website is a useful resource.

The MLA also offers a British Locksmiths Institute (BLI) General Locksmithing Course at their training centre. As part of this course, candidates will study for the City & Guilds award in Basic Locksmithing. To apply for training you must be a member of the BLI. Individuals over the age of 16 can apply for Student membership without any prior experience. Advanced Student membership is for those who have 12 months' practical training in locksmithing and have passed the entry exam.

An NVQ in Providing Security, Emergency and Alarm Systems (Levels 2 and 3) and City & Guilds vocational courses in security and alarm systems are also available.

What the work involves

You will sell, install and fix the locks of houses, cars and businesses for your customers.

You will use specialist machinery to cut replacement keys for locks.

Advising on, repairing and installing security and closed-circuit television systems may be part of your job.

Type of person suited to this work

As a locksmith you will have to be calm and patient – reassuring your customers, who may be distressed, whilst providing a prompt and reliable service. Good communication skills are important in this job.

Your customers and employer will also expect you to be totally trustworthy and honest.

To do this job you will have to enjoy using your hands, different tools and equipment. You should enjoy practical tasks and be able to offer solutions to security problems. Carpentry or general engineering skills are also helpful.

Working conditions

If you work in a shop you will probably have a 40-hour Monday–Saturday week. Self-employment is possible.

If you or your employer offer a 24-hour call-out service, you could be working at all times of the day or night. Where you work will depend on your customers and could include working outdoors in all weathers.

You will mainly operate from a van that holds your tools so a driving licence is essential.

Future prospects

Employers include independent small locksmiths, larger national companies offering a 24-hour call-out emergency service, specialist security companies, DIY hardware stores and shoe repairers that offer a key-cutting service.

Progression for locksmiths is mainly achieved by becoming self-employed and building up a profitable business. It is also possible to progress into more specialist areas of work such as safe engineering.

Advantages/disadvantages

This can be a varied job as your work and location will change with each customer.

You will have the opportunity to meet many people and have the satisfaction of helping them.

Working unsocial hours/during the night can affect your personal life.

Call-outs to replace locks after burglaries can be distressing.

Money guide

Trainee locksmiths can expect a starting salary of about £13,000.

As you gain experience, you could achieve earnings of up to £25,000 per year.

You will usually receive bonuses or higher rates for emergency call-outs.

Self-employed locksmiths establish their own rates based upon their company's success and reputation.

Earnings can vary with geographical location.

Related opportunities

- Carpenter/Joiner p79
- Glazier p101
- Shoe Repairer p493

Further information

British Locksmiths and Key Cutters Association
www.blka.co.uk

Master Locksmiths Association
www.locksmiths.co.uk

Skills for Security
www.skillsforsecurity.org.uk

MANUFACTURING/PRODUCTION ENGINEER

Qualifications and courses

The most common entry route is with a relevant degree in an engineering subject. For degree entry, you will need 3 A levels/Highers (including maths and physics) and 5 GCSEs/S grades (A*–C/1–3). It is becoming increasingly common for candidates to obtain a master's degree; this is the quickest way to become a Chartered Engineer.

HNDs in similar subjects are also considered by employers, but you will have to undertake further study towards degree level qualifications whilst working. The most direct way to reach Incorporated Engineer (IEng) status is through obtaining a relevant degree, but it can also be achieved through a HNC or Foundation degree in engineering or an appropriate NVQ4 or SVQ4 qualification.

Academic qualifications are not always considered essential, but you must be able to show good problem-solving and project management skills, leadership, an ability to work to deadlines and have an awareness of health and safety issues in the workplace.

You could start as an apprentice and train to be a technician. To apply you will need at least 3 GCSEs/S grades (A*–C/1–3), including English, maths and science. GCSEs in engineering or design and technology may also be useful.

What the work involves

Manufacturing engineers design, implement and maintain manufacturing processes. You will be consulting with other professionals, such as design engineers, in order to produce high quality products efficiently and with minimum cost.

You could work in a variety of industries, including food and drink, fashion, and pharmaceuticals. You could work widely across a project, from design and research to after-sales care. Therefore, you will be using a variety of manufacturing equipment and computer systems on a daily basis.

Type of person suited to this work

You should be able to work as part of a team, as you will be liaising with other professionals on a daily basis to discuss product ideas and manufacturing solutions.

You should be good at analysing and solving problems in order to understand and stay ahead of potential manufacturing issues. The ability to prioritise your workload is also beneficial.

Strong numerical skills are essential.

Working conditions

You will usually work 37 hours per week, but this often includes evening and weekend work. Extra or unsocial hours can be expected when a new production process is being tested, or if the company you are working for operates a shift system.

You will divide your time between office based work, meetings and time spent on the shop floor or in the factory. When on the shop floor, you might have to wear safety equipment or protective clothing.

Future prospects

It is encouraged that you join your relevant professional body, dependent on your specialism, once you have qualified. These include the Institution of Mechanical Engineers (IMechE) and the Institution of Chemical Engineers (IChemE). This also lets you keep your training up to date through the continuing professional development (CPD) courses many of them run. You could work in a variety of manufacturing sectors, building diverse experience that will help you move across industries and sectors within manufacturing, taking up managerial or marketing roles.

Alternatively, you could specialise in a certain area (such as pharmaceuticals or clothing) and move into production management or consultancy; here you would draw upon your knowledge and experience to motivate and advise others.

There are also numerous short-term contracts available for manufacturing engineers, which would allow you to become self-employed.

Advantages/disadvantages

Manufacturing engineers enjoy one of the most creative roles in the engineering sector, with great input into product design and final function.

If you work in a large company, there may be opportunities to travel.

You may work evenings and weekends on a regular basis.

Money guide

The average graduate starting salaries on completion of initial training range from £24,000 to £28,000.

With 5–10 years' experience, you could earn up to £40,000.

Senior manufacturing engineers can expect to earn in excess of £55,000.

Related opportunities

- Electrical Engineer p219
- Mechanical Engineer p233
- Textile Operative p245

Further information

Institution of Engineering and Technology
www.theiet.org

Institution of Mechanical Engineers
www.imeche.org.uk

Semta
www.semta.org.uk

ENGINEERING, MANUFACTURING AND PRODUCTION

CRCI: G

Qualifications and courses

Many employers ask for GCSEs (A*–C/1–3) in English, maths and a science or related subject. Sometimes employers will ask for further qualifications, or even set an aptitude test.

It is possible to enter this profession by doing an apprenticeship in the ship-building industry. You can take an engineering-related vocational course at college, such as an NVQ or BTEC, which will enable you to apply for an Advanced Apprenticeship.

You can undertake a mixture of on-the-job and classroom-based training, which most employers will be willing to fund. Training usually starts with health and safety regulations and an induction course, followed by basic skills including selecting materials, interpreting drawings, how to use relevant tools and developing skills.

Possible boat-building qualifications you can take include NVQs in Boat Production and Support Services, Boat Building and Maintenance, and a City & Guilds Certificate in Boat Building, Maintenance and Support. You could also take a specialist degree in Leisure Boat Design and Construction.

What the work involves

A marine craftsperson takes part in the building and repair of many different kinds of ships and boats.

Repairers and shipbuilders work with big vessels such as ferries, dredgers, tugs, submarines, tankers and warships. Boat builders work with smaller boats, such as wooden dinghies, sailing boats, narrow boats and powerboats.

Both crafts require you to work from a design to create the ship or boat. This has usually been created on a computer, and you work at marking and cutting out shapes, welding, and cutting and bending steel and other materials.

Type of person suited to this work

You should be a good teamworker, and a good communicator.

A practical, logical and problem-solving mindset is essential, as you will not only be required to interpret drawings and plans but will also need to solve problems on the job quickly and intelligently.

You should also be good with numbers, and have good eyesight and good physical fitness.

Working conditions

Marine craftspeople tend to work a normal 37 hour week, but overtime is usually available. Some urgent repair jobs may take place overnight and during weekends, but this is relatively rare.

Working at heights is normal, and you will probably spend the majority of your time indoors.

Future prospects

As you gain experience, it may be possible to progress to a position such as supervisor or inspector. You could also work towards becoming workshop manager.

Another option is to use your experience to become self-employed in areas such as boat building and repair.

Some people choose to gain further qualifications and become a marine engineering technician.

Advantages/disadvantages

If you have an interest in practical work and building things, and in ships and maritime matters, then this job can be really enjoyable. It can be really satisfying to create something you are passionate about.

The grubby working conditions might not sit well with everybody, so if you want to work in a clean and tidy environment your skills may be better suited elsewhere.

Money guide

Starting salaries range from around £13,000 to £17,000 per year.

Once qualified you could earn up to £23,000 a year.

As a senior craftsperson you could earn more than £25,000 a year.

Related opportunities

- Civil/Construction Engineer/Civil Engineering Technician p83
- Marine Engineer p231
- Merchant Navy Engineering Officer p605

Further information

British Marine Federation
www.britishmarine.co.uk

Semta
www.semta.org.uk

The Institute of Marine Engineering, Science and Technology
www.imarest.org

MARINE ENGINEER

Qualifications and courses

Entry to this career is usually with a degree or a or BTEC HNC/HND in a relevant subject. Useful subjects would be marine engineering, marine technology, naval architecture or general engineering courses. Entry to a degree course usually requires at least 5 GCSEs/S grades (A*–C/1–3) and 3 A levels/4 H grades, including maths and a science subject. Entry requirements for an HND course are usually 1 A level/Higher or a BTEC National Certificate in a relevant subject.

You could undertake an Apprenticeship as a marine engineering technician and work towards becoming a marine engineer, undertaking additional training and qualifications on the job.

The Merchant Navy Training Board offers a number of training and sponsorship schemes for entrants at GCSE, S grade, A level, Higher, undergraduate or graduate stages of their education. Graduate applicants must have degrees in a scientific subject.

The Royal Navy accepts applications for engineering officers from candidates in their final year of university.

What the work involves

Marine engineers design, construct and maintain ships' seafaring equipment, as well as developing and preserving offshore systems.

You could work in a shipbuilding company, on-board ships and submarines, in marine surveying, in an oil company or in the leisure industry.

You will work across a range of engineering disciplines, including electrical, construction and mechanical. You will work closely with naval officers, architects, other professionals and team members.

Type of person suited to this work

You will need excellent communication skills, both verbal and written, in order to manage and lead your team as well as liaise with other professionals and clients.

Excellent maths and ICT skills are essential, as is an ability to solve problems under pressure. Prioritising your workload through careful planning and project management is also very important.

You should be good at working within a team, especially as you might have to live and work with colleagues in confined areas when undertaking projects on boats or submarines.

Working conditions

You could work anywhere from an office to a boatyard, or even on a submarine, and many jobs involve a combination of office-based and onsite work.

If you are working on projects on a ship or offshore installations, living accommodation can be tight and you will probably need to spend time away from home.

The job involves climbing and lifting equipment so you will need to be physically fit.

Future prospects

Prospects are good for marine engineers. You could work for a variety of companies, from small shipping businesses, to leisure cruise liners, through to joining the Royal Navy.

When you have gained skills and experience, you could go on to specialise in project management or marine research, or even work as a consultant.

There are plenty of opportunities to work abroad.

Advantages/disadvantages

There are a huge variety of employment options available to you, from conservation projects to defence systems.

You will work in numerous diverse areas, and with many different people, so the work will always be interesting and fresh.

You may be working in cramped, uncomfortable conditions for long periods of time. This includes living and working with colleagues 24 hours a day on certain projects.

Money guide

As a graduate marine engineer, you could expect to earn around £20,000.

With a few years' experience, this can rise to £36,000.

Experienced and highly skilled marine engineers can expect to earn over £50,000.

Related opportunities

- Electrical Engineer p219
- Marine Craftsperson p230
- Mechanical Engineer p233

Further information

Engineering Council UK
www.engc.org.uk

Merchant Navy Training Board
www.mntb.org.uk

The Institute of Marine Engineering, Science and Technology
www.imarest.org

ENGINEERING, MANUFACTURING AND PRODUCTION

CRCI: GG

Qualifications and courses

There are no formal entry qualifications needed to work as a meat processor. However, GCSE/S grades in English and maths are useful, particularly if you want to move up to supervisory, inspection or technical level.

There are also a number of apprenticeships available. The most relevant are the Improve Proficiency Apprenticeship in food and drink (Meat and Poultry Industry Skills) and the Improve Proficiency Apprenticeship in Food and Drink (Food Manufacturing Excellence).

You can also work towards NVQs/SVQs at Levels 2–3 in Meat and Poultry Processing or Food Manufacturing Excellence and then on to an NVQ/SVQ at Level 4 in Meat Processing Management. The Meat Training Council offers other courses.

To work at an abattoir you must be aged 18 or over, and be licensed by the Meat Hygiene Service (MHS), a division of the Food Standards Agency.

What the work involves

Meat process workers do everything from herding animals, to slaughtering, to cutting up carcasses, to packaging and grading meat and ensuring it is free from contamination and ready to sell to the public. A meat process worker could specialise in either of the following roles.

Abattoir operative

You will slaughter animals for food.

After the animals have been humanely killed, you will separate the edible meat from the waste.

Meat manufacturing operative

You will manufacture meat products.

You may also weigh, wrap and label the meat.

Type of person suited to this work

This can be distressing work, so you should be prepared to cope with blood and mess.

As you will have to do lots of lifting and operating machinery, you will need to be physically fit.

You should have a responsible attitude as you may use dangerous knives and machinery. You also need to be aware of your personal cleanliness as you are part of a food production process.

Working conditions

Refrigerated areas are cold and all areas need frequent cleaning and so may be wet. You will be expected to wear protective clothing, including footwear and hairnets.

You will normally do a 40-hour week, usually from 7.30am to 3.30pm although shift and part-time work are possible.

Future prospects

Abattoir operative

With experience you could apply for senior positions or look to move to related areas such as butchery, retail or food marketing. Other options are jobs in quality control, health and safety consultancy or self-employment.

Meat manufacturing operative

With experience you could apply for supervisory, quality control and management jobs or move into related areas of work such as retail butchery.

With the right experience, qualifications and training you may be able to progress into work on the meat inspection teams employed by the Meat Hygiene Service (MHS) – part of the Food Standards Agency.

Advantages/disadvantages

This can be cold, smelly and dirty work. The job can be repetitive and monotonous.

You will be part of a team and often there is a good working atmosphere.

Money guide

Abattoir operative

The minimum salary for trained adults is around £12,000 per year (although apprenticeships may be less). With experience this can rise to between £15,000 and £20,000 a year.

Meat manufacturing operative

The starting salary is usually between £10,000 and £15,000 per year. Experienced meat manufacturing operatives earn up to £18,000 per year.

Related opportunities

- Butcher p478
- Kitchen Assistant/Supervisor p145
- Meat Hygiene Inspector p486

Further information

Department for Environment, Food and Rural Affairs
www.defra.gov.uk

Food Standards Agency
www.foodstandards.gov.uk

Meat Training Council
www.meattraining.org.uk

Qualifications and courses

Most employers require a foundation degree, BTEC HNC/HND or degree in a relevant subject such as mechanical, nuclear, aeronautical, civil or computer-aided engineering. For entry to a degree course you will need at least 5 GSCEs/S grades (A*–C/1–3) and 2/3 A levels/Highers, including maths and physics.

However, it is also possible to start as a technician which you can enter via an apprenticeship. To apply for an apprenticeship you will need GCSEs/S grades (A*–C/1–3) in English, maths and science. You will work towards an NVQ Levels 1–3 in Performing Engineering Operations, Mechanical Manufacturing Engineering or Technical Services. In order to progress however you will need to take a top-up course to convert to degree level.

What the work involves

Mechanical engineers design, develop and maintain the moveable parts of all equipment, ranging from those in small household appliances up to large machinery or vehicles.

You will probably work on a project from conception to completion, so will be involved with all aspects from design and development through to final manufacture.

You could work in a number of industries, including manufacturing, sport, medicine or transport.

You will also have to manage budgets, resources and people on each project.

Type of person suited to this work

You will need an exceptionally high level of scientific knowledge and technical ability in order to design mechanisms and solve practical problems as they occur in the development process.

Good communication skills, both verbal and written, are essential for dealing with colleagues, other professionals and clients on a daily basis. You will also be required to produce detailed reports and occasional presentations.

Excellent organisational skills and the ability to work under pressure are a must, as are good ICT skills including knowledge of computer-aided design (CAD).

Working conditions

You will usually be required to work longer hours than those of the average working week, but evening or weekend work is rare.

You will be based mainly in an office although you will also spend a good amount of time on site, whether in a factory, workshop, hospital or other building. Despite this travel, overnight absence from home is uncommon.

You will need to wear a smart suit or similar whilst in the office, but appropriate safety equipment when on site.

Future prospects

Job opportunities for mechanical engineers are found throughout the UK, particularly in larger towns and cities. There are also excellent opportunities for working abroad.

With experience, you will be able to qualify for Chartered Engineer (CEng) status. You could become self-employed and undertake freelance work which will give you greater flexibility over your work–life balance. Alternatively, you could go on to increasingly senior engineering posts, or even set up your own consultancy.

Some engineers choose to move into a more business-orientated role within their company such as sales or HR.

Advantages/disadvantages

It is exciting to be at the forefront of creating new products and finding solutions to mechanical problems across numerous industries. You will be working on a variety of projects and meeting a range of people, so the work is rarely boring.

There are excellent opportunities for career development, including the option of working overseas.

You may have to work long hours to meet project deadlines.

Money guide

Starting salaries for mechanical engineers can range from £19,500 to £22,000 a year.

With experience, your salary could increase to between £26,000 and £39,000.

Engineers with chartered status/10–15 years' experience can earn over £40,000.

Within engineering, salaries vary greatly according to location (London usually yields the highest wages) and the size of the company that you work for.

Some companies also offer excellent benefit packages and bonus schemes in addition to a basic salary.

Related opportunities

- Clinical/Biomedical Engineer p296
- Electrical Engineer p219
- Marine Engineer p231

Further information

Engineering Council UK
www.engc.org.uk

Institution of Mechanical Engineers
www.imeche.org.uk

ENGINEERING, MANUFACTURING AND PRODUCTION

CRCI: GH

Qualifications and courses

Although you do not need any formal qualifications to begin training as a motor vehicle technician, most employers (especially the larger companies) prefer you to have at least 4 GCSEs/S grades (A*–C/1–3) including English, maths and a science.

There are several ways to enter the industry at a trainee level. You could undertake the Intermediate or Advanced Apprenticeship in Vehicle Maintenance and Repair. This scheme involves learning on the job whilst gaining qualifications at college. Alternatively, some larger employers have dedicated training facilities for their employees where you can learn the required skills.

Another option is to study for relevant qualifications. Many colleges have links with local employers which could be a route into work experience or employment. City & Guilds provide the NVQ in Automotive Maintenance and Repair, Body and Paint, Vehicle Fitting and Roadside Assistance (Levels 1–3). IMI Awards offer the NVQ in Vehicle Maintenance and Repair (Level 2) specialising in either Motorcycle or Auto Electrical and the NVQ in Vehicle Fitting Operations (Level 3). Those who wish to pursue higher qualifications could take the BTEC National in Vehicle Technology (Level 3) or the BTEC Higher National in Automotive Engineering (Levels 4 and 5).

What the work involves

Motor vehicle technicians are responsible for the maintenance and repair of all vehicles, including cars, motorbikes, lorries and coaches.

You will need to carry out routine jobs, such as servicing a vehicle, and identify technical problems, advising customers as to which repairs are necessary and the costs involved.

You will work on a variety of different mechanical and electrical systems and use a range of tools and equipment.

Type of person suited to this work

You need an excellent technical and mechanical knowledge of most motor vehicles and you will be expected to build on this knowledge throughout your career to ensure that you are familiar with technological changes.

Strong communication skills are required for advising customers and you must be able to work well within a team of colleagues.

Full colour vision, a good level of fitness and the ability to think quickly and work methodically are all essential. You will also need good IT skills in order to understand and fix the computerised equipment in vehicles.

Working conditions

You will usually work 40 hours per week, just above the national average. Most of your work will involve regular hours but occasionally, depending on your employer, you may be expected to work shifts, weekends and overtime.

If you specialise in repairing broken down vehicles, you might have to travel to their location at any time of the day or night.

You will usually work in a garage which can be noisy and very cold in winter. You will need to wear overalls and use other safety equipment to protect you whilst you work.

Future prospects

Being a motor vehicle technician provides good career opportunities as demand is relatively high all over the UK. This means you could work in a large city or a small village, for a large company or a tiny independent garage.

Within a larger organisation, you could progress to a senior or supervisory level as a technician, or alternatively move into a management or training role.

There is also the option of setting up your own repair business, although the initial costs of hiring and equipping premises can be high.

Advantages/disadvantages

There is demand for technicians throughout the UK so you should be able to find a job in the location of your choice.

The hours are fairly regular and it is unlikely that your work will involve absences from home.

You may have to work in cold, damp or cramped conditions which can be unpleasant.

Money guide

Trainee motor vehicle technicians may have a starting salary of £10,500–£11,000.

Once qualified, you could expect £15,000–£20,000 a year.

Those with extensive experience in the industry can achieve in excess of £25,000.

Garage owners and self-employed technicians can earn considerably more.

Related opportunities

- Electrician p92
- Highways Maintenance/Road Worker p103
- Sheet Metal Worker p242

Further information

GoSkills
www.goskills.org

Institute of the Motor Industry
www.motor.org.uk

NUCLEAR ENGINEER

Qualifications and courses

The most common entry qualification is a degree in mechanical, electrical or chemical engineering but you could enter with a related degree such as maths, physics or science. Some universities offer specialist degrees in nuclear engineering and the Nuclear Industry Association (NIA) provides further information on these courses. For degree entry you will need at least 5 GCSEs/S grades (A*–C/1–3) and 2 A levels/3 H grades including maths and a science subject.

You can also enter the industry with an HND in a relevant subject such as general engineering, civil engineering, maths or physics. Entry requirements are usually 1 A level/2 H grades or a BTEC National Certificate in a relevant subject.

Graduate Apprenticeships or training schemes may also be available which combine study at degree or postgraduate level with work-based learning. Entry requirements are usually a 2.2 degree in a relevant subject.

Nuclear engineers with an MEng can apply for Chartered Engineer (CEng) status with the Engineering Council and those with a bachelor's degree are eligible for Incorporated Engineer (IEng) status.

What the work involves

Nuclear engineers work mainly in the large-scale production of nuclear energy, although they can be involved in smaller industrial or medicinal projects.

Alternatively, you could work in developing effective nuclear waste management systems.

You might lecture and train other people on the subject of nuclear power.

Type of person suited to this work

You will need excellent communication skills, both verbal and written, in order to manage and lead your team, and liaise with other professionals and clients. The ability to work effectively as part of a team is also important.

You should possess an analytical mind and a logical approach to problem-solving. Excellent maths and IT skills are also essential.

As you will be working with nuclear hazards, you must be able to take responsibility for your own safety and that of your colleagues.

Working conditions

You will usually work a normal 37-hour week, although you may be required to work additional hours as project deadlines approach. If you work in a nuclear power station, your hours will usually adhere to a 7-day shift system.

The majority of the work will be indoors in a power plant, laboratory, office or factory.

You may have to work in hot, cramped conditions and you will have to wear protective clothing in certain situations. As you will be working with radioactive substances, you will also need regular medical check-ups.

Future prospects

Prospects are good for nuclear engineers, especially given the government's new drive to increase nuclear power production in the forthcoming years.

The majority of nuclear engineers work in large power plants and companies, although you could work in medical research or nuclear waste disposal. With continued study and increased experience, you can move into more senior positions within any company or discipline.

Advantages/disadvantages

Nuclear power is a growing industry so employment opportunities will increase accordingly.

You have the opportunity to work freelance after building significant experience so you can achieve a suitable work–life balance.

You will be working in an environmentally controversial industry which could potentially upset your friends and family.

Money guide

Graduate nuclear engineers typically have a starting salary of £20,000–£25,000.

With increased experience, earnings rise to between £30,000 and £50,000.

Senior engineers with chartered status could achieve £55,000–£65,000.

Some companies offer excellent benefit packages and bonus schemes.

Related opportunities

- Aerospace Engineer p212
- Chemical Engineer p217
- Mechanical Engineer p233

Further information

Nuclear Industry Association
www.niauk.org

Semta
www.semta.org.uk

Qualifications and courses

There are no formal entry qualifications, but having GCSEs/S grades (A*–C/1–3) in English, maths and science will help.

You can start straight from school, working your way up and training on the job as an apprentice. If you hold an HNC or HND in a subject such as engineering you could enter the profession at a higher level.

You could study towards an NVQ in a subject such as Engineering or Combined Working Practices. There are also courses in paper technology. You will be expected to keep up with the latest developments in the industry and relevant techniques. The Paper Industry Technical Association (PITA) runs several courses and conferences, so membership is advised to improve your future prospects as far as possible.

What the work involves

Paper manufacturers work with the equipment and systems that turn wood pulp and other materials into many different kinds of paper.

Your role can vary greatly depending on which sector you decide to work for within the paper mill. You might be operating the machine that breaks down the raw materials, managing what is going on inside, adding chemicals, checking consistency or adjusting the controls.

You could also be managing the steam system that dries the paper, controlling it in reels or overseeing the packaging process.

Type of person suited to this work

You need to be good with your hands, and good at teamworking and communication with others.

Being able to act on your own initiative is important, and you should have an accurate and methodical mindset.

Following plans and diagrams is a big part of the job, so you should be confident in this, and the ability to work with chemicals is also important.

A lot of the work will involve using computerised machinery. You must be capable of adapting to new equipment and learning to use it safely and accurately.

Working conditions

This kind of work usually takes place in shifts. You could be working daytimes, evenings, nights or weekends depending on your company, and it may well be a combination of them all.

It is normal for you to work 38 to 40 hours per week. Overtime is usually available and often encouraged.

You will be working on the factory floor most of the time or in the control room. This is so that you can monitor the processes being carried out by the machines you are looking after.

It will sometimes be necessary to work outdoors in order to load and unload delivery wagons.

Future prospects

There are opportunities for progression within the industry. With experience you can apply for positions at technician and supervisor level, which can turn into engineering roles.

If you choose to you can also move around in the industry, changing to a career such as management or sales.

Roles and jobs such as these might require additional qualifications which you may be able to pursue.

Advantages/disadvantages

Opportunities to progress are good in this job, and even if you come straight from school and work on the factory floor, you could move up to sales or management relatively quickly.

The work may be a little mundane to start with.

Conditions inside the factory can be noisy, hot and humid.

Money guide

Trainees earn around £12,000 a year, but this can be boosted with overtime.

This can increase to between £14,000 and £22,000 once you have gained sufficient experience.

Papermaking supervisors can earn up to £50,000.

Related opportunities

- Chemical Engineer p217
- Manufacturing/Production Engineer p229
- Textile Operative p245

Further information

Confederation of Paper Industries
www.paper.org.uk

Paper Industry Technical Association
www.pita.co.uk

Proskills UK
www.proskills.co.uk

Qualifications and courses

Most entrants to this profession have a first degree in a related subject. This could be polymer science, materials engineering, materials technology or materials science. For entry to a degree course you will need at least 5 GCSEs/S grades (A*–C/1–3) and 2–3 A levels/H grades including chemistry, maths or physics. A 1-year Foundation degree may be available for those who wish to take a relevant degree but do not have the required scientific subjects.

It is also possible to gain entry to this profession with an HNC/HND in polymer technology or manufacturing engineering. Candidates with relevant industry experience could study for an HNC/HND while they work.

Work placements may be available for those on sandwich courses and graduates have the option to apply for company training schemes.

Postgraduate courses in materials engineering or polymer technology may be available after you have taken a first degree in engineering or science.

The British Plastics Federation (BPF) provides professional development for those within the industry, offering both short courses and the master's level Materials for Industry (MfI) programme.

What the work involves

Polymer technologists use polymer materials, such as plastics, rubber, adhesives, resins and fibres, to manufacture products. You will utilise these materials to make a wide range of products including toys, casings for mobile phones, medical devices, tyres, wetsuits and hoses.

You might also use composite polymer materials when manufacturing car bodies or aircraft wings instead of traditional materials such as metal.

You will be responsible for developing the moulds used to form materials during manufacture. This is a job that requires specialist skills as a minor flaw could ruin an entire batch of products.

Type of person suited to this work

You should have a strong interest in materials science, chemicals, engineering and design technology. A good understanding of manufacturing processes and construction methods is also important.

Familiarity with computer-aided design and developed IT skills would be beneficial.

Analytical and numeracy skills are required for analysing projects or problems that arise.

You must be able to communicate effectively with people as you will be working within, and possibly leading, a team.

You should be able to take initiative, use your creativity and find a solution when you are confronted with a problem.

Working conditions

You will work between 35 and 40 hours per week, Monday to Friday. It may be necessary for you to work additional hours to meet deadlines. Overtime and weekends will increase your pay accordingly.

Your time may be divided between the office, the laboratory and the factory. As you will be required to travel, it would be useful to have a driving licence.

You will be expected to wear protective clothing in some of your working environments.

Future prospects

Polymer science is a growing industry with a shortage of qualified staff. As new uses are found for plastic, rubber and composite materials, the industry will continue to develop. There are many opportunities for promotion within the field.

You could work for a variety of companies including manufacturers of medical equipment, toy companies and aerospace engineering firms.

You could choose to specialise in a specific area such as vehicle manufacturing, aviation or medical equipment.

Advantages/disadvantages

You may have the opportunity to travel locally and abroad as part of your work.

The factory or laboratory conditions that you work in may sometimes be noisy and messy.

Money guide

A starting salary for a polymer technologist is around £14,000–£18,000.

As you gain experience, you can expect to earn £20,000–£25,000.

Those who reach a senior level or work as a specialist technologist can achieve £35,000–£40,000.

Related opportunities

- Aerospace Engineer p212
- Chemical Engineer p217
- Manufacturing/Production Engineer p229
- Materials Scientist p524

Further information

British Plastics Federation
www.bpf.co.uk

Institute of Materials, Minerals and Mining
www.iom3.org

ENGINEERING, MANUFACTURING AND PRODUCTION

CRCI: NI

237

Qualifications and courses

Most entrants to this profession have prior experience in a relevant industry. For example, you might have started your career in a production role and then progressed to the level of quality control inspector. Employers usually seek applicants with 4 GCSEs/S grades (A*–C/1–3) including maths, English and a science subject.

As a quality control inspector you could specialise in a particular sector such as aerospace or pharmaceuticals. For this you may require A levels/H grades, a BTEC/SQA National qualification, an HNC/HND or a degree in science or technology.

Engineering Apprenticeships which could be useful for this career are the Intermediate Apprenticeship in Improving Operational Performance or the Intermediate and Advanced Apprenticeships in Food and Drink. You will be able to learn on the job and you may be entitled to study for professional qualifications.

With experience as a quality control inspector you can take courses to increase your skills. City & Guilds offer a vocational qualification in Quality Assurance (Level 4) or the Chartered Quality Institute (CQI) have a Certificate in Quality Management which enables you to apply for associate membership of the CQI.

What the work involves

Quality control inspectors work in a variety of industries such as engineering, food, pharmaceuticals and clothing, where manufacturing procedures must be monitored to ensure that products meet specified standards.

You will test products as they go through each stage of production by observing, measuring and weighing samples, and comparing results to specified requirements. You will also work to ensure that quality and safety standards are maintained by checking and testing materials sourced from external suppliers.

You will write reports on the tests that you carry out and help to come up with solutions to any problems or inconsistencies that arise.

Type of person suited to this work

As you will be regularly inspecting products and manufacturing processes, you must be highly organised, methodical and have a keen eye for detail.

You should be responsible, thorough and able to solve problems efficiently.

You will have an aptitude for communicating with others and for advising and persuading people to improve standards.

Good written communication skills are required for writing up reports on testing methods and results.

You should have an interest in the science and technology of the industry that you are monitoring.

You also need a keen awareness of health and safety issues and procedures.

Working conditions

You will work 35–40 hours per week and this will often include shift work, weekends and nights.

You could be based in a laboratory or an office. You will also frequently visit factories or warehouses to monitor production processes or meet with staff. These locations may be clean and bright or noisy and dirty. Protective clothing is often required.

Future prospects

The number of available jobs in this field is falling as sophisticated equipment is developed to identify faults and inconsistencies in products.

However, there are opportunities to work in many different sectors such as cosmetics, textiles and electrical goods.

When you have some experience you may progress to become a team leader, supervisor or quality manager. You could also move into technical sales or production management.

Advantages/disadvantages

There may be opportunities to travel and work abroad as a quality control inspector.

You could become self-employed.

Owing to developments in technology, companies are increasingly using advanced equipment to monitor quality standards.

Money guide

Starting salaries for quality control inspectors can range from £14,000 to £20,000.

Those with experience can expect to earn around £25,000 a year.

As you gain responsibility you can earn from £30,000 to £35,000, depending on the sector in which you work.

Related opportunities

- Laboratory Technician p522
- Quality Manager p58
- Trading Standards Officer p496

Further information

Chartered Quality Institute
www.thecqi.org

Semta
www.semta.org.uk

QUARRY MANAGER

Qualifications and courses

You will need a degree or HND. Subjects such as minerals engineering, environmental sciences, geology or mining engineering are very useful. You will typically need at least 2 A levels/H Grades in sciences and 5 GCSEs/S grades (A*–C/1–3). Master's degrees are also available in quarry management. You could also take a year-long industrial placement with a big organisation as part of your degree.

Graduate management schemes with large organisations typically look for a degree in quarry engineering, IT or business. Work experience on a quarry site would be very useful.

The Mineral Products Qualifications Council (MPQC) offers many useful qualifications in risk assessment, supervising safety in quarries, quarry safety inspections and understanding quarries regulations. Entrants will typically acquire professional accreditation with the Institute of Quarrying or the Institute of Materials, Minerals and Mining.

What the work involves

Quarrying involves opencast mining to extract minerals and other materials to manufacture goods such as chemicals. Your job will involve managing all the staff in the office and the quarries.

On-site, you will inspect the quality of the minerals and other products mined, ensure production is on schedule and check equipment.

In the office you will manage the sales department, look after the budget, produce performance reports and plan changes to the production system when different materials are needed.

Type of person suited to this work

You will need to have good communication skills as you will be liaising with a wide range of people. You must also have a good technical knowledge of the production system in quarries. You should be business minded with excellent management skills.

You will need to be aware of health and safety legislation as well as government regulations and ensure that these are followed on-site. It is important to have a good understanding of technical drawings and plans.

Working conditions

You will be on-call in case of emergency.

You will typically spend 2 days on-site and 3 days based in an office.

You must wear protective clothing such as helmets and ear protectors when on site and be prepared to work in all weathers.

Future prospects

After gaining experience, it might be possible to progress into a managerial role in area operations.

There is also the possibility of working abroad.

It would be helpful to become a member of the Institute of Quarrying. It has a professional development system which ranges from student to fellowship levels. Career prospects can be improved by further qualifications in management and quarry legislation. It will be necessary to take jobs at different quarries to improve career progression, unless you work for a big company. However, personal development generally remains in the hands of the individual.

Advantages/disadvantages

You will have a high level of responsibility.

You will spend time working outdoors. Long hours, including work at weekends, are common in this industry.

Working conditions on sites are dirty, dangerous and noisy, with sites often based in rural areas.

Money guide

Salaries will depend upon the location of the site and the employer. Bonuses can boost salaries.

A new assistant quarry manager can earn £23,000 or more.

£35,000 is a typical starting salary for a quarry manager.

A unit manager who is in charge of a number of quarries or a big quarry can earn £50,000 or more.

Related opportunities

- Construction Operative p86
- Demolition Operative p90
- Quarry Worker p240

Further information

Institute of Materials, Minerals and Mining
www.iom3.org

Institute of Quarrying
www.quarrying.org

Proskills UK
www.proskills.co.uk

ENGINEERING, MANUFACTURING AND PRODUCTION

CRCI: GI

QUARRY WORKER

Qualifications and courses

This job does not have any formal educational requirements. However, employers generally look for at least 5 GCSEs/S grades (A*–C/1–3). Relevant subjects include English, maths, science and technology.

The Diploma in Engineering or Construction and the Built Environment could be useful. Apprenticeships in Extractive and Mineral Processing Operations may be on offer in your area.

You can also take a Level 3 Certificate or Diploma in the Extractives and Mineral Processing Industries.

Once on the job, you could also work towards NVQs at Levels 1–3 in Mineral Processing Industries, Level 2 in Plant and Operations (Extractives), Levels 1–2 in Specialized Plant and Machinery and Level 2 in Drilling Operations.

An NVQ at Level 3 in Blasting Operations or equivalent is needed to work with explosives. Courses are also available from the Mineral Products Qualifications Council (MPQC). A LGV licence would be helpful, but some vehicles can be driven on a full catergory B driving licence.

What the work involves

There are many types of quarry worker. A machine operator controls heavy equipment whilst a plant and process operator is focused on the screening plant.

Shotfirers are responsible for explosives and drillers are responsible for creating holes for explosives and investigation.

Truck drivers, maintenance workers and laboratory technicians are also needed to undertake quality control and investigate samples from the site.

Type of person suited to this work

You need to be strong, fit and active to do this job.

You must also follow safety regulations at all times owing to the dangers that could arise when using heavy machinery.

You need to be able to work well with others as teamwork is a big part of this job.

An interest in mechanical work is also crucial. Quarry workers should enjoy working outdoors and be prepared to do so in all weathers.

Working conditions

You will often work in shifts, which will include early mornings and late nights. Floodlights will be switched on during these periods.

You should be prepared to travel for long periods of time to reach sites, as they are predominantly located in rural areas.

Working conditions are often dirty, noisy, muddy and dangerous. Protective clothing such as helmets and ear protectors must be worn at all times. Work will often include a lot of carrying and climbing.

Future prospects

Roughly 1000 quarries exist in the UK. Although each local authority will have a quarry, the majority of them are located in the East Midlands and south-west of England.

After gaining experience, you may be able to progress into a role as supervisor or manager.

With further study, you can apply for jobs as laboratory or quality control technicians.

Drivers, mechanics and fitters can undergo training to become drillers or shotfirers.

Advantages/disadvantages

You could use powerful machines such as drills and excavators or explosives.

You will work outdoors. Working conditions are muddy, noisy and dangerous.

Travel times to work can be fairly long as sites are often located in remote, rural areas.

Money guide

Salaries will depend upon the location of the site and the employer. They can also be boosted by extra payments from overtime, bonuses and shift work.

The starting salary for an operator is about £13,000.

After gaining experience and training this could rise to £28,000.

If you are a specialist with significant experience, or progress to a role as a manager, you can earn in excess of £40,000.

Related opportunities

- Construction Operative p86
- Demolition Operative p90
- Quarry Manager p239

Further information

Institute of Materials, Minerals and Mining
www.iom3.org

Institute of Quarrying
www.quarrying.org

Proskills UK
www.proskills.co.uk

Qualifications and courses

The typical entry route to this profession is through an Apprenticeship/Skillseekers scheme. The Advanced Apprenticeship in Rail Traction and Rolling Stock Engineering is available. Entry requirements are usually 3–5 GCSEs/S grades (A*–C/1–3) including English, maths, science and technology. Rail engineering firms, Network Rail and train operating companies also offer their own training schemes.

The selection process for employment involves a medical exam to test physical fitness, eyesight and hearing. An aptitude test may also be set to assess your existing skills and knowledge.

Whilst many entrants train on the job, it would be very beneficial if you have experience working as a mechanical fitter, electrician or craftsperson in another industry.

Relevant qualifications include the NVQ in Rail Transport Operations (Level 2) and the NVQ in Railway Engineering (Traction and Rolling Stock) at Levels 2 and 3.

An ability to drive and access to personal transport is often required.

What the work involves

A mechanical fitter will maintain and service the traction and rolling stock, plant, machinery and passenger coaches.

You could also repair station equipment such as customer lifts and hoisting equipment.

An electrical fitter will work alongside mechanical fitters and other engineers, specialising in the electrical side of the maintenance and servicing work on the traction and rolling stock, plant machinery and passenger coaches.

A multi-skilled fitter will possess the skills held by both mechanical and electrical specialists so they will be able to work in all aspects of railway maintenance.

Type of person suited to this work

You should enjoy working with your hands, diagnosing faults and working out solutions. You will be comfortable using different hand tools and equipment and enjoy working in a team alongside other fitters.

Physical fitness is important as you will be on your feet, working at your bench or directly within the various railway stock.

You should be happy to follow verbal and written instructions, be able to read and understand technical drawings and diagrams and have a responsible attitude to health and safety.

Working conditions

Much of your work will take place within heated workshops or depots. Sometimes you will have to visit jobs which are outdoors, for example near to railway sidings or within a station. On these occasions it might be cold and dark.

As many of the work places are in remote areas, it is often essential to have your own transport.

You will have to wear protective clothing and be prepared to work in cramped places, engaging in lots of bending and lifting.

You will have a 37-hour working week with shifts that cover early, late, evening and weekend hours. You might also need to be on-call for emergencies that occur outside your working hours.

Future prospects

The rail industry is beginning to expand so demand for new recruits will increase.

Well-developed promotional and in-service training programmes exist which help fitters to progress to supervisor, technician, team leader and management levels.

Many specialist maintenance companies carry out work for operating companies and engineering companies, making new traction units and carriages.

Advantages/disadvantages

Owing to the range of jobs within the railway industry, it is possible to move sideways into other related job areas.

Working on the railway tracks is hazardous so you must be aware of health and safety procedures.

Money guide

Trainees will usually earn £12,000–£15,000 per year.

Those with experience and relevant qualifications can achieve a salary ranging from £18,000 up to £30,000.

Further benefits include increased pay for working overtime and free or discounted rail travel.

Related opportunities

- Mechanical Engineer p233
- Rail Signalling Technician p610
- Rail Track Maintenance Operative p611

Further information

Engineering Council UK
www.engc.org.uk

GoSkills
www.goskills.org

Network Rail
www.networkrail.co.uk

ENGINEERING, MANUFACTURING AND PRODUCTION

CRCI: GE

Qualifications and courses

Entry to this profession is usually via a training scheme. The Apprenticeship in Engineering Manufacture (Craft and Technician) is available at Advanced Level. You will need to have at least 5 GCSEs/S grades (A*–C/1–3) including maths, English and a science subject.

Alternatively, the Engineering Construction Industry Training Board (ECITB) offers a fast-track Advanced Apprenticeship under the National Apprenticeship Scheme for Engineering Construction (NASEC). This scheme takes about 3 years to complete, with up to a year of college-based learning, followed by practical work on-site and study for professional qualifications.

Relevant courses for sheet metal workers include the NVQ in Fabrication and Welding Engineering (Levels 2 and 3) and the BTEC National in Manufacturing Engineering (Level 3).

What the work involves

Sheet metal workers produce parts for a number of important items ranging from vehicles and aeroplanes, through to electrical equipment and common domestic appliances.

You will be using complex engineering drawings as a guide for marking out and cutting each piece.

You will also be operating a variety of machines including hand-powered tools, cutting and pressing devices and computer numerically controlled (CNC) devices.

Type of person suited to this work

You should have good communication skills and be able to build strong relationships with colleagues as you will be working within a team.

Good numerical skills and the ability to interpret complicated technical drawings are essential for making accurate calculations and creating precise parts. You should also have good IT skills as computer-operated machinery is increasingly being used in this role.

You need a fairly high level of fitness as you will be expected to lift large items and operate heavy machinery. Good eyesight and excellent practical skills are also required in order to use tools and equipment safely.

Working conditions

You will usually work a 37–39 hour week but shift work and overtime is common. If you are producing bespoke items for a customer to a tight deadline, you may be required to work overnight on occasion.

Work is usually undertaken in a factory or workshop. You will spend the majority of your time at a bench so you will be bending over for most of the day. The work also involves lifting and spending hours on your feet.

You will be required to wear appropriate safety clothing at all times.

Future prospects

Prospects are good for sheet metal workers.

Once your initial training is completed, you could work towards qualifying as an engineering technician.

Alternatively, you could become a supervisor/manager of an engineering workshop which would increase your responsibility and salary.

Owing to demand, opportunities are available on small and large projects both in the UK and overseas.

Advantages/disadvantages

You will work with a variety of materials and tools, enabling you to build specialist understanding and knowledge quickly.

With overtime, it is likely that you will work considerably longer than the average working week.

Money guide

Starting salaries for trainees within this sector are usually £12,000–£14,000.

With experience, you can expect to earn between £17,000 and £20,000.

Workers with supervisory responsibilities or those who are highly skilled in using computer-controlled equipment can achieve in excess of £25,000.

Shift allowances and overtime can increase earnings.

Related opportunities

- Assembler p213
- Blacksmith p214
- Welder p248

Further information

Engineering Construction Industry Training Board
www.ecitb.org.uk

Semta
www.semta.org.uk

Qualifications and courses

The main route into tailoring or dressmaking is straight from school. No experience is necessary as all training is provided on the job by more experienced colleagues. However, a demonstrable aptitude for design, sewing and art is usually sought by employers, as are GCSEs/S grades (A*–C/1–3) in English, maths, textiles or art.

If you are specifically looking to train as a prestigious Savile Row tailor, you could join the Bespoke Tailoring Apprenticeship Programme run by Newham College in partnership with Savile Row Bespoke. This scheme teaches all the skills and knowledge you need to become a top tailor, including pattern cutting, garment construction and sewing by both machine and hand. The number of opportunities is limited so competition for places is very strong

A number of courses are available on a full- or part-time basis or via distance learning. These include the City & Guilds Award/Certificate/Diploma in Creative Techniques in Fashion (Levels 1–3), the ABC Awards in Fashion and Textiles, the BTEC First in Art and Design (Level 2), the BTEC National in Art and Design (Level 3) and the BTEC Higher National in Fashion and Textiles (Levels 4 and 5).

What the work involves

Tailors and dressmakers design and make made-to-measure, bespoke items of clothing.

Tailors usually make structured items such as suits, jackets and coats. Dressmakers can make a range of clothing, from day dresses and casual trousers to ball gowns and wedding dresses.

You will be working with numerous materials including silk, linen, cotton and polyester and you will also use equipment such as sewing machines, scissors, tape-measures and pins.

Type of person suited to this work

Since you will be dealing with a range of people, including clients and suppliers, you will need to have excellent interpersonal and verbal communication skills.

Understanding how different cuts, styles and colours flatter various shapes and figures is important for customer satisfaction, as is maintaining a smart/fashionable appearance.

You must be creative and innovative to produce fashion designs.

Working conditions

You can expect to work 37–40 hours a week. Saturday and weekend work is common as that is when most of your clients will be available for meetings and fittings. You could be situated in a workshop, small factory or work from home if you are self-employed.

A reasonable level of physical fitness and flexibility is required, as you will be bending and kneeling when measuring customers and fitting clothes. You may also need to lift and carry heavy rolls of fabric.

A lot of the work is very detailed so you will need a high level of accuracy and good eyesight.

Future prospects

You could work for a small or large company and create high fashion or more classic pieces. You can also opt to be self-employed.

In larger companies, you may be promoted to a supervisory position and there may also be the opportunity to diversify into pattern cutting or design.

There are opportunities to travel and work overseas, especially if you are involved in fashion and haute couture tailoring or dressmaking.

Advantages/disadvantages

You will be undertaking very creative work with lots of scope to use your talent and imagination on a daily basis.

Fashion is a fast-paced, interesting and potentially lucrative industry to be working in.

Making clothes requires many hours of concentration and patience.

Money guide

The average starting salary for both tailors and dressmakers ranges from £11,500 to £13,000.

With experience, your salary could rise to £14,000–£18,000.

Senior tailors or dressmakers, especially those located on Savile Row or who work in high fashion, could earn up to £50,000.

Self-employed tailors establish their own rates based upon their experience and reputation.

Related opportunities

- Costume Designer p170
- Fashion Designer/Milliner p171
- Textile Operative p245

Further information

ABC Awards
www.abcawards.co.uk

Newham College of Further Education
www.newham.ac.uk

ENGINEERING, MANUFACTURING AND PRODUCTION

CRCI: NB

ENGINEERING, MANUFACTURING AND PRODUCTION

CRCI: GE

Qualifications and courses

Most employers require a relevant degree in a subject such as telecommunications, electronic engineering, electronic and communication engineering, computer science, physics or maths.

It is possible to enter this sector with an HND in a relevant engineering subject but you will only be able to work at technician level. With an accredited HND you could take a 'top-up' course to convert it into a degree or you may be able to supplement your on-the-job experience with further qualifications at degree level.

Many employers also look for candidates who have a postgraduate qualification such as an MEng or suitable MSc. Those with master's level qualifications are eligible for Chartered Engineer (CEng) status which could improve long-term career prospects. Alternatively, you can work to become an Incorporated Engineer (IEng) if you have a bachelor's degree.

A PhD could help you to enter the industry at a more senior level or specialise in a particular area as a technical expert.

Gaining relevant work experience through a sandwich course or vacation placement is a useful way to develop your skills and build contacts within the industry.

What the work involves

Telecommunications engineers are responsible for designing, testing and overseeing the installation of all telecommunications equipment and facilities.

You could work across a variety of engineering fields, including electronics and construction, providing technical guidance and offering solutions to other professionals and clients.

You will be responsible for the management of telecommunications projects which includes planning budgets, recruiting a team and implementing on-site safety. You will also produce written reports and verbal presentations in order to keep both your team and your clients up to date on how each project is progressing.

Type of person suited to this work

Good communication skills are essential for managing and briefing your team, as well as negotiating with clients and explaining complex technical information to them in a clear and simple manner.

You should have an analytical mind and be excellent at problem-solving. The ability to work efficiently under pressure and organise your workload effectively is also essential.

Working conditions

You will usually work a normal week of about 37 hours from Monday to Friday. Occasionally additional hours may be required, particularly as you progress to more senior positions.

Your working hours may be fairly flexible and you will not always be office based as the industry is seeking to promote working from home and part-time opportunities.

You will sometimes work on site, checking and overseeing the installation of telecommunications equipment. In these instances, you may find yourself working outdoors or in cramped conditions. You will usually be required to wear appropriate safety equipment as well.

Future prospects

As the telecommunications industry is continually expanding and improving, job prospects for engineers in this sector are good.

Working in this fast-paced industry will require you to undertake further training throughout the course of your career in order to stay up to date with new products, techniques and developments.

As you gain experience, you could move into increasingly senior positions.

Advantages/disadvantages

Hours are generally regular and there are increasing opportunities to work from home or undertake part-time hours.

In such a rapidly changing industry, you will be learning continually throughout your career.

You will have to spend time on site which may involve working in cold, muddy conditions, at heights, or in cramped and uncomfortable surroundings.

Money guide

Starting salaries for graduate trainees are typically £20,000–£25,000.

With experience, you could expect to earn £30,00–£40,000.

If you reach a senior level and gain chartered status, you can achieve up to £60,000.

Some companies also offer excellent benefit packages and bonus schemes.

Related opportunities

- Civil/Construction Engineer/Civil Engineering Technician p83
- Electrical Engineer p219
- Electrician p92

Further information

Institution of Engineering and Technology
www.theiet.org

TEXTILE OPERATIVE

ENTRY LEVEL 1

Qualifications and courses

There are no specific entry requirements for this position and training usually takes place on the job. The best way to get a position would be to apply directly to textile manufacturers.

There are several courses available that would build valuable understanding of the industry and what the role would involve. Courses include GCSE art and design (including a textiles module), Edexcel BTEC Introductory Certificate/Diploma in Art, Design and Media, and Edexcel Level 1 BTEC First Certificate in Art and Design. The Textile Centre of Excellence also offers a Technical Certificate in Textiles that provides a flexible, distance learning programme.

The Textile Institute (TI) also offers a range of qualifications for professional development for those already working in the sector from Licentiate to Fellow level. Alternatively, ABC offers a variety of courses in sewing, manufacturing and textiles, as do City & Guilds at Levels 1–3.

Apprenticeships with textile manufacturers may also be available.

What the work involves

Textile operatives manufacture carpets, prepare the yarns of fibres to be woven or knitted (which may involve carding and combing or chemical processing), spin yarn on a machine or even make fabric on a loom.

You will carry out basic maintenance on your machinery, make sure you have a supply of raw materials and keep your work area clean and tidy in accordance with health and safety regulations.

You may also work on finishing processes such as dyeing or waterproofing fabrics.

Type of person suited to this work

You will need to be practical in order to operate the machinery skilfully and responsibly. In keeping with this, you should have good concentration as you will be doing repetitive tasks for long periods of time.

Manual dexterity and good spatial awareness, coupled with excellent eyesight and in the majority of cases full colour vision, are also requirements for carrying out tasks such as spinning or weaving textiles.

A reasonable level of personal fitness, an understanding of, and adherence to, work place health and safety rules, and enjoyment of working in a team are also attributes.

Working conditions

Although you will work an average 37 to 40 hours per week, you will usually be doing shift work which is likely to involve early mornings or later evenings. Overtime and part-time work is also available.

You will usually work in a textile factory, which should be light and well ventilated, although the machines can be noisy and you will have to wear relevant safety equipment at all times.

It can be physically tiring, as you will spend the majority of your time standing over your machine or walking between the various pieces of equipment you are using.

Future prospects

The opportunities for textile operatives are good, as there has been increasing demand for textile production in recent years so a larger number of people are gaining employment at entry level and progressing more quickly to supervisory or managerial positions.

If you gain experience in using a variety of machines and performing a range of tasks, you will find your prospects improve accordingly.

You could also choose to move into quality control or sales once you have gained a full knowledge of the textile industry.

Advantages/disadvantages

You will be putting your practical skills to good use creating a range of textiles for various purposes.

The work can become monotonous.

Hours can involve unsociable shift work in the early morning or evening.

Money guide

Starting salaries for new entrants range from £12,000 to £13,000.

With a couple of years of experience and increasingly diverse skills, you could earn between £13,000 and £17,000.

Once you have become a multi-skilled senior operative you could earn up to £20,000.

If you work shifts, or undertake overtime, earnings could be higher. Piecework payments (awarded for high production volume) can also boost earnings.

Related opportunities

- Costume Designer p170
- Fashion Designer/Milliner p171
- Tailor/Dressmaker p243

Further information

Society of Dyers and Colourists
www.sdc.org.uk

Textile Institute
www.textileinstitute.org

ENGINEERING, MANUFACTURING AND PRODUCTION

CRCI: NK

TOOLMAKER

Qualifications and courses

You will need to have at least 5 GCSEs/S grades (A*–C/1–3) or equivalent, including maths, English, science and technology.

Most people start on the Advanced Apprenticeship in Engineering scheme on completion of school or college. You will spend several months at a training centre and then spend 2 or 3 years working within your company whilst also attending college.

If you have difficulty finding an apprenticeship, there is also the option of taking an NVQ that is related to engineering.

Entry opportunities for adults are limited unless you have significant previous experience, as companies generally train up existing employees when necessary. Many companies aim to train multi-skilled craftspeople rather than specialists. Apprentices may learn fabrication skills (welding and metalwork), computer-aided design (CAD) or computer-aided manufacturing (CAM). Only exceptional trainees are encouraged to focus completely on toolmaking.

What the work involves

Toolmakers make specialist tools and devices that are used to cut, shape, mould and form various materials for use in the production of all items; ranging from domestic appliances to aeroplanes. You will work with a range of materials, including metals and plastics.

You will also be using complex engineering drawings as a guide to marking out and cutting each piece.

You will be operating a variety of machinery including drills, grinding and milling machines, cutting and pressing devices and, increasingly, computer numerically controlled (CNC) equipment.

Type of person suited to this work

Good hand-to-eye coordination and a keen eye for detail will be beneficial, both when operating machinery and to check the quality of the tools produced. You will be making extremely precise devices, so it is essential to be able to spot any faults or errors before the tools are despatched to customers.

Good numerical skills and the ability to interpret complicated technical drawings are essential, both for making accurate calculations and creating precise parts.

Finally, you should have good ICT skills as computer-operated machinery is increasingly used in this role.

Working conditions

You will usually work 39 hours per week from Monday to Friday. Although some larger companies operate shift patterns so evening and weekend work may be necessary.

Work is usually undertaken in a tool room within a factory or workshop. This means that you will be working in a fairly quiet environment, away from the main factory machinery.

You will normally stand for the duration of your working day, which can be tiring. You will be required to wear appropriate safety equipment at all times.

Future prospects

Prospects for toolmakers are good, there are employment opportunities in most parts of the UK.

After gaining 5 to 10 years' experience as a toolmaker, you could move into a supervisory role within a company. This would involve overseeing production within a tool room or workshop. This could then lead into a management position.

You could also undertake further qualifications in order to work towards employment as an engineering technician. This could then lead to you undertaking a degree course in order to become an engineer of some kind.

Advantages/disadvantages

You will be making tools which are vital for the construction of important equipment; these range from aeroplanes to washing machines.

You will be using both your practical skills and your mental abilities daily.

The work can be physically exhausting, as you will spend the majority of your day on your feet.

Money guide

Starting salaries for toolmakers range from £15,500 to £17,500 a year.

With a few years' experience, you could expect to earn around £25,000.

Highly skilled toolmakers, who are fully competent with using computer-controlled equipment, can earn up to £35,000.

Related opportunities

- Motor Vehicle Technician p234
- Sheet Metal Worker p242
- Welder p248

Further information

Engineering Council UK
www.engc.org.uk

Semta
www.semta.org.uk

Qualifications and courses

Vehicle maintenance patrollers are qualified vehicle technicians, and as such must hold NVQ Levels 1 and 2 in motor vehicle maintenance and repair along with having a minimum of 3 years of relevant experience in motor vehicle repair.

You will need a clean driving licence, and will have to pass a driving assessment, aptitude test and medical exam. Most employers will expect you to have at least 4 GCSEs/S grades (A*–C/1–3), including English, maths and science.

NVQs are available in roadside assistance and recovery, which encompass all aspects of the job including assessing the vehicle and carrying out minor repairs at the roadside.

Some of the larger organisations offer induction programmes that allow new entrants to train on the job and learn skills such as customer service techniques, alongside building their technical knowledge. They may also support study for relevant NVQs.

What the work involves

Vehicle maintenance patrollers travel to motorists who have broken down in order to diagnose the problem with the vehicle and fix it if possible. If repair is not possible, you will need to tow the vehicle to the nearest garage.

You will be responding to urgent calls from a central control centre, and may need to reassure worried or shaken motorists.

You will be driving a van or truck, and operating a range of electronic equipment alongside general tools and car parts.

Type of person suited to this work

You will need excellent communication skills in order to explain to motorists what is wrong with their vehicle and what can be done to fix it. You may be required to reassure people who are distressed or upset following an accident.

The ability to think quickly when assessing vehicles at the roadside is necessary.

You should be good with your hands as you will be operating various tools and machines and undertaking fiddly jobs from time to time.

Working conditions

An average working week comprises 39 hours, usually worked on a shift system including evening and weekend work. You may also be required to remain on standby on occasion.

Since the majority of work is undertaken on the road, a driving licence is essential. Depending on the vehicle you drive, you may also need an additional HGV or LGV licence. You will be working on the roadside in all conditions, including hazardous weather such as snow and fog, so must wear relevant safety equipment at all times.

Future prospects

Vehicle maintenance patrollers enjoy a variety of employment options. You could work for a large, well known national organisation such as the Royal Automobile Club (RAC) or the Automobile Association (AA), or for a smaller garage providing a localised breakdown service.

With experience you may progress to a supervisory role in a larger organisation, in which you will oversee and develop the performance of a number of breakdown engineers across a region.

In larger organisations, you could also move into a managerial or senior administrative position.

Advantages/disadvantages

You will be providing a valuable and well appreciated service to people every day.

There is great job satisfaction in being able to repair a vehicle at the roadside and send a happy customer on their way.

You will spend long periods of time on your own, which can get boring and lonely.

Money guide

The starting salary for a qualified vehicle breakdown engineer is around £13,000 to £18,000 per year.

With 3 to 5 years of experience, you could expect this to rise to between £26,000 and £30,000.

The specialist skills you acquire, such as the ability to use lifting equipment to move a stranded vehicle, are likely to increase your pay.

Related opportunities

- Assembler p213
- Highways Maintenance/Road Worker p103
- Motor Vehicle Technician p234

Further information

Institute of Vehicle Recovery
www.theivr.com

Royal Automobile Club
www.rac.co.uk/careers/

The Automobile Association
www.theaa.com

ENGINEERING, MANUFACTURING AND PRODUCTION

CRCI: GF

WELDER

Qualifications and courses

Most employers expect you to have least 5 GCSEs/S grades (A*–C/1–3) or equivalent, including maths, English and a science subject.

You could enter this career through an Apprenticeship or Advanced Apprenticeship in engineering.

Alternatively, you can take related NVQs or BTEC Certificates and Diplomas at college in order to gain knowledge prior to entering the industry. Relevant qualifications include NVQ Level 2 in Fabrication and Welding Engineering, NVQ Level 3 in Welding (pipework) and Welding (plate), the Welder Approval Certificate which is the industry-recognised qualification, a BTEC in Manufacturing Engineering, or completing Vocationally Related Qualifications (VRQs) in Welding at Levels 1, 2 and 3.

Most of the training will take place at work and there will likely be opportunities to study for NVQs and other related qualifications while you work.

What the work involves

Welders work with metals and heavy duty plastics, which they join together using heat to form plates, pipes and other items.

You could use a number of welding techniques that are either classed as manual, semi-automatic or fully mechanised. You will most likely specialise in one of these areas as opposed to working across all three.

You may have to work from technical drawings, using them as a guide by which to weld components together.

Type of person suited to this work

You will need good hand-to-eye co-ordination, coupled with manual dexterity, to successfully operate your tools and machinery.

You should be willing to work responsibly within strict health and safety guidelines, and to look out for the safety of others in your team. This will prove especially important when you are called upon to work unsupervised.

Working conditions

Hours are usually 37 per week, and often operate on a shift pattern. Opportunities for overtime work are common.

You could find yourself working in almost any location, from standard factory or workshop roles to onsite jobs which could be outdoors or even under the sea. This means you might have to work in confined spaces which can be uncomfortable.

You will also need to wear safety equipment, including protective goggles to shield your eyes from UV light and sparks, and also fire-resistant aprons and gloves.

Future prospects

There are excellent employment opportunities for welders throughout the UK, although the majority are found in fairly industrial areas.

Employers are mostly small and medium-sized firms, although some larger companies do also employ welders. There is also the option to be self-employed.

As you gain experience within a company, you could move into a supervisory role. Alternatively, you could undertake further qualifications in order to specialise in a particular area of welding, or work towards a career as an engineer.

Advantages/disadvantages

Practical work, where you can see the result of your efforts, is extremely rewarding.

Career prospects are good, with opportunities throughout the UK.

You will be operating machinery that is potentially dangerous.

Money guide

Starting salaries are usually between £12,500 and £17,000 but will vary depending on location.

With experience you could earn in the region of £26,000 a year.

If you are working as a specialist welder you could earn over £30,000 a year.

Related opportunities

- Blacksmith p214
- Civil/Construction Engineer/Civil Engineering Technician p83
- Sheet Metal Worker p242

Further information

Engineering Construction Industry Training Board
www.ecitb.org.uk

The Welding Institute
www.twi.co.uk

Environment, Animals and Plants

Jobs in this sector are perfect for those of you who do not want to spend every day behind a desk in an office, although this is not to say that you will not need to spend time writing reports and keeping a log of research findings or clients' information. Workers in this sector are passionate about animals or about caring for and maintaining the environment. You should also have brilliant people skills especially if you find yourself responsible for the welfare of someone else's animal. You should be someone who is very observant and interested in the natural world, not just from a welfare point of view but also from an economic one; many jobs in this sector involve using the environment for financial gain but increasingly industry is interested in doing so responsibly.

The jobs featured in this section are listed below. For similar jobs to the ones in this section turn to *Leisure, Sport and Tourism* starting on page 377.

Organisation profile
CAPEL MANOR COLLEGE

Some people were just born to be hands-on, and sitting in a classroom and learning from a textbook makes them feel ensnared rather than inspired. But when that person is given the chance to put theory to practical use, a whole world of discovery opens up before them. Our aim at Capel Manor is to make the theory come alive.

Capel Manor College is the largest land-based college in London, offering courses and apprenticeships for those interested in the environment and animals, or working with plants, trees and flowers. Our students regularly win awards and many study at Level 3 (equivalent to 3 or 4 AS/A levels), leading to higher education, and go on set up their own businesses or have fulfilling careers in the green sector. We cater for a mix of ages and abilities and offer a safe and supportive learning environment including study skills support, free, impartial and confidential careers advice, counselling by qualified therapeutic counsellors and enrichment activities.

Subjects on offer include: gardening, landscape construction, animal care, balloon artistry, floristry, flower arranging, garden design, arboriculture (the study of trees), countryside and environment studies, and saddlery. Tuition is free for those aged 16 to 18 years old, and those that have already completed A levels are still entitled to another free year's education on a full-time course, as long as they are still 18 on 31 August 2013.

With our apprenticeships, you gain real work experience and train at the same time, earning a regular income, supported by an assessor that visits you in the workplace and helps keep you on-track. Subjects include horticulture, arboriculture, environmental conservation, sports turf and animal care.

Ofsted lists our strengths as:

• excellent standards of work in horticulture and landscaping, garden design and floristry
• highly qualified and vocationally experienced teachers
• excellent specialist teaching resources.

With five centres in central, north, south, east and west London, we are within reach of anyone with a passion for the great outdoors. We run open days twice a year and advice evenings throughout the year, offering you the opportunity to come in and see the college for yourself and talk to our expert tutors. Visit www.capel.ac.uk for more information or ring 08456 122122.

Case study

CAPEL MANOR COLLEGE

Trees and Timber apprenticeship: Tom Uridge

20-year-old Trees and Timber apprentice, Tom Uridge, did A levels at school but was keen to get out of the classroom and into the world, where he could earn money and learn a trade. He was taken on by company CSG Ushers, tree work contractors and consultants as one of two apprentices, and attended Capel Manor College on a block release basis to study for his Level 2 Trees and Timber apprenticeship. Capel Manor is one of only a handful of colleges across the country to offer this apprenticeship.

'I've got a good understanding of how to carry out tasks instead of just learning about them in a classroom because I have gained the experience first hand. I really like working for CSG Ushers, everyone is really nice and helpful. Because it is such a large firm I have worked with lots of different people and have been able to pick up a variety of techniques from watching what my colleagues do. I used to be quite a shy person but working
with so many different people has made me come out of my shell.'

Level 3 Diploma in Horticulture: Shanice McClymont

After leaving school Shanice McClymont, 19, first considered following in her sister's footsteps and becoming a psychologist. She started A levels in science subjects but found that she couldn't focus on her future career. Instead, having had a childhood passion for plants and gardening, she joined Capel Manor to take a Level 3 National Diploma in Horticulture. She has now been offered a place at Aberystwyth University to do a degree in botany.

'I'd enjoyed school up to sixth form but then most of my friends left and being quite shy I found it difficult to fit in. Now I love my course – it's much more grown-up than school. Before I found out about gardening I didn't know you could do a course in it or that it could offer career options. Capel Manor College has built my confidence. It has made me focus on what I really want to do in life.'

Qualifications and courses

The entry requirements vary depending on the specific role you wish to apply for. Some employers will expect you to have A levels or equivalent qualifications and at least 2 years' relevant work experience. It would be particularly useful to have a background or qualifications in science, technology or engineering.

For other roles you will be required to hold a degree or equivalent professional qualification. Subjects which may be beneficial for this career include environmental health, engineering and science. For degree entry you usually need a minimum of 2 A levels/3 H grades and 5 GCSEs/S grades (A*–C/1–3) including maths and English.

Once you have secured employment, training is provided on the job, usually over a 2-year period in which you accompany experienced inspectors on-site visits and attend short courses.

Relevant professional qualifications include the NVQ in Occupational Health and Safety (Levels 3–5) and the BGAS-CSWIP Agricultural & Environmental Inspector course offered by TWI Training.

To work in a specialist sector, such as the Sea Fisheries Inspectorate, you may need relevant industry qualifications.

What the work involves

You will be responsible for monitoring standards within agriculture and ensuring that regulations are followed. You are likely to be employed as one of the following.

Health and Safety Executive (HSE) inspector

You will be concerned with occupational health and safety and required to visit premises to check machinery, investigate accidents, write reports and at times give evidence in court cases.

Department for Environment, Food and Rural Affairs (DEFRA) inspector

You will enforce UK and EU legislation. This will involve collecting and analysing data, issuing certificates and planning for the prevention and control of animal and poultry disease.

Food assurance scheme inspector

You will check that agricultural practice meets the Assured Food Standards. You will also inspect the health and living conditions of livestock.

Type of person suited to this work

You must have knowledge and experience of agriculture and be able to carry out the inspections with impartiality, consistency and sound judgement. You need up-to-date knowledge of relevant laws.

Much of your job will involve monitoring others so observational and problem-solving skills are essential.

You will also need good written and spoken communication skills, as well as confidence using IT.

Working conditions

Normal working hours will be 9am to 5pm, Monday to Friday, although extra hours will sometimes be necessary.

You will have an office base but at least half your time will be spent visiting workplaces. You will therefore travel often and overnight stays may sometimes be required.

The job can involve a great deal of pressure as it will be your responsibility to ensure that legal requirements are followed effectively within agriculture. Your actions could determine the health and welfare of both people and livestock.

Future prospects

Once you have several years' experience, you could progress to a senior position or work as a consultant in occupational health.

With enough experience and training, you could move into education, becoming a lecturer in occupational health and safety.

Alternatively, you could work in public health or conservation.

Advantages/disadvantages

The job involves inspecting others and pointing out violations of the law so you may encounter confrontation.

It will be rewarding to know that you have ensured that livestock are treated correctly and people are working in a safe environment.

Money guide

Trainee inspectors could expect a starting salary between £18,000 and £26,000.

As you gain experience, your salary may increase to £35,000.

Those working in a specialist area could achieve up to £50,000.

Related opportunities

- Countryside Ranger p259
- Farm Manager p261
- Farm Worker p262

Further information

Assured Food Standards
www.redtractor.org.uk

Department for Environment, Food and Rural Affairs
www.defra.gov.uk

Health & Safety Executive
www.hse.gov.uk

Qualifications and courses

To enter this profession you will need a degree in a subject such as agriculture, biological science, horticulture, soil science or animal nutrition. Entry requirements for a degree are typically a minimum of 2 A levels/3 H grades, including maths and chemistry or another science, as well as 5 GCSEs/S grades (A*–C/1–3) including English, maths and science. Equivalent qualifications may also be accepted.

It can be useful to have a postgraduate qualification in a specialist area, for example, a master's degree in animal production, soil science, poultry science or seed and crop technology.

It will also be necessary to have some work experience on a farm or in horticulture. The City & Guilds Certificate/Diploma in Agriculture (Levels 2 and 3) may be useful.

Those with an accredited master's degree and at least 4 years of work experience may be eligible to become a Chartered Scientist (CSci), a qualification which provides international recognition of your experience and expertise within your field.

What the work involves

Agricultural scientists carry out research to improve current farming techniques in crop production and the breeding and managing of livestock.

Using biology, biochemistry or chemistry, you will become a specialist in an area such as the study of soil, viruses, fungi, pests or genetics.

You will conduct tests, analyse the information and write reports. You could also teach farmers and companies that sell seeds or chemicals about your findings.

Type of person suited to this work

You must have an aptitude and a passion for science and the environment, especially biology and chemistry.

You will need strong communication skills as you will liaise with farmers and other growers to find out about their agricultural problems. You should be innovative and have strong research skills as you will spend much of your time in a laboratory or in the field, developing new solutions.

It is important to be patient, methodical and organised as progress in some research projects can take a very long time.

Working conditions

You will work 35–39 hours a week. It may be necessary to work early mornings, late evenings and weekends.

You will be based in either an office or a laboratory. Shift work could be needed when conducting experiments in the laboratory.

This job may be unsuitable for those with hayfever, dust allergies or animal allergies. A driving licence would be helpful as you might have to travel to farms or greenhouses.

Future prospects

Opportunities for general research are declining, although they are rising in some fields like genetic engineering. There is strong competition for jobs.

Vacancies are available with local and national governments, research organisations, and manufacturers of animal feed, fertilisers and chemicals.

After gaining experience, you could become a lecturer in a university, school or college. You may be able to move into sales-related work for production companies.

Advantages/disadvantages

This job is perfect for those with a passion for plants and wildlife.

Conducting scientific research and practical work can be interesting and varied.

Job opportunities are falling in some areas.

It can take a long time to see any progress in some research projects.

Money guide

Salaries will depend on your location and employer.

Certain private companies and the majority of public organisations have a structured pay scale.

The starting salary for an agricultural scientist is £17,000–£22,000.

With experience, earnings can increase to £26,000–£35,000.

Those in a senior role, possibly with chartered status, could earn considerably more.

Related opportunities

- Botanist p506
- Chemist p507
- Ecologist p512

Further information

Department for Environment, Food and Rural Affairs
www.defra.gov.uk

Institute of Biology
www.iob.org

Lantra
www.lantra.co.uk

ENVIRONMENT, ANIMALS AND PLANTS

CRCI: HA

AGRONOMIST

Qualifications and courses

You will need a degree in a relevant subject such as agronomy, crop science or agriculture.

Typical entry requirements are a minimum of 2 A levels/H grades, including a science and GCSEs/S grades including science.

It can be useful to have a postgraduate qualification such as a master's degree in soil science or seed and crop technology.

On-the-job training is provided. Work experience on a farm is very useful. The Diploma or Certificate in Agriculture may be helpful. A driving licence is often needed.

Alternatively, you can enter the profession in other ways, including as a field trials officer. As part of your career progression you can, with experience and training, become a senior field trials officer, assistant agronomy assistant, eventually rising to become a fully fledged agronomist. As with an agronomist, a degree in a related subject is needed, and although entry with a Foundation degree/HND is limited, it does allow you enter a post as a technician which can be an excellent way of gaining experience in the industry.

What the work involves

As an agronomist you will develop and implement production systems for the maximum economical production of high quality crops without harming the environment.

You will become an expert in areas such as irrigation, drainage, plant breeding, soil classification, soil fertility and wood control.

You will study any factors which could affect the crop, including the weather and water supply. You will carry out experiments, examine the results and then complete reports.

As a field trials officer you will need to organise different trials, either in the field or laboratory. You will be expected to write research proposals, record trial results accurately, developing experiments and ensuring government legislation is correctly followed. Other duties in support of the agronomist will also be expected.

Type of person suited to this work

You need to be good at problem-solving and have excellent research skills. You should be comfortable working on your own and as part of a team.

You must have strong analytical and communication skills in order to turn your research into practical solutions and explain them to farmers or businesses. It is important that you are methodical, practical and patient as it may take a long time to conduct successful experiments.

Working conditions

You will spend a lot of time working outdoors. You will also carry out experiments and tests in laboratories and write up reports in an office.

Hours are generally between 9am and 5pm, Monday to Friday, although you might have to work extra hours to complete some experiments.

Travelling to different locations such as farms can be necessary for some agronomists. Protective clothing is needed as you will probably work with hazardous equipment. This job may not be suitable for those with pollen or dust allergies. Good colour vision may be needed for certain jobs.

Future prospects

Job prospects are better for agronomists in certain fields such as genetic engineering.

A lot of agronomists work for the government, research organisations and agricultural development organisations as well as businesses that produce seeds, chemicals or food products.

After gaining experience, it is possible to become self-employed and work as a consultant. Lecturing in universities is another option. You could also progress to a role such as a manager in a research agency or a project supervisor.

Advantages/disadvantages

You will have the opportunity to work outdoors.

Scientific research and practical work are combined in this role.

Conducting successful experiments can take a long time and requires patience.

You will often have to wear protective clothing.

Money guide

Salaries vary according to the location and type of employer.

The starting salary for an agronomist and similar roles including a field trials officer is around £16,000 to £20,000.

After gaining experience, salaries can range from £25,000 to £35,000.

If you progress to a senior role, you can expect a salary of up to £45,000.

Related opportunities

- Botanist p506
- Chemist p507
- Ecologist p512

Further information

British Agrochemical Standards Inspection Scheme (BASIS)
www.basis-reg.com/

Department for Environment, Food and Rural Affairs
www.defra.gov.uk

Institute of Biology
www.iob.org

Lantra
www.lantra.co.uk

Qualifications and courses

To qualify as an animal physiotherapist, you can complete a degree in human physiotherapy and become a chartered physiotherapist in human physiotherapy.

You will need the highest level A levels/H grades in maths and science for entry. Upon completion of the degree you then can choose to spend a further 2 years (at least) gaining work experience with a practising animal physiotherapist.

Alternatively, you can choose to complete an animal physiotherapy course, such as a certificate in animal physiotherapy offered by the National Association of Veterinary Physiotherapists (NAVP). Entry requires a suitable first degree such as equine sciences of at least a 2.1 Honours standard; veterinary nurses with four years' experience are also considered. This programme lasts 2 years.

The College of Animal Physiotherapy also offers a diploma in animal physiotherapy. This course lasts 1 to 2 years part time. If you successfully complete this course you will be accepted into the International Association of Animal Therapists.

What the work involves

Animals suffer from joint and muscular pain in the same way that humans do. As a result, animal physiotherapy has become a regular part of animal care.

You would be used by many domestic pet owners and even more so by horse owners.

Techniques you will use may include soft tissue mobilisation, ultrasound (including long-wave), neuromuscular stimulation, joint mobilisation, magnetic field therapy, hydrotherapy and massage.

Type of person suited to this work

This job involves working with the owner so you will have to be able to communicate with people too!

Working with animals can be messy and smelly, so you must be prepared to get dirty. You should expect the work to be occasionally distressing, especially if the animal is injured or dies.

You will need to have good dexterity and be physically fit. You should have experience of working with animals and the ability to match treatments with problems.

Working conditions

You will be working in clinics, clients' homes, farmyards and/or stables. You could be indoors or outside in all weathers.

A driving licence is essential for some posts and you will normally wear protective clothing. This job will probably involve some heavy lifting and you will need to be physically fit.

Some assignments will involve evening and weekend work, especially if you visit your clients and animals in their own homes. As most animal physiotherapists are self-employed, working hours must be flexible to suit the client.

Future prospects

This profession is extremely competitive and employs very small numbers. Work experience will improve your chances of employment.

Some of the larger animal welfare charities and veterinary surgeries employ animal physiotherapists; however most are self-employed running their own practices. To be successful you will need to build up a client list and have good business skills. There is not a structured career path in place.

With experience you could work as a lecturer or consultant.

Advantages/disadvantages

You will be working with animals, perhaps helping them to have a better quality of life. Some aspects of the job may be messy and smelly.

There is the opportunity for self-employment.

Some heavy lifting will be required.

Money guide

Many working in this area are self-employed; average fees are around £20.00 to £70.00 for each consultation of 1 hour.

The average starting salary is about £18,500 per year; this can increase to around £20,000–£25,000 with experience.

As a senior animal physiotherapist or consultant you could earn up to £65,000 a year.

Related opportunities

- Pet Behaviour Counsellor p279
- Physiotherapist p330
- Veterinary Surgeon p283

Further information

Association of Chartered Physiotherapists in Animal Therapy
www.acpat.org

National Association of Veterinary Physiotherapists
www.navp.org.uk

The College of Animal Physiotherapy
www.tcap.co.uk

ENVIRONMENT, ANIMALS AND PLANTS

CRCI: HC

ANIMAL WELFARE OFFICER

Qualifications and courses

There are no formal entry requirements for this position but it would be an advantage to have experience working with animals. Opportunities for voluntary work with animals are available on the Do-it website and through the RSPCA and the SSPCA.

City & Guilds offer the Award/Certificate/Diploma in Work-Based Animal Care (Levels 1–3) which may be a useful pre-entry qualification or could be studied whilst you work. The NVQ in Animal Care and Management (Level 4) is also available.

To be recruited by the RSPCA you will need a full UK driving licence and 5 GCSEs/S grades (A*–C/1–3). Physical fitness is as important as academic qualifications; you must be able to swim 50m fully clothed. The RSPCA has its own training course which covers animal welfare legislation, basic veterinary training, rescue situation techniques, interview and communication techniques, animal handling and public speaking.

The entry requirements for the SSPCA are the same as above and ideally you should also have a qualification in an animal-related discipline.

What the work involves

You will work for an animal protection organisation or local authority offering a 24/7 service. You will undertake rescue work but you will also visit and advise pet and animal owners. You may need to investigate cases of abuse.

You will be on-call to collect stray and injured animals or animals at risk from dangerous situations.

You will promote animal welfare in your area and you may be responsible for caring for any animals taken in by the organisation you work for.

Type of person suited to this work

You will find yourself in situations that could be potentially dangerous so you will have to be aware of your own, the public's and the animals' health and safety. Some work will be distressing, especially if the animal is in pain or has been mistreated.

Although you will often work on your own, you may well work within a team, especially in rescue situations.

Strong interpersonal skills are one of the RSPCA's key requirements and you must be able to handle confrontational situations in a calm and assertive manner. Accurate report writing ability is also important.

Working conditions

Each day will be different; you could be in a factory, private house, animal establishment or outdoors up to your waist in water.

You will spend a lot of time travelling around the local area in a van so a driving licence is essential. You will probably have to work shifts including evenings and weekends.

Animals can bite and kick, especially when they are frightened, so you will have to use your skills to make sure they remain safe and that you do not put yourself at risk. You will not be able to do this work if you suffer from animal or dust-related allergies.

Future prospects

You could work for a number of animal charities such as the RSPCA, SSPCA or the Blue Cross, or for a local authority. Within the RSPCA you can be promoted from animal welfare officer to inspector, with increased responsibility for animal cruelty cases. Further progression to chief inspector or superintendent level is possible.

You may be able to work overseas, providing support to local people in disastrous events such as earthquakes or informing local people about animal welfare.

You can also move into other related jobs as a local authority dog and animal warden, or kennel and cattery work.

Advantages/disadvantages

You will have the satisfaction of rescuing animals that are being abused and improving their quality of life.

There will be opportunities to work with a range of wild animals, farm animals and pets.

Some people will be abusive and you may encounter dangerous situations.

Money guide

Starting salaries for a trainee animal welfare officer are around £15,000.

Once qualified, you will earn about £18,000.

After several years' experience, you could achieve up to £28,000.

Related opportunities

- Dog Trainer/Handler p260
- Veterinary Nurse p282

Further information

Royal Society for the Prevention of Cruelty to Animals
www.rspca.org.uk

Scottish Society for the Prevention of Cruelty to Animals
www.scottishspca.org

ENVIRONMENT, ANIMALS AND PLANTS

CRCI: HC

ARBORICULTURAL WORKER/ TREE SURGEON

Qualifications and courses

There are no set academic requirements for this job but some employers do prefer people to have some GCSEs/S grades. Entry is through a combination of work experience, on-the-job training and qualifications.

There are NVQs/SVQs available in Forestry and Arboriculture at Levels 1 and 2, which include workplace assessments. BTEC National qualifications in Forestry and Arboriculture and the Royal Forestry Society Level 2 Certificate in Arboriculture are also available and The National Proficiency Training Council offers a Level 2 Certificate in Competence to Climb Trees and Perform Aerial Rescue.

Short part-time and full-time courses are available at colleges of further education in chainsaw use, maintenance of equipment, health and safety and climbing techniques. A Competency Certificate from the National Proficiency Training Council or Scottish Skills Testing Service is needed to work on your own or with machinery. The Royal Horticultural Society also offers short courses leading to Arboricultural Association certificates and Lantra-accredited apprenticeships.

The National Trust can help in organising work experience placements. The Woodland Trust and the British Trust for Conservation Volunteers also provide volunteer opportunities.

What the work involves

You will carry out all kinds of work on the trees, shrubs and hedgerows in private and public gardens, parks, roadsides and on paths.

You will be responsible for planting new trees and shrubs, taking direction from a landscaper or garden designer.

Using chainsaws, hand tools, ladders and other specialised climbing equipment, you will use your knowledge of trees to make them safe, help them grow or increase the light available for other species.

Type of person suited to this work

You must have practical skills and be happy using potentially dangerous machinery and tools. You will also have to be interested in trees and the problems that can occur with them and be good with your hands.

This job is physically demanding and will include lifting, cutting and climbing so you will need to be strong and agile and good with heights. You will need to observe health and safety rules and be happy working in a team or on your own.

You will need excellent communication skills to deal with customers and explain what work needs to be done.

Working conditions

You will be outdoors in all weathers, hanging from ropes and using dangerous tools like a chainsaw.

If you suffer from pollen and dust allergies or vertigo, this work will be difficult for you.

You will have to wear protective clothing and be very safety conscious.

Future prospects

Demand for experienced workers has risen owing to greater public interest and concern for the environment. Opportunities are available with the National Trust, contractors, landowners or private employers.

With further qualifications you could enter senior or managerial positions, but this might involve moving to larger organisations.

With experience you could set up your own business.

Advantages/disadvantages

The work can be hazardous so you must obey safety regulations.

You will be outside working in all weathers.

You could do very long hours in the summer and shorter hours in the winter, which may affect your earnings.

Money guide

Salaries will depend on whether you are working for a contractor or are self-employed.

You will probably earn more in the south-east of England.

Starting salaries are around £16,000 per year. This rises to around £18,000–£24,000 with experience. Those who are self-employed can earn in excess of £30,000.

Related opportunities

- Countryside Ranger p259
- Gardener/Garden Designer p271
- Horticultural Worker/Manager p274

Further information

Institute of Chartered Foresters
www.charteredforesters.org

Lantra
www.lantra.co.uk

Royal Forestry Society
www.rfs.org.uk

ENVIRONMENT, ANIMALS AND PLANTS

CRCI: HB

COUNTRYSIDE MANAGER/ OFFICER

ENVIRONMENT, ANIMALS AND PLANTS

CRCI: HB

Qualifications and courses

Most entrants have completed a degree; however it is possible to enter this profession with a HND, Foundation degree, A levels or equivalent. A postgraduate qualification would be beneficial as this field is highly competitive. Subjects such as environmental science, biological sciences (such as zoology), environmental conservation, countryside management and earth sciences (such as geography) would all be relevant.

Generally degree programmes require applicants to have achieved at least 2 A levels/3 H grades and 5 GCSEs/S grades (A*–C/1–3).

You will also have to demonstrate your commitment to this career, which you can do by completing work experience placements within conservation groups or wildlife trusts such as the National Trust.

An alternative route into this industry is to start as a ranger or warden, gather experience and then apply for a countryside officer post. There are Apprenticeships available through which it is possible to do this and groups such as The Countryside Management Association or The National Trust offer a range of short courses and events – ranging from ecology and habitat management to the identification of fungi – to help you gain expertise and develop your career.

What the work involves

Countryside officers/managers preserve and protect important wildlife areas, including nature reserves and sites of special scientific interest. You will achieve this through methods such as raising awareness of the issues that affect the natural environment, monitoring species to see which require protection, and gathering evidence of pollution.

You will advise authorities and communities on the effect developments will have on the natural environment. Managers are responsible for the hiring, training and supervising of staff. You will also be in charge of the way budgets are spent.

Type of person suited to this work

In order to pursue this career you must have an interest in, and a passion for, environmental conservation.

You should have strong observational skills. You will also need to be physically fit. You should be capable of conducting research, of have strong communication and negotiation skills, both in person and on paper, and the ability to speak in public.

You might have to be involved in enforcing environmental laws and so you will have to be able to remain calm and logical.

Working conditions

You will spend some of your time in an office environment and the rest working outdoors.

Working hours will vary depending on the season, but the average is about 40 hours a week. This is not a 9am to 5pm job; working weekends, evenings and bank holidays is common.

You might be required to travel between sites and so a driving licence may be useful. As an officer you may be provided with protective clothing.

Future prospects

Officers may progress into a managerial position, for example countryside manager or senior officer. In order to gain this kind of promotion you will need to gather qualifications and experience. However, promotion opportunities can be hard to come by.

You may also be able to specialise in a specific area of conservation such as rivers, coasts or access and recreation for the general public. Each of these could increase your employment potential.

Advantages/disadvantages

You will have to work outside in all weathers.

This job has many elements to it and so every day will be different.

You will have to enforce environmental legislation which might place you in heated situations.

Money guide

These figures will vary depending on location, employer and sector.

Your salary will increase as you gain responsibility.

The average starting salary for a countryside officer is between £19,500 and £21,500 a year.

With experience this can increase to between £24,000 and £32,000.

Those who excel in the field can earn up to £36,000.

Related opportunities

- Countryside Ranger p259
- Landscape Architect/Designer p276
- Landscaper/Landscape Manager p277

Further information

BTCV
www.btcv.org.uk

The Countryside Management Association
www.countrysidemanagement.org.uk

COUNTRYSIDE RANGER

Qualifications and courses

There are no set entry qualifications, but GCSEs/S grades or higher-level qualifications in science and geography may be required.

Relevant courses include NVQs/SVQs at Levels 2 and 3 in Environmental Conservation and BTEC/SQA National Certificates and Diplomas in Practical Conservation and Countryside Management, Countryside Skills or Countryside Management. You will require 1 A level/ Higher and relevant work experience to gain entry to these.

Most training is done on the job. Courses for professional development are provided by Lantra National Training Organisation.

A driving licence is essential. Employers prefer applicants aged 21 or over. This can be a very competitive area to enter so unpaid experience can be vital. Volunteering may be possible at the Wildlife Trust, the National Trust and Groundwork.

What the work involves

By patrolling the countryside throughout the year you will monitor the success and progress of the plants/animals and the integrity of the fencing and buildings in your care.

You will be responsible for the safety and enjoyment of any visitors, answer their queries and help them get the most from their visit.

You will keep a record of any work that is carried out, along with inspections, accidents and incidents.

Type of person suited to this work

You will need to enjoy being outdoors and have a strong interest in wildlife and the countryside.

To ensure the future of your area you will need to provide information to the public which could include talking to potential funding organisations or local politicians. You will therefore have to be confident speaking in public and have excellent written and spoken communication skills. You might have to write reports and sometimes undertake research.

To find work you might have to start with some voluntary or community-based work, so it is important that you are keen and willing.

Working conditions

Most of your work will be outdoors, driving or walking around your area. You will be working in all weathers and despite protective clothing you will be, at times, cold and wet or hot and dusty. This is physically demanding work and is likely to involve walking over difficult terrain.

You are likely to work longer hours during the spring and summer, especially if there are animals or plants that require protection.

This work can be difficult if you suffer from pollen or dust allergies.

Future prospects

Once employed within the industry it is likely that you will need to move from employer to employer in order to progress.

Many jobs are offered on temporary contracts or on a seasonal basis.

After gaining experience, it is possible to enter lecturing, consultancy or research work. You could also progress to the role of officer or a more managerial position, which would be more office based. You might choose to move to leisure management, agriculture or horticulture work.

Advantages/disadvantages

You will spend a lot of time in the open air combining your interest in the countryside with work!

You could be working in remote areas.

Money guide

Initial salaries are between £9,000 and £13,000 per year. With experience this can rise to around £20,000 a year. The most senior countryside rangers can earn over £25,000 per year.

You may also be given additional payments if you are required to work unusual hours.

Related opportunities

- Countryside Manager/Officer p258
- Farm Manager p261
- Gamekeeper p270

Further information

BTCV
www.btcv.org.uk

Lantra
www.lantra.co.uk

Natural England
www.naturalengland.org.uk

ENVIRONMENT, ANIMALS AND PLANTS

CRCI: HB

Qualifications and courses

Dog handler

Dog handling is usually a second career. Employers such as the UK Border Agency, the police, the army and the fire service expect you to start in mainstream work in the service before applying.

You could start as an apprentice and work towards a Diploma in Work-Based Animal Care. There is also an ASET Level 2 National Award for General Purpose Security Dog Handlers. You are required by law to have a Security Industry Authority (SIA) licence.

Dog trainer

After working as a handler you can then apply to become a trainer. Some organisations, such as the police, require 3 GCSEs/S grades (A*–C/1–3), including English and maths. Voluntary work is recommended.

Foundation degrees and degrees are available in animal behaviour and training and animal studies. It is also recommended that as a dog trainer you join a professional body through which you can continue your continuing professional development (CPD) and keep up to date with new techniques as they arise.

What the work involves

Dog handler

Working as a team, you will search buildings, vehicles and open spaces for such things as people, illegal drugs, firearms or evidence. You may protect property including private property or military establishments.

You might attend large-scale disturbances to control crowds or search for casualties at disaster scenes.

Dog trainer

You could support security staff, the police force or animal charities such as the Guide Dogs for the Blind. Your work will be divided between training the dogs and their human carers.

You might run one-to-one and group classes on obedience training for dogs.

Type of person suited to this work

You may need to house and care for your dog from puppyhood right to the time it retires 7–10 years later. You will require a stable home environment.

Most police dog work involves attending incidents, so you will need to be able to stay calm in an emergency. You will need to be patient, self-confident, alert and observant.

Much of your time will be spent on your feet and may involve running, so a high level of fitness is required.

Dog trainer

You will need to be patient and a good teacher. You will need to have a good imagination to make classes fun and also be physically fit.

Working conditions

If you work with domestic owners you will probably be self-employed and work from a community setting like a village hall.

Dogs are used in dangerous situations and so you will be at risk of injury.

Future prospects

The main employers are the police, Armed Forces and customs and excise. Some other organisations employ a few dog handlers, for example the fire service, security companies and search and rescue services.

This job is fiercely competitive as many handlers stay in the job for life.

There is also the option of self-employment or lecturing on dog training courses.

Advantages/disadvantages

There is the possibility of self-employment.

You may at some point be bitten or scratched.

You will form a strong bond with your dog. It is really rewarding when the dog you have trained catches a criminal, or finds dangerous drugs or explosives.

Money guide

On average dog handlers earn between £15,000 and £25,000 a year depending on experience.

Extra allowances are paid when the dog lives with and is cared for by you.

Domestic dog trainers earn around £15,000 a year. Police dog trainers make about £21,000 which can rise to £30,000 with experience. If you are self-employed your earnings will depend on your success.

Related opportunities

- Pet Behaviour Counsellor p279
- Police Officer p551
- Racehorse Trainer p280

Further information

Army
www.army.mod.uk/join

Association of Pet Dog Trainers
www.apdt.co.uk

Police Recruitment
www.policecouldyou.co.uk

FARM MANAGER

Qualifications and courses

There are no formal entry requirements but most people who enter this area do so with an HND, degree or other higher level qualification.

Courses are available in agriculture, agricultural science, land and property management, and agricultural engineering. A levels/H grades or their equivalent, often including a science subject will be required. Postgraduate courses are also available which will require a relevant degree or HNC/D and experience.

It is possible to enter with an NVQ/SVQ in Agriculture Crop Production or Livestock Production Level 3, Agriculture (Livestock Management) Level 4 or Agricultural and Commercial Horticulture (Crop Management) Level 4.

Candidates should also have previous experience of farm work, and most degree-level courses include sandwich placements for this purpose. A driving licence is essential.

What the work involves

You will be responsible for the overall running of a farm. This includes making the decisions about which crops to grow or livestock to raise. You will supervise the work of your staff, keep up to date with farming developments and oversee the economic side of the business.

You will have to communicate with government officials, farming suppliers and feed merchants and your customers who could be major supermarkets or small local shops.

You will keep farm records up to date such as the budget and where crops and livestock are sold to and bought from.

Type of person suited to this work

You should have a passion for science, the environment and business, combined with a strong understanding of farming and a desire to learn.

You will also need an appreciation of health and safety and the ability to recruit, develop and retain your staff, as well as run the business of the farm.

You should be capable of motivating staff, be computer literate and work well when under pressure.

Working conditions

Farm managers tend to work long hours, with particular times of year being exceptionally busy. This includes harvest or lambing season and involves early mornings.

Managers will spend a lot of their time doing accounts and making sure the farm is operating profitably, but will also need to participate in general farm work during busy periods. On smaller farms this may be a regular occurrence. The outdoors work will involve heavy lifting and will be dirty, smelly and/or dusty.

Future prospects

Competition for jobs is intense and career progression is likely to involve moving between farms and from one part of the country to another.

With substantial experience and qualifications it is possible to progress into other related areas of agriculture; such as plant breeding, crop protection, plant trials or genetics. These opportunities are available within private companies or academic/research organisations.

Training or research opportunities are also possible and there could be the chance to work abroad.

Advantages/disadvantages

You will spend a lot of time in the open air caring for living and growing things. You will get to combine business acumen and an understanding of nature.

At some times of the year your social life may be restricted.

Your future can depend on factors outside of your control such as bird flu or foot and mouth disease.

Money guide

There is a set minimum wage, decided upon by the Agricultural Wages Boards for England and Wales, Scotland and Northern Ireland.

Average salaries are around £16,000 a year.

With experience this can increase to between £24,000 and £30,000. Managing a large farm, once enough experience has been gathered, may increase this to over £50,000.

Some jobs include rent-free accommodation and a vehicle.

Related opportunities

- Farm Worker p262
- Fish Farmer p268
- Parks Officer p278

Further information

Department for Environment, Food and Rural Affairs
www.defra.gov.uk

Lantra
www.lantra.co.uk

National Federation of Young Farmers' Clubs
www.nfyfc.org.uk

ENVIRONMENT, ANIMALS AND PLANTS

CRCI: HA

Qualifications and courses

There are no set entry requirements for this job but many employers will expect you to have work experience. GCSEs/S grades in English, maths and science may be useful for gaining promotion and higher pay. An Advanced Apprenticeship in Agriculture may also be helpful.

Livestock
Lantra offers a variety of livestock courses including Herdsman Foot Trimming, Sheep (lambing) and Dairy (calf-rearing). You can train while on the job and work towards NVQs Levels 1–3 in Livestock Production or a Diploma in Animal Care.

You may choose to do an HNC in Poultry Production at the Scottish Agricultural College. Poultry husbandry courses are also available at many other colleges.

Crops
The Royal Agricultural College offers degrees in crops, sustainable soil management and agricultural science. You could also take a National Proficiency Tests Council accredited course in Tractor Driving or Pesticide Use.

Many employers will allow you to train on the job and you can work towards NVQs Levels 1–3 in Agriculture, Mixed Farming and Crop Production.

What the work involves

Livestock
You will work on farms or estates caring for livestock such as cows, sheep, poultry and pigs. You will need to feed and handle the animals, clean their living spaces, and load and unload livestock for transport. You may need to milk cows and shear sheep.

You will tend to ill livestock, give them proper medication and help out with birthing procedures. You may also be required to keep track of animals' breeding cycle and care for the animals through pregnancy and the birthing process.

Crops
You will work on arable farms, ploughing, planting, sowing, fertilising, spraying and harvesting a variety of crops. You will either handpick crops or use machinery.

You could work with crops such as wheat, barley and oats, non-food crops such as linseed and flax, or energy crops used for heat and power generation. You will also be responsible for general maintenance and upkeep of the farm.

Type of person suited to this work

You should be practical and have a passion for the outdoors and environmental issues. You should be strong, active and adaptable and prepared to work very long hours.

A good knowledge of plant and/or animal care is important. You may need to work out weights and other calculations so good numeracy skills are also useful. You also need to be able to follow instructions and work with care and caution.

Working conditions

Farm work is seasonal so you will be busier at certain times of the year, when you may need to work 16 hour days.

You will normally work 40 hours a week, including evenings, early mornings and weekends. You will work in all weathers and will often be expected to live on or near the farm.

The work on livestock farms can be dirty so you will need to wear protective clothing and footwear.

Future prospects

You could be promoted to supervisory roles or train further and become farm manager. Most farms are small so you might need to move farms in order to be promoted. There are also opportunities to work overseas.

Livestock farms are mostly found in western parts of the UK. A rise in farmers' markets means that demand for meats is high and interest in organic foods has left ample opportunity.

Crop farms are mostly found in eastern parts of the UK. You could specialise in non-food crops such as pharmaceuticals, oils or materials such as hemp.

Advantages/disadvantages

You will work in all weathers. Working on a farm, especially during busy seasons, can be exhausting and at times dirty.

It is an amazing experience to tend to and watch an animal give birth and rewarding to reap an abundant harvest.

Money guide

If you start out as a trainee aged 16, you may earn around £9,977 a year. If you are 18 or older you may earn between £12,000 and £16,690. When you reach 20 this may increase to £20,000.

Many farm workers are paid per hour on a flexible or part-time basis. You can earn from £6.25 to £9.00 per hour. Apprentices earn between £139 and £232 per week.

Many employers will provide you with free or low-rent accommodation. Overtime pay is also common.

Related opportunities

- Farm Manager p261
- Fish Farmer p268
- Gamekeeper p270

Further information

Department for Environment, Food and Rural Affairs
www.defra.gov.uk

Lantra
www.lantra.co.uk

National Federation of Young Farmers' Clubs
www.nfyfc.org.uk

Organisation profile
BRIDGWATER COLLEGE

BRIDGWATER
COLLEGE

Getting a land-based education

The Cannington Centre at Bridgwater College has been delivering land-based education for almost 100 years. Somerset Farm Institute, as it was first known, opened its doors in 1921, and as Cannington College, it went on to achieve a national reputation as one of the leading providers in the sector. In 2004, it merged with local tertiary education provider Bridgwater College, a move which secured a substantial investment package to significantly improve the facilities.

The countryside location of the Cannington Centre makes it an ideal choice for students wanting to pursue a land-based education. The rural environment creates a calm and relaxed atmosphere, which students find very satisfying and conducive to learning. The teaching facilities consist of a range of purpose-built accommodation within beautifully maintained grounds. Many students opt to live on site and the College recently achieved an overall rating of 'outstanding' in its recent Social Care inspection by Ofsted. The inspectors summarised, 'The College provides excellent support for learners while they are living in residence. Arrangements for safeguarding are outstanding reflecting the College priorities for the safety of learners.'

The Student Liaison Team makes sure there is plenty of entertainment for day and residential students. Typical activities might include paintball and laser quest trips, DVD nights, various sports activities, pool competitions, College parties and the College Young Farmers' Club. The common room has a pool table, jukebox, games machines and much more. The team is on duty 24 hours a day, Monday to Friday, providing help and support to all students.

Facilities at the Centre include a 200 hectare farm with a new £1 million milking parlour, a £2 million new animal management centre with dog grooming salon, a fully refurbished BHS approved equestrian centre, beautiful walled gardens and botanical glasshouse, new activity centre with high and low rope challenges, a nine hole, 18 tee golf course – and much, much more.

There is also a dedicated Learning Resources Centre, with a library and access to over 20,000 books, journals, newspapers, DVDs and CDs, and a careers library. Our Virtual Learning Environment allows students 24 hour access to course materials, assignments and other resources. The Centre has its own restaurant offering breakfast, lunch and dinner, with a College shop selling groceries and stationery.

The provision is comprehensive – offering everything from agriculture to sports turf management, and from floristry to equine studies. Class sizes and tutor groups are usually small, which allows every student to have individual attention from their lecturers and tutor groups tend to form strong units and many lasting friendships are established.

The College hosts regular open days and evenings throughout the year, which are ideal opportunities to view the facilities, find out more about the courses, and speak to staff and students.

For more information, contact us:

Bridgwater College
Bath Road
Bridgwater
Somerset
TA6 4PZ

Call: 01278 441216
Email: enquiries@bridgwater.ac.uk
Visit: www.bridgwater.ac.uk

You can also keep up-to-date with new events and information by following Bridgwater College on Facebook, Twitter and Flickr.

Case study
BRIDGWATER COLLEGE

Which course are you studying?

I am studying a BTEC Level 3 Extended Diploma in Agriculture at Bridgwater College's Cannington Centre in Somerset.

Why did you choose this course?

I have lived on the family farm all my life and wanted to get a qualification to prepare me to take on the family business in the future.

What would you usually do in a typical day?

The College has its own fully operational farm so there is always something to get stuck in to. There is a theory element to the course but lessons are very practical and hands on, no two days are the same! I live on-site and so some mornings I can be up at the crack of dawn for milking duties or lambing – it's good practice for work in the agriculture industry.

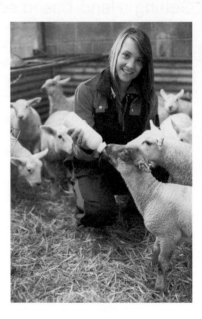

What do you enjoy most about the course?

The College farm is really different from my family farm and through studying at the Cannington Centre I get a completely different insight into farming. Sometimes I return home and suggest different methods and approaches to my dad; it's great to be able to put my learning into practice.

What are the main benefits of studying a course in agriculture?

The course is brilliant for anyone wanting to get into the agriculture industry. You don't even need to have had previous experience of farming – the course is tailored to students of all levels. The skills I have learnt are adaptable to all types of farming and the course has opened my eyes to lots of new ideas that I'd like to take back to my family farm.

What do you hope to progress on to on completion of this course?

On completion of this I am going to progress on to the Foundation Degree in Agricultural Management at Bridgwater College before returning to work on the family farm.

FARRIER

Qualifications and courses

To train as a farrier you must be at least 16 years old and will need to take an Advanced Apprenticeship with a training farrier approved by the Farriers Registration Council. You will need a minimum of 4 GCSEs/S grades (A*–C/1–3), including maths and English language, to be accepted for the Advanced Apprenticeship.

You will also need to pass a medical examination and look for an Approved Training Farrier (ATF) to recommend you to the Farrier Training Agency and complete the apprenticeship with. The apprenticeship takes 4 years and 2 months.

The course combines on-the-job training with periods at a FTA-approved college. At the end you will also be awarded a NVQ Level 3 in Farriery and the Diploma of the Worshipful Company of Farriers. To work as a farrier you must register with the Farriers Registration Council. A driving licence is required.

A Foundation degree in farriery at Myerscough College is also available for those who are already qualified and working. Additionally it is possible to learn farriery as a trade whilst serving with the army.

What the work involves

Farriers shoe, trim and care for the feet of horses.

As well as the skills of removing and fitting new shoes, you will have to keep up to date with new practices and know about horse anatomy and illnesses that can affect horses' feet.

You would often work in partnership with vets to treat leg and joint problems.

Type of person suited to this work

You should enjoy being around horses and have the right temperament to handle them. You will need to get on with your customers and deliver high-quality care to them and their horses.

You will have to enjoy being outdoors working in all weathers, often in a muddy environment.

This work is both practical and physical, so you will need to be strong to do manual work using lots of hand tools and have good metalworking skills.

Working conditions

Weekend work is common and emergency cover can be needed at any time.

Your days will involve driving to each customer, working with the horses and returning to your forge to prepare shoes and collect materials. In the summer months your hours will be long, especially when more people are riding their horses. This can be hot, tiring work, especially if fitting shoes to a difficult horse.

You could work from a blacksmith's forge or travel to farms and stables and work out of a mobile workshop.

Future prospects

Riding is a very popular activity and there are stables all around the country.

There are about 2500 farriers who are mostly self-employed. There is high competition for each apprenticeship. Larger riding schools, stables and horse breeders can offer permanent jobs. You could progress to become a senior farrier or into a managerial role.

Some farriers supplement their earnings by undertaking blacksmithing whilst they build up their farriery client list.

Advantages/disadvantages

This is a great job if you want to work with horses without riding.

Using your hands is a satisfying skill to have.

The work is physically demanding and can result in back injuries.

Money guide

When starting out you can expect a salary of around £8,500 per year.

Once qualified, you can earn between £10,000 and £20,000, depending on your success and the number of customers you have.

Some experienced and popular farriers can earn over £35,000.

Related opportunities

- Farm Manager p261
- Pet Behaviour Counsellor p279
- Racehorse Trainer p280

Further information

Farriery Training Agency
www.farrier-reg.gov.uk

Worshipful Company of Farriers
www.wcf.org.uk

ENVIRONMENT, ANIMALS AND PLANTS

CRCI: HC

Organisation profile

FARRIERY

What is farriery?

Farriery, or the shoeing of horses and similar animals, is an ancient craft. It is defined in the Farriers (Registration) Act 1975 as 'any work in connection with the preparation or treatment of the foot of a horse for the immediate reception of a shoe thereon, the fitting by nailing or otherwise of a shoe to the foot or the finishing off of such work to the foot'.

A farrier is a skilled craftsperson with a sound knowledge of both theory and practice of the craft, capable of shoeing all types of feet, whether normal or defective, making shoes to suit all types of work and working conditions and of devising corrective measures to compensate for faulty limb action. Farriery is hard work and it is practised on animals, some of which may be fractious. Care should be taken that young people have realistic expectations of the nature of employment within the sector – idyllic stereotypes seldom last long!

The Court of Aldermen of the City established a Livery Company of the City of London, known as the Worshipful Company of Farriers, in 1356 during the reign of Edward III. It was given statutory responsibility for securing adequate standards of competence and conduct among Farriers by the Farriers (Registration) Act 1975, together with advancement of the art and science of farriery and education in connection with it. The Farriers Registration Council, through Investigating and Disciplinary Committees, exercises a continuing surveillance of professional conduct.

A farrier should not be confused with a blacksmith. farriers and blacksmiths both work with metal but only a farrier is permitted to fit shoes to horses.

How to become a farrier

To become a farrier it is necessary to qualify for entry onto the Register of Farriers. To achieve this requires completion of a course of training approved by the Farriers Registration Council (FRC), passing the Diploma of the Worshipful Company of Farriers Examination (DipWCF) and completion of an adequate period of experience.

Eligibility for registration in the Register of Farriers is obtained during the course of an Advanced Apprenticeship, which satisfies the requirements of the FRC. Registration, once secured, is maintained by payment of a retention fee on 1 January each year for as long as farriery is practised.

How to become an apprentice

Candidates cannot apply directly for an Apprenticeship, and must be proposed by an Approved Training Farrier (ATF).

1. Check you have the minimum academic entry requirements.
2. Write to ATFs from the list published by the NFTA to find one to propose you as a candidate and employ you for the Period of Apprenticeship. It may be necessary to look outside your local area for such an ATF, and you may need to be prepared to live away from home during the Apprenticeship Period.
3. The ATF will then propose you as a candidate for an apprenticeship, in accordance with the timetable of events for each intake.

Further information can be found at www.farrierytraining.co.uk or by phoning 01733 319770.

Case study
FARRIER

Beckie Mabbutt: West Sussex

Beckie is a farrier working in West Sussex. She has been self-employed since completing her farriery apprenticeship.

Beckie was determined to be a farrier from 8 years old, after seeing her own horse shod. She worked with a couple of farriers whilst still at school and then completed the pre-farriery course to give her a route into the job she loves, before starting the apprenticeship.

In an average week, Beckie works 4 days for herself, shoeing around 6 horses a day and doing trims on a wide variety of horses. She continues to develop her training working one day a week with another farrier at Liphook Veterinary Hospital. Says Beckie, 'This has really opened my eyes to the things you don't see out on the road. Repeating procedures on seriously lame horses and having the facilities of MRIs, X-rays etc has really accelerated my learning. Dave has really helped me to learn and has put me in contact with other great farriers and vets.'

Beckie believes the apprenticeship gave her the confidence both with theory and practical work. 'Learning all of the anatomy at college was excellent, as was teaching on how to run an effective business and deal with customers. However, I think that the on the job training was most beneficial, as you can clock up experiences a lot easier than you could by just attending a college course. It also gave me the chance to become known amongst the horse owners in Sussex. I wouldn't be in a position to run my own business if I hadn't learnt the skills of the trade.'

Although Beckie initially found it challenging to be accepted in a male dominated job, she quickly made sure that her gender was not an issue. 'I had to prove I was better than a male rather than equal to gain the same respect, some thought I would be too weak so I made sure that I kept fit and regularly visited the gym. I now have a business that is prospering; I was fully booked up within 2 months.' Beckie now sends her customers a monthly newsletter to educate them on different topics and share ideas.

The rewards of the job are plentiful for Beckie. 'I enjoy helping horses to move better and more comfortably and helping customers with options as to how we can develop their horse's action. I've also found it very rewarding making so many good friends such as vets, other farriers and owners.'

'I would definitely encourage others to start a career in farriery. All I would say is that you've got to really want to do it. I've learnt that you need to be very understanding of not only the horse's needs, but your customer's too. It's a tough job but very rewarding. I would encourage more females to enter the profession, as there is a definite niche for us.'

FISH FARMER

Qualifications and courses

Applicants do not necessarily need formal educational qualifications but most employers require GCSEs/S grades (A*–C/1–3). A BTEC First Certificate/Diploma in Fish Husbandry (Level 2) is available to those with 4 GCSE/S grades (A*–C/1–3). Students can then progress to the BTEC National Certificate/Diploma in Fish Management. SQA also offer a National Progression Award (NPA) in Aquaculture (Levels 4 and 5).

Training can be done on the job with attendance at short courses. Entrants may study via distance learning for the Certificate or Diploma in Fisheries Management offered by the Institute of Fisheries Management (IFM).

Those who would like to begin their career as a manager or assistant manager may require a degree in a relevant subject such as aquaculture and fishery management, biology or marine and freshwater biology.

Once you are employed in this sector, you may be expected to take industry recognised qualifications in emergency first aid, food hygiene and sea survival.

What the work involves

As a fish farmer you will raise fish from small (juvenile) fry until they reach saleable size. The most common fish to raise are salmon and trout. You will feed them, check for disease and protect them from predators. The final stage of the process is to net the catch and pack them for market.

Some farms specialise in producing the breeding stock – the tiny fish that other farmers bring to saleable size – known as fingerlings. Some shellfish farms in coastal locations also produce oysters, scallops and mussels.

Type of person suited to this work

You must be a practical person, willing to get wet and dirty. You need a good knowledge of fish which you will develop throughout your career. Much of this work is scientific in approach, so you should have good observational skills to be able to identify anything that might affect the quality and success of the fish in your care.

You should be patient, hard working and able to persevere in challenging situations. This work is difficult and long-term security is not guaranteed.

Entrants to this profession must be comfortable working within a team and independently.

If you become a manager you will also require good business and administrative skills.

Working conditions

Working with fish is the same as any animal-based work, which means they need care and attention 24/7. You are likely to work on a rota basis with 2 days off every week. You will work very long hours including early mornings, late evenings and weekends.

You will be outdoors in damp, cold conditions having to cope with all types of weather.

Some of the work will be unpleasant and will involve the sight of blood.

Future prospects

Fish farming is becoming quite important owing to the problems with sea fish stocks.

Like other farming enterprises, fish farms are vulnerable to price fluctuations, so predicting the future is difficult. Around 7500 people are employed in the industry, most of whom are based in Scotland. There are 300 trout farms located in Scotland, North Yorkshire, and southern and central England.

With experience you may move into a research-related role involving scientific and technical work. You could also start up your own fish farm or work abroad.

Advantages/disadvantages

You will spend a lot of time in the open air.

You will have the satisfaction of producing an in-demand product.

There are only limited areas of the UK where the work is available.

Having to work unsocial hours could interfere with your personal life.

Money guide

Fish farm workers may have a starting salary of £10,000–£13,000.

As you gain experience, you could expect to earn around £18,000.

Experienced managers of a fish farm can achieve up to £38,000.

Related opportunities

- Countryside Ranger p259
- Farm Manager p261
- Skipper/Deckhand p281

Further information

British Trout Association
www.britishtrout.co.uk

Institute of Fisheries Management
www.ifm.org.uk

Qualifications and courses

Forest worker

There are no formal entry requirements but at least 2 GCSE/S grades (A*–C/1–3) or a forestry qualification would be an advantage. These include the City & Guilds Certificate and Diploma in Forestry and Arboriculture (Levels 2 and 3), the City & Guilds Diploma in Work-based Trees and Timber (Levels 2 and 3), the BTEC National in Forestry and Arboriculture (Level 3) and the BTEC National in Countryside Management (Level 3). Alternatively, the Apprenticeship in Trees and Timber is available at Intermediate and Advanced Level.

The National Proficiency Tests Council (NPTC) and Lantra award certificates of competence in skills such as operating chainsaws and carrying out chemical spraying.

Forest officer

Entry is with a Foundation degree, HND, degree or postgraduate qualification in forestry, land management, horticulture or environmental science. For entry to a degree a minimum of 2 A levels/3 H grades, normally including maths or a science is required. At least 1 A level/H grade or equivalent is required for entry to an HND or Foundation degree. It may be useful to gain some experience before applying for a course.

What the work involves

Forest worker

Work includes planting and felling trees, managing weeds, maintaining fencing and carrying out tree surgery. In addition, you will use tools, drive vehicles and repair any broken fences.

Forest officer

You will plan and manage the annual programme of your forest. This includes organising the clearing of areas, planting and felling trees, and overseeing general maintenance.

Type of person suited to this work

Forest worker

It is important that you can follow instructions and safety procedures as the work is dangerous. You should enjoy being outdoors.

Forest officer

You must be organised as you will plan jobs months in advance. You need both technical skills and theoretical knowledge of forests and wildlife.

Working conditions

Forest worker

You will probably work a standard Monday–Friday week with overtime and weekend work during the busier summer months. You will have to be aware of health and safety legislation as this can be dangerous work, using potentially hazardous tools.

Forest officer

Much of your time will be spent outdoors but you will also work indoors planning duties for your staff. You are likely to do a lot of travelling whilst you check the different areas under your responsibility. A driving licence would be helpful as many of these places are isolated.

Future prospects

The range of employers includes the Forestry Commission, private landowners and estates, local authorities and large companies.

Career progression is likely to involve relocating as promotion is rare unless you work for a large company. Many contracts are short term so you need to have a flexible approach to employment opportunities.

With significant experience, self-employment as a consultant or trainer is possible.

Advantages/disadvantages

It is a perfect job if you love the outdoors.

As with all land-based careers, you are often at the mercy of the weather.

Money guide

Forest worker

You are likely to earn around £12,000 per year when starting out in this career.

With experience, salaries increase to around £18,000.

A supervisor could earn up to £26,500.

Forest officer

Starting salaries for this role are usually between £16,000 and £21,000.

An experienced forest officer could achieve in excess of £35,000.

Forest workers and officers employed by private estates may have accommodation provided.

Related opportunities

- Countryside Ranger p259
- Gardener/Garden Designer p271
- Rural Property/Practice Surveyor p117

Further information

Forestry Commission
www.forestry.gov.uk

Institute of Chartered Foresters
www.charteredforesters.org

ENVIRONMENT, ANIMALS AND PLANTS

CRCI: HB

GAMEKEEPER

Qualifications and courses

No formal qualifications are needed for this role. However, 3 GCSEs/S grades (A*–C/1–3) may be an advantage. Voluntary or relevant work experience is very useful. Training is generally on the job, but there are some courses available to applicants who wish to progress.

City & Guilds offer the National and Advanced National Certificate in Countryside and Environment Management, National Certificate in Gamekeeping Level 2 and the Certificate in Land-based Studies Level 1.

NVQs/SVQs are available in Gamekeeping and Wildlife Management at Levels 2 and 3. A BTEC National Award is available in Gamekeeping. A BTEC National Diploma in Countryside Management is also available. An HNC in gamekeeping with wildlife management is another possibility. Candidates would need practical experience and/or the National Award in Gamekeeping.

Foundation degrees are available in countryside and environment (gamekeeping) at several colleges. These generally require a National Diploma or 2 or more A levels/H grades for entry. Apprenticeships/Skillseekers could be available for those aged between 16 and 24.

What the work involves

As a gamekeeper you will work on a large country estate, where shooting for sport is part of the estate business. You will also play an important role in managing the land.

You will be responsible for providing birds and other animals such as deer or hares for the clients to shoot, or possibly fish to catch. This is achieved by raising game birds and releasing them into the wild once they are mature enough, and protecting game from its natural predators such as magpies and rats.

You may also plant and protect crops, clear the land, and keep rivers clean.

Type of person suited to this work

You must have an unsentimental approach to wildlife as this job involves the killing of animals for sport.

To enable the clients to get the most from their day, you will need to be a good communicator and be able to offer advice about gun usage and how to hit targets successfully.

Physical fitness and stamina are essential. You must be alert and possess excellent practical skills. You must be happy to work on your own for long periods of time.

Working conditions

You will be outdoors in all weathers and seasons. Your hours will be flexible and will involve weekend working and late or early starts. You will spend long periods of time on your own, doing lots of walking to check the estate and the progress of the game.

You will be handling and using guns, traps and poisons so will have to be confident using them and very aware of your own safety and that of others.

This work will be difficult for those who suffer from allergies to animals, pollen or dust.

Future prospects

Most of this work is within remote parts of the country or on large country estates.

There is strong competition for jobs, so it is best to take a few training courses before applying.

With further skills in shoot or land management you can be promoted to head of estate, with experience and dedication you can advance from trainee to head keeper quickly.

Advantages/disadvantages

This job combines outdoor physical work with lots of practical skills.

You will spend a lot of time alone.

You might be provided with a house.

Money guide

Starting salaries for new entrants are around £11,000 per year.

With experience you may earn between £13,000 and £18,500.

Head gamekeepers can expect up to £21,500.

Related opportunities

- Countryside Ranger p259
- Farm Manager p261
- Farrier p265

Further information

British Association for Shooting and Conservation
www.basc.org.uk

Game and Wildlife Conservation Trust
www.gct.org.uk

National Gamekeepers' Organisation
www.nationalgamekeepers.org.uk

Qualifications and courses

Gardener

There are no set requirements for entry to this career. GCSEs/S grades (A*–C/1–3) would be useful. Courses are available to those who wish to progress and include NVQs/SVQs in Environmental Studies. The Royal Horticultural Society (RHS) have a general examination, which allows entry onto the Advanced National Certificate in Horticulture.

Garden designer

Although there are no formal requirements for this job, a design-orientated qualification is an advantage. Many garden design courses are offered at land-based colleges and some art colleges too. Courses include NVQs/SVQs. Degrees in garden design and related subjects are also available. The Institute of Gardening offers a Diploma in Horticulture which can be studied at home.

What the work involves

Gardener

Gardeners work in a wide range of settings, from large gardens such as those in stately homes and National Trust properties, to small urban parks and private gardens.

Garden designer

You will advise clients on how to improve the look and planting of their garden. You will present your ideas as a series of plans, and supervise a landscape contractor to turn your design into reality.

Type of person suited to this work

Gardeners need to be physically fit and confident in using hand tools.

You must be creative and able to picture how a piece of bare or neglected ground can be transformed into something beautiful.

As a garden designer, drawing and ICT skills will be useful, as will an extensive knowledge of plants and the environments they need.

Working conditions

Gardeners mostly work outdoors. There will be a lot of physical work, lifting large pots and bags of peat, and digging and clearing beds.

Garden designers will spend most of their time in a studio designing and researching garden plans. You will spend some time outdoors overseeing practical tasks.

Future prospects

Gardener

Many gardeners are self-employed offering services to both the public and private sectors. If you work for a local authority, with experience, you could move on to supervisor or manager jobs, especially if you gain further qualifications. Gardeners can also train to be garden designers.

Garden designer

Half of all designers work in private practice. Some specialise in certain types of design such as planting, landscaping, etc. Some designers choose to be self-employed offering services to private home owners.

Advantages/disadvantages

Designers can mix creative, practical and outdoor work.

Your work will depend on the weather.

You may work in beautiful places (or create them if you are a designer).

Money guide

Gardener

Gardeners working for a local authority start at around £11,000–£12,000 per year. With experience this can rise to £20,000+, especially if you have management duties. If self-employed you will agree an hourly rate with your customer.

Garden designer

As a guide, trainee rates start at between £10,000 and £15,000 per year. Designers' pay will depend entirely on how well they can market themselves and generate work; many are self-employed and charge around £30–£60 per hour.

Related opportunities

- Groundsperson/Greenkeeper p273
- Horticultural Worker/Manager p274
- Landscape Architect/Designer p276

Further information

Royal Horticultural Society
www.rhs.org.uk

ENVIRONMENT, ANIMALS AND PLANTS

CRCI: HB

GROOM/STABLE HAND/ STUD HAND

Qualifications and courses

Groom/stable hand

You must be at least 16 years of age and ideally you should have experience working with horses. Qualifications which may be useful include the NPTC NVQ in Horse Care (Levels 1–3), the City & Guilds Certificate and Diploma in Horse Care and Management (Levels 2 and 3), the BTEC First in Horse Care (Level 2) and the BTEC National in Horse Management (Level 3). The Association of British Riding Schools (ABRS) offers the Grooms Certificate and Grooms Diploma, and the British Horse Society (BHS) have exams in Horse Knowledge Care and Riding at stages 1–4.

Stud hand

There are no formal entry requirements. Some knowledge of stable work and horse care is expected. The National Stud in Newmarket offers a free Apprenticeship for school leavers. This involves 10 weeks of training at a residential centre and the opportunity for a 10-month placement. Those over the age of 18 with experience working with horses can apply for the free Diploma in Stud Practice and Management with the National Stud. Students spend 5 months undertaking practical training, attending lectures and workshops, and completing projects and exams.

What the work involves

Groom/stable hand

You will be responsible for the health and welfare of the horses in your care. You will groom, feed, muck out and tack up the horses. You could be based within a riding school, competition or livery yard, racing stable or veterinary hospital.

Stud hand

This is a specialised area of work as you will be working with stallions, brood mares and young stock. You will use your understanding and knowledge of breeding lines to help owners breed a foal that meets their requirements.

Type of person suited to this work

You must be comfortable and competent riding and working with horses. Good observation skills and patience are essential when caring for animals.

You need strong communication and team-working skills to work with your colleagues, the horse owners and stable visitors.

You should be a practical person, physically fit and willing to work in messy conditions.

Working conditions

You will spend most of your time outdoors lifting heavy bags of feed, hay and bedding. You will carry tack, clean up the yard or ride. In the summer the work can be hot, dusty and smelly. In the winter it is cold, wet and muddy.

You will wear protective clothing and, as this work can be dangerous, you must be aware of your own and others' safety. Horses can kick and bite.

You can expect to work 24/7, including some holidays and weekends, especially if you live-in.

A driving licence is useful.

Future prospects

Groom/stable hand

With experience it is possible to specialise. Competition grooms (show-jumping, dressage and eventing) are in demand. Gaining your HGV driving licence can increase opportunities. Most grooms progress to more successful yards that compete internationally or keep more expensive and quality horses.

Stud hand

Interest in breeding quality British horses and ponies has increased owing to European competition. Stud work is therefore rising in importance and those with skills are in demand.

Advantages/disadvantages

This is the perfect job for a horse lover.

The pay is relatively low for such a demanding job.

Injury risks are high in all horse activities and this could affect your long-term career security.

Money guide

The horse industry has a reputation for low salaries and long hours.

Starting salaries are usually around £12,500.

With experience, you could earn £14,000–£16,000.

A head groom could achieve up to £20,000.

Free or supplemented accommodation is common for those living on the premises.

Related opportunities

- Farm Manager p261
- Farrier p265
- Racehorse Trainer p280

Further information

British Horse Society
www.bhs.org.uk

GROUNDSPERSON/ GREENKEEPER

Qualifications and courses

There are no set entry qualifications for this role and training generally takes place on the job. The Apprenticeship in Horticulture is available at Intermediate and Advanced Levels.

Relevant qualifications offered by City & Guilds are the Award/Certificate/Diploma in Work-Based Horticulture (Levels 1–3), the Certificate in Sports and Amenity Turf Maintenance (Level 2) and the Certificate and Diploma in Horticulture (Levels 2 and 3). Other courses include the BTEC First in Horticulture (Level 2), the BTEC National in Horticulture (Level 3) and the BTEC Higher National in Horticulture (Sports Turf Management) at Levels 4 and 5.

Degrees and Foundation degrees in sports turf and golf course management are available. Entry requirements are 2 A levels/3 H grades and 5 GCSEs/S grades (A*–C/1–3) including English and maths.

The Institute of Groundsmanship (IOG) offers short courses in areas such as generic sports turf management, basic lawn care and synthetic surfaces.

The British and International Golf Greenkeepers Association (BIGGA) also have a range of qualifications, including the Master Greenkeeper Certificate for those with experience and expertise.

What the work involves

Your main role will be to prepare and maintain the grounds used for different sports. Although you might work on synthetic surfaces for games like hockey, most of the time you will be working with grass. You will cut, treat, weed and prepare the surface before each game, match or event.

You will be responsible for outlining the playing areas with tape or marking compound, ensuring that they adhere to the regulations of the appropriate governing body.

You will put up posts, nets and other equipment where needed.

Type of person suited to this work

You need specialist horticultural knowledge, combined with an understanding of the different sports and what the competitors of each sport need.

You should be good with your hands and have a working knowledge of machinery maintenance.

You will require lots of stamina and physical fitness to do a variety of jobs.

Working conditions

You will have to work flexible hours including evenings and weekends.

The role involves a lot of physical labour such as carrying heavy items and bending. This work may be unsuitable for those who suffer from hay fever or allergies to chemicals.

You will spend a lot of your time working outdoors, although you will probably be in a workshop when repairing and maintaining the equipment. You will need to wear protective clothing.

Future prospects

The range of potential places for you to work is increasing and demand for staff is growing. You could work in a professional sports club, local authority education or sports and leisure department, hotel, university or college.

With additional qualifications and experience you could apply for promotion to team leader or supervisor, head groundsperson and then area manager. Bigger companies offer greater promotion opportunities.

It is possible to progress into a position in leisure management or estate management.

Advantages/disadvantages

This job provides the satisfaction of knowing that your work will be seen by thousands of people.

Sports fans will have the opportunity to work in a sector that they are passionate about.

You will spend most of your time working outside in all weather conditions.

Money guide

A trainee groundsperson could have a starting salary of £10,000–£11,000.

Once qualified, you can expect to earn £14,000–£18,000 a year.

An experienced and skilled groundsperson/greenkeeper could receive between £18,000 and £24,000.

A head groundsperson could achieve £25,000–£33,000.

Staff responsible for major sporting venues can receive higher salaries.

Employers may also offer on-site accommodation or bonuses for overtime.

Related opportunities

- Countryside Ranger p259
- Gardener/Garden Designer p271
- Horticultural Worker/Manager p274

Further information

British and International Golf Greenkeepers Association
www.bigga.org.uk

Institute of Groundsmanship
www.iog.org

HORTICULTURAL WORKER/ MANAGER

ENTRY LEVEL 2

Qualifications and courses

There are no formal entry requirements for horticultural work, but certain employers look for GCSEs/S grades (A*–C/1–3) including science, or a BTEC First Diploma in Horticulture.

There are a number of vocational qualifications that could be useful, including qualifications in horticulture from the Royal Horticultural Society at Levels 1–3. There are also Foundation degrees and degrees in horticulture. A Kew Diploma from the Royal Botanical Gardens can be obtained after 3 years. They also offer a 3-year Kew Apprenticeship.

In addition to those courses above you could gain NVQs/ SVQs in Management or Supervisory Management. The Royal Botanical Gardens at Kew offer International Diploma courses in Botanic Garden Management.

What the work involves

You will undertake a variety of horticulturally related tasks and have a number of different responsibilities such as mowing lawns and tidying flowerbeds. You will also need to maintain equipment and tools and look after plants by checking for disease, feeding, watering, pruning and spraying them. To produce new stock, you will plant out cuttings and seedlings. You will also pot-up and pack plants.

As a manager you will supervise, train and recruit staff and look after the day-to-day running of the organisation. You will decide which plants to grow, manage the budgets, ensure deliveries are despatched on time and develop a business plan for now and in the future.

Type of person suited to this work

Much of your day will involve carrying, bending and working with the plants, so you will need to be physically fit.

You will be outdoors for much of the time working in all weathers, doing dirty work.

These jobs could be difficult if you suffer from pollen or dust allergies.

Working conditions

You will normally work a 40-hour week and could be based at a garden centre, plant nursery or in a park or public garden. You will often have to work weekends and late evenings.

Work could be seasonal with more hours required at certain times of the year. You will spend much of your time outdoors, in all weathers.

Future prospects

There is a constant demand for workers, especially for those with experience.

Horticultural jobs are available within major plant producers, national parks, public gardens and local and national garden shops/nurseries.

After gaining experience and qualifications you could progress to a role as supervisor or manager, freelance work or start up your own shop. There is the opportunity to undertake training to help career development. The British Agrochemical Standards Inspection Scheme (BASIS) offers a number of courses on a range of technical subjects including fertilisers, pesticides and cultivation.

Advantages/disadvantages

There is a good mix of practical and managerial work.

These jobs combine lots of skills and can be very rewarding.

This is an expanding market with lots of opportunities.

Money guide

Starting salaries are around £12,000 to £15,000 per year. With experience, this rises to around £18,000 to £20,000.

Salaries for a mangerial role are around £16,000 per year, rising to £21,000 for graduates.

Qualified and experienced managers can earn between £30,000 and £40,000.

Related opportunities

- Arboricultural Worker/Tree Surgeon p257
- Gardener/Garden Designer p271
- Groundsperson/Greenkeeper p273

Further information

British Agrochemical Standards Inspection Scheme (BASIS)
www.basis-reg.com/

Institute of Horticulture
www.horticulture.org.uk

KENNEL WORKER

Qualifications and courses

There are no formal educational requirements although some employers will favour candidates with GCSEs/S grades (A*–C/1–3) in English and/or maths. NVQ/SVQ Levels 1–3, BTEC National Qualifications in Animal Care and the City & Guilds Advanced National Certificate in Animal Care and Management may be useful.

The Animal Care College also offers training programmes which may prove helpful. The Guide Dogs for the Blind Association can provide work experience for applicants aged over 18. Hearing Dogs for the Deaf also recruit volunteer puppy socialisers from people who have experience of looking after young dogs and have an approved home.

Lantra have developed several Apprenticeship/ Skillseekers schemes for those aged between 16 and 24. Training takes place on the job and is given by the manager or an experienced staff member.

What the work involves

There are lots of types of kennels including boarding, pet sanctuary, breeding and quarantine kennels for animals brought from overseas.

Administrative skills may be useful, you might need to answer the phones, take payments and keep records when medicine is administered or if any behavioural problems are displayed. As well as cleaning the kennels, you will feed, exercise and check on the general health of the dogs and cats.

In a pet sanctuary you might be required to show prospective owners around and answer any questions they have on animal care.

Type of person suited to this work

You will need to enjoy spending time outdoors and not mind getting dirty. Some of the animals you will be working with might have behavioural problems or nervous dispositions and so you will need to be calm and patient. A good knowledge of small pet care is vital.

You will require a good level of fitness as you will spend a large part of the day being active.

You should have strong communication skills and the ability to work well alone or as part of a team.

Working conditions

This is physically demanding work involving walking dogs and cleaning the kennels. You may work shifts and your hours will probably include evenings, weekends and public holidays.

Many animals will be frightened and confused so they could be aggressive, you will therefore have to be aware of not only your own, but the safety of those around you.

You will spend a lot of time outdoors in all weathers and the work can be smelly, dirty and noisy.

Future prospects

There are approximately 3500 kennels in the UK, but with recent changes in quarantine laws numbers employed within this job have reduced. However, you could work for national charitable organisations such as the RSPCA, Guide Dogs for the Blind Association or a private breeder.

The army and police recruit service and civilian kennel staff.

In larger kennels there may be the opportunity to progress to the position of supervisor or manager.

Advantages/disadvantages

This is not a 9am–5pm job and the unusual hours may affect your social or family life.

There is the possibility of being attacked by an animal.

There is an opportunity to become self-employed by opening your own kennels.

Money guide

Pay will depend on the nature of your employer.

If you are working for a private kennels £12,000–£16,000 is likely. For animal charities and larger organisations you may get more. The RSPCA offers a minimum of £10,500 to its kennel workers (known as Animal Care Assistants).

You may be provided with accommodation and extra pay could be offered for overtime.

Related opportunities

- Dog Trainer/Handler p260
- Veterinary Nurse p282
- Zookeeper p285

Further information

Animal Care College
www.animalcarecollege.co.uk

Guide Dogs for the Blind Association
www.guidedogs.org.uk

Lantra
www.lantra.co.uk

Royal Society for the Prevention of Cruelty to Animals
www.rspca.org.uk

ENVIRONMENT, ANIMALS AND PLANTS

CRCI: HC

Qualifications and courses

You will need a degree in landscape architecture or a relevant first degree followed by a postgraduate qualification, accredited by the Landscape Institute (LI).

In order to gain entry to a degree course you will usually need at least 2 A levels/3 H grades and 5 GCSEs/S grades (A*–C/1–3), or a diploma in an environmental or land-based subject. In order to gain entry to a postgraduate course you will usually need to complete an Honours degree in a relevant subject. It is not possible to gain accreditation with only a HND or Foundation degree.

Entrants who have completed a course accredited by the Landscape Institute (LI) can work towards chartered membership of the LI through the Professional Practice Examination.

Courses are also available at land-based colleges of further education, which offer a range of BTEC National qualifications in relevant subjects.

Practical experience in a landscape-related field is very useful when applying to postgraduate courses.

The profession welcomes mature applicants.

What the work involves

You will design or develop a new or existing outside space. You will then make a plan, saying what plantings should be included, and calculate the cost. You will then see the project through to completion by supervising the work on-site.

Although you will understand garden design, you will also have an understanding of civil engineering, horticulture and planning law.

You could work on projects aimed to regenerate towns and cities and developments to help combat climate change.

Type of person suited to this work

You will have to enjoy being outdoors and want to make a difference to the environment. You will need to be happy in the open in both the summer and the winter and be prepared to spend time away from home on some jobs.

You will be interested in making, building and constructing hard landscaping but will appreciate and understand the impact that different plants can have.

You should be physically strong and able to use machinery and hand tools. You must be creative, artistic and have strong computer skills. You should have solid communication and negotiation skills.

Working conditions

Landscape architects spend a lot of time in the design studio sitting at a computer and drawing board or attending meetings on-site at clients' premises.

You could spend about a quarter of your time at the project site, supervising operations. Some of your time will also be spent on the phone dealing with contractors and suppliers.

Site work will involve being outdoors in all weather. Average hours are about 37 per week Monday to Friday. You may spend some time away from home.

Future prospects

Owing to the impact of home improvement programmes, designing and developing gardens is now a popular and growing business. However, it can be a competitive area so many choose self-employment.

Organisations who recruit landscape staff include local authorities, botanical gardens, large private estates, the National Trust, English Heritage, building contractors and landscape design houses.

If you choose to become self-employed your success will depend upon finding customers, the quality of your work and how quickly you can build your reputation.

Advantages/disadvantages

There is a good mix of practical hands-on work with planning, design and meeting people.

You will get satisfaction from knowing your work will have an impact on future generations.

You could get wet, cold, hot and dusty.

You will not be able to do this work if you suffer from pollen or dust allergies.

Money guide

Starting salaries for a graduate landscape architect are around £20,000 per year.

Once you have become fully qualified as a chartered landscape architect salaries could range from £25,000 to £45,000 a year.

If you work in private practice these figures could increase substantially, especially if you become partner.

Related opportunities

- Architect p70
- Landscaper/Landscape Manager p277
- Town Planner/Planning Technician p127

Further information

Landscape Design Trust
www.landscape.co.uk

Landscape Institute
www.landscapeinstitute.org

Qualifications and courses

Landscaper

There are no required qualifications but relevant GCSEs/S grades, National Proficiency Tests Council Certificates (NPTC), BTEC and RHS Certificates/ Diplomas in Horticulture are useful.

A driving licence is often required.

Landscape manager

Although there are no set qualifications this is still an extremely competitive industry. A HNC/HND, degree or postgraduate qualification in a relevant subject such as garden design would prove valuable.

The Landscape Institute has accredited some degree courses.

For both positions it is possible to obtain a ROLO card. This entitles you to membership of the Register of Land Based Operatives. To qualify for this you will need a Work Based Diploma (a new NVQ course), Level 2 or 3 and accredited health and safety training. More information is available on the British Association of Landscape Industries (BALI) website.

What the work involves

Landscaper

You will do the practical work of turning a landscape architect's plan into reality.

You will operate machinery, carry out planting schemes, put up fences, create ponds, lay paths, construct decking and make terraces.

Landscape manager

You will use your specialist knowledge to advise others on the development and maintenance of a wide range of landscapes such as historic gardens, motorway verges and public parks. You will decide where to place features like footpaths and play areas, oversee the people contracted to carry out work, complete reports and manage budgets.

Type of person suited to this work

You must enjoy working outdoors and want to make a difference to the environment. You will be interested in making, building and constructing hard landscaping but will also appreciate and understand the impact that different plants can have.

You will need to be physically strong and able to use machinery and hand tools.

An understanding of the laws surrounding the environment and the countryside is essential.

Working conditions

Landscaper

You will be outdoors in all weathers creating the design and working on landscape maintenance. There is a lot of physical labour involved such as heavy lifting, operating machinery and digging. You will need to wear protective clothing.

Landscape manager

You will work in an office for a lot of your time, but you will also go out for meetings to check and supervise work on-site. On average you will work 37 hours a week, though overtime may be required. You may need to spend time away from home.

Future prospects

Landscape staff work for local authorities, botanical gardens, large private estates, the National Trust, English Heritage, building contractors and landscape design houses.

Landscape managers in government can follow a structured career path, in other organisations you may find yourself moving companies in order to progress.

Self-employment is also an option.

Advantages/disadvantages

You will get satisfaction from knowing your work will have an impact on future generations.

You could get wet, cold, hot and dusty.

You will not be able to do this work if you suffer from pollen or dust allergies.

Money guide

Landscaper

Starting salaries are around £15,000 per year increasing to £19,000–£20,500 for those with experience.

Landscape manager

Starting salaries are around £20,000 rising to between £25,000 and £45,000 with experience.

Related opportunities

- Gardener/Garden Designer p271
- Groundsperson/Greenkeeper p273
- Landscape Architect/Designer p276

Further information

British Association of Landscape Industries (BALI)
www.bali.org.uk

Landscape Institute
www.landscapeinstitute.org

ENVIRONMENT, ANIMALS AND PLANTS

CRCI: HB

PARKS OFFICER

ENVIRONMENT, ANIMALS AND PLANTS

CRCI: HB

Qualifications and courses

No formal qualifications are required for this work although 5 GCSEs/S grades (A*–E/1–5) will be helpful. The Advanced Apprenticeship in Horticulture provides a good route to training as a parks officer.

Many people begin their career as gardeners/ horticulturists. NVQs/SVQs in Amenity Horticulture (Levels 1 and 2) are available and are useful qualifications to take at the early stages of your career. City & Guilds offer several relevant courses such as the Award/ Certificate/Diploma in Practical Horticulture Skills (Level 1), the Award/Certificate/Diploma in Work-Based Horticulture (Levels 1–3) and the Certificate and Diploma in Horticulture (Levels 2 and 3).

Other training options include the BTEC First in Horticulture (Level 2), the BTEC National in Horticulture (Level 3) and the BTEC Higher National in Horticulture (Levels 4 and 5).

The Royal Horticultural Society (RHS) provides courses from entry to degree level, such as the Award in Practical Horticulture (Level 1), the Diploma in the Principles and Practices of Horticulture (Levels 2 and 3) and the Master of Horticulture (RHS) Award.

What the work involves

You will supervise the gardeners and horticulturists who maintain and look after local parks, sports and recreation centres, gardens and public places. As well as planning new planting schemes you will organise staffing rotas and annual work programmes. You will be responsible for the recruitment and monitoring of your team, as well as budget control.

You will have to liaise with your employer (normally your local government) and other department colleagues.

Type of person suited to this work

To do this work you must be organised, able to plan ahead and capable of managing people. You will need technical and practical horticultural skills, an understanding of budgets and you should be an effective negotiator.

You must have a good understanding of plants and how to present outside spaces so they look good throughout the year.

To do this job you will need to be physically fit and passionate about your work.

Working conditions

You will normally work Monday–Friday but at busier times, particularly in the spring and summer, you may do extra hours.

You will be provided with protective clothing and you will have to ensure that health and safety rules are followed by your teams. This work might be unsuitable if you suffer from asthma, pollen allergies or some skin conditions.

A small part of your job will involve working in an office at a computer where you will spend time ordering plants and materials.

Future prospects

Most parks officers are employed by a local or county council. A small number work for companies who win park management contracts.

It is likely that you will start your career as a gardener or horticulturist and then progress to a parks officer role once you have gained sufficient experience.

You may also move into department or divisional management within local/county authorities.

Advantages/disadvantages

This is a mixture of indoor and outdoor work, using a variety of skills.

You will use your experience and knowledge to make a difference in your local community.

You might have to wait for opportunities to become available or be willing to relocate to progress in this career.

Money guide

Your earnings depend on the size and location of your local authority employer, and the number of staff and sites that you are responsible for.

Starting salaries are usually around £17,000.

Experienced parks officers could earn up to £27,000.

Those employed in a senior role could achieve in excess of £30,000.

Related opportunities

- Countryside Ranger p259
- Groundsperson/Greenkeeper p273
- Horticultural Worker/Manager p274

Further information

Convention of Scottish Local Authorities
www.cosla.gov.uk

Institute for Sport, Parks and Leisure
www.ispal.org.uk

Local Government Careers
www.lgcareers.com

Qualifications and courses

There is no specific route into this career but a degree is required to join the Association of Pet Behaviour Counsellors (APBC) or to be registered as a Certified Clinical Animal Behaviourist (CCAB). Candidates are advised to take a degree in one of the following subjects: biological science, behavioural science, animal behaviour or equine science. The Association for the Study of Animal Behaviour (ASAB) and APBC provide lists of approved courses.

Typical entry requirements for an appropriate Honours degree are 2 A levels/3 H grades (which should include biology and/or another science subject).

Those who are already employed within the animal care industry, for example as an animal welfare officer, may be able to progress into a role in pet behaviour counselling. Short training courses and diplomas are available from the Canine & Feline Behaviour Association (CFBA) and VetNet's Courses in Animal & Veterinary Education (CAVE).

It is essential that all entrants to this profession have practical experience working with animals. Opportunities to volunteer with animals in your local area are available on the Do-it website and through the RSPCA, SSPCA and the Blue Cross.

What the work involves

Pet behaviour counsellors advise owners whose pets have developed inappropriate and dangerous behaviour.

Although working with all domestic animals, you will probably focus on dogs, cats and horses. Typical problems include aggressive behaviour, soiling or destructiveness. You will also aid owners in achieving general control over their pets.

You could be connected to a veterinary practice, work in kennels, catteries and welfare societies or be freelance.

Type of person suited to this work

You will need a strong interest in animals, their care and welfare. As this job also involves working with the owner, you will have to be able to communicate with people too! You need to be tactful but also assertive.

Working with animals can be messy and smelly work, so you must be prepared to get dirty. You will also need to have lots of patience and the ability to remain calm.

You should be good at science, especially biology, and have a certain degree of business acumen along with the ability to keep records and accounts.

Working conditions

This work takes place in clinics and often in clients' homes so a driving licence would be beneficial. You could be indoors or outside in all weathers.

Some jobs will involve evening and weekend work, especially if you visit your clients and animals in their own homes. Most pet behaviour counsellors are self-employed and set their own hours.

The work can be dusty, dirty and physically demanding, so you will need to be fit and active. This profession is unsuitable for those with animal allergies.

Future prospects

Although demand across the canine and equine areas has increased owing to television programmes and press coverage, there are still very limited career opportunities for this job.

Some of the larger animal welfare charities are starting to employ staff with these skills but most pet behaviour counsellors are self-employed and running their own practices.

Other options include lecturing and writing papers on animal behaviour.

Advantages/disadvantages

You will have the satisfaction of working with animals and improving their quality of life.

Some owners may be resistant to change the way they deal with their pets which could be challenging.

This job offers the opportunity for self-employment but it can be difficult to establish a client list.

Money guide

Most pet behaviour counsellors are self-employed and charge fees of £85–£250 per consultation, depending on their experience and the size of the business.

Newly qualified pet behaviour counsellors can expect to earn around £15,000 per year.

With experience, you could achieve £25,000–£35,000.

Few people make a full-time living from this industry. Many supplement their income by lecturing or writing articles.

Related opportunities

- Animal Physiotherapist p255
- Animal Welfare Officer p256
- Dog Trainer/Handler p260
- Veterinary Surgeon p283

Further information

Association for the Study of Animal Behaviour
www.asab.nottingham.ac.uk

Association of Pet Behaviour Counsellors
www.apbc.org.uk

ENVIRONMENT, ANIMALS AND PLANTS

CRCI: HC

RACEHORSE TRAINER

ENTRY LEVEL 3

ENVIRONMENT, ANIMALS AND PLANTS

CRCI: HC

Qualifications and courses

Racehorse trainers need to be licensed with the British Horseracing Authority. There are 3 types of licence: a Combined Licence (which permits the training of horses for both flat and jump races), a Jump Only Licence and a Flat Only Licence.

All candidates for a Trainers Licence must have the QCF Level 3 Diploma in Work Based Racehorse Care and Management and they need to attend 3 week-long courses in Racehorse Management, Business Skills for Racehorse Trainers and Staff Management.

The British Horseracing Authority also requires all applicants to have at least 5 years' experience working in training establishments which should include at least 2 years in a senior position, such as assistant trainer in a racing yard. Those who have been a successful jockey will often become a racehorse trainer later in their career.

What the work involves

Trainers usually own or lease their stables and train horses for owners as well as owning horses themselves. Most trainers start as jockeys or assistant trainers and progress to running their own yard.

You will have to prepare the horses for races by increasing their stamina, technique and fitness. In order to do this you will have to create training regimes.

To be successful you will work closely with everyone in your team including other professionals such as vets and farriers.

Type of person suited to this work

You should have a strong interest in horse racing, a flair for business and an inherent talent for training horses. You will need the ability to communicate well and be a strong leader and manager of people.

This role is ideal for people who love caring for horses, have the right temperament to work with them and plenty of patience.

You will need to enjoy working outside in all weathers as this is where most of your duties will take place. You should be a practical person who is willing to get their hands dirty. You will require a certain level of physical fitness.

Working conditions

Much of your work will take place outdoors. In the summer months it may be hot, smelly and dusty, whereas in winter it could be cold, wet and muddy. You will also spend some time in an office environment.

When riding you will wear a hard hat and a body protector. Horses can be unpredictable and so there is a certain level of risk involved.

The hours are long and include weekends. There will also be some travel involved if you are required to attend race meetings. A driving licence would be useful.

Future prospects

There are around 500 licensed trainers in the UK.

Before you are granted a licence, you need several years' experience as an assistant trainer. Your success will then depend on attracting and retaining the owners of good quality horses, and lots of luck! You will need to build up a strong client base in order to progress.

Managing your own successful yard may enable you to employ staff to complete some of the more mundane tasks.

Advantages/disadvantages

This can be an extremely lucrative profession if you are successful.

Injury risks are high in all animal-related careers. This could affect your long-term career security.

Looking after horses is not a 9am–5pm job and the hours may affect your social or family life.

Money guide

As you are likely to be self-employed, your earnings will depend on the size, success and reputation of your yard.

You will establish your own fees and these will be influenced by a variety of factors including costs and the market rates.

As a guide, a trainer can earn anything from £15,000 per year to over £50,000 if they are very experienced and have a good record of winning.

Related opportunities

- Farm Manager p261
- Farrier p265
- Groom/Stable Hand/Stud Hand p272

Further information

Association of British Riding Schools
www.abrs-info.org

British Horse Society
www.bhs.org.uk

British Racing School
www.brs.org.uk

Qualifications and courses

There are no formal academic requirements to become a deckhand but you must be at least 16 years old. School leavers have the option to apply for the Apprenticeship in Sea Fishing. Alternatively, Seafish offer the Introduction to Commercial Fishing course and the Maritime Skills Alliance run a Sea Fishing Apprenticeship programme.

New entrants must take the Marine Coastguard Agency (MCA) approved basic safety training course. This programme consists of 4 days of training in sea survival, first aid, fire fighting and basic health and safety.

To become a skipper, you must have at least 2 years' experience working as a deckhand. Those who wish to be a limited area skipper (working around the UK coastline) must be over the age of 20 and have Seafish's Deck Officer (Fishing Vessel) Class 2 certificate. To work as an unlimited area skipper (fishing beyond UK coastal waters) you need to be at least 21 years old and study for Seafish's Deck Officer (Fishing Vessel) Class 1 certificate.

For those who wish to develop further skills and knowledge, Seafish offer various short courses on topics such as basic seamanship, net mending, navigation, engineering and stability awareness.

What the work involves

Deckhands are crew members on sea-going fishing vessels. You will spend anything from a few days to several weeks at sea. You will drop the nets, wind them in, sort the catch and then box it up. If your vessel has the facilities on-board, you might help to process fish by gutting and filleting. You might keep watch, steer the ship and use winching gear. Duties may also include vessel maintenance and cooking.

Skippers are in charge of fishing vessels. Their role includes overseeing health and safety, navigation, paperwork and crew management. They also manage the business arrangements to ensure that fishing trips return a profit.

Type of person suited to this work

This work is suited to someone with practical skills and a high level of physical fitness. You should be able to cope with challenging conditions while remaining positive and focused.

A deckhand needs teamwork skills and the ability to follow instructions. Skippers should be comfortable managing people.

Working conditions

This is a very tough outdoor job. You will work in cold, wet and rainy conditions during the winter and hot weather during the summer.

Fishing is the most dangerous industry in the UK, with big machinery and rough seas producing a combination of risks which must be treated with great caution.

You will have to work long hours at sea, often for substantial periods away from home, and conditions below deck may be basic and cramped. There could also be some heavy lifting and carrying.

Future prospects

The career progression route is from deckhand to ship's mate and then skipper.

Jobs are located around the coasts of Scotland and the south-west and east of England.

Many jobs are within family-owned businesses which have been in existence for generations, making it difficult to find work. Some are seasonal, meaning long-term security can be difficult.

Advantages/disadvantages

This job is ideal for those who love working outdoors.

You will have the opportunity to develop strong relationships with the other crew members.

Your social and family life may be difficult as you could be away at sea for extended periods of time.

Jobs are limited to certain locations in the UK.

Money guide

Earnings from fishing can vary extensively as you are often paid a share of the total value of the catch. For this reason, pay depends upon the type of boat you work on, the amount of fish caught and the weather conditions.

New entrants can expect to receive around £10,000 per year as a starting salary.

With experience, earnings can rise to £25,000.

Skippers are generally self-employed so their earnings depend on the success of their team.

Skippers who work for large companies could achieve up to £65,000.

Related opportunities

- Coastguard Watch Assistant/Officer p542
- Fish Farmer p268
- Merchant Navy Deck Officer/Rating p604

Further information

Maritime and Coastguard Agency
www.mcga.gov.uk

Scottish Fishermen's Federation
www.sff.co.uk

ENVIRONMENT, ANIMALS AND PLANTS

CRCI: HA

Qualifications and courses

You usually enter this profession through work-based training. For those aged 16–24, the Apprenticeship in Veterinary Nursing is available at Advanced Level.

Alternatively, you can study for the Level 3 Diploma in Veterinary Nursing from the Royal College of Veterinary Surgeons (RCVS). This can be completed on a full-time basis or alongside work in a veterinary practice. Qualifying takes 2–3 years and involves practical training and college-based learning.

Entry requirements for the RCVS scheme are 5 GCSEs/S grades (A*–C/1–3) including English, maths and 2 science subjects. Trainees must be at least 16 years old and there is strong competition for places. For those without these qualifications, an alternative route may be through the ABC Certificate for Animal Nursing Assistants (Level 2), the City & Guilds Diploma for Veterinary Care Assistants (Level 2) or the BTEC National in Animal Management (Level 3).

You could also complete an RCVS-approved veterinary nursing degree or Foundation degree. Entry requirements are 2 A levels/3 H grades, ideally in biology and chemistry.

Work experience with a veterinary practice or an animal charity would be helpful.

What the work involves

Veterinary nurses assist vets in their work by helping to treat animals suffering from disease and injury. Most nurses also undertake the day-to-day care of animals recovering from treatment within veterinary hospitals.

As well as carrying out simple procedures, such as changing dressings and nail trimming, you will also examine blood and urine samples, give injections, prepare and help in the theatre and sterilise the instruments after use. You might also work in reception, giving an initial assessment of animals, ordering drugs and arranging future appointments.

Type of person suited to this work

You will have to be passionate about animals and want to help them. You need the capacity to learn scientific information about different diseases and treatments.

Although lots of animals recover, some of this work will be distressing. This means you will have to work in a practical and unsentimental way.

As you will work closely with the animals' owners, you will also need to have excellent communication skills to explain what is happening.

You may need administrative and IT skills to complete duties on reception.

Working conditions

Depending on the type of practice you are employed by, your role may involve working with small animals, horses, farm animals, or even zoo animals.

Most of your work will take place indoors, possibly in a treatment room, operating theatre or on the reception desk. If you work with large animals, you may have to travel to visit farms or zoos.

Working with animals can be noisy and dirty. This job would be unsuitable for those with animal allergies or a fear of blood. You will usually be provided with a uniform and you will be expected to wear protective clothing during some procedures.

Future prospects

You could be employed by zoos, wildlife centres, animal welfare centres, veterinary hospitals and charities such as the People's Dispensary for Sick Animals (PDSA).

With experience, you could progress to become a supervisor, practice manager or head nurse, or move into related areas such as research.

You could also lecture, specialise in an area such as animal behaviour or become a representative for a veterinary drugs company.

Advantages/disadvantages

Helping sick animals is very rewarding.

The role is interesting, with lots of variety and the chance to meet many people and animals.

You will deal with illness and death which can be stressful and upsetting.

You may have to work irregular hours which will affect your social life.

Money guide

You can expect a starting salary of £10,500–£14,000.

As you gain experience, your earnings can increase to £22,000.

Head nurses or supervisors can achieve £25,000 or more, depending on the size and type of the practice they work for.

Related opportunities

- Dog Trainer/Handler p260
- Veterinary Surgeon p283
- Zookeeper p285

Further information

British Veterinary Nursing Association
www.bvna.org.uk

Qualifications and courses

In order to practise as a vet, all candidates are required to have a degree in veterinary science/veterinary medicine and registration with the Royal College of Veterinary Surgeons (RCVS). Degrees approved by the RCVS are currently available at 7 institutions in the UK. Normal minimum entry requirements for a degree are 3 A levels/4 H grades including biology and 1 or 2 from chemistry, physics or maths. Depending upon the individual university, you will be expected to have either 2 A grades and a B or 3 A grades (or equivalent). A good range of GCSE/S grades (A*–C/1–3) are required.

Degree courses usually last 5 years but courses may include an optional additional year in which students gain an Honours degree in a related science subject. All courses include the 38 weeks of practical experience required by RCVS.

All universities expect applicants to demonstrate their passion for animals and commitment to a career as a veterinary surgeon by undertaking relevant work experience. Candidates could work on farms, in stables, kennels or vets and opportunities to volunteer with animals are available on the Do-it website or through the RSPCA, SSPCA and the Blue Cross.

What the work involves

Vets treat animals that are suffering because of disease or injury. They administer vaccinations, prescribe drugs and deliver newborn animals. They also advise owners on caring for their animals. You might carry out surgical operations and be involved in the inspection of livestock and meat.

You could work in local practices and become a specialist carrying out complex surgery on a certain part of the anatomy or become an expert on a particular animal.

Type of person suited to this work

You must have the capacity to learn large amounts of complex scientific information and apply this in a practical way to treat animals.

Some of your work will be sad or distressing, so you will have to work in a practical and unsentimental way. You must have good communication skills to talk to the owners.

Working with large animals is physically demanding so you will need to be in good health. This job will not suit those who dislike the sight of blood or suffer from animal allergies.

Working conditions

Your working conditions will depend on the type of practice that employs you. In veterinary practices for small animals, you will spend a lot of time in the surgery. Working with farm livestock and horses, you will travel to visit your patients.

Some of this work will be unpleasant or smelly and involve travelling long distances. A driving licence is required.

Your job may be dangerous as animals can be unpredictable. You will work long hours and be on-call to cover emergencies 24/7.

Future prospects

This sector has become increasingly competitive owing to the current economic situation.

As a graduate, you will normally join an established practice. With experience, you could progress to become a partner (effectively part-owner) of a practice.

There are around 20,000 registered vets in the UK. The majority of these work in private practice. Some vets work for the government or for firms researching and producing animal pharmaceuticals.

Advantages/disadvantages

The training is long and very competitive to enter. In this career you will never stop learning – more experience will make you a better vet.

It can be a very stressful but rewarding job, with lots of responsibility.

You will have to deal with the death of some of the animals you treat, including times when you put them down.

Money guide

Salaries vary according to experience, specialisations, and the size, type and location of the practice you work in.

Newly qualified vets have a starting salary of £20,000–£30,000.

As you gain experience, your earnings can range from £35,000 up to £48,000 for a senior vet.

A senior partner in a veterinary practice can achieve in excess of £50,000.

Employers may include accommodation and a company car within your benefits package.

Related opportunities

- Farm Manager p261
- Hospital Doctor p312
- Veterinary Nurse p282

Further information

British Veterinary Association
www.bva.co.uk

Royal College of Veterinary Surgeons
www.rcvs.org.uk

ENVIRONMENT, ANIMALS AND PLANTS

CRCI: HC

ENVIRONMENT, ANIMALS AND PLANTS

CRCI: HA

Qualifications and courses

In England and Wales, there are no set requirements for those wishing to become water bailiffs. In Scotland, there is a training module that you need to pass, set by the Institute of Fisheries Management. In Northern Ireland, you need at least 5 GCSEs/S grades at C/3 grade or above, and these have to include English and maths.

Medical examinations usually need to be passed, and many people work their way into the industry by working unpaid for angling clubs to begin with.

This is a popular second career, and if you want to get into the field then any experience you can gain in gamekeeping, security work, police work or farm work will be advantageous.

The Scottish IFM offers a course in Fisheries Management. You can choose between a 1-year certificate or a 2-year diploma, covering all aspects of working with fish and pondlife. You can also follow an NVQ in Fisheries Management if you choose to do so.

What the work involves

Water bailiffs work outdoors, maintaining lakes or rivers and everything that lives in them, for the purpose of legitimate recreational use.

You will confront 2 main problems in your work; breaches of the law and ecological problems.

You will basically be a gamekeeper for water. Water bailiffs have the same powers of search and arrest as police officers. You would mostly be looking out for poachers and lawbreakers, and you will be granted a warrant by the Environment Agency.

Type of person suited to this work

Ideally, you should be a friendly yet firm person, able to deal with members of the public effectively and politely, sometimes in difficult disciplinary situations.

An interest in the environment and working outdoors is really useful, as is knowledge of waterways. You need to be aware of the main environmental threats, understand the basics of how ecosystems maintain themselves and know about fish diseases and biology.

You also need to know about fishery law, not only in the UK (although this is most useful), but also at EU level. Be aware that it may even be different at local level, for example if you live in Scotland.

Working conditions

You will spend the majority of your time outside, patrolling areas either in a car, by boat or on foot.

You will usually work between 37 and 39 hours per week, which will involve night shifts and weekends. Part time or seasonal work is also available.

The work is physical and tiring. You may have to pursue offenders across rough terrain on foot, and could find yourself wading through cold rivers and ponds. For this reason, you will probably spend your days in waterproofs, wellies and even lifejackets.

Future prospects

Once you are working for the Environment Agency, many possibilities arise. You will have the opportunity to become a team leader within the agency, and this may lead to promotion and managerial opportunities.

Another option would be to move into related areas of work, such as fish farming or gamekeeping. Once you have a little experience in the area it will be possible to choose what interests you most, and in which direction you want your career to progress.

Advantages/disadvantages

This can be a really satisfying and exciting job, and if you enjoy being outside, you will probably thoroughly enjoy the job.

It can be lonely, and conditions can be hard if you are not naturally a country person.

You need to be prepared for all weather conditions, and work can be cold, wet, and tiring.

Money guide

Salaries vary, and can range from £14,500 to £26,500 upwards per year.

With 10 to 15 years' experience you can expect to be earning up to £34,000.

Those in the most senior positions earn around £40,000 per year.

Related opportunities

- Countryside Ranger p259
- Fish Farmer p268
- Gamekeeper p270

Further information

Environment Agency
www.environment-agency.gov.uk

Institute of Fisheries Management
www.ifm.org.uk

Qualifications and courses

No specific qualifications are required although GCSEs/S grades (A*–C/1–3), especially in English and science subjects, will be useful. However, it is becoming increasingly necessary to gain qualifications as this is a very competitive area.

Experience, proven interest and interaction with animals is incredibly important, sometimes favoured over qualifications, but often a requirement of application. Volunteering at a zoo or animal sanctuary would stand you in good stead. Apprenticeships may be available if you are aged 16–24.

General animal care and management courses available include the City & Guilds Level 2 National Certificate in Animal Care, Advanced National Certificate in the Management of Zoo Animals and Advanced National Diploma in Animal Management at Level 3. Alternatively you could take BTEC Awards, Certificates and Diplomas at Level 3 in Animal Management or ABC Awards and Diplomas in Work-based Animal Care at Levels 1 to 3.

Foundation degrees or BSc Honours degrees in subjects like zoology are also available. Sparsholt College in Hampshire offers a Foundation degree in Zoo Resource Management for people in relevant employment.

What the work involves

You could work in a zoo, safari, wildlife or birdlife park or aquarium where you will care for animals (ranging from mammals to birds, reptiles to amphibians, fish to invertebrates etc.) and their environmental surroundings.

You will provide food, water and fresh bedding for the animals in your care. You will clean out enclosures and check the animals for signs of injury or disease, keeping records of feeding, health and behaviour and informing veterinary staff if there are any issues.

Many zoos stress the importance of conservation and education and some of your work may involve leading tours and giving presentations to visitors.

Type of person suited to this work

You need to be passionate about the care and well-being of animals in your care. This requires patience, observation and the desire to handle and be around animals.

Most of this work is done outdoors and can be physically demanding so a fit, active person who is not afraid of physical work would be well suited to the job.

Some animals you will work with could be dangerous, so you will have to respect them and be aware of your own and others' safety.

Working conditions

Animals require 24/7 care so you will be expected to work 5–6 days a week. This is normally organised on a shift system which includes early mornings, late evenings, weekends and bank holidays, especially during busy periods.

Your work will be physically demanding and often dirty. A uniform will be provided. If you suffer from allergies, this work will be difficult for you.

Work could be seasonal as some centres close for part of the year.

Future prospects

There are 350 zoos and animal parks throughout the UK employing around 3000 people full time. Jobs can be harder to find and competition for employment will be high so be prepared to move for work or promotion.

You may choose to specialise and work with one species. You could also be promoted to senior keeper or head keeper. You may also choose to move into related work such as becoming an RSPCA inspector.

Advantages/disadvantages

This can be difficult work to enter and progress in and the financial rewards can be small.

You will be working with some unusual or exotic animals, with some opportunity to specialise.

A variety of day to day tasks with lots of different animals can keep the job interesting.

The role of zoos as centres of breeding and supporting conservation has increased recently, so you could undertake important work.

Money guide

Pay will depend on your location and type of animal park. Many jobs include free or subsidised accommodation.

Trainees can start at about £10,000–£13,000 per year.

With experience, this can rise to £16,000.

Senior keepers earn around £17,000–£30,000 a year.

Related opportunities

- Animal Welfare Officer p256
- Dog Trainer/Handler p260
- Veterinary Surgeon p283

Further information

Association of British Wild Animal Keepers
www.abwak.co.uk

British and Irish Association of Zoos and Aquariums
www.biaza.org.uk

ENVIRONMENT, ANIMALS AND PLANTS

CRCI: HC

Healthcare

If you are keen to pursue a career in healthcare you must be compassionate and enjoy either caring for people or deciding what treatment they should receive. There is such a wide variety of jobs available in this sector simply because you can specialise in absolutely any aspect of human healthcare. Many jobs require a lot of training and you can expect to work in some highly pressurised and sometimes distressing situations. Workers in healthcare are extremely dedicated and enthusiastic about their careers, which rarely constitute a 9am–5pm job.

The jobs featured in this section are listed below. For similar jobs to the ones in this section turn to *Science, Mathematics and Statistics* on page 501 and *Social Work and Counselling Services* on page 567.

ACUPUNCTURIST

Qualifications and courses

Careers in acupuncture are open to all graduates and diplomates although a degree or HND in a related subject such as life or medical sciences may increase your chances of employment.

Degrees are not compulsory though and experience and the right aptitude is just as important. Previous experience of advice work or counseling may enable entry into the profession.

Acupuncture is currently only regulated by voluntary agreement but the British Acupuncture Council (BacC) works with the British Acupuncture Accreditation Board (BAAB) to offer training courses. The courses generally take 2–3 years to complete full time. Entry onto one of the courses requires at least 5 GCSEs/S grades and 2 or 3 A levels/Highers. Science subjects are preferred.

These accredited training courses lead to professional membership of the British Acupuncture Council which offers protection and public liability insurance.

Courses vary, but generally cover topics such as anatomy and physiology, techniques and acupuncture points, ethical issues, clinical experience, and advice on setting up a practice.

Some courses are even available at postgraduate and doctorate levels.

What the work involves

Acupuncturists work from ancient Chinese holistic guidelines. They treat medical illnesses and imbalances of energy by inserting very fine needles into identified pressure points on the human body.

You will need to talk to patients about their problems, taking plenty of notes, in order to explore their lifestyle and emotional state, and then assess all of these factors to determine a suitable treatment.

In addition you may carry out procedures such as burning herbs on needles, and passing small electric currents through them.

Type of person suited to this work

You must be very personable, with excellent communication skills in order to elicit trust and personal information from your patients, as well as being able to explain the techniques you are using to them.

You will need an analytical mind in order to understand each patient's problem and formulate a beneficial course of treatment. Being comfortable with close and physical contact is also important when examining and treating your patients.

As you will probably be running your own business, you will need excellent business acumen in order to successfully take on aspects such as marketing, accounting, and administrative tasks.

Working conditions

Hours vary and tend to fit around the needs of clients. This usually involves evening and weekend work.

You could work from your own rented treatment room, from home, in your patients' homes, or in hospices, health clinics and addiction treatment centres. As you may work across a number of locations, a driving licence is really useful.

You will usually be working on your feet, standing and bending a lot. Conditions have to be clean and sterile, and there are strict health and safety guidelines to adhere to.

Future prospects

If you are self-employed, the success of your career depends on your reputation and marketing skills. If you build up a strong client base there are plenty of opportunities for expansion and even setting up your own health clinic.

Many practising acupuncturists choose to teach their subject, or carry out research and write articles for books and magazines.

You could work abroad, although qualifications for practice vary from country to country.

Advantages/disadvantages

This can be a really rewarding career, especially if you like being with people and enjoy helping them.

You may hear distressing stories and have insight into some upsetting personal lives, so you need to be able to leave work at work.

Money guide

Earnings in acupuncture depend a lot on your situation, marketing ability, experience and how many patients you treat. As a newly qualified acupuncturist starting up your own practice, you will probably earn around £12,000 per year.

Once you have started to build up clients and gain experience, you can expect to earn up to £30,000 a year.

If you grow your business into a large established practice, your earnings may rise to about £40,000 a year.

Per session, acupuncturists charge around £40, although this can rise to up to £90 in London.

Related opportunities

- Chiropractor p295
- Counsellor p569
- Homeopath p311

Further information

British Acupuncture Accreditation Board
www.baab.co.uk

British Acupuncture Council
www.acupuncture.org.uk

The Acupuncture Society
www.acupuncturesociety.org.uk

ADULT NURSE

Qualifications and courses

You must hold a degree in adult nursing which has been approved by the Nursing and Midwifery Council (NMC). Minimum entry requirements for a degree are usually 5 GCSEs/S grades (A*–C/1–3) including English, maths and a science subject and 2–3 A levels/H grades, ideally including a science-based subject. All applicants must obtain clearance from the Criminal Records Bureau (CRB) before commencing their training.

If you do not have the required GCSEs/A levels, some universities will accept other qualifications, such as a BTEC National Diploma in Health and Social Care (Health Sciences) or an Access to Higher Education Diploma in a science or health-related subject.

Graduates with a degree in a health-related subject such as human biology, life and medical sciences or biomedical science, may be eligible to enter the nursing profession by taking an accelerated 2-year programme which leads to an MSc or postgraduate diploma.

You are eligible to register as a nurse with the NMC once you have completed an approved nursing degree. Nurses are expected to engage in continuing professional development (CPD) throughout their career to keep their skills and knowledge up to date.

What the work involves

Adult nurses assess the needs of each patient in order to plan a care programme for them. You will observe how they progress on this treatment plan and modify it as necessary. You will also give patients practical care such as administering medicines and injections, changing dressings and checking blood pressure.

You could work in a variety of positions, such as a community nurse, occupational nurse or healthcare assistant.

Type of person suited to this work

You will be working with patients from all parts of the community who will have a wide range of problems, so it is essential to remain non-judgemental and sympathetic. A clear understanding of confidentiality is essential.

You will need excellent communication skills in order to interact with patients, explain care plans and illnesses, and calm those who are angry or distressed.

You will also need to be very practical with good manual dexterity for undertaking precision jobs such as taking blood.

Working conditions

You will usually work 37.5 hours per week but overtime is available for those who want it. If you are working in a hospital, these hours will include night and weekend shifts.

You could work in a number of locations including hospitals, GP surgeries, prisons, hospices and in patients' homes. If you are required to travel around in the local community, a driving licence is useful.

Adult nurses in hospitals work in specific wards, such as intensive care or accident and emergency.

Future prospects

There is currently a shortage of trained adult nurses so employment prospects are very good. The majority of job opportunities lie within the NHS, although other employers include private hospitals, the Armed Forces, hospices and nursing homes, and the prison service.

With experience and additional qualifications, you could specialise in a subject of interest such as neurology or cardiology, and go on to become a nurse consultant.

UK nursing qualifications are recognised across the globe so there are opportunities to work abroad.

Advantages/disadvantages

Helping a wide range of people to get better or become more independent is both rewarding and enjoyable.

There are opportunities to work flexible hours or part time. Career breaks are common and the NHS runs specialist courses to get nurses who have had a break back up to speed quickly.

You may have to deal with distressed, angry or violent patients.

Money guide

A newly qualified nurse can expect a starting salary of £21,200.

As you gain experience, your earnings can increase up to about £28,000.

Those who take on a senior position with additional responsibilities can achieve £30,000–£40,000.

If you specialise in a particular area and undertake the training to become a nurse consultant, you could earn up to £56,000.

Related opportunities

- Hospital Doctor p312
- Learning Disabilities Nurse p314
- Mental Health Nurse p317

Further information

NHS Careers
www.nhscareers.nhs.uk

Nursing and Midwifery Council
www.nmc-uk.org

Royal College of Nursing
www.rcn.org.uk

CRCI: JI HEALTHCARE

ANAESTHETIST

Qualifications and courses

Candidates must first train as a hospital doctor by completing a medical degree which is approved by the General Medical Council (GMC). Entry requirements for medical school are very high A level/H grade results including relevant subjects such as science and maths.

After completing a medical degree, candidates undergo 7 years of specialist postgraduate training. Stage 1 involves a 2-year Foundation Programme of general training. This acts as the bridge between medical school and specialist training. The second stage is 3 years of core training in acute care and candidates then move on to the final stage: higher specialty training in anaesthesia, intensive care medicine and pain management.

After successfully completing the higher specialty stage, trainees receive a Certificate of Completion of Training (CCT) and become eligible to join the GMC Specialist Register.

Anaesthetists must engage in continuing professional development (CPD) throughout their career to ensure that their skills and knowledge are up to date. The Royal College of Anaesthetists provides information on available training.

What the work involves

Anaesthetists are qualified hospital doctors who have undergone further training in anaesthesia. You will prepare and administer drugs to make patients unconscious and pain free during surgery. You will monitor patients during the procedure and bring them back to consciousness afterwards. You will also give local anaesthesia to specific areas of the body.

In addition, you will give pain relief after surgery to seriously ill patients or during procedures such as childbirth. Anaesthetists also work in intensive care, resuscitation and pain management.

Type of person suited to this work

Anaesthetists need excellent communication skills: you must be reassuring and a good listener in order to gain patients' trust and explain procedures to them. You should work well in a team and be able to give and follow instructions.

You must be able to stay calm in an emergency and make decisions under pressure. You will need the confidence and skill to use complicated equipment and administer powerful drugs safely and accurately. You should have a strong sense of the responsibility involved in this job.

You will need to be prepared to undergo a long programme of education and training in order to gain the in-depth knowledge and skills necessary to become an anaesthetist.

Working conditions

Anaesthetists work in operating theatres, wards, clinics and accident and emergency departments within hospitals.

You will work shifts as part of an on-call rota, which includes working at nights, weekends and on bank holidays.

You will handle potentially dangerous drugs and equipment.

Future prospects

There are opportunities throughout the UK, mainly within the NHS but also in private hospitals and clinics.

Promotion to consultant posts is very competitive. Anaesthetists may work in sub-specialities such as paediatrics, obstetrics, cardiac surgery, resuscitation or intensive care.

Once fully qualified you will probably be expected to teach and examine students and trainees and to carry out research.

Advantages/disadvantages

Being responsible for the safety of patients in your care and dealing with emergency situations makes this a very demanding job.

It is rewarding to be able to help patients through surgery and other medical procedures by providing pain relief.

Money guide

Salary levels in the NHS may vary in different locations.

Junior doctors have a starting salary of £22,000–£28,000 during the 2-year Foundation Programme.

When undertaking the specialty training, you can expect to earn between £28,000 and £46,000 a year.

Consultant anaesthetists can achieve salaries ranging from £74,000 up to £170,000 for those in the most senior positions.

Earnings are often higher in private practice work.

Related opportunities

- Doctor (GP) p305
- Hospital Doctor p312
- Pathologist p325

Further information

Association of Anaesthetists of Great Britain and Ireland
www.aagbi.org

British Medical Association
www.bma.org.uk

The Royal College of Anaesthetists
www.rcoa.ac.uk

AROMATHERAPIST

Qualifications and courses

There are no formal academic requirements for aromatherapists. Professional training courses are the standard method of entry and you usually have to be at least 18 years old to enrol.

The General Regulatory Council for Complementary Therapies (GRCCT) has devised National Occupational Standards (NOS) for aromatherapy. If you wish to operate as a professional aromatherapist, you must ensure that you choose a course which meets the NOS. Courses which conform to the standards are offered at diploma, Foundation degree or degree level. Short courses are only advised for those with a personal (rather than professional) interest in aromatherapy. The Aromatherapy Council provides information on choosing a course. Prior experience in a related profession, such as massage, will help your application.

Most courses include modules on anatomy, physiology, pathology, therapeutic relationships and the theory and practice of aromatherapy. You will also consider the practicalities of being a professional aromatherapist, covering topics such as legal and ethical issues and business studies.

Once qualified, you can improve your career prospects by registering with the Complementary & Natural Healthcare Council (CNHC).

What the work involves

Aromatherapists use essential oils to improve the health and wellbeing of clients.

You will be required to look into the medical history of all your clients, discussing their lifestyle, diet, exercise, allergies and stress levels. Using the information gathered, you will decide on blends and mixes of oils appropriate for the needs of the client.

You will administer oils to the skin by massage, provide instructions for aftercare and maintain records of each of your clients.

Type of person suited to this work

You must be very personable with excellent communication skills in order to explain the techniques you are using and elicit trust and personal information from your patients. Being comfortable with close and physical contact is also important when examining and treating your patients.

You need an analytical mind in order to understand each patient's problem and formulate a beneficial course of treatment.

As you will probably be self-employed, you need excellent business acumen to undertake marketing, accounting and administrative tasks.

Working conditions

Aromatherapists tend to run their own business so working conditions vary. You could rent a treatment room in a health clinic, gym or leisure centre, work from home or travel to patients' homes to provide treatment. Hours depend on individual schedules and the needs and demands of clients. You should expect to work evenings and weekends. Part-time hours are a possibility.

Rooms and workspaces must be clean and quiet, and most aromatherapists tend to wear white clothes.

You will be bending, stretching and spending most of the day on your feet.

Future prospects

Success in aromatherapy depends on effective business skills. If you build a strong client base and market your services well, your practice will grow into a successful business.

You could train in another relevant therapy such as homeopathy, reflexology or counselling, which could attract more clients.

If you like the idea of working abroad, you could take your skills overseas. You must ensure that the country you choose recognises your qualifications.

Advantages/disadvantages

This can be a really rewarding career, especially if you are sociable and enjoy helping people.

There is a lot to remember in aromatherapy so it requires a calm and intelligent person to be familiar with all the oils and administer them carefully.

Money guide

Most aromatherapists are self-employed and charge a fee of between £25 and £60 per session.

Income will depend upon your experience, reputation and the number of clients you treat.

During the process of building up your practice, earnings can be quite low – possibly ranging from £2,000 to £10,000 a year.

With experience and an established business, you could achieve between £15,000 and £30,000.

Related opportunities

- Acupuncturist p288
- Beauty Therapist p455
- Homeopath p311

Further information

General Regulatory Council for Complementary Therapists
www.grcct.org

Institute for Complementary and Natural Medicine
www.i-c-m.org.uk

CRCI: JA   HEALTHCARE

ART THERAPIST

Qualifications and courses

To work as an art therapist you must complete a postgraduate qualification approved by the British Association of Art Therapists (BAAT). It is also possible to specialise in music or drama therapy and for these roles you would need to complete a course by their specific approved association.

Although arts-based first degrees are preferred for entry to postgraduate courses, other subjects such as psychology, education and nursing are all acceptable.

You must be at least 23 years old at the time of entry. To apply for a master's you will need a strong portfolio, and at least a year's experience in working in health, education or social care.

A master's degree course lasts 2 years full time, or 4 years part time. Many areas are covered, including psychodynamics, psychopathology of art, contemporary art therapy and practice skills.

You will have to have therapy yourself as part of training, and will also be expected to spend 120 days on clinical placement during the course.

Once you have qualified, you need to register with the Health Professions Council (HPC).

What the work involves

Therapists use a range of mediums of art to help clients who may have difficulty in expressing themselves through words.

You may work closely with people suffering from mental health problems, emotional problems, or those with drug and alcohol addiction, helping them to recover. People with speech and language difficulties also benefit from art therapy.

You will create a safe environment where patients feel free to express themselves and their feelings and move on positively.

Type of person suited to this work

If you want to work with people with emotional and psychological difficulties, you need to be a calm, caring, understanding and trustworthy person. You will need a lot of patience, excellent communication skills, and a very sensitive nature.

These skills need to be combined with strong artistic ability: you have to be a creative thinker prepared to take on the responsibility of helping clients who may be in a great deal of emotional pain. An interest in all forms of art is also essential.

If you plan on starting your own business, you will need good marketing and accounting skills.

Working conditions

Conditions depend on who you choose to work for. If being employed by the NHS appeals to you, you are likely to work 37.5 hours per week, with weekends free. If you work in private practice, your hours will vary and will probably include evenings and weekends.

As a therapist, you will probably have to travel around to give therapy, so a driving licence is really useful. You could work in hospitals, prisons, clinics and community centres.

Surroundings for therapy must always be warm, light and comfortable, so you can expect this to be your working environment.

Future prospects

If you work for yourself, you can grow and expand your business by building up a solid client base and making good contacts.

If you choose to work for the NHS, you could be promoted to management positions; becoming a specialist, head of profession, or consultant.

You might decide to specialise within a particular area, such as mental health or palliative care. Alternatively, you could combine art therapy with another complementary treatment such as psychotherapy.

Advantages/disadvantages

If you have both a love of art and a desire to help people this will prove a very rewarding career.

Opportunities for progression are good, and experiences can be enriching and very fulfilling; there will never be a boring day at work.

You will have to deal with people who are in pain or mentally unstable, which can be extremely upsetting.

Money guide

As a newly qualified art therapist working for the NHS your salary will range from £25,472–£34,189.

If you set up your own practice your intial salary will probably be less.

As you gain experience this figure can rise to about £40,000 a year.

If you get into a management or supervisory role, you can earn around £46,600 a year.

Related opportunities

- Clinical/Health Psychologist p568
- Counsellor p569
- Learning Disabilities Nurse p314

Further information

British Association of Art Therapists
www.baat.org

Health Professions Council
www.hpc-uk.org

NHS Careers
www.nhscareers.nhs.uk

AUDIOLOGIST

Qualifications and courses

The professional qualification for audiologists is a 4 year BSc degree in audiology. The entry requirements for an audiology degree are 3 A levels/5 H grades or equivalent including at least one science subject, maths or psychology.

You will spend the first 2 years of the course at university. During year 3, you will work in a placement in an audiology setting. The final year will be spent back at university learning about more advanced aspects of audiology.

It is also possible to enter this profession with a degree in another appropriate subject if you complete an MSc in audiology. Most people who follow this route work towards registering as audiological scientists.

If you want to practise as an audiological scientist or clinical scientist in audiology you will need to undertake a Higher Training Scheme (run by the British Academy of Audiology (BAA)). This involves on-the-job training and clinical supervision.

You will be expected to partake in continuing professional development (CPD) and to conduct ongoing research.

No pre-entry experience is required for audiology but experience working with young and elderly people is an advantage.

What the work involves

Audiologists examine patients to identify and assess hearing and balance disorders. Audiologists usually work in one of four main areas: paediatrics, adult assessment and rehabilitation, special needs groups, and research and development.

As an audiologist, you will use specialist equipment to test patients and assess their problems and needs.

You will also fit hearing aids and give treatment and advice to patients on how to improve and manage their conditions.

Type of person suited to this work

As an audiologist you will need to speak clearly and be easily understood by people who are lip reading. You should also be flexible and able to work as part of a team.

You will need to be a caring person with excellent communication skills to deal sensitively with patients of all ages and backgrounds, listening to them and explaining the tests and procedures you are doing.

You will need to be practical to operate specialist equipment and take a logical, scientific approach to your work and be able to assess patients' needs and conditions correctly, keep accurate records and provide solutions and practical help.

Working conditions

Most audiologists work as part of a hospital team but you could also be based in a clinic or visit patients in their homes or in care homes or schools.

You could also be involved in teaching and research work in a university.

You will probably work Monday to Friday but could have to be on-call and cover shifts including nights, weekends and bank holidays.

Self-employment or freelance work, part-time hours and career breaks are all possible.

Future prospects

Audiology is a rapidly developing area of healthcare, there is a shortage of qualified staff so job prospects are good. There are opportunities within the NHS throughout the UK. There are also jobs available in research and in private hospitals.

You could specialise in one area such as paediatrics or adult rehabilitation.

Within the NHS you could progress to higher grades, where you will have more responsibility including managing and training others.

Advantages/disadvantages

You may need to deal with people suffering from an illness or disorder, such as those with dementia, and this can be emotionally draining at times.

It is fulfilling to know that you are using your skills to improve people's hearing and balance, providing them with a better quality of life.

Money guide

The NHS sets rates for audiologists. There are extra payments available, for example, if you work in London.

Trainees start on NHS band 5 which ranges from £21,176 to £27,625 per year. Once qualified and registered as an audiological scientist this rises to band 7, £30,460–£40,157.

Senior posts have a salary range at bands 8 to 9 of £38,851–£97,478.

Related opportunities

- Occupational Therapist p319
- Physiotherapist p330
- Speech and Language Therapist p338

Further information

British Academy of Audiology
www.baaudiology.org

British Society of Audiology
www.thebsa.org.uk

NHS Careers
www.nhscareers.nhs.uk

HEALTHCARE

CRCI: JF

CHILDREN'S NURSE ENTRY LEVEL 5

Qualifications and courses

All nurses must hold a degree in child nursing which has been approved by the Nursing and Midwifery Council (NMC). Minimum entry requirements for degree courses are usually 5 GCSEs/S grades (A*–C/1–3) including English, maths and a science subject and 2–3 A levels/H grades, ideally including a science-based subject. All applicants must obtain clearance from the Criminal Records Bureau (CRB) before commencing their training.

If you do not have the required GCSEs/A levels or S/H grades, some universities will accept other qualifications, such as a BTEC National Diploma in Health and Social Care (Health Sciences) or an Access to Higher Education Diploma in a science or health-related subject.

Graduates with a degree in a health-related subject such as human biology, life and medical sciences or biomedical science, may be eligible to enter the nursing profession by taking an accelerated 2-year programme which leads to an MSc or postgraduate diploma.

You are eligible to register as a nurse with the NMC once you have completed an approved nursing degree. Nurses are expected to engage in continuing professional development (CPD) throughout their career to keep their skills and knowledge up to date.

What the work involves

Children's nurses work specifically with babies and young people up to the age of 18. You will also work closely with the parents and families of your patients, providing support, education and advice on treatment and care plans.

You will take medical histories from children and their families, devise a care plan for them with the help of other medical professionals and record their treatment procedures and outcomes in detailed records. You will also have to carry out procedures such as checking blood pressure, taking temperatures, dressing wounds and taking blood samples.

Type of person suited to this work

You will need to be a very warm, approachable person in order to gain the trust of young patients and their families. At the same time, you must be highly professional and authoritative to deal with difficult children and situations.

You should be patient when teaching others, as you will need to demonstrate treatment techniques to both your patients and their parents or carers. You will also need to motivate them to continue treatment at home.

You must be observant, capable of making decisions and able to respond quickly to changes in children's health.

Working conditions

On average, you will work 37.5 hours per week and this will usually include early morning, evening, night and weekend work as part of a shift-based rota. Part-time and flexible hours are often available.

You could work in children's wards within NHS hospitals, specialist hospitals, hospices and GP surgeries. You may also work throughout the local community, visiting patients at home, in care homes or at school.

You will usually be required to wear a uniform and suitable sterile clothing, such as gloves and an apron, for certain procedures.

Future prospects

As you gain experience, you can undertake further training and specialise in a particular area such as neurological or cardiovascular conditions in children. You could eventually become a nurse consultant.

Alternatively, you could apply for team leadership roles such as staff nurse or sister. You could also move into general NHS management.

Advantages/disadvantages

Working with children, helping them to get better, managing their treatment and easing their suffering is extremely rewarding.

There are plenty of opportunities to work part time in order to fit your job around your family commitments.

It can be upsetting to deal with distressed or very ill children.

Money guide

A newly qualified nurse can expect a starting salary of £21,200.

As you gain experience, your earnings can increase up to about £28,000.

Those who take on a senior position with additional responsibilities can achieve £30,000–£40,000.

If you specialise in a particular area and undertake the training to become a nurse consultant, you could earn up to £56,000.

Related opportunities

- Adult Nurse p289
- Learning Disabilities Nurse p314
- Speech and Language Therapist p338

Further information

NHS Careers
www.nhscareers.nhs.uk

Nursing and Midwifery Council
www.nmc-uk.org

Royal College of Nursing
www.rcn.org.uk

CHIROPRACTOR

Qualifications and courses

Entrants must complete a degree course that has been accredited by the General Chiropractic Council (GCC). There are currently 3 institutions in the UK offering the GCC-recognised Masters in Chiropractic (MChiro) which takes 4–5 years to complete. Upon graduation, candidates are eligible to register with the GCC, which is a legal requirement for anyone wishing to practise as a chiropractor.

You must be at least 18 years old to start training. Minimum entry requirements are 3 A levels/H grades or equivalent including biology and another science subject. For candidates who do not meet these requirements, year-long preliminary chiropractic courses are available as an entry route to the full degree.

More mature applicants looking to move into chiropractic as a second career are considered for degree courses without the usual entry qualifications, providing they have relevant experience or knowledge of science.

You must undergo a Criminal Records Bureau (CRB) check prior to training as you will be working with children and vulnerable adults.

Registered chiropractors must undertake continuing professional development (CPD) throughout their career.

What the work involves

Chiropractors work with joints, bones and muscles, using their hands and other physical tools, as opposed to drugs, in order to treat patients. Techniques include massage, movement and applying ice or heat to troublesome areas.

You could treat a variety of ailments including back and neck problems, joint stiffness, postural and muscular complaints, headaches and sports injuries.

You will also need to carry out full patient examinations, listen to their concerns and complaints, and record detailed notes of each consultation.

Type of person suited to this work

You should have exceptional communication skills as you will need to listen to patients carefully in order to understand their complaint and to explain the techniques you are using to treat it.

You will need to be professional and approachable in order to inspire confidence and trust in your patients.

Good organisation and commercial awareness are essential if you are to run your own business.

Working conditions

Working hours are usually 9am–5pm, Monday to Friday, although some flexibility may be required to suit the needs of clients. Many clinics and practitioners are increasingly offering early morning, evening and weekend appointments.

Most chiropractors work either in a specialist clinic, a doctor's surgery, at home or at the homes of their clients. This means you could be working alongside other chiropractors/healthcare professionals or alone.

It is a physically demanding job so you will have to ensure that your own fitness levels remain high in order to avoid work-related injuries.

Future prospects

The chiropractic profession is gaining medical credibility and growing rapidly so there are increasing opportunities within the sector. However, there are also many graduates competing for clients.

Most chiropractors are self-employed or work in private practice. A few are employed by the NHS.

Numerous options are open to you as you gain experience. You could choose to specialise in a specific area, such as children or sports injuries, you could set up your own practice or you could teach.

Advantages/disadvantages

Each day you will meet new people and relieve their physical aches and ailments which gives great job satisfaction.

Being self-employed can be extremely stressful as you are responsible for your own business administration and your earnings are dependent on the number of clients you attract.

Money guide

Most chiropractors are self-employed so their earnings depend upon the size, location and reputation of their practice, as well as how many clients they have.

Newly qualified chiropractors can expect a starting salary of £20,000–£22,000.

With experience, your earnings could rise to £40,000.

Once you are in a senior position within your own practice, you could achieve £50,000–£70,000.

Related opportunities

- Massage Therapist p315
- Osteopath p323
- Physiotherapist p330

Further information

British Chiropractic Association
www.chiropractic-uk.co.uk

General Chiropractic Council
www.gcc-uk.org

HEALTHCARE

CRCI: JB

Qualifications and courses

You will need either a 1st or 2.1 degree in a subject such as mechanical, electronic or electrical engineering or biomedical science/engineering. You should choose a degree which is accredited by the Institution of Engineering and Technology (IET) or the Institution of Mechanical Engineers (IMechE). For degree entry you will need at least 3 A levels or equivalent including maths and physics.

Mature students without relevant qualifications may be considered if they have significant work experience in this area or complete an Access to Higher Education course.

Those who wish to work in the public sector can apply for the graduate NHS Scientist Training Programme (STP) which is offered in conjunction with the Institute of Physics and Engineering in Medicine (IPEM). Training takes 3–4 years and involves both work-based learning and studying for a master's degree in your chosen specialism.

You will need to commit to a programme of continuing professional development (CPD) throughout your career.

What the work involves

Clinical engineers design and maintain medical equipment such as scanners, X-ray machines, pacemakers, heart rate and blood pressure monitors, equipment for surgery and instruments used in medical research.

All kinds of engineers, from physicists to computer scientists, work on many different parts of the process.

You would test equipment and collaborate with hospital staff, installing equipment and teaching them how to use it.

Type of person suited to this work

If you are looking to go into this field, you need to have a natural interest in both electronic and mechanical engineering, and in health and medical issues. You must also be skilled in engineering and have in-depth knowledge of your subject.

You should be good at problem-solving and willing to keep up to date with developments in science, medicine and engineering.

You need organisational skills to effectively prioritise and plan your workload and the ability to work within a budget.

Communication and teamwork skills are also essential.

Working conditions

You could work in a hospital or laboratory, depending on the nature of the work.

Those working in hospitals might have to work shifts and are often on standby for call-outs. Laboratory hours tend to be more fixed.

The usual working hours for clinical engineers are Monday to Friday and you would normally be working 37.5 hours a week.

Future prospects

There are good opportunities for progression and promotion for clinical and biomedical engineers.

With the right experience, you can move into management and senior management jobs, and if you work for the NHS you could be promoted to consultant level.

For those who do not wish to work for the NHS, other opportunities may be available in the private sector. For example, you could be employed by a medical equipment manufacturer.

Advantages/disadvantages

This career requires very skilled and well-educated professionals, and building up this knowledge, studying for your degree and putting it into practice can be a really rewarding experience.

You will be doing a worthwhile job as you will help many people by building and maintaining medical equipment.

The role can be stressful at times and involve high levels of pressure.

Working in a hospital environment will not suit everyone.

Money guide

Starting salaries for those on the NHS graduate training scheme are about £25,500.

Experienced and qualified clinical engineers can expect to earn up to £40,000.

An engineer with chartered status, who is employed by the NHS in a senior position, can achieve £49,000–£61,000.

Salaries may be higher for those employed in the private sector.

Related opportunities

- Biotechnologist p505
- Clinical Scientist p509
- Medical Physicist p316

Further information

Association of Clinical Scientists
www.assclinsci.org

Clinical Scientist Recruitment Centre
www.nhsclinicalscientists.info

CRITICAL CARE TECHNOLOGIST

Qualifications and courses

There are currently no formal entry requirements but most employers expect a good general education and may prefer 4 GCSEs/S grades (A*–C/1–3).

Many candidates enter with higher qualifications, such as A levels, Advanced Highers or a BTEC National qualification in Applied Science (Medical Science) or Electrical/Electronic Engineering.

In the future, critical care technology will become a degree-entry career. A degree in clinical physiology (specialising in critical care technology) will be the preferred option. Alternatively, graduates of degrees in life sciences, science, maths or electronics can take vocational training and some modules from the clinical physiology degree to supplement their knowledge. Entry to a degree usually requires 3 A levels/H grades including maths, physics and another science subject.

Those who enter the profession without a degree train on the job with colleagues and senior members of staff. You will attend college/university by day or block release to study for relevant qualifications.

What the work involves

Critical care technologists support other medical staff caring for critically ill patients by maintaining and operating life-support equipment in intensive care units.

You will work with equipment such as ventilators, brain monitors, blood filtration machines, electrocardiograms (ECGs) and infusion devices. Your job will involve setting up this equipment, taking readings, checking the equipment is working correctly, repairing it and ordering more supplies.

You will use diagnostic techniques to help the medical team assess a patient's needs and condition. You will also be required to keep detailed reports of all your work for patients' records.

Type of person suited to this work

You should have an interest in electronics, science and medicine, with a willingness to keep your skills and knowledge up to date.

You must be a practical person with good technical skills and the ability to work accurately and precisely when under pressure. Good problem-solving and decision making skills are essential. You should have a responsible attitude to your work as patients' lives will depend on you.

You will need compassion and excellent communication skills to work with patients and their relatives at a time of intense stress, and to be able to explain things simply and clearly.

Working conditions

Critical care technologists work as part of a team in the intensive care unit of a hospital using specialist equipment and machinery.

You will need to follow strict health and safety regulations to ensure that infections and diseases are safely contained.

You will normally work shifts which include nights, weekends and bank holidays.

Future prospects

This is a small but growing profession with opportunities to work for the NHS throughout the UK. Job prospects are good as there is a shortage of applicants for job vacancies.

You could specialise in a particular area such as cardiology or respiratory units.

Many critical care technologists are involved in research and teaching, as well as in practice.

Advantages/disadvantages

Working under pressure in emergency situations will be emotionally and physically demanding.

It is extremely rewarding to help patients recover from illnesses.

You will have a varied working day which will involve using your technical skills and having contact with patients.

Money guide

The NHS sets pay rates for critical care technologists.

Starting salaries range from £21,200 to £27,500.

Once qualified and with experience, earnings can rise to £40,200.

If you work in London, you may receive an additional allowance.

Working overtime or being on-call can increase your earnings.

Wages may be higher in the private sector.

Related opportunities

- Audiologist p293
- Operating Department Practitioner p320
- Sterile Services Technician p340

Further information

NHS Careers
www.nhscareers.nhs.uk

Skills for Health
www.skillsforhealth.org.uk

Society of Critical Care Technologists
www.criticalcaretech.org.uk

HEALTHCARE

CRCI: JF

Qualifications and courses

To practise as a dental hygienist you will need to register with the General Dental Council (GDC) and have completed a GDC-approved course. This can be either a 2-year full-time Diploma in Dental Hygiene and Therapy or a 3-year full-time BSc degree in Oral Health Science.

Minimum entry requirements for these courses are 5 GCSEs/S grades (A*–C/1–3), including English, maths and a science related subject, plus 2 A levels/Highers. Some schools may accept a GDC recognised qualification in Dental Nursing in place of A levels.

As you will work with children and vulnerable adults you will need a Criminal Records Bureau check prior to training.

What the work involves

Dental hygienists are predominantly concerned with oral hygiene and help prevent tooth decay and gum disease in their patients.

Your work will include scaling and polishing teeth, putting in temporary fillings, taking impressions and X-rays, and applying protective coatings to teeth to prevent decay.

You will be using a range of instruments, including scraping devices and drills. You will instruct patients on the appropriate way to floss and brush as well as advise them on their diet.

Type of person suited to this work

You will need to have excellent communication skills and be warm and reassuring as you treat patients of all ages, advising them on oral care.

You will need to combine good scientific knowledge with a personable approach to your work in order to motivate patients and convince them to stick to dental routines. A genuine desire to help people is essential.

You will need good eyesight and precise manual skills so that you can carry out detailed dental work with delicate instruments. An ability to stay focussed for long periods of time is also important.

Working conditions

You will usually work a 37-hour week from Monday to Friday, although occasional evening and Saturday morning work may be required according to practice opening hours. Part-time work is also available.

If you work for a community dental service you may travel to see patients in various locations such as schools and residential homes. You may also work out of a mobile clinic.

Surgeries are clean and well lit. You will need to wear a white coat, surgical gloves, a face mask and eye protection for various procedures.

Future prospects

Although the majority of hygienists work in dental surgeries, you could also work for a community dental service, in a hospital or for the Defence Dental Agency (DDA), providing dental treatment for the British Armed Forces around the world.

You may be promoted to practice manager or go on to become an orthodontic therapist.

You could also become self-employed and work across several practices, undertaking part-time hours in each or teach a dental hygiene training course.

Advantages/disadvantages

You will meet all kinds of people, which can create a diverse and interesting working day.

It is satisfying to see a patient's condition improve based on your advice.

You may come across anxious patients who are difficult to calm down.

Money guide

Recent graduates working in an NHS practice may earn up to £25,000 per year in their first few years as a dental hygienist.

Once you have gained several years' experience, you could earn between £26,000 and £34,000 per year.

If you work in private practice, have considerable experience and a good reputation, you could earn up to £48,000 per year.

Related opportunities

- Dental Therapist p301
- Dentist p302
- Orthodontist p322

Further information

British Dental Association
www.bda.org

British Society of Dental Hygiene & Therapy
www.bsdht.org.uk

General Dental Council
www.gdc-uk.org

NHS Careers
www.nhscareers.nhs.uk

Qualifications and courses

Typically there are no academic entry requirements to work as a trainee dental nurse but in order to progress you will need to study a recognised qualification in dental nursing before becoming a dental nurse. These qualifications need to be approved by the General Dental Council (GDC) and many of these courses require GCSEs/S grades (A*–C/1–3) in English, maths and a science subject for entry.

Qualifications recognised by the GDC are the Certificate of Higher Education in Dental Nursing, City & Guilds Level 3 Award in Dental Nursing, SQA Level 3 in Dental Nursing, National Examining Board for Dental Nurses (NEBDN) National Certificate or a Certificate of Proficiency in Dental Nursing from a recognised dental hospital.

The Armed Forces also offer several routes into dental nursing.

What the work involves

Dental nurses assist dentists in all aspects of clinical work and patient treatment.

You will be expected to prepare the surgery each day and for each patient, ensuring that all instruments are to hand and sterilised ready for use. You will also assist in dental procedures by holding suction devices in the patient's mouth, ensuring that they are comfortable throughout their treatment, and giving patients pre- and post-operative advice.

You may also take responsibility for the day-to-day running of the surgery, including maintaining stock and ordering equipment, and undertaking some administrative duties.

Type of person suited to this work

You should have excellent interpersonal skills as you will be dealing with patients on a daily basis, many of whom may be anxious about forthcoming treatment and in need of kindness and reassurance.

Good eye-sight and manual dexterity are helpful when aiding in procedures, as is a calm approach to jobs and the ability to react quickly and calmly to unforeseen situations. As you will be working closely with a dentist and other colleagues, you will need to enjoy being part of a team environment.

Good time management and organisational skills are necessary in order to fulfil the range of duties you will be expected to undertake.

Working conditions

You will usually work from 8am to 5.30pm Monday to Friday, and some evening or weekend work may be required. Part-time work is often available. If you work in a hospital, you may be asked to remain on-call over weekends and provide emergency cover at any time of day or night.

Dental nurses are also employed by the Salaried Primary Care Dental Service (SPCDS) to work in local communities, assisting with patient care in various locations such as mobile clinics, schools and residential homes.

You will have to wear a uniform, and relevant safety equipment such as surgical gloves and a face mask.

Future prospects

Once qualified, you could continue your studies in order to gain further qualifications that will allow you to take on additional responsibilities such as sedation of patients and radiography.

Another option is to train to become a specialist orthodontic dental nurse, or a dental hygienist.

Some dental nurses also move into teaching roles and train student nurses.

Advantages/disadvantages

You will be working in pleasant, clean environments helping to treat patients and maintain a high standard of dental care across the UK.

Hours are usually standard and regular, with the opportunity to work part time for a better work–life balance.

Money guide

These salaries are based on those listed by the NHS, and they may vary according to your employer and the location in which you work.

Student dental nurses can start on a salary of £15,860–£18,827.

Once qualified, you could expect this to increase to £18,402–£21,798.

If you reach a more senior position, such as team leader or nurse specialist, your earnings could rise to £25,528–£34,189.

Related opportunities

- Adult Nurse p289
- Dental Hygienist p298
- Dentist p302

Further information

British Association of Dental Nurses
www.badn.org.uk

General Dental Council
www.gdc-uk.org

HEALTHCARE

CRCI: JC

DENTAL TECHNICIAN

ENTRY LEVEL 4

Qualifications and courses

You will need to register with the General Dental Council (GDC) prior to working as a dental technician, and to do this you need to pass a qualification that is recognised by it. These include the BTEC National Diploma, a Foundation degree, or a BSc in Dental Technology.

Entry requirements for the BTEC National Diploma are at least 4 GCSEs/S grades (A*–C/1–3) or equivalent, including English, maths and a science. For a Foundation degree in dental technology, you will need 4 GCSEs/S grades (A*–C/1–3) and an A level/Higher. Entry requirements for a degree course are 5 GCSEs/S grades (A*–C/1–3) and 2 or 3 A levels/3 H grades including a science.

You can work as a trainee in a laboratory or hospital whilst you study to obtain a relevant qualification that will enable you to register as a practising dental technician.

The Armed Forces also recruit dental technicians, but you will need to be fully qualified at the time of applying, and be under 33 years of age.

It is important to commit to a programme of continuing professional development (CPD) to keep your skills up to date.

What the work involves

Dental technicians make and repair dental accessories such as braces, crowns and false teeth. You could work across all three areas, or specialise in just one.

You will follow detailed prescriptions, written by a doctor or dentist, in order to create individual, patient-specific appliances.

You will use a variety of materials for crafting each device, including gold, steel, porcelain and plastic. You will also use numerous technical instruments in order to accurately carve, mould or wire each accessory.

Type of person suited to this work

You will be producing extremely delicate, precise devices so you will need excellent manual dexterity, good eye-sight and full colour vision. It also helps to have some artistic ability so that you can make items such as false teeth and crowns look as natural and aesthetically pleasing as possible.

You will need to be able to concentrate on a task for lengthy periods of time, and maintain a high level of accuracy throughout.

You should also be comfortable understanding and interpreting complex technical instructions in order to create them as 3D devices.

Working conditions

You should expect to work between 37 and 40 hours per week. Hours usually fall on weekdays but if you work in a hospital dental unit you might have to work evenings and weekends to cover emergency clinics.

You will be working in a laboratory, either within a hospital, dental practice, or independent commercial facility.

You will be expected to wear protective clothing and safety equipment when undertaking certain tasks.

Future prospects

Dental technicians usually work for commercial laboratories that produce equipment for a number of different practitioners in an area. These range in size from smaller businesses to large companies.

Other employers include hospital dental units, the Royal Army Dental Corps (RADC), the RAF, and the Royal Navy. There is also the option to be self-employed, although this is relatively uncommon.

Within larger companies, prospects for promotion are good.

Advantages/disadvantages

You will have job satisfaction in knowing you are producing high quality dental devices to improve a patient's dental health or appearance.

It is not a very sociable job. Although you will be working in a laboratory with other professionals, you will be responsible for your own projects and have no patient contact.

Money guide

As a newly qualified dental technician you could expect to earn in the region of £21,200.

With experience, and often through specialising, you could earn between £34,000 and £40,000.

Dental lab managers can earn up to £67,000.

Related opportunities

- Dental Hygienist p298
- Dental Nurse p299
- Dental Therapist p301

Further information

British Institute of Dental and Surgical Technologists
www.bidst.org

General Dental Council
www.gdc-uk.org

DENTAL THERAPIST

Qualifications and courses

You will need to register with the General Dental Council (GDC) prior to working as a dental therapist. To do this, you will need either a Diploma in Dental Therapy (often combined with a Diploma in Dental Hygiene) or a degree in Oral Health Sciences approved by the GDC.

Minimum entry requirements for these courses are 5 GCSEs/S grades (A*–C/1–3), including English, maths and biology, plus 2 or 3 A levels/Highers. Some schools may accept a GDC recognised qualification in Dental Nursing in place of A levels.

In addition to all of the training applied to a dental hygienist you will also need clinical skills training in how to do fillings and extract deciduous (milk) teeth. As a student you can join the British Association of Dental Therapists (BADT) which can give you access to relevant job adverts as well as help you network.

As you will work with children and vulnerable adults you will need a Criminal Records Bureau check prior to training.

What the work involves

Dental therapists, or oral health practitioners, perform both clinical and educational dental tasks.

You will not only perform a hygienist's role such as scaling and polishing teeth, but you will also remove plaque from the root surface of the teeth and carry out fillings and nerve treatments on both adult and deciduous teeth.

You will educate patients on proper diet and ways to brush and floss their teeth. You could also need to administer a supervised local anaesthetic.

Type of person suited to this work

As you will treat everyone from children to the elderly you will need to be adaptable, good-natured and encouraging. Your patients must feel comfortable with you and trust you.

You need to be a clear and motivational communicator in order to educate patients on proper dental care.

It is essential to have both a solid understanding of biology as well as a sincere interest in the wellbeing of your patients. You will need endurance, the ability to focus for long periods of time and a precise hand for carrying out detailed procedures.

Working conditions

You will work in a clean and bright environment. Your hours will be standard Monday to Friday but you might need to work the occasional Saturday morning or evening surgery. It might be possible to work freelance or on a part-time basis.

You might need to travel to schools or residential homes to visit patients if you are employed by a community dental service. This may include working from a mobile clinic.

For most procedures you will need to wear protective gloves, a facemask and uniform.

Future prospects

Good job opportunities exist for dental therapists throughout the UK. You may be employed by a general practice (private or NHS), a dental school, a cosmetic surgery, a Salaried Primary Care Dental Service or with a Primary Care Trust.

You could be promoted to a dental practice manager or become a researcher or lecturer. With further training you could also specialise in health promotion.

You might choose to set up your own dental practice.

Advantages/disadvantages

It is rewarding to see a patient satisfied at the end of their treatment.

Your work will be varied as each patient's case will be unique.

The job can be demanding as you must deal with the public all day and you might find it difficult to win a patient's trust.

Money guide

Starting out as a therapist in the NHS you can earn between £21,200 and £27,500 a year. As a specialist you may earn up to £35,000 a year.

Advanced therapists may earn up to £40,000 a year.

Your salary may increase based on your employer and where you live. If you are self-employed you will be able to negotiate your fees.

Related opportunities

- Dental Hygienist p298
- Dental Nurse p299
- Dentist p302

Further information

British Association of Dental Therapists
www.badt.org.uk

General Dental Council
www.gdc-uk.org

NHS Careers
www.nhscareers.nhs.uk

HEALTHCARE

CRCI: JC

Qualifications and courses

There are six dental schools offering degrees approved by the British Dental Association with the standard programme lasting 5 years. You will need at least 3 good A levels or equivalent, including chemistry and biology and 5 GCSEs/S grades (A*–C/1–3).

If you have good A level/H grade results, but not in the required subjects, you can apply for a 6 year programme that includes an initial 30-week course that will get you up to speed in chemistry, physics and biology.

If you already have a degree in another subject it is possible to take an accelerated degree lasting only 4 years. To qualify you will need a 2.1 first degree, and have relevant qualifications in biology and chemistry.

Once you have completed your degree you will have 1 year of vocational training and will also need to commit to a programme of continuing professional development (CPD) to remain registered with the General Dental Council.

What the work involves

Dentists are trained to recognise, diagnose and treat all problems that affect the teeth, gums and mouth.

You will examine teeth and carry out appropriate treatments, such as fitting or replacing fillings, scraping away plaque, polishing and removing teeth, as well as educating patients about good oral habits in order to prevent disease or decay.

You will also need to keep detailed dental records for each patient, alongside managing your staff and, if you are a practice manager, looking after the practice budget.

Type of person suited to this work

You will need to have excellent communication skills in order to inspire your team and build good relationships with your patients, who will represent all ages and backgrounds.

You should also be compassionate and sympathetic, as you will encounter patients who are nervous or anxious about their treatment and you will need to be able to soothe and reassure them.

You will need good eyesight, concentration and manual dexterity to successfully carry out complicated and delicate procedures. If you intend to run your own practice, you will also need good business acumen.

Working conditions

If you work in a dental surgery, you should have regular Monday to Friday hours, and may even enjoy some flexibility within this framework. Dentists who work in hospitals will usually work longer hours, including weekends, and will have to adhere to an on-call rota.

You could work across the community, travelling to provide treatment in locations such as schools and retirement homes.

You will need to wear protective, hygienic clothing such as a white coat and surgical gloves when dealing with patients.

Future prospects

Most dentists are self-employed, working in general practice across the UK. Some work for the NHS, and some take on a mixture of private and NHS patients.

A recent surge in dental graduates has increased competition in this sector. There is still demand for graduates across the UK, but this is mostly within the NHS which is viewed by some as a less lucrative career move than private practice.

You could undertake further training to specialise in a field such as orthodontics or maxillofacial surgery.

Advantages/disadvantages

The majority of dentists are self-employed and work in the private sector, so you have a good amount of control over the hours you work and the patients you see.

There are excellent opportunities for rapid career progression or further training if you want to specialise in a specific area.

You will mainly be undertaking routine check-ups and very standard procedures, so work can feel monotonous at times.

Money guide

Salaries for recently graduated, trainee dentists in general practice start at around £30,000 per year. If you start your career in the NHS, your salary will be slightly lower.

Experienced dentists in general practice can earn between £50,000 and £110,000. However, even more is available, especially if they run their own surgery.

If you reach consultant level working for the NHS, your salary could exceed £100,000.

Related opportunities

- Dental Hygienist p298
- Dental Therapist p301
- Orthodontist p322

Further information

British Dental Association
www.bda.org

General Dental Council
www.gdc-uk.org

NHS Careers
www.nhscareers.nhs.uk

CRCI: JC   HEALTHCARE

DIETITIAN

Qualifications and courses

To become a dietitian, an approved degree or postgraduate qualification (PgDip/MSc) in dietetics or human nutrition and dietetics is required. You must then register with the Health Professions Council in order to practise. You will need 2–3 A levels/3 H grades including chemistry and another science and GCSEs/S grades (A*–C/1–3) including English and maths, or equivalent, for entry to a degree in dietetics.

Entry requirements for a postgraduate diploma are typically an Honours degree in a science subject with an acceptable level of biochemistry and human physiology, along with a good command of spoken and written English.

Both routes involve practical training in a hospital or community setting.

Mature applicants can complete an Access course in science to be accepted into a degree programme.

Some institutions expect applicants to have visited a dietetic department before applying for a place.

The approved degree is usually a full-time course that lasts 4 years, while the postgraduate diploma is 2 years long. Both routes include practical training in a hospital or community setting.

If you don't have an approved degree or postgraduate diploma, entry is only available at assistant level.

What the work involves

Dietitians use their scientific knowledge of food to provide advice and information about diet and nutrition. Dietitians might work in industry developing food products and even in the media.

You will give advice to a broad range of people, such as hospital patients, caterers, sports professionals and the general public.

You will help people improve their health and prevent disease by making changes in their diet.

Type of person suited to this work

You will need expert knowledge of the science of food and nutrition, and how this relates to the body.

You must have excellent communication skills to be able to give practical information and advice to a range of people, from school children to food manufacturers. You will need to be caring, supportive and non-judgemental, and able to understand the needs and issues of individuals, especially if you are working with sick people.

You should have good motivational skills so that people can follow your advice and make the changes that you recommend.

Working conditions

You could work in a range of locations such as hospitals, laboratories, offices and sports centres.

You are likely to work a standard working week from Monday to Friday, although in hospitals you may be called in to work at weekends and on bank holidays.

In most jobs you will be working directly with people who can be ill, distressed or reluctant to take your advice.

Future prospects

The British Dietetic Association has over 5000 members, and the profession is growing. There are opportunities across the UK and abroad, but competition for jobs is fierce.

Most dietitians work in the NHS, but there are also many opportunities in areas such as sports nutrition, the food and pharmaceutical industries, scientific research, education and journalism. You could become self-employed working as a consultant or see private clients.

In the NHS, you could go on to specialise in areas such as cancer care, or with particular groups such as children or the elderly. You could also move into management.

Advantages/disadvantages

People might be unable or unwilling to take on your advice, which can be frustrating.

It is rewarding to see improvements in people when they put into practice the information and advice you have given them.

Money guide

The starting salary for an NHS dietitian is band 5, £21,176–£27,534 per year.

Once you are working at a specialist level, salaries increase to band 6, £25,472–£34,189.

Salaries for senior grade dietitians working at band 7 can be between £30,460 and £40,157.

There are higher grades for chief members of staff, or for work outside the NHS, although salaries are not necessarily higher in private work.

You may earn more if you work in London or the south-east of England. In addition, salary premiums are offered where there are recruitment issues or for specialist positions.

Related opportunities

- Food Scientist/Technologist p515
- Health Promotion/Education Specialist p306
- Health Visitor p309

Further information

British Dietetic Association
www.bda.uk.com

NHS Careers
www.nhscareers.nhs.uk

Skills for Health
www.skillsforhealth.org.uk

Qualifications and courses

You must be registered with the General Optical Council (GOC). To qualify, you must complete an appropriate training course, pass the Professional Qualifying Examinations of the Association of British Dispensing Opticians (ABDO), and undergo a pre-registration year working under the supervision of a qualified optician.

You could take a 3-year degree course in optical management, ophthalmic dispensing or a related area. Alternatively, 2-year diploma courses or Foundation degrees in ophthalmic dispensing are available.

Typical entry requirements for a degree or Foundation degree are 2 A levels/3 H grades, normally including relevant science subjects, and 5 GCSEs/S grades (A*–C/1–3) including English, maths and science. For a diploma, you will need at least 5 GCSEs (A*–C) including English, maths and a science, or equivalent.

You could start as a trainee with a qualified optometrist and work part time towards qualifications. ABDO offers a 3-year distance learning course and certain colleges offer a 3-year day-release programme for those in suitable employment.

What the work involves

Dispensing opticians use prescriptions from optometrists to supply and fit glasses.

The work you will do includes measuring the patient's face to ensure the glasses will fit and advising on lenses and frame styles to suit them and their prescription. You will check that the finished glasses meet the original specifications and supply them to the patient. You will also do repairs.

Some dispensing opticians take further training to supply and fit contact lenses.

Type of person suited to this work

Interpreting prescriptions requires specific scientific expertise.

You will be advising and listening to customers of many different ages and backgrounds, and working as part of a team with other professionals, so you will need excellent communication skills. It will be your responsibility to take measurements and repair glasses so manual skills are necessary.

You will need to be business minded if you choose to set up your own practice.

Working conditions

Most dispensing opticians work in high-street opticians. Financial and management challenges may arise if you are self-employed.

You may work 35–40 hours a week from Monday to Saturday (with some time off during the week instead).

You may have to work on Sundays and bank holidays or in shifts, including weekends, in big chains.

Future prospects

Most dispensing opticians work for high-street companies. Some work is available in hospitals. Registration with the GOC will allow you to work in other countries.

With experience, you may specialise, for example in supplying and fitting contact lenses or low vision aids. You could also train new entrants.

You may also be promoted into a management position within a high-street optical chain. With experience, some opticians choose to run their own practices. However, increasing numbers of dispensing opticians are choosing to work for franchises rather than run an independent practice owing to the growing threat from big high street chains.

Advantages/disadvantages

It can be stressful having to meet sales targets in some opticians.

If you enjoy combining scientific knowledge with working with the public, this job could be good for you.

Money guide

Salary levels vary enormously and are usually higher for opticians with management responsibility.

Starting salaries are around £12,000–£17,000 per year.

Practice managers or those who are qualified to fit contact lenses can earn between £28,000 and £35,000 per year.

Related opportunities

- Optometrist p321
- Pharmacist p326
- Sales/Retail Assistant p492

Further information

Association of British Dispensing Opticians
www.abdo.org.uk

General Optical Council
www.optical.org

NHS Careers
www.nhscareers.nhs.uk

DOCTOR (GP)

Qualifications and courses

To become a GP you must first take an undergraduate degree in medicine with the standard programme lasting 5 years. You will need at least 3 good A levels/Highers or equivalent, including chemistry and biology. Some medical schools also require applicants to sit the UK Clinical Aptitude Test (UKCAT).

If you do not have science A levels, some universities offer a 6 year programme that includes an initial 'pre-medical' 30-week course that will get you up to speed. If you already have a 2.1 degree in another subject, some medical schools offer an accelerated degree in medicine lasting only 4 years.

Once you have a degree in medicine, you will need to complete a foundation programme and specialist training in general practice before you can qualify as a GP.

To complete the foundation programme takes 2 years and you will work in a range of different medical settings. At the end of the foundation programme you would choose to train in general practice. This second stage of specialist training takes around 3 years to complete and will include at least 12 months working as a GP registrar in the NHS.

What the work involves

General practitioners (GPs) diagnose various health problems, physical or emotional, within their local community.

You will be talking to and examining patients in order to find out what is wrong with them, and then deciding on how to treat them. This could include giving them advice, prescribing medicine or referring patients to a specialist doctor.

You may occasionally have to perform minor surgery such as removing moles or warts. You are responsible for educating your patients about how to live a healthy lifestyle and prevent illness.

Type of person suited to this work

You will need to have excellent communication skills in order to gain the trust of your patients and build good relationships with them. You should be able to put them at their ease quickly whilst maintaining a professional attitude.

You must have excellent scientific and medical knowledge in order to assess problems quickly and reach a suitable diagnosis, all within the time limit of a 10 minute appointment.

You should have an enquiring mind as you will need to continually update your knowledge and learn about new techniques and medicines in order to keep up to date in this fast moving discipline.

Working conditions

You will usually work normal hours from Monday to Friday, although increasingly surgeries are offering evening and weekend appointments which you might have to cover on a rota basis. You may also have to spend some time on-call, visiting patients at home at any hour of the day or night.

GPs are practice based in small or large surgeries within cities, towns and rural areas.

GPs have to adhere to time and budget constraints, which can make the work stressful and demanding.

Future prospects

As a general practitioner you will be able to work anywhere in the UK, in a larger practice with healthcare professionals from a number of disciplines, or a smaller surgery.

You could undertake work for the NHS, enjoy the freedom of self-employment, or opt for a combination of the two.

Advantages/disadvantages

The training period prior to qualifying as a GP is, on average, 10 years.

Dealing with a number of patients with varying complaints each day can be stressful, but helping them to recover is rewarding.

The work is varied and you will meet lots of different people on a daily basis.

Money guide

Once you are on the foundation programme you will earn between £33,300 and £41,300 a year.

On starting the vocational general practitioner training you could earn between £44,100 and £69,400 a year.

As a fully-qualified GP your earnings could be between £53,250 and £80,350 a year.

If you are self-employed this could rise to £80,000–£120,000.

Related opportunities

- Hospital Doctor p312
- Pharmacist p326
- Surgeon p341

Further information

British Medical Association
www.bma.org.uk

General Medical Council
www.gmc-uk.org

Royal College of General Practitioners
www.rcgp.org.uk

CRCI: JH   HEALTHCARE

Qualifications and courses

Entrants need a degree. Courses in health promotion, health studies, public health, social science, environmental health or related subjects provide an advantage. Entry requirements for degrees are usually a minimum of 2 A levels/3 H grades and 5 GCSEs/S grades (A*–C/1–3) or alternatives such as BTEC qualifications in health and social care. More senior posts generally require a postgraduate diploma or MSc in health promotion. If you have a nursing diploma or a related Foundation degree, there is the option to take a BSc top-up course in health promotion.

It may be possible to train on the job for recognised qualifications. The Open University offers a certificate in Promoting Public Health. Some colleges run a Health Studies Access Course for candidates without the necessary entry requirements.

It is possible to enter the profession through related fields. It is advisable to undertake relevant voluntary work or short courses in areas such as stopping smoking and working with patient groups.

The Society of Health Education and Health Promotion Specialists maintains a voluntary register for specialists in this field, and recommends degree and postgraduate courses to its members.

What the work involves

Health promotion/education specialists aim to promote and improve public health in line with national recommendations.

You could work with organisations such as schools or directly with individuals, groups or communities.

Your work might include advising individuals on how to make lifestyle changes such as taking more exercise or giving up smoking, encouraging organisations like workplaces, schools and hospitals to improve diets and promote health and developing partnerships with communities to improve public health. Your role might also involve liaising with the press and compiling features to encourage healthy living.

Type of person suited to this work

You must be able to encourage individuals and communities to change their lifestyles. It is important to have excellent communication and negotiation skills as a large part of your job will involve dealing with people from all age groups and all walks of life.

You will need to be creative to find different ways of persuading people and organisations to make changes. Good research and writing skills are also necessary in order to put together clear reports.

You will need to be supportive and non-judgemental and able to relate to the needs of a wide range of people, communities and cultures. You must have good organisational skills to run and manage projects.

Working conditions

You could work in many different places such as health centres, local authority buildings, hospitals, workplaces and fitness centres.

You are likely to have a normal working week, Monday to Friday. Some employers offer flexible working schemes.

Travel within a working day is common as you will need to attend meetings, for example at local schools or community groups.

Future prospects

This is a very competitive industry and you will probably need to do work experience.

Most health promotion/education specialists work for the NHS, health promotion agencies, local authorities or in social and community settings.

You can progress to management roles or go into research and lecturing in health promotion.

Advantages/disadvantages

Changing people's habits can be difficult and take a long time.

Working to tight deadlines and targets can be very stressful.

Seeing improvements in public health when people put into practice the information and advice you have provided is very rewarding. You will have the opportunity to work with many different people.

Money guide

Salary levels are largely dependent on which health sector you work in and for whom. In the NHS starting salaries when qualified are between £21,200 and £27,500 per year.

More experienced and senior staff can earn between £32,000 and £43,000, with managers earning in excess of £60,000.

With some employers, there may be extra payments available, for example if you work in London.

Related opportunities

- Dietitian p303
- Health and Safety Adviser p41
- Youth and Community Worker p585

Further information

Faculty of Public Health
www.fphm.org.uk

NHS Careers
www.nhscareers.nhs.uk

HEALTH RECORDS CLERK

ENTRY LEVEL 2

Qualifications and courses

Most employers require candidates to have at least 5 GCSEs/S grades (A*–C/1–3) or equivalent, including English and maths.

Apprenticeships might enable you to enter this role for candidates aged 16–24. Previous administrative experience will give you an advantage.

As you will be working with children and vulnerable adults, you will need to pass a Criminal Records Bureau (CRB) check.

Training is done on the job; you may also be offered the chance to study for extra qualifications such as the NVQ Level 2 in Support Services in Healthcare and Level 3 in Business Administration. The Institute of Health Record and Information Management offers several courses in healthcare administration including the Certificate of Technical Competence.

What the work involves

Health administrators and records clerks are responsible for preparing and maintaining records of patients' medical notes, including details about the medicines they take and any other care needs.

You will be collating, organising and archiving relevant notes and documents in each patient's file, and also ensuring that they are easily accessible for other healthcare professionals.

You will be working with both paper documents and electronic records, which will include using equipment such as computers, photocopiers and scanners. You will also undertake other administrative duties, such as making and rearranging patients' appointments, sorting incoming correspondence and covering reception from time to time.

Type of person suited to this work

You will be working within a team of healthcare professionals as well as dealing with patient enquiries, so you should be personable and have excellent communication skills.

You will need good numeracy and ICT skills. As you will be dealing with a variety of tasks each day, you will also need good organisational skills and the ability to prioritise your workload.

You will be working with confidential information so you must be discreet.

Working conditions

You could work in an office, a reception area, filing room, medical records library or a hospital ward. You will usually work a 37 hour week from Monday to Friday, although

occasionally some jobs require employees to work shifts. Part-time opportunities are common.

As you will be moving and transporting large, heavy piles of paper files around the hospital or practice, you will need to be reasonably strong and fit.

The majority of the work is office based, although you might need to courier documents to various departments within your building. You will be expected to look fairly smart, although a business suit is unnecessary.

Future prospects

Although the NHS is the biggest employer of administrative staff, there are also opportunities in private hospitals and voluntary organisations.

Increasingly, the NHS is providing a more structured career path for administrators. This means you could progress to a supervisory or managerial role within your department, move on to another branch or hospital, or move into supporting a specialist area such as neurology or gastroenterology.

Advantages/disadvantages

You will be providing an essential service to both patients and other healthcare professionals by ensuring the smooth running of behind-the-scenes operations.

You can expect to have a heavy workload at times.

Hours are regular and there is plenty of opportunity for part-time work which fits in around family commitments.

Money guide

The salary for a health records clerk usually starts at £13,000–£17,000.

As you gain experience over a few years, this should rise to between £16,000 and £19,000.

Team leaders can earn up to £22,000.

If you move into a more senior supervisory or management position, you can expect to earn up to £30,000.

Salaries do vary according to your employer and where you work in the UK.

Some employers offer additional benefits such as a pension scheme.

Related opportunities

- Adult Nurse p289
- Health Visitor p309
- Pharmacy Technician p328

Further information

Institute of Health Record and Information Management
www.ihrim.co.uk

HEALTHCARE

CRCI: JE

307

HEALTH SERVICE MANAGER

ENTRY LEVEL 3

HEALTHCARE

CRCI: JE

Qualifications and courses

You could start as an administrator and progress to a management role. For entry level positions 5 GCSEs/S grades (A*–C/1–3) or, more commonly, 2–3 A levels or equivalent are needed.

Once you are in an administrative post you can study for relevant management training courses, such as those offered by the Institute of Healthcare Management (IHM). The Association of Medical Secretaries, Practice Managers, Administrators and Receptionists (AMSPAR) offer a Certificate and Diploma in Primary Care and Health Management (Level 5) in association with City & Guilds.

One of the most direct routes into health service management is through the NHS Graduate Management Training Scheme. There is a choice of 4 specialisms: finance management, general management, HR management or health informatics management. Entry is with a 2.2 degree in any subject or equivalent qualifications that are health or management-related, including the NVQ in Management (Level 5) and the Diploma in Management Studies (DMS). The recruitment process is quite competitive and involves tests and interviews.

The private sector also has graduate management schemes. With BUPA and BMI healthcare you need a 2.1 in any degree or equivalent to enter.

What the work involves

You will help run GP surgeries, hospitals and other health centres, either working for the NHS or within the private sector.

Your job will be varied; you might be controlling finances, managing staff, producing reports on performance, overseeing buildings and buying equipment.

There are specific areas that managers can work in, such as clinical, financial, human resources, IT and facilities. You could also be a practice manager who runs GP surgeries.

Type of person suited to this work

Strong leadership skills and a likable personality will be essential for managing your team. Good communication skills are important as you will be interacting with a variety of people including professionals and patients.

You should be comfortable making important decisions, be logical in your approach to problems and have good negotiation skills.

You must have excellent written communication skills to produce detailed reports and you should be comfortable working with figures, as you may be responsible for budgets and resources.

Working conditions

You will work standard office hours, Monday to Friday, but you could be on-call for emergencies or required to work weekends.

Most of your time will be spent in an office within hospitals, GP surgeries or health centres.

As a manager, you will be expected to dress smartly.

It is useful to have a driving licence as you might travel between sites or to attend meetings.

Future prospects

There is a structured career path if you are employed by the NHS: promotion is gained by moving into different departments and areas of management.

The NHS Gateway to Leadership is available for managers with substantial experience. This fast-track programme enables you to become a chief executive within 5 years. In private healthcare there are stages of promotion which can also be followed.

With experience you may choose to take your managerial skills into another industry or become a consultant.

Advantages/disadvantages

You will be in a very responsible position which could be daunting and stressful.

You will gain valuable management skills which are transferable to many other industries.

Meeting and helping lots of different people provides a strong sense of job satisfaction.

Money guide

Graduates on the NHS training scheme have a starting salary of about £22,000.

Once qualified, you could earn between £27,000 and £37,000 a year.

Those in the most senior positions could achieve £70,000–£100,000.

Salaries in the private sector could be higher.

Related opportunities

- Accountant p16
- Archivist/Records Manager p346
- Human Resources/Personnel Officer p42

Further information

Institute of Healthcare Management
www.ihm.org.uk

NHS Careers
www.nhscareers.nhs.uk

NHS Graduate Management Training Scheme
www.nhsgraduates.co.uk

HEALTH VISITOR

Qualifications and courses

All health visitors must be registered nurses or midwives with at least two years' post-qualification experience. To become a nurse or midwife, you must complete a degree in nursing or midwifery that is recognised by the Nursing and Midwifery Council. Generally, you will need 5 GCSEs/S grades (A*–C/1–3) or equivalent, and 2 A levels or equivalent. The degree course lasts 3 or 4 years.

Once you have completed your training as a nurse, you will need to undertake a further degree-level course in public health nursing. This lasts 1 year full time, or can be studied as a 2 year part time option.

What the work involves

Health visitors work with people of all ages, backgrounds and cultures in various settings such as residential homes, schools, GP surgeries and village halls.

You will provide advice on issues ranging from problems in children's sleep or feeding patterns, to postnatal depression, bereavement or relationship problems and your primary patients will be parents with babies and young children.

You will also be involved in organising community events designed to promote health and wellbeing.

Type of person suited to this work

You will be working closely with patients so you will need excellent communication skills.

You must be trustworthy, understanding, reassuring and professional in order to inspire confidence in your patients, mainly parents, and allow them to share their problems and concerns with you openly. You should also be able to motivate them to make important lifestyle changes on occasion.

You must be able to prioritise a heavy workload, and maintain discretion when dealing with confidential information.

Working conditions

You will usually work a 37 hour week from Monday to Friday, and flexible hours or part-time work are often available.

You will work in a variety of locations, including schools, GP surgeries, health centres and residential homes. Because this will require a good deal of travelling within the local area, a driving licence is usually required.

You will encounter patients who are extremely difficult or distressed at times, which can be upsetting.

Future prospects

All health visitors work for the NHS, and they can be based in larger areas such as cities and towns, or work across villages and rural communities.

Career progression could take the form of managing a team of health visitors, moving into a role as a consultant nurse, specialising in a particular area of nursing, education or research, or even taking up a position in general management within the NHS.

Advantages/disadvantages

You will be offering healthcare advice and treatment across the community, including to those who may otherwise not be able to reach a doctor or hospital very easily such as the elderly.

There are opportunities to work part time or on a job share basis, which would allow you to work around other commitments.

You may have to deal with difficult, potentially threatening patients, which can be frightening and upsetting.

Money guide

The starting salary for a newly qualified health visitor is £24,800.

Once you have gained a few years' experience, this could rise to £33,500.

Senior health visitors, who have supervisory or managerial duties across a team, can earn up to £39,300.

Related opportunities

- Adult Nurse p289
- Children's Nurse p294
- Midwife p318
- Occupational Therapist p319
- Paramedic p324

Further information

Nursing and Midwifery Council
www.nmc-uk.org

Royal College of Nursing
www.rcn.org.uk

CRCI: JH   HEALTHCARE

Qualifications and courses

There are no fixed entry qualifications for this job. Previous experience caring for people, either through paid or voluntary work, may be expected by some employers.

All entrants to this profession will be required to obtain clearance from the Criminal Records Bureau (CRB).

The Apprenticeship in Health and Social Care, which is available at both Intermediate and Advanced Levels, offers an ideal route into this career for school leavers.

You can study for a range of relevant courses full time at school or college, prior to entry. The BTEC National in Health and Social Care (Level 3) and the A level in health and social care are 2-year courses. For entry, candidates usually require 4 GCSEs/S grades (A*–C/1–3) or a BTEC First Diploma.

Once you secure employment as a healthcare assistant, you will receive on-the-job training covering topics including hygiene, health and safety, personal care and communication skills. You may also have the option to work towards relevant NVQs/SVQs. You could go on to take a Foundation degree or degree in a subject such as nursing, mental health or applied health and social care.

What the work involves

Healthcare assistants help people who find it difficult to look after themselves with everyday tasks. Your clients could be children, elderly people or people with disabilities living in residential care or in their own homes.

You will help them to bathe, dress and use the toilet or commode, as well as assisting them with eating, washing, ironing, cleaning and shopping.

Part of your time will be spent talking to your clients, helping them to write letters, budget their money or pay bills.

Type of person suited to this work

Healthcare assistants need to be cheerful, outgoing and friendly, as their clients may be lonely or depressed.

As the job involves working with people who need individual support, you will have to work out what help they need and provide it in a sympathetic and tactful way.

You must be trustworthy, discreet and able to keep clients' confidential information private, as you will handle money, and write and read personal/business letters.

The job usually includes domestic work so you need to be happy and skilled at doing housework and laundry.

Working conditions

Most of your work is indoors but you may go out with people, for example to hospital appointments or on outings. You might have to live in for some jobs.

You will usually work on a shift system which will include early mornings, evenings, weekends and bank holidays.

You need to be physically fit and capable of heavy lifting as you may need to help people who are unable to move around themselves.

You will be expected to be very careful about health and safety issues, such as fire and hot water.

Future prospects

There are over a million healthcare assistants in the UK and demand is increasing. Many healthcare assistants work in residential homes and day-healthcare centres, but more people are being cared for in their own homes.

The main employers are health authorities, social services, private homes and voluntary agencies.

Promotion depends on qualifications and experience. With experience in healthcare work, you could train for related jobs such as social work or nursing.

Advantages/disadvantages

It can be satisfying to help people in need.

Working on public holidays, such as Christmas Day, can interfere with your personal life.

Some jobs can be messy and unpleasant.

Money guide

Salaries start at about £14,150.

With experience and relevant qualifications, you can expect to earn approximately £17,250 a year.

Those with additional responsibilities and promotion to a more senior post can receive up to £19,000 per year.

Allowances for working shifts and unsocial hours can increase your income.

Related opportunities

- Adult Nurse p289
- Childminder p567
- Social Worker p579

Further information

General Social Care Council
www.gscc.org.uk

NHS Careers
www.nhscareers.nhs.uk

Qualifications and courses

Although it is not compulsory to hold a qualification, most patients would not feel comfortable seeing you if you are not registered with one of the UK regulatory bodies, the best known of which is the Society of Homeopaths.

In order to register, you will need to complete an accredited degree or diploma which leads to the qualification of Licentiate in Homeopathy.

Entry requirements are usually 5 GCSEs/S grades (A*–C/1–3) or equivalent and a degree will need the above and at least 2 A levels/3 H grades. Degree courses can be taken full time over 3 years, or part time over 4.

Qualified healthcare professionals can undertake shorter accredited courses in homeopathy at various universities, each of which is regulated by the Faculty of Homeopathy.

What the work involves

Homeopaths use highly diluted doses of natural remedies to treat patients for a variety of ailments, ranging from simple headaches to complicated emotional issues, addiction and disease.

You will need to take into account not only patients' physical symptoms, but also their psychological and emotional state, as well as their lifestyle.

You will be working with a variety of patients of all ages, backgrounds and cultures. You could undertake general cases, or specialise in areas such as fertility and drug addiction.

Type of person suited to this work

You will need excellent communication and listening skills in order to quickly build a rapport with patients and encourage them to discuss their problems and concerns honestly.

As you will need to build your own practice and find clients from scratch, you must have good business acumen, confidence and motivation.

You should also be well-organised and methodical, as you will need to undertake your own administration and keep detailed, informative patient notes.

Working conditions

You will be self-employed and reliant on your clients, so will find that you mainly work at evenings and weekends (especially when newly qualified) in order to fit around their lifestyles.

You could work in a clinic with other healthcare professionals, in an alternative therapy centre, in your own home, or you could travel to see patients in their homes.

Patient appointments can take anywhere between 45 minutes and an hour and a half, so the work is mentally and emotionally draining. Because of this, most homeopaths only work part time.

Future prospects

Alternative therapy has increased in popularity in recent years. This means that there are more people willing to explore it as a means of treatment, but also that there are an increasing number of practising homeopaths. Competition for clients, especially in the early years, can be great.

The majority of homeopaths are self-employed, although there are opportunities in independent surgeries, private hospitals and in 1 of the 5 homeopathic NHS hospitals in the UK.

With experience you could use your knowledge to teach in a university or college, or write related books and articles.

Advantages/disadvantages

Spending time talking to patients about their concerns and alleviating their ailments is extremely rewarding.

If you are self-employed, overheads such as renting clinic space and buying remedies and other equipment will eat into your earnings.

You must be commercially aware in order to successfully market your business, and be prepared to do your own complicated tax forms.

Money guide

Most homeopaths charge their patients directly by appointment. They usually ask between £30 and £100 per hour.

A newly qualified homeopath who is just starting to build a reputation and attract clients could earn between £6,000 and £10,000 a year.

With experience this can rise to between £10,000 and £15,000.

For top earning homeopaths with lots of experience, salaries can rise to £30,000.

Related opportunities

- Aromatherapist p291
- Chiropractor p295
- Osteopath p323

Further information

Alliance of Registered Homeopaths
www.a-r-h.org

British Homeopathic Association
www.trusthomeopathy.org

Society of Homeopaths
www.homeopathy-soh.org

CRCI: JB   HEALTHCARE

Qualifications and courses

To become a hospital doctor, all entrants need to hold a degree in medicine which has been accredited by the General Medical Council (GMC). Courses normally last 5 years and entry requirements are usually at least 3 very high A levels/H grades including chemistry and biology, and good GCSEs/S grades (A*–C/1–3) or equivalent including English, maths and science. Competition for places on medical degrees is very high. Undertaking relevant pre-entry work experience may benefit your application.

For those without the relevant A levels or equivalent, some universities offer a 6 year medical degree, in which the first year is a preliminary course in chemistry, physics and biology lasting 30 weeks.

Graduates of a science-related subject can apply for a 4-year, fast-track medical degree programme. Some universities will consider applications from non-science graduates.

Upon completion of your degree in medicine, you need to complete 2 further stages of vocational training to qualify as a senior doctor or consultant in your chosen field. The first stage is the 2-year foundation programme which forms the bridge between medical school and specialist/general practice training. The second stage is specialist training in an area of medicine which particularly interests you and the length of time this takes depends upon the area you choose.

What the work involves

Hospital doctors work in either NHS or private establishments, diagnosing illnesses, treating patients and monitoring their care.

You may treat patients yourself or, having assessed them, refer them to their GP or another healthcare professional. You will work in one of over 60 specialisms which include cardiology, general medicine, paediatrics, orthopaedics and psychiatry.

You will also be required to carry out surgical operations within your specialism, for example, fitting a pacemaker if you are in cardiology. You may be responsible for teaching medical students.

Type of person suited to this work

You must have excellent communication skills as you will be dealing with patients and healthcare professionals on a daily basis. When handling patients, you should be empathetic, non-judgemental, professional and calm. You should be good at working under pressure, making sensible, bust sometimes difficult, decisions and solving problems.

Working conditions

Generally you can expect to work longer hours than in most other professions, although new guidelines prohibit junior doctors from working more than a 48-hour week. You will usually work on a shift pattern of days and nights which will sometimes involve being on-call.

You will work in a consulting room, on the wards and in operating theatres. Conditions are usually quiet and clean, although things can get very fast paced during times of emergency.

You will also be required to attend numerous meetings and conferences across the UK, Europe and perhaps worldwide.

Future prospects

Junior doctors can choose to specialise in an area such as gastroenterology or geriatric medicine. Once they have completed a training programme in their specialism and passed the necessary exams, they will become a consultant.

Increasingly, senior level hospital doctors undertake managerial responsibilities, alongside teaching and mentoring work with students or junior doctors.

Advantages/disadvantages

You will be responsible for helping patients get better and making them comfortable throughout their illness which is very rewarding.

Hours can be long and unpredictable so it can be difficult to get a satisfactory work–life balance.

Constant developments in medicine and medical technology mean that you will be continually learning and developing throughout your career.

Money guide

Salary levels in the NHS may vary in different locations.

Earnings are often higher in private practice work.

Junior doctors have a starting salary of £22,000–£28,000 during the 2-year foundation programme.

When undertaking the specialty training, you can expect to earn between £28,000 and £46,000 a year.

Consultants can achieve salaries ranging from £74,000 up to £170,000 for those in the most senior positions.

Related opportunities

- Children's Nurse p294
- Doctor (GP) p305
- Surgeon p341

Further information

British Medical Association
www.bma.org.uk

NHS Careers
www.nhscareers.nhs.uk

HOSPITAL PORTER

Qualifications and courses

There are no formal entry requirements for this job, but applicants must be literate and have good all-round communication skills.

There is no set minimum age, but most applicants are at least 18 years old, and there are good opportunities for mature entrants.

Candidates usually have to pass a medical examination, and may be required to take a physical fitness test.

Experience of volunteer hospital work, or previous work with the public, can be useful. A health and safety qualification would also be beneficial.

A driving licence may be required so that you can work at a range of different sites.

You will undergo a short induction once you start and then training is generally on the job. You could work towards NVQ Level 2 in Support Services in Health Care.

What the work involves

Hospital porters transport patients, equipment and other items to where they need to go within the hospital.

One of your main tasks will be to move frail and ill patients between departments and wards, while keeping them safe and comfortable.

You will transport patients using wheelchairs and trolleys.

You may also have a variety of other tasks such as delivering mail and moving medical equipment and supplies.

Type of person suited to this work

Hospital porters need to be responsible and reliable with a positive attitude to make sure that people and equipment are transported to the correct part of the hospital on time.

You should be able to follow instructions and work well as part of a team.

Patients may be distressed or in pain so you must be caring and sympathetic and be able to reassure them and keep them comfortable. You must be able to cope with sickness and death.

Physical fitness is important, because you will walk long distances during your shift and you will have to lift and move patients and equipment.

Working conditions

You will work with patients and other staff, mainly indoors, although you might need to travel to other hospital sites to make deliveries.

You will need to pay attention to health and safety when lifting and handling people and equipment.

Porters usually wear a uniform and often need to work shifts, which includes working nights, weekends and bank holidays.

You may assist with hospital security which could involve working on reception.

Future prospects

Most jobs are within NHS hospitals, although there are also posts within private hospitals.

There are opportunities throughout the country but they can be competitive in some areas.

With experience you could become a supervisor and then take management qualifications for promotion to head porter or porter manager.

You could also do further training to move into related careers, such as healthcare assistant or ambulance work.

Advantages/disadvantages

The work can be physically demanding and stressful at times.

You will meet a variety of people and the job is active and busy.

It is satisfying to play a vital role within a hospital; without porters a hospital would not be able to function.

Money guide

The NHS sets national pay rates for hospital porters.

Earnings start at around £13,600 per year.

With experience this can rise to around £16,700. Team leaders or senior porters can earn up to £18,500.

Extra payments are available for working additional hours.

Salaries in private hospitals are similar to that of the NHS.

Related opportunities

- Hotel Porter p141
- Paramedic p324
- Sterile Services Technician p340

Further information

NHS Careers
www.nhscareers.nhs.uk

Skills for Health
www.skillsforhealth.org.uk

HEALTHCARE

CRCI: JI

Qualifications and courses

All learning disabilities nurses must hold a degree in nursing which has been approved by the Nursing and Midwifery Council (NMC). Minimum entry requirements for degree courses are usually 5 GCSEs/S grades (A*–C/1–3) including English, maths and a science subject and 2–3 A levels/H grades, ideally including a science-based subject. All applicants must obtain clearance from the Criminal Records Bureau (CRB) before commencing their training.

If you do not have the required GCSEs/A levels or S/H grades, some universities will accept other qualifications, such as a BTEC National Diploma in Health and Social Care (Health Sciences) or an Access to Higher Education Diploma in a science or health-related subject.

Graduates with a degree in a health-related subject such as human biology, life and medical sciences or biomedical science, may be eligible to enter the nursing profession by taking an accelerated 2-year programme which leads to an MSc or postgraduate diploma.

For this branch of nursing, you will usually be required to have relevant experience working with people with learning disabilities. Opportunities to volunteer may be available through the Charity Choice website.

What the work involves

Learning disabilities nurses work with people with learning disabilities in order to teach them new skills and support them in becoming as independent as possible.

You will be assessing patients and devising suitable care plans for them, as well as supporting their families or carers by helping them implement development strategies and arranging for them to take a break from their responsibilities when necessary.

You will work in a range of locations, including patients' homes, care homes and schools.

Type of person suited to this work

You will need excellent communication skills in order to develop a good relationship with patients and colleagues alike. To successfully help people to learn new skills, you must be a patient teacher.

You should be compassionate and empathetic in understanding your patients' feelings and frustrations, whilst maintaining a professional attitude so that you can distance yourself from your work at the end of the day.

You will need both physical and mental stamina to support your patients fully.

Working conditions

You will usually work 37 hours a week including evening, night and weekend work. Part-time work and flexible hours are frequently available.

As you will be working in the community, you will spend time travelling to and from patients' homes, schools, clinics and residential homes. A driving licence would be useful.

You may also accompany and support clients as they undertake everyday tasks such as going to the shops or the gym, booking a holiday, travelling on public transport or even going to work.

Future prospects

Most learning disabilities nurses are employed by the NHS, although there are also opportunities in the private sector and with local authority healthcare teams.

You may undertake further training that could allow you to specialise in an area that particularly interests you, such as education or cognitive disability.

You could go on to become a team leader, supervisor, or even a nurse consultant. Alternatively, you could move into research or teaching.

Advantages/disadvantages

You will be providing a life enhancing service for a number of people in your local community.

There are good opportunities for career development or diversification, as well as the option of flexible working hours to suit your lifestyle and family commitments.

You may encounter difficult or abusive patients which can be distressing and unpleasant.

Money guide

A newly qualified nurse can expect a starting salary of £21,200.

As you gain experience, your earnings can increase to about £28,000.

Those who take on a senior position with additional responsibilities can achieve £30,000–£40,000.

If you specialise in a particular area and undertake the training to become a nurse consultant, you could earn up to £56,000.

Related opportunities

- Adult Nurse p289
- Children's Nurse p294
- Health Visitor p309

Further information

NHS Careers
www.nhscareers.nhs.uk

Nursing and Midwifery Council
www.nmc-uk.org

Qualifications and courses

There are no set requirements to enter this profession, but many professional bodies recommend you take an in-depth course of at least 6 months full time or 12 months part time. You should have at least 5 GCSEs/S grades to enrol on a course.

The course you choose will need to be recognised by the General Council for Massage Therapy, and include beauty therapy, Swedish massage, holistic massage, and anatomy and physiology. Awarding bodies include the International Therapy Examination Council (ITEC) and Vocational Training Charitable Trust (VTCT). Once you start training, you will cover not only massage itself, but also first aid, health and safety, employment law, and assessing clients.

You could begin on the path to massage by following an apprenticeship in beauty therapy. If you already have experience of work in health and beauty, you can enter this field as a second career; many people choose to do this.

Once you are fully qualified you can choose to become a member of a professional body and register with the General Council for Massage Therapy. This will keep you up to date with developments in the field, and you may receive additional training. You can also expand your repertoire by studying related areas of massage such as sports therapy.

What the work involves

A massage therapist uses massage as a therapy to relieve clients of pain or stress. Some practitioners specialise in specific areas of the body, whilst others work on the entire body. Many practitioners are self-employed and either work from home or run their own salons.

As a massage therapist, you are trained in techniques and movements that have proven therapeutic effects and aid the healing process.

Type of person suited to this work

You will need to be good with people and have a reassuring friendly manner.

You will need to be able to explain what you are doing clearly, and have to be able to respond to your client effectively and calmly. You should be very comfortable with close physical contact, and have good manual dexterity.

You should have excellent concentration skills, as the work demands great physical and mental energy. You will also need good organisational skills, as you may well end up running your own business. This will also require confidence and good business acumen.

Working conditions

If you work in a beauty clinic, you will usually do a 40 hour week, whilst self-employed massage therapists can opt for fewer hours. Either way, you will have to work around your clients' lifestyles, which means working evenings and weekends.

You could work in hospitals, beauty salons, health spas, care homes, leisure centres, and clients' homes. You could also work from home, or even set up your own clinic.

Treatment rooms should be (and usually are) clean, warm and peaceful. You may often play calming music or use aromatherapy oils to add to the experience.

Future prospects

Once you have gained some experience, you can think about setting up your own practice, provided you have the business sense to do so.

You might also decide that you would like to learn about a similar profession such as reflexology or aromatherapy so that you can offer your clients a wider range of services.

You could even teach massage, if you are prepared to study for a teaching qualification.

Advantages/disadvantages

If you like working with and helping people you should really enjoy this work.

It is a good opportunity to use your skills, and you can really see the results.

The work can be tiring, and you need to be physically fit to do a good job and enjoy it properly.

Money guide

Starting out you could earn between £12,000 and £18,000 a year.

This can increase to around £30,000 once you are more established and have a large client base.

If you work your way up to specialist and work in a private practice, you could earn over £40,000 a year.

Related opportunities

- Acupuncturist p288
- Aromatherapist p291
- Physiotherapist p330

Further information

CIBTAC
www.cibtac.com

Complementary and Natural Healthcare Council
www.cnhc.org.uk

General Council for Massage Therapy
www.gcmt.org.uk

ITEC
www.itecworld.co.uk

HEALTHCARE

CRCI: JA

MEDICAL PHYSICIST

Qualifications and courses

Candidates will need a 1st or 2.1 degree in subjects such as physics, medical physics or electrical engineering. Entry to a relevant degree course requires at least 3 A levels/H grades, usually including physics and maths, plus 5 GCSEs/S grades (A*–C/1–3), including English and maths. An MSc, PhD or industrial experience may also be useful to enter this career.

Candidates go into the profession as trainees. The NHS Scientific Training Programme (STP) has replaced the previous NHS Clinical Scientist Training Scheme. The new training programme lasts 3 years, and includes study for an MSc in medical physics. If you already have an MSc qualification, you need only to complete a 15 month training period based in a hospital.

Advanced trainee medical physicists undertake 2 years of training in a specialist field. On completion, candidates are eligible for registration with the Health Professions Council to work in the NHS and apply for Membership of the Institute of Physics and Engineering in Medicine.

What the work involves

Medical physicists use their expert knowledge of physics to diagnose, prevent and treat disease.

You will be using specialist equipment and techniques to investigate patients' illnesses, this includes X-rays, radiography, ultrasounds, MRI machines, radiotherapy, and laser therapy.

You may be designing, developing and maintaining equipment, and advising medical staff on its use or planning the correct treatment for a patient using specific equipment. Your role may also involve patient contact, explaining procedures and results.

Type of person suited to this work

Medical physicists need to have expert skills in physical sciences and the ability to use their skills to solve problems and improve the diagnosis and treatment of disease.

You should have excellent research skills, be able to work accurately and be willing to take responsibility for decisions which will have a direct effect on patients.

You will need good communication skills to explain complex procedures clearly to patients, and to work as part of a team. You must also be prepared to keep up with the latest developments and continue to learn new skills.

Working conditions

Most medical physicists work in hospitals and laboratories and some have contact with patients on wards or in clinics.

You will need to work safely with equipment and chemicals in the laboratory, some of which can be hazardous.

You will normally work from Monday to Friday, but work outside normal hours and travel to conferences will sometimes be necessary.

Future prospects

The number of medical physicists is increasing, although trainee posts are competitive and you might have to relocate for some specialist roles.

Most jobs are in the larger NHS hospitals throughout the UK. There are also some opportunities in the medical equipment industry, private hospitals and medical research institutes.

Within the NHS there is a recognised career path and you could even reach consultant level. Employment in the private sector is less structured.

There are plenty of opportunities for Continuing Professional Development (CPD) which will improve your career prospects. IPEM also offers formal development courses in skills such as management, and once these have been completed you will have the opportunity to become a Chartered Scientist (CSci).

Advantages/disadvantages

Some of the work could be routine at times.

You will be playing an important role in the overall healthcare of the patients, as you will be contributing to the diagnosis and treatment of their diseases.

Money guide

As a trainee you could expect a starting salary of between £27,000 and £34,000 per year rising to around £40,000 after several years' experience and training.

Senior posts can have a salary of around £50,000 and even in excess of £80,000.

Related opportunities

- Physicist p531
- Radiographer p336
- Radiologist p337

Further information

Institute of Physics and Engineering in Medicine
www.ipem.ac.uk

NHS Careers
www.nhscareers.nhs.uk

Skills for Health
www.skillsforhealth.org.uk

MENTAL HEALTH NURSE

Qualifications and courses

All nurses must hold a degree in mental health nursing which has been approved by the Nursing and Midwifery Council (NMC). Minimum entry requirements for degree courses are usually 5 GCSEs/S grades (A*–C/1–3) including English, maths and a science subject and 2–3 A levels/H grades, ideally including a science-based subject. All applicants must obtain clearance from the Criminal Records Bureau (CRB) before commencing their training.

If you do not have the required GCSEs/A levels or S/H levels, some universities will accept other qualifications, such as a BTEC National Diploma in Health and Social Care (Health Sciences) or an Access to Higher Education Diploma in a science or health-related subject.

Graduates with a degree in a health-related subject such as human biology, life and medical sciences or biomedical science, may be eligible to enter the nursing profession by taking an accelerated 2-year programme which leads to an MSc or postgraduate diploma.

For this branch of nursing, it would be useful to have relevant experience working with people who use mental health services.

What the work involves

Mental health nurses care for people with mental health problems both in hospitals and within the wider community. They help patients come to terms with their problems and overcome their limitations by listening to them as they discuss their illness and anxieties.

You will also work with a patient's friends and family where possible to create a stable and proactive network around the individual and also to provide support to those closest to him/her.

You could encounter patients with problems including stress-related conditions, eating disorders, drug and alcohol dependency, and personality disorders.

Type of person suited to this work

You will need excellent communication skills in order to develop a good relationship with patients, their families and other healthcare professionals.

You must be extremely observant so that you can spot any minor changes in a patient's condition and manage them before they trigger undesirable results.

You should be non-judgemental and empathetic in order to understand your patients' feelings and frustrations. In a difficult situation, you must be able to remain calm and assertive.

Working conditions

You will usually work 37 hours a week, including evenings and weekends.

You could work in a hospital, in the community, or undertake a mixture of both.

If you work across the community, you will travel to a variety of places including patients' homes, hostels, day centres and drug dependency units. A driving licence may be required.

Future prospects

Most mental health nurses are employed by the NHS, although there are also opportunities in the private sector and in local social services teams.

You may undertake further training to specialise in an area that particularly interests you, such as drug abuse.

You could go on to become a team leader, supervisor or nurse consultant, or you may progress to a general management position within the NHS. Alternatively, you could move into research or teaching.

Advantages/disadvantages

Providing a life enhancing service for a number of people in your local community is highly rewarding.

After gaining a few years' experience, you should have the option of flexible working hours that will suit your lifestyle and personal commitments.

You may encounter difficult or abusive patients which can be distressing and unpleasant.

Money guide

A newly qualified nurse can expect a starting salary of £21,200.

As you gain experience, your earnings can increase up to about £28,000.

Those who take on a senior position with additional responsibilities can achieve £30,000–£40,000.

If you specialise in a particular area and undertake the training to become a nurse consultant, you could earn up to £56,000.

Related opportunities

- Health Visitor p309
- Learning Disabilities Nurse p314
- Occupational Therapist p319

Further information

NHS Careers
www.nhscareers.nhs.uk

Royal College of Nursing
www.rcn.org.uk

HEALTHCARE

CRCI: JI

317

MIDWIFE

Qualifications and courses

All midwives must hold a degree in midwifery which has been approved by the Nursing and Midwifery Council (NMC). Entry requirements for degree courses depend upon the individual university but you will usually need 5 GCSEs/S grades (A*–C/1–3) including English, maths and a science subject and 2–3 A levels/H grades, ideally including a science-based subject. All applicants must obtain clearance from the Criminal Records Bureau (CRB) before commencing their training. A degree in midwifery lasts 3 years when studied on a full-time basis.

If you do not have the required GCSEs/A levels, some universities will accept other qualifications, such as a BTEC National Diploma in Health and Social Care (Health Sciences) or an Access to Higher Education Diploma in a science or health-related subject.

Those who have already qualified as an adult nurse and are currently registered with the NMC have the option of taking a shorter 18-month course to become a midwife.

You are eligible to register as a midwife with the NMC once you have completed an approved midwifery degree. Midwives are expected to engage in continuing professional development (CPD) throughout their career to keep their skills and knowledge up to date.

What the work involves

Midwives help and support women and their partners from early pregnancy, through the antenatal period, during the labour and birth, and also for up to a month after the baby has been born.

You will be responsible for monitoring your patient throughout her pregnancy, providing advice and support on issues including nutrition, methods of childbirth and breastfeeding.

You will deliver babies or assist in the birthing process. You will also be responsible for identifying high risk pregnancies and arranging specialist care and provisions where necessary.

Type of person suited to this work

You must be an excellent communicator as it is essential to form a good relationship with patients, their partners and other healthcare professionals. You need to be friendly and caring in order to gain the trust and confidence of the women under your guidance.

As childbirth is strenuous, messy and unpredictable, you should be able to stay calm under pressure, think on your feet and have good mental and physical stamina.

You need careful attention to detail when carrying out your work and completing patient notes.

Working conditions

You will usually work 37 hours a week and these will include evening, night and weekend work. You may also be on-call at times. Part-time work and flexible hours are frequently available.

You could be based in the maternity unit of a hospital or in a birth centre. Midwives are also increasingly affiliated with GP surgeries and other health centres.

You will probably spend time travelling from your place of work to your patients' homes so a driving licence would be helpful.

Future prospects

Midwives can progress to a senior level as a team leader or midwife consultant. You could take further training which would allow you to specialise in an area that particularly interests you, or to move into a related profession such as neonatal nursing.

Other opportunities include undertaking research, or training and teaching student midwives.

Advantages/disadvantages

Supporting women and families through pregnancy and childbirth is both rewarding and fulfilling.

This job can be distressing as you will have to deal with complications in pregnancy and labour.

Money guide

The starting salary for a newly qualified midwife is between £21,176 and £27,625.

As you gain experience, you can expect earnings of £25,528–£34,189.

Those in a senior position, such as a midwife team manager, typically earn £30,460 to £40,157.

If you specialise or become a midwife consultant, you could earn up to £67,000.

Salaries are usually higher in London.

Allowances for on-call duties can increase earnings.

Related opportunities

- Adult Nurse p289
- Children's Nurse p294
- Occupational Therapist p319

Further information

Nursing and Midwifery Council
www.nmc-uk.org

Royal College of Midwives
www.rcm.org.uk

OCCUPATIONAL THERAPIST

Qualifications and courses

To become an occupational therapist, you need a degree or postgraduate diploma in occupational therapy approved by the Health Professions Council (HPC). You must also be registered with the HPC in order to practise in the NHS.

For degree entry, you will normally need at least 2 A levels/3 H grades including a science, preferably biology, human biology or psychology and 5 GCSEs/S grades (A*–C/1–3), or equivalent. The Advanced Diploma in Society, Health and Development may also be relevant.

A degree in occupational therapy normally takes 3 years. An accelerated 2-year diploma programme is available for graduates in other subjects who have experience in health or social care.

In-service courses are available for those employed as occupational therapy support workers or technical instructors. Courses are studied part time and lead to professional qualification as an occupational therapist.

Before you can register with the HPC, you must undergo a Criminal Records Bureau (CRB) background check.

What the work involves

Occupational therapists help people overcome physical, psychological or social problems arising from illness or disability.

You could see patients with problems stemming from conditions such as multiple sclerosis or Parkinson's, those with physical and mental disabilities or issues, and those who are affected by drug and alcohol use.

You will help patients with everyday tasks such as washing, cooking and even going to work. Your care will focus on what patients can achieve, rather than on their disabilities. Your job will also include writing treatment plans, giving advice on practical issues such as disability equipment, teaching coping strategies and using activities to stimulate your patients.

Type of person suited to this work

You must have excellent interpersonal skills as you will need to inspire trust and confidence in patients with a range of problems, including some who are difficult, anxious or unpredictable. You will need to be patient, caring, and sensitive to your patients' needs, concerns and expectations.

You should have both mental and physical stamina as you will need to provide hands-on support to patients as well as coping with their emotional issues.

You should be a natural problem-solver with a flexible and creative approach to your work. The ability to motivate your patients and other professionals is also essential.

Working conditions

Most occupational therapists work a normal working week from Monday to Friday, although you might have to work evenings and weekends to provide a 24 hour community service.

You could work in a variety of locations, such as hospitals, a patient's home, residential homes, prisons and workplaces, so a driving licence would be useful.

Future prospects

Demand for occupational therapists is high, but you may still find that there is competition for jobs in certain areas.

You could be employed by the NHS, private hospitals, local authorities, charities or voluntary agencies. There are also opportunities to work abroad.

With experience, you could move into a more clinical position or take up a research post. Alternatively you could progress to a managerial role within the NHS, or opt to teach within your field.

Advantages/disadvantages

It is very rewarding to be able to help people to overcome difficulties and achieve their goals.

You could specialise in a variety of areas such as rehabilitation, learning disabilities or paediatrics.

The work can be emotionally and mentally demanding.

Money guide

Starting salaries for newly qualified occupational therapists are around £20,000 to £27,000.

As a specialist this can rise to around £34,000 increasing to around £39,000 with further experience.

In a more senior role that includes supervisory and managerial responsibilities or consultancy your earnings could rise to £37,000–£50,000.

Related opportunities

- Health Visitor p309
- Learning Disabilities Nurse p314
- Mental Health Nurse p317

Further information

British Association of Occupational Therapists and College of Occupational Therapists
www.cot.org.uk

NHS Careers
www.nhscareers.nhs.uk

OPERATING DEPARTMENT PRACTITIONER

Qualifications and courses

Entry into this work requires a Diploma of Higher Education (DipHE) in Operating Department Practice approved by the Health Professions Council (HPC). Courses are available throughout the UK and generally last 2 or 3 years. The normal minimum entry requirements are 5 GCSEs/S grades (A*–C/1–3) preferably in English, maths and/or a science based subject or equivalent, but some institutions might require AS levels or A levels/H grades.

It is also necessary to undergo a medical test, an occupational health screening and a Criminal Records Bureau (CRB) check.

The minimum age for entry is 18, and mature entry is common. Access courses may be taken prior to diploma programmes.

Entrants often have experience of other types of hospital work, for example as a healthcare assistant, and apply to become operating department practitioners later.

What the work involves

Operating department practitioners work alongside surgeons, anaesthetists and other staff before, during and after operations.

Before surgery you will help calm a patient's anxiety, plan treatment, sterilise equipment and bring the patient to the operating theatre. During surgery you will monitor effects of the anaesthetic, pass tools to surgeons, take care of surgical wounds and dispose of soiled dressings.

After surgery you will bring patients to the recovery unit, monitor their wellbeing, provide pain relief and evaluate care.

It will be your responsibility to anticipate the needs of your colleagues and respond effectively.

Type of person suited to this work

You will need the scientific knowledge and practical skills to prepare specialist equipment and drugs. You will be helping with operations so you cannot be squeamish.

You must pay close attention when monitoring patients because their lives depend on it. You need to be able to react quickly and accurately if the patient experiences any complications.

Excellent communication skills are essential and you will need to be caring and sensitive.

Working conditions

You will mainly work in operating theatres, anaesthetic areas and recovery rooms in hospitals. However, operating department practioners are increasingly being recognised for their skills in other critical areas.

You will need to follow hygiene procedures closely, wear a sterile gown and gloves during operations and be able to stand for long periods.

You will usually work shifts which may include working at nights, at weekends and on bank holidays. You might also have stand-by or on-call duties.

Future prospects

There is a shortage of trained operating department practitioners, so job prospects are excellent.

Most employment is available with the NHS throughout the UK. There are also opportunities in private hospitals.

You could progress into higher grade posts which involve more responsibility for managing and training others. It is possible to become a senior operating department practioner or run your own theatre.

There are also opportunities to enter research or teaching.

Advantages/disadvantages

The work can be stressful at times and you will see some unpleasant things.

It is rewarding to be part of a team improving people's health and saving lives.

You could work in a range of areas, such as resuscitation, intensive care or day surgery.

Money guide

Starting salaries for qualified staff in the NHS are between £18,402 and £21,798 per year.

With experience you can earn up to £25,528.

It is possible for a higher-level theatre practitioner to earn up to £34,189.

Related opportunities

- Critical Care Technologist p297
- Paramedic p324
- Sterile Services Technician p340

Further information

College of Operating Department Practitioners
www.codp.org.uk

NHS Careers
www.nhscareers.nhs.uk

Skills for Health
www.skillsforhealth.org.uk

discover
risk
.co.uk

Do you have an

ENQUIRING mind?

Have you got an enquiring mind?

Do you ask more questions than you can answer?

Want to know more?

Considering a career in flooring?

A job within the flooring industry is a trade to be proud of and often very lucrative. Whether it be fitting floors in residential or commercial environments, the opportunities for individuals with good practical skills and an eye for detail are endless.

Whilst school leavers should, wherever possible, gain their skills from formal programmes like apprenticeships, they can also choose to supplement this through organisations such as FITA, the Flooring Industry Training Association, www.fita.co.uk, who offer practical training courses to suit all levels of experience, from real beginners just getting started in the industry to upskilling courses aimed towards the more seasoned professional.

The Contract Flooring Association (CFA) and the National Institute of Carpet and Floorlayers (NICF) offer guidance on all aspects of floor fitting to companies and individuals. For more information on the world of flooring from the leading trade associations representing the commercial and domestic markets visit their websites at www.cfa.org.uk and www.nicfltd.org.uk.

Whatever path you choose, from laying that perfect floor to estimating, planning and even self employment, with experience and skills the future is bright in flooring!

For further information or advice contact:

The Contract Flooring Association (CFA)
Telephone 0115 941 1126

The Flooring Industry Training Association (FITA)
Telephone: 0115 950 6836

The National Institute of Carpet & Floorlayers (NICF)
Telephone: 0115 958 3077

CONTRACT FLOORING ASSOCIATION

cfa

fita
THE FLOORING INDUSTRY
TRAINING ASSOCIATION

n i c f
national institute of carpet & floorlayer

Tomorrow

Today

ee where a Rolls-Royce apprenticeship could take you.

a Rolls-Royce apprentice you'll carry out mission-critical work, rning while you learn from the engineers and scientists behind e world's most important power systems. Like our revolutionary

LiftFan technology and a swivelling jet pipe, which together allow the F-35B fighter to land vertically. Join the team that sets the standard.

Trusted to deliver excellence

Rolls-Royce

Creative and enjoy meeting people?

Like science and mad about animals?

Passionate about trees and the environment?

Want to create beautiful green spaces?

Enjoy the outdoors and interested in plants?

Capel Manor College
Living learning in London

Capel Manor College is the largest land-based college in London, offering courses and apprenticeships for those interested in the environment, animals or working with plants, trees and flowers.

Our training leads to nationally recognised qualifications and our students regularly win awards. Many study at level 3 (equivalent to 3 or 4 AS/A levels) leading to higher education and go on to set up their own businesses or have fulfilling careers in the green sector.

Subjects include **gardening, landscape construction, animal care, balloon artistry, floristry, flower arranging, garden design, arboriculture (the study of trees), countryside and environment studies,** and **saddlery.**

With five centres in central, north, south, west and east London, we are within reach of anyone with a passion for the great outdoors.

Ofsted lists our strengths as:

- Excellent standards of work in horticulture and landscaping, garden design and floristry.
- Highly qualified and vocationally experienced teachers.
- Excellent specialist teaching resources.

For further details visit **www.capel.ac.uk**, ring **08456 122122** or email **enquiries@capel.ac.uk**

Enfield: Bullsmoor Lane, Enfield EN1 4RQ

Apprenticeships

Landex
Land Based Colleges
Aspiring To Excellence

Combining qualifications with experience

LSIS
BEACON

OPTOMETRIST

Qualifications and courses

The only route into optometry is through professional qualifications and registration with the General Optical Council (GOC).

Degrees accredited by the GOC are offered at 8 universities. Entry requirements may vary according to the institution. Candidates are normally expected to have 5 GCSEs/S grades (A*–C/1–3), including English, maths and physics or double award science, and 3 A levels/H grades including at least 2 from biology, maths, physics and chemistry, or equivalent. You will need to gain at least a 2.2 Honours degree.

After graduation, new entrants must follow a pre-registration year of supervised clinical experience. You will need to achieve the GOC's Stage 1 competencies to progress to this supervised year. If you have not fully achieved these competencies you can complete the GOC's optometry progression scheme. Before qualification you must achieve the GOC's Stage 2 competencies. After qualification, trainees are eligible to register with the GOC and as a Member of the College of Optometrists.

There are many advanced courses that allow qualified optometrists to specialise in other areas. Courses can include paediatric vision, vision therapy and sports vision.

What the work involves

Optometrists examine the eyes of their patients for disease or abnormalities and carry out vision tests.

Your work will include shining a light on the retina, and using reading charts and other instruments to diagnose the needs of the patient.

You will determine prescriptions and may also supply and fit glasses or contact lenses. You will look out for signs of diabetes and eye diseases and refer patients to surgeons when needed.

Type of person suited to this work

Examining eyes and diagnosing problems requires a high level of scientific knowledge and a high attention to detail. Fitting contact lenses and handling instruments requires good technical skills.

You need to have excellent communication and listening skills to deal with patients of all ages and backgrounds. You will need to put patients at ease and explain procedures simply and clearly to them.

You should have good interpersonal skill as you will have to work as part of a team with other professionals.

Working conditions

Optometrists work in high-street opticians and hospitals, in examination rooms which usually have no natural light and often have to be quite dark.

You will undertake 10 to 20 half-an-hour eye examinations per day.

You will probably have a normal working week from Monday to Friday, but may need to work on Saturdays as well.

Future prospects

Job prospects are good but vary throughout the UK.

You may work for a chain of opticians, an independent practice or a hospital. You could also do related work with lens manufacturers.

With experience you may specialise, for example, in children's vision, low vision or contact lenses. You could choose to run your own practice. There are also opportunities to move into research and university teaching.

Advantages/disadvantages

The work can be routine and repetitive at times.

If you enjoy combining scientific knowledge with working with the public, this job could be good for you.

Working closely with patients can be demanding.

Money guide

Trainees during their one year pre-registration period may earn between £17,000 and £21,000 per year. This can be more if working for a private practice.

Qualified and experienced optometrists may earn around £25,000 to £44,000.

Consultants can earn up to £75,000 in NHS hospitals and more in the private sector.

Related opportunities

- Dentist p302
- Dispensing Optician p304
- Hospital Doctor p312

Further information

College of Optometrists
www.college-optometrists.org

General Optical Council
www.optical.org

HEALTHCARE

CRCI: JI

ORTHODONTIST

Qualifications and courses

All orthodontists must first qualify as a dentist. The standard degree programme lasts 5 years and you will need at least 3 good A levels/H Grades or equivalent qualifications, including chemistry and biology. GCSE/S grade results may also be taken into account, and at least 8 passes (A*–C/1–3) are required for consideration.

If you have good A level/H Grade results, but not in the required subjects for entrance onto the degree course, you can apply for a 6-year programme that includes an initial 30-week course that will get you up to speed.

Once you have qualified as a dentist, you will need to gain 2 years of clinical experience before applying for a place on an orthodontic course. Orthodontic training combines academic study with hands-on training in a hospital, and lasts 3 years full time. You will then sit the Membership in Orthodontics (MOrth) exam to qualify as an orthodontist.

If you are looking to progress to become a hospital consultant, you will need to undertake a further 2 years training and pass the Intercollegiate Specialty Fellowship Examination.

What the work involves

Orthodontists are concerned with the growth of teeth and jaws, specifically correcting irregularities or abnormalities in either area.

You will be responsible for rectifying cosmetic and physical problems in your patients, resulting in a considerable improvement in their quality of life.

The most common procedures that you will carry out involve fitting and maintaining fixed or removable braces, and extraction of teeth. You may occasionally have to carry out jaw surgery. You will also need to examine the mouths and teeth or your patients, take X-rays and impressions, and keep detailed medical records of their treatment.

Type of person suited to this work

You will need to have excellent communication skills in order to gain the trust of your patients and build good relationships with them.

You will be working with and possibly managing other professionals, so you should also enjoy working in a team environment and motivating those around you.

Good eyesight and manual dexterity are essential for undertaking fiddly tasks such as fitting and tightening braces or performing jaw surgery. The ability to maintain your concentration during occasionally lengthy procedures is also important.

Working conditions

If you work in private practice you can generally expect to do normal office hours, although some orthodontists choose to work evenings and weekends to suit their patients' lifestyles.

Those working in hospitals must be more flexible, occasionally undertaking emergency shifts and being on-call.

You will need to wear protective clothing, along with surgical gloves and a mask when working on patients in order to maintain high levels of hygiene and safety.

Future prospects

There is a constant demand for orthodontists in both the private and public sector, so career prospects are good.

Jobs can be found across the UK in both large cities and smaller towns. You could work in the NHS or as a self-employed professional.

There are opportunities to specialise in certain areas of orthodontics, such as adult cosmetic dentistry or children's corrective orthodontics.

Advantages/disadvantages

The majority of orthodontists are self-employed and work in the private sector, which gives you greater control over your working hours and salary.

You will be correcting physically obvious imperfections in your patient's teeth and jawline, and seeing the subsequent improvements in their health and happiness will be rewarding.

A lot of your patients are likely to be children, who may well be anxious and frightened of many procedures which can be upsetting.

Money guide

Generally, salaries start at around £28,000 to £30,000.

Working in a specialist private practice, you could earn anything from £40,000 to £90,000.

If you run your own practice you could earn in excess of £150,000.

Related opportunities

- Dental Hygienist p298
- Dentist p302
- Surgeon p341

Further information

British Dental Association
www.bda.org

British Orthodontics Society
www.bos.org.uk

NHS Careers
www.nhscareers.nhs.uk

Qualifications and courses

All osteopaths must be registered with the General Osteopathic Council (GOsC) before they are legally allowed to practise. In order to register, you must hold a recognised qualification in osteopathy.

Most recognised courses are at Honours or master's level. Each takes 4 years when studied full time, and 5 on a part-time basis. For entry onto these courses, most of the universities require at least 5 GCSEs/S grades (A*–C/1–3) or equivalent and a minimum of 2 A levels/Highers, with chemistry or biology preferred. If you do not have a science degree or appropriate A levels, you may still be considered but will have to take an intensive science course before beginning to train.

Many people train in osteopathy as a second career. If you have relevant experience in healthcare or hold medical-related qualifications prior to commencing your degree, you may be exempt from parts of the course. Short courses are available for fully qualified healthcare professionals.

What the work involves

Osteopaths work on the musculo-skeletal system of patients, rectifying problems with all areas of the body including the circulatory, gastro-intestinal and nervous systems.

You will focus on understanding the problem of each patient by talking to them, observing their movements and carrying out physical examinations.

You will then rectify the problem using a series of manipulative techniques on the muscles and bones of your patient, such as stretching the muscles, mobilising the joints and realigning bones.

Type of person suited to this work

You will need a highly developed sense of touch and strong observational skills in order to identify points of slight weakness or pain in your patients. Logic and problem-solving abilities will also help you diagnose correctly and treat the problem creatively where necessary.

Excellent communication skills are also essential to develop a good relationship with patients and in order to explain their treatment to them.

The work can be very physical, so you should also have a good level of fitness.

Working conditions

You could practise in a variety of locations including leisure centres, therapy centres, private clinics, hospitals and even your own home. You will probably have a treatment room in which to see patients.

Most professionals offer evening and weekend appointments as well as those during the day, as these tend to be more convenient for patients.

Future prospects

As awareness of osteopathy grows, there is increasing demand for qualified and registered professionals, so career opportunities are correspondingly positive.

Most osteopaths are self-employed, and usually start out by working as an associate in a practice to establish a reputation and solid client base. After a few years, many then go on to set up their own practice.

You could also choose to specialise in an area of particular interest to you, such as treating sports injuries or problems resulting from childbirth.

Advantages/disadvantages

You will be providing a highly effective, natural alternative to drugs and surgery for your patients.

You will work with a variety of people and encounter a wide range of new complaints and challenges on a daily basis.

If you are self-employed this can be stressful as your income is not predictable and you have to handle all your own marketing, accounts and expenses.

Money guide

As the majority of osteopaths are self-employed and work varying hours, it is difficult to predict an exact level of earnings at any stage. Generally, most charge between £25 and £50 for a 30–45 minute session.

Newly qualified osteopaths in a practice can expect to earn £15,000–£20,000 in their first couple of years. With experience, you could see this increase to around £40,000.

If you run your own practice or work in a well-established one, your salary could rise to £50,000 per year.

Related opportunities

- Acupuncturist p288
- Chiropractor p295
- Physiotherapist p330

Further information

British Osteopathic Association
www.osteopathy.org

British School of Osteopathy
www.bso.ac.uk

General Osteopathic Council
www.osteopathy.org.uk

HEALTHCARE

CRCI: JB

Qualifications and courses

There are two approved routes you can follow. You could apply to an ambulance service trust for a role as a student paramedic, and they will put you through an approved course. Training takes between 2 and 5 years to complete. You will need at least 5 GCSEs/S grades (A*–C/1–3) or equivalent including English and maths.

Alternatively you could apply for an approved degree in paramedic science which can take from 2 to 4 years. Entry requirements are usually at least 2 A levels/H grades or equivalent and 5 GCSEs/S grades (A*–C/1–3) including English and maths or a science subject.

A full clean driving licence, that allows you to drive larger vehicles and carry passengers, will be required. You will need to pass a Criminal Records Bureau check, fitness test, and medical assessment.

If you are working in the NHS you will need to be registered with the Health Professions Council (HPC).

What the work involves

Paramedics provide a rapid response to 999 calls reporting medical emergencies.

You will usually be the first healthcare professional to reach a patient and as such must assess their condition and administer immediate treatment.

You will need to stabilise patients using a variety of methods and equipment, including life support techniques, oxygen, drugs and occasionally performing minor operations such as tracheotomies. You will also have to make notes of all the treatments administered so you can brief hospital staff.

Type of person suited to this work

You must have good communication skills and a caring disposition to successfully soothe and comfort patients. You should be mature, responsible and non-judgemental so that you can relate to people from a wide range of ages, backgrounds and cultures.

You must be able to keep calm in a crisis, as you will be making life and death decisions on a fairly regular basis.

A good level of physical fitness is required for lifting and carrying both patients and equipment. Mental stamina is also essential for coping with occasionally horrific and frightening circumstances.

Working conditions

You will work 37.5 hours a week on rotational shifts. This means you will work nights, weekends and on public holidays regularly. Part-time work is commonly available.

You will either work for a local ambulance service or be based at a hospital, but you will travel to a range of locations in response to emergency calls. You should be prepared to undertake treatment of patients in unfamiliar and potentially dangerous situations.

Because you will be responsible for full or shared driving responsibilities of your vehicle, you need a full, clean driving licence.

Future prospects

Career prospects for paramedics are good. Once you have completed your training and gained 3–5 years' experience you could be promoted to a team leader.

Further promotion can take you into management posts within the ambulance service, although you will need to supplement your work experience with further relevant qualifications to achieve this level.

You could also move into related careers such as nursing or occupational therapy.

Advantages/disadvantages

Providing rapid response in emergency situations means that you really will be responsible for saving lives on a weekly basis.

You could find yourself confronted with very difficult patients; those who are frightened, angry or under the influence of drugs and alcohol may be violent and hostile to treatment.

You will have to work unsocial hours fairly regularly.

Money guide

Salaries for student paramedics vary depending on the ambulance trust you train with.

Once qualified, salaries range from £21,176 to £27,625.

As a team leader you could earn up to £34,000.

Related opportunities

- Adult Nurse p289
- Hospital Doctor p312
- Midwife p318
- Occupational Therapist p319

Further information

Ambulance Service Network
www.nhsconfed.org/networks/ambulanceservice

British Paramedic Association
www.britishparamedic.org

NHS Careers
www.nhscareers.nhs.uk

Qualifications and courses

Candidates must initially train as a hospital doctor by completing a medical degree which is approved by the General Medical Council (GMC). Entry requirements for medical school are very high A level/H grade results including relevant subjects such as science and maths. Competition for places on medical degrees is very high. Undertaking relevant pre-entry work experience will benefit your application.

After studying for a medical degree, graduates undertake the 2-year foundation programme of general training which acts as the bridge between medical school and specialist training. Candidates then progress to 5–6 years of specialty training in a particular area of pathology, such as histopathology or chemical pathology.

After successfully completing the specialty stage, trainees receive a Certificate of Completion of Training (CCT) and become eligible to join the GMC Specialist Register. It is then possible to apply for a post as a consultant.

Pathologists must engage in continuing professional development (CPD) throughout their career to ensure that their skills and knowledge are up to date. The Royal College of Pathologists provides information on available training.

What the work involves

Pathologists are doctors who have undergone further training to specialise in pathology.

As a pathologist you will detect and diagnose diseases, help to identify sources of disease and reduce the risk of them spreading further.

You will spend a lot of time in a laboratory but you will also work directly with patients.

You could work in one of many branches including haematology (studying diseases of the blood), histopathology (studying tissue samples removed for diagnosis, and determining cause of death by performing post-mortems and autopsies) and immunology (studying diseases and conditions of the immune system).

Type of person suited to this work

To be a pathologist you should be able to use your medical knowledge and training to diagnose patients' conditions. You must have problem-solving skills and pay close attention to detail when carrying out laboratory assessments.

You should be kind and caring in order to gain your patients' trust. Excellent communication skills are required to listen to patients carefully and explain their conditions and treatments in a clear, simple way.

Working conditions

You will normally work within a hospital as part of a medical team, working both in a laboratory and with patients.

You will need to work safely in the laboratory and wear protective clothing such as a lab coat and gloves.

There will be long hours and you are likely to work shifts and be on an on-call rota, which includes working at nights, weekends and on bank holidays.

Future prospects

Most pathologists work within the NHS throughout the UK. There are also opportunities in industry, working for private companies.

You could decide to specialise further in particular areas of the work such as forensic pathology or transfusion medicine. You could also move into academic work, carrying out research or teaching students.

There are also similar careers in pathology for clinical and biomedical scientists but they do not treat patients.

Advantages/disadvantages

The work can be emotionally demanding because it involves dealing with patients who have life-threatening conditions.

As your role is to find accurate and early diagnoses for patients, you will help to save their lives.

Money guide

Salary levels in the NHS may vary in different locations.

Earnings are often higher in private practice work.

Junior doctors have a starting salary of £22,000–£28,000 during the 2–year foundation programme.

When undertaking the specialty training, you can expect to earn between £28,000 and £46,000 a year.

Consultant pathologists can achieve salaries ranging from £74,000 up to £170,000 for those in the most senior positions.

Related opportunities

- Anaesthetist p290
- Psychiatrist p330
- Radiologist p337

Further information

NHS Careers
www.nhscareers.nhs.uk

Royal College of Pathologists
www.rcpath.org

Skills for Health
www.skillsforhealth.org.uk

HEALTHCARE

CRCI: JH

PHARMACIST

Qualifications and courses

All candidates who wish to become pharmacists need to study for a 4-year Master of Pharmacy (MPharm) degree. Throughout the UK there are 26 pharmacy schools offering degrees which have been accredited by the Royal Pharmaceutical Society (RPS).

Most universities require a minimum of 3 A levels/H grades or equivalent including chemistry and one from biology, maths or physics, and at least 5 GCSEs/S grades (A*–C/1–3) including English, maths and science.

It is not possible to start work as a pharmacist with an HND only but you could gain employment as a pharmacy technician. This would enable you to build up experience whilst you study for an MPharm degree.

Once students have completed their pharmacy degree, they need to apply for a 1-year pre-registration training course in a community or hospital pharmacy. This enables you to train on the job with experienced professionals. Candidates must then pass the General Pharmaceutical Council (GPhC)'s registration examination to become a fully qualified, registered pharmacist.

What the work involves

Pharmacists work in one of three areas: hospital, community or industry.

Hospital pharmacists are responsible for buying, manufacturing, dispensing and supplying medicines to in and out-patients. You will ensure that patients receive the most appropriate treatment in the correct dosage.

Community pharmacists work in high-street pharmacies both in large cities and small rural villages. You will supply medicines over the counter, prepare doctors' prescriptions and advise people on general health-related queries.

Industrial pharmacists work for pharmaceutical companies. You will be discovering, developing, manufacturing, testing and marketing new drugs.

Type of person suited to this work

You should be a strong communicator as you will be advising patients on medications and explaining how to administer them. You must be comfortable working in a team with other pharmacy staff or healthcare professionals.

You need in-depth medical knowledge and problem-solving skills in order to identify treatment solutions and prepare medications for patients. You should be committed to keeping your knowledge up to date. Accuracy and attention to detail are essential when selecting, preparing, measuring and labelling medicines.

Working conditions

Hours will depend on where you work. Community and industrial pharmacists will usually work 39 hours per week from Monday to Friday, although Saturday work is increasing in order to meet patients' requirements. Hospital pharmacists may need to work shifts in order to provide a 24-hour service. There are opportunities to work part time.

You could be working in a shop, hospital or laboratory and you may occasionally be required to travel to nursing homes and community health centres/clinics.

Future prospects

Opportunities to find work as a pharmacist are good as there is currently a shortage, particularly in hospitals.

You will have the option of working in a range of different environments including community shops and large hospitals.

As you gain experience, you could choose to combine your work with other responsibilities such as teaching. You could also go on to research or write about pharmaceutical matters.

Advantages/disadvantages

Your role will be varied and rewarding as you endeavour to help a diverse range of patients.

You may have to work unsocial hours which could disrupt your personal life.

Money guide

Pharmacists employed by the NHS during their pre-registration training have a starting salary of £21,176.

Once qualified, you can expect earnings ranging from £25,528 to £34,189.

Those employed in a senior or managerial role could achieve between £38,000 and £67,000.

Pharmacist consultants could earn up to £80,000 a year.

Those who are employed by smaller, independent pharmacies may receive lower salaries.

Related opportunities

- Biochemist p503
- Pharmacologist p327
- Pharmacy Technician p328

Further information

NHS Careers
www.nhscareers.nhs.uk

Royal Pharmaceutical Society
www.rpharms.com

PHARMACOLOGIST

Qualifications and courses

Owing to the scientific nature of this work, most entrants to pharmacology have a relevant degree in a subject such as pharmacology, biomedical sciences, biochemistry, molecular and cell biology, physiology or microbiology. Entry for a degree requires 3 A levels/H grades or equivalent including chemistry and biology, and at least 5 GCSEs/S grades (A*–C/1–3) or equivalent.

It is sometimes possible to enter this sector with a relevant HND but this is uncommon. You would have to start in a lower position and gain qualifications as you work if you wanted to progress to a pharmacologist role.

Competition for jobs within this industry is high so candidates may benefit from a postgraduate qualification such as an MSc in pharmacology or a relevant PhD. Qualifications at this level are likely to be essential for a research and development role or to gain employment with a major pharmaceutical company. Undertaking a PhD gives candidates essential lab experience which is viewed favourably by employers.

Pre-entry work experience within a pharmaceutical company is also desirable as it demonstrates your enthusiasm and commitment. A sandwich degree with a year-long placement would enable you to make industry contacts.

What the work involves

Pharmacologists study the effect of drugs on the body. Their work includes discovering, researching, developing and testing new drugs and medicines.

You will study the actions of drugs via computer simulations, in biological tests in cells and tissues, or in animals and human volunteers.

You could specialise in a number of areas including neuropharmacology or clinical pharmacology.

Type of person suited to this work

You should be a strong communicator with the ability to work within a team whilst also leading and motivating your colleagues in order to drive projects forward.

You will need excellent analytical skills as you will be gathering and interpreting complex information. Since the majority of equipment used to undertake experiments is computer-based, it is essential to have good IT skills.

To design and modify experiments, you will require problem-solving skills, creativity and flexibility. Patience and perseverance is essential as projects may involve many months of research and change.

Working conditions

You will normally work from 9am to 5pm during the week. Occasionally you may have to work evenings and weekends in order to monitor the more complex experiments.

You will work in a laboratory environment, usually within a university, government or commercial research centre, or a pharmaceutical company. The environment is generally clean and quiet, and you may be required to wear protective clothing when undertaking certain experiments.

Future prospects

Although the industry is competitive, once you have gained a position as a pharmacologist the opportunities for career progression are good.

You could work within a university, undertaking research and gaining a PhD, and then perhaps moving into a position as a lecturer.

Within commercial laboratories, experience will lead to increased responsibility and managerial opportunities.

Advantages/disadvantages

Gaining an entry level position in this competitive industry is difficult but once you have secured a job, prospects are excellent and career progression rapid.

You will have the satisfaction of knowing that the new drugs you develop will enhance the quality of life for thousands of people worldwide.

You will have to experiment on animals which may be upsetting and controversial.

Money guide

Starting salaries range from £21,000 for those with a first degree to £28,000 for those with a PhD.

As you gain experience, you can expect to earn £30,000–£40,000.

Pharmacologists employed in senior roles can achieve between £35,000 and £80,000.

Commercial pharmaceutical companies tend to offer higher salaries than academic institutions.

A PhD will increase your earning potential by approximately 25%.

Related opportunities

- Biochemist p503
- Pharmacist p326
- Toxicologist p534

Further information

British Pharmacology Society
www.bps.ac.uk

CRCI: JK   HEALTHCARE

Qualifications and courses

Most employers ask for 5 GCSEs/S grades (A*–C/1–3) or equivalent including English, maths and at least 1 science subject.

The Pharmacy Services Apprenticeship is available at Advanced Level for those who wish to become a pharmacy technician. The Apprenticeship typically lasts 2 years and involves training on the job with a practising pharmacist whilst studying for relevant qualifications.

Another route is to obtain a trainee post within either a community pharmacy or a hospital.

To register as a qualified pharmacy technician you must meet the requirements of the General Pharmaceutical Council (GPhC). Entrants must complete one of the GPhC-accredited competency-based qualifications, such as the NVQ in Pharmacy Services (Level 3), and one of the knowledge-based qualifications, such as the City & Guilds Certificate in Pharmacy Services (Level 3). Candidates must also complete 2 years of work experience with a qualified pharmacist before they are eligible for GPhC registration.

All pharmacy technicians are required by the GPhC to undertake continuing professional development (CPD) throughout their career to keep their knowledge up to date.

What the work involves

Pharmacy technicians work under the supervision of a qualified pharmacist, helping to prepare, supply and dispense medications, whilst also providing advice on how to take them.

You could work in a retail environment as a community pharmacy technician, within a hospital or in a commercial pharmaceutical lab. You will be responsible for monitoring stocks of medicines, checking expiry dates and reordering supplies as necessary.

You will be working with a variety of healthcare professionals including pharmacists, doctors and nurses, and you will also have considerable contact with patients and customers.

Type of person suited to this work

You will need to be a strong communicator as you will advise patients on medications and clearly explain how to administer them. You will also need to be comfortable working in a team and following instructions.

You should be good with numbers and calculations. Accuracy and attention to detail are essential to ensure that you are making and labelling medications correctly, and keeping detailed records of each patient's medication needs.

You must be mature, tactful and non-judgemental when dealing with patients, who will present a variety of unusual complaints.

Working conditions

Hours will depend on where you work. Community pharmacy technicians usually work 39 hours a week from Monday to Saturday. Industry and hospital technicians work a 37-hour week but may be required to cover evening and weekend shifts on occasion.

You could work in a shop, hospital or laboratory and you may occasionally be required to travel to nursing homes or community health centres and clinics.

Future prospects

You could work in a community context, within a small local pharmacy or a larger well-known chain. Alternatively, you could be employed by an NHS or private hospital, be based in a prison or work for the Armed Forces.

If you work in a hospital you could move into a specialised, supervisory role after gaining a few years' experience.

Additionally, many clinical pharmacy technicians in hospitals are now more involved with patients, undertaking ward rounds and other such duties.

Advantages/disadvantages

You will meet and help a range of patients and colleagues so your work will be varied and rewarding.

You can choose to work in a more relaxed retail environment, in the bustle of a hospital or in a professional industrial setting.

You may have to work evenings and weekends in order to provide a good level of service to patients and healthcare professionals.

Money guide

Starting salaries for pharmacy technicians are usually around £18,000–£22,000.

Experienced pharmacy technicians employed in a senior position could expect earnings of £21,000–£28,00.

If you become a team manager within the NHS, your salary could reach £40,000.

Related opportunities

- Health Records Clerk p307
- Pharmacist p326
- Sterile Services Technician p340

Further information

Association of Pharmacy Technicians UK
www.aptuk.org

Royal Pharmaceutical Society
www.rpharms.com

PHLEBOTOMIST

ENTRY LEVEL **2**

Qualifications and courses

There are no formal entry requirements for this job, but 4 or more GCSEs/S grades (A*–C/1–3), including English, maths and science, or equivalent, may be an advantage, and are essential for more advanced work.

Training is usually done entirely on the job. After training, you may be awarded a Certificate of Competence, which will allow you to work without close supervision throughout the hospital. You will be trained to National Occupational Standards.

Phlebotomists may be able to work towards related qualifications, such as NVQ/SVQ Medical Assistance Level 2.

The National Association of Phlebotomists offers short training courses and workshops.

What the work involves

Phlebotomists are specialist medical laboratory assistants who collect blood samples for analysis to help diagnose diseases.

You will take blood samples from patients as painlessly as possible, label samples and make sure they are taken promptly and safely to a laboratory for examination.

You will need to keep accurate records and enter data in a computer system. It is your responsibility to ensure samples are not mixed up or contaminated.

Type of person suited to this work

Phlebotomists need to be practical and good with their hands to take blood without harming the patient or disturbing nursing care.

Good colour vision is essential.

You need to pay close attention to detail and work carefully as any errors could affect results.

It is important that you are able to communicate well with a range of people from children to the elderly. Some people are scared of having their blood taken, so you need to be able to reassure them.

Working conditions

You will carry out your work in hospital wards, out-patient departments and in the community. You will also spend time working in laboratories.

You will need to pay close attention to health and safety to prevent infection, and will wear a uniform and protective clothing such as gloves.

You are likely to work a normal working day during the week, but you may also need to work at weekends.

Future prospects

Most employment is available in NHS hospitals throughout the UK. There is also similar work available in blood transfusion services, government research departments and university laboratories. Currently there is a shortage of phlebotomists in certain areas including London.

Phlebotomists can progress into managerial and senior roles.

Although there is no route for phlebotomists to progress to a career as a biomedical scientist, you may be encouraged to gain the qualifications that you need to train as one. You can also train to enter other areas of healthcare, such as nursing.

Advantages/disadvantages

Some of your patients will be scared of blood and needles which can make your job difficult.

It can be rewarding to work with patients and play a vital role in helping to diagnose illnesses.

Money guide

The NHS sets national pay rates for phlebotomists each year; those listed below are a guide only.

Salaries start at £13,300 per year and generally go up to £16,300. Seniors can earn between £17,700 and £21,400. Managers can earn up to £33,500.

If you work in the private sector or in London you may be paid more.

Related opportunities

- Biomedical Scientist/Medical Laboratory Assistant p504
- Immunologist p521
- Laboratory Technician p522

Further information

National Association of Phlebotomists
www.phlebotomy.org

NHS Careers
www.nhscareers.nhs.uk

Skills for Health
www.skillsforhealth.org.uk

HEALTHCARE

CRCI: JF

329

PHYSIOTHERAPIST

Qualifications and courses

All chartered physiotherapists must hold a degree in physiotherapy that has been recognised by the Health Professions Council (HPC). Full time and part time courses are available. Once you have completed your degree you are then eligible to apply to be a member of the Chartered Society of Physiotherapy (CSP).

Entry requirements vary according to the university, but you will usually need 3 A levels (A*–C) or equivalent, including biology or similar. You will also need at least 5 GCSEs/S grades (A*–C/1–3) or equivalent, including English, maths and science. You may also be considered for a university place if you hold a BTEC National Diploma/Certificate in science, applied science, or health sciences or an NVQ Level 3 in a related subject.

Graduates with a related science degree could opt for a 2 year fast-track postgraduate course, and Access courses are available for entry onto a degree programme for candidates without the relevant science qualifications.

It is recommended to get work experience prior to applying for your degree, as universities look favourably on this and physiotherapy courses are very competitive.

What the work involves

Physiotherapists treat patients with problems affecting their muscles, bones, heart, circulation and lungs that have been caused by accident, illness or aging.

You will assess patients, then decide on an appropriate course of treatment for them. This could include exercise, movement, hydrotherapy, massage or manipulation.

Sports physiotherapists use the same techniques as those above, but focus solely on treating sports-related injuries.

Type of person suited to this work

You must have excellent communication skills as you will be dealing with both patients and other healthcare professionals on a daily basis. When treating patients, you will need to be able to listen to their concerns, explain the best course of treatment, and motivate them to persevere with their programme.

You will need to have a practical, logical mind in order to think around problems and solve unusual complaints in a creative way.

You must be physically fit, as much of the work can be strenuous and involve a good deal of hands-on contact and muscle manipulation.

Working conditions

You will generally work a 37 hour week, although you should expect to work evenings and weekends to fit in with your clients' lifestyles.

You could be employed by the NHS, private practices and health centres, residential homes, or sports centres and specialist clinics. A good number of physiotherapists opt for self-employment and work in a mixture of locations.

You will need to wear practical clothes, and certain employers may require you to wear a uniform.

Future prospects

Sixty per cent of physiotherapists are employed by the NHS, although this number is significantly lower for those who have specialised in sports physiotherapy. There are opportunities with numerous other employers such as health clinics and sports centres, and you can be self-employed.

You could go on to specialise in an area such as orthopaedics or geriatric care, or pursue more senior positions. The NHS now offers consultant-level posts for experienced physiotherapists.

Advantages/disadvantages

You will have a great deal of contact with patients and other healthcare professionals so the job is varied and rewarding.

If you opt for self-employment, you have control over your working hours and the patients you decide to take on.

It is physically demanding work, and working with injured or ill people can also prove emotionally draining.

Money guide

Starting salaries for newly qualified physiotherapists depend on your employer, or whether you are self-employed but private sector salaries are generally quite similar to the NHS.

In the NHS, physiotherapists start at band 5 which ranges from £21,176 to £27,534.

With a few years' experience, this can rise to between £25,472 and £34,189.

For specialist and advanced physiotherapists, salaries are between £30,460 and £40,157.

Consultant physiotherapists in the NHS earn in excess of £50,000, and those who have specialised in sports physiotherapy can earn up to £55,000.

Related opportunities

- Acupuncturist p288
- Chiropractor p295
- Hospital Doctor p312

Further information

Chartered Society of Physiotherapy
www.csp.org.uk

Health Professions Council
www.hpc-uk.org

NHS Careers
www.nhscareers.nhs.uk

PODIATRIST

ENTRY LEVEL 5

Qualifications and courses

To work as a podiatrist, you need to have gained a BSc (Honours) degree in podiatry (lasting 3 or 4 years) approved by the Health Professions Council (HPC).

There are currently 13 institutions in the UK offering approved courses. For degree entry you are generally required to have a minimum of 5 GCSEs/S grades (A*–C/1–3) or equivalent and 3 A levels/4 Highers, one of which should be a science subject, preferably biology. Competition for places on podiatry courses is fierce so demonstration of your commitment to the subject through some work experience could be beneficial to your application.

You must be registered with the Health Professions Council in order to practise as a registered podiatrist.

What the work involves

Podiatrists (also commonly known as chiropodists) are healthcare practitioners responsible for assessing, diagnosing and treating problems relating to the feet and lower limbs.

The work involves using medical braces to correct deformities, administering local anaesthetics to enable pain free specialist foot treatment, wound care, neurological assessment, skin, nail and bone surgery, care planning and health promotion.

You will treat a variety of people including those with disabilities and long-term illnesses, children and people with sports related injuries.

Type of person suited to this work

Podiatrists need to be caring and understanding. You should be able to reassure patients of all ages who could be in pain and explain their treatment clearly and simply.

You will also need good communication skills to be an effective part of a healthcare team. You should be able to apply your skills and knowledge to diagnose and solve problems.

You should be good with your hands as you will be using a range of equipment and techniques.

Working conditions

You will most likely work in a clinic but may visit patients in their own homes or in residential care homes at times. You might also need to attend sporting events to treat injured players.

If employed by the NHS you will work 37 hours per week, Monday to Friday. Self-employed podiatrists can work flexible hours, including evenings and weekends.

Future prospects

Podiatry offers excellent employment flexibility with the opportunity to work in the NHS, private practice, commerce, leisure, education and occupational health sectors to name but a few.

With experience you might choose to specialise in one area of podiatry such as biomechanics (musculoskeletal disorders), forensic podiatry, working with children or surgery.

You could also go on to teach and research in a university or move into management. Many podiatrists even set up their own small private practices.

Advantages/disadvantages

The idea of working with other people's feet and lower limbs may not appeal instantly, but podiatrists generally get great satisfaction from their work.

You will have to deal with people who may be badly injured, very ill and in pain, which could be distressing.

You will be helping people to deal with pain and issues that could be affecting their mobility which can be rewarding.

Money guide

A new graduate in podiatry would have a starting salary of around £21,000 in the NHS.

NHS podiatrists can earn up to £40,000 at advanced level and as a consultant.

Private podiatrists can charge hourly, but their income is dependent on the number of patients they have and the location of their practice but earnings should be similar to, or possibly more than, earnings in the NHS.

Related opportunities

- Doctor (GP) p305
- Physiotherapist p330
- Prosthetist/Orthotist p334

Further information

NHS Careers
www.nhscareers.nhs.uk

Skills for Health
www.skillsforhealth.org.uk

Society of Chiropodists and Podiatrists
www.feetforlife.org

CRCI: JG   HEALTHCARE

Organisation profile

 The Society of Chiropodists and Podiatrists

THE SOCIETY OF CHIROPODISTS AND PODIATRISTS

Interesting facts about The Society of Chiropodists and Podiatrists

- The Society of Chiropodists and Podiatrists came into being in 1945 when five United Kingdom chiropody organisations amalgamated. The oldest of the constituent bodies and the first such organisation in Europe was founded in 1912.
- The Society of Chiropodists and Podiatrists is the largest organisation representing the podiatry profession. It has an educational as well as trade union function. While the society acts as the focus for the corporate identity of practitioners, the college maintains and develops the systematic body of knowledge and skills that define the profession and on which the practice of podiatry is based. It does this by accrediting undergraduate honours degree courses in podiatry which are offered at 13 universities.
- Podiatrists are also required to keep themselves abreast of developments in their particular field. The college helps them by providing opportunities to update their skills and knowledge and developing postgraduate training and qualifications, for example in local anaesthesia, medicines and podiatric surgery. The college therefore not only reflects the established traditions and contemporary definitions of podiatry education and research in the UK, but offers opportunities for continuing professional development.
- The head office is in London and there are currently 25 members of staff, some of who work in other locations around the country including an office in Edinburgh.
- The society is governed by a council who are responsible for the conduct of the business of the society. The council is made up of 24 members, all chiropodists/podiatrists elected by members of the society.
- The council meets four times a year. Members of the council are working clinicians, educators and managers who work in the NHS, private practice, higher education and other areas of practice.
- The mission of the society is 'looking after the interests of members, enabling them to practise more effectively'. The society's five year strategic plan for 2007–2012 focuses on growing our presence and influence, developing the profession, improving member services and extending democracy in the organisation.
- The key roles of the society are education, guidance on professional practice, raising foot health awareness, representing members on a wide range of national bodies, influencing the influencers, working with other professional bodies, trade unions and membership organisations. The society offers a range of membership services including professional indemnity insurance, legal advice, trade union support, a monthly journal and e-newsletter and a website that reports all the latest podiatry and society news together with an extensive library of resources.
- The majority of members are practising chiropodists and podiatrists working in both the public and private health care sectors in clinical, educational or managerial capacities. The society also offers associate membership to orthotic technicians and podiatry assistants.
- The society has an active student body and almost all students graduating from the 13 recognised courses run by universities join the society on completion of the honours bachelor degree in podiatry.

www.careersinpodiatry.com

The Society of Chiropodists and Podiatrists
1 Fellmongers Path
Tower Bridge Road
London
SE1 3LY
www.feetforlife.org/careers

Case study
PODIATRIST

The Society of
Chiropodists and
Podiatrists

Here's Joe Parker's story

After graduating from his BSc in Podiatric Medicine, Joe started out as a community podiatrist working in a local health centre dealing with the foot disorders and complaints of the local community. He did this for three years before being moved on to a promoted post where he specialises in children, working in different health centres and hospitals.

What the job entails

'Working with children is a specialist area which covers a variety of foot and gait (walking) complaints. I get referrals from health visitors, GPs, physiotherapists and other podiatrists. My referrals include children with in-grown toenails, verrucae and curly toes, but mostly I get children who have flat feet, in-toeing gait or other unusual walking/development problems. I also go out to schools and give health promotion talks to pupils on foot health.'

A bad day in the office for Joe

'When a child comes into the clinic with a really sore toe and it's so sore that they don't want you to even touch it. Most children don't like getting an injection so won't let you give them a local anaesthetic and it can take you a long time to try and persuade them that you will be able to make them feel better. The parents can put pressure on you also as they know how sore it has been and know that it has become infected.'

What makes Joe good at his job

'You need to be very patient and sympathetic towards the children to make them feel relaxed with you to allow you to assess and treat them. Good communication skills are vital to be able to decipher what is wrong. Problem solving skills help you to be able to come up with a management plan that suits you, the patient and the parents.'

What Joe personally gets out of it

'It is really rewarding working with children, when that crying child with the sore toe comes back to you smiling as the pain has gone and their foot is better it makes it all worthwhile. Also working as part of a team with the health visitors, GPs, physiotherapist etc. is interesting as you are all working together to help your patient.

'No two days are the same in this job, there is always something different to do, i.e. one day you could be treating ingrowing toenails, the next you are giving exercises to help correct a child with an in-toeing gait. You could also be in the lab making specialist insoles to fit into someone's shoes then going off to give a talk to children in a primary school – there is never a dull moment!'

The Society of Chiropodists and Podiatrists
1 Fellmongers Path,
Tower Bridge Road,
London
SE1 3LY
www.feetforlife.org

Qualifications and courses

Training to become a prosthetist and orthotist takes 4 years, leading to a BSc (Honours) degree recognised by the British Association of Prosthetists and Orthotists and the Health Professions Council. Approved degrees are offered by either the University of Strathclyde or the University of Salford.

Entry requirements are usually 240 UCAS points with 3 A levels/Highers, including maths or physics as well as either biology or chemistry, plus 5 GCSEs/S Grades (A*–C/1–3). Entry could be granted with qualifications such as AS levels, BTEC Nationals and Higher Nationals or the International Baccalaureate.

Graduates can either specialise in one area or practise both specialities but must register with the HPC.

What the work involves

Prosthetist

Prosthetists design and fit artificial limbs for patients who have lost a limb, have a deformity or who were born without a limb.

Work will include taking a cast of the area where the artificial replacement limb will fit and modelling it so that it will be safe and comfortable for the patient. You will also fit and adjust the replacement limb and teach the patient how to use it.

Orthotist

Orthotists provide surgical appliances such as arm and leg braces, collars, splints and special footwear for patients.

Work will include assessing the patient's problem, designing, fitting and adjusting the orthosis, and helping the patient to use it.

Type of person suited to this work

You must have a good technical knowledge and aptitude of biomechanics and movement. You need to have excellent manual skills in order to take measurements, design devices and do fittings and make adjustments.

You should be practical and have a high attention to detail as each device is made to perfectly fit each patient.

It is important to have excellent communications skills and be caring and tactful as you will have to reassure, encourage and explain procedures to your patients.

Working conditions

Opportunities are available in hospitals, clinics and centres for people with disabilities.

Some time will be spent in workshops where the prostheses and orthoses are made.

You will generally work normal hours from Monday to Friday, although extra hours are required at busy times. A driving licence is useful if you are working in many different locations

Future prospects

With a shortage of prosthetists and orthotists, job prospects are generally excellent across the UK. Most prosthetists and orthotists work within the NHS but there are also opportunities in private practice, in charities such as the Red Cross and with commercial companies that make devices for NHS hospitals.

With experience, you may specialise in an area such as upper or lower limb prosthetics or spinal orthotics; you could also move into management or carry out research and teaching.

There are also many opportunities to work all over the world – especially in the US. Prosthetic and orthotic work is especially important in development programmes which work with communities affected by war.

Advantages/disadvantages

Working with patients who are upset and in pain can be emotionally demanding.

It is satisfying to be able to see the positive effects that the artificial limbs and surgical appliances have on people's lives.

Money guide

There is no set salary scale for NHS prosthetists and orthotists, but salaries tend to be similar to those in commercial companies.

The starting salary for prosthetists and orthotists is around £21,200–£27,500 per year.

Experienced prosthetists and orthotists can earn £30,000–£40,000.

Some senior practitioners in the NHS or those who work for manufacturers can earn up to £67,000.

Earnings are generally higher in London.

Related opportunities

- Medical Physicist p316
- Occupational Therapist p319
- Physiotherapist p330

Further information

British Association of Prosthetists and Orthotists
www.bapo.com

Skills for Health
www.skillsforhealth.org.uk

PSYCHIATRIST

Qualifications and courses

Candidates must initially train as a hospital doctor by completing a medical degree which is approved by the General Medical Council (GMC). Entry requirements for medical school are very high A level/H grade results including relevant subjects such as science and maths. Competition for places on medical degrees is very high. Undertaking relevant pre-entry work experience may benefit your application.

After studying for a medical degree, graduates undertake the 2-year foundation programme of general training which acts as the bridge between medical school and specialist training. Candidates then progress to 5–6 years of specialty training in a particular area of psychiatry, such as general adult psychiatry, forensic psychiatry or old age psychiatry.

After successfully completing the specialty stage, trainees receive a Certificate of Completion of Training (CCT) and become eligible to join the GMC Specialist Register. It is then possible to apply for a post as a consultant.

Psychiatrists must engage in continuing professional development (CPD) throughout their career to ensure that their skills and knowledge are up to date. The Royal College of Psychiatrists provides information on available training.

What the work involves

Psychiatrists are doctors who have undergone further training in psychiatry.

As a psychiatrist, you will diagnose mental health problems by talking to patients and carrying out tests. You will then decide on a course of treatment which could include prescribing drugs and talking to patients to help them deal with their problems.

You will treat people with a range of mental health problems. These include depression, schizophrenia, eating disorders, anxieties, phobias, drug and alcohol abuse, and post-traumatic stress disorder.

Type of person suited to this work

As a psychiatrist you need to be patient and caring. You will need excellent communication skills to listen carefully to people who might be confused or withdrawn. You will help them discuss and come to terms with their problems or illness and you should be able to explain their conditions and treatment in a clear, simple way.

You will work with relatives and carers, and as part of a team with other medical staff such as psychiatric nurses and occupational therapists.

Working conditions

You could work in a range of locations including hospitals, patients' homes, schools, residential homes and prisons.

Some psychiatrists have standard office hours. Others work shifts and are on an on-call rota which includes working nights, weekends and on bank holidays.

You will work as part of a team of healthcare professionals.

Future prospects

Most psychiatrists work within the NHS throughout the UK. There is also a small amount of work available in private hospitals, care homes and rehabilitation centres. The Armed Forces also employ psychiatrists.

There are six specialist areas of psychiatry that you may work in: adult psychiatry; child and adolescent psychiatry; forensic psychiatry; the psychiatry of learning difficulties; old age psychiatry and psychotherapy. Entry to psychotherapy is competitive.

You could move into academic work, either carrying out research or teaching medical students.

Advantages/disadvantages

Your patients could be confused or aggressive with a range of difficult problems so the work can be demanding.

It is rewarding to be able to make a difference to people's lives by helping them to regain their self-respect and happiness.

Money guide

Salary levels in the NHS may vary in different locations.

Earnings are often higher in private practice work.

Junior doctors have a starting salary of £22,000–£28,000 during the 2-year foundation programme.

When undertaking the specialty training, you can expect to earn between £28,000 and £46,000 a year.

Consultant psychiatrists can achieve salaries ranging from £74,000 up to £170,000 for those in the most senior positions.

Related opportunities

- Doctor (GP) p305
- Hospital Doctor p312
- Psychoanalyst/Psychotherapist p576

Further information

British Medical Association
www.bma.org.uk

NHS Careers
www.nhscareers.nhs.uk

HEALTHCARE

CRCI: JH

RADIOGRAPHER

Qualifications and courses

All radiographers need a degree approved by the Health Professions Council (HPC). You must decide which branch of radiography you wish to practise in before university as they require different qualifications.

Most universities expect you to have previous work experience in a radiography department. All radiography degrees involve spending 50% of your time doing academic work and 50% undertaking practical placements. Courses usually last 3 years. Minimum entry requirements for a degree are usually 2–3 A levels/H grades including a science-based subject (preferably biology or physics).

Diagnostic radiographer
You must hold a degree in diagnostic radiography. Radiography assistants who wish to qualify as radiographers could study for in-service or foundation degrees.

Therapeutic radiographer
You will need a degree in radiotherapy or therapeutic radiography. Alternatively, those who already have a degree in a science or health-related subject, such as life and medical sciences, biology or health studies, may be eligible for a 2-year postgraduate training course.

What the work involves

Diagnostic radiographer
You will help doctors and surgeons to diagnose diseases and injuries as an essential step towards treating a patient. You may use a variety of methods such as X-ray, computed tomography (CT) scanning and ultrasound to create images of body parts and organs.

Therapeutic radiographer
Working with an oncology team, you will use doses of radiation to control or kill cancerous cells. You will be involved in every aspect of the treatment, including pre-treatment preparation, planning, the delivery of the radiation and follow-up care of patients.

Type of person suited to this work

You should be warm, understanding and adaptable. You must be able to work with both children and adults who are extremely ill. Communication skills are vital for listening to patients and explaining their treatments.

You need to be a quick thinker and be detail-oriented in order to produce accurate images. Confidence to operate sophisticated computerised equipment is essential.

Working conditions

Diagnostic radiographer
You will be based in accident and emergency, operating theatres, wards or imaging units.

These departments need to be staffed 24 hours a day so you will work a shift system including nights and weekends. You should work a total of 37.5 hours a week.

Therapeutic radiographer
You will be based in radiotherapy or oncology centres, outpatient units or at charities such as Macmillan Cancer Support.

Future prospects

You could work for the NHS in a clinic, hospital or oncology centre, or work for the Armed Forces or a private practice.

You could be promoted to management roles or become an instructor or researcher. UK radiography qualifications are recognised internationally so you could choose to work overseas.

Diagnostic radiographer
You could specialise in areas such as MRI, ultrasound or nuclear medicine.

Therapeutic radiographer
You could specialise in anything from quality management to treatment planning or palliative care.

Advantages/disadvantages

Each of your patients will be unique, keeping your work interesting.

It is satisfying when you capture the best image possible and contribute to your patients' wellbeing.

Rota work can be difficult as you may be required to work bank holidays and nights.

Money guide

Starting salaries for NHS radiographers are between £21,176 and £27,625.

An experienced specialist could earn £25,528–£34,189.

Senior radiographers can achieve up to £40,000 and consultants could reach £67,000.

Salaries may be higher in private practice.

Related opportunities

- Critical Care Technologist p297
- Medical Physicist p316
- Radiologist p337

Further information

Radiography Careers
www.radiographycareers.co.uk

Society and College of Radiographers
www.sor.org

RADIOLOGIST

ENTRY LEVEL 5

Qualifications and courses

To become a radiologist, you must initially train as a hospital doctor by completing a medical degree which is approved by the General Medical Council (GMC). Entry requirements for medical school are very high A level/H grade results including relevant subjects such as science and maths. Competition for places on medical degrees is very high.

After studying for a medical degree, graduates undertake the 2-year foundation programme of general training which acts as the bridge between medical school and specialist training.

Candidates then register as Members of the Royal College of Radiologists (RCR) and begin 5 years of specialty training in clinical radiology. At least 4 years of the training are spent in clinical posts and 6 months' research in any aspect of diagnostic imaging is also included. Trainees must pass all three parts of the Fellowship of the Royal College of Radiologists (FRCR) examination. After successfully completing the specialty stage, trainees receive a Certificate of Completion of Training (CCT) and become eligible to join the GMC Specialist Register.

RCR operate a continuing professional development (CPD) scheme for qualified radiologists to update their knowledge and skills.

What the work involves

Radiologists are doctors who have undergone further training in radiology. Radiologists increasingly perform interventional procedures such as biopsies using image guidance.

As a radiologist, you will diagnose patients' diseases by using information gained from images such as X-rays, and computed tomography (CT) or magnetic resonance imaging (MRI) scans.

You will also play an important role in identifying sources of disease and reducing the possible risks of them spreading further.

Type of person suited to this work

As a radiologist, you must care about patients and be sensitive to their situation. You need strong communication skills to explain things to patients simply and clearly so that they understand their health conditions and any treatments they may require. You must be comfortable working as part of a team with other medical staff.

Scientific and technical knowledge and an ability to diagnose patients' conditions accurately are also necessary. You should be willing to continue learning throughout your career.

You will need good eyesight and excellent attention to detail so that you can interpret images. Practical skills are required when caring for patients and operating equipment.

Working conditions

You will work within a hospital, mainly in the radiology department but you will also spend time visiting patients on their wards.

You will use a range of sophisticated equipment and you will be required to wear protective clothing when operating it.

Your working hours will vary and you will be expected to work shifts, evenings and weekends in order to provide a 24-hour service for patients.

Future prospects

Career prospects are excellent owing to an international shortage of radiologists.

Most radiologists work within the NHS throughout the UK. There is also some work available in private hospitals.

You may decide to specialise further in a particular area or you could progress to a management role. You could also move into academic work, either carrying out research or teaching medical students.

Advantages/disadvantages

The role can be emotionally demanding because you will be dealing with patients who have life-threatening conditions.

Your work is vital in finding an accurate and early diagnosis for patients, which can help to save lives.

Money guide

Salary levels in the NHS may vary in different locations.

Earnings are often higher in private practice work.

Junior doctors have a starting salary of £22,000–£28,000 during the 2–year foundation programme.

When undertaking the specialty training, you can expect to earn between £28,000 and £46,000 a year.

Consultant radiologists can achieve salaries ranging from £74,000 up to £170,000 for those in the most senior positions.

Related opportunities

- Anaesthetist p290
- Hospital Doctor p312
- Radiographer p336

Further information

British Medical Association
www.bma.org.uk

NHS Careers
www.nhscareers.nhs.uk

Royal College of Radiologists
www.rcr.ac.uk

CRCI: JH   HEALTHCARE

CRCI: JG   HEALTHCARE

Qualifications and courses

All speech and language therapists must be registered with the Health Professions Council (HPC). In order to qualify for registration, you must either have a Speech and Language degree accredited by the Royal College of speech and language Therapists (RCSLT) or complete postgraduate study (relevant work experience is necessary for a postgraduate application).

For entrance onto a degree course you will need 3 A levels or equivalent, and 5 GCSEs/S grades (A*–C/1–3) including English, science and maths.

There are also Foundation courses available for those who do not have the relevant qualifications to go straight onto a degree programme, and accelerated 2 year degree courses for students who already have a health-related degree. All courses comprise a balance between academic study and on-the-job training.

Because you will be working with children and vulnerable adults, you will need to undergo a Criminal Records Bureau check. You will also need to undergo a medical screening.

What the work involves

Speech and language therapists work with patients who have problems speaking, chewing or swallowing.

You will be responsible for assessing patients, and prescribing a suitable course of treatment.

You will work with a range of patients including children who need help in developing their speech, people with a speech defect such as a stammer, and those who have trouble eating because of an accident or illness. You will also work with each patient's family, partner or carer in order to show them how to support your patient at home.

You will liaise with professionals in education and social services.

Type of person suited to this work

You will need excellent communication skills in order to develop a good relationship with patients and colleagues alike. You will also need to be a patient teacher in order to successfully help your patients learn new skills to overcome their problems.

You should be mature and non-judgemental in your approach to patients as you will be dealing with people of varying ages, backgrounds and cultures.

You will work both on your own and within a wider team of healthcare professionals, so you must have plenty of initiative coupled with a good approach to working within a team.

Working conditions

Speech and language therapists usually work 37.5 hours per week from Monday to Friday. Evening, weekend or shift work is rare.

There are plenty of opportunities to work part time.

You could work in one or several of a variety of locations, including hospitals, schools, residential homes, health centres, young offenders' institutions and in patients' homes. Since local travel in the community is required, it is useful to have a driving licence, particularly in rural areas.

Future prospects

There is a current shortage of registered speech and language therapists, so job opportunities outweigh the number of candidates.

Most therapists are employed by the NHS and work throughout their local community. Others work for social services, local education authorities, charities and schools. There is a growing trend amongst therapists to be self-employed and treat patients privately.

You could progress to more senior supervisory positions, specialise in an area that particularly interests you, or move into research.

Advantages/disadvantages

Speech and language therapists are in great demand, so you will have a greater choice of job opportunities open to you than in some other health-related professions.

Working closely with patients and seeing them improve under your care and guidance is rewarding.

You may have to work with difficult patients in unfavourable conditions on occasion, such as young offenders' institutions or prisons.

Money guide

As a newly qualified speech and language therapist, you could expect to earn around £21,000. This is line with the National Health Service pay scale – which consists of 9 bands.

This usually rises quickly to £27,000, and then, as you gain experience, it can increase up to £34,000.

Senior therapists start at around £35,000 and can earn up to £46,374. If you take on significant supervisory and management responsibilities as well you could expect to earn in excess of £50,000.

Other employers, outside of the NHS, such as charities and local education authorities, offer comparable pay.

Related opportunities

- Health Visitor p309
- Learning Disabilities Nurse p314
- Occupational Therapist p319

Further information

NHS Careers
www.nhscareers.nhs.uk

Royal College of Speech and Language Therapists
www.rcslt.org

SPORTS AND EXERCISE SCIENTIST

Qualifications and courses

Most entrants to this profession have a degree in sports science, but it's also fine if you take a degree in psychology or any kind of physical education.

To follow a degree in sports science, you usually need good GCSEs/S grades and 3 A levels/H grades or equivalent. Some of these should be in sciences, especially biology. There's also the option of following an Access course before taking a degree, or doing a postgraduate degree in sports science after an degree in a related subject.

Once you have a relevant degree, you can seek accreditation through the British Association of Sport and Exercise Sciences (BASES), which can help improve job prospects.

After completing your degree, it may be necessary to gain some relevant practical experience in the fitness or leisure industry to increase your chances of employment.

Continuing professional development (CPD) and keeping your skills up to date is really important, and there are plenty of opportunities to do this through the BASES.

What the work involves

Sports scientists work either with athletes to help build their performance or with people who need or wish to improve their health. Clients may also be recovering from illness or injury.

As a sport or exercise scientist, you require a lot of scientific knowledge, including an understanding of biology, biomechanics and physiology. You also need to have an understanding of psychology, as you might have to assess the mental state of some athletes, and you will also spend time on performance analysis (usually done with video footage).

You'll spend some time outside, and also conduct research.

Type of person suited to this work

If you want to be a sports and exercise scientist, above all you need to be a good communicator. Your work will centre on building relationships with people, and you have to be good at listening and aware of your clients' needs.

Aside from this, you need to have a clear writing style to communicate findings, and be good at research and problem-solving.

You should be good with numbers and statistics, well organised, accurate and good with computers.

You will also need a scientific and analytical mind to help your clients improve their sporting potential.

Working conditions

You will usually work in leisure and sports centres and gyms, for around 38 hours a week.

If you are a sports scientist, some clients may require you outside regular working hours, and part-time work is also available.

You will also spend a lot of time outdoors, and probably travel too. For this reason, a driving licence is an advantage.

Future prospects

Although there is no specific career path for this job, progression is possible.

Building a list of contacts is important, and with the right experience you may be able to work your way up to helping people who play sport at an international level.

You could also teach, or, if you are an exercise scientist you might be able to move into a specific area such as cardiology.

Advantages/disadvantages

This job is really rewarding for those who are interested in exercise and science, and like to be out and about being active rather than sitting still.

You have to use your brain and your body, and the job is unlikely to become boring as you will be working with so many different people.

It can be tiring, and you need quite specialist knowledge that has to be constantly maintained.

Money guide

As a newly qualified sports and exercise scientist, you'll probably earn around £20,000 a year.

As you gain experience, this may rise to about £40,000.

If you work with top athletes in competitive sport, you might earn in excess of £60,000 a year.

Related opportunities

- Leisure Centre Assistant/Manager p385
- Sports Coach p388
- Sports Development Officer p389

Further information

British Association of Sport and Exercise Sciences
www.bases.org.uk

English Institute of Sport
www.eis2win.co.uk

SkillsActive
www.skillsactive.com

CRCI: JG   HEALTHCARE

Qualifications and courses

There are no set minimum qualifications to begin work in this position. However, employers will expect you to have a good general standard of education, to have strong reading skills and neat handwriting (for labelling materials and equipment clearly and correctly).

Some employers may prefer you to have 5 GCSEs/S grades (A*–C/1–3). Qualifications such as the BTEC National Certificate in Applied Science (Level 3) or the BTEC National Diploma in Applied Science (Medical Science) at Level 3 could also be an advantage.

Once you secure a position as a sterile services technician, training is provided on the job by experienced colleagues. You may also be encouraged to study for an ASET Certificate in the Control of Infection and Contamination (Level 2) or an NCFE Prevention and Control of Infection Award (Level 2).

Becoming a member of the Institute of Decontamination Sciences (IDSc) may help you to progress in your career and gain a management position. IDSc also offer training programmes which may be useful.

What the work involves

Sterile services technicians work as part of a team responsible for helping to prevent the spread of infections by making sure that hospital equipment is sterile.

Your work will involve collecting and cleaning a range of instruments. You will have to operate a steam sterilising machine, such as an autoclave.

You will dismantle and examine certain instruments through a microscope before sterilising them and then reassembling and testing them. Once the equipment is reassembled and sufficiently cleaned, you will follow set procedures to repackage, seal and label the equipment.

You will work to national standards, operating highly technical machines, and you must keep accurate records of your work.

You will also be expected to deliver sterile supplies by trolley to wards and departments and restock supplies of items such as dressings, needles and syringes.

Type of person suited to this work

You will need to be good with your hands, work accurately, pay attention to detail and follow instructions and set procedures carefully.

Sterile services technicians should be very vigilant about hygiene and interested in keeping hospitals and equipment clean and safe for patients and staff.

You will work in a team so you will need good communication skills. You should also be well organised and able to keep clear, detailed records.

You will be collecting and dismantling machinery so you will need to be physically fit.

Working conditions

You will work in a hospital as part of a team and will have contact with doctors, nurses and other staff.

Based in the sterile services department, you will collect equipment from all parts of the hospital and this will involve lifting and pushing trolleys.

You will have to wear protective clothing and you may have to work shifts.

Future prospects

Most jobs are in NHS hospitals throughout the UK but you could also work in a private hospital. Opportunities are good as there is a shortage of applicants for vacancies.

With experience, you could be promoted to senior technician or supervisor. You could then take professional qualifications and become a sterile services manager. As a manager you could move into management in other areas of the NHS.

Advantages/disadvantages

The work can be routine and physically demanding.

The working conditions can be humid and uncomfortable as protective clothing is essential and steam sterilising machines are often required.

You will be making a vital contribution to controlling the spread of potentially deadly infections which is very rewarding.

Money guide

Starting salaries for sterile services technicians are between £14,153 and £17,253.

Those employed as a supervisor can expect to earn £16,110–£19,077.

Related opportunities

- Biomedical Scientist/Medical Laboratory Assistant p504
- Hotel Porter p141
- Operating Department Practitioner p320

Further information

Institute of Decontamination Sciences
www.idsc-uk.co.uk

NHS Careers
www.nhscareers.nhs.uk

Skills for Health
www.skillsforhealth.org.uk

Qualifications and courses

To become a surgeon, you must initially train as a hospital doctor by completing a medical degree which is approved by the General Medical Council (GMC). Entry requirements for medical school are very high A level/H grade results including relevant subjects such as science and maths. Competition for places on medical degrees is very high. Undertaking relevant pre-entry work experience may benefit your application.

After studying for a medical degree, graduates undertake the 2-year foundation programme of general training which acts as the bridge between medical school and specialist training. Candidates then progress to 5–6 years of specialty training in a particular area of surgery, such as neurosurgery, paediatric surgery or plastic surgery.

After successfully completing the specialty stage, trainees receive a Certificate of Completion of Training (CCT) and become eligible to join the GMC Specialist Register. It is then possible to apply for a post as a consultant surgeon.

Surgeons must engage in continuing professional development (CPD) throughout their career to ensure that their skills and knowledge are up to date. The Royal College of Surgeons of England provides information on available training.

What the work involves

Surgeons work in hospitals, operating on patients in order to remove or prevent the spread of disease, treat injuries, and fix other complaints.

You will specialise in operating on specific conditions or diseases relating to a particular system of the body, such as neurological, gastrointestinal or cardiovascular. You will also be responsible for diagnosing problems, taking case histories, talking patients through surgical procedures and advising them on post-operative care.

You will see patients on ward rounds and in outpatient clinics, as well as undertaking administrative work such as updating patient records.

Type of person suited to this work

You need excellent communication skills in order to develop a good relationship with patients and colleagues alike. You will be required to direct your team through complex surgical procedures in the operating theatre, as well as explaining them to patients in simple terms.

You should have excellent manual and technical skills in order to operate with precision and confidence. As you will be working under immense pressure, you should also be able to think quickly and clearly when solving problems.

You must be prepared to break bad news to patients and relatives on occasion, which requires sensitivity and diplomacy.

Working conditions

Surgeons work extremely long hours which often include nights and weekends.

Most of your work will take place in hospitals, working with health professionals including other surgeons, nurses, anaesthetists and GPs. You could work in the NHS or in private hospitals, although the majority of surgeons divide their time between the two.

The work is mentally and physically exhausting as you will need to concentrate for hours at a time and spend a lot of time on your feet.

Future prospects

There are many opportunities to work abroad, particularly in conjunction with specialist charities operating in developing countries.

You will continue to train and learn new skills throughout your career as technology and techniques develop, change and improve.

Once you have qualified as a surgeon, you can become a consultant and work within the NHS or in private practice, both of which are lucrative options.

Advantages/disadvantages

You will be personally responsible for transforming and saving a number of lives throughout your career.

The training period is extremely long, often in excess of 12 years, so you have to be extremely dedicated.

You will work long and unpredictable hours which can have an adverse effect on your personal life.

Money guide

Salary levels in the NHS may vary in different locations.

Junior doctors have a starting salary of £22,000–£28,000 during the 2–year foundation programme.

When undertaking the specialty training, you can expect to earn between £28,000 and £46,000 a year.

Consultant surgeons can achieve salaries ranging from £74,000 up to £170,000 for those in the most senior positions.

Related opportunities

- Dentist p302
- Doctor (GP) p305
- Hospital Doctor p312

Further information

British Medical Association
www.bma.org.uk

NHS Careers
www.nhscareers.nhs.uk

Royal College of Surgeons of England
www.rcseng.ac.uk

CRCI: JH   HEALTHCARE

Qualifications and courses

The main route into trichology is to complete the Institute of Trichologists' 2-year training course. There are no set minimum entry requirements but the course is academic and scientific in nature and the progress of students is closely monitored through exams and practical placements.

Successful completion of the Institute's course makes you eligible for admission as an Associate Member of the Institute (AIT). Progression to full membership (MIT) is available upon further study and a minimum of 2 years' professional practice as a trichologist.

Another option is to study for the Diploma in Pure-Trichology offered by the Trichological Society. This is a distance learning course which lasts up to 3 years and involves practical clinical experience, a dissertation and an oral exam.

Those who already have medical qualifications may be eligible to take shortened versions of the above courses.

To become a doctor (dermatologist), candidates must complete a medical degree recognised by the General Medical Council (GMC).

What the work involves

Trichologists diagnose and treat diseases and disorders of the scalp and hair, such as hair loss and dandruff.

You will talk to patients about their medical history, health and diet, and closely examine their hair and scalp.

You will give advice and recommend treatment, such as using special creams or shampoos. You might also refer patients to other healthcare professionals if appropriate.

Type of person suited to this work

Trichologists need excellent communication skills to speak to patients about their problems and explain the treatments they have recommended.

You should be sympathetic, tactful and able to reassure patients, put them at their ease and gain their trust.

You will need to have a methodical approach to your work and pay close attention to detail so that you can assess patients' conditions accurately and plan appropriate treatment.

Working conditions

Most trichologists work in clinics treating patients and if you are self-employed you will rent your own premises.

You will usually have normal working hours from Monday to Friday. If you work in private practice you might need to work in the evenings or occasionally at weekends to treat people at times that suit them.

The work involves close contact with patients and hands-on treatment.

You are likely to wear a uniform and those employed in a research role may need protective clothing for laboratory work.

Future prospects

Dermatologists are doctors who have trained in trichology and are usually employed in hospitals.

Some trichologists will become involved in research or teaching and will work in universities and colleges (often in hair and beauty departments) or pharmaceutical and cosmetics companies.

There are also a number of opportunities to work in research for pharmaceutical and cosmetics companies.

Advantages/disadvantages

Working with patients who are distressed can be challenging and stressful.

It is rewarding to be able to use your knowledge to treat patients successfully.

Money guide

Most trichologists are self-employed and charge clients by the session.

Earnings vary widely, depending on your location, experience and the number of clients you have.

Newly qualified practitioners may charge about £30 per consultation.

Experienced practitioners may earn up to £90 for a session.

For NHS doctors/dermatologists, you must complete a medical degree and your salary will be in line with that of a hospital doctor.

Related opportunities

- Dietitian p303
- Hairdresser/Barber p465
- Hospital Doctor p312

Further information

Institute of Trichologists
www.trichologists.org.uk

The Trichological Society
www.hairscientists.org

Languages, Information and Culture

The jobs in this family are quite varied in terms of whether you would work with other people or by yourself. You could find yourself working in a range of different places, from museums to antiques fairs to conferences as an interpreter. Some of the jobs in this family are more unusual and are perfect for those of you who want a fascinating job that allows you to indulge in your passion for historic artefacts and artwork or languages and foreign countries. To excel in this sector you should have an inquisitive mind, be meticulous in your work and enjoy carrying out research.

The jobs featured in this section are listed below. For similar jobs to the ones in this section please see *Design, Arts and Crafts* on page 167 and *Marketing, Advertising, Media, Print and Publishing* on page 395.

ANTHROPOLOGIST

Qualifications and courses

Entry to this area is usually gained with a relevant degree or postgraduate qualification. Voluntary or paid work experience can be useful. There are limited opportunities to gain qualifications in this area before degree level. A level/H grade sociology and GCSEs/S grades cover some aspects of anthropology. For biological anthropology, an A level/H grade in biology may be useful.

Access and degree courses in this area cover subjects such as social anthropology and physical/biological anthropology. Anthropology can also be studied as part of a combined Honours degree with subjects such as archaeology or psychology. It is also possible to study for a master's or other postgraduate degree in anthropology following a first degree in any subject.

The Association of Social Anthropologists based at the University of Birmingham runs seminars and conferences, and has information on bursaries and awards for anthropology students.

Professionals using their anthropology training in another area such as archaeology are likely to have gained a qualification or degree in their specialist subject. Researchers in this area are often required to have a relevant postgraduate qualification or the equivalent practical experience. Higher education lecturers are usually required to have, or be working towards, a PhD in addition to this and are expected to have experience in, or show potential for, teaching.

What the work involves

You will study and research the origin and cultural, physical and social developments of humans. You will investigate human culture across the world, in terms of its beliefs, values, traditions, social structure and language.

You will also apply specialist knowledge and research skills to find out about the differences between human cultures.

Anthropologists undertake their research in a wide range of areas such as archaeology, the arts, the environment, biology and religion.

Type of person suited to this work

Whatever job you do as an anthropologist, you will need a strong interest in people and a respectful, flexible attitude to other people's beliefs and customs. You should also enjoy meeting new people and entering different social situations.

Good communication skills are also very important. Strong research skills and an organised approach are useful. ICT skills and a good level of numeracy are also helpful.

You will need an observant approach with an interest in a wide range of subjects.

Working conditions

For research-based work, you might need to visit and stay in different areas. Spending time in other places means that anthropology is not generally a 9am to 5pm office-based job.

The work can involve travel in the UK and overseas.

Some physical or biological anthropologists work in laboratories analysing and researching samples.

Future prospects

You could gain employment as a researcher on specific projects. Many anthropologists progress within academia by undertaking research and teaching around their specialist interests.

You could also work for government bodies and charities. There are some opportunities to work overseas.

Anthropologists also apply their research skills and training to their work in other areas such as social care, teaching and the health service.

Advantages/disadvantages

This job can provide opportunities to develop and research theories about people and cultures.

Anthropology can also provide the chance to meet a variety of people and visit different places.

Field research can be physically demanding and spending time away can be difficult if you have family commitments.

Money guide

Anthropologists work in a range of sectors, so salaries vary.

Starting salaries for graduates are around £21,000 per year, rising to £26,000 for research assistants/researchers.

Between £33,000 and £43,000 per year is usual for lecturers, with between £28,000 and £55,000 the norm for senior lecturers.

Related opportunities

- Archaeologist p345
- Archivist/Records Manager p346
- Historian p351

Further information

Association of Social Anthropologists
www.c-sap.bham.ac.uk

Royal Anthropological Institute of Great Britain and Ireland
www.therai.org

ARCHAEOLOGIST

Qualifications and courses

Most professional archaeologists have a degree, BTEC HND, or postgraduate qualification. Degree entry usually requires 2 A levels/3 Higher Grades, although there are no specific subject requirements. Archaeology can be studied as a single Honours degree or in combination with another degree subject. A small number of Foundation degrees are available in archaeology. Entry to postgraduate courses requires a good first degree.

A number of different degrees, ranging from geography or history to computer science and geology can be good preparation for a career in achaeology. Skills with computer-aided design (CAD) or geographical information systems (GIS) software could be very useful owing to the increasing use of technology in archaeology.

It is possible to enter this profession without a degree, although this is becoming increasingly uncommon. The Diploma in Environmental and Land-based Studies could be useful. NVQs at Levels 3 and 4 in Archaeological Practice are also available.

Voluntary experience on digs is very useful. The key professional bodies can provide details of holiday work experience opportunities. The Archaeology Training Forum (ATF) develops and offers short courses in Continuing Professional Development (CPD), and similar options are offered by the Society for the Protection of Ancient Buildings (SPAB).

What the work involves

Using your specialist knowledge and skills you will investigate and record physical evidence of the past.

You will provide practical support on archaeological excavations or 'digs', which might include undertaking basic digging work, project-managing a team or researching evidence found on sites.

You will develop public understanding of history through presentations, the publication of your findings or teaching in universities or schools. You could also provide information and advice on how to protect and maintain historical sites.

Type of person suited to this work

You will need a strong interest in history and past cultures.

For practical work you will need a patient and careful approach. You should also be observant with an eye for detail. A good level of physical fitness and manual dexterity will be needed when working on digs and handling objects.

The ability to work as part of a team is useful. In more senior jobs, you will need to explain your work to others so communication skills are important. Writing skills will help you to be able to write up reports and keep detailed records. ICT skills are also useful.

Working conditions

Archaeologists often work on sites or digs that are outdoors. Varying weather conditions and the nature of the work make this job physically demanding.

Some archaeologists are based in offices within government bodies, heritage organisations and museums.

Much of your work will be on temporary contracts.

Future prospects

Whatever route you follow, this is a very competitive area in which to develop a career.

You will need to gain practical experience on a voluntary or paid basis. With further experience you could project-manage site excavations or work as a researcher analysing excavation findings.

Some archaeologists work for heritage organisations to help preserve historic monuments and buildings. Others go into teaching or follow an academic career.

Advantages/disadvantages

It is likely that you will need to move around different geographical areas to gain practical experience.

There are opportunities to work overseas.

It's rewarding to discover artefacts that can shed ground-breaking light on the past.

Money guide

Salaries can vary dependent on location, employment sector and size of the specific organisation for which you work.

The starting salary in a purely excavatory role is between £13,000 and £17,000 per year.

Experienced archaeologists with the relevant qualifications can earn around £30,000.

Senior archaeologists can expect a salary of around £47,000.

Related opportunities

- Archivist/Records Manager p346
- Conservator/Restorer p349
- Further Education Lecturer p195

Further information

Council for British Archaeology
www.britarch.ac.uk

Creative and Cultural Skills
www.ccskills.org.uk

Institute of Field Archaeologists
www.archaeologists.net

Society for the Protection of Ancient Buildings
www.spab.org.uk

CRCI: K   LANGUAGES, INFORMATION AND CULTURE

Qualifications and courses

Archivist

Entrants to this profession need a 2.1 Honours degree followed by a postgraduate qualification in Archives and Records Management or Archival Studies. Useful subjects include history, classics, languages and information science. You will need at least 2 A levels/3 H grades and 5 GCSEs/S grades (A*–C/1–3) for degree entry. Your postgraduate degree must be recognised by the Society of Archivists.

Relevant work experience is an advantage and is considered a necessity for entry onto a postgraduate course. This experience must be of good quality and cannot be undertaken in a library. See the Society of Archivists website for opportunities.

Records manager

You will normally require both an Honours degree and a postgraduate qualification in Records Management or in Archives and Records Management. You will need at least 2 A levels/3 H grades and 5 GCSEs/S grades (A*–C/1–3) for degree entry. Relevant experience is also important. Visit the Society of Archivists website for opportunities.

Both archivists and records managers may start out as assistants without a degree but will need to study for a degree and postgraduate qualification in order to become professionals.

What the work involves

Archivist

You will manage and organise stored sets of archives, including records such as documents, maps, films and other items.

Many archivists deal with information enquiries and advise on the availability of records. You will ensure that archives are maintained in an appropriate way. You may also conserve documents and prepare them for storage.

Records manager

You will be responsible for organising records and information and advising your organisation as to which should be classified, stored or destroyed. You could be dealing with paper based or electronic records.

Type of person suited to this work

Both records managers and archivists manage information, so a well-organised and methodical approach is essential. They need strong analytical and IT skills.

Archivists will need an interest in preserving historical records. You may provide information and advice to members of the public, so strong communication skills are useful.

Working conditions

Record/archive centres can be modern and spacious, but if based in older buildings, space may be limited.

Accessing records from cramped storage rooms or high shelves can be physically demanding. This job may not suit people with dust allergies.

In dealing with enquiries from visitors, the working environment can be very busy.

Future prospects

Archivist

Public records offices, private companies and other organisations need skilled information professionals.

With experience, you could progress from an assistant archivist role into senior management.

Records manager

Records managers may need to change employers in order to progress. Consultancy work is an option.

Advantages/disadvantages

Archivist

This job allows you to preserve and protect historical documents.

Employers often offer short-term contracts which can create job instability.

Records manager

You may have to change employers in order to progress.

You will constantly be learning as computer software and legislation are always changing.

Money guide

A salary of between £17,000 and 24,000 a year is typical for starting salaries (before gaining a professional qualification).

When qualified and with some experience you could earn between £27,000 and £30,000.

As a senior archivist it is possible to earn between £55,000 and £60,000.

Records managers receive a starting salary of between £17,000 and £27,000.

With some experience this can increase to £40,000.

With substantial experience and within a large enough team you could earn around £80,000.

Related opportunities

- Antiques Dealer p474
- Bookseller p476
- Librarian/Library Assistant p354

Further information

Society of Archivists
www.archives.org.uk

Qualifications and courses

There are no specific entry requirements, but most arts administrators have a degree or HND in an arts subject or business studies.

At degree level, arts management can be studied on its own, or in combination with a related subject such as events management and heritage management. The minimum entry requirements are 2 A levels/3 H grades.

Postgraduate courses in arts administration/arts management are available. A degree and/or relevant work experience is required for entry to these programmes. NVQs are available in Cultural Venue Operations and Support at Level 2 and Cultural Venue Administration or Cultural Heritage Operations at Level 3, Cultural Heritage at Level 4 and Cultural Heritage Management at Level 5. Another possible entry route is a creative Apprenticeship as it covers community arts management.

Experience in the arts, in administration or business, and good ICT skills will be an advantage. It is crucial to gain experience in the arts sector by undertaking work experience, voluntary work, internships or temporary work.

What the work involves

You will support the development and operation of activities and events in areas such as visual arts, drama and music.

You will undertake a range of administrative tasks including coordinating facilities and office management. You may be responsible for booking artists, refreshments, security and ticket sales. Your job could also involve managing funding applications and budgets or writing press releases.

Arts administrators are employed in many different organisations; including arts centres, museums, community arts groups, local authorities and theatre companies. If you work for a bigger organisation, you will probably specialise in one administrative field such as public relations or sponsorship.

Type of person suited to this work

Enthusiasm for the arts is essential for this role. You will need a committed approach and be able to take initiative. A good range of administrative, office and ICT skills are also essential.

You should be able to communicate well in person and in writing. As you will probably have to manage project budgets, numeracy skills are also useful.

Good organisational and multi-tasking skills are essential. You should enjoy working with a range of people, including artists and members of the public. You should be able to work equally well independently or as part of a team.

Working conditions

Working hours can vary but it is likely that you will need to work some evenings and weekends to attend events.

Working environments vary according to employer. You might be based in a spacious office or have to work in more cramped conditions.

You might be required to travel to meet with artists and to attend performances.

Future prospects

This is a competitive area to get into. Developing expertise in a specific area such as community arts or theatre can be helpful.

With experience, you could progress from an assistant administrator role into a more senior job such as general manager or director.

With higher levels of experience, you could provide freelance support or specialise in a particular area such as arts marketing.

Advantages/disadvantages

This job provides the satisfaction of working in the arts.

Many roles are available on a part-time or on a project by project basis which can create job insecurity.

You may have to move geographic areas to gain work.

Money guide

Salary levels vary according to the type of organisation you work for.

£12,000 a year is a normal starting salary for an assistant or trainee.

When qualified this can rise to £21,000.

With experience you could earn up to £30,000.

Senior managers could earn between £30,000 and £55,000.

Salaries are higher in London and in other large cities.

Related opportunities

- Events and Exhibition Organiser p404
- Museum/Art Gallery Curator p355
- Personal Assistant p56

Further information

Arts Council England
www.artscouncil.org.uk

Scottish Arts Council
www.scottisharts.org.uk

LANGUAGES, INFORMATION AND CULTURE

CRCI: K

Qualifications and courses

To work as a bilingual secretary it is necessary to be fluent in at least one foreign language. The majority of entrants have this language as their mother tongue. For those who are not native speakers, employers will usually expect you to have at least an A level/H grade in your chosen foreign language. A degree in languages or a joint Honours degree in languages and business studies may be useful but is not essential. Degree entry requirements are usually 5 GCSEs/S grades (A*–C/1–3) and at least 2 A levels/H grades including a foreign language.

Employers may also look for qualifications in administration or secretarial skills such as the NVQ/SVQ in Business and Administration (Levels 1–4). An Advanced Apprenticeship in Business and Administration is also available for those seeking to develop the required secretarial skills. A GCSE/S grade in business studies could be useful.

The ABC Awards in Practical Languages and the OCR qualifications in Asset Languages are aimed at those looking to use their language skills in a work-based context. The LCCI International Qualifications and the Chartered Institute for IT (BCS)'s European Computer Driving Licence (ECDL) may also give entrants an advantage.

What the work involves

Bilingual secretaries use their language skills to provide administrative support to professionals.

You will deal with incoming and outgoing telephone calls, emails and faxes in a foreign language, translate reports and take on the role of an informal interpreter.

It will also be your responsibility to coordinate travel arrangements for visits overseas and make arrangements for foreign visitors.

Type of person suited to this work

You must have the ability to write and speak fluently in English and at least one foreign language, as well as having a good grasp of spelling and grammar. It is necessary to have excellent IT and keyboard skills.

You should be extremely organised, able to multitask and have good attention to detail. You must be friendly, helpful and polite and be able to work well as part of a team or independently. You should be able to remain calm under pressure.

Working conditions

You will work standard office hours but overtime may be required during busy periods. You could find part-time or temporary work. Job sharing is also available.

Bilingual secretaries share an office and spend a lot of time on the phone, working on a computer, and reading and translating documents. It could be your responsibility to deal with members of the public.

At senior levels, you might get the opportunity to travel abroad.

Future prospects

Western European languages such as Spanish, French and German are most sought after by employers, although there is growing demand for other languages including Chinese, Arabic and Japanese.

You could work for an international organisation or any companies which conduct business abroad, although most vacancies are in London and big cities.

You can progress to working for a more senior member of staff or to a supervisory role in a bigger company. This job can be a stepping stone into a career in marketing or human resources. You could also work overseas. After gaining more qualifications, you could become a translator or interpreter.

Advantages/disadvantages

You will get the opportunity to use your language skills on a daily basis.

It is possible to use the experience you have gained in a specific company or department to gain a promotion.

This job can be repetitive.

Tight deadlines and a heavy workload can be stressful.

Money guide

Salaries vary with geographical location and are likely to be highest in London.

Jobs in banks or other financial organisations tend to be higher paid than those in the media or charity sectors.

Bilingual secretaries can expect a starting salary of £18,000–£20,000.

Those with experience can earn between £20,000 and £35,000.

Taking on additional responsibilities may increase your salary further.

Related opportunities

- Personal Assistant p56
- Receptionist p59
- Secretary p64

Further information

Institute of Chartered Secretaries and Administrators
www.icsa.org.uk

Institute of Professional Administrators
www.inprad.org

LANGUAGES, INFORMATION AND CULTURE

CRCI: AD

Qualifications and courses

The most common route into this profession is through a degree or postgraduate qualification in conservation. Entry requirements for a degree are 2 A levels/3 H grades including chemistry. Some candidates may choose to take a Foundation degree in an art or furniture-related subject before their undergraduate degree and entry requirements are GCSEs/S grades (A*–C/1–3).

Graduates from relevant disciplines such as fine art, textile technology, ceramics, art history or chemistry can also enter this profession but they will need a postgraduate qualification in conservation. Details of approved courses are available from the Institute of Conservation (ICON).

An alternative route for school leavers looking to specialise in stonemasonry conservation or other crafts is to apply for an Apprenticeship.

Work experience in a museum or gallery is useful and opportunities to volunteer are available through the National Association of Decorative and Fine Arts Societies (NADFAS).

Restorers/conservation officers can work towards NVQs in Cultural Heritage (Levels 2, 3 and 5) or the EDI Diploma in Conservation (Level 4) offered by the Victoria & Albert Museum.

What the work involves

You will manage the preservation of historical objects and artwork, as well as the care of historic houses and stately homes, applying your specialist knowledge of subjects such as textiles and furniture.

You will undertake conservation work, treating objects to protect them against wear and tear or restoring objects to as close to their original state as possible.

Your job might involve managing freelance restorers/ conservators.

Type of person suited to this work

The role of preserving valuable collections or buildings requires a sound knowledge of culture and history. You will need good practical skills, attention to detail and normal colour vision. You should have a patient and methodical approach to your work.

Strong communication skills, the ability to clearly explain complex issues and confidence speaking at public events are important. You should be comfortable working both independently and as part of a team. Those who are self-employed need business and administration skills.

Working conditions

Your work is likely to involve handling and treating fragile objects and you will usually be based in a clean workshop or laboratory. Conservators of stonework or other outdoor exhibitions may have to work outside in all weather conditions.

If you are employed by a museum or gallery you will work regular office hours Monday to Friday. Some conservators/ restorers are self-employed and may have to work additional or flexible hours to suit the needs and deadlines of their client.

You might have to work with specialist materials and equipment which can affect people with skin conditions.

Future prospects

Restoration/conservation officers work in museums, galleries and historic houses, often with alternative job titles such as collections manager or curator. Many will have worked as craft conservators/restorers or have gained extensive experience in caring for collections.

You have the opportunity to work anywhere in the world. A willingness to be geographically mobile may improve your career prospects.

With experience, you could progress to managing a historic house or managing a team in a museum or gallery. It is also possible to become self-employed.

Advantages/disadvantages

This type of work offers the chance to care for valuable and rare historical collections and artwork.

Most galleries/museums employ only one person in this role so you might have to relocate to progress in this career.

Money guide

Starting salaries are usually between £18,000 and £22,000.

Once you have gained experience, you can expect earnings of £23,000–£30,000.

Those who are employed in a senior or managerial role can achieve up to £40,000.

Salaries vary according to the quality of your work and your employer.

Earnings are likely to be higher in London and large cities.

Related opportunities

- Architect p70
- Archivist/Records Manager p346
- Museum/Art Gallery Curator p355

Further information

Creative and Cultural Skills
www.ccskills.org.uk

Institute of Conservation
www.icon.org.uk

National Association of Decorative and Fine Arts Societies
www.nadfas.org.uk

LANGUAGES, INFORMATION AND CULTURE

CRCI: K

GENEALOGIST

Qualifications and courses

Most entrants have a degree, and knowledge of social and local history sources is necessary. Training in palaeography (the study of ancient writing and scripts) and Latin is also essential.

Direct entry to this profession is unusual. Entrants normally have qualifications and experience in a related field such as archive administration, librarianship or historical research.

A history degree provides a useful first step into this profession. Blackpool and The Fylde College runs a Foundation degree in history and heritage management studies at Lancaster University and the course has the option to study modules in genealogy.

The Society of Genealogists offers short courses in genealogy and palaeography both for beginners and for those already working in the field. The Institute of Heraldic and Genealogical Studies (IHGS) provides qualifications including a Certificate, Higher Certificate and Diploma in Genealogy. Those over the age of 25 who have completed the Diploma and have at least 5 years of experience in research are eligible to apply for Licenciateship of the IHGS.

What the work involves

You will organise and plan research into the history or ancestry of individual families (genealogy) and write reports from your findings.

You will work with a range of historical information such as newspapers and directories to trace specific facts about family histories. Your work could also involve liaising with or supervising the work of researchers.

Meeting with clients and keeping them updated with your research would also be part of your job.

Type of person suited to this work

As you will be investigating family history, a strong enthusiasm for historical research is essential. You will also need excellent research skills and the ability to understand detailed information.

IT skills will help you work with information management software. You will also need writing skills to produce reports.

You should enjoy meeting a range of people. You will need a good knowledge of historical resources and subject areas. An organised, thorough approach to your work is important. Working with unique historical documents demands careful handling skills.

Working conditions

Most genealogists are self-employed and work from home or in offices. However, they spend a lot of their time undertaking research in public records buildings.

The job can involve travel, for example to visit archive collections. A driving licence would be useful.

You will spend a lot of time reading and assessing detailed information.

Future prospects

Genealogy is usually followed as a hobby rather than as a profession. The number of opportunities for work are small so there is a lot of competition.

Most genealogists work on a self-employed basis whilst a small number work for specialist research companies.

You can develop knowledge on a specific subject or geographical area and then undertake additional work such as teaching.

Advantages/disadvantages

There are very few job opportunities.

As the work is often project based, it can create some job insecurity.

This work gives the satisfaction of providing people with information about their family history and it can be both fascinating and rewarding to tell people the information you find out.

Money guide

Freelance genealogists are usually paid at an hourly rate which can range from £15 to £35.

You could also charge a fixed rate for each piece of information you find.

For more complex projects you may charge a total fee between £35 and £100 per hour.

Genealogists with a postgraduate qualification can expect to earn £26,500–£35,000 per year.

Related opportunities

- Archivist/Records Manager p346
- Librarian/Library Assistant p354
- Registrar of Births, Deaths, Marriages and Civil Partnerships p62

Further information

Creative and Cultural Skills
www.ccskills.org.uk

Institute of Heraldic and Genealogical Studies
www.ihgs.ac.uk

Society of Genealogists
www.sog.org.uk

HISTORIAN

Qualifications and courses

An MA in history or historical archaeology is usually required for work as an archival or historical researcher.

Entry requirements for postgraduate degrees are a first degree in history or related subject such as ancient world studies or politics. Entry requirements for first degrees are generally 3 A levels/H grades (A*–C) including history.

For a position in a university faculty, a PhD is usually required.

Training courses in historical research are available through the Institute of Historical Research, the Society of Genealogists and the Institute of Heraldic and Genealogical Studies.

What the work involves

You will undertake historical research using ICT, paper-based information and other resources to broaden public and academic understanding of the past.

You can choose to teach and lecture on specific historical subjects.

You could also write articles for professional journals and other publications.

Heritage organisations sometimes employ historians for research purposes.

Depending on your specialism, you could spend a lot of time searching for, and analysing primary documents in achives and museums.

Professional historians can specialise in a specific area of history such as women's history, ancient history or modern history.

Type of person suited to this work

You will need a strong enthusiasm and love for history. You should also have a good knowledge of your specialist subjects.

ICT and research skills are essential. You should pay close attention to detail and be accurate in your work.

Excellent verbal communication skills are important for explaining facts to people. Good writing skills are needed for writing up research and articles.

Historians need to consider a wide range of theories, so an open-minded approach is important.

You should also be well organised to manage and plan your research.

Working conditions

You will spend time in libraries and archive centres. This will involve reading and assessing information.

Some historical researchers are based in public records offices.

Historians in an academic role are based in universities.

You can also become the specialist historian for wide variety of organisations, businesses or groups such as a football club, a military formation or think tank.

Undertaking historical research on a self-employed basis can create some job insecurity.

Future prospects

As a professional historian you could go into historical research or follow an academic career path.

Many historians combine both roles; they write, teach and carry out research on their specialist area of interest. Others combine historical research with other related areas such as genealogy.

A small number of historians are employed by heritage organisations to provide expert advice and support.

Advantages/disadvantages

This type of work provides the satisfaction of undertaking original research and finding out about the past.

It takes time and dedication to get established as a specialist on a specific historical period or subject.

Money guide

Earnings vary according to your job. Historical researchers usually charge by the hour; rates vary from £16 to £50.

Starting salaries for academic posts range from £21,000 to £25,000 per year.

With experience this rises to around £35,000.

At senior academic levels this could increase to between £35,000 and £55,000.

Related opportunities

- Archaeologist p345
- Genealogist p350
- Museum/Art Gallery Curator p355

Further information

Creative and Cultural Skills
www.ccskills.org.uk

Institute of Historical Research
www.history.ac.uk

Royal Historical Society
www.royalhistoricalsociety.org

LANGUAGES, INFORMATION AND CULTURE

CRCI: K

Qualifications and courses

Most professional information officers (sometimes called information scientists) are graduates. The fastest route to professional qualification is via a first degree in subjects such as information management, information studies and information and library studies, which are accredited by the Chartered Institute of Library and Information Professionals (CILIP).

An alternative route to professional qualification is via a degree in any subject, followed by a CILIP-approved postgraduate qualification. Experience of information-related work is advantageous, and may be a requirement for some postgraduate courses. Graduate training opportunities are available for people who wish to pursue a career in this area, and need to gain relevant experience before studying for a postgraduate qualification. Details are available through CILIP.

It is also possible to become a qualified information scientist from a library/information assistant post. CILIP offers a certification scheme for people with five years' experience of information work, or two years' experience plus relevant work-based training.

Entrants through both the educational and certification routes may have the opportunity to work towards Chartered membership of CILIP. Candidates for Chartership must have completed an approved period of professional experience.

What the work involves

You will develop, manage and coordinate both electronic and paper-based information systems for a range of organisations and companies.

Your job will involve cataloguing, indexing and archiving information. You will also respond to research enquiries, manage intranets and ensure all of your information is up to date.

You could work in a range of sectors, including law, education and business and be employed in a variety of roles. For example you could be an analyst or a librarian. You will produce reports, graphs and briefings based on your findings.

Type of person suited to this work

You should be able to work with different forms of information such as databases, the internet and paper resources.

You may provide information for members of the public or staff within an organisation so strong communication skills are important. An interest in customer service is useful.

Writing skills and ICT skills are increasingly important. Managing information demands an organised, methodical approach. A good level of numeracy can be useful. You will need to be resourceful and pay close attention to detail.

Working conditions

Information scientists work in offices, resource centres, libraries and other sites.

You will be working standard hours, Monday to Friday, and can also be hired on short-term contracts for specific projects.

You could work face to face with members of the public or staff within your organisation. You could also deal with information enquiries over the phone and through email.

Self-employed or freelance work is possible.

Future prospects

Information science is a very broad area. You could begin in an assistant or junior information job and with experience you could progress to working in a management role.

With experience you could specialise and work on a consultancy basis. At the moment there is a demand for specialists in science and computer science.

There are also opportunities to work abroad.

Advantages/disadvantages

Depending on the sector you work in, this job can be very fast paced.

Information science skills are transferable to a wide range of job areas.

Money guide

Salaries range quite widely for this role. Starting salaries vary between £18,000 and £28,000 per year.

With experience or at senior level this rises to between £28,000 and £55,000.

£70,000+ is possible at senior levels in large organisations, particularly private sector companies such as legal and finance sectors and sometimes in consultancy.

Specific salary guides for some sectors are available from the Chartered Institute of Library and Information Professionals (CILIP).

Information consultants can earn around £400–£500 a day.

Related opportunities

- Archivist/Records Manager p346
- Media Researcher p409
- Museum/Art Gallery Curator p355

Further information

Arts and Humanities Research Council
www.ahrc.ac.uk

Association for Information Management
www.aslib.com

Chartered Institute of Library and Information Professionals
www.cilip.org.uk

INTERPRETER

Qualifications and courses

Fluency in English and at least one foreign language is a prerequisite for those looking to work as an interpreter. Most entrants have a degree in modern languages, translation and interpreting, or British Sign Language (BSL) and interpreting. Entry requirements for a degree are usually 5 GCSEs/S grades (A*–C/1–3) and 2 A levels/H grades or equivalent including a modern language. A postgraduate diploma or master's degree in interpreting techniques is normally required.

Degrees in science, engineering, the environment, business or politics can be useful for jobs where you will be expected to understand specialist vocabulary and concepts.

The Chartered Institute of Linguists (IoL) offers vocational qualifications including the Certificate in Bilingual Skills (Level 3), the Diploma in Public Service Interpreting (Level 6) and the Diploma in Translation (Level 7). Candidates are expected to have achieved the required level of competence in their language. CILT, the National Centre for Languages, has developed National Occupational Standards for professional linguists.

Qualified interpreters can work towards membership of the IoL or the Institute of Translation and Interpreting (ITI). These professional bodies provide further training and development opportunities.

What the work involves

Interpreters convert words spoken in one language into conversation or speech in another language. Using your knowledge of foreign languages, you will enable speakers of different languages to communicate with each other.

You could interpret while a person speaks or make notes and then interpret their statements.

Interpreters provide services for international political conferences, court hearings, business meetings and public services.

Type of person suited to this work

You must be fluent in at least 1 or preferably 2 foreign languages. It is also important to be aware of the culture of these languages. You must have excellent listening skills and the ability to speak clearly.

Interpreting at courts and conferences requires a confident manner. You should keep up to date with current affairs as you will interpret on subjects including business and law.

Dealing with confidential information may be part of your job so you will need discretion.

Working conditions

Interpreters have to concentrate continuously for long periods which can be physically demanding.

You will need to travel to different locations at fairly short notice, either abroad or within the UK.

Interpreters work in a range of environments, including high-profile conferences and formal meetings.

Hours vary according to clients' needs and are likely to include evening and weekend work. Freelance interpreters may find the demand for work irregular.

Future prospects

This area of work is very competitive with a limited number of full-time opportunities. A small number of interpreters work for international or European agencies. Others are employed by local governments and interpret in courts, hospitals and police stations.

You can choose to work within community organisations, helping people gain access to public services. Many interpreters work on a freelance basis.

There is a greater demand for Chinese, Urdu, Punjabi and eastern European languages.

Advantages/disadvantages

This type of work provides the opportunity to travel and live abroad.

Owing to tight schedules and extensive travelling, this can be a pressured and demanding job.

Freelance interpreters often need to take on additional work to support themselves.

Money guide

Newly qualified interpreters can expect a salary of around £17,000–£20,000 per year.

With experience, your earnings can rise to between £26,000 and £35,000.

Senior interpreters working for international or European agencies can achieve up to £60,000.

Many interpreters work freelance and charge a daily rate between £110 and £500, depending on their experience, the level of demand for the language they speak and the type of interpreting required.

Related opportunities

- Importer/Exporter p601
- Secretary p64
- Teacher of English to Speakers of Other Languages p205

Further information

Chartered Institute of Linguists
www.iol.org.uk

CILT, the National Centre for Languages
www.cilt.org.uk

Institute of Translation and Interpreting
www.iti.org.uk

Qualifications and courses

The entry requirements to become a library assistant are usually at least 5 GCSEs/S grades (A*–C/1–3) or equivalent including English. Commercial or industrial libraries may require A levels/H grades. The Apprenticeship in Libraries, Archives, Records and Information Management Services is available at Intermediate and Advanced Level.

The fastest route to becoming a qualified librarian is via a degree in librarianship or information management which is accredited by the Chartered Institute of Library and Information Professionals (CILIP). The usual entry requirements are 2 A levels/3 H grades in any subjects but people with experience as library assistants are often admitted to the degree courses with vocational qualifications.

An alternative route is via a degree in another subject followed by a CILIP-accredited postgraduate qualification in librarianship or information management. Prior experience of library or information work is advantageous and some institutions will expect you to have up to 1 year's experience in a role such as library assistant.

Senior library assistants can study for a librarianship qualification (degree or postgraduate qualification) accredited by CILIP if they wish to progress to librarian level.

What the work involves

Librarian

You will manage collections of books, newspapers, documents and IT resources in libraries and information services to make them available to visitors. You may choose new resources to suit the library or information service you work in. You will also help visitors look for information and use IT and other resources.

Library assistant

You will organise and reshelve books and other resources. You may also work on the library counter to help visitors with enquiries and check books in and out of the library. You might deal with petty cash, catalogue new library resources and maintain databases.

Type of person suited to this work

You should have good customer care skills and enjoy helping people with enquiries. The ability to undertake research and use resources to locate information is essential. You must be able to work with IT software, the internet and databases and be confident in explaining these to others.

Librarians should be comfortable working in a team and managing people. Financial skills will help you monitor budgets. You will need an organised approach to your work.

Working conditions

You are likely to work face to face with members of the public or staff within an organisation.

Working on a counter, dealing with information enquiries and lifting and carrying books can all be physically demanding.

Library work can be pressured as you will need to locate and provide information to meet specific requests.

Future prospects

Librarians could progress to a senior level, meaning they would manage a branch library or department.

Some librarians move into information management roles within public services or private companies.

Library assistants are employed in library and information services in businesses, community library services and government. Larger organisations provide opportunities to progress into senior roles and take on additional responsibilities. Library closures and budget cuts could, however, affect job opportunities and prospects.

Advantages/disadvantages

You will be able to exercise your creativity by thinking up ways to promote the library and its resources.

You may need to move geographic locations to develop your career.

This type of work provides the satisfaction of helping people access information and other services.

Money guide

Salaries vary according to the sector in which you are employed and CILIP provide recommendations for minimum salaries.

Most library assistants start on £15,000 a year.

With experience, earnings can increase to £18,000.

Senior assistants earn over £20,000.

Starting salaries for librarians range from £20,000 to £24,000.

At chartered librarian level, you could expect earnings of £24,000–£33,000.

A senior librarian can receive up to £40,000.

A head of service can achieve £55,000+

Related opportunities

- Archivist/Records Manager p346
- Arts Administrator/Manager p347
- Information Officer p352

Further information

Chartered Institute of Library and Information Professionals
www.cilip.org.uk

Qualifications and courses

Entrants to this profession are required to have a relevant degree in a subject such as archaeology, history of art, heritage management, fine art or archive and museum studies. Most universities expect candidates to have achieved 2 A levels/3 H grades and 5 GCSEs/S grades (A*–C/1–3).

As competition for entry level jobs is very high, many candidates increasingly hold a postgraduate qualification in museum, gallery or heritage studies. To study at this level you will need at least a 2.1 in your undergraduate degree.

Employers will also require you to have relevant paid or voluntary work experience. Details of opportunities to volunteer are available through the Museums Assocation, the National Trust and English Heritage.

Many curators continue their studies while working and undertake a master's degree or PhD in their specialist area. Short training courses and professional development schemes are often provided by museums and galleries. Once employed you may also wish to study for the NVQ in Cultural Heritage (Levels 2, 3 and 5).

What the work involves

You will manage and maintain collections of artworks, historical objects or documents. Curators usually have specialist knowledge of a specific historical or cultural field such as women's history, textiles or archaeology. You will research and write about the collections in your care.

You might be responsible for thinking of ways in which you can gain funding for your museum/gallery. You will also organise exhibit loans with other museums/galleries.

You will work with other museum/gallery staff to plan exhibitions using items and information from your collection. You may also give talks to members of the public at special events.

Type of person suited to this work

You will need a good knowledge of history and of your specialist area of art/culture. You must be a ble to communicate this information to other staff and be a confident public speaker. You may lecture at educational events so enthusiasm for your subject is essential.

You will need good written communication skills for writing reports. IT skills are increasingly important in this area, for example when managing collection information through specialist databases. You should be organised, careful and have good attention to detail.

Working conditions

Curators generally work 37 hours a week, however these hours may be extended for special exhibitions and private showings.

This job will probably involve weekend or evening work. You may have to be on-call to respond to emergencies at the gallery/museum.

Working environments vary depending on the size, location and popularity of the gallery/museum. You will work indoors on a daily basis. There may be some heavy lifting and carrying involved when exhibits need to be moved.

Future prospects

Museum/gallery work is a competitive area in which to develop a career but it offers a variety of interesting roles.

You could work your way up in some larger organisations but often you will need to move employers or geographical location in order to move up the career ladder.

From working as an assistant curator, you could progress into a curator's role. You could then move on to work as a senior curator or go into managing museums/galleries or historic buildings.

Advantages/disadvantages

This job provides the satisfaction of working closely with works of art and historical objects, some of which can be very valuable.

You will help create exhibitions and then watch the public enjoy them.

Gaining necessary funding may be difficult.

Money guide

Salaries vary according to the location, size and type of employer.

A museum or art gallery curator can expect a starting salary of £16,000–£23,000.

Once you have gained experience in the role, you could earn between £26,000 and £37,000 a year.

A senior curator with high levels of responsibility could achieve up to £60,000.

Related opportunities

- Arts Administrator/Manager p347
- Events and Exhibition Organiser p404
- Museum/Art Gallery Technician p356

Further information

Museums Association
www.museumsassociation.org

LANGUAGES, INFORMATION AND CULTURE

CRCI: K

Qualifications and courses

Experience of working with the public and enthusiasm for museums/galleries are often valued more by employers than academic requirements. However, many large galleries/museums will require at least 4 GCSEs/S grades (A*–C/1–3) and some may expect A levels or equivalent.

Studying for a Foundation degree or degree in museum and gallery studies may improve your career prospects. Other useful subjects are history of art, heritage management and arts and cultural management. You will need at least 2 A levels/3 H grades and 5 GCSEs/S grades (A*–C/1–3) for entry to a degree.

The Apprenticeship in Cultural and Heritage Venue Operations is offered at Advanced Level and provides school leavers with the opportunity to train for a museum assistant position. Once employed, you could then work your way up to technician level.

Relevant work experience is recommended and may help you secure a permanent position. Details of volunteering opportunities are available from the Museums Association.

You might be able to gain NVQs/SVQs in Heritage Care and Visitor Service (Level 2) and Cultural Heritage Venue Operations (Levels 2 and 3) whilst working.

What the work involves

You will help prepare gallery and museum spaces for temporary exhibitions and collection displays.

Your work will involve installing audio-visual equipment to suit specific exhibitions. You will also transport objects and artworks to and from exhibition spaces. You will provide general technical support to the museum/gallery team as required.

You might be responsible for maintaining files, mending and cleaning exhibitions, and labelling and storing specimens.

Type of person suited to this work

You will need a good range of technical skills to meet the varied practical demands of a museum/gallery environment.

As well as providing support in setting up new exhibitions, you will have to deal with practical problems as they arise. The ability to handle fragile or valuable objects and artworks carefully is essential.

You will need a good knowledge of building security and maintenance. You may also be responsible for the fire safety of the gallery/museum. You will be a good team player and have a strong interest in helping people get the most out of their visits to galleries and museums.

Working conditions

Although you may spend some time in an office environment, the majority of your work will take place around the museum/gallery.

Generally technicians work about 36 hours a week but you might have to be on-call to respond to emergencies at the gallery/museum. You might also have to work longer hours when setting up or dismantling exhibitions. You may have to work some weekends, evenings and bank holidays.

You will usually be required to wear a uniform and/or name badge.

Future prospects

Whilst museum/gallery work is a competitive area in which to develop a career, it offers a variety of interesting roles.

You could work your way up in some larger organisations but often you will need to change employers/relocate in order to move up the career ladder.

It is possible to progress to working as a senior or head technician. In larger organisations, you could manage a team of technicians.

Advantages/disadvantages

This job provides the satisfaction of working closely with works of art and historical objects, some of which can be very valuable.

This is a competitive area of work so you might have to change jobs to gain a promotion.

You may have to work some unsocial hours which could disrupt your social or family life.

Money guide

These figures are only approximate and may vary depending on location and employer. Larger galleries and museums may pay a higher rate.

Starting salaries are between £13,000 and £16,000.

With experience, you can expect to earn about £19,000 a year.

Senior technicians with additional responsibilities can achieve up to £25,000.

Related opportunities

- Archaeologist p345
- Events and Exhibition Organiser p404
- Museum/Art Gallery Curator p355

Further information

Association of Independent Museums
www.museums.co.uk

Creative and Cultural Skills
www.ccskills.org.uk

Museums Association
www.museumsassociation.org

TRANSLATOR

Qualifications and courses

Most translators have a relevant degree. These include degrees in one or more foreign languages (preferably applied), a foreign language combined with a specialist subject such as business, law, engineering, computer studies, Asian or European studies, or translation or interpreting.

For modern language degrees, 5 GCSEs/S grades (A*–C/1–3) and a minimum of 2 A levels/3 Highers, with one in a language, or equivalent qualifications are normally required.

Postgraduate courses in translation are available, and usually require a degree in a modern language. The Chartered Institute of Linguists (IoL) offers vocational qualifications in a wide range of languages, including the Certificate in Bilingual Skills (equivalent to A level/H grade), the Diploma in Public Service Interpreting at QCF Level 6, and the Diploma in Translation at Level 7. Examinations are open entry, but candidates are expected to have achieved the required level of competence before sitting an exam.

Fluency in two or more languages is required to work as a translator. Qualified translators can work towards membership of the IoL or Institute of Translation and Interpreting. These professional bodies provide further training and development opportunities.

What the work involves

You will convert written text such as letters, reports, leaflets and brochures from one language to another. You will ensure that your translation matches the tone and style of the original text and has a high standard of grammar.

Your work will also involve meetings with employers to agree projects.

Translators provide services to specialist translation agencies, private companies, local government bodies and international organisations.

Type of person suited to this work

Translators must work to a high standard of accuracy, so attention to detail is important.

The ability to write in your chosen languages in a range of styles is essential. You should also be able to understand and translate complex documents. ICT skills are very useful.

Discretion is important as you may translate confidential information. Being well organised will help you to meet project deadlines. You will need a confident approach to work on a freelance basis and promote your services. Numeracy skills are also useful.

Working conditions

Translators are usually self-employed and based in offices at home, but there are opportunities for translators in companies.

You might attend meetings with employers and colleagues.

This type of work involves close working at a computer and the use of resources such as dictionaries and technical reference books.

Future prospects

As a translator you could work for a variety of employers, translating medical, technical, legal and other documents.

Many translators work on a freelance basis.

There are opportunities to work for private companies and international organisations on a permanent basis, in the UK or abroad. Demand for translators is growing, especially owing to large multi-national events such as the Olympic Games and G-20 Summits.

Advantages/disadvantages

This area of work can provide opportunities to travel and work abroad.

Working on a self-employed project-by-project basis can create some job instability.

Translation can be very demanding owing to short deadlines and the constant demand for accuracy.

Money guide

Translators may be paid between £75 and £180 per 1000 words, depending on the language they are translating.

Most positions pay between £18,000 and £21,000 per year.

With experience, generalist translators earn around £30,000 and senior translators can earn up to £60,000.

Related opportunities

- Importer/Exporter p601
- Secretary p64
- Teacher of English to Speakers of Other Languages p205

Further information

Chartered Institute of Linguists
www.iol.org.uk

CILT, the National Centre for Languages
www.cilt.org.uk

Institute of Translation and Interpreting
www.iti.org.uk

LANGUAGES, INFORMATION AND CULTURE

CRCI: K

357

Legal and Political Services

If you find the law a fascinating subject and you feel you would enjoy a challenging career where the rewards are a good salary and a real sense of achievement when your hard work pays off, a job in this sector could be what you are looking for. Workers in this sector are fiercely passionate about their careers and have more often than not, completed a lot of training and worked hard to establish themselves in this competitive field. You need to be driven and thrive on pressure and tight deadlines; this is a sector for someone who is ambitious and very talented at working tactfully with people.

The jobs featured in this section are listed below. For similar jobs to the ones in this section turn to *Administration, Business, Office and Financial Services* on page 15.

Qualifications and courses

Employers prefer candidates to have 5 GCSEs/S grades (A*–C/1–3), including English and maths. Applicants must be aged between 21 and 62 but mature candidates, without a criminal record or debt, are often preferred because their life experience may help them deal with difficult situations. A Diploma in Public Services could be helpful.

To become a certificated bailiff, candidates need to obtain a Bailiff's General Certificate. This is issued by a circuit judge. The necessary legal knowledge can be gained by taking the examinations of the Certificated Bailiffs' Association (CBA).

In Scotland, to be commissioned as a sheriff officer, candidates need to pass the examinations of the Society of Messengers-at-Arms and Sheriff Officers. The minimum age to be commissioned is 20, but training, which normally takes 3 years, can begin earlier.

You will need a security bond up to the value of £10,000, plus 2 references for insurance purposes.

In England and Wales training is done mostly on the job. However it is possible, upon gaining enough experience and having passed the relevant exams, to join the Association of Civil Enforcement Agencies (ACEA) or the Enforcement Services Association (ESA) in order to aid continuing professional development.

In Scotland, training is done under an appointed mentor. After 2 years of experience has been gained you can apply to become a messenger-at-arms.

What the work involves

Court bailiffs deliver legal documents such as court summonses to people who owe money and might also take steps to ensure payment. Certificated/private bailiffs visit people in debt to recover the money they owe, arranging for removal of their property where necessary.

In Scotland, officers of court deliver legal documents to people who owe money and take all the legal steps required to get the money paid.

You might also give advice on how to pay debts.

Type of person suited to this work

As there are strict legal procedures connected with recovering debt, you will need to be sure you are completely up to date with legislation to conduct your work correctly and within legal guidelines.

The work will bring you into contact with many different people, so it's important that you are able to deal with all members of the public.

You will need to be assertive to deal with people's resistance and be persistent to get the job done. Being tactful and able to cope with people under stress is also essential.

Working conditions

You will spend a lot of time travelling and so will need a clean driving licence.

Although you will be based in an office, you might have to visit people's homes in the evenings and early mornings to make sure that someone is there.

If you have to remove furniture in payment of debt, you could have to do a lot of heavy lifting, so you will need to be physically fit.

In England and Wales, court bailiffs generally work for the county courts and private bailiffs with magistrates' court orders.

In Scotland, officers of court are called sheriff officers in the sheriff court and messengers-at-arms in the Court of Session.

Future prospects

If you work for the county court you can progress into management or switch to a private firm in which you would also have opportunities to progress into management roles.

Advantages/disadvantages

The work is varied and in different locations; no two days will be the same.

You will meet many different people, some of whom may be difficult to deal with and threatening.

The hours can be long and unsocial.

Money guide

Starting salaries are around £14,000 per year if you are uncertified.

If you are newly certified this rises to between £20,000 and £25,000.

A top rate of £50,000 is possible for the very capable and highly experienced.

Private firms may pay you a basic salary plus some form of commission or commission only.

In Scotland you could start at around £17,000.

With experience this can rise to between £26,000 and £28,000.

Related opportunities

- Police Officer p551
- Police Support Worker p552
- Security Officer/Manager/Door Supervisor p563

Further information

Association of Civil Enforcement Agencies
www.acea.org.uk

Enforcement Services Association
www.ensas.org.uk

Society of Messengers-at-Arms and Sheriff Officers
www.smaso.org

Qualifications and courses

England and Wales

You will need either an approved law degree or another degree (minimum 2.1 Honours for both), followed by a postgraduate law conversion course, known as the Common Professional Examination, or a Graduate Diploma in Law.

For vocational entry, you must become a member of one of the four Inns of Court and undertake the Bar Vocational Course. You must also complete 2 6-month pupillages (a mix of work and training, in chambers). Training for the 'bar' continues for 3 years, working in one of the Inns of Court.

Once you have qualified, you will be required by the Bar Standards Board (BSB) to undertake at least 45 hours of continuing professional development (CPD) per year. This must include at least 9 hours of advocacy training and 3 of ethics. Once 3 years have passed you need only complete 12 hours of CPD per year.

Scotland

You will need either an Honours degree in Scottish Law from a Scottish university (minimum 2.1 Honours); an Ordinary degree in Scottish Law from a Scottish university with an Honours degree from a UK university (minimum 2.1 Honours); or a Scottish Ordinary degree with distinction. You must also undertake a 1-year full-time postgraduate Diploma in Legal Practice at a Scottish university.

For vocational entry, you will need to work for 12–21 months in a solicitor's office and 'devilling' (training with) a member of the bar for nine and a half months, before taking the entry examinations of the Faculty of Advocates.

Advocates will normally practise as a solicitor for 10 years, prior to acting as an advocate.

What the work involves

Barristers/advocates give legal advice to solicitors and other professionals and act for clients in certain cases in the high courts. You will research information and past cases before giving advice to solicitors on whether a case should go to court.

In court, you will examine witnesses and present the case for the prosecution or the defence.

You will also act for clients at tribunals or enquiries if asked to do so by a solicitor.

Type of person suited to this work

You will need to research large amounts of information before giving legal advice. You will need to be able to think logically to work out what is important in the case and apply the law to it.

You will need to be confident to speak in court, to convince a jury with your arguments, and able to think quickly when questioning witnesses or defendants.

Good writing and speaking skills are needed to prepare your case. Keeping an open mind is important and you must be able to gain people's confidence.

Working conditions

Barristers usually work in offices called 'chambers', and advocates in groups known as 'stables' in the Advocates' Library in Edinburgh.

If you specialise in criminal law, you will spend more time in court than civil law specialists would.

As you will travel widely, a driving licence is useful.

Future prospects

Most barristers/advocates are self-employed and it can take around 5 years to establish a practice and become known.

After 10–15 years' experience you can apply to 'take silk' to become a Queen's Counsel. This is essential if you want to become a judge in the higher courts.

Some people work in central or local government where there is a clear promotion structure.

Advantages/disadvantages

The work is varied and you will get satisfaction when you win a case.

Some cases may put you under pressure, particularly if they attract media attention.

You will sometimes work long hours to meet deadlines.

Money guide

During training or pupillage, between £11,000 and £18,500 per year is usual.

Earnings between £28,000 and £60,000 are normal in the Crown Prosecution Service in England and Wales.

As an advocate in Scotland you may start at around £11,000; moving up to between £24,000 and £56,000 in the Procurator Fiscal Service.

The majority of barristers in England and advocates in Scotland are self-employed. Earnings can be up to £300,000 or sometimes more. This is dependent on experience, location and reputation.

In private practice top earnings can be in excess of £750,000.

Related opportunities

- Barrister's/Advocate's Clerk p362
- Crown Prosecutor/Procurator Fiscal p368
- Paralegal p373

Further information

Faculty of Advocates
www.advocates.org.uk

Skills for Justice
www.skillsforjustice.com

The Bar Council
www.barcouncil.org.uk

Qualifications and courses

In England and Wales, barristers' clerks usually require a minimum of 4 GCSEs/S grades (A*–C/1–3), including maths and English. A levels are an advantage and relevant work experience would benefit you greatly.

You may join the Institute of Barristers' Clerks (IBC). The IBC offers a 1 year BTEC Advanced Award in Chambers Administration for Barristers' Clerks which is aimed at clerks with 5 years' service in chambers. Upon completion you can apply for qualified membership of the IBC. Graduates do not need to take the BTEC but must have 3 years' service in chambers.

The IBC also offers a number of topical seminars and an annual conference which it is important to attend as you must maintain a firm grasp on current legal issues.

In Scotland, advocates' clerks require a minimum of an H grade in English and evidence of computer literacy and numeracy. More advocates' clerks are now entering with a HNC/HND or degree. Most training is on the job but you are encouraged to take courses organised by Faculty Services Ltd.

What the work involves

Clerks manage the day-to-day work for a group of barristers (England and Wales) or advocates (Scotland).

An important task will be liaising with solicitors to encourage them to give work to your business. You will estimate how much work is involved in a case to see how much time it will take, allocate cases to barristers/advocates and negotiate fees.

When you first enter this career, you will mainly be preparing accounts, filing and photocopying, and answering the phone.

Type of person suited to this work

As your work will involve meeting lots of people, you will need excellent speaking skills. Good writing skills are needed for writing letters and preparing notes and reports.

Being good with figures is essential when negotiating fees and preparing accounts. You will need to be business-like and have good negotiating skills to bring in work, and confidence to deal with solicitors, court officials and clients.

Your work will involve handling confidential information, which means discretion and tact are necessary. It is also important to be a good teamworker and flexible in your approach to work.

Working conditions

You will work mainly indoors in an office, using computers and spending a lot of time on the telephone. However, you might travel in connection with your work so a driving licence is useful.

As you will also be meeting other professionals, you will have to be smartly dressed at all times.

Some chambers are based in historic buildings with difficult working conditions and limited access.

You will typically work standard office hours, Monday to Friday. However, you might have to work evenings and weekends during busy periods.

Future prospects

Competition is fierce for entry to this profession.

One clerk will serve more than 1 barrister with most offices in London or other large cities. Advocates work in groups known as 'stables' in the Advocates' Library in Edinburgh.

You would start as a junior clerk and progress to clerk with experience. Training will be ongoing throughout your career. With experience you could train for another legal profession or move into general administrative work.

Advantages/disadvantages

Your work will be interesting and varied and you will have a lot of responsibility.

Work in the evenings and long hours are necessary when deadlines are approaching.

After further training, you can move into other legal careers.

Money guide

Starting salaries are quite low, ranging between £12,000 and £14,000 for a junior clerk or clerk's assistant.

This rises considerably with experience. Clerks with more than 5 years' experience can earn between £25,000 and £55,000. Senior clerks with a high level of responsibility, in busy chambers, can earn up to £100,000.

There is also the opportunity for bonuses directly related to the income of the barristers.

In Scotland you can earn between £22,000 and £28,000. As a senior clerk, you can earn up to £45,000.

Most opportunites are in London.

Related opportunities

- Barrister/Advocate p361
- Court Administrative Officer p365
- Paralegal p373

Further information

Faculty of Advocates
www.advocates.org.uk

Institute of Barristers' Clerks
www.barristersclerks.com

Skills for Justice
www.skillsforjustice.com

CONSTITUENCY AGENT/POLITICAL RESEARCHER

Qualifications and courses

There are no set academic requirements but entry is very competitive and many employers expect candidates to have a 2.1 degree or above. Subjects such as politics, law, social policy, economics, marketing, public relations or journalism may prove valuable. You will need at least 2 A levels/3 H grades and 5 GCSEs/S grades (A*–C/1–3) for degree entry.

A postgraduate qualification such as an MSc in public affairs and lobbying, an MPhil in politics or an MA in political communications would also be helpful.

Experience of working for the party on a voluntary basis is very important and demonstrates your commitment to the organisation. It is also possible to develop relevant skills through other opportunities, for example, involvement with a trade union, holding office in a students' union or campaign work for a charity group.

In general, candidates must be at least 20 years of age.

What the work involves

Constituency agent
Your job will be to organise the running of the constituency for your political party, including election campaigns. You will arrange meetings, coordinate PR and marketing, and deal with enquiries.

As secretary to the local office, your duties will include managing local membership, fundraising and organising volunteers.

Political researcher
You will research information on political subjects and provide your employer with a coherent briefing of your conclusions. Your duties may include helping to write political speeches, finding sources of expertise on a specific issue and monitoring parliamentary reports.

Type of person suited to this work

You will need a solid understanding of the political system, along with a genuine interest in and love of politics. It is important to have strong political opinions whilst understanding that sometimes you must look at the bigger picture.

Key skills for constituency agents are communication, information handling, IT, money management, teamwork and leadership and supervisory skills.

Key skills for political researchers include tact, resourcefulness, debating abilities, IT and research skills, resilience, communication, articulation and analytical abilities.

Working conditions

Constituency agent
Most of your work will be based in the party office which will be open to the public. However, you will be expected to do lots of travelling both locally and nationally, so a driving licence and car would be useful. You could work evenings, weekends or during the day. Hours could increase during national or local events like elections.

Political researcher
You will be working in an office, normally 9am–5pm although some longer hours might be required to meet specific deadlines. You may need to travel.

Future prospects

Constituency agent
Your prospects could depend on the size of the party you support. Later, you could become a local councillor or Member of Parliament.

Political researcher
This is an excellent starting point for a career in politics. Progression may include becoming an MP. You could take on extra responsibilities and move between public affairs firms in order to achieve promotion.

Advantages/disadvantages

You will get considerable job satisfaction as your work will make a difference to citizens and the local community.

You may find this career stressful, particularly when you have to meet project deadlines or when there are elections.

Money guide

Constituency agent
Your starting salary is likely to be about £19,000.

With experience and increased responsibilities, you could earn £25,000–£31,000.

Political researcher
Starting salaries range from £17,000 to £22,000.

Those with considerable experience can achieve £27,000–£35,000.

Related opportunities

- Media Researcher p409
- Politician p375
- Welfare Benefits Adviser/Welfare Rights Caseworker p584

Further information

Association of Professional Political Consultants
www.appc.org.uk

Chartered Institute of Public Relations
www.ipr.org.uk

CORONER

Qualifications and courses

Candidates must be qualified solicitors, barristers or medical practitioners with at least 5 years' experience. The usual entry route is to find a coroner who will appoint you as their deputy or assistant deputy coroner.

Following the Coroners and Justice Act 2009, the coroner service is undergoing reforms regarding the recruitment and training of coroners. New coroners will need law qualifications. Up-to-date information is available from the Ministry of Justice.

To train as a lawyer you need either an approved law degree, or a non-law degree followed by the Common Professional Examination (CPE), the Postgraduate Diploma in Law (PgDL) or the Senior Status Law degree. Candidates must then complete a Legal Practice Course (LPC). To be accepted onto a law degree you will usually require 2–3 A levels/H grades and 5 GCSEs/S grades (A*–C/1–3) or equivalent.

In order to qualify as a doctor you must complete an undergraduate course which leads to a degree in medicine. To do this you will need very high results in 3 A levels/H grades including chemistry and biology, and good GCSEs/S grades (A*–C/1–3). Entry requirements differ between universities.

Aldermen and councillors of local authorities are not eligible for appointment as coroners in their counties or districts until 6 months after the end of their service.

What the work involves

You will investigate sudden and suspicious deaths, determining if an inquest or post-mortem is necessary. Coroners preside at inquests and make decisions on whether or not further action is required.

You will need to work with police and medical services in order to conclude whether or not a person died of natural causes and keep detailed records of all proceedings.

Once you have completed your investigations you must provide families or the relevant authorities with your report.

Type of person suited to this work

Preparing cases involves looking at statements and reports so you need to be able to read and analyse large amounts of information. You might need to check points of law and request further information so you must pay attention to detail.

Much of your work will involve talking to people and writing reports so you need to have excellent verbal and written communication skills. Being confident to speak in court and argue logically are also important.

You must be organised, able to meet deadlines and handle distressing situations calmly.

Working conditions

You will work both indoors and outdoors, as you will primarily be based in an office but will also spend time in court, at crime scenes and in hospitals.

You will usually work normal office hours but you will also fulfil on-call duties as each district is required to provide a 24-hour service.

Most coroners work part time and spend the rest of their time working in private legal practice.

Future prospects

Coroners are appointed and paid for by local councils but hold office under the crown.

Once employed as a deputy or assistant deputy coroner, with experience you can progress to coroner level. Although there is currently no further promotion route, the Coroners and Justice Bill has proposed that posts such as senior coroner and chief coroner should be made available in the future.

Advantages/disadvantages

The work is varied, carries responsibility and can be satisfying.

You will have the opportunity to meet a wide range of people.

The role involves extensive administration and paperwork.

You will be on an on-call rota for evenings, weekends and bank holidays.

Money guide

If you work full time as a deputy coroner, your starting salary will be around £25,000.

As a full-time coroner you can expect earnings between £91,000 and £99,000 a year, depending on the population size of the area you cover.

Part-time coroners are paid in proportion to the amount of cases they undertake. As a guide, you would receive £9,900 for 200 cases and £50,500 for 2000 cases a year.

Related opportunities

- Barrister/Advocate p361
- Hospital Doctor p312
- Solicitor/Notary Public p376

Further information

Coroners' Society of England and Wales
www.coronersociety.org.uk

Ministry of Justice
www.justice.gov.uk

COURT ADMINISTRATIVE OFFICER

ENTRY LEVEL 2

Qualifications and courses

Qualification requirements vary within different regions and according to the type of court. Most employers expect candidates to have a good general education, with 5 GCSEs/S grades (A*–C/1–3) including maths and English.

Some areas require administrative, typing, office or computing experience while others also expect a minimum of 1 year of relevant office-based experience. City & Guilds offer several courses which enable candidates to develop their administrative skills such as word processing, typing and shorthand.

Applicants without formal qualifications but with relevant administrative experience may be able to sit an aptitude test to gain entry to this profession.

New recruits tend to hold A levels/H grades or equivalent qualifications such as the NVQ/SVQ in Business and Administration (Levels 1–4). An alternative route is the Apprenticeship in Court, Tribunal and Prosecution Administration which is available at Intermediate Level.

The NVQ/SVQ in Court Tribunal Administration (Level 2) may be beneficial for those already working as an administrative assistant and looking to progress to the role of officer.

What the work involves

You will organise all the papers and information for a court hearing so that everything is ready for the judge or magistrate when the court session begins.

Booking dates, times and courtrooms for court hearings will be part of your job and you will prepare the timetable for each day. You will ensure that everyone arriving at court knows where to go and receives the relevant paperwork.

After the hearings, you will carry out court orders such as endorsing driving licences, writing adoption orders or collecting fines.

Type of person suited to this work

As you will be responsible for making sure that court hearings run smoothly and everything is ready on time, it is important to be methodical, organised and pay close attention to detail.

You must be polite and helpful so that you can put people at ease and explain things clearly to them. Tact and an understanding of confidentiality are essential.

If you are working in a finance section, you must have good numeracy skills to be able to calculate fines and costs. You should be confident using IT.

Working conditions

Most of your time will be spent indoors in courtrooms and offices in the court. You may have to travel to different courts so a driving licence is useful.

You will be working around 37 hours a week, however overtime may be necessary if there is a hearing in the evening or at the weekend. Part-time work is often possible.

Future prospects

Court administrative officers in England and Wales are employed by Her Majesty's Courts Service (HMCS) and move through promotion grades. In Scotland they are often known as court officers and are employed by the Scottish Court Service.

Most training is on the job. It is possible to start as a court administrative assistant and work your way up to officer level.

You may have to move courts to widen your experience. You could move into similar work in the legal field, such as legal executive roles, or into general administrative work. Promotion to senior administration roles is possible.

Advantages/disadvantages

The work is varied and no two days will be the same.

You will meet and work with many different people.

Some people may be aggressive and threatening, which you could find frightening.

You may have to start early or work late at busy times.

Money guide

Salaries vary depending on your employer and geographical location.

Those beginning their career as an administrative assistant can expect to earn between £12,824 and £14,912 a year.

An administrative officer will have a starting salary of about £14,551.

Earnings can increase to £19,200 as you gain experience.

If you progress to become a senior clerk or team leader you could earn in excess of £22,000 per year.

Related opportunities

- Barrister's/Advocate's Clerk p362
- Civil Service Administrative Officer p27
- Court Usher/Officer/Macer p367

Further information

HM Courts and Tribunals Service
www.justice.gov.uk

Scottish Court Service
www.scotcourts.gov.uk

CRCI: L   LEGAL AND POLITICAL SERVICES

365

Qualifications and courses

Candidates are usually required to have 3–5 GCSEs/S grades (A*–C/1–3) including English. Many entrants also have A levels/H grades. Thorough knowledge of the English language and a high standard of spelling, grammar and punctuation is expected.

To begin work as a court reporter in England and Wales, you must be certified as competent by the British Institute of Verbatim Reporters (BIVR). The requirements for approval by the BIVR are to learn how to use shorthand machines, to reach a speed of at least 180 words per minute on a shorthand machine and to gain experience as a trainee court reporter.

Sorene Court Reporting & Training Services offer a distance learning course which lasts 1–2 years and teaches candidates how to use the stenotype machine. Training is also provided in real-time reporting and Speech-to-Text (STT) reporting.

In Scotland, all training is undertaken on the job with a mentor and regular tests will be set to monitor progress.

It is possible after training and 3 years' experience to become a member of the BIVR by taking an examination. Members of the BIVR with deaf awareness training can become accredited STT Reporters.

What the work involves

Your job could involve attending court hearings, listening and reporting on what is said. Using a stenotype machine, or sometimes other recording equipment, you will write down everything a witness says. You may edit other speakers to correct the grammar.

Mostly you will work on your own but in complex cases where lawyers may want a daily transcript of proceedings, you will work in a team of 3 on a rota basis.

You could also record proceedings within other legal meetings such as industrial tribunals.

Type of person suited to this work

You need to have excellent listening skills and the ability to concentrate for long periods of time. A fast typing speed, strong attention to detail and a good grasp of punctuation and grammar are needed to ensure that your record is accurate. Manual dexterity and keyboard skills are essential for operating the stenotype.

You must speak clearly when reading back what you have written. If you do not hear what is said or you fall behind in your transcription, you must have the confidence to stop proceedings or ask for something to be repeated.

Working conditions

You will operate a stenotype machine with computer aided transcription systems, a machine with a keyboard layout which enables whole words and phrases to be typed with one stroke.

There is a growing trend in Scotland for court cases to be taped and transcribed afterwards.

You might have to travel to different courts so a driving licence is useful.

Future prospects

You could attend criminal cases in the crown courts or civil cases in the high courts. You will also be present at other events, including industrial tribunals, public enquiries and in Parliament to record proceedings for Hansard.

Most court reporters are self-employed and there is no defined promotion ladder. Others work for companies contracted to service courts.

In England and Wales there is a shortage of trained staff. In Scotland vacancies may decrease owing to the shift to taping court proceedings.

Reporters also have the option to work in the media industry, providing subtitles for viewers with hearing impairments.

Advantages/disadvantages

You will have contact with a wide range of people.

You will have to concentrate for long periods so the work is demanding.

Work in the evenings is possible to complete reports for the next day.

Money guide

Starting salaries are around £10,000–£15,000 per year.

With experience, your earnings can increase to £17,000–£24,000.

Many court reporters work on a freelance basis so earnings vary according to the number of days worked.

Daily rates can range from £40 to £200.

Real-time reporters are likely to earn more and could receive £300 a day for private sector work.

Related opportunities

- Court Administrative Officer p365
- Paralegal p373
- Receptionist p59

Further information

British Institute of Verbatim Reporters
www.bivr.org.uk

Sorene Court Reporting & Training Services
www.sorene.co.uk

COURT USHER/OFFICER/ MACER

Qualifications and courses

Whilst no formal qualifications are required, a minimum of at least 2 GCSEs/S grades (A*–C/1–3) including English is strongly recommended.

A background in the police or Armed Forces can be an advantage. Experience working with the public would also be helpful.

Training is conducted on the job and new entrants will work alongside an experienced usher. Employers may also provide short courses covering topics such as equality awareness, security and dealing with challenging situations.

It is possible to study for the NVQ/SVQ Diploma in Court Tribunal Operations (Levels 2 and 3).

You will need to obtain clearance from the Criminal Records Bureau (CRB) before becoming a court usher.

The stated minimum age for entry to this profession is 21 (16 in Scotland), but most courts prefer to recruit mature people under the age of 63 (60 in Scotland).

What the work involves

Court ushers make sure that everything in the courtroom is ready for proceedings to begin, for example that all papers are ready, glasses and water are on tables, and fire exits are clear.

When people arrive at court, you will meet them and direct them to the right courtroom. In court, you will tell people to stand when the judge comes in, call witnesses and administer the right oath to them. You will have to label the evidence and give it to the judge and jury. You will also pass messages between lawyers and legal advisers.

In Scotland, you will be known as a court officer in the sheriff court and a macer in the supreme courts.

Type of person suited to this work

As courtrooms must be prepared at the beginning of the day, court ushers need to be thorough in their work and pay attention to detail. You must be logical and organised.

You need to be able to work with people of all ages and backgrounds. Some may be nervous so it is important to have good communication skills to explain what is happening and put them at ease. You will also need to be confident and sound in control in court.

It is important to stay calm at all times and be impartial when dealing with people from both sides of a case. You will come into contact with a great deal of confidential information so trustworthiness and professionalism are essential attributes.

You need to be able to work well as part of a team to ensure the smooth running of the court case.

Working conditions

You will spend most of your time in a courtroom but you might also have an office in the courthouse, as your job will involve entering data into the computer system, filing and photocopying.

In certain jury cases, you might have to stay away from home overnight. A driving licence would be useful if you are required to travel between courts.

You must be smartly dressed at all times.

Future prospects

There are few jobs for court ushers and entry to the career can be competitive.

You can be promoted to senior and supervisory grades. You could also progress into other administrative jobs within the legal profession or another sector.

Advantages/disadvantages

The job will be varied and no two days will be the same.

You might have to stay late or start early if proceedings overrun.

You will meet many different people, some of whom may be difficult to deal with.

Money guide

Earnings vary with location and tend to be higher in London.

Starting salaries for court ushers in England and Wales are between £13,000 and £16,000.

A court officer in Scotland is likely to earn £13,274 to £14,878 a year.

At a senior level it is possible to achieve up to £22,000.

You may receive overtime payments for late nights or early starts.

Related opportunities

- Bailiff/Enforcement Agent p360
- Civil Service Administrative Officer p27
- Court Administrative Officer p365
- Receptionist p59

Further information

HM Courts and Tribunals Service
www.justice.gov.uk

Scottish Court Service
www.scotcourts.gov.uk

Skills for Justice
www.skillsforjustice.com

LEGAL AND POLITICAL SERVICES

CRCI: L

Qualifications and courses

Crown prosecutor
If you are a qualified solicitor or barrister then you can apply directly to the Crown Prosecution Service (CPS). Lawyers must have completed their Legal Practice Course (LPC) and 2-year training contract and barristers must have finished their Bar Professional Training Course (BPTC) and 12-month pupillage.

Alternatively, law students can apply for the CPS Legal Trainee Scheme (LTS) in the year that they are owing to complete their vocational training. The CPS offers 15 candidates a training contract each year.

Procurator fiscal
Candidates are solicitors qualified in the Scottish legal system. An LLB degree in Scottish law (or 3 years of pre-diploma training and a pass in the Law Society of Scotland's exams) is required, followed by a Diploma in Professional Legal Practice (PEAT 1) and a 2-year training contract with a practising solicitor in Scotland (PEAT 2).

Alternatively, those who have completed an LLB at a Scottish university can apply for one of 25 places available on the 2-year traineeship offered by the Crown Office and Procurator Fiscal Service (COPFS).

What the work involves

Crown prosecutor
You will look at reports from the police and other agencies and decide whether or not crimes in England and Wales should be prosecuted.

You will take statements from witnesses before a trial and examine witnesses in court, guiding them through their evidence. You will then sum up the case for the prosecution.

Procurator fiscal
You will work in the Scottish legal system, carrying out similar duties to crown prosecutors in England and Wales. In Scotland, the Crown Office and Procurator Fiscal Service (COPFS) investigates and prosecutes all crime.

Type of person suited to this work

Preparing cases involves looking at statements so you must be able to read and analyse a lot of information. Attention to detail is essential.

You must have excellent verbal and written communication skills as you will deal with other professionals and the public. You should be confident making clear and logical arguments in court and have the ability to make unbiased decisions.

Working conditions

You will be based in an office but you will also spend time in court. You might also work outdoors at scenes of crime and accidents.

You will work 37–42 hours a week, including covering weekends and bank holidays on a rota system.

Future prospects

Crown prosecutor
There is a clear promotion structure within the service but very few posts at the most senior levels. Competition in the CPS is high.

Procurator fiscal
Candidates start as deputes, working under the guidance of senior colleagues and gradually taking more responsibility. After a few years, they can apply to become procurator fiscals but promotion is not automatic.

Crown prosecutors and procurators fiscal can transfer into other areas of law such as private practice.

Advantages/disadvantages

The job is interesting, carries responsibilities and can be rewarding.

You will have contact with many different types of people, some of whom may be difficult to deal with.

Working on a rota system may disrupt your personal life.

Money guide

Crown prosecutor
Crown prosecutors have a starting salary of £27,722–£31,374.

As a senior crown prosecutor, you can earn up to £42,224.

Procurator fiscal
During your traineeship you can expect £15,965 in your first year and £19,107 in your second year.

With experience and qualifications, your salary will be between £39,000 and £46,365.

A senior procurator fiscal can achieve £45,084–£52,540.

Related opportunities

- Barrister/Advocate p361
- Paralegal p373
- Solicitor/Notary Public p376

Further information

Crown Office Scotland
www.crownoffice.gov.uk

Crown Prosecution Service
www.cps.gov.uk

JUDGE/SHERIFF

Qualifications and courses

Candidates looking to become a judge must be qualified solicitors or barristers who have 5–7 years' legal experience. The Lord Chancellor requires that candidates should normally have previous judicial experience in a part-time role such as deputy district judge, recorder or tribunal judge. District or circuit judges are usually appointed after 10–15 years' court experience and applications are made through the Judicial Appointments Commission (JAC).

To qualify as a solicitor or barrister, you will need either an approved law degree, or a non-law degree followed by the Common Professional Examination (CPE), the Postgraduate Diploma in Law (PgDL) or the Senior Status Law degree. Solicitors must then complete a Legal Practice Course (LPC) followed by a 2-year training contract and barristers must undertake the Bar Professional Training Course (BPTC) and a 12-month pupillage.

In Scotland, candidates for a sheriff's position must be a fully qualified solicitor or advocate with at least 10 years' experience. Applications are made through the Judicial Appointments Board for Scotland.

To become qualified in the Scottish legal system it is necessary to have an LLB degree in Scottish law (or 3 years of pre-diploma training and a pass in the Law Society of Scotland's exams), followed by a Diploma in Professional Legal Practice (PEAT 1) and a 2-year training contract with a practising solicitor in Scotland (PEAT 2).

What the work involves

Judges (sheriffs in Scotland) preside over courts and make judgements on what should happen based on the evidence from 2 opposing parties. You will listen to all the evidence and decide on procedures, including whether a piece of evidence can be used, whilst keeping order in court.

In jury cases, you will instruct and advise the jury on the strength of the evidence before the jury leaves court to consider the verdict.

You will decide on penalties in criminal courts and on settlements in civil cases.

Type of person suited to this work

As judges make the final decision in a court case, it is important to be able to grasp facts quickly and analyse the evidence to help make your decision. Judges must think logically and not become emotionally involved.

You should have excellent communication and public-speaking skills. You also need to be a good listener and pay careful attention to the evidence.

It is important to have the confidence to make difficult decisions and stand by them. Discretion is needed to deal with confidential information.

Working conditions

You will spend much of your time in court but you will also have an office with support staff to help you. You will travel between courts and may have to spend time away from home.

You will dress smartly at all times and wear robes in court. Courts are very formal and have traditions which you must observe.

Future prospects

There are very few openings for judges and sheriffs, which means entry is competitive. Successful candidates have normally followed a long career in law as a barrister/advocate or solicitor.

Most judges work in one type of court, such as a Crown Court or Court of Appeal. Senior positions, such as Lord Chief Justice and Master of the Rolls, are made on the recommendation of the Prime Minister.

In Scotland, most sheriffs work in sheriff courts. A few with experience become supreme court judges in the High Court of Justiciary or the Court of Session.

Judicial office holders are legally required to retire at the age of 70.

Advantages/disadvantages

The work is varied and no two days will be the same.

This is a very responsible job which requires a high amount of intellect and dedication.

You will meet many different people and hear some cases which will have a high media interest or involve distressing evidence.

Some courts work into the evenings.

Money guide

The starting salary for a district judge is about £102,921.

You could earn £128,296 as a circuit judge.

As a High Court judge you can achieve in excess of £170,000.

The Lord Chief Justice, the highest legal position in England and Wales, earns £239,845 a year.

In Scotland, sheriffs have a salary of £128,296–£138,548.

Related opportunities

- Barrister/Advocate p361
- Crown Prosecutor/Procurator Fiscal p368
- Legal Executive p370

Further information

Judicial Appointments Commission
www.judicialappointments.gov.uk

Judicial Communications Office
www.judiciary.gov.uk

Skills for Justice
www.skillsforjustice.com

LEGAL AND POLITICAL SERVICES

CRCI: L

LEGAL EXECUTIVE

Qualifications and courses

You need to undertake academic and practical training to be a legal executive. These examinations are set by the Chartered Institute of Legal Executives (the Institute of Legal Executives (ILEX) was awarded the Royal Charter in 2012).

There are 2 stages of training to complete – the CILEx Level 3 Professional Diploma in Law and Practice and the CILEx Level 6 Professional Higher Diploma in Law and Practice. In addition, you will need to gain 5 years' working experience to become a fully qualified Chartered Legal Executive.

The minimum requirements for the Level 3 training are 4 GCSEs/S grades (A*–C/1–3), including English. City & Guilds/ILEX Level 2 Certificate in Legal Studies is a suitable alternative.

Students will train for Level 3 under the supervision of a solicitor or senior legal executive and study is carried out on day release or at evening classes. The Diploma takes 1 to 2 years to complete.

Full training at Level 6 takes 2 years (while working full time) and leads to CILEx Membership. CILEx qualifications can also be taken as part of a Modern Legal Apprenticeship scheme.

Some qualifications such as a law degree may provide exemption from some academic parts of the qualifications. People with relevant experience can also apply to have their experience approved by CILEx.

In Scotland, there is no direct equivalent to legal executive; staff are known as paralegals or solicitors' assistants. Generally 4 GCSEs/S grades (A*–C/1–3) including English and maths, followed by office experience are required.

What the work involves

Legal executives work with solicitors, preparing complex cases for them and dealing with straightforward cases themselves.

You will interview clients, asking questions to help you give them legal advice and explain legal points to them clearly. You will write letters on their behalf, draft contracts and wills and prepare other documents.

In certain cases, you may represent clients in court or at tribunals.

Type of person suited to this work

Excellent written and verbal communication skills are essential.

Clients will give you confidential information so it is important to be discreet and tactful. You will also need patience as legal points can be difficult to grasp.

When preparing cases, you will be handling large amounts of information, which means it is useful to be a thorough and well-organised worker.

Working conditions

Most legal executives work 37 hours a week, Monday to Friday but you will probably be expected to work additional hours on a regular basis including evenings and weekends.

You will be based in an office but you may attend court. You will be expected to dress smartly.

You might have to travel to visit clients or legal libraries, so a driving licence is useful.

Future prospects

You could work for solicitors in private practice or in local and central government and industry. Legal executives usually specialise in one area, for example property or business law.

You can train to qualify as a legal executive advocate or as a solicitor, which allows you to follow a case right through to court.

This is a very competitive career, and the majority of entrants are now graduates.

Advantages/disadvantages

You will have the chance to work in a legal environment while studying part time and earning a good salary.

You might have to work under pressure to meet deadlines and work unsociable hours.

Money guide

Starting salaries for trainee legal executives vary from £15,000 up to £28,000 per year of training.

Once you have the CILEx qualifications you can earn up to £38,000, depending on where you work.

Legal executives with more experience (it takes 5 years to become a fully qualified Legal Executive) can earn between £35,000 and £55,000 and in big city firms the salary potential is even higher.

Owing to increasing demand for Legal Executives the salary range has broadened considerably depending a lot on experience, skills and location.

Related opportunities

- Barrister's/Advocate's Clerk p362
- Civil Service Administrative Officer p27
- Solicitor/Notary Public p376

Further information

Institute of Legal Executives
www.ilex.org.uk

Law Society of England and Wales
www.lawsociety.org.uk

Law Society of Northern Ireland
www.lawsoc-ni.org

Qualifications and courses

England and Wales

Candidates must pass the Council for Licensed Conveyancers (CLC) training and exams. To begin training applicants must have 4 GCSEs (A*–C), including English and an A level in law is useful. You may be accepted without minimum qualifications if you have relevant work experience with a solicitor or licensed conveyancer's office.

Many applicants will hold a law degree or might have undertaken the Chartered Institute of Legal Executives course or the Legal Practice Course for trainee solicitors. They must have at least 2 years' practical training with a 'qualified employer' and pass the CLC examination. Many students take this as a correspondence course. It is also offered on a part-time basis.

Candidates can then apply for a limited licence. After a further 3 consecutive years you can apply for a full licence. An Apprenticeship in Business, Administration and Law may also be available.

Scotland

Entrants require a degree in law from a Scottish university or a Diploma/Certificate in legal studies which takes at least 2 years.

They then undertake a 1 year training contract with an independent qualified conveyancer. After six months of training, a Professional Competence Course, which comprises 36 hours of core requirements and 18 hours of electives, must be completed.

For law degrees you need 5 GCSEs/S grades (A*–C/1–3) and 3 A levels/H grades. Some universities require applicants to take the National Admissions Test for Law.

Northern Ireland

The job of a licensed conveyancer is carried out by a solicitor. Solicitors must complete an Apprenticeship programme of 2–4 years, combined with a vocational course. You can complete either a Certificate in Professional Legal Studies or a Postgraduate Diploma in Professional Legal Practice.

What the work involves

Licensed conveyancers deal with the legal side of buying, selling, renting and mortgaging of houses, flats, business premises and other property.

You will draw up the legal documents, known as contracts, that buyers and sellers exchange to make a sale legal.

Other work includes liaising with lawyers and estate agents involved in the sale and researching details in the contract.

Type of person suited to this work

You will need excellent communication skills to explain complicated legal matters to clients. Being a good teamworker is useful to liaise with others involved in a contract.

As legal contracts must be completely accurate, you must be thorough and able to process large amounts of information.

You will need good organisational skills to deal with several properties simultaneously.

Working conditions

You will work standard office hours, but may be required to work some late evenings or weekends to meet clients.

Your job may be salaried or commission only.

Many licensed conveyancers are self-employed.

Future prospects

There are only around 1000 licensed conveyancers in England and Wales, and very few qualified conveyancers in Scotland. Job opportunities are mainly with legal practices, although since the recession there are fewer places for trainees.

Training is ongoing to cover developments in property law. You could progress into other legal professions, a managerial role or run your own business.

Changes in the law now allow conveyancers to take an additional qualification, to add to their licence, and deal with probate. Probate is the legal procedure of administering the money, property and possessions of a person after they die.

Advantages/disadvantages

The work is varied. You will meet different people, though some may be difficult.

You will get satisfaction when clients get their dream home.

You might find it stressful when trying to meet deadlines or clients feel things are moving too slowly.

Money guide

A trainee salary would start around £14,000 per year.

With further experience, this rises to £25,000–£40,000 per year.

At the more senior levels you might earn £35,000–£55,000 per year.

It is possible to earn in excess of £60,000 per year as a partner or an owner of a conveyancing firm.

Related opportunities

- Barrister/Advocate p361
- Estate Agent p95
- Surveying Technician p124

Further information

Council for Licensed Conveyancers
www.conveyancer.org.uk

Law Society of Scotland
www.lawscot.org.uk

LEGAL AND POLITICAL SERVICES

CRCI: L

Qualifications and courses

Magistrates' court legal adviser (England and Wales)

Candidates must be fully qualified as either a barrister or solicitor. You will start as a trainee legal adviser following a structured on-the-job induction programme organised by the associated court.

You need an approved law degree, or a non-law degree followed by the Common Professional Examination (CPE) or a Graduate Diploma in Law (GDL). You should then have completed either the Legal Practice Course (LPC) or the Bar Professional Training Course (BPTC).

Sheriff's clerk (Scotland)

There are no minimum entry requirements but it would be helpful to have S grades (1–3) in maths and English. You could start as an administrative officer and then progress to a role as sheriff's clerk.

Fast-track entry to a position as sheriff's clerk deputy is sometimes available to those with a law degree, the Diploma in Legal Practice and 2 years' training with a solicitor.

What the work involves

Magistrates' court legal adviser (England and Wales)

You will be a qualified solicitor or barrister with responsibility for advising magistrates in court.

You will advise on points of law, procedures, penalties and other issues.

Sheriff's clerk (Scotland)

You might advise on points of law and procedures in any court (civil or criminal).

You could have a more general administrative role such as handling court complaints and providing statistics for court staff.

Type of person suited to this work

You must have a strong interest in the law and excellent communication skills as you will be expected to advise on a wide range of issues.

You must be organised, reliable and able to work quickly and accurately under pressure.

It's important to be impartial and remain detached from emotionally demanding cases. You will need to be discreet to deal with confidential information.

Working conditions

You will normally be located in one court building and will generally work a 37-hour week, from Monday to Friday.

However, your working hours may, at times, be irregular owing to complex cases.

Some courts also open as early as 8.00am and you might need to work weekends.

You might travel to different courts so a driving licence is useful.

Future prospects

Her Majesty's Court and Tribunal Service has a set career structure. You could progress to a role as a justices' clerk or a justices' chief executive. You could go on to a role where you train magistrates or manage a team of legal advisers.

In Scotland, sheriff's clerks are employed by the Scottish Court Service. Small rural courts may have only one clerk, while a court in a big city will have several.

There is a clear promotion structure within the Scottish Court Service.

Advantages/disadvantages

The work is varied and no two days will be the same.

You might have to work unsocial hours at times.

You might find it hard not to be the decision maker.

Money guide

You can expect around £20,500 as a trainee adviser, having completed either the LPC or the BPTC.

Those who have completed a training contract in addition, can expect to earn around £29,000.

An experienced magistrates' legal adviser can earn between £30,000 and £43,000.

Starting salaries for sheriffs' clerks are about £12,211. This can rise to between £28,000 and £35,000.

Related opportunities

- Barrister/Advocate p361
- Legal Executive p370
- Solicitor/Notary Public p376

Further information

HM Courts and Tribunals Service
www.justice.gov.uk

Scottish Court Service
www.scotcourts.gov.uk

LEGAL AND POLITICAL SERVICES

CRCI: L

PARALEGAL

Qualifications and courses

You do not need any specific qualifications to become a paralegal, and can start work straight from school. However, most employers prefer you to have some relevant qualifications, for example GCSEs (A*–C), a BTEC/HNC in Legal Studies, an NVQ in Business Administration or a Foundation degree in law.

Some employers ask for a HND or degree in law, and others even request the LPC (Legal Practice Course) postgraduate qualification. Becoming a paralegal is also a popular option with those who graduated in law but do not have a training contract to become a solicitor.

Training usually takes place on the job, and you will be supervised by experienced lawyers. Employers may well encourage you to follow courses in legal training; these are widely available. They might include BTEC Level 2 and 3 qualifications in law and legal work or City & Guilds Level 2 Award/Certificate/Diploma in Legal Studies.

Membership of the Institute of Paralegals or the NALP offers the opportunity to work towards a degree-level qualification and provides increased recognition in the industry. As a member, you must take part in continuing professional development (CPD) programmes.

What the work involves

A paralegal is somebody who is not a qualified lawyer, but whose job involves dealing with a lot of legal issues.

You may have legal training or experience, and will work in a law firm or similar organisation. Your duties will be varied, but will probably involve legal research and drafting documents, as well as other administrative tasks.

You will also interview witnesses and clients, and appear in court, often acting on behalf of lawyers. You might specialise in a specific area of law.

Type of person suited to this work

You should have a natural interest in law and current affairs, and be discreet in your work, as you may frequently be dealing with confidential information.

Attention to detail is essential. Equally, a good command of English and the ability to communicate well with everybody, from the lawyers you will be working with to all of their clients, is vital. You should also be patient, understanding, tactful, sympathetic and be able to work well under pressure.

Organisational skills are essential, as is computer literacy, excellent concentration and a good memory. You also need to be able to understand and absorb a lot of information.

Working conditions

You'll probably be working in an office for about 37 hours a week. However, some of these will be spent visiting clients, which means that a driving licence is useful.

You may spend time in police stations and court, occasionally out of office hours.

You may be required to work weekends and bank holidays.

Future prospects

Future prospects for a paralegal are good. You can use the knowledge you gain on the job to develop your legal career.

If you have the necessary qualifications, you can become a solicitor or barrister, and even work your way up to partner.

With experience, you can take on additional responsibilities and move up within the firm. You may choose to move on to freelance work.

Advantages/disadvantages

Working as a paralegal is stimulating and rewarding, especially if you have an interest in or study law.

It can really give your law career a nudge in the right direction, and is a great option if, for example, you are training to be a solicitor and want to take a gap year or year out.

Occasionally tasks may be a little mundane and meeting with clients can be stressful.

Money guide

As a paralegal who is starting out, you may earn between £18,000 and £25,000 a year.

This can grow, with experience, to £40,000.

As a senior paralegal, you might be earning over £70,000 a year.

Related opportunities

- Barrister's/Advocate's Clerk p362
- Court Administrative Officer p365
- Legal Executive p370

Further information

Institute of Legal Executives
www.ilex.org.uk

Institute of Paralegals
www.instituteofparalegals.org

National Association of Licensed Paralegals
www.nationalparalegals.com

LEGAL AND POLITICAL SERVICES

CRCI: L

Qualifications and courses

Patent attorney

All patent attorneys need a degree related to science, engineering or maths. Entry is with at least 5 GCSEs/S grades (A*–C/1–3) including English and maths, and at least 2 A levels or equivalent. Entry is competitive and most employers look for a minimum of a 2.1 Honours degree.

Patent attorneys receive specialist training in intellectual property law. Qualified solicitors with experience of working in an intellectual property department or those training to become patent agents may apply to join the Chartered Institute of Patent Attorneys (CIPA).

A high level of skill in the English language is required, and fluency in foreign languages, especially French and/ or German, is a bonus. This is a requirement in order to become a European patent attorney.

A training period and the successful completion of examinations is required for admission to the Register of Patent Attorneys and the Register of Trade Mark Attorneys. It usually takes 4 to 5 years to qualify. The Certificate in IP Law, offered by several universities (typically a 1 to 3 month course), gives exemption from all the Foundation Papers of the CIPA examinations.

Examiner

You must have a good Honours degree in science, maths, engineering or technology. An equivalent professional qualification or corporate membership of a relevant major professional institution may be accepted. It is also essential that you meet the nationality and residency requirements as specified by the civil service.

What the work involves

Patent attorney

You will advise clients on the law of intellectual property.

The work involves checking that an invention is a new one and does not already exist.

You will prepare specifications for the Patent Office, carrying out any negotiations required and representing the client before the patent examiner.

Examiner

You will examine patent applications submitted by patent agents for new inventions, trademarks or designs.

You must ensure that patents are granted for new inventions.

You will conduct a study of each application to check that it is clear and that it meets legal requirements.

Type of person suited to this work

You will need a thorough knowledge of applying intellectual property to inventions and of the laws regarding this sector.

You should have strong research skills and a high attention to detail. You must have excellent communication skills in order to explain complex legal issues to your clients.

You must be highly organised, decisive and able to multi-task.

Working conditions

You will be based in an office, although patent agents do some travelling in the UK and abroad; a driving licence would be useful.

The majority of your time will be spent researching and writing reports on the computer.

Future prospects

Roughly 750 patent attorneys are registered in the UK. Around 80% work in private practices, mostly in the larger towns and cities. Around 20% work with industrial companies or local government agencies.

Patent examiners are civil servants, mostly based in the Patent Office in Newport with a few working in London.

The civil service has a formal promotion structure culminating in the successful candidate becoming a senior patent examiner.

Advantages/disadvantages

This job has a high level of responsibility and is intellectually demanding.

You will get satisfaction from helping new inventions become recognised and being involved from an early stage in the process of creation.

Money guide

The starting salary for a trainee is around £20,000, rising to £30,000 per year with experience.

Technical assistants can earn £28,000 and progress to £48,000.

Once qualified you could earn between £50,000 and £70,000, reaching in excess of £100,000 for senior partners in private practices.

Related opportunities

- Barrister's/Advocate's Clerk p362
- Legal Executive p370
- Solicitor/Notary Public p376

Further information

Chartered Institute of Patent Attorneys
www.cipa.org.uk

Intellectual Property Office
www.ipo.gov.uk

POLITICIAN

ENTRY LEVEL 1

Qualifications and courses

Any British citizen may stand for election as long as they are over 18 years old. There are no formal minimum educational requirements. Commitment to a political party is the most important criterion.

However, owing to the competitive nature of this field, many Members of Parliament (MPs) are graduates or hold other professional qualifications. Relevant subjects to study include politics, business, law or economics.

Active involvement in a political party is essential and experience as a trade union activist may be useful. Some people work their way up from being a politician's assistant or political researcher. Many people enter politics after a career in medicine, law or education.

There are a series of selection interviews before candidates can be 'adopted' by their party and their local constituency to stand for election. Candidates must then carry out a successful campaign and be elected by the votes of the local people.

Those disqualified from standing for election are undischarged bankrupts, prisoners of more than 1 year, members of the House of Lords and people holding offices listed in the House of Commons Disqualification Act 1975.

What the work involves

MPs represent the people in their local constituencies in Parliament, usually as a member of a political party. You will hold 'surgeries' in your local constituency and deal with issues raised by local people at local and national level.

MEPs (Members of the European Parliament) deal with European legislation. In Parliament, you will join committees, attend meetings and take part in debates. You will also vote on new policies or laws.

You may specialise in a particular area and you may hold office in the government or for the opposition.

Type of person suited to this work

You should be passionate about politics and have strong social beliefs, along with a desire to represent the people of your constituency. Key skills include: communication, decision making, information handling, supervisory and management skills. A pleasant manner and the ability to gain people's confidence are also important.

You will be expected to keep up to date with party policies and legislation, which requires being able to process large amounts of information quickly and thoroughly.

Working conditions

Your time will be divided between your local constituency and Parliament/Scottish Parliament/Welsh Assembly. MEPs spend 1 week a month in Strasbourg and much of their remaining time in Brussels.

Politicians tend to work very long hours when parliament is sitting. From the end of July to the beginning of October parliament breaks so that politicians can spend time in their constituencies. This is an extremely demanding job with a great deal of responsibility.

There is a lot of travel involved both at home and overseas.

Future prospects

Your job in any parliament will depend on being re-elected, which means it is important to have another career option to fall back on.

Although most MPs represent the local people in their constituencies, they are also involved in the government of their country.

You could be offered a post in a ministry, which may lead to appointment as a minister in a particular area. In exceptional circumstances, you could become the leader of your party and maybe even the Prime Minister.

Advantages/disadvantages

The work is varied and challenging, and no two days will be the same.

You will get a sense of satisfaction if your party is in power but also frustration when votes are not in your favour.

You will need plenty of stamina to cope with the long hours and high levels of pressure.

Money guide

Earnings depend on your level of responsibility. Additional allowances/expenses are available for travel and communications.

The basic salary for an MP in the House of Commons is £65,738.

You could earn £134,565 as a cabinet minister.

The Prime Minister currently takes an annual salary of £142,500.

MEPs are paid the same salaries as national MPs in their own countries.

Related opportunities

- Public Relations Officer p416
- Trade Union Official p581
- Welfare Benefits Adviser/Welfare Rights Caseworker p584

Further information

National Assembly for Wales
www.wales.gov.uk

Scottish Parliament
www.scottish.parliament.uk

UK Parliament
www.parliament.uk

CRCI: L LEGAL AND POLITICAL SERVICES

375

Qualifications and courses

England and Wales

You will need either an approved law degree, or a non-law degree followed by the Common Professional Examination (CPE), the Postgraduate Diploma in Law PgDL) or the Senior Status Law degree. Candidates must then complete a Legal Practice Course (LPC) followed by 2 years of training with a solicitor.

Candidates without a degree can take examinations to become Members or Fellows of the Chartered Institute of Legal Executives.

Scotland

You will need either an approved Scottish law degree, or a good non-law degree followed by a 2-year graduate law degree. Entry is usually with 5 Highers (grades A–B) including English.

Candidates without a degree can take 3 years' pre-Diploma training with a Scottish solicitor and pass the Law Society of Scotland's exams.

All entrants must complete a 26-week Diploma in Professional Legal Practice followed by a 2-year training contract with a practising solicitor in Scotland.

Northern Ireland

Candidates must complete an apprenticeship programme combined with a vocational course. This takes 2–4 years, depending upon whether you have a degree. You can choose to do either a Certificate in Professional Legal Studies or a Postgraduate Diploma in Professional Legal Practice.

Notary public

In England and Wales, qualified solicitors must take a Postgraduate Diploma in Notarial Practice and be approved by the Master of the Faculties to act within a specific area. In Scotland and Northern Ireland, solicitors can apply to be enrolled as notaries once qualified.

What the work involves

Solicitor

A major part of your job will be advising clients on legal matters, making a will or setting up a business.

In certain circumstances you may represent clients in court, or you might have to instruct a barrister or advocate to act for your client.

Notary public

Your main job will be to certify deeds and other documents so that they will be accepted by judicial and public authorities as authentic and legally binding. Notaries public are generally solicitors who combine this function with other legal work.

Type of person suited to this work

You must be able to examine and analyse vast amounts of information and pay close attention to detail.

You will need to possess good communication and interpersonal skills.

You will need to be discreet when dealing with confidential information. It is important to remain impartial.

Working conditions

Most of your work will be in an office.

You might spend time in court or have to visit clients, therefore you will need to dress smartly.

You will often be under a lot of stress to meet deadlines.

Future prospects

There is keen competition for traineeships, but when you are qualified as a solicitor there there are good prospects in private practice, government and industry.

You will usually specialise in one area of law and may eventually become a partner in a firm or even become a judge.

As a notary public you may decide to start your own company.

Advantages/disadvantages

The work is varied and no two days will be the same.

You might have to work long hours.

Some people may be difficult and unpleasant to work with.

Money guide

As a trainee, you can earn £16,650 per year in England and Wales; in Scotland you start at £15,965 for the first year rising to £19,107 in the second. In Northern Ireland, your salary will start at a minimum of £12,480.

Experienced solicitors can earn between £25,000 and £75,000.

Salaries will be higher in London and large cities.

An experienced senior partner in a legal practice can earn in excess of £150,000.

Notaries public are paid set fees for work on individual cases, reflecting the responsibilities of their professional role.

Related opportunities

- Barrister/Advocate p361
- Crown Prosecutor/Procurator Fiscal p368
- Legal Executive p370

Further information

Law Society of England and Wales
www.lawsociety.org.uk

Law Society of Northern Ireland
www.lawsoc-ni.org

Law Society of Scotland
www.lawscot.org.uk

Leisure, Sport and Tourism

This sector relies on a motivated, up-beat and out-going workforce for its success. You will need to show that you can work very well with other people, providing them with an excellent service when they want to enjoy themselves on holiday or if they are keen to improve their fitness and sporting ability. If you are keen to work with professional sports players or become one yourself you should be very aware of how to keep the body fit while avoiding injury. You should be warm and friendly but also able to maintain a high level of professionalism at the same time. You should also demonstrate you have patience and tact with people of all ages and be clued up on health and safety regulations.

The jobs featured in this section are listed below. For similar jobs to the ones in this section turn to *Catering and Hospitality* on page 133.

Qualifications and courses

There are no formal entry requirements although many betting shop chains may ask for a GCSE/S grade (A*–C/1–3) in maths. You may have to take a basic maths test as part of the recruitment process, focusing on the calculation of percentages, odds and payments. By law, you must be 18 years of age to work in a betting shop and at least 20 years old to start as a manager.

Experience working in a customer service role is an advantage. Betting shop employees may have opportunities to work towards the City & Guilds Award in Principles of Customer Service in Hospitality, Leisure, Travel and Tourism (Level 2) or the NVQ in Customer Service (Levels 1–4). Other relevant qualifications are the City & Guilds Award in Working within Gambling Legislation (Level 2), the NVQ in Gambling Operations (Levels 2 and 3) and the NVQ Diploma in Gambling Operations – Betting (Levels 2 and 3).

Training is provided on the job and covers areas such as calculating betting odds and payouts, administration, customer service, business skills, managing staff, betting laws and company policies.

Some entrants to trainee management positions have a degree, HND or Foundation degree while others work their way up from cashier level.

What the work involves

You will take bets from customers on the outcomes of sporting events and contests, and pay out winnings. You will work out betting odds (the chance of winning or losing) for your customers.

Cashiers will update display boards with betting opportunities, oversee betting terminals, balance the books at the end of each shift and look out for fraud.

Managers ensure that the shop meets Gambling Commission regulations, deal with disputes and complaints, and control profits and costs.

Type of person suited to this work

You need to be alert to gather vital information about race entrants' recent performance ratings and handicaps. You should have a good understanding of sports.

Customers will keep coming back to place bets in your shop if you are friendly and service-oriented. You need to be good with numbers and money.

Confidence and good verbal and negotiation skills are vital in order to handle difficult customers. Being able to work well under pressure is essential.

Working conditions

You will most likely work up to 40 hours a week although part-time work may be available. Betting shops are open 7 days a week year-round and are usually open until 10pm. Your busiest day will be Saturday and you will need to be prepared to work evenings, weekends and holidays.

You will need to wear a uniform or dress smartly.

An independent bookmaker will travel long distances to attend all major sporting events and much of the work will be outdoors.

Future prospects

You have the opportunity to work for a chain, an independent shop, a bookmaker business at a racecourse or a national regulatory body such as the Gambling Commission. With experience, you can be promoted from cashier to manager.

You could become a multi-site manager of about 15 shops within a city or even an area manager looking after 50 or more shops.

Successful bookmakers often prefer to move into self-employment and may work well beyond normal retirement age.

Advantages/disadvantages

Being involved with people taking risks can create a high-pressure atmosphere and may lead to confrontations.

The long hours may disrupt your personal life and commitments.

You have the opportunity to build a good rapport with customers which can make for an enjoyable workplace.

Money guide

Starting salaries for a cashier are between £10,500 and £14,000.

Deputy managers can expect about £15,000.

Betting shop managers usually earn £20,000–£30,000.

An area manager for a large chain could achieve £45,000 plus bonuses.

If you are a self-employed bookmaker your salary will depend on racing conditions, the number of entrants and gamblers, and the number of events in the calendar.

Related opportunities

- Accounting Technician and Accounts/Finance Clerk p18
- Croupier p380
- Entertainment Manager p382

Further information

Association of British Bookmakers Ltd
www.abb.uk.com

Gambling Commission
www.gamblingcommission.gov.uk

National Association of Bookmakers
www.nab-bookmakers.co.uk

CINEMA PROJECTIONIST

Qualifications and courses

There are no formal academic requirements for entry to this career. Owing to film classification laws, you must be at least 18 years of age to work as a projectionist.

Many employers expect applicants to have some knowledge or experience of working with electronics, cameras or sound equipment. This could be gained by working as an assistant projectionist for a few months.

All employers look for candidates who can demonstrate a real enthusiasm for the moving image. Joining a film club can help to develop your knowledge of film formats and projection equipment. Working part time in a cinema will give you further insight into the industry while you wait for a trainee projectionist role to become available.

There are also short and part-time courses available which could give you the experience needed to go straight into employment as a projectionist. The Moving Image Society (BKSTS) offer courses in both film-based and digital cinema projection.

What the work involves

Projectionists work in cinemas and are responsible for operating film screening equipment, ensuring that everything runs smoothly throughout the feature.

You will also be required to monitor other technical equipment in the cinema, including lighting, heating and ventilation systems, and electrical and gas supplies. You may be responsible for ensuring that all fire alarms and extinguishers are in good working order.

You may work with traditional 20-minute reels of film or modern digital versions that are stored on a hard drive. You will be expected to check that the sound on each film is operating properly and the volume is correct.

Type of person suited to this work

You should enjoy working independently and have a strong interest in film and cinema, as the majority of your time will be spent alone operating machinery in the projection room. You will need good IT skills in order to use increasingly complicated film screening technology and equipment.

You must be alert and observant so you can identify problems quickly, and also have the practical skills and knowledge to solve these issues effectively and under pressure. Good eyesight, hearing and coordination are essential.

You should be able to adhere to the strict timings given on schedules to ensure that each film runs according to plan.

Working conditions

You will work 5 days a week but hours are generally long and irregular as most cinemas screen films from the afternoon up until late in the evening.

Shift work and overtime are common.

You will spend most of your time in a projection room. Most of these do not have windows but in modern cinemas they are usually air conditioned. You will be working alone in the projection room for the majority of your shift.

Future prospects

Opportunities can be found in large cinema chains or in smaller and often more specialist independent theatres.

In larger organisations, you could be promoted to senior projectionist or an administrative role.

Small independent cinemas offer scope for experienced staff to become more involved with the running of the business.

Advantages/disadvantages

If you love cinema, you will enjoy being able to watch films for free.

You will have the opportunity to work for a number of employers, ranging from large multiplexes screening major blockbusters, to small independent cinemas which may specialise in art-house or international films.

You will be working alone for the majority of the time.

Your hours will be unsocial, including evenings and weekends.

Money guide

Starting salaries for cinema projectionists tend to be around £12,000.

With a few years' experience, your earnings could rise to £17,000.

Chief projectionists in larger cinemas can achieve up to £22,000 a year.

Related opportunities

- Actor p430
- Arts Administrator/Manager p347
- Lighting Technician p440

Further information

BKSTS
www.bksts.com

British Film Institute
www.bfi.org.uk

LEISURE, SPORT AND TOURISM

CRCI: MA

Qualifications and courses

You must obtain clearance from the Criminal Records Bureau (CRB) as you are unable to work as a croupier if you have a criminal conviction. All entrants to this profession need to apply for a personal functional licence (PFL) from the Gambling Commission. You must be 18 years old to work in a casino but there are no specific academic requirements. Prospective employers may set assessments at interview, including maths and manual dexterity tests.

Most major casino operators run training schemes for entrants, both in-house and externally. To gain the NVQ at Level 2 in Gambling Operations (Casino), entrants may attend an 18-week course available at Blackpool and The Fylde College, the London Gaming College and North Warwickshire and Hinckley College.

As a croupier with 2 years of experience, you can progress to supervising a number of gaming tables after undertaking further training. Floor managers have additional security responsibilities in counting, checking and locking away all the money taken by close of business so experience or training in security may be useful.

The National Gaming Academy offers a Foundation degree in Gaming Technology which could improve your long-term career prospects.

What the work involves

Croupiers work in casinos and are responsible for setting up gaming tables, preparing packs of cards and selling gaming tokens to customers.

You will be greeting customers, inviting them to join games of roulette, blackjack or baccarat and explaining the rules if necessary. Spinning the roulette or money wheel, shuffling and dealing cards, shaking mini dice cages and encouraging players to place their bets will be part of your role.

You will also be responsible for announcing and paying out wins, and collecting in lost bets.

Type of person suited to this work

You should have an engaging personality, good interpersonal skills and possess the ability to make customers feel happy and relaxed. Confidence in front of an audience is essential. Appearance is highly important. You must be smartly dressed, clean and manicured, with immaculately groomed hair.

There might be difficult moments when people are distressed or angered by losing so you must be confident and assertive.

Fluency in another language is an asset.

Working conditions

Casinos open 7 days a week and on bank holidays from noon to 6am. Many are now open 24 hours a day. This means that staff work shifts including evenings, weekends and bank holidays.

On cruise liners, croupiers spend up to 12 months on-board, with about 6 weeks' vacation. Casinos close when in port so you do get time ashore in exotic locations!

Future prospects

The number of casinos across Britain is increasing so prospects are good. Gambling has become better regulated in recent years and employers really value good staff.

Significant numbers of croupiers are needed to fill jobs on cruise liners and this can be a favourite choice for experienced croupiers seeking management-level experience.

With further training, you can progress to inspector, pit boss and, finally, manager of a casino.

Advantages/disadvantages

If you are quick and ambitious, you can make rapid progress from croupier to casino manager.

Standing for hours and concentrating on running the games without error, while talking to customers, can be tiring.

Casino-goers drink alcohol which exacerbates the emotional tension during gaming. Arguments often break out which you must be able to handle according to the rules and regulations governing gaming.

Money guide

Starting salaries for croupiers outside of London are between £11,500 and £13,500. Within London, a trainee croupier can expect to earn £17,000-£18,500.

Those with experience who are employed in a senior position can achieve £25,000–£30,000. In London, a highly experienced croupier could reach earnings of £40,000 a year.

Pay scales on cruise liners are similar, however meals and accommodation are provided and the opportunity for tips may boost your salary.

Related opportunities

- Cruise Ship Steward/Purser p595
- Entertainment Manager p382

Further information

British Casino Association
www.britishcasinoassociation.org.uk

DIVER

Qualifications and courses

There are no formal academic requirements to become a professional diver or diving instructor but you must meet the Diving at Work Regulations 1997 (DWR) established by the Health & Safety Executive (HSE). Before you begin training, you must obtain a valid certificate of medical fitness to dive from a doctor approved by the HSE. You must also pass a medical every year during your diving career.

Entrants must ensure that the training course they undertake is approved by the HSE. Organisations offering recognised diving qualifications include the Professional Association of Diving Instructors (PADI) and the British Sub-Aqua Club (BSAC). Employers also require divers to have specialised First-Aid training. Divers who intend to work offshore must pass the Basic Offshore Induction and Emergency Training (BOSIET).

Professional divers should ideally already possess the technical skills that are relevant to their industry. For example, divers involved in an archaeology project may require a degree in archaeology.

What the work involves

As a diver you will work either at sea or inland in rivers, lakes, canals and reservoirs. Your tasks will depend on the industry you choose to work in and the type of diving you specialise in.

You could choose to become a diving instructor. Diving instructors teach a wide variety of skills from entry level diver training for beginners to technical diving for more experienced divers. They often operate from dedicated dive centres at coastal sites or through hotels in holiday resorts or local swimming pools.

Professional divers are often used in several industries, such as offshore oil and gas, civil engineering, fish farming, media, scientific research, underwater archaeology or police diving, and undertake a variety of specialist tasks.

A civil engineer diver is employed for underwater repairs and demolition. Divers employed in media will be required to participate in stunts or underwater filming. Police divers are responsible for searching for and recovering missing persons or evidence. Offshore divers recruited in the oil and gas industries will be employed for exploration and surveying, or building and maintaining drilling rigs and pipelines.

Scientific diving is the use of diving techniques by scientists to study underwater what would normally be studied by scientists on land. Examples of disciplines pursued include underwater archaeology, marine biology and geology.

Type of person suited to this work

You must be fit, active and a very strong swimmer as diving is extremely physically demanding.

You must be able to follow health and safety regulations. You should work well in a team and on your own.

You need to be able to concentrate and cope with diving conditions that could be dangerous and have quick reactions to deal with emergencies.

Working conditions

Underwater working conditions are cold, dark and may be cramped. It is necessary to wear protective clothing and breathing apparatus.

Working hours for divers are irregular and depend on the job. A lot of divers work just 120–180 days per year. Jobs may be located abroad.

Future prospects

Divers who pursue higher education have good advancement potential because they can combine subject expertise with practical skill. For example a diver with a qualification in forensics would be more likely to be involved with police diving.

Experienced, senior divers may become self-employed, either as contractors or as operators of diving schools or equipment stores.

The growth of offshore wind farms and the oil and gas sector has led to a huge rise in the demand for experienced offshore divers around the world. However, finding work as an offshore diver may be hard at first as employers favour divers with experience.

Advantages/disadvantages

There is a strong demand for experienced, offshore divers.

The high levels of fitness and health needed for diving can make this a short career.

There is a risk of accidents when underwater and there are potential long-term health hazards which include a number of specific acute and chronic medical conditions.

Money guide

The majority of divers are paid daily. Earnings can be between £120 and £1,000 a day, depending on the type of diving and work involved.

A recreational diving instructor can expect a starting salary of £16,000.

Experienced commercial, Armed Forces or police divers may earn between £22,500 and £40,000.

Offshore divers receive about £30,000 a year.

Related opportunities

- Marine Engineer p231
- Royal Navy Officer p561
- Sports Coach p388

Further information

Health & Safety Executive
www.hse.gov.uk

International Marine Contractors Association
www.imca-int.com

PADI
www.padi.com/scuba

Underwater Centre
www.theunderwatercentre.co.uk

LEISURE, SPORT AND TOURISM

CRCI: MA

Qualifications and courses

There are no formal entry requirements for this career. Experience, enthusiasm and personality can be more important than qualifications. Some employers may expect you to have previous experience working in the entertainment industry or a relevant sector such as hospitality, customer service or events management.

Useful courses at further and higher education level include hospitality management, leisure management, events management, marketing, and travel and tourism. The minimum entry requirements for a degree are 2 A levels/3 H grades and 5 GCSEs/S grades (A*–C/1–3) or equivalent, and for an HND or Foundation degree, 1 A level/2 H grades and 4 GCSEs/S grades (A*–C/1–3).

People working in the industry can study for the NVQ in Cultural Heritage Venue Operations (Levels 2 and 3) or the City & Guilds Award in Principles of Customer Service in Hospitality, Leisure, Travel and Tourism (Levels 2 and 3). The Educational Development International (EDI) offer the Certificate in Supporting Live Events and Promotion (Level 2) and the Diploma in Live Events and Promotion (Level 3). Alternatively, the NCFE Award/Certificate/Extended Certificate in Music Technology (Level 2) and the Certificate in Event Planning (Level 2) are available.

What the work involves

Entertainment managers take responsibility for the schedule of visiting entertainers to a venue, achieving a balance of activities that engage the age, gender and cultural interests of the audience.

You will plan, organise, advertise and oversee the running of a full calendar of social events.

You will contact acts and agents, and negotiate the best possible prices with them. When the events listing is finalised, you will promote the programme on a weekly and daily basis. You will also be responsible for costing out the entertainment.

Type of person suited to this work

Entertainment managers are people who enjoy life, can think on their feet and can make audiences cry with laughter, if need be.

You will need excellent interpersonal and communication skills. Confidence speaking in public is essential.

Your organisation depends on you to find reliable acts, possibly at short notice. You have to make quick appraisals to drive home a deal. You need persuasive powers, imagination and considerable personal initiative.

Working conditions

You could be permanently based in a grand hotel or located in a popular resort, on a cruise liner, or with a large company that frequently entertains important clients.

Entertainment managers work in an office during the day and emerge after 6pm to manage the flow of evening entertainment and introduce the artists.

There is seasonal work for entertainment managers in all the major holiday centres. Travel may be required so a driving licence would be useful.

Future prospects

As the travel and tourism industry is still growing at a fast rate, there will be increasing need for evening entertainment for holidaymakers.

A willingness to be geographically mobile could be important if you are looking to progress in this career.

With experience, you could move into other managerial roles within the hospitality industry.

You will have the opportunity to travel both around the UK and overseas. Those employed on a cruise liner may spend extended periods of time away from home.

Advantages/disadvantages

You will meet some interesting and entertaining artists.

You will have to work evenings, weekends and bank holidays.

Pressure can build if an act does not show up so you might occasionally need to fill a gap and prevent the audience from getting irritable.

Money guide

Generally, travel and recreation work is not well paid.

Trainee entertainment managers can expect a starting salary of £12,000–£15,000.

With experience, you may receive £18,000–£20,000 per year.

If you are an entertainment manager for a large international company, pay and prospects could be much higher, with possible earnings of £25,000–£35,000.

Related opportunities

- Croupier p380
- Holiday Representative p384
- Theme Park Assistant/Manager p391

Further information

NCFE
www.ncfe.org.uk

People 1st
www.people1st.co.uk

FITNESS INSTRUCTOR/PERSONAL TRAINER

Qualifications and courses

No formal academic qualifications are required for this career but you do need an industry-recognised qualification in order to be placed on the Register of Exercise Professionals (REPs). Before you can work as an instructor, you will need to hold public liability insurance, a first aid certificate and Criminal Records Bureau (CRB) clearance if you intend to work with children or vulnerable adults.

The preferred REPs-approved qualification is the Level 2 Certificate in Fitness Training available from City & Guilds. During this course you can choose to specialise in gym-based exercise, exercise to music, water-based exercise or exercise and physical activity for children. Once you have gained considerable experience as a fitness instructor, you can then study for the Level 3 Certificate in Personal Training and progress to a role as a personal trainer.

An alternative route is to take the Instructing Exercise and Fitness Apprenticeship which is available at both Intermediate and Advanced Level.

Other approved qualifications include degrees in sports science or human movement studies, and an HNC/HND in Fitness, Health and Exercise. For degree entry you will need at least 2 A levels/H grades including biology and 5 GCSEs/S grades (A*–C/1–3). HNC/HND courses require 1 A level and 5 GCSEs (A*–C) or equivalent.

What the work involves

Fitness instructors/personal trainers teach people how to exercise in a safe and effective manner, whilst also helping them work towards personal fitness targets.

You could provide a one-on-one service to your clients, direct and choreograph group fitness activities and classes, or undertake a mixture of the two. You could work in a health club, community gym, leisure centre or private gym.

Other duties may include writing individual training programmes for clients, showing them exercise techniques and how to use equipment, and offering advice on nutrition and other lifestyle-related issues.

Type of person suited to this work

You will need excellent interpersonal skills so that you can attract new business opportunities, chat to clients and advise them on fitness and dietary requirements, and build good relationships with other team members.

You must be very enthusiastic about training and fitness in order to motivate your clients and persuade them to persevere with exercise. You should look smart and fit yourself to promote a good image to existing and potential clients.

You must be innovative in your approach to keeping fit, thinking up new routines for classes or creating diversity in one-on-one clients' training programmes so people remain enthused and interested in their activities.

Working conditions

Fitness instructors work longer than average hours – between 38 and 40 hours per week – and these often include early mornings, evenings and weekends to suit the needs of their clients.

Most instructors work on a part-time basis and are affiliated to one or a number of gyms in their local area.

Future prospects

As society has become increasingly aware of health and fitness issues, the demand for fitness instructors has grown. This trend is set to continue for the foreseeable future so employment prospects are good.

In certain areas and in popular high street gyms, competition for jobs can be tough.

With experience, you could move into roles such as fitness manager or sports facility manager. Alternatively, you could build your own fitness consultancy.

Advantages/disadvantages

You will play an active role in enhancing many people's lives by introducing them to exercise and ensuring they continue with it.

You will see tangible results of your efforts and guidance as people become fitter and slimmer during the course of your work with them.

You will have to work unsocial hours.

Money guide

Earnings usually depend on your reputation, client base and location.

Fitness instructors usually have a starting salary of about £13,000.

With experience, earnings can increase up to £20,000.

Freelance instructors may charge an hourly rate of £10–£20.

Personal trainers can receive a salary ranging from £18,000 up to £40,000.

Self-employed personal trainers are likely to earn £20–£40 an hour.

Those working with high profile clients can achieve an hourly rate of £50–£100.

Related opportunities

- Leisure Centre Assistant/Manager p385
- Outdoor Pursuits Instructor p387
- Sports Coach p388

Further information

Register of Exercise Professionals
www.exerciseregister.org

HOLIDAY REPRESENTATIVE

Qualifications and courses

Academic qualifications are not essential as most employers place higher value on customer service experience. However, GCSEs (A*–C) or equivalent in subjects such as English, maths and geography can be useful as competition for entry to this industry is high. Competency in a foreign language, such as Spanish, French, Italian, Portuguese, Greek or Turkish would be particularly beneficial.

Relevant qualifications include the NCFE Award for Resort Representatives (Level 2) and the NVQ in Travel and Tourism Services (Levels 2 and 3) available from City & Guilds. It may also be useful to study for a BTEC First in Travel and Tourism (Level 2), a BTEC National in Travel and Tourism (Level 3) or a BTEC Certificate in Travel Services (Levels 2 and 3).

Training is usually provided on the job, both in the UK and at the holiday resort.

In some roles you might need specialist knowledge in an area such as archaeology, scuba diving or history, in which case a relevant qualification would be essential.

To work with children, you will need at least 6 months of practical experience, a childcare qualification and clearance from the Criminal Records Bureau (CRB).

What the work involves

Holiday representatives meet holidaymakers at airports and other terminals, helping them to locate their luggage and directing them towards the transport that will take them to their accommodation. You will be responsible for checking all the details of each passenger's transport and accommodation to ensure that everything is in place for their stay.

You will inform customers of important information, including local bus routes, recommended restaurants and sites of interest. You will also sell excursion tickets. You may be expected to accompany tourists on expeditions and provide them with holiday entertainment.

Type of person suited to this work

You will need to look smart and have a pleasant, approachable attitude so that holidaymakers are comfortable speaking to you. You will need to be sociable and very patient as you will deal with guests 24 hours a day for the duration of the holiday season.

You should have a methodical approach to your work and excellent organisational skills as you will be coordinating lots of details for numerous people at one time.

Fluency in the language of the country in which you are working is also an asset.

Working conditions

Working hours vary from day-to-day but are usually long and unpredictable. Most representatives only have 1 day off a week and even then they will be on-call in case of an emergency.

The work is seasonal, although there are opportunities all year round with beach holidays in the summer months and ski work during winter. You could work indoors or outdoors. You will usually have to wear a uniform.

Future prospects

Although there are many vacancies for holiday representatives each year, competition is tough as it is a very popular job.

You could work for a large international travel company or a smaller, more specialist firm. Most opportunities are overseas, although there are a few jobs available in the UK.

With experience, you could move into a supervisory or managerial position. Some representatives also branch out into another area of travel and tourism, such as hotel management or working on a tourist board.

Advantages/disadvantages

You will have plenty of opportunities to work abroad in a number of diverse and exciting areas.

You will deal with a range of people from all ages and backgrounds on a daily basis, making the work diverse and challenging.

You will have to work long hours which can make the job both physically and mentally exhausting.

Money guide

Starting salaries for holiday representatives are usually around £12,000.

With experience, representatives can expect to earn £16,000 a year.

If you move into a supervisory or managerial role, your earnings could increase to £18,000.

Holiday representatives are usually provided with free accommodation and insurance. You may earn commission for selling tours or excursions to guests.

Related opportunities

- Air Cabin Crew p588
- Tour Guide/Manager p392
- Travel Agent p394

Further information

Career in Travel
www.careerintravel.co.uk

Qualifications and courses

Assistant

Although there are no formal entry requirements, many employers prefer applicants with GCSEs/S grades (A*–C/1–3) in maths, English and a science and A levels/ Highers or a BTEC National qualification in sport or leisure. Previous experience working in customer service is also helpful.

Training is often given on the job, although many courses are offered by the Institute for the Management of Sport and Physical Activity (IMSPA). Normally, assistants try for an instructor or coach award in their preferred activity and could be expected to gain a Lifeguard's Certificate. You can also study towards NVQs in Instructing Exercise and Fitness or take an Apprenticeship in Active Leisure and Learning. A First Aid certificate would be useful.

It is possible to work towards supervisory qualifications.

Manager

A trainee manager will usually have at least 5 GCSEs/S grades (A*–C/1–3) and 2 A levels/Highers, an NVQ Level 2 in Sport, Recreation and Allied Occupations or a Diploma in Sport and Active Leisure. Many employers also require an NVQ Level 3 in Leisure Management or a BTEC National Certificate/Diploma in Sport. You can also work and study for the IMSPA Supervisory Management Certificate.

Foundation degrees, degrees and HNDs are also available in sport and leisure management and sports science. Graduate training programmes are often available at large organisations.

It is also possible to begin as an assistant and work your way up to a managerial position by completing the relevant qualifications whilst you work.

What the work involves

Assistant

You will help run sports activities, set up equipment and demonstrate its safe use to leisure centre users.

You will also work on the reception desk issuing tickets, taking bookings, answering enquiries and performing other tasks specified by your manager.

Manager

You will oversee the day-to-day work and recruitment of all leisure centre staff, and deal with queries.

You will meet with company or council reps to discuss budgets, funding sources, marketing issues, and new developments.

Type of person suited to this work

You will need to be friendly and helpful with excellent interpersonal skills.

A role as manager will require proven leadership skills. As you will be working within or leading a team you must be able to communicate well.

Assistants should be fit and active.

Working conditions

Most of your time will be spent indoors – at the poolside, in a sports hall, at reception or in the office.

You should expect to work unsocial hours – early starts and late finishes.

Future prospects

Owing to a growing trend in healthy living, interest in leisure centres is high.

You could progress from a role as an assistant to supervisor and then become a manager. After gaining more experience, you could go on to become an area or regional manager.

There are greater opportunities for promotion in large organisations.

Advantages/disadvantages

Most leisure centres have a relaxed working atmosphere.

It is possible to work a variety of shifts and hours can be flexible.

Earnings can be low, unless you start on the trainee management route.

Money guide

Starting salaries for leisure centre assistants are around £12,500 per year rising to £19,000 with qualifications and experience.

This can be boosted by overtime and bonuses related to membership as well as weekend and shift work.

The starting salary for managers is between £17,000 and £25,000 a year.

Managers at senior levels can earn in excess of £35,000.

Salaries vary according to the size of the organisation.

Related opportunities

- Fitness Instructor/Personal Trainer p383
- Lifeguard p386
- Outdoor Pursuits Instructor p387

Further information

Institute for the Management of Sport and Physical Activity
www.imspa.co.uk

LEISURE, SPORT AND TOURISM

CRCI: MA

Qualifications and courses

Pool lifeguard
You must be over 16, physically fit and a strong swimmer to qualify to become a poolside lifeguard.

Lifeguards must be in possession of a National Pool Lifeguard Qualification (NPLQ) from the Royal Life Saving Society UK or a NaRS Pool Rescue Qualification from the Swimming Teachers Association (STA).

The NPLQ training covers 2 assessed units: The Principles of Lifesaving and Swimming Pool Supervision, and The Application of Supervision and Rescue in a Swimming Pool. This training can only take place in a centre approved by the Institute of Qualified Lifeguards.

Both the NPLQ and NaRS qualifications are valid for 24 months. After this you must have your lifesaving and First Aid skills assessed before your qualification is renewed.

Beach/ocean lifeguard
You must be aged over 18, physically fit and a strong swimmer to qualify to become a beach lifeguard.

Lifeguards must be in possession of the National Beach Lifeguard Qualification (NBLQ) from the Royal Life Saving Society UK or the NaRS Beach Lifeguard Award run through clubs by the Surf Life Saving Association of Great Britain. These courses cover practical ocean rescue skills involving the use of boards and tubes.

Training is also provided by the Royal National Lifeboat Institution. Apprenticeships are also available to entrants aged 16–24.

All lifeguards need to hold a valid First Aid Worker Certificate. Lifeguard qualifications must be renewed every 2 years.

What the work involves

Lifeguards are responsible for patrolling and monitoring the water and weather conditions where people are swimming, surfing or boating. You will keep watch on public swimming pools or stretches of shoreline to reduce the risk of tragic accidents occurring and taking rapid action to alert the public to danger.

Your role could involve rescuing people at risk from drowning, assisting them ashore and administering First Aid including mouth-to-mouth or CPR (cardiopulmonary resuscitation).

You will also be involved in informing the public about water safety.

Type of person suited to this work

You must be fit and active, with an interest in canoeing, sailing, swimming or surfing. You should also have a full understanding of the level of danger in all water activities.

You should be a strong swimmer (able to cover 400 metres of a pool in less than 8 minutes) and have good vision and hearing. The ability to work within a team is also essential. It's important to be observant and be able to respond quickly.

You must be assertive in order to take command and manage dangerous incidents and be able to stay calm in emergencies.

Working conditions

You will either work on the beach or poolside. Either way, you will need to cover early morning and later shifts as part of your hours in order to provide a full emergency service to water users.

You must keep alert and vigilant at all times as when emergency strikes, you have to be ready to act in seconds – not minutes.

Overseas work is possible with holiday companies.

Future prospects

Interest in water sports has grown dramatically and so lifeguards are in great demand.

You could progress into a managerial role such as a pool supervisor, duty manager or general pool manager.

You could also qualify as a swimming teacher.

Advantages/disadvantages

Pools and beaches have a relaxed, upbeat atmosphere.

There can be periods of boredom that you have to work through, maintaining vigilance. Accidents can happen at any time.

If working outdoors you could be in danger of overexposure to sunlight.

Money guide

Pay levels vary, depending on employer and patrol times involved.

Starting salaries for full-time lifeguards are around £11,500–£14,000 per year. With experience, pay can rise to £15,000+ per year.

Many lifeguards work for local authorities on a part-time basis and rates of pay can vary from £6 to £10 per hour.

Related opportunities

- Fitness Instructor/Personal Trainer p383
- Outdoor Pursuits Instructor p387
- Sports Coach p388

Further information

Royal Life Saving Society UK
www.lifesavers.org.uk

Saltwater Training
www.saltwatertraining.com

Surf Life Saving Great Britain
www.slsgb.org.uk

Swimming Teachers Association
www.sta.co.uk

OUTDOOR PURSUITS INSTRUCTOR

Qualifications and courses

No formal academic qualifications are required to work as an outdoor pursuits instructor and requirements will vary depending on the role and the employer. Many employers usually expect applicants to hold 2 or more relevant proficiency or coaching awards in their chosen sporting field.

These qualifications should be recognised by the national governing body for the sport, and include courses such as Sports Leaders UK Basic Expedition Leadership Award (BEL), British Canoe Union Level 1 Coach, and the Mountain Leader Training UK Single Pitch Award. Full-time college courses and degrees are also available that provide relevant qualifications.

As well as holding suitable qualifications, candidates are expected to be able to demonstrate a history of leading and taking responsibility for others.

You will need to be 18 years old before you can work as an instructor. You will also need to undergo a Criminal Records Bureau check as you could be working with children and vulnerable adults from time to time.

What the work involves

Outdoor pursuits instructors lead groups of people through a range of challenging activities, designed to help them bond, have fun, learn more about themselves and develop new skills.

You will work with people of all ages and backgrounds, including those with disabilities, children with special needs, adult recreation groups, and business professionals. You will be responsible for guiding these groups though a range of activities.

You will also be responsible for checking safety equipment, ensuring that group members are comfortable with each activity, and giving practical demonstrations.

Type of person suited to this work

You should have strong leadership skills as you will be required to persuade a group of people who have never met you before to undertake activities that are frightening and push them out of their comfort zone.

You must have an excellent level of physical fitness, alongside good eyesight and hearing.

You must be responsible and maintain continual awareness of the safety of both yourself and those around you. You should have good communication skills and a personable manner to explain activities clearly.

Working conditions

Hours are generally long and irregular, usually falling over evenings and weekends, including bank holidays. Much of the work is seasonal. Part-time hours are commonly available.

Many outdoor pursuits centres are located in the countryside, so a driving licence may be useful in order to travel to and from work with ease. Holding a licence for a passenger carrying vehicle (PCV) may also be helpful.

You should expect to be working outdoors in all weather conditions. Long treks may also involve spending evenings away from the centre, camping in a tent.

Future prospects

Although the outdoor leisure industry is growing, there is still a lot of competition for jobs.

Most opportunities are in independently run activity centres, or those owned by local authorities and charities. There are also jobs available with expedition companies who organise overseas excursions.

Many instructors specialise in a particular discipline, such as canoeing or abseiling, and work freelance across several activity centres.

Advantages/disadvantages

You will be helping people to break down boundaries and overcome fear, which will increase their self-reliance and self-confidence.

You will be working with a wide range of people, from all backgrounds and ages, which will give great diversity to your working day.

You will have to work unsociable hours.

Money guide

As an outdoor pursuits instructor, you could expect to earn around £12,000 as a starting salary.

As your experience grows, this could increase to around £18,000.

Once you have reached the level of a more senior instructor, perhaps also developing specialist skills, you could earn up to £25,000.

As a freelancer you would be paid a daily rate depending on the regularity of the activities you lead. This could be between £80 and £110 a day plus expenses.

Related opportunities

- Holiday Representative p384
- Sports Coach p388
- Sports Development Officer p389

Further information

British Activity Holiday Association
www.baha.org.uk

Institute for Outdoor Learning
www.outdoor-learning.org

LEISURE, SPORT AND TOURISM

CRCI: ME

SPORTS COACH

Qualifications and courses

All sports coaches must hold a qualification that has been accredited by the National Governing Body (NGB) of their chosen discipline. You can start working towards recognised qualifications at the age of 16, but must be 18 or over to work as an independent coach.

Accredited courses are available directly from the NGB, or you can undertake a college or university course. NGB qualifications are equivalent to studying for NVQs Level 1–4, and no academic qualifications are required. They are usually studied on a part-time basis.

Relevant courses at college or university include: BTEC National Certificate/Diploma in Sports Coaching or Leisure Studies; entry requirements are 4 GCSEs/S grades (A*–C/1–3) or equivalent; BTEC HNC/HND in Leisure Studies, requires 1 A level/H grade and 4 GCSEs/S grades (A*–C/1–3) or equivalent; Foundation degree in sports coaching, entry requirements vary; degrees in sports science/studies, coaching, and physical education, usually requiring 2 A levels/H grades and 5 GCSEs/S grades (A*–C/1–3) or equivalent, including English and maths.

Some employers may require a First Aid certificate, and if you intend to work with children you must first obtain Criminal Records Bureau clearance.

What the work involves

Sports coaches provide specialist support, motivation and knowledge to athletes in order to help them attain their best performances and achieve personal goals.

As a competitive coach, you could work with a variety of levels of athlete, ranging from children's football or netball teams, through to professional and even world class sports professionals.

At a non-competitive level, you will focus on providing fun and accessible exercise sessions for participants with a range of abilities and fitness levels.

You will usually coach one specific sport.

Type of person suited to this work

You will need excellent communications skills. You will also need to have good motivational abilities in order to inspire and encourage sports players to push themselves.

You will need an in-depth knowledge of your chosen sport, and an understanding of nutrition and physiology is also useful.

It is also essential that you understand a variety of training methods and principles so that you can provide an informed and beneficial service to your clients. Patience and determination are also vital qualities.

Working conditions

You will usually work early mornings, evenings and weekends. This is when the majority of your athletes will be available.

If you are working in a seasonal sport such as cricket or football, you might have to supplement your income with another job during the quiet months.

You will spend hours on your feet, and might also have to undertake activity in order to demonstrate methods and principles to athletes.

Future prospects

The vast majority of sports coaches working in the UK work on a voluntary or part-time basis. Competition for full-time positions is fierce.

Career prospects will depend on the level of success you achieve in your work. If you gain credibility, you could move into a related development or management position.

You could be self-employed, work for a local authority, or in a school, gym or professional sports club.

Advantages/disadvantages

You will be teaching the sport you love to a range of people and developing their interest in it.

You may have the opportunity to work with talented athletes.

You will have to spend long periods of time standing outside in all weather conditions.

Money guide

As a newly qualified coach working for an employer, you could earn between £15,000 and £25,000.

Experienced coaches who work for a NGB or professional association can earn between £30,000 and £35,000.

If you work at the highest level of your sport, such as coaching Premiership football players, you could earn in excess of £100,000.

Related opportunities

- Fitness Instructor/Personal Trainer p383
- Outdoor Pursuits Instructor p387
- Sports Professional p390

Further information

SkillsActive
www.skillsactive.com

Sports Coach UK
www.sportscoachuk.org

SPORTS DEVELOPMENT OFFICER

Qualifications and courses

Although there are currently no specific academic requirements, new entrants to the profession are usually graduates. If you hold coaching qualifications you may be able to start out as an assistant and move your way up.

Relevant first degree subjects include sports science/studies, physical education, recreation/leisure management, and health and exercise sciences. Most universities require candidates to have 2 A levels/H grades, one in a related subject such as biology, and 5 GCSEs/S grades (A*–C/1–3), including English, maths and a science. Some employers will also accept entrants with relevant BTEC or HNC/HND qualifications in sport, sports science, sports development or another related subject.

Most employers will also require you to have 2 years' experience in sports development, for example at a leisure centre, a holiday camp or summer school.

What the work involves

Sports development officers are responsible for ensuring that sports and related activities are available to people of all ages and abilities. You will be promoting the benefits of exercise and encouraging people to live a healthy lifestyle by devising simple but effective strategies that increase participation in sport.

You will work within the local community, liaising with schools, gyms and social clubs, and also have involvement with larger agencies such as sports national governing bodies (NGBs).

You may work closely with groups who are usually excluded from sports-related activity, such as disadvantaged youths, prisoners and disabled people.

Type of person suited to this work

You will need a positive attitude, coupled with a commitment to sport, that will help you to persuade local community members and service providers to back your initiatives.

You will need excellent verbal and written communication skills in order to illustrate your objectives to other professionals. This includes strong persuasive and negotiating skills.

Good ICT and administrative ability will be essential for creating reports, producing material to support your ideas, and keeping accurate records.

Working conditions

You will usually work a 36 hour week within normal office hours. Flexible hours and overtime are often available.

It is not unusual to have to work additional hours during evenings and weekends, attending meetings or networking events.

You will work in an office environment, and also spend time at local schools, clubs and community venues. Since a good deal of travelling is required each day, a driving licence can be helpful.

Future prospects

You will most likely be working for a local authority, county sports partnership, or NGB. A few opportunities are available in specialist sports colleges.

Career progression for sport-specific development officers is fairly limited; you could be promoted to the role of sports development manager, or become more involved with other community initiatives. The Institute for the Management of Sports and Physical Activity (IMSPA) offers a number of different courses aimed at continuing professional development (CPD) and similar courses are available through Sports Coach UK.

Advantages/disadvantages

You will play an active role in enhancing many people's quality of life by providing them with access to sport in their local area.

You will be liaising with a variety of people on a daily basis, which should make the work dynamic and interesting.

You will need a resilient approach to your work, as suggestions and plans will often be knocked back or fall through.

Money guide

The starting salary for a newly qualified sports development officer is usually around £20,000 per year.

With a few years of experience, your wages could rise to about £35,000.

If you reach a management position, you could earn up to £40,000.

Related opportunities

- Fitness Instructor/Personal Trainer p383
- Outdoor Pursuits Instructor p387
- Sports Coach p388

Further information

Institute for the Management of Sport and Physical Activity
www.imspa.co.uk

Sports Coach UK
www.sportscoachuk.org

Sports Leaders UK
www.sportsleaders.org

LEISURE, SPORT AND TOURISM

CRCI: ME

Qualifications and courses

You do not need any academic qualifications for most sports. The only exception to this rule is golf, in which the Professional Golfers' Association requires players to have 4 GCSEs/S grades (A*–C/1–3) or equivalent. Aptitude and enthusiasm for your sport are the key requirements to become a sports professional. Joining a club or amateur organisation would be beneficial as you will receive instruction and training.

Talented athletes aged 16–18 could apply for the Advanced Apprenticeship in Sporting Excellence. This structured training and development programme leads to an NVQ Level 3 and qualifies you to study for a sports-related degree.

Across the UK, there are opportunities to gain additional help and support if you are a promising young athlete. In England, the Talented Athlete Scholarship Scheme (TASS) awards funding of up to £3,500 for sports training to those over the age of 16. Nominations for the TASS awards are made by the individual sporting National Governing Bodies (NGBs). Details of NGBs are available from the Sport England website.

Scotland and Wales provide similar assistance to young sports stars through the Athlete Support Scheme and Elite Cymru.

What the work involves

Sportsplayers are paid professionals who compete across the globe in their chosen sport, often in front of an audience. You could compete individually in sports such as boxing, swimming, golf and athletics, or alternatively with a team in sports like football, hockey, cricket and rugby.

You will need to spend a great deal of time training in order to maintain a high standard of general fitness, alongside honing your skills in your chosen sport.

You may also be required to attend social events, give interviews and promote the companies that provide you with sponsorship.

Type of person suited to this work

First and foremost, you will need to have an outstanding natural ability in your chosen sport. You must also have the necessary commitment and self-discipline to maintain a continuous training schedule and strict eating regime.

You will need to have a highly competitive nature but also a polite and pleasant manner in order to get on with team members, fellow players and coaches.

As well as being physically fit, you must be mentally stable so that you can cope with the pressure of competition, defeat and disappointment.

Working conditions

Competitions and matches usually fall on weekends, although qualifying rounds may take place during the week.

You will usually need to travel to reach competitions, which may involve overnight absence from home. If you are competing at an international level, you could be away for weeks at a time.

You will need to train most days and if you are supplementing your professional sports income with a regular job, this will mean exercising either early in the morning or in the evening.

Future prospects

Most professional sportsplayers are spotted at an early age by a talent scout or coach. From this point, they build up skills and a reputation through competitions.

Unfortunately, the majority of professionals cannot earn a living playing their chosen sport alone, so you might have to supplement your income with full- or part-time work.

Sports professionals rarely continue to compete once they have reached their mid-30s but there are plenty of opportunities to work as a coach or manager, commentator, or even earn money as a TV personality.

Advantages/disadvantages

Pursuing your dream as a professional sportsplayer is much more exciting than a conventional job.

The hard work and dedication you put in should be repaid in the form of sporting achievements and acclaim.

One bad injury could ruin your career at a very early stage.

Money guide

If you start your professional career as an apprentice, you will earn about £6,000. You may also receive accommodation and food allowances.

Once you are established as a professional, competing in and winning competitions regularly, you should earn £20,000+.

Highly successful sports professionals working in well-supported sports, such as tennis and football, can earn anything from £100,000 to over £5,000,000.

Related opportunities

- Fitness Instructor/Personal Trainer p383
- Outdoor Pursuits Instructor p387
- Sports Coach p388

Further information

SkillsActive
www.skillsactive.com

Talented Athlete Scholarship Scheme
www.tass.gov.uk

THEME PARK ASSISTANT/MANAGER

Qualifications and courses

You have to be at least 18 years old to start work in a theme park. No formal academic qualifications are required but if you intend to become a supervisor or manager then it would be beneficial to have some GCSEs/S grades in maths, English, IT and possibly design technology and sports education.

Once you are employed you will receive on-the-job training, in areas such as customer care and health and safety, from more experienced staff.

You could study for the Level 2 NVQ in Mechanical Ride Operations (Leisure Parks, Piers and Attractions) offered by City & Guilds. NVQs/SVQs and other qualifications in customer care, catering and sales could also be relevant.

With experience as a theme park assistant, you could progress to a role as a team leader or manager if you take relevant qualifications, such as those offered by the Chartered Institute for the Management of Sport and Physical Activity (CIMSPA).

If the theme park you work for is registered with the British Association of Leisure Parks, Piers and Attractions (BALPPA) then you may be able to attend specialist training schemes and seminars.

What the work involves

As a theme park assistant you will greet customers, check ticket holders' ages and heights, and operate and supervise rides. You may also sell merchandise.

You must always observe safety rules and ensure that there are no hazards. Assistants are also required to carry out repairs and maintenance on machines each morning and evening.

If you are a manager you will need to oversee all the different operations within a theme park, ensuring the smooth running of the amusements and catering facilities. You will be responsible for the maintenance, cleaning and surveillance of the park.

You will also be involved with recruiting and training staff, managing the budget of the park and handling any problems that arise.

The manager must inspect the whole site before opening time, taking responsibility for checking that all the necessary safety checks have been done and that the rides and other facilities are fully staffed.

Type of person suited to this work

Theme park workers should be comfortable talking to the public and keen to ensure that they have an exciting and memorable time.

You must be trustworthy and dependable, with good practical and mechanical skills, and the ability to follow instructions

carefully. Awareness of health and safety practices is essential.

Working conditions

Theme parks are open 7 days a week and on bank holidays. You are likely to work shifts and have 1 full day off each week. This work may be seasonal and could involve travelling to different locations.

As a theme park assistant, you will work outdoors in a variety of weather conditions. Managers will spend some of their time in an office environment.

Assistants may be required to wear a uniform and managers should dress smartly.

Future prospects

There is always a high turnover of staff in theme parks but a core group of workers stay on, benefiting from training and increased responsibility which allows them to gain certificates as evidence of their skills.

There is more work in Europe for trained, experienced theme park workers. Speaking a foreign language would be useful.

Advantages/disadvantages

This is a specialised line of entertainment and leisure work so it may be difficult to progress to roles in other sectors.

You have the opportunity to work anywhere in the world such as Legoland Denmark or Disneyland USA.

Money guide

If you are aged 18–21, you can expect a starting salary of about £9,000.

With experience as a theme park attendant, you may earn over £12,000.

Managers are likely to have a salary between £18,500 and £30,000.

Experienced managers in the large theme parks could achieve £35,000–£75,000 a year.

Employees may receive additional benefits such as overtime pay, free health insurance and a cash bonus at the end of the season.

Related opportunities

- Customer Services Assistant/Manager p480
- Entertainment Manager p382
- Leisure Centre Assistant/Manager p385

Further information

British Association of Leisure Parks, Piers and Attractions
www.balppa.org

EQ
www.thinkeq.org.uk

LEISURE, SPORT AND TOURISM

CRCI: MA

Qualifications and courses

Most tour guides and managers are aged 18 or over. Although no formal academic qualifications are required, some GCSEs (A*–C) or equivalent might be useful, particularly in subjects such as English, maths and languages.

Fluency in another language is important if you intend to work abroad, or work with foreign tourists in the UK.

You can do an Apprenticeship or Advanced Apprenticeship in Travel and Tourism Services. Tour guides can also study towards a number of professional qualifications, which include NVQ Level 2 and Level 3 in Travel and Tourism.

Professional courses for tour managers include full-time HND and degree courses in Travel and Tourism Management, City & Guilds HLQ Level 4 in Travel and Tourism, and a range of related Northern Advisory Council for Further Education (NACFE) certificates.

What the work involves

Tour guides are responsible for meeting and greeting parties of people who are taking a holiday, trip, cultural visit or tour together. You will accompany the sightseers on their journey and inform them of the historical/environmental/cultural interests of the area they are visiting. You will also assist them if they encounter problems or difficulties.

Tour managers are responsible for putting together proposals for day trips and excursions in order to attract holidaymakers to the company.

You will visit destinations to assess their potential as a tour venue, and may also assist tour guides with the delivery of the trip itself.

Type of person suited to this work

Tour guides and managers both need excellent communication skills in order to convey enthusiasm and interest for venues to both customers and potential clients. You will need good stamina in order to keep up a high level of energy and interest throughout tours.

You will also need to have excellent customer relation skills in order to soothe any disgruntled holiday-makers and reach amicable solutions to problems.

Tour managers should also be methodical in order to put together logistically plausible, suitably detailed plans for excursions.

Working conditions

You may work long hours, and when out on a tour you will be on-call for customers 24 hours a day should they need anything.

You could work for a large international company, or a small independent tour provider, but either way your focus will be on promoting the company image and following their tour policies carefully.

You will be expected to wear a uniform when on duty, which usually includes a shirt and tie.

Future prospects

The travel and tourism industry is in a period of expansion, so job prospects for tour guides are good.

You could work in a large international company that runs tours throughout the UK and overseas, or a smaller provider that focuses on specific tourist areas in the UK such as Bath or London.

Competition for work as a tour manager is tough, but if you have built up good skills and knowledge as a tour guide first, you will be in a good position for promotion.

Advantages/disadvantages

You will be dealing with a variety of people of all ages and backgrounds on a daily basis, educating them about areas in which you have an interest.

It can get monotonous as you will be repeating the same spiel over and over again for weeks, months and even years.

Money guide

Tour guides can expect to start on around £10,000, and with experience this could rise to up to £25,000.

Tour managers generally start on about £16,000, and with experience this rises to around £20,000.

Particularly experienced or specialised tour managers can earn up to £28,000.

Related opportunities

- Holiday Representative p384
- Tourist Information Centre Assistant p393
- Travel Agent p394

Further information

Institute of Travel and Tourism
www.itt.co.uk

International Association of Tour Managers Limited
www.iatm.co.uk

TOURIST INFORMATION CENTRE ASSISTANT

Qualifications and courses

No formal educational qualifications are required for this career. Personal qualities are usually more important. Acute listening and clear speaking skills are essential, and it is very helpful if assistants can use ICT to research information and respond to enquiries sent via the internet.

Applicants who have GCSEs/S grades (A*–C/1–3) might be at an advantage. A number of tourist information centres (TICs) are close to international airports or in popular destinations for overseas visitors. In these centres it is valuable if one or more TIC assistants have modern foreign language skills to help newly arrived tourists, business travellers and foreign visitors. British Sign Language will also be an advantage.

Working as an assistant, you can be assessed for NVQs/SVQs in Tourist Information and Customer Service. Many employees within tourist information centres work towards these awards.

There are also the part-time HLQ Level 4, BTEC or SQA HNC qualifications in Leisure and Tourism which might be useful for career progression to become a TIC manager. However, it is possible to move into supervisory and managerial positions simply with extensive experience.

What the work involves

You will be answering questions in person, over the phone or via the internet from UK and foreign tourists, business people, local young people and researchers.

You will provide information, make bookings and reservations, locate accommodation, restaurants or sites of interest. You will also be expected to inform people about forthcoming shows and events in the local area.

You will hand out leaflets and sell maps, postcards and items of interest from the local area and region. You could also operate a bureau de change.

Type of person suited to this work

You need to have an interest in local matters and in promoting your local area. Good, up-to-date knowledge about places of interest is useful. You should be friendly with good interpersonal skills.

A methodical approach to researching difficult questions is an asset. Relevant skills include customer-service experience, the ability to research information using the internet and good verbal communication skills.

It is important to be a good team player and assist your colleagues, even if you are busy.

Working conditions

You will usually work shifts which include the weekends and bank holidays.

Tourist information centres are modern, bright spaces that make pleasant work surroundings.

There is quite a lot of standing at the counter and moving to and from storage areas with piles of information, leaflets and stock items. You may spend some hours sitting at a computer, researching routes or B&B facilities in distant locations.

Future prospects

Tourist information centres are located across the whole of the UK, so you should have one local to you.

You could move from a part-time contract into a full-time one and with experience progress to a managerial or supervisory post. You could also choose to become a travel agent or tour guide.

Advantages/disadvantages

There are both busy and quiet times at the counter in tourist information centres.

You could spend a long time on the phone which could get dull.

You will play an important role in promoting both the local region and helping its economy.

Money guide

The starting salary for full-time staff is around £16,000 per year.

With experience, this can rise to £20,000.

You can earn up to £30,000 as full-time manager of a tourist information centre.

Your salary will most likely be higher in and around London.

Related opportunities

- Holiday Representative p384
- Tour Guide/Manager p392
- Travel Agent p394

Further information

VisitBritain
www.visitbritain.org

VisitScotland
www.visitscotland.com

LEISURE, SPORT AND TOURISM

CRCI: MC

Qualifications and courses

Although no formal educational qualifications are needed, it is useful to have a good standard of education with GCSEs/S grades (A*–C/1–3) in English and maths as a minimum. Skills in geography and IT, and experience working in a customer service or sales role would also be beneficial.

The Apprenticeship in Travel Services is available in the Leisure and Business pathway, which trains entrants for a customer-facing role as a travel agent, or the Tour Operator (Head Office) pathway, where you would be based at a call centre and assist customers with booking their holiday over the phone.

Training is provided on the job by employers but you could take relevant qualifications to help you secure a position. City & Guilds offer the Award, Certificate and Diploma in Introduction to the Travel and Tourism Industry (Level 1), the Award in Principles of Customer Service in Hospitality, Leisure, Travel and Tourism (Levels 2 and 3) and the NVQ in Travel and Tourism Services (Levels 2 and 3).

Full-time A level courses in Travel and Tourism make an excellent starting point for this work. Alternatively, the BTEC First in Travel and Tourism (Level 2) and the BTEC National in Travel and Tourism (Level 3) are available.

What the work involves

You will sell holiday packages to the public and try to meet your company's sales targets. You could be based in a high street travel agency or work in a call centre, assisting customers with online and telephone bookings.

You will put together individual holidays for an independent customer or for an organisation that seeks travel, accommodation and entertainment arrangements that are distinct from the travel companies' normal holiday packages.

You will need to contact airline, ferry and rail sales operatives to arrange transport and make reservations for accommodation, meals, hire cars and entertainment, both in this country and abroad. There are numerous details to check over the phone and tickets, booking confirmations and insurance notes to post out to customers.

Type of person suited to this work

You will need excellent administrative and research skills to quickly track down, assemble and book all the parts needed for each customer's ideal journey or holiday. You must have excellent listening and questioning skills in order to find the right holiday package for each individual customer.

If you are friendly, communicative and methodical, with excellent IT skills, you will suit both your customers' and your employers' needs. It helps if you have a real interest in exploring new places yourself.

Working conditions

You will work indoors, mainly at a desk or behind a counter. Almost all the work is done using a computer and telephone.

All travel agents tend to work 35–40 hours a week. If you work in a travel agency, it can be very busy at lunchtimes, near to closing time and on Saturdays, particularly leading up to the peak holiday season. Those working in a call centre are likely to work shifts including evening and weekend work.

Travel agencies usually provide staff with a uniform.

Future prospects

The travel industry has changed considerably in recent years, as increasing numbers of people book holidays on the internet. For this reason, many travel agents work in call centres, selling holiday packages over the phone and assisting customers with online bookings and queries.

Opportunities do still exist in high street travel agencies as some customers prefer to book a holiday face-to-face with an agent's help. With experience, you could progress to a managerial position.

You can move into other areas of tourism work, such as holiday repping or working as a tour guide, which may enable you to travel the world.

Advantages/disadvantages

A perk of this career is that you may receive free or discounted holidays.

Working to meet performance targets can be stressful.

It can be satisfying knowing that you have helped a customer to find and book their ideal holiday.

Money guide

Starting salaries are usually £11,000–£15,000.

With experience, your earnings can increase to £15,000–£25,000.

Senior travel agents can achieve over £30,000.

Benefits can include target-based commission and discounted holidays.

Related opportunities

- Holiday Representative p384
- Tour Guide/Manager p392
- Tourist Information Centre Assistant p393

Further information

Association of British Travel Agents Limited
www.abta.com

Institute of Travel and Tourism
www.itt.co.uk

Marketing, Advertising, Media, Print and Publishing

Do you consider yourself to be a great communicator? Are you interested in working in an exciting and often fast-paced environment with passionate, driven and ambitious individuals? If so, a career in this industry could be right for you. People who work in this sector are exceptionally motivated and are willing to put in long hours often on low starting wages because of their love of the job. You should have a great sense of creativity and imagination and be good at putting your ideas on paper, but you will often also need strong business acumen as many of your decisions will be made from an economic point of view as well as a creative one.

The jobs featured in this section are listed below. For similar jobs to the ones in this section turn to *Design, Arts and Crafts* on page 167 and *Performing Arts* on page 429.

Qualifications and courses

Most entrants to this profession are graduates as advertising is a very competitive sector. Large agencies usually expect candidates to have a degree or HND. A range of courses are available at universities and colleges at HND, Foundation degree, Honours degree and postgraduate levels. Relevant subjects include advertising, marketing, English, communications and business/management.

Entry without a degree is sometimes possible in smaller or specialist agencies. Applicants will be expected to have relevant work experience. It is likely that you will be employed in a junior administrative role and work your way up to account executive level.

Work experience is an excellent way to develop your knowledge and build a network of industry contacts. Vacation work, job shadowing or taking a sandwich degree course are all useful.

Training tends to be done on the job. Employers may encourage you to study for qualifications offered by the Chartered Institute of Marketing (CIM), the Institute of Practitioners in Advertising (IPA) and the Communication, Advertising and Marketing (CAM) Education Foundation.

What the work involves

You will plan and develop strategies for campaigns to suit different clients' requirements, working for advertising, PR or media agencies.

You will use a variety of different tactics from TV, newspapers, posters, radio and direct mail to viral and online marketing. It will be your responsibility to ensure that all the campaigns run smoothly, to budget and on schedule.

Your work will involve liaising between clients and the agency staff, including designers and budget planners. Identifying, approaching and engaging potential clients will also be important.

Type of person suited to this work

As much of your work involves discussions with clients and agency staff, you will need to be flexible with good communication skills. Having a well-organised approach is essential because you could be running a number of campaigns at the same time.

You will need a strong creative flair and a resourceful attitude. A key ability will be to manage clients' campaigns within budget.

Being a confident team player with an enthusiastic attitude and strong negotiating skills is essential.

Working conditions

You will be based in an office, spending a lot of time at your computer. However, your job will also involve travelling to visit clients and attend meetings.

It is almost certain that at times you will have to work under pressure to complete projects within limited time scales. You will work standard office hours but during busy periods you will have to work late if required.

Future prospects

Owing to the popularity of this sector, competition for jobs is tough. You will need to have particular skills or work experience that make you stand out. It can be difficult to progress owing to a lack of higher-level opportunities. The majority of agencies have fewer than 100 employees.

The speed and extent of your career progression will depend on the outcome of your different advertising strategies. With experience, it is possible to progress into a role as account manager and then to account director, where you would have control of the account management department. Another option would be to work as a freelancer or open your own agency.

Your training will be relevant to the related industries of marketing, market research, business or retail and commerce.

Advantages/disadvantages

The job is fast paced with hectic periods of work.

There are opportunities to meet and work with a wide range of people.

It can be rewarding when your clients' campaigns are successful.

Money guide

Earnings vary according to employer and geographical location, with the highest salaries in London.

Starting as a graduate you can expect to earn £18,000–£25,000 a year.

An experienced account executive is likely to receive £30,000–£35,000.

Those employed at a senior level, as an account manager or account director, can achieve between £45,000 and £90,000.

Related opportunities

- Advertising Art Director p397
- Advertising Media Planner p399
- Marketing Manager/Director p408

Further information

Advertising Association
www.adassoc.org.uk

Communication, Advertising and Marketing Education Foundation
www.camfoundation.com

Institute of Practitioners in Advertising
www.ipa.co.uk

Qualifications and courses

While there are no specific entry requirements, art directors usually have an HND, degree or postgraduate qualification in graphic design, advertising design, illustration or fine art.

For degree entry, students generally require at least 2 A levels/3 H grades, 5 GCSEs/S grades (A*–C/1–3) and a portfolio of work. Foundation courses in an art-related subject are also available.

Work experience is an excellent way to develop your knowledge and build a network of industry contacts. Vacation work, job shadowing or taking a sandwich degree course are all useful. Employers look for a strong portfolio of your design work and ideas, which should include both print and digital work.

The Design & Art Direction (D&AD) run workshops in which participants develop relevant skills and build up a portfolio. Once employed, you may wish to take a course offered by the Institute of Practitioners in Advertising (IPA).

What the work involves

You will design and create effective brand styles and images for advertising campaigns in accordance with clients' requirements.

Working with specialist software, you will develop new designs, often at short notice, to convey the required mood or tone of a particular campaign. In close collaboration with colleagues, especially copywriters and reprographic specialists, you will make sure your ideas are realised.

You might also be involved in selecting photographers and other professionals to create additional visuals for use in a campaign.

Type of person suited to this work

You will need visual design skills and creative strengths but also the skills to develop commercial ideas. The capacity to adapt to a client's requirements is also important.

As you will be using software to create new designs, you will need to have up-to-date computer skills.

Much of your time will be spent working in a team so you will need excellent communication and people skills. Your ideas could be rejected or changed so a flexible yet confident attitude is essential.

It is important to be able to work to exacting standards, paying close attention to detail.

Working conditions

Most of your tasks will be office based, sometimes in a studio. Your job will also involve travelling to visit clients and attend shoots.

You will be seated for long periods at a workstation using a number of computers and you may often be on the phone.

The majority of your work will be done in normal office hours. However, there will be pressure to complete jobs as you near deadlines and at these times you will be expected to work late.

Future prospects

This is a highly competitive area of work to enter. Although newer agencies exist in some of the larger cities (Manchester, Bristol and Newcastle), the number of creative art directors employed is still low. Job opportunities are increasing at the fastest rate in digital/viral marketing.

Normally agencies hire a team consisting of a copywriter and an art director so finding a good partner is essential. You will start as a junior creative team member and then could progress to becoming a middleweight art director.

With experience you could move up to senior art director level. Some established art directors go on to work on a freelance basis.

Advantages/disadvantages

This job is rewarding as it offers individuals the chance to influence the images of major companies and brands.

The constant need to develop new ideas can be stressful at times.

Money guide

Earnings vary according to employer and location. The highest salaries are normally in London.

Starting salaries at junior art director level are around £18,000–£25,000 per year.

With experience and a track record of successful campaigns, earnings can range from £25,000 to £50,000.

Those employed in the most senior positions can achieve a salary between £45,000 and £120,000.

Related opportunities

- Advertising Media Planner p399
- Copywriter p403
- Graphic Designer p175

Further information

Communication, Advertising and Marketing Education Foundation
www.camfoundation.com

Institute of Practitioners in Advertising
www.ipa.co.uk

Qualifications and courses

Most entrants are graduates of degree or diploma programmes. Relevant subjects include marketing or communications, media studies, statistics and business management. Entry to an HND is with 1 A level/2 H grades and 4 GCSEs/S grades (A*–C/1–3). Requirements to study for a degree are 2 A levels/3 H grades and 5 GCSEs/S grades (A*–C/1–3).

Foreign language skills are helpful, especially for jobs with international companies.

Building up a portfolio of work experience through work placements or volunteering will increase your chances of getting your first job, develop your skills and give you invaluable experience in media buying, negotiation and sales.

What the work involves

Advertising media buyers research, identify and negotiate the purchase of media space (eg advertising time on television or radio).

Working for an advertising agency, you will work from a brief laid out by your clients, taking into consideration target audiences, media events and activities, schedules and budgetary constraints.

You will present proposals, advise creative teams, estimate costs and profits, and monitor and keep records of the progress of your media campaigns.

You will make media contacts and liaise with other media companies in order to get the best deal and most exposure on behalf of your client.

Type of person suited to this work

You should have a keen interest in media, marketing and advertising and be constantly thinking of new creative ways to approach your work. As you will need to have a good understanding of your target audiences and markets, you should also be interested in the reasons why people purchase certain products or use certain media channels.

You must have good communication skills as you will have to make presentations, draw up proposals and correspond with contacts on a regular basis. You should have strong organisational skills and be able to work under pressure and within tight deadlines.

You will need to have initiative, drive and be able to work in a team.

Working conditions

You will work around 40 hours a week, Monday to Friday. You may have to work longer hours to meet deadlines. Part-time work or flexible hours may be possible.

You will be mainly office based but as you gain experience you will spend more time meeting with clients, making presentations and discussing proposals. You may have to travel away from home with some overnight stays.

The majority of your correspondence with media owners and companies is conducted on the phone, by email or by socialising.

Future prospects

You will usually progress to a permanent position after 1 year in a junior role. Your promotions will depend largely on personal performance and successful campaigns. You may have to move between agencies in order to progress.

You can take postgraduate qualifications to increase your knowledge about specific aspects of your job such as business or marketing.

After 3–5 years you may gradually take on more account management and responsibilities or you may take a position in data management or account planning.

Advantages/disadvantages

Advances and changes in the media industry mean that you will find new and exciting opportunities to work with multimedia technologies.

This is a highly competitive industry and your work may involve long and stressful hours.

Money guide

Earnings vary with the size of the agency and geographical location. Salaries in London are usually higher.

As a junior advertising media buyer, your starting salary may be £18,000–£22,000.

After you have gained several years' experience in the role, your earnings may increase to between £25,000 and £35,000.

At a senior level you can achieve up to £50,000 a year.

Related opportunities

- Advertising Account Executive p396
- Market Research Executive p406
- Marketing Manager/Director p408

Further information

Account Planning Group
www.apg.org.uk

Institute of Practitioners in Advertising
www.ipa.co.uk

The Advertising Association
www.adassoc.org.uk

Qualifications and courses

Although there are no minimum educational requirements for a role as an advertising media planner, competition is high and most entrants will have a degree. It is rare to get into the profession with less than an HND. Relevant subjects include media studies, business management, marketing, advertising and English.

Most agencies tend to require relevant work experience and undertaking a sandwich course can be a particular advantage. Work experience in media, marketing or advertising companies will help you to develop skills, knowledge and industry contacts.

Training tends to be done on the job. New account planners may train with the Account Planning Group (APG) or the Market Research Society (MRS).

Employers may encourage you to study for qualifications offered by the Institute of Practitioners in Advertising (IPA) and the Communication, Advertising and Marketing (CAM) Education Foundation.

What the work involves

You will research public opinion and interest in a client's product or service to develop new advertising and media campaigns. Market research, both positive and negative, will form a starting point from which you will plan and develop new advertising strategies for your clients.

You will need to be very clear when interpreting your clients' intentions. The work will require close cooperation with your clients and your creative team in order to create strong and successful advertising.

Type of person suited to this work

As you will be developing new advertising ideas, you will need a high level of creativity.

To understand and make use of a range of facts and figures in support of your work, you will need an ability to interpret and analyse trends in data.

As you will have to make presentations to your clients and colleagues at progress meetings, excellent verbal and written communication skills will be essential. Being self-motivated and confident is also important.

Good business skills are helpful and you will need to use clear verbal reasoning when stating your point of view.

Working conditions

Most of your work will be undertaken in an office or at clients' premises. You will be expected to dress formally and be well presented at all times.

Although you will mainly work normal office hours, you can expect to work overtime and at weekends during busy periods.

You will have to travel to attend meetings on a regular basis, perhaps staying overnight.

Future prospects

The majority of job opportunities in advertising are based in London, although the number of companies in other large cities is growing. Despite this, there are still only around 21,000 people working within the sector of advertising and media, making entry highly competitive. Realistically, account planning makes up only a very small part of the overall advertising/media sector.

If employed by one of the few larger companies – with over 300 employees – it is occasionally possible to work abroad in areas such as Europe.

With experience, you could work on a freelance basis or move into market research, design or management.

Advantages/disadvantages

This type of work can provide the opportunity to work for high-profile companies with a Europe-wide or global reach.

You will have to develop new ideas, often at relatively short notice.

This is a very competitive career and only the most determined will succeed.

Money guide

Earnings vary with employer and geographical location. Salaries tend to be higher in London.

Starting salaries for a junior media planner range from £18,000 to £24,000 per year.

Experienced advertising media planners can earn between £25,000 and £45,000.

Those employed in the most senior positions can achieve £60,000–£80,000.

Some employers provide bonuses if you develop successful campaigns or gain new business.

Related opportunities

- Market Research Executive p406
- Marketing Manager/Director p408
- Media Researcher p409

Further information

Account Planning Group
www.apg.org.uk

Communication, Advertising and Marketing Education Foundation
www.camfoundation.com

Institute of Practitioners in Advertising
www.ipa.co.uk

CRCI: D

MARKETING, ADVERTISING, MEDIA, PRINT AND PUBLISHING

Qualifications and courses

Most entrants will have a degree but enthusiasm, good industry knowledge and the ability to make good contacts is equally important. For entry onto a degree you will usually need a minimum of 3 A levels/H grades and 5 GCSEs/S grades (A*–C/1–3).

Most entrants to this work will have previous experience and qualifications in related fields such as sales, business, music, performing arts or publishing.

It is also possible to start out as an assistant or administrator and then work your way up to an agent or manager.

Contract law knowledge and a second language may be useful in the negotiation of rights deals.

What the work involves

Agents represent and promote artists and creatives in the film, television, radio, theatre, music and publishing sectors. They can also play a similar role for sporting professionals. You will be expected to work proactively to enhance your client's career by securing work and negotiating to ensure that the client attains the best work at the highest fee.

Literary agents are responsible for assessing the quality and commercial potential of manuscripts submitted by authors.

You will also have to develop publication and rights agreements with publishers and TV, radio and film producers on their behalf.

Type of person suited to this work

As you will be acting as the link between your client and the world they work in, you will need excellent communication skills. The ability to develop good contacts and a name for reliability is essential. It is also important to develop good working relationships with clients.

You should have a good head for business and an assertive approach will be helpful when it comes to agreeing contracts on behalf of clients.

You should have a good knowledge of the law and how it applies to your client's sector, as they will rely on you for professional advice in this area.

Working conditions

Agents are office based and can be self-employed or work for agencies.

Although, theoretically, they could work anywhere, most agents are based near London. Literary agents can also be found in Edinburgh, which is an important centre for the UK publishing industry.

Travel is common and you should expect to work 30–40 hours a week, including evening and weekends, as some of your work will involve attending performances and social events to network and raise the profile of your clients.

Future prospects

This is a diverse and extremely competitive area. Agencies are constantly being set up but few stand the test of time. However publishers increasingly prefer to respond to new publication ideas through agents.

Your success will be determined partly by the standard of the clients you represent but, also, by the quality of the advice you can provide to them.

With sufficient experience you might have the opportunity to work abroad in entertainment and publishing hubs such as New York.

Advantages/disadvantages

You will have the satisfaction of supporting new artists and helping them to succeed.

As you will earn your income from commissions, you will be under pressure to identify and promote new artists.

Unsociable hours and extensive travelling can affect your personal life.

Money guide

Salaries vary widely according to the nature of the agent, the number of artists they work with and the success they have in their field.

Literary agents are paid commission which is usually between 10% and 25% of authors' earnings.

New entrants can expect to earn £15,000 in a large agency, progressing to £30,000 with experience.

Top agents with prestigious clients can earn in excess of £100,000.

Related opportunities

- Marketing Manager/Director p408
- Public Relations Officer p416
- Publisher/Commissioning Editor p417

Further information

Association of Authors' Agents
www.agentsassoc.co.uk

The Agents' Association (Great Britain)
www.agents-uk.com

AUTHOR/ SCRIPTWRITER

Qualifications and courses

Authors/scriptwriters are not required to have any specific qualifications. Some, however, are graduates and it may be useful to have a degree in English, journalism, media studies or performing arts.

There are a variety of English and creative writing courses available. These range from degree and postgraduate courses to evening classes designed to improve a writer's technique. Above all it is essential to have a good command of the English language, imagination and originality.

This is a fiercely competitive profession and few authors progress to attain mass-market appeal and a high level of commercial success. For this reason it is often necessary to obtain a second job in order to supplement income.

It is important to be proactive and establish a good network of contacts to aid self-promotion.

Arts Council grants may be available to new authors for work in literature and drama. It is necessary to request such a grant by way of a written proposal.

What the work involves

Authors write the text for books, magazines, ICT resources and more. This can involve developing initial ideas to create a complete piece, or simply rewriting sections.

Scriptwriters create text for TV, film, radio and theatre productions.

As part of the work, you will undertake research using resources such as the internet and libraries.

Authors often specialise in a particular subject area such as technical writing, science, medicine, cookery, travel or education. A small number of authors write and publish creative works of fiction, poetry or drama.

Type of person suited to this work

It is essential to have an excellent command of the English language and the ability to write with your audience in mind. Having a good imagination and a creative approach is important.

As you will be explaining project ideas to publishers and producers/directors, you will need strong communication skills. However you should also be able to cope with working alone for much of the time.

Many authors work on a self-employed basis, so business awareness and numeracy skills are very helpful. You will also need to be able to handle rejections from publishers.

Working conditions

The majority of authors and scriptwriters are self-employed and work from home. Most of your time will be spent researching and writing, whilst sitting at a computer for long periods.

It may be necessary to juggle deadlines with other part-time employment taken on to supplement income. Most authors/ scriptwriters are employed on a project-by-project basis, so the work provides very little job security.

Most of your work will be undertaken alone, which can be isolating.

Future prospects

Making a living as a professional author can be challenging, and it takes time to develop your writing expertise and specialist areas.

Having an established network of contacts helps.

A variety of support groups, writers' groups and courses exist to help people develop their writing skills. There are opportunities to write and share your work in amateur dramatic groups and writers' circles, some of which publish work on the internet.

At present, short dramas for radio broadcast are actively sought.

Advantages/disadvantages

This type of work can provide the satisfaction of being creative and seeing your work in print and in the public domain.

Not all authors succeed in publishing their work and you might need to take on other types of work to make a living.

Money guide

Earnings vary widely depending on the nature of the writing project, your experience, and your popularity as a writer.

Publishers may give a one-off payment for a piece of work or will pay you royalties (a percentage of the sales income of the book).

Salaries can be £15,000–£30,000 for authors employed in a commercial environment. You may have a higher income if you are well known and your work is popular.

Related opportunities

- Copywriter p403
- Journalist p405
- Technical Author/Medical Writer p419

Further information

BBC Writersroom
www.bbc.co.uk/writersroom

Society of Authors
www.societyofauthors.org

Writers and Artists
www.writersandartists.co.uk

COPY EDITOR/SUB-EDITOR/ PROOFREADER

Qualifications and courses

Although there are no set formal entry qualifications, most copy editors are graduates. Relevant degree subjects include English, publishing, media and journalism. For financial journalism a business studies degree would be useful and to work in technical publishing a science-related degree is recommended. You will need at least 2 A levels/3 Highers and 5 GCSEs/S grades (A*–C/1–3) for degree entry.

Candidates could be taken on as editorial assistants or trainees to gain experience. Building a portfolio of work and experience is important.

It is also possible to study for a postgraduate qualification in publishing (PgDip or MA).

The Society for Editors and Proofreaders and the Publishing Training Centre offer introductory and advanced training courses on topics such as copy editing and grammar skills. The National Council for the Training of Journalists also offers an introductory sub-editing qualification.

What the work involves

Copy editors prepare manuscripts for publication by checking for grammatical and punctuation errors, spelling mistakes and inconsistencies in style. You might also be responsible for checking the legality of the text.

Sub-editors are copy editors who work in newspapers and magazines. You may also create headlines and captions and manipulate text to fit a word count.

Proofreaders carry out the final quality checks on texts before publication. You will use a recognised set of symbols and normally mark changes on a hard copy, but sometimes make alterations on screen using specialist software.

Type of person suited to this work

As you will be responsible for preparing texts for publication, you will pay great attention to detail and take pride in your work. An excellent knowledge of the English language and strong writing and communication skills are expected. Patience and a methodical approach to your work are also helpful.

If you are working in-house for a publishing or other company, you will need good team-working skills. In addition you will need to be able to deal tactfully with people, for example when explaining changes to authors' manuscripts.

The ability to manage budgets is useful, as is the ability to work to tight deadlines and cope with pressure.

Working conditions

These jobs tend to be largely solitary. Most copy editors work within offices or are self-employed and work from home.

You can spend some time attending meetings with authors, designers, printers, illustrators and colleagues.

At the busiest times you might have to work late to meet copy or production deadlines, but mostly you will work normal working hours.

Future prospects

This is a very competitive area and many copy editors start off in an administrative or related role and work their way up.

It may be necessary for in-house copy editors to change their job frequently to aid career progression. With experience you could become a project manager or commission new publications.

Increasingly, copy editors work on a freelance basis for a number of clients.

Advantages/disadvantages

The work provides the satisfaction of shaping and improving the style and tone of manuscripts.

You will work with many different types of people.

As you will be making sure a publication is produced on time, this can be a high-pressured job.

Money guide

Earnings vary according to employer and geographic location.

Starting salaries are between £16,000 and £22,000 per year.

Salaries for experienced editors employed in-house vary between £23,000 and £35,000.

The most senior editors can earn up to £60,000.

Freelance rates vary between £12 and £25 an hour, with higher rates for more complex project management editorial work.

As a freelancer you may charge a page or word rate.

Related opportunities

- Copywriter p403
- Journalist p405
- Publisher/Commissioning Editor p417

Further information

National Union of Journalists
www.nuj.org.uk

Society for Editors and Proofreaders
www.sfep.org.uk

MARKETING, ADVERTISING, MEDIA, PRINT AND PUBLISHING

CRCI: PD

COPYWRITER

Qualifications and courses

There are no formal entry requirements to be a copywriter, but most entrants have a degree or HND. Relevant subjects include advertising design, English, journalism, communications or media. A postgraduate qualification in copywriting or creative advertising, such as the West Hertfordshire College PG Diploma in Copywriting, can be useful for graduates without a relevant background.

Students generally require at least 2 A–levels/3 H grades and 5 GCSEs/S Grades (A*–C/1–3) to get a place on a degree course. Foundation courses are also available.

You will require determination to enter the profession and you will probably need to complete several unpaid work experience placements as a copywriter before being taken on. The most common entry route involves producing a high-quality portfolio and showing this to agencies.

What the work involves

Copywriters create informative, well-constructed text (or 'copy') on a wide range of subjects, from a range of perspectives and for a variety of audiences.

Advertising copywriters produce text for TV, film, radio, press and internet advertisements. You will create copy for websites, company magazines/publications, direct mail, brochures and product information guides.

Design companies, sales promotion organisations and other companies employ copywriters to write text that promotes their services or products and helps to increase sales.

Type of person suited to this work

As you will be writing copy for a range of uses, you will require excellent writing skills, a strong creative flair and a good imagination. The ability to describe a subject concisely can also be important.

In discussing innovative ideas with your colleagues and clients, you will make valuable use of your strengths in verbal and written communication skills. You will have to be flexible and willing to alter what you think are good ideas to meet clients' requirements.

It is essential to have good organisational skills, to be able to work well under pressure and to meet tight deadlines.

Working conditions

Many copywriters work on a freelance basis for a number of employers. In-house copywriters will work 9am–5pm from Monday to Friday, within an office or studio environment.

You will spend long periods of time sitting typing, which can be tiring. You will also be expected to attend client meetings, which may involve overnight travel. You will have to work long hours to meet project deadlines, which can be stressful.

Advertising copywriters normally work with an art director, who creates the visual aspect of the campaign.

Future prospects

There are interesting opportunities available, particularly in the website domain, as an increasing number of organisations require innovative copy for service and product promotion.

Competition is fierce but with good contacts, a strong writing style and knowledge of your market, it is possible to make a living in this area.

With experience, some copywriters become freelancers or set up agencies in partnership with other 'creatives'. Other copywriters go on to work in related areas such as public relations and publishing.

Advantages/disadvantages

This job provides the satisfaction of seeing your work in print and in the public domain.

You will be working alongside imaginative colleagues, which can be stimulating.

Copywriting can be stressful because of the need to produce new ideas to tight deadlines.

There may be some job instability if working on a self-employed basis.

Money guide

Earnings vary according to employer and project.

Self-employed copywriters may charge hourly rates, by the day, or for individual projects.

Starting salaries are around £18,000–£25,000 per year.

With 3 to 5 years' experience, you could earn between £25,000 and £40,000.

Senior level salaries can range between £45,000 and £100,000. More is possible for Creative Directors who have won campaign awards.

Related opportunities

- Author/Scriptwriter p401
- Journalist p405
- Technical Author/Medical Writer p419

Further information

Institute of Copywriting
www.inst.org/copy

Institute of Practitioners in Advertising
www.ipa.co.uk

CRCI: O   MARKETING, ADVERTISING, MEDIA, PRINT AND PUBLISHING

403

Qualifications and courses

There are no set entry requirements for this profession, but many entrants have degrees and postgraduate qualifications. There are relevant courses offered by over 50 higher education institutions in areas such as events management, conference and exhibition management, and hospitality management. Other relevant courses include marketing, tourism, and business. A Diploma in Hospitality is also available.

For entry to one of these courses, you will need 5 good GCSEs/S grades (A*–C/1–3), including English and maths and 2 A levels/3 H grades. A foreign language A level or equivalent is also recommended.

The Northern Council for Further Education Certificate in Events Management is also relevant, and is good if you want to work at a supervisory level or if you are already in the industry and want to develop your career.

The best advantage you can have when you are looking to enter the industry is to gain as much experience as you can of organising events. Try to help with organising charity events, local festivals or anything similar. It will also give you an idea of whether the job suits you. Once you are in the industry, there are many training courses available including planning techniques, marketing and crowd safety.

What the work involves

As an events and exhibition organiser, you will be planning and organising events of varying sizes and ensuring that they run to plan on the day. You could find yourself organising anything from conferences, seminars and meetings to parties, ceremonies or weddings.

The nature of your role will depend on the event itself, but you might be researching, planning, marketing the event, setting the budget, and sorting out all of the little details that go into planning an event.

Hours can be late and involve working at weekends – but you may get to attend a free party or two.

Type of person suited to this work

You need to be incredibly well organised. Work can be tough and stressful, so you need energy and stamina: you should relish taking on a heavy workload, not crumple beneath it.

You should be a team player who is really good at communicating with others.

You need to be creative and have a good imagination, but also have a business mind. Your project management and problem-solving skills should be very good, and you must be able to market, sell and negotiate.

Working conditions

You will be extremely busy and rushing to and from various locations.

You will usually work office hours, although additional hours are common when events require extra last minute work

Your time will be divided between the office, events venues, and client meetings. You may well have to travel away from home, sometimes abroad.

You will be working both indoors and outdoors, and may find yourself in hotels, museums, castles, showgrounds. . . the list is endless.

Future prospects

By starting off in roles such as assistant events organiser, you are paving the way and can aim towards positions such as event organiser or manager. From this level you can progress to event director, or even start up your own company.

It is often necessary to move company more than once to progress in this industry.

Advantages/disadvantages

This is an exciting job, and the sense of achievement when an event you have planned is a success is a great feeling.

Planning an event can be stressful, and you might have to work flat out to meet deadlines and make your event a success, sacrificing your evenings and weekends in the process.

Money guide

As you start out, you might earn between £17,000 and £21,000 a year.

With experience this can grow to between £25,000 and £40,000.

As an event manager you might earn around £60,000 or even more at the most senior levels.

Related opportunities

- Catering/Restaurant Manager/Maître d'Hôtel p135
- Entertainment Manager p382
- Hotel Manager p140

Further information

Association for Conferences and Events
www.aceinternational.org

Association of British Professional Conference Organisers
www.abpco.org

Qualifications and courses

The most common route into this career is with pre-entry qualifications. The National Council for the Training of Journalists (NCTJ), the Broadcast Journalism Training Council (BJTC) and the Periodicals Training Council (PTC) accredit HNDs, Foundation degrees, degrees and postgraduate courses. Alternatively, you could complete an unrelated degree, followed by an accredited 1-year postgraduate course or a fast-track postgraduate course lasting 18–20 weeks.

The NCTJ offers the Diploma in Journalism, a new qualification aiming to prepare trainees for multimedia journalism. Those looking to work in the magazine sector could take professional qualifications from the Professional Publishers Association (PPA). The NCTJ also runs distance-learning courses in both newspaper and magazine journalism.

Those with 18 months' work experience who have passed the Diploma in Journalism can take the NCTJ's National Certificate Examination (NCE) which enables candidates to achieve senior status as a journalist.

It is advisable to get as much work experience as possible, either within the industry or for student newspapers and magazines, and to build up a portfolio of your writing. Broadcast journalism is fiercely competitive and entrants should have a strong showreel and work experience in student or community media.

What the work involves

Journalists research and write stories on subjects such as current affairs, business, health and culture. Broadcast journalists also digitally present these features on radio, television or the internet.

These stories can immediately become live news articles or features for local and national newspapers, magazines, TV, radio and online broadcasts.

You will be planning, writing and editing articles in accordance with a house style, usually to very tight deadlines.

Type of person suited to this work

As you will be producing articles on a regular basis, you will need to thrive on working under pressure.

Strong IT, written and verbal communication skills are essential for this job and broadcast journalists should have a clear and professional voice.

You should be a highly organised multi-tasker with a good instinct for a potential story and the ability to undertake research through interviews and contacts. You will be expected to research difficult stories and meet hostile people, which can be stressful.

Working conditions

Your work will be dictated by the story you are following. You could visit a range of locations in the working day, often at short notice as news stories unfold.

Overnight travel is often part of this job when chasing a story or undertaking research. You will have to work long, sometimes irregular hours in order to meet publication deadlines.

Whilst you may be part of a wider team, you could work alone for much of the time, or in the company of a photographer.

Future prospects

This is a highly competitive area to enter and many people undertake unpaid work experience before they secure a job. Approximately a third of all journalists work freelance. Many full-time journalists started work as freelancers to establish their reputations.

It is possible to cross over from newspaper/magazine journalism into broadcast journalism as a reporter or presenter.

There may be opportunities to work abroad.

Advantages/disadvantages

You will create features that could be read, heard or seen by thousands of people – often beyond the UK.

This profession offers exciting, varied work.

Owing to short deadlines, you will have to regularly produce work under pressure.

You might have to get information or photographs to support sad and distressing stories, which could make you unpopular.

Money guide

Starting salaries for trainee journalists are usually £15,000–£18,000.

An experienced newspaper or magazine journalist can expect to earn between £22,000 and £35,000.

In broadcast journalism, you can achieve up to £40,000, depending on your experience.

The highest earners in this sector, such as newspaper editors and television newsreaders, can receive up to £100,000.

Related opportunities

- Copywriter p403
- Media Researcher p409
- Newspaper/Magazine/Web Editor p411

Further information

Broadcast Journalism Training Council
www.bjtc.org.uk

National Council for the Training of Journalists
www.nctj.com

National Union of Journalists
www.nuj.org.uk

MARKETING, ADVERTISING, MEDIA, PRINT AND PUBLISHING

CRCI: PB

Qualifications and courses

There are no set qualifications for this role but you will most likely be expected to have an HND or degree. Useful subjects are those which develop skills in communication and analysis, such as English, maths, psychology, statistics and social sciences.

Employers also perceive an outgoing personality and enthusiasm for the job to be equally as important as academic qualifications.

Undertaking voluntary or vacation work experience in research, statistical data analysis or interview techniques would be useful pre-entry experience.

The Market Research Society (MRS) offers the Advanced Certificate in Market and Social Research Practice and, at a higher level, the Diploma in Market and Social Research Practice for those with experience in the industry. Once candidates have completed the Diploma, they are eligible for full membership of the MRS.

An NVQ in Marketing (Levels 2–4) is available and some companies may support further study. An MA is not required but may improve your long-term career prospects. Courses include marketing management (specialising in market research) and applied social and market research.

What the work involves

You will undertake research to obtain people's opinions on specific products, services or issues and then analyse the results.

Developing surveys to analyse public opinion on a wide range of subjects or issues will be part of your job. You may also interview small groups of people, known as focus groups or panels, to assess their views on a specific topic in more detail.

You will compile the results of your research in the form of detailed reports or summary analyses to be used by your clients, businesses and other organisations.

Type of person suited to this work

This job is all about people and their opinions, so verbal communication skills are essential. You will also need strong writing skills to create surveys, plan interviews and write reports.

You will need to understand exactly what your client wants to know and think up ways to get this information. A logical and deductive approach to your work is important. You should be interested in human psychology and behaviour.

Also, as you will be working with a lot of paperwork, you will need to be well organised. Confidence working with numbers will be useful in helping you to perform statistical analyses.

Being aware of the marketplace and what sells is also important.

Working conditions

Market researchers work from offices and attend meetings, presentations and interviews. You could work in a specialist market research agency or a marketing department within a larger organisation. Some market researchers work freelance.

The job can involve frequent daily and overnight travel. You will usually work standard office hours, Monday to Friday, with occasional overtime if necessary to meet project deadlines.

Future prospects

The market research industry is worth over £1 billion a year. As well as businesses, many other organisations increasingly depend on market researchers to provide up-to-the-minute facts and figures concerning public opinion on everything from train services to trainers!

After gaining experience as a market research interviewer, you can move up to research executive, and then progress to senior research executive.

With sufficient experience you could enter a senior management role or set up your own agency.

Advantages/disadvantages

The role is interesting as you will work on a variety of projects and meet many different types of people.

The public may not want to speak to you and getting the required information needed may be difficult.

This job is fast paced and can involve high levels of pressure near deadlines.

Money guide

Starting salaries are typically between £18,000 and £25,000.

With experience, earnings increase to £25,000–£35,000.

A very experienced market researcher employed in a senior position could achieve £40,000 to £80,000.

Related opportunities

- Marketing Manager/Director p408
- Media Researcher p409
- Statistician p533

Further information

ESOMAR
www.esomar.org

International Marketing Research Information
www.imriresearch.com

Market Research Society
www.mrs.org.uk

MARKETING ASSISTANT/ EXECUTIVE

Qualifications and courses

Marketing is highly competitive. While you may become an assistant/executive with relevant work experience or a dynamic personality, you will have an advantage if you are a graduate. A degree, Foundation degree or HND in a relevant subject such as marketing, communications or business/management may improve your chances of securing employment. Entry requirements vary between universities but are usually 5 GCSEs/S grades (A*–C/1–3) and 2–3 A levels/H grades.

BTEC offer the Certificate in Principles of Marketing (Levels 2 and 3) which may be useful. School leavers and graduates of non-related disciplines could take the Introductory Certificate in Marketing provided by the Chartered Institute of Marketing (CIM).

Owing to the competitive nature of this sector, you are advised to undertake vacation work or an internship in order to build a network of contacts and develop your skills and experience.

Once you have worked in the industry for a few years, you may wish to study for a professional qualification provided by CIM or the Communication, Advertising and Marketing (CAM) Education Foundation to improve your career and promotion prospects.

What the work involves

Marketing assistants/executives (under the direction of a marketing manager or director) need to promote and raise the profile of ideas, products and services for their clients or organisation.

You will use a variety of techniques to do this including writing press releases and brochures, advertising, developing promotional material for the web or for TV and radio, poster campaigns or events. Use of social media is becoming increasingly important within this field.

You will need to conduct market research which could involve implementing customer surveys and focus groups. You will network (sourcing new clients and gaining contacts) regularly and update customer databases with new client details.

Type of person suited to this work

You must be commercially aware and in-tune with consumer behaviour. It is important to understand what motivates people. Imagination and initiative are essential when developing innovative marketing techniques.

Excellent communication and persuasion skills are necessary. You need to be confident, adaptable and ambitious in order to succeed.

You should be organised as many projects will require you to multi-task, working quickly and to a high standard.

Working conditions

You will spend most of your time in an office working normal hours from Monday to Friday. However, you might need to work evenings and weekends when running events and campaigns. Most companies will provide you with time off in lieu for working overtime.

You will travel to meet clients and attend exhibitions or launches. You will probably be expected to dress formally.

Future prospects

The majority of marketing vacancies are centred in cities such as London, Manchester and Birmingham.

You will work either in-house with a company or for a specialist agency.

With 3–10 years' experience you may be promoted to marketing manager. You could also choose to focus on a particular area such as social media, public relations or advertising. It may be necessary to transfer to a new company in order to increase your chances of promotion.

Advantages/disadvantages

You will be inspired working alongside lively and creative people.

It is rewarding when your campaigns are successful and impact the public or profit your company.

A deadline-driven environment can be stressful and demanding.

You could have many campaigns running at once which can be difficult to balance.

Money guide

Salaries vary with geographical location and tend to be higher in large cities.

As a marketing assistant, you can expect to earn £18,000–£22,000.

Salaries rise to between £25,000 and £40,000 as you gain experience.

Salaries tend to be lower in the public sector.

Bonuses can increase your earnings.

Related opportunities

- Advertising Account Executive p396
- Marketing Manager/Director p408
- Public Relations Officer p416

Further information

Chartered Institute of Marketing
www.cim.co.uk

Communication, Advertising and Marketing Education Foundation
www.camfoundation.com

MARKETING, ADVERTISING, MEDIA, PRINT AND PUBLISHING

CRCI: O

MARKETING MANAGER/DIRECTOR

ENTRY LEVEL 5

MARKETING, ADVERTISING, MEDIA, PRINT AND PUBLISHING

CRCI: O

Qualifications and courses

For entry to management positions, employers want to see a good track record and previous experience in marketing. Most managers begin as marketing assistants or executives and work their way up to a senior level.

Most employers prefer candidates to have completed the 1-year Professional Diploma in Marketing from the Chartered Institute of Marketing (CIM). This course is aimed at those wishing to pursue marketing management. For entry to the Diploma you will need either a degree in marketing or the CIM Professional Certificate in Marketing.

If you want to work at a strategic, directorate level then a postgraduate qualification may be useful. CIM offers the Chartered Postgraduate Diploma in Marketing. Entry requirements are a degree in marketing or the CIM Professional Diploma in Marketing, and significant experience working as a manager.

Alternatively, the Institute of Direct and Digital Marketing (IDM) provides relevant courses such as the IDM Diploma in Direct and Digital Marketing and an MSc in marketing management.

NVQs/SVQs in Marketing (Levels 2–4) are also available from City & Guilds.

What the work involves

You will analyse markets and evaluate the competition in order to develop marketing strategies that will promote and increase sales of products, services or ideas. You will also oversee branding.

You will be responsible for post-campaign evaluations and assessing past strategies. This information will help you to come up with innovative campaigns in the future. You will also be in charge of product development and budgeting.

You will oversee a team of assistants and executives.

Type of person suited to this work

In order to work at a strategic level, you must have vision and be a confident and creative decision-maker. You should be diplomatic and persuasive in order to manage your team effectively.

Good business sense and consumer knowledge are essential. You need to have excellent communication and presentation skills. Enthusiasm and imagination will help you to stay ahead of your competitors.

Analytical and numerical skills are also important as you will be responsible for a project's success and ensuring it is within budget. You must be able to cope under pressure.

Working conditions

You will usually work a 37-hour week, Monday to Friday, but you may often work overtime in order to meet deadlines.

As the manager of a campaign you will be in regular contact with the press, printers and designers and will need to travel often. International travel may also be required and you may spend long periods of time away from home. Otherwise you will be office based, developing strategies and supervising staff.

Future prospects

With 10–15 years of experience you may be promoted from marketing manager to marketing director.

Taking postgraduate qualifications or moving to another company could increase your chance of promotion.

Directors may choose to become self-employed or work as freelance marketing consultants. Alternatively, if you work for a global organisation you may choose to take up a leadership role in an office overseas.

Advantages/disadvantages

It is rewarding to see your strategies and campaigns increase profits and raise awareness for your clients.

You have the freedom to be creative and innovative in your role.

Clients might dislike your ideas and can be difficult to please.

Working overtime to meet deadlines is stressful and demanding.

Money guide

The starting salary for a marketing manager is around £25,000.

As you gain experience in the role, your earnings can increase up to £40,000.

Senior managers and marketing directors can achieve £50,000–£75,000.

Earnings are higher if you work in the private rather than public sector.

Many companies offer benefits such as bonuses, medical insurance and a company car.

Related opportunities

- Advertising Account Executive p396
- Marketing Assistant/Executive p407
- Public Relations Officer p416

Further information

Chartered Institute of Marketing
www.cim.co.uk

Communication, Advertising and Marketing Education Foundation
www.camfoundation.com

408

MEDIA RESEARCHER

Qualifications and courses

There are no formal educational requirements to become a media researcher but owing to the competitive nature of this industry, many entrants have a degree or HND. Relevant subjects include journalism, English, media studies and broadcasting. Depending on the type of programmes you will be working on, a degree in a specialist subject, such as politics, history or legal studies may be useful.

Those without a degree could start their career as a production assistant or runner and work their way up to become a researcher. Personal qualities, confidence and relevant skills are often valued as much as academic qualifications.

Pre-entry work experience is essential. Volunteering for student film/TV productions, hospital or community radio stations, local newspapers or TV/radio production companies would be useful. A good knowledge of current affairs and media practice can be an advantage.

Many researchers gain experience as print or broadcast journalists first. If you have undertaken research in a non-media field, such as social or political research, then your skills would also be relevant.

What the work involves

Researchers develop TV and radio programmes and documentary films by gathering and checking information on specific subjects, people or places.

You will use the internet and phone, conduct face-to-face interviews and visit different locations to do your research. It will be your job to research guests and programme contributors as well as to find relevant images, film clips and music. You could also write and edit programme scripts.

You will brief the production team on the specific subjects covered by your research in preparation for filming.

Type of person suited to this work

The ability to find accurate, relevant information quickly is central to this role. You will need to be creative and resourceful in order to find the best story angles possible. Strong IT skills are required.

You should be persistent, confident and an excellent communicator. You will work to strict deadlines and must be able to stay calm under pressure. A flexible approach will help you balance varied tasks and unsocial hours.

Organisational skills are also important. As you will be responsible for gaining permission to access and make use of information, you will need a clear understanding of the law.

The ability to network and build good relationships with contacts is essential.

Working conditions

You will be based in offices or studios to undertake desk research. You will also spend time on research trips to locations in the UK or overseas. A driving licence would be useful.

The hours tend to be long and it is likely that you will have to work weekends and evenings on a regular basis.

Future prospects

Whilst this is a competitive area to get into, researchers are employed in many areas of the media including radio, production companies, TV and film companies.

Although the number of roles in terrestrial TV companies has dropped, jobs in the smaller cable and satellite sector are on the rise.

With experience, you could progress into a role as an assistant producer and then on to working as a producer/programme director. Many researchers work freelance, getting paid on a contract-by-contract basis.

Some specialise in areas such as documentaries on wildlife, architecture, social history or travel, whilst others concentrate on picture research.

Advantages/disadvantages

You will have to work long and often unsocial hours, which can affect your personal life.

This is a varied job in a fast-moving industry.

You could get the opportunity to travel to a range of places.

Money guide

Starting salaries are usually £18,500–£22,000.

An experienced media researcher can expect to earn £29,000–£32,500.

Many researchers work on a freelance basis and could receive £650 a week, depending on their employer and the number of hours worked.

Related opportunities

- Archivist/Records Manager p346
- Historian p351
- Journalist p405

Further information

Creative Skillset
www.creativeskillset.org

TRC media
www.trcmedia.org

MARKETING, ADVERTISING, MEDIA, PRINT AND PUBLISHING

CRCI: PA

MODEL

Qualifications and courses

There are no formal entry qualifications, but you will need to possess the right 'look' and a portfolio of photographs is normally required for modelling agencies. You should not have to pay an upfront fee to join an agency and be wary of paying for portfolio pictures; most reputable agencies will cover these costs if they think you have potential.

Female models should be at least 5 feet 8 inches (1.72m) tall and should measure no more than 34–24–34 inches (86–61–86cm). Male models should be at least 6 feet (1.83m) tall and have a 38–40 inch chest (97–102cm) and a 30–32 inch waist (76–81cm). However, some photographic models are required to be smaller or larger than the usual sizes, depending on employer requirements.

There are modelling courses which focus on diet, health, deportment, fashion coordination, grooming, catwalk turns and movements, photographic modelling techniques and how to work with agents.

What the work involves

You could be involved in different types of modelling, such as fashion, photographic or demonstration work. You could work in a studio, on location outdoors, at fashion shows or at events such as car shows or conventions.

It is necessary to build a good portfolio of your work and establish a good reputation within the industry.

Your job will be to show off new clothing or products to their best advantage in order to help potential customers visualise them being worn or in use.

Type of person suited to this work

This is a very competitive area to find work. You will have to be determined and prepared to deal with disappointment if contracts do not come your way.

Most fashion model agencies have set physical requirements that you will have to meet before you are accepted onto their books. There is also scope for models with one particularly good feature, such as hands, feet, eyes or hair, to model specific items.

During your work you will meet different types of people, so you will have to be confident and have good communication skills.

Working conditions

The places you will work will depend on the type of modelling that you do and the nature of the contracts you are offered. You might work indoors within a studio, or you could be on location doing catalogue work. This can involve many hours of work to get the correct shot.

You will be on your feet for long periods at a time and will always have to look your best, even if you have been travelling.

The work can be physically demanding; hours spent walking back and forth and posing in awkward positions for long periods can take their toll.

Future prospects

Only the most successful models are always in work. Most are self-employed and have to take up temporary or part-time work when necessary.

To build your reputation, you will have to create a portfolio of work using photos from previous contracts. Your portfolio will need to have a distinct edge to help you win contracts and work.

While top models are very famous and can be rich, there are hundreds more who work for smaller companies and businesses who may earn a lot less. Most models finish their career in their early 30s.

Advantages/disadvantages

Only a few models get the top contracts.

You could get to travel around the world.

You will be posing for long periods which could be tiring.

Modelling can be a very glamorous and confidence boosting career although you will also have to take criticism.

Money guide

You will probably be self-employed so your earnings will depend on your success in finding regular, well-paid work.

Most agencies keep 20% of earnings as commission.

You can expect to start on around £50–£200 per booking, rising to up to £1,000 per booking for models with experience.

Models working for particular fashion houses can earn between £12,000 and £18,000 a year.

Well known models can earn very high wages.

Related opportunities

- Beauty Consultant p454
- Fashion Designer/Milliner p171
- Wardrobe Assistant p451

Further information

Alba Model Information
www.albamodel.info

Association of Model Agents
www.associationofmodelagents.org

Equity
www.equity.org.uk

London College of Fashion
www.fashion.arts.ac.uk

Qualifications and courses

Most newspaper, magazine or web editors have extensive experience in journalism. To become a journalist you usually need an HND, Foundation degree or degree accredited by the National Council for the Training of Journalists (NCTJ) or the Periodicals Training Council (PTC). Alternatively, you could complete an unrelated degree, followed by an accredited 1-year postgraduate course or a fast-track postgraduate course lasting 18–20 weeks. Editors of specialist publications may have qualifications or experience in that particular field, for example, a degree in science or art.

The Diploma in Journalism offered by the NCTJ, distance-learning courses in newspaper and magazine journalism from the NCTJ and professional qualifications from the Professional Publishers Association (PPA) may be useful.

Those with 18 months' work experience who have passed the Diploma in Journalism can take the NCTJ's National Certificate Examination (NCE) which enables candidates to achieve senior status as a journalist.

Developing a strong portfolio by writing for student publications, local newspapers or online magazines is important. As you gain experience and contacts, you could secure a journalism position and eventually become an editor.

What the work involves

Newspaper/magazine/web editors are responsible for the coordination of each aspect of a publication or website.

You will understand the readership of the publication or website and include informative, newsworthy articles, entertaining features and high quality images. You will work with the editorial, design and advertising departments, as well as journalists, printers, web developers and publishers.

Tasks include editing and proofreading articles and features, assigning journalists to cover stories, commissioning freelance writers for features, meeting with photographers and conducting interviews.

Type of person suited to this work

You should be able to demonstrate excellent writing skills and a creative flair. You must have a strong interest in current affairs.

You will have a practical approach to problem-solving and remain calm in a stressful situation. You need to show initiative, persistence and decisiveness. You must pay attention to detail, be meticulous in your organisation and time management, and be able to work to a deadline.

You must have excellent communication skills to be able to delegate tasks and persuade others to meet deadlines.

Web editors must possess good IT skills and feel comfortable using a content management system, monitoring online message boards and dealing with enquiries. You must also keep track of developments within web technology and legal requirements.

Working conditions

You will probably work around 40 hours a week which may include early starts, late nights and weekend work to cover a breaking story. Some large newspapers may offer shift work.

You will mainly be based in an office which could be noisy and busy. You may be required to meet with other editors, journalists or photographers outside the office.

Future prospects

Journalism is a very competitive industry to break into. Work experience, published articles and evidence of commitment to journalism are as important as qualifications.

The typical route to becoming a newspaper/magazine/web editor is to begin in a junior role as a journalist or editorial assistant and work your way up through the editorial department until you are in charge of the content of the magazine, website or newspaper.

You could move across and work in PR, website development or on a freelance basis.

Advantages/disadvantages

Your work will be diverse and stimulating as it will involve constantly creating new content.

You may work in a highly stressful environment, working long and unsocial hours.

Money guide

Earnings depend on the type, size and location of your employer.

The salary for a newspaper or magazine editor can range from £30,000 to £50,000.

A web editor is likely to earn between £25,000 and £38,000.

Those with extensive experience working for the largest publications can achieve up to £80,000.

Related opportunities

- Copy Editor/Sub-editor/Proofreader p402
- Publisher/Commissioning Editor p417
- Website Developer p165

Further information

National Council for the Training of Journalists
www.nctj.com

Newspaper Society
www.newspapersoc.org.uk

MARKETING, ADVERTISING, MEDIA, PRINT AND PUBLISHING

CRCI: PD

Qualifications and courses

There are no set academic requirements to become a photographer but the following courses may be useful: A level/Higher in photography; City & Guilds Levels 1–3 in Photo Imaging and Photography; the Diploma in Creative and Media; and an HNC/HND in Art and Design. The content of a photography degree and other programmes can vary significantly, with some having greater emphasis on an artistic aspect and others more focused on commercial concerns.

Given that photography has become an increasingly competitive field, a postgraduate qualification in a related aspect may be advantageous. It is generally accepted that prior work experience is necessary to entering the industry, with perseverance and patience essential. Applicants will also need a strong portfolio of work comprising between 10 and 15 shots.

Candidates wishing to pursue careers as police, medical or press photographers will need 5 GCSEs/S grades (A*–C/1–3) including English and maths. It is necessary for medical photographers to have a degree or postgraduate certificate in clinical photography and forensic photographers to have 1 A level/H grade in science.

The British Institute of Professional Photography's qualifying exam requires an HND or a degree. Apprenticeships in Photo Imaging are available through Skillset.

BIPP provides a variety of 1-day courses run by experts which cover a wide range of photography disciplines and business skills. This may be very useful in order to learn skills such as financial management, should you choose to become freelance or set up your own photography business.

What the work involves

Photographers create photographic images using technical lighting and equipment. Using your eye for design and knowledge of photographic techniques you will create images for a specific brief.

Many photographers work with digital enhancing techniques to modify and improve, or add interest and illusions to the images they produce.

Type of person suited to this work

You will need a strong visual sense and an eye for what makes a good picture. You will need the technical knowledge and skills to get the most from lighting, studio set-ups and, of course, camera equipment. The use of editing software means that ICT skills are increasingly important.

Strong communication skills and a flexible attitude come in useful when discussing projects with clients, or putting nervous subjects at ease.

To work on a freelance basis, business skills and self-confidence are essential.

Working conditions

You will either be studio or location based. In a studio you could work with still life and portraiture. Lighting equipment can be heavy and the work can be physically tiring as you will be on your feet for long periods.

If you work outdoors you could record images for advertising and photo-journalism. This may require patience if the weather or light conditions are not correct for your shot.

Commercial photography is completed to tight deadlines, which can be stressful.

Future prospects

In order to gain the essential skills and an understanding of your specialist type of photography, you could work as a photographer's assistant. Nowadays, positions are even more limited as digital photography has reduced the work of professionals.

With experience you could progress into freelance work or specialise in a particular area such as press, medical or food photography.

Advantages/disadvantages

You will have the satisfaction of using your creativity and technical skills to create original images, which may end up in the public eye.

It takes time in this competitive industry to develop contacts, so if you work on a freelance basis you might need a second job to support yourself.

Money guide

As a trainee assistant photographer you can expect to earn about £12,000 per year.

This rises to between £18,000 and £20,000 with experience.

In excess of £60,000 is possible at senior levels.

Earnings will vary if you are self-employed or freelance. You are likely to earn between £150 and £600 per day. You may have periods of inactivity and many people have a second job, in an area such as teaching, to supplement their income.

Related opportunities

- Graphic Designer p175
- Illustrator/Technical Illustrator p176
- TV and Film Camera Person/Operator p420

Further information

Association of Photographers
www.the-aop.org

British Institute of Professional Photography
www.bipp.com

PHOTOGRAPHIC STYLIST

Qualifications and courses

There are no formal qualifications for becoming a photographic stylist. Many people who go into the role will have art or design related qualifications though or experience as a photographer's assistant. If you want to work in food styling then you should have a background in catering.

Several relevant further education courses are available, for instance the London College of Fashion offers a Foundation degree in Fashion Styling and Photography. BTEC National Diplomas in fashion or photography may also be useful.

Only a few degree courses are directly related to this area, but many fashion or photography courses include the relevant module. The skills and disciplines used in interior or exhibition design or home economics (food styling) could be useful. Some courses include a period of time in work placements.

Qualifications alone will not secure you work so it is essential that you secure as much relevant work experience as possible. It is useful to compile a portfolio of any work you do. Training is on the job.

What the work involves

Photographic stylists work closely with photographers to design the look and mood of a photo shoot.

It would be your responsibility to arrange and dress the set, to find appropriate props and to organise any work that needs to be done behind the scenes.

Typically, you would receive a brief from the photographer or director of the shoot and then come up with creative ideas to fulfil the brief. Sometimes you will have a lot of freedom for your own ideas and input but other times the brief will be very strict.

It is useful to build up a collection of accessories that you can bring to shoots.

Most stylists specialise in a particular area, such as fashion, food or interior photography.

Type of person suited to this work

You will need to be creative with a good eye for design and understand what makes a good picture. You will also need to have a sound understanding of photography and lighting.

Good communication skills are essential as you will need to coordinate with a range of people on each shoot.

You must be able to stay calm under pressure.

An understanding of the latest fashion trends is important as is commercial awareness.

Working conditions

You will need to have an office base but will spend the majority of your time out on location and in photography studios.

Working hours will be varied and days will often be long and often extremely pressurised. You will probably need to work some evenings and weekends.

It is useful to have a full driving licence as you will need to drive between shoots and transport props which could be large or delicate.

Future prospects

You will probably work freelance and as you build up contacts and experience you may secure work with magazines, consultancies, photography studios, agencies and design houses. It is a very competitive industry though so you will need to make sure your portfolio is really strong.

You can advertise your services through a number of directories for creative professionals or it may be possible to join an agency.

Advantages/disadvantages

Working as a photographic stylist is a very creative job where you can see your ideas brought to life on camera.

Hours are long and the work can be stressful as you will have to work to very tight deadlines.

Pay can be low to start with and competition is fierce.

Money guide

Starting salaries vary, but are typically around £12,000. With experience, this can rise to up to £35,000 a year.

Top stylists who have built up a reputation can earn considerably more.

Daily rates vary between £200 and £400.

As most stylists work freelance, incomes vary considerably depending on how much work you have.

Related opportunities

- Fashion Designer/Milliner p171
- Photographer p412
- TV and Film Camera Person/Operator p420

Further information

Association of Photographers
www.the-aop.org

British Display Society
www.britishdisplaysociety.co.uk

British Institute of Professional Photography
www.bipp.com

MARKETING, ADVERTISING, MEDIA, PRINT AND PUBLISHING

CRCI: PC

Qualifications and courses

Although there are no set entry requirements for this career, GCSEs/S grades (A*–C/1–3) in English, maths, science and technology are an advantage.

Many people enter these professions by means of an apprenticeship. The Diploma in Manufacturing and Product Design might be useful. In addition you can study a relevant college course prior to entry.

Machine printer

Most employers will expect a good level of education, particularly GCSEs or equivalent in English, maths, science and IT. You also need to have good colour vision.

As an introduction to the sector you can take a 10-day course run by the Institute of Paper, Printing and Publishing. You can also work towards NVQs Levels 1–3 in subjects such as machine printing, mechanised print finishing and binding, digital print production, envelope manufacture and carton manufacture.

Screen printer

You can choose to do a college course in printing and graphic communications, printmaking skills, screen printing, graphic printmaking or print media. It is also possible to attain City & Guilds Certificates in Printing and Graphic Communications at Levels 2 and 3, an NVQ in Screenprinting at Levels 2 and 3, an ABC Level 3 Award in Printmaking Skills, Screen Printing and Screen Printing Skills. The Digital and Screenprinting Association, and specialist schools such as London College of Communication also run relevant courses.

The majority of training takes place on the job.

Bookbinder

On-the-job training is usually provided to be a bookbinder. GCSEs (or equivalent) particularly in English or maths are also useful.

NVQs are available in mechanised print finishing and binding at Levels 2 and 3 and hand binding at Level 3. It is also possible to enter the profession through an apprenticeship scheme.

To work as a craft bookbinder you will need to have certain skills. Craft bookbinding is often a second career path. Courses, degrees and diplomas are available in fine bookbinding and repair.

Print production planner

Many print production planners have a degree or diploma in a related subject such as print management, graphic communications, business studies or publishing although the job is open to all graduates and diploma students.

You can also study for an NVQ in Print Administration at Level 3, which includes modules on health and safety.

It is also possible to enter without a degree or HND and employers are willing to provide release from work for training. This job requires maturity and practical industry experience. It is possible to commence as a machine printer and work your way up to this position.

What the work involves

Machine printer

Machine printers oversee the production of printed items on machines of various sizes for products such as newspapers, posters, books, etc. You will set up the printing press correctly for the specific job. This includes ensuring that the appropriate plates, paper and inks have been selected.

You will trial the print run, check for errors and ensure that the quality is up to standard.

Screen printer

Screen printers create visual images by organising and operating hand- or power-driven screen printing machines which print graphics onto fabrics and paper by forcing ink through a delicate mesh overlay of the stencil design.

You will be required to prepare the stencils, inks and print processes.

Bookbinder

Bookbinders are responsible for transforming the printed material into the finished product. Nowadays the majority of bookbinding is a machine orientated process, which involves stitching, stapling, collating, cutting, binding and coating.

Print production planner

Print production planners are responsible for workflow in the printing firm and ensuring that the efficiency is maximised by checking orders, creating schedules, allocating work, supervising and quality control. It will be your responsibility to liaise with other production departments.

Type of person suited to this work

Printing requires good teamwork and communication skills. It is usual that your work will involve computers and other types of machinery and equipment so you will need good practical skills and an understanding of ICT.

It is important to have normal colour vision, good hand-to-eye co-ordination and a high level of physical fitness.

You should have a meticulous eye for detail, and you will need to demonstrate art and design skills to convince customers that you can make aesthetically pleasing finished products, from CD covers to pages of pure text or full-colour brochures.

As print runs do not always go smoothly you will need to be adept at problem-solving, have a long concentration span and the ability to work under pressure.

Furthermore you should be flexible as some print companies run 24 hour operations and you might have to work shifts at night and at the weekends. Print production managers should also have good multi-tasking skills, a good head for numbers and the ability to influence people.

Working conditions

In smaller print companies you will normally work office hours, that is 9am to 5pm, but during busy periods you could do additional hours in order to ensure that projects are completed on time. Larger companies tend to run 24 hour operations and you will be expected to work shifts and weekends. Overtime is widely available.

Bookbinders may also have the opportunity to work part time.

Your working environment will depend on your role and the size of the firm. Printshops can be dirty and noisy when machines are functioning. Hazardous chemicals are used in finishes and to wash inks from the press but there is good ventilation to cope with the resulting fumes.

You will be required to adhere to health and safety regulations at all times and use protective gear such as overalls, boots, gloves and ear protectors.

It is necessary to have a good level of physical fitness as you will be standing for long periods of time. Upper body strength is also important as you may be required to carry out some heavy lifting.

Print production planners will work in an office but will also carry out work on the production floor and may have to travel to attend meetings with clients.

Future prospects

At present in the UK there are about 10,000 print companies, which employ about 140,000 people. There are about 30,000 machine printers and bookbinders and 15,000 print production planners.

The majority of the industry comprises small, family-owned enterprises. The industry is sensitive to wider economic issues, such as cheaper rates from foreign print companies, increasing use of electronic resources and seasonal order variations.

Opportunities will depend on your skills and the size and type of your company. Although printers cover all the stages of production, the job of folding machine operator (at the finishing end of the process) is becoming a skills shortage area.

With experience and additional design skills, you could work for a specialist press production company, a design or reprographic house or general printers. To run a printing business takes a high level of business skills, including accounting and sales.

Advantages/disadvantages

This job combines creative and artistic skills with technical and computer aided design.

There are good entry opportunities for some printing jobs such as specialist print finishers, which have become skills shortage areas.

Owing to the nature of the industry, you might have to move to other parts of the country for promotion.

Many companies now produce high quality publications in-house, so printers need to work with large volumes or specialist niche markets to make a profit.

Money guide

Machine printer
Newly qualified printers can expect to earn between £16,000 and £19,000 a year.

More experienced machine printers can earn up to £40,000.

Additional payments for shift allowances and bonuses are also possible and the highest salaries in this profession can be up to £60,000.

Screen printer
Screen printers can expect to start on £16,000, rising to £24,000 with experience.

Top earners can reach salaries of up to £36,000.

Bookbinder
Bookbinders can expect to earn a relatively low starting salary of £14,000.

This can rise to between £16,000 and £30,000, including shift bonuses, with experience.

Those with extensive experience and who lead a team can earn up to £35,000.

If you are a self-employed craft bookbinder earnings can vary depending on the amount of work you have.

Print production planner
New entrants can expect to earn between £20,000 and £25,000.

With experience, print production planners can earn between £30,000 and £40,000.

Senior planners (with at least 10 or 15 years in the role) can earn up to £56,000.

Related opportunities

- CAD Draughtsperson p216
- Publisher/Commissioning Editor p417
- Quality Control Inspector p238
- Signwriter/Signmaker p184

Further information

British Printing Industries Federation
www.britishprint.com

Institute of Paper, Printing and Publishing
www.ip00.org.uk

Scottish Print Employers Federation
www.spef.org.uk

Society of Bookbinders
www.societyofbookbinders.com

Qualifications and courses

There are no formal academic requirements but most entrants to this profession are graduates. A degree in a relevant subject, such as public relations, marketing, business, English or media studies may be useful.

Entry is highly competitive and a postgraduate qualification may improve your career prospects. Employers often expect candidates to undertake pre-entry work experience in PR, communications or marketing. You could also develop relevant skills by volunteering at a charity or writing for a student newspaper.

The Chartered Institute of Public Relations (CIPR) offers professional qualifications. Entry requirements for the CIPR Advanced Certificate in Public Relations are a first degree or 2 years' PR experience and 5 GCSEs/S grades (A*–C/1–3) including English language.

The Diploma in Marketing Communications available from the Communication, Advertising and Marketing (CAM) Education Foundation could also be beneficial.

The Public Relations Consultants Association (PRCA) have a range of qualifications at different levels suitable for new entrants, experienced PR officers or managers.

What the work involves

You will manage the image and reputation of organisations by writing publicity materials, studying and advising clients, and responding to enquiries or complaints.

It will be important that you develop and maintain positive working relationships with the local, national and relevant trade press and TV news reporters.

Public relations (PR) officers work in public relations or communications departments in large organisations and for PR companies. Some work on a freelance basis.

Type of person suited to this work

PR is all about maintaining a positive image so you must be confident and have a smart appearance.

You need to have strong communication skills and enjoy liaising with a wide range of people. Written communication and research skills are essential, as are good IT skills.

You must be able to work effectively to tight deadlines and be flexible when managing several projects at once. Financial management skills are also useful.

Working conditions

Most of your work will be within an office where you will have a workstation with a computer, access to office equipment and a phone.

Although you will work normal office hours, longer hours are common in this job, particularly in busy periods.

You will have meetings with clients, colleagues or other professionals. You will need to travel to attend meetings, special events and presentations on a regular basis. Working for global companies or high-profile charities may mean some overseas travel.

Future prospects

PR is a growing industry. However, there is strong competition, often with hundreds of well-qualified applicants for one post.

You will start as a PR assistant and then progress to a role as an account executive, followed by a move into a senior role.

It is possible to work abroad either within an existing organisation or by moving to one based overseas or with offices abroad. With experience, some PR professionals set up their own companies or work freelance for other organisations.

Advantages/disadvantages

You can be part of high-profile campaigns.

This job can be pressured owing to the speed of information releases and the range of activities you will have to juggle.

If working for a high-profile organisation, you might have to be on-call to respond to unexpected situations or emergencies.

Money guide

Earnings vary with location and tend to be higher in London and the south-east of England.

Those working in the private sector usually earn more than public sector employees.

Starting salaries are around £16,000 to £20,000.

An experienced public relations officer can expect to earn between £20,000 and £40,000.

Those employed in the most senior positions can achieve £80,000–£100,000.

Related opportunities

- Advertising Account Executive p396
- Advertising Media Planner p399
- Journalist p405

Further information

Chartered Institute of Public Relations
www.ipr.org.uk

Communication, Advertising and Marketing Education Foundation
www.camfoundation.com

International Public Relations Association
www.ipra.org

PUBLISHER/COMMISSIONING EDITOR

Qualifications and courses

The majority of new entrants have gained a degree. You will need at least 2 A levels/3 Highers and 5 GCSEs/S grades (A*–C/1–3) for degree entry. A relevant postgraduate qualification, such as an MA or MSc in publishing, is not essential but is advantageous given the competition for places. A 2.1 or higher degree is needed for entry to a postgraduate course.

As this is a senior role, it is unlikely that a new graduate would start as a publisher/commissioning editor. Most entrants begin as an editorial assistant before being promoted to an editor position and then going on to secure a publisher/commissioning editor role.

Specialist training centres such as the Publishing Training Centre provide short courses on different areas of publishing. The Society of Young Publishers can also offer advice and support to those wanting to enter this field or who are just starting their careers.

Entry into the industry is highly competitive and it is important to learn as much as possible about publishing from trade magazines or people in the industry before applying. Experience of writing or editing at a non-professional level can be useful.

What the work involves

Publishers/commissioning editors plan and manage ranges or lists of books, magazines or ICT resources produced by their department or company. This could include researching consumers' needs and identifying gaps in the company's list of publications.

You will develop ideas for new publications and respond to proposals from authors. You will also oversee the entire process of developing new publications from an original idea to completed manuscript.

In a small organisation you might also be responsible for liaising with copy-editors and proofreaders. You may also be responsible for developing marketing strategies to increase publication sales.

Type of person suited to this work

You will need a strong interest in producing books and publications that have extensive commercial appeal.

As you will liaise closely with authors and colleagues, you should enjoy meeting and working with a variety of people.

You will also need strong written and verbal communication skills and the ability to encourage people to complete tasks to deadlines. You must be well organised and able to plan ahead.

Working conditions

Most of your work will involve attending meetings or working at a computer within the office of a company or organisation.

You will be expected to liaise with authors, colleagues, designers, ICT specialists and printers either face to face, by email or on the phone.

Although your working week will comprise normal office hours, you can expect to work late at times in order to meet strict publication deadlines or to attend evening events. Business trips, including overnight stays, are a possibility and you could travel abroad.

Future prospects

This is a competitive profession to enter. The main employers are publishing houses, specialist businesses, professional and educational companies.

Sales and marketing experience can facilitate entry to this sector. It is possible to set up your own publishing company, although the market is well covered and profit margins narrow.

Currently, the area of greatest expansion is that offered by the internet and digital publishing.

Advantages/disadvantages

You will meet and work with an interesting cross-section of people.

You will be responsible for creating strategies to increase sales of publications, which can be stressful.

Developing new publications can be a lengthy process and requires patience.

Seeing the finished publication that you have helped to develop is highly satisfying.

Money guide

Salaries can vary depending on the size and type of employer.

Starting salaries in editorial roles can be around £16,000–£28,000 per year (depending on the role).

With experience you could earn up to £35,000 as a commissioning editor.

Senior managers and directors of large publishing companies can earn between £48,000 and £80,000.

Related opportunities

- Copy Editor/Sub-editor/Proofreader p402
- Copywriter p403
- Newspaper/Magazine/Web Editor p411

Further information

Publishers Association
www.publishers.org.uk

Publishing Training Centre
www.train4publishing.co.uk

MARKETING, ADVERTISING, MEDIA, PRINT AND PUBLISHING

CRCI: PD

Qualifications and courses

There are no specific qualifications, although formal music training of some kind is recommended. Work experience and voluntary work for a studio and record companies are vital.

Courses that may help you develop skills and experience include Foundation degrees and degrees in music production, music technology, music practice and music industry management. These include the BTEC National Diploma in Music Technology: Level 3, or the HNC/HND in Music Production: Level 5. You will need at least 2 A levels/3 H grades and 5 GCSEs/S grades, (A*–C/1–3), for degree entry.

Short music courses are available for young professionals beginning in the music industry such as the BPI seminar, 'Music, It's the Business'. The Music Producers' Guild (MPG) have created a Knowledge Band and Members' Directory to encourage debate and facilitate future recording industry producers' networking within the industry. The MPG, in association with the Association of Professional Recording Services (APRS), has set up the Joint Audio Media Education Services (JAMES) to allow new entrants to learn from experienced professionals.

What the work involves

Recording industry producers are employed by the Artists and Repertoire (A&R) department of a recording company to work with artists to produce successful music tracks or demos.

You will discuss ideas with artists and their management, plan new projects, listen to existing tracks and identify areas for improvement.

You will be involved in the organisation of each stage of the recording process, including rehearsal time, recruitment of sound engineers, booking studio time, directing the artists and suggesting alterations that will produce the desired sound.

Type of person suited to this work

You must have excellent communication skills to give instructions to others, persuade people to try your ideas and to build up a good network of contacts.

As you will have to spend long hours in the studio you should have a good ear for music, high stamina, self-discipline and patience.

You should also have good planning skills to work out budgets, organise time scales for recording studios and estimate production and post-production costs.

Working conditions

You will work long, irregular hours. This may include working late into the night and at the weekends.

Your work may not always be constant and you might have to find other methods of earning money.

You may have to travel within the UK and abroad.

Future prospects

You will probably progress to a production position after several years of working in an assistant sound engineer or engineer roles.

At first, you will approach A&R departments with your services until you establish your reputation, usually by producing music that is commercially successful.

Advantages/disadvantages

You may have the opportunity to work with a diverse range of artists and to be a part of the creative process of making music.

You may produce music which becomes very successful and gains you national, or even international, acclaim.

Prolonged exposure to loud music may damage your hearing.

Artists can be independent-minded and sometimes difficult.

Money guide

You can expect a starting salary of around £16,000 per year. With experience and constant work you can earn from £30,000 or more. The top recording industry producers can earn in excess of £100,000.

You may be paid 'on spec' if you work with an unsigned band. This means that you will be paid if and when the artist is successful.

Usually you will be paid a flat fee, but this will also be supplemented by an agreed percentage of the sales income. This can be minimal or thousands of pounds.

Related opportunities

- DJ p438
- Musician p442
- Sound Engineer p446

Further information

BPI The British Recorded Music Industry
www.bpi.co.uk

Music Producers Guild UK Ltd
www.mpg.org.uk

TECHNICAL AUTHOR/MEDICAL WRITER

ENTRY LEVEL 4

Qualifications and courses

It is possible to enter this profession without an HND or degree but a demonstration of extensive specialist knowledge will be required.

Many entrants have a degree or qualification in English, journalism or media studies. Others have qualifications in the area that they wish to specialise in, for example engineering or computer science. Minimum degree entry requirements are usually 2 A levels/3 H grades and 5 GCSEs/S grades (A*–C/1–3).

Coventry University offers a BA Honours degree in Communication, Culture and Media with an incorporated work placement. In addition, the University of Portsmouth offers an MA in Technical Communication which is useful for graduates in science and technology who wish to improve their writing skills. The Institute of Scientific and Technical Communicators (ISTC) provides a further list of approved specialist courses.

It is common for mature adults to enter this profession as it necessitates expert knowledge. There is the possibility to take an open-learning course in Communication of Technical Information at the ISTC, which may be beneficial for mature entrants.

What the work involves

Technical authors/medical writers interpret technical information and communicate it in written language which the intended audience can understand. Technical authors work in various sectors from medicine and defence to business and finance.

You will create content, commission images, organise and design the layout of any given document.

You should be an expert in your specialist sector, but your audience may be novices as well as specialists. For example, you may write mass market instructions for a mobile phone or a medical writer may create a report on clinical trial results for the medical community.

Type of person suited to this work

It is essential to have an excellent command of English and the ability to write concisely and convincingly, with your audience in mind. You should also be detail driven and have a good eye for design.

Having a passion for your specialist sector and an inquiring mind is a necessity. The ability to solve problems, multi-task and to work to deadlines is also important.

Good communication and teamworking skills are required as you will have to work closely with technical colleagues, such as doctors, as well as liaising with suppliers including printers and translators.

Working conditions

The majority of work will take place at a computer within normal office hours. However, supplementary hours may be required in order to meet tight deadlines. Also, you might have to travel to meet clients.

Having gained experience, many people decide to start up their own business or go freelance, especially as the pay is more attractive.

Future prospects

At present there are 5000–10,000 technical authors working in the UK in a variety of sectors.

There are jobs all over the nation, but more in England than elsewhere. In addition more positions are available in technological clusters eg defence in the south west of England.

It is helpful to establish a network of useful contacts, and mature entry is common as being an expert in your chosen sector is a necessity.

Advantages/disadvantages

This type of work can provide the satisfaction of seeing your completed work in print and, sometimes, in the public domain.

This profession is likely to be particularly sensitive to the effects of the recession, and many technical authors may lose their positions to developers.

Money guide

Earnings vary widely depending on the technical writer's specialist sector and the size of the employer. However software and telecommunications currently offer particularly attractive salaries.

New entrants can expect to earn between £18,000 to £20,000 per year.

With experience, this can rise to £40,000.

Top earners in senior roles with extensive experience can achieve in excess of £50,000.

Related opportunities

- Copy Editor/Sub-editor/Proofreader p402
- Journalist p405
- Publisher/Commissioning Editor p417

Further information

British Association of Communicators in Business
www.cib.uk.com

e-skills UK
www.e-skills.com

Institute of Scientific and Technical Communicators
www.istc.org.uk

MARKETING, ADVERTISING, MEDIA, PRINT AND PUBLISHING

CRCI: PB

Qualifications and courses

To be a TV/film camera operator you do not need any specific academic qualifications. GCSEs/S grades (A*–C/1–3) in English, maths, science or other relevant subjects might be useful. However, the majority of camera operators have higher level qualifications, such as HNDs, Foundation degrees or degrees. Relevant subjects include media production, photography and media studies.

Courses which may help you to develop the necessary skills are the City & Guilds Diploma in Media Techniques (Level 3), the BTEC First in Creative Media Production (Level 2), the BTEC National in Media Production – Television and Film (Level 3) and the BTEC Higher National in Creative Media Production – Moving Image (Levels 4 and 5).

You will start as a trainee, runner or camera operator's assistant and learn on the job. You could apply for a place on the Advanced Apprenticeship in Creative and Digital Media which offers training to become an assistant to the camera crew.

Large companies, such as the BBC, offer work experience placements that provide opportunities to work with camera equipment or in a set-up studio. Experience with community film projects or working for a camera equipment hire company could also be useful.

What the work involves

Camera operators use digital, electronic and film cameras to capture images for use in films, TV programmes or other broadcasts.

You will work closely with a director or director of photography and will be helped by a 'grip' (a camera assistant) and other crew members such as pullers, clappers, sound engineers and lighting technicians.

You will understand the technical and creative aspects of filming, including how to work with a script or list of shots, planning shots and shooting images.

You will have an in-depth knowledge of the equipment you work with and how best to use, maintain and repair it.

Type of person suited to this work

You must be interested in photography, camera technology and video, film and TV production.

You will be required to have a certain amount of physical fitness as your work may involve carrying heavy equipment for long periods of time.

As you will be working in a creative environment, you will need to have a good imagination and at times an abstract approach to problem-solving.

You should be patient, have good concentration and work well under pressure.

Working conditions

Your working hours will vary greatly. You may be required to work early mornings, late nights and on the weekend. Shooting may be long and run over planned schedules.

Your work may be affected by weather, for example some shoots may be cut short, or extended, if they depend on natural light.

You may have to work with cameras on cranes, scaffolding, in moving vehicles or in venues such as concert halls, theatres and sports grounds.

Future prospects

Skillset and regional screen agencies run schemes for those who have some experience and wish to work on a freelance basis within the industry.

Camera operators usually learn most of their skills on the job. However, constantly changing technology means that continuing professional development (CPD) is essential. Regular training in health and safety is also required.

Advantages/disadvantages

You may work on a variety of exciting projects, including big budget films or breaking news programmes.

Working on location may be dangerous at times, especially if it involves shooting footage for news broadcasts.

Money guide

A starting salary for a camera operator is around £13,800.

With experience, earnings can increase from £22,000 up to £40,000.

Most camera operators work on a freelance basis so rates of pay vary according to the type of production you are working on.

As an example, you could earn £276 for working a 1 0-hour day on a TV drama or £411 for a 10-hour day filming commercials.

The Broadcasting Entertainment Cinematograph and Theatre Union (BECTU) set recommended rates of pay.

Related opportunities

- Lighting Technician p440
- Photographer p412
- TV, Film and Radio Director p421

Further information

BBC Training and Development
www.bbctraining.com

Qualifications and courses

There are no specific entry requirements but most entrants have a drama or media-related degree or postgraduate qualification.

You can take GCSEs/S grades or A levels/H grades in media, film and TV or you can study at BTEC National, HND, degree or postgraduate level.

The Creative Skillset website provides details of institutions offering the highest quality education in film and television studies. Entry requirements are usually 2 A levels/3 H grades and 5 GCSEs/S grades (A*–C/1–3) for a degree. For an HND, you should have an A level/H grade in an art and design-related subject.

Practical work experience is essential and most budding directors create a showreel of self-funded projects to promote their work. Directors often begin as runners and work their way up to become floor managers or assistant directors. Some production companies, such as the BBC, offer work experience placements which could lead to full-time employment.

Specialist postgraduate courses in directing are offered at the National Film and Television School (NFTS). You will need a showreel of work for entry. Funding may be available from organisations like the UK Film Council.

What the work involves

Directors manage the process of creating films, radio and TV programmes. This involves commissioning each project and overseeing the work and schedules of the entire production team.

You will define the presentation and style of films and productions by making decisions about content, scripting, camera work, editing and acting.

You will also be required to handle any problems with presenters, actors or production staff, as well as editing the final 'cut' of the show you have directed.

Type of person suited to this work

Working in these competitive sectors can be very demanding and stressful. You should be confident and able to react quickly and calmly to any crises that may arise.

Good verbal communication, interpersonal and teamwork skills are important, especially as you could be away from home on location for weeks at a time.

In addition, you should have good organisational skills to ensure that projects are carried out on time and within budget.

Working conditions

A good level of physical stamina and fitness is required as this job involves lengthy days spent standing up and carrying, lifting and assembling heavy equipment.

In TV and film you will work on set and on location. You will have to cope with changeable outdoor conditions.

You will also be expected to be flexible and work at night and weekends, both during and post-production.

Future prospects

In the UK there are around 110,000 people working in TV and radio, many of whom are freelancers.

Recent financial unrest has resulted in a slow-down in the TV industry with fewer new productions scheduled. The British film industry is coping well but obtaining financial backing to develop larger productions may be challenging.

Entry to the industry is very competitive and excellent technical skills are expected from all applicants.

Advantages/disadvantages

This role provides the satisfaction and excitement of seeing your work in the public sphere.

The work is fast paced and varied.

Directors are often employed on a freelance or contract basis which can lead to job instability.

Contrary to popular belief, this is not glamorous work!

Money guide

Earnings in this sector vary greatly according to media, location, employer and project.

New entrants can expect to earn about £20,000 per year.

As you gain experience, your salary can rise to £40,000.

The most successful directors can earn anything up to £200,000.

Many directors are employed on a freelance or contract basis.

Rates of pay are established by the Broadcasting Entertainment Cinematograph and Theatre Union (BECTU).

Related opportunities

- Artistic/Theatre Director p432
- TV, Film and Radio Producer p424
- TV, Film and Radio Production Assistant/Runner p426

Further information

BBC Careers
www.bbc.co.uk/jobs

Creative Skillset
www.creativeskillset.org

MARKETING, ADVERTISING, MEDIA, PRINT AND PUBLISHING

CRCI: PA

Industry profile

LONDON SCHOOL OF
FILM, MEDIA & PERFORMANCE

CREATIVE AND ENTERTAINMENT INDUSTRIES

New Talent in Constant Demand

Sector growth

Even before the Government's publication of its 2008 document 'Creative Britain: New Talents for a New Economy', the popularity, influence and employment opportunities of the global creative media industries could not be denied. In the UK this sector employs over two million people and contributes 7.3% to Gross Domestic Product.

Leaps forward in digital video, on-demand TV, streaming video and the internet have seen the creative and entertainment industries expanding twice as fast as the rest of the UK economy; recent predictions indicate that it will soon contribute 10% to the national economy.

Globally the picture is equally strong: according to the World Bank, the global creative industries account for more than 7% of the world's economy and are growing by 10% per year.

Contrary to current employment trends, this sector continues to develop and recruit. Its rapid and continuing growth represents huge opportunities for well educated, creative and market-responsive graduates who are in tune with consumer demands.

Indeed, as technological developments continue to integrate entertainment and the media ever more seamlessly into our lives, the demand for high quality content has never been greater. New talent is in constant demand to create high quality, engaging content for viewers to experience across both traditional and newly developing platforms.

British contribution to film and television

Throughout the history of the screen as a cultural and commercial artistic pursuit, British film and television have been recognised worldwide for their record of continued excellence. In quality and cultural influence the UK has always been and continues to be widely respected as exhibiting the highest standards of creativity, discernment, commercial wisdom and, perhaps most tellingly of all, originality.

The topical relevance of these qualities and the growing successes at international awards ceremonies are further testament to these claims. Indeed, the UK is now the world's second-biggest exporter of television programmes. In film also it stands second, with 16% of US sales and 20% of European. UK cinema box office sales for 2008 were the highest since records began.

London – a creative hub

London is not only recognised as a creative and cultural hub but is at the heart of the world's fastest-developing general media and specific screen disciplines. Ideas, projects and products that have gone around the world have had their beginnings in this city, often in quite insignificant and unpromising circumstances.

In visual and performance art London has a worldwide reputation which is second to none, and students have access to opportunities which they could never have elsewhere with the same quality of provision and experience.

How to get ahead

A weakness of many graduates with degrees in media and the creative industries is a lack of understanding of the business of the media, and how their own creative work will be commissioned, developed and marketed. It's important to consider this when choosing a course; a programme that includes professional skills and industry placements will give you the head start you need.

By David Hanson,
Head of London School of Film, Media & Performance

TV, FILM AND RADIO EDITOR

Qualifications and courses

There are no specific academic requirements but this is a competitive industry so many entrants have a degree or postgraduate qualification. Relevant subjects include film, IT, media studies and visual art. You will need 2 A levels/3 H grades and 5 GCSEs/S grades (A*–C/1–3) for degree entry.

It is common to start out as a runner or editing assistant. Practical work experience is essential and you will need a showreel to promote your work.

When choosing a course, you should make sure it uses the most advanced equipment and offers work experience placements which will help you to gain industry contacts. Creative Skillset lists approved degrees, courses and opportunities on their website.

You could take an entry level training course offered by the BBC or an independent organisation such as Cyfle, Creative Scotland or Screen Yorkshire.

Other relevant qualifications include the City & Guilds Diploma in Advanced Media Techniques (Level 3), the BTEC National in Creative Media Production specialising in Radio or Television and Film (Level 3) and the BTEC Higher National in Creative Media Production specialising in Moving Image or Radio (Levels 4 and 5).

What the work involves

Editors play a key role in the post-production process by assembling the final product from captured footage and additional sound and graphics. They are also responsible for storing the footage.

You will fulfil a brief and liaise closely with the director. You will create the flow and pace of a production by using specialist IT editing equipment to put shots together in a smooth sequence.

You will ensure the continuity and order of these productions, which may include TV and radio programmes, films, music and corporate videos, and advertisements.

Type of person suited to this work

It is essential to be creative and to have a passion for your chosen medium.

You should have good attention to detail, plenty of patience and the ability to identify good storytelling techniques.

You will be expected to be well versed in the latest technological advances in the field, as well as possessing advanced IT skills and a willingness to try new techniques.

Working conditions

Hours vary depending on workload but are typically 9am–5pm, Monday to Friday. However, your personal life may be affected by long and unpredictable hours which are common in order to meet tight deadlines.

The majority of the work takes place at a computer in an editing suite and may be carried out alone or with a director.

Freelance editors with their own equipment may work from home.

Future prospects

At present there are about 11,000 people working in post-production roles in the UK. This profession is fast paced and there is fierce competition for entry level positions.

The majority of roles are based in London in post-production companies, independent production firms, broadcasters, and companies in the film and computer software sectors.

Having gained experience, many editors choose to go freelance. This involves working on several projects simultaneously and the workload may be irregular, with both busy and quiet periods.

Advantages/disadvantages

You will have the satisfaction of seeing the results of your work in the public domain.

This is a fast-moving and varied industry with exciting opportunities.

Editors are often employed on a freelance or contract basis which can lead to job instability.

Money guide

Earnings in this sector vary greatly according to employer and project.

New entrants can expect to earn £18,000–£25,000.

Salaries for experienced editors are £20,000–£35,000.

Those employed in the most senior positions can achieve up to £70,000.

The majority of editors are employed on a freelance or contract basis.

Rates of pay are set by the Broadcasting Entertainment Cinematograph and Theatre Union (BECTU).

Related opportunities

- Media Researcher p409
- TV and Film Camera Person/Operator p420
- TV, Film and Theatre Special Effects Technician p450

Further information

Broadcasting Entertainment Cinematograph and Theatre Union
www.bectu.org.uk

Creative Skillset
www.creativeskillset.org

Qualifications and courses

There are no specific academic requirements but producers need extensive experience in both the creative and business sides of the industry. Most will have worked their way up the ladder starting out as runners, broadcast assistants or journalists.

Gaining experience in a junior role provides a well-rounded view of the industry, invaluable knowledge and the opportunity to develop a network of contacts. You should create a showreel/portfolio of projects you have been involved in to show prospective employers.

Many entrants hold a Foundation degree, degree or HND. Useful subjects include film production, communications, broadcasting, media studies and drama. You will need at least 1 A level/2 H grades and 4 GCSEs/S grades (A*–C/1–3) for entry to a Foundation degree or HND and 2 A levels/3 H grades and 5 GCSEs/S grades (A*–C/1–3) for a degree. Details of approved qualifications are available from Creative Skillset and the British Film Institute (BFI).

If you are a radio producer working on news and current affairs shows you will need to have journalistic training. The Broadcast Journalism Training Council (BJTC) provides further information on accredited institutions and courses.

What the work involves

A producer originates ideas, employs pivotal team members, has creative input, gets involved in casting decisions and script editing, and generally oversees the complete production. Many producers also play a financial role, approaching initial backers, securing rights and managing the budget throughout production.

You will be the lead person in TV, film and radio production. Producers have a detailed knowledge of the industry, coupled with sound business skills. You may also be expected to oversee the final editing process, as well as marketing and distribution plans.

Type of person suited to this work

It is essential to have a strong creative flair and a passion for your chosen medium. A well-rounded knowledge of your sector, spanning technical, creative and commercial aspects is also required.

Excellent communication skills are important and you should have the ability to provide inspiration and motivation for team members. You should be a competent problem solver who works well under pressure.

You also need strong negotiation, numeracy, multi-tasking and organisational skills to ensure that projects are carried out on time, within budget and as requested.

Working conditions

Producers work in a variety of environments including offices, studios and external filming locations.

This role requires a great deal of flexibility. During production, hours can be long and erratic, and travel is often required to assess venues and attend meetings.

Future prospects

At present there are 18,000 TV and film producers in the UK and vacancies tend to be centred in major cities such as London, Manchester and Glasgow.

The main employers are well-known broadcasters such as the BBC, TV and film production firms, and production and facilities houses.

Entry to the industry is very competitive. It is essential to establish good contacts – many jobs are never advertised and are awarded based on the reputation of the producer.

Advantages/disadvantages

You will have the satisfaction of seeing the results of your work in the public domain.

This is a fast-moving and varied industry which can provide exciting opportunities.

Producers are often employed on a freelance or contract basis which can lead to job instability.

Money guide

Earnings in this sector vary greatly according to your experience and the media, employer and project.

New entrants can expect to earn £18,000–£25,000 per year.

Salaries for those with experience can range from £30,000 up to £55,000.

Senior producers can achieve £60,000–£80,000.

Almost half of all producers in the industry are freelancers and daily rates are typically between £237 and £437.

Rates of pay are set by the Broadcasting Entertainment Cinematograph and Theatre Union (BECTU).

Related opportunities

- Media Researcher p409
- TV Floor Manager p427
- TV, Film and Radio Production Assistant/Runner p426

Further information

BBC Careers
www.bbc.co.uk/jobs

Creative Skillset
www.creativeskillset.org

UK Film Council
www.ukfilmcouncil.org.uk

Organisation profile

LONDON SCHOOL OF FILM, MEDIA & PERFORMANCE

The London School of Film, Media & Performance is part of Regent's College London, the largest college of private higher education in the UK.

LSFMP is ideally situated to provide invaluable practical, hands-on work placements at TV, film and theatre production companies in the heart of London's media-land. With the support of academic staff – media industry practitioners and recognised specialists in creative production – you will develop your skills, make valuable industry connections and enhance your employability.

Our programmes will undoubtedly foster your creative development, but will also ensure that you gain the necessary business skills to succeed in these fast-paced industries. With your unique combination of creativity and business acumen, you will be well placed to produce and market your creative product, liaising and negotiating with a diverse range of individuals across the creative and media sectors.

London is vibrant and dynamic; it is one of the world's great entertainment and creative industry hubs. It's an inspiring place to live and to study. LSFMP is only minutes away from Soho, the West End and live music hotspot Camden, allowing you to get involved in all that London has to offer.

We offer the following three year degree courses in the creative and media Industries:

- BA (Hons) Creative Industries
- BA (Hons) Screenwriting & Producing
- BA (Hons) Film, TV & Digital Media Production

All degrees include an industry placement. Scholarships are available for academically strong students, up to a maximum of 50% of tuition fees.

BA (Hons) Creative Industries

The BA (Hons) Creative Industries degree will develop transferable producing skills which can be applied across the creative media sector. It will also educate you in the mechanics and practices of the creative industries – allowing you to work in both creative and decision-making management roles.

BA (Hons) Screenwriting & Producing

The BA (Hons) Screenwriting & Producing degree will help you to become part of the next generation of writers and producers for the screen. You will develop key skills which are essential for the career success of a writer or producer, learning not only how to write effectively but also gaining insight into the commercial and production side of the screen industry.

BA (Hons) Film, TV & Digital Media Production

The BA (Hons) Film, TV & Digital Media Production is a new degree and the only course of its kind in the UK. Created and taught by media professionals, you will learn about '360-degree broadcasting', alongside the traditional skills of drama, documentary, studio and outside broadcast training.

For more information on creative and media courses at the London School of Film, Media & Performance, scholarships and how to apply, please contact:

LSFMP@regents.ac.uk
www.regents.ac.uk/lsfmp
Tel: +44 (0)207 487 7505

TV, FILM AND RADIO PRODUCTION ASSISTANT/RUNNER

ENTRY LEVEL 3

MARKETING, ADVERTISING, MEDIA, PRINT AND PUBLISHING

CRCI: PA

Qualifications and courses

Runner
There are no formal entry requirements and this role is often a key starting point in the TV and film industry. It may be advantageous to have a degree in TV/film/radio production or a media-related subject. Enthusiasm is essential and it would be beneficial to have gained work experience, for example on student film/TV productions or community radio. The Apprenticeship in Creative and Digital Media may be available.

Production assistant
No formal qualifications are required but entry is highly competitive and many entrants are graduates. An understanding of the production process is very important and relevant experience is advantageous. Many production assistants begin as runners and work their way up. The BTEC National in Creative Media Production (radio or TV and film) may be useful.

As vacancies in this field are rarely advertised, it is important to be proactive and network to aid self-promotion.

In a bid to create a formal entry path and provide industry-specific education, the UK Film Council and Creative Skillset have collaborated to open specialist training academies and offer advice on professional development.

What the work involves

Runner
You will provide a wide range of practical help and support to all members of the production team. As well as some administrative work, you will pass messages on and carry equipment and scripts between offices and sets – often with no prior notice.

Production assistant
Production assistants provide support to the producer and director to help ensure that productions run smoothly and to schedule. You will manage a range of key administrative activities, such as organising scripts and filming updates, booking hotels and hiring equipment. You may also be responsible for managing budgets for productions.

Type of person suited to this work

It is essential to be enthusiastic, possess a willingness to learn and a passion for your chosen medium.

You should be interested in learning about all areas of the field and be well versed in recent trends in the industry.

You should also enjoy problem-solving and have the ability to work well under pressure and adhere to strict deadlines.

Working conditions

There are no standard hours in this profession as they vary depending on the project you are working on. During production, hours can be long and unpredictable, including evening and weekend work. Shift work is common and you may be required to be on-call at all times. Many employees are freelancers.

You will work in offices, studios and editing suites, as well as on location.

Future prospects

Most opportunities are in London and the south-east of England, where over half of the TV and film industries are based.

This profession is fast paced and there is fierce competition for entry level positions. Any relevant work experience will help to secure employment.

There are many freelancers in this sector. This involves working on several projects simultaneously and the workload may be irregular, with both busy and quiet periods.

Advantages/disadvantages

This is a fast-moving and varied industry with exciting opportunities.

Entry level positions are demanding and unglamorous.

Money guide

Earnings in this sector vary greatly according to experience, media area, employer and project.

Many people are employed on a freelance or contract basis.

Runner
New entrants can expect to earn £10,000–£12,000 per year.

With experience, salaries can rise to £20,000.

Production assistant
Starting salaries are typically £14,000–£16,000.

Those with experience can expect £20,000–£25,000.

Senior production assistants can achieve up to £30,000.

Related opportunities

- TV and Film Camera Person/Operator p420
- TV Floor Manager p427
- TV, Film and Radio Producer p424

Further information

Broadcasting Entertainment Cinematograph and Theatre Union
www.bectu.org.uk

Creative Skillset
www.creativeskillset.org

426

TV FLOOR MANAGER

Qualifications and courses

There are no set academic qualifications. It might be useful to have GCSEs/S grades (A*–C/1–3) and A levels/H grades in subjects such as maths, English, languages or theatre and drama studies.

Degrees or HNDs in relevant subjects such as media studies, drama, photography, film and television will give you an advantage as competition is fierce. You will need 2 A levels/3 H grades and 5 GCSEs/S grades (A*–C/1–3) for degree entry. Other qualifications that may help include the BTEC First in Creative Media Production (Level 2), the BTEC National in Creative Media Production – Television and Film (Level 3) and the City & Guilds Diploma in Media Techniques (Level 3).

Creative Skillset have formed a network of Media and Film Academies which offer film and television training, with the option to work towards vocational qualifications. The BBC and Channel 4 also run training schemes. See websites for further information.

Employers seek candidates with a proven commitment to the job and the industry. It is advisable to undertake voluntary pre-entry work experience with a production company or local TV station. You will probably start your career as a runner, production assistant, or in a technical role.

What the work involves

TV floor managers are responsible for the coordination of many aspects of the filming process.

You will ensure that all sets, props and technical equipment are working, in place and set up correctly.

In situations where the director is away from the set (in the gallery or a broadcast vehicle) you will wear headphones to relay instructions from the director to the crew, actors or audience members. You will make sure that everyone involved in the production process knows what to do so that everything runs according to schedule.

Type of person suited to this work

You must be passionate about the media industry and TV production in particular.

You should be very organised and able to work under pressure and to a tight schedule.

As you will be working with a variety of people, from directors to the most junior crew members, you will need to have good communication skills to create an efficient working environment.

You must have an understanding of the technical and creative aspects of production to ensure that you can deal with problems encountered during the filming or recording stage.

Working conditions

Hours are likely to be long and irregular, including early starts, late nights and weekend work. If you work on feature films, 6-day weeks are common.

You will probably work on a freelance basis, which may involve periods of unemployment between jobs.

You will spend most of your time at work on your feet. You will mainly work in studios but sometimes you may be required to work outdoors in all weather conditions.

You might have to travel within the UK or abroad, at short notice and for varying periods of time.

Future prospects

You may find opportunities to move up to a position as first director and eventually become a producer or director.

You could move across into other aspects of the industry such as production or broadcasting.

As you will be working on a freelance basis most of the time, you will depend on having a strong portfolio of your work, an excellent reputation and good contacts within the industry to guarantee work.

Advantages/disadvantages

Your work will involve a diverse range of projects including creative, practical and technical tasks.

Your working hours may be long, stressful and unsocial which could disrupt your personal life.

Money guide

Earnings vary with geographical location and tend to be higher in London.

Starting salaries are usually between £15,000 and £22,000.

Those with experience can expect to earn in excess of £25,000.

Many floor managers work on a freelance basis and receive an hourly, daily or weekly rate.

Daily rates could range from £150 to £400.

Related opportunities

- TV and Film Camera Person/Operator p420
- TV, Film and Radio Director p421
- TV, Film and Radio Production Assistant/Runner p426

Further information

Creative Skillset
www.creativeskillset.org

National Film and Television School
www.nftsfilm-tv.ac.uk

Performing Arts

This job family contains a wide range of exciting jobs for those of you who want to work in theatre, music, on screen or behind the scenes. People working in this sector do so because they are passionate and creative and love the arts. Jobs can be scarce, so you will need to demonstrate that you are willing to work very hard but the rewards of being part of a fantastic production can be huge. There are also jobs available in this sector for those of you who are more technically minded – sound and lighting engineers also play a vital role in this industry as do people who have trained in fashion and textiles.

The jobs featured within this section are listed below. For similar jobs to the ones in this section turn to *Design, Arts and Crafts* on page 167 *and Marketing, Advertising, Media, Print and Publishing* on page 395.

Qualifications and courses

Although there are no specific requirements to enter this profession, it is very competitive and a lot of actors now have some formal training. There are a number of different routes for entering the profession.

The National Council for Drama Training (NCDT) and the Conference of Drama Schools accredit full-time 3-year vocational drama school courses and degrees. Graduates of NCDT-accredited courses who are legally entitled to work in the UK are eligible for Equity membership. Part-time courses and more academic degrees in, for example, drama or theatre studies, are not accredited. Entry is by audition, and A levels, Highers or a BTEC National Diploma in Performing Arts are often required.

You can do a degree in acting (or a related subject such as drama or performing arts). Acting degrees are offered by drama schools and by universities. Further study, such as an MA or Postgraduate Diploma in acting, is also available, and can offer more opportunities to make contacts and develop your skills.

However, experience in the industry is more beneficial than qualifications. It can be helpful to join a local amateur dramatics group and undertake relevant work experience. The BBC, for instance, runs a number of work placements schemes which provide an insight into how the industry works.

Some actors gain experience working at holiday camps in entertainer roles. This is a good way of getting paid work and experience at the same time.

Networking is extremely important as a lot of actors secure roles through contacts they have made.

What the work involves

Actors perform in front of audiences and this can sometimes include dancing and singing as part of the role. There are opportunities for parts in dramatic plays, comedies and musicals on stage as well as on TV and in films.

You will research your characters, rehearse lines and attend auditions.

You will also attend costume fittings and make-up sessions.

Type of person suited to this work

Acting is a very competitive area so you should be truly dedicated to this career path. A good memory is important as you will have to learn lines.

There will be many times when you will be rejected at auditions mainly because you are just not the right face for the part, and so you will need to be able to cope with this and keep trying.

Adaptability, self-confidence and creativity are essential.

Working conditions

You will work mainly indoors, in theatres, halls and sometimes studios.

Your hours will be long and irregular, including evenings and weekends.

You could have to travel to different venues for your performances where you might spend time waiting for your part in the performance.

Future prospects

Prospects for success as an actor depend on talent, hard work and a bit of luck.

Some actors go on to work as writers or directors, while others train to teach drama in schools and colleges.

Advantages/disadvantages

Sometimes work can be irregular so you will not neccessarily have a stable income.

The nature of the work means that you will experience a lot of rejection which may be hard to take.

It is a tough, demanding career to enter and to stay in, but once you get regular work it can be very satisfying.

Money guide

Basic rates of pay depend on experience and reputation. It is important to join Equity, the union for the world of entertainment – as this can help you negotiate fair rates of pay, terms and conditions. Union-negotiated pay scales are on the Equity website.

The minimum pay for theatre workers (as set by Equity) is £373 per week although this can increase if the actor has to relocate. The salary in the West End tends to be higher and you are guaranteed a minimum salary of nearly £500 a week. The wages for TV and film work vary considerably and are dependent on how well known you are as an actor. As you become a recognised name, your income could be quite considerable, but it may take many years and continuous employment is uncommon.

Although there are a few (very famous) actors who earn huge salaries, the majority of actors have to take on second employment to support themselves and raise their income. Only 6% of actors receive more than £30,000.

A lot of actors have an agent to help them secure work but also to help them negotiate higher wages. However, although agents can obtain higher wages they will also take a cut of your earnings, generally between 10% and 25%.

Related opportunities

- Artistic/Theatre Director p432
- Dancer p436
- Entertainer p439

Further information

Creative and Cultural Skills
www.ccskills.org.uk

Equity
www.equity.org.uk

National Council for Drama Training
www.ncdt.co.uk

Royal Academy of Dramatic Art
www.rada.org

PERFORMING ARTS

CRCI: Q

Organisation profile

LONDON SCHOOL OF
FILM, MEDIA & PERFORMANCE

LONDON SCHOOL OF FILM, MEDIA & PERFORMANCE

The London School of Film, Media & Performance is part of Regent's College London, the largest college of private higher education in the UK. We are a new, vibrant school led by media industry practitioners, academics and recognised specialists in creative production.

Our stunning location in Regent's Park, central London is to be envied, and is fully integrated into our programmes.

Immerse yourself in London's vibrant theatre culture – you will have the opportunity to undertake theatre visits, walks and backstage tours, and will explore London on both a professional and personal basis.

Small classes will nurture your creative development, and will allow for close attention and guidance. Tutors on our Performing Arts courses are experienced professionals from the London theatre community.

We offer the following courses in Performing Arts:

- Acting Foundation Course (1 year)
- BA (Hons) Acting & Global Theatre (3 years)

Acting Foundation Course

This 1 year, intensive Acting Foundation course has been designed to build key acting skills in a relatively short period, as a solid preparation for further study – either at drama school, or university-level study (for example, our 3 year BA (Hons) Acting & Global Theatre).

The course will develop your confidence, will give you industry knowledge, and will prepare you for future auditions as you progress in your career.

The course is structured over two academic semesters. You will be in class for 20 hours per week from Monday to Friday, between 10:00 and 16:00; additional study time will be needed for out-of-class rehearsals, independent study and theatre visits/field trips.

BA (Hons) Acting & Global Theatre

This 3 year degree allows you to develop both your practical acting skills, and your knowledge of the theatre industry through an exciting study of theatre cultures of the world.

This course draws upon the wide range of theatrical expertise of practitioners from both Western and non-Western traditions. You will enjoy Masterclasses, theatre visits and fieldwork. Workshops, practical exercises, scene work, and tutorials develop your performance skills.

You will work under the guidance of a director to explore how a play is structured, issues of potential audience and intended communication, rehearsal strategies, and, above all, creative collaboration between actors, designers and director.

In your second year you will broaden your international understanding of theatre and performance during a Study Abroad Semester at one of the partner universities affiliated with Regent's College; options include Australia, Chile, the Czech Republic and the USA.

In addition to subject-specific training, students develop strong transferable skills in team-working, communication, project management, problem-solving, presentation and interpersonal relations.

For more information on Performing Arts courses at the London School of Film, Media & Performance, scholarships and how to apply, please contact:

LSFMP@regents.ac.uk
REGENTS.AC.UK/LSFMP
Tel: +44 (0)207 487 7505

Qualifications and courses

Most artistic directors hold a relevant degree in English, creative/performing arts, drama or theatre studies on entry to the industry. HNDs and Foundation degrees in creative/performing arts or drama/theatre studies are available and may also be useful qualifications to hold prior to entering the theatre.

If you are looking to move into the industry after completing your first degree, Birkbeck College, RADA and Mountview offer postgraduate courses in theatre direction.

Entry without any FE/HE qualifications is possible as the industry is reliant on reputation which you can gain through experience in acting, directing, writing and producing.

Of equal importance to professional qualifications are practical skills, acquired through work experience and involvement in school, college or university productions. Since few theatre companies offer in-house training, gaining this practical experience prior to applying for positions is vital.

The Arts Council England runs assistant director schemes for new entrants to the profession, and a few theatres and regional arts councils also offer training bursaries for candidates with exceptional potential. Competition for the bursaries is fierce.

What the work involves

Artistic and theatre directors have control over the artistic interpretation of plays, ballets, operas and other performances.

You will be responsible for coordinating all the creative elements of each production, including set and costume design, stylistic presentation, the interpretive work of artists, and any musical or choreographic sequences.

You will liaise with a number of other professionals on a daily basis, including producers, musical directors, technicians, theatre managers, financial backers, performing artists and writers.

You will select each production, oversee casting, and appear at performances and press events to help generate publicity around each show.

Type of person suited to this work

You will need fantastic artistic and creative vision, that you are able to express both verbally and in written documents. You will also need to have the courage and tenacity to make your vision a reality and present it to an audience.

You must be an excellent leader with the ability to inspire and motivate others. Being able to negotiate with writers, actors and other professionals is an asset.

You should have an in depth knowledge of the theatre, including productions past and present, theatrical trends, and the history of the industry.

Working conditions

Hours can be irregular and you will be employed on a freelance basis through which contracts can be short. Longer fixed-term contracts are available, but they usually only last 3–5 years.

You will be mainly working in theatres and other performance venues. Although the final production may take place on a large stage, you could spend a great deal of time directing scenes from small, offsite rehearsal rooms.

You will mainly work indoors, although certain venues will require you to work outdoors in occasionally inhospitable conditions.

Future prospects

Competition in the theatrical industry is fierce, so you will need talent, dedication, good qualifications and experience.

Since the majority of theatrical work takes place in London you can expect to work there at some period in your career. The city is a base for most freelance directors, although there are opportunities in regional theatres.

As an experienced and admired artistic director, you could set up your own theatre company through which you can stage your performances. Other directors move from theatre into film or television work.

Advantages/disadvantages

Your creative ability will be the driving force behind the production of visually and technically beautiful or unusual performances.

The industry is extremely competitive so you might have to spend long periods of time working for free or at a minimal wage in order to build enough experience to work as an artistic director.

Money guide

Salaries are dependent upon the length and type of contract, for example if you were working freelance, touring or repertory.

Theatre directors who are working regularly can earn around £19,000.

Reaching the level of artistic director should increase your salary to about £23,000.

Well-established artistic directors who have built up a good reputation and are in demand across the industry can earn in excess of £40,000.

Related opportunities

- Actor p430
- Stage Manager p447
- Stagehand p448

Further information

Arts Council England
www.artscouncil.org.uk

Directors Guild of Great Britain and Directors Guild Trust
www.dggb.org

CHOREOGRAPHER

Qualifications and courses

There are no formal academic entry requirements for this career. GCSEs/S grades and AS/A levels/H grades are available in dance, and some institutions offer a BTEC National Diploma in Performing Arts.

Most choreographers have experience as dance performers prior to becoming choreographers.

Choreography can be studied as an option on some full-time vocational dance courses accredited by the Council for Dance Education and Training, as part of a degree course in dance or as a postgraduate course. Institutions which offer these options include the University of Winchester and Northumbria University.

Work experience alongside an experienced practitioner offers a good introduction to choreography and will certainly be taken into account if applying for a dance or choreography-related course.

What the work involves

As a choreographer, you will create and develop new dance movements for productions such as ballets, opera and musicals.

Creating a dance means planning the way dancers move to perform beautiful and exciting routines which interpret the music.

Choreographers work closely with performance artists, musical directors, ballet dance teachers and trainers.

Type of person suited to this work

You will need to have a keen, lively interest in music and movement, and a very well-developed sense of rhythm and timing.

To develop new ballets, dances and shorter dance routines requires an excellent knowledge of past and present pieces, complete understanding of how the body works and of possible movements within dance and the creative imagination to interpret the significance of events and mood changes through physical expression.

Choreographers have the responsibility of developing and teaching complicated movements and routines. You will need a good memory, clear communication skills, patience and an ability to get on well with others.

Working conditions

You will mainly work indoors in dance studios, theatres, TV or film studios.

Your initial contacts are likely to be producers, directors and musical conductors. Some choreographers work directly with modern composers, interpreting their music.

As production plans progress, you will start working directly with the performers. To do this you will travel frequently.

Future prospects

Jobs and opportunities can be limited as this is a highly competitive area of work, where experience counts.

It is possible to find opportunities outside mainstream ballet; for example in modern dance companies and developing international venues.

Opera and musicals are becoming reinvigorated through audience demand and both performance areas require choreographers to interpret dance music and contextual pieces as dance routines. You may choose to set up your own dance company.

Advantages/disadvantages

Many hours are spent travelling to different venues – even overseas.

Seeing your finished routine beautifully performed will boost your morale.

Enthusiastic reviews will help your career progression.

It will be hard going, and you will need patience and enthusiasm to get the best from dancers.

Money guide

Equity, the performing arts union, recommends a minimum daily sum of up to £130.

You could earn round £12,500 per year if you have just finished at a dance college, completed a degree or other college courses.

Your salary could reach £20,000 if you have moved into choreography as an experienced dancer.

Experienced, well-known choreographers can earn £50,000, but good salaries will depend on your skills and experience.

Related opportunities

- Artistic/Theatre Director p432
- Dancer p436
- Make-up Artist p441

Further information

Council for Dance Education and Training
www.cdet.org.uk

Creative and Cultural Skills
www.ccskills.org.uk

Dance UK
www.danceuk.org

Qualifications and courses

Useful qualifications include GCSE/S grades and A levels/ H grades in music, BTEC National Diplomas in music practice or popular music, and relevant degree courses.

For entry onto a BTEC National Diploma you will need 4 GCSEs/S grades (A*–C/1–3) including music or equivalent qualification. Degree courses usually require 5 GCSEs/S grades, (A*–C/1–3), and at least 2 A levels/3 Highers, preferably with one in music or a related subject. Candidates who have reached grade 8 in an instrument as classified by the Associated Board of the Royal Schools of Music are usually preferred.

A wide variety of postgraduate courses are also available. If you are looking to break into the world of classical composition, you are strongly advised to attain a postgraduate qualification.

It is possible, but extremely rare, to achieve success without having undertaken some of the relevant qualifications for this industry.

What the work involves

Composers and songwriters create original music for a variety of uses.

You could use a variety of tools and instruments when composing or writing, from a pen and paper to advanced computer software programs.

You may also perform your compositions and songs, although this is most common for composers who are just starting out and those writing for individuals or small groups.

Type of person suited to this work

You will need to have outstanding musical or lyrical talents.

You will need dedication, determination and self-discipline as the music industry is extremely tough and disappointment may well be frequent.

You should have a flexible attitude to your work and be willing to take on a range of commissions and assignments in order to build up your experience and reputation.

Working conditions

Composers and songwriters (the former in particular) can expect to work long and unsocial hours writing, rehearsing and performing their work.

As most musical events take place over evenings and weekends, you are most likely to work during these hours.

Most composers and songwriters have other jobs in order to fund themselves whilst they establish a name in the music industry.

Future prospects

The music industry is highly competitive, so it can take a long time to gain any recognition for your work. This makes composing a challenging profession to choose and you will need to be extremely resilient.

Most composers or songwriters are self-employed. Although opportunities are available with theatrical companies, music publishers and universities.

You could gain great critical acclaim and commercial success, although the majority of work completed by composers and songwriters stems from smaller commissions within the media. This can include writing for TV, film and radio.

Advantages/disadvantages

You will be working in a job that you are passionate about, which will be immensely satisfying.

If you gain recognition the personal and financial rewards can be excellent.

The industry is highly competitive and chances of success are relatively slim.

Money guide

It is very hard to gauge salaries in this industry as so many composers and songwriters are freelance.

If you are commissioned by a large company or orchestra, as a composer you can expect to earn around £500–£1000 for each minute of music you create.

Songwriters could earn around £300 per minute. For title music, jingles and commercials both composers and songwriters can earn about £350 per minute.

You could also be entitled to royalties from your work.

Related opportunities

- Conductor p435
- Musician p442
- Singer p445

Further information

Arts Council England
www.artscouncil.org.uk

British Academy of Songwriters, Composers and Authors
www.basca.org.uk

British Music Information Centre
www.soundandmusic.org

CONDUCTOR

Qualifications and courses

Entry to this profession is usually with a degree in music. Most universities require at least 5 GCSEs/S grades and 3 A levels/4 H grades, as well as the ability to play an instrument to grade 8. Upon completion of a degree, the majority of candidates study for a postgraduate qualification in conducting.

Those who achieve good marks may be eligible for a scholarship offered by institutions such as the Royal Opera House, the Royal College of Music and the Guildhall School of Music and Drama.

Whilst studying, it is advisable to seek work experience as a deputy or assistant conductor. Working as a répétiteur in opera may also be beneficial, as you can watch and learn from highly skilled and experienced conductors.

Most conductors speak at least 2 European languages. The most useful are English, German, French and Italian.

Attending seminars run by the Association of British Orchestras (ABO) is a useful way to learn about current areas of interest in the sector. Qualified conductors are expected to engage in continuing professional development (CPD) throughout their careers to ensure that their knowledge of music theory and practice is up to date.

What the work involves

Music conductors work with musicians and singers to help shape their performance and make sure each musical piece is performed the way it should be.

You will be responsible for preparing musical scores for the performance and making decisions about how each musical piece should sound.

You need to understand the role of each performer and make sure every musician knows which part to play and does so correctly.

You may work with a wide variety of musicians, both amateur and professional, and these could include choirs and choruses, music students, youth groups and professional artists.

Type of person suited to this work

You must have a strong interest in music and extensive knowledge of the subject. You need to be able to play an instrument, preferably the piano, to a very high standard.

Good communication skills are vital, as is the ability to work flexibly and with lots of different creative people.

You should also have the ability to speak an additional European language.

You must be comfortable performing in front of an audience and remain calm under pressure.

Working conditions

Working hours for conductors are varied, and you must be prepared to work whenever and wherever the opportunity arises. Hours include evenings and weekends for both rehearsals and performances.

You will divide your time between working in rehearsal rooms, concert halls, churches, theatres, opera houses and other venues.

Conductors often spend a lot of time away from home, both within the UK and abroad. The places where you stay will vary in standards.

A driving licence is useful as travel is often required.

Future prospects

Succeeding in conducting is all about building up your reputation.

You may begin your career conducting small community or youth orchestras.

Once you have proved yourself and become established, opportunities to conduct large, high profile orchestras may become available.

Advantages/disadvantages

This job is ideal for those who are musically talented and like a balance between working with people and independently.

Producing a performance that audiences enjoy is incredibly satisfying.

In the early stages of your career it may be difficult to secure work and you could experience a sense of job instability.

Money guide

Conductors tend to be paid a fee for each concert.

At the start of your career, you may earn about £380 per concert.

With experience, you are likely to receive approximately £1000 per concert.

The most successful conductors can achieve up to £5000 per concert.

Related opportunities

- Composer/Songwriter p434
- Musician p442
- Private Music Teacher p200

Further information

Association of British Orchestras
www.abo.org.uk

Incorporated Society of Musicians
www.ism.org

International Artist Managers' Association
www.iamaworld.com

PERFORMING ARTS

CRCI: Q

435

DANCER

Qualifications and courses

Most professional dancers take classes in at least 1 form of dance from a very young age. Entrants to this career usually undertake a 3-year vocational Diploma, National Diploma or degree at a specialist school such as the Royal Academy of Dance (RAD). Entry is by audition, interview and a medical, and 5 GCSEs/S grades (A*–C/1–3) are usually needed. For ballet, there are also physical requirements, including height and body proportion requirements.

The Council for Dance Education and Training (CDET) accredits full-time courses at vocational dance schools.

You can do a degree in dance at a university or college of higher education. A levels/H grades are usually required and candidates attend an audition. For those without the relevant qualifications, the BTEC National in Performing Arts – Dance (Level 3) may be accepted instead. Postgraduate courses in professional dance or musical theatre are also available.

Some courses include a teacher training element. RAD and the Imperial Society of Teachers of Dancing (ISTD) provide specialist teacher training programmes. The British Ballet Organisation (BBO) and the British Theatre Dance Association (BTDA) also offer qualifications in dance and teacher training.

What the work involves

Dancers use the movement and language of their bodies as a way of expressing ideas and emotions to an audience, often accompanied by music.

You will focus on any number of styles including street, cultural, modern, contemporary, classical ballet, jazz or tap dance.

You might find work in theatres, cabaret clubs, cruise ships or video/TV studios. In addition to performing, you may use dance as a form of education or therapy.

Type of person suited to this work

Anyone entering this area of work must enjoy performing and be very talented to succeed. You must be dedicated to improving your technique through daily practice – sometimes for as long as 10 hours each day.

To be a successful dancer, you need a good sense of rhythm and timing. Being creative and imaginative with routines and choreography is desirable.

It is important that you can cope with setbacks and remain positive and focused.

The majority of your time will be spent dancing in a group so you must enjoy working with others.

Working conditions

Most of your rehearsals and performances will take place indoors in studios, schools, theatres or other venues.

The job is physically demanding and requires working long hours, including evenings and weekends. Frequent travel is often required.

Future prospects

Your future prospects as a dancer will largely depend on talent, hard work and luck; competition is always strong. Only a few individuals become top performance artists in solo roles.

If you are employed by a dance company you can progress from chorus to solo parts, but this will depend on your skills and dedication.

Although dancing is a career for younger people, dance teachers can continue long after they finish as professional performers, and many leave dancing to set up private dance schools.

Advantages/disadvantages

Dance can be a fantastically rewarding career.

A career as a top soloist can be finished by the age of 30.

You will need to stay fit and healthy as injuries can necessitate a complete career change.

Money guide

Salaries for dancers depend on the length, type and location of the job.

Dancers usually work on a freelance basis.

Most dancers are members of Equity, the trade union for the performing arts.

Equity have established minimum weekly rates of £400 for dancers.

Experienced dancers can expect to earn £450–£500 a week.

Those working on a West End show can achieve a weekly rate of £550.

Dance teachers are mainly self-employed and receive salaries dependent on the type and size of dance school they work in.

Related opportunities

- Actor p430
- Choreographer p433
- Stagehand p448

Further information

Council for Dance Education and Training
www.cdet.org.uk

Royal Academy of Dance
www.rad.org.uk

Royal Ballet School
www.royal-ballet-school.org.uk

Industry profile

THINKING ABOUT A CAREER IN THE PERFORMING ARTS?

Do you love singing, dancing and acting? Are you on top of the world when you're on stage and in the limelight?

Have you been in a drama club, or perhaps been in your very own High School Musical?

Then you might be thinking about a career in the performing arts.

Despite the seemingly overnight success of those on *Britain's Got Talent* and *The X-Factor*, a career in the performing arts requires long-term commitment, determination, self-awareness and a talent for making the most of opportunities. To lay the foundations, many people undertake specialised training.

Getting started

- Not sure if this is the right choice for you? Then consider a 1-year Foundation course. This gives you a taste of the kinds of performance styles in your chosen area. Choose from acting, drama, dance, popular music and creative industries.
- A 2-year BTEC will give you more in-depth experience of the performing arts.
- A 3-year BA degree course at a university or college of higher education combines performing with academic study, and will equip you for a variety of careers in the creative industries.
- Vocational training takes place in a drama school or a music conservatory. There are fewer than 1000 places for the 22 drama schools in the Conference of Drama Schools (CDS). These courses prepare students exclusively for careers in theatre, television, orchestras, opera, film, radio and allied fields.

What job might I do after graduation?

Actor: your performance work may be on stage, screen, TV, radio and in voice-over work. Work is largely freelance and can be very irregular, with long periods of 'resting' between jobs.

Arts Marketing: you develop the publicity material to promote your arts event; you can work freelance or for a company.

Choreographer: the choreographer creates and structures dance pieces for solo performers or group, either as a freelance artist or member of a company.

Dancer: trained in dance styles such as ballet, jazz, contemporary, street dance or modern, a dancer works as a member of a company, as a solo performer and for special events.

Drama Animateur: you work for a theatre company or arts organisation, developing workshops and other drama related events.

Lighting and Sound Design: graduates with a degree in technical theatre and theatre design, they create the complex lighting and sound effects for theatre, film, and music events.

Musician: whether classical, jazz, rock or pop, musicians work as solo artists as well as in groups and orchestras; you may also find work composing or performing for events, films, or theatre.

Production Assistant: you work alongside a director, designer, or film-maker. Your work is enormously varied as you undertake the different tasks to keep the production running smoothly.

Stage Manager: the stage manager works with the theatre director, recording the staging and serving as the liaison between the rehearsal room and the other members of the production team.

Theatre Designer: graduates with a degree in fine art or theatre design, they create the sets, costumes, and props for theatre productions.

Dr Valerie Kaneko-Lucas
Programme Director, Theatre & Performance Studies
London School of Film, Media & Performance

Qualifications and courses

There is no specific entry route to this job and no formal qualifications are required.

The BTEC National in Music Technology specialising in DJ Technology (Level 3) is offered at some colleges of further education. The normal entry requirements are 4 GCSEs/S grades (A*–C/1–3). The BTEC National in Creative Media Production specialising in radio (Level 3) and the BTEC National in Performing Arts (Level 3) are also available.

Other qualifications which may be useful include the City & Guilds Certificate and Diploma in Sound and Music Technology (Levels 1–3), the NCFE Award and Certificate in Music Technology (Levels 1 and 2) and the NCFE Award, Certificate and Diploma in Radio Production (Levels 1–3). Training in radio skills is also offered by CSV Media which runs Media Clubhouses around the UK.

Work experience is highly advisable. Those looking to work in radio can gain practical experience by volunteering at student, hospital or community radio stations. To work as a club DJ you need to develop your skills using decks, mixers and sampling equipment. Some top DJs offer masterclasses or allow work-shadowing. You need to produce a demo CD to showcase your DJ-ing abilities and style.

What the work involves

You will play and mix music for audiences at live venues or on the radio. You could use vinyl, CDs, MP3s, turntables, mixers, microphones and amplifiers.

Club DJs keep people dancing in bars and clubs. You will create your own sounds and mixes and use lighting and visual effects in time to the beats.

Mobile DJs play at weddings and other social occasions.

As a radio DJ, you will work in a studio playing records and chatting to listeners.

VJing (Video Jockeying) is an alternative form of artistic expression, using a good PC and software to mix/inter-splice sounds with images from video clips and loops, in real time.

Type of person suited to this work

You must have a passion for music, excellent coordination, good communication and listening skills, and a lively outgoing personality.

You need advanced technical skills as DJs use the latest in turntables, amplifiers and multimedia, and practise techniques such as mixing, scratching and cross fading to make their performance interesting.

Hard work and persistence are key to success. As most DJs are self-employed, basic business skills are an advantage.

Working conditions

As a DJ, you could work in clubs, on radio, in hotels, in holiday camps or at festivals and gigs. You will work long, irregular hours including weekends.

You will be required to travel to different venues so a driving licence is useful.

High noise levels are an occupational hazard for DJs; you need to take steps to protect your hearing.

Future prospects

Some DJs stay in the job only a short time before moving on. Many work part time alongside a daytime job.

You have to be a self-starter and seek out opportunities as jobs are rarely advertised. Experienced DJs can get seasonal work in holiday camps. Some move into careers in music production or retail.

Increasingly, DJs are finding opportunities working with VJs who create pop videos.

Advantages/disadvantages

It is rewarding to know that you have provided entertainment and made people happy.

There can be heavy equipment to move around, often in the early hours.

Set-up equipment costs over £1,000.

Money guide

Your earnings will depend on the event, venue and your reputation and experience.

At the start of their career, DJs often do unpaid work to gain experience.

Your earnings could range from £50 to £300 per session.

Very established and experienced DJs can earn £500–£1,000 for a session.

Top club DJs with celebrity status can achieve an annual salary in excess of £100,000.

Many DJs have another job to supplement their income.

Related opportunities

- Musician p442
- Private Music Teacher p200
- Sound Engineer p446

Further information

Access to Music
www.accesstomusic.co.uk

SAE Institute
www.sae.edu

ENTERTAINER

Qualifications and courses

Entertainers do not need to hold any academic qualifications as the most important requirement is to have a skill or talent that will entertain audiences. Training and courses may be beneficial in developing your skills and proving your ability and commitment to potential employers.

Entry routes are numerous and varied and could include entering talent competitions, working in holiday centres, performing in local clubs and bars or undertaking professional training courses.

Courses that will lead to useful qualifications include the BTEC First in Performing Arts (Level 2), the BTEC National in Performing Arts (Level 3) and the BTEC Higher National in Performing Arts (Levels 4 and 5). You could also take an HNC/HND in Acting and Performance or a Foundation degree/degree in performing arts. BTEC entry requirements are usually 4 GCSEs/S grades (A*–C/1–3). All degree courses require at least 2 A levels or equivalent, with one in a related subject.

If you are intending to work with children and/or vulnerable adults, you will also be required to obtain clearance from the Criminal Records Bureau (CRB) before entering this profession.

What the work involves

Entertainers perform amusing or amazing acts in front of audiences. They include comedians, circus performers, street artists, cabaret performers, dancers, musicians and magicians.

You could specialise in one area or skill, or you might have several skills that you can combine into one act.

You will have to source your own props and costumes, attend regular auditions, book venues, rehearse your routine and also carry out your own promotional work.

Type of person suited to this work

You will need natural confidence and a very outgoing nature in order to present a lively and entertaining act to your audience. You will need to be extremely talented in your chosen field.

You should be good with a wide range of people, as your audience could include members of all ages and backgrounds.

You should have good business awareness and a creative approach to marketing yourself in order to attract interest in your act and increase your bookings. You must be extremely punctual and reliable so as not to disappoint or annoy a venue or your audience.

Working conditions

Working hours vary. Most performances take place during evenings and weekends, with occasional daytime work. You can choose to work full time if you have a number of bookings, or part time in order to supplement your income with another job.

You could have regular weekly, fortnightly or monthly jobs but a great deal of work is on a one-off basis.

You may work across numerous venues throughout the UK (and abroad) so a driving licence would be useful.

Future prospects

The majority of entertainers are self-employed, although there are employment opportunities with circuses, theme parks, holiday parks and cruise ship companies.

Some may also work with one or more agents, who help with promotion and finding bookings in return for a small fee or commission from earnings.

Overseas work is possible, especially if you work for a cruise ship company or if you have an act that is appreciated across a variety of cultures.

Advantages/disadvantages

You will travel across the UK, and even the world, showcasing your talent to a variety of people to entertain and amaze them.

If you are self-employed, you have the opportunity to choose your hours and bookings to fit around other commitments.

The industry is competitive and few entertainers are able to pursue their career on a full-time basis.

Money guide

Salaries for entertainers vary depending on your act, reputation and level of success.

New entrants who have regular work can expect around £10,000 a year.

With experience, you could earn between £12,000 and £20,000.

Well established entertainers, such as those with regular bookings at reputable venues, or regular TV appearances, can earn over £30,000.

Related opportunities

- Dancer p436
- Musician p442
- Singer p445

Further information

Circus Space
www.thecircusspace.co.uk

Spotlight
www.spotlight.com

Qualifications and courses

All lighting technicians must be fully qualified electricians. The Advanced Level Electrotechnical Apprenticeship may be available or you could study for the NVQ in Electrotechnical Services (Level 3) or the NVQ in Electrotechnical Systems and Equipment (Level 3).

Colleges, universities and drama schools offer courses in subjects such as lighting technology, lighting design and technical theatre, theatre design and theatre production, which include the study of lighting. Many of these are accredited by the National Council for Drama Training (NCDT).

A BA (Hons) in Theatre Practice specialising in production lighting is available at the Central School of Speech and Drama and Rose Bruford College offers degree programmes in lighting design or creative lighting control.

The Association of British Theatre Technicians (ABTT) provides professional qualifications for technical theatre electricians. An alternative route which may be available is the Apprenticeship in Technical Theatre at both Intermediate and Advanced Levels.

The BBC offers a work experience scheme but places are limited. Volunteering with student or community film projects, theatres or concert venues would be useful.

What the work involves

Lighting technicians are responsible for creating stage lighting effects, working closely with the set designer and producer. It is important to visit venues before productions start and watch rehearsals to get the lighting effects right for live performances.

You will do lighting for advertising sets, in video production, theatre and broadcasting work.

You will be responsible for rigging and setting up the lighting, and plotting and programming the lighting requirements.

Type of person suited to this work

Anyone entering this career must have an interest in electrical work and electronics, combined with a strong interest in theatre and performance or live concerts.

Lighting technicians need to have a creative flair as the main aim of this job is to create the atmosphere required by the producer.

You will also need to be physically fit and work well in a team.

In some situations, for example changing or operating spotlights, the tasks could involve working at heights, and would not suit a person who suffers from vertigo.

Working conditions

You will work indoors and outdoors, usually working afternoons, evenings and weekends.

You will work with lots of heavy equipment and you may sometimes need to wear protective steel toe-capped boots.

You may have to work in cramped spaces with computerised control systems.

You will often be away from home for weeks and months if you are travelling with a roadshow.

Future prospects

Theatre lighting is usually provided by specialist companies who employ technicians on a short-term contract basis.

However, once you are experienced and known in the trade, your opportunity to join the backstage crew of a particular theatre group increases.

Progression as a lighting technician relies on skills and dedication. When in demand, you can become a senior or chief lighting technician and, in some cases, technical manager.

Advantages/disadvantages

You will have irregular working hours, including evening and weekend work, and you will frequently be away from home.

Seeing your skills and experience light up a set or production will be a great confidence booster.

Money guide

Trainee technicians start on around £9,500 per year.

Experienced lighting technicians working in theatre can earn between £15,000 and £25,000.

Earnings are higher in film/TV and you could receive up to £30,000.

Many lighting technicians work on a freelance basis, earning a daily or weekly rate.

The Broadcasting Entertainment Cinematograph and Theatre Union (BECTU) recommends a daily rate of £250.

Related opportunities

- Electrician p92
- Stage Manager p447
- TV, Film and Theatre Special Effects Technician p450

Further information

Association of British Theatre Technicians
www.abtt.org.uk

National Electrotechnical Training
www.net-works.org.uk

MAKE-UP ARTIST

Qualifications and courses

Make-up artists in theatre/TV/film are usually trained in beauty therapy or both hairdressing and make-up. Relevant qualifications are the NVQ Certificate in Beauty Therapy (Level 1), the NVQ Diploma in Hairdressing and Beauty Therapy (Level 1) or the NVQ Diploma in Beauty Therapy specialising in make-up (Levels 2 and 3). The BTEC First in Beauty Therapy (Level 2) and the BTEC National in Beauty Therapy (Level 3) are also available.

There are a range of specialist further education courses in theatrical and/or media make-up, including both short courses and diplomas. Relevant qualifications are available from the Vocational Training Charitable Trust (VTCT), the International Therapy Examination Council (ITEC) and the National Association of Screen Make-Up Artists and Hairdressers (NASMAH). City & Guilds offer a Diploma in Hair and Media Make-Up (Levels 2 and 3).

A number of universities and colleges run HND courses in theatrical and media make-up or make-up artistry. A Foundation degree in Hair and Make-Up for Film and TV and a BA (Hons) in Make-Up and Prosthetics for Performance are available at the London College of Fashion. Degrees and diplomas in subjects such as fine art, visual art, fashion design or graphic design can be useful.

What the work involves

Your work will involve applying make-up and arranging hair to produce the right look for male and female artists and performers in films, TV and stage productions. You will need to listen to the director in order to create the desired look for the individual characters or troupe.

You could be employed in TV, by a video production company, as a specialist in wedding and occasion make-up, by a theatre or film company, or be self-employed, perhaps as part of a backstage team.

Type of person suited to this work

Anyone who considers doing make-up work needs to be creative, with the imagination to visualise the finished effect. You will have to pay great attention to detail. The job requires excellent communication skills, as you will need tact to advise colleagues or clients on their image.

At times, there will be many people needing to be made up for a particular scene and you could be working under intense pressure. Self-confidence and an outgoing personality are positive factors in building relationships and succeeding at work.

Working conditions

Most of your work will be undertaken indoors in theatres, studios, beauty salons and, at first, possibly in retail outlets.

Long hours and weekend work are common. Doing make-up involves spending extended periods of time standing over customers and you will need to be physically fit.

If you are self-employed, you will probably need to provide your own cosmetics. You will carry all your equipment and materials with you.

A driving licence would be useful for travelling to different jobs.

Future prospects

Although this is not a huge area for employment, there will always be a demand for make-up artists. The larger towns and cities present the best opportunities. Although limited, some work could be available in hotels or on cruise ships.

Once you have gained experience, you can secure regular work in TV or video, on a cruise ship, in a hotel, a retail store or with a theatre company. You could set up your own beauty salon.

Competition is strong and progression depends upon the reputation, contacts and talent of the individual.

Advantages/disadvantages

Working hours may be irregular and unsocial, especially if you do make-up both before and during performances.

It is highly satisfying to see your work on stage or set, or to make people look nice for a special occasion.

Money guide

Most make-up artists work on a freelance basis and their earnings depend on their reputation, experience and the project they are working on.

Recommended rates of pay are set by the Broadcasting Entertainment Cinematograph and Theatre Union (BECTU).

A make-up artist's assistant should earn £178–£198 for a 10-hour day.

The daily rate for a make up artist is between £206 and £257.

A chief make-up artist can achieve £268–£289 for a 10-hour day.

Related opportunities

- Beauty Consultant p454
- Beauty Therapist p455
- Hairdresser/Barber p465

Further information

British Association of Beauty Therapy and Cosmetology
www.babtac.com

Greasepaint
www.greasepaint.co.uk

Make Up Artist magazine
www.makeupmag.com

Qualifications and courses

Classical musicians undertake extensive musical training and academic qualifications. Most take graded examinations in their chosen instrument/s, as well as further related courses. These include GCSE/S grade or A level/H grade music and the BTEC First, National or Higher National in Music or Music Technology (Levels 2–5). BTEC entry requirements are usually 4 GCSEs (A*–C) or equivalent.

Some musicians also pursue music degrees at university, specialist courses at music colleges (conservatoires) and relevant postgraduate qualifications. For entry to a music degree you usually need 2–3 A levels/H grades including music and grade 8 in your chosen instrument or voice. Postgraduate programmes require entrants to hold a relevant first degree.

Popular musicians do not need to hold any qualifications for entry to the industry. However, undertaking training may prove your ability and dedication to prospective employers. Any of the qualifications mentioned above would be useful for popular musicians. There is also the option to study for a degree in popular music.

Armed Forces musicians do not need to hold any formal qualifications and aptitude in your chosen instrument/s will be assessed during an audition.

What the work involves

Whether you work as a classical, popular or Armed Forces musician, your main responsibility will be to perform to and entertain an audience.

You will spend the majority of your time practising in order to develop and strengthen your ability on the instrument/s you play.

You could compose your own material or play existing music from a variety of genres.

Type of person suited to this work

You must be extremely musical, particularly if you are looking to work as a classical musician. You will need to be very confident in yourself and your abilities, as well as having considerable stage presence to hold the attention of an audience.

Throughout the music industry, there is intense competition for jobs. You will need determination, tenacity and resilience in order to cope with knock-backs and persevere.

Working conditions

You must be prepared to work long, unsocial hours in a variety of environments including clubs and bars. You may have to work away from home for long periods of time.

Classical musicians tend to work in locations such as concert halls, theatres, parks and recording studios.

Musicians employed by the Armed Forces usually perform for military parades, regimental dinners, state occasions, sporting events and other special occasions.

Future prospects

Classical musicians may rise to enjoy success as solo artists or may work in group ensembles, such as orchestras, in which there are chances for promotion. Diversifying into teaching is also common.

Prospects for popular musicians are varied and depend a great deal on how successful you become. Many decide to move into a business role, for example as a manager or representative for a recording company.

Armed Forces musicians usually move across various bands throughout their career, whilst also progressing up through the standard ranks as they gain relevant management, leadership and military skills.

Advantages/disadvantages

As a musician, you could work in a variety of disciplines and with a range of different people, so the job will be stimulating and interesting.

Competition is intense in the music industry so you will have to work incredibly hard.

Money guide

Classical musicians employed by an orchestra usually receive a salary of £22,000–£28,000.

Principal players in an orchestra can earn from £25,000 up to £45,000.

Session musicians could receive £120–£350 for a 3-hour job.

Solo musicians can achieve £500 to £2,000 a week, depending on their popularity.

Armed forces musicians have a starting salary of about £14,000, rising to £18,000 upon completion of training.

Army musicians on a fast-track scheme can earn over £23,000 after 2 years.

Pay in the army will increase as you gain experience and promotions.

Related opportunities

- Composer/Songwriter p434
- Entertainer p439
- Singer p445

Further information

Arts Council England
www.artscouncil.org.uk

Associated Board of the Royal Schools of Music
www.abrsm.org

Royal Military School of Music
www.army.mod.uk/music

PROPS MAKER/ ASSISTANT

Qualifications and courses

There is no standard route into this career and it is possible to enter without academic qualifications. However, to be employed as an assistant you will be expected to have at least GCSEs/S grades (A*–C/1–3) in English, maths and art. You will also need a good history of relevant work experience, possibly from student productions or amateur theatre, and a lot of talent and dedication.

Most prop makers have relevant qualifications, such as the BTEC National in Production Arts (Level 3), specialising in Stage Management or Set Design and Construction, or the BTEC Higher National in Performing Arts specialising in Production (Levels 4 and 5). The Royal Academy of Dramatic Art (RADA) offers a specialist course in Property Making and the Central School of Speech & Drama provides a BA (Hons) in Theatre Practice (Prop Making).

Degrees, Foundation degrees and postgraduate courses are available in set design, prop making and stage management. Other useful subjects include art and design, fine art, 3D design and model making. Entry requirements for a degree are usually at least 2 A levels/4 H grades including art.

Most course providers also ask candidates to present a portfolio of work for entrance assessment.

What the work involves

Props makers and their assistants are responsible for designing, changing, making and finishing the props used in theatre, video, film, TV or circus work.

You will be working with different materials, such as wood, fibreglass, fabric and metal, and you will use a range of practical skills including carpentry, modelling and painting.

You will spend a considerable amount of time researching the historical and cultural background of the props to ensure that they fit the era they represent.

Type of person suited to this work

You will need to have a mixture of practical and artistic skills in order to have the vision to design props and the ability to make them yourself.

You will be taking direction from theatre/TV producers, so you must be able to listen carefully to their briefs and ideas, and translate them into actual props. You will need good problem-solving skills so that you can balance meeting people's expectations and working to a budget.

The ability to use a variety of IT packages, including CAD, is useful.

Working conditions

Working hours vary but you can expect to work long hours over evenings and weekends in order to meet deadlines now and again. You will be working in small studios and prop rooms and these locations can often be cramped.

You may also spend time visiting suppliers for equipment and travelling to libraries and museums to carry out research.

You will have to wear relevant safety equipment when dealing with materials such as wood, metal, fibreglass and any chemical products.

Future prospects

The majority of props makers are freelance so you will be employed on short-term projects most of the time. These could be for film studios, theatres, TV companies or museums.

Career progression is dependent upon building a good reputation and an excellent portfolio of work.

With experience, you could move into set design or take a more general role in stage management.

Advantages/disadvantages

Working in a creative industry such as theatre or film provides challenging, exciting work opportunities.

You will be using a mixture of artistic, practical and intellectual skills which will be tiring but rewarding.

Working freelance can create a sense of job instability and it can be difficult when you have a period of time without work.

Money guide

As an assistant to a props maker, you can expect to earn about £12,000.

Props makers who are just starting in the industry usually receive an annual salary of around £15,000.

If you gain a good reputation and start to work on large productions with big budgets, you could earn £40,000+

Many props makers work on a freelance basis and negotiate fees dependent on the project and their reputation.

Related opportunities

- Make-up Artist p441
- Stage Manager p447
- Wardrobe Assistant p451

Further information

Creative and Cultural Skills
www.ccskills.org.uk

Royal Academy of Dramatic Art
www.rada.org

Stage Management Association
www.stagemanagementassociation.co.uk

PERFORMING ARTS

CRCI: Q

ROADIE

Qualifications and courses

There are no formal entry qualifications. Most people enter this career through experience of working with a friend or other contacts. If you are under 18 you may not be able to work in some licensed premises.

If you are planning to do the more technical work, formal qualifications would set you apart in a very competetive industry. The Creative & Cultural department of the National Skills Academy provides courses in music technology, video work and sound production. More technical courses such as 'Music Rigging' and specialised 'Festival Stage Side Days' are available in festival season.

The majority of roadies will learn the trade from working with other more experienced people.

Useful skills and qualifications include a First Aid certificate and the ability to speak one or more foreign languages. The Production Services Association (PSA) operates a Safety Passport scheme that deals with issues including manual handling, transport and general safety precautions.

A full driving licence is helpful and a large goods vehicle (LGV) licence or passenger carrying vehicle (PCV) licence could be useful if you need to drive the tour bus or larger vehicles to transport heavy equipment.

What the work involves

Roadies are responsible for setting up a range of equipment for music concerts and events including amplification systems, electrical cabling, stage and special effects lighting.

You will have to move and set up heavy equipment, load and unload vans and trailers and do lots of driving around. You will need to maintain and fine-tune your equipment on a regular basis.

Your work could include handling pyrotechnics, laser displays, computer/live film feeds and video links.

Type of person suited to this work

You will need to have a strong interest in music, technology and electronics. It is essential to have good communication skills and an interest in people, be creative and practical.

Physical fitness and stamina will be essential, with a sense of humour a bonus. Sets will have to be assembled and disassembled safely in tight deadlines so you should be able to work whilst under pressure.

As most roadies are self-employed, a well-organised person with some business skills will do well by maintaining their accounts and keeping records of bookings.

Working conditions

You will have exceptionally long working hours, mainly evenings, nights and weekends. If you are on a tour you might be working 7 days a week. Three month contracts are typical in this line of work.

The work is very physical and there is lots of heavy lifting involved. Sometimes you could be working at heights on electrical cabling.

Future prospects

There is strong competition for jobs. The work is unpredictable and you might need another job to boost your income. Work can be seasonal, with more roadies needed for summer events.

Marketing your services will be essential for getting gigs; many roadies now use websites to advertise.

A wide range of technical skills such as stage lighting and management or sound engineering will improve your chances of employment and could enable you to secure lighting or sound jobs in film, television or theatre.

Advantages/disadvantages

Roadies work long unsociable hours and there is lots of travelling.

Very loud sounds will damage your hearing if your ears are unprotected.

You will get to attend many gigs and concerts for free.

Money guide

Most roadies work freelance and your pay will depend on the gig, your experience and general availability of roadies.

As a starter, with regular work, you could earn around £12,000 per year.

A roadie with electrical, audio or video skills can earn in excess of £21,000.

With excellent technical skills, pay can rise to £30,000.

On contract to a big touring band, you could earn in excess of £35,000.

Related opportunities

- Large Goods Vehicle Driver p602
- Lighting Technician p440
- Sound Engineer p446

Further information

National Access and Scaffolding Confederation
www.nasc.org.uk

National Skills Academy for Creative & Cultural
www.nsa-ccskills.co.uk

Production Services Association
www.psa.org.uk

Stage Management Association
www.stagemanagementassociation.co.uk

SINGER

Qualifications and courses

Academic qualifications are not strictly required in order to become a singer, but they quite often demonstrate talent, commitment, and the necessary expertise to succeed in the music industry to potential employers or clients.

Relevant qualifications include GCSEs and A levels/S and H grades in music, BTEC courses in music, performing arts, music performance, music practice and music technology, HNC/HND courses in music-related subjects, and a degree in popular music or similar. Entry requirements for these courses vary; BTECs usually require 4 GCSEs/S grades (A*–C/1–3) or equivalent, whilst HNC/HND programmes require an additional A level/H grade, and degree programmes require at least 2 A levels/H grades, (often including music).

Building up singing experience, through performing with choirs, in amateur productions or in talent contests, is also important in order to help you develop as a rounded performer who can hold the attention of an audience.

Classical singing is generally formally taught at a number of different institutions. As part of a much longer preparation process, singers take postgraduate courses in either opera or oratorio, dependent on their repertoire, alongside short courses.

What the work involves

Singers perform in front of an audience in clubs, at gigs, on television or radio, in a recording studio, or in an opera house. They work as solo artists, or as part of a backing group, choir or chorus.

You will spend many hours practising in order to develop and strengthen your breathing and vocal ability. You will need to have good diction, and be able to pronounce songs written in a variety of languages including Latin and French.

You will work with a variety of musicians and music industry professionals, including orchestras, bands, session musicians, sound engineers, and maybe a manager.

Type of person suited to this work

You will need to have an exceptional talent for singing in order to get noticed in the music industry.

Owing to the intense competition in this area, you will also need determination, self-discipline and resilience in order to cope with disappointments and to persevere in order to achieve your goals.

You will need to be very confident in yourself and your abilities. It is difficult to hold an audience without stage presence and charisma.

Working conditions

As a singer you can expect to work long and unsociable hours, over evenings and weekends, as this is when the majority of your audience will be free.

You may have to travel long distances for gigs and rehearsals.

You could work in a variety of locations, from small clubs and theatres, to large concert halls and even outdoor venues.

Future prospects

Singing is a highly competitive industry, and opportunities for full time work are extremely limited. Most professionals supplement their income with another job, so you could look into teaching or writing songs and jingles for other artists.

Most successful singers move to London to pursue their careers, as this is where the majority of opportunities lie.

You may well work with an agent or manager at some point in your career. Their purpose is to offer you career advice and to find you singing opportunities.

Advantages/disadvantages

You will be fulfilling a passion whilst also doing your job, which is rare and satisfying.

You will be bringing pleasure to the people in your audience, no matter how big or small.

You will have to work long and unsociable hours.

You will have to be resilient in order to persevere despite negative feedback on occasion.

Money guide

As a solo singer, you could earn between £150 and £450 per concert. Chorus singers usually earn between £70 and £100. Backing singers on albums are paid £110 or more for a 3-hour recording session.

If you go on to perform in the theatre, there are set rates of pay that employers must adhere to. For example, chorus members command £650 per week for performances onstage in London's West End.

Related opportunities

- Composer/Songwriter p434
- Entertainer p439
- Musician p442

Further information

BRIT School for Performing Arts and Technology
www.brit.croydon.sch.uk

Creative and Cultural Skills
www.ccskills.org.uk

PERFORMING ARTS

CRCI: Q

Qualifications and courses

It is possible to become a sound engineer without gaining any relevant qualifications, as many companies take on trainees as runners or assistants, and you can build your knowledge whilst you work.

Larger studios and companies do prefer candidates to hold relevant qualifications. These could include: BTEC National Certificates in live sound, stage sound, or light and sound; HNDs in sound technology or sound engineering and electronics; Foundation degrees and degrees in music production or audio technology.

Postgraduate qualifications are also offered by a limited number of providers. The University of Westminster runs a Master of Arts course in Audio Production, and the National Film and Television School offers a Diploma in Sound Recording for Film and Television or a Master of Arts degree in Sound Design for Film and Television.

For theatre sound engineers, many drama schools offer courses in theatre lighting and sound which may be useful. All good programmes are accredited by the National Council for Drama Training.

What the work involves

Sound engineers set up, operate and maintain a range of technical equipment that is designed to capture, magnify and manipulate words and music.

Theatrical sound engineers create 'sound plots', choose equipment and insert sound effects according to the instructions of the director of the production.

Sound engineers working in the recording industry capture speech, music and other sound effects and modify them using sophisticated electronic equipment for a number of purposes including creating pop songs, adverts,or computer game soundtracks to name but 3 possible outlets for your work.

Type of person suited to this work

You will need a good musical ear and excellent sense of timing in order to put together pleasing and appropriate soundtracks/background audio to a range of productions.

You should also have knowledge of both electronics and ICT systems.

Recording industry sound engineers must also have a good knowledge of both recording and post-production processes.

Working conditions

Sound engineers working in both theatre and the recording industry should expect to work varied hours that will encompass day, evening and weekend commitments.

Theatre sound engineers will spend the majority of their working day confined to a small control box which may be cramped and often is plunged into semi-darkness.

Recording sound engineers work in studios, some of which are large and air-conditioned, whilst others can be small and cramped. You will usually be working in artificial light and the atmosphere can be stressful when working against deadlines.

Future prospects

Competition for jobs is intense, and you may spend a long while proving your credentials as a runner or gofer.

You could work for a variety of employers, including theatres, opera and ballet houses, commercial recording studios or media post-production departments.

Theatre sound engineers may go on to become sound designers with greater creative input in productions, whereas many recording sound engineers move into roles as producers.

Advantages/disadvantages

You will work with a variety of people on diverse projects, so each day will bring new challenges and rewards.

Theatre and media are exciting industries to work in as there is constant cultural and technical development.

You will have to work long hours that will often fall over evenings and weekends.

Money guide

Starting salaries for sound engineers, whether they work in theatre or the recording industry, range from £15,000 to £18,000 per year.

With experience, this could rise to £30,000.

Sound engineers working on large productions, with big companies or well-known artists, can earn in excess of £40,000.

Related opportunities

- Lighting Technician p440
- Musician p442
- TV, Film and Theatre Special Effects Technician p450

Further information

National Film and Television School
www.nftsfilm-tv.ac.uk

Professional Lighting and Sound Association
www.plasa.org

Qualifications and courses

Practical experience is key to obtaining work as a stage manager and is valued over academic qualifications. You could gain this by volunteering at local theatres or participating in student productions.

Drama schools such as the Royal Academy of Dramatic Art (RADA) and the London Academy of Music and Dramatic Art (LAMDA) offer Foundation degrees in technical theatre and stage management. The National Council for Drama Training (NCDT) accredits vocational stage management courses.

You can complete a BTEC National in Production Arts specialising in Stage Management (Level 3) which lasts 2–3 years when studied full time. The selection process involves an interview and providing a portfolio of your practical work.

Some universities offer degrees and HNDs in technical theatre or theatre production which include study of stage management. Entry requirements for a degree are usually 5 GCSEs/S grades (A*–C/1–3) and 2–3 A levels/H grades, as well as a demonstrable interest in theatre production.

The Stage Management Association (SMA) runs a variety of short courses for people already working as stage managers or assistant stage managers.

What the work involves

Stage managers work with designers, directors and producers, assessing and discussing what props, lighting and other stage support are needed for the production.

You are the link between the artistic and technical aspects of all productions, as you are in charge of everything that happens on stage including calling actors, giving technical cues and moving scenery.

You could work on numerous types of production, such as theatrical performances, opera, ballet and even music festivals.

Type of person suited to this work

You will need to have artistic flair, be practical, communicate instructions clearly and manage others confidently.

Good time management skills are crucial.

The work is demanding as the successful running of the backstage support for the performance rests with you. A cool head and a sense of humour – while still being assertive – will make the work easier for you. An excellent stage manager can help create a good team atmosphere backstage between artists, props manager and stagehands.

Working conditions

You will spend long hours in theatres and studios, sometimes working into the night to meet deadlines. In addition, you will have to travel to different venues so a driving licence would be useful.

Finding work is not easy and can take up a huge amount of your time, so you should be prepared for rejection and periods without work.

Future prospects

The employment demand for stage managers has remained stable for some years. This is a competitive area of work and the opportunities for employment are not extensive. Work can be found in theatre companies, opera, theatre in education and touring companies.

You could be promoted to a nationally recognised position or become a company stage manager where you would do publicity and finance work as well.

You could also choose to move into TV or film, becoming a director or producer.

Advantages/disadvantages

You will work long, unpredictable hours to meet production deadlines.

Permanent contracts are difficult to find so you may experience a sense of job insecurity.

The work is both creative and practical.

There is a great sense of achievement at the end of a successful run when everything has operated smoothly.

Money guide

Starting out as a trainee or assistant stage manager, you will earn about £16,000–£18,000 per year.

With experience, your annual salary can rise to £20,000–£26,000.

The most successful and experienced stage managers can achieve up to £40,000.

Many stage managers work on a freelance basis.

Minimum rates of pay are negotiated by Equity, the performers' and entertainment workers' trade union.

Related opportunities

- Entertainment Manager p382
- Props Maker/Assistant p443
- Wardrobe Assistant p451

Further information

EQ
www.thinkeq.org.uk

Stage Management Association
www.stagemanagementassociation.co.uk

PERFORMING ARTS

CRCI: Q

Qualifications and courses

There are no formal qualifications necessary to work as a stagehand.

The majority of the time, you will begin casual work backstage and you are more likely to secure this work if you have previous experience and some practical skills. It would therefore be useful to have worked backstage at school or college, or as part of an amateur dramatics society.

Skills such as carpentry, electrics or sound and lighting are all advantageous for securing work.

If you eventually want to progress into stage management, there are some relevant courses that may be useful, including BTECs from Levels 2–4 in Production Arts and Performing Arts.

What the work involves

Stagehands (also known as stage technicians or crew) work backstage as part of the production team.

You will provide assistance with props, scenery and special effects in either theatres, concert halls or at TV/film studios.

Your tasks will involve handling the equipment, helping to assemble and move scenery, opening and closing the theatre curtain between acts (when working on live plays or shows) and clearing the stage or studio at the end of each performance.

The work is normally completed as part of a team of stagehands under the supervision of the stage manager.

Type of person suited to this work

You will need to be physically fit to work as a stagehand as the work will involve a lot of heavy lifting. It will also be important to have good stamina as working hours will be long and you will probably work 6 days a week on a show.

As the work is normally team based, you will need to work well as part of a team and have a flexible attitude as you may be required to do a wide range of tasks, some at short notice. You must also be able to cope under pressure as the shows will be live and things can go wrong.

You must have a head for heights as well as a good understanding of health and safety.

A passion for theatre and live performance, as well as for stage and set design, is also essential.

Working conditions

You will be working irregular hours, including evenings, weekends and bank holidays.

You must be prepared to work at short notice and work overtime as productions can overrun.

You may be based in one venue, or have to travel to different venues if the production goes on tour.

You should wear black, comfortable clothing for making scenery changes during a production.

Future prospects

This is a popular and competitive area to work in.

With experience, you could go on to a supervisory or management role, leading a crew of stagehands.

You could also specialise in a certain area such as carpentry and become a production carpenter.

Eventually, after working your way up, it may be possible to progress to tour manager or stage manager.

Advantages/disadvantages

The work is often quite casual, so you may not have a steady income.

You will work irregular and unsocial hours as most performances will be in the evening and at weekends and you may have to work away from home on location for days or weeks at a time.

Working in theatre is an exciting and challenging job role; you will get to be part of a glamorous industry.

Money guide

The salary for stagehands is fairly low.

Starting salaries are around £12,000 and could rise to £15,000 with experience.

The majority of stagehands work on a freelance or casual basis though so pay rates vary considerably. You may be able to negotiate a higher rate if you have extensive or specialist experience.

Related opportunities

- Artistic/Theatre Director p432
- Stage Manager p447
- TV, Film and Radio Producer p424

Further information

Association of British Theatre Technicians
www.abtt.org.uk

Creative Skillset
www.creativeskillset.org

National Council for Drama Training
www.ncdt.co.uk

Stage Management Association
www.stagemanagementassociation.co.uk

CRCI: Q

PERFORMING ARTS

STUNT PERFORMER

Qualifications and courses

There are no academic entry requirements for this work but you must be over the age of 18. Equity (the trade union for the performing arts) recommends that film and TV producers only employ stunt performers who are on the Joint Industry Stunt Committee (JISC) Stunt Register.

To join the JISC register you are required to prove that you have at least 1 year of experience and qualifications in a minimum of 6 sports across the following categories: fighting, falling, riding/driving, agility/strength and water. You must have experience in at least 4 of these categories and you cannot have more than 2 sports from the same category. For example, you could be skilled in martial arts, high diving, horse riding, gymnastics, rock climbing and swimming.

When registering these qualifications they must not be more than 5 years old. You will also need to give the JISC evidence that you have spent a minimum of 60 days in front of the camera either as an actor or walk-on artist.

Organisations such as the British Academy of Dramatic Combat (BADC), the British Academy of Stage and Screen Combat (BASSC) and YoungBlood offer a range of courses, workshops and classes in stage combat for practising actors.

What the work involves

Stunt performers plan, design, practise and perform stunts in areas such as motorbike riding, car driving, diving, flying, paragliding, bungee jumping, skiing and horse riding.

Standing in for actors in TV, film or video productions, you will enter flaming buildings, crash vehicles, drive at speed or do dangerous stunts at sea. Sometimes, performances are in front of live audiences.

You could advise other performers on health and safety issues.

Type of person suited to this work

Being skilled in a range of sports including gymnastics, trampolining, parachuting, wrestling, fencing and some of the well-known martial arts is often useful.

Stunt performers are dedicated to their art and committed to ensuring that their skills are highly developed. A high level of stamina and fitness is essential. You should be a risk taker with an adventurous spirit.

You need to be happy to practise every aspect of your stunts over and again until they are reproducible in all aspects, so you must be a perfectionist. You must always be aware of the dangers you face, practising long hours to make the performance appear easy!

Working conditions

Part of your working day could be spent within a studio, on location or on a film set.

You could be working indoors or out, in cramped spaces, at heights or sometimes in bad weather conditions.

The hours will be very long, often up to 16 hours per day depending on the production, with frequent weekend work and travel to distant places.

Future prospects

Opportunities for live stunt work are decreasing, as digital graphics and new media can simulate stunts, so competition for work is growing increasingly fierce.

Stunt artists work anywhere in the world, with the main employers being film, TV and video production companies.

You could progress into advisory work, helping film directors or advising and training other stunt artists. You could also direct action scenes.

Advantages/disadvantages

You will have the opportunity to travel the world and no two days will be the same.

Seeing the finished product on screen is rewarding.

This is difficult, dangerous work involving many risks.

Entry to this sector is very competitive.

Money guide

There is no formal pay scale for stunt performers and income varies greatly.

Equity establishes minimum rates for stunt work with TV companies and independent producers.

Recommended daily rates are £250–£370 for TV work and £425 a day for film work.

Although the majority of stunt artists are freelance, you might enter full-time employment with a salary of about £12,000.

A very experienced performer may earn £25,000+ per year.

Related opportunities

- Actor p430
- Choreographer p433
- Entertainer p439

Further information

British Academy of Stage and Screen Combat
www.bassc.org

EQ
www.thinkeq.org.uk

YoungBlood
www.youngblood.co.uk

Qualifications and courses

There is no specific entry route into this profession. Employers like to see degrees and diplomas in art subjects, especially stage crafts and animation, but a degree is not essential.

Degree courses are available in areas such as technical arts and special effects and you will need at least 5 GCSEs/S grades (A*–C/1–3) and 2 A levels/Highers for entry. Most applicants take a Foundation art and design course prior to entry.

There are some courses available to improve your skillset, for example the Association of British Theatre Technicians runs day courses in specialised subjects such as pyrotechnics.

There are very few permanent posts with large broadcasting houses, usually in London, so relevant work experience is essential for learning new skills and gaining contacts. These skills can be in any aspect of special effects, from theatre stage crafts to pyrotechnics and working with explosives.

When you gain employment, you will be trained whilst shadowing an experienced technician. This trainee period often lasts 5 years, though this is reduced to 2 for visual effects.

What the work involves

As a technician you'd work to create special effects in the TV and film industry. You might work with either physical effects, pyrotechnic, or visual. The first involves robotics, the second explosions, and the third superimposes images after filming.

You'll work with colleagues to plan effects, create them, test them, and oversee their staging during filming.

You will adhere to strict health and safety regulations, update detailed logbooks of work done and the methods used and prepare the work area by setting up explosives for a gun battle or preparing materials for prosthetic work for example.

Type of person suited to this work

An interest in films and TV is useful for this profession. You need to be creative and imaginative, but at the same time practical and logical.

A visual mind is important as you'll need to imagine how things will look on screen as well as having a sense of drama and the desire to create a feeling of authenticity in screen shots through detailing. You should also be resourceful as you'll be working to a budget.

A strong awareness of health and safety issues is paramount as you will be working with props and explosives that can pose a threat to others if used improperly. You will often have to help with the equipment and this often includes heavy lifting so a level of fitness would be required.

You'll be working under pressure, both with others and on your own, so need to be good at coping with all of these scenarios. You should be adaptable and capable of coping with criticism.

Working conditions

Hours are flexible, and you should be prepared to fit around filming schedules. This may mean late nights, early mornings, and weekends.

You could work freelance, which may well mean you are very busy for a while, then unemployed for a long period of time. When you're working, you could be travelling anywhere, sometimes for quite a while. Be prepared to stay away from home often.

Work takes place wherever filming takes place – in a studio or workshop, outdoors in the sunshine, outdoors in the rain, on location etc.

Future prospects

Once you've been working for about 10 years, you can advance to a senior technician position.

With 5 years' more experience, you can move into a supervisor role.

Progression is much easier when you've built a list of contacts, and vacancies in this industry are often only advertised internally.

Advantages/disadvantages

This is a really exciting job, and seeing your hard work on the big screen can be really rewarding.

It's a fiercely competitive profession, and you might have to face periods of unemployment.

Money guide

As a trainee, you can expect to earn between £200 and £500 a week, depending on how advanced your skills are.

Once you're a technician this can rise to about £1,250 for a week of work.

If you make it to a senior technician role, this might rise to between £3,000 and £4,000 a week.

Related opportunities

- Animator p168
- Lighting Technician p440
- Props Maker/Assistant p443

Further information

Association of British Theatre Technicians
www.abtt.org.uk

Broadcasting Entertainment Cinematograph and Theatre Union
www.bectu.org.uk

WARDROBE ASSISTANT

Qualifications and courses

There are no formal entry requirements for this career but it is an absolute necessity that you possess the practical skills of hand and machine sewing, pattern cutting, dress making. The best way to get a job is to gain practical experience; applying to local theatre companies or to student productions as a volunteer is a good place to start.

As competition is fierce many people study for qualifications in costume related subjects. Courses include City & Guilds Certificates and Diplomas at Levels 1, 2 and 3 in Creative Techniques, BTEC Level 3 Certificate and Diploma in Production Arts (Costume) or Level 2 Certificate and Diploma in Fashion and Clothing. Also available are Foundation degrees in Fashion and Costume Craft and degrees in Costume for the Stage and Screen. Entry to a degree is with 5 GCSEs/S grades (A*–C/1–3) and 2 A levels/4 H grades.

Apprenticeships are available within large corporations such as the BBC and regional screen agencies but again competition is very fierce. Details of available schemes can be found on the Creative Skillset website.

Most training is done on the job, under the supervision of a senior wardrobe assistant. It is important to develop your skills by taking short courses in costume assembling or by joining a professional association.

What the work involves

You will be responsible for assembling and sourcing the costumes needed for TV, film and theatre productions. You will be buying or hiring accessories and costumes and making sure they are correctly stored and transported.

You will be responsible for altering, repairing, cleaning and fitting costumes as well looking after them in between scenes/takes.

You will need to keep a detailed record of the different costumes worn by each performer and make sure they are ready to be worn for each stage of the production.

Type of person suited to this work

You will need to be organised, accurate and be able to remain calm under pressure, especially when dealing with costume emergencies during a live performance when you must use your initiative.

It is important to have good communication and interpersonal skills as you will be working with a range of people; colleagues and professionals.

A good eye for detail, practical sewing skills and creative flair are all useful when assembling costumes. A solid working knowledge of design, fashion and fashion periods will be advantageous.

Working conditions

You will be working unsocial and long hours the majority of the time. In film and television most of the work is during the daytime whereas in theatre you will be expected to work before and after both matinee and evening performances, usually 6 days a week.

Film and television production companies may need you to work away from home for long periods of time.

You will be sitting down, sewing and fitting costumes or running around a set helping to dress performers.

Future prospects

Most work can be found in London and other major cities with theatres, touring companies and film/TV production companies. It is important to gain as many contacts as possible by undertaking work experience and working for free as competition for jobs is fierce.

You can gain promotion to wardrobe supervisor and short courses are available which can enable you to have the right skills to switch between theatre and film/TV work; you usually start off specialising in one area.

Some wardrobe assistants move into specialist areas such as costume/set design or stage management.

Advantages/disadvantages

This is an exciting job in a glamorous industry; no two days will be the same and you may get to work with celebrities.

The pay is low for such an important role.

You can gain good insight and experience into a competitive industry enabling you to progress to senior positions.

Money guide

You could start out doing work experience where only travel expenses or lunch are paid for; £30 per day is the average amount.

Your starting salary may be around £12,000. Senior wardrobe assistants could earn £28,000+.

Freelance rates do vary greatly depending on the job you are doing and your reputation.

Related opportunities

- Costume Designer p170
- Fashion Designer/Milliner p171
- Museum/Art Gallery Curator p355

Further information

Costume Society of Great Britain
www.costumesociety.org.uk

Creative Skillset
www.creativeskillset.org

Society of British Theatre Designers
www.theatredesign.org.uk

Personal and Other Services including Hair and Beauty

This is a very wide job family and covers everything from hairdressing and beauty to cleaning to wedding consulting. You can enter this career sector with a host of different skills and qualifications. What all of the jobs have in common is that they provide a particular service that a customer has asked for so you need to be good at listening to others and giving customers exactly what they want – people in this sector have a brilliant way with people. You should also demonstrate creativity and strong practical and technical skill as many of the jobs in this family require you to use specialist equipment and to have knowledge of health and safety.

The jobs featured in this section are listed below. For similar jobs to the ones in this section turn to *Catering and Hospitality* on page 133.

Qualifications and courses

Although formal qualifications are not generally required, GCSEs/S grades (A*–C/1–3) may prove useful, particularly in maths and English. Previous experience in a retail, sales or customer service role would be beneficial. You must be over 18 years old if you wish to be self-employed.

The Vocational Training Charitable Trust (VTCT) offers a Certificate in Cosmetic Make-Up and Beauty Consultancy (Level 2), and NVQs/SVQs are available in Retail Skills, Beauty Therapy (general or specialising in make-up) and Customer Service (Levels 1–3). City & Guilds and BTEC both provide a Certificate in Retail Knowledge (Beauty) at Level 2. These courses may be taken prior to employment or while working. Although they are not essential, they will help to show prospective employers that you are committed to the industry.

An alternative training route to becoming a beauty consultant is to apply for the Beauty Therapy Apprenticeship at Intermediate Level.

Once you secure employment, training is generally provided in-house and may cover topics such as sales techniques, skincare and make-up techniques, and stock recording and ordering.

What the work involves

You will work in department stores and other public locations, promoting and selling beauty products on behalf of cosmetics companies.

You will provide product demonstrations to individual customers or groups, including facials, make-up applications and manicures. You will give advice and information on cosmetic products. Your work may involve selling items and taking payments, managing stock levels and keeping the demonstration area attractive and presentable.

If you are self-employed, you will have to control every aspect of your business including sales, finances and marketing.

Type of person suited to this work

A sociable and professional approach is important because you will meet many customers. You should have a smart appearance.

Working on a store counter can be fast paced so you should be able to stay calm in busy situations. You will use your communication skills to encourage customers to find out more about your products.

You should also have a strong interest in helping people make the best of themselves. For applying make-up and other products, you will need an eye for design and good practical skills. Numeracy skills will help you manage stock and take payments. You should enjoy the challenge of working towards sales targets.

Working conditions

You could work between 37 and 40 hours a week, with some weekend and evening hours. If you are self-employed, the majority of your hours will be in the evening.

You may have to do some lifting and carrying from the stockroom.

Depending on where you work, you may wear a uniform and you will normally be expected to wear the cosmetics that you are selling.

Future prospects

Beauty consultancy offers a flexible career for people who want to combine their interest in beauty with working in sales.

As well as employment within department stores, there are opportunities to work in airports and hotels. You may choose to promote and sell products from your own home.

With experience, you could progress to working as a team manager and then move on to an area management role. Progression might involve changing employers and moving to a larger company.

Advantages/disadvantages

This type of work is often available on a part-time or flexible basis which would suit people with other commitments.

You might spend a lot of time on your feet which could prove tiring.

You may receive a product allowance of either discounted or free cosmetic products.

Money guide

Starting salaries are usually £12,000–£13,000.

Experienced beauty consultants can expect to earn £19,000–£23,000.

Those employed in a senior or managerial position could achieve up to £30,000 a year.

Many beauty consultants receive commission based upon their sales figures.

Related opportunities

- Beauty Therapist p455
- Hairdresser/Barber p465
- Nail Technician p466

Further information

Hairdressing and Beauty Industry Authority
www.habia.org

Skillsmart Retail
www.skillsmartretail.com

BEAUTY THERAPIST

Qualifications and courses

To work as a fully qualified beauty thearapist, you need at least a Level 3 qualification. Candidates are also usually required to have some GCSEs/S grades (A*–C/1–3).

Suitable courses include the City & Guilds Diploma in Beauty Therapy Techniques, the NVQ Diploma in Beauty Therapy, the BTEC National in Beauty Therapy, the Vocational Training Charitable Trust (VTCT) Diploma in Beauty Therapy Treatments and the International Therapy Examination Council (ITEC) Diploma in Advanced Beauty Therapy.

An alternative route for those aged 16–24 is to take the Apprenticeship in Beauty Therapy which is available at Intermediate and Advanced Levels.

Universities and higher education colleges offer HNCs/ HNDs, Foundation degrees and degrees in cosmetic science or beauty therapy and spa management. Degree programmes usually require applicants to have at least 5 GCSEs/S grades (A*–C–/1–3) and 2 A levels/3 H grades.

Beauty therapists often extend their knowledge into holistic or alternative treatments such as massage and aromatherapy. The International Federation of Professional Aromatherapists (IFPA) accredits courses at private schools and colleges in the UK.

What the work involves

You will provide a range of face and body treatments. These could include facials, massages, electrolysis and waxing treatments.

Beauty therapists provide services in beauty salons, health clubs and hotels. They also work on a self-employed basis in rented treatment rooms or from their homes.

Your work will involve cleaning and tidying the treatment room before and after each client.

You may also have to complete some administrative duties and keep client records.

Type of person suited to this work

People often choose to have a beauty therapy treatment to help them relax so you will need a calm, confident approach.

An interest in helping people with a range of therapies is essential. You will need good communication skills when advising clients about the treatments they can have.

A well-presented appearance and a good level of physical fitness are also important. You will work to a high standard of health and hygiene.

Working conditions

You will generally work between 37 and 40 hours a week, including some weekends and evenings to accommodate customers' needs.

Therapy rooms or cubicles are private, clean and warm. You could visit clients in their homes. You will spend the majority of your day standing and bending.

Beauty therapists usually wear a uniform. People with allergies to beauty products may not be suitable for this role.

Future prospects

More people than ever before are seeking specialised beauty treatments so future prospects in this line of work are good.

Your location can vary from being based in a beauty salon to working in a hotel or spa. With experience you could progress into a management role. You may choose to set up your own beauty therapy business or, with further experience, move into training and lecturing in beauty therapy.

There are opportunities to work on cruise ships and in resorts overseas.

Advantages/disadvantages

Therapists working in health and beauty companies or clubs may be provided with free club membership and discounted treatments.

You might find some treatments difficult to carry out if you are not comfortable seeing people's bodies.

You can feel proud knowing that you have made a customer happy after completing their chosen treatment.

Money guide

Salaries vary depending on location and employer.

Once qualified as a beauty therapist, you could receive a starting salary of £11,000–£12,000.

With experience, earnings increase to about £17,000 a year.

In a senior or managerial position, you could achieve in excess of £20,000 per year.

Tips and commission from the sale of products can supplement your income.

Related opportunities

- Beauty Consultant p454
- Hairdresser/Barber p465
- Nail Technician p466

Further information

British Association of Beauty Therapy and Cosmetology
www.babtac.com

Hairdressing and Beauty Industry Authority
www.habia.org

Qualifications and courses

No formal qualifications are required for entry to this job. Car valets are usually aged 17 or over as a full driving licence is often required. Qualifications in practical or technical subjects, or previous experience in the motor trade, industrial/office cleaning or dry cleaning can be an advantage.

Once you secure employment, you will undertake training on the job, learning about cleaning techniques and health and safety procedures from an experienced colleague. You may also be sent on short courses run by the manufacturers of cleaning products.

The British Institute of Cleaning Science (BICSc) provides a Car Valeting Certificate scheme. Topics covered include interior cleaning, exterior cleaning, engine cleaning, pressure washing, stain removal, upholstery cleaning and polishing and waxing.

The City & Guilds Certificate and Diploma in Vehicle Valeting Principles (Levels 1 and 2) is also available for those who wish to take a relevant qualification.

Apprenticeships in Cleaning and Environmental Services, Vehicle Body and Paint Operations, and Vehicle Maintenance and Repair may equip you with relevant skills and knowledge for this career.

What the work involves

Car valets clean and finish car exteriors and interiors using specialist equipment.

You could work for vehicle service centres, new and used car centres, garages, crash repair centres and valeting companies.

You may clean a vehicle both internally and externally or you might clean the exterior only. You could also clean the engine and help prepare cars for bodywork repairs.

You will clear the interior of rubbish and polish the surfaces and windows. You will also clean the seats and remove any stains. For exteriors, you will clean the wheels and polish and wax the bodywork.

Type of person suited to this work

You should be physically fit as jobs can take between 1 and 4 hours and involve a lot of bending, stretching and lifting.

You should be able to use different types of cleaning equipment and apply your knowledge of health and safety to your work.

As you will be providing a service to customers, you will need to be a quick but thorough worker with good attention to detail.

You need strong people skills and the ability to work both independently and as part of a team.

You should be able to cope with dirty working conditions.

Working conditions

The work is very hands on and can be tiring because it involves spending a lot of time on your feet.

You might be based outside cleaning cars on a forecourt, potentially working in poor weather conditions.

This job requires regular contact with cleaning chemicals, so it might not suit people with allergies or skin conditions. Sometimes you will be required to wear protective clothing including gloves and safety glasses.

Future prospects

Car valeting is a key part of the sales and services sector of the motor vehicle industry.

You could work for a large vehicle repair company or service centre as part of a valeting team.

With experience, you could progress to a supervisory or managerial role.

You could choose to set up your own valeting company. Some professional car valets offer a mobile service, going out to visit customers at their premises.

With experience and further training, you could progress into a technical or sales role.

Advantages/disadvantages

Car valeting jobs may include regular travel, either when providing services to customers on their premises, or when returning vehicles to customers.

This type of job offers the chance to work in close contact with a range of cars and other vehicles.

Money guide

Starting salaries begin at £12,000 per year.

With experience as a car valet you could earn £15,000–£18,000.

Overtime and shift payments can increase your income.

Related opportunities

- Cleaner p460
- Motor Vehicle Technician p234
- Vehicle Parts Operative p497

Further information

Asset Skills
www.assetskills.org

British Institute of Cleaning Science
www.bics.org.uk

CARETAKER

Qualifications and courses

No formal qualifications are required for entry to this job. Some GCSEs/S grades (A*–C/1–3), particularly English, maths and practical subjects, may be an advantage. However, hands-on skills and experience in basic DIY, carpentry or painting and decorating are more important. Experience in maintenance or security work is useful, as is a driving licence. Within some areas, for example schools, you will need to pass a CRB check.

Maturity is an advantage and employers often prefer older applicants with relevant experience.

Caretakers are trained on the job. It may be possible for entrants to work towards an NVQ Level 1 and 2 in Cleaning and Support Service. Caretakers can also work towards the Cleaning Supervisory Skills Certificate offered by the British Institute of Cleaning Science. A Diploma in Construction and the Built Environment could also be useful.

Studying for a NVQ Level 3 in Property and Caretaking Supervision can speed up career progression. Caretakers can also work towards the Chartered Institute of Housing and the Chartered Institute of Building Level 3 Certificate in Housing Maintenance.

What the work involves

Caretakers manage the security, cleaning and general maintenance of sites such as schools, colleges and office blocks.

In some jobs, you would combine caretaking with other roles such as cleaner, gardener, porter or security attendant.

You will be responsible for opening and locking the premises and checking building security. You will repair broken equipment and reorder supplies. Your work could also involve some gardening. You could also clean parts of the site or manage the work of the site cleaners.

Type of person suited to this work

Caretakers need good communication skills, because they interact closely with the people based on their premises. You may be responsible for the security of an entire site, so it's important to have a mature, honest attitude and a full understanding of emergency procedures.

The ability to work independently is essential, for example when repairing broken equipment. You should also be able to work as part of a team.

Physical fitness is essential for work such as moving equipment and gardening. You will work to a high standard of health and safety at all times.

Working conditions

A 37 hour working week, which could encompass early mornings, evenings and weekends, is normal in this line of work.

Caretaking work is physically demanding. You might work outside using ladders and other tools.

Caretakers work with cleaning chemicals and wear protective clothing such as overalls. The job might not suit people with allergies or skin conditions.

Future prospects

Many locations only employ one caretaker, so you might need to move to a bigger site to progress.

In larger establishments, senior caretakers have the responsibility of managing a small team of caretakers or other staff like cleaners.

You could progress to a management position in a private cleaning contract company.

Advantages/disadvantages

As the premises keyholder, you could be on-call for emergencies.

This job can be sociable and caretakers often build up a good working relationship with the people based on their premises.

Money guide

The starting salary for an assistant caretaker is £12,000 per year. With experience this rises to £16,000 per year.

You could earn £25,000 as a senior or mobile caretaker.

In some work areas, such as education, caretakers are offered on-site subsidised housing as part of their contract.

Related opportunities

- Cleaner p460
- Hotel Porter p141
- Refuse and Recycling Operative p468

Further information

Chartered Institute of Housing
www.cih.org

The Caretakers' website
www.thecaretakers.net

Qualifications and courses

There are no formal qualifications for this career. It might be helpful to have basic numeracy and literacy skills for measuring quantities of chemicals and writing quotes for customers. You will usually be trained on the job, and told about health and safety regulations.

Your employer may encourage you to take further training; there are NVQs available at Levels 1 and 2 in Cleaning and Support Services with one unit specifically for carpet and soft furnishings, a City & Guilds Level 2 Certificate in Cleaning Principles and the British Institute of Cleaning Science's Cleaning Operators Proficiency Certificate.

The National Carpet Cleaners Association has regular specialist cleaning courses such as Advanced Spot and Stain Treatment and Removal.

Apprenticeships/Skillseekers may be available for people aged between 16 and 24 in cleaning and support services.

What the work involves

Carpet and upholstery cleaners clean soft furnishings and carpets using specialist equipment. They work in a variety of private and public buildings.

Soft furnishings include curtains, tapestries, antique fabrics, rugs and seat covers. These fabrics and carpets need special cleaning to remove dirt, smoke and grease that build up on them daily.

You will visit the cleaning site first to assess what needs to be cleaned, and what sort of equipment and chemicals you might need. You will write an assessment of the job and what it will cost for the customer.

Type of person suited to this work

It is important to understand how fabrics and carpets are constructed as this will assist if finding ways to remove stubborn stains.

You will also need good practical skills to be able to use specialist cleaning equipment and an understanding of the different types of chemicals you can use.

Excellent communication skills will be essential for talking to customers and colleagues. You should be able to work equally well alone or as part of a team.

Working conditions

You may need to work evenings and weekends. Most of your time will be spent on your feet and carrying around heavy equipment. You will normally be based indoors, in people's homes or public buildings.

You are likely to need to drive around to work at different locations so a driving licence will be useful. You should also be physically fit.

You might have to wear protective clothing to protect you from dust and chemicals which may irritate your skin.

Future prospects

Carpet and upholstery cleaners are needed throughout the UK, meaning there will be lots of job opportunities wherever you live.

You might work for a general or specialist cleaning company or be self-employed.

With experience, you can move into managerial or training roles or start your own cleaning business.

Advantages/disadvantages

This work brings good job satisfaction; you will be pleasing people by restoring their carpets and upholstery to perfect condition.

You could find some aspects of cleaning messy or dirty which could be unpleasant.

You have the opportunity to work for yourself and run your own business.

Money guide

The starting salary is around £12,000 per year.

With experience this can increase to £14,500.

You may be able to earn up to £25,000 if you specialise in antique or tapestry cleaning.

Related opportunities

- Car Valet p456
- Caretaker p457
- Cleaner p460

Further information

British Institute of Cleaning Science
www.bics.org.uk

National Carpet Cleaners Association
www.ncca.co.uk

CHIMNEY SWEEP

Qualifications and courses

There are no formal entry requirements but basic qualifications in English and maths are useful. Previous experience of manual work such as construction is an advantage. You would normally be trained on the job by an experienced chimney sweep.

Trainee chimney sweeps can work towards membership of the National Association of Chimney Sweeps (NACS) or the Guild of Master Chimney Sweeps. NACS offers a 3-day induction course which covers basic chimney sweeping techniques and health and safety. On completion of the training, candidates become probationary members of NACS until they have gained sufficient experience and on-site training to work as professional sweeps. NACS also provides an NVQ Level 2 in Chimney Engineering.

Alternatively, the Guild of Master Chimney Sweeps runs a 2-day intense training course covering theory and practical elements.

Once employed as a chimney sweep, you could take short courses in particular areas of the work which are offered by both NACS and the Guild of Master Chimney Sweeps. To be qualified to carry out inspections and work on gas appliances, you need to gain a certificate of competence through the Accredited Certification Scheme (ACS), leading to registration with Gas Safe.

What the work involves

Chimney sweeps help prevent chimney fires and dangerous fuel emissions by inspecting and cleaning chimney and flue systems, heating appliances and vents.

Your work will involve using brush and vacuum equipment to clear chimneys and vents of blockages.

You will provide information and advice to customers on the repair and maintenance of their chimneys.

Type of person suited to this work

Chimney sweeps combine their professional knowledge with practical skills to protect public safety. You will need a good knowledge of different types of chimney and flue systems.

Operating brush and vacuum chimney cleaning equipment requires good manual skills.

You will visit customers in their homes so you should have a friendly, professional attitude. A good level of physical fitness and stamina is essential as the work is demanding and potentially strenuous. You should be comfortable working at heights and able to work independently without supervision.

Working conditions

Most of your work will take place at people's homes but you could also work on heating systems in commercial or industrial premises.

Travel to different locations is a regular part of the work so a driving licence is essential.

When clearing chimneys, you will wear protective clothing, such as overalls, gloves, a helmet, eye guards and respiratory protection.

You will usually work normal hours Monday to Friday but you may also be required to work unsocial hours, including weekends and evenings, to suit customers.

Future prospects

Chimney sweeping is a specialist but essential service. After gaining the relevant experience and professional qualifications, you could set up your own business, providing services within your local area.

Most chimney sweeps build up a network of loyal and regular customers.

You could also offer additional roofing or ventilation services. There may be opportunities to work with another professional or to join a small specialist company.

Advantages/disadvantages

Most chimney sweeps work on a self-employed basis, which can lead to some job insecurity, particularly at the start of their careers.

You will have the opportunity to meet a variety of people.

Money guide

The majority of chimney sweeps are self-employed and establish their own rates of pay for each job they undertake.

Earnings vary according to the hours spent on a task and the speed at which you work.

You could charge between £35 and £55 for a full sweep.

For a more specialist task, you could receive £70–£75.

Those working full time can expect to earn between £16,000 and £25,000 per year.

Related opportunities

- Cleaner p460
- Roofer p116
- Steeplejack p121

Further information

Guild of Master Sweeps
www.guild-of-master-sweeps.co.uk

National Association of Chimney Sweeps
www.chimneyworks.co.uk

PERSONAL AND OTHER SERVICES INCLUDING HAIR AND BEAUTY

CRCI: RB

459

CLEANER

Qualifications and courses

There are no formal qualifications required for this job. It may be helpful to have basic literacy and numeracy skills. School leavers could apply for the Intermediate Apprenticeship in Cleaning and Environmental Services.

Cleaners receive on-the-job training in health and safety and how to use the necessary cleaning materials and equipment. Once you are employed, you could study for relevant qualifications, such as an NVQ in Cleaning and Support Services (Levels 1 and 2) or a City & Guilds Award, Certificate or Diploma in Cleaning Principles (Level 2). The British Institute of Cleaning Science (BICSc) offers a Cleaning Operators Proficiency Certificate.

Experienced cleaners who wish to progress to a supervisory level can study for an NVQ in Team Leading (Level 2) or the BICSc Cleaning Supervisory Skills Certificate. City & Guilds offer a Diploma in Cleaning Services Supervision (Level 3) or an Award, Certificate and Diploma in Cleaning Supervision Skills (Level 3).

If your job involves contact with hazardous waste, such as sharps and syringes, you will need vaccinations against hepatitis B and C. This is most likely to be necessary if you work in a hospital.

What the work involves

You will be responsible for cleaning and tidying a variety of places including people's homes and places of work.

Industrial cleaners work in public buildings such as hospitals, prisons, schools and health centres and work to the highest standards to reach health and safety requirements.

Domestic cleaners work in people's homes and may have additional tasks such as ironing and washing up.

You will use a range of cleaning materials and equipment such as hoovers, mops, dusters and brooms.

Type of person suited to this work

You will need to be honest and trustworthy, as you will be entering people's homes and workplaces where valuables could be on display.

Being fit and mobile is important, as you will be on your feet for long periods, bending, stretching and carrying heavy equipment.

Good communication skills are required to interact with colleagues and clients, especially if you run your own cleaning business.

You will need a good knowledge of the cleaning chemicals you use and the ability to decide which chemical should be used in each situation. It will also be necessary to adhere to health and safety regulations when using hazardous chemicals.

Working conditions

You will usually work 35–40 hours a week in a full-time job but hours vary. You may be required to work weekends, evenings and early mornings when public places or offices are closed. If you clean private homes, you will normally work during the day when the owner of the home is out. Hospitals need to be kept clean 24/7 so shift work is common. Part-time work is often available.

Many cleaners are self employed and work for several different clients in one day. It would be useful to have a driving licence. Most cleaners wear a uniform or protective clothing.

Future prospects

There is a great demand for cleaners in all sectors.

You could choose to work for a cleaning company or be self-employed.

Many cleaners decide to set up their own small business or move into other roles as a caretaker or supervisor of a team of cleaners.

Advantages/disadvantages

You can work different shifts that fit in well with other jobs or family commitments.

You can progress to being the owner of your own cleaning business.

Owing to the chemicals used in cleaning, this job would not be suitable for those with breathing problems or skin allergies.

Money guide

Earnings vary according to your employer and the number of hours you work.

Most cleaners are paid hourly, with rates ranging from the National Minimum Wage to £10 an hour.

If you are employed on a full-time basis you can expect a starting salary of £11,000–£12,000.

Earnings are higher for specialist cleaners or those employed in a supervisory role.

Related opportunities

- Caretaker p457
- Pest Control Technician p467
- Window Cleaner p472

Further information

Asset Skills
www.assetskills.org

British Institute of Cleaning Science
www.bics.org.uk

Qualifications and courses

There are no formal entry requirements for this type of work, and training is done on the job.

Good reading and writing skills are important though and basic administrative and computer skills are useful.

Trainees follow the Crematorium Technicians' Training Scheme (CTTS) provided by the Institute of Cemetery and Crematorium Management (ICCM). The scheme consists of a BTEC Intermediate Certificate and a BTEC Advanced Certificate.

Employees may also work towards NVQ/SVQ Level 2 in Amenity Horticulture (Cemeteries and Graveyards).

Another work-based training route is provided by the Federation of Burial and Cremation Authorities' (FBCA) TEST scheme.

If your work involves ground maintenance you may also receive training in practical areas such as how to safely use chainsaws and pesticide sprayers.

Experienced crematorium technicians can progress to management roles. Once you have the relevant experience you may be able to work towards ICCM qualifications for crematorium managers. The qualifications are in three stages: ICCM Certificate for Cemetery and/or Crematorium Management, ICCM Diploma and finally ICCM Diploma with Honours. These can be studied for via distance learning.

The ICCM also operates a Continuing Professional Development scheme for crematorium staff at all levels.

What the work involves

Crematorium technicians assist with the running of the crematorium and cemetery premises.

Your work will involve operating cremation equipment to a high standard of health and safety. You will ensure that the cremated remains are stored and disposed of correctly. You will help manage the chapel and cemetery and attend cremation ceremonies.

You will also assist with other cemetery duties, such as excavating graves and grounds maintenance. However, grave digging work is mostly undertaken by contractors working for local authorities.

Type of person suited to this work

Meeting and working with bereaved people requires a mature, sympathetic attitude. You will use your communication skills to liaise with people in the process of cremation ceremonies.

A good level of physical fitness is helpful in a role that covers a wide range of activities.

You will need to keep accurate records so must have good attention to detail.

It's important that cremations are undertaken to a high standard of health and safety, so you should be able to follow strict working guidelines. The ability to work as part of a team is also useful.

Working conditions

This can be a tiring job owing to the range of activities involved and the physical requirements of operating cremation machinery. You will be on your feet for long hours.

You will need to be smartly dressed when facing the public and your outfit will usually be provided for you.

When operating machinery you will need to wear protective clothing.

You will normally work 37–40 hours a week, with some overtime including Saturdays.

You will be out working in all weather conditions.

Future prospects

Owing to changing public attitudes, the number of cremations is increasing, as is the demand for skilled professionals.

Crematorium technicians are usually employed by local councils.

There is also the opportunity to progress into an administrative position within the cemetery.

With experience, you could progress to working as a senior crematorium technician and manage a team of technicians.

Advantages/disadvantages

This role provides the opportunity to provide support to people at an important and challenging time.

The nature of the job means this work can sometimes be distressing.

Money guide

Starting salaries vary between £11,000 and £13,000 per year.

With experience you could earn between £16,000 and £17,000.

At senior/management level you could earn £20,000+.

Salaries are often dependent on local authority rates so may be higher in areas such as London where living costs are deemed more expensive.

There may be the opportunity for additional money through overtime.

Related opportunities

- Cleaner p460
- Embalmer p463
- Funeral Director p464

Further information

Federation of Burial and Cremation Authorities
www.fbca.org.uk

Institute of Cemetery and Crematorium Management
www.iccm-uk.com

Local Government Careers
www.lgcareers.com

The Cremation Society of Great Britain
www.crematorium.org.uk

PERSONAL AND OTHER SERVICES INCLUDING HAIR AND BEAUTY

CRCI: RA

461

DRY CLEANER

Qualifications and courses

There are no formal qualifications needed for this work, although good numeracy and literacy skills will be helpful. It may be useful to have some previous experience working in a laundry or cleaning. Customer service and/ or retail skills would also be an advantage.

You will be trained on the job by an experienced dry cleaner. Many employers offer opportunities to study for qualifications part time. These include the NVQ in Dry Cleaning Operations (Level 2), the Edexcel NVQ Certificate in Textile Care Services (Level 2) and the BTEC Certificate in Laundry and Dry Cleaning Technology (Level 2). The Skillsfirst QCF Award in Retail Skills (Levels 1 and 2) may also be useful.

The Guild of Cleaners & Launderers (GCL) awards Certificates as part of the Qualification Star Scheme. Candidates can undertake exams in Retail Sales, Stain Removal, Garment Finishing, Dry Cleaning Practice and Wet Cleaning.

The SATRA Technology Centre also provides dry cleaning courses at their training centre in Kettering.

All dry cleaners who intend to use solvents must be registered and hold a permit.

What the work involves

You will be cleaning clothes and fabrics which are delicate or sensitive to being washed in water; you will use chemicals and steam to clean garments instead. You might be cleaning specialist fabrics or garments such as wool, suede, bridal wear, suits and beaded fabrics.

You will look for any stains and treat them individually before cleaning the item. You might use potentially hazardous chemicals, although many dry cleaners now use safe and environmentally friendly products. You will press and package the garments after cleaning.

You will assist customers at the counter, take payments, complete paperwork and work the cleaning machinery.

Type of person suited to this work

You will need to have good communication skills for dealing with customers and practical skills for handling the cleaning machinery.

A good level of fitness would be helpful for bending, carrying heavy items of clothing and organising cleaned garments.

You will be dealing with payments and paperwork so it is important to have good numeracy skills and an organised approach to your work.

Working conditions

You will work standard hours from Monday to Saturday, usually with 1 day off during the week. Increasingly, dry cleaners are staying open in the evenings and Sundays. You are likely to work shifts to accommodate these hours. Part-time work is often available.

You will be working in the store, both at the counter and with the cleaning machines.

You might be exposed to some chemical fumes and there is a danger of burning yourself on pressing machines. This work would not be suitable for people with skin allergies.

Most stores will supply you with a uniform.

Future prospects

There are jobs available across the UK in high street dry cleaning stores or industrial cleaning plants which clean for hospitals or factories. There is currently a shortage of dry cleaners, with more vacancies than applicants.

You can progress from an assistant position to a supervisory or managerial role; gaining a qualification in team leading might help you to progress more quickly.

After developing extensive experience and knowledge of dry cleaning, you could choose to open your own store.

Advantages/disadvantages

This is a good career if you enjoy practical work and providing a service.

You could be affected by the chemical fumes which would be unpleasant.

There are opportunities to run your own business.

Money guide

The starting salary for a dry cleaner is usually around £12,000.

Once you have undertaken training and gained experience, you can expect to earn approximately £14,500 a year.

If you are employed in a senior or managerial position, your salary could range from £15,000 to £30,000, depending on the reputation and performance of the store.

Related opportunities

- Car Valet p456
- Cleaner p460
- Textile Operative p245

Further information

Guild of Cleaners and Launderers
www.gcl.org.uk

Textile Services Association
www.tsa-uk.org

EMBALMER

Qualifications and courses

There are no formal entry requirements for working as an embalmer but GCSEs/S grades in English, maths, chemistry, biology and religious studies may be useful.

To achieve professional qualifications, you must first secure a job and register with a tutor approved by the British Institute of Embalmers (BIE). You will then undertake on-the-job training, with part-time or distance learning tuition from your tutor.

Most embalmers work for qualifications awarded by the International Examinations Board of Embalmers (IEBE). The IEBE training is modular and trainees must pass the foundation unit before proceeding with the rest of the training. You are eligible to register with the BIE as a student member upon completion of the foundation unit.

The main IEBE training involves modules in anatomy, physiology, bacteriology and practical embalming. Assessment is via exams and practical work. Once you have passed these modules, you can apply for full membership of the BIE.

You could develop your skills by taking courses in facial reconstruction, hair and make-up or air brushing. Some embalmers train to work in specialist areas, for example with the bodies of disaster victims.

What the work involves

Embalmers prepare the bodies of deceased people for funerals and for viewing by their relatives. They preserve the body in the most life-like way.

You will wash and disinfect the deceased person's body. You will use specialist equipment to remove all liquids and gases from the body and replace these with injected preservatives which help prevent infection.

Part of preparing the body will involve washing and arranging the person's hair and applying cosmetics. If the deceased has any injuries, you will use plaster of Paris or wax to restore their body.

Your work will also include setting up and cleaning the embalming equipment and treatment area.

Type of person suited to this work

You must be able to cope with working with the bodies of deceased people. A respectful approach to your work is essential. You might have to deal with distressing sights so a mature, detached and down-to-earth attitude is very important.

Embalming work involves presenting a deceased person in the most positive way for grieving relatives. A creative flair and attention to detail will help you to achieve this. You should be senstive to people's feelings.

Working conditions

Embalmers work in operating rooms within funeral parlours. These are maintained to a very high standard of hygiene and kept at a low temperature.

Whilst embalming you will wear protective clothing such as latex gloves, rubber boots and a theatre gown. Regular contact with chemicals means that this job may not suit people with skin conditions or allergies. You will spend most of the day on your feet and the work is physically demanding.

You will usually work normal hours from Monday to Friday, with occasional weekend and overtime work during busy periods. Some employers will require you to be on-call for emergency work.

Future prospects

There are around 1300 qualified embalmers in the UK but the industry has a slow turnover of staff and entry to the career can be difficult.

Embalming is an integral part of the funeral care process, so qualified workers will always be needed. You could gain employment with a funeral care company or you may choose to work on a self-employed basis, providing services to a number of funeral companies. There are opportunities to work abroad.

With extensive experience, you could go into teaching or training.

Advantages/disadvantages

You have the option of working on a freelance basis for a number of employers at the same time.

There are opportunities to work overseas.

This can be distressing work, so you will need to be able to stay detached and professional.

Money guide

Starting salaries are typically around £12,000.

With experience, an embalmer could earn £17,000 per year.

Very experienced embalmers, or those who offer specialist services, can achieve in excess of £30,000.

Related opportunities

- Crematorium Technician p461
- Funeral Director p464
- Hospital Porter p313

Further information

British Institute of Embalmers
www.bioe.co.uk

Federation of Burial and Cremation Authorities
www.fbca.org.uk

FUNERAL DIRECTOR

Qualifications and courses

There are no minimum academic qualifications to work as a funeral director. You will normally start as an assistant and undertake on-the-job training.

For funeral operatives/assistants with driving duties, a driving licence is essential.

The National Association of Funeral Directors (NAFD) offers work-based vocational qualifications for those who are currently employed in the funeral industry. The Advanced Certificate in Funeral Service is an entry-level course suitable for funeral assistants, funeral operatives, drivers and bearers. Those who have progressed to a role as a funeral arranger or administrator can study for the Advanced Diploma in Funeral Arranging and Administration.

NAFD also have a Certificate of Training in Funeral Service Awareness which is aimed at people considering joining the funeral service.

The British Institute of Funeral Directors (BIFD) provide several qualifications, ranging from entry level courses to a Diploma in Funeral Service Management.

A Foundation degree in funeral services is available at the University of Bath.

What the work involves

Funeral directors coordinate funeral arrangements for burials and cremations.

You will liaise with the family of the deceased, offering advice and taking note of the details they would like included in the ceremony.

You will arrange the date and location of the funeral, transport and death notices. You will also attend the funeral and ensure that everything runs smoothly during the ceremony.

You might undertake embalming work and prepare the body for the funeral.

Type of person suited to this work

You need to have a sensitive and mature attitude to your work. Excellent communication skills and a high standard of health and safety are essential. You must also be well organised with a good eye for detail.

For liaising with local authorities and completing paperwork you will need a good knowledge of the relevant legal issues.

If you are self-employed, you will require good office and budgeting skills.

A thorough knowledge of different cultures and religions is also helpful.

Working conditions

Funeral directors work in funeral homes or centres based within high-street outlets or other areas. Attending funerals will involve working outdoors in all weather conditions.

Your working hours will vary. Most of your administrative work will be undertaken during office hours from Monday to Friday but you may need to visit clients at weekends and in the evenings. You will also have to be on-call, possibly working on a rota system. You may be required to work extra hours during busy times.

Funeral directors must dress smartly.

Future prospects

Most people start a career in this area by gaining experience as a funeral operative or assistant. They learn the varied aspects of the job from more experienced colleagues and work towards professional qualifications.

You could work for one of the large funeral services companies or for a smaller independent firm.

With experience, you could work as a funeral director abroad. After several years in the industry, you could set up your own funeral services company.

Advantages/disadvantages

Depending on the size of the funeral company you work for, you may be on-call on a regular basis, which can affect your personal life.

Providing a professional and sympathetic service to people experiencing a very difficult time can be rewarding.

Money guide

Earnings usually vary from year to year.

Starting salaries are typically £14,000–£15,000 per year.

With experience in the sector, you can expect to earn £19,000–£25,000.

Those employed in a senior position can achieve £30,000 a year.

Self-employed funeral directors could earn considerably more.

Related opportunities

- Crematorium Technician p461
- Embalmer p463
- Management Consultant p51

Further information

British Institute of Funeral Directors
www.bifd.org.uk

National Association of Funeral Directors
www.nafd.org.uk

HAIRDRESSER/ BARBER

Qualifications and courses

You can either train as a hairdresser full time at college or you can start as an assistant/trainee in a salon and attend college on day release. You could take an NVQ Certificate in Hairdressing and Barbering (Level 1), an NVQ Diploma in Hairdressing (Levels 2 and 3) or an NVQ Diploma in Barbering (Levels 2 and 3). Those who wish to specialise in African-Caribbean hair could take the NVQ Diploma in Hairdressing (Combined Hair Types).

Another route into this career is to apply for an Apprenticeship, either in Hairdressing or Barbering, both of which are available at Intermediate and Advanced Levels.

Those with NVQ Level 2 can register as a State Registered Hairdresser with the Hairdressing Council (HC). The Freelance Hair and Beauty Federation (FHBF) runs courses for hairdressers on establishing and managing their own business, as well as continuing professional development (CPD) courses.

Qualified hairdressers can take more specialised courses through part-time study, such as the BTEC HNC/HND in Hair and Beauty Management (Levels 4 and 5) or Level 4 qualifications in salon management from City & Guilds. Degrees and Foundation degrees in hairdressing and salon management are also available.

What the work involves

Hairdressers shampoo, cut and style clients' hair to a range of modern or classic looks. You could also provide dry or wet shaves to male clients.

You will discuss hair treatments with clients and may carry out colouring, tinting, perming and fixing hair extensions. You will also give advice on general haircare and hair products.

At senior levels, you could provide training to junior hairdressers.

Type of person suited to this work

Cutting and styling hair involves close personal contact with clients so hairdressers need good communication skills and a friendly manner.

You should have an interest in fashion, a creative flair and an eye for detail. You will need manual dexterity when using specialist chemicals and equipment required to style, perm and colour customers' hair. You should be willing to learn new techniques and methods throughout your career.

Sometimes you may work on reception, booking appointments and taking cash, so you will have to be efficient, confident and numerate.

Some salons require staff to be able to offer a wider choice of services, such as nail and beauty treatments.

Working conditions

Most hairdressers and barbers are based in salons in high streets and other areas. Some work as mobile hairdressers, providing services to clients in their own homes, so a driving licence would be required.

You will do a 40-hour week, which may include working Saturdays. A lot of salons remain open in the evening once or twice a week. Certain salons also open on Sunday. Part-time work is often available.

Hairdressing involves bending over customers for long periods of the day so you will need to be physically fit.

Future prospects

In a salon, you could progress to a role as senior stylist or manager. Alternatively, you could set up your own business.

As a mobile hairdresser, you could provide services to people in hospitals, care homes or prisons, as well as private clients.

There are opportunities to work on cruise ships. With further beauty therapy training you could work in film, TV or theatre.

Advantages/disadvantages

This is a very sociable job which allows you to express your creativity.

Regular contact with beauty products and chemicals means that this type of work may not suit people with skin conditions or allergies.

Money guide

As a trainee you can expect to earn the National Minimum Wage, which varies according to your age.

Trainee hairdressers are likely to receive a starting salary of £8,000–£12,000.

Fully qualified and experienced hairdressers can expect to earn up to £20,000 a year.

Top professional hairdressers can achieve in excess of £30,000.

Earnings vary with employer and geographical location.

Related opportunities

- Beauty Therapist p455
- Image Consultant p483
- Nail Technician p466

Further information

Hairdressing and Beauty Industry Authority
www.habia.org

Qualifications and courses

There are no formal entry requirements for this career. However, in many areas nail technicians require a licence from the environmental health department of their local council. To obtain a licence you will need to have nationally recognised qualifications and you should check which qualifications your local council will accept.

Relevant courses include the City & Guilds NVQ Diploma in Nail Services (Levels 2 and 3), the Vocational Training Charitable Trust (VTCT) Certificate in Nail Technology (Level 2) or Certificate in Nail Treatments (Level 2) and the VTCT Diploma in Nail Technology (Level 3).

You could also complete a Certificate in Nail Technology (Level 2) or Diploma in Nail Technology (Level 3) from the International Therapy Examination Council (ITEC). The Confederation of International Beauty Therapy & Cosmetology (CIBTAC) offers a Certificate in Nail Technologies (Level 3) and a Diploma in Nail Tech Services (Level 3).

An option for those aged 16–24 is to apply for the Apprenticeship in Nail Services which is available at Intermediate and Advanced Levels.

What the work involves

Nail technicians provide a range of nail treatments to clients, including manicures, nail extensions, nail art and nail jewellery. Depending on the treatment you are providing, you will work with a range of beauty products and equipment such as brushes, stencils and airbrushes.

You will discuss with clients their intended treatment and check their hands for skin or nail disorders. You will provide advice about aftercare and recommend products for nail care and maintenance.

Your work will also include cleaning and tidying the treatment area before and after each client.

Type of person suited to this work

Nail technicians work with many people so you should have good communication skills. A professional appearance is also important. It will also be important that you are able to maintain a high standard of hygiene at all times.

You will need excellent manual handling skills to undertake nail design work. A good knowledge of nail and beauty products is important. An eye for design and an interest in fashion are essential.

If you work as a freelance technician you will need good business skills.

Working conditions

Nail technicians work in nail or beauty salons and other locations. Mobile nail technicians provide treatments to clients in their own homes. A driving licence would be useful for travelling to your clients.

Salon-based technicians usually work between 30 and 40 hours a week with some evening/weekend work.

Nail technicians come into regular contact with chemicals so the job might not suit people with skin conditions or allergies.

Future prospects

Nail technology is a popular area of beauty and treatments are now available in nail salons, department stores, and beauty and hairdressing salons.

You could work as a freelance nail technician, providing services to care homes and hotels as well as private clients. If you gain additional professional qualifications you could offer other therapies.

There are opportunities to work abroad or on cruise ships.

You could choose to teach nail treatments or become an NVQ assessor.

Advantages/disadvantages

Working as a freelancer can involve unsocial hours which may disrupt your personal life.

Benefits available from working in a salon include bonus schemes, commission payments for product sales and free or discounted beauty treatments.

Money guide

Starting salaries in this career are between £8,000 and £12,000.

With increased experience, your earnings will rise to about £16,000.

At senior/management level, you could receive £18,000–£25,000 a year.

Some nail technicians either work on a freelance basis or are self-employed and charge per job.

Rates vary from £10 to £50 depending on the type of treatment.

Related opportunities

- Beauty Therapist p455
- Hairdresser/Barber p465
- Make-up Artist p441

Further information

British Association of Beauty Therapy and Cosmetology
www.babtac.com

International Therapy Examination Council
www.itecworld.co.uk

Qualifications and courses

A good standard of education is required, with GCSEs/S grades (A*–C/1–3) in English, maths and science being useful (although not essential). You will need to be able to study for pest control qualifications and be able to measure correct dosages.

Because the job involves using specialist equipment and dangerous substances, some employers prefer candidates to be over 18 years old.

Training is undertaken on the job, supervised by an experienced technician. There might also be opportunities to attend training courses. Some larger companies have an in-house training programme.

The entry-level qualification for the industry is the British Pest Control Association/Royal Society for the Promotion of Health Certificate in Pest Management, which equates to NVQ Level 2.

NVQs/SVQs are available in Pest Control Supervision at Level 3. The British Pest Control Association also offers specialist short courses in fumigation, rodents, insects, bird management and field biology, and a Technical Inspector Certificate.

The Property Care Association offers short courses covering insect infestation. The National Proficiency Training Council (NPTC) offers Certificates in Competence in the use of pesticides in rural areas.

Once qualified, you can join a professional registration scheme such as the NPTA Professional Pest Technician Registration Scheme (PPTRS) where you can document your level of training.

What the work involves

Pest control technicians protect public health by treating and eradicating infestations of insects and vermin such as cockroaches and rats. Pest control technicians work in private homes, offices, shops and other sites.

Your job may involve investigating or monitoring a site to check for pests. You will use a range of specialist chemicals and equipment. Your work might involve fitting traps or spraying areas with chemicals.

In some situations you will provide advice to customers on the prevention of pest problems.

Type of person suited to this work

This job is all about protecting public health so you should be able to work to a high standard of health and safety. Working with chemical treatments and specialist equipment demands a professional approach.

You will need to be calm when dealing with large numbers of insects and rodents. A strong stomach will also help you cope with working in unpleasant conditions.

Physical fitness and good manual handling skills are essential. You will need to be able to communicate and have a tactful

approach when providing advice to customers. You will use your writing skills to keep records and write reports.

Working conditions

Whilst not all pest control work is unpleasant, dealing with dirty or unhygienic situations is a likely part of the job.

You will travel to different locations on a regular basis. A driving licence is essential.

Pest control technicians must wear protective clothing, such as overalls and eye goggles. They work with a range of chemicals, so the job might not suit people with skin conditions or allergies.

You may choose to specialise in one type of pest once you have gained some experience.

Hours will normally be longer during the summer months when there are more problems with pests.

Future prospects

Pest control technicians provide an important service to domestic homes, factories, offices and other locations in cities and rural areas.

You could run your own business or work with local councils or specialist companies.

With experience you could progress to supervising teams of staff, managing a large pest control company or working in a management role for local councils.

Advantages/disadvantages

This type of work is sometimes available on a flexible basis.

Your day-to-day work will be varied.

The work is quite solitary; you will often drive alone to jobs in a van containing the specialist equipment.

You might be faced with unpleasant situations.

Money guide

As a trainee you could start at between £13,000 and £16,000 per year.

With experience and qualifications, this rises to £25,000.

There may be the opportunity for additional income, depending on your employer, such as commission, bonuses or petrol allowance.

Related opportunities

- Environmental Health Practitioner/Officer p36
- Refuse and Recycling Operative p468
- Toxicologist p534

Further information

British Pest Control Association
www.bpca.org.uk

National Pest Technicians Association
www.npta.org.uk

REFUSE AND RECYCLING OPERATIVE

ENTRY LEVEL **1**

Qualifications and courses

There are no formal academic entry requirements but you will need to be at least 18 years old and drivers must hold a large goods vehicle (LGV) licence. When you secure employment you will receive on-the-job training in health and safety, manual handling and the disposal of hazardous items.

The Apprenticeship in Sustainable Resource Management, available at both Intermediate and Advanced Levels, offers an ideal route into this career. The Apprenticeship in Driving Goods Vehicles may also equip you with useful skills.

Those who wish to gain relevant qualifications could take the NVQ in Waste Management Operations (Levels 1 and 2) or the NVQ in Recycling Operations (Levels 1 and 2).

People looking to progress to supervisory or managerial roles could study for the NVQ in Waste Management Supervision (Level 3), the NVQ in Managing Waste Collection Operations (Level 4) or the NVQ in the Management of Recycling Operations (Level 4).

What the work involves

You will collect rubbish and unwanted items and take them to an official rubbish tip or recycling depot.

Working as part of a team, you will travel around your area emptying bins, removing plastic sacks of waste or picking up recyclable waste.

Recycling operatives may have additional duties, such as sorting rubbish or collecting hazardous waste. Recycling technicians also work in recycling facilities, sorting through recycled materials in preparation for re-use.

Type of person suited to this work

A strong stomach is useful when dealing with rubbish. You should also be able to cope with getting your hands dirty.

Most companies are required to complete their rounds to deadlines so you should be able to work under pressure. You will also need manual handling skills to lift and move recycling collections. For work in a recycling sorting facility, you will require good eyesight and attention to detail.

Excellent people skills are necessary as you will work as part of a team and encounter members of the public.

Working conditions

You will wear protective clothing, such as gloves and overalls, and you will come into contact with dirt and rubbish on a regular basis. The work will involve nasty smells and some unpleasant sights.

The hours are generally around 6am–3pm from Monday to Friday. You may be required to work overtime during busy holiday periods when the amount of rubbish increases.

You will work outdoors in all weather conditions and the role involves bending, lifting and carrying heavy rubbish bags.

This type of work might not suit people with skin conditions or allergies.

Future prospects

Loaders will always be in demand as even recyclable rubbish has to be collected. You could work for a contracting company providing services for a local authority and there are some jobs with specialist companies who collect paper or food waste.

It is likely that there will be a growth in the number of recycling jobs in local councils and contracting companies providing services to councils and recycling companies.

With experience, you could progress to supervisory or management work.

Advantages/disadvantages

Your working day usually finishes early so you will have your entire evening free.

The work is physically demanding and potentially unsafe.

Money guide

Starting salaries usually range from £11,000 to £14,500.

With experience in the role, you could expect to earn £16,500–£18,000 a year.

Drivers receive slightly higher earnings, usually between £18,000 and £20,000.

A recycling or refuse collection manager can achieve up to £25,000 per year.

There are usually opportunities to increase your income by working overtime or during holiday periods.

Related opportunities

- Delivery Driver p596
- Large Goods Vehicle Driver p602
- Removals Operative p613

Further information

Waste Management Industry Training and Advisory Board
www.wamitab.org.uk

PERSONAL AND OTHER SERVICES INCLUDING HAIR AND BEAUTY

CRCI: RB

468

Qualifications and courses

Spa therapists need qualifications in the treatments or therapies they wish to offer and they are often trained in a combination of therapies.

One route into this career is to take the Apprenticeship in Spa Therapy. This is an Advanced Apprenticeship so candidates are required to have completed a Level 2 qualification in another subject, such as beauty therapy or nail services.

If you wish to take the NVQ Diploma in Spa Therapy (Level 3) offered by City & Guilds, you will also need to hold a Level 2 qualification in a related subject or have work experience in a spa or salon.

You could study for a BTEC First in Beauty Therapy (Level 2) or a BTEC National in Beauty Therapy (Level 3). The Vocational Training Charitable Trust (VTCT) offers an Award in Spa Treatments (Level 3) and a Diploma in Spa and Body Treatments (Level 3). A Diploma in Spa Treatments (Level 3) is also available from the International Therapy Examination Council (ITEC).

If you wish to progress into management then a Foundation degree/degree in beauty and spa management will give you an advantage. ITEC also offer a Diploma in Spa and Salon Management (Level 4).

What the work involves

Spa therapists provide various treatments which are designed to enhance appearance, reduce stress or improve wellbeing.

The treatments you offer could include facials, manicures and pedicures, massage, body treatments such as wraps, and exfoliation and specialist treatments like light therapy and lymphatic drainage.

You will be required to talk to your clients in order to discover their specific health needs and personal expectations. You will ensure that they are comfortable at all times and provide them with any necessary aftercare advice.

You will also be expected to keep the salon clean and tidy.

Type of person suited to this work

You will need a caring manner and the ability to make people feel at ease. You should be discreet and understand the role of confidentiality within the industry.

It is important that you are able to work effectively as part of a team. You should have excellent dexterity, outstanding attention to detail and good time management skills.

You will need to have strong personal hygiene and a smart appearance. A sound understanding of health and safety requirements would also prove beneficial.

Working conditions

Most of the work will be based in private treatment rooms which will be warm and clean but you may be required to complete some treatments in wet rooms.

A great deal of time will be spent standing and bending. Some products may irritate your skin, particularly if you are prone to such reactions. Most spa therapists wear a uniform.

Full-time hours are usually between 37 and 40 hours a week and often include evening and weekend work.

Future prospects

You will have the possibility of working in various beauty-related professions.

You may choose to progress to a supervisory or management post. You could decide to combine the more practical aspects with administrative work. There is also the option of becoming a trainer or lecturer.

There are numerous opportunities for overseas work, for example on a cruise ship or in a hotel.

Advantages/disadvantages

The unusual working hours may prove inconvenient.

Opportunities within this industry are varied so you will have many options regarding which environment you wish to work in.

Being on your feet all day could be tiring.

You may receive bonuses, discounted/free products and the use of spa facilities.

Money guide

Salaries vary depending on location, employer and number of hours worked.

Starting salaries for spa therapists are usually £12,000–£14,000.

With several years' experience, earnings can increase to between £15,000 and £19,000.

If you progress to become a spa manager, you can achieve £20,000–£30,000.

Related opportunities

- Beauty Consultant p454
- Beauty Therapist p455
- Nail Technician p466

Further information

Guild of Professional Beauty Therapists
www.beautyguild.com

PERSONAL AND OTHER SERVICES
INCLUDING HAIR AND BEAUTY

CRCI: RC

469

TATTOOIST

Qualifications and courses

It is usual to become a tattooist through an apprenticeship which can last between 1 and 3 years. The only way to do this is by approaching a working tattoo artist and applying for the position. There are no formal qualifications required to become a tattooist's apprentice. It is advisable to compile a portfolio of any artwork and experience you have to present to any future employers.

Over time, greater responsibility will be granted, until you can tattoo unsupervised. You will then become a trainee tattooist. It can take about five years to become fully competent and able to carry out the various styles of tattooing.

Once your teacher deems you ready, a licence to practice must be obtained from your local Environmental Health Department and then you will be qualified to work as a professional tattooist. Working without a licence incurs a heavy penalty.

You can get details of registered tattooists from the Tattoo Club of Great Britain or from the Environmental Health Department of your local council.

Some Environmental Health Departments also offer short training courses for experienced and practising tattooists.

What the work involves

Tattooists, also referred to as body artists, apply permanent images onto their clients' bodies. They use needles and ink to draw images, symbols or words onto the skin.

As a tattooist you will have to advise clients on suitable tattoos, ensuring that the chosen design is exactly what the client wants and that they understand the permanent nature of a tattoo.

You will create the tattoo either by drawing freehand on the customer's skin or by using a transfer.

When not tattooing, you will clean and sterilise tattoo equipment and work areas, keeping up to date with the latest health and safety procedures and devise new and interesting designs.

Type of person suited to this work

A tattooist ought to possess a flair for design, raw talent as an artist and an excellent attention to detail.

You must have good hand–eye coordination, a steady hand and feel comfortable using different equipment depending on the type of tattoo. Tattooists should also possess the ability to communicate with customers both in the consultation process and during the tattoo itself.

Owing to strict regulation, tattooists must maintain high standards of cleanliness and constant awareness of the need for hygiene and an up-to-date knowledge of health and safety.

Working conditions

You will generally work 5 or 6 days a week, including Saturdays. Studio hours are usually 9am to 5pm, but you may schedule your work into short sessions during the day because of the level of concentration and attention to detail you need.

Tattoo artists usually work from a tattoo studio, which must be registered by the local Environmental Health Department.

Tattoo studios are fitted out with books of designs, all the hygiene equipment necessary and dedicated work and preparation spaces, whilst tattooists must provide their own inking equipment.

Future prospects

Once a subject of taboo, the alternative culture of tattoos has become more mainstream and tattooing is increasingly regulated, creative and popular.

You could work as a tattooist in tattoo studios around the UK. Some of these are part of beauty salons offering other similar services such as body piercing.

Once you have experience as a tattooist you could become self-employed.

Advantages/disadvantages

The job is very artistic and poses new challenges of creation with each customer.

As a tattooist you will come into contact with many different people; some of these may be difficult to deal with.

Hours are long and mistakes are out of the question, so working as a tattooist can be mentally exhausting.

Money guide

Many tattoo artists are self-employed and renumeration varies widely depending on the amount of trade they receive. Summer months are traditionally the busiest.

As an apprentice you are likely to work for free and some tattoo studios require apprentices to pay for their training. Apprentices must also provide their own equipment and sterilising kit.

A trainee tattooist can earn around £12,000 a year.

An experienced tattooist can earn between £15,000 and £30,000.

A tattoo artist owning his or her own business and employing others could earn in excess of £50,000 although again, this varies considerably.

Related opportunities

- Cartoonist p169
- Computer Games Designer p151
- Fine Artist/Sculptor p172
- Graphic Designer p175

Further information

Arts Council England
www.artscouncil.org.uk

Tattoo Club of Great Britain
www.tattoo.co.uk

Qualifications and courses

There are no set entry requirements for this career. A background in hospitality, event planning, design, catering or marketing is useful, especially if you want to work for a large events company. Degrees, Foundation degrees and HNDs in events or hospitality management may help you.

An alternative way to start a career in the industry is to work your way up from an administrative position in a wedding planning or event management company then progress as your experience grows.

Those with proof of more than 3 years' business trading, three client references and a satisfactory quality inspection can become members of the National Association of Professional Wedding Services which offers an Advanced Certification in Wedding Design and Management.

The UK Alliance of Wedding Planners' 2-day course with an optional work placement may also be helpful.

What the work involves

Wedding planners organise ceremonies, receptions and other events to suit a client's plans and budget. You will negotiate prices, book and confirm with all suppliers and keep a detailed record of costs. For example you will liaise with florists, caterers, photographers, musicians, venues and hair stylists.

You will help come up with creative ideas and themes, as well as advise the couple on wedding customs and etiquette. You will also help organise transport, stag and hen weekends, wedding attire and accommodation for out-of-town guests.

Type of person suited to this work

You need to be enthusiastic and approachable. You should be a good listener and always take into account your client's ideas and wishes. You will also need the initiative and creativity to develop these dreams into a reality. A good sense of style and attention to detail is essential.

It's important to have both financial and crisis management skills. It's your job to ensure the wedding stays within budget and runs smoothly so you should be confident and effective in negotiations.

In order to keep track of multiple clients and the variety of tasks involved you must possess strong organisational skills and be adept at multi-tasking.

You will have to be able to work with sensitivity if your client's wishes are unrealistic or not feasible for their budget and be able to offer suitable alternatives.

Working conditions

It is common to work 12-hour days, especially in the period leading up to the wedding. Although you can generally plan your own hours you will most likely need to meet your clients during evenings and weekends.

The busiest months for weddings are February, June and December. During peak wedding season you will often work at weekends, attending clients' weddings to ensure the day runs smoothly.

You could work from home or out of an office but most of your time will be spent visiting venues, suppliers and clients. A driving licence is essential.

Future prospects

Thanks to many Hollywood films profiling wedding planners the market is growing. You might work for a hotel or event-management company and start out temping as an assistant. You could also offer to plan weddings for friends, helping you to build up a portfolio.

Most wedding planners are self-employed. Your success will depend on your reputation and how well you market yourself.

You could choose to specialise in destination weddings or work overseas.

Advantages/disadvantages

This is a glamorous and creative role.

It's rewarding when you make a bride and groom's dream wedding come true.

You will be under a lot of pressure to deliver perfection.

Money guide

If you work for a wedding and events planning company you can earn between £16,000 and £20,000 a year starting out.

With experience this can rise to £25,000–£40,000.

If you're freelance you can charge either a percentage of the total cost of the wedding, an hourly rate or a flat fee.

Your salary will be dependent on how many weddings you organise a year.

Related opportunities

- Entertainment Manager p382
- Events and Exhibition Organiser p404
- Image Consultant p483

Further information

National Association of Professional Wedding Services
www.theweddingassociation.co.uk

UK Alliance of Wedding Planners
www.ukawp.com

PERSONAL AND OTHER SERVICES INCLUDING HAIR AND BEAUTY

CRCI: O

Qualifications and courses

There are no formal qualifications needed for this job, although basic numeracy skills for calculating prices are useful. Most training is done on the job by a senior window cleaner. Health and safety issues will need to be understood.

If you are using ropes and access equipment you will need to be insured. The Industrial Rope Access Trade Association offers rope Access courses.

The British Window Cleaning Academy offers courses covering window cleaning skills, water-fed pole instruction and health and safety. The NVQ at Level 2 in Cleaning and Support Services may be helpful.

With some experience you might want to study for NVQs in Team Leading or First Line Management at Levels 3 and 4.

What the work involves

You will be cleaning windows and other glass surfaces in private and public buildings, using detergents.

You will be using ladders to reach high windows or platforms and ropes for very tall office buildings. Recently the use of water pumping poles has reduced the use of ladders for health and safety reasons.

Customers may ask you to complete other tasks, alongside cleaning their windows. This could involve clearing gutters and cleaning paintwork or UPVC window frames.

If you are self-employed you might need to organise paperwork and collect payments.

Type of person suited to this work

Practical skills are very important for this job as you will be working at heights and with equipment. Having a good level of fitness will help with lifting and carrying heavy equipment.

You need to be aware of health and safety issues and you will have to learn to safely use power-operated lifting equipment for high level cleaning.

It is important to respect your customers' privacy especially when cleaning windows at people's homes.

Good communication skills are needed for dealing with customers, in particular if you want to run your own business. Running your own business will also require you to be organised, as you will have to plan your own work to schedule. You must also be able to keep your accounts in order, which requires completing paperwork. In order to maintain a successful business, you must be capable of advertising your services, which will require you to be persuasive.

Working conditions

The hours you work will vary greatly. You may be contracted to work about 40 hours a week, in daylight hours, or if self-employed, you can choose which jobs you take.

Be prepared to work in all weathers and at great heights. It is useful to have a driving licence and access to your own vehicle.

Future prospects

There are jobs available across the UK, with a great demand in towns and cities. Smaller rural areas also require window cleaners, so job prospects are good.

Health and safety regulations have been introduced to help prevent accidents at great heights.

If you have access to stabilising equipment it can help you win large contracts and more work.

Advantages/disadvantages

You may have to work in poor weather conditions or at great heights which could be demanding.

You will get to meet all types of people and establish contacts.

You can set up and run your own business.

Money guide

If you are employed by a contract cleaning company, you could earn between £15,000 and £20,000.

If you are a self-employed window cleaner your earnings will depend on how many customers you have and your reputation. With a good reputation you could earn over £20,000.

Related opportunities

- Car Valet p456
- Caretaker p457
- Pest Control Technician p467

Further information

Asset Skills
www.assetskills.org

Federation for Window Cleaners
www.f-w-c.co.uk

Retail, Sales and Customer Services

Jobs in this sector are suited to those of you who are very good at communicating with others and are interested in making your customers happy. Maybe you are interested in working with food and want to give your customers high quality, fresh produce. Your interest may lie in fashion retail and you could spend your time providing style advice. You should also be commercially minded and think about how your work relates to the success of the company you work for. Jobs in this sector also involve maintaining standards such as safety and quality to ensure guidelines are met, so a practical outlook can be useful.

The jobs featured in this section are listed below. For similar jobs to the ones covered in this section turn to *Administration, Business, Office and Financial Services* on page 15.

ANTIQUES DEALER

ENTRY
LEVEL 1

Qualifications and courses

No formal qualifications are needed, but enthusiasm and sales skills are useful. GCSEs/S grades (A*–C/1–3) in art, design and history are an advantage.

Entry is normally through work experience or as a trainee. Many auction houses will employ people as general workers or assistants. An NVQ/SVQ in Retail Operations can be an advantage. Auctioneers Sotheby's, Christie's and Bonhams take on graduate trainees, from a relevant degree such as history or art.

The University of Central Lancashire offers a Master's degree by distance learning in Antiques. There are also some privately-run courses available from institutions such as Christie's and Sotheby's. Information and advice about careers in antiques dealing and current vacancies with dealers may be available from the British Antique Dealers Association (BADA) or the Association of Art and Antique Dealers (LAPADA).

What the work involves

You will be buying and selling things such as furniture, clocks, jewellery and pictures, which are either old or which people collect. You will go to auctions and fairs to buy things to sell in shops, markets or antique salerooms.

You will need to develop specialist knowledge so that you can assess the age of an object, value and whether it will sell at a profit.

You will advise customers on the value of their antiques.

Type of person suited to this work

You should be fascinated by antiques and working out where they come from and what they are worth.

You will need to be interested in history and dedicated enough to travel and visit fairs and auctions all over the country, and possibly abroad, searching out bargains and objects to sell. You will need to develop good specialist knowledge, know what is likely to be popular and sell quickly at a profit.

Antiques do not have fixed prices, so you will need to be able to make quick decisions and cope with the stress of buying things at auction. You will need to have good all round business skills.

Working conditions

You will work in a shop, in an antiques saleroom or on a market stall. You could be outside in all weathers and will probably have to travel to different markets.

You could be dealing with heavy objects like furniture or dusty and dirty things such as clothes and books.

Your working hours will vary a lot. Shops and stalls will be open at fixed times and on public holidays, and you could be visiting auctions or customers at any time.

Future prospects

Most antique dealers are self-employed or work in a family business, but you could start in an auction house or as a sales assistant in a larger shop.

Once you have developed contacts and knowledge of antiques and their value, you could work for yourself, perhaps starting with a market stall and expanding your business from there.

Most dealers specialise in a particular period of history or type of antique.

Advantages/disadvantages

You will be working with things that you love and have the thrill of finding bargains or rare items.

It can be a very uncertain business and prices will rise and fall as things go in and out of fashion. You can make a lot of money, but you can also lose a lot.

Money guide

An assistant earns around £15,000 per year.

Between £20,000 and £30,000 is usual for a dealer with a flair for the trade and considerable experience.

In excess of £50,000 is possible for successful dealers, or people with a high level of specialist knowledge.

Related opportunities

- Auctioneer p475
- Museum/Art Gallery Curator p355
- Sales/Retail Assistant p492

Further information

British Antique Dealers Association
www.bada.org

Sotheby's
www.sothebys.com

AUCTIONEER

Qualifications and courses

There are no set entry requirements, but most employers prefer candidates with good communication skills and sound GCSEs/S grades (A*–C/1–3).

You can enter the profession by working as a salesroom assistant and progressing to the position of auctioneer. If you want to go into property auctioneering, you could start out by gaining experience in valuation work. Some employers will be willing to take you on as a trainee.

The Royal Institution of Chartered Surveyors accredits some degree courses in property and valuation. You can also follow a Foundation degree in auctioneering and valuation, or a degree in the arts market (offered at Wolverhampton and Kingston universities). Sotheby's Institute of Art also offers an MA in art business.

If you want to work for an international auction house you will need a degree in a subject related to fine arts, for example, history of art. For entry onto these courses, you will need GCSEs/S grades (A*–C/1–3) and at least 2 A levels/3 H grades. Training is done on the job and you will shadow an experienced auctioneer.

What the work involves

Auctioneers sell items at auctions, getting the best market price possible for the items they're selling.

It is your responsibility to make sure the item sells for the best price, both by selling well on the day and by organising and publicising sales in advance. You will be inspecting and valuing items and coming to price agreements with the sellers, making sure that reserves are appropriate.

On auction days, you will run through the items on sale, observe customers, and take bids. You may specialise in a particular area, and could be working on anything from antiques and property to livestock and motors.

Type of person suited to this work

You will need to be good with people and communicate well, so that you can interact with customers and successfully sell goods. In addition, you should be outgoing and confident, with excellent knowledge of what you're selling.

You should have excellent observational skills and a good attention to detail; valuing objects is also a big part of the job. For this reason you also need to be able to think on your feet, and work well under pressure.

You must have shrewd business sense and a good head for figures, as much of your day will revolve around numbers.

Working conditions

You'll usually be working in an auction house, or an office or auction room within. Normal working hours are 9am–5.30pm Monday to Saturday, but be prepared to carry out viewings and valuations during evenings and weekends.

A driving licence is useful as travel may be necessary, for example if you're selling the contents of a large house clearing.

You may also sell livestock and motors outdoors.

Future prospects

Career development relies on building up a list of contacts, and working towards moving to larger more prestigious auction houses.

You may want to become self-employed, or work towards a management position or partnership.

You may also have the chance to travel, as some auction houses have offices abroad.

Advantages/disadvantages

This work is stimulating and challenging, and especially rewarding if you choose to work with items or goods you have a genuine interest in.

Every day will be different, and you will constantly be interacting and communicating with people.

It can be tiring work, and much of the day will be spent on your feet. As the person leading an auction, you have to be 100% alert all the time.

Money guide

Starting salaries for trainees can be between £18,500 and £20,000 a year.

As you gain experience, this may rise to between £30,000 and £40,000.

If you become a business partner, you might earn over £60,000.

Related opportunities

- Antiques Dealer p474
- Chartered Surveyor p82
- Rural Property/Practice Surveyor p117

Further information

Livestock Auctioneers' Association Limited
www.laa.co.uk

National Association of Valuers and Auctioneers
www.nava.org.uk

National Federation of Property Professionals
www.nfopp.co.uk

RETAIL, SALES AND CUSTOMER SERVICES

CRCI: SB

475

Qualifications and courses

There are no formal qualifications to enter this work, but most employers look for GCSEs/S grades (A*–C/1–3) in English and maths. A degree in English or a degree/HND/Foundation degree in retail, business management or retail marketing can also be an advantage.

Relevant FE courses include NVQs/SVQs in Retail Operations at Levels 2 and 3, Customer Service at Levels 2, 3 and 4, Visual Merchandising at Level 2 and BTEC First and National qualifications in Retail/SQA National qualifications in Retail and Distribution.

Apprenticeships/Skillseekers might be available to those aged 16–24.

What the work involves

Front of house duties often include serving customers, taking money, answering enquires, giving advice and ordering books. You might also be expected to liaise with publishers and stockists, ordering books and keeping stock information up to date.

You will be expected to undertake shop floor work which will include stock replenishment, recommending books to customers, arranging displays and keeping shelves tidy. Depending on the size and type of shop you may also be responsible for shop maintenance and undertake cleaning duties after hours.

Behind the scenes you will also have to deal with deliveries, update the stock list, repackage returns and cash up the till. You might work with local colleges or universities to make sure you have got the books needed for their courses and sometimes organise book sales and events with them.

Type of person suited to this work

You need to have a genuine interest in books and be able to keep up to date with new publications, so that you can help and advise customers.

You will need excellent communication skills for dealing with customers and sales representatives. You will work as part of a team, but should also be able to use your own initiative. It is important to remain calm and polite when the shop is busy.

Basic numeracy and ICT skills will be useful when using the tills for payments and computers for stock orders.

You should be able to use your initiative, especially when ordering stock. You should be able to identify customer demand for certain titles and order books accordingly.

Working conditions

You will be working in either a small private bookshop or in one which is part of a chain of bookshops.

You will be on your feet all day, at a till, carrying heavy books and assisting customers.

You will work 39–40 hours a week, which may include weekends and evenings on a rota basis.

Future prospects

A lot of smaller book shops have closed owing to competition from larger stores and the internet, so the majority of opportunities are with the big chains.

You can progress to a supervisor role or be in charge of a specific section of books. You can go on to management level or to work for head office.

With considerable experience and good finances you might open your own shop or choose to specialise in certain types of books such as antique or second hand.

Advantages/disadvantages

You will be using your knowledge and love of books to help other people and to keep up to date with new publications.

You could develop specialist knowledge, for example in children's books.

You will be dealing with the public, which can be rewarding but also stressful.

Money guide

Salaries vary a lot depending on the size of the shop. With large chains, you may get bonuses for high levels of sales or for meeting targets.

You can expect £12,000–£16,000 per year when you start.

With experience this can rise to £20,000 per year.

A manager of a large bookshop with specialist departments can earn between £20,000 and £40,000 per year.

Related opportunities

- Librarian/Library Assistant p354
- Publisher/Commissioning Editor p417
- Sales/Retail Assistant p492

Further information

Booksellers Association
www.booksellers.org.uk

British Shops and Stores Association Limited
www.british-shops.co.uk

Qualifications and courses

Although there are no entry requirements most employers prefer applicants to have some GCSEs, including English and maths.

Previous experience within the construction industry or retailing is beneficial, as many employers view experience and personality as being more important than academic qualifications. However, the BTEC Diploma Level 1 in Construction might be a useful qualification for this job.

You can choose to do an Apprenticeship in subjects such as business and administration, customer service, retail, team leading and management or warehousing and storage.

The Builders' Merchants Federation (BMF) offers specialist courses in areas such as central heating, bricks, mortar and bathrooms as well as a Diploma in Merchanting.

What the work involves

You will be dealing with building materials and bathroom fittings. You will keep track of stock using computer or paper systems, order new stock and take deliveries.

You will supply goods to building firms and individual builders – plumbers, electricians or plasterers – and members of the public. As part of this you will take payyments and use tills.

Assistants will work for a builders' merchant looking after the stock.

Assistants will also handle a range of building materials, take deliveries, store deliveries properly, keep the yard clean and deal with customers.

Type of person suited to this work

You will need to have a certain level of physical fitness for both of these positions, as there will be heavy lifting and carrying involved. Asthma and allergies to dust and chemicals may be a problem.

You will need solid communication skills for dealing with customers and suppliers. You should have good numeracy and computer skills and the ability to handle money and paperwork efficiently.

Customer service skills will also be useful.

Working conditions

You will work about 40 hours a week, usually on Saturdays and sometimes Sundays. You may start at about 7.30am so that builders can buy their materials on the way to their work.

You may also need to use a forklift truck and climb ladders, which could be dangerous. You will be wearing overalls and protective boots or shoes.

You could be working outside in all weathers.

Future prospects

There are job opportunities in all areas of the country, but these vary depending on the strength of the building trade. At present there are good opportunities.

The number of builders' merchants has increased with a lot of stores on out-of-town retail sites.

You can work part time, and if you work for large merchants or a chain you could become a supervisor or manager. You could also work for a supplier or as a sales representative.

Advantages/disadvantages

The work can be a great way of using your interest in building and knowledge of materials, tools and equipment.

There is a lot of paperwork involved in keeping track of the stock.

You could be starting early in the morning and working outside.

Money guide

An assistant at a builders' merchant could start on around £12,500 a year.

Once you have built on your experience and have additional responsibilities you can expect to earn up to £20,000.

Delivery van drivers can earn around £16,500 a year.

You could earn more as the manager of a department or store. Managers of large companies could earn in excess of £50,000.

Related opportunities

- Building Surveyor p77
- Sales/Retail Assistant p492
- Warehouse Worker/Manager p619

Further information

Builders' Merchants Federation
www.bmf.org.uk

RETAIL, SALES AND CUSTOMER SERVICES

CRCI: SD

BUTCHER

Qualifications and courses

There are no formal qualifications required to become a butcher and most people train on the job. Many employers will however want proof of a certain level of literacy and numeracy. They may require employees to have acquired English, maths and a science GCSE (A*–C) or even set aptitude tests. Work experience in the food and drink industry is also beneficial.

A good way to begin in this career is through an Apprenticeship scheme. Many employers provide entrants with the opportunity to work towards qualifications including food safety qualifications and NVQs/SVQs in Meat and Poultry Processing at Levels 1 and 2.

The MTC (Meat Training Council) offers a range of qualifications which include the Intermediate Certificate in Meat and Poultry, the Intermediate Certificate in Management and the Intermediate Certificate in Hazard Analysis Critical Control Points (HACCP).

You could become a member of the professional body for butchers, the Worshipful Company of Butchers, according to your qualifications.

What the work involves

You might prepare an assortment of meat and poultry products. This could involve cutting, de-boning, trimming and slicing. You could offer advice to customers about varieties of meat available and preparation techniques involved with them. Some butchers offer a delivery service.

You will take part in the everyday running of the business, visiting markets, ordering stock, taking deliveries from suppliers, organising displays and selling the products.

Butchers can also work in the wholesale area of the industry, receiving the meat from the abattoir, then preparing and storing it for sale to the retailers or wholesale customers.

Type of person suited to this work

You will have to be meticulous and practical. You will need to have a strong understanding of and a professional approach to health and hygiene. Owing to the fact you will be using sharp tools and machinery you need to be safety conscious.

You should be personable, maintaining a high level of customer service. You need to have an outstanding knowledge of the various products and cuts of meat.

You should have cash handling skills.

Working conditions

A retail butcher works in a shop environment with a chilled storage area. You will be expected to prepare meat in front of customers, using knives, cleavers and saws and will therefore be required to wear protective clothing, such as disposable gloves and an apron. Wholesale butchers also work in chilled environments and wear protective clothing.

This profession involves a great deal of standing, lifting and carrying as butchers are required to transport joints of meat.

Average working hours are between 39 and 40 a week, including Saturdays and sometimes evenings and Sundays. Work starts as early as 7am.

Future prospects

With a large number of local butchers having closed down and the ones left being small businesses, prospects are becoming somewhat limited. Supermarkets have however resurrected the idea of the meat counter over simply selling packaged meats and promotion opportunities within these chains are plentiful.

Once you have gained experience there is the option of setting up your own retail outlet. Other options include making the move into meat catering, meat hygiene, meat wholesale or meat-product manufacture.

Advantages/disadvantages

You will have a great deal of customer contact and the opportunity to share your knowledge.

The amount of time spent on your feet, heavy lifting and in cold temperatures may cause discomfort.

Money guide

On average, a butcher will earn a starting salary of around between £12,000 and £15,000 a year.

With experience, earnings will increase to between £16,000 and £22,000 a year.

A butchery manager could make up to £30,000 per year.

If an individual chose to open their own shop this may increase further.

Related opportunities

- Food Processing Operative p224
- Kitchen Assistant/Supervisor p145
- Meat Process Worker p232

Further information

Meat Hygiene Service
www.food.gov.uk/foodindustry/meat/mhservice

CALL CENTRE OPERATOR

Qualifications and courses

There are no formal entry qualifications but employers generally look for at least 5 GCSEs/S grades (A*–C/1-3) including English and maths. You can enter and train in this career with qualifications at Levels 1 or 2. Previous experience of working with the public or in a customer service role is helpful.

You could study for a BTEC Award in Introduction to Contact Centres (Level 1), a BTEC Award in Contact Centre Skills (Level 2) or a BTEC Award in Contact Centre Supervisory Skills (Level 3). City & Guilds also offer relevant qualifications such as the Certificate for Introduction to the Contact Centre (Level 1) and the Technical Certificate in Contact Centre Operations (Levels 2 and 3).

Once you have found employment in a call centre, you may wish to undertake further study to enhance your career progression prospects. City & Guilds provide the NVQ Award, Certificate and Diploma in Contact Centre Operations (Levels 1–4), the NVQ for Contact Centre Professionals (Levels 2–4) or the NVQ in Sales and Telesales (Levels 2–4).

The Chartered Institute of Marketing (CIM) offers a 1-day course in the Fundamentals of Outbound Calling.

What the work involves

You will be dealing with customers over the phone and using a computer to log details or find information. You might do telesales or telemarketing, selling, mail ordering, banking, or promoting goods and services, which could involve 'cold calling'.

You could be doing market research, asking about people's buying habits or what services they would like from a company.

You might be providing a service – receiving calls from customers who are ordering goods, making a complaint or accessing their bank accounts.

Type of person suited to this work

You should have good spoken English, with a clear voice and good hearing. You will need excellent customer service skills and you must be polite and calm when dealing with difficult callers.

For telesales or telemarketing, you will need to be motivated, persuasive and persistent. Good IT skills are also important.

You will probably work to targets and you are likely to be very busy, so you must be comfortable working under pressure and using your initiative. The ability to work successfully as part of a team is also required.

Working conditions

You will be office based, usually working 38–40 hours a week. You might work shifts which could include nights, weekends and evenings.

Call centre staff have their own workstations with a headset and computer and work as part of a team.

You will be given targets which you are expected to meet. For this reason, calls are often monitored by supervisors and staff turnover can be fairly high.

Future prospects

There has been a huge growth in call centres recently as more services are available over the phone – such as mail order and banking – and more companies are using telesales and marketing to sell their goods and services.

You could become a team leader or supervisor.

You could also work abroad or establish new contact centres.

Advantages/disadvantages

There are lots of job opportunities and flexible working hours are possible.

You could utilise your customer service and sales skills to move into related areas such as marketing or human resources.

Trying to reach sales targets can be stressful and the work can be repetitive.

Money guide

Earnings vary with employers and financial services call centres tend to pay the highest wages.

Starting salaries for call centre operators range from £12,000 to £15,500.

With increased experience, you can expect to earn £17,000–£18,000.

A team leader is likely to receive £18,000–£24,000 a year.

Those employed in a managerial role usually earn in excess of £25,000.

If you meet your targets you may receive commission on sales or bonuses which will increase your income.

Related opportunities

- Customer Services Assistant/Manager p480
- Marketing Assistant/Executive p407
- Sales/Retail Assistant p492

Further information

Institute of Customer Service
www.instituteofcustomerservice.com

Institute of Direct Marketing
www.theidm.com

RETAIL, SALES AND CUSTOMER SERVICES

CRCI: SA

479

Qualifications and courses

Assistant

You can enter this profession without any formal qualifications. However, certain employers look for at least 3 or 4 GCSEs/S grades (A*–C/1–3) including maths and English.

Progression to a senior role or entry to a customer services manager training scheme might be faster if you have at least 4 GCSEs/S grades (A*–C/1–3) or A levels/H grades.

The most important entry requirement is to have strong people skills, and any experience dealing with people, either face to face or over the phone, would be useful.

Once you secure employment, you could study for the NVQ in Customer Service (Levels 1–3) on day release.

Manager

A degree or Foundation degree can increase your chances of entry onto a management training scheme and employers usually accept any subject.

Many entrants start as a customer services assistant and progress to a role as manager, obtaining qualifications while they work. You could study for the NVQ in Customer Service (Level 4).

What the work involves

Assistant

You will be liaising with customers, either face to face or by phone and email, in order to sell products and services such as retail goods, insurance or holiday packages. You could be responsible for dealing with customer enquiries, problems or complaints.

Manager

Your role will include hiring and training customer services assistants. You will need to establish targets and implement different motivational techniques to ensure that staff reach them.

Type of person suited to this work

Assistant

You need to have good people skills and be polite and helpful. You must remain calm and patient when faced with difficult customers. You should be able to work well as part of a team and independently.

Manager

A manager needs to have excellent leadership skills and be able to motivate his or her team. Managers must also be organised, decisive and able to work under pressure.

Working conditions

You will typically work a 37-hour week, although this could be on a rota system that includes early mornings, evenings or weekends. If your company provides 24-hour assistance, you might have to work nights. There is also the opportunity to work part time.

You could spend the majority of your time dealing with customers face to face, or at a desk with a computer or telephone headset.

Future prospects

Vacancies are available throughout the UK, especially in big cities and towns. You could work in a wide range of different organisations including shops, call centres, banks, airports or tourist information centres.

Assistant

After gaining experience and further qualifications, you could progress into a role as team leader, supervisor and then manager.

Manager

You could move into a head office role or take a job with a higher salary and responsibility. You can go on to train staff or take further qualifications and work as a staff assessor.

Advantages/disadvantages

Difficult customers or problems can make the work stressful.

This job can be repetitive.

There are good prospects for promotion within this sector.

You will deal with a wide range of people.

Money guide

Bonuses or commission can increase your income.

Assistant

Starting salaries are about £12,000–£14,000.

With experience, you could earn £16,000–£19,000 a year.

Manager

Starting salaries for trainee customer services managers are typically £16,000–£23,000.

Those with experience as a manager can expect to earn £25,000–£45,000.

Senior managers who work for large organisations can achieve up to £60,000.

Related opportunities

- Receptionist p59
- Retail Manager p490
- Sales/Retail Assistant p492

Further information

Institute of Customer Service
www.instituteofcustomerservice.com

Qualifications and courses

You do not need any formal qualifications to enter this industry. However, most employers will expect a good standard of general education including English and maths. The Apprenticeship in Retail offers an ideal route into this career and is available at both Intermediate and Advanced Levels. Competition for places is fierce so good GCSEs/S grades (A*–C/1–3) would be beneficial.

People normally begin at counter assistant level and train on the job. Whilst working you will need to attain your basic food hygiene certification, followed by Hazard Analysis and Critical Control Point (HACCP) training.

It may be useful to work towards the City & Guilds Award/Certificate/Diploma in Retail Skills (Levels 1 and 2) or the Certificate/Diploma in Retail (Sales Professional) at Level 3. These qualifications have a wide selection of optional units so you can choose to specialise in relevant areas.

The Billingsgate Seafood Training School offers 1-day courses on topics such as Introduction to Fishmongering, Get into Fishmongering and Knife Skills. The City & Guilds Seafood Profile of Achievement is a 2-day course which equips candidates with skills in cutting, displays, selling techniques and quality assessment.

What the work involves

Fishmongers prepare and sell fish, offering advice to customers on how to store and cook it. They can work in various environments including shops, supermarkets and market stalls.

You will be required to provide customers with information such as how the fish was caught, the sustainability of its stock and whether it has been previously frozen.

You will buy fish from the wholesaler and prepare it for retail sales. This preparation includes removing bones, skin and scales then gutting the fish and maybe cutting it into portions.

Type of person suited to this work

You will require good hand–eye coordination as you will be using sharp knives to complete detailed jobs such as filleting and taking out small bones. You will have to carry out messy tasks such as cleaning and gutting fish.

You should be able to stand for long periods of time. You need a strong level of personal hygiene and an awareness of food safety procedures.

You will need to be personable as customer service is extremely important for this role.

Working conditions

The conditions in this industry can be cold and wet. You will be expected to spend a great deal of time on your feet, moving between the counter and storage areas.

Most fishmongers work for approximately 40 hours a week. Your working week will usually include Saturdays, with a day off during the week to compensate.

You will frequently have to work early mornings to sign for stock deliveries.

Protective clothing and footwear are required. If you suffer from skin allergies then this work may not be suitable for you.

Future prospects

Fishmongers work in many different environments including supermarkets, small local stores and mobile fish units so you may choose to move between them.

You may have the opportunity to work overseas.

Other possibilities for progression might involve supplying fishmonger stores with fresh fish or moving into other industries which require food preparation, for example working with meat.

You can also work your way up to a management position or open your own shop.

Advantages/disadvantages

You will have to work early mornings.

You will have the opportunity to be creative, both in the preparation of the fish and in providing customers with advice on how best to prepare or cook it.

Spending all day on your feet and in cold temperatures can be uncomfortable.

Money guide

Pay rates vary depending on location and employer.

Fishmongers usually have a starting salary of £11,000–£14,000.

With experience in the role, earnings increase to about £20,000 a year.

Fishmongers who are self-employed and own a shop are likely to have a higher income.

Related opportunities

- Butcher p478
- Kitchen Assistant/Supervisor p145
- Shopkeeper p494

Further information

Billingsgate Seafood Training School
www.seafoodtraining.org

Sea Fish Industry Authority
www.seafish.org

RETAIL, SALES AND CUSTOMER SERVICES

CRCI: SB

FLORIST

Qualifications and courses

There are no specific academic qualifications for this career. Candidates can either find work and train on the job or study at college prior to securing employment. Those seeking work in a florist shop should demonstrate an interest in floristry, possibly through joining a local flower arranging club or doing a course in flower arranging.

Available qualifications include the BTEC First in Floristry (Level 2), the BTEC National in Floristry (Level 3), the City & Guilds Award, Certificate and Diploma in Floristry (Levels 2 and 3) and the City & Guilds Advanced National Certificate in Floristry (Level 3). Those who are currently working at a florist shop could study for the City & Guilds Diploma in Work-based Floristry (Levels 2 and 3).

The entry requirements for these courses vary, however GCSEs/S grades (A*–C/1–3) in subjects such as English, maths and arts and crafts would be beneficial. Any other relevant experience and skills might be taken into account. Work experience in a florist shop would also be valuable.

Another option is the Apprenticeship in Floristry which is available at both Intermediate and Advanced Levels. With experience, you could study for a Foundation degree or degree in floristry.

What the work involves

Florists combine creativity with knowledge of plants and flowers to design and create floral displays. These are sold via shops and market stalls.

You will be responsible for ordering and caring for the plants and flowers, aiding customers in choosing flowers suitable for specific occasions and creating floral displays. You may also be required to deliver flowers to customers and set up displays at events.

You will be expected to handle money, complete regular stock takes and help with the day to day running of the business.

Type of person suited to this work

You will need to be extremely creative, with an understanding of shape, colour and design. As a great deal of this job is hands-on, you must be dexterous.

A strong knowledge of plants and flowers and the care required for them is essential, along with a desire to expand your knowledge. You should be patient, with good customer service skills and sensitivity to the needs of the client.

You will be expected to have brilliant telephone communication skills and the ability to work within tight deadlines. Administration and sales skills are also important.

Working conditions

Florists usually work inside in a shop environment. Those who work on a floristry stall will spend most of their time outdoors.

This job involves a great deal of standing at the work bench/counter.

Working hours usually vary between 35 and 40 hours per week, and shop opening hours are normally 9am to 5pm. Some travel may be required when making deliveries so a driving licence might be needed.

Some shops provide uniforms or aprons. This job may not be suitable for people who suffer from pollen allergies.

Future prospects

Those with experience may progress to a managerial role. Once you have the required skills, there is also the possibility of becoming self-employed and opening your own business.

Another progression option is to work as a freelance florist for a variety of businesses on a contract basis.

You could also teach floristry or become a professional demonstrator.

Advantages/disadvantages

You can combine creativity, skill and knowledge to create floral displays.

You will be on your feet for a great deal of time and those who work on florist market stalls will be outdoors in all weathers.

Every day will be different as you will work with a wide range of customers for a variety of events.

Money guide

Earnings vary depending on location and employer.

At the start of their career, a florist usually receives the National Minimum Wage. Details of the current rates are available from the Directgov website.

As you gain experience as a florist, you can expect to earn £16,000–£18,000 a year.

Those employed in a managerial role can achieve up to £25,000.

Related opportunities

- Gardener/Garden Designer p271
- Landscaper/Landscape Manager p277
- Visual Merchandiser p187

Further information

British Florist Association
www.britishfloristassociation.org

Flowers and Plants Association
www.flowers.org.uk

Qualifications and courses

While there are no set academic qualifications for this career, related experience in areas such as fashion, hair, beauty, retail or public relations is useful.

The City & Guilds Diploma in Beauty Consultancy (Level 2) or the BTEC Certificate/Diploma in Retail Beauty Consultancy (Level 2) may be a good starting point. Some entrants hold a Foundation degree, HND or degree in a subject such as beauty therapy, cosmetic sciences, business studies or sales and marketing. For HND courses you will need at least 4 GCSEs/S grades (A*–C/1–3) and for degree entry you are required to have 5 GCSEs/S grades (A*–C/1–3) and 2 A levels/H grades.

Entrants to this profession are recommended to take a course in image consultancy approved by the Federation of Image Professionals International (FIPI). Courses involve training in the 4 core areas of image consultancy: colour analysis, women's style, men's style and cosmetic application and tuition. Upon completion of this training, you can become a Registered Affiliate of FIPI.

To improve your skills and marketability, you could work towards the FIPI/City & Guilds Masters Certification Award in Image Consultancy. You are eligible to become a Master of FIPI once you hold this qualification.

What the work involves

You will advise individuals and companies on branding, impact and appearance. This can include style analysis, make-up advice, wardrobe management and personal shopping. Part of your job might involve speaking on the radio as a way of promoting your business.

When working with private clients you will discuss fabrics, styles, patterns and colours that will suit your client's body shape, hair and eye colour and skin tone.

When working with corporate clients you may advise on body language, etiquette, first impressions and branding. You could also coach executives and run workshops.

Type of person suited to this work

You must be aware of current fashion trends, possess a good sense of style and a great eye for colour and detail. Creativity and communication skills are essential in order to inspire clients to believe in their image. You want clients to trust you so you should be easy to talk to, uplifting and sensitive.

Self-motivation is important when running your own business. You should be able to budget well and to organise your time effectively.

The ability to network and market your brand is essential.

Working conditions

You can choose to work from home or out of a studio. Your hours will vary depending on how many clients you see and could include evenings and weekends.

You will need to travel at times to a client's home or company so a driving licence would be useful.

You should dress smartly when meeting clients.

Future prospects

You could be an independent image consultant or work for an organisation such as First Impressions who will provide you with business support.

With experience, you can progress from working solely with private clients to corporate work.

You might specialise in one area, such as working with brides. You could also move into life coaching, retail or hairdressing. Opportunities to work abroad are available.

Advantages/disadvantages

It is rewarding to help clients with low self-esteem gain confidence in their personal or professional brand.

The job can be glamorous as you may work with well-known people.

Setting up your own business and building up a client base can be difficult.

You might need to supplement your income when first starting out.

Money guide

Whilst establishing your business, you could earn between £10,000 and £15,000 per year.

Once you gain experience and a regular client base, you may earn up to £30,000.

If you work in the corporate sector you could earn £40,000+

As most image consultants are self-employed, your income will depend on your location, skills and how well you market yourself.

You could charge anywhere between £50 and £350 per session.

Related opportunities

- Beauty Consultant p454
- Fashion Designer/Milliner p171
- Make-up Artist p441

Further information

Federation of Image Professionals International
www.tfic.org.uk

Hairdressing and Beauty Industry Authority
www.habia.org

Skillsmart Retail
www.skillsmartretail.com

RETAIL, SALES AND CUSTOMER SERVICES

CRCI: SC

483

JEWELLER

Qualifications and courses

Although there are no specific entry requirements, many employers will expect GCSEs/S grades (A*–C/1–3), including English, maths, art or design and technology. Previous work experience in a retail or customer services role would be beneficial.

Candidates looking to take relevant qualifications could consider the City & Guilds Award/Certificate in Retail Principles (Level 2), the City & Guilds Award/Certificate/Diploma in Retail Skills (Levels 1 and 2) or the City & Guilds Certificate/Diploma in Retail (Sales Professional) at Level 3.

The Apprenticeship in Retail, available at both Intermediate and Advanced Levels, may equip you with relevant skills to work as a retail jeweller.

The National Association of Goldsmiths (NAG) offers the Professional Jewellers' Diploma (JET 1 & 2), an 18-month course which covers topics such as design, manufacture, hallmarking, gemstones, silverware, horology, antiques, legal matters, repair handling, selling techniques and window displays.

Senior staff, managers and business owners may wish to extend their knowledge by studying for the NAG Business Development Diploma (JET Pro).

What the work involves

Retail jewellers work in shops, selling jewellery and sometimes watches, clocks and silverware to customers. Other services they offer might include valuation, alteration and repair.

You will advise customers on the available products and help them to choose an appropriate item. You will package the customer's goods and process their payment.

As part of the day to day running of the shop, you will arrange window displays, ensure that the shop is presentable and carry out stock control procedures.

You may work for a company which specialises in selling a particular gemstone, such as diamonds. You could focus on one area, for example casting or enamelling, or learn a variety of techniques.

Type of person suited to this work

An interest in precious metal, gemstones, jewellery or fashion is essential.

As you will be interacting with customers, you need excellent communication skills, with a polite and friendly manner. You should be comfortable working independently and as part of a team.

You must be extremely trustworthy and conscious of security procedures when handling valuable goods. Numeracy skills are important for processing payments and dealing with money.

If your role involves carrying out repairs or alterations, you should have practical skills, patience and good attention to detail.

Working conditions

Retail jewellers work indoors in shops and spend the majority of the day standing up.

You will work 37 to 40 hours per week including weekends. Sometimes you may be required to work overtime during evenings and bank holidays. Part-time work is often available.

You will be expected to look smart and some stores may provide a uniform.

Future prospects

There are opportunities to work for independent jewellers or large high street chains. You could progress to become a supervisor, assistant manager or even a manager.

Specialist skills can improve your prospects, so learning how to value or alter items may lead to higher paid roles.

With extensive experience, you could open your own jewellery shop.

Advantages/disadvantages

You will have the opportunity to meet a wide range of people and help them choose jewellery for special occasions.

Working on your feet all day can be demanding and tiring.

Money guide

Your starting salary could range from the National Minimum Wage up to £16,000.

With experience and progression to a managerial level, you can expect to earn £25,000–£30,000.

Those employed by luxury jewellery retailers in the most senior positions can achieve up to £60,000.

Your income will be increased if you earn commission for your sales.

Related opportunities

- Gold/Silversmith/Engraver p174
- Jewellery Designer p178
- Sales/Retail Assistant p492

Further information

British Jewellers' Association
www.bja.org.uk

The Goldsmiths' Company
www.thegoldsmiths.co.uk

Qualifications and courses

There are no formal entry requirements but you will need to have basic maths and English skills. Your personality and ability as a salesperson are the most important attributes. Any previous experience working in a retail or customer service role would be useful.

Most of the training is done on the job, learning from more experienced market traders. Markets have their own culture and jargon which your employer will teach you.

There are some short courses you can take, usually run by the local authority, and the National Market Traders Federation (NMTF) can give advice. Small business advice services provide short courses on starting or running your own business which you could take.

If you are selling things that you have made, you will probably need to do a specialist course in the relevant craft, for example jewellery making or a fashion course at university.

To become a market trader you must be 17 or 18 years old and you are likely to need a driving licence, a vehicle/van and public liability insurance. The NMTF can provide appropriate insurance. You will also need to apply for a market licence and a pitch from your local authority.

What the work involves

Market traders buy goods from a wholesaler or manufacturer and then sell them from a market stall which they rent in an open-air or covered market. You might sell things you have made yourself at specialist craft markets.

You will be dealing with customers, encouraging them to buy items on your stall, weighing and wrapping goods, and taking money and possibly cheques, credit and debit cards.

As well as setting up the stall in the morning, arranging your things and keeping the stall clean and tidy, you will also pack up and clear away in the evenings.

Type of person suited to this work

You will need to be friendly, outgoing and enjoy working with the public in an informal way, persuading them to buy your goods.

Market traders have to be fit and active to transport their goods, be on their feet all day and then pack up when the market closes.

When you are buying goods, you need to know what will sell and negotiate a good price. If you make your own products, you should be creative and able to produce attractive items.

You must have good numeracy and business skills for dealing with money and, if you are self-employed, doing your accounts. You should also be self-motivated and hardworking.

Working conditions

You will probably have a very early start and work from about 5am to 6pm. You will usually work Saturdays and often Sundays.

You could work on your own or with a few other people. You might work at the same market every day or move round to several different markets during the week. You will work outdoors in all weather conditions.

You might have to travel to a wholesale supplier to buy your goods and transport them to your stall so a driving licence is essential.

Future prospects

It can be hard to do well with a market stall: there is a lot of competition and you will need good products.

At craft markets, it can be difficult to sell things at a competitive price.

Most market traders are self-employed and you could expand by taking on staff to run extra stalls or opening a shop.

Advantages/disadvantages

You will be your own boss, working outside in an active, practical job with lots of contact with the public.

The hours can be long and strenuous.

Money guide

When starting your career as an employee on a market stall, you are likely to earn the National Minimum Wage.

As an experienced market trader who runs a stall several days a week, your earnings can range from £12,000 up to £26,000 a year.

Market traders who sell specialist goods tend to have a higher income.

The most successful traders can achieve £30,000–£50,000 a year.

You will be required to pay for your stall rent, stock and vehicle out of your income.

Related opportunities

- Customer Services Assistant/Manager p480
- Sales/Retail Assistant p492
- Shopkeeper p494

Further information

British Shops and Stores Association Limited
www.british-shops.co.uk

National Market Traders' Federation
www.nmtf.co.uk

RETAIL, SALES AND CUSTOMER SERVICES

CRCI: SB

485

Qualifications and courses

To qualify as an official meat inspector, you are required to hold the Royal Society for Public Health (RSPH)'s Level 2 Certificate for Proficiency in Poultry Meat Inspection and the Level 4 Certificate for Proficiency in Meat Inspection. For entry to these qualifications you will need to have at least 5 GCSEs/S grades (A*–C/1–3) including English and either maths or a science. In order to complete the RSPH courses, you need access to practical work placements.

An NVQ in Food Manufacture Meat and Poultry Processing Skills (Levels 1–3) is available and can equip you with relevant skills and knowledge for this profession.

The RSPH also provides a Level 3 Award in Food Safety Supervision for Manufacturing and a Level 4 Award in Food Safety Management for Manufacturing.

The Apprenticeship in Food and Drink is available at Intermediate, Advanced and Higher Levels and involves both on-the-job and off-the-job training to develop the required technical and practical skills.

What the work involves

Meat hygiene inspectors visit slaughterhouses and meat stores to check that meat is being processed and produced safely and hygienically, following relevant laws and regulations.

You will check that live animals and poultry are healthy and disease free, and do post mortems on diseased carcasses. You will check that animals are cared for and transported safely, that meat plants and deliveries are run safely and hygienically, and that unwanted meat or carcasses are destroyed properly.

You will write detailed reports and make sure that any action you have recommended is carried out quickly and to the right standards.

Type of person suited to this work

You will be dealing with people in lots of different organisations and at all levels, so you will need to be able to establish good working relationships and deal with problems calmly.

You must have strong written and communication skills, good attention to detail and the ability to understand and apply laws and regulations.

It is a fairly active job so you will need to be fit and healthy, practical and good with your hands.

Working conditions

You will spend most of your time travelling to farms and processing plants so a driving licence is usually required.

You will be wearing protective clothing, using tools and equipment and handling heavy meat carcasses.

Slaughterhouses can be cold, noisy and smell strongly, and on farms you will be working outdoors in all weathers.

Meat inspectors usually work normal office hours but might need to work evenings, weekends and at short notice if there is a hygiene emergency.

Future prospects

Most meat inspectors work for the Meat Hygiene Service which is part of the government's Food Standards Agency. Others work for companies producing or selling food and meat products.

You will need experience in the industry before you can become an inspector. You can then progress to be a supervisor or manager for the Meat Hygiene Service or go into management in a large food company.

Advantages/disadvantages

You need to be flexible with your working hours as you may be asked to respond to an emergency at any time.

You will feel satisfied that you are doing an important job in ensuring that food standards are met and the meat is safe for the public.

Money guide

You can expect to earn £16,000–£17,000 per year as a trainee inspector.

Once you have qualified and gained experience in the role, your salary is likely to be £20,000–£25,000.

Those employed as a senior meat inspector can earn between £25,500 and £32,300.

Related opportunities

- Butcher p478
- Health and Safety Adviser p41
- Trading Standards Officer p496

Further information

Food Standards Agency
www.foodstandards.gov.uk

Meat Hygiene Service
www.food.gov.uk/foodindustry/meat/mhservice

MERCHANDISER

Qualifications and courses

Competition for entry to this career is fairly high so most entrants have a degree, Foundation degree or HND. Larger companies will accept degrees in any subjects, although retail management, marketing, business studies, economics or maths would be useful. Entry requirements for a degree are usually 5 GCSEs/S grades (A*–C/1–3) including English and maths and 2–3 A levels/H grades.

The London College of Fashion offers a 2-year Foundation degree in Fashion Buying and Merchandising or a 15-week Postgraduate Certificate in Fashion: Buying and Merchandising.

Those aged 16–24 may gain entry to a trainee post through a relevant Apprenticeship, for example in Purchasing and Supply Management. However, competition for a position would be very high and you would usually need retail experience.

NVQs in Supply Chain Management (Levels 2–5) and an ABC Diploma in Buying and Merchandising for Fashion Retail (Level 4) are also available and may prove beneficial.

Merchandisers are trained on the job and can work towards professional qualifications from the Chartered Institute of Purchasing and Supply (CIPS) or the Chartered Institute of Marketing (CIM).

What the work involves

You will ensure that stores are stocked with products at the right quantity and price.

You will work with retail buyers who choose different lines and then calculate the quantities of products required and the amount of money to be spent. It will be your responsibility to decide upon the selling prices of goods and any special offers.

You will put together budgets and sales targets, analyse sales trends, negotiate with suppliers and ensure that goods are displayed and presented in an attractive way that is consistent throughout the company.

Type of person suited to this work

You will need to be interested in your product and in predicting what will sell and how best to display it. Merchandisers must be creative and self-motivated, with initiative and confidence, because they make decisions involving large amounts of money and have to present their ideas to managers and staff.

You should be able to work well in a team and deal with people at all levels, for example when negotiating prices and arranging deliveries. The job involves analysing statistics and sales figures and working under pressure to meet targets and deadlines.

Working conditions

You will mainly be based in an office in a large store or in a head office, and you will probably visit other stores in your region.

You will also travel to suppliers and manufacturers, possibly staying away from home regularly. It is necessary to have a driving licence.

You will probably work normal office hours but you might have to work much longer at busy times.

Future prospects

Most opportunities are in the south-east of England and big cities such as London.

You will usually start as an allocator, distributor or merchandise administrative assistant and advance to a role as an assistant merchandiser and then to merchandiser. In a large company, you could progress to a role as senior merchandiser and then possibly manager or director.

Progression depends on the talent of the individual. After gaining experience, you could become self-employed and work as a retail consultant, or you could move into a related role such as a business analyst.

Advantages/disadvantages

This job can be stressful as you will be making decisions which will directly affect the image of your company and what the public can buy.

Keeping your finger on the pulse of fashion and future trends is exciting.

Money guide

Salaries depend on the size and location of the employer, and are typically higher in high street chains.

Starting salaries for assistant merchandisers are usually £18,000–£20,000.

With experience, your earnings can increase to between £20,000 and £40,000.

A senior merchandiser is likely to receive a salary of £45,000 to £65,000.

Those employed in the most senior positions, as a head or director of merchandising, can achieve up to £85,000.

Related opportunities

- Purchasing/Procurement Manager p609
- Retail Buyer p489
- Retail Manager p490

Further information

British Shops and Stores Association Limited
www.british-shops.co.uk

Chartered Institute of Marketing
www.cim.co.uk

RETAIL, SALES AND CUSTOMER SERVICES

CRCI: SB

POST OFFICE CLERK

Qualifications and courses

There are no set requirements for this role. Most people enter directly into employment. Training is done on the job and involves 2 weeks in a training centre followed by 2 supervised weeks at the counter.

Despite the lack of formal academic entry requirements it would be preferable to have achieved some GCSEs/S grades at A*–C/1–3, particularly in English and maths. A Higher Diploma may also be a valid qualification as this offers a mixture of academic and work related study.

An aptitude for languages would also be beneficial.

Any experience of working in a customer service industry would be advantageous, as would experience of handling money. This experience might involve working in a shop as a sales assistant, working in a restaurant as a waiter/waitress or maybe as an assistant in a launderette.

What the work involves

Post office clerks provide customers with a variety of postal services along with banking services, bill payment, lottery sales, passport applications and offering advice to customers on these services.

Tasks you will complete on a daily basis include sending important and expensive mail, selling stamps, weighing, measuring and mailing letters and parcels and dispatching mail abroad.

You might also be required to complete administrative work such as keeping accounts.

Type of person suited to this work

A post office clerk should be able to work within a team and without supervision. You should have excellent communication skills, being both polite and helpful with the ability to adjust to the needs of each client.

You should have a certain level of numeracy and be able to handle money with confidence and accuracy. You will be able to cope under pressure.

You should have an interest in the numerous services you will be offering along with a willingness to learn about the various forms that clients may require information on. You should have a keen eye for detail and the ability to sustain concentration.

Working conditions

If you work for a sub-post office you might be working in a newsagent, stationer or village shop. WH Smith has opened franchise Post Offices in many of its high street stores. You will be working mainly at a counter but could also do some behind the scenes work in an office environment.

You may be required to wear a uniform. The job will probably involve some lifting of heavy parcels.

You will usually work between 35 and 36 hours per week, Monday to Friday and occasionally Saturday mornings. Part-time and flexible working hours may be arranged.

Future prospects

You could progress to the role of postmaster or training officer.

Experienced post office clerks may have the opportunity to work on the post office helpline. Within this role you would answer any queries customers or sub-postmasters/mistresses had regarding the products and services that the Post Office Ltd offers.

The skills you acquire in this role stand you in good stead to move on to careers within other industries such as banking.

Advantages/disadvantages

You may, at times, find this role stressful particularly when the post office is especially busy.

You might be able to work flexible hours which suit you.

There may be some heavy lifting involved.

Money guide

The rate of pay will vary depending on the location and the employer.

Post office clerks generally start on a salary of around £13,000. After experience this may increase to £18,000 a year.

A promotion to the role of postmaster or training officer would result in a pay increase. Post Office managers can earn around £24,000.

Related opportunities

- Accounting Technician and Accounts/Finance Clerk p18
- Bank Cashier/Customer Adviser p23
- Customer Services Assistant/Manager p480

Further information

Royal Mail
www.royalmail.com

Royal Mail Group
www2.royalmailgroup.com

Skillsmart Retail
www.skillsmartretail.com

RETAIL, SALES AND CUSTOMER SERVICES

CRCI: SA

488

RETAIL BUYER

Qualifications and courses

Entry is usually by degree, though an HND or equivalent can also be acceptable. Useful subjects include business, management, purchasing, logistics and marketing. Some specialist degrees are available in fashion buying.

The minimum entry requirements for a degree course are normally 2 A levels or equivalent. Entry into retail fashion requires a relevant qualification. It is possible to take a 2-year Foundation degree in Fashion Buying and Merchandising at The London College of Fashion. An Apprenticeship in Retail is also available.

Retail buyers are sometimes required to study for the professional qualifications of the Chartered Institute of Purchasing and Supply (CIPS). CIPS offers a Certificate and Advanced Certificate for people employed in purchasing at a clerical level. Entrants with an HND or degree study towards the CIPS Graduate Diploma. CIPS-accredited degrees in purchasing or business are available at some institutions, and give exemption from part or all of the Graduate Diploma.

People employed in buying can work towards NVQs at Levels 2–5 in Supply Chain Management and the Level 4 Diploma in Buying and Merchandising for Fashion Retail. Some companies offer their own graduate training schemes, but only take on a few candidates each year.

What the work involves

You will probably work in the merchandising and marketing team of a large retail company, looking for products which fit the company image and will appeal to its customers. You will be responsible for reviewing current stock and sourcing new stock to ensure the products sold by your company remain competitive.

You will visit manufacturers and suppliers to negotiate prices and decide on quantities and colours. You will also check on the quality of the products.

You will help to predict and set trends. This could involve analysing sales figures and researching competitors to see what customers are buying and why.

Type of person suited to this work

You will need to be confident and decisive because you will be dealing with large budgets. You will need to be assertive with good communication skills to negotiate prices and make presentations to staff.

Numerical skills are important as you will need to be able to analyse figures and use them to set prices and targets and check stock levels.

You should be creative, well organised and good at planning ahead, and have an eye for detail.

Working conditions

You will be office based but spend a lot of time visiting suppliers and manufacturers in this country and abroad, so will probably have to spend time away from home.

You will work standard hours but will need to work late at busy times and to meet deadlines.

Future prospects

There are job opportunities all over the country but most will be in London and the south-east of England.

In a small company there may not be much chance of promotion, but in a larger company prospects are good. You could progress to senior retail buyer, trading manager or buying controller.

It is possible to work as a buyer in other areas, including manufacturing, the civil service and local government.

Advantages/disadvantages

This can be an exciting job and the decisions you make will affect what the public can buy and the image of the stores.

You will have a lot of responsibility and tight deadlines which can be very stressful.

Money guide

Junior retail buyers typically earn between £18,000 and £25,000 a year.

Experienced buyers can earn between £35,000 and £60,000 a year.

Senior buyers can earn between £55,000 and £70,000, more if working for large organisations with multiple retail outlets.

Salaries will vary depending on the size and location of the company you work for and your buying specialism.

Related opportunities

- Marketing Assistant/Executive p407
- Purchasing/Procurement Manager p609
- Retail Manager p490

Further information

British Shops and Stores Association Limited
www.british-shops.co.uk

Chartered Institute of Marketing
www.cim.co.uk

Chartered Institute of Purchasing & Supply
www.cips.org

RETAIL, SALES AND CUSTOMER SERVICES

CRCI: SB

Qualifications and courses

There are no set requirements but many stores will require 5 GCSEs/S grades (A*–C/1–3) including maths and English. Previous experience of working in retail is important.

You may pursue an Edexcel BTEC Certificate in Retail or a Foundation degree or degree in retail management. Management degrees are offered by universities across the country. Advanced Apprenticeships in Retail Management are also available.

Many retailers offer graduate trainee management schemes and if you have a suitable degree you could pursue this fast-track option.

NVQs/SVQs are available in Retail Operations at Levels 2 and 3. Other qualifications include BTEC Retail qualifications at Levels 2 and 3 and the City & Guilds Higher Professional Diploma in Retail Management at Level 4.

What the work involves

Unlike a shopkeeper who owns the store and deals with manufacturers, you will be running the shop on a day-to-day basis. This could be a small or a large department store, chain, independent store or a supermarket. Managers recruit, train and supervise staff, encouraging them to develop their skills and meet targets.

You will monitor sales looking at ways of improving them and oversee supplies by checking stock, placing orders and making sure you do not run out or over-order.

The store manager has overall responsibility for everything that happens in the shop and must deal with any problems or complaints.

Type of person suited to this work

As you could be dealing with customers and complaints you will need excellent negotiation skills. You will also need to motivate, train and sometimes discipline staff.

You should be energetic, able to take responsibility and make quick decisions. You will need an understanding of business and of relevant laws.

You should be able to analyse sales figures and have creative ideas for selling and promoting goods to improve profits. You will have to be organised whilst working to targets and deadlines.

Working conditions

Many stores are open long hours, at weekends and overnight, so you will probably have to work shifts, usually over 5 days.

You will be on your feet a lot as well as doing administration and paperwork.

You may be based in one store, or be visiting several that you have responsibility for.

Future prospects

There are many opportunities but trainee posts with large chains can be very competitive. With a large retail chain your prospects can be good and you can quickly take on more responsibilities.

You could move into other areas of the company, for example, marketing or buying and might be able to work abroad.

You could work for yourself, but will need money to start up your own store.

Advantages/disadvantages

Retail is an expanding, developing business and so can offer you an exciting career with good promotion prospects.

You will have a lot of responsibility quite early in your career.

Working with the public can be demanding and stressful.

Money guide

Wages vary with the company and the size of the store.

You could earn between £15,000 and £18,000 per year when you start as a non-graduate trainee with a large chain.

A trainee with a smaller company can expect to earn between £11,000 and £12,500.

With experience this could rise to between £21,000 and £28,000.

In excess of £45,000 is possible if you are working for a large company with a lot of responsibility. This could reach £60,000 if you are a manager in a large superstore.

You will probably also get discounts, commission and bonuses related to sales.

Related opportunities

- Distribution Manager p597
- Merchandiser p487
- Retail Buyer p489

Further information

British Shops and Stores Association Limited
www.british-shops.co.uk

Chartered Institute of Purchasing & Supply
www.cips.org

Qualifications and courses

There are no specific entry requirements for sales reps but if you are working in pharmaceutical or engineering sales a related degree will probably be required. However, employers are often more interested in your sales and communication skills and track record than formal qualifications.

In entering the profession it might be useful to take a qualification from a professional body such as the Institute of Sales and Marketing Management (ISMM) which offers Awards, Certificates and Diplomas from Levels 1–6 in Sales Skills and Sales/Marketing.

NVQs are available at Levels 2–4 in Sales and you may be able to earn experience through an Apprenticeship scheme.

A full driving licence is essential for most positions.

What the work involves

You will be responsible for selling your company's products or services to existing clients and creating relationships with new clients.

You will most likely specialise in a particular market, such as pharmaceuticals, medical equipment, engineering or consumer goods.

Your responsibilities will include meeting with customers and maintaining good relationships with them, promoting new products, meeting sales targets, and reporting sales trends.

You will be in charge of agreeing sales, organising the delivery and signing of contracts as well as checking payments have been made. You will also be responsible for providing after-care sales service by recording orders, advising customers about delivery schedules and receiving feedback.

Type of person suited to this work

You must have good people skills as much of your success will depend on how you interact with customers and your ability to maintain relationships with them.

Excellent communication and negotiation skills are essential, as are organisational and time management skills as much of your work will be self-motivated.

You must have the ability to gain and maintain an in-depth knowledge of the product you are selling and the markets you are selling to.

You must also be able to deal with rejection.

Working conditions

You will most likely be working for a large company.

As much of your work will involve meeting with customers, you may be able to choose your hours to a certain extent, as long as you are meeting sales targets.

You will usually be responsible for sales in a geographic area, and will spend a lot of time driving to meet customers in that area.

You may have to put in long hours, depending on your appointment schedule and travel time. When not in transit, you could be based in an office or at home.

Future prospects

Opportunities are available throughout the UK as the work is often based on a geographical area.

With experience and success, you could be promoted to sales team leader or a national sales manager.

You could also be headhunted from one company or region to another.

Advantages/disadvantages

Your job will vary from day to day, and you will be constantly interacting with people.

Your performance will be tangibly rewarded through commission bonuses.

You will spend a lot of time travelling which can be lonely and increase the time you spend away from home.

Money guide

You will often earn a basic salary plus commission, which will be based on meeting targets.

You could start at around £15,000–£20,000 per year plus commission.

This can rise to up to £40,000 plus commission, with experience.

Top salespeople can make over £100,000 per year.

Some companies will include a company car and petrol allowances in your salary.

Related opportunities

- Customer Services Assistant/Manager p480
- Recruitment/Employment Agency Consultant p60
- Retail Buyer p489
- Sales/Retail Assistant p492

Further information

Institute of Sales & Marketing Management
www.ismm.co.uk

Managing and Marketing Sales Association
www.mamsasbp.org.uk

RETAIL, SALES AND CUSTOMER SERVICES

CRCi: O

SALES/RETAIL ASSISTANT

Qualifications and courses

There are no minimum entry requirements for this work. Training is provided by employers. However, larger companies may ask for 2–4 GCSEs/S grades (A*–C/1–3). You might have to pass tests in basic maths and English.

You could do a retail Apprenticeship if aged 16–24.

Sales assistants can also work towards City & Guilds, Edexcel and OCR certificates and diplomas Level 1 and 2 in retail skills. The Level 3 certificate/diploma also includes modules on management, visual merchandising or sales professional.

Degrees in business or retail management are also available and can speed up entry into management roles.

What the work involves

Shops range from small specialist outlets to huge department stores, so your duties will vary. You will deal with customers, offering them a polite, helpful and speedy service and sell them a range of goods.

You will help keep the shop tidy and well stocked, answer questions, deal with complaints and give suggestions and advice.

When you are working on the till, you will take payments, give change, deal with refunds, wrap goods and arrange orders and deliveries.

Type of person suited to this work

You will need to be well presented, outgoing, friendly, polite, and be able to deal with awkward customers and stay calm when you are busy. Sales assistants have to learn about the things they are selling, which could involve in-house training, and they must be able to help and advise customers to find what they want.

You could be working to targets and earning bonuses according to how much you sell, so will need to be persuasive but not pushy.

You should be responsible and trustworthy, and fit and active to cope with being on your feet all day. You should be able to work within a team and on your own when required.

Working conditions

In small shops you could spend most of the time at the till/checkout. In large stores you could be working on the shop floor, helping and advising customers and fetching goods from stockrooms.

You might have to carry heavy items. You will keep the shop clean and tidy and might wear a uniform.

You could work early or late shifts and at weekends and evenings. There are many opportunities for part-time work.

Future prospects

There are shops in all areas of the country, though large retail parks and shopping centres have meant that some smaller shops in town centres have closed.

Working in a small shop you may get to know your regulars well and be given responsibility quite quickly, but promotion prospects can be limited.

In large stores and chains you will probably get training and can quickly become a supervisor and then move into management jobs. Depending on your employer, you might have to move around from shop to shop gaining experience within different-sized shops and departments.

With significant retail experience, some sales assistants progress to occupations like merchandising or buying.

Advantages/disadvantages

There are lots of opportunities and you will be meeting new people.

The hours can be long.

The work can be stressful if you have to reach sales targets.

You will have very busy times and very quiet times.

Money guide

Wages vary a lot depending on the type and size of the shop and its location.

Salaries at entry level are around £11,000 to £15,000 per year.

As a supervisor you could earn up to £20,000.

You will get discounts and may get bonuses and commission on what you sell. You may also get more money for working shifts.

Related opportunities

- Bank Cashier/Customer Adviser p23
- Customer Services Assistant/Manager p480
- Receptionist p59

Further information

British Retail Consortium
www.brc.org.uk

British Shops and Stores Association Limited
www.british-shops.co.uk

SHOE REPAIRER

Qualifications and courses

There are no minimum qualifications for this job but you should be able to take measurements, handle money and work with numbers. Some employers require entrants to take an aptitude test to assess their abilities in English, basic maths and practical skills. Experience in a retail/customer services role or any qualifications in leatherwork would be useful.

Training is done on the job, working alongside an experienced shoe repairer. It is also possible to work towards relevant qualifications, such as the BTEC Certificate in Apparel, Footwear, Leather or Textile Production (Level 2) or the BTEC Diploma in Apparel, Footwear or Leather Production (Level 3).

ABC Awards also provide useful courses including the Level 2 Certificate in Apparel, Footwear, Leather or Textile Production and the Level 3 Diploma in Apparel, Footwear or Leather Production. For those employed in a shoe repair shop offering several services, the ABC Level 2 Certificate in Shoe Repair, Key Cutting and Associated Multi Services would be appropriate.

The City & Guilds Award/Certificate in Retail Principles (Level 2) or the Award/Certificate/Diploma in Retail Skills (Levels 1–3) may also be beneficial.

What the work involves

Shoe repairers mend and repair shoes and other footwear. They also repair belts, bags and briefcases using tools and materials including nail and staple guns and stitching machines. A lot of shoe repairers use specialist machinery to cut keys and do metal engraving.

You will replace soles and heels by stitching or gluing on new ones and finishing them off neatly.

You will be serving customers, labelling the shoes they leave, issuing customers with tickets, taking payments, using a till and probably selling things like shoe dyes and polishes.

Type of person suited to this work

It is important to be practical, good at working with your hands and able to do detailed work quickly and neatly. As the machinery and tools can be dangerous, you will need to be responsible, able to work safely and happy to get your hands dirty. You might be dyeing shoes so good colour vision is essential.

You should enjoy meeting people and be able to cope with working whilst customers wait for their repairs. You must be comfortable working on your own or in a small team, and be able to work out costs and deal with money and payments. You will need to have good communication skills and, if you are self-employed, business skills.

Working conditions

You will be on your feet a lot, using a range of tools, equipment, dyes and glues. The work can be noisy and dirty with strong smells so you will wear overalls.

Shoe repairers usually work around 40 hours a week, including weekends.

You will typically be based in a small high street store. Some shoe repairers work in factories repairing goods which customers have returned.

Future prospects

There are around 8000 shoe repairers in all areas of the country but job opportunities can be limited as most are small shops only employing a few people. Shoe repairers also work in small outlets in supermarkets or department stores.

You will learn at least one skill, and possibly more, so you would be equipped to open your own business. You would need some money to start up and business skills to plan your work and keep accounts.

In a large chain you could progress to management roles.

Advantages/disadvantages

You do not need qualifications and you will be doing a practical, hands-on job.

You could work for yourself, running your own shoe repair outlet.

The work can be repetitive and fiddly.

Money guide

Those entering this profession can expect a starting salary of around £12,000.

With experience, your earnings could be between £13,000 and £17,000.

A shop manager is likely to receive £21,000 per year.

Many shoe repairers are self-employed so income depends upon the size, location and success of the shop.

Some employers offer a target-based bonus scheme.

Related opportunities

- Locksmith p228
- Sales/Retail Assistant p492
- Shopkeeper p494

Further information

MultiService Association
www.msauk.biz

SHOPKEEPER

Qualifications and courses

There are no formal academic requirements but it is essential that you have strong numeracy, business and people skills. Experience working in a customer services, sales, administrative or managerial role would be beneficial.

One route into this career is to undertake the Apprenticeship in Retail, which is available at both Intermediate and Advanced Levels, and then work your way up to become a shopkeeper.

Relevant qualifications include the NVQ/SVQ in Retail Skills (Levels 1–3), the NVQ in Customer Service (Levels 1–4) and the City & Guilds Award/Certificate in Retail Principles (Level 2). City & Guilds also offer an Award/Certificate/Diploma in Retail Skills (Levels 1 and 2) and a Certificate/Diploma in Retail Management (Level 3).

Those who wish to study at a higher level could consider a Foundation degree or degree in retail management.

Some local colleges offer evening courses in marketing and sales skills. Local training facilities also provide courses in all aspects of self-employment including starting up a business, marketing and VAT. You could consult an organisation such as the National Enterprise Network or Business Link for advice.

What the work involves

A shopkeeper owns or manages one or more shops, such as greengrocers, bakeries, newsagents, supermarkets, fishmongers, dry cleaners, fashion retailers, jewellers and florists.

You will find manufacturers and suppliers in order to stock your shop with products. For stores that sell foodstuffs, this may mean sourcing local produce and purchasing it for the best price.

As well as keeping the shop tidy and well stocked, you will pay staff wages and keep books and accounts.

Type of person suited to this work

You need to be determined and motivated, with a real interest in what you are doing. You should also be prepared to work long hours and to travel in order to find stock and suppliers.

You will need to be able to sell and market your goods and be confident about finding products that people want to buy.

Excellent communication skills are essential. Having good business sense and the ability to plan your finances and keep accounts is also important. You should be well organised and have some marketing, business and sales skills to succeed in this area of work.

Working conditions

Your hours and conditions will depend on what you are selling and how well you do.

Shops usually open at weekends and often in the evenings, with newsagents and convenience stores opening early and closing late.

Shops vary in size and appearance, and how pleasant the working environment is will depend on its staff and clientele.

You might wear a uniform and do some heavy lifting.

Future prospects

The trend towards large shops has meant that lots of smaller shops have closed. This is a very competitive sector so you will need to find products that sell well in your chosen location and demographic.

One option is to operate a franchise, such as a local convenience store, paying a larger company to use their name and sell their products.

If you are successful, you could expand by opening more or larger stores.

Advantages/disadvantages

There is a lot of freedom and satisfaction in being your own boss: you do not have to answer to anyone else and you can make all your own decisions.

You will need to develop good business skills as success will depend on your abilities.

Money guide

Earnings vary significantly and depend upon your success and reputation, the size and location of the business, and the products you sell.

When you first enter this profession, you may have a relatively low salary of £13,000–£15,000.

With experience, you are likely to earn up to £34,000.

Related opportunities

- Merchandiser p487
- Retail Buyer p489
- Sales/Retail Assistant p492

Further information

British Franchise Association
www.thebfa.org

National Enterprise Network
www.nationalenterprisenetwork.org

STOCK CONTROL/REPLENISHMENT ASSISTANT

Qualifications and courses

No formal qualifications are necessary, however some employers might expect applicants to have GCSEs/S grades (A*–C/1–3) in maths and English. Most employers will want candidates to have solid communication skills, a can-do attitude and a basic level of numeracy to know how much of each item needs to be restocked.

Previous experience dealing with the public within a relevant industry such as retail would prove beneficial when applying for a post in stock control/replenishment.

Training is done on the job and most retailers expect employees to complete an induction course and training programme. Training may be in a formal, traditional manner or individually on specially designed computer programs. A number of different subjects are normally covered, including health and safety, company policies, customer care, pricing or stock rotation. You may work towards a Diploma in Retail Skills or Customer Service.

What the work involves

You will work in a supermarket or retail environment refilling the shelves. You must be aware of where each product is, both for when you need to restock it and for when a customer inquires about the whereabouts of an item.

Your duties will include checking to see which goods need replacing, adding labels to products, tidying the display areas and shelves and transporting goods from the stockroom.

You may be required to order stock, take deliveries and serve customers.

Type of person suited to this work

This role involves physical activity and so you will need to have a certain level of fitness.

You will be expected to, at times, work alone and unsupervised and so you must be trustworthy. You will also spend some time working as part of a team so you will need to be comfortable working with others.

You must have an approachable and friendly disposition as you might need to advise customers. You might use a BHT (battery-hand terminal) or HHT (hand-held terminal) in order to keep track of stock or print labels and so you should be comfortable working with computerised equipment.

Working conditions

You will be working in a retail environment; your surroundings will vary depending on which area you choose to work in. Supermarkets can sometimes be cold.

You will be on your feet for most of the day; you will be lifting and transporting sometimes heavy stock.

Average working hours are about 37 to 40 a week; you will probably be on a rota and so could be working at any time of the day or night. Part time work and flexitime are available. You might wear a uniform.

Future prospects

Working in stock control/replenishment stands you in good stead to move into other retail positions such as sales assistant or checkout operator. Your skills will be transferable to other retail environments. However, if you have not completed any qualifications progression may prove difficult.

You might be able to complete extra training whilst working which would enhance your chances of promotion.

There is a possibility, with training and/or qualifications, that you could progress into a supervisory or managerial position.

Advantages/disadvantages

You may find the physical nature of this job tiring.

This job has a social element as it allows you to meet people from all walks of life every day.

You might find this role repetitive.

Your job will allow you to be active.

Money guide

These figures are only approximate and will vary depending on location and employer.

On average the starting salary for this role will be around £10,000 per year. This amount could increase to approximately £15,000 with experience.

If you reach the role of supervisor you can expect to earn up to £18,000 per year.

Related opportunities

■ Retail Manager p490
■ Sales/Retail Assistant p492

Further information

British Retail Consortium
www.brc.org.uk

British Shops and Stores Association Limited
www.british-shops.co.uk

Qualifications and courses

To become a qualified trading standards officer, you need a Diploma in Consumer Affairs and Trading Standards (DCATS) awarded by the Trading Standards Institute. You must be working for a local authority to achieve this.

Prior to this, you can follow a relevant degree course, such as the trading standards degree and Foundation degree. The normal entry requirements for a degree in trading standards or consumer protection are 2 A levels/3 H grades or equivalent. The degree provides exemption from certain parts of the DCATS.

Graduates from an unrelated degree subject can apply to do a Graduate Diploma in Trading Standards at Manchester Metropolitan University. A 2.2 Honours degree in any subject is a minimum requirement.

Non-graduates can join a Trading Standards authority within the department of a local authority as an enforcement officer or consumer adviser and follow the Accreditation of Prior and Experiential Learning route (APEL) before studying for the DCATS. The Trading Standards Institute also offers a Diploma in Consumer Affairs for people employed in these positions.

What the work involves

Trading standards officers work for local government to protect consumers. You will check that any individual or company selling products or services is keeping to the law and providing a fair service.

You will be working with a range of people and organisations. You will travel to check premises, or to follow up on a complaint from the public.

You will be enforcing the law, leading to prosecutions but also giving help and advice to companies and consumers.

Type of person suited to this work

You will be enforcing laws and regulations so will need to be able to take in and apply a lot of complex information. You must have an eye for detail and make sure the reports you write are accurate because they could be used in court.

Excellent communication skills are vital because you will be dealing with lots of different people, advising them and enforcing the law. You will need to be forceful but not aggressive.

You will need to be efficient at using computers and be good at maths as you will be dealing with lots of statistics.

Working conditions

You will probably work for local government but could work for private industry advising on relevant legislation.

You will be office based but will spend time visiting places such as shops, factories, pubs and clubs which could be dirty or cold.

Trading standards officers work normal office hours, Monday to Friday and possibly evenings and weekends. This is largely dependent on when different business premises are open.

Future prospects

There are jobs all over the country and the work varies from cities to rural areas. You could move from local government to central government or into retail and manufacturing companies.

There is a shortage of qualified staff but trainee jobs are competitive.

It might be possible to progress to senior officer and managerial positions. As relevant laws and regulations are increasing, opportunities in private industry are growing.

Advantages/disadvantages

This can be an interesting and satisfying job where you are helping the public to get a fair deal.

You could be dealing with difficult or aggressive people.

Money guide

As a new enforcement officer or a trainee, you could expect between £16,000 and £22,000 per year, although employed apprentices earn less.

You would start on between £24,000 and £34,000 when newly qualified.

You could go on to earn between £35,000 and £50,000 as a senior trading standards officer.

Depending on the size of the local authority from which you work, in excess of £70,000 is possible for the head of a service.

Related opportunities

- Environmental Health Practitioner/Officer p36
- Police Officer p551
- Quality Control Inspector p238

Further information

Trading Standards Institute
www.tscareers.org.uk

Qualifications and courses

There are no formal entry requirements for this work but GCSEs/S grades (A*–C/1–3) in English, maths, IT and science are useful.

Those aged 16–24 could apply for the Vehicle Parts Apprenticeship which is available at both Intermediate and Advanced Levels. Apprentices will have the opportunity to achieve NVQs/SVQs at Levels 2 and 3.

Trainee parts operatives can study for the Institute of the Motor Industry (IMI) Awards Certificate in Vehicle Parts (Level 2) and Diploma in Vehicle Parts Principles (Level 3). Alternatively, those who have secured employment could work towards the NVQ in Vehicle Parts Operations (Levels 2 and 3) or the NVQ in Automotive Maintenance and Repair, Body and Paint, Vehicle Fitting and Roadside Assistance (Levels 1–3).

It may also be beneficial to take the IMI Awards Certificate in Customer Service for the Automotive Industry (Level 2) and Certificate in Customer Service for the Motor Industry (Level 3).

What the work involves

This job involves ordering and looking after vehicle parts and accessories and selling them to the public, garages and mechanics. You need specialist knowledge of stock, and when ordering or supplying parts you have to know the exact make, model and year of the vehicle.

You will undertake stock control using computerised systems or possibly keeping paper records, and reorder from warehouses or manufacturers when stocks are low. You will check off parts that arrive against delivery notes before placing them in a stock room.

As well as processing deliveries and taking orders over the phone and in person, you will use tills, take payments and sometimes invoice customers.

Type of person suited to this work

You should be interested in cars, know about a wide range of parts and accessories, and which makes of vehicles they are for. You will need to be well organised and able to research where to find more unusual parts.

You will also deal with the public over the phone and in person, so you will need the ability to explain technical information clearly and simply.

You must have strong communication skills, be a good team player and able to work on your own. The job involves being on your feet a lot so you will need to be fit and active.

Working conditions

You could be working in a large shop open to the public or a warehouse used by the motor trade. You could be in a fairly small, local garage or work for a large dealership.

You might have to lift heavy parts, move trolleys and climb ladders to reach high shelves. You will work with the public and staff from the motor trade.

Normal hours are Monday to Friday from 8.30am to 6.00pm but you may be expected to work evenings and weekends with time off in lieu.

Many employers provide a uniform.

Future prospects

If you work for a smaller company your promotion prospects might be limited but in larger companies you could get additional responsibilities more quickly and move into supervisory and managerial roles.

You could become a trainee manager in other areas of the retail trade or move into car sales.

Advantages/disadvantages

This is a skilled job which enables you to undertake training and use your knowledge of, and interest in, cars and the motor trade.

There is a lot of information to remember and the work can be repetitive.

This is an ideal career for those wanting to work with vehicles who do not want to be mechanics.

Money guide

During your training you can expect to earn between £6,000 and £10,000.

Once you are qualified and have gained experience, your salary could range from £14,000 to £18,000.

Those employed as a senior vehicle parts operative can achieve in excess of £25,000 a year.

Overtime work and sales-based bonus schemes may increase your income.

Related opportunities

- Motor Vehicle Technician p234
- Stock Control/Replenishment Assistant p495
- Vehicle Sales Executive p498

Further information

Retail Motor Industry Federation
www.rmif.co.uk

RETAIL, SALES AND CUSTOMER SERVICES

CRCI: SB

VEHICLE SALES EXECUTIVE

Qualifications and courses

You do not need formal qualifications to enter and train in this career but employers will expect GCSEs/S grades (A*–C/1–3) in maths and English.

Most entrants to this profession are at least 21 years old, as insurance companies will not insure younger people to do test drives.

The Apprenticeship in Vehicle Sales, available at both Intermediate and Advanced Levels, offers an ideal route into this career.

Car salespeople receive on-the-job training and may also work towards NVQs/SVQs in Vehicle Sales (Levels 2 and 3) or the IMI Awards Certificate (Level 2) and Diploma (Level 3) in Vehicle Sales. Upon completion of the Certificate you can apply for the grade of Licentiate Member of the Institute of the Motor Industry (IMI) and those who achieve the Diploma are eligible to become an Associate Member.

Once employed, you may also have the opportunity to attend short courses run by vehicle manufacturers.

Those who have studied to degree level have the option to apply for a graduate training scheme run by one of the larger car manufacturers. Entry is usually with good A level/H grades and at least a 2.1 in your degree.

What the work involves

You will be selling new or used cars, motorbikes or vans. Your role will involve greeting customers, advising them, explaining different models, features and prices, and demonstrating cars by going out on test drives.

Your job will include arranging finance for customers and doing paperwork for the sale and the finance.

Garages promote their cars through advertising, special events and direct contact with customers, which may also be part of your work. Sales staff help keep the forecourt, salesroom and cars clean and tidy.

Type of person suited to this work

You will need to be smart, confident and outgoing with a polite, friendly manner. You must have the ability to deal with all types of people and be persuasive without being pushy. You will need good negotiation and numeracy skills. You should be able to work without supervision.

You must be interested in cars, know a lot about the ones you are selling and be able to explain technical features clearly and simply.

Your wages will depend on how much you sell so you will need to be motivated, determined and able to deal with stress and pressure. You need good attention to detail to complete forms and paperwork accurately.

Working conditions

You could be working in a small, local garage selling used cars or for a large dealership. You will be based in a showroom but will also be outside on the forecourt and going on test drives. A driving licence is essential.

You will usually work a 40-hour week which includes evening and weekend work.

Future prospects

There are currently good opportunities in all parts of the country. However, this is a popular industry with strong competition for jobs, especially with the main dealers.

In larger dealerships you can progress to senior salesperson, sales manager or dealer principal. At management level you will probably earn bonuses linked to the sales of the whole team.

With extensive experience, you could establish your own dealership.

Advantages/disadvantages

It can be rewarding when you persuade a customer to buy a car.

You can progress well in this industry and earn a high salary.

Working on commission and having to meet targets can be very stressful and often requires long working hours.

Money guide

Wages vary considerably.

Employees in this sector usually receive a basic salary which is supplemented by commission on sales and bonuses for achieving sales targets.

You could expect to earn between £9,000 and £15,000 as a starting salary.

With experience, you are likely to receive £17,000–£25,000 a year.

The most successful vehicle sales executives can achieve £35,000–£40,000.

In a senior role, you could earn up to £50,000.

Related opportunities

- Customer Services Assistant/Manager p480
- Motor Vehicle Technician p234
- Retail Manager p490

Further information

Institute of the Motor Industry
www.motor.org.uk

Retail Motor Industry Federation
www.rmif.co.uk

WINE MERCHANT

Qualifications and courses

There are no formal academic requirements but many new entrants have a degree or vocational qualification. Some employers prefer candidates to have 5 GCSEs/S grades (A*–C/1–3) and experience in the retail industry. You must be at least 18 years old to sell wine.

It is possible to study for the Wine and Spirit Education Trust (WSET) qualifications, which range from the Level 1 Award in Wines to the Level 5 Honours Diploma.

Other relevant qualifications include the BTEC HNC/HND in Hospitality Management specialising in Licensed Retail (Levels 4 and 5) and a Foundation degree in wine business or hospitality management. It is also possible to take a degree in hospitality and licensed retail management.

To become an independent wine merchant, you will need a premises licence and a personal licence to sell alcohol. In England and Wales, candidates are required to take the Level 2 Award for Personal Licence Holders from the British Institute of Innkeeping Awarding Body (BIIAB). In Scotland, you must take the BIIAB Scottish Certificate for Personal Licence Holders (SCPLH).

What the work involves

You will use your knowledge of wine to buy from vineyards and suppliers and sell to the public or shops, pubs and restaurants. If you manage your own shop or an off-licence, you will also be responsible for supervising staff and maintaining profitability. If you sell wine over the internet or by mail order, you could be doing your own deliveries.

You could also act as a buyer for a supermarket or wine retailer. You will probably spend a lot of time abroad finding and tasting new wines, agreeing prices and checking quality.

As an independent merchant, you will probably go to wine tastings to make selections and buy wine from companies who ship it into the country.

Type of person suited to this work

Wine merchants are keen to develop their knowledge, find new wines and growers, and keep up to date with developments and tastes.

A good sense of taste and smell is needed to judge the quality of a wine. You should be able to advise people on specific wines to complement different foods.

You must have excellent communication and customer service skills as dealing with the public and negotiating prices with growers and suppliers will be an important part of your job.

Working conditions

If you are self-employed, you will have freedom and flexibility but you will probably work long hours. If you work in retail, wine shops are often open until 10pm so you might work shifts including weekends. You will be on your feet a lot and could be lifting heavy boxes.

If you become a buyer you may travel frequently, both within the UK and abroad, or you could be based in a head office.

You could be working with the public, sometimes even travelling to people's homes to sell wine. A driving licence is essential.

Future prospects

As supermarkets have become the biggest retailers of wine, it is increasingly difficult for small shops to succeed.

Large chains offer good promotion prospects. You could progress to a store manager role and then to area manager.

To start your own business you will need experience, a good knowledge of wine and money to buy stock and premises.

Advantages/disadvantages

This job will allow you to use your expertise and passion for wine.

You might get to travel and work abroad.

There are few vacancies for buyer positions and competition is high.

Money guide

Starting salaries for this profession are typically about £17,000.

With experience, you can expect to earn between £18,000 and £28,000.

Wine merchants who are self-employed or employed in a senior position by the largest companies can achieve in excess of £35,000.

Related opportunities

- Bar Manager/Licensee/Publican p134
- Importer/Exporter p601
- Retail Buyer p489

Further information

British Shops and Stores Association Limited
www.british-shops.co.uk

Wine & Spirit Education Trust
www.wset.co.uk

RETAIL, SALES AND CUSTOMER SERVICES

CRCI: SD

499

Science, Mathematics and Statistics

Do you have a very mathematical brain? Are you logical in how you approach tasks? Maybe you are fascinated by scientific advances and would like to be involved in future discoveries? People who work in this sector can spend long periods of time carrying out meticulous research. You may find yourself working for a variety of employers, from the health service to a cosmetics company or even a charity. You should be willing to work on your own but also be happy to present your findings in reports to others. People in this sector are very highly skilled individuals who have often been through a lot of training, and possess a questioning and inquisitive mind.

The jobs featured in this section are listed below.

Qualifications and courses

Most entrants to this profession are graduates. Relevant degrees include acoustics, maths, physics, environmental science, mechanical engineering and subjects related to construction. For degree entry, you usually need 5 GCSEs/S grades and at least 3 A levels/H grades including maths and a numerate science/physics. There are also specialist postgraduate courses available in subjects such as environmental or architectural acoustics.

The Institute of Acoustics offers a postgraduate Diploma in Acoustics and Noise Control for graduates with a degree in a science, engineering or construction-related subject. The Certificate of Competence in Workplace Noise Risk Assessment and the Certificate of Competence in Environmental Noise Measurement are also available.

Once you secure employment, you will usually undertake a training programme or graduate scheme.

You can also become a member of the Institute of Acoustics and take part in their continuing professional development (CPD) scheme. There are several levels of membership, ranging from student members to Fellows, who are over the age of 35, have at least 7 years' experience working in acoustics and have made a significant contribution to the industry.

What the work involves

As an acoustician you will manage, regulate and control sound and vibrations in various environments. You could work on projects for defence, music, healthcare or telecommunications.

Your work can include many kinds of noise, from building acoustics, architectural acoustics and aerodynamic noise to electroacoustics, environmental issues and even therapeutic uses of ultrasound, as well as diagnostic techniques.

In your daily work you could be doing anything from advising on sound insulation to researching new ways to adapt the noise levels created by machinery. You might use computer modelling software to design ways to reduce or eliminate noise.

Type of person suited to this work

If you want to be an acoustician, you should have an interest not only in how sound behaves, but also in problem-solving and environmental science. You need to understand sound and acoustics, and be good at physics and maths.

You must be creative and innovative in your approach to problem-solving. You will require good skills in technology for testing and planning any designs that you or others create. You should be organised, with the ability to design and plan projects methodically.

Excellent communication, project management and people skills are essential.

It is important that you understand environmental legislation and standards. IT, budgeting and negotiation skills are also required for this role.

Working conditions

Working conditions and hours vary depending on the sector in which you work.

Those employed in a research role in a laboratory will usually work 9am to 5pm but unsocial hours may be required when working on some projects.

You will mainly work at a desk with a computer but you will also frequently visit laboratories, studios and sites.

The work involves standing and bending, and you may occasionally be required to lift and install heavy instruments.

You may spend time away from home and travel both within the UK and abroad.

Future prospects

Registering with the Institute of Acoustics could significantly improve your career prospects.

Possibilities for promotion include moving into supervisory or managerial roles, or specialising in a particular area. You could work freelance, or even consider setting up your own company.

Advantages/disadvantages

This is an ideal career option for those who are interested in science and sound.

You will have the opportunity to travel to some very interesting locations but this means that you will frequently be away from home.

Money guide

When you start out, you can expect to earn between £20,000 and £25,000 a year.

With increased experience in the role, your salary could rise to about £35,000.

Senior acoustics consultants can achieve in excess of £50,000 a year.

Related opportunities

- Aerospace Engineer p212
- Physicist p531
- Sound Engineer p446

Further information

EngineeringUK
www.engineeringuk.com

Institute of Acoustics
www.ioa.org.uk

Semta
www.semta.org.uk

ASTRONOMER

Qualifications and courses

A degree in physics, maths, astrophysics, geophysics or a related science is required. Specialist degrees are available in astronomy, astrophysics and space science, and you often have the option to study for either a single Honours degree or a joint Honours combined with a related subject such as maths, physics or another science. The Royal Astronomical Society (RAS) provides details of relevant degree courses.

Entry requirements for a first degree are usually 3 A levels/H grades, including physics, maths and another science, as well as 5 GCSEs/S grades (A*–C/1–3), including English and possibly chemistry.

Most entrants to this career also have a master's degree or a PhD. Taught postgraduate courses in astronomy are available at some universities for graduates with a degree in physics, maths or a related area.

To work as a research astronomer, candidates should have a 1st or 2.1 Master of Science (MSci) or Master of Physics (MPhys), followed by further study for a PhD in their specialist area of interest. University physics departments may include astronomical research groups and some universities offer MPhil/PhD programmes specifically in astronomy.

What the work involves

Astronomers investigate and study the universe. Astronomy covers a wide range of areas and astronomers usually focus on a specific subject, such as planets or stars.

You will mainly use maths, physics and specialist computer software to examine the pictures and information collected by observatories.

You will plan and coordinate projects using specialist equipment, such as telescope systems, to observe the skies and collect information. Your work can include constructing new observational instruments and software to improve your knowledge about the universe.

Type of person suited to this work

As a professional astronomer you should have a keen interest in the natural world. You will also need a good understanding of the sciences. Whether you are observing the skies or analysing detailed information, you should be able to take in a range of facts and figures.

You will use your decision-making skills to make informed conclusions from the information you work with.

A patient, logical and organised approach to your work is essential as projects can last several years. You should be confident in working with computers to complete a range of tasks. You will also need strong communication skills and an aptitude for numbers.

Working conditions

Late or antisocial working hours can often be a feature of this type of work, whether you are based in a university, observatory or research centre. You will spend a great deal of your time working with computers.

The job may involve frequent work away from home as many of the major telescopes are in remote locations.

Close observation is often part of this job so it may be unsuitable for people with visual impairments.

Future prospects

Employment as a professional astronomer is very competitive and demands a great deal of academic study. If you followed the academic route, you could undertake original research combined with a PhD-level qualification and then progress to lecturing.

You may choose to work as part of a technical team providing support for astronomy research projects.

You could progress into related jobs such as a software or electronics engineer.

Advantages/disadvantages

This job provides the opportunity to increase public understanding of the natural world.

You might have to spend a lot of time undertaking observations which requires patience and commitment.

Carrying out research on site can be physically tiring.

Money guide

A junior researcher can expect to earn between £20,000 and £30,000 per year.

With experience in a postdoctoral research post, your salary can increase to £36,000.

Senior researchers and lecturers can achieve £50,000–£60,000 a year.

Related opportunities

- Geophysicist p519
- Mathematician/Mathematics Research Scientist p525
- Physicist p531

Further information

British Astronomical Association
www.britastro.org

Institute of Physics
www.iop.org

Royal Astronomical Society
www.ras.org.uk

Qualifications and courses

To work as a bacteriologist, a 1st or 2.1 degree in a relevant subject such as biochemistry, physiology or microbiology is required. Entry to a degree is usually with a minimum of 2 A levels/3 H grades and 5 GCSE/S grades (A*–C/1–3). Entry may also be possible by completing a Foundation degree course in science. This normally requires 1 or 2 A levels/H grades, or the equivalent.

An MSc or PhD is an advantage as a postgraduate qualification is required for entry to an academic research post. Applicants without a PhD may start as a research assistant and work towards a PhD.

Alternatively you could enter as a laboratory assistant; for this you will need a minimum of 4 GCSEs/S grades including 2 sciences, maths and English.

Bacteriologists are given regular on-the-job training to learn new laboratory techniques, and keep up to date with IT developments and health and safety regulations. You might also receive training for personal development, management or supervisory responsibilities.

What the work involves

Bacteriologists study and analyse single-celled micro-organisms, particularly ones that cause disease. Their research provides important information on protecting against illnesses and caring for people with specific kinds of diseases.

In industry bacteriologists work in companies manufacturing pharmaceuticals, agrochemicals, food and drink, home and personal care products, and consumer goods.

Research bacteriologists study a particular genus or species. This work may be new and untried, and often techniques are selected by the researcher. Researchers may work in hospitals, universities and private companies.

In all areas the work involves the interpretation and analysis of findings, and will include designing and conducting experiments, making observations and drawing conclusions from your findings. You must enjoy writing reports and scientific papers and presenting them to other scientists.

Type of person suited to this work

You need to be scientifically capable. You need to be meticulous, practical and logical in your approach to work and should be patient as you may have to repeat tests.

You should have an enquiring mind and good problem-solving skills and be able to work to tight deadlines when required.

You must also be able to work well alone and as part of a team, have good communication skills and be highly safety conscious.

Working conditions

You are likely to work in a multidisciplinary team with other scientists, including geneticists, microbiologists and chemical engineers.

You will usually work from 9am to 5pm, Monday to Friday. Evening and weekend work may be required for fieldwork or some experiments.

You will work in laboratories or factories or out on location. You must wear protective clothing in laboratories. Microbes are classified as bio-hazardous substances so you must follow strict health and safety regulations. The job might require you to travel to meetings and conferences.

Future prospects

Promotion prospects vary depending on the type of organisation. Some bacteriologists may need to change employer to gain promotion.

Career prospects may be improved with additional qualifications.

There may be opportunities to work abroad, especially for clinical bacteriologists involved in healthcare projects.

Advantages/disadvantages

There are opportunities to visit different types of outside locations on research trips.

Employers such as the National Health Service can offer the chance to gain experience in different departments and provide well-structured career paths.

You will be handling potentially dangerous substances and experiments can take a long time to complete and some aspects might become tedious.

Money guide

If you begin your career as a laboratory assistant you can expect to earn between £13,000 and £19,000 a year.

Newly qualified bacteriologists can expect between £20,000 and £38,000 a year.

Top salaries for bacteriologists are about £65,000 a year.

Related opportunities

- Biochemist p503
- Clinical Scientist p509
- Microbiologist p528

Further information

Health Professions Council
www.hpc-uk.org

Institute of Biomedical Science
www.ibms.org

NHS Careers
www.nhscareers.nhs.uk

SCIENCE, MATHEMATICS AND STATISTICS

CRCI: TD

BIOCHEMIST

Qualifications and courses

A degree in biochemistry or a related subject is required for entry to this profession. Many posts also require a postgraduate qualification. A levels/H grades including chemistry and/or biology are required for entry to a biochemistry degree. Some universities offer Foundation or bridging years as pre-degree courses for applicants who do not have the required qualifications.

Biochemists with a degree and relevant work experience are eligible to join a professional body, the Biochemical Society or the Society of Biology. Biochemists continue their training in service. Those with a first degree are often encouraged to study part time for an MSc or PhD.

If you want to work with the NHS you will need a 1st or 2.1 degree and and may need to follow the Scientist Training Programme. This is a 3-year work-based learning programme that leads to a master's degree in your specialist subject. You will also need to register with the Health Professions Council (HPC).

What the work involves

You will research a range of living organisms and processes, using specialist equipment. Your work may involve collating detailed information and producing reports.

Biochemists investigate the chemistry of living organisms. They use their investigations to plan experiments and solve problems.

Biochemists apply their knowledge and skills in many areas, including food and nutrition, agriculture, medicine, plant research and brewing.

Type of person suited to this work

You will need to be curious about biological organisms and interested in improving systems and products. You will constantly use problem-solving skills in this job. Your excellent observational skills will also be very useful. You should enjoy working as part of a team.

You will be confident in using a range of scientific equipment to gain information. You will need a patient and methodical approach for sometimes repetitive but important activities. Your strong communication skills will help you explain and record your work. Confidence in working with numbers and detailed information is also essential.

Working conditions

You would normally work in a laboratory as part of a team. You may also do some of your work in an office environment. In some sectors, biochemists work on a shift system.

The job involves the regular use of specialist equipment which requires good manual handling skills.

As you become more senior, it is likely you will be involved with managing staff or projects.

Future prospects

Many of the products you use on a daily basis have been developed by biochemists. Biochemists have an important role in organisations ranging from research institutes to multinational companies.

If you go into research and development, you would start by working as part of a team. With experience, you would progress to planning and managing experimental work.

You may choose to undertake academic research and go into lecturing or teaching.

Advantages/disadvantages

You may have to work very long hours in this job.

This type of work is often project based which provides job variety.

Biochemistry offers a wide range of areas in which to specialise.

Money guide

Starting salaries for biochemists are typically between £21,000 and £27,000.

With experience your salary could increase to between £33,000 and £40,000.

At senior/management/consultancy level you can earn in excess if £60,000.

Salaries tend to be higher in industry compared with the NHS and universities, especially at junior levels.

Related opportunities

- Biomedical Scientist/Medical Laboratory Assistant p504
- Biotechnologist p505
- Chemist p507

Further information

Association of Clinical Biochemists
www.acb.org.uk

Biochemical Society Membership Office
www.biochemistry.org

Institute of Biomedical Science
www.ibms.org

SCIENCE, MATHEMATICS AND STATISTICS

CRCI: TD

505

Qualifications and courses

Biomedical scientist

To become a biomedical scientist you must register with the Health Professions Council (HPC). Requirements for registration are an Honours degree accredited by the Institute of Biomedical Science (IBMS), 1 year's training in a laboratory (which could be undertaken as part of a sandwich degree), and completion of the Registration Training Portfolio to achieve the IBMS Certificate of Competence.

Alternatively, those with A levels or equivalent in life sciences can start work as a trainee biomedical scientist if their employer is willing to allow them to study part time for a relevant degree. Entry requirements for a biomedical science degree are 5 GCSEs/S grades (A*–C/1–3) including maths and English, plus 3 A levels/H grades, preferably including biology and chemistry.

Medical laboratory assistant

There are no formal entry requirements but 4 or more GCSEs/S grades (A*–C/1–3) in English, maths and a science, or an equivalent qualification such as a BTEC First in Applied Science (Level 2) may be valuable. Laboratory assistants can work towards qualifications such as NVQs/SVQs.

What the work involves

A biomedical scientist carries out laboratory tests on bodily fluid and tissue in order to help doctors assess what is wrong with their patients. They use a range of specialist equipment to carry out tests.

Medical laboratory assistants support the work of biomedical scientists. As a medical laboratory assistant, you will carry out a variety of tasks including sorting and labelling tissue samples, sterilising and disinfecting equipment, making up chemical solutions, separating blood serum and plasma from samples, and recording and analysing information.

Type of person suited to this work

Biomedical scientist

You must be interested in science and medicine and have strong scientific skills. You should be practical and responsible, with good IT skills. You need the ability to supervise junior members of staff and to follow complex instructions.

Medical laboratory assistant

You need a careful, methodical approach to your work. You should be able to concentrate and pay attention to detail. You will work accurately under pressure to meet deadlines. Solid communication skills are essential.

Working conditions

You will mainly work in pathology laboratories within hospitals but sometimes you will have direct contact with patients.

You will work a 37-hour week which could involve shift, evening, weekend and on-call work.

You will be required to wear protective clothing.

Future prospects

Biomedical scientist

You will probably specialise in a specific area. You might need higher qualifications in order to progress. Within the NHS, you could move up to a managerial role.

Work abroad is a possibility, especially within developing countries.

Medical laboratory assistant

Most employment is available in NHS hospitals. You may specialise or move to a related career such as a pharmacy technician. To train as a clinical or biomedical scientist you will need to study for a relevant degree which may be available for part-time study.

Advantages/disadvantages

Providing an essential service within a hospital, by helping to diagnose patients' illnesses, is incredibly rewarding.

You may have to deal with angry doctors/patients who want results sooner than you can deliver them.

Money guide

Rates of pay in this sector are established by the NHS.

A medical laboratory assistant will have a salary of £16,110–£19,077.

A biomedical scientist will have a starting salary of £21,176–£27,625.

As a team leader or specialist, you could earn £25,528–£34,189.

Those who reach an advanced level or are employed as a team manager can achieve £30,460–£40,157.

Related opportunities

- Chemist p507
- Clinical Scientist p509
- Laboratory Technician p522

Further information

Institute of Biomedical Science
www.ibms.org

NHS Careers
www.nhscareers.nhs.uk

SCIENCE, MATHEMATICS AND STATISTICS

CRCI: TD

BIOTECHNOLOGIST

Qualifications and courses

A degree in either biotechnology, bioscience or a related subject, such as microbiology, biochemistry or chemical engineering, is required for entry to this profession. Requirements for a degree are usually 5 GCSEs/S grades (A*–C/1–3) including English, maths and science, and at least 2 A levels/H grades including chemistry or biology.

For research posts you will be expected to have a postgraduate qualification and experience working in the sector, and be studying for a PhD. Entry to a postgraduate course is with a minimum of a 2.1 in a relevant undergraduate degree and courses typically last 1–3 years.

Although rare, it is possible to become a biotechnologist with an HND or Foundation degree in chemical or manufacturing engineering by working your way up from trainee technician level.

The majority of employers look for relevant work experience, such as a vacation placement or a sandwich degree course with a year in industry.

Once you have secured employment, you will learn on the job, possibly through a structured in-house training programme. NVQs/SVQs in Laboratory and Associated Technical Activities (Levels 2–4) are also available.

What the work involves

You will use biological organisms and processes to develop and adapt products. Biotechnologists work in a range of areas such as genetic engineering, electronics, food science and microbiology. Biotechnology provides the scientific basis for agriculture, pharmaceuticals, waste management, food and medical care.

You could work in research and development or in aspects of production such as quality control.

Your work might involve enhancing existing products or developing new types of organisms.

Type of person suited to this work

You will need a keen interest in science for working in any area of biotechnology. Strong observational skills and an organised approach are also essential.

You should be confident working with scientific equipment and computers to manage information and undertake research. Most biotechnologists are employed as part of a group so the ability to work within a team is helpful.

If you work as a technician, you should be able to cope with undertaking routine but required testing activities. Biochemists in industry also need to understand the commercial applications of their work.

Working conditions

Biotechnologists usually work in a laboratory or research centre in sterile conditions to undertake experimental and testing work.

You will work normal office hours but you may occasionally be on-call during evenings and weekends. Protective clothing is needed when working with micro-organisms and dangerous chemicals.

Your work is likely to involve using microscopes and electronic testing equipment, and spending time on a computer doing analysis work.

Future prospects

You could work within government research institutions or play a central role in developing and enhancing products in commercial biotechnology companies.

You could progress to a supervisory role.

There is also the option to develop an academic career – this may provide additional opportunities to undertake commercial research. You can use this research to move into sales, marketing or production roles.

Advantages/disadvantages

Laboratory work, particularly at technician level, can be time consuming and requires a lot of patience.

You will be researching and learning new things every day.

Job prospects are good as there are a range of sectors in which you can work.

Money guide

Earnings vary according to the type of employer and tend to be highest in industry.

Starting salaries for graduates are usually £19,000–£24,000 per year.

With experience, you can expect to earn between £30,000 and £45,000.

Those employed in a senior position with high levels of responsibility can achieve up to £60,000 a year.

Related opportunities

- Biochemist p503
- Biomedical Scientist/Medical Laboratory Assistant p504
- Chemist p507

Further information

BioIndustry Association
www.bioindustry.org

Biotechnology and Biological Sciences Research Council
www.bbsrc.ac.uk

Institute of Biology
www.iob.org

BOTANIST

Qualifications and courses

Botanists may enter this career as laboratory technicians or technical assistants. Most entrants have a degree. Relevant degree subjects include botany, plant biology, plant science, environmental science and ecology. Entry into a degree programme requires 5 GCSEs/S grades (A*–C/1–3) and 2 or 3 A levels/H grades in biology and another science, often chemistry.

It may also be a good idea to complete some voluntary work in relevant organisations and to acquire relevant skills such as plant identification.

To work as a researcher, a postgraduate qualification is required. Candidates may enter with a MSc, PhD or enter as a trainee researcher in a university department and work towards a PhD. In order to apply for a postgraduate qualification you will need to successfully complete an undergraduate degree.

What the work involves

Botanists study all kinds of plant life and plant biology. They are increasingly employed within industry and research in areas such as plant-cell technology and genetic engineering.

Your work could involve managing rare plant collections, environmental conservation, horticulture, agriculture and other areas. You will use specialist equipment such as electron microscopes and satellite imaging technology.

You might look into how human activity affects plants in farming, or you may try and discover useful chemicals produced by plants.

Type of person suited to this work

As a botanist you should have a real interest in science and plants. This interest should stretch to a particular field of work such as conservation.

This profession will involve detailed analysis so you will need strong observational skills. You must also have a methodical approach to your work activities.

You should be comfortable working with a range of scientific equipment. However you will also need to be happy undertaking practical research work, sometimes in unpleasant weather conditions. You may also need to be a good leader as you might be in charge of junior staff, students and volunteers.

Working conditions

You could be working in one or more of the following environments: laboratories, classrooms, lecture theatres, offices and outdoors. Hours will vary, but within research and higher education you will work about 37 hours a week.

Fieldwork takes place in all weather conditions and you may find it physically demanding.

Whilst working in a laboratory you will be using specialist equipment and might be required to wear protective clothing. A driving licence may be required if you need to travel between locations.

Future prospects

Within conservation and fieldwork, progression would entail taking on more responsibility and possibly managing others.

Within the higher education sector there is a set career path leading from researcher to head of department or professor.

Within industry there is the possibility of promotion. You also have the option of working as a freelance consultant and therefore being self-employed. There is the potential to work overseas in most areas of botany.

Advantages/disadvantages

There are opportunities to visit different types of outside locations on research trips.

Research jobs are often offered on a short-term basis, which can create job insecurity.

You will have the opportunity to combine your love of plants with your passion for science.

Money guide

These figures will vary depending on location, sector and employer. Salaries within private industry will vary considerably.

Starting salaries are around £22,000 a year.

Botanists in research jobs can expect to earn up to £30,000 a year.

In a senior role, such as a senior lecturer at a university, you could earn around £55,000 per year.

Related opportunities

- Ecologist p512
- Entomologist p513
- Microbiologist p528

Further information

Botanical Society of the British Isles
www.bsbi.org.uk

BTCV
www.btcv.org.uk

Society of Biology
www.societyofbiology.org

CHEMIST

Qualifications and courses

You will usually require a degree in chemistry, applied or analytical chemistry, biochemistry or a related scientific subject. For entry to one of these degrees you will need 5 GCSEs/S grades (A*–C/1–3) including maths, 2 sciences and English and 2 or 3 A levels/H grades in chemistry and 1 other science or maths.

Many institutions offer 1-year Foundation courses for candidates without the necessary scientific background.

The majority of chemists also have a postgraduate qualification in chemistry or in a specialist area such as materials chemistry, medicinal chemistry or pharmaceutical chemistry. You can also work towards professional membership of the Royal Society of Chemistry.

Alternatively, it is possible to enter as a technician with a minimum of 4 GCSEs/S grades (A*–C), including English, maths and 2 sciences. A levels/H grades, a National Certificate/Diploma or HNC/HND in a science subject may be required.

What the work involves

Chemists work in many different sectors, undertaking the analysis and use of complex scientific processes and substances on a detailed molecular level.

As well as research and development, chemists also check that products are developed to a safe standard.

Professional chemists are employed in a wide range of sectors, including the oil industry, pharmaceuticals, medical research and academia.

Type of person suited to this work

Chemists need strong observational, numerical and technical skills. You must have an enquiring mind with a logical approach and desire to solve complex scientific problems.

You will have good manual handling abilities for undertaking research with a range of scientific equipment. The ability to interpret and analyse data is vital and you must have good written and verbal communication skills to translate complex problems.

Often you will be working as part of a team so you must be comfortable working with other people as well as having the patience and confidence to take the lead within certain projects.

Working conditions

The average chemist works about 37 hours a week. Your job could involve working in a laboratory as part of a research centre, but you may also undertake research outdoors on-site.

You may have to wear protective clothing such as lab coat, protective glasses and gloves.

If you are employed by a private company you may be required to work shifts organised by a rota. At senior levels, you may be involved with business development and managerial activities.

Future prospects

Professional chemists play an important role in developing and updating products and systems.

Public research institutes, academic institutions and private companies employ chemists. There are also opportunities in government research, health and education. Some chemists move into areas such as law, IT, science journalism and marketing.

With experience you could enter a supervisory role. There are also opportunities to teach in schools and universities. Postgraduate qualifications may improve your chances for progression.

Advantages/disadvantages

Low numbers of entrants taking chemistry degrees means that there are many opportunities.

Laboratory tasks can sometimes be repetitive and time-consuming.

Many large companies employ chemists, so promotion can be possible without moving employers.

Money guide

These figures are only approximate and will vary depending on sector, employer and location.

Salary levels should increase with the level of academic qualification. At graduate entry you can earn between £16,000 and £22,000 per year.

With experience, and when established, you can expect £35,000 a year.

With added responsibility, such as if you are in charge of a team or project, you could expect to earn between £35,000 and £60,000 a year.

Related opportunities

- Biochemist p503
- Biotechnologist p505
- Cosmetic Scientist p511

Further information

Association of the British Pharmaceutical Industry
www.abpi.org.uk

Royal Society of Chemistry
www.rsc.org

Qualifications and courses

An Honours degree in genetics, biomedical or biological sciences is required. In order to become a clinical geneticist with the NHS you will need a 2.1 Honours degree or better in genetics or another life science. For entry to relevant degree courses 2 or 3 science A levels/H grades are normally required. Chemistry and/or biology may be specified. You will also need 5 GCSEs/S grades (A*–C/1–3).

As of 2011, the Clinical Scientist Training Scheme was replaced by the Scientist Training Programme (STP). This takes 3 years and candidates are attached to an NHS trust and undertake a mixture of formal learning and practical training. A postgraduate qualification is desirable and you are given the opportunity to study for a master's degree as part of the qualification. Training is undertaken in an accredited genetics laboratory.

It is also possible to enter the profession at technician or trainee level with GCSEs/S grades, A levels/H grades, or equivalent qualifications in subjects such as biology, maths, science and English.

What the work involves

Clinical geneticists test samples from patients, record their findings and draw a conclusion from them. They also supervise the work of others. This profile focuses on clinical geneticists who are responsible for identifying and diagnosing genetic disorders. There are 2 main jobs in this field: cytogeneticists (studying chromosomes which contain genes) and molecular geneticists (studying DNA).

Geneticists analyse and modify human, animal or plant DNA. If working as a human geneticist, you could be involved with medical genetics or human genetic research.

You could undertake genetic engineering in agricultural research.

Type of person suited to this work

You should be an excellent communicator, both verbally and in writing. You will need to be able to work accurately and meticulously, whilst keeping to deadlines.

You must have a good understanding of computers. You will need to be discreet as you will be dealing with confidential medical information.

You should be able to work effectively as part of a team and be able to take on the role of a supervisor when training junior staff. You must have strong problem-solving skills.

Working conditions

You will be based in a sterile laboratory. You will have to wear protective clothing such as overalls, laboratory glasses and gloves.

You will also have to ensure that you reach all health and safety standards.

As a clinical geneticist within the NHS you will be working about 37.5 hours per week, from Monday to Friday. There may also be a rota in place which covers bank holidays and weekends.

Future prospects

Genetics is a fast-developing area of science that offers the chance to work directly with patients as a medical geneticist within the NHS or directly within research in research centres and universities.

You could also go on to work in research and development in industry.

In order to be promoted you will need to gather experience, responsibility and training. Once you have worked for 2 or 3 years as a registered geneticist you can begin to apply for more senior positions.

Advantages/disadvantages

You may have to repeat procedures which could become tedious.

This job contains a great deal of responsibility.

You will be working with a wide range of samples and so every day will be different.

Money guide

These figures will vary depending on sector, location and employer.

The average starting salary for a graduate clinical scientist trainee is about £24,000 per year.

Once registered, you can expect to earn between £29,000 and £38,352.

If you reach the level of principal clinical scientist you could earn up to £44,527.

As a consultant this can increase to as much as £93,098.

You may also receive an additional allowance if you work in London.

Related opportunities

- Clinical Scientist p509
- Forensic Scientist p516
- Laboratory Technician p522

Further information

British Society of Human Genetics
www.bshg.org.uk

Genetics Society
www.genetics.org.uk

NHS Careers
www.nhscareers.nhs.uk

SCIENCE, MATHEMATICS AND STATISTICS

CRCI: TD

Qualifications and courses

Entrants to this profession require a 1st or 2.1 class degree in a relevant subject, such as biochemistry, biology, chemistry, engineering, genetics, microbiology, physics or physiology. Entry to a degree typically requires a minimum of 2 A levels/3 H grades, including appropriate science subjects as well as 5 GCSEs/S grades (A*–C/1–3) including English and maths.

Equivalent qualifications, such as the International Baccalaureate, Foundation degrees in Science, BTEC National and BTEC Higher Nationals and science Access to Higher Education courses may also be relevant.

An MSc or PhD in your specialist area is an advantage. In order to apply you usually require a 1st or 2.1 in your first degree.

Clinical scientists start as Grade A trainees. The training lasts 2–3 years. On completion, candidates are eligible for state registration, and can apply for Grade B posts. In-service training continues, and many clinical scientists work towards membership of professional bodies or a PhD. Scientists can register with the Health Professions Council (HPC).

Once qualified, clinical scientists are encouraged to undertake continuing professional development (CPD), through workshops, conferences, private research or meetings.

What the work involves

Clinical scientists work mainly for the NHS but are also employed in the Health Protection Agency, research centres and industry.

Your work may involve supporting doctors, suggesting suitable tests for diagnosing patients, reporting on results and recommending treatments. You may also research and test new methods of treatment and make recommendations on the best equipment or test materials.

You might specialise in a particular area such as clinical embryology (the study of infertility), or clinical microbiology (identifying infections in patients caused by bacteria, fungus or parasites).

Type of person suited to this work

You should have a keen interest in medicine and science, alongside a desire to help others. You should have excellent observational skills.

You need technical skills and the ability to use scientific equipment to get results. You will need an organised approach for undertaking practical work and the ability to work to set deadlines. You should be able to interact well as part of a team.

As a scientist you will get results by combining a logical approach with a creative flair. You should have strong computer skills.

Working conditions

You might work around 37.5 hours a week, usually from Monday to Friday, although these hours could vary depending on your specialism. You may need to work some evenings and weekends if you are on-call.

You will usually work in a laboratory or within a specialist department. You may have some contact with patients.

You will be working in a sterile environment, which may demand that you wear protective clothing. You might need to use ionising radiation.

Future prospects

As progression is performance based, you will need to accept more responsibility and/or take part in research and development projects to reach a more senior level.

As a consultant, you would be responsible for a large department and have the chance to make important contributions to your area of expertise.

There is also the option of moving between departments to gain further training. You could move into lecturing or training. There is the possibility of working abroad.

Advantages/disadvantages

You will be helping to diagnose patients and suggest treatments which will improve their quality of life.

Mistakes could lead to an incorrect diagnosis and so you will be working under a lot of pressure.

Money guide

Salaries vary depending on employer and location. If you work in London you will be given an additional allowance.

As a trainee clinical scientist within the NHS you could earn about £21,000 per year.

Once registered, you could earn between £30,000 and £40,000.

This could increase to £97,478 if you become an advanced practitioner, clinical scientist or consultant clinical scientist.

Related opportunities

- Hospital Doctor p312
- Medical Physicist p316
- Radiographer p336

Further information

Association of Clinical Scientists
www.assclinsci.org

Clinical Scientist Recruitment Centre
www.nhsclinicalscientists.info

Federation of Clinical Scientists
www.acb.org.uk/federation

SCIENCE, MATHEMATICS AND STATISTICS

CRCI: TD

Qualifications and courses

For entry, you will be expected to have a HNC/HND or degree in a relevant subject such as consumer studies/science, food studies/science, food and nutrition, food and marketing or food technology. Degrees are also available in specialist areas of consumer science, such as consumer protection or consumer psychology.

To gain acceptance to an HNC/HND course you will usually require at least 4 GCSEs/S grades (A*–C/1–3) and 1 A level/Higher. Most degree courses expect candidates to have at least 5 GCSEs/S grades (A*–C/1–3) and 2 or 3 A levels/Highers. These requirements may vary so be sure to check with the institution.

Some employers may also prefer you to have a postgraduate qualification in a relevant subject such as health promotion or consumer behaviour. For entry on a postgraduate course you will need a good undergraduate degree.

Experience in the food manufacturing industry or within market research can also offer an alternative way of entering the field or act as an advantage when applying for jobs.

What the work involves

Consumer scientists or home economists provide support, information and specialist services related to healthy living and eating.

You will be the point of communication between consumers and manufacturers. You will study what the consumer needs and provide advice on how to develop it. Your work could involve developing new food products, educating people about healthy eating or assessing new cookery equipment.

Jobs are available within quality assurance, marketing, media and journalism, food product development, education, government, product and service development and catering.

Type of person suited to this work

You will need to have strong communication skills, which allow you to talk to people of all ages and backgrounds.

You should also have an interest in food and how people live their lives within the home environment.

You should have solid computer skills and a knack for describing information in a clear way, both orally and in writing. You must be creative and have proficient design skills.

Working conditions

This role may involve travelling to meetings, conferences and other environments in the UK and abroad.

Your working environment will vary according to which industry you work within. You could be in an office, kitchen, classroom, laboratory or a selection of these.

You will be working about 35 to 40 hours per week, usually from Monday to Friday. You might also have to complete reports in your free time.

Future prospects

Consumer scientists can move between industries as their services are always required. Specific industries include retail chains, marketing bodies, local authorities, magazines, television and newspapers, health authorities, producers of food, advisory and consumer organisations, hotels and restaurants, consumer pressure groups, schools, colleges and universities and many others.

In most areas there is the opportunity to progress to managerial level.

Promotion may involve moving to a new location within the country.

Advantages/disadvantages

You may find it frustrating when asked to complete tests in the later stages of the factory process.

This profession will give you the opportunity to move into a number of industries, such as retail or food manufacturing, which will aid your career progression possibilities.

You may have to complete reports in your free time.

Money guide

Salary levels vary according to employer, sector and location.

Starting salaries range from £17,000 to £22,500 per year.

With experience, you could earn up to £30,000 a year.

Managers at a senior level earn between £40,000 and £50,000 per year.

Consumer scientists working on a consultancy basis can earn £150–£500 a day.

Related opportunities

- Dietitian p303
- Environmental Health Practitioner/Officer p36
- Market Research Executive p406

Further information

Improve Ltd
www.improveltd.co.uk

Institute of Food Research
www.ifr.ac.uk

Institute of Food Science & Technology
www.ifst.org

Qualifications and courses

Career entry can be achieved at more than one level, including a relevant degree (cosmetic science, chemistry, chemical engineering, biology, microbiology, physics, medicine and pharmacy), Foundation degree or HNC/D. Most degree courses require applicants to have achieved a minimum of 2 A levels/H grades, which should include relevant sciences (particularly chemistry) and 5 GCSEs/S grades (A*–C/1–3), including English and maths.

Many colleges include a 1-year introductory (Access) course for students who have not studied the requisite science subjects at A level/H grade. For Foundation degrees and HNC/HND qualifications, applicants are normally expected to have achieved at least 1 A level (or equivalent).

The Diploma in Cosmetic Science can be attained by distance learning, after approximately 300 hours of study. The Principles and Practice of Cosmetic Science course is a shorter course, which is particularly useful for those who have been in the industry for a while and are looking to move into supervisory or managerial roles and/or who are taking on a new field of expertise.

What the work involves

The cosmetics industry requires scientists to help develop, test and produce new and existing cosmetics and beauty products, such as make-up, perfumes and haircare products.

There are various elements to this profession, including researching new ingredients, developing cosmetic products, developing the processes used to create the product, quality control, safety testing, packaging development and regulatory affairs which involves ensuring the product meets all legal requirements.

Most work takes place in a sterile, laboratory environment.

Type of person suited to this work

You will have an interest in the science of cosmetics, along with knowledge and skill in chemistry and biology. You will need to be meticulous, but also able to work at speed.

You will need to understand statistics and have the ability to use the relevant computer software. You should have an extremely methodical approach to your work and the ability to follow instructions effectively.

You must have strong communication skills, to convey information to your colleagues and clients effectively.

Working conditions

Most of your work will take place in a sterile, laboratory environment. Your job may involve handling potentially dangerous materials, so you would need to wear protective clothing.

This job might involve repetitive analysis work in the laboratory, which can be physically demanding.

In addition to hands-on experimental work, your work may include using computers. Your job might involve travelling to meetings, conferences and other events in the UK and abroad.

Future prospects

Progression generally comes in the form of moving to a supervisory or managerial role, which could allow you to spend more time with the client.

Alternatively, you might consider changing departments and moving into a sales or marketing position, where the scientific knowledge you have acquired would be extremely relevant.

There is also the option of self-employment, working as a consultant, providing specialist support to cosmetic companies. You might also consider lecturing on cosmetic science courses.

Advantages/disadvantages

You may find some elements of the job extremely repetitive and monotonous.

Your work will be directly influenced by the fashion industry; you will be working to predict the latest trends, which could be exciting.

This profession can be fast paced and you may find it stressful.

Money guide

Salary levels will vary according to employer, sector and location. Starting salaries are roughly between £16,000 and £23,000 per year.

With experience and training this will increase and you could earn from £25,000 to £45,000 a year.

At senior levels, such as within management, it is possible to earn over £50,000 a year.

Related opportunities

- Biochemist p503
- Laboratory Technician p522
- Pharmacologist p327

Further information

Cosmetic Toiletry and Perfumery Association
www.ctpa.org.uk

Royal Society of Chemistry
www.rsc.org

Society of Cosmetic Scientists
www.scs.org.uk

SCIENCE, MATHEMATICS AND STATISTICS

CRCI: TD

Qualifications and courses

Entrants normally require a degree in a relevant subject such as ecology, environmental biology/management, conservation and marine biology. Additionally, many employers seek experience (as a research assistant or a conservation project volunteer), and postgraduate qualifications are increasingly an advantage. A driving licence may also be useful when travelling to conduct fieldwork.

A levels/H grades in sciences are required for entry to degrees in ecology or biological sciences. Biology A level or equivalent is a required or preferred subject for some degrees.

NVQs/SVQs are available in Environmental Conservation at Levels 2 and 3 and Environmental Management at Level 4.

Ecologists with relevant qualifications and experience can become members of the Institute of Ecology and Environmental Management (IEEM). Different levels of membership are available depending on qualifications and experience. The IEEM also provides short professional development courses for its members.

What the work involves

Ecologists help to protect the natural world by investigating the relationship between living organisms and their environment.

You will undertake ecological surveys of animals and plants and monitor the state of urban and rural environments. You may also write reports and analyse statistical information.

You may also advise on legal regulations, manage wildlife conservation areas and present your research at conferences or educational seminars.

Type of person suited to this work

A keen interest in the natural world is essential. It's important to be observant and methodical in your work. You will also need to be organised and work to a high standard of accuracy when collating statistics.

You will need to be comfortable working outdoors, sometimes in poor weather conditions. You must have a good knowledge of environmental policies and legislation. Good manual handling skills are important.

You will be presenting your research on a regular basis so excellent communication skills are essential.

Working conditions

Ecologists work in laboratories or research centres when undertaking analysis activities.

You would work outside in all kinds of weather conditions when undertaking fieldwork such as surveys of plants or animals.

For fieldwork you would need a good level of physical fitness and good observational skills. This may make the job unsuitable for people with visual impairments.

Future prospects

Ecology offers a wide range of job opportunities; you can shape your career according to your interests. However, there is strong competition for jobs; some are available only on a contract basis and it can take time to find a permanent role.

Many types of organisations employ ecologists. You could go into scientific research, environmental management, teaching or conservation for organisations such as environmental consultancies, research bodies and private companies.

Advantages/disadvantages

This job provides the satisfaction of having a positive impact on the natural environment.

You may need to move around employers to develop your career.

You can choose to work in your specialist area, and develop your career around something you love learning about.

Money guide

Salaries vary according to the type of organisation you work for.

Starting salaries range from around £20,000 to £27,000 per year.

With experience you could earn £35,000–£40,000.

Senior or management roles in larger organisations can pay in excess of £45,000.

Related opportunities

- Countryside Manager/Officer p258
- Countryside Ranger p259
- Environmental Scientist p514

Further information

British Ecological Society
www.britishecologicalsociety.org

Institute of Ecology and Environmental Management
www.ieem.net

Institution of Environmental Sciences
www.ies-uk.org.uk

ENTOMOLOGIST

Qualifications and courses

An Honours degree in a relevant subject is required for entry to this profession. There are no entomology degree courses available but biology, zoology, environmental science and biological sciences would all be appropriate as these typically include modules in entomology. For entry to a degree course, candidates usually need at least 2 A levels/3 H grades including biology and 5 GCSEs/S grades (A*–C/1–3). Entry requirements vary between universities.

Many employers will also expect applicants to have a postgraduate qualification in entomology. Postgraduate courses are available at several universities throughout the UK and you must have achieved a minimum of a 2.1 in your first degree to be eligible for a place. To secure a research post you will need to have or be studying for a PhD.

Entry at technician level requires GCSEs/S grades and A levels/H grades. Useful subjects include biology (and other sciences), maths, English, geography and geology. Foreign language qualifications may also prove beneficial.

Experience within the field is valued by employers and candidates can develop relevant skills through voluntary work in museums or with conservation organisations.

What the work involves

Entomology is the study of insects, including how they live and how they interact with their environment. Entomologists also observe the behaviour of insects to gain valuable information on the state of specific natural areas.

As an entomologist, you could analyse and assess the effects of insect life on agriculture. Entomologists are also employed to undertake research in medicine or to support ecological and environmental conservation work.

Work in the field might include searching for new species or studying insect ecology. In the laboratory, you could be developing insecticides or classifying insects.

Type of person suited to this work

You should have a methodical, logical and meticulous approach to your work and the ability to be patient and persevere when you encounter problems. You will also require good communication, computer and leadership skills.

You must be able to work effectively both alone and within a team. As you will need to remember a great deal of information, such as insect names and classifications, you should have an excellent memory.

Working conditions

Working hours and environments will depend upon the area of entomology you work in.

Entomologists working in research and higher education usually work regular hours from Monday to Friday. In a research post, you will spend your time in a laboratory, whilst a lecturer will also work in classrooms, lecture theatres and an office. Those working in conservation or field research will often work irregular hours and be outdoors in all weather conditions.

Future prospects

Entomologists work in a wide range of areas, including agricultural research and development, ecological protection and conservation, forensics and pest control. Others go on to develop their research interests as academic professionals after gaining postgraduate qualifications.

Progression within conservation and field research will depend on merit and responsibilities such as managing others. Within universities there is a progression path from researcher to head of department. Within industry, promotion opportunities to senior positions are available.

Self-employment is a possibility.

Advantages/disadvantages

It could be frustrating when an experiment or investigation does not go according to plan.

Your work could take you all over the world.

There are a wide variety of career options available.

If you work in the field or within conservation, you might have to live and work in inhospitable environments.

Money guide

Salaries vary depending on location, sector and employer.

Starting salaries for entomologists are around £16,000.

With experience, you should expect to earn £35,000 a year.

The most senior and highly regarded entomologists can achieve over £60,000 per year.

Related opportunities

- Agricultural Scientist p253
- Ecologist p512
- Environmental Scientist p514

Further information

British Entomological and Natural History Society
www.benhs.org.uk

Natural History Museum
www.nhm.ac.uk

Royal Entomological Society
www.royensoc.co.uk

SCIENCE, MATHEMATICS AND STATISTICS

CRCI: TD

Qualifications and courses

Most employers expect candidates to have completed an environmental science degree. However, other degrees may be considered and relevant subjects include sustainable development, environmental management, chemistry, geophysics and environmental engineering. Graduates with a first degree in a science subject can take a postgraduate course in a specialist area of environmental science.

For entry to an undergraduate degree, most universities require applicants to have 2 A levels/3 H grades and 5 GCSEs/S grades (A*–C/1–3). Relevant subjects at A level include biology, chemistry, physics, geography, English, maths and geology. Some admissions tutors will also favour foreign languages.

Candidates without a degree may gain entry to this profession by starting as a technician and working their way up to an environmental scientist position. In order to do this you will need at least 4 GCSEs/S grades (A*–C/1–3), which should include 2 sciences, English and maths or technology. Equivalent qualifications, for example a BTEC First in Applied Science (Level 2), might be considered. Many technicians also complete A levels/H grades.

Relevant work experience would be beneficial and some degree courses include a placement.

What the work involves

Environmental scientists apply scientific techniques to study and protect the natural environment. You might look for ways to ensure sustainable development by discovering and experimenting with methods to reduce the damage caused to the world and our natural resources.

You could work in pollution monitoring, conservation, energy, engineering, environmental consultancy and research or other areas.

You will probably be advising colleagues and clients, some of whom may not have a scientific background, on the damage particular developments could cause to the environment.

Type of person suited to this work

To work in this industry you should have an interest in geography, science and environmental issues.

You will need to be practical and methodical, as well as having the ability to think outside the box in order to solve problems. You must be meticulous in your approach to work, as the results you find could have an impact on whether developments go ahead.

You should be comfortable working independently and as part of a team. Communication, presentation and IT skills are required.

Working conditions

Your working hours and conditions will depend on the specific role you take and the sector you are employed in. Some environmental scientists work 9am to 5pm, Monday to Friday, but others involved in fieldwork will have to work overtime in order to meet deadlines.

For fieldwork you will be outside in all weather conditions and are likely to travel both within the UK and abroad. You will also spend a considerable amount of time in an office and/or laboratory.

Future prospects

There is a growing demand for environmental scientists, mainly owing to the increasing concern about climate change, global warming and other environmental issues.

You can progress to team manager or project manager, which will involve taking on more responsibilities. You could also become self-employed, working as a consultant and advising clients on a variety of environmental issues.

You might consider lecturing in environmental science.

Advantages/disadvantages

Your work will have a positive impact on the environment.

There could be opportunities to work abroad in unusual environments, such as rainforests and deserts.

You might face animosity if you refuse to approve a development.

You will often be required to spend time away from home which could disrupt your personal life.

Money guide

Earnings typically vary depending on sector, employer and location.

Starting salaries range from about £15,000 to £22,000.

With increased experience and training, you could expect up to £30,000 a year.

As a senior environmental scientist with managerial duties, it is possible to earn between £35,000 and £50,000.

Related opportunities

- Botanist p506
- Environmental Health Practitioner/Officer p36
- Oceanographer p529

Further information

Environment Agency
www.environment-agency.gov.uk

Institution of Environmental Sciences
www.ies-uk.org.uk

StudentForce for Sustainability
www.studentforce.org.uk

Qualifications and courses

Entrants to this profession usually have a degree, HNC/ HND or Foundation degree in a subject such as food science or food technology. For degree entry you will need 3 A levels/4 H grades, including chemistry and biology, and 5 GCSEs/S grades (A*–C/1–3). HNC/HND programmes usually require 1 A level/2 H grades and 3 GCSEs/S grades (A*–C/1–3).

Graduates with a degree in an unrelated subject could take a postgraduate course in food safety or food quality management. Some food technologists have a postgraduate diploma or an MSc in food sciences.

You can enter this profession with lower qualifications as a laboratory technician/assistant. Typical entry requirements are 4 GCSEs/S grades (A*–C/1–3), including English, maths, chemistry and biology, or an A level in applied science. Technicians can work towards an NVQ in Food Manufacture (Levels 1–3) or an NVQ in Laboratory and Associated Technical Activities (Levels 2–4).

They can also study part time for an HND or degree to gain promotion to a role as a food technologist. Once qualified, candidates can apply for registration with the Institute of Food Science and Technology (IFST).

The Apprenticeship in Food and Drink may also equip you with relevant skills.

What the work involves

Food scientists undertake research, production and quality assurance work in all areas of the food industry. You could apply your knowledge of food, chemistry, biology and nutrition to analyse food products, set up manufacturing processes and develop food labelling.

Your research may involve ensuring that food is safe to eat by testing it under different conditions. Alternatively, you might decrease the risk of contamination by analysing the food safety systems.

You will be using both laboratory and computer equipment to carry out your work.

Type of person suited to this work

You will need to have a high level of ability in biology and chemistry and an interest in food and its production. You should also possess a good knowledge of maths and physics.

You will require strong communication and teamwork skills. You should be meticulous, with a keen eye for detail. You will need to be organised and able to prioritise and manage your workload.

Good problem-solving skills are key and you will need to be extremely logical. You should be able to follow strict health, safety and hygiene rules.

Working conditions

You could be working in research units, laboratories or in a factory within the quality department. The working environment will always be clean to prevent the food being contaminated and you will be required to wear protective clothing.

You will typically work between 35 and 40 hours per week and if your employer operates a shift system, you might need to work weekends.

This role may include travel to warehouses, factories and distribution centres. A driving licence would be useful.

Future prospects

You might be offered the opportunity of promotion to team leader, technical director or project coordinator if you work within a larger organisation. If you work for a smaller employer, you might need to change companies in order to progress.

Your skills would be transferable to several related sectors such as production management, marketing and buying raw materials. You could also become a specialist in a certain area.

Working abroad may be a possibility, especially within larger companies.

Advantages/disadvantages

You will be able to combine your love of food with your scientific background.

You may find some aspects of the job tedious, for example if you need to repeat the same tests over a period of time.

This career has the possibility of leading to roles in a number of areas.

Money guide

Earnings vary depending on sector, location and employer.

Starting salaries range from £20,000 to £25,000.

With several years' experience and increased responsibilities, you could expect to earn £30,000–£45,000 a year.

Those employed in a senior management role can achieve £55,000–£65,000.

Related opportunities

- Chef/Sous Chef p137
- Dietitian p303
- Microbiologist p528

Further information

Food and Drink Federation
www.fdf.org.uk

Improve Ltd
www.improveltd.co.uk

Institute of Food Science & Technology
www.ifst.org

SCIENCE, MATHEMATICS AND STATISTICS

CRCI: TA

FORENSIC SCIENTIST

Qualifications and courses

You will need a good Honours degree in biology, chemistry, forensic science or a related subject. Some employers may accept an equivalent professional qualification. The Forensic Science Society accredits university courses. For degree entry you will usually require at least 2 A levels/3 H grades including biology and/or chemistry, and 5 GCSEs/S grades (A*–C/1–3) including maths, English and science.

Many entrants to this profession also have a postgraduate, master's or PhD qualification in forensic science or a related subject. Employers sometimes expect you to have experience working in a laboratory.

To enter as an assistant forensic scientist in England and Wales, you will need 4 GCSEs (A*–C), including English, biology, chemistry or maths, and 1 A level in chemistry or biology. In Scotland, a Higher National qualification in chemistry, biology or a related subject is normally required. Assistant forensic scientists often have a degree or postgraduate qualification and you will be unable to progress to a role as a forensic scientist without qualifications at this level.

Once you secure employment as a trainee forensic scientist, you will receive on-the-job training from experienced colleagues.

What the work involves

You will use your skills to provide important scientific information and help resolve legal and criminal cases. By analysing samples and assessing accident and crime scenes, you will support the work of police and lawyers.

Your role will involve identifying anything that may be used as evidence from a crime scene, including organs, blood, bodily fluids, illegal drugs, fire arms and explosives, DNA and even paint or fragments of glass. You will carry out the necessary tests to extract the information required by the police.

You will use techniques including photography, DNA profiling, chromatography and metallurgy.

Type of person suited to this work

You need strong scientific skills and the desire to help solve crimes. Confidence is essential, as you might have to make court appearances.

You should be able to handle distressing situations well. You will need to pay great attention to detail whilst in the field, in the laboratory and when producing reports.

You will require the ability to clearly explain scientific findings to people without a scientific background. You should be able to use statistics to interpret your findings. You must be a great communicator.

Working conditions

You will spend the majority of your time in the laboratory but you will also need to visit crime scenes. You might have to deal with unpleasant or upsetting sights.

You may also be outdoors in all weathers. You could be standing or crouching for long periods of time to examine evidence. You might have to travel with some absences from home.

The average forensic scientist works about 35 to 37 hours per week. You may also have to spend time on-call.

Future prospects

As an assistant forensic scientist with an appropriate degree, you can progress to become a forensic scientist.

Forensic scientists employed in the Forensic Science Service (FSS) could move up to reporting officer level, delivering reports in court.

Promotion to management is generally based on appraisal reports and experience. You could become self-employed by working as a forensic consultant. You might also have the opportunity to work abroad.

Advantages/disadvantages

You will be using your scientific knowledge to help the police catch criminals, which would be extremely rewarding.

This job comes with a lot of responsibility as your evidence may be the reason someone gets convicted.

This is a varied job and no two cases will be the same.

Money guide

Earnings vary according to employer and location.

Starting salaries for trainee or assistant forensic scientists are between £16,000 and £20,000.

Once you have gained 2–3 years' experience earnings can increase to £25,000–£35,000 a year.

As a senior forensic scientist you could achieve £45,000 to £60,000 a year.

Related opportunities

- Biomedical Scientist/Medical Laboratory Assistant p504
- Clinical Scientist p509
- Microbiologist p528

Further information

Forensic Science Service
www.forensic.gov.uk

Forensic Science Society
www.forensic-science-society.org.uk

Skills for Justice
www.skillsforjustice.com

GEOGRAPHER

Qualifications and courses

An Honours degree or above in geography or a related field is required. Geography degrees cover varied aspects of human, economic and physical geography, but it is also possible to gain an undergraduate degree in one particular aspect, such as oceanography or global change.

Entry requirements for geography degrees vary but are usually 5 GCSEs/S grades (A*–C/1–3) and 2 A levels/ 3 H grades including geography. For science-based geography courses (BSc), A levels/H grades in science might be needed.

Graduates who wish to secure a role as a researcher in academia will need to continue their studies to master's and PhD level. You will need a minimum of a 2.1 in your first degree to progress to a master's. To obtain funding for a PhD, you will be required to have achieved a high level in your master's.

The Royal Geographical Society (RGS-IBG) offers opportunities for A level/H grade students to carry out sponsored fieldwork, and also provides gap year scholarships and several short courses.

What the work involves

You will be undertaking research, using IT, fieldwork and paper-based resources to broaden public and academic knowledge of your specific field of geography.

You can choose to specialise in either physical geography – the study of the earth, rivers, climate, land formation and oceans – or human geography – the study of humans in their environment. There are also several other branches of geography within these 2, including environmental, health, historical, geomatics and pedology.

You could use your skills and the research you have collected in a range of industrial fields, from government bodies to private consulting firms. As a researcher for a university, you will also lecture and contribute as a writer to geographical journals or articles while studying for a PhD or similar.

Type of person suited to this work

You need to have a good knowledge of your area of geography, with a genuine interest in and love for what you study. You will need excellent research and communication skills to be able to thoroughly understand and lecture on your chosen area of study.

Being flexible, approachable and hardworking will assist your progression to becoming an expert in your specialist geographical subject.

You will need a good level of physical fitness for fieldwork, as you will be working long hours in unusual conditions, spending a lot of time on your feet.

Working conditions

You could be based in a research centre, university, office or on location during fieldwork. Travel within the UK and abroad is frequently required.

You might need to work unsocial hours and weekends during fieldwork. Lecturing and office-based research tend to have more standard working hours, Monday to Friday.

You will have access to a computer and a library to assist with research. You might need to use special equipment while in the field.

Future prospects

It is important to get some work experience in a research position before applying for a fully paid job, as the competition for research positions can be fierce. You can progress from research assistant to head researcher.

If you are following an academic route, you can start off as an assistant lecturer and progress to professor after completing a PhD and contributing significantly to your field of geography.

Advantages/disadvantages

You can work overseas, often for long periods of time, when doing field-based research.

The work is interesting and varied.

You will be required to constantly keep up to date with any changes or developments in your geographical field of expertise.

Money guide

Earnings vary according to your experience and employer.

As a research assistant, you can expect a starting salary between £17,000 and £26,000.

With increased experience and acknowledgement in your chosen area of expertise, your earnings could rise to £30,000–£45,000.

Professors contributing significantly to their field can earn in excess of £50,000.

Related opportunities

- Planning and Development Surveyor p110
- Secondary School Teacher p203
- Town Planner/Planning Technician p127

Further information

Geographical Association
www.geography.org.uk

Royal Geographical Society with IBG
www.rgs.org

Qualifications and courses

Geologist

To enter this profession you need a degree in a relevant physical science subject such as geology, geophysics or geochemistry. Requirements for a degree course are 5 GCSEs/S grades (A*–C/1–3) including English and 3 A levels/H grades from subjects such as physics, chemistry, biology, geology and maths. The Geological Society provides details of approved courses which meet the first stage requirements for becoming a Chartered Geologist (CGeol).

Many entrants will have studied for a master's or PhD in a relevant area of geoscience. As competition for jobs is strong, a postgraduate qualification may improve your career prospects.

Geological technician

The usual minimum entry requirements for a junior technician are 4 GCSEs/S grades (A*–C/1–3) including science and maths, and some employers may also require A levels/H grades. A BTEC National in Applied Science (Level 3) may be accepted.

Once you secure employment, it is possible to work towards further qualifications, such as a degree, HND or the NVQ in Laboratory and Associated Technical Activities (Levels 2–4).

What the work involves

Geologist

Geologists analyse and study the planet Earth, including its materials, structure and history. Your work may involve organising practical field and laboratory research to gain specific information. You may use your skills to support development work, for example mineral mining and the oil industry.

Geological technician

You will work closely with geologists, undertaking practical research work in the field and laboratory. You will collect and examine samples and produce test results. You will use other sources, for example surveys, to provide detailed information on specific geological features and aspects.

Type of person suited to this work

You should have the ability to pay close attention to detail. You will need to be meticulous, practical and logical in your approach to work. You will have to work with technical equipment so you should have high levels of dexterity. You must be able to uphold health and safety regulations.

Geologists need to be able to make important decisions and communicate well, both verbally and in writing. A geological technician requires good graphical skills, including computer-aided design, to help produce maps.

Working conditions

The hours and working conditions of a geologist will vary considerably depending on the sector they work in.

Geological technicians normally work 9am–5pm, Monday–Friday, with some exceptions when they have approaching deadlines.

Future prospects

Geologists could progress to a managerial role, although this may involve relocating. There is also the possibility of becoming self-employed if you work as a consultant. Alternatively, you could work as a university lecturer.

There are more promotion opportunities for geological technicians within larger organisations. If you choose to work for a smaller company, you might need to change employers to progress. Training to become a geologist is possible.

Advantages/disadvantages

You may have difficulty gaining enough money to fund your research or projects.

There are job opportunities within multinational corporations which would allow you to use the latest technology and travel.

Employers generally prefer applicants who have completed postgraduate study.

Money guide

Geologist

Starting out as a graduate you can expect a salary of £20,000–£30,000.

With experience, you could earn £40,000–£50,000 a year.

Senior geologists with extensive experience can receive a salary ranging from £70,000 to over £100,000.

Geological technician

Starting salaries are between £12,800 and £18,500.

With experience, you can expect £20,000–£32,000 a year.

At senior levels, salaries can increase to £40,000.

Related opportunities

- Ecologist p512
- Geophysicist p519
- Oceanographer p529

Further information

British Geological Survey
www.bgs.ac.uk

Cogent Sector Skills Council Limited
www.cogent-ssc.com

GEOPHYSICIST

Qualifications and courses

A degree in geophysics, geology, physics or a related subject is required for entry to this profession. For a geophysics degree, you will usually need 3 A levels/H grades including maths and physics and 5 GCSEs/S grades (A*–C/1–3). Other useful subjects to study at A level/H grade are biology, chemistry, geography and geology.

Many entrants also have a postgraduate qualification and relevant courses include an MSc in petroleum engineering, petroleum geoscience or exploration geophysics. It is also possible to achieve a PhD in a specialist area of geophysics.

Pre-entry work experience, from a vaction placement or internship, is desirable and will provide opportunities to make contacts within the industry.

For entry at technician level, an A level/H grade in physics is normally required. It may be possible to enter with an SQA National in Physics at Intermediate 2 or a BTEC National Certificate/Diploma in Applied Science (Level 3).

The Apprenticeship for Laboratory and Science Technicians is available at both Intermediate and Advanced Levels. For entry to an Apprenticeship you will need 4 GCSEs/S grades (A*–C/1–3).

What the work involves

Geophysicists apply physics-based investigation techniques to analyse the nature of the rocks, structures and minerals below the Earth's surface. You will spend a lot of time undertaking practical work and writing up results.

Most geophysicists and field seismologists are involved with helping companies locate oil and gas. You will plan and organise exploration work and interpret detailed geological information.

Geophysicists work in research in universities, research institutes and for companies involved in oil and mineral exploration. You will work as part of a team of geologists, engineers and/or engineering geologists.

Type of person suited to this work

You should have an interest in rock structures and a desire to travel. Your scientific and technical skills will be of a high quality. You should pay excellent attention to detail and have a methodical and meticulous approach to solving problems.

You will need to have strong numeracy skills and the ability to use software packages which may be extremely complex. You should be able to communicate well, both in person and in writing.

Working conditions

You will spend some time in an office or laboratory and the rest in the field. If you are involved in data collection you will travel the world, operating from base camps.

You might also work offshore (at sea) on oil or gas platforms or ships. This work will involve being away from home for long periods of time in a confined space, living and working with the same people.

In a UK office-based role, hours are generally 9am–5pm but you will be expected to be flexible. At sea, the working day is 12 hours. You may also be called on during your free time if there is an urgent need.

Future prospects

Skilled geophysics professionals are in demand with construction, fuel and mineral exploration and development organisations within the public and private sectors.

Developing a career in industry may involve moving around to gain the relevant professional experience. In some jobs you might work overseas.

As you develop appropriate contacts, you have the option of becoming self-employed or doing consultancy/freelance work.

Advantages/disadvantages

The work can be physically demanding and may involve visiting potentially hazardous sites.

You may have the opportunity to study and observe the natural world in a variety of locations.

Some employment in this area is offered on a short-term basis, which can lead to job insecurity.

Money guide

Earnings vary depending on location, employer and the sector you work in.

Graduates with a first degree have a starting salary of £22,000–£25,000, whilst those with an MSc/PhD can expect £24,000–£30,000.

With experience, you could earn between £30,000 and £45,000 a year.

In a senior position, you could achieve over £60,000 per year.

Related opportunities

- Energy Engineer p221
- Environmental Scientist p514
- Oceanographer p529

Further information

British Geological Survey
www.bgs.ac.uk

British Geophysical Association
www.ras.org.uk

Geological Society
www.geolsoc.org.uk

SCIENCE, MATHEMATICS AND STATISTICS

CRCI: TB

HYDROLOGIST

Qualifications and courses

The minimum requirement for entry to this profession is an Honours degree in a subject such as geography (focusing on physical science), environmental science, civil engineering or environmental management. For degree courses, students usually need a minimum of 2 A levels/3 H grades and 5 GCSEs/S grades (A*–C/1–3). Useful subjects to study at A level/H grade include maths, science, geography and geology.

Owing to the high level of competition for positions in this sector, a postgraduate qualification is strongly recommended. Possible subjects to study are water resources, engineering hydrology and water management. Entry is with a minimum of a 2.1 in a relevant first degree.

The Chartered Institution of Water and Environmental Management (CIWEM) accredits a number of undergraduate and postgraduate courses in the field.

Pre-entry work experience is a useful way to develop your skills and build contacts within this competitive industry. You should consider completing placements during your holidays or as part of a sandwich degree.

Hydrologists are expected to engage in continuing professional development (CPD) throughout their career.

What the work involves

As an invaluable natural resource, water needs to be monitored and managed by hydrologists. You will help ensure that safe drinking water is available when and where it is needed.

Your work could involve measuring river flows, rainfall, evaporation and groundwater. You may assess water use in agriculture and forestry, or deal with water-management emergencies, for example in droughts.

Your research might involve working out potential flood risks, designing water supply systems or developing resources such as reservoirs. You will work with civil engineers, freshwater ecologists, chemists and other professionals.

Type of person suited to this work

You will need to have an interest in environmental protection and management, and an understanding of how a water supply affects a society. You should have strong geographical, scientific, mathematical and technical capabilities.

This role requires the ability to think creatively and solve problems. You will also need to be confident in using and creating maps and other ways of portraying a landscape.

The job demands excellent observational skills and attention to detail. You must be able to work with detailed factual information and communicate your findings.

Working conditions

Most hydrologists work conventional hours within an office environment. If there is an emergency or a deadline approaching, you might need to work some evenings and weekends.

You might also be required to spend time in the field. You will be working outdoors in a variety of weather conditions and using heavy equipment, so you will need to have a certain level of physical stamina.

This job might involve travel within the UK and abroad.

Future prospects

The opportunities available for promotion will vary according to the organisation and employer. Progression also depends on experience, skills, responsibility and merit. You may be able to increase your chances of promotion by moving to another team or geographical location. To progress, you should be able to manage people, projects and budgets.

Self-employment is possible if you become a consultant and there are many opportunities to work overseas for international organisations.

Advantages/disadvantages

You can live and work abroad while you undertake research work.

You may have to work outdoors in the wind and rain.

Some employment in this area is offered on a short-term basis, which can lead to job insecurity.

If you work within consultancy, you will have a wide variety of work available to you.

Money guide

Earnings vary according to sector, location and employer.

Starting salaries range from £17,000 to £25,000.

With experience, your earnings can rise to £23,000–£32,000 a year.

Those employed in a senior role can earn £35,000–£45,000.

Related opportunities

- Geophysicist p519
- Meteorologist p527
- Oceanographer p529

Further information

British Hydrological Society
www.hydrology.org.uk

Chartered Institution of Water and Environmental Management
www.ciwem.org

IMMUNOLOGIST

Qualifications and courses

All immunologists hold a relevant degree in immunology or a related science subject such as medical microbiology, biomedical science, or genetics. Most institutions require at least 5 good GCSEs/S grades and 2 A levels/Highers (including biology) for entrance.

You will need at least a 2.1 degree and a postgraduate qualification is required for many NHS positions. You can also enter the profession through working in a pathology laboratory straight from school (ie after A levels/Highers), but this route is less common.

You can enter this profession as a mature student, and there are Access courses available which can help those who are out of practice at education prepare for a degree.

Once you are in the industry, there is plenty of training on offer. Many employers train you in house, and with the NHS you can apply to the Scientist Training Programme. Some programmes lead to a master's degree, and contribute to the requirements for membership of professional bodies.

In an academic setting it is normally encouraged for you to complete a PhD as part of your ongoing training. Outside of academia there are technical courses to attend.

What the work involves

Immunologists work with the body's immune system. They study functions and use the knowledge gained to treat and control illness and disease.

You might work on developing vaccines against diseases such as HIV or meningitis.

You could also find yourself studying the causes of allergies and looking at ways to stop the human body rejecting transplanted organs.

Type of person suited to this work

If you are thinking of becoming an immunologist, you naturally need to be interested in medicine and healthcare, and the way the body works.

You should have a logical, scientific mind and be good at solving problems, as well as being good at biology and science subjects in general. You may spend years researching one area or topic, and so will need to be patient and enjoy in-depth research work.

You will often have to work in teams, so you should enjoy this but equally be able to use your initiative and work independently. If you choose to lecture, your communication skills need to be excellent.

Working conditions

Working hours will vary depending on your employer, but will generally fall into the average 9am–5pm Monday to Friday pattern. During busy periods you may be required to work overtime.

Work tends to take place in a laboratory environment, often in sterile conditions. You will probably be required to wear appropriate clothing, and this often includes a white coat, face mask and rubber gloves.

If you choose to lecture, the environment will be very different, and you will spend most of your time in classrooms and lecture theatres.

Future prospects

If you choose to work as a lecturer, once you are a researcher, you can work your way towards a promotion to lecturer, then senior lecturer and so forth, up to professor and head of department.

If you follow the NHS pathway, the career progression structure is very clear. You basically work your way up the grades, from A to B to C.

Other options to consider include scientific writing and publishing, or working on drugs trials and quality assurance. You could also progress to sales, finance and management positions within the biotechnology industry.

Advantages/disadvantages

This is a skilled profession, and training and progression can be really rewarding, especially in such an interesting job.

There is also the added advantage that you will be helping people.

The job can be stressful and demanding, and the work is by no means easy.

Money guide

As a new graduate in an NHS training post you will start on band 6 which is £25,528 a year. After considerable experience this can gradually rise to a band 9 salary which is up to £97,478 a year.

Outside of the NHS, starting salaries range from £22,000–£30,000. Once you gain experience, this rises to between £28,000 and £37,000 and senior immunologists can earn between £40,000 and £60,000 a year.

Salaries vary between sectors.

Related opportunities

- Biomedical Scientist/Medical Laboratory Assistant p504
- Clinical Scientist p509
- Hospital Doctor p312

Further information

British Society for Immunology
www.immunology.org

NHS Careers
www.nhscareers.nhs.uk

SCIENCE, MATHEMATICS AND STATISTICS

CRCI: TD

Qualifications and courses

Entrants need at least 4 GCSEs/S grades (A*–C/1–3), including English, mathematics and a science. Equivalent qualifications such as a BTEC First Certificate or Diploma in Science may be accepted.

Qualifications at a higher level such as A levels, a BTEC National qualification, a HNC/HND or a degree in a science subject might be required.

Laboratory technicians are trained on the job, and may be able to study towards NVQs at Levels 1–4 in Laboratory and Associated Technical Activities or Level 2 in Clinical Laboratory Support.

You could take the Institute of Science & Technology's Certificate in Laboratory Technical Skills at Levels 1–3 or their Higher Diploma in Analytical Chemical, Biochemical or Microbiological Laboratory Techniques.

What the work involves

You will analyse samples of different types of substances and materials using specialist equipment. You could specialise in a particular area, such as microbiology or clinical chemistry.

Your work may involve recording detailed information and developing and maintaining microbiological or other cultures.

Laboratory technicians apply their scientific analysis and measurement skills in organisations such as the military services, the NHS, industry and scientific research institutions.

Type of person suited to this work

You will provide important factual information, so must work to a high standard of accuracy. Your patient attitude will help you undertake sometimes repetitive but important laboratory activities.

Good manual handling skills will be needed to organise laboratory equipment. You will also need good communication skills and normal colour vision.

Good ICT skills will help you record and analyse a range of information. As your work may involve potentially dangerous situations, like handling bacteria and working with radiation, you must work to a good standard of health and safety at all times.

Working conditions

You will most likely have standard working hours, although some employers do work on a shift or rota basis which includes early mornings, evenings and weekends. Your working day will be spent in a clean and sterile laboratory.

You will work with specialist computer software to complete your research and record activities.

You could also have to carry out fieldwork at various sites outside the laboratory.

Future prospects

You will play an important role in protecting public health and help make safe, high-quality products that many of us use every day.

Scientific laboratory technicians are employed within industry, health service organisations, public research and other areas. With further experience, you could progress to supervising a team of technicians or managing a laboratory.

Medical laboratory technicians can advance into a role as an education laboratory technician, phlebotomist, cardiographer or physiologist.

Advantages/disadvantages

Laboratory tasks can be repetitive, time-consuming and require patience.

Because of the transferable nature of lab skills, you could move from one organisation to another quite easily.

In some organisations you would work on a shift basis.

Money guide

Starting salaries are generally between £14,000 and £19,000 per year.

With experience and qualifications, you could earn up to £20,000.

As a very experienced laboratory technician, team leader or laboratory manager, it is possible to earn between £30,000 and £40,000.

Related opportunities

- Biochemist p503
- Biomedical Scientist/Medical Laboratory Assistant p504
- Pharmacy Technician p328

Further information

Biochemical Society Membership Office
www.biochemistry.org

Science Council
www.sciencecouncil.org

Semta
www.semta.org.uk

SCIENCE, MATHEMATICS AND STATISTICS

CRCI: TD

MARINE BIOLOGIST

Qualifications and courses

To enter this profession you require a degree in a relevant subject such as marine biology, marine science and oceanography. These subjects could be usefully combined with subjects such as maths and statistics. Minimum entry requirements for a degree are usually 3 A levels/H grades in relevant science subjects such as biology along with 5 GCSEs/S grades (A*–C/1–3). A levels in maths, technological subjects or languages would also be beneficial.

Although not essential, a postgraduate qualification is a distinct advantage in this field. For postgraduate study you will normally require a minimum of a 2.1 in your first degree.

If you want to apply for a technological support role you should have achieved A levels/H grades in biology, maths or geography and another science subject.

What the work involves

You will undertake practical research and analysis into animal and plant life in the world's seas and oceans. As well as academic research, you could apply your skills in fisheries, research or fish-farming development.

You may undertake research trips above or below the sea's surface and keep detailed research records. By increasing understanding of the sea you will be able to make predictions about the effects man will have on the marine ecosystem and how it will cope with these changes.

You may provide specialist advice to organisations such as governments or environmental pressure groups.

Type of person suited to this work

You should have a strong interest in science and a particular interest in marine life. You will require both a scientific understanding and practical ability. You will need to be meticulous and extremely patient.

You should have good numerical and computer-based skills. You must be observant and have a questioning mind. You will need to be able to analyse and interpret data effectively. You should have a certain level of physical stamina.

You will need a desire to travel and not mind being at sea. You should be highly organised and able to work autonomously and as part of a team.

Working conditions

You will spend time in an office environment, laboratory and researching in the field. Whilst in the laboratory or office you will usually work normal office hours, however some projects and deadlines may require overtime.

When working on projects at sea you will probably be working longer hours. Operating at sea might mean you are away for long periods of time, in cramped and possibly uncomfortable conditions.

You will be living and working with the same people.

Future prospects

There can be a lot of competition for jobs. Gaining a good level of practical experience in addition to the relevant training shows commitment and provides useful skills. Once you have gathered enough field experience you could go freelance or alternatively, set up your own consultancy.

You could lecture students, which you could combine with completing your own research.

Working abroad is a distinct possibility.

Advantages/disadvantages

A lot of your research in the field will depend on the tides and weather conditions, which could slow down your progress.

You will use your skills and knowledge to increase public understanding of the natural environment.

Finding funding for your projects may prove problematic.

Money guide

Starting salaries for graduates are usually between £19,000 and £24,000 although they vary greatly depending on the employer and location of the work.

With experience, and for those with a PhD, salaries could increase to £26,000–£34,000.

The highest earning marine biologists, who are at the top of their field, can earn around £50,000 a year.

Related opportunities

- Ecologist p512
- Environmental Scientist p514
- Oceanographer p529

Further information

Centre for Environment, Fisheries and Aquaculture Science
www.cefas.co.uk

Marine Biological Association
www.mba.ac.uk

National Oceanography Centre, Southampton
www.noc.soton.ac.uk

Qualifications and courses

Candidates typically hold a relevant degree, often in metallurgy, materials science/technology or materials engineering. It is also possible to enter with a degree in a general science subject. A Foundation year is available at some institutions for candidates without the required scientific background.

Most degree courses expect applicants to have achieved at least 2 A levels/3 H grades, including maths and science, and 5 GCSEs/S grades (A*–C/1–3), including maths and English. You could take NVQs or an Apprenticeship in Engineering and Manufacturing Technologies.

To become a chartered materials engineer, you need to have studied a 4-year MEng degree or a 3-year BEng or BSc followed by a period of professional development. Postgraduate courses are available, and may be studied prior to entry, or through company training schemes. In order to be accepted you must have successfully completed a first degree. Many employers prefer candidates to have an MSc or to be working towards a PhD.

It may be possible to enter the profession at technician level, as a research assistant for example. Often technicians are studying part time for their PhD.

What the work involves

Materials scientists measure, define and process materials. They help decide the types of materials to use in engineering, construction and product processing work.

You will use your knowledge of the properties of metals and alloys, glass, ceramics and other materials in many areas of industrial research, development and production. You will research how and why materials react to certain conditions and how they can be used in our everyday lives.

You will use technology and computer equipment to carry out tests on different materials, keep records of your findings and draw conclusions from the results.

Type of person suited to this work

You will need to have creative flair and you should have an inquisitive and logical mind. You will need to be meticulous.

You will be able to write coherent reports and be a good public speaker, as you might need to give presentations. You will need solid computer skills. You should work well in a team environment.

You should have dexterity as you will be working with a range of test equipment. You will need good eyesight (including colour vision for some projects).

Working conditions

Materials scientists in industry work normal office hours or shifts, however the more senior your role is, the longer you will have to work.

You could be working in a sterile laboratory or an industrial environment. The most common working environments for materials scientists are laboratories and offices.

There is a possibility you will have to complete work in the field. You may have to wear protective clothing.

Future prospects

You will have the option to change industries and purchase raw materials, work in sales, management or marketing. You could progress to become a project manager or a technical director, meaning you would be leading people in developing new products.

Alternatively, you could move into a career in teaching.

Opportunities for self-employment are limited but you could work in NDT (non-destructive testing) or failure analysis. There may be the possibility to work abroad.

Advantages/disadvantages

You will have the opportunity to apply your skills and knowledge to develop new products and provide new scientific information.

Scientists are constantly in demand in most areas of industry.

This can be a highly lucrative career.

Money guide

On entering this career as a graduate you can expect to earn around £21,000 per year.

Entry salaries tend to be higher with a postgraduate qualification at £25,000–£35,000 per year.

Once you have reached a senior role, as a professor for example, you could earn in excess of £50,000 per year.

Salaries are usually higher within large companies in the private sector.

Related opportunities

- Biochemist p503
- Chemist p507
- Laboratory Technician p522

Further information

Institute of Materials, Minerals and Mining
www.iom3.org

Semta
www.semta.org.uk

UK Centre for Materials Education
www.materials.ac.uk

Qualifications and courses

A degree in maths is essential to work as a professional mathematician in industry, business/finance, education or research.

Degrees are available in general maths or in specific areas, for example, financial maths or business maths. Entry onto maths degree courses usually requires at least 2 A levels/H grades including maths, and 5 GCSEs/S grades (A*–C/1–3), including English and maths. Science and or computing-related subjects are also viewed favourably.

Maths graduates are recruited directly by some companies. Most mathematicians have postgraduate qualifications, which require a first degree in mathematics, physics or another subject with a high mathematical content. Entry is possible with an undergraduate degree only but progression is significantly limited unless you hold a further qualification, particularly within academia.

It is possible to become a Chartered Mathematician with the Institute of Mathematics and its Applications after gaining an Honours degree in maths or a degree with more than two-thirds maths content, and 3 years in employment.

What the work involves

Research is conducted using mathematical theory in order to solve problems in areas such as science, engineering, finance, government and ICT. You could work at all levels of industry, research and education and help to inform the work of different organisations.

You could study and teach pure mathematics in an academic environment or work in job roles requiring mathematical skills and knowledge, for example actuary, operational researcher or statistician.

Your work may involve undertaking research and analysis, setting up research programmes and assessing research findings. In a business, you will work on a specific project such as predicting future trends in population growth or financial markets.

Type of person suited to this work

You must have a strong interest in working with numerical information to solve complex problems. You need to be logical and methodical, as well as flexible and innovative to analyse a range of problems.

Your work could help shape the activities of your company so you must have good attention to detail and be able to record your work accurately.

Strong communication skills will help you explain mathematical ideas to people without a maths background. As maths-related research can take time to set up, a patient attitude can be helpful.

Working conditions

For many roles, you would work in an office and use computers to analyse information. Long hours are common in this role.

If you work in education, you will spend time teaching in classrooms and in lecture rooms. You could also spend time undertaking research.

Mathematicians who work in business, such as accountants, will spend time in meetings with their clients.

Future prospects

There is a high demand for professional mathematicians in areas such as business, finance or industry, and in companies that develop new products such as new computer software and pharmaceuticals.

After gaining experience, you could progress into a managerial role.

In an academic environment, progression depends on your research accomplishments.

Advantages/disadvantages

Mathematical skills apply to many different sectors, so you could move across a range of areas.

A shortage of qualified mathematicians means that there are a variety of opportunities.

A second degree could be needed to follow your chosen career.

Tight deadlines and the uncertainty in being able to find a solution to problems can make this line of work stressful.

Money guide

Salary levels vary widely according to employer and sector, although on average larger companies will pay more than smaller companies.

Starting salaries range from £25,000 to £35,000 per year.

With several years' experience you could earn £29,000–£38,000 per year.

At senior level, expected earnings would be from £30,000 up to £70,000, depending on sector and level of responsibility. These figures apply to professors within academic settings and team leaders within industrial settings.

Related opportunities

- Actuary p19
- Stockbroker p66
- Systems Analyst p161

Further information

Institute of Mathematics and its Applications
www.ima.org.uk

Mathematical Association
www.m-a.org.uk

Maths Careers
www.mathscareers.org.uk

SCIENCE, MATHEMATICS AND STATISTICS

CRCI: TC

METALLURGIST

ENTRY LEVEL 5

Qualifications and courses

The usual entry qualification for a metallurgist is a degree. Degrees are available in metallurgy and in materials science, materials technology and materials engineering. It is also possible to enter with a degree in a general science subject, including physics or chemistry.

Entry to a relevant degree course usually requires a minimum of 2 A levels/3 H grades and 5 GCSEs/S grades (A*–C/1–3). BTEC/SQA National qualifications might be offered as alternatives.

For those seeking entry to the profession by first becoming a technician or with an HNC/HND or Foundation degree (in a subject such as metallurgy and materials, metals technology, manufacturing engineering or applied science) then at least 1 science A level/H grade will be required.

You can apply for a graduate training programme offered by many employers which can lead to membership of a professional institution, such as the Institute of Cast Metals Engineers (ICME), and could increase job prospects.

Once you have qualified, continuing professional development (CPD) is actively encouraged. Once you have gained 2 years of relevant experience you will be given the opportunity to join the Institute of Materials, Minerals and Mining (IOM³). Membership will give you an opportunity to attend conferences and network with others in the industry. If you have a relevant master's degree and 4 years' experience you will be able to become a 'professional' member of IOM³. You can then apply to gain charted engineer status (CEng).

What the work involves

Metallurgists apply their materials science and engineering knowledge to support product and process development in areas such as aerospace, rail, construction and oil and gas.

You may be involved with the metal extraction process, managing projects or researching metals and materials. You might help develop practical solutions for production problems.

Whatever job you do, it is likely that your role will involve aspects of quality control, project management and process/product development.

Type of person suited to this work

Metallurgists need an excellent knowledge of metals and related materials, whatever area they work in. They must also be able to understand the uses for different materials.

You will need to have good communication and teamworking skills. But you will also have to be confident in making decisions that could affect major industrial processes and understand the commercial impact of your work.

Your flexible approach and attention to detail will help you adapt to the changing demands of different projects. Your ICT and numeracy skills will also be important. Because you could work with potentially dangerous materials you must have a good knowledge of health and safety.

Working conditions

You might have to work in a noisy location if you are employed by a large manufacturing company. In other roles you could be based in a laboratory-style setting.

Hours vary from employer to employer, but they can be long especially if you are working to complete a specific project to a set deadline.

In many roles, you will be part of a team and could also meet with clients on a regular basis. In some roles you may be required to write detailed reports.

Future prospects

Many industries are quite literally built on metals and related materials so there are all kinds of job opportunities.

You could undertake project management for individual companies. You could choose to work for companies that develop materials for industries such as automotive and aerospace engineering.

There may be the opportunity for you to directly manage the process of mining and extracting materials.

Advantages/disadvantages

The role can provide the satisfaction of developing new products and materials.

There are opportunities to work and live abroad.

You might need to work unsocial hours for various projects.

Money guide

Starting salaries range from around £18,500 to £28,000 per year. Those with CEng status are likely to earn more.

With experience and at a senior level it is possible to earn £40,000.

As a senior manager and with chartered engineer status and considerable experience you could earn in excess of £50,000.

Related opportunities

- Aerospace Engineer p212
- Laboratory Technician p522
- Materials Scientist p524

Further information

Engineering Council UK
www.engc.org.uk

Institute of Cast Metals Engineers
www.icme.org.uk

Institute of Materials, Minerals and Mining
www.iom3.org

METEOROLOGIST

Qualifications and courses

Entrants to this profession need a degree and often a postgraduate qualification. Degrees in meteorology are available, but other suitable subjects are physics, maths, computer science, oceanography and environmental science. Employers may also require A levels/H grades in maths and physics.

Relevant taught postgraduate courses are available. Subject areas include meteorology, climatology and atmospheric science. There are also opportunities to do a research PhD at some institutions.

The Met Office provides initial training for new entrants without a postgraduate qualification. The training consists of an 18-week Initial Forecasting Course, followed by practical training at a weather station, and a 3 week Forecasting Consolidation Course. You will generally need a 1st or 2.1 and a good grade in at least A level/H grade physics to apply for a post at the Met Office.

You can also enter work at the Met Office in a support role, for which you will generally require at least an HNC/D or 2 A levels/H grades at grade C or above in maths and physics. Relevant work experience would be extremely valuable.

What the work involves

Information gained from observing the sky, the atmosphere and natural phenomena gives a picture of everyday weather conditions.

As well as providing weather forecast information that is used throughout the media and to inform industries such as fishing, meteorologists undertake research into the earth's atmosphere. You could be employed by the Royal Navy, the RAF, the Met Office and other employers.

You will be using specialist computer programs and mathematical techniques to gather information, which you will combine in order to form a weather picture. Within meteorology you can work as a forecaster or a researcher.

Type of person suited to this work

You should have a strong interest in the environment, science, research and climate change. You will need to excel in maths and physics.

The job calls for the ability to problem-solve and think creatively to resolve specific issues. You should be happy to work in various locations, however remote. The job demands excellent observational skills and attention to detail.

You should be able to comprehend and evaluate complex information. You must be able to communicate effectively, both in person and on paper. You will be computer literate, and work well as part of a team.

Working conditions

You will generally conduct your work from an office environment, using specialised computers.

When you are working in the field you could be living and working in extremely isolated areas with basic living conditions.

Researchers generally work ordinary office hours. Forecasters and observers however will usually work in shifts. When working in the field you will not usually have set hours.

Future prospects

There are 3 main areas that a meteorologist can work in; these are forecasting, research and teaching. You may wish to move between them in order to progress.

Once you have gained experience as a forecaster you might be able to move into broadcasting, research or consultancy work.

There are careers available at the Met Office, within utility companies, shipping, insurance companies and in the Armed Forces. There could be the possibility of working abroad.

Advantages/disadvantages

You may have the opportunity to study and observe the natural world in a variety of locations.

You might have to work inconvenient shifts.

There is a wide variety of work within this industry so you shouldn't get bored.

Employers increasingly require applicants to have a postgraduate qualification in a relevant subject.

Money guide

Starting salaries are usually between £21,000 and £27,000 per year.

Experienced meteorologists can earn between £25,000 and £35,000 a year.

AS a manager, £38,000 rising to £60,000 is possible.

Related opportunities

- Geophysicist p519
- Oceanographer p529
- Physicist p531

Further information

Met Office
www.metoffice.gov.uk

Royal Meteorological Society
www.rmets.org

Qualifications and courses

Most entrants have a degree in microbiology or another biological science. To get on to a degree in microbiology you will usually need 5 GCSEs/S grades (A*–C/1–3) including science, English and maths, plus at least 2 A levels/3 H grades including biology and preferably chemistry. An MSc or PhD in microbiology is advisable as there are more opportunities for more highly qualified candidates. Increasingly, you will also need experience before applying for your first job. You may be able to get this through a work placement as part of a sandwich degree course, or by arranging work experience with companies during the holidays. Your university or local NHS Trust may be able to give you further advice about voluntary opportunities.

It is also possible to get into microbiology by working your way up from laboratory technician. This involves studying part time for a relevant degree for which you will need 4 GCSEs/S grades (A*–C/1–3) including 2 sciences (or double science), maths and English and at least 2 A levels/ H grades. NVQs/SVQs are available in Laboratory and Associated Technical Activities at Levels 2 to 4.

Once you are working as a microbiologist, you will usually receive on-the-job training from your employer in areas such as lab techniques and technology and management skills.

To qualify as a clinical scientist (specialising in microbiology), you need a further 2 years' experience after a 3-year programme working towards an MSc in the lab before you can apply for the Association of Clinical Scientists Certificate of Attainment.

What the work involves

Microbiologists study microorganisms such as bacteria and viruses.

As a clinical microbiologist in a healthcare setting, you would aim to identify diseases and protect the community from the spread of infection. Alternatively, you could work in research and development for the pharmaceutical and food industries, in agriculture, the environment or in education.

Duties include presenting the findings of your research, supervising the work of support staff and carrying out administrative work. If you worked as a researcher and lecturer in a university or teaching hospital, you would also be involved in tutoring, mentoring and supervising students.

Type of person suited to this work

You will need to be scientifically capable. You must also have good problem-solving skills and the ability to work with statistics and relevant computer packages.

You will require a high level of dexterity and need to be meticulous, practical and logical in your approach to work. You should also be patient as you might find you have to repeat tests.

Microbiologists should be able to work equally well independently or as part of a team. They must be able to keep careful records and to communicate their ideas and findings to others.

Working conditions

Most microbiologists spend at least part of their time in laboratories. Some microbiologists spend part of their time in classrooms and offices.

The work week for many microbiologists is generally 40 hours. Some overtime may be necessary when a project must be completed or when an experiment must be monitored around the clock.

Microbiologists usually spend some time reading and studying to keep up with the newest findings of other scientists.

Future prospects

There is considerable competition for research positions. Nonetheless, increased public awareness in preserving the environment, providing sanitary food production and storage, and finding cures for such diseases as AIDS, cancer, and heart disease are likely to provide the stimulus for increased spending by private companies.

Opportunities for those with doctoral or master's degrees in microbiology are expected to be better than the opportunities for those with bachelor's degrees.

Advantages/disadvantages

There are opportunities to visit different types of outside locations on research trips.

Experiments can take a long time to complete and some aspects might become tedious. You will also be handling potentially dangerous substances.

Employers such as the National Health Service can offer the chance to gain experience in different departments and provide well-structured career paths.

Money guide

If you begin your career as a laboratory assistant you can expect to earn between £13,000 and £19,000 a year.

Newly qualified microbiologists can earn between £20,000 and £35,000 per year.

Top salaries for microbiologists can reach £60,000 a year.

Related opportunities

- Biochemist p503
- Immunologist p521
- Pharmacologist p327

Further information

NHS Careers
www.nhscareers.nhs.uk

Society for General Microbiology
www.socgenmicrobiol.org.uk

OCEANOGRAPHER

Qualifications and courses

The majority of entrants will hold a degree. Degrees are available in oceanography and related areas, such as marine biology. Other relevant subjects include biology, chemistry, physics, mathematics and geology. For degree entry, candidates usually require 3 relevant A levels such as maths and science subjects and 5 GCSEs/S grades (A*–C/1–3). Relevant GCSE/S grade subjects include sciences, English and maths along with foreign languages, IT and geography.

Most employers expect candidates to hold an A level/H grade in maths. It is possible to join the Merchant or Royal Navy without a degree and then undertake the necessary studying and training to become an oceanographer.

A postgraduate qualification in oceanography will increase employability. Taught courses are available in oceanography and related/specialist areas. In order to be accepted onto a master's degree you will usually need a first degree in a science-based subject. Some master's programmes will accept graduates without a scientific background, though this is very uncommon. It is also possible to do research for an MPhil or PhD.

Entry without a degree or HND/HNC qualification is possible but support and technical roles are rare and a willingness to partake in further study later on would be expected.

What the work involves

Oceanographers investigate how ocean organisms and structures work together.

Your work could involve undertaking fieldwork above and below the surface of the sea. You may also interpret the information you find and write research reports.

The information you produce could be used by government and/or industry.

You could specialise as a marine geologist (studying the ocean floor), marine chemist (studying the chemical composition of water and/or sediment), marine physicist (measuring the properties of currents etc), or a marine biologist (studying the plants and animals in the sea).

Type of person suited to this work

You will require a passion for the environment and ocean life, along with an interest in maths, science and engineering. You will need to be prepared to travel and spend time working at sea.

As you may be working in the field you will need to be physically fit. You should have strong verbal and written communication skills. You will be carrying out detailed research and so will need to be meticulous, logical and practical.

You will also need to be able to present your findings in front of an audience and so should have a certain level of confidence. Good teamwork is essential.

Working conditions

Much of your time will be spent working in a laboratory or an office, with typical office hours from Monday to Friday.

Fieldwork may be carried out at sea or along the coastline.

When working at sea you might be required to spend 6 weeks or more away from home. You will be living and working with the same people.

Future prospects

Most oceanographic work is structured around fixed, short-term contracts and so progression can prove tricky.

You might find that you have to move between employers in order to achieve a promotion. Progression is based on merit and taking on more responsibilities, such as leading a team.

It is possible to become self-employed and work as a consultant. Another option might be university lecturing, where progression opportunities are easier to come by.

Advantages/disadvantages

You will be able to combine your love of the environment with your scientific ability.

Some employers may expect candidates to hold a postgraduate qualification.

You will have the opportunity to travel.

Money guide

These figures are only approximate as salaries will vary depending on location, sector and employer.

Starting salaries begin at between £18,000 and £22,000 per year; with a PhD you could start on between £20,000 and £25,000.

Once you have gained experience as an oceanographer you could earn between £33,000 and £44,000 a year.

As a senior oceanographer, with management responsibilities, you could earn £60,000.

Related opportunities

- Diver p381
- Ecologist p512
- Marine Biologist p523

Further information

Centre for Environment, Fisheries and Aquaculture Science
www.cefas.co.uk

National Oceanography Centre, Southampton
www.noc.soton.ac.uk

SCIENCE, MATHEMATICS AND STATISTICS

CRCI: TB

Qualifications and courses

The entry requirement for this profession is a 2.1 Honours degree or higher in a relevant subject such as maths, statistics, economics, management science or business studies. Specialist degrees in operational research are available at some institutions and are usually offered as a joint Honours degree with a subject such as maths or statistics.

Entry to a relevant degree course is with a minimum of 2 A levels/4 H grades including maths. It may be possible to become an operational researcher with a degree in a non-mathematical subject if you have a good A level/H grade in maths.

Some employers will expect candidates to have a postgraduate qualification, for example a master's in operational research or management science.

Opportunities for graduates are available through the Civil Service Fast Stream programme. The Government Operational Research Service (GORS) recruits candidates with a minimum of a 2.1 in a numerate degree or a postgraduate degree in operational research.

The Operational Research Society organises an annual careers open day for undergraduates who are considering working in this sector. The Society also offers a wide range of training courses and in-house training services.

What the work involves

Operational researchers use mathematical, scientific and other analytical methods to help improve the performance of organisations in business, industry and government.

You will work closely with managers and other staff to create practical solutions to different management and organisational issues.

You will develop analytical models or strategies to improve a specific area or aspect of an organisation. You might also be involved with putting your ideas into practice within companies.

Type of person suited to this work

Operational research is all about getting practical results from in-depth analysis. Consequently, you should enjoy solving problems and applying your analytical and mathematical abilities to find solutions.

You will have a strong interest in helping organisations develop and you will put your understanding of each company to practical use. You will need excellent communication skills for working closely with managers and other staff.

Your flexible approach will help you cope with the varied demands of each project. While you will need strong IT skills, a creative flair can also benefit you in this job.

Working conditions

You will usually work a 37-hour week, Monday to Friday, with some overtime near deadlines.

You will undertake most of your work in an office setting and meetings with managers, technical specialists and staff are likely to be a regular part of your job. You will also be required to visit clients so a driving licence would be useful. Travel both within the UK and abroad is possible.

Future prospects

Operational researchers help many different organisations to develop successfully. There are increasing opportunities in manufacturing, finance and other sectors.

You could move into managing an operational research team or work in areas such as marketing. With more experience, you could develop a career as a consultant.

The civil service offers a well-structured career path and a range of opportunities in operational research.

Advantages/disadvantages

Strong demand in many sectors means that you can develop your career in various types of companies.

Operational research work is fast moving and you will always be learning something new.

Resolving production, resource or staffing problems for a company can be stressful and confrontational.

Money guide

Salary levels depend on location, the sector you work in and your academic background.

Earnings tend to be highest for those employed by management consultancies.

Starting salaries range from £20,000 to £28,000.

With experience and a more senior position, you can expect to earn between £40,000 and £80,000.

At operational research consultant level, you could achieve up to £100,000 a year.

Related opportunities

- Actuary p19
- Mathematician/Mathematics Research Scientist p525
- Statistician p533

Further information

Government Operational Research Service
www.operational-research.gov.uk

Operational Research Society
www.theorsociety.org.uk

PHYSICIST

Qualifications and courses

For entry to this profession you need to have a relevant degree in physics or applied physics. Requirements for a degree course are usually at least 2–3 A levels/3–4 H grades including physics and maths, and 5 GCSEs/S grades (A*–C/1–3) including English, maths and science.

Some employers may also expect you to have a relevant postgraduate qualification such as an MSc, MPhil or PhD and entry is with a minimum of a 2.1 in your first degree.

Many institutions offer 1-year science foundation courses for candidates without the necessary scientific background.

Physicists are trained on the job and often study for a PhD or the membership exams of relevant professional bodies. For example, medical physicists must work towards the Clinical Science Diploma of the Institute of Physics and Engineering in Medicine (IPEM).

For entry at technician level, an A level/H grade in physics, or an equivalent qualification such as a BTEC National in Applied Science/SQA National in Science is required. Some technicians may hold a science-based degree. Technicians who have secured employment can take the NVQ in Laboratory and Associated Technical Activities (Levels 2–4).

What the work involves

Physicists apply their understanding of the relationship between matter and energy to their work in industry, government research, academia and medicine.

You could use your specialist skills and knowledge to investigate diverse subjects, including space research, nuclear energy, electronics, defence technology and materials for industrial use.

You might be involved with research and development work or with designing projects and experiments. Your role could also include developing products and systems in areas such as computing, aeronautics, transport and medicine.

Type of person suited to this work

Physicists must combine their scientific knowledge with strong problem-solving skills.

You will need the confidence to work with complex numerical information. You should have excellent attention to detail and a patient approach for undertaking research.

IT skills are also important. Good written and verbal communication skills are needed to be able to explain your work clearly.

Working conditions

You will usually work Monday to Friday from 9am to 5pm. If you are employed by the NHS as a medicial physicist, you are likely to work shifts and fulfil on-call duties.

You will be based in a laboratory, workshop or office, using specialist equipment and computers. This work can involve handling dangerous chemicals so you will need to wear protective clothing.

For some jobs you will be required to travel to meetings and conferences so a driving licence would be useful. If you are undertaking research in the field, you may be away from home for extended periods of time.

Future prospects

Physicists work at the cutting edge of science and industry. They apply their skills in areas as varied as electronics, power, communications and defence. They are employed by research institutions, government bodies and private companies to improve and develop products and systems.

You will be able to progress to supervisory or management roles, or enter into the training and teaching of physics.

Advantages/disadvantages

Physics offers the chance to develop public understanding of important scientific questions.

Working with detailed information for long periods of time can be very tiring.

You might have the chance to work abroad.

Money guide

Salary levels vary according to employer and sector.

Holding a relevant PhD may increase your income.

Starting salaries are usually £21,000–£25,000.

A qualified and experienced research physicist can expect to earn between £24,000 and £35,000.

Senior physicists with increased responsibilities typically receive a salary of £40,000–£50,000.

In academia, a senior higher education lecturer can achieve £55,000–£60,000 a year.

Related opportunities

- Aerospace Engineer p212
- Astronomer p501
- Meteorologist p527

Further information

Institute of Physics
www.iop.org

Institute of Physics and Engineering in Medicine
www.ipem.ac.uk

Physics World
www.physicsworld.com

SCIENCE, MATHEMATICS AND STATISTICS

Qualifications and courses

Depending on their interests, seismologists can come from the fields of geology, geophysics, physics or applied mathematics.

A university undergraduate degree is necessary, and a master's degree or doctoral work are significant assets for more advanced research. A seismologist typically initiates the route of their career with an undergraduate programme in science. This usually includes courses in geophysics, computer science, chemistry, and other mathematical and science subjects.

While lecturers and researchers often continue with their studies at the postgraduate level, seismologists who work for private companies will often undertake additional specialised training in the area required.

Continuing professional development (CPD) is advised once you have qualified, but there are no formal methods through which to do so. Membership of a relevant professional body, such as the Society of Exploration Geophysicists (SEG), may be advantageous as it would allow you to keep up to date with the latest developments in your chosen specialism. Initial training is usually provided on the job. This includes health and safety, field training and data entry. There may be a probationary period during which you will be mentored by a more experienced colleague.

What the work involves

Seismologists are earth scientists, specialists in geophysics, who study seismic waves in geological materials. Their research aims at interpreting the geological composition and structures of the earth. In the case of earthquakes, seismologists evaluate the potential dangers and seek to minimise their impact through the improvement of construction standards.

Some of a seismologist's typical tasks may include monitoring, maintaining, testing and operating seismological equipment, documenting data, supervising preparation of test sites, managing inventory on equipment and maintaining safety standards.

Most seismologists work for petroleum or geophysical companies, and data processing centres. Government jobs in geology and earthquake surveying are also available. Some seismologists even teach, or work on their own as private consultants.

Type of person suited to this work

As with any earth scientist, curiosity and a thirst for knowledge are essential to the seismologist. You will also need a meticulous nature and an interest in computer science. In certain cases, an interest in outdoor activities would also be advantageous.

Though often called upon to work alone, seismologists must also be able to work within teams to solve problems.

Developed written and oral communication skills are important in order to communicate the results of their research.

Working conditions

Hours of work may vary depending on your role.

A scientist who specialises in earthquake seismology may work in a university or a laboratory, keeping a standard work week. Alternatively, a seismologist who works for an earthquake monitoring facility or a petroleum company may work hours that vary.

Some seismologists may even be on-call, which requires their availability at a moment's notice.

Future prospects

Though the need for experts in earthquake seismology is typically slim, employment prospects for seismologists are generally strong in the oil and gas industries.

Seismologists who acquire a postgraduate degree are often able to secure employment more easily than those who with only a bachelor's degree.

Growing needs in the fields of resource management, environmental protection, and energy may also increase the demand for seismologists.

Advantages/disadvantages

You must live and work closely with a small team of scientists and other staff away in the field or offshore for long periods of time.

Freelance consultancy or setting up your own consultancy are possible through contacts.

It may be possible to move between seismology and engineering geology or hazard prediction.

Money guide

Salaries vary depending on the industry. The typical starting salary for a seismologist is between £20,000 and £22,000 with a first degree.

This can increase to between £24,000 and £26,000 with an MSc/PhD.

Salary levels will be between 10% to 30% higher in commercial companies, such as oil service companies.

With experience, the typical salary of a senior level seismologist, where the post holder is in charge of one or more major projects, is between £40,000 and 60,000.

Related opportunities

- Cartographer p80
- Geologist/Geological Technician p518
- Hydrologist p520

Further information

British Geophysical Association
www.ras.org.uk

Energy and Utility Skills
www.euskills.co.uk

Qualifications and courses

The usual entry qualification is a degree in statistics or another quantitative subject such as maths, economics or operational research. Requirements for a degree are 5 GCSEs/S grades (A*–C/1–3) and 2 A levels/3 H grades including maths. A master's in statistics may be an advantage and entry is with a 2.1 or above in your first degree.

The professional examinations of the Royal Statistical Society (RSS) provide an alternative entry route for mature candidates or those already in relevant employment. Courses are available at 3 levels and can be studied by day-release, at evening classes or by distance learning. The Graduate Diploma is the highest level qualification and is equivalent to an Honours degree.

The Government Statistical Service (GSS) offers a Fast Stream recruitment programme. Candidates must have at least a 2.1 in a numerate degree with a high statistical content or a postgraduate qualification in statistics.

Chartered Statistician (CStat) status is awarded by the RSS to those with an approved degree and a minimum of 5 years' experience in the field. Graduates of an approved degree who have not yet undertaken the required training and experience are eligible for Graduate Statistician status.

What the work involves

Statistics involves the use of mathematical techniques to collect, analyse and present large quantities of factual information.

You will plan and undertake surveys using a range of mathematical research methods. You could apply your skills to investigate diverse subjects such as population levels, patterns of illness or national shopping habits.

Statistical research plays a vital role in informing the activities of many areas such as government, advertising, medicine and scientific research.

Type of person suited to this work

Strong mathematical skills are essential for producing and analysing a range of statistical information. You will also need excellent problem-solving abilities to create practical solutions and collect information on specific issues.

Excellent IT skills are needed as it is likely that you will use specialist computer software.

Your findings could help to shape the work of different organisations, so you must have a high standard of accuracy and pay close attention to detail at all times.

The ability to communicate with managers, staff and clients is essential.

Working conditions

You will be based in an office environment and spend a lot of time using computers. Depending on the sector you are employed in, you may undertake practical projects in a laboratory or research centre. You will sometimes be required to travel to meet colleagues and clients so a driving licence would be useful.

You will usually work 37–40 hours a week from Monday to Friday, with some overtime as project deadlines approach.

Future prospects

Statisticians investigate and research issues within the environment, medicine, business, social science and many other areas.

You could develop a career in the Government Statistical Service. There are many opportunities in scientific and medical research and pharmaceutical development. Alternatively, you could choose to work in academia, researching and lecturing on statistics. Self-employment as a consultant is also possible.

Advantages/disadvantages

Working to a high level of accuracy at all times can be very demanding.

You are likely to need a postgraduate qualification for roles in environmental or forensic statistics.

As the job is often project based, it offers a lot of variety.

Money guide

Earnings vary depending on your location, employer, qualifications and experience.

The highest salaries are offered in London.

Employees in the private sector tend to earn more than those working in the public sector.

Starting salaries typically range from £22,000 to £30,000.

With experience, you can earn between £30,000 and £50,000.

Those employed in the most senior positions can achieve up to £70,000 a year.

Related opportunities

- Actuary p19
- Economist p34
- Mathematician/Mathematics Research Scientist p525

Further information

Office for National Statistics
www.statistics.gov.uk

Royal Statistical Society
www.rss.org.uk

SCIENCE, MATHEMATICS AND STATISTICS

CRCI: TC

Qualifications and courses

You will need an Honours science degree to become a toxicologist. Relevant subjects include pharmacology or biochemistry. For entry to a degree course, you will need at least 2 A levels/3 H grades, including maths and chemistry and 5 GCSEs/S grades (A*–C/1–3).

Following your degree, it may be possible to take up a post that offers training as you work, but the usual route is to take a postgraduate qualification. Entry requirements are at least a 2.1 classification for your undergraduate degree.

After completing a master's degree, you could choose to study for a PhD or MPhil by carrying out research into toxicology. There are diplomas offered by many institutions across the UK in the subject, and you could even choose to go into ecotoxicology and may wish to study pollution or pesticide science.

There are many societies that provide qualifications in toxicology, and these include the British Toxicology Society and Federation of European Toxicologists.

What the work involves

As a toxicologist, you will study the effects of chemicals on the environment and everything within it, from humans and animals to plants. Some toxicologists work for the government.

Work is very varied. You may find yourself working on the development of products, on testing new drugs, or lecturing and carrying out your own research.

You may deal with poisons and drugs, or study the effects of chemicals on the environment or on human health.

Type of person suited to this work

You should have a strong interest in the environment, science, and public health and safety. For forensic toxicology, an interest in law is also useful.

Your level of scientific and technical knowledge should be high, and you need an excellent eye for detail as well as the ability to work carefully and accurately.

You should be able to apply scientific knowledge to practical work, and have excellent communication skills in order to explain technical and scientific information to others both verbally and in written reports. You will also need good ICT skills.

Working conditions

The hours worked by toxicologists tend to follow the standard 9am to 5pm, Monday to Friday working week pattern. This does not tend to vary too much. However, if you are carrying out experimental work you might be expected to be more flexible. You might be on-call on occasional weekends and evenings in case emergencies occur.

You will spend most of your time working in a laboratory, but may sometimes have to visit scenes where incidents have taken place.

Expect to wear protective clothing most of the time, and be prepared to work occasionally with animals.

Future prospects

You can work towards being promoted to a more senior position such as project manager. This will involve spending less time with hands-on toxicology, and more carrying out tasks such as administration and supervision.

If you decide that this does not suit you, it's also possible to become self-employed and/or work on a freelance basis.

Advantages/disadvantages

Toxicology is an interesting and challenging profession, and you may be involved in exciting cases. You will constantly be learning and expanding your knowledge.

It can be difficult, and you may see some distressing things. You also need to be constantly alert and cannot afford to make mistakes.

Money guide

When you start out in toxicology, you can earn about £21,500 to £26,500 a year.

This can increase to around £40,000 with experience.

In clinical toxicology salaries can rise to up to £65,000 and in other fields this can reach £100,000.

Related opportunities

- Biochemist p503
- Chemist p507
- Clinical Scientist p509

Further information

Association of the British Pharmaceutical Industry
www.abpi.org.uk

British Toxicology Society
www.thebts.org

Council for the Registration of Forensic Practitioners
www.crfp.org.uk

ZOOLOGIST

Qualifications and courses

The most common route into this profession is to obtain a degree in zoology or a related subject, such as wildlife biology, marine biology, parasitology, animal behaviour, animal ecology or wildlife conservation. The typical entry requirements for a degree course are 5 GCSEs/S grades (A*–C/1–3) and 2 A levels/3 H grades including biology. Some courses also require an A level/H grade in chemistry.

Many candidates have a postgraduate qualification and entry is with at least a 2.1 in your first degree. To work in research, you would initially secure a post as a trainee researcher within a university research department and work towards a PhD in your specialist area.

It is also possible to enter the profession at technician or trainee level with GCSEs/S grades, A levels/H grades or equivalent qualifications, including biology, maths and English.

Some people undertake a degree after gaining practical experience working as a zookeeper or laboratory technician. Admissions tutors often grant these candidates a place, regardless of their formal qualifications.

Zoologists engage in continuing professional development (CPD) throughout their career.

What the work involves

Zoologists classify, study and research all kinds of animal life. You could be involved with protecting endangered species through practical work and raising public awareness.

Some zoologists work within industry, developing pharmaceuticals or enhancing agricultural products. Others are involved with research in their specific area of interest in academic or research institutions.

You may choose to specialise in an area such as mammalogy (mammals), entomology (insects) or herpetology (amphibians and reptiles). You could work in a variety of environments including safari parks, wildlife centres and zoos.

Type of person suited to this work

You will need to have a passion for environmental issues and a love of science.

For some roles in this sector, you will need to feel comfortable dissecting dead animals. You must be meticulous, logical, practical and patient in your approach to your work.

The ability to solve problems is a key feature of this role. Communication skills are important as you might need to share your findings with people who lack scientific knowledge. Leadership and computer skills are also essential.

Working conditions

If you are working in the field, you will have to base your hours upon the animals you are studying, for example, you will have to work nights if you are researching nocturnal animals.

Your working environment will also vary depending on your area of interest.

Many zoologists spend the majority of their time in laboratories or teaching in lecture theatres but outdoor work is also common.

Future prospects

Whilst this is a specialist area, zoologists work for a variety of organisations such as environmental consultancies, conservation bodies, animal charities and local authorities. Others go into research and development in industry.

Many choose to work in universities which have a set progression path from researcher to head of department. Promotion within industry and government is also clearly defined. Within other areas such as conservation, progression is more limited and you may need to change employers in order to achieve promotion.

Advantages/disadvantages

There are opportunities to travel and visit various locations on research trips.

You will use your skills and knowledge to increase public understanding of many aspects of the natural environment.

When undertaking fieldwork, you may find yourself in inhospitable environments.

Money guide

Earnings vary depending on sector, location and employer.

Having a PhD may increase your income.

Your starting salary will probably be in the region of £17,000 to £20,000.

With experience, earnings can increase to between £25,000 and £35,000 a year.

As a senior zoologist, you could achieve in excess of £50,000 per year.

Related opportunities

- Ecologist p512
- Veterinary Surgeon p283
- Zookeeper p285

Further information

British and Irish Association of Zoos and Aquariums
www.biaza.org.uk

Institute of Biology
www.iob.org

Institute of Zoology
www.zsl.org

SCIENCE, MATHEMATICS AND STATISTICS

CRCI: TD

Security, Emergency and the Armed Forces

Working in security and the Armed Forces may give you many incredible experiences and opportunities not open to most people. You need to be an excellent team player and in some instances you may find yourself in a potentially dangerous situation, therefore it is essential that you are a great communicator. Working in this sector you can expect to spend your day absolutely anywhere! Some roles involve a lot of office work whereas others can involve spending a lot of your time on the road, or even at sea. If you are looking for a job that will be exhilarating but are able to remain calm and professional under pressure this sector could offer you a lot of opportunities.

The jobs featured in this section are listed below. For similar jobs to the ones in this section turn to *Legal and Political Services* on page 359.

ARMY OFFICER

ENTRY LEVEL 3

Qualifications and courses

Entrants must have at least 2 A levels/H grades as well as GCSEs/S grades in English, maths and science or a foreign language. Entrants must be aged between 17 years and 9 months and 28 years. Age restrictions are higher for those with professional qualifications.

Over 80% of the cadets accepted each year are university graduates but personal qualities are also important and a degree is not usually a requirement although some regiments and corps, such as the medical corps, might request a particular degree for entry. The University Officers Training Corps (UOTC) can help with degree funding by offering paid experience with the Army during your years at university.

You will need to pass vigorous medical and fitness entrance tests, as well as a range of interview and written tests during the selection process.

Upon entry, you will undertake intensive training in areas such as weapons handling, leadership, tactics and fitness at Sandhurst for 44 weeks. Once you have completed your initial training, you'll go on to specialist training depending on your skillset.

There is the opportunity for certain professionals, such as dentists, nurses, lawyers, physiotherapists and chaplains to become officers via fast track training which lasts 10 weeks. Professionally Qualified Officers (PQO) can expect to enter at a higher rank and receive a higher pay grade.

What the work involves

Army officers lead, command and train a team of soldiers on day-to-day activities, either on training exercises or on a range of combat, peacekeeping, humanitarian operations or disaster-relief missions.

Your platoon's training, welfare and discipline will be entirely your responsibility. You will work within a specific professional or skill area such as medicine, dentistry, engineering, intelligence or combat.

Type of person suited to this work

You will need to have excellent self-discipline, confidence, and a natural ability to lead and motivate your team, which will consist of soldiers, non-commissioned officers and junior officers.

You must be able to keep a clear head and make sensible decisions under pressure in order to take responsibility for the safety of your team.

Initial training, with its physical and mental challenges, often comes as a shock. You will need to have determination, courage and resilience as well as a good level of physical fitness in order to get through.

Working conditions

Your hours will depend upon which specialism you have chosen to work in. Some officers work within a normal office timeframe, whilst others are required to work shifts. Hours may also be long and irregular when away on training or taking part in field-based operations.

You could be stationed anywhere in the world, and have to travel to destinations at short notice.

Officers must wear a uniform at all times.

Future prospects

Only around 1000 officer cadets are recruited each year for the training programme at Sandhurst, so entry is competitive.

Throughout your career, you will undertake further training and study for professionally recognised qualifications in order to be promoted through the ranks.

After 5 years in service (or 3 years if you have a degree) you can expect to be promoted to the rank of captain.

Although prospects for new and existing recruits may be affected by defence budget cuts, there are still good opportunities if you meet the selection criteria.

Advantages/disadvantages

You will be working within a close-knit team of professionals, so will build strong personal and working relationships within the job.

You may be involved in implementing large-scale peace initiatives which would be rewarding.

You may be posted overseas for long periods of time which can be disruptive to your personal life.

Money guide

Starting salaries vary depending on whether you hold a degree or not.

Officer cadets joining the programme straight after their A levels can expect to earn a starting salary of £16,073 rising to £24,615 with experience and once you are commissioned as a second lieutenant.

Graduate entrants start on £24,615 and can earn a minimum of £29,586 once they leave Sandhurst.

Salaries gradually increase as you rise through the ranks and, after 15–20 years with the Army, you could earn up to £100,963 per year if you get promoted to Brigadier.

In addition to a basic salary, you will receive subsidised accommodation and food, medical and dental care, discounted rail fares and subsidised nursery facilities.

Related opportunities

- Army Soldier p539
- Police Officer p551
- Royal Navy Officer p561

Further information

Army
www.army.mod.uk/join

Welbeck College
www.welbeck.mod.uk

SECURITY, EMERGENCY AND THE ARMED FORCES

CRCI: UA

Qualifications and courses

There are no formal qualifications for entry as a soldier, although some technical jobs require certain GCSEs/S grades. You must be between 16 and 32 years and 11 months on the day you enlist and meet the army nationality and residency requirements (applicants under 18 must have parental consent). Some jobs such as vehicle mechanic have specific entry requirements.

You will need to complete the Army Entrance Test (known as BARB) and undergo an interview. Once these stages are done, you will take a physical assessment, medical, and a further interview over 2 days at the Army Development and Selection Centre (ADSC). Entrants aged 16 or 17 enter as a junior recruit and have to complete phase 1 training at Bassingbourn or the Army Foundation College Harrogate before going to the Infantry Training Centre (ITC) to complete phase 2 training.

Entrants who are aged 18 or over will attend training programmes according to the regiment they wish to join. Adult infantry soldiers go to the Infantry Training Centre to complete a 24 week Combat Infantryman's Course (CIC).

Those planning to join the Royal Engineers, Household Cavalry, Royal Armoured Corps or Royal Artillery attend an Army Training Regiment (ATR) where they undertake a 14-week course in skill at arms, fitness training, qualities of a soldier, military knowledge, battlefield casualty drills, individual health and education. They then join their chosen regiment to undertake further, more specific training.

What the work involves

The army is responsible for defending the UK and its allies across the world, as well as taking part in peacekeeping and humanitarian operations.

You will be involved in regular training exercises to ensure you maintain a high level of fitness and military skills so that you are ready for combat at any time.

You will also choose to train and work within one of more than 130 different trades. You may be posted to dangerous areas and inhospitable environments at any time, whether for peacekeeping and aid missions, or to engage in warfare.

Type of person suited to this work

You should be able to work within a team, reacting quickly to orders, working on your own initiative where necessary, and supporting other team members both professionally and emotionally at times.

You must be extremely disciplined and responsible, with the ability to think and act logically under pressure.

You must be physically fit with excellent stamina. You should be practical, with good manual dexterity, so that you will be able to operate various machines and equipment.

Working conditions

Some soldiers work normal office hours, whilst others are expected to undertake shifts that encompass night and weekend work.

You could be stationed in the UK or overseas, and must be prepared for life in a number of environments including deserts, war torn cities, and mountains.

Future prospects

Although prospects for new and existing recruits may be affected by defence budget cuts, there are still good opportunities if you meet the selection criteria.

You will sign up for an open engagement lasting 22 years, but you can leave after serving 4 years. You must give 12 months notice prior to leaving.

All soldiers start as a private, and are awarded promotion according to their increasing levels of skill and commitment.

Advantages/disadvantages

You will be meeting new challenges each day and adapting to unusual and inhospitable situations, which will ensure the work never gets dull.

You will be working within a close knit team, supporting their work both in training and actually out on operations.

You are continually on-call, and could be sent anywhere in the world at a moment's notice.

Money guide

Whilst training, soldiers can expect to receive £272 per week and this rises to a minimum of £17,514 per year once you are qualified as a private.

Some roles receive additional specialist pay, which can be up to an extra £19 a day.

If you move up the ranks to corporal or sergeant, you can expect to earn £26,400–£33,223.

All staff receive an annual salary increase, regardless of promotion or additional responsibilities. There is also a scheme which offers additional pay for spending longer than 7 days away from your base. You will be entitled to an allowance of up to £28.24 per day with a further £18.16 if conditions are unpleasant.

In addition to a basic salary, you will receive subsidised accommodation and food, medical and dental care, discounted rail fares and subsidised nursery facilities.

Related opportunities

- Army Officer p538
- Royal Air Force Airman/woman p557
- Royal Marines Commando p559

Further information

Army
www.army.mod.uk/join

Welbeck College
www.welbeck.mod.uk

BODYGUARD

Qualifications and courses

There are no formal entry requirements but since 2006 there is a legal requirement for all bodyguards to hold a Security Industry Authority Licence (SIA) which lasts for 3 years and covers other security sectors that also require a license, such as security guarding and door supervision.

To obtain a SIA license you must be over 18, hold a recognised First Aid certificate, have a clean identity and criminal record and a Level 3 SIA-approved qualification.

Approved SIA courses include a Level 3 Certificate in Protective Security Management from Buckinghamshire New University, an Edexcel Certificate in Close Protection Operations or a City & Guilds Certificate in Close Protection. They all cover areas like risk assessment and surveillance.

A driving licence will also be necessary.

What the work involves

You will be guarding your client or group, keeping them safe from harm or unwanted attention. You might also be known as a personal protection officer or a close protection officer (CPO).

Protecting an executive on a business trip to a dangerous region of the world, an overseas royal visiting the UK, or a celebrity during an autograph-signing session could all be part of your work.

You will be responsible for making a preliminary sweep of premises before your client arrives, setting up surveillance equipment, assessing potential threats and driving your client around. It is possible to be a specialist in areas such as close protection, surveillance or defensive driving.

Type of person suited to this work

This is not a first job – most have related experience and the most lucrative contracts go to those who have worked in the Special Forces or specialist close-protection police units. Most of the work is on a self-employed basis, so you need to have a flair for business because you will need to network and keep your accounts.

Exceptional planning skills and quick responses are essential to ensure that your client is free from harm or unwanted attention. You will also need to be confident, physically fit to cope with the demands of the work, and have good eyesight and hearing.

Your appearance, diplomacy and communication skills also need to be top level, because you will be with your client and need to blend into the background to observe at high profile events.

Working conditions

Your work will be wherever your client goes and so this could mean lots of travelling.

You could be at risk as you would protect your client if necessary with your own body – but this is more an issue when working in dangerous areas of the world.

You will work long and irregular hours during a contract as some clients may need 24 hour protection and there will be long periods of inactivity.

Future prospects

You can progress to become a leader of a team of CPOs on assignment or establish your own business.

Very few officers are in long-term employment. The vast majority are self-employed. There is an increasing demand for good female officers.

Some progress into more mainstream security work, for example security guard or security manager. There may be opportunities to specialise in areas such as driving and residential security.

Advantages/disadvantages

You will get to enjoy a fast-paced lifestyle and travel frequently.

Training courses are residential and expensive.

The work can be dangerous.

Money guide

Most bodyguards are self-employed, earning daily or hourly rates for specific contracts. These could range from £100–£150 a day for low risk work to £400–£500 a day in a very hostile environment or for protecting a key principal.

For those bodyguards contracted to a particular company, a new entrant can earn over £18,000 per year.

With experience this can rise to £24,000–£30,000 per year.

In high risk areas, with considerable experience, you could earn up to £100,000 per year.

Related opportunities

- Army Officer p538
- Police Officer p551
- Royal Marines Officer p560

Further information

British Security Industry Association
www.bsia.co.uk

Security Industry Authority
www.sia.homeoffice.gov.uk

Qualifications and courses

There are no specific entry requirements for employment as a Civil Enforcement Officer though your employer will provide introductory training on the job which must be completed. Training will cover on-street enforcement activity, car park patrolling and enforcement, clamping and tow-away and CCTV operation.

In order to further your career or improve employability you could complete a relevant course such as a NVQ Level 2 qualification in Controlling Parking Areas or City & Guilds Level 2 Award for Civil Enforcement Officers (Parking). On completion you could work towards a Level 3 course in Parking Management/Supervision or an NVQ Level 3 in Parking Clerical Work.

Some employers look for at least 4 GCSEs/S grades (A*–C/1–3), including English and maths as well as experience working with the public.

A full driving licence is also needed for some positions.

What the work involves

You will be enforcing parking regulations for a local authority or contractors working on their behalf, patrolling and checking for illegal parking and non-payment of parking fees.

Using a hand-held computer you will regularly check details of vehicles parked in limited-stay parking areas and issue fixed penalty tickets. You will take pictures of any illegally parked vehicles.

You will need to arrange for vehicles to be clamped or sent to the pound. You will attend court to give evidence if any prosecution results from your work. You will have to report any suspected abandoned or stolen vehicles to the police.

Type of person suited to this work

All employers look for a polite but firm manner as well as good communication skills. You will need to be very good at dealing with people, many of whom could be feeling irate about the ticket you have just given them.

You need to be a good observer and able to follow rules and instructions. You will have to watch out at all times for illegal parking and enforce the rules.

You will meet a lot of people but you will also be working unsupervised and independently so you need to be confident, self-disciplined and reliable.

Working conditions

You will be working in the streets, in all seasons and weathers.

You will need to wear a uniform and carry a hand-held computer.

You will work shifts to a total of 37–40 hours a week, including early mornings and late evenings. You might also have to work at weekends.

Future prospects

Civil enforcement officers are now carrying out most of the duties that were formerly assigned to traffic wardens.

Parking contractors are working with over 100 local authorities to enforce parking legislation. Vacancies are available with numerous main contractors.

With experience, progression is possible into a role as supervisor or trainer and then into management if suitable. However, prospects may be more limited in more rural areas.

Advantages/disadvantages

You will keep fit, walking an average of ten miles a day, five days a week carrying a 5kg pack (including your computer, printer and radio).

There is no doubt that civil enforcement officers are not always popular and you might have to deal with some aggressive people.

Illegal parking can cause real problems for most law-abiding motorists and many attendants feel a sense of satisfaction from keeping the roads clear.

Money guide

Starting pay is about £12,000 per year. In certain places, supervisors' salaries can reach up to £18,000.

The hourly wage is £7–£10.

Civil enforcement managers can expect £26,000–£30,000 a year.

Related opportunities

- Bailiff/Enforcement Agent p360
- Police Community Support Officer p550
- Train Conductor/Guard p617

Further information

British Parking Association
www.britishparking.co.uk

Institute of Parking Professionals
www.theipp.co.uk

SECURITY, EMERGENCY AND THE ARMED FORCES

CRCI: UA

COASTGUARD WATCH ASSISTANT/OFFICER

Qualifications and courses

Most people join HM Coastguard as a coastguard watch assistant (CWA).

There are no minimum entry qualifications, but GCSEs (A*–C)/S grades including English and maths, and Key Skills in Communication and Numeracy, are useful.

Most CWAs start as volunteers and you must be aged 16 or over to apply. A few join at coastguard watch officer level (CWO).

You will need a good standard of hearing and eyesight and a high level of fitness. You must have significant search and rescue experience and either a Coastal Skipper Certificate or a Yachtmaster Certificate from the Royal Yacht Association.

Training is initially for seven weeks at the Coastguard Training Centre. Training is then on the job with a further short course after 10–12 months. You must then pass a series of exams.

What the work involves

You will work as part of a team responding to vessels and people in distress.

You will be dealing with 999 coastguard calls and radio distress calls, and will direct the efforts of the volunteer coastguard rescue officers. You may also work alongside the services of the Royal National Lifeboat Institution (RNLI).

You will keep records of all activity and weather conditions, giving information to vessels and reporting anything unusual.

Type of person suited to this work

You must have excellent computer skills, the ability to concentrate for long periods and a clear voice to make sure that you send rescuers to the right place.

Active search and rescue work involves carrying heavy equipment, climbing and working out at sea, all of which require a high level of physical fitness.

Watch officers need good management and teaching skills to lead and train groups of auxiliary coastguards.

Working conditions

You will be located in an operations centre, using a computer and talking to others using hands-free communications equipment.

Search and rescue work involves working outside in dangerous conditions.

Coastguards operate 24/7 – you will be working shifts that include evenings and weekends and will often work over a 42-hour week.

Future prospects

This is a competitive job to enter.

You could work up to officer or sector management level. However, a limited number of senior jobs exist in this fairly small service.

It is also expected that numbers will continue to drop in some areas of the service in the next few years.

If you have experience and a degree, you could take a job in marine surveying within the Maritime and Coastguard Agency.

Advantages/disadvantages

With the use of satellite technology, it is possible to co-ordinate the rescue of someone hundreds of miles away from your control centre.

The sea is dangerous and you may arrive too late, which is an upsetting event for the whole team.

Money guide

When starting out you could earn £15,000 per year as a coastguard watch assistant. After gaining experience, this can rise to £17,800.

The starting salary of a coastguard watch officer is £18,100 and can increase to £23,200.

On-call allowances, plus overtime pay, can increase earnings at every level of experience.

Additional allowances are paid to those working in the Scottish Islands.

Related opportunities

- Air Traffic Controller p589
- Merchant Navy Deck Officer/Rating p604
- Royal Navy Officer p561

Further information

Maritime and Coastguard Agency
www.mcga.gov.uk

Maritime Skills Alliance
www.maritimeskills.org

Port Skills and Safety Ltd
www.portskillsandsafety.co.uk

Qualifications and courses

While individual police forces will all have different entry requirements, most are now requiring applicants to have a degree. Various universities offer degrees or Foundation degrees in subjects such as forensic science and criminology. A bachelor's degree in crime scene science is available at the University of Teesside. You will need at least 2 A levels or equivalent, 1 being in science, for these degrees.

Work experience is usually required, ideally in a related area such as photography or scientific work. Previous work dealing with the public would also be an advantage.

You will need a medical exam and a background security check for this role. You will also usually need a driving licence and must have full colour vision.

In some forces you would start as an assistant crime scene investigator (CSI) or scenes of crime officer (SOCO) before undertaking further training to become fully qualified.

Once in the job you will have an introductory period with your force, followed by a 1-month course with the National Police Improvement Agency. Upon completion you are qualified to undertake volume crime scene investigation. It is then possible to do a further 5-week training programme which qualifies you as a full CSI/SOCO.

Specialist and refresher courses are also on offer and you will be expected to attend a course at least once every 5 years.

What the work involves

You will be collecting, storing and recording evidence such as fibres, hair and blood to help investigate crimes like burglary, accidents and suspicious deaths.

You will use equipment and materials to lift, package and preserve evidence, such as biological samples, paint, tyre marks and fingerprints.

Your job will involve taking photographic and video evidence of both crime scenes and victims of crime. You will also need to keep thorough records and attend court when required to give evidence.

Type of person suited to this work

Sifting through evidence is the main aspect of this job so you will need to be able to pay attention to detail. You will also need to be methodical and patient.

This job can be very distressing. You will need to be able to distance yourself emotionally from the crime, and be able to record the scene and collect evidence in an analytical, scientific way. Good teamworking skills are essential as you may be working on a project with many others.

An interest in science and technology is essential. You will need to keep up to date with developments in forensic science and technology as they will affect how well you do your job.

Working conditions

You will work both outside at crime scenes and inside at base.

You will do a 37-hour working week, including shifts, but hours might be longer at times. You could also be on-call 24-hours.

Conditions at crime scenes can be very difficult and unpleasant but you will be provided with protective clothing. You will need a driving licence.

Future prospects

Crime scene investigators are recruited by all regional police forces. Some forces only recruit civilians to do this work but a few also recruit specialist police officers. There are currently about 1800 crime scene investigators in the UK. Competition for vacancies is high.

It is possible to move into more specialised areas of work, such as the investigation of suspicious fires, or scenes where firearms have been used.

There may be opportunities for promotion to senior investigator with management responsibilities. You can study for further qualifications and become a forensic scientist or specialise in fingerprint technology.

Advantages/disadvantages

Although this job has an exciting image, fuelled by popular television shows, the work can be routine, repetitive and quite shocking at times.

You will have the satisfaction of working with a team of investigating officers and forensic scientists to gather evidence needed to trace, arrest and convict offenders.

Money guide

Starting salaries for assistants are around £16,000.

Once fully qualified, salaries vary from £17,000–£26,000 per year.

This rises to in excess of £30,000 for experienced and senior investigators, depending on your local police force and responsibility level.

Related opportunities

- Forensic Computer Analyst p547
- Forensic Scientist p516
- Private Investigator p555

Further information

Forensic Science Service
www.forensic.gov.uk

National Policing Improvement Agency
www.npia.police.uk

Police Recruitment
www.policecouldyou.co.uk

SECURITY, EMERGENCY AND THE ARMED FORCES

CRCI: UG

Qualifications and courses

For an officer grade you will need 5 GCSEs/S grades (A*–C/1–3) including English and maths, and 2 A levels/H grades.

If you have a degree at 2.2 or above, you could join the fast-track graduate recruitment scheme although opportunities may not be specifically for customs officer roles and the application may be for other roles in Her Majesty's Revenue & Customs (HMRC).

All candidates must be UK nationals.

What the work involves

You will be working as a civil servant for the Home Office, enforcing tax regulations on all goods entering and leaving the country and all goods bought and sold in the UK.

You could specialise in customs: checking for anyone either not paying tax or smuggling in illegal items and substances.

You could specialise in excise work: visiting traders, manufacturers and importers to check licences and accounts to make sure that the right duties are being paid on goods like petrol, alcohol and tobacco.

You could specialise in VAT: visiting businesses to check their accounts and that the right amount of VAT is being collected.

Type of person suited to this work

If you are part of front-line detection work, investigating the entry of illegal goods into the UK, you will be involved in observing, questioning and challenging people.

You will need top-notch communication and observation skills. You must be intuitive and persistent. Knowledge of or a willingness to learn a foreign language is useful.

If you work in VAT or excise, an aptitude for numbers and computers is a must, because you will be checking business accounts and watching out for sometimes quite sophisticated cover-ups.

Working conditions

Customs and immigration officers mainly work in airports, seaports and freight terminals but also may need to do outdoor surveillance work. You will wear a uniform if you are a front-line detective.

Excise and VAT officers are based in offices but also travel around their local areas carrying out checks and interviews. You will generally work office hours, Monday to Friday.

Customs officers work shifts.

Future prospects

There are about 23,000 staff based all over the country.

Customs specialist staff are mainly located at air- and seaports and the Channel Tunnel.

It is possible to move on to senior or management posts. There are also specialist areas within customs, for example in detection, operations and intelligence units and dog units.

Advantages/disadvantages

When dealing with front-line detection work you might have to question or detain angry or abusive people. It can be a high-pressure job at peak times.

No two days are ever the same, especially in detection work.

It can be very rewarding to know that you have prevented dangerous items such as drugs and firearms getting into the country.

Money guide

Starting out at administrative or assistant level you could earn between £12,734 and £18,716 a year.

As an officer you could be earning between £19,587 and £25,206 a year.

After promotion to higher officer grades salaries increase to between £24,513 and £38,099 a year.

Related opportunities

- Army Officer p538
- Civil Service Executive Officer p28
- Police Officer p551

Further information

Chartered Institute of Taxation
www.tax.org.uk

General Fast Stream Programme
www.faststream.gov.uk

Qualifications and courses

All graduates are eligible to apply to work in this profession although some degree subjects such as emergency planning and disaster management are considered more desirable in candidates applying for their first job in the field. Many of the courses that are more directly related to the industry will be sandwich courses to give students the chance to spend a year working in the sector and gain valuable experience.

There are also more specific courses available which are geared towards a job in emergency planning but these do not guarantee a job in the sector.

For individuals without a relevant degree, a postgraduate qualification will be required, such as the MSc in Disaster Management.

Candidates who have extensive previous experience of working in this sector or a related career may be able to enter the industry without the usual necessary qualifications.

Individuals who enter the profession as an assistant will take part in a lot of training on the job as well as complete several external courses, many of which are run by the Emergency Planning Society. The courses available allow individuals to specialise in certain areas of emergency planning as well as to gain more general professional skills.

What the work involves

Emergency planners and managers work primarily in local government as part of a larger team to help maintain public safety, especially at times when this is threatened by an external force.

You will be required to respond quickly to and learn from emergency situations that have arisen from natural disasters, outbreaks of serious contagious diseases, industrial accidents and terrorism.

You will compile reports from lengthy research and planning on the most efficient ways to protect the general public should an emergency situation arise.

You will carry out risk assessments, write safety briefs to train emergency response services and help with the recovery process after an incident has occurred.

Type of person suited to this work

You will need to enjoy working in a high pressure situation as part of a large team. You should be enthusiastic about helping to provide better public safety.

You will also need to respond quickly and calmly in an emergency and keep a level head in what may be a dangerous situation.

The job requires someone willing to work long hours, sometimes at unsociable times as well as a neat and organised person who can take comprehensive notes and present their findings accurately.

Working conditions

You may often find yourself in a highly pressured situation especially in the aftermath of a major incident so you could find yourself in danger or not knowing when you will finish the job.

You can expect travel to feature heavily as part of your job with many trips away from home a distinct possibility.

Future prospects

If you enter the career as an assistant you can expect to progress, with experience, to a management or senior role if you show signs of willingness to go where the work takes you and put in long hours.

Once you reach a more senior role you will not be working in such a hands-on environment but would provide more managerial support to your team.

Advantages/disadvantages

Your future prospects could take you all over the world to work with individuals who enjoy working as part of a close knit team.

The work has the potential to be highly distressing especially as you could be one of the first people on the scene after a major natural disaster or a terrorist attack.

Money guide

A typical starting salary in the profession is likely to be £24,000–£33,000.

You can expect this to progress to around £27,000–£33,000 after 3–5 years of experience.

Senior roles come with a lot of responsibility but you could expect to earn £46,000–£70,000 at this level.

The profession is still relatively new so salaries vary widely between jobs. Private sector jobs are often more highly paid than the public sector.

Related opportunities

- Environmental Health Practitioner/Officer p36
- Firefighter p546
- Police Officer p551

Further information

Emergency Planning Society
www.the-eps.org

The Emergency Planning College
epcollege.com

Qualifications and courses

To be considered for selection as a firefighter you must be at least 18 years old and a full UK driving licence is preferable. Firefighters need a good general education and a reasonable level of fitness. Some brigades may ask for specific GCSEs/S grades and some entrants have A levels/H grades or a degree.

Entrance is dependent on performance within practical and written tests as well as an interview. Some colleges offer a Fire Service Pre-Recruitment Access Course as a way to prepare candidates for the entrance tests.

As a new firefighter you will be required to undergo full-time induction training which lasts between 12 and 18 weeks. You will be required to pass certain rigorous physical and job-related tests (such as working within confined spaces and at heights) as well as written and psychological tests. You will also be required to undergo strict medical examinations to make sure you are fit enough to undertake demanding firefighting duties.

What the work involves

You will be dealing with a range of emergencies, not only fires but also helping at other incidents such as rescuing trapped animals and people, handling chemical spillages and assisting at road, rail or air crash scenes.

If your team arrives on the scene before the paramedics you will have to give First Aid.

You might give advice to organisations on fire safety and check that buildings or public events meet fire regulations.

Type of person suited to this work

You will need to stay calm in dangerous situations. People in danger tend to react in extreme ways and you will need to be good at talking to them, giving instructions, reassuring them and leading them to safety.

You need to be an excellent team player. You will be assigned to a 'watch' (a team) and need to work together to keep yourself and others safe.

You will need to be able to deal with very stressful and disturbing situations.

Working conditions

You will be based at a fire station but will go out to attend incidents. Fire stations have good facilities for eating and resting.

Working conditions can often be unpleasant and dangerous. You will wear a uniform and, when needed, protective clothing and equipment.

You will work an average of 42 hours per week, which will be divided into day and night shifts. You can also work as a retained firefighter which means you will be on-call. Many retained firefighters have other full-time or part-time occupations.

Future prospects

The main employers are regional fire services which employ about 41,000 firefighters. Airports, the Ministry of Defence, the RAF and the Royal Navy also recruit firefighters.

Some firefighters start their career as retained firefighters to gain experience. Entry is competitive.

You could move into driving fire trucks by taking a large goods vehicle (LGV) licence. Promotion to supervisory and management roles is by clear grades and given on ability, but exams must also be passed.

Advantages/disadvantages

This job can be very stressful and you cannot just leave an emergency situation if your shift has ended.

You will get to know your watch very well; firefighters say they really enjoy the team spirit at work.

You need to pass demanding training successfully to qualify, and keep up a rigorous fitness and training schedule.

Money guide

As a trainee you will earn around £21,000 per year; with experience this can increase to £28,200.

Crew managers earn around £31,000 per year and station managers earn £36,000–£40,100 per year.

Retained (on-call) firefighters earn a fee of around £2,500 per year. They also receive additional payments, according to their rank, for attending fires and carrying out extra duties.

Related opportunities

- Paramedic p324
- Police Officer p551
- Royal Navy Officer p561

Further information

Defence Fire Training and Development Centre
www.dftdc.org

Fire Gateway
www.fire.gov.uk/careers

Fire Service Recruitment Information
www.fireservice.co.uk

Qualifications and courses

Most people who enter this career have completed a degree in IT (or equivalent computing subject). If your degree is not IT based you can take an IT conversion course. However, it is becoming more and more necessary to have a specific degree in forensic computing and information security. In order to gain a place on a degree course you will normally require at least 2 A levels/Highers and 5 GCSEs/S grades (A*–C/1–3). Computing, maths and science subjects are all relevant A level/Higher subjects.

You could alternatively complete a Foundation degree in an IT subject. These courses generally require applicants to have attained at least 1 A level and about 4 GCSEs grades A*–C (or equivalent). There is also a Diploma in Information Technology which might be of interest.

A postgraduate degree would be extremely valuable. Entry to postgraduate programmes is reliant on the successful completion of a first degree.

Members of police staff can complete specialist training with the National Policing Improvement Agency (NPIA). There are a number of courses on offer, including a Master's in Cybercrime Forensics at Canterbury Christ Church University. Also, given the ever increasing amount and effectiveness of software, ensuring that you undertake regular continuing professional development (CPD) and keep up to date with developments is advised.

What the work involves

You will be responsible for inspecting computers (and other technology such as mobile phones) for criminal activity. You might be looking for evidence of identity theft, child abuse, hacking, phishing and other illegal activity.

Even if evidence of the crime has been deleted or corrupted you will need to retrieve it without altering it in any way.

You might be using specialist software and working with the police to look through files, photographs, emails and phone conversations in order to discover evidence of criminal activity. You may need to appear in court to relay your findings.

Type of person suited to this work

You will need to have a certain level of skill using computers, as well as an interest in detecting and preventing crime.

You should be a patient and determined person as some investigations may take place over a long period of time. You might come across unpleasant or even horrific material and you must be able to distance yourself and deal with it objectively.

You will need to be able to record your findings in a clear, coherent and logical manner. You should be able to understand the law in relation to IT crime. Articulateness and strong communication skills are essential.

Working conditions

You will spend most of your time in an office using a computer.

You will generally work standard office hours (9am–5pm from Monday to Friday).

You might need to be on-call over weekends and public holidays or work overtime to meet deadlines. You might also have to attend court to give evidence.

Future prospects

Postgraduate qualifications will enhance your chances of promotion (particularly if you work within the commercial world).

You could progress to the level of supervisor or line manager.

You may have to change employers in order to progress. Jobs are available with the police force, MI5, government, the Serious and Organised Crime Agency and IT firms which specialise in computer security.

Advantages/disadvantages

Your workload will be varied and opportunities are available in many different sectors.

You will spend a lot of time hunched over a computer.

If you work within a police or government sector you might help to send criminals to jail.

Money guide

These figures are only approximate and will vary depending on location, sector and employer.

As a trainee you can expect to earn around £20,000 a year. After some experience, this can rise to somewhere between £25,000 and £35,000 per year.

A senior forensic analyst might earn in the region of £40,000 to £60,000.

Related opportunities

- Forensic Scientist p516
- Information Officer p352
- Software Engineer p160

Further information

BCS, The Chartered Institute for IT
www.bcs.org

National Policing Improvement Agency
www.npia.police.uk

Skills for Justice
www.skillsforjustice.com

SECURITY, EMERGENCY AND THE ARMED FORCES

CRCI: UG

Qualifications and courses

Applicants for the role of assistant immigration officers have to sit a literacy and numeracy test and must attend an assessment day.

Immigration officers need no formal qualifications although most employers expect entrants to be educated to A level standard. Assistant immigration officers can apply for promotion to this level.

Applicants with a minimum of a 2.2 Honours degree can apply for fast-stream entry. This is for entry into all civil service departments and although a preference can be expressed, entry into Immigration is not guaranteed. All fast-stream candidates must be UK nationals. For all other entrants, you must be a European Economic Area national, EU national or Commonwealth citizen. Swiss nationals, although Switzerland is not an EEA country, are also eligible to apply for non-reserved posts.

After a period of 10 weeks' initial training, entrants are placed with more experienced officers, usually at Dover, Heathrow or Gatwick. Financial support may be available for officers wishing to learn a foreign language.

What the work involves

You will be working as a civil servant for the Home Office; you will be controlling the entry of people into the UK by checking the passports and visas of passengers arriving at ports, airports or via the Channel Tunnel. You could ask questions to find out more about them and, if suspicious, conduct a more detailed interview.

As an assistant officer you would refer to a more senior officer if you are concerned about documentation or answers to questions.

You might work in an office processing immigration applications, dealing with appeals and conducting intelligence-based activities.

Type of person suited to this work

You will need to be confident, assertive, have the ability to work under pressure and to deadlines.

You will need to be well organised, reliable and have good report-writing skills. You will need an ability to get on with people from across the world.

You should enjoy investigating and collecting information. You will need the ability to write up and pass on your concerns to others in your team or colleagues from other professions.

Working conditions

You could work in a range of places such as ports and airports where you will have access to a desk, PC, phone and interviewing area.

Some immigration officers have to undertake surveillance duties and work with other intelligence officers, but normally you will check documents and interview individuals within your office or interviewing booth.

You will work shifts that will include out-of-office hours and weekends.

Future prospects

Half of all immigration staff are employed in London and the south-east of England, at Heathrow, Gatwick and the Channel ports.

The numbers of people entering the UK and asking for asylum has increased over recent years. This has impacted on the service, which has grown in numbers. Entry is competitive at officer level and the majority of entrants are graduates.

It is possible to enter at assistant grade and work up to officer grade. Placements are also possible, for example, to Immigration Visa sections at the British Deputy High Commissions overseas or to police forces around the UK.

Advantages/disadvantages

You will play an important role in helping protect national security.

This job is part of the civil service, so entry can be competitive.

The civil service offers excellent conditions of service and training.

Money guide

When starting out as an assistant officer, you earn around £16,000 a year.

With experience you can earn £20,500, later rising to £26,000.

Salaries for immigration officers start at around £22,000 increasing, with experience, to £38,000.

All staff working shifts or unsocial hours are paid additional allowances. Those working in and around London receive an additional allowance.

Related opportunities

- Civil Service Executive Officer p28
- Equality and Diversity Officer p37
- Police Officer p551

Further information

Civil Service Jobs
www.civil-service.gov.uk/jobs

General Fast Stream Programme
www.faststream.gov.uk

Home Office
www.homeoffice.gov.uk

Qualifications and courses

Applicants for any post within MI5, MI6 or GCHQ must be a British citizen and one or both of your parents must also be British or have substantial ties to the UK. You normally have to have been resident in the UK for 10 years prior to your application.

MI5 applicants must be aged 18 or over. MI6 applicants must be aged 21 or over and A levels/H grades or degrees may be required by some organisations. The agencies may consider significant work experience within an intelligence environment in lieu of a degree qualification though many applicants will have first degrees or postgraduate qualifications.

Graduates from a wide range of disciplines are considered. Specialist areas may require more precise subject choices, for example linguistics or computer software development. Useful degrees include criminology and criminal intelligence and analysis.

Each applicant is considered individually during the rigorous vetting procedure, known as Developed Vetting (DV) clearance. This includes medical and security clearance and may include background checks on family and friends. Recruitment can take many months.

What the work involves

In most cases you will work for one of the UK's 3 intelligence and security agencies: Government Communications Headquarters (GCHQ), Security Service (MI5) and the Secret Intelligence Service (MI6).

Your job is to protect the UK from attack and terrorism, to protect its economic wellbeing as well as to prevent organised crime such as drug trafficking. You may be involved in helping to build up intelligence pictures by identifying targets, evaluating the reliability of source information and validating data, and then formally delivering information to the Government.

You will also develop expertise in particular areas.

You might be involved in military operations, counter-espionage, detecting weapons of mass destruction, and identifying agents and targets.

Type of person suited to this work

This job requires you to use your initiative and be aware of the big picture, sometimes across agencies. You should be a confident decision-maker, flexible and adaptable with an exceptional eye for detail. You must be persevering, diligent and work well under pressure.

Motivation, inquisitiveness and cultural sensitivity are essential. You need to be able to recall events accurately and analyse information and data efficiently with the ability to convey your findings effectively.

Some of your work will include informing and working alongside professionals from other national and international security services so you should be a good team player.

You must keep up to date on current affairs and communications technologies.

Working conditions

Some of the posts operate shifts, which might include weekends.

Starting out you will be required to work at headquarters. GCHQ is based in Cheltenham and MI5 and MI6 are based in central London. You could also be required to travel both nationally and internationally. It might be possible to work from home for some posts.

This job can become more of a way of life than a career so you should be completely dedicated and be able to keep information totally confidential.

Future prospects

You will usually work for up to 3 years in your first role. Based on your performance and your potential you may be promoted to a more specialist role which will include more responsibility.

You could be responsible for a wider geographical region or for specific analytical techniques. You could also move into policy work, projects, personnel or finance.

Advantages/disadvantages

It's satisfying to know you are helping to protect national security.

Background checks in the recruitment process can be long and very intrusive.

The secrecy of the job may be difficult and sometimes lonely as you will not be allowed to talk about your work with friends and family.

Money guide

Outside of working for MI5, MI6 or GCHQ a junior analyst will earn around £16,000 a year.

With experience this can rise to £18,000–£26,000 and once you reach senior/management level you can expect a salary in excess of £30,000.

However, if you work for MI5, MI6 or GCHQ your salary will start at around £24,000.

With 5–10 years of experience you could earn up to £43,000. In addition to pay, there are excellent benefits including leisure and fitness facilities, childcare vouchers and travel assistance.

Related opportunities

- Army Officer p538
- Customs and Excise Officer p544
- Private Investigator p555

Further information

GCHQ
www.gchq.gov.uk

MI5 Careers
www.mi5careers.co.uk

Secret Intelligence Service
www.sis.gov.uk

Qualifications and courses

There are no specific entry requirements, and applicants from a diverse range of backgrounds are encouraged to apply in order to get a good representational mix across the force. You can apply for the role at 17 years old but cannot take up appointment until you are 18.

Some employers may view your application more favourably if it demonstrates some commitment to community service schemes, or if you have undertaken a relevant course such as an NVQ Level 2, BTEC National Diploma, HNC/D in Public Services, or a Foundation degree in police studies or public services.

During the application process, you will be required to sit written, fitness and role-play tests, as well as undergo medical, financial and security checks.

Upon entry, you will undertake between 3 weeks and 3 months of classroom training. Areas covered will include relevant areas of law, self-defence, First Aid, interviewing skills, and using police communication equipment.

It is possible to go on to become a police officer after gaining experience as a community support officer.

What the work involves

Police community support officers are uniformed members of the force whose role is to work within their local community, supporting the activities and initiatives of police officers.

You will be part of the group of officers that provides visible police presence on the streets and in other public areas. You will be on the frontline, offering help and advice to members of the public, as well as tackling anti-social behaviour.

Everyday duties could include crowd-control and traffic directing, dealing with minor offences, checking out abandoned vehicles, or imposing fines for acts such as littering or dog fouling.

Type of person suited to this work

You will need to be an excellent communicator, as you will encounter a range of people in your work. You must also be able to remain calm but authoritative when confronted with potentially difficult or violent members of the public.

You must be able to work effectively within a team. This means you should be able to take orders and act on your own initiative when necessary.

You should have good, accurate writing skills, as you will need to produce reports on events and deal with complex paperwork at times.

Working conditions

You will work up to 40 hours on a shift basis, encompassing night and weekend work. Flexible or part-time hours are available.

Although you will be based at a police station, you will work in a variety of locations including patrolling the streets, within people's homes, or in public places such as train stations.

You will be required to wear a uniform, which includes a high visibility jacket and protective hat. Additional protective equipment may need to be worn or carried on occasion.

Future prospects

Competition for entry to become a PCSO can be fierce, depending on the force you are applying to.

Experienced PCSOs are often responsible for teaching, training and guiding new recruits. There are also opportunities to move into supervisory or managerial roles within the PCSO contingent.

It is also a good role to start in if you would like to become a police officer. Prospects for this role may be affected by defence budget cuts.

Advantages/disadvantages

You will play a direct role in protecting your local community and finding solutions to problems and crime in the area.

There are good opportunities for career development, including progression to become a police officer.

You may be confronted with difficult and dangerous situations, which can be both frightening and unnerving.

Money guide

As a new recruit to the force, you could expect to earn around £16,000 (although those working in London will earn considerably more).

If you are working specifically for the British Transport Police, your starting salary will be slightly higher at £18,500.

Once you have gained a few years' experience, you can expect to earn £21,500.

If you reach a supervisory or managerial role, your earnings will reach about £25,000.

Similar to police officers, community support officers are eligble for certain benefits such as free London travel, flexible hours and key worker living benefits.

Related opportunities

- Army Soldier p539
- Police Officer p551
- Prison Officer/Instructor p554

Further information

Police Recruitment
www.policecouldyou.co.uk

Qualifications and courses

There are no specific academic requirements, but you must be aged 18 years or older, and be a UK, European Union or Commonwealth citizen or a citizen from any country who has been granted indefinite leave to stay in the UK.

You could also take a relevant qualification to enhance your application. These include BTEC qualifications at Levels 1–3, a HND/C in public services as well as a degree or Foundation degree in police studies or criminology.

Other useful experience is to gain voluntary police work as a special constable. Specials work unpaid (with expenses covered) but after full training have the same powers as regular police officers.

The police force operates an intensive selection process, and you will need to pass medical, fitness, eyesight, literacy and numeracy tests. You will also be assessed using a variety of scenario exercises by which your communication, decision-making and problem-solving skills will be judged.

You will need to pass a Criminal Records Bureau check.

Upon entry, you will be a probationary officer for 2 years while you undergo further officer training through the Initial Police Learning and Development Programme (IPLDP).

What the work involves

Police officers are responsible for safeguarding communities from crime by apprehending criminals and maintaining order.

You will spend your time on patrol, responding to any situation that occurs whilst you are on shift. You will keep records, take statements, and write reports. You may need to give evidence in court on occasion, and may also give educational talks in community venues.

Once trained, you could specialise in a department such as CID, Mounted Police, Child Protection, Drugs Squad or Traffic Police.

Type of person suited to this work

You must have excellent communication skills in order to deal with a variety of people on a daily basis whose position could range from that of a criminal who needs restraining, to a victim who needs careful treatment.

You will need to be non-judgemental, and have the ability to view situations from different perspectives.

You will need courage, initiative, and common sense in order to deal with many of the circumstances you will be presented with. You will also need to have good problem-solving skills.

Working conditions

You will be required to work 40 hours a week, covering early, late and night shifts 7 days a week. Part-time or flexible working hours can usually be accommodated.

You will be based at a police station, but the majority of your time will be spent on patrol, either on foot or by car. This means you will be out in all weather conditions, and will travel to many different locations.

Future prospects

You can move upwards to the level of sergeant and inspector, and these promotions are subject to examination and interview. To progress further you must demonstrate your skills to a board of judges.

Prospects for this role may be affected by defence budget/local government cuts.

Advantages/disadvantages

You will be meeting new challenges each day and adapting to unusual environments, which will keep you mentally and physically alert and ensures the work never gets dull.

You will be responsible for promoting safety and wellbeing in the local community, which is rewarding.

You will be required to work unsociable hours including nights and weekends.

You will have to deal with difficult, distressed, and occasionally violent members of the public.

Money guide

The starting salary for police officers varies between forces (salaries tend to be higher in the Metropolitan Police, for instance).

A typical starting salary is £22,680, however once you have completed your initial training this rises to £25,317.

For senior officers, such as sergeants and chief inspectors, salaries can rise to between £35,610 and £53,919.

London weighting of up to £6,501 is available for all ranks and key benefits can include free London travel, flexible hours and key worker living benefits.

Related opportunities

- Police Support Worker p552
- Road Safety Officer p614
- Security Officer/Manager/Door Supervisor p563

Further information

Civil Nuclear Constabulary
www.cnc.police.uk

Police Oracle
www.policeoracle.com

Police Recruitment
www.policecouldyou.co.uk

SECURITY, EMERGENCY AND THE ARMED FORCES

CRCI: UG

POLICE SUPPORT WORKER

Qualifications and courses

There are no specific academic requirements for entry to the police force, but most employers prefer that you are educated to GCSE standard or equivalent. You must also be aged 18+, a UK or European Union national, or come from within the European Economic Area.

There are several qualifications that would be viewed favourably by employers. These include an NVQ Level 2 or BTEC First Diploma in Public Services, and the BTEC National Diploma in Uniformed Public Services. Entry requirements for these courses are usually 5 GCSEs/S grades (A*–C/1–3) or equivalent, including English and maths.

If you reach interview stage, you will need to have medical, criminal record and other background checks to assess your suitability for the role. You must declare any previous convictions prior to this stage.

Once you have been accepted onto the force, your training will be provided by a more experienced support worker and you will learn on the job. Training usually lasts between 3 weeks and 3 months.

What the work involves

Police support workers are the first point of contact for members of the public in a police station.

You will be responsible for answering and directing calls, passing walk-ins to appropriate members of staff, and carrying out general administrative tasks within the station.

You will be on the front desk, so will receive firearms, knives, driving licences and any other paraphernalia seized by police whilst on patrol. You will also be the first point of contact for missing persons and lost property enquiries. You will need to look after victims and witnesses when they come into the station, which may require providing First Aid on occasion.

Type of person suited to this work

You must have excellent communication skills in order to deal with a wide variety of people on a daily basis, ranging from victims to aggressive detainees. Assertiveness, confidence and sensitivity are all desirable personality traits.

You should be happy working within a team, supporting your colleagues, taking directions, and working on your own initiative when required.

You will also need to adhere to confidentiality, diversity and data protection issues.

Working conditions

You will usually work a 37 hour week based on a shift pattern, which will require early morning and weekend work. There are usually part time opportunities.

You will be based within a police station, and will spend most of your time on the front desk answering queries or updating information on a computer. It is unlikely that you will need to travel in the course of your working day.

Stations can get very busy at times, so you should expect to work in pressurised and potentially stressful conditions at times.

Future prospects

The police force operates throughout the length and breadth of the UK, so there are opportunities in all regional forces.

Opportunities for promotion within a station are limited to its size. Larger establishments may have room to move you to a more senior, supervisory role whereas the smaller one will not be able to.

You could move to a more specialised area of support work, such as manning the crime helpdesk, or working in an enquiry centre. It is possible to train as a police officer from a support role.

Advantages/disadvantages

You will be working within a close-knit team, so your support work will be essential to the successful running of the station.

Part-time and flexible working hours are commonly available.

You will have to deal with difficult, distressed, and occasionally violent members of the public.

Money guide

The starting salary for an entry level police support worker is about £15,500 per year.

With a couple of years' experience, this should rise to around £19,000.

If you pursue promotion and attain a high level administrative role, or become a police officer, you could earn in excess of £40,000.

Related opportunities

- Civil Service Administrative Officer p27
- Police Community Support Officer p550
- Secretary p64

Further information

Police Oracle
www.policeoracle.com

Police Recruitment
www.policecouldyou.co.uk

Qualifications and courses

Most prison governors enter the profession as a prison officer. Generally, expectations for candidates include good health and physical fitness, Commonwealth, British or European Union nationality, and that you have Criminal Records Bureau clearance if you are going to work with inmates under 18 years of age.

Training is largely on the job and would be tailored to individual needs to take into account any previous and relevant work experience.

Once you have gained experience as a prison officer you will need to work your way through supervisory and senior positions, taking relevant work-related qualifications as you go, in order to become a prison governor.

The National Offender Management Service (NOMS) provides an alternative route into the profession for graduates only, and is designed to encourage rapid progression through the grades into a management position. To follow this route you will need at least a 2.1 degree.

On the NOMS graduate programme, you would complete full prison officer training, followed by up to a year as a prison officer. You may then progress to a senior role with responsibility for other staff members and could then take up an operational management post.

What the work involves

Prison governors/operational managers are responsible for the overall running and security of the establishment.

You will supervise security measures, make inspections, carry out disciplinary procedures, and advise both staff and inmates on behavioural standards and guidelines. You will also be dealing with each prisoner's casework and administration. This will include processing parole applications and complaints, and require liaison with other social and healthcare professionals.

You will be working within strict parameters set out by the government, and must ensure that you meet their targets on service, health and safety, and prisoner welfare and development.

Type of person suited to this work

You will need excellent communication skills, including confidence, assertiveness and a motivational ability, all of which will be essential when managing and inspiring staff, and also for building effective relationships with inmates.

You must have integrity and be committed to working with vulnerable people with various social issues. This should include respect for those in your care, and for the other professionals working around you.

Working conditions

You will be expected to work on a shift basis, including night and weekend hours, in order to meet the 24 hour needs of the prison. On average, you will work a 39 hour week.

You could work in a modern prison with excellent facilities, or an older, more austere establishment that will come with maintenance problems and perhaps a less comfortable working environment.

Future prospects

Prisons are located in large cities, towns, and very rural locations, so you have a good range of options regarding the working conditions that would most suit you.

Prison governors are at the top of their sector, so only sideways movements are possible. You could opt to work in a specialist institution, such as one dealing with inmates with specific medical needs. Extra qualifications may be required for this.

Advantages/disadvantages

You could be responsible for turning the lives of inmates around, both by providing them with opportunities whilst serving their sentence, and also by encouraging them to pursue better lives when they leave.

You may have to control difficult and violent situations at times.

Money guide

Prison officers start on around £18,000.

Once you have worked through the grades and get to senior or principal officer level your salary could increase to between £30,000 and £35,000.

With experience, and on gaining the full title and responsibilities of a prison governor, you could earn between £40,000 and £79,000.

Related opportunities

- Police Community Support Officer p550
- Police Officer p551
- Prison Officer/Instructor p554

Further information

HM Prison Service
www.hmprisonservice.gov.uk

Scottish Prison Service
www.sps.gov.uk

SECURITY, EMERGENCY AND THE ARMED FORCES

CRCI: UI

555

Qualifications and courses

Entry requirements for roles as a prison officer vary throughout the UK. Generally, expectations for candidates include good health and physical fitness, Commonwealth, British or European Union nationality and that you have Criminal Records Bureau clearance if you are going to work with inmates under 18 years of age.

If you meet all of the criteria above, you may be asked to attend an assessment day at which employers will observe how you react to the prison environment and work-related simulations, in order to see if you would be suitable for the role.

Candidates hoping to become a prison instructor must hold a relevant qualification in the subject they wish to teach, such as a degree, NVQ, or City & Guilds Advanced Certificate. You will also need to hold a qualification in health and safety, and be able to demonstrate teaching or supervisory experience.

What the work involves

Prison officers are responsible for supervising inmates within a secure institution. Prison instructors undertake the same duties as prison officers, but are also responsible for training prisoners in order to help them develop new skills and qualifications.

You will need to build positive relationships with the prisoners in your care in order to educate and encourage them to pursue a law-abiding life.

You could work with a variety of inmates, ranging from high risk criminals in top security institutions, to those with minor offences in low security prisons.

Type of person suited to this work

You should have excellent communication skills and be a confident person so that you can interact positively with inmates whilst also retaining your authority when necessary.

You must be non-judgemental and have respect for the prisoners in your care. The ability to remain calm in pressurised or uncomfortable situations is also an asset.

Prison instructors should be approachable and patient. You will need to be understanding and encouraging in order to help prisoners learn and progress.

Working conditions

You will usually work 39 hours a week. Prison officers will work on a shift basis including night and weekend shifts, but prison instructors usually only work during the week.

Most work is indoors and within a prison. Prison officers will also be responsible for supervising outdoor exercise and patrolling the prison grounds. Prison instructors will work in a setting suitable for their subject, for example a workshop within the prison, or in the grounds if they are teaching horticulture.

Some travel between prisons may be expected to provide extra staffing on occasion. Prison officers may also have to escort prisoners to and from court appearances.

Future prospects

Opportunities for promotion are good, and both prison officers and prison instructors can move into a position as a senior officer or principal officer of a prison. Promotion is based solely on merit, so the more you put in the more you can get out of this career.

Advantages/disadvantages

Helping to rehabilitate and educate prisoners can be rewarding, and you will be providing an important public service.

Working in a prison environment can be claustrophobic and stifling.

You may be faced with difficult and occasionally violent prisoners, which can be both stressful and unpleasant.

Money guide

New officers and instructors typically earn around £18,000 in England and Wales. Wages in Scotland are slightly lower at £16,000.

If you become a senior prison officer, after gaining several years of experience, your salary should rise to about £29,000.

Principal officers could earn up to £31,000.

Senior prison instructors may earn £31,169, while principal instructors may earn up to £33,537.

Related opportunities

- Police Officer p551
- Police Support Worker p552
- Social Worker p579

Further information

HM Prison Service
www.hmprisonservice.gov.uk

SECURITY, EMERGENCY AND THE ARMED FORCES

CRCI: UI

Qualifications and courses

There are no formal entry qualifications for this work. However, many entrants have degrees or advanced level qualifications. You will need a driving licence and most successful Private Investigators (PIs) work in a related job such as the police, law, customs and excise or security work first.

Applicants new to the role would benefit from having a relevant qualification, which may include an NVQ Level 3 in Intelligence Analysis, membership qualifications from the Association of British Investigators (ABI), the Level 3 Award for Professional Investigators from the ABI or a degree in an appropriate subject. You could also take the Institute of Professional Investigators (IPI) Foundation Course for Investigators or the BTEC Advanced Diploma in Private Investigation.

Your training should be accepted by the Security Industry Authority (SIA), and include the topics of the law, investigative methods and equipment. A scheme is being introduced whereby a government licence issued by the SIA will be required to practise. Check with the SIA for the latest developments.

Courses are available from a number of private companies and listed by the ABI. Topics such as theft, court work, investigation and surveillance are offered.

What the work involves

You will be collecting information for a private client or a solicitor by asking questions, researching, obtaining evidence and making sense of what you find out.

PIs do a variety of different jobs such as surveillance, tracing people, serving legal documents or investigating road accidents, suspected fraud and employee backgrounds.

You could be recording your findings using a computer, and you may be asked to present your findings in court or to a large company. You will probably take witness statements, attend court hearings and give evidence.

Type of person suited to this work

Much of the day-to-day work of this exciting sounding job is actually quite routine, so you will need to be patient and persistent and be happy with your own company.

You need to be interested in learning about the law.

You will need to have excellent communications skills, both spoken and written in order to write reports and take witness statements. You may need to calm down anxious or aggressive people when you serve legal papers or repossess their car to pay a debt.

Working conditions

Most of your working hours will be spent driving or walking around. You could be in your vehicle for hours or out in all weathers.

Hours are irregular and in some cases they could be long and include evening and weekend work.

You will be at risk of assault from aggressive individuals who you are serving with legal papers.

Future prospects

With the introduction of licensing there may be more opportunities for those with licences. A lot of the work is for legal, insurance or financial companies.

Some private investigators go on to take further qualifications and specialise in areas such as commercial piracy or insurance fraud. A few set up their own agencies and others move into supervisory or security management work.

There is the opportunity to progress into a managerial or senior investigator role at bigger agencies.

Advantages/disadvantages

PIs are usually self-employed and so need to buy their own equipment. Licences and training will also add to the expense.

A lot of the work is routine, but PIs say that there is a lot of satisfaction when after months of patient work you manage to find the evidence your client needs.

Money guide

Starting salaries range between £12,500 and £15,000 per year.

Experienced investigators could earn up to £25,000.

Well-qualified specialists working in corporate investigation can earn between £50,000 and £100,000 per year.

Related opportunities

- Forensic Computer Analyst p547
- Police Officer p551
- Store Detective p564

Further information

Academy of Professional Investigation
www.pi-academy.com

Association of British Investigators
www.theabi.org.uk

Institute of Professional Investigators
www.ipi.org.uk

Security Industry Authority
www.sia.homeoffice.gov.uk

SECURITY, EMERGENCY AND THE ARMED FORCES

CRCI: UK

PROBATION OFFICER

Qualifications and courses

New recruitment procedures have been in place from April 2010, meaning you will need to work as a probation service officer (PSO) before becoming a probation officer.

You will also need to have an Honours degree in community justice in order to apply for a position as a probation officer. If you have graduated in the last five years with a relevant degree, in a subject such as police studies or community justice, it is possible to take the Vocational Qualification Level 5 Diploma in Probation Practice. Both qualifications are studied for whilst training and working as a PSO.

Experience working with offenders or time in a public facing role can be useful in becoming a PSO. Local trusts recruit PSOs as needed, so you should check their websites frequently. A graduate training scheme is also available.

In Scotland, in order to join the Probation Service you must complete a 4-year course in social work and gain relevant experience. Alternatively a postgraduate scheme is available. Northern Ireland has a similar approach, with candidates first becoming social workers before moving into probation.

Continuing professional development (CPD) is actively encouraged. Each trust provides its own staff development, and you can undertake courses in a variety of areas including dealing with sex offenders or those who have committed hate crimes.

What the work involves

Probation officers protect the public by assessing the risk that offenders pose to the community and working out how to limit that risk.

You will work with offenders before, during and after their sentencing. This will include ensuring they carry out their punishment, making them aware of the consequences of their offences and helping them back into the community. You will construct and deliver programmes to change offenders' behaviour and attitude.

You will prepare pre-sentence reports (PSR) to advise judges on sentencing and prepare risk assessments for prisons and parole review boards, which may then contribute towards a decision on the early release of an offender.

Type of person suited to this work

You will need to have the ability to gain the trust and confidence of offenders and have a fair and non-judgemental approach. Good communication skills will be helpful.

Organisational skills are essential as you will often be planning your own workload. An ability to write clearly and accurately will be needed for reports and risk assessments. Employers also look for good teamwork skills and experience of the criminal justice system.

As you may face stressful situations and setbacks, strong motivation and commitment is important.

Working conditions

Typically you will work between 37 and 40 hours a week. Hours are not always regular and you may have to work in the evenings and at weekends, but you will usually get extra time off to make up for unsocial hours.

You will work from an office but will also be expected to travel to courts and prisons and community programmes on a regular basis.

Future prospects

You can specialise in areas such as managing approved premises, which provide accommodation for people on bail, or drug treatment and testing orders. Probation officers are offered frequent opportunities for training.

With experience there is a possibility of moving to a managerial role as a senior probation officer. Eventually you may become an area manager.

Recruitment may be affected by budget cuts.

Advantages/disadvantages

You will meet a wide range of people.

Providing a public service and helping to rehabilitate prisoners can be deeply rewarding.

You may meet difficult or violent offenders which could be stressful or distressing.

Money guide

Salaries differ between probation trusts, but typically probation service officers earn between £19,000 and £26,000 a year.

With time and experience this can rise to £35,000.

Salaries for assistant chief officer posts start at around £50,000.

Related opportunities

- Prison Officer/Instructor p554
- Social Worker p579
- Victim Care Officer p582

Further information

Ministry of Justice
www.justice.gov.uk

Probation Board for Northern Ireland
www.pbni.org.uk

Skills for Justice
www.skillsforjustice.com

Qualifications and courses

Entry requirements to become an RAF airman/woman vary according to the specialist trade you are looking to work in. Most trades require entrants to be at least 15 years and 9 months old whilst others set a higher age limit with the maximum age of entry being 29.

To become an RAF Regiment gunner, you do not need any formal qualifications. Most other fields require 2–5 GCSEs/S grades (A*–C/1–3) or equivalent. If you are looking to enter as a student nurse or similar, then you will need 2 A levels or equivalent. You will need to pass a rigorous medical and fitness entrance test, as well as a range of interview and written tests during the selection process.

It is also essential that you have been registered as a citizen of the UK, Commonwealth or Republic of Ireland since birth.

Once accepted into the RAF, you will complete an 11-week training course at RAF Halton in Buckinghamshire which will cover fitness and weapons training. On completion of these general elements, you will then start on more specialised training for your chosen trade, and this can take between 3 weeks and 18 months.

What the work involves

The Royal Air Force is responsible for protecting UK airspace, performing search and rescue missions offshore and on land, transporting aid to the victims of war and natural disaster, and pursuing military action in a war situation. Opportunities include positions in catering, aircrew, engineering, protection and medical support.

You will work within a team of other RAF professionals, under the guidance of an officer.

You will also be expected to undertake general military duties, such as guarding RAF bases, and taking part in training exercises and military initiatives.

Type of person suited to this work

You should be able to work well within a team. This includes being able to follow orders, work calmly under pressure, support colleagues and use your own initiative when necessary.

You should be self-disciplined in order to maintain high levels of fitness, mental agility and a positive attitude to your work.

You should be good at interpreting and analysing information, both verbal and written.

Working conditions

Airmen/women usually work regular office hours, but you are required to be available for duty at all times in case of an emergency. There are also occasional social functions or other duties that need to be fulfilled over weekends.

You will be stationed at an RAF base, many of which have all the amenities of a small town.

You should be prepared to be posted overseas at short notice, and to spend long periods of time away from friends and family.

Future prospects

On joining the RAF as an airman/woman, you sign up for a minimum length of service that ranges from 12 months for non-commissioned aircrew, up to 9 years for other specialisations.

After 6 months or on completion of specialist training, you should be promoted to leading aircraftman/woman, and from there you can work up the ranks to the position of corporal or higher. Promotion is based on merit, so you will be rewarded for the hard work that you put in.

Although prospects for new and existing recruits may be affected by defence budget cuts, there are still good opportunities if you meet the selection criteria.

Advantages/disadvantages

You will work on diverse assignments within a supportive team environment, so each day will be both diverse and interesting.

There are good training schemes and potential for promotion and career progression within the RAF.

You may have to enter war situations, which can be traumatic and stressful.

Money guide

Pay during training is around £13,900 per year.

On completion of your initial 6 months of training, your salary will increase to £17,265.

Senior level airmen/airwomen will earn between £17,735 and £28,989 per year.

Corporals can expect to earn between £26,404 and £33,182.

Sergeants can expect to earn £30,012–£36,929.

Related opportunities

- Air Traffic Controller p589
- Army Soldier p539
- Royal Air Force Officer p558

Further information

RAF Careers
www.raf.mod.uk/careers

RAF Halton
www.raf.mod.uk/rafhalton

SECURITY, EMERGENCY AND THE ARMED FORCES

CRCI: UA

559

Qualifications and courses

In order to qualify to train as an RAF officer you must be 17 years and 6 months or older, be a UK, Commonwealth, or Republic of Ireland citizen since birth and have at least 2 A levels/Highers or equivalent, and 5 GCSEs/S grades (A*–C/1–3) or equivalent, including English and maths.

For a role as an intelligence officer, you must have been a British citizen from birth.

Some specialisations (including engineering, legal, and the medical divisions) require a relevant degree. For entrance onto related degree courses, you will need 3 A levels/Highers or equivalent, as well as at least 5 GCSEs/S grades (A*–C/1–3) or equivalent, including English, maths and science.

If you meet the entrance criteria, you may be invited to attend the 3-day selection event held at the RAF College Cranwell, in Lincolnshire. During this process, you will have to undertake interviews, fitness and health assessments and various aptitude tests. The RAF also offers sponsorship to sixth form and university students.

As a new recruit you will have to complete a 30-week initial officer training course at Cranwell where you will be taught a variety of skills such as service knowledge and leadership skills. If you join the RAF with a professional qualification this initial training may be reduced to 12 weeks. After this you will go on to specialise.

What the work involves

The RAF is responsible for protecting UK airspace, performing search and rescue missions offshore and on land, transporting aid to the victims of war and natural disaster, and pursuing military action in a war situation.

RAF officers are responsible for managing, leading and inspiring a team of airmen.

You will occupy a specialist post within the RAF, such as that of a pilot, engineer, catering manager or medical officer.

You will be involved in planning and implementing various procedures from rescues to humanitarian aid drops.

Type of person suited to this work

You must have excellent communication skills as you will be responsible for briefing, leading and motivating your team. This also includes being able to listen and get on with all team members.

You will be called upon to make difficult decisions in highly pressurised situations, so must be able to think on your feet in order to reach mature, responsible conclusions.

You must be physically fit and mentally alert.

Working conditions

Officers usually work regular office hours, but you are required to be available for duty at all times in case of an emergency. There are also occasional social functions or other duties that need to be fulfilled over weekends.

You will be stationed at an RAF base, many of which have all the amenities of a small town, including shops, banks, a gym and childcare facilities.

You should be prepared to be posted overseas at short notice, and to spend long periods of time away from friends and family.

Future prospects

On joining the RAF as an officer, you sign up to a minimum length of service. This can range from 6 to 12 years according to your specialisation.

There is defined career progression through the ranks from flying officer, to flight lieutenant, squadron leader, wing commander, group captain and further if you wish.

The training, qualifications and personal skills that come with being an RAF officer are easily transferred to a number of civilian positions.

Although prospects for new and existing recruits may be affected by defence budget cuts, there are still good opportunities if you meet the selection criteria.

Advantages/disadvantages

You will be responsible for training and organising a team that will carry out essential defence and humanitarian functions for the UK and the world.

You may have to enter combat situations which can be distressing and unpleasant.

Money guide

If you enter the RAF without a degree, as a pilot officer you can expect to earn £24,615 as a starting salary.

If you hold a degree and enter as a flying officer, your starting wages will be £29,586–£32,702 per year.

On promotion to flight lieutenant, your salary will increase to £37,915–£45,090 per year.

If you become a squadron leader with experience, you could earn between £47,760 and £57,199.

Related opportunities

- Air Traffic Controller p589
- Royal Air Force Airman/woman p557
- Royal Navy Officer p561

Further information

RAF College Cranwell
www.raf.mod.uk/rafcranwell

ROYAL MARINES COMMANDO

ENTRY LEVEL 1

Qualifications and courses

There is a rigorous selection process. You will need to attend an interview and pass a medical examination and aptitude tests.

You will also have to undertake the Potential Royal Marines Course. This lasts 2.5 days and is designed to test your fitness, determination, stamina and mental ability. This is a gruelling assessment designed to push you to your limits, so you will have to train and prepare for it for a number of months.

You must be male and between 16 and 32 years of age to apply to the Royal Marines.

You will need to have British, Irish, Commonwealth or British dual citizenship to be considered for entry.

There are no academic qualification requirements for entry but a career in the Royal Marines offers the opportunity to gain qualifications related to your area of specialism as your career progresses.

What the work involves

The Royal Marines are a specialist, highly trained, amphibious division of the Royal Navy. They carry out operations on land, in the sea or in the air. They operate in combat, peacekeeping and humanitarian situations, and also as a law enforcement agency at sea.

You will be a commando and rifleman, working within an operational commando unit. You will be ready to take immediate action in any emergency or threat to national security, and this means performing to a very high standard at all times whether on land or at sea.

You will specialise either in general duties, or in one of 26 trades which include assault engineer, mountain leader or swimmer canoeist.

Type of person suited to this work

You will need high levels of fitness, discipline, commitment and self-confidence in order to get through one of the most demanding and gruelling training programmes in the Armed Forces prior to qualifying as a commando.

You must be able to work well within a team and also use your own initiative when required. The ability to lead and motivate others is also an asset.

You should be level-headed and be able to react quickly and logically when under pressure. Courage and determination are also necessary in order to head into combat situations.

Working conditions

You will usually work 37 hours a week, unless you are on an operation or in training. In these instances, you could expect to work long, unpredictable hours. Even if you are not at work, though, you will always be on-call in case of emergency.

You could be stationed or deployed anywhere in the world at short notice, including undertaking operations in areas of desert, jungle, and even out in the Arctic.

You will be expected to wear a uniform.

Future prospects

Within the UK, you are most likely to be stationed within the south-west of England or in Scotland, as that is where the majority of naval bases are located.

You will be expected to serve with the Royal Marines for 22 years, although you can leave at any point after completing the minimum three years of service and giving 12 months' notice.

You will be promoted on merit, so hard work should be rewarded. You could move up the ranks from lance corporal right up to warrant officer 1.

Although prospects for new and existing recruits may be affected by defence budget cuts, there are still good opportunities if you meet the selection criteria.

Advantages/disadvantages

You will be operating at your optimum level of mental and physical fitness, meeting new challenges each day and adapting to unusual and inhospitable situations.

You will be working within a close knit team, providing essential services such as delivering aid or maintaining order in areas across the globe.

You are continually on-call, and could be sent anywhere in the world at a moment's notice.

Money guide

New entrants to the Royal Marines as a general duties marine receive a starting salary of around £13,377 rising to £16,681 a year after you complete your initial training.

With increasing experience and promotion you could expect to earn about £28,300.

If you move up the ranks and reach the level of warrant officer 1 you should earn £45,836.

Related opportunities

- Army Officer p538
- Army Soldier p539
- Royal Marines Officer p560

Further information

Royal Marines
www.royalnavy.mod.uk/royalmarines

SECURITY, EMERGENCY AND THE ARMED FORCES

CRCI: UA

561

Qualifications and courses

Although most applicants are graduates, the minimum entry criteria are at least 2 A levels/Highers or equivalent, and 5 GCSEs/S grades (A*–C/1–3) including English and maths.

Only men can serve as Royal Marines officers, and you must be between 17 and 25 years old to enter. You must also have British or dual British nationality and have lived in the UK for a minimum of 5 years.

You will attend a 3-day Potential Officers Course, which is a gruelling assessment designed to push you to your limits. If you successfully complete the 3-day assessment, you will be invited to attend a further 2.5-day interview process, during which you will sit further tests in maths, reasoning, accuracy, written communication, spatial orientation, leadership, and problem-solving and undergo a series of interviews.

If you are selected to train as an officer, you will then have to complete a further 15 month programme prior to being given your own team to lead.

What the work involves

The Royal Marines carry out operations on land, in the sea or in the air. They operate in combat, peacekeeping and humanitarian situations, and also as a law enforcement agency at sea.

You will be responsible for leading and managing a team both on training operations and on real missions including combat situations and peace keeping tasks. You will be in charge of training your team, keeping them disciplined, and looking out for their welfare.

You will be given the opportunity to specialise in 1 of 10 areas, including weapons training, signals, physical training, or as a pilot.

Type of person suited to this work

You will need high levels of fitness, discipline, commitment and self-confidence in order to get through the demanding and gruelling training programme prior to qualifying as an officer.

You must be able to lead and motivate your team, looking out for their welfare and making decisions for them in dangerous and stressful conditions.

You should be able to focus on the operations you undertake fully in order to function at your maximum level of mental and physical capacity.

Working conditions

You will usually work 37 hours a week, unless you are on an operation or in training. In these instances, you could expect to work long, unpredictable hours. Even if you are not at work, you are always on-call in case of emergency.

You could be stationed or deployed anywhere in the world at short notice, including undertaking operations in areas of desert, jungle, and even out in the Arctic.

You will be expected to wear a uniform, and specialised clothing when required.

Future prospects

Competition for entry as a Royal Marines officer is fierce. You will be expected to join on a 12 year commission, and must serve at least 3–5 years of this. 12 months' notice is required prior to departure.

You will normally move appointments every other year, so you will be able to experience numerous areas of work in various locations throughout your career.

Promotion is awarded on merit, and you could work through the ranks from 2nd lieutenant right up to major-general.

Although prospects for new and existing recruits may be affected by defence budget cuts, there are still good opportunities if you meet the selection criteria.

Advantages/disadvantages

You will be operating at your optimum level of mental and physical fitness, meeting new challenges each day and adapting to unusual and inhospitable situations.

You will be working within a close knit team, leading them through essential operations such as delivering aid or maintaining order in areas across the globe.

Money guide

Entrants who do not have a degree can expect a starting salary of £15,268 at the start of their training, rising to £24,132 12 months after completing their initial training.

Graduates can expect a starting salary of between £29,006 and £32,061.

Related opportunities

- Army Officer p538
- Army Soldier p539
- Royal Marines Commando p559

Further information

Royal Marines
www.royalnavy.mod.uk/royalmarines

ROYAL NAVY OFFICER

Qualifications and courses

You will need to be at least 151.5cm tall and be of proportionate weight. Upon application you must be no younger than 15 years and 9 months. A medical, with strict eyesight standards, must be passed, and you must meet the Royal Navy nationality and residence requirements. Women will be able to serve as submariners from 2014.

The minimum requirements for officer entry are 5 GCSEs (or equivalent) at grades A–C, including English and maths and a minimum of 180 UCAS points (each subject must be allocated at least 45 UCAS points).

The Defence Sixth Form College (Welbeck) focuses on gaining entry to the Armed Forces.

If you then want to study for an Honours degree (funded by the Royal Navy) there are a number of sponsored options including the Defence Technical Undergraduate Scheme (DTUS). The most commonly sponsored subject is engineering and specific and relevant units are agreed before you commence the course. All candidates undergo a selection interview and medical examination before the Admiralty Interview Board (AIB).

It is also possible to enter directly as a Royal Navy officer after completing a degree independently.

What the work involves

You will command and train ratings, looking after their welfare, development and discipline.

Your day-to-day work will involve you managing operations in 1 of 4 areas of duty: as a warfare officer, engineer officer, supply officer or specialist officer (for example chaplain, doctor or dentist).

Your ship may be sent into combat or on peacekeeping duties.

You may be tasked to do a specific job such as policing the North Sea fishing grounds or helping out in a disaster situation.

Type of person suited to this work

Officers especially need top-level leadership and communication skills as well as good judgement.

You will be required to inspire ratings, be resourceful and have excellent communication skills. You should have good levels of physical fitness and stamina. You may need to work in combat zones.

You should also have a very strong sense of responsibility as your decisions may impact upon your colleagues' safety as well as your own. You should display a very high level of personal awareness and a keen sense of personal safety.

Working conditions

Most of your work will be on-board a ship or submarine, or at land-based establishments in Britain or overseas. At sea, conditions can be cold, cramped and damp. You will need to wear a uniform, and protective clothing when necessary.

Hours vary but you will usually work 8-hour turns of duty on a shift rota including weekends and holidays.

You may find yourself working in a dangerous or highly unpredictable situation.

Future prospects

There are over 7500 officers in the Royal Navy. There are annual vacancies but some specialisms are more competitive than others.

A naval college entrant usually starts out as midshipman rising to sub-lieutenant after 2 years. A graduate starts as sub-lieutenant rising to lieutenant commander by their early 30s. If you have got the right qualities you can progress on to the ranks of commander, captain and, for a few, admiral.

Although prospects for new and existing recruits may be affected by defence budget cuts, there are still good opportunities if you meet the selection criteria.

Advantages/disadvantages

You will be trained to a high level and will be offered a resettlement package to help you find work in civilian life when you leave.

You will be living in cramped conditions with lots of other people. However, most officers say that they enjoy the feeling of camaraderie on-board and make life-long friendships.

Money guide

Entering this career (without a degree) you can expect to start on £16,073 per year.

Upon completion of a degree, starting salaries for officers are £28,216.

As you rise through the ranks and gain experience, your salary can range from £24,616 to £89,408 per year.

Related opportunities

- Army Officer p538
- Royal Marines Officer p560
- Royal Navy Rating p562

Further information

Royal Navy Careers
www.royalnavy.mod.uk

Welbeck College
www.welbeck.mod.uk

ROYAL NAVY RATING

Qualifications and courses

There are no formal qualifications for entry, but holding at least 2 GCSEs/S grades (A*–C/1–3) or equivalent is helpful. Some specialist trades have entry requirements and a higher age for admission. Typically, you must be 16 to 36 years of age to apply.

Selection takes place at local Armed Forces careers offices, where you will be required to take several tests including numeracy, English language, reasoning and mechanical comprehension. If you are successful, you will be invited for an interview. You must also pass a medical assessment and fitness test.

You will join the Royal Navy on a Full Career, which lasts 18 years. You can leave after completing 2.5 years' training but must give 12 months' notice.

Upon entry you will undertake 9 weeks' basic training, followed by specialist training in your chosen trade.

What the work involves

The Royal Navy protects the UK's ports and coastline, and also undertakes international missions such as delivering humanitarian aid, entering combat, and enforcing the law on the seas.

Royal Navy ratings work on-board a ship, submarine or onshore, and are responsible for operating, maintaining and repairing technical equipment.

You will specialise in 1 of the 6 main trades; medical, warfare, logistics, engineering, fleet air arm, or submarine. You will also take part in naval exercises and operations both in UK and overseas waters.

Type of person suited to this work

You should be able to work within a team, reacting quickly to orders, working on your own initiative where necessary, and supporting other team members both professionally and emotionally at times.

You must be responsible and decisive and find solutions to problems under difficult or pressurised circumstances. You should also have a methodical and logical approach to your work.

You will need to have a good level of fitness, including the ability to swim and tread water for a number of minutes.

Working conditions

You will usually work 37 hours a week, which can include weekends and public holidays. You will also be on-call at all times, in case of an emergency.

You could be based at sea on a ship or submarine, or in a naval station onshore. Living conditions on ships and submarines tend to be basic, and men and women always sleep in separate accommodation.

You will have to spend long periods of time away from friends and family, and may be posted overseas at a moment's notice.

Future prospects

The career progression for a Royal Navy rating is clearly mapped out. Promotion is awarded on merit so the harder you work the faster you will progress. The grades that you will move upwards through are able rating, leading rating, petty officer, chief petty officer and warrant officer.

If you have the necessary qualifications, you could apply to become an officer. This is a popular route of career progression amongst ratings.

Although prospects for new and existing recruits may be affected by defence budget cuts, there are still good opportunities if you meet the selection criteria.

Advantages/disadvantages

You will be meeting new challenges each day and adapting to unusual and inhospitable situations, which will keep you mentally and physically alert and ensures the work never gets dull.

You will be working within a close knit team, supporting them both in training and when out on real operations.

As you are continually on-call you could be sent anywhere in the world at a moment's notice.

Money guide

You will enter the Royal Navy as a rating on a starting salary of £14,145.

Once you have completed your training and have qualified as an able rating, you could earn between £17,515 to £28,940.

If you are promoted to the role of leading rating, your salary will increase to between £27,592 and £33,182.

Related opportunities

- Army Soldier p539
- Royal Air Force Officer p558
- Royal Marines Commando p559
- Royal Navy Officer p561

Further information

Royal Navy Careers
www.royalnavy.mod.uk

Qualifications and courses

Officer

All security guards must have an industry licence, approved by the Security Industry Authority (SIA). The licence is awarded to candidates who pass the 2-part assessment process, usually delivered over 4 days.

For a licence you will need a City & Guilds Level 2 Certificate for Security Guards, a BTEC Level 2 Award or an EDI Level 2 Certificate in Security Guarding. If the role involves monitoring CCTV, you may need a SIA public space surveillance (CCTV) licence.

Manager

In addition to the SIA licence specialist managers may need specific training and experience, for example in security systems, legislation and anti-terrorist work.

Door supervisor

You will need an SIA licence which requires you to be over 18 years old, have an SIA-approved Level 2 Certificate in Door Supervision and pass a Criminal Records Bureau check.

What the work involves

Security work is about protecting organisations, people, places, valuable goods or money.

Officer

You might work at reception monitoring visitors and deliveries or you might patrol a site, checking for intruders or fire risks.

Manager

You will manage a team and be responsible for their work, training and supervision. You will do security surveys, give advice on improvements and liaise with other organisations such as the emergency services.

Door supervisor

You will stand at the entrance to a building and help control people entering and leaving, judging whether or not they should be allowed on the premises. You could also search bags and assist the police if trouble breaks out.

Type of person suited to this work

You will need to be a mature, responsible and honest person. You should be keen on technology and keep up to date with new security systems. You will also have to keep records of all incidents, so you must be happy to do paperwork.

To become a manager you will need a great deal of experience in security work as well as a talent for motivating a team of staff.

Working conditions

If you are a door supervisor you will be based in 1 location which could be inside, or outside in all weathers. Many security officer/manager jobs involve driving and you will spend a lot of time in a security van.

You will probably be working shifts of up to 12 hours covering days, nights and weekends. Some door supervisors or security officers work permanent nights. You may work a 48-hour week although part-time work is available.

Future prospects

This work will increasingly use sophisticated technology, computer security systems and also biometrics (fingerprint recognition systems) to control access to buildings and other secure areas.

With the right training and technical ability you are likely to be in demand in this growing industry.

Advantages/disadvantages

Your promotion and earnings prospects are excellent.

You could often work alone and be put in vulnerable situations.

Money guide

Officer

Starting out, officers are paid between £12,000 and £15,000 a year. With experience this can rise to £20,000.

Manager

On entry, managers earn between £26,500 and £28,500 per year. This can rise to in excess of £35,000 with experience.

Area managers can earn in excess of £50,000.

International security managers can earn up to £70,000.

Door supervisor

Door supervisors earn up to £13 per hour; up to £17,000 per year full time.

With experience this can rise to £15 per hour for a part-time supervisor, equating to £28,000 per year for the full-time equivalent.

Related opportunities

- Bodyguard p540
- Police Officer p551
- Prison Officer/Instructor p554

Further information

Security Industry Authority
www.sia.homeoffice.gov.uk

SECURITY, EMERGENCY AND THE ARMED FORCES

CRCI: UK

Qualifications and courses

There are no formal entry requirements, but you will need to be able to write clearly and accurately. A GCSE/S grade in English or a Key Skill in Communication would be useful.

You will have to undergo a police check. Some employers may also do an employment history and credit check. Previous relevant work experience is preferred, especially within the police, prison or security industry.

Training is primarily done through courses or on the job with the support of a more experienced store detective. Most companies run an induction course for new employees covering topics such as relevant criminal law and principles of investigation.

The Security Institute and the International Professional Security Association both offer courses by distance learning. The Security Industry Authority (SIA) now has a requirement for you to be licensed to operate as a store detective. Store detectives can work towards NVQ Level 2 in Providing Security Services and cover important areas such as loss prevention, customer care and defusing potentially volatile situations.

Previous experience in a related field including the police or armed services would be advantageous.

What the work involves

You will be preventing and detecting theft or fraud in a retail outlet. You might need to chase the suspected offender, search them and make arrests. You will then need to contact the police and describe your observations.

Working undercover, wearing plain clothes, you will merge with shoppers, looking out for suspicious behaviour or theft.

Using a radio you will call for assistance and listen for alerts from other staff about known offenders entering the store.

You will make notes of any incidents and may need to use these if a decision is made to prosecute. Occasionally you will have to give evidence in court.

You may also be involved with preventing the use of stolen credit cards.

Type of person suited to this work

You need to have excellent communications skills as it will be your responsibility to deal with customers who have become anxious or aggressive when challenged.

Your written reports will be used in court if you prosecute and you will need to be fluent and precise to get a conviction.

You must have good observation skills in order to spot suspicious behaviour and also remember the faces of known shoplifters.

You should be able to plan and think ahead so that when a situation happens you can act quickly.

You will need to be mature, responsible and be able to handle difficult situations sensitively.

Working conditions

You will spend the majority of your time on your feet, in the store.

A 40-hour week is common and you may work shifts to cover long opening hours and weekends.

You might wear a uniform but the majority wear their own clothes to blend in.

Future prospects

Shoplifters cost stores more than £2 billion a year so most large stores in the UK employ store detectives to minimise their losses.

Some retail chains employ their own detectives, while others use agencies on a contract basis.

After gaining experience, you could become a supervisor or move into more general security management.

Advantages/disadvantages

Apprehending shoplifters can be dangerous.

This job can be a good stepping stone into jobs such as security management.

Money guide

Starting wages are usually between £12,500 and £16,500 per year.

Experienced store detectives can earn up to £20,000.

Over £28,000 is possible for top earners.

Related opportunities

- Police Officer p551
- Private Investigator p555
- Security Officer/Manager/Door Supervisor p563

Further information

British Security Industry Association
www.bsia.co.uk

Security Industry Authority
www.sia.homeoffice.gov.uk

Social Work and Counselling Services

People who work in this sector are dedicated to caring and talking through people's problems and anxieties to improve their general wellbeing and their future prospects in life. The work requires a lot of patience, an open mind and a friendly and approachable personality. You could be helping people who are distressed and need help and guidance but equally you may be helping people who want to move on to the next stage in their careers or educational choices. Either way, you should be someone who enjoys helping people change their lives for the better. If you are interested in working in this field you need to show that you are compassionate and very good at communicating with people from all walks of life and of all ages. You should also be someone who can maintain a strong sense of professionalism as you could be in a position of trust and you must be very respectful of your clients' privacy.

The jobs featured in this section are listed below. For similar jobs to the ones covered in this section turn to *Healthcare* on page 287 and *Education and Training* on page 189.

- Careers Adviser p566
- Childminder p567
- Clinical/Health Psychologist p568
- Counsellor p569
- Debt Counsellor/Money Advice Caseworker p570
- Educational Psychologist p571
- Forensic Psychologist p572
- Fundraiser p573
- Life Coach p574
- Occupational Psychologist p575
- Psychoanalyst/ Psychotherapist p576
- Rehabilitation Officer p577
- Residential Support Worker p578
- Social Worker p579
- Substance Misuse Worker p580
- Trade Union Official p581
- Victim Care Officer p582
- Volunteer Manager p583
- Welfare Benefits Adviser/ Welfare Rights Caseworker p584
- Youth and Community Worker p585

ENTRY LEVEL 4

Qualifications and courses

There are two main routes into this profession: the Qualification in Careers Guidance (QCG) or the work-based route.

The QCG is a 1-year full-time or 2-year part-time course that combines academic study with work-based learning and leads to the Postgraduate Diploma in Careers Guidance. You normally need a degree to take this course but applicants with significant and relevant work experience would also be able to follow this route.

If you follow the work-based route you could study for the OCR Level 3 Award for Supporting Clients to Overcome Barriers To Learning and Work, OCR Level 4 Diploma in Career Information and Advice and OCR Level 6 Diploma in Career Guidance and Development.

You do not need a professional careers qualification to work as a careers adviser in higher education, although most successful candidates do have a qualification or have experience working in higher education. A specialist qualification for higher education careers advisers, the Certificate/Diploma in Careers Education, Information and Guidance in Higher Education (CEIGHE), is available.

What the work involves

Researching information about job opportunities in different sectors from newspapers, books, the internet or through visits to employers is all part of the role.

You will help people make realistic choices about education, training and work by listening to their ideas, discussing their interests and skills, and providing information on different jobs. Advisory work is often one to one, but you could also work with large groups. Increasingly advice is being delivered over the phone or via email and instant messaging services.

Careers advisers work with young people in schools/colleges, but also with higher education students or adults.

Type of person suited to this work

Since much of the work involves talking and listening to people, careers advisers need to have excellent communication skills. You will need to be impartial, allowing people to come to their own decisions rather than making up their minds for them.

Careers information and guidance is largely ICT-based, so computer skills are essential, along with the ability to write reports and perform administrative tasks.

You will need to enjoy researching, as you will need to keep up to date with any changes in skills and opportunities available, and with any new qualifications and training routes.

Working conditions

Most of your work is office based, either in a careers centre open to the public or an educational establishment. You would normally work 9–5, Monday to Friday but occasional evening work may also be required.

You will travel between different educational establishments and visit employers and training organisations, which means that a driving licence may be required.

Future prospects

Careers advisers work in schools, colleges, universities and adult guidance services – some will be based in 1 institution, others will work for several organisations.

You could move into a managerial-level post in a careers service, work for a large company as a careers manager or you could become self-employed as a consultant or researcher.

Ongoing professional development is essential.

Advantages/disadvantages

The work is varied and can be highly satisfying.

You will work some evenings or weekends to attend school/college parents' evenings and for careers events.

The job also includes a great deal of administrative work.

Money guide

Starting salaries range from £18,000 to £20,000 a year.

With experience and qualifications salaries can increase to £20,000–£27,500.

As a senior manager you could earn around £35,000.

Related opportunities

- Counsellor p569
- Debt Counsellor/Money Advice Caseworker p570
- Youth and Community Worker p585

Further information

Careers Research and Advisory Council
www.crac.org.uk

Institute of Careers Guidance
www.icg-uk.org

CHILDMINDER

Qualifications and courses

Qualifications in childcare are useful. Candidates must be aged 18 or over. They, and everyone in their households over 16, must be police checked.

You could study for BTEC Certificates and Diplomas in Children's Care or Learning and Development, the Diploma in Society, Health and Development and the Oxford Cambridge and RSA Examinations (OCR) Entry Level certificate in Child Development. A City & Guilds qualification in Early Years Foundation Stage Practice is also available.

You could also take an Apprenticeship in Children's Care, Learning and Development or NVQ at Levels 2–5 in Children's Care, Learning and Development.

Childminders must register with Ofsted in England, the Care Commission in Scotland, the Care and Social Services Inspectorate in Wales and the local Health and Social Services board or trust in Northern Ireland. You need to take an introductory childminding training course and be prepared for a registration visit.

What the work involves

You will care for children in your own home, ensuring they are comfortable and happy. You will plan the children's day and keep parents informed about what they have done during the day, what they have eaten and if there have been any problems.

You could accompany children to and from playgroup, nursery or school.

For children aged under five, you will have to follow the guidelines set by the Early Years Foundation Stage for play-based learning.

Type of person suited to this work

As a childminder you must be patient and caring. Creativity is needed to plan varied activities for children of different ages. You must also be adaptable and prepared to change your plans at short notice to meet the changing needs of the children in your care.

You need to share information with parents on a daily basis which means that good observation and communication skills are important.

As you will be self-employed, you will need to be organised, with good administrative and numeracy skills to work out tax and invoices. ICT skills are useful.

Working conditions

You are allowed to care for up to 6 children, including your own, under the age of 8 providing that only 3 are less than 5 years old.

You will work in your own home which may have to be altered to meet childminding standards by fitting equipment such as stairgates and socket covers.

A driving licence is useful as you may take children to playgroup or school. You will do a lot of lifting and clearing up. A working day of 8am to 6pm is usual and you will need to do other administrative tasks outside of this time.

Future prospects

Although the minimum age for entry is 18, most childminders are older and are parents themselves or have experience of care work.

The demand for childminders can vary regionally and at different times of the year.

Childminders can become care assistants or home care assistants, or can go on to train for similar work as a nursery nurse or registered nurse.

Advantages/disadvantages

The work will be varied and fun.

Working from home often suits people who have young children themselves.

Some jobs can be messy and unpleasant.

The hours can be very long and it can sometimes be hard work for low pay.

Money guide

Most childminders charge an hourly rate for each child of between £3 and £6 an hour. Your income can vary at different times of the year: for example, your hours might go up or down during school holidays.

You can expect around £6,000–£10,000 per year when starting out, rising to £15,000 when experienced.

Top hourly rates are charged in London where experienced, full-time childminders can earn up to £20,000 a year.

Your earnings will depend on how many children you care for at any one time.

Related opportunities

- Children's Nurse p294
- Early Years Specialist/Nursery Nurse p192
- Play Worker/Hospital Play Specialist p198

Further information

National Childminding Association of England and Wales
www.ncma.org.uk

Northern Ireland Childminding Association
www.nicma.org

Scottish Childminding Association
www.childminding.org

SOCIAL WORK AND COUNSELLING SERVICES

CRCI: V

Qualifications and courses

Entrants must have Graduate Basis for Chartered Membership (GBC) with the British Psychological Society (BPS). Graduate Basis for Registration (GBR) can be obtained by taking a BPS-accredited degree in psychology or a non-accredited degree plus a conversion course.

Additional postgraduate training is usually required to specialise.

Clinical psychologist

To specialise, you need to follow a BPS-accredited 3 year postgraduate training course, which is mostly hospital based. As a rule, you normally need a degree with a 2.1 classification or above but some courses will accept a 2.2 with a master's degree. It is not possible to enter with only a HND. This is full-time only and will lead to a Doctorate in Clinical Psychology.

To start training you will need lots of experience (normally a minimum of 2 years) which can take a range of forms including working as a psychological assistant or volunteering with the NHS.

Health psychologist

A BPS-accredited master's in Health Psychology and 2 years of appropriate supervised experience are essential for professional recognition. If you want to achieve chartered status and your course is not BPS accredited it is still possible to do this if you sit the BPS qualifying examination which would give you GBR.

To use the title health psychologist you will need to register with the Health Professions Council (HPC). Some universities offer a doctorate programme which enables you to become an eligible Chartered Member.

What the work involves

Clinical psychologist

You will work with people whose health problems affect their behaviour, to learn what they do and why they do it.

Health psychologist

This is a new and rapidly growing field of applied psychology which promotes changes in people's attitudes, behaviour and thinking about health.

Type of person suited to this work

An interest in people, their personalities, abilities and interests is essential.

The work involves contact with many different types of people which means you must be good at relating to others and have excellent communication skills.

Psychologists must think logically, analyse data and statistics, and work in an organised and methodical way. They need administrative and ICT skills for writing reports and analyses, and presenting information at case conferences or company meetings.

Working conditions

Clinical psychologist

Your work will take you to schools, colleges, hospitals and health centres. You may find yourself working with social services or with adolescent and child mental health services. Most clinical psychologists are employed by the NHS.

Health psychologist

Health psychologists work in a number of settings, such as hospitals, academic health research units, health authorities and university departments.

Future prospects

Entry to psychology degrees is competitive and it takes a long time to become a chartered psychologist. For both clinical and health psychology the jobs available tend to be within government services, education and health, in the public and private sectors. Ongoing professional development will be important throughout your career.

Advantages/disadvantages

The work is varied, interesting and challenging.

You will meet many different types of people.

Some people may be aggressive or even violent and you may sometimes have difficulty remaining impartial.

Money guide

Clinical psychologist

Trainee clinical psychologists can expect to earn £26,528, which is the current NHS band 6 salary. Once qualified, this rises to roughly £30,500. As you gain experience salaries can rise to £46,621 and in top-level positions you can earn in excess of £80,000.

Health psychologist

You can expect to start on around £17,000 if you start work as an assistant. Pay rises with experience to between £27,500 and £40,000 and as a senior health psychologist with the NHS salaries can reach £60,000.

For both positions, the NHS pays a London high cost area supplement.

Private hospital and practice salaries vary.

Related opportunities

- Educational Psychologist p571
- Occupational Psychologist p575
- Psychoanalyst/Psychotherapist p576

Further information

British Association for Counselling and Psychology
www.bacp.co.uk

Health Professions Council
www.hpc-uk.org

NHS Careers
www.nhscareers.nhs.uk

COUNSELLOR

Qualifications and courses

Counselling is open to graduates and those with an HND qualification, but requirements are flexible for certificate-level courses and it is possible to gain entry to these without a degree or HND.

A pre-entry certificate qualification in counselling is more or less essential for entry on to a diploma or master's in counselling and usually takes 1 year to study for part time.

Candidates then need to study for a Diploma/Advanced Diploma lasting 1 year full-time or 2–3 years part time. There are a number of counselling diplomas available but those accredited by the British Association for Counselling and Psychotherapy are the most widely recognised.

You will also need to obtain a certain number of hours in practice.

Counselling is often a second career, and maturity and experience are beneficial. It is rare for someone to enter a full-time position in this field before their mid 20s. Entrants might have worked as teachers/lecturers, personal tutors, careers advisers, social workers or nurses, or in other fields

What the work involves

Counsellors listen to what their clients say and ask questions in response, to help them explore, talk about and eventually resolve their problems.

You will help your clients to see things more clearly, perhaps from a different point of view. You will not tell people what to do but will help them work out their next steps themselves.

You might work with people with a range of problems or specialise in a particular area, such as bereavement, gambling, relationship difficulties or eating disorders.

Type of person suited to this work

As most of the work involves talking and listening to people, excellent communication skills are essential.

Counselling workers may not always agree with the views held by their clients, which means they have to be open-minded and tolerant. You must also be highly discreet as you will be given a lot of confidential information.

You need to be interested in how the mind works, and in people's welfare.

Working conditions

You will work indoors, usually sitting in a quiet, comfortable room in places such as advice centres, schools, colleges, outpatient clinics and health centres. If you are self-employed, you might work from home, visit your clients at home, or both. Some counselling work is done exclusively over the phone.

You will work mainly with people on a one-to-one basis but also, on occasions, with couples, families or groups. Most counselling sessions last 50 minutes.

You may work in the evenings and at weekends and many counsellors work part time.

Future prospects

Most people gain voluntary experience before moving into part-time paid work. They usually have experience in a career such as social work, nursing or teaching.

While the demand is increasing, there is keen competition for full-time posts and many people combine counselling work with another role.

You could work in education or health, or with a specialist agency. Experienced counselling workers can become self-employed or train for a specialist area.

Advantages/disadvantages

The work can be very rewarding but also highly stressful.

Starting salaries can be low, until you are fully trained and have gained some experience.

You must be able to take constructive criticism from an experienced counselling worker, therapist or psychoanalyst – both during and after completing training.

Some clients may become dependent on therapy or analysis sessions and will have to be carefully assisted to refocus.

Money guide

Starting salaries range from £19,000 to £26,000 per year when newly qualified (but this can vary considerably).

Experienced counsellors or those with supervisor or managerial responsbility can earn between £30,000 and £40,000.

Counsellors are paid £30–£50 an hour in private practice.

A lot of counsellors combine part-time employment with private practice and voluntary work.

Related opportunities

- Careers Adviser p566
- Debt Counsellor/Money Advice Caseworker p570
- Mental Health Nurse p317
- Psychoanalyst/Psychotherapist p576

Further information

British Association for Counselling and Psychotherapy
www.bacp.co.uk

Counselling and Psychotherapy Central Award Body
www.cpcab.co.uk

Qualifications and courses

There are no fixed entry requirements but it is preferable to have a good standard of general education; usually a minimum of 5 GCSEs/S grades (A*–C/1–3) including English and maths. Strong people skills are the most important attribute for those seeking to enter this profession. In certain areas, it could be an advantage to be fluent in a minority language, such as an Eastern European or South Asian language.

Many applicants have training and/or experience in finance or accounting, consumer advice or have worked as a volunteer for at least a year in an advice centre.

Money advisers need a detailed knowledge of the relevant laws. Short courses in specialist areas such as court procedures, housing law or bankruptcy are available.

Once you have secured employment, you could study for an NVQ Certificate (Level 3) and Diploma (Level 4) in Advice and Guidance. Alternatively, you could take a diploma, Foundation degree or degree in advice or legal advice work.

The Money Advice Trust (MAT) and the Citizens Advice Bureau (CAB) also provide training programmes for debt counsellors.

What the work involves

It will be your responsibility to give free, impartial and confidential advice to people in serious debt.

You will have to guide your clients through the legal procedures and represent them if they are being taken to court.

To ensure that clients are claiming available tax allowances and benefits, you will list clients' income and expenditure, then help them plan their spending by devising a budget.

By liaising with creditors, you will try to arrange realistic repayments over a reasonable timescale.

Type of person suited to this work

People experience money problems for reasons such as unemployment and bad money management. You will need to work with very different people and be non-judgemental about their circumstances. You will require good communication skills and a confident manner so that people trust you.

Much of the work involves figures, so you should have strong numeracy skills. It is important to be a quick-thinking negotiator to get the best deal for your clients.

Good time management is essential, as are excellent IT skills. This job suits people who have worked in financial services.

Working conditions

You could meet your clients face to face in an office or advise them through a telephone helpline. You could also spend time in court or at meetings.

You might travel around locally so a driving licence is useful.

You will usually work 9am to 5pm from Monday to Friday. In order to suit your clients' needs, you will sometimes have to work Saturdays and evenings, perhaps doing shift work.

Future prospects

Although money advisers are in demand, there are more applicants than jobs. Most openings are town or city based, in the Citizens Advice Bureau, advice centres or money advice units.

As funding is supported by local authorities or voluntary organisations, the majority of vacancies are for 2-year contracts.

You could move into specialist casework. If you work for a large company, there could be opportunities for progression into a role as team leader or supervisor. You could enter other social care jobs or change to work in the financial sector.

Advantages/disadvantages

Helping clients to manage and get rid of their debt can be rewarding.

You may have to deal with rude and difficult people.

Evening and weekend work is possible in this job, but there may also be opportunities for part-time work.

Money guide

Starting salaries are usually between £17,000 and £20,000.

An experienced caseworker can expect to earn £22,000–£24,000.

Those employed in a senior position as a supervisor or manager can achieve £28,000–£30,000 a year.

Earnings vary with location and tend to be higher in London.

Related opportunities

- Accountant p16
- Financial Adviser p40
- Welfare Benefits Adviser/Welfare Rights Caseworker p584

Further information

Advice UK
www.adviceuk.org.uk

Citizens Advice Bureau
www.citizensadvice.org.uk

Financial Services Skills Council
www.fssc.org.uk

SOCIAL WORK AND COUNSELLING SERVICES

CRCI: V

Qualifications and courses

To become a qualified educational psychologist you will need an Honours degree in psychology accredited by the British Psychological Society (BPS). If your degree is not in psychology, you can complete a BPS-approved conversion course. You can then achieve the Graduate Basis for Chartered Membership (GBC) required to progress to the next stage of training.

For entry to a degree course, you will need at least 5 GCSEs/S grades (A*–C/1–3) including maths and 2 A levels/3 H grades including a science.

Upon completion of a degree, candidates must study for a BPS-accredited doctorate in educational psychology. In Scotland, you will need an approved master's degree in educational psychology and the BPS Qualification in Educational Psychology (Stage 2).

To be accepted onto a postgraduate course you will require a 2.1 or higher in your first degree and at least 1 year's relevant experience working with children in an educational, childcare or community setting.

You are eligible to register as an educational psychologist with the Health Professions Council (HPC) when you have completed your doctorate.

What the work involves

You will work with children with social, behavioural or learning difficulties to assess their progress and their academic and emotional needs. You will give help and guidance, and design activities which will enable them to learn.

Your role will also involve working closely with parents and teaching professionals to broaden their understanding of children's psychological needs and the difficulties they face.

You will carry out research and you will be required to remain up to date with new government policies and measures that have been brought in with regard to assessing a child's psychological progression.

Type of person suited to this work

You must enjoy working closely with children. You will need to be sensitive and tactful, yet assertive and persuasive. You should be prepared to work with pupils who are finding school difficult and may not be very receptive to your help.

You will need excellent communication skills as you will be working regularly with both children and adults. You should ensure that you are good at explaining procedures and assessment methods in a way that is easy to understand.

You need administrative and IT skills for writing reports and analyses, and presenting information.

Working conditions

You will usually work 35–37.5 hours a week from Monday to Friday, with some evening work required to attend parent–teacher meetings.

You will spend time in an office, as well as visiting schools and colleges, meeting clients, writing reports and assessing your findings. You will also run training sessions for parents and teachers.

You will probably have to travel between different locations so a driving licence is useful.

Future prospects

Most educational psychologists work for local authorities but an increasing number are self-employed as independent consultants. You will be more restricted in the way you can progress whilst working for a local authority as there are only a certain number of positions you can work up to. However, you may become a senior officer in a local authority children's services department.

Being an independent consultant will give you greater opportunity to branch out into different areas of psychology such as occupational psychology.

Advantages/disadvantages

The work is varied and interesting.

Helping children to learn and develop is incredibly rewarding.

Dealing with difficult children, and parents who are not willing to accept that their child has a psychological problem, can be stressful and challenging.

Money guide

As a graduate trainee you can expect to earn between £21,800 and £29,700 per year.

Once qualified, your annual salary can range from £34,000 to £46,000.

Senior educational psychologists can achieve £50,000–£60,000 a year.

Earnings vary with location and tend to be higher in London.

Related opportunities

- Clinical/Health Psychologist p568
- Counsellor p569
- Youth and Community Worker p585

Further information

Association of Educational Psychologists
www.aep.org.uk

Children's Workforce Development Council
www.cwdcouncil.org.uk

Educational Psychology Postgraduate Grant Scheme
www.lge.gov.uk

SOCIAL WORK AND COUNSELLING SERVICES

CRCI: V

Qualifications and courses

To become a qualified forensic psychologist you will need an Honours degree in psychology accredited by the British Psychological Society (BPS). If your degree is not in psychology, you can complete a BPS-approved conversion course. You can then achieve the Graduate Basis for Chartered Membership (GBC) required to progress to the next stage of training.

For entry to a degree course, you will need at least 5 GCSEs/S grades (A*–C/1–3) including maths and 2 A levels/3 H grades including a science.

Upon completion of a degree, candidates must study for a BPS-accredited master's degree in forensic psychology. They then undertake 2 years of supervised practice to obtain the BPS Qualification in Forensic Psychology (Stage 2).

To be accepted onto a postgraduate course you will require a 2.1 or higher in your first degree and relevant experience, such as voluntary work within a prison, mental health service or victim support charity.

You are eligible to register as a forensic psyschologist with the Health Professions Council (HPC) when you have completed the Stage 2 BPS qualification.

What the work involves

You will apply psychology to the criminal and civil justice systems. Your job will involve direct contact with offenders to carry out assessments and you may design programmes to help in their rehabilitation.

You may be required to present your findings on a criminal case in court.

Your work will also include carrying out detailed research into what provokes people to carry out crimes. You will analyse the behavioural patterns and personality traits of offenders.

Type of person suited to this work

You need brilliant communication skills and the ability to work with people from a wide variety of backgrounds. You must be prepared to work with criminals and be enthusiastic about helping them during their rehabilitation process. You should not be a judgemental person and you must hold no prejudice against the people you are working with, even if they have committed an awful crime.

You should be very good at reading people's subconscious behaviour and taking detailed notes of your findings to present in reports. You must be organised and able to manage your workload. Research and IT skills are necessary.

Working conditions

You will spend a lot of time working in prisons, secure hospitals, police stations and mental health rehabilitation units. You may be employed by a variety of organisations; from the NHS to Her Majesty's Prison Service to the police force. If you are working in a prison you will need to become adjusted to the conditions and regulations.

A driving licence would be useful for travelling between locations.

You will typically work a 37-hour week from Monday to Friday and some evening/weekend work will be expected. Part-time work may be available.

Future prospects

As this is a fairly new and emerging sector, there are many opportunities to progress and branch into different areas of psychology and forensics once you have some experience.

If you achieve chartered status as a forensic psychologist, you may have the chance to move into a senior role. In this position, you could be in charge of creating a complete rehabilitation scheme for a certain type of offender.

With experience, you will have the option of working for a consultancy.

Advantages/disadvantages

You may find yourself working with people who have committed very serious crimes which can be distressing.

Helping to rehabilitate offenders back into society can be immensely rewarding.

You will learn new things all the time which will make the job exciting and fulfilling.

Money guide

As a trainee forensic psychologist, you can expect a starting salary of around £20,000.

Once fully qualified, you are likely to earn between £27,000 and £45,000.

Those with extensive experience who are employed in a senior position can achieve up to £65,000 a year.

Earnings vary with location.

Related opportunities

- Clinical/Health Psychologist p568
- Counsellor p569
- Forensic Computer Analyst p547

Further information

Division of Forensic Psychologists
www.bps.org.uk/dfp

HM Prison Service
www.hmprisonservice.gov.uk

National Probation Service
www.probation.homeoffice.gov.uk

FUNDRAISER

Qualifications and courses

There are no specific entry requirements but this is a popular and competitive sector so many entrants are graduates. Useful degree subjects include business studies and sales and marketing. For entry to a degree course you will need at least 2 A levels/3 H grades and 5 GCSEs/S grades (A*–C/1–3) including English and maths.

Most entrants undertake voluntary fundraising experience to demonstrate their commitment to the not-for-profit sector and to help develop a network of industry contacts. The majority of charities run unpaid internships and large organisations, such as Cancer Research UK, offer graduate training schemes.

Employers will consider those without a degree or academic qualifications if they have relevant experience in marketing, sales, public relations, events management or charity work.

If you are trying to enter the sector from another field, you may choose to do a course run by Fundraising Training Ltd. The Institute of Fundraising (IoF) provides qualifications ranging from an Introductory Certificate in Fundraising to an Advanced Diploma in Fundraising for experienced professionals.

Short courses for people working as fundraisers/ fundraising managers are also available.

What the work involves

Fundraisers raise money for their charity by targeting donors and organising activities such as publicly sponsored events, membership schemes with various benefits and corporate sponsorship.

You will represent your charity at public events such as dinners, giving talks to possible supporters.

You will write strategies, reports for trustees and donors, and proposals for grants.

You will prepare publicity material and liaise with the media, always keeping your charity in the public eye.

Type of person suited to this work

It is essential that you are enthusiastic and committed to your charity. You must be good with all types of people. You should be an excellent communicator and an engaging and confident public speaker, able to persuade people to support your charity.

You will need to be a good negotiator, with excellent writing skills to produce effective publicity material. You will have to be imaginative and creative to come up with innovative fundraising ideas.

You must be able to organise your time and workload so you can keep running costs down to a minimum and save money for your charity.

Working conditions

You will normally be based in an office working on a computer, but you can be based at home, particularly if you work for a very small charity. You might spend time outdoors at fundraising activities.

You will work about 35-40 hours a week and weekend/ evening work is common when arranging and attending events.

There could be pressure to meet fundraising targets and deadlines for organising events.

You will travel fairly widely so a driving licence is useful.

Future prospects

It is not usual to become a charity fundraiser straight from school – most entrants have experience in sales or marketing and voluntary fundraising.

Most jobs are with charities, pressure groups and other not-for-profit organisations, including hospitals.

It may be necessary to move around – possibly to larger organisations – to progress in your career. With experience you could move into management, become self-employed or offer consultancy advice.

Advantages/disadvantages

It is satisfying to see your charity flourish with the money that you have helped to raise.

People who do not support your charity can be unpleasant at times.

You will need to work evenings and weekends.

Money guide

Earnings vary according to the size and location of the charity.

Starting salaries are usually between £18,000 and £23,000.

With experience and increased responsibilities, your earnings could range from £24,000 up to £40,000.

If you head up a fundraising department in a large charity, you could achieve £50,000–£70,000 a year.

Related opportunities

- Advertising Account Executive p396
- Events and Exhibition Organiser p404
- Public Relations Officer p416

Further information

Association of Chief Executives of Voluntary Organisations
www.acevo.org.uk

Directory of Social Change
www.dsc.org.uk

Institute of Fundraising
www.institute-of-fundraising.org.uk

CRCI: V   SOCIAL WORK AND COUNSELLING SERVICES

Qualifications and courses

Although there are no specific requirements to enter this area of work, you need to have gained a great deal of life experience and to have tasted many different approaches to conducting business and managing an organisation's workforce performance and delivery.

A degree in human resources work, organisations and structures, sociology or psychology would be helpful starting points.

There are a number of private agencies and academies offering training in life coaching, for example the Coaching Academy, where you can take a 2-day fast-track course by distance learning to focus on corporate or individual (personal performance) life coaching. The Chartered Institute of Personnel and Development offers an Advanced Certificate in Coaching and Mentoring, aimed at people with experience which could be useful.

Continuing professional development (CPD) is also important and membership of the Association for Coaching could give you access to courses to help your development in this field.

You could also work towards accreditation from one of the recognised bodies for life coaches, such as the International Coach Federation (ICF) which would give you greater credibility with clients.

What the work involves

You will help people – independent clients or employees – to recognise and develop their special attributes and skills.

You will coach individuals to become more successful in career matters, fitness levels, financial affairs or personal relationships. You will also help in boosting self-esteem.

You will discuss values, attributes and beliefs and set goals with your clients for them to work towards. At a later stage you will review and revise the action plans you have created.

Type of person suited to this work

Once a bond of trust is established – that you are non-judgemental and hold personal information in strictest confidence – individuals will reveal their present feelings and frustrations, their future ambitions and their perceived restrictions to progress.

Besides integrity and discretion, life coaches need excellent interpersonal skills, patience and perseverance to allow clients the time to set themselves goals for change.

Working conditions

You will agree timetables with clients for coaching sessions and hold one-to-ones at their work-base or in a neutral location. Later sessions are often by phone or email.

Many life coaches work with busy, highly successful chief executives, usually outside normal business hours.

Coaching sessions can be weekly, fortnightly or monthly; the frequency may change.

Future prospects

Life coaching is a relatively new field, but interest has increased as more attention is paid to developing the whole person – both within and outside the workplace.

Life coaches work as independent consultants or for business consultancy agencies. If you network and market yourself well you can build up a substantial client base.

You could choose to specialise in one area such as spiritual coaching or executive coaching.

Advantages/disadvantages

There is great satisfaction in observing changes in your clients.

If clients fail to implement action plans, it can be dispiriting and frustrating.

You could have long-term coaching relationships with clients who want to work on different aspects of their lives.

Money guide

Life coaches earn an agreed rate per session.

Working for an agency, you can earn around £60 per session plus expenses. Rates for private clients could be £50–£100 for a coaching session lasting an hour.

You could charge up to £250 a session if you are working with corporate clients.

It is possible to earn the full-time equivalent income of between £18,000 and £24,000.

Life coaches who become well known and sought after can charge higher fees for periods of life coaching lasting 6 months or longer.

Related opportunities

- Careers Adviser p566
- Counsellor p569
- Social Worker p579

Further information

Association for Coaching
www.associationforcoaching.com

Chartered Institute of Personnel and Development
www.cipd.co.uk

International Coach Federation
www.coachfederation.org.uk

The Coaching Academy
www.the-coaching-academy.com

Qualifications and courses

Entrants must be graduates with Graduate Basis for Chartered Membership (GBC) with the British Psychological Society (BPS). Graduate Basis for Registration (GBR) can be obtained by taking a BPS-accredited degree in psychology or a non-accredited degree plus a conversion course. For entry to a degree course, you will need 2 A levels/3 H grades including maths.

Additional postgraduate training is usually required to qualify in a specialist area.

Psychology graduates need to gain an accredited MSc followed by 2 years of supervised practice, or 3 years' supervised practice and the BPS Postgraduate Certificate in Occupational Psychology, to become fully qualified.

If you want to achieve chartered occupational psychologist status you will have to complete Stage 2 of the Qualification in Occupational Psychology. One way to do this is with the BPS or alternatively you can keep a log book of your work carried out under the supervision of a qualified chartered occupational psychologist. This should demonstrate your progression and the knowledge that you have built up. This will then be assessed by the Division of Occupational Psychology who will decide whether to award you chartered status.

What the work involves

You will explore how organisations function and how people behave at work to improve an organisation's efficiency and employees' job satisfaction.

You will help managers plan how they recruit and train staff. You will give advice on matters concerning communication between individuals in the workplace, the most effective working environment and coping with change.

Part of your job may involve helping to recruit the right person for a particular role as well as offering support to those facing redundancy. You will also be working with bosses and managers to help them to understand the psychological needs of their staff, so that they can maintain a stress-free environment for them as much as possible.

Type of person suited to this work

You should have a great interest in how organisations function and what makes people tick in the workplace.

You should be comfortable working with adults and also be happy to help them progress professionally.

You must be a brilliant communicator and it will also be very useful for you to have strong business skills because you will have been employed to improve the overall efficiency of a company. Additionally, your personal safety awareness should be very good.

Working conditions

Much of your work will take place in offices and business premises of the companies you are working for. This may involve working by yourself or as part of a team.

You can expect to work around 37 hours a week from Monday to Friday but you may run or attend courses that require you to travel away and stay overnight.

There is the opportunity to be self-employed but this is often after working for an organisation and building up your work experience.

Future prospects

Occupational psychologists work in large companies in the public and private sectors.

They can work with government and public services as private consultants.

Some specialise in a certain area, for example ergonomics (the interaction of people with where they work), or health and safety – studying the causes of accidents and how to prevent them.

Once you have progressed to a senior role you may set up your own consultancy.

Advantages/disadvantages

Your work will really make a difference to people's day to day lives at work which will be very rewarding.

You may be working with unmotivated or stressed individuals.

You may find that bosses are not willing to take on your advice for their staff.

Money guide

As a trainee occupational psychologist you can earn around £18,000 as your starting salary.

This can progress to between £35,000 and £55,000 with experience in a senior position.

Salaries vary in the private sector but in senior positions can be in excess of £70,000.

Related opportunities

- Educational Psychologist p571
- Health and Safety Adviser p41
- Recruitment/Employment Agency Consultant p60

Further information

Association of Business Psychologists
www.theabp.org.uk

Health Professions Council
www.hpc-uk.org

Occupational Psychology Services
www.opsltd.com

CRCI: V

SOCIAL WORK AND COUNSELLING SERVICES

Qualifications and courses

Psychoanalyst

Most people enter psychoanalysis as a second career after they have gained experience in a related field such as psychology, psychiatry, counselling or social work.

To qualify as a psychoanalyst, candidates must undertake a training course approved by the International Psychoanalytical Association (IPA). Training takes 4 years and entry is with a first degree and relevant experience in psychology, medicine, nursing, social work or teaching. For a first degree you will need at least 2 A levels/3 H grades and 5 GCSEs/S grades (A*–C/1–3).

Psychotherapist

Useful subjects to study at degree level include psychology, nursing, medicine, social work or sociology. A postgraduate qualification in psychotherapy which is approved by the UK Council for Psychotherapy (UKCP) or the British Psychoanalytic Council (BPC) is also required. Pre-entry experience working with vulnerable children or adults is expected.

Training courses usually last 4 years when studied on a part-time basis and include personal therapy, theory and supervised clinical work.

What the work involves

Psychoanalyst

You will help people uncover their buried, unconscious thoughts and behaviours which are disrupting and negatively affecting their daily life. You will see your patients 4–5 times a week over an extended period of time. You will listen during the sessions and then write down your observations after your patient has left. Your goal is to help patients achieve self-awareness.

Psychotherapist

You will explore a person's inner conflicts and feelings in order to help alleviate their distress. Your goal is to help patients feel happy or better. Your treatment will be non-medical, focussing on talking through problems. Your treatment approach may include cognitive behavioural therapy, hypno-psychotherapy and psychodynamic therapies.

Type of person suited to this work

You need to be positive, empathic and a great listener. You want to build a good bond with your patients so you should respect confidential information.

Your work can be intense and you will need to sympathise with your patients' problems whilst remaining emotionally resilient. You should be observant and have a genuine interest in feelings and emotions.

Working conditions

You will work in a consulting room that is comfortable, quiet and furnished with a couch or chair for your patients.

You will most likely work Monday to Friday but you may need to work weekends and evenings to suit your clients' needs. You can choose your own hours if you work for a private practice.

This work can be emotionally demanding and you are advised to be involved in a support network, especially if you are self-employed.

Future prospects

Psychoanalyst

Most psychoanalysts are self-employed and you may choose to work part time for a prison, school or child guidance clinic. You could become a lecturer, train graduate entrants or specialise in a particular area such as adolescent psychoanalysis.

Psychotherapist

With experience, you could go on to become a manager or supervisor of other psychotherapists, although this will mean you will have less clinical work. You could also become a consultant for community organisations or specialise in an area such as psychodrama.

Advantages/disadvantages

It is rewarding to see a patient overcome their problems.

You will constantly be learning more about the human mind which can benefit you as well as your patients.

Your patients might struggle with upsetting issues and this can be emotionally taxing for you.

Money guide

Psychoanalyst

You can expect a starting salary of £40,000 when you are newly qualified.

With experience, you can achieve £50,000–£60,000 a year.

Psychotherapist

NHS trainees can earn between £21,200 and £27,500 a year.

Once qualified and with experience, your salary can range from £35,000 to £47,000.

Related opportunities

- Counsellor p569
- Educational Psychologist p571
- Psychiatrist p330

Further information

British Association of Psychotherapists
www.bap-psychotherapy.org

Qualifications and courses

Visually impaired

You will need a qualification in rehabilitation work (visual impairment). A relevant 2-year Foundation degree is available and involves both work-based training through an employer and distance learning. Entry requirements are at least 1 A level/2 H grades and 3 GCSEs/S grades (A*–C/1–3).

If you already have a job volunteering with visually impaired people, you can study via distance learning for the BTEC Professional Diploma in Rehabilitation Studies (Levels 4 and 5).

Hearing impaired

There are no set entry requirements for this career. However, most employers will look for GCSEs/S grades (A*–C/1–3) and relevant experience. It might help to have the Signature Level 1 Award in British Sign Language (BSL). The Apprenticeship in Health and Social Care may also equip you with relevant skills for this profession.

Training is on the job, with the chance to study for further qualifications such as the Advanced Diploma in Technical and Rehabilitation Work with Deaf People (Level 3) and the City & Guilds Certificate in Supporting Users of Assistive Technology (Level 2).

What the work involves

Rehabilitation officers train people with visual and hearing impairments to use their existing skills in new ways that will help them lead a normal life.

You will assess your patients' needs before making a detailed action plan to teach them new skills. You will also provide financial and employment information and advice.

Part of your role will be liaising with other medical professionals to follow up on reports you have made about your patients' standard of living. You might also be responsible for providing training to other social and healthcare workers about sensory loss and awareness.

Type of person suited to this work

You will need to be aware of the issues that affect visually and hearing impaired people. It is important to have good communication skills as your patients may rely on other senses to understand you.

You will be in contact with people of all ages and backgrounds, so it is essential that you are friendly and approachable. Good organisational, problem-solving and assessment skills are required for report writing and devising action plans for patients.

Working conditions

You will divide your time between working in an office and visiting patients' homes to assess their living space and daily routines. It is useful to have a driving licence as you might be travelling around on a regular basis.

You might need to work outdoors when training a patient to use a new piece of assistive equipment or if you are escorting them somewhere.

You will work around 40 hours a week, Monday to Friday, although you might need to visit your patients during the evenings and weekends.

Future prospects

Most positions are with local authority social care departments, voluntary services such as the Royal National Institute for the Blind (RNIB) and educational institutions.

Although there is no set career path in rehabilitation work, you can be promoted to supervisory and managerial roles in sensory support or you can choose to train other people. There are postgraduate qualifications available which would speed up your career progression.

Advantages/disadvantages

This is a very rewarding career as you will be helping people who are in a vulnerable position.

You need to stay emotionally detached from your patients, which could be difficult as you will be spending a lot of time with them.

Money guide

Visually impaired

Starting salaries are around £18,000–£23,000.

With experience, you can expect £24,000–£30,000 a year.

Those in more senior positions can earn in excess of £35,000.

Hearing impaired

Your starting salary could range from £16,000 to £22,300.

Earnings can increase to £27,000 with experience.

Team leaders can achieve up to £35,000 a year.

Related opportunities

- Careers Adviser p566
- Healthcare Assistant p310
- Social Worker p579

Further information

Royal National Institute for Deaf People
www.rnid.org.uk

Royal National Institute of the Blind
www.rnib.org.uk

Skills for Care and Development
www.skillsforcareanddevelopment.org.uk

SOCIAL WORK AND COUNSELLING SERVICES

CRCi: V

RESIDENTIAL SUPPORT WORKER

Qualifications and courses

There are no particular qualifications necessary to become a residential support worker but it is necessary to have previous experience of caring for people, such as nursing or working with the disabled, elderly or homeless.

It is possible to study for qualifications in health and social care, youth work or childcare. For instance, it may be helpful to complete the BTEC National Certificate or Diploma in Health and Social Care.

NVQs/SVQs in care, as well as a First Aid certificate, are also useful.

If you will be working with children or vulnerable adults you will need to undergo a Criminal Records Bureau (CRB) check.

What the work involves

Residential workers look after the welfare of people living in supervised accommodation, including the elderly, people with disabilities, temporary hostel residents, students and young people.

You will make sure that meals are organised, cooked and served at set times, and that cleaning and maintenance are up to standard.

It will be your responsibility to make sure health and safety standards are met, insurance is up to date and that security is effective. You will also collect rents and fees and organise social events, and sort out any disputes.

Type of person suited to this work

As you may be responsible for the accommodation of many different groups of people, it is important to be friendly and outgoing. You will also need to be understanding, patient and tolerant.

There are likely to be crises in the job so it is important to be able to cope under pressure and make decisions quickly. problem-solving skills are useful in these situations.

If you are dealing with rents and fees, being good with figures is helpful. There will be a lot of administrative work which needs a well-organised and methodical approach.

Working conditions

Most of your work will be indoors, but you may handle maintenance and repair work, using tools and climbing ladders.

Many residential support workers live on-site or in the grounds, but you might travel locally, so a driving licence is useful. You will be constantly on the go, responding to alarm calls at any hour of the day or night.

You will use ICT for administration and record-keeping.

Future prospects

Although there are opportunities throughout the UK, there are few vacancies for residential workers. Most jobs are in cities and major towns.

The main employers are local authorities, housing associations, private companies, voluntary organisations, universities and colleges.

Promotion is likely to be to a senior worker. You might have to move jobs to progress your career. It is also possible to move into management positions or other caring jobs such as social work.

Advantages/disadvantages

The work is varied and no two days will be alike.

You will get great job satisfaction from helping people.

Some residents may be difficult to deal with.

You will work long hours, evenings and weekends, and may have to live on-site.

Money guide

Starting salaries are between £13,000 and £18,000 per year.

Senior support workers can earn between £19,000 and £24,000 a year.

Hourly rates vary between £7 and £14 an hour.

Accommodation and food may also be provided.

Related opportunities

- Caretaker p457
- Cleaner p460
- Hotel Manager p140

Further information

Chartered Institute of Housing
www.cih.org

General Social Care Council
www.gscc.org.uk

Scottish Social Services Council
www.sssc.uk.com

SOCIAL WORKER

Qualifications and courses

You will need an Honours degree or postgraduate degree in social work approved by the General Social Care Council (GSCC) in order to be employed. For entry to a degree you will need at least 2 A levels/3 H grades and 5 GCSEs/S grades (A*–C/1–3), including English and maths. You will need a 2.2 Honours degree for entry onto a postgraduate course. Relevant subjects include social sciences, education, psychology and nursing.

A Diploma in Society, Health and Development may be useful. If you want to work with children and families, a Diploma in Children and Young People's Workforce or an Apprenticeship in Children's Care, Learning and Development may be helpful.

You will need to pass a Criminal Records Bureau check and a medical test. You must also be registered with the GSCC.

All social workers must renew their qualifications every 3 years.

What the work involves

Working at a senior level, you will interview your clients and assess their complex problems and needs.

You will then advise on the best package of care for your client.

Your goal is to support people to live independently and thrive in their surroundings. This might involve helping families to stay together, protecting vulnerable people or helping the excluded to be a part of their community.

You will keep detailed records of all your work.

Type of person suited to this work

You should be culturally aware, non-judgemental and able to engage with clients of all ethnicities, religions and backgrounds.

Caseloads can be heavy, so you need to be organised and able to multi-task effectively. Excellent communication skills are important.

At times your clients may become difficult and you must be confident at resolving conflict. You also need to remain professionally detached in emotionally tense circumstances.

Working conditions

You will often work within a team from other disciplines including psychologists and therapists and will be office based. Most of your time however will be spent visiting clients at their homes.

A driving licence is essential.

You will work 37 hours a week but this may include evenings, early mornings and weekends.

Future prospects

There is currently a demand for qualified social workers so job prospects are high. You will most likely work for a local authority social services department or for children or adult service departments within the NHS. Jobs may also be available with Armed Forces support groups.

After gaining experience you can vary your role by changing your specialism or by moving on within your specialism. For example you could move from child protection into foster care.

You could also become a senior practitioner or manager but this will mean you will deal more with finances and politics rather than directly with clients. Lecturing and self-employment opportunities are also possible.

Advantages/disadvantages

No two cases will be the same, keeping your work interesting.

It is rewarding to see people reach their full potential, solve their own problems and improve their lives.

Social work systems can be bureaucratic and frustrating at times.

Your work can be emotionally distressing and may put you in vulnerable situations.

Money guide

Starting salaries vary between £19,500 and £25,000 a year.

With experience and depending on location, you could earn up to £35,000.

Managers can earn in excess of £42,000.

Many employers offer additional benefits such as car allowances and child care.

Related opportunities

- Counsellor p569
- Healthcare Assistant p310
- Youth and Community Worker p585

Further information

British Association of Social Workers
www.basw.co.uk

Skills for Care
www.skillsforcare.org.uk

SUBSTANCE MISUSE WORKER

ENTRY LEVEL 3

Qualifications and courses

Entry requirements vary based on the type of user you work with: with young people you will need the Common Core of Skills and Knowledge for the Children's Workforce; with adults you will need an NVQ Level 3 in Health and Social Care.

You could choose to do an Advanced Apprenticeship in Community Justice and follow the drug and alcohol pathway. Many colleges offer a Northern Advisory Council for Further Education (NCFE) Certificate in Drug Awareness.

Voluntary experience is recommended and most employers will want to see evidence of this. Given the importance of maturity and life experience in this post, most employers will not consider you for a position unless you are at least 21 years old.

If you want to specialise in certain methods of treatment such as medicine you will need to qualify first as a nurse. For psychological intervention you will need to qualify first as a counsellor.

You will need to pass a Criminal Records Bureau (CRB) check.

What the work involves

You will help people who misuse harmful substances, including drugs and alcohol, to overcome their dependencies.

You could provide support in one-to-one or group sessions This can include counselling and care planning.

You could offer drug treatment options to prisoners, advise on detox methods in a rehabilitation centre, prescribe drugs and give medical advice in a clinic or run educational workshops in schools and youth centres. You could also help substance users find housing and temporary accommodation. You might accompany police patrols around clubs doing street outreach work.

Type of person suited to this work

You want your clients to trust you so you should be understanding, warm and a good listener. You need to be patient and non-judgemental as it may take substance users a long time to recover. If your clients know that you believe in them, they will develop confidence to change.

You could work with many clients at any given time and should be organised. An ability to stay calm under pressure and to maintain professional boundaries is essential.

Good communication skills are important as your role may involve educating others about the dangers of substance abuse.

Working conditions

You could be based in a drop-in centre, a clinic, prison or other community site. However a lot of your time will be spent visiting substance users in their homes or other venues. Sometimes you will be visiting shelters as many clients may be homeless. A driving licence will be useful.

You will most likely work 35 to 40 hours a week but these could be irregular hours including evenings and weekends. You might need to be on-call throughout the night.

Part-time work is available.

Future prospects

Your job prospects are high as there are a variety of opportunities across the UK for substance misuse workers. You could work for Connexions services, drop-in centres, local authorities, housing agencies, private rehabilitation centres, the NHS, prisons, police services, charities or drug and alcohol organisations.

With experience, you could become a supervisor or manager.

You could also specialise in one area of treatment such as psychological intervention or drug and alcohol testing or even specialise in one user group such as young people.

Advantages/disadvantages

You have the opportunity to build meaningful relationships with clients and colleagues.

It's rewarding when you help a client overcome an addiction.

You might need to be on-call 24 hours a day which can be demanding.

It can be frustrating to work with uncooperative clients who don't believe they have a problem.

Money guide

In your first job, you may start out earning between £15,000 and £20,000 per year.

With experience and team leader responsibilities you can earn between £21,000 and £28,000 a year.

As a project manager you may earn in excess of £40,000.

Related opportunities

- Adult Nurse p289
- Counsellor p569
- Social Worker p579

Further information

Federation of Drug and Alcohol Professionals
www.fdap.org.uk

National Treatment Agency for Substance Misuse
www.nta.nhs.uk

Qualifications and courses

To become a paid official at a union's branch or regional office, candidates normally have previous experience working unpaid as a local representative, shop steward or administrator. There are no formal entry requirements.

There is the opportunity to work as a paid Union Learning Representative without completing unpaid experience first if you have an adult education or training and development background.

If you want to work at national head office level, you would need experience in a specialist area of work or a degree in a relevant area in which you wish to specialise, for example law, politics, industrial relations, labour studies, social policy or economics.

Alternatively, it is possible to work your way up from branch or regional level to national office.

Training is mainly on the job. The Trades Union Congress and commercial training organisations run regular short training programmes in a range of different skills.

What the work involves

Trade union officials negotiate with employers over pay, working conditions, health and safety, dismissal and redundancy.

Working in regional offices, you will recruit members, train shop stewards, support local officials and negotiate individual cases with employers. At head office, you will work on national policies and negotiate at national level.

At all levels your role will be to bring about the best deal for the workforce by finding common ground between employers and employees.

Type of person suited to this work

It is important to have a genuine interest in people's welfare and to believe in the aims of your union. You will need to see issues from different view points.

You will spend time dealing with individuals or groups, which requires good speaking, listening and negotiating skills. Speaking in public requires confidence.

Union matters involve problem-solving and negotiation which needs a patient, methodical approach and the ability to research and analyse information.

Working conditions

As a local shop steward you will have another job and attend to union business part time. Paid officials at regional and national level are office based.

You could travel quite extensively to meetings, tribunals and conferences so a driving licence is useful.

You will make maximum use of ICT and will probably have a lot of phone work – some after normal work hours.

Future prospects

Your prospects depend very much on the size of the union, ie they are greater with the large unions which are never out of the news.

Head-office posts are usually in London. After gaining experience it is possible to progress to a regional role, as organiser or secretary, or a national role.

Some people move from union work into politics by becoming councillors or MPs.

Advantages/disadvantages

The work is varied, but you may be working on one theme in preparation for a meeting.

Negotiating better pay and working conditions can be very rewarding.

Some people might be unpleasant and sometimes you have to support people you do not agree with.

You might have to work long and unsocial hours.

Money guide

Local shop stewards/union representatives are generally unpaid. As a paid official you can expect between £20,000 and £25,000 per year on entry.

As an experienced regional or national official you could earn £30,000–£50,000.

In senior positions such as a general secretary, salaries rise to as much as £80,000.

Related opportunities

- Equality and Diversity Officer p37
- Health and Safety Adviser p41
- Human Resources/Personnel Officer p42

Further information

Directgov
www.direct.gov.uk

Scottish Trades Union Congress
www.stuc.org.uk

Trades Union Congress
www.tuc.org.uk

CRCI: V   SOCIAL WORK AND COUNSELLING SERVICES

Qualifications and courses

Formal qualifications are not essential to enter this field as experience is more highly valued. However related degree subjects include psychology, counselling and criminal justice and law.

You can volunteer with Victim Support, the largest charity in this field, to gain experience. You will need 2 references and it may also be useful to be fluent in a foreign language.

As a volunteer you may work on the Victim Supportline, support witnesses at court or work with victims in your community, which will help develop your listening and communication skills.

Although working as a volunteer is not essential to become a victim care officer, employers will expect you to have a similar level of experience and knowledge of the issues surrounding victims of crime.

A Criminal Records Bureau (CRB) check will be made if you are volunteering and if you are applying for paid work.

NVQs exist in Witness Care at Level 3 and Community Justice: Work with Witnesses, Survivors and Victims at Levels 3 and 4. You may also be expected to have good IT, administration and organisational skills.

What the work involves

Victim care officers help victims to deal with the aftermath of crime and come to terms with events.

Your work may be focused on a particular group such as victims of domestic abuse, serious sexual assault or anti-social behaviour.

You will listen carefully to victims and provide objective support. You may provide information on legal procedures and relevant services and agencies.

Practical support for victims may involve arranging visits from a police community support officer (PCSO), organising repairs to damaged property or obtaining a personal attack alarm for the victim.

Type of person suited to this work

You will need to be patient, understanding and possess the ability to remain objective and to relate to people from all walks of life.

Excellent listening and communication skills, including telephone skills, are imperative.

There may be tight deadlines which you will have to meet, so organisational skills are important.

You will need to have the energy and ability to assess clients' needs and be able to create solutions for them.

The ability to keep strict confidentiality is essential.

Working conditions

You will work from 37 to 40 hours a week and may often work in the evening and at weekends as required by clients.

Support of victims may take place over the telephone. You may also visit the victim at their home.

Future prospects

With time and experience as a victim care officer you may become a victim care team leader and eventually a victim care manager.

Recruitment for this role may be affected by local authority budget cuts.

Advantages/disadvantages

You will have the satisfaction of helping people through difficult stages and experiences in their lives.

If the victim has not spoken about their feelings before, a lot of emotions may come to the surface, such as distress, confusion or anger, which may become directed at you.

Money guide

Starting salaries for victim care officers working full time are between £15,000 and £20,000.

This can rise to between £22,000 and £24,000 a year with experience.

Related opportunities

- Counsellor p569
- Police Support Worker p552
- Social Worker p579

Further information

Skills for Justice
www.skillsforjustice.com

Victim Support
www.victimsupport.org.uk

VOLUNTEER MANAGER

Qualifications and courses

No formal qualifications are needed to enter this career but employers are likely to require 5 GCSEs/S grades (A*–C/1–3) including English and maths. Relevant experience organising and managing people or working as a volunteer is valuable.

You could begin as a volunteer, then move into voluntarily managing other volunteers before progressing to a paid role as a manager.

Some employers may expect you to have a degree or professional qualification. Useful subjects include community development, business studies, social care and human resource management.

A postgraduate degree could offer you an advantage, especially if you are working in the creative industries or for an international development project, as these fields are becoming increasingly popular.

The National Council for Voluntary Organisations (NCVO) has established Working for a Charity, a project which provides training for those in the not-for-profit sector. A Foundation Course of seminars and an online course in Effective Voluntary Sector Management are available.

What the work involves

You will recruit, train and organise volunteers to assist charities, hospitals, social service departments and other volunteer organisations.

After interviewing volunteers, you will match them to the kind of work that would suit them. Once you have selected the volunteers, you will provide them with training and mentor them in their position. You will then offer ongoing advice and support.

You will deal with administration, budgets, correspondence and report writing.

You could also prepare publicity material and liaise with other agencies.

Type of person suited to this work

You will work with volunteers from many different backgrounds so you must be personable, as well as a good motivator.

You will need tact and patience, as not all volunteers are suited to the kind of role they wish to have.

It is essential to be confident and have good communication skills to sell placements to volunteers and volunteers to placements. You will need to be flexible and adaptable.

The job will demand a good deal of administration and record-keeping, which requires excellent organisational and time-management skills.

Working conditions

You could work out of an office or from home, depending on the size of the organisation.

You will need to travel locally to arrange placements and visit volunteers, so a driving licence will be useful.

You will most likely work 40 hours a week from Monday to Friday but you may need to work evenings and weekends to meet deadlines.

Future prospects

You are unlikely to enter this career straight from school.

Opportunities are increasing but there is keen competition for jobs and you might have to move to another organisation or charity to gain promotion. A willingness to be geographically mobile would be useful.

Volunteer management provides useful experience if you would like to transfer into a career such as social work or other management posts in the not-for-profit sector.

You will have opportunities for further training, mainly through short courses.

Advantages/disadvantages

This work is varied and challenging.

The job is fulfilling; by helping volunteers find placements you will be making a difference to people in need.

You might have to work long hours.

As with any management role, some people may be hard to work with and difficult to please.

Money guide

Starting salaries are usually between £18,000 and £21,000.

With experience, you can expect to earn £25,000–£30,000.

Senior staff who have substantial supervisory experience and are employed in large organisations can achieve £40,000–£45,000 a year.

Related opportunities

- Fundraiser p573
- Social Worker p579
- Substance Misuse Worker p580
- Welfare Benefits Adviser/Welfare Rights Caseworker p584
- Youth and Community Worker p585

Further information

Association of Chief Executives of Voluntary Organisations
www.acevo.org.uk

Directory of Social Change
www.dsc.org.uk

National Council for Voluntary Organisations
www.ncvo-vol.org.uk

Scottish Council for Voluntary Organisations
www.scvo.org.uk

SOCIAL WORK AND COUNSELLING SERVICES

CRCI: V

Qualifications and courses

There are no set minimum entry requirements but a good standard of education with GCSEs/S grades (A*–C/1–3) in English and maths is desirable. Life experience is essential and applicants typically have a background in working with people.

Many entrants to this profession begin their career as a volunteer in an advice centre. Undertaking training with the Citizens Advice Bureau (CAB) or other community advice centres would equip you with relevant skills. Once you have gained experience in general advice, you can choose to specialise in welfare rights and benefits.

Although a degree or professional qualification is not a formal requirement, applicants are often graduates. Relevant subjects to study include social policy, community work, law and sociology.

It will help if you have experience in advising/counselling work, communication, information handling, IT skills, money management, problem-solving or working with others.

Once you have secured employment, you will attend in-house training and continuing professional development (CPD) courses. The NVQ Certificate (Level 3) and Diploma (Level 4) in Advice and Guidance are available from City & Guilds.

What the work involves

In this sector, you will help people to cope with problems by listening, asking questions and giving impartial and confidential advice.

Benefits advisers may represent their clients at tribunals or act as advocates in a court of law.

Welfare rights caseworkers explain people's rights on matters such as tenancy, employment, conflicts with neighbours, consumer law and finance; sometimes referring clients to other professionals.

You will help people fill in forms to claim benefits and make phone calls on their behalf.

Type of person suited to this work

As the work is mainly about dealing with people, you must have excellent interpersonal skills and the ability to remain impartial and non-judgemental. In order to explain issues very clearly to your clients and help them to complete forms and documents, you will need excellent verbal and written communication skills.

You will be handling large amounts of information, often to find answers to queries, which means you must enjoy research and be able to grasp facts and analyse data quickly.

You need to be understanding and tactful when dealing with clients who are upset and stressed.

Working conditions

Benefits advisers are based in an open-access centre within a local community, town or city. You will see clients on a one-to-one basis by appointment and you will also liaise with colleagues and other professionals, such as social workers and solicitors.

You will usually work standard office hours from Monday to Friday with occasional shift work including Saturdays and evenings.

You will use IT to consult client records, access email and the internet, and undertake research.

Future prospects

Advice centre work is not open to school-leavers – it suits mature people who are experienced in other fields. Entry is competitive; you should gain experience in helping people through voluntary work.

Most jobs are with local authorities or charities. There are a few paid jobs with the Citizens Advice Bureau but many posts are voluntary. Training will be given in areas such as counselling skills and benefits.

Promotion prospects are limited, although every advice centre has a manager.

Advantages/disadvantages

You will get the opportunity to work with many different people.

You will have to deal with angry and upset clients; some may even have mental health problems.

Helping clients resolve their problems can be personally rewarding.

Money guide

Earnings vary with location and employer.

Starting salaries are usually around £19,000–£20,000.

With experience and increased responsibilities, you are likely to earn between £22,000 and £30,000 per year.

Team leaders or managers can achieve in excess of £30,000.

Related opportunities

- Counsellor p569
- Equality and Diversity Officer p37
- Solicitor/Notary Public p376

Further information

Advice UK
www.adviceuk.org.uk

Citizens Advice Bureau
www.citizensadvice.org.uk

Citizens Advice Scotland
www.cas.org.uk

YOUTH AND COMMUNITY WORKER

Qualifications and courses

Entry to this profession is with a BA Honours degree in Youth or Community Work which has been approved by the Joint Negotiating Committee (JNC) for Youth and Community Workers. The requirements for a degree course are usually 5 GCSEs/S grades (A*–C/1–3) and 2 A levels/3 H grades. Entry requirements may be waived for mature applicants with relevant experience.

Graduates with a degree in a non-related subject can gain entry to this profession by studying for a postgraduate certificate, diploma or MA approved by the JNC.

These qualifications vary in length, are available in full-time or part-time study options and include work placements. The National Youth Agency (NYA) supplies a list of universities offering the validated youth and community work qualifications on its website.

Additional aptitudes which are needed include caring for people and high level skills in communication, managing and organising, and working with others.

You will need to pass a disclosure check from the Criminal Records Bureau (CRB).

What the work involves

Youth workers are mainly involved with young people while community workers try to make sure that people of all ages in the local community have access to opportunities.

You will work with people in their local area, encouraging them to take part in learning opportunities and community activities.

You could be in charge of a community centre, arranging activities for people of all ages, such as youth clubs, over-60s lunch clubs and playgroups.

You will keep records, manage budgets and try to obtain grants and funding.

You will work alongside other professionals including social workers, teachers, probation officers and the police.

Type of person suited to this work

As the work involves contact with all sorts of people, it is important to be able to get on with everyone and earn their trust. You also need to be genuinely interested in the local community and in equal opportunities.

Local people have a say in what they want in their area, so you must be a good listener, with the ability to balance the ideas of the community with local and national government policies.

Working conditions

You might be based in a community centre or in an area office. Depending on your job, you could also work in a school, college or Connexions centre.

You will work where young people go, including drop-in centres, cafés and youth clubs.

You will usually work 35 to 37 hours a week and this includes attending evening and weekend sessions.

Youth/community workers often travel around their local area so a driving licence is useful.

Future prospects

Youth and community work is a growth area. As well as roles in youth club and community centre management, there are new strands to the work with developing music, drama, art or sporting groups.

Local lifelong learning adult centres also require youth and community workers.

Local authorities have a defined promotion structure but in some jobs you might have to move around to widen your experience. You could progress to working for voluntary organisations or for a specific young people's service, such as Connexions.

Advantages/disadvantages

This work provides variety and challenge.

You will play a major part in developing your local community and/or the lives of young people.

You might have to work evenings, weekends and public holidays.

Money guide

Earnings vary with location and tend to be higher in London.

Starting salaries for qualified youth and community workers are usually £19,000–£22,000.

With experience, you can expect to earn £24,000–£29,000.

Those employed in managerial positions are likely to receive up to £36,000 a year.

Related opportunities

- Education Welfare Officer p194
- Further Education Lecturer p195
- Social Worker p579

Further information

Council for Wales of Voluntary Youth Services
www.cwvys.org.uk

National Youth Agency
www.nya.org.uk

Transport and Logistics

The jobs in this sector are immensely varied because of the wide range of transport and communication links that exist today to keep our lives running. You could need a high level of technical knowledge in this sector especially for jobs such as a pilot or a train driver. But you could also be great at keeping attention to detail and maintaining schedules if logistics is more where your interest lies. Jobs in transport and logistics require very efficient and practical people to ensure that our infrastructure continues to run smoothly and safely. You may need to cope well in pressurised situations as well as be very good at communicating so that any problems can be sorted out quickly.

The jobs featured in this section are listed below. For similar jobs to the ones in this section see *Security Emergency and the Armed Forces* on page 539 and *Leisure, Sport and Tourism* on page 377.

AIR CABIN CREW

Qualifications and courses

Entry requirements depend on the individual airline. Employers often expect 3–5 GCSEs/S grades (A*–C/1–3) including English and maths.

You will need to be at least 18 years old, physically fit and within height and weight restrictions. You will also need a valid passport allowing unrestricted world travel. Most airlines will expect you to be able to swim at least 25 metres. Previous experience in a customer service role, the ability to speak another language or training in First Aid would all be beneficial.

Relevant entry qualifications include a GCSE in Leisure and Tourism and an AS/A level in Travel and Tourism. BTEC offer Level 2 qualifications in Travel and Tourism, Customer Service and Preparation for Air Cabin Crew Service. Other useful Level 2 courses include the City & Guilds Award/Certificate/Diploma in Air Cabin Crew (New Entrant) and the Northern advisory Council for Further Education (NCFE) Certificate in Introduction to Cabin Crew. NVQs are available in Hospitality, Travel and Tourism, Customer Service and Aviation Operations in the Air - Cabin Crew.

Once accepted by an airline you will take part in their 4–6 week training course which covers areas such as First Aid, safety and emergency procedures, security regulations and customer care.

What the work involves

When you have prepared the cabin, you will welcome your passengers on-board and make sure that they are comfortable.

You will be responsible for checking that customers are wearing their safety belts and that their bags are stored away. You will demonstrate safety procedures before take-off.

During the flight you will help to care for any young children and sick passengers, giving First Aid if needed. You will also serve food and drinks, sell duty free items, ensure that passengers are ready for landing and see them all safely off the plane.

Type of person suited to this work

You will need to be welcoming, friendly, well-groomed, confident and caring.

You should be happy working in a team with the rest of the crew.

Common sense and tact are important when dealing with a variety of situations ranging from nervous or unruly passengers to medical emergencies. It is essential to stay calm under pressure and to have a reassuring attitude.

Working conditions

You will work in a cabin, which can sometimes be cramped and unstable. You will spend the majority of your time standing up which may affect your health, for example ear pain from cabin pressure or jet lag from long flights.

Planes fly 24/7 which means unsocial working hours. You will work different shifts on a rota system. You might work on short flights within the UK/Europe or you could fly long-haul with frequent periods of time away from home.

You will be provided with a uniform and you must have a smart appearance at all times.

Future prospects

There is fierce competition for jobs and the number of vacancies available for new entrants has declined in recent years.

With experience, you could progress to working as a purser (looking after a particular cabin such as first class) and then to cabin service director or crew controller.

You could also go on to train new cabin crew.

Advantages/disadvantages

You will travel to dream destinations, but on short flights you will not always get off the plane!

No two working days will be the same.

While working with people can be very rewarding, you might have to deal with difficult passengers.

Money guide

Starting salaries for air cabin crew are usually between £11,000 and £14,000.

With experience, earnings rise to £15,000–£21,000.

Senior members of the crew can achieve up to £25,000 a year.

Benefits include meals, free or discounted flights and allowances for working unsocial hours/working away from home.

Air cabin crew can often boost their income with commission on in-flight sales.

Related opportunities

- Holiday Representative p384
- Tour Guide/Manager p392
- Travel Agent p394

Further information

EAL
www.eal.org.uk

NCFE
www.ncfe.org.uk

AIR TRAFFIC CONTROLLER

Qualifications and courses

To enter this profession you must complete a training course approved by the Civil Aviation Authority (CAA) in order to obtain the required Air Traffic Controller's (ATCO) Licence. Course providers include Resource Training, Global ATS and National Air Traffic Services (NATS).

Applicants for an air traffic control course must be at least 18 years old and have a minimum of 5 GCSEs/S grades (A*–C/1–3), or equivalent, including English and maths. You will need a good standard of health, hearing, colour vision and a clear voice.

There is strong competition for places and the application process involves attending assessment days and a formal interview, completing online and written tests, and receiving security and medical clearance.

It takes 3–4 years to become fully qualified. Candidates will initially learn in the classroom and through practical exercises using computer simulators. There are ongoing exams and assessments throughout the course which you need to pass in order to progress to the next stage. After graduation, trainees go on to an operational air traffic control unit for validation training under the supervision of an experienced instructor. The ATCO Licence is awarded upon successful completion of the training.

What the work involves

Air traffic controllers issue pilots with instructions and advice to ensure that planes take off, fly and land safely.

When using radar, you will be in control of a specific section of airspace, keeping air traffic flying safely and expeditiously. In a control tower, you will be responsible for the safe movement of aircraft on the ground both arriving and departing from an airport.

You will have to make quick but safe decisions at all times, particularly in emergencies or difficult weather conditions.

Type of person suited to this work

You must speak clearly and confidently when passing instructions to pilots. It is essential to stay alert at all times and pay close attention to detail. You must be able to make quick and logical decisions and stay calm in an emergency situation.

Whilst controlling you will need to have good spatial awareness and the ability to multitask and operate safely in a 3D environment.

The technology and software used is regularly upgraded to improve safety, so you will need to be willing to train on new equipment and procedures during your working life.

Working conditions

You will work around 40 hours a week at an air traffic control centre or in an air traffic control tower. As this is a 24/7 job, you will work shifts including early mornings, nights, weekends and public holidays. Hours are strictly regulated to provide rest periods during your shifts.

You will use radar displays, radio headphones and computer tools. The lighting in the control room is kept at the right level to help you read the radar screens.

Future prospects

Most UK air traffic controllers are employed by the NATS. Most of the NATS controllers work in one of two main area control centres (Swanwick near Southampton and Prestwick in Scotland) and others work at airports where NATS are contracted to provide air traffic control.

Air traffic controllers are also employed by other companies/councils, at other airfields.

There are regular trainee vacancies as air traffic continues to increase, although entry is very competitive.

With experience, you could manage and train other air traffic controllers.

Advantages/disadvantages

No two working days are the same and your job will remain interesting and challenging.

You will be paid well for the level of responsibility you take on.

This job can involve high levels of stress.

Money guide

During your college training, your salary will be around £10,000 a year.

Whilst undertaking the validation training you can expect to earn between £15,000 and £19,000.

Once you are fully qualified as an air traffic controller you will receive an annual salary of £40,000–£50,000.

Those employed in a senior position can achieve up to £90,000 a year.

Related opportunities

- Airline Pilot p590
- Helicopter Pilot p600
- Royal Air Force Officer p558

Further information

Civil Aviation Authority
www.caa.co.uk

National Air Traffic Services Ltd
www.nats.co.uk

AIRLINE PILOT

Qualifications and courses

You must be aged at least 16 to begin training for a 'frozen' Airline Transport Pilot Licence (ATPL) which allows you to become a co-pilot. After you have accumulated enough flying hours, you can unfreeze your licence and work towards becoming a captain. You need to be over the age of 21 to hold a full ATPL.

There are various entry routes to getting an ATPL: you can train full time over 2 years with a flying school. Entry is with at least 5 GCSEs/S grades (A*–C/1–3) in English, maths and a science. Another option is to undertake modular training: the first stage is to apply for a Private Pilot's Licence (PPL) and then gain an extra 150 hours' flying experience to be eligible for an ATPL.

You could train as a pilot in the Armed Forces, serve for a time and then take a conversion course to get a commercial pilot's licence.

You may do a degree course in pilot training at a university which will take you to frozen ATPL status.

Training can be expensive – up to £60,000 for a full-time course. Sponsorship is possible and organisations such as the Air League offer scholarships. You will have a medical to assess your physical fitness, hearing, eyesight and colour vision.

What the work involves

You will be responsible for the safety of your passengers, crew and cargo and will need to carry out a range of safety, route and fuel checks before each flight.

When flying you will keep in radio contact with air traffic controllers, inform and direct the crew, plan your route and use computer systems to control and monitor the aircraft.

After each flight you will need to write a report and record any problems that occurred.

Type of person suited to this work

You will need to be confident and responsible enough to take charge of your aircraft and follow the exact instructions of air traffic control. You must have the ability to read maps and 3D displays.

Good communication and teamwork skills are essential.

You must stay composed under pressure and in emergency situations. Quick thinking and good coordination are also important.

Once you have earned your full licence, you will still be regularly assessed on your health, skills and competencies so you must be keen to keep on learning.

Working conditions

You will wear a uniform and carry company ID at all times.

You will work shifts which will include weekends, nights and public holidays. If a flight is delayed you may work much longer hours than anticipated. The hours you are allowed to work are strictly regulated.

You must be prepared for jetlag and spending time away from home if piloting a long-haul flight. You will spend the majority of your time sitting in a small flight deck.

Future prospects

Competition for vacancies for new pilots is intense but openings for experienced pilots are increasing.

You could be promoted to co-pilot on a long-haul flight after you have about 5 years of experience as a short-haul pilot. In order to be promoted to captain level, you will need to fly 5000 hours and this can take up to 10 years to achieve.

You could become a manager or an instructor or even work up to a senior position within a major airline.

Advantages/disadvantages

You will be at the mercy of the weather and you may not always be able to minimise turbulence.

You will have the opportunity to travel to exotic locations.

The training to qualify as a pilot is incredibly expensive.

Flying a plane is a thrilling experience so your day-to-day work will be exciting.

Money guide

As a co-pilot, you may start out earning between £20,000 and £43,000 per year.

A captain usually has an annual salary ranging from £55,000 to £80,000.

Captains who have around 20 years' experience can achieve up to £100,000 a year.

Benefits include free or discounted flights.

Related opportunities

- Air Traffic Controller p589
- Helicopter Pilot p600
- Royal Air Force Airman/woman p557

Further information

British Airline Pilots' Association
www.balpa.org.uk

Guild of Air Pilots and Air Navigators
www.gapan.org

AIRPORT BAGGAGE HANDLER

Qualifications and courses

There are no minimum entry requirements for this job but employers often expect a good standard of literacy and numeracy. You will usually need to be at least 18 years old, be physically fit and pass a medical, vision and Criminal Records Bureau (CRB) check. You will also need a clean driving licence and in some cases a large goods vehicle (LGV) or forklift licence. Previous experience working in a warehouse may be an advantage.

The Apprenticeship in Aviation Operations on the Ground is available at both Intermediate and Advanced Levels and may equip you with relevant skills for this profession.

Once you secure employment, you will receive training from an experienced colleague in areas such as health and safety, security procedures, using luggage conveyor belts and lifting equipment, and driving airport vehicles.

You can also study for relevant qualifications whilst you work. City & Guilds offer a Diploma in Aviation Operations on the Ground (Levels 2 and 3) and an NVQ in Aviation Operations on the Ground (Levels 2 and 3). A BTEC Certificate in Aviation Operations on the Ground is also available at Levels 2 and 3.

What the work involves

You will be responsible for safely loading, unloading and transporting baggage, cases and freight.

By checking the baggage against flight lists, you will sort items to make sure you get the baggage to the right place on time. You will then lift the baggage onto the ramp or conveyor belt to move it onto the plane or into the baggage hall.

If you spot any unusual or suspicious baggage, you will need to report it immediately.

Type of person suited to this work

You need to be alert and pay close attention to detail when checking labels against flight lists and looking out for suspicious baggage. As you will be handling passengers' belongings, you must be honest and reliable.

In order to get aircraft loaded and unloaded on a short timescale, you will need to be physically fit, fast moving and accurate.

Flexibility and a willingness to get your hands dirty are also vital, as you might need to carry out jobs such as cleaning the aircraft and keeping runways free of hazards such as snow and birds. You should enjoy working as part of a team.

Working conditions

You will mainly work outdoors in all weathers, as well as in cramped spaces such as cargo holds.

You will work around 39 hours per week on a shift system which includes evenings, weekends and public holidays. It is advisable to live near the airport and have your own transport so that you will arrive on time for early shifts.

Working near aircraft can be noisy but you will wear ear protectors.

Your job will involve a lot of bending, lifting and carrying and you will be required to wear protective boots and a high visibility jacket.

Future prospects

Most of the 5000 baggage handlers in the UK work for large airlines or handling agents at the biggest airports but there are vacancies at many regional airports as well.

Seasonal work is also on offer during busy holiday periods.

You may be promoted to a supervisory role or manage ground transport on the runways. With further training and qualifications, you could also work in cargo services or aviation management.

Advantages/disadvantages

This is a very active, fast-paced and busy role.

If you are working for an airline, one of the perks may be subsidised travel.

You may have to work outside in poor weather conditions.

Money guide

Starting salaries are usually between £10,000 and £15,000 per year.

With experience in the role, you could expect to earn about £16,000.

Baggage handlers with supervisory duties can earn in excess of £18,000.

Some workers are paid by the hour and rates are typically between £6 and £8.

Allowances for shift work and overtime pay can increase your income.

Related opportunities

- Hotel Porter p141
- Removals Operative p613
- Warehouse Worker/Manager p619

Further information

International Air Transport Association
www.iata.org

Royal Aeronautical Society
www.aerosociety.com

Qualifications and courses

There are no specific academic requirements for entry to this profession. Some employers will expect you to have a good standard of literacy and numeracy.

You must hold a passenger carrying vehicle (PCV) licence and obtain the Driver Certificate of Professional Competence (Driver CPC). You need to be at least 18 years old to train for your PCV licence and you must be over the age of 21 to drive on major bus and coach routes.

If you already have a full EU driving licence then most companies are willing to employ you and fund your training for the PCV licence.

PCV training lasts between 1 and 6 weeks and includes both a theory and practical driving test, as well as a medical.

During your training period, your company will teach you about customer care, disability awareness, defensive driving and health and safety. You also have the option to study for an NVQ Level 2 in Passenger Carrying Vehicle Driving (Bus and Coach) or a BTEC Level 2 Certificate in Transporting Passengers by Bus and Coach.

What the work involves

Bus/coach drivers provide a transport service for passengers making short or long journeys.

You will be responsible for the safety and comfort of your passengers throughout their journey, which includes ensuring that passengers are safely on or off your vehicle before pulling out, and that they are wearing seatbelts when applicable.

If you do not have a conductor, you might have to work out passenger fares and issue tickets and passes. You will also be responsible for checking your vehicle, coping with breakdowns and other emergencies, and driving safely at all times.

Type of person suited to this work

You will need to be an extremely competent driver.

You should have a polite and approachable manner when dealing with passengers, but have the confidence to handle disagreements or other situations which may arise on journeys.

You will need good eyesight and excellent concentration in order to remain alert for very long periods of time. Quick reactions are also useful in case you need to respond to an unforeseen event on the road.

You should be a punctual person as you will have to adhere to a strict timetable.

Working conditions

You will work on a shift pattern including evening, overnight and weekend work. You cannot work more than 56 hours a week, or 90 hours over 2 weeks. You are also required, by law, to take a 45 minute break every 4.5 hours.

Coach drivers are expected to provide assistance to disabled travellers and help passengers with luggage so your role could involve heavy lifting. You will have to wear a uniform.

Future prospects

There is a continuous shortage of bus/coach drivers so job opportunities are good. Over 80% of the workforce is employed by 1 of 6 companies: Stagecoach, First, National Express, Transdev, Arriva and Go-Ahead.

You could work anywhere in the UK, undertake long distance tour driving or provide a transport service for specific groups such as the elderly or disabled.

You can progress to become a supervisor, service controller or instructor within your company.

Advantages/disadvantages

You will be providing an essential public service.

Part time and flexible hours are available so you can fit your work around other commitments.

You may have to deal with difficult or distressed passengers.

Driving the same route or for long periods of time can become monotonous.

Money guide

As a trainee driver working towards your PCV licence, you could expect to earn between £11,000 and £14,000 a year.

With experience, your salary is likely to be £15,000–£20,000.

Coach drivers for specialist tours can earn around £25,000 a year.

You could supplement your income with overtime and shift work.

Related opportunities

- Driving Instructor p598
- Large Goods Vehicle Driver p602
- Taxi Driver p616

Further information

Driving Standards Agency
www.dsa.gov.uk

CHAUFFEUR

Qualifications and courses

You do not need any specific academic qualifications to become a chauffeur. The only necessity is that you hold a full driving licence. Most employers will expect this to be clean, but some do consider candidates with penalty points. You may benefit from holding an advanced driving certificate, details of which can be found through the Institute of Advanced Motorists. This demonstrates an enhanced driving ability and additional skills that may be valued by some employers.

It is beneficial to have several years' driving experience. Not only does this demonstrate a proven ability behind the wheel, but if you are over 21 years old you will cost your employer less to insure.

There are professional courses that you could take to enhance your application and understanding of the job. These include NVQs in Road Passenger Vehicle Driving, and the ASET Level 2 Certificate in Defensive Driving. The British Chauffeurs Guild also offers a Security Chauffeur Training Course which covers the fundamental areas of chauffeuring; theory, practice, protocol, security and etiquette.

Some employers may also require you to pass a medical assessment, and a Criminal Records Bureau check, prior to taking you on.

What the work involves

Chauffeurs are responsible for driving their client to and from appointments or events, as well as the maintenance of the vehicle.

You will have to clean the vehicle regularly, inside and out, and also undertake any minor maintenance work when necessary, or book it in to see a mechanic.

You will be providing a personal service to your passengers, including opening and closing doors for them, assisting them in and out of the vehicle, and carrying and loading their luggage or shopping. You might also be required to provide a low level of security protection to your client, as well as maintaining confidentiality at all times.

Type of person suited to this work

You must be an excellent driver who observes the law and keeps cool under pressure, even when faced with endless traffic jams or unpredictable clients. You will also need to have a good awareness of safety and security, both on the road and with regard to your client.

You should have excellent interpersonal skills. You must be punctual, respectful and polite.

Good map reading skills, knowledge of basic vehicle maintenance, and a reasonable level of fitness are also helpful.

Working conditions

It is unlikely that you will work regular hours as a chauffeur, as most clients will require your services during the evenings and at weekends. Split shifts are common, where you will find yourself with 2 or 3 free hours in between appointments.

You may be required to spend nights away from home on occasion.

You will need to wear a uniform in most instances.

Future prospects

Most chauffeurs are employed by limousine companies, but there are opportunities with hotel groups, car-hire companies, park and ride schemes, tour operators, businesses and private employers.

The British Chauffeurs Guild operates a specialist employment agency for their members, through which they can find suitable opportunities.

With experience, you can command a higher salary, or you could branch into a related career such as that of a taxi driver or driving instructor.

Advantages/disadvantages

You could work for some interesting, high profile clients.

The work offers some flexibility with hours.

There is a lot of waiting around for clients, which can get boring and frustrating.

Money guide

Salaries vary depending on your employer, but on average the starting wage for a chauffeur is usually around £16,000. With 3–5 years' experience, this could rise to £25,000.

An experienced chauffeur, especially one with advanced driving or additional security qualifications, could earn £30,000+.

Related opportunities

- Driving Instructor p598
- Motor Vehicle Technician p234
- Taxi Driver p616

Further information

British Chauffeurs Guild
www.britishchauffeursguild.co.uk

Institute of Advanced Motorists
www.iam.org.uk

Qualifications and courses

You will need to be at least 17 years old – many driver couriers are over 21 because of high insurance costs for young drivers. School leavers could start as bicycle couriers. Employers ask for a full UK driving licence for driver couriers and motorcycle couriers will need the CBT qualification issued by the DVLA. Motorcycle and bicycle couriers usually use their own bikes.

Key Skills in Communication and Working with Others are useful. Apprenticeships/Skillseekers are available for candidates aged 16–24.

You might be able study for an NVQ/SVQ at Level 2 in Carry and Deliver Goods and an NVQ at Levels 2 and 3 in Driving Goods Vehicles when employed.

What the work involves

You will collect fragile, valuable or urgent letters and packages and deliver them within an agreed time limit.

Once you have been allocated your job, you will travel to a collection point for pick-up. You will load up the goods and then take them to the drop-off point where you will obtain a signature for delivery. You will need to check the lights, brakes and tyres of your motorbike, van or bicycle regularly.

Motorcycle couriers may travel long distances and van couriers carry larger parcels in a town or city.

Type of person suited to this work

Map-reading skills are essential. You may only be paid for the number of deliveries you do so you need to be quick and know where you are going.

You will be in constant contact with customers; collecting items, asking for instructions and getting signatures for deliveries, so you need to be good with people.

You should also be reliable – you may be dealing with high value or very urgent items.

Working conditions

You will spend a lot of time travelling but with regular stops to make deliveries. Long distance or overseas deliveries might mean time away from home.

Motorcycle and bicycle couriers will be out in the weather at all times.

Courier services operate 24/7 and many couriers work on overnight deliveries.

You might have to provide your own car or van. Motorcycle and bicycle couriers usually use their own bikes.

Future prospects

The continued growth of online shopping and customer online tracking means that the demand for same and next day courier delivery is growing. However the recession has affected the industry making fewer vacancies available.

Promotion generally depends on the size of the courier company – large companies may have sales and management opportunities.

It might be possible to become self-employed and start your own courier service. You could also train further and move into a related area such as large goods vehicle driving or distribution.

Advantages/disadvantages

Pay rates are good but if you are using your own transport you will have running, insurance and maintenance costs.

Making up to 20 journeys a day and possibly working 50-hour weeks make this a stressful job.

Most couriers take up the job because they are attracted to the freedom of travel. However most couriers do lots of repeat deliveries in a small, often congested, urban area.

Money guide

Couriers are often self-employed and paid for each delivery they make, so earnings vary.

Employed couriers can earn £14,500 a year (£18,000 in London).

Experienced couriers can earn up to £20,000 a year (£23,000+ in London).

Couriers travelling by air may be employed by airlines on a one-off basis, receiving reduced cost flights instead of wages.

Related opportunities

- Airport Baggage Handler p591
- Delivery Driver p596
- Warehouse Worker/Manager p619

Further information

Driving Standards Agency
www.dsa.gov.uk

Institute of Couriers
www.ioc.uk.com

CRUISE SHIP STEWARD/PURSER

ENTRY LEVEL **1**

Qualifications and courses

Steward
There are no formal entry requirements for this work, but relevant experience in the leisure and hospitality industry is normally required.

Training is provided on the job, and covers subjects such as safety, health, environment, survival and rescue, fire, First Aid, etc, as well as company-specific training.

Purser
A levels/H grades or equivalent are normally required, and many employers prefer a degree in a related subject such as hospitality or travel and tourism. The normal entry requirements for a degree in a travel or hospitality subject are 2 A levels/3 H grades, or equivalent. No specific A level subjects are required.

Related experience is normally required. For senior positions, managerial experience or a degree in hotel management may be required.

Knowledge of a language other than English is an advantage.

What the work involves

Steward
You will be responsible for keeping the public and private areas on a cruise ship clean and serviced to a very high standard. Duties may include making beds and vacuuming.

You may serve passengers drinks in the bar area, wash glasses and keep the bar stocked and tidy.

Purser
Pursers provide the administrative support necessary to ensure the ship operates smoothly and that passengers have a good holiday. You might work in the reception area, do secretarial duties or order various items of stock.

As well as providing passenger services you might also support crew members by paying their salaries or updating and maintaining immigration records.

Type of person suited to this work

As you will have contact with passengers, you should be happy meeting, talking with and helping people of all nationalities.

You should be polite and happy to help, and have good customer service skills.

You will need to be a dedicated employee as the work can be hard at times.

Working conditions

You will be expected to work long shifts, which for some posts can last up to 10 hours. Although cruise ships appear to be glamorous, you might work in cramped conditions or during rough weather.

You might have to share your accommodation with other members of staff.

Short-term, holiday and summer work is available.

Future prospects

In the last 7 years the cruise ship industry has become the second fastest growing sector in the UK and USA, so prospects are good.

There is a clear process of career progression. You will start as a member of crew then rise to officer as you gain skills and responsibilities.

The skills gained on-board will also be useful on land in many areas of hospitality and catering (steward) or the business sector (purser).

Advantages/disadvantages

You might be away from home for months at a time.

You will be able visit lots of places around the world.

Your accommodation could be cramped and you might have to share with other crew members.

Pay is very good; accommodation and food are free while on-board, and usually your salary is tax free if on a 6 month contract or longer.

Money guide

Salaries for all on-board positions are higher than for comparable jobs ashore. Salaries vary with company and liner, so contact companies directly for their earnings guide.

Stewards typically earn around £12,000 per year; this may increase slightly with experience. Free accommodation and food, as well as tips from passengers, boost the value of earnings.

The purser can expect a varying salary dependent on experience and responsibility. Salaries generally start from £19,000 to £21,000 per year as an assistant purser.

With experience and increased responsibility as the administration purser, this can increase to between £33,000 and £37,000.

A chief purser can earn between £45,000 and £55,000.

Related opportunities

- Holiday Representative p384
- Housekeeper/Accommodation Manager p144
- Tourist Information Centre Assistant p393

Further information

International Cruise Services
www.cruiseservices.co.uk

TRANSPORT AND LOGISTICS

CRCI: WF

DELIVERY DRIVER

Qualifications and courses

No specific academic qualifications are required for delivery drivers, but some employers prefer candidates with some GCSEs (A*–E) or equivalent, including English and maths.

You will need to hold a good driving record and the appropriate driving licence for work as a delivery driver. You might also find holding a licence for category C1 useful as it will allow you to drive vehicles that weigh between 3.5 and 7.5 tonnes. For this you will need to take a large goods vehicle (LGV) theory and C1 practical test.

If you plan to work for a company that transports large sums of money or valuable items, you will also need a Security Industry Authority (SIA) licence. This can be obtained on completion of the National Open College Network (NOCN) Level 2 Award in Cash and Valuables Transit.

What the work involves

You could be responsible for the safe transportation and delivery of a variety of goods, including food and drink, parcels, and domestic appliances.

You will be loading and unloading goods from your vehicle, and making sure that your load is secure prior to starting on your journey. You will also be responsible for ensuring that your van is well maintained and roadworthy.

You will need to organise your own delivery schedule in order to meet strict distribution times each day.

Type of person suited to this work

You will need to be an extremely competent driver and be able to focus for long periods of time.

You should have a polite manner in order to build good relationships with colleagues and customers. You should be physically fit, as you might need to load and unload heavy items from your van.

Good map reading and navigational skills are helpful for finding your way round new and unfamiliar areas on a delivery. It is also important to be reliable and to stay calm in hazardous situations.

Working conditions

You might need to work 37–40 hours in shifts over evenings and weekends. Other companies will only deliver goods during standard working hours. Part-time work is often available.

You might work on your own or with another person who will help navigate and plan your route, and assist with loading and unloading goods.

You will spend the majority of your time in the van, and will have to drive and meet time-restricted schedules no matter what the weather. You might have to wear a uniform.

Future prospects

The rise of internet shopping has resulted in an increase in opportunities for delivery drivers; however the recession has affected the number of vacancies available.

There is demand for drivers all over the UK, so you could work anywhere, although most opportunities are found in larger towns and cities.

You could work for a variety of companies, including retail, manufacturing and supermarkets, or you could opt for self-employment. You could also move into a related area in transport, such as an administrative or transport manager post.

Advantages/disadvantages

Part-time and flexible hours are available so you can fit work around other commitments.

You will be providing a valuable service to people, either delivering food or appliances to their homes, or transporting parcels or money safely around the UK.

The work can be quite lonely as you may work for long periods on your own.

Money guide

Starting salaries for full-time van drivers are usually around £13,000.

With experience this could rise to between £15,000 and £26,000.

Most van drivers earn around £19,000. You can increase your wage by working overtime.

Related opportunities

- Chauffeur p593
- Large Goods Vehicle Driver p602
- Train Driver p618

Further information

Driving Standards Agency
www.dsa.gov.uk

National Open College Network
www.nocn.org.uk

DISTRIBUTION MANAGER

Qualifications and courses

There are no specific entry requirements and it is possible to work your way up from a transport clerk position by gaining relevant NVQ qualifications or professional qualifications. Apprenticeships in the traffic office, logistics operations management or warehousing and storage are also available.

However, many candidates hold a HNC/HND, Foundation degree or degree. Courses are available in areas such as logistics, geography, transport management and supply chain management. Normally, at least 5 GCSEs/S grades (A*–C/1–3) and 2 A levels/3 H grades or equivalent are required for a degree course. Entry for HNC/D requires a minimum of 4 GCSEs/S grades (A*–C/1–3) and 1 A level/2 H grades, a related BTEC National Certificate/Diploma or equivalent.

People working in the industry can study for the Chartered Institute of Logistics and Transport's (CILT's) professional qualifications. The Introductory Certificate is suitable for employees new to the profession. The Certificate is aimed at supervisors and first line managers. The Professional Diploma is intended for middle managers, including recent graduates, and fulfils the requirements for membership of the Institute. Senior distribution managers can take the CILT Advanced Diploma or study for a master's in logistics. Distribution managers might find it helpful to take the Certificate of Professional Competence of the Department of Transport.

What the work involves

You will be responsible for overseeing the control and movement of goods or raw materials held in stock.

Using ICT, you will manage stock levels and monitor the ordering and storage of goods.

You will also manage staff and carry out their recruitment and training.

Type of person suited to this work

Distribution is a fast-moving industry and ICT is at its centre, so you will need excellent computer skills. Like the computer programs you will use, you will need to be systematic and logical.

Brilliant communication skills are also a necessity as you will have to deal with people at different levels. It might be that the goods you have to order come from far-flung places. This means that the supply chain you will be managing might be very complex.

You will also need to able to deal with the stress of making sure that you get the goods at the best price and supply them in the right condition.

Working conditions

Most of your work will be in an office, but you will also travel to meetings with suppliers or customers and visit storage depots.

Your hours will be mainly office hours, Monday–Friday, but you might have to do shift work or work weekends and evenings on a rota system.

There could be travel away from home and, for some, travel overseas.

Future prospects

There are more than 86,000 distribution managers working for a wide range of companies, including warehouse and distribution firms but also manufacturers, major retail companies, the Armed Forces and central and local government.

With experience, you could progress into a senior role in business development or undertake consultancy work.

Advantages/disadvantages

As a key figure in your company, you will have the satisfaction of making sure your supply chain works and that your customers are happy.

The demands of coordinating vehicles, products, people and tight deadlines, can make this a stressful role.

Money guide

Salaries start around £15,000 per year.

Experienced managers earn from £30,000.

Senior distribution managers responsible for transport schedules can earn around £60,000 per year.

Related opportunities

- Freight Forwarder p599
- Importer/Exporter p601
- Warehouse Worker/Manager p619

Further information

Chartered Institute of Logistics and Transport
www.ciltuk.org.uk

Freight Transport Association
www.fta.co.uk

TRANSPORT AND LOGISTICS

CRCI: WB

Qualifications and courses

You must be registered with the Driving Standards Agency as an Approved Driving Instructor (ADI). You will need to be aged over 21 and have held a full clean driving licence for 4 out of the last 6 years, with no criminal or motoring convictions.

The ADI examination is in 3 parts: an IT-based multiple choice theory test and a video-based hazard perceptions test; a practical driving test; and a practical teaching test. Parts 2 and 3 must be completed within a 2 years of part 1. Applicants must pass the practical driving test within 3 attempts.

As training can be very expensive, the majority of entrants join a training organisation or an organisation which provides franchise prospects if you complete the training.

An NVQ at Level 3 in Driving Instruction is available.

What the work involves

You will teach people how to drive safely, and well enough to pass their driving test. You will explain basic motor and road skills as well as safe and courteous driving.

Your role will include making your pupils aware of all aspects of the Highway Code, helping to develop observation skills and teaching manoeuvres such as reverse parking.

It will be your responsibility to plan driving lessons to suit your pupil and give constructive criticism.

Type of person suited to this work

Not only will you need to be a good, safe driver, you will also need teaching skills. People learning to drive are often stressed and anxious, so you will need to be calm, steady and patient.

Instructors need to plan lessons to cover individual weaknesses. You will need to have quick reactions in order to prevent your pupils from causing any accidents.

As many instructors are self-employed, you will need to have a good business sense and the ability to manage your own finances.

Working conditions

Instructors can spend more than 8 hours a day sitting in the car ready to operate the dual controls to avert problems.

Early morning, evening and weekend work is common as you will teach lessons at times that suit your pupils.

Instructors with lots of experience can work a 35 to 40 hour week. However, you might have to work longer hours to keep a steady income. This can restrict the times and lengths of holidays for self-employed or franchised instructors.

Future prospects

Driving instructors could work for driving schools, operate under a franchise, or have their own businesses. Opportunities are also available with big transport companies, the emergency services, local authorities and the Armed Forces.

Around 80% of instructors are self-employed. There are no restrictions on the numbers of instructors meaning there is sometimes strong competition for pupils.

You could undertake fleet driver training and instruction in driving large goods or passenger-carrying vehicles. You could also progress to a role as a trainer for new driving instructors or a driving examiner.

Advantages/disadvantages

It can be very rewarding to enable learners to become safe, qualified drivers.

Many driving instructors are self-employed.

If you run your own car to give lessons you will have to pay for your fuel, insurance and maintenance costs.

It may be a challenge to maintain a steady income.

Money guide

Instructors charge £15–£27 per hour for a driving lesson.

Full time driving instructors could earn £16,000 as a starting salary. With several years' experience this can rise to around £25,000. Your income will be reduced by the costs of running and maintaining your vehicle or paying a franchise fee.

Full-time, experienced driving instructors can earn over £30,000. Salaries are higher in London.

Related opportunities

- Chauffeur p593
- Taxi Driver p616
- Work-based Training Instructor p207

Further information

Driving Instructors Association
www.driving.org

Motor Schools Association of Great Britain Ltd
www.msagb.co.uk

UK Driving Instructors Confederation
www.ukdic.co.uk

Qualifications and courses

Entry requirements vary with employer and could range from a minimum of 4 GCSEs/S grades including English and maths, to A levels/H grades, to the BTEC Level 3 Certificate in Road Freight Logistics. Language skills or office experience would be advantageous.

Larger employers may expect a degree, HND or Foundation degree in a related subject such as logistics, supply chain management, international transport or transport management. Some companies have graduate training schemes. Entry to degree courses will require a minimum of 2 A levels/3 H grades and 5 GCSEs/S grades (A*–C/1–3). For HNC/HND courses, you will normally need at least 1 A level/2 H grades and 4 GCSEs/S grades (A*–C/1–3) or equivalent. An alternative entry route is the Apprenticeship in International Trade and Logistics.

Key Skills qualifications in Communication, IT, problem-solving and Working with Others are useful.

Training on the job includes the NVQ in Traffic Office (Levels 2 and 3). City & Guilds offer a Certificate in International Trade and Logistics Operations (Level 2). The British International Freight Association (BIFA) and the Institute of Export (IOE) also provide specialist training and qualifications in international trade.

What the work involves

You will organise the transport of goods across the world for importers and exporters. Your role will involve working out if the freight needs special handling and whether it should go by sea, road or air.

Arranging the packing, carriage, collection and storage of the goods will be part of your job.

You will be responsible for dealing with paperwork, applying for customs clearance and calculating insurance, transport and customs costs.

Type of person suited to this work

As you will deal with lots of different customers, some of whom may not speak fluent English, you must have excellent communication skills.

You need to be determined and have excellent bargaining skills to get the best prices and terms. You will also be a good problem-solver. For example, you might have to work out how to transport a valuable racehorse from Hong Kong to the UK.

You will require strong basic maths skills as you will be asked to calculate exchange rates, or work out if a large piece of cargo will fit into the cargo hold of a small aircraft.

Working conditions

Most of your work will be in an office at a workstation using a telephone, computer and fax machine. You will also need to travel to meet customers and contractors, within the UK and possibly abroad, so you will sometimes be away from home. A driving licence would be useful.

Depending on your employer, you might work normal office hours from Monday to Friday or you might work shifts and extra hours to cover urgent deliveries and world time zones.

Future prospects

Freight forwarding offices are usually in cities and near airports and ports. Opportunities are growing but it is a competitive industry and it helps if you have related work experience.

As you progress, there are opportunities to specialise in specific countries and industries. You could work within the entertainment industry, shipping film and concert sets around the world, or with medical and pharmaceutical supplies.

After gaining experience, you could progress to become a senior freight forwarder and then to a managerial role such as export office manager.

Advantages/disadvantages

This role offers varied opportunities – you could specialise in moving film and TV crews and their equipment or handling perishable goods such as fruit.

You might get a chance to travel or work overseas.

Working to meet tight delivery deadlines can be stressful.

Money guide

Starting salaries range from £15,000 to £21,000.

With experience, you could expect to earn £25,000–£27,500 a year.

As a senior freight forwarder, manager or director you could achieve £30,000–£40,000 per year.

Related opportunities

- Distribution Manager p597
- Importer/Exporter p601
- Warehouse Worker/Manager p619

Further information

Chartered Institute of Logistics and Transport
www.ciltuk.org.uk

Institute of Export
www.export.org.uk

TRANSPORT AND LOGISTICS

CRCI: WB

Qualifications and courses

In order to fly commercially and charge for your services, you must be over the age of 18 and hold a CPL(H) (Commercial Pilot Licence) issued by the Civil Aviation Authority (CAA).

There are 2 main routes to obtaining a CPL(H). The integrated course involves training full time for 12 months to complete 500 hours of theoretical study, 135 hours of flight training, 9 exams and a flight skills test. Alternatively, if you already have a PPL(H) (Private Pilot's Licence), you could undertake modular training and qualify for your CPL(H) after 155 hours of flying experience, 500 hours of theoretical study, a 35-hour commercial flying course and 9 exams.

For both of these routes you will need at least 5 GCSEs/S grades (A*–C/1–3) including English, maths and a science (preferably physics). You need to pass a medical exam and raise money for training as sponsorships for helicopter pilots are rare. Courses can cost up to £50,000.

It is also possible to train as a pilot by joining the Armed Forces and then taking a conversion course to get a commercial licence.

To pilot a 2-crew helicopter you will need an ATPL(H) (Advanced Airline Transport Pilot Licence).

What the work involves

You will most likely pilot a helicopter alone and you will be responsible for the safety of your passengers. You will carry out fuel, weather and route checks before taking off and you will keep in contact with air traffic controllers whilst navigating and monitoring the helicopter during the flight.

After landing you will record your hours and details from the flight.

You may fly for a variety of purposes including searching for missing persons, emergency work, crop spraying, photography, leisure trips or ferrying supplies.

Type of person suited to this work

You must be good with maths and physics, an excellent problem solver and a quick thinker in order to control your helicopter in all weather conditions and emergency situations. Strong communication and teamwork skills are essential.

Good coordination, spatial awareness and attention to detail are also important. You could be flying long hours and you will need stamina, forward-thinking skills and the ability to stay focused on your work.

As a pilot you are responsible for other people's safety so you must be reliable.

Working conditions

Helicopter pilots are usually provided with a uniform. If you fly over the sea for emergency services you will wear a survival suit. Most of your time will be spent sitting alone in a small space.

Your helicopter will be single or multi-engine and it will take time to adjust to the noise and sensation.

If you are a pilot within the leisure and tourism industry, you will most likely work during the daytime only. Emergency and business services may require you to fly through the night and on weekends. If you undertake long journeys, you may spend time away from home.

Future prospects

There are opportunities to work in emergency services, the Armed Forces and for commercial companies but competition is intense for newly qualified helicopter pilots.

With 1000 hours of flight experience and 350 hours as 'pilot in command', you can go on to get your ATPL(H) (Advanced Airline Transport Pilot Licence). You can then fly multi-engine, multi-pilot helicopters for commercial air transport.

You could also set up your own air taxi service company or become self-employed.

Advantages/disadvantages

Helicopter training is expensive and you will need to raise a lot of money if you are unable to gain sponsorship.

No two days will be the same and it is exciting to be unaware of what each flight will hold.

Money guide

Newly qualified commercial helicopter pilots can earn between £20,000 and £25,000 a year.

With a few years' experience, you could expect a salary of around £30,000.

Pilots with extensive experience who captain passenger-carrying helicopters can achieve between £45,000 and £65,000 a year.

Related opportunities

- Air Traffic Controller p589
- Airline Pilot p590
- Royal Air Force Airman/woman p557

Further information

British Helicopter Association
www.britishhelicopterassociation.org

Civil Aviation Authority
www.caa.co.uk

IMPORTER/EXPORTER

Qualifications and courses

There are no set minimum qualifications to enter this industry but most employers will expect 4 GCSEs/S grades (A*–C/1–3) including English and maths. Others will require A levels or equivalent qualifications while many large companies ask for an HND, Foundation degree or degree. Useful subjects include logistics, supply chain management, international transport, business or languages. Some companies offer graduate training schemes.

Apprenticeships in Logistics Operations Management, Business and Administration or Sales and Telesales are available and may equip you with relevant skills for this profession.

The Institute of Export (IOE) offers professional qualifications in international trade. The Advanced Certificate in International Trade leads to Associate membership of the IOE and Graduate membership is granted to those with the Diploma in International Trade. These qualifications are offered at colleges of further education and by distance learning. Candidates must be at least 18 years old with 4 GCSEs/S grades (A*–C/1–3) and 1 A level/H grade or equivalent.

Other relevant courses include the City & Guilds Certificate in International Trade and Logistics Operations (Level 2) and the IOE's Introduction to Importing and Introduction to Exporting seminars.

What the work involves

You will organise all aspects of exporting or importing goods for companies who source or sell them overseas.

Liaising with shipping and forwarding companies, you will get the best prices, sources, quality and delivery services.

You will deal with all the necessary financial paperwork, including invoicing and checking, and issuing letters of credit so that payment can be made. You will also work out accurate costings, customs duties, insurance and forwarding charges.

Type of person suited to this work

You should have an interest in business and trade, as well as other countries and cultures.

As you will be making arrangements with a wide range of customers, you need to be confident, tactful and an excellent communicator. Language skills are a real advantage.

Dealing with numbers will be another of your key strengths because you will be responsible for working out currency exchanges and import and export duties.

You must be a good negotiator as you will need to bargain with shipping and distribution companies, as well as your customers and suppliers.

In addition, problem-solving, IT and organisational skills are vital.

Working conditions

Most of your work will be in an office using the telephone, computer and fax machine.

You will usually work standard office hours from 9am to 5pm, Monday to Friday. You might need to work early mornings or late evenings if your customers or suppliers operate in a different time zone.

You may travel to meet suppliers or customers. At a senior level, you are likely to work overseas on a regular basis in order to maintain your network of business contacts.

Future prospects

As more products are bought and sold in a global market, the number of companies employing an import/export specialist has increased.

Freight-forwarding, industrial, retail and specialist companies such as flower, jewellery or fruit distributors all offer potential jobs.

Vacancies are competitive and usually require work experience in a related area.

Some import/export specialists move into overseas sales management or take up consultancy work.

Advantages/disadvantages

This job is satisfying as you are helping to make the global supply chain work.

You could be under a lot of stress to meet tight deadlines and budgets.

You might have the opportunity to travel overseas.

Money guide

Starting salaries at clerk level range from £11,000 to £15,000 per year.

Experienced staff with increased responsibilities can expect to earn up to £35,000.

Import or export managers of companies with global interests can achieve between £40,000 and £65,000 a year.

Related opportunities

- Freight Forwarder p599
- Road Transport Manager p615

Further information

Institute of Export
www.export.org.uk

Qualifications and courses

Most employers prefer candidates who have GSCEs/S grades (A*–E/1–5) in English and maths, although no formal academic qualifications are required.

You need to be over 18 years old, have a full clean UK driving licence, pass a medical exam and hold an large goods vehicle (LGV) licence. There are 3 categories of LGV licence: a C1 licence which allows you to drive a truck up to 7.5 tonnes, a C licence for vehicles of 3.5–32 tonnes, or a C+E licence for vehicles up to the legal maximum weight of 44 tonnes.

In order to obtain an LGV licence you need to pass both a theory and practical driving test, and train for the Driver Certificate of Professional Competence (Driver CPC). To keep your licence, you are required to do 35 hours of training every 5 years.

If you want to carry dangerous goods you will need to undertake training to obtain an International Carriage of Dangerous Goods by Road (ADR) certificate, which is valid for 5 years before it must be renewed.

The Apprenticeship in Driving Goods Vehicles, which is available at both Intermediate and Advanced Levels, would provide an ideal entry route into this career.

What the work involves

You will transport thousands of tonnes of cargo in your LGV. You could carry loads such as livestock, fuel, chemicals, food or construction equipment.

Your job is to deliver the cargo to its destination on time. To do this you will figure out the best route with your transport manager. You also need to calculate your mileage.

You will sometimes help load and unload cargo, keep the goods safe, and refuel and clean your lorry after each journey.

Type of person suited to this work

You must be an excellent driver with good maths skills as you will be navigating long distances. You should be able to use your initiative and follow safety precautions.

Quick reactions, good eyesight and colour vision are useful in case you need to respond to an unforeseen event on the road. It is essential that you can stay alert for long periods of time.

Overall, you need to be an experienced, confident and punctual driver. You should be polite when dealing with customers and also be content working on your own.

Working conditions

LGV cabs are cosy and quiet, equipped with cooking facilities, bunks, air conditioning and heating. These comforts are important as you will spend hours by yourself in your lorry, eating and sleeping in the cab.

On average, you will work 48 hours per week and legislation prevents you from exceeding 60 hours. Ten hours of night driving is the maximum you may do in a 24-hour period.

Your shifts will include evenings, nights and weekends.

Future prospects

If you work for a road haulage firm you will transport loads for multiple companies. You could also work for farms, transporting livestock, or move sporting goods for retailers. You could be employed by manufacturers, for example moving fleets of cars.

You could be promoted to a supervisor, become an instructor or move into driving hazardous goods. With further training you could become a manager or start up a company, operating your own lorry.

Advantages/disadvantages

You have freedom and flexibility in your work.

The job can be adventurous as you travel to different locations.

You might need to spend long periods of time away from home which can be difficult.

It can be frustrating when you are stuck in traffic and have a deadline to meet.

Money guide

Earnings vary according to geographical location and employer.

Starting salaries are typically £14,000–£17,000.

With experience and increased responsibilities, you could expect to earn £25,000–£30,000 per year.

If you choose to drive a specialist fuel or chemical tanker then your salary can increase up to £35,000.

Overtime pay can increase your income.

Related opportunities

- Driving Instructor p598
- Taxi Driver p616
- Train Driver p618

Further information

Driving Standards Agency
www.dsa.gov.uk

Freight Transport Association
www.fta.co.uk

Road Haulage Association
www.rha.uk.net

LIFT TRUCK OPERATOR

Qualifications and courses

There are no minimum entry qualifications for this job but basic maths is useful to work out safe loads and weights. You may have to pass a medical exam and an aptitude test as part of the application process. Direct entry to this career is possible but it may be advantageous to have experience working in a warehouse.

You will need to be at least 18 years old to work without supervision, although you can start training at the age of 16. A driving licence is required if the truck is to be used on public roads.

Before starting work you will need to have a Construction Plant Competence Scheme (CPCS) card. To qualify you will need to pass the NVQ Level 2 in Plant Operations, as well as the ConstructionSkills Health and Safety Test.

Lift truck operators can work towards the National Proficiency Tests Council (NPTC) Level 2 Certificate of Competence in Forklift Truck Operations or an NVQ/SVQ in Specialised Plant and Machinery Operations (Level 2).

An Apprenticeship in Warehousing and Storage may provide you with relevant skills for this career and would lead to NVQs/SVQs at Levels 2 and 3.

What the work involves

Operating a lift truck with a special fork and carrying platform, you will load, unload, move and stack heavy goods.

You will activate the controls so that your fork or lifting gear is under the load, usually stored in pallets, cages or cases, to raise it safely. This may require manoeuvring at considerable heights.

You will then drive the goods, being careful not to damage them, to their destination. This could be a transport vehicle, a depot or a warehouse. You will also need to perform routine maintenance checks to your truck.

Type of person suited to this work

An aptitude for driving is vital. You will need to be focused and alert when manoeuvring your truck in narrow spaces, always on the lookout for potential hazards. A responsible, mature outlook is required for working to strict safety rules. You will need to be physically fit and have good coordination.

Although you will operate the truck on your own, you will also need to be a team player, working alongside warehouse operatives and large goods vehicle (LGV) drivers.

Working conditions

At times you will work inside a warehouse or factory and at other times outside in loading bays. While some trucks will have cabs offering protection from the weather, most of the time you need to be prepared to get cold and wet.

Operating your equipment will mean sitting in a driving seat for long periods.

Hours vary depending on your employer. You may work regular hours from Monday to Friday, but many jobs include shift work covering evenings and weekends.

Future prospects

You may be employed by the manufacturing, transport, haulage, warehouse or retail industries. There are about 100,000 lift truck operators in the UK.

With experience, you can move into supervisory or management roles in areas such as warehousing. You could go on to train new lift truck operators.

Some large employers may train you to become an LGV driver or instructor.

Advantages/disadvantages

You might work outside in poor weather conditions.

If you are keen on driving, large employers might give you the chance to progress to LGV driver training.

It can be stressful to get a load out quickly but it is very satisfying when transport leaves on time.

Money guide

Starting wages are about £12,000–£13,000 per year.

With some experience, you could expect to earn £14,000–£16,000.

The most experienced operators can achieve a salary of £20,000–£22,000.

Shift allowances and the opportunity to do overtime can increase your income.

Related opportunities

- Airport Baggage Handler p591
- Construction Plant Operator p87
- Delivery Driver p596

Further information

Association of Industrial Truck Trainers
www.aitt.co.uk

National Plant Operators Registration Scheme
www.npors.com

TRANSPORT AND LOGISTICS

CRCI: WB

Qualifications and courses

To become a rating, you will need to have gained GCSEs (A*–C) or equivalent, in both maths and English. You must also pass the merchant navy medical.

Entrants wishing to become officers can pursue 1 of 3 routes, each of which requires sponsorship by a shipping company.

You could choose to take an HND in nautical science, or alternatively a Foundation degree/SQA professional diploma in nautical science or marine operations. The third option is undertaking a degree in nautical science or merchant ship operations, for which you will need to hold 2 A levels (including maths or physics) or equivalent, in addition to your GCSE grades.

Completion of a training course leads to the Maritime and Coastguard Agency Officer of the Watch Certificate of Competency.

If you have previous relevant experience or were a former Royal Navy officer you may also be considered for the role.

What the work involves

The merchant navy consists of thousands of civilian ships, operated by individual shipping companies. They include fuel tankers and cargo ships, as well as ferries and cruise liners.

Merchant navy deck officers are responsible for navigating ships, as well as being involved in communications and cargo handling.

Deck ratings are responsible for supporting the ship's officers by helping to navigate and steer the ship, as well as carrying out maintenance tasks and helping to load and unload cargo.

Both jobs will involve using satellite and radar systems to navigate the ship, maintaining machinery and safety equipment, and training and support of junior officers and ratings.

Type of person suited to this work

Both officers and ratings need to have good social skills in order to work successfully as part of a team. You will also need to be calm and logical in the face of emergency situations.

In addition, officers will need to have excellent numeracy skills and be able to use complex technology in order to successfully make navigational calculations.

Officers will also need to have good leadership qualities, so that they inspire respect and dedication from their crew members.

Working conditions

You will expect to work shifts, known as 'watches'. These can vary in length from 4 hours on and 4 hours off, to 6 hours on and 6 hours off, or even 12 hours on and 12 hours off at times. These shifts can take place at any time.

Ratings can expect to live in close proximity to their colleagues, often in fairly cramped accommodation. Officers have their own private, en-suite cabin.

Generally, good leisure facilities are provided on-board so that crew can make the most of their time off.

Future prospects

With over 20 UK shipping companies in operation, and a predicted increase in shipping activity over the next few years, prospects for merchant navy officers and ratings are good.

As a rating, you could gain promotion to Seaman (Grade 2), or even take a conversion course in order to progress to a position as an officer.

Officers may move into related onshore work, including shipbuilding, maritime law and ship and fleet management.

Advantages/disadvantages

You will be working within a strong team environment, so will build excellent relationships with colleagues from a variety of backgrounds.

Shift work can be exhausting.

You will have to spend long periods of time away from your family. This could encompass months as well as weeks.

Money guide

Trainee merchant navy ratings can expect to earn between £15,000 and £16,000. This can increase to up to £30,000 with experience.

Newly qualified deck officers may have a starting salary of £20,000–£23,000. With experience, this should increase to around £35,000.

For senior officers salaries can rise to £50,000.

Related opportunities

- Marine Engineer p231
- Merchant Navy Engineering Officer p605

Further information

Marine Society & Sea Cadets
www.ms-sc.org

Merchant Navy Association
www.mna.org.uk

Merchant Navy Training Board
www.mntb.org.uk

MERCHANT NAVY ENGINEERING OFFICER

Qualifications and courses

There are a number of training routes to become a merchant navy engineering officer, depending on the level of your qualifications. You must be at least 18 years old when you start training, pass a medical and eyesight test and secure sponsorship from a shipping company who will provide you with work placements whilst you're at sea.

To study via the HND route, you will need to gain 4 GCSEs/S grades, including science, maths and English. The training programme then lasts 3 years, leading to a HND.

To study for a Foundation degree (the most common route to this profession) you will need the GCSEs/S grades detailed above plus 2 A levels/3 H grades.

To complete the undergraduate route, your degree will need to be in either marine engineering, nautical studies or marine operations.

It is also possible to enter an accelerated version of the training programme as a graduate, as long as you have a science-based degree.

Whichever training route you follow, you will need to take and pass an exam for the Certificate of Competency (also known as the Officer of the Watch certificate), which is distributed by the Coastguard and Maritime Agency.

What the work involves

The merchant navy consists of thousands of civilian ships, operated by individual shipping companies. They include fuel tankers and cargo ships, as well as ferries and cruise liners. Merchant navy engineering officers work with all the mechanical and electrical equipment onboard ships.

You will work on areas of the ship such as the engines, the computer-controlled engine management systems, and the pumps and fuel systems.

Engineering officers are based in the engine control room of a ship. They are responsible for assisting engineering officers in the repair and servicing of technical equipment.

Type of person suited to this work

You will need to be interested in working with very high-tech machinery and enjoy learning about new, state-of-the-art technology.

You will also need to be very practical and logical so that you can work quickly and efficiently to rectify problems that occur with the equipment.

You should enjoy working as part of a close-knit team and have a high level of self-discipline. Impeccable communication skills are essential for these roles.

Working conditions

You will expect to work shifts, known as 'watches'. These can vary in length from 4 hours on and 4 hours off, to 6 hours on and 6 hours off, or even 12 hours on and 12 hours off at times. These shifts can take place at any time, day or night.

You will spend the majority of your time in the engine control room or the engine room itself, where it will be hot and noisy. As an engineering officer you could be responsible for all of the ship's systems.

Generally, good leisure facilities are provided on-board so that crew can make the most of their time off.

Future prospects

There are fewer people applying to become trainee engineers now so your chances of success are good.

The large shipping companies that recruit trainees are recruiting more people than they used to.

Officers may rise through the ranks to reach the level of chief engineer. Alternatively, there are also opportunities in related areas such as ship surveying or ship management.

Advantages/disadvantages

You will be working within a strong team environment, so will build excellent relationships with colleagues from a variety of backgrounds.

The relentless nature of shift work can be exhausting.

You will have to spend long periods of time away from your family. This could encompass months as well as weeks.

Money guide

Sponsored trainee salaries are roughly £8,000 per year.

Once qualified, this jumps significantly to around £25,000 a year.

With experience, this should increase to between £26,000 and £50,000 depending on rank.

Chief engineers can earn up to £65,000.

Whilst at sea, your food and accommodation will be paid for by your employer.

Related opportunities

- Marine Engineer p231
- Royal Marines Commando p559
- Royal Marines Officer p560

Further information

Merchant Navy Association
www.mna.org.uk

Merchant Navy Training Board
www.mntb.org.uk

PASSENGER CHECK-IN OFFICER

Qualifications and courses

Entry requirements vary, but many employers prefer applicants with 3–5 GCSEs (A*–C)/S grades (1–3), including English and maths. Minimum age for entry varies from 16 to 20 years of age. You will need to be physically fit, and there may be height and weight restrictions. It's an advantage to be able to speak another language.

Key Skills in Communication and Information Technology are useful, as is work experience with the public in a caring, catering or travel agency job.

You could study a related college or university course; for example, a BTEC/SQA National Certificate/Diploma or HNC/D in travel and tourism, a GCSE/A level in Leisure and Tourism, NVQ in Aviation Operations or a degree in Travel and Tourism. Once accepted you will be trained for 4 to 8 weeks in all aspects of the job.

NVQs/SVQs in Handling Aircraft Passengers at Levels 2 and 3 may be available for further study.

What the work involves

You will be responsible for making sure that passengers and their baggage board the right aircraft.

You will greet passengers, provide information, ask security questions and check tickets and passport details.

Once you have weighed and put luggage on the conveyor belt, you will issue boarding passes and prepare paperwork for customs. You could also work at the flight gate, making announcements and checking boarding cards.

Type of person suited to this work

As the public face of your airline, you will need a pleasant, confident and helpful manner with a well-groomed appearance.

You need to be confident with IT. You will use a sophisticated computer system to allocate seats, print boarding cards and baggage labels and produce post-flight figures.

You must be friendly and approachable as you will be helping passengers, including those with disabilities and unaccompanied children, from check-in, through security, and on to their flight. You will also need to be able to deal with difficult situations. Good communication skills are essential for working with your colleagues and other airport staff.

Working conditions

You will wear a uniform and work indoors at an airport. When you are working at the check-in desk you may sit behind a counter for long periods.

If you are escorting passengers or helping with boarding at a gate, you will spend periods of time on your feet, sometimes walking quite long distances and carrying luggage.

Hours will include shifts covering evenings, weekends and holidays. This is done to cover all the times the airport is open.

Future prospects

Employers are either airlines or the ground handling companies that work on behalf of airlines.

About 70% of passenger handling work takes place at the 4 main airports – Heathrow, Gatwick, Stansted and Manchester – so there are more opportunities if you live within travelling distance of 1 of the big 4. There is a lot of competition for jobs, many of which are seasonal.

You could progress to be a member of the air cabin crew, or a supervisor within passenger services.

Advantages/disadvantages

You will get to meet all types of new people from across the world.

If there is a delay to their flight, you might have to deal with difficult or demanding passengers.

If you are keen to work as a member of air cabin crew or similar role, experience in this work will be a big advantage.

Money guide

Starting salaries are between £12,000 and 14,000 per year. Experienced customer service agents can earn between £15,000 and £20,000.

In a supervisory or management post you could earn up to £25,000.

Shift allowances are usually paid. There may be opportunities to earn overtime pay. Some airline companies also grant their employees concessions on flight costs.

Related opportunities

- Air Cabin Crew p588
- Holiday Representative p384
- Tour Guide/Manager p392

Further information

GoSkills
www.goskills.org

Royal Aeronautical Society
www.aerosociety.com

PASSENGER TRANSPORT CLERK

Qualifications and courses

There are no formal qualifications required to enter this profession. However GCSEs/S grades in English, maths or any relevant subjects (A*–C/1–3) will be useful.

You will learn largely on the job, although some training might be provided.

Many companies will provide their own in-house training, or day-release training for clerical staff.

If you are going into a position as a rail passenger transport clerk or a member of telephone enquiry bureau staff, you will be trained in fare structures, customer care, railway geography and computerised ticket systems.

You may also be provided with training from bus and coach companies which may be provided in-house. This will involve learning how to use timetables, ticket systems, price structures and customer care information.

What the work involves

As a passenger transport clerk you will deal with customer enquiries regarding departure times, fares, routes, connections and disruptions on bus and rail services.

You will use computerised systems to organise the purchase or refund of tickets and in order to issue travel cards.

You will research the best rail or coach fares for a customer and ensure that their transport is as efficient and affordable as possible.

You may specialise in either sales or customer enquiries but usually members of staff share these responsibilities amongst themselves.

Type of person suited to this work

You should be friendly and polite and have a genuine interest in working with the public.

Some maths and ICT skills will be necessary as you will be dealing with fares and payments.

You must be able to work quickly and efficiently so that passengers are not delayed getting to their train/bus.

As you might have to deal with customers in busy times or times when there are unexpected delays you need to have patience and the ability to deal with frustrated or angry customers.

You should also have an interest in travel and customer service.

Working conditions

You will work an average of 37 to 40 hours each week. This may include shift work, evenings, weekends and even public holidays.

You may have the opportunity to work part time, overtime and flexible hours.

You will be based in stations or travel centres which will function essentially as an office but you will deal with customers on the phone or as they come to the ticket office or information desk you are based at.

Future prospects

You may gain NVQs as you work in order to progress to supervisory and managerial roles.

You may be employed by any bus or coach operator or private rail companies, train operating companies throughout the UK, the London Underground or Eurostar.

Advantages/disadvantages

You will have the opportunity to work in an ever-changing environment as bus and rail services are constantly updated and new customers use them each day.

At times your work may be repetitive.

Money guide

Your starting salary as a transport clerk may be around £14,500 a year.

With some experience this can increase to £17,000.

With several years' experience and qualifications, you can earn between £19,500 and £22,500.

Related opportunities

- Customer Services Assistant/Manager p480
- Passenger Check-In Officer p606
- Train Conductor/Guard p617
- Travel Agent p394

Further information

Customer Contact Association
www.cca.org.uk

GoSkills
www.goskills.org

POSTAL DELIVERY WORKER

ENTRY LEVEL 1

Qualifications and courses

No specific qualifications are required for this job. Candidates should be aged 18 or over, and selection is by an aptitude test, a fitness assessment and interview. You might need to pass a medical examination or test to ensure that you can read addresses properly and spot any mistakes.

The ability to ride a bicycle and/or possession of a driving licence with no more than 6 penalty points may be required.

Apprenticeships are available from the Royal Mail.

You will receive induction training. Further training is chiefly on the job, lasting 18 months, and can include the chance to work towards an NVQ in Mail Services at Level 2. Once you have gained a minimum of 1 year of experience, you can seek advancement to supervisory or managerial levels.

What the work involves

You will sort and deliver mail to homes, shops, factories and offices in your area.

Your day will start at the sorting office, getting your mail ready for delivery and packing your bag in the best order for your route.

You will then deliver your mail by foot, bicycle or, in rural areas, by van. If working in a rural area you may also be responsible for delivering other goods such as milk. You might also be responsible for mail collections from post boxes and places of work.

Type of person suited to this work

Your round could include several hundred addresses and cover several miles a day so you will need to be fit, especially if you are doing the job on foot or by bicycle. You should also enjoy being outdoors as you will be expected to deliver the mail in all weathers.

Honesty and reliability are vital qualities in this job. You will be carrying lots of valuable and urgent mail around and you will be responsible for delivering it to the right place.

Good customer service skills and a friendly attitude are important.

Working conditions

Most of your work will be outside in all weathers. A uniform, footwear and protective clothing will be provided. If on foot, you might have to carry your mail in bags, though there will be

arrangements to transport you and your mail out to the start of your route.

Shift work with an early morning (5am) start or late evening (10pm) finish is usual. You will often work on a Saturday.

You might have to walk a couple of miles in a single day or walk up steep hills and deal with minor hazards.

Future prospects

Postal delivery workers mainly work for the Royal Mail.

Recruitment tends to be steady and there are opportunities in urban and rural areas throughout the UK. Some workers start out with temporary work over the Christmas period and are retained.

It is possible to move into parcel deliveries, supervisory or managerial work.

Advantages/disadvantages

With a regular round you will really get to know your customers.

There might be some hazards on your round; you will soon learn what to avoid!

All the walking or cycling will keep you fit.

Although you will have to start work by 5am if you are on the early shift, you will finish at around lunchtime.

Money guide

Starting pay for staff over 18 is £13,312 a year.

After 1 year's experience you can expect to earn between £14,820 and £16,172.

With further experience postal delivery workers outside of London can expect to earn £19,280 and £20,405 is common for those working within London.

There are additional payments for overtime and sometimes for shift work which takes place during unsocial hours.

Related opportunities

- Courier p594
- Delivery Driver p596
- Freight Forwarder p599

Further information

Royal Mail Group
www2.royalmailgroup.com

Skills for Logistics
www.skillsforlogistics.org

TRANSPORT AND LOGISTICS

CRCI: WB

610

PURCHASING/PROCUREMENT MANAGER

Qualifications and courses

Employers usually ask for a degree or HND qualification. It may be possible to enter at a lower level and progress with experience and on-the-job training. The Chartered Institute of Purchasing and Supply (CIPS) accredits some degree courses in business (with purchasing options), logistics and supply chain management, and purchasing and supply chain management.

To progress you will need the CIPS professional qualifications. You can study for a Level 2 Introductory Certificate up to a Level 7 Executive Diploma in Purchasing and Supply. These can be studied full time or part time at college, or by distance learning. The Introductory Certificate has no formal entry requirements. Once completed, you can progress to the Advanced Certificate.

After working for 3 years and completing the Level 6 Graduate Diploma, you can become a full member of CIPS. You will need at least 2 A levels and 3 GCSEs (A*–C), or equivalent qualifications, or be over 21 years old with relevant work experience. Many employers in this field will look upon any applicant more favourably if they have full membership of CIPS.

You can take NVQ at Levels 2, 3 and 4 in Supply Chain Management as an alternative route. Some universities offer postgraduate courses in purchasing, supply management and logistics.

What the work involves

You will be responsible for buying the goods or services needed by a business, and providing the best value for money.

Your first job is to find out what your employer wants to buy and how much the budget is.

An important aspect will be to find the best suppliers and negotiate with them to get products or services at the right conditions and price. You will then be responsible for quality checks to make sure that the goods or services provided are of the standard agreed.

Type of person suited to this work

You must have excellent negotiation and communication skills in order to get the best quality and lowest priced goods and services for your company.

ICT and numerical skills are essential for researching, calculating costs and managing a budget.

You will need to be organised and analytical and have a good business-sense.

Working conditions

You will work Monday to Friday, from 9am to 5:30pm although there can be longer hours if you work in the manufacturing industry.

If your suppliers are in a different time zone to the UK, this can mean early mornings or late nights.

You will be located in a busy office, although you may travel to meet suppliers and customers which can mean time away from home.

Future prospects

Jobs are available in nearly all areas of the business sector including manufacturing, retailers, wholesale, and government organisations. Purchasing administrative jobs are competitive, but there is a shortage of qualified applicants for purchasing manager jobs.

Some buyers move into specialist areas, for example construction or chemicals. ICT purchasing is a new specialism and is predicted to grow with the expansion of e-business.

Promotion prospects are good, especially in large organisations. It may be possible to progress to a role as director. Increasing numbers of experienced managers are choosing to become self-employed and work as consultants or contract workers.

Advantages/disadvantages

If successful, you can reach high levels of responsibility, and even travel overseas, early in your career.

This job is stressful. Businesses spend over half their money on the goods and services they need to buy, so mistakes could be expensive.

Money guide

Starting pay for a trainee is between £18,000 and £25,000 per year.

For experienced purchasing administrators the salary range is between £25,000 and £40,000.

In excess of £80,000 is possible for senior managers and directors.

Related opportunities

- Distribution Manager p597
- Importer/Exporter p601
- Warehouse Worker/Manager p619

Further information

Chartered Institute of Purchasing & Supply
www.cips.org

Skillsmart Retail
www.skillsmartretail.com

TRANSPORT AND LOGISTICS

CRCI: WC

RAIL SIGNALLING TECHNICIAN

Qualifications and courses

Network Rail operates a large Apprenticeship programme for those aged between 16 and 24, as do many other employers of rail signalling technicians. Employers usually require candidates to have 3 to 5 GCSEs/S grades (A*–C/1–3) or equivalent, including English, maths and science. A double GCSE in engineering or a related technical subject would also be helpful.

Apprentices work towards an NVQ Level 3 in Railway Engineering (signalling), undertaking a mixture of classroom-based and on-the-job learning.

Most employers operate their own selection process on top of these academic requirements. This usually consists of a medical test, which will assess your fitness, eyesight and hearing, as well as drug and alcohol screening. Occasionally, you may also have to sit an aptitude test.

You could undertake a full-time or part-time course prior to looking for work as a rail signalling technician. Relevant courses include the BTEC National Certificate in Electronics and Railway Signals/Telecommunications.

What the work involves

Rail signalling technicians are responsible for installing and repairing all of the signalling and telecommunications systems that are used to support the railways.

Equipment that you will be working on will include signal boxes, warning systems, manual lever frame boxes and coloured light signals.

You will also install new signalling equipment, such as GSM-R communication masts, and update existing systems.

Type of person suited to this work

You should have good manual dexterity in order to operate a range of tools and machines.

A logical approach to your work will help when tracing faults, as will the ability to understand technical drawings and engineering instructions when repairing systems. You will need good eyesight and full colour vision.

You should have a reasonable level of numeracy and good ICT skills so that you can operate computerised machinery. You will also need to be physically fit, as the work can include lifting and carrying heavy equipment, as well as working up ladders or in awkward places.

Working conditions

You will work around 37 hours a week, most likely in a shift pattern that could include early morning, evening and weekend work. You may also be expected to work overtime fairly regularly.

Your time will be divided between working outside, carrying out repairs trackside, and undertaking maintenance near signal boxes or within stations. You should be prepared to work in any weather conditions.

You may well have to travel to various different locations each day; overnight absence from home is common.

Future prospects

You could be employed by Network Rail, working on the UK's commercial railway tracks, or by a number of underground, metro or light rail operators such as London Underground, Metronet, Translink and the Docklands Light Railway.

With experience, you can become a member of the Institution of Railway Signal Engineers, which offers a route into becoming a registered engineering technician.

Promotion opportunities are good, and you could end up as a team manager, or even move into a consultancy role when you have built up significant experience.

Advantages/disadvantages

You will be playing an essential role in maintaining and developing the infrastructure of the UK.

Promotion opportunities are good, and there is also the chance to undertake extra training to drive forward your career.

Working in all weather conditions and cramped surroundings can be uncomfortable and extremely unpleasant at times.

Money guide

Your salary as an apprentice rail signalling technician will be about £14,000 per year.

As you gain experience, this should increase to between £22,000 and £30,000.

If you become a senior technician, or move into a consultancy role, your salary could reach in excess of £40,000.

Related opportunities

- Electrician p92
- Electricity Distribution Worker p220
- Telecommunications Technician p163

Further information

Railway-technology.com
www.railway-technology.com

TRANSPORT AND LOGISTICS

CRCI: WD

612

RAIL TRACK MAINTENANCE OPERATIVE

Qualifications and courses

Network Rail and most other employers look for candidates with a minimum of 4 GCSEs/S grades (A*–C/1–3) or equivalent, including English and maths. A technical subject is also desirable.

Qualifications in related subjects, such as a GCSE or A level in Engineering, or the City & Guilds NVQ Level 1 in Basic Track Maintenance, may be helpful in demonstrating your enthusiasm for the role and securing you employment.

You will have to be fit, and most employers will ask you to take a medical assessment to measure your fitness, stamina, and also test your hearing and eyesight. You will also have to take tests for drugs and alcohol.

Some employers also require candidates to go through a Criminal Records Bureau (CRB) check, as the role of a maintenance operative is critical in ensuring railway safety. Experience in a similar construction or engineering related role may be beneficial, but is not essential.

Network Rail operates a large Apprenticeship programme for those aged 16–24.

What the work involves

Rail track maintenance workers are responsible for building, repairing and maintaining the rail track network across the UK.

You will use a variety of manual and automated tools including welding equipment, clamping machines, and cement mixers.

You will also be responsible for inspecting the track in order to spot potential faults, which will involve walking along live tracks, with trains passing nearby.

Type of person suited to this work

You will need to be fit and strong to undertake this work, as you will be lifting and moving heavy pieces of track, as well as operating powerful machinery at times. You should also have good manual skills in order to use tools effectively and safely.

You must be a good communicator so you can work effectively within a team. You should be able to listen to instructions and take direction, whilst also having the confidence to use your own initiative and help colleagues when necessary.

You should have a good awareness of onsite safety practice and a responsible attitude to your work.

Working conditions

You will work an average of 35 hours per week on a shift system. You will have to work nights and weekends regularly, as these are the times at which maintenance work causes least disruption to the train timetable.

Work usually takes place outdoors, in all weather conditions. You should be prepared to get cold and wet working in muddy conditions, and also extremely hot in the summer months.

You will have to wear protective clothing; including a hard hat, high visibility jacket and reinforced boots.

Future prospects

Network Rail employs almost all the rail track maintenance workers in the UK, and they continuously update track all around the country.

There are also opportunities with rail employment agencies, who recruit workers for specific projects managed by rail engineering contractors.

With experience, you could progress to a supervisory role, or become a specialist in a technical area such as line-laying or welding.

Advantages/disadvantages

The work is physically tiring but rewarding, as you will be working towards maintaining the infrastructure of the UK.

You will be working in a team, so the job will be sociable and you will build strong relationships with your colleagues.

Working in all weather conditions can be uncomfortable and extremely unpleasant at times.

Money guide

Your starting salary as an apprentice rail track worker will be between £12,000 and £14,000 per year.

Once you have spent a few years in the role and built up your skills, you could be earning £18,000.

Rail track workers with additional supervisory responsibilities can earn up to £30,000.

Related opportunities

- Bricklayer p74
- Rail Signalling Technician p610
- Stonemason p122

Further information

Institute of Mechanical Engineers
www.imeche.org

Network Rail
www.networkrail.co.uk

Qualifications and courses

You must be at least 18 years of age. Good communication skills and numerical ability are viewed as extremely important by employers, so most train operating companies (TOCs) require candidates to have 4 GCSEs/S grades (A*–C/1–3) or equivalent, including English and maths. You may also be required to pass medical assessments, which will include eyesight, colour vision and hearing tests, as well as those for drugs and alcohol use.

Employers favour candidates who have previous experience in customer relations roles, whether paid or voluntary.

Apprenticeships may be available for entrants aged 18–21.

Once employed as a railway station assistant, you will have to undergo a training period that will encompass classroom-based learning programmes including health and safety, customer care, railway operating systems and coping in emergency situations. This will be followed by practical training in the station. Some TOCs also encourage employees to work towards an NVQ Level 2 in Rail Services as part of their training.

What the work involves

Railway station assistants work within train stations, assisting customers, dealing with queries, and ensuring that passengers are happy.

You may work behind a ticket desk, on an information stand, or on the station platforms so that you are accessible to passengers.

You will need to provide assistance to wheelchair users and other people who require help boarding or disembarking from a train. You will check tickets, and be on the look out for any security threats or other problems within the station.

Type of person suited to this work

You will need to be a confident communicator so that you can impart information to passengers, and also field any negative comments that might be directed towards you.

You should be polite and approachable, and maintain a clean, smart appearance. You will need good hearing and eyesight, as well as a high level of fitness in order to physically assist customers and move around the station quickly when necessary.

You should be able to work well within a team, taking instructions and helping colleagues, but also enjoy working autonomously and using your initiative.

Working conditions

You will usually work 37 hours per week, and this will include early morning, late night and weekend shifts.

There are usually opportunities to undertake paid overtime work.

You will also be working within ticket offices or passenger information areas in the station. You will have to wear a uniform so that you are easily recognisable to passengers.

Future prospects

You could either work for a train operating company or for Network Rail, within large or small train stations across the UK.

There are also opportunities to work for underground or metro operators in some cities.

You could progress as a conductor or driver, move upwards to become a customer services manager, or even reach the position of station manager.

Advantages/disadvantages

You will be working in a variety of roles each day so work should not get monotonous.

You will spend a lot of time on freezing station platforms in the winter.

You may have to deal with aggressive passengers at times.

Money guide

Your starting salary as a railway station assistant is likely to be about £13,000. As you gain experience and knowledge, this should rise to £18,500. If you are promoted to team leader, your salary will increase to £21,000+.

Overtime is always available, so your wages can be increased if you are willing to work extra hours.

Related opportunities

- Rail Track Maintenance Operative p611
- Train Conductor/Guard p617
- Train Driver p618

Further information

Network Rail
www.networkrail.co.uk

Qualifications and courses

No formal educational qualifications are needed, although GCSEs/S grades (A*–E/1–5) in English and maths are useful. While some firms will accept you at 16 years old, many specify a minimum age of 18 or even 21.

To work as a removals operative driver, you will need a large goods vehicle (LGV) licence, as well as a Driver Certificate of Professional Competence (Driver CPC). You must be at least 18 years old to train for an LGV licence and you will be required to undertake both a theory and a practical driving test.

Edexcel offer an Award, Certificate and Diploma in Commercial Moving (Levels 1–3) which may be useful. You can also enter this job through the Intermediate Apprenticeship in Carrying and Delivering Goods.

Most entrants are trained on the job by experienced colleagues. Some firms send employees on courses run by the British Association of Removers (BAR). Statutory training covers topics such as health and safety, manual handling and risk assessment, while skills training is offered in areas including fragile, commercial and specialist packing. You may be able to take NVQs in Warehousing and Storage (Levels 1 and 2) or Driving Goods Vehicles (Levels 2 and 3).

What the work involves

Removals operatives move furniture, garden, household and office items into storage or to new sites. This involves carefully packing goods and taking apart large items to fit into the removals van.

You must plan how you will pack the van in advance to make the most of the space and to prevent damage to the goods during transit. You will also need to unload and unpack once you have driven the items to their destination.

This could involve putting furniture and other items back together again and placing them where the customer directs.

Type of person suited to this work

Your customers will most likely be stressed about moving and will rely on you to remain calm and cheerful. You should be friendly and personable.

An honest and careful approach to your work is vital as you will be dealing with valuable and fragile items on a regular basis. You should also be a team player and able to follow instructions.

It is important that you are physically fit and enjoy practical work. You will be lifting and carrying large items and sometimes removing door or window frames to get items out of or into a property.

Working conditions

You will spend the majority of your time in the cab of your van. Your job may sometimes involve overnight and long-distance journeys and you should be prepared to spend time away from home.

Removals operatives usually work a 40 hour week but some days will require working overtime until the job is finished. A lot of moves take place at weekends.

All the lifting, carrying and bending involved may put you at risk of back injury.

Future prospects

Although you will find removals companies throughout the UK, urban areas are the best place to look for vacancies as thousands of people and businesses are constantly on the move in these hubs.

You may find that drops in the housing market can affect the number of jobs available.

With further training, such as the management courses offered by BAR, you may be promoted to a specialist packer, supervisor or manager.

You could also buy or lease a van and set up your own removals service.

Advantages/disadvantages

You might need to start early and work late, especially when legal processes can delay house removals.

You will be satisfied by your efforts and professionalism when you finish a move.

Happy customers may reward you with tips!

Money guide

Starting salaries range from £10,000 to £15,000.

With experience, you can expect to earn around £20,000 a year.

Senior staff can receive up to £30,000 per year.

Overtime pay, shift allowances and tips can increase your income.

Related opportunities

- Airport Baggage Handler p591
- Delivery Driver p596
- Roadie p444

Further information

British Association of Removers
www.bar.co.uk

Skills for Logistics
www.skillsforlogistics.org

TRANSPORT AND LOGISTICS

CRCI: WG

Qualifications and courses

Although there are no formal entry requirements to this job, most entrants are graduates. Useful subjects include transport management and transport safety. However, experience and personal qualities are equally as important to employers as academic qualifications. A driving licence is essential.

The Manchester College (MANCAT) is the only college in the UK that offers a BTEC Professional Development Diploma in Accident and Safety Management. For entry to the course you will need at least 1 A level/H grade and GCSEs/S grades (A*–C/1–3) in maths and English. It is also possible to work towards an NVQ/SVQ in Transportation at Levels 3–5.

The National Staff Training Group offers a training programme for road safety officers. Phase 1 provides training for newly appointed officers, phase 2 consists of a residential short course and phase 3 involves a series of seminars. Completion of phase 2 training can lead to Associate Membership of the Institute of Road Safety Officers (IRSO).

Requirements for becoming a member of IRSO are a relevant degree, a BTEC Professional Development Diploma in Accident and Safety Management, or NVQ/SVQ Levels 3/4 in Road Safety.

What the work involves

You will be working to reduce the number of motorists, cyclists and pedestrians injured or killed on the roads in your area.

You will educate the public by giving presentations to groups such as children. Promoting national road safety campaigns by distributing leaflets and running exhibitions could also be part of your job.

You will collect information about traffic accidents and make recommendations about how to prevent them.

Type of person suited to this work

As this job involves a lot of marketing and persuading, you will need to be an excellent communicator. You will use these skills to develop publicity materials and encourage people to behave more responsibly on the roads.

Self-confidence is vital to build good working relationships with safety engineers, police officers and local councillors.

To persuade others, you will need teaching skills and to be able to work with all age groups. You could give advice on fitting child car seats outside supermarkets, or teach small groups of young children how to cross the road safely.

Working conditions

Most of your work will be office based, but you will also visit schools and other locations. You will usually work 37 hours a week, Monday to Friday. Some evening work is required.

When working on-site with engineers, or when investigating accidents, you must wear high visibility clothing.

Your office work will involve using a computer to collect and analyse information.

Future prospects

Road safety officers are usually employed by local authorities. Some jobs are temporary as they are paid for by short-term government funding.

You could be promoted to manager or to a specialist post, for example, in publicity or working with schools. You might also find a job coordinating national safety and environmental initiatives, for example, the National Walk to School Campaign.

Prospects for this job may be affected by local authority budget cuts.

Advantages/disadvantages

You will receive great satisfaction in saving lives and seeing death and injury figures reduced in your area.

There might be delays or obstacles to putting in place the safety improvement work you have recommended, which can be frustrating.

Money guide

Newly qualified officers earn £18,000.

With experience you can earn up to £25,000 a year.

Officers with management responsibility can earn £40,000.

If you are a senior manager this can rise to over £50,000.

Local authorities may offer essential car user allowances as well as bonuses.

Related opportunities

- Community Education Officer p190
- Health and Safety Adviser p41
- Police Officer p551

Further information

Employers' Organisation for Local Government
www.lgcareers.com

Institute of Road Safety Officers
www.irso.org.uk

Qualifications and courses

It is possible to enter the transport industry with qualifications ranging from a few GCSEs/S grades, including English and maths, to a degree. Some companies offer Apprenticeships/Skillseekers in Logistics Operations Management.

Some companies recruit graduates to management positions. It is possible to enter with a degree in any subject although there are specialist degrees and postgraduate courses in transport management, transport planning and logistics available. Once working you can study for a variety of qualifications, including NVQ/SVQ Levels 2 and 3 in Road Passenger Transport (passenger work) and Traffic Office (freight work).

Postgraduate study is available as well. The Chartered Institute of Logistics and Transport (CILT) offers master's programmes in partnership with different universities.

The essential qualification to become a road transport senior manager is the Certificate of Professional Competence (CPC) of the Department of Transport (or Department of the Environment in Northern Ireland). This course is roughly equivalent to NVQ Level 3.

What the work involves

You will work for a business that moves goods or passengers, planning the routes and work timetables of your drivers.

You will oversee the day-to-day movement of your vehicles, checking that they are in the right places at the right times.

Putting health and safety regulations into place, and monitoring compliance, will be part of your role. Your job will include checking costs to make sure that your company makes a profit.

Type of person suited to this work

Planning timetables, journeys and loads means that you will need to be organised. You should also be logical and enjoy using computers to manage and develop information.

You will cost up journeys, work out timetables and stick to a strict budget, so you must enjoy working with figures.

You will need to have motivational and leadership skills, as it is your responsibility to take care of your drivers.

Working conditions

Most of your work will be based in an office. You will also spend time at vehicle depots, and might need to travel to carry out spot checks on your drivers.

Transport is a 24/7 business, so you might need to work shifts and weekends, or be called out in emergencies.

A passenger carrying vehicle or large goods vehicle licence will be useful.

Future prospects

Transport is a growing industry. You could work for a range of employers such as logistics and distribution companies, road haulage firms, manufacturers, retail chains or coach and bus operators.

It is possible to be promoted to area or general manager. Prospects are better if you are flexible about moving to a larger company or into other modes of transport. With multinational companies there may be opportunities to work abroad.

Transport planning is currently a severe skill shortage area, and it is possible to move into it with management experience in the transport sector.

Advantages/disadvantages

No two days are the same – traffic levels, problems and weather conditions vary from day to day.

You will have the satisfaction of seeing an instant result when you make decisions. The way you manage a problem can mean happier customers.

Money guide

Starting salaries are usually between £14,000 and £21,000 per year.

Experienced mangers can earn can earn between £25,000 and £35,000, though this is largely dependent on the size of your employer.

Senior managers earn up to £65,000, but the economic climate has reduced opportunities at this level.

Allowances are usually paid for shift work and unsocial hours.

Related opportunities

- Distribution Manager p597
- Freight Forwarder p599
- Warehouse Worker/Manager p619

Further information

Chartered Institute of Logistics and Transport
www.ciltuk.org.uk

TRANSPORT AND LOGISTICS

CRCI: WE

TAXI DRIVER

Qualifications and courses

It is not necessary to have any formal qualifications in order to become a taxi driver, but you must fulfil the conditions set out by your local licensing authority prior to them granting you a licence to work.

Criteria vary across the licensing authorities but all require applicants to pass an enhanced Criminal Records Bureau (CRB) check. You must have held a full driving licence for at least 12 months (3 years in London), you need to pass a medical assessment and you must be over the age of 21 (18 in Northern Ireland.)

The strictest local licensing authority is London, which requires all registered taxi drivers to pass an extensive geographical test known as 'The Knowledge'. It takes an average of 34 months to accumulate and learn all the necessary road information to pass.

The Driving Standards Agency (DSA) has developed a Hackney Carriage/Private Hire Test Assessment, which some licensing authorities use.

What the work involves

Taxi drivers pick up and transport passengers between destinations in a licensed vehicle for an agreed fee.

You could either drive your own black cab (also known as a hackney carriage) or operate a private hire vehicle (more commonly called a minicab).

If you drive a black cab, you will be able to pick up people who are waiting at a taxi rank, in the street, or those who have pre-booked. Minicabs are only allowed to carry pre-booked passengers. You will also need to assist passengers in and out of your vehicle, and help them with bags as necessary.

Type of person suited to this work

You will need to be personable and pleasant to passengers but also have the confidence to handle difficult or aggressive customers should the need arise. You should be numerate, as you will be handling money regularly and you will need to ensure that you give passengers the correct change.

You must have an extensive knowledge of the local area in which you operate so you will need a good memory and sense of direction.

Working conditions

Your working hours will vary according to your employer. If you work for a company, you may undertake shifts that include night and weekend hours. Self-employed drivers can choose their own hours.

Most work is available in larger towns and cities, and taxi drivers are busiest on Friday and Saturday night when people are looking to go home after a night out.

You will spend the majority of your time in your vehicle, either driving passengers to their destination, or waiting for a job to come up.

Future prospects

Taxi usage is growing at a rapid rate so job opportunities in the industry are plentiful.

Although you can work anywhere in the UK, the majority of work is focused within the larger towns and cities.

Many taxi drivers are self-employed, and with experience and knowledge you could gain an operator's licence and build up your own company.

Advantages/disadvantages

You will be dealing with a variety of people on a daily basis so the work is sociable and interesting.

You will be confined to your vehicle for most of your working day, and you may spend long periods of time waiting around in-between jobs.

You will occasionally have to deal with drunk, aggressive or distressed passengers.

You often have the freedom to choose your own hours.

Money guide

Taxi drivers who are just starting out usually earn about £11,000–£14,000 a year.

If you work around 40 hours a week and take a good amount of fares, you could earn between £15,000 and £20,000.

Taxi drivers in London and other very busy cities can achieve up to £30,000 a year but you must be prepared to work long hours.

Figures will vary for those working part time, or undertaking significant overtime.

Related opportunities

- Chauffeur p593
- Driving Instructor p598
- Tour Guide/Manager p392

Further information

Driving Standards Agency
www.dsa.gov.uk

Licensed Taxi Drivers Association
www.ltda.co.uk

Qualifications and courses

Although there are no set qualifications for entry to become a train conductor, almost all train operating companies (TOCs) look for candidates with 5 GCSEs/S grades (A*–C/1–3) or equivalent, including English and maths.

You will need to be 18 years of age before you are legally allowed to work on-board a train. You can work within a railway station from the age of 16, which could help to build up the customer services skills that employers desire in candidates applying for conductor roles.

When you apply, you will need to pass a series of tests in order to assess your suitability. These include a full medical to gauge your level of fitness, eyesight, colour vision, and hearing. You might also need to pass memory, comprehension and concentration tests. There is also a strict safety policy with regard to drugs and alcohol abuse for anyone working on a train and you may be asked to take random drugs tests throughout your career.

Apprenticeships may be available for those aged 16–24.

What the work involves

Train conductors work on passenger trains, checking and issuing tickets, and ensuring that passengers are enjoying a comfortable and pleasant journey.

You will mainly focus on providing an excellent level of customer service to those riding the train. This will include fielding any queries or complaints, and handling rowdy passengers at times.

You will be responsible for making announcements to notify passengers about approaching stations, times of arrival, and any delays in the journey. You may also need to look after passengers with special requirements, such as assisting the elderly and disabled, and keeping an eye on children travelling alone.

Type of person suited to this work

You must have excellent interpersonal skills in order to advise passengers about their journey, answer queries, deal with complaints calmly and professionally, and to maintain authority when dealing with aggressive or difficult passengers.

You should be very confident, as you will be working alone as the first point of contact for all train passengers.

You must be able to quickly and effectively deal with a number of unexpected situations. It is also beneficial to be medically fit, and have good eyesight and hearing.

Working conditions

You will usually work 37 hours per week, according to a shift rota that will include early morning, night and weekend work. Overtime opportunities are regular. If you work on long distance routes, you may be required to stay overnight at the destination on occasion.

Although most of your time is spent walking through the train, you will usually also have a small, private office onboard. This will have equipment for making announcements, CCTV and usually a computer terminal.

You will be expected to wear a uniform and maintain a clean, smart appearance at all times.

Future prospects

Job opportunities for conductors have decreased slightly in recent years with the introduction of driver-only trains on shorter routes. Nowadays, roles are concentrated on cross-country trains.

Most train conductors are employed by a TOC that specialises in passenger transportation. TOCs operate throughout the UK, so there are opportunities in most towns and cities.

Promotions can include titles such as senior conductor or train manager, and there may also be opportunities to move into general management within the rail sector.

Advantages/disadvantages

You will be dealing with a variety of people on a daily basis, so work is rarely monotonous or boring.

You will be providing an important and valuable service to railway passengers.

You may have to deal with drunk, aggressive or distressed passengers from time to time.

Money guide

The starting salary for a trainee conductor is about £12,000.

Once you have qualified, this will rise to around £18,000–£21,000.

With experience, and having gained extra supervisory responsibilities, this could increase to £25,000.

Related opportunities

- Air Cabin Crew p588
- Rail Signalling Technician p610
- Train Driver p618

Further information

National Rail Enquiries
www.nationalrail.co.uk

TRANSPORT AND LOGISTICS

CRCI: WD

TRAIN DRIVER

Qualifications and courses

Although there are no set qualifications for entry to train as a driver, almost all train operating companies (TOCs) look for candidates with 5 GCSEs/S grades (A*–C/1–3) or equivalent, including English, maths and a science subject.

You will need to be 21 years of age before you are legally allowed to train as a driver, but you can build up rail-related experience from the age of 16 working within a station, and from 18 onboard trains. This way, you can gain beneficial experience of dealing with railway passengers and understand how the industry works prior to applying to be a trainee driver.

When you apply, you will need to pass a series of tests in order for your suitability to be assessed. These include operating hand and foot controls, concentration skills, basic mechanical knowledge, and staying calm under pressure. You will also need to pass a medical assessment that will encompass fitness, hearing, eyesight and colour vision.

Once you have gained a position as a trainee driver, you will undergo 9–18 months of training prior to becoming a qualified driver. This will take the form of both classroom-based learning, and practical experience of driving trains.

What the work involves

Train drivers are responsible for safely operating trains that carry both passengers and goods around the UK.

You will drive the train on set routes aiming to arrive punctually at your destination, as long as there are no interferences with signalling or other unforeseen problems.

You must check your route carefully prior to setting off to ensure that it is still viable. You should also carry out safety-related checks on the train itself. You will provide a safe and efficient service by observing railway signs, signals and speed limits, and staying alert at all times.

Type of person suited to this work

You will need to have excellent concentration and good observational skills, coupled with a responsible attitude towards safety, so that you can effectively operate a train. You must be happy working alone for long periods of time.

You will need good eyesight and hearing, as well as quick reactions in order to respond to unexpected situations. Being able to keep calm under pressure is also an asset as difficult circumstances can arise during journeys.

You should have some mechanical or engineering knowledge so that you can carry out the necessary safety checks on the train.

Working conditions

You will usually work 35–40 hours per week on a shift system, which will include early morning, late night, and weekend work. Overtime is commonly available, and part time work can be an option.

Occasionally you might need to stay overnight at a destination if it is a long way from home, although this is more common for freight train drivers than those providing passenger services.

You will usually work alone, operating the train from the driver's cab. You may occasionally have company in the form of a driver inspector or trainee driver.

Future prospects

Most train drivers are employed by a TOC, of which there are 24 in the UK. These consist of passenger operators, light rail companies that provide underground services, freight companies, and engineering supply organisations.

With experience, you could become a trainer or an inspector of other drivers. Your company would probably fund your studies towards gaining a professional qualification in this area.

It may also be possible to move into a management role within your company or the rail sector.

Advantages/disadvantages

It can be very peaceful and pleasant driving through the British countryside on journeys.

You may have to work nights and weekends on a fairly regular basis.

It can get quite lonely being on your own in the driver's cab for long periods of time.

Money guide

Starting salaries for trainee drivers are usually about £17,500.

Once you are fully qualified, this should rise to £30,000.

With 5–7 years' experience, you could earn £35,000. If you work on mainline/high-speed passenger services this could increase further to £40,000.

Related opportunities

- Delivery Driver p596
- Rail Signalling Technician p610
- Train Conductor/Guard p617

Further information

National Rail Enquiries
www.nationalrail.co.uk

Qualifications and courses

For employment as a warehouse worker you will need to be physically fit and a medical may be required. The Apprenticeship in Warehousing and Storage may be available for those aged 16–24. You could have the option to study for an NVQ in Warehousing and Storage (Levels 1 and 2) or a City & Guilds Certificate in Logistics Operations (Levels 2 and 3). 3 GCSEs/S grades (A*–C/1–3) might be required including maths and English.

Most training takes place on the job. The National Proficiency Tests Council (NPTC)'s Level 2 Certificate of Competence in Forklift Truck Operations may be offered by employers.

It is possible to start as a warehouse worker, gain NVQs/SVQs or the professional qualifications of the Chartered Institute of Logistics and Transport (CILT), and progress to supervisory or management roles. Some employers may require qualifications such as A levels/H grades for management positions. Degrees are on offer in related subjects such as logistics and supply chain management.

New or aspiring senior warehouse managers can take the CILT Advanced Diploma or study for an MSc in international transport and logistics. You can also work towards an NVQ Level 3 in Logistics Operations Management or a Foundation degree in logistics or transport.

What the work involves

Warehouse workers are responsible for making sure that goods from a delivery or dispatch are in the right condition and quantity. They then input details into a hand-held computer terminal. If trained, you may also drive a lift truck.

Managers will be in overall charge of the warehouse, responsible for maintaining stock levels, storing the goods safely, and dispatching them onwards when needed. You will have to manage a team of staff and ensure that they adhere to health and safety regulations.

You will use a computer to monitor stock levels and orders, and to check the times when deliveries are due in and dispatches due out of your warehouse.

Type of person suited to this work

You must be honest and security conscious as warehouses often store valuable stock. You will need to work well in a team to get goods in and out of the warehouse quickly.

The use of machinery to move and stack goods at heights can be dangerous, so you should be able to follow or implement safety regulations.

You will need excellent IT skills as deliveries and dispatches are recorded and monitored on the warehouse's computer tracking system.

Working conditions

You will work a 37–40 hour week. Shift work and overtime is typical and includes working nights and weekends.

Workers spend a lot of time on their feet and might need to lift heavy items and climb ladders. Managers work at a computer in an office and out in the warehouse.

Future prospects

Warehouses are owned and managed by companies who either store large quantities of goods for their own businesses, or charge customers to store their goods. The biggest employers of warehouse staff are retail and manufacturing companies, logistics and distribution service providers and specialist freight and haulage companies.

Warehouses are becoming more computerised and some of the heavier work is being automated. This is likely to change the job in the future. Some warehouses will have fewer operatives and some are already 'lights out' warehouses with no human workers at operative level.

After gaining experience, you can progress to a role as team leader or supervisor. With additional qualifications, you can move into warehouse management.

Advantages/disadvantages

You will be working to tight deadlines which can be stressful.

Working together to finish a job can foster an excellent team spirit.

Heavy workloads are common at certain periods such as Christmas, although you will receive overtime pay.

Money guide

Starting salaries for workers are usually £12,000–£14,000.

With experience, you can earn up to £17,000.

Warehouse managers start on between £17,000 and £22,000.

Experienced managers can achieve £28,000–£36,000 a year.

Bonuses and overtime pay can increase your income.

Related opportunities

- Airport Baggage Handler p591
- Distribution Manager p597
- Freight Forwarder p599

Further information

Chartered Institute of Logistics and Transport
www.ciltuk.org.uk

United Kingdom Warehousing Association
www.ukwa.org.uk

TRANSPORT AND LOGISTICS

CRCI: WG

621

INDEX OF LEVELS

Level 3

Level 4

Level 5

Level 6

Level 7

Level 8

INDEX

INDEX

629

INDEX OF ADVERTISERS

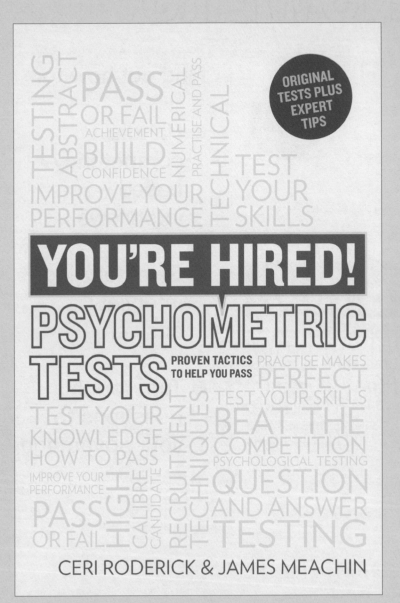

HEAP
Degree Course Offers Online!

We've launched a brand new website so students can access the most up-to-date information on degree courses and find the course and university right for them.

The site contains ALL the information you'll find in *HEAP* but delivered in a new and interactive format, enabling students to:

✓ Use predicted UCAS tariff points to search for courses and filter results

✓ Access *HEAP's* unique and invaluable advice to help make their application successful

✓ Search by location, courses or university

✓ Save searches online and access them again at any time

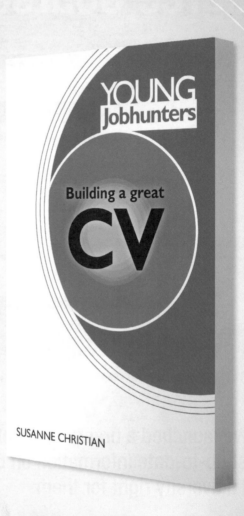